T0213421

Lecture Notes in Computer Science 10524

Commenced Publication in 1973
Founding and Former Series Editors:
Gerhard Goos, Juris Hartmanis, and Jan van Leeuwen

More information about this series at http://www.springer.com/series/7407

Julian M. Kunkel · Rio Yokota
Michela Taufer · John Shalf (Eds.)

High Performance Computing

ISC High Performance 2017 International Workshops
DRBSD, ExaComm, HCPM, HPC-IODC, IWOPH, IXPUG,
P^3MA, VHPC, Visualization at Scale, WOPSSS
Frankfurt, Germany, June 18–22, 2017
Revised Selected Papers

Editors
Julian M. Kunkel
Deutsches Klimarechenzentrum (DKRZ)
Hamburg, Hamburg
Germany

Rio Yokota
TITECH
Tokyo
Japan

Michela Taufer
Department of Computer Science
University of Delaware
Newark, DE
USA

John Shalf
Lawrence Berkeley National Laboratory
Berkeley, CA
USA

ISSN 0302-9743 ISSN 1611-3349 (electronic)
Lecture Notes in Computer Science
ISBN 978-3-319-67629-6 ISBN 978-3-319-67630-2 (eBook)
https://doi.org/10.1007/978-3-319-67630-2

Library of Congress Control Number: 2017955780

LNCS Sublibrary: SL1 – Theoretical Computer Science and General Issues

Printed on acid-free paper

This Springer imprint is published by Springer Nature
The registered company is Springer International Publishing AG
The registered company address is: Gewerbestrasse 11, 6330 Cham, Switzerland

Preface

A separate workshop day attached to the ISC High Performance, formerly known as the International Supercomputing Conference, was first added to the Technical Program in 2015 under the leadership of Bernd Mohr (Forschungszentrum Jülich GmbH). ISC High Performance has renewed and further extended the workshop program this year welcoming 646 attendees to 21 workshops. This year Michela Taufer (University of Delaware, USA) served as workshop chair and led the workshop organization with workshop deputy chair John Shalf (Lawrence Berkeley National Laboratory). Julian Kunkel (German Climate Computing Center) served as the proceedings chair and managed the organization of proceedings for the workshops with Rio Yokota (Tokyo Institute of Technology) as the proceedings deputy chair.

The 21 workshops at ISC High Performance provided a focused, in-depth platform with presentations, discussion, and interaction on topics related to all aspects of research, development, and application of large-scale, high-performance experimental and commercial systems. Workshop topics included HPC computer architecture and hardware; programming models, system software, and applications; solutions for heterogeneity, reliability, power efficiency of systems; virtualization and containerized environments; big data and cloud computing; as well as international collaborations. Workshops were selected with a peer-review process by an international committee of 12 experts in the field from Europe, the United States, and Asia.

As in 2016, ISC High Performance provided a platform for workshops with their own call for papers and an individual peer-review process through an early deadline in December 2016. In all, 11 workshop proposals were submitted before this deadline from organizers all over the world; because of their high quality, all proposals were accepted by the committee (seven full-day and four half-day workshops) after a rigorous review process in which each proposal received at least three reviews. Additionally, each reviewer was given the possibility to discuss all the submissions.

Workshops without a call for papers were invited to submit their proposals in February 2017. For this second deadline, 15 workshop proposals were submitted and 10 workshops (one full-day and nine half-day workshops) were accepted by the committee with the same rigorous peer-review process as for workshops with proceedings.

The 21 workshops were held on Thursday, June 22, 2017, at the Frankfurt Marriott Hotel with 646 registered attendees, about 170 presentations, and over a dozen panel discussions. Workshop organizers were asked to collect the slides of all presentations at their workshops. PDF versions of the presentation slides were included in the ISC 2017 online proceedings, which were made available online to conference attendees a few days after the conference.

The workshop proceedings volume collects all accepted papers of the workshops received after the call for papers and a handful of invited papers. Each chapter of the book contains the accepted and revised papers for one of the workshops. For some workshops, an additional preface describes the review process for the workshop and provides a summary of the outcome.

June 2017

Julian M. Kunkel
Michaela Taufer
Rio Yokota
John Shalf

Organization

ISC High Performance Workshops Chair

Michela Taufer — University of Delaware, USA

ISC High Performance Workshops Deputy Chair

John Shalf — Lawrence Berkeley National Laboratory, USA

ISC High Performance Workshops Committee

Rosa M. Badia	Barcelona Supercomputing Center, Spain
François Bodin	IRISA, France
Bronis R. de Supinski	Lawrence Livermore National Laboratory, USA
Jay Lofstead	Sandia National Laboratories, USA
Naoya Maruyama	Lawrence Livermore National Laboratory, USA
Simon McIntosh-Smith	University of Bristol, UK
Bernd Mohr	Jülich Supercomputing Centre, Germany
Marie-Christine Sawley	Intel, France
Seetharami Seelam	IBM T.J. Watson Research Center, USA
John Shalf	Lawrence Berkeley National Laboratory, USA
Michela Taufer	University of Delaware, USA
Carsten Trinitis	Technische Universität München, Germany
Antonino Tumeo	Pacific Northwest National Laboratory, USA
Didem Unat	Koç Universitesi, Turkey
Rio Yokota	Tokyo Institute of Technology, Japan

ISC High Performance Workshops Proceedings Chair

Julian Kunkel — DKRZ, Germany

ISC High Performance Workshops Proceedings Deputy Chair

Rio Yokota — Tokyo Institute of Technology, Japan

Experiences on Intel Knights Landing at the One-Year Mark

Organizing Committee

Estela Suarez	Jülich Supercomputing Centre, Germany
Michael A. Lysaght	ICHEC, Ireland

Simon J. Pennycook	Intel, USA
Richard Gerber	NERSC, USA

Program Committee

Damian Alvarez	Jülich Supercomputing Centre, Germany
Carlo Cavazzoni	CINECA, Italy
Gilles Civario	DELL, USA
Doug Doerfler	Lawrence Berkeley National Laboratory, USA
Richard Gerber	Lawrence Berkeley National Laboratory/NERSC, USA
Clayton Hughes	Sandia National Laboratories, USA
Balint Joo	Thomas Jefferson National Accelerator Facility, USA
Rakesh Krishnaiyer	Intel, USA
Michael A. Lysaght	ICHEC, Ireland
Simon McIntosh-Smith	University of Bristol, UK
Andrew Mallinson	Intel, UK
David E. Martin	Argonne National Laboratory, USA
Hideki Saito	Intel, USA
Thomas Steinke	Zuse Institute Berlin, Germany
Estela Suarez	Jülich Supercomputing Centre, Germany
Zhengji Zhao	Lawrence Berkeley National Laboratory, USA

HPC I/O in the Data Center

Organizing Committee

Julian Kunkel	DKRZ, Germany
Jay Lofstead	Sandia National Laboratory, USA
Colin McMurtrie	CSCS, Switzerland

Program Committee

Wolfgang Frings	Jülich Supercomputing Center, Germany
Javier Garcia Blas	University Carlos III of Madrid, Spain
Rob Ross	Argonne National Laboratory, USA
Carlos Maltzahn	University of California, Santa Cruz, USA
Thomas Bönisch	HLRS, Germany
Sai Narasimhamurthy	Seagate, UK
Jean-Thomas Acquaviva	DDN, France
Julian Kunkel	DKRZ, Germany
Jay Lofstead	Sandia National Laboratory, USA
Colin McMurtrie	CSCS, Switzerland

Workshop on Performance and Scalability of Storage Systems (WOPSSS)

Organizing Committee

Jean-Thomas Acquaviva	DDN, France
Jalil Boukhobza	Université de Bretagne Occidentale, France
Philippe Deniel	CEA/DIF, France
Massimo Lamanna	CERN, Switzerland
Pedro Javier García	University of Castilla-La Mancha, Spain
Allen D. Malony	University of Oregon, USA

Program Committee

Julien Bigot	CEA, France
Jason Chun Xue	City University of Hong Kong, Hong Kong, SAR China
Stefano Cozzini	CNR, Italy
Jesus Escudero-Sahuquillo	University of Castilla-La Mancha, Spain
Maria E. Gomez	Polytechnic University of Valencia, Spain
Pilar Gonzalez Ferez	Universidad de Murcia, Spain
Denis Gutfreund	ATOS, France
Julian Kunkel	DKRZ, Germany
Duo Liu	Chongqing University, China
Manolis Marazakis	Forth, Greece
Lars Nagel	Johannes Gutenberg-Universität Mainz, Germany
Ramon Nou	BSC, Spain
Juan Piernas Cánovas	Universidad de Murcia, Spain
Rekha Singhal	Tata Consultancy Services, India
Josef Weidendorfer	TUM, Germany
Soraya Zertal	University of Versailles, France

ExaComm: Third International Workshop on Communication Architectures for HPC, Big Data, Deep Learning and Clouds at Extreme Scale

Organizing Committee

Hari Subramoni	The Ohio State University, USA
Dhabaleswar K. (DK) Panda	The Ohio State University, USA

Program Committee

Taisuke Boku	University of Tsukuba, Japan
Ron Brightwell	Sandia National Laboratories, USA
Hans Eberle	NVIDIA, USA
Jesus Escudero-Sahuquillo	University of Castilla-La Mancha, Spain
Ada Gavrilovska	Georgia Institute of Technology, USA
Brice Goglin	Inria, France
Dror Goldenberg	Mellanox Technologies, Israel
R. Govindarajan	Indian Institute of Science, India
Ryan Grant	Sandia National Laboratories, USA
Hai Jin	Huazhong University of Science and Technology, China
Sven Karlsson	Technical University of Denmark, Denmark
Nectarios Koziris	National Technical University of Athens, Greece
Takeshi Nanri	University of Kyushu, Japan
Dimitrios Nikolopoulos	Queen's University of Belfast, UK
Antonio Pena	Barcelona Supercomputing Center, Spain
Sebastien Rumley	Columbia University, USA
Smruti Ranjan Sarangi	Indian Institute of Technology, India
Martin Schulz	Lawrence Livermore National Laboratory, USA
John M. Shalf	Lawrence Berkeley National Laboratory, USA
Tor Skeie	Simula Research Laboratory, Norway
Sayantan Sur	Intel, USA
Xin Yuan	Florida State University, USA
Jidong Zhai	Tsinghua University, China

12th Workshop on Virtualization in High-Performance Cloud Computing (VHPC'17)

Organizing Committee

Michael Alexander	scaledinfra technologies, Austria
Anastassios Nanos	OnApp, UK
Balazs Gerofi	RIKEN, Japan

Program Committee

Stergios Anastasiadis	University of Ioannina, Greece
Jakob Blomer	CERN, Europe
Ron Brightwell	Sandia National Laboratories, USA
Eduardo César	Universidad Autonoma de Barcelona, Spain
Julian Chesterfield	OnApp, UK
Stephen Crago	USC ISI, USA
Christoffer Dall	Columbia University, USA
Patrick Dreher	MIT, USA

Robert Futrick	Cycle Computing, USA
Maria Girone	CERN, Europe
Kyle Hale	Northwestern University, USA
Romeo Kinzler	IBM, Switzerland
Brian Kocoloski	University of Pittsburgh, USA
Nectarios Koziris	National Technical University of Athens, Greece
John Lange	University of Pittsburgh, USA
Che-Rung Lee	National Tsing Hua University, Taiwan
Giuseppe Lettieri	University of Pisa, Italy
Qing Liu	Oak Ridge National Laboratory, USA
Nikos Parlavantzas	IRISA, France
Kevin Pedretti	Sandia National Laboratories, USA
Amer Qouneh	University of Florida, USA
Carlos Reaño	Technical University of Valencia, Spain
Thomas Ryd	CFEngine, Norway
Na Zhang	VMWare, USA
Borja Sotomayor	University of Chicago, USA
Craig Stewart	Indiana University, USA
Anata Tiwari	San Diego Supercomputer Center, USA
Kurt Tutschku	Blekinge Institute of Technology, Sweden
Yasuhiro Watashiba	Osaka University, Japan
Nicholas Wright	Lawrence Berkeley National Laboratory, USA
Chao-Tung Yang	Tunghai University, Taiwan

Visualization at Scale: Deployment Case Studies and Experience Reports

Organizing Committee

Glendon Holst	KAUST, Saudi Arabia
Thomas Theussl	KAUST, Saudi Arabia
Julien Jomier	Kitware, France
Joachim Pouderoux	Kitware, France

Program Committee

Second International Workshop on Performance Portable Programming Models for Accelerators (P^3MA)

Organizing Committee

Sunita Chandrasekaran	University of Delaware, USA
Graham Lopez	ORNL, USA

Program Committee

Samuel Thibault	Inria, University of Bordeaux, France
James Beyer	NVIDIA, USA
Wei Ding	AMD, USA
Saber Feki	KAUST, Saudi Arabia
Robert Henschel	Indiana University, USA
Eric Stotzer	Texas Instruments, USA
Amit Amritkar	University of Houston, USA
Guido Juckeland	Helmholtz-Zentrum Dresden-Rossendorf, Germany
Will Sawyer	ETH, Zurich
Sameer Shende	University of Oregon, USA
Costas Bekas	IBM, Zurich
Toni Collis	University of Edinburgh, UK
Adrian Jackson	University of Edinburgh, UK
Henri Jin	NASA, USA
Andreas Knuepfer	TU Dresden, Germany
Steven Olivier	Sandia National Laboratory, USA
Suraj Prabhakaran	TU Darmstadt, Germany
Bora Ucar	ENS De Lyon, France
Veronica Vergara Larrea	ORNL, USA
Manisha Gajbe	Intel, USA
Daniel Tian	PGI, USA

Second International Workshop on OpenPOWER for HPC (IWOPH'17)

Organizing Committee

Dirk Pleiter	Jülich Supercomputing Centre, Germany
Jack Wells	Oak Ridge National Laboratory, USA

Program Committee

Nishant Agrawal	TCS, India
Carlo Cavazzoni	CINECA, Italy
Norbert Eicker	Jülich Supercomputing Centre, Germany
Holger Fröning	University of Heidelberg, Germany
Christoph Hagleitner	IBM Research, Switzerland
Oscar Hernandez	Oak Ridge National Laboratory, USA
Guido Juckeland	Helmholtz-Zentrum Dresden-Rossendorf, Germany
M. Graham Lopez	Oak Ridge National Laboratory, USA
Lena Oden	Jülich Supercomputing Centre, Germany
Dirk Pleiter	Jülich Supercomputing Centre, Germany
Swaroop Pophale	Oak Ridge National Laboratory, USA

Tiago Quintino	ECMWF, UK
Sebastiano F. Schifano	University and INFN Ferrara, Italy
Sameer Shende	University of Oregon, USA
Tjerk Straatsma	Oak Ridge National Laboratory, USA
Xiaonan Tian	NVIDIA, USA
Piero Vicini	INFN, University of Rome Sapienza, Italy
Jack Wells	Oak Ridge National Laboratory, USA
Michael Wolfe	PGI, USA
Bronis de Supinski	Lawrence Livermore National Laboratory, USA

First International Workshop on Data Reduction for Big Scientific Data (DRBSD-1)

Organizing Committee

Ian Foster	National Laboratory/University of Chicago, USA
Scott Klasky	Oak Ridge National Laboratory, USA
Gary Liu	New Jersey Institute of Technology, USA
Mark Ainsworth	Brown University/Oak Ridge National Laboratory, USA

Program Committee

Frank Cappello	Argonne National Laboratory, USA
Peter Lindstrom	Lawrence Livermore National Laboratory, USA
Tamara Kolda	Sandia National Laboratory, USA
Todd Munson	Argonne National Laboratory, USA
George Ostrouchov	Oak Ridge National Laboratory, USA
Scott Klasky	Oak Ridge National Laboratory, USA
Mark Ainsworth	Brown University/Oak Ridge National Laboratory, USA
John Wu	Lawrence Berkeley National Laboratory, USA
Todd Munson	Argonne National Laboratory, USA
Eric Suchyta	Oak Ridge National Laboratory, USA
Martin Burtscher	Texas State University, USA

Contents

Workshop on Performance and Scalability of Storage Systems (WOPSSS)

The 1st International Workshop on Data Reduction for Big Scientific Data (DRBSD-1)

Toward Decoupling the Selection of Compression Algorithms from Quality Constraints

Julian Kunkel[1(✉)], Anastasiia Novikova[2], Eugen Betke[1], and Armin Schaare[2]

[1] Deutsches Klimarechenzentrum, Hamburg, Germany
kunkel@dkrz.de
[2] Universität Hamburg, Hamburg, Germany

Abstract. Data intense scientific domains use data compression to reduce the storage space needed. Lossless data compression preserves the original information accurately but on the domain of climate data usually yields a compression factor of only 2:1. Lossy data compression can achieve much higher compression rates depending on the tolerable error/precision needed. Therefore, the field of lossy compression is still subject to active research. From the perspective of a scientist, the compression algorithm does not matter but the qualitative information about the implied loss of precision of data is a concern.

With the Scientific Compression Library (SCIL), we are developing a meta-compressor that allows users to set various quantities that define the acceptable error and the expected performance behavior. The ongoing work a preliminary stage for the design of an automatic compression algorithm selector. The task of this missing key component is the construction of appropriate chains of algorithms to yield the users requirements. This approach is a crucial step towards a scientifically safe use of much-needed lossy data compression, because it disentangles the tasks of determining scientific ground characteristics of tolerable noise, from the task of determining an optimal compression strategy given target noise levels and constraints. Future algorithms are used without change in the application code, once they are integrated into SCIL.

In this paper, we describe the user interfaces and quantities, two compression algorithms and evaluate SCIL's ability for compressing climate data. This will show that the novel algorithms are competitive with state-of-the-art compressors ZFP and SZ and illustrate that the best algorithm depends on user settings and data properties.

1 Introduction

Climate science is data intense. For this reason, the German Climate Computing Center spends a higher percentage of money on storage compared to compute. While providing a peak compute performance of 3.6 PFLOPs, a shared file system of 54 Petabytes and an archive complex consisting of 70,000 tape slots is provided. Compression offers a chance to increase the provided storage space or to provide virtually the same storage space but with less costs. Analysis has

J.M. Kunkel et al. (Eds.): ISC High Performance Workshops 2017, LNCS 10524, pp. 3–14, 2017.
https://doi.org/10.1007/978-3-319-67630-2_1

shown that with proper preconditioning and algorithm, a compression factor of roughly 2.5:1 can be achieved with lossless compression, i.e., without loss of information/precision [1]. However, the throughput of compressing data with the best available option is rather low (2 MiB/s per core). By using the statistical method in [2] to estimate the actual compression factor that can be achieved on our system, we saw that LZ4fast yield a compression ratio[1] of 0.68 but with a throughput of more than 2 GiB/s on a single core. Therefore, on our system it even outperforms algorithms for optimizing memory utilization such as BLOSC.

Lossy compression factors can yield a much lower ratio but at expense of information accuracy and precision. Therefore, users have to carefully define the acceptable loss of precision and properties of the remaining data properties. There are several lossy algorithms around that target scientific applications.

However, their definition of the retained information differs: some allow users to define a fixed ratio useful for bandwidth limited networks and visualization; most offer an absolute tolerance and some even relative quantities. The characteristics of the algorithm differs also on input data. For some data, one algorithm yields a better compression ratio than another. Scientists struggle to define the appropriate properties for these algorithms and must change their definition depending on the algorithm decreasing code portability.

In the AIMES project we develop libraries and methods to utilize lossy compression. The SCIL library[2] provides a rich set of user quantities to define from, e.g., HDF5. Once set, the library shall ensure that the defined data quality meets all criteria. Its plugin architecture utilizes existing algorithms and aims to select the best algorithm depending on the user qualities and the data properties.

Contributions of this paper are: (1) Introduction of user defined quantities data precision and performance; (2) Description of two new lossy compression algorithms; (3) The analysis of lossy compression for climate data.

This paper is structured as follows: We give a review over related work in Sect. 2. The design is described in Sect. 3. An evaluation of the compression ratios is given in Sect. 4. Finally, in Sect. 5 a summary is provided.

2 Related Work

The related work can be structured into: (1) algorithms for the lossless data compression; (2) algorithms designed for scientific data and the HPC environment; (3) methods to identify necessary data precision and for large-scale evaluation.

Lossless algorithms: The LZ77 [3] algorithm is dictionary-based and uses a "sliding window". The concept behind this algorithm is simple: It scans uncompressed data for two largest windows containing the same data and replaces the second occurrence with a pointer to the first window. DEFLATE [4] is a variation of

[1] We define compression ratio as $r = \frac{\text{size compressed}}{\text{size original}}$; inverse is the compr. factor.

[2] The current version of the library is publicly available under LGPL license: https://github.com/JulianKunkel/scil.

LZ77 and uses Huffman coding [5]. GZIP [6] is a popular lossless algorithm based on DEFLATE.
Lossy algorithms for floating point data: FPZIP [7] was primarily designed for lossless compression of floating point data. It also supports lossy compression and allows the user to specify the bit precision. The error-bounded compression of ZFP [7] for up to 3 dimensional data is accurate within machine epsilon in lossless mode. The dimensionality is insufficient for the climate scientific data. SZ [8] is a newer and effective HPC data compression method. Its compression ratio is at least 2x better than the second-best solution of ZFP. In [1], compression results for the analysis of typical climate data was presented. Within that work, the lossless compression scheme MAFISC with preconditioners was introduced; its compression ratio was compared to that of standard compression tools reducing data 10% more than the second best algorithm. In [9], two lossy compression algorithms (GRIB2, APAX) were evaluated regarding to loss of data precision, compression ratio, and processing time on synthetic and climate dataset. These two algorithms have equivalent compression ratios and depending on the dataset APAX signal quality exceeds GRIB2 and vice versa.
Methods: Application of lossy techniques on scientific datasets was already discussed in [10–15]. The first efforts for determination of appropriate levels of precision for lossy compression method were presented in [16]. By doing statistics across ensembles of runs with full precision or compressed data, it could be determined if the scientific conclusions drawn from these ensembles are similar.

In [2], a statistical method is introduced to predict characteristics (such as proportions of file types and compression ratio) of stored data based on representative samples. It allows file types to be estimated and, e.g., compression ratio by scanning a fraction of the data, thus reducing costs. This method has recently been converted to a tool[3] that can be used to investigate large data sets.

3 Design

The main goals of the compression library SCIL is to provide a framework to compress structured and unstructured data using the best available (lossy) compression algorithms. SCIL offers a user interface for defining the tolerable loss of accuracy and expected performance as various quantities. It supports various data types. In Fig. 1, the data path is illustrated. An application can either use the NetCDF4, HDF5 or the SCIL C interface, directly. SCIL acts as a meta-compressor providing various backends such as the existing algorithms: LZ4, ZFP, FPZIP, and SZ. Based on the defined quantities, their values and the characteristics of the data to compress, the appropriate compression algorithm is chosen[4]. SCIL also comes with a pattern library to generate various relevant synthetic test patterns. Further tools are provided to plot, add noise or to compress CSV and NetCDF3 files. Internally, support functions simplify the development of new algorithms and the testing.

[3] https://github.com/JulianKunkel/statistical-file-scanner.

[4] The implementation for the automatic algorithm selection is ongoing effort and not the focus of this paper. SCIL will utilize a model for performance and compression ratio for the different algorithms, data properties and user settings.

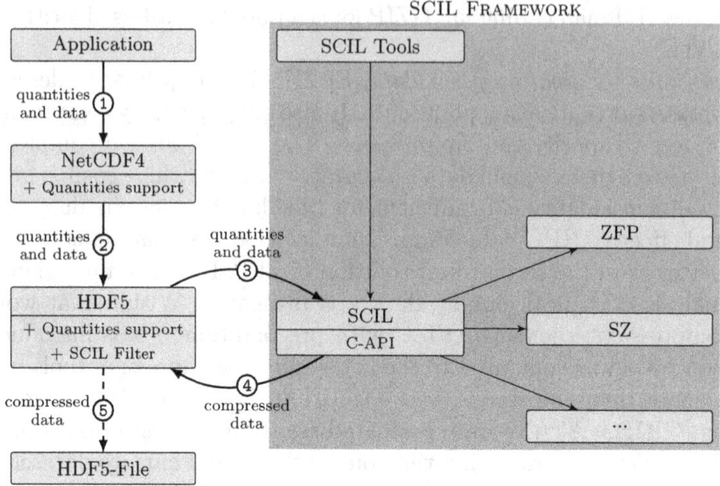

Fig. 1. SCIL compression path and components

3.1 Supported Quantities

The tolerable error on lossy compression and the expected performance behavior can be defined. Quantities define the properties of the residual error ($r = v - \hat{v}$):

- **absolute tolerance**: compressed value $\hat{v} = v \pm \text{abstol}$
- **relative tolerance**: $v/(1 + reltol) \leq \hat{v} \leq v \cdot (1 + reltol)$
- **relative error finest tolerance**: used together with rel tolerance; absolute tolerable error for small v's. If relfinest $> |v \cdot (1 \pm reltol)|$, then $\hat{v} = v \pm \text{relfinest}$
- **significant digits**: number of significant decimal digits
- **significant bits**: number of significant digits in bits

Additional, the performance behavior can be defined for both compression and decompression (on the same system). The value can be defined according to: (1) absolute throughput in MiB or GiB; or (2) relative to network or storage speed. Thus, SCIL must estimate the compression rates for the data. The system's performance must be trained for each system using machine learning.
An example for using the low-level C-API:

```
#include <scil.h>
int main(){
  double data[10][20]; // our raw data, we assume it contains sth. useful

  // define the quantities as hints, all specified conditions will hold
  scil_user_hints_t hints;
  hints.relative_tolerance_percent = 10;
  hints.absolute_tolerance = 0.5;
  hints.significant_digits = 2;
  // define permformance limit on decompression speed
  hints.decomp_speed.unit = SCIL_PERFORMANCE_GIB;
  hints.decomp_speed.multiplier = 3.5;
  // ... add more limitations if desired
  // create a compression context for a given datatype
```

```
  scil_context_t* ctx;
  scil_create_context(&ctx, SCIL_TYPE_DOUBLE, 0, NULL, &hints);

  // the multi-dimensional size of the data, here 10x20
  scil_dims_t dims;  scil_initialize_dims_2d(& dims, 10, 20);

  // the user is responsible to allocate memory for the output/tmp
      buffers
  size_t buffer_size = scil_get_compressed_data_size_limit(& dims,
      SCIL_TYPE_DOUBLE);
  byte * compressed_data = malloc(buffer_size);

  size c_size; // will hold the number of bytes of the compressed buffer
  scil_compress(compressed_data, buffer_size, data, &dims, &c_size, ctx);
  // now do something with the data in compressed_data
```

3.2 Algorithms

The development of the two algorithms sigbits and abstol has been guided by the definition of the user quantities. Both algorithms aim to pack the number of required bits as tightly as possible into the data buffer. We also consider these algorithms useful baselines when comparing any other algorithm.

Abstol. This algorithm guarantees the defined absolute tolerance. Pseudocode for the Abstol algorithm:

```
compress(data, abstol, outData){
  (min,max) = computeMinMax(data)
  // quantize the data converting it to integer, according to abstol
  tmp[i] = round((data[i] - min) * abstol)
  // compute numbers of mantissa bits needed to store the data
  bits = ceil(log2(1.0 + (max - min) / abstol))
  // now pack the neccessary bits from the integers tightly
  outData = packData(tmp, bits)
}
```

Sigbits. This algorithm preserves the user-defined number of precision bits from the floating point data. One precision bit means we preserve the floating point's exponent and sign bit as floating point implicitly adds one point of precision. All other precision bits are taken from the mantissa of the floating point data. Note that the sign bit must only be preserved, if it is not constant in the data. Pseudocode for the Sigbits algorithm:

```
compress(data, precisionBits, outData){
  // preserve the exponent always
  (sign, min, max) = computeExponentMinMax(data)
  // compute numbers of bits needed to preserve the data
  bits = sign + bits for the exponent + precisionBits - 1
  // convert preserved bits into an integer using bitshift operators
  tmp[i] = sign | exponent range used | precisison Bits
  // now pack the bits tightly
  outData = packData(tmp, bits)
}
```

3.3 Compression Chain

Internally, SCIL creates a process which can involve several compression algorithms. Algorithms may be preconditioners to optimize data layout for subsequent compression algorithms, converters from one data format to another, or, on the final stage, a lossless compressor. Floating point data can be first converted into integer data and then into a byte stream. Intermediate steps can be skipped. Based on the basic datatype that is supplied, the initial stage of the chain is entered. Figure 2 illustrates the chain.

3.4 Tools

SCIL comes with tools useful for evaluation and analysis: (1) To create well-defined multi-dimensional data patterns of any size; (2) To modify existing data adding a random noise based on the hint set; (3) To compress existing CSV and NetCDF data files.

4 Evaluation

In the evaluation, we utilize SCIL to compress the data with various algorithms. In all cases, we manually select the algorithm. The test system is an Intel i7-6700 CPU (Skylake) with 4 cores @ 3.40 GHz.

4.1 Test Data

A pool of (single precision floating point) data is created from several synthetic patterns generated by SCIL's pattern library such as constant, random, linear steps, polynomial, sinusoidal or by the OpenSimplex [17] algorithm. An example is given for the Simplex data in Fig. 3; original data and the compressed data for the Sigbits algorithm preserving 3 bits from the mantissa.

Additionally, utilize the output of the ECHAM atmospheric model [18] which stored 123 different scientific variables for a single timestep as NetCDF. This scientific data varies in terms of properties and in particular, the expected data locality. Synthetic data are kept in CSV-files.

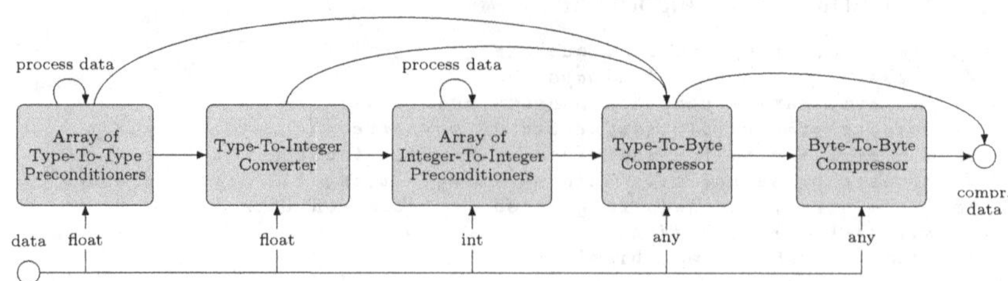

Fig. 2. SCIL compression chain. The choice of blocks and the resulting data path depend on input data.

4.2 Experiments

For each of the test files, the following setups are run[5]:

- Lossy compression preserving T significant bits
  - Tolerance: 3, 6, 9, 15, 20 bits
  - Algorithms: zfp, sigbits, sigbits+lz4[6]
- Lossy compression with a fixed absolute tolerance
  - Tolerance: 10%, 2%, 1%, 0.2%, 0.1% of the data maximum value[7]
  - Algorithms: zfp, sz, abstol, abstol+lz4

In each test, only one thread of the system is used for the compression/decompression. Each configuration is run 10 times measuring compression and decompression time and compression ratio.

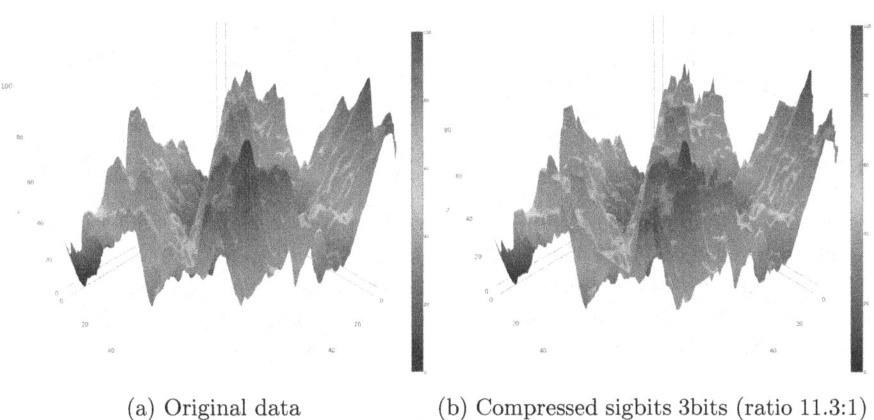

(a) Original data (b) Compressed sigbits 3bits (ratio 11.3:1)

Fig. 3. Example synthetic pattern: Simplex 206 in 2D

4.3 Compression Ratio Depending on Tolerance

Firstly, we investigate the compression factor depending on the tolerance level. The graphs in Fig. 4 show the mean compression factor for all scientific data files varying the precision for the algorithms ZFP, SZ, Sigbits and Abstol. The mean is computed on the pool of data, i.e., after compression, a factor of 50:1 means the compressed files occupy only 2% of the original size.

With 0.2% absolute tolerance, the compression ratio of abstol+lz4 is better than our target of 10:1; on average 3.2 bits are needed to store a single float. The SZ algorithm yields similar results than abstol+LZ4. The LZ4 stage boosts the factor for Abstol and Sigbits significantly.

[5] The versions used are SZ from Mar 5 2017 (git hash e1bf8b), zfp 0.5.0, LZ4 (May 1 2017, a8dd86).

[6] This applies first the Sigbits algorithm and then the lossless LZ4 compression.

[7] This is done to allow comparison across variables regardless of their min/max. In practice, a scientist would set the reltol or define the abstol depending on the variable.

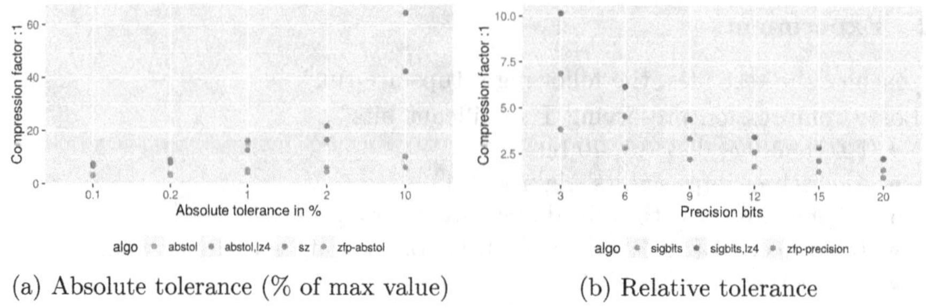

(a) Absolute tolerance (% of max value)

(b) Relative tolerance

Fig. 4. Mean harmonic compression factor based on user settings

For the precision bits, when preserving three mantissa bits, roughly 9:1 could be achieved with sigbits+LZ4. Note that in roughly half the cases, ZFP could not hold the required precision, as it defines the number of bits for the output and not in terms of guaranteed precision[8].

4.4 Fixed Absolute Tolerance

To analyze throughput and compression ratio across variables, we selected an absolute tolerance of 1% of the maximum value.

Mean values are shown in Table 1. Synthetic random patterns serve as baseline to understand the benefit of the lossy compression; we provide the means for 5 different random patterns. For abstol, a random pattern yields a ratio of 0.229 (factor of 4.4:1) and for climate data the ratio is slightly better. But when comparing SZ and Abstol+LZ4, we can observe a decrease of the compression ratio to 1/3rd of the random data. Compression speed is similar for random and climate data but decompression improves as there is less memory to read.

The results for the individual climate variables are shown in Fig. 5; the graph is sorted on compression ratio to ease identification of patterns. The x-axis represents the different data files, each point in the synthetic data represents one pattern of the given class created with different parameters. It can be observed that Abstol+LZ4 yields mostly the best compression ratio and the best compression and decompression speeds. For some variables, SZ compresses better, this is exactly the reason why SCIL should be able to automatically pick the best fitting algorithm below a common interface.

4.5 Fixed Precision Bits

Similarly to our previous experiment, we now aim to preserve 9 precision bits for the mantissa. The mean values are shown in Table 2. Figure 6 shows the ratio and performance across climate variables. The synthetic random patterns yield a compression factor of 2.6:1. It can be seen that Sigbits+LZ4 outperforms ZFP mostly, although ZFP does typically not hold the defined tolerance.

[8] Even when we added the number of bits necessary for encoding the mantissa to ZFP.

Table 1. Harmonic mean compressing with an absolute tolerance of 1% max

Algorithm	Ratio	Compr. MiB/s	Decomp. MiB/s
abstol	0.19	260	456
abstol,lz4	0.062	196	400
sz	0.078	81	169
zfp-abstol	0.239	185	301

(a) For ECHAM data files

Algorithm	Ratio	Compr. MiB/s	Decomp. MiB/s
abstol	0.194	265	482
abstol,lz4	0.151	226	456
sz	0.165	74	147
zfp-abstol	0.295	161	266

(b) For 5 different random patterns

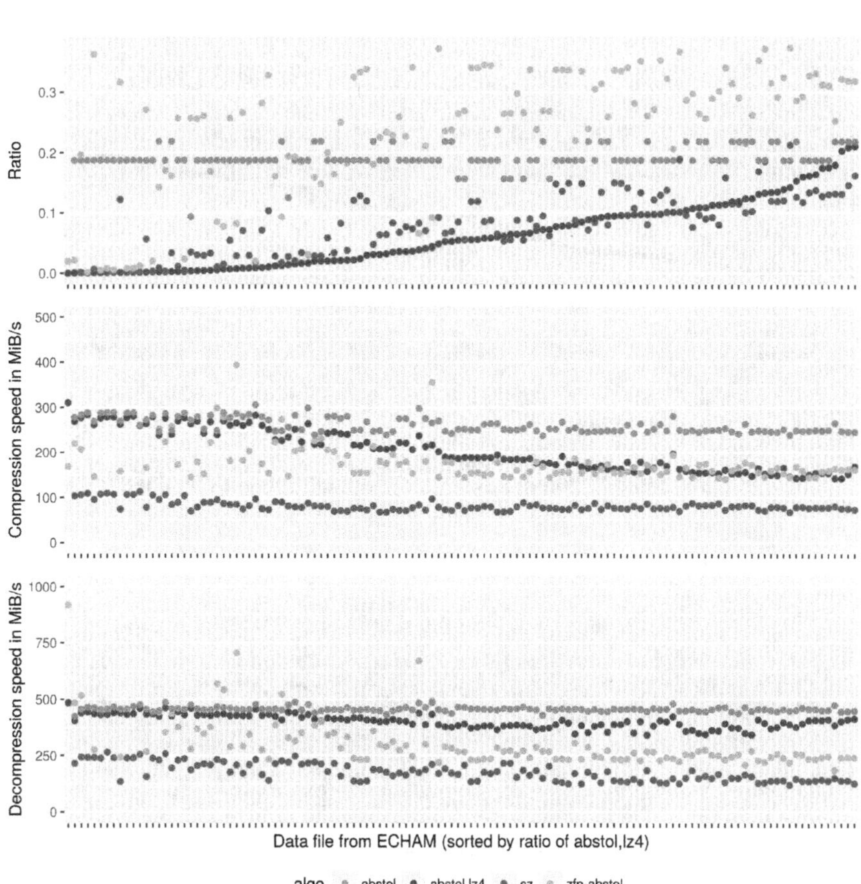

Fig. 5. Compressing various climate data variables with abstol of 1% max

Table 2. Harmonic mean compressing with 9 precision bits

Algorithm	Ratio	Compr. MiB/s	Decomp. MiB/s
sigbits	0.448	462	615
sigbits,lz4	0.228	227	479
zfp-precision	0.299	155	252

(a) For ECHAM data files

Algorithm	Ratio	Compr. MiB/s	Decomp. MiB/s
sigbits	0.369	528	672
sigbits,lz4	0.304	466	599
zfp-precision	0.232	175	314

(b) For 5 different random patterns

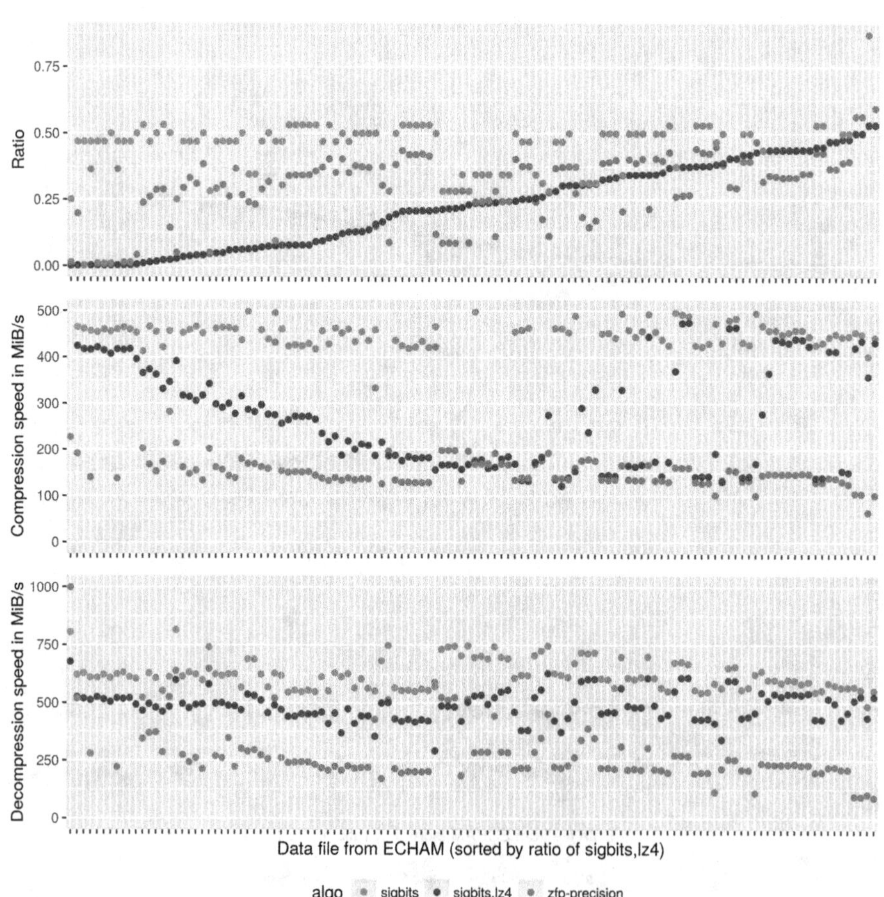

Fig. 6. Compressing various climate data variables with 9 Bits precision

5 Summary

This paper introduces the concepts for the scientific compression library (SCIL) and compares novel algorithms implemented with the state-of-the-art compressors. It shows that these algorithms can compete with ZFP/SZ when setting the absolute tolerance or precision bits. In cases with steady data, SZ compresses better than abstol. Since SCIL aims to choose the best algorithm, it ultimately should be able to take benefit of both algorithms. Ongoing work is the development of a single algorithm honoring all quantities and the automatic chooser for the best algorithm.

Acknowledgements. This work was supported in part by the German Research Foundation (DFG) through the Priority Programme 1648 "Software for Exascale Computing" (SPPEXA) (GZ: LU 1353/11-1).

References

1. Hubbe, N., Kunkel, J.: Reducing the HPC-Datastorage Footprint with MAFISC - Multidimensional Adaptive Filtering Improved Scientific data Compression. Computer Science - Research and Development, pp. 231–239 (2013)
2. Kunkel, J.: Analyzing Data Properties using Statistical Sampling Techniques - Illustrated on Scientific File Formats and Compression Features. In Taufer, M., Mohr, B., Kunkel, J., eds.: High Performance Computing: ISC High Performance 2016 International Workshops, ExaComm, E-MuCoCoS, HPC-IODC, IXPUG, IWOPH, P3MA, VHPC, WOPSSS, 130–141. Number 9945 2016 in Lecture Notes in Computer Science. Springer, Heidelberg (2016)
3. LZ77. https://cs.stanford.edu/people/eroberts/courses/soco/projects/data-compression/lossless/lz77/example.htm. Accessed 04 Oct 2016
4. DEFLATE algorithm. https://en.wikipedia.org/wiki/DEFLATE. Accessed 04 Oct 2016
5. Huffman coding. A Method for the Construction of Minimum-Redundancy Codes. Accessed 04 Oct 2016
6. GZIP algorithm. http://www.gzip.org/algorithm.txt. Accessed 04 Oct 2016
7. Lindstrom, P., Isenburg, M.: Fast and efficient compression of floating-point data. IEEE Trans. Visual Comput. Graphics **12**(5), 1245–1250 (2006)
8. Di, S., Cappello, F.: Fast error-bounded lossy HPC data compression with SZ (2015)
9. Hübbe, N., Wegener, A., Kunkel, J.M., Ling, Y., Ludwig, T.: Evaluating lossy compression on climate data. In: Kunkel, J.M., Ludwig, T., Meuer, H.W. (eds.) ISC 2013. LNCS, vol. 7905, pp. 343–356. Springer, Heidelberg (2013). doi:10.1007/978-3-642-38750-0_26
10. Bicer, T., Agrawal, G.: A compression framework for multidimensional scientific datasets. In: 2013 IEEE 27th International Parallel and Distributed Processing Symposium Workshops and PhD Forum (IPDPSW), pp. 2250–2253 (2013)
11. Laney, D., Langer, S., Weber, C., Lindstrom, P., Wegener, A.: Assessing the effects of data compression in simulations using physically motivated metrics. Super Computing (2013)

12. Lakshminarasimhan, S., Shah, N., Ethier, S., Klasky, S., Latham, R., Ross, R., Samatova, N.F.: Compressing the incompressible with isabela: in-situ reduction of spatio-temporal data. In: Jeannot, E., Namyst, R., Roman, J. (eds.) Euro-Par 2011. LNCS, vol. 6852, pp. 366–379. Springer, Heidelberg (2011). doi:10.1007/978-3-642-23400-2_34
13. Iverson, J., Kamath, C., Karypis, G.: Fast and effective lossy compression algorithms for scientific datasets. In: Kaklamanis, C., Papatheodorou, T., Spirakis, P.G. (eds.) Euro-Par 2012. LNCS, vol. 7484, pp. 843–856. Springer, Heidelberg (2012). doi:10.1007/978-3-642-32820-6_83
14. Gomez, L.A.B., Cappello, F.: Improving floating point compression through binary masks. In: 2013 IEEE International Conference on Big Data (2013)
15. Lindstrom, P.: Fixed-Rate Compressed Floating-Point Arrays. IEEE Trans. Visualization Comput Graphics 2012 (2014)
16. Baker, A.H., et al.: Evaluating lossy data compression on climate simulation data within a large ensemble. Geosci. Model Dev. **9**, 4381–4403 (2016)
17. OpenSimplex Noise in Java. https://gist.github.com/KdotJPG/b1270127455a94ac5d19. Accessed 05 Feb 2017
18. Roeckner, E., Bäuml, G., Bonaventura, L., Brokopf, R., Esch, M., Giorgetta, M., Hagemann, S., Kirchner, I., Kornblueh, L., Manzini, E., et al.: The Atmospheric General Circulation Model ECHAM 5. Model description, PART I (2003)

On the Scalability of Data Reduction Techniques in Current and Upcoming HPC Systems from an Application Perspective

Axel Huebl[1,2(✉)], René Widera[1], Felix Schmitt[2,3], Alexander Matthes[1,2], Norbert Podhorszki[4], Jong Youl Choi[4], Scott Klasky[4], and Michael Bussmann[1(✉)]

[1] Helmholtz-Zentrum Dresden – Rossendorf, Dresden, Germany
{a.huebl,m.bussmann}@hzdr.de
[2] Technische Universität Dresden, Dresden, Germany
[3] NVIDIA ARC GmbH, Berlin, Germany
[4] Oak Ridge National Laboratory, Oak Ridge, TN, USA

Abstract. We implement and benchmark parallel I/O methods for the fully-manycore driven particle-in-cell code PIConGPU. Identifying throughput and overall I/O size as a major challenge for applications on today's and future HPC systems, we present a scaling law characterizing performance bottlenecks in state-of-the-art approaches for data reduction. Consequently, we propose, implement and verify multi-threaded data-transformations for the I/O library ADIOS as a feasible way to trade underutilized host-side compute potential on heterogeneous systems for reduced I/O latency.

1 Introduction

Production-scale research simulation codes have been optimized in the last years to achieve maximum compute performance on leadership, heterogeneous computing systems such as the Titan supercomputer at Oak Ridge National Laboratory (ORNL). With close to perfect weak scaling domain scientists can increase spatial and temporal resolution of their simulation and explore systems without reducing dimensionality or feature resolution.

We present the consequences of near-perfect weak-scaling of such a code in terms of I/O demands from an application perspective based on production runs using the particle-in-cell (PIC) code PIConGPU [8,17]. PIConGPU demonstrates a typical use case in which a PFlops/s-scale, performance portable simulation [29,30] leads automatically to PByte-scale output even for single runs.

This project has received funding from the European Unions Horizon 2020 research and innovation programme under grant agreement No. 654220. An award of computer time was provided by the Innovative and Novel Computational Impact on Theory and Experiment (INCITE) program. This research used resources of the Oak Ridge Leadership Computing Facility at the Oak Ridge National Laboratory, which is supported by the Office of Science of the U.S. Department of Energy under Contract No. DE-AC05-00OR22725.

J.M. Kunkel et al. (Eds.): ISC High Performance Workshops 2017, LNCS 10524, pp. 15–29, 2017.
https://doi.org/10.1007/978-3-319-67630-2_2

1.1 PIConGPU

PIConGPU is an electro-magnetic PIC code [5,14] implemented via abstract, performance portable C++11 kernels on manycore hardware utilizing the Alpaka library [29,30]. Its applications span from general plasma physics, over laser-matter interaction to laser-plasma based particle accelerator research.

Since its initial open-source release in 2013 with CUDA support, PIConGPU is reportedly the fastest particle-in-cell code in the world in terms of sustained peak Flops/s [8]. We achieved this by not only porting the bottlenecks of the PIC algorithm to new compute hardware but the complete code, thus minimizing data transfer. PIConGPU data structures are tiled and swapping of frequently updated data residing on device memory over low-bandwidth bottlenecks such as the PCI bus is avoided [6].

The overall simulation is spatially domain decomposed and only nearby border areas need to be communicated across compute nodes (and accelerators) inbetween iterations. Iterations in PIConGPU are performed with a frequency of about 10 Hz on current accelerator architectures (GPUs) when simulating 3D spatial domains and up to 60 Hz for two-dimensional domains. Each iteration updates electro-magnetic fields and plasma particles, which together constitute the simulation's state.

1.2 Physical Observables

We will define primary observables as variables directly accessible and iterated within the simulation. In terms of an electro-magnetic PIC code these are electric field, magnetic field and plasma particles' properties such as position, momentum, charge to mass ratio and weighting. Primary observables are convenient for the domain expert for exploration, of limited use for theories and models and nearly always inaccessible directly in experiments.

We define secondary observables as computable on-the-fly, PIC examples being the electric current density, position-filtered energy histograms or projected phase space distributions. In practice, analysis of a specific setup needs multiple additional, study-specific derivations from already derived observables which we summarize as tertiary observables. Examples in the domain of plasma physics are integrals over phase-space trajectories, time-averaged fields, sample trajectories or particle distributions in gradients of fields, flux over time, growth-rates, etc. Usually, observables accessible by experiments fall in this last category and can be compared to theoretical model predictions.

1.3 Two Example Workflows to Explore Complex Systems

In daily modeling work we usually iterate between two operational modes while investigating a new physical system. We start with an exploratory phase guided by initial hypotheses, looking at primary observables via visualizations or utilizing existing analysis pipelines to iterate over the result of strongly reduced secondary and tertiary observables. During this phase, we develop new study-specific analysis steps and working hypotheses.

The second phase continues with a high-resolution, high-throughput scan of an identified regime of the physical system to prove or falsify our working hypotheses. Due to higher resolution and full physical modeling, new observations will emerge from that step. Research is then about iterating both steps in a refined manner until a system is well understood and a model is found to describe the complex processes of interest.

1.4 Structure of This Paper

As our guiding example, we describe the Titan and Summit systems at ORNL and their I/O bandwidth hierarchies from the special perspective of a fully GPU-driven, massively parallel PIC code. We then evaluate the performance of PIConGPU's I/O implementation, the overhead it introduces and mitigation strategies via on-the-fly data reductions. We address issues in current state-of-the-art compression schemes for our application and compare them to self-implemented compression schemes that make optimal use of underutilized hardware components. More specifically, we integrated the meta compression library blosc [2] into ADIOS, thereby for the first time enabling multi-threaded compression within ADIOS.

2 ORNL Titan and Summit Systems

With the launch of the Titan supercomputer to the public in 2013, manycore powered supercomputing finally became accessible on large-scale installations. Since then, the share of accelerator hardware in the TOP 100 systems has risen to one third [24]. Such heterogeneous systems concentrate their compute performance in the accelerator component, usually outnumbering the host system's compute potential by an order of magnitude, a trend that seems to continue on upcoming systems such as Summit.

2.1 I/O Limitations in State-of-the-Art Systems

The parallel file system Atlas at ORNL, partitioned in two islands of 14 PBytes each, provides an overall design parallel bandwidth of $B_{\text{parallel}} = 1$ TByte/s. It is worth noting that *if* a hypothetical application would be constantly writing at this maximum parallel bandwidth, Atlas would run out of disk memory in less than 9 hour. We managed to write within each 8 hour production run of our plasma simulation code PIConGPU about 1 PByte of (zlib) compressed data, sampling the full system state every 2000 iteration steps. PIConGPU thus presents a realistic use case that can consume a significant fraction of those resources. With the upper limit of shared storage in mind, it is clear that data reduction comes with great value. Additionally, fast migration to and from tape storage and a strictly imposed short data lifetime on Atlas also encourage users to avoid occupying disk memory for too long.

An equally severe limitation for I/O besides maximum data size is the overall time $t_{\mathrm{I/O}}$ for file I/O compared to one iteration of the simulation, including data preparation time t_{prep}. Compared to the time $t_{\mathrm{without\,I/O}}$ one iteration takes without I/O this $t_{\mathrm{I/O}}$ introduces an overhead to the application run time, so that the single iteration runtime with I/O becomes $t_{\mathrm{with\,I/O}} = t_{\mathrm{without\,IO}} + t_{\mathrm{I/O}}$. When considering applications scaling to the full Titan system, reaching TByte/s overall throughput results in a maximum node-average throughput of 55 MByte/s. Applications with near perfect scaling can generate GPU data at two-digit Hz levels amounting to data rates as high as 10×6 GiByte/s (device global memory) on a node-local level, outnumbering the file system performance by three orders of magnitude. Asynchronous I/O lowers this dramatic gap temporarily, but still throttles the application at least to 1/10th of the bandwidth of the CPU-GPU interconnect, not accounting for data reorganization from tiled GPU memory to per-node contiguous memory as expected by parallel I/O APIs.

2.2 Staging, Burst Buffers and I/O Backlog

Even at moderate data rates, asynchronous writing can quickly overlap with the next consecutive write period. Staging [1,10], if operating off-node, can reduce that data pressure but is similarly limited by another order of magnitude gap in throughput as soon as the interconnect is accessed.

Systems such as NERSC's Cori recently introduced so-called burst-buffers [4]. Located either off-node similar to I/O nodes or in-node as with the upcoming Summit system, overall size of those burst buffers is usually similar to that of the global host RAM with access bandwidth ranging between network-interconnect and parallel filesystem bandwidth.

Burst buffers provide an interesting mean for temporary checkpointing and error-recovery. Coupled applications that only act as either a data sink or a source for the main application are also major beneficiaries of burst buffers. A prominent example in HPC are in situ visualizations copying on demand snapshots [3,28] or accessing the primary observables directly [21,23,25].

Nevertheless, with the current absolute sizes of burst-buffers it is close to impossible to keep data between application lifetime and parallel filesystem data lifetime, simply because they cannot store a useful multiple of primary observables. As soon as a single stage in the I/O hierarchy is not drained as fast as it is filled, a backlog throughout all previous stages is inevitable even when buffers are used.

3 I/O Measurements

PIConGPU implements I/O for outputs and checkpoints within its plugin system. Plugins are tightly coupled algorithms that can register within the main application for execution after selected iterations. They share full access to primary observables (read and write) of the application.

I/O modules implemented are parallel HDF5 [27] and ADIOS (1.10.0) [20]. In order to tailor domain-specific needs for particle-mesh algorithms, libSplash is used as an abstraction layer [16]. Data objects are described by the meta-data standard openPMD [15] in human- and machine-readable markup, allowing for cross-application exchangeability as needed in post- and pre-processing workflows.

3.1 Preparation of PIConGPU Primary Observables for I/O

In preparation of GPU device data for I/O libraries, PIConGPU field data are copied from device to host via CUDA 3D memory copies while plasma particle attributes stored in tiled data structures are copied via the mallocMC [11] heap manager. Subsequently, scalar particle attributes are concatenated in preparation for efficient parallel I/O in a parallelized manner using OpenMP. The single GPU data size needed for saving a complete system state is typically $S = 4$ GiByte (assuming $^2/_{3^{\text{rd}}}$ of device global memory for primary observables). The overall time for preparing these 4 GiByte of data for one GPU is typically $t_{\text{prep}} = 1$ s on the systems considered in this publication.

3.2 I/O Performance in a Realistic Production Scenario

Measurements of the I/O performance are based on one of the default benchmarks implemented in PIConGPU, a simulation of the relativistic Kelvin-Helmholtz Instability [8,12]. Starting from two spatially homogeneous, counterpropagating neutral plasma streams, a shear flow instability develops. This scenario shows good load-balancing due to nearly homogeneous data distribution across all GPUs with data size per output and GPU of $S = 4$ GiByte. We thus assume in our following analysis for sake of simplicity that indeed each node has the same output size, the same bandwidth and I/O operations have the same impact on all N nodes of a system.

Our benchmark systems are Titan (ORNL) and the K20 queue of Hypnos (HZDR), see Table 1. We choose the second system intentionally, since it has roughly the same age, similar ratio of Flops/s between CPU host an GPU device, multiple GPUs per node as in upcoming systems, even less CPU cores per GPU and an even higher single node average filesystem bandwidth compared to Titan. All measurement input and results of the following sections are available in the supplementary materials [18] and all software used is open source.

Most relevant from an application point of view is the absolute overhead $t_{\text{I/O}}$ in seconds caused by enabling I/O since it equals 'wasted' computing time that could be otherwise spent to iterate the problem further or in higher resolution. We define the effective parallel I/O throughput T_{eff} in GiByte/s as

$$T_{\text{eff}} \equiv N \times \frac{S}{t_{\text{with I/O}} - t_{\text{without I/O}}} = \frac{N \times S}{t_{\text{I/O}}} \tag{1}$$

Table 1. PIConGPU I/O benchmark systems, both commissioned in 2012/13: relevant system characteristics and single node average filesystem throughput T_{FS}, defined as the design parallel bandwidth $B_{parallel}$ divided by N nodes

	Titan	Hypnos (queue: 'k20')
GPUs/node	1× K20x	4× K20m
CPUs/node	1× AMD Opteron 6274	2× Intel Xeon E5-2609
CPU-cores/GPU	16 (8 FP)	2
GPU/CPU Flop/s (DP)	9.3 : 1	7.6 : 1
File system	Spider/Lustre	GPFS
$B_{parallel} = T_{FS} * N$ [GiByte/s]	1000	20
T_{FS} [GiByte/s]	0.055	1.25
CPU T_{memcpy} [GiByte/s]	6.0	6.1
Maximum number of nodes N_{max}	18000	16

with the number of nodes N, the data size per node S and the difference between execution time with I/O $t_{\text{with I/O}}$ and without I/O $t_{\text{without I/O}}$ as $t_{I/O}$. Besides the (included) correction for intrinsic overheads in scaling the application, all measurements are performed as a weak scaling of PIConGPU, which is near-perfect up to the full size of Titan [8]. We average over 11 outputs within 2000 iterations with an average application iteration frequency of one Hertz.

In the following we model the I/O time per node by

$$t_{I/O}^{\text{simple}} \equiv t_{\text{prep}} + t_{\text{off RAM}} = t_{\text{prep}} + \frac{S}{T_{FS}} \tag{2}$$

defining t_{prep} as the time to concatenate data into large, I/O-API compatible chunks and $t_{\text{off RAM}} \equiv S/T_{FS}$ as the time to synchronously send the data off RAM. This preparation time can potentially be lowered by reorganizing data on the accelerator, where RAM is usually in full utilization from the application alone, while asynchronous (non-blocking) writes that hide data transfer latency require large enough temporary buffers to avoid backlog (see discussion in Sect. 2.2) and I/O library support. It is thus S/T_{FS} that will dominate overhead compared to iterations without I/O.

Figure 1 shows the achieved effective parallel I/O throughput T_{eff} on Titan. We noticed HDF5 I/O overhead getting prohibitively large for production runs as its parallelism is currently limited by the number of allocatable Lustre OSTs ($\leq$160) on which one global file needs to be strided over. After optimizing HDF5 performance with MPI-I/O and HDF5 hints, first manually via best-practices and later using T3PIO [22], we turned down the strategy of parallel output in one global file (June 2014) and started adopting ADIOS aggregators, which enable transparently striding on subgroups of processes over a limited number of OSTs

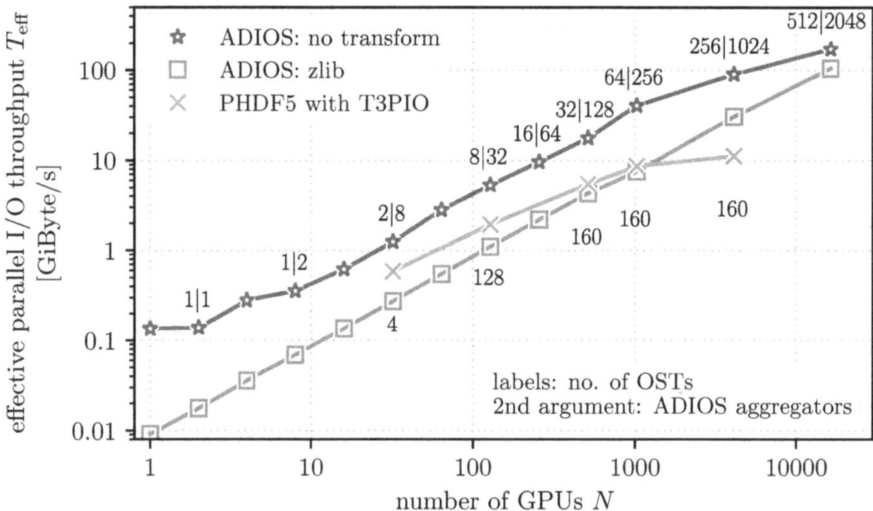

Fig. 1. PIConGPU I/O weak scaling on Titan from 1 to 16384 K20x GPUs (nodes). Zlib was only supported serially with compression mode fast. MPI_Info hints for parallel HDF5 set via T3PIO (v2.3). For ADIOS, labels denote number of *OSTs|aggregators*, resulting for $N \geq 32$ in a striping of each aggregated process group over four OSTs. Lustre filesystem limits enforced 160 OSTs for (single-file) parallel HDF5 writes.

(latest benchmark: September 2015). When using ADIOS in this manner, we were able to reach an overall application throughput close to 280 GByte/s, see Fig. 2. We are not aware of substantial changes in the Atlas filesystem during this period of time, expecting both benchmarks to be comparable.

It is important to note that measuring the I/O throughput indirectly via introduced overhead masquerades the actual filesystem bandwidth B_{FS} which is always higher than the previously defined effective parallel throughput T_{eff} for raw, untransformed data as seen by the application. This is very important to keep in mind as the effective parallel throughput determines the application performance in most realistic scenarios.

As mentioned in Sect. 2.1, absolute I/O size during production runs quickly becomes a show-stopper. Compressing data streams on the fly seems to suggest itself as data reduction technique, either lossless or lossy, depending on application needs. In ADIOS, compression schemes are implemented transparently for the user as so-called data transforms. One would not only expect a reduction in data size but also an increase in effective bandwidth since the size of the compressed data S_{C} written to the filesystem is lowered by a compression ratio $f_{\text{C}} \equiv {}^{S_{\text{C}}}/_{S} \leq 1$ compared to the initial size S. We observed that this expectation could not be fulfilled using even the fastest compression algorithm implemented at the time in ADIOS, zlib, see Fig. 1.

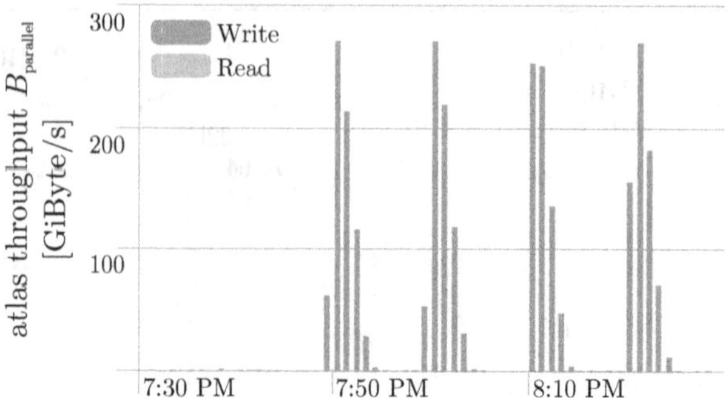

Fig. 2. Actual filesystem throughput as seen by Atlas 2 (ORNL) during run no. 2489794 (Sep 23rd, 2015) on 16384 nodes according to user support (data: DDNTool, Splunk).

We therefore expanded our model to account for the time $t_{\text{reduce}} \equiv S/\mathcal{T}_{\text{C}}$ it takes to reduce the data by compression or other means and copy it from an application-side buffer to an I/O library buffer. Up to now, data transforms in ADIOS are performed before starting to send the data off-node, while parallel HDF5 does not yet support data compression[1]. In order to account for data reduction, Eq. (2) needs to be extended to add synchronous reduction overhead by

$$\begin{aligned} t_{\text{I/O}}^{\text{reduce}}(t_{\text{reduce}}) &\equiv t_{\text{prep}} + t_{\text{reduce}} + f_{\text{C}} \times t_{\text{off RAM}} \\ &= t_{\text{prep}} + \frac{S}{\mathcal{T}_{\text{C}}} + \frac{f_{\text{C}} \times S}{\mathcal{T}_{\text{FS}}} \\ &= t_{\text{prep}} + \frac{S}{\mathcal{T}_{\text{C}} \times T_{\text{memcpy}}} + \frac{f_{\text{C}} \times S}{\mathcal{T}_{\text{FS}} \times T_{\text{memcpy}}} \\ f_{\text{C}} \equiv \frac{S_{\text{C}}}{S} \quad \mathcal{T}_{\text{C}} &\equiv \frac{T_{\text{C}}}{T_{\text{memcpy}}} \quad \mathcal{T}_{\text{FS}} \equiv \frac{T_{\text{FS}}}{T_{\text{memcpy}}}. \end{aligned} \tag{3}$$

$\mathcal{T}_{\text{C}}$ and $\mathcal{T}_{\text{FS}}$ characterize throughput for compression and filesystem writes, respectively, normalized to in-node memory copy throughput T_{memcpy}. We acknowledge that $t_{\text{reduce}} + f_{\text{C}} \times t_{\text{off RAM}}$ could in principle be lowered by copying the data to an I/O stage immediately and performing compression there, again within the limits of the discussion in Sect. 2.2.

Consequently, for a given normalized per-node filesystem throughput $\mathcal{T}_{\text{FS}}$ any data reduction algorithm C needs to fulfill the relation

$$\frac{\mathcal{T}_{\text{C}} \times (1 - f_{\text{C}})}{1 - \mathcal{T}_{\text{C}}} > \mathcal{T}_{\text{FS}} \tag{4}$$

in order to not only reduce data size by f_{C} but also perceived write time. This inequality arises from Eq. (3) assuming a reduce operation that is as fast as

[1] An experimental development preview with compression support in parallel HDF5 was announced after our measurements in February 2017.

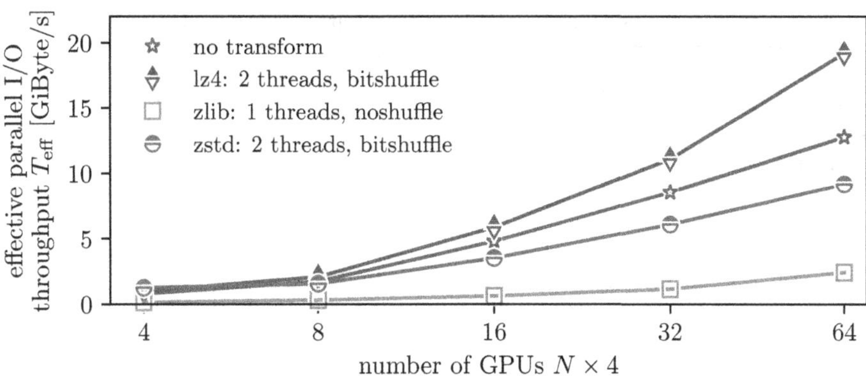

Fig. 3. Weak scaling of PIConGPU with implemented I/O methods on Hypnos from 4 to 64 K20m GPUs (16 nodes). In contrast to Titan and Summit nodes, on Hypnos only two physical CPU cores are available per GPU, resulting in I/O performance with zlib and zstd [9] below the untransformed output.

possible by setting the second term of the sum $t_{\text{reduce}} \equiv t_{\text{memcpy}}$ and thus comparing $t_{\text{I/O}}^{\text{reduce}}(t_{\text{reduce}}) < t_{\text{I/O}}^{\text{reduce}}(t_{\text{memcpy}})$. The left-hand side of Eq. (4), which we call the *break-even threshold* for a given data transform algorithm and single (parallel) I/O stage, is discussed in greater detail in the following section.

In order to confirm this observation, we measured I/O performance on the K20 queue of the HZDR compute cluster Hypnos, see Fig. 3 (data points 'no transform' and 'zlib'). Following Eq. (4) it should be even harder for a compression algorithm, lossless or lossy, to fulfill the requirements for break-even on Hypnos. Therefore, an improvement in the latter case will be automatically favorable for Titan or a Summit-like system.

3.3 Measurement of Compression Performance

In the interest of exploring feasible compression methods for PIConGPU data, we performed ex situ benchmarks on generated data. Visualized in Fig. 4, such a measurement directly allows a prediction for individual systems and user data when comparing to our model, Eq. 4.

PIConGPU currently only utilizes one host thread per GPU, so we decided to implement and explore compression throughput for blosc as an example for a multi-threaded algorithm and compare it to other, previously implemented compression algorithms. Blosc provides several bitshuffle pre-conditioners, which we found of great importance for floating-point compression performance in agreement with recent studies [7]. Further benchmarks with four threads on Hypnos' K20 queue, limited to two host threads per GPU without oversubscription, indicated that on Hypnos application throughput would benefit from more physical CPU cores per GPU since the recent filesytem upgrade to GPFS.

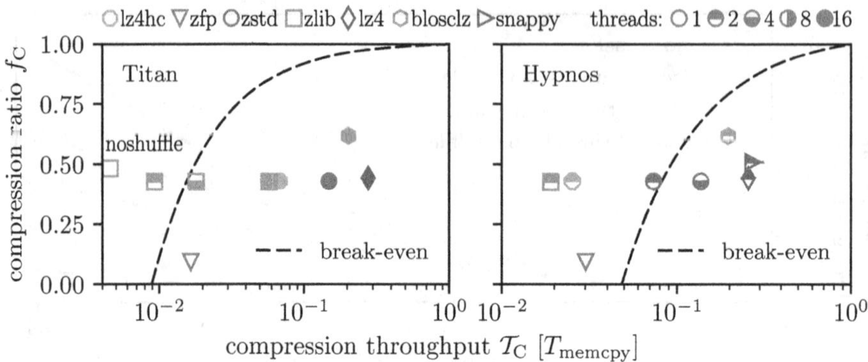

Fig. 4. Compression throughput $\mathcal{T}_C$ and ratio f_C measured on PIConGPU particle data (32 Bit floating point and integers). Lower f_C and higher $\mathcal{T}_C$ is better. All operations performed on contiguous, aligned, none-page-locked memory. The blosc [2] compression level is 1 (fast). From available pre-conditioners (none, shuffle, bitshuffle), the latter is shown due to the observed positive influence on f_C with small impact on $\mathcal{T}_C$ for floating point data which otherwise could not be compressed with LZ4 (v1.7.5) and snappy [13]. Zfp (v0.5.1) was used in fixed-precision mode with three uncompressed bits per scalar [19].

4 Analysis

Fully accelerator driven applications can use 'the last 10% of system performance' on the host side in order to trade compute performance for I/O latency. The Titan system provides up to 16 physical CPU cores per GPU and Summit is expected to allow for an order of magnitude higher parallelization on the host. This section explores the limits to data reduction methods in terms of data reduction ratio and throughput for an individual I/O stage independently of the method of data reduction and only exemplified for compression methods.

4.1 Overhead of Compression in Parallel I/O

From Eq. (3) the relative I/O performance ratio Γ when using data reduction instead of direct pass-through in an I/O stage follows as:

$$\Gamma \equiv \frac{t_{\text{I/O}}^{\text{reduce}}(t_{\text{reduce}})}{t_{\text{I/O}}^{\text{reduce}}(t_{\text{memcpy}})} = \frac{C_{\text{prep}} + \frac{f_C}{\mathcal{T}_{\text{FS}}} + \mathcal{T}_C^{-1}}{C_{\text{prep}} + \mathcal{T}_{\text{FS}}^{-1} + 1} \tag{5}$$

$$C_{\text{prep}} \equiv \frac{t_{\text{prep}}}{S} \times \mathcal{T}_{\text{memcpy}}$$

where we assume that the time for reducing the data $t_{\text{reduce}} \geq t_{\text{memcpy}}$ at minimum is as long as for copying data from node RAM to I/O buffer. It is clear that in terms of I/O throughput reduction algorithms are beneficial if $\Gamma < 1$ compared to I/O without reduction. Cases of $\Gamma \geq 1$ and $f_C < 1$ can still be

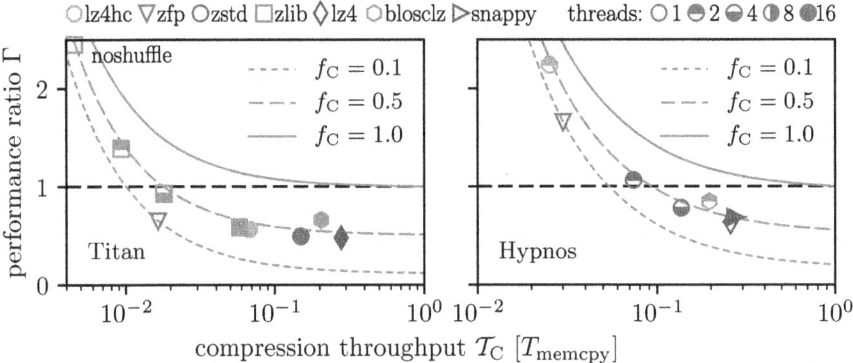

Fig. 5. Visualization of Eq. (5) predicting the relative I/O overhead $\Gamma > 1$ (gain $\Gamma \leq 1$) of compression during parallel I/O. The break-even threshold discriminates between feasible and overhead-adding compression algorithms at $\Gamma = 1$ (dashed line). Lower Γ and higher $\mathcal{T}_C$ is better. Iso-compression lines for user data are plotted for individual systems (see Table 1) and compared to measured ex situ compression performance on PIConGPU user data (see Fig. 4).

relevant in case of limited disk space. Note, that decreasing C_{prep} would increase the gradient of Γ, but not affect the position $\mathcal{T}_C$ for which we expect break-even.

Figure 5 shows the effect of threaded compression, keeping the compression ratio along iso-compression lines. Following the graph to the right, the higher the throughput of a compression algorithm the less importance it has on Γ compared to the compression ratio f_C. Thus, an important limit to Γ is the high-throughput limit $\mathcal{T}_C \rightarrow 1$ for fast compression algorithms below the break-even threshold. For such, the performance ratio over non-compressed I/O can barely be improved further via throughput but solely by compression ratio.

Exactly the opposite is true for any reduction algorithm with low throughput $\mathcal{T}_C$, to the left of the graph. Above the break-even threshold (dashed line at $\Gamma = 1$), data reduction quickly becomes impractical for medium to high-throughput tasks for a specific system, as the relatively wasted computing time never reaches $\Gamma \leq 1$ even for small f_C.

Following the last argument one can further derive from Eq. (4) with ‘perfect reduction’ $f_C \rightarrow 0$: For *any* given I/O stage with write and reduction throughput $\mathcal{T}_{FS}, \mathcal{T}_C$ the effective time an application spends in (synchronous) I/O can only be reduced, if the data reduction operation provides at least a throughput of

$$\frac{\mathcal{T}_C}{1 - \mathcal{T}_C} > \mathcal{T}_{FS}. \tag{6}$$

5 Summary and Outlook

We implemented and benchmarked parallel I/O methods on top of state-of-the-art I/O libraries for the massively parallel, fully-manycore driven, open source

PIC code PIConGPU. We outlined performance bottlenecks for medium to high-throughput applications in general and the possibility to overcome these with general data reduction techniques such as compression. We then derived and verified a scaling law that gives limits to expected application speed up when using data reduction schemes for medium- to high-throughput applications. With this we were able to derive a system- and application-specific break-even threshold that allows for predicting when reducing data is benefitial in terms of I/O throughput compared to I/O without reduction.

5.1 Compression Algorithms

For the special case of compression algorithms, future designs to soften I/O bottlenecks first and foremost need to improve throughput for floating point data. Even for a relatively large gap between local memory and filesystem throughput as on the current Titan system, many single-threaded compression algorithms that are still in use today do not fulfill the break-even threshold in Eq. (4).

Existing high-throughput compression algorithms would benefit from research improving the compression ratio f_C instead of throughput $\mathcal{T}_C$ [7,26]. This case is of importance since, due to high entropy in HPC applications' primary observables (e.g. floating point), only lossy compression algorithms are likely to bridge the upcoming throughput gaps between node-local high-bandwidth memory and storage accessible longer than application lifetime.

For ADIOS we proposed, implemented and benchmarked for the first time host-side multi-threaded transform methods as a feasible step to reach the break-even threshold. With that, we successfully traded unused compute performance within a heterogeneous application for overall I/O performance.

5.2 I/O Libraries

Burst-buffers are identified as enablers to reduce blocking time of the application caused by synchronous transformations within I/O libraries, but are vulnerable to backlog. Nonetheless, burst-buffers alone cannot cover the gap that will arise between expected I/O on system today and in the future. Further applications of burst-buffers are coupled multi-scale simulations, in situ processing and checkpointing and not in the scope of this paper.

Nevertheless, for both explorative-qualitative and medium- to high-throughput quantitative studies I/O libraries need to act now to provide transparent and easily programmable means for multi-stage I/O. For any practical application, the first I/O stage should immediately start with a maximum-throughput memcopy from user RAM to I/O buffer, ideally asynchronously, while later stages need to follow fully asynchronously. Copied memory (in unutilized RAM or burst-buffers) will need several off-node user-programmable transformations which are finally staged transparently through a subsequent non-blocking data reduction (compression) pipeline. In each I/O stage, the break-even threshold derived in this paper needs to be fulfilled or backlog will occur for successive outputs and the overall application will be throttled by that specific bottleneck. With deeper memory hierarchies, user-programmability of stages will be a human bottleneck and needs to be addressed with easy and fast turnaround APIs to design application- and study-specific stages, e.g. via Python/Numba.

In conclusion, introducing data reduction for I/O will be necessary because of limited medium to long term storage size expected for future systems. Our analysis and measurements show that even today one should however not expect I/O performance gains when using reduction. Parallelization of reduction algorithms is one way to gain overall I/O performance but requires compute resources in addition to those used by the application. Even for fully GPU accelerated applications one should not assume resources to be 'free' for I/O and analysis tasks, since loosely coupled application workflows and models that depend heavily on hardly-parallelizable aspects such as atomic data lookups will in the future be more widespread and compete for the exact same resources.

References

1. Abbasi, H., Wolf, M., Eisenhauer, G., Klasky, S., Schwan, K., Zheng, F.: Datastager: scalable data staging services for petascale applications. Clust. Comput. **13**(3), 277–290 (2010). doi:10.1007/s10586-010-0135-6
2. Alted, F.: blosc 1.11.4-dev, March 2017. https://github.com/Blosc/c-blosc
3. Ayachit, U., Bauer, A., Geveci, B., O'Leary, P., Moreland, K., Fabian, N., Mauldin, J.: ParaView catalyst: enabling in situ data analysis and visualization. In: Proceedings of the First Workshop on In Situ Infrastructures for Enabling Extreme-Scale Analysis and Visualization, ISAV2015, pp. 25–29. ACM (2015). doi:10.1145/2828612.2828624
4. Bhimji, W., Bard, D., Romanus, M., Paul, D., Ovsyannikov, A., Friesen, B., Bryson, M., Correa, J., Lockwood, G.K., Tsulaia, V., et al.: Accelerating science with the NERSC burst buffer early user program. In: Proceedings of Cray Users Group (2016)
5. Birdsall, C., Langdon, A.: Plasma physics via computer simulation. The Adam Hilger series on plasma physics. McGraw-Hill, New York (1985). ISBN 9780070053717
6. Burau, H., Widera, R., Honig, W., Juckeland, G., Debus, A., Kluge, T., Schramm, U., Cowan, T.E., Sauerbrey, R., Bussmann, M.: PIConGPU: a fully relativistic particle-in-cell code for a gpu cluster. IEEE Trans. Plasma Sci. **38**(10), 2831–2839 (2010)
7. Burtscher, M., Mukka, H., Yang, A., Hesaaraki, F.: Real-time synthesis of compression algorithms for scientific data. In: SC16: International Conference for High Performance Computing, Networking, Storage and Analysis, pp. 264–275, November 2016. doi:10.1109/SC.2016.22
8. Bussmann, M., Burau, H., Cowan, T.E., Debus, A., Huebl, A., Juckeland, G., Kluge, T., Nagel, W.E., Pausch, R., Schmitt, F., Schramm, U., Schuchart, J., Widera, R.: Radiative signatures of the relativistic Kelvin-Helmholtz instability. In: Proceedings of the International Conference on High Performance Computing, Networking, Storage and Analysis, SC 2013, pp. 5:1–5:12. ACM (2013). doi:10.1145/2503210.2504564
9. Collet, Y., Skibinski, P., Terrell, N., Purcell, S.: Contributors: Zstandard (zstd) 1.1.4 - fast real-time compression algorithm, March 2017. https://github.com/facebook/zstd

10. Docan, C., Parashar, M., Klasky, S.: DataSpaces: an interaction and coordination framework or coupled simulation workflows. In: Proceedings of 19th International Symposium on High Performance and Distributed Computing (HPDC 2010), June 2010. doi:10.1007/s10586-011-0162-y
11. Eckert, C.H.J.: Enhancements of the massively parallel memory allocator scatter-alloc and its adaption to the general interface mallocMC, October 2014. doi:10.5281/zenodo.34461
12. Grismayer, T., Alves, E., Fonseca, R., Silva, L.: dc-magnetic-field generation in unmagnetized shear flows. Phys. Rev. Lett. **111**, 015005 (2013). doi:10.1103/PhysRevLett.111.015005
13. Gunderson, S.H., Evlogimenos, A.: Contributors: Snappy 1.1.1 - a fast compressor/decompressor (2011). https://github.com/google/snappy
14. Hockney, R., Eastwood, J.: Computer Simulation Using Particles. Taylor & Francis, Bristol (1988). ISBN: 9780852743928
15. Huebl, A., Lehe, R., Vay, J.L., Grote, D.P., Sbalzarini, I., Kuschel, S., Bussmann, M.: openPMD 1.0.0: a meta data standard for particle and mesh based data, November 2015. doi:10.5281/zenodo.33624
16. Huebl, A., Schmitt, F., Widera, R., Grund, A., Schumann, C., Eckert, C., Bukva, A., Pausch, R.: libSplash: 1.6.0: SerialDataCollector filename API, October 2016. doi:10.5281/zenodo.163609
17. Huebl, A., Widera, R., Grund, A., Pausch, R., Burau, H., Debus, A., Garten, M., Worpitz, B., Zenker, E., Winkler, F., Eckert, C., Tietze, S., Schneider, B., Knespel, M., Bussmann, M.: PIConGPU 0.2.4: Charge of bound electrons, openPMD axis range, manipulate by position, March 2017. doi:10.5281/zenodo.346005
18. Huebl, A., et al.: Supplementary materials: On the scalability of data reduction techniques in current and upcoming HPC systems from an application perspective, April 2017. doi:10.5281/zenodo.545780
19. Lindstrom, P.: Fixed-rate compressed floating-point arrays. IEEE Trans. Vis. Comput. Graph. **20**(12), 2674–2683 (2014). doi:10.1109/TVCG.2014.2346458
20. Liu, Q., Logan, J., Tian, Y., Abbasi, H., Podhorszki, N., Choi, J.Y., Klasky, S., Tchoua, R., Lofstead, J., Oldfield, R., et al.: Hello ADIOS: the challenges and lessons of developing leadership class I/O frameworks. Concurr. Comput. Pract. Exp. **26**(7), 1453–1473 (2014)
21. Matthes, A., Huebl, A., Widera, R., Grottel, S., Gumhold, S., Bussmann, M.: In situ, steerable, hardware-independent and data-structure agnostic visualization with ISAAC. Supercomputing Frontiers and Innovations **3**(4) (2016). http://superfri.org/superfri/article/view/114
22. McLay, R., James, D., Liu, S., Cazes, J., Barth, W.: A user-friendly approach for tuning parallel file operations. In: Proceedings of the International Conference for High Performance Computing, Networking, Storage and Analysis, SC 2014, pp. 229–236. IEEE Press (2014). doi:10.1109/SC.2014.24, https://github.com/TACC/t3pio
23. Meredith, J.S., Ahern, S., Pugmire, D., Sisneros, R.: EAVL: The extreme-scale analysis and visualization library. In: Childs, H., Kuhlen, T., Marton, F. (eds.) Eurographics Symposium on Parallel Graphics and Visualization. The Eurographics Association (2012). doi:10.2312/EGPGV/EGPGV12/021-030
24. Meuer, H.W., Strohmaier, E., Dongarra, J., Simon, H., Meuer, M.: November 2016 — TOP500 Supercomputer Sites, June 2016. https://www.top500.org/lists/2016/11/. Accessed 22 Mar 2017
25. Corporation, N.: NVIDIA IndeX 1.4. https://developer.nvidia.com/index

26. Tao, D., Sheng, D., Chen, Z., Cappello, F.: Significantly improving lossy compression for scientific data sets based on multidimensional prediction and error-controlled quantization. In: IPDPS 2017: Proceedings of the 31th IEEE International Parallel and Distributed Processing Symposium, May 2017
27. The HDF Group: Hierarchical data format version 5 (C-API: 1.8.14) (2000–2017). http://www.hdfgroup.org/HDF5
28. Whitlock, B., Favre, J.M., Meredith, J.S.: Parallel in situ coupling of simulation with a fully featured visualization system. In: Kuhlen, T., Pajarola, R., Zhou, K. (eds.) Eurographics Symposium on Parallel Graphics and Visualization. The Eurographics Association (2011). doi:10.2312/EGPGV/EGPGV11/101-109
29. Zenker, E., Widera, R., Huebl, A., Juckeland, G., Knüpfer, A., Nagel, W.E., Bussmann, M.: Performance-portable many-core plasma simulations: porting PIConGPU to openpower and beyond. In: Taufer, M., Mohr, B., Kunkel, J.M. (eds.) ISC High Performance 2016. LNCS, vol. 9945, pp. 293–301. Springer, Cham (2016). doi:10.1007/978-3-319-46079-6_21
30. Zenker, E., Worpitz, B., Widera, R., Huebl, A., Juckeland, G., Knüpfer, A., Nagel, W.E., Bussmann, M.: Alpaka-an abstraction library for parallel kernel acceleration. In: 2016 IEEE International on Parallel and Distributed Processing Symposium Workshops, pp. 631–640. IEEE (2016)

Toward a Multi-method Approach: Lossy Data Compression for Climate Simulation Data

Allison H. Baker(✉), Haiying Xu, Dorit M. Hammerling, Shaomeng Li, and John P. Clyne

The National Center for Atmospheric Research, Boulder, CO 80305, USA
{abaker,haiyingx,dorith,shaomeng,clyne}@ucar.edu

Abstract. Earth System Model (ESM) simulations are increasingly constrained by the amount of data that they generate rather than by computational resources. The use of lossy data compression on model output can reduce storage costs and data transmission overheads, but care must be taken to ensure that science results are not impacted. Choosing appropriate compression algorithms and parameters is not trivial given the diversity of data produced by ESMs and requires an understanding of both the attributes of the data and the properties of the chosen compression methods. Here we discuss the properties of two distinct approaches for lossy compression in the context of a well-known ESM, demonstrating the different strengths of each, to motivate the development of an automated multi-method approach for compression of climate model output.

1 Introduction

The Community Earth System Model (CESM) [9] is a popular earth system model code based at the National Center for Atmospheric Research (NCAR). A high-resolution CESM simulation can easily generate over a terabyte of data per compute day (e.g., [22]), outputting time slices of data for hundreds of variables at hourly, daily, and monthly sampling rates. In fact, the raw data requirements for CESM for the current Coupled Model Comparison Project (Phase 6) [19] are expected to exceed 10 petabytes [20]. The massive data volumes generated by CESM strain NCAR's resources and motivated the work in [2], a first step in advocating for the use of lossy data compression on CESM output. In [2], errors in reconstructed CESM data (data that had undergone compression) resulting from multiple lossy compression methods were evaluated primarily in the context of an ensemble of simulations. The idea was that the effects of lossy compression on the original climate simulation should not, at a minimum, be statistically distinguishable from the natural variability of the climate system. Preliminary results indicated that this requirement could be met with a respectable compression rate with the *fpzip* compressor [18].

A more recent study in [1] applied *fpzip* lossy compression to a subset of the data from the CESM Large Ensemble (CESM-LE) Community Project [12], which was made available to climate researchers to examine features of the

J.M. Kunkel et al. (Eds.): ISC High Performance Workshops 2017, LNCS 10524, pp. 30–42, 2017.
https://doi.org/10.1007/978-3-319-67630-2_3

data relevant to their interests (e.g., extremes, variability patterns, mean climate characteristics). The results from several of these studies are discussed in [1], and the authors conclude that while it is possible to detect compression effects in the data in some features, the effects are often unimportant or disappear in post-processing analyses. For this study, each CESM output variable was assessed individually to maximize compression such that the reconstructed data passed the ensemble-based quality metrics in [2]. This costly "brute force" approach required the generation of multiple ensembles and exhaustive testing of the compression algorithm's parameter space.

Our goal is to simplify the process of determining appropriate compression for a given CESM dataset that both maximizes data reduction and preserves the scientific value of the data. Therefore, we must be able to detect problematic compression artifacts with metrics that do not require ensemble data. Further, because a single compression algorithm cannot obtain the best compression rate (and quality) on every CESM variable, we explore applying multiple types of compression methods to a CESM dataset. Once a particular method has been matched to a variable, then the amount of compression (i.e., parameters) must be chosen inexpensively as well. In this work, we progress toward identifying which type of compression method to use based on a variable's characteristics and determining the strengths and weaknesses of different types of lossy compression algorithms in the context of CESM output. We also demonstrate the potential of a multi-method compression approach for CESM.

2 Challenges

Our ultimate goal is to develop an automated tool to integrate lossy compression into the CESM workflow. Given a CESM dataset, this tool must be able to *efficiently* determine which compression algorithm(s) to apply and evaluate the impact of the information loss. These two capabilities are particularly challenging for CESM simulation output due to the diversity of variables, and a variable's characteristics determine how effectively it can be compressed. CESM variables may be smooth, constant, or contain abrupt changes. Variables may have large ranges of data values, artificial "fill" values, unpredictable missing values, or large numbers of zero values. Further, the same variable field may "look" different at different spatial and temporal resolutions.

The work in [2] customizes how aggressively each CESM variable is compressed by adjusting algorithm-specific parameters that control the amount of compression. However, here we further suggest using different compression algorithms on different variables. The benefit of a multi-method approach is that, for example, a compression method that does poorly on data with sharp boundaries but extremely well on smooth data would not be excluded from consideration, but simply applied only to smooth variables. The challenge of a multi-method approach is that determining the rules to automate the process of matching variables to appropriate lossy compression algorithms requires a thorough understanding of the features of each variable, the strengths and weaknesses of each compression method, and the evaluation metrics in the context of CESM data. Further, once a lossy compression method has been chosen, method-specific parameters must be optimized as well.

Determining appropriate metrics to evaluate the impact of information loss is also challenging due to the diversity of data (e.g., smooth data may be easier to compress, but perhaps there is less tolerance for error). However, a second issue stems from not knowing in advance how a large publicly-available CESM dataset will be analyzed. Indeed, if we know how data will be analyzed, compression can be tailored to well preserve features of interest (e.g., top of the atmosphere surface radiation balance) in the reconstructed data. Finally, computational cost is a consideration. While the ensemble-based quality metrics that leverage the climate model systems's variability were needed to establish the feasibility of applying lossy compression to CESM output in [2], an ensemble-based approach is expensive. On the other hand, simple metrics such as the root mean squared error (RMSE) or peak signal-to-noise ratio (PSNR) are insufficient for detecting features potentially relevant to climate scientists.

3 Lossy Compression Algorithms

Lossy compression algorithms for general floating-point scientific data have received attention recently (e.g., [3,4,6,11,14–18,21]) due to their ability to compress much more agressively than lossless approaches. A few studies have focused on applying lossy algorithms to climate simulation data in particular (e.g., [2,8,25]). Compression schemes can be described in terms of their modeling and encoding phases, and available compression algorithms differ in how these phases are executed. Predictive schemes and transform methods are common choices for the modeling phase in lossy compression algorithms. We focus on a representative algorithm of each type to explore how the two different types of compression algorithms differ in the context of CESM data. While not discussed in this work, note that algorithm performance and ease-of-use are important and desirable lossy compression method properties for CESM data are discussed in [2].

The *fpzip* compressor [18] models the floating-point numbers via predictive coding; as the data are traversed, values are predicted based on data already visited. The idea behind a predictive method is that the residual between the actual and predicted floating-point value is smaller than the original value and, therefore, can be encoded with fewer bits. The *fpzip* compressor [18] may be lossless or lossy depending on whether all bits are retained (or a number of least significant bits are truncated) before the floating-point values are converted to integers. Integer residual values are then encoded by a fast entropy encoder. In lossy mode, because discarding of bits effectively rounds toward zero, some introduction of bias is possible [15].

A tranform compression method aims to model the original data with a relatively small number of basis coefficients (i.e., those with the largest magnitudes) and then encode those coefficients. The compressor that we refer to as *SPECK* uses a discrete wavelet basis and encodes with the set partitioned embedded block coder algorithm [10]. In this research we adopted the *SPECK* implementation from QccPack [7], with the CDF 9/7 wavelet transformation [5]. For 2D variables, a 2D transform was applied to each horizontal slice; for 3D variables, an additional 1D transform was applied along the Z axis. Normally a transform method cannot support a lossless option due to floating-point inaccuracies associated with the transform, and *SPECK* is no exception. The amount of compression with *SPECK* is controlled by specifying a target bit per voxel (i.e., a fixed rate). For example, for single precision data (32-bits), specifying a bit per voxel of 8 would yield a compression ratio (CR) of approximately 0.25, where (CR) is defined as the ratio of the size of the compressed file to that of the original file. Other examples of transform approaches include JPEG2000 (e.g. [25]) and *zfp* [17], the latter of which targets numerical simulation data.

4 Metrics

Three of the four metrics in [2] for evaluating information loss in CESM due to lossy compression are ensemble-based. We move away from ensemble-based metrics in this study largely due to cost considerations, though a second hinderance to automation with ensemble-based metrics is that variable properties across the ensemble cannot be known in advance to determine allowable error. For example, if a variable is constant across the ensemble, then there may be no tolerance for any error no matter how small. Therefore, for our comparison of the two lossy approaches here, we use the three metrics described next, as well as the Pearson correlation coefficient as in [2]. We do not claim that the following metrics (and tolerances) are comprehensive (notably absent are multivariate metrics and temporal considerations), but they reflect our evolution in terms of suitable metrics that measure different aspects of the data and illustrate the differences between the two lossy approaches that we compare in this work. Indeed, determining comprehensive and efficient metrics is a subject of on-going long-term research.

We consider a single temporal step for our analysis and denote the original spatial dataset X as $X = \{x_1, x_2, \ldots, x_N\}$, with x_i a scalar and i the spatial index, and the reconstructed dataset $\tilde{X}$ by $\tilde{X} = \{\tilde{x_1}, \tilde{x_2}, \ldots, \tilde{x_N}\}$. The range of X is denoted by R_X. The normalized maximum pointwise error (e_{nmax}) is the maximum norm, normalized by R_X, and the normalized RMSE ($nrmse$) is the RMSE between the original and reconstructed data, normalized by R_X.

Pearson correlation coefficient: The Pearson correlation coefficient (PCC) indicates the strength of the linear relationship between the original and reconstructed data, and a value of one indicates a perfect (positive) correlation. Lossy compression should not degrade this relationship, and as such, we require that $PCC \geq 0.99999$ as the acceptance threshold for this test [2]. The PCC is useful as it is sensitive to outliers in the data (but is invariant to mean shifts).

Kolmogorov-Smirnov Test: The two-sample Kolmogorov-Smirnov (KS) test detects a potential shift in the distribution. The KS test is a nonparametric hypothesis test for evaluating whether two datasets are drawn from the same probability distribution (the null hypothesis) and is based on the supremum distance between two empirical cumulative density functions (CDFs). We use the SciPy statistical functions package two-sample KS test at the 5% confidence level. Note that the KS test benefits from large sample size, which we have here, making it more accurate/sensitive. This test should detect smoothing, skew, or other distribution-changing features in the reconstructed data. For example, if many points with the same value in the distribution are systematically under- or overestimated (by even a tiny amount), this test will fail even if the discrepancy is undetectable in the sample mean and standard deviation.

Spatial relative error: While checking the maximum norm of the error gives a minimum guarantee of precision, the error may only be large at one single point. On the other hand, a measure of average error (e.g., RMSE) can hide an error at a single or a few point(s). To better describe the spatial extent of the error, we determine the percentage of spatial grid locations at which the relative error is greater than a specified tolerance δ. In particular, for each variable X at each grid point, we calculate the relative error: $re_{x_i} = (x_i - \tilde{x}_i)/x_i$ (if $x_i == 0$, then we calculate the absolute error). If percentage of grid points with $re_{x_i} > \delta$ exceeds 5%, this test will fail. We are compressing single-precision (32-bit) data in CESM, and for our experiments we use $\delta = 1e^{-4}$.

Structural similarity index: The structural similarity Index (SSIM) was developed to measure the perceived change in structural information between two images, as the commonly used RMSE is typically not well suited to such a task [23]. Data visualization is a key component in many climate simulation post-processing analyses, as evidenced by the popularity of the Atmosphere Working Group Diagnostics Package (AMWG-DP). Clearly, visual evidence of information loss due to compression in post-processing image analysis would be problematic, particularly if scientific conclusions are affected. Computing the SSIM for 2D slices of the original and reconstructed data provides an indication as to whether the difference is noticeable. An SSIM score of one indicates that two images are identical, while lower scores indicate some degree of difference. Most threshold values for minimum allowable SSIM for compression in the medical imaging research field, which focuses on "diagnostically lossless" [13], range from .95 to .99. While an appropriate SSIM threshold is clearly application dependent (and requires further research for CESM), we use .98 in this study as it is commonly cited as the level of visual indistinguishability (e.g., [24]).

5 Multi-method Comparison

We limit our investigation to output from the atmospheric model component of CESM, the Community Atmosphere Model (CAM), evaluating the same data as in [2], which were annual averages obtained from the 1.1 release version of CESM, using a spectral element (SE) dynamical core on a cubed-sphere 1-degree global grid (48,602 horizontal grid-points and 30 vertical levels).

Table 1. Representative CESM variable characteristics

Variable name	Description	Dim.	x_{min}	x_{max}	% zeros
H2O2	H_2O_2 concentration	3D	9.44e-13	3.55e-9	0.1
FSNTC	Clearsky net solar flux (top of model)	2D	4.57e1	3.80e2	0.0
TS	Surface temperature	2D	2.15e2	3.04e2	0.0
TAUY	Zonal surface stress	2D	−2.66e-1	2.44e-1	0.0
CLOUD	Cloud fraction	3D	0.0	8.95e-1	22.3
PRECSC	Convective snow rate	2D	0.0	6.80e-9	75.8
TOT_ICLD_VISTAU	Total in-cloud visible sw optical depth	3D	0.0	6.75e1	27.3
PRECCDZM	Convective precipitation rate (ZM deep)	2D	0.0	2.39e-7	4.6
OMEGAT	Vertical heat flux	3D	−2.74e2	2.01e2	0.0
FLNS	Net longwave flux at surface	2D	1.14e1	1.50e2	0.0
VQ	Meridional water transport	3D	−9.21e-2	1.07e-1	0.0
NUMLIQ	Grid box averaged cloud liquid num	3D	1.00e-12	1.10e8	43.1
WSUB	Diagnostic sub-grid vertical velocity	3D	2.00e-1	1.30e0	0.0

CESM data are written to single-precision (truncated from double-precision), and we use all 198 default output variables, 101 of which are two-dimensional (2D) and 97 three-dimensional (3D). We define fpzip_Y as *fpzip* where Y indicates the number of bits to retain before quantization, and we evaluate with $Y = \{8, 12, 16, 20, 24, 28, 32\}$. Therefore, fpzip_8 is the most aggressive and fpzip_32 is lossless. We define speck_M as *SPECK* where M indicates the bit target rate and evaluate with $M = \{1, 2, 4, 8, 12, 16, 24, 32\}$. Therefore, speck_1 is the most aggressive and speck_32 is the least (closest to lossless). Note that because the CAM SE data is output as a 1D array for each horizontal level (space-filling curve ordering), we reorder the CAM data to be spatially coherent data before applying the transform method. In particular, the original 48,602 horizontal grid points were mapped to the six cubed-sphere faces (91x91x1), and *SPECK* is applied to each face independently (3D variables have 91x91x30 input arrays). *SPECK* also takes two additional parameters related to the wavelet transform levels; given that the wavelet transform kernel size is 9, we set XY-level to 4 ($log_2(91/9) + 1$) and Z-level to 2 ($log_2(30/9) + 1$).

Table 2. A list of the lowest CR variants of *SPECK* and *fpzip* for each representative CESM variable

Variable name	*SPECK*				*fpzip*				DWT→IDWT
	Variant	e_{nmax}	$nrmse$	CR	Variant	e_{nmax}	$nrmse$	CR	Max. abs. error
H2O2	speck_2	2.47e-4	2.47e-5	0.06	fpzip_20	2.56e-4	2.05e-5	0.23	0.0
FSNTC	speck_8	1.75e-4	2.08e-5	0.26	fpzip_24	2.33e-5	1.18e-5	0.36	0.0
TS	speck_4	1.46e-3	1.95e-4	0.13	fpzip_24	8.71e-5	4.95e-5	0.28	0.0
TAUY	speck_12	8.04e-6	1.24e-6	0.38	fpzip_24	1.41e-5	7.92e-7	0.54	0.0
CLOUD	–	–	–	–	fpzip_24	1.70e-5	2.42e-6	0.36	8.88e-16
PRECSC	–	–	–	–	fpzip_16	4.01e-3	1.97e-4	0.12	2.53e-24
TOT_ICLD_VISTAU	–	–	–	–	fpzip_24	2.68e-5	5.84e-7	0.38	8.88e-15
PRECCDZM	speck_24	7.44e-9	1.61e-9	0.77	fpzip_16	3.89e-3	4.16e-4	0.24	5.29e-23
OMEGAT	speck_16	2.24e-8	3.11e-9	0.51	fpzip_24	1.09e-5	2.04e-7	0.52	0.0
FLNS	speck_12	1.38e-5	2.72e-6	0.38	fpzip_24	2.81e-5	5.19e-6	0.42	0.0
VQ	speck_16	3.50e-9	3.82e-10	0.51	fpzip_24	9.53e-6	6.52e-7	0.48	0.0
NUMLIQ	–	–	–	–	fpzip_32	0.0	0.0	0.46	5.96e-8
WSUB	–	–	–	–	fpzip_32	0.0	0.0	0.43	0.0

5.1 Detailed Investigation of Representative Variables

We examine a subset of the variables in detail (Table 1). For each variable, we determine the most aggressive (i.e., lowest CR) variant of *SPECK* and *fpzip* that pass the four tests described in Sect. 4 (see Table 2). Comparing *SPECK* to *fpzip* is complicated by the fact that *SPECK* uses a fixed-rate specification and *fpzip* does not. Values for e_{nmax} and $nrmse$ are listed in Table 2, but are not used as selection metrics, and the rightmost column is discussed in Sect. 6.

The top section in Table 2 lists four variables, H2O2, FSNTC, TS, and TAUY, which have a lower CR with *SPECK* than with *fpzip*. These variables all have either very few or no zeroes. Each variable is also quite smooth (intuitive for surface temperature, TS). For H2O2, while the range is a bit larger overall, the range within each horizontal level is smaller. Note that *fpzip* does not do poorly

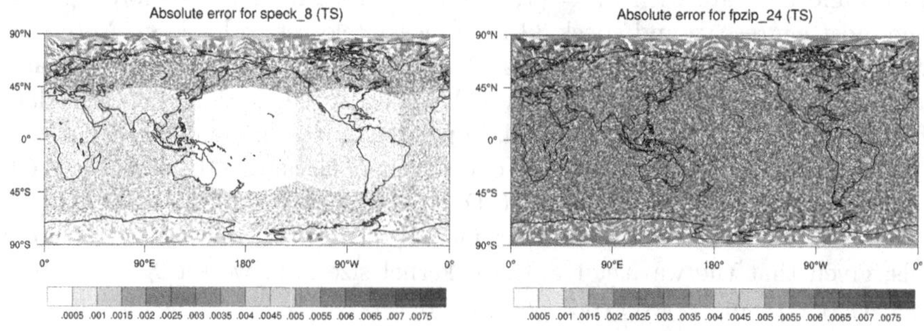

Fig. 1. Absolute error between the original and reconstructed data with speck_8 (left) and fpzip_24 (right) for variable TS. Both methods shown attain a similar CR.

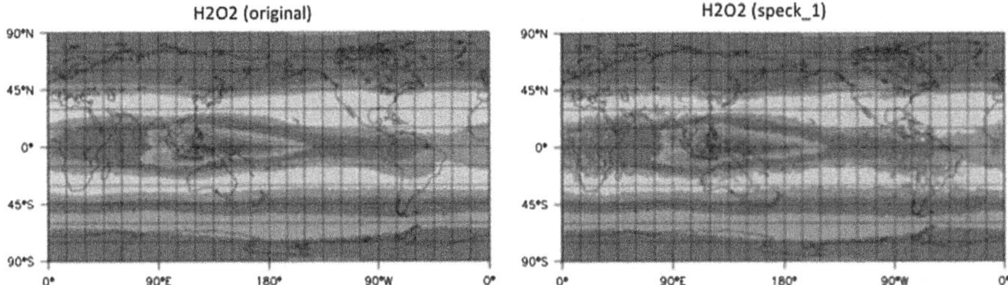

Fig. 2. Variable H2O2 (level 7) in original data (left) and after speck_1 compression (right). The SSIM index for the images is below the 0.98 threshold. Colorbars for these two plots have been omitted as they are identical and do not contribute information.

on these four variables, but *SPECK* compresses more aggressively. Figure 1 illustrates the difference in the two methods via the absolute error for TS with speck_8 (left) and fpzip_24 (right), which achieve a similar *CR* of .26 and .28, respectively. The error with *SPECK* is uniformly smaller at this same compression ratio, which makes sense given that more aggressive compression via speck_4 is acceptable (Table 2). Note that the cubed-sphere faces are evident in Fig. 1. For FNSTC, TS, and TAUY, more aggressive variants of the two compressors fail the spatial relative error test. For H202, though, the more aggressive variant of *SPECK* fails the SSIM test, which can be visually confirmed by the noticeable difference in Fig. 2 along the contour between blue and light blue.

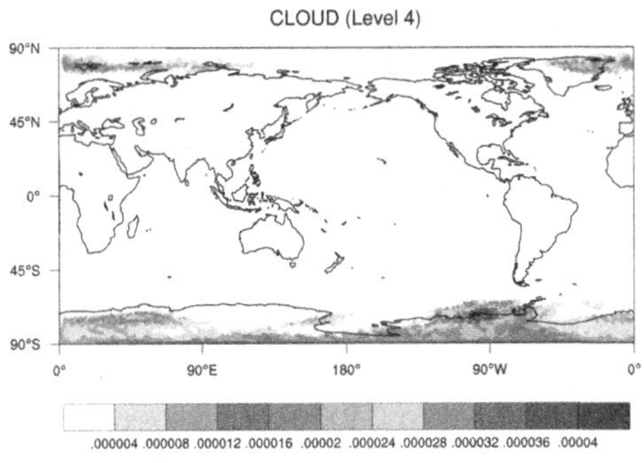

Fig. 3. Variable CLOUD (level 4) in the original data.

The second section in Table 2 lists four variables that achieve a lower *CR* with *fpzip*. The first three of these variables (CLOUD, PRECSC, TOT_ICLD_VISTAU) contain sizable percentages of zeros, which *SPECK* typically does not exactly preserve. Even the least aggressive *SPECK* variant, speck_32 (which does not reduce the file size) cannot pass the KS test, which detects the shift in distribution caused by reconstructing zero values in the original data as very small values (positive and negative). These fields also contain

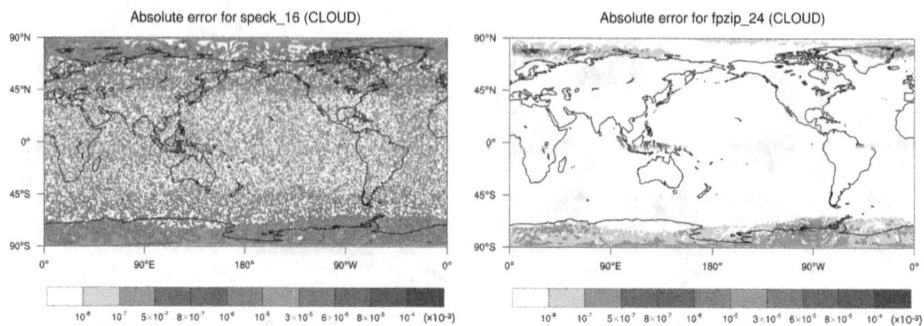

Fig. 4. Absolute error between the original and reconstructed data with speck_16 (left) and fpzip_24 (right) for variable CLOUD (level 4).

more abrupt jumps in the data, which are not favorable to a transform method. For example, the 3D variable CLOUD contains many zero values, very small numbers, and large ranges. Some levels have ranges of eight orders of magnitude, half of the levels have no zeros, the surface level (level 0) has all zeros, and level 4 (Fig. 3) is 95% zeros with a range of five orders of magnitude. Figure 4 shows the absolute error for CLOUD on level 4 with fpzip_24 ($CR = .36$ and passes all metrics) and speck_16 ($CR = .51$ and does not pass), and it is clear that this variable is challenging for a transform method. The fourth variable, PREC-CDZM, has fewer zeros but a large range, and can be compressed with *SPECK*, but not as aggressively as *fpzip*. More aggressive variants of *SPECK* and *fpzip* on PRECCDZM fail the KS test and correlation coefficient test, respectively.

The third section in Table 2 contains variables for which both approaches achieve a similar CR. These variables all fail the spatial relative error test if compressed more aggressively with either method. Note that while the CR is similar, both $nmrse$ and e_{nmax} are notably smaller with *SPECK* for variables OMEGAT and VQ. Finally, the bottom of Table 2 lists two variables for which only lossless compression can pass the metrics. Lossy compression of NUMLIQ (which has both a huge range and a high percentage of zeros) resulted in KS and SSIM test failures for both *SPECK* and *fpzip*. In contrast, WSUB does not have a large range, but it does have a large number of non-zero constants (29% of the data values are equal to 0.2). Neither lossy approach preserved this prevalent constant, resulting in KS test failures indicating a shifted distribution. We note that *fpzip* lossless compression is slightly better than NetCDF4 lossless compression (essentially *gzip*), which results in CR of 0.48 for both variables. Lossless compression achieves a respectable CR on these two variables due to their large numbers of constant values.

5.2 Full Set of Variables

Now we look at all 198 variables and divide them into five categories according to which lossy compression approach passes the Sect. 4 metrics with a lower CR (Table 3). We find that 87 variables do better with *SPECK* than *fpzip*, and the

Table 3. All variables (198) categorized by method with lowest CR.

Category	Number of Variables	*SPECK* averages			*fpzip* averages		
		e_{nmax}	$nrmse$	CR	e_{nmax}	$nrmse$	CR
SPECK better	87	4.23e-4	5.62e-5	0.16	1.35e-4	2.25e-5	0.30
fpzip better	12	4.26e-7	5.91e-8	0.45	7.76e-4	1.09e-4	0.37
fpzip/*SPECK* similar	24	5.31e-6	9.58e-7	0.32	2.59e-4	1.18e-5	0.32
fpzip (*SPECK* fails)	63	–	–	–	1.38e-3	6.71e-5	0.29
lossless (fpzip_32)	12	–	–	–	0.0	0.0	0.50

average CR and error measurements for that subset of variables is given in the first row of Table 3. The average CR is approximately a factor of two smaller with *SPECK* for these variables. The second and third row of Table 3 show that *fpzip* outperforms *SPECK* on only 12 variables and that they perform similarly in terms of CR on 24 variables. However, in both of these cases the *SPECK* average errors are a couple of orders of magnitude smaller, indicating that traditional error metrics may be insufficient for identifying certain problematic features. Finally, for the remaining 75 variables (rows 4 and 5), *SPECK* is not an option as it fails the metrics even with its least aggressive variant. Of these, twelve of the variables cannot pass with *fpzip* in lossy mode either and require the lossless variant of *fpzip* (fpzip_32).

6 Characterizing Data

The two lossy compression approaches that we evaluated have different strengths. Unsurprisingly, transform methods are challenged by CESM datasets with abrupt changes and large ranges of values. They can also be problematic when zeros or constants must be preserved for post-processing analyses. However, for smooth CESM data, our results indicate that transform methods can compress more aggressively and more accurately than a predictive method like *fpzip*. On the other hand, *fpzip*'s general utility and effectiveness is valuable; it can be applied successfully to every CESM variable and its lossless option is a necessity.

An automated tool for a multi-method approach must be able to assess easily measurable properties of a variable's data to determine which type of compression approach will be most effective. Our experimental results with *SPECK* and *fpzip* indicate that if the least aggressive variant of *SPECK* (speck_32) is able to pass the metrics, then the "best" (i.e., lowest CR that passes metrics) *SPECK* variant is likely to be as good or better than that of the best *fpzip* variant. When speck_32 fails on CESM variables, the reason is a KS test failure. CESM variables with many zero values (or many constants in general) are particularly problematic as zeros are frequently reconstructed as small (positive or negative) values, causing the underlying distribution to shift and the KS test to fail.

In an attempt to predict *SPECK* effectiveness, we looked at a variety of variable properties (range, gradient, number of zeros, etc.) and investigated the cause of the speck_32 failures. We found that the key to the failures was *SPECK*'s CDF 9/7 wavelet transformation (DWT), which can suffer from floating-point computation induced-error. We refer to the process of applying DWT followed immediately by an inverse DWT (IDWT) as DWT→IDWT, which is lossless in infinite precision. In practice, DWT→IDWT was lossless for some CESM variables and lossy for others, as indicated by the maximum absolute error between the original data and the data after DWT→IDWT in the rightmost column in Table 2 (e.g., a zero value indicates lossless). For all but 4 of the 198 total variables, we found that variables with non-zero absolute errors after DWT→IDWT indicate that *SPECK* is not appropriate for these variables. Note that WSUB in Table 2 is an exception as it requires lossless despite its zero DWT→IDWT error (and is a target of future study). Therefore, applying a standalone DWT→IDWT test (e.g., via QccPack) is promising method for automating the decision as to whether to use a wavelet transform method such as *SPECK*.

7 Concluding Remarks

Transform methods are enticing due to their ability to compress both aggressively and accurately. Unfortunately, *SPECK* was unsuitable for 38% of the variables in our test CESM dataset (though issues with preserving zeros or other constants could conceivably be addressed by a pre-processing step). However, the 2x improvement of *SPECK* over *fpzip* indicates that an automated multi-method approach is worth pursuing. Indeed, large climate simulations commonly produce data volumes measured in hundreds of terabytes or even petabytes, and even a modest reduction in CR is quite significant in terms of data reduction and impact on storage costs. Future work includes more research on appropriate metrics, as the selection of the most appropriate type of compression scheme must now be followed by a specification of the parameters that control the amount of compression. Further, we note that we chose rather conservative tolerances for our metrics that, if relaxed, would likely be more favorable to a transform method.

References

1. Baker, A.H., Hammerling, D.M., Mickleson, S.A., Xu, H., Stolpe, M.B., Naveau, P., Sanderson, B., Ebert-Uphoff, I., Samarasinghe, S., De Simone, F., Carbone, F., Gencarelli, C.N., Dennis, J.M., Kay, J.E., Lindstrom, P.: Evaluating lossy data compression on climate simulation data within a large ensemble. Geosci. Model Dev. **9**(12), 4381–4403 (2016). http://www.geosci-model-dev.net/9/4381/2016/
2. Baker, A., Xu, H., Dennis, J., Levy, M., Nychka, D., Mickelson, S., Edwards, J., Vertenstein, M., Wegener, A.: A methodology for evaluating the impact of data compression on climate simulation data. In: Proceedings of the 23rd International Symposium on High-Performance Parallel and Distributed Computing, HPDC 2014, pp. 203–214 (2014)

3. Bicer, T., Yin, J., Chiu, D., Agrawal, G., Schuchardt, K.: Integrating online compression to accelerate large-scale data analytics applications. In: International Parallel and Distributed Processing Symposium, pp. 1205–1216 (2013)
4. Burtscher, M., Ratanaworabhan, P.: FPC: a high-speed compressor for double-precision floating-point data. IEEE Trans. Comput. **58**, 18–31 (2009)
5. Cohen, A., Daubechies, I., Feauveau, J.C.: Biorthogonal bases of compactly supported wavelets. Commun. Pure Appl. Math. **45**, 485–560 (1992)
6. Di, S., Cappello, F.: Fast error-bounded lossy HPC data compression with SZ. In: 2016 IEEE International Parallel and Distributed Processing Symposium, IPDPS 2016, Chicago, IL, USA, 23–27 May 2016, pp. 730–739 (2016). http://dx.doi.org/10.1109/IPDPS.2016.11
7. Fowler, J.E.: Qccpack: An open-source software library for quantization, compression, and coding. In: International Symposium on Optical Science and Technology, pp. 294–301. International Society for Optics and Photonics (2000)
8. Hübbe, N., Wegener, A., Kunkel, J.M., Ling, Y., Ludwig, T.: Evaluating lossy compression on climate data. In: Kunkel, J.M., Ludwig, T., Meuer, H.W. (eds.) ISC 2013. LNCS, vol. 7905, pp. 343–356. Springer, Heidelberg (2013). doi:10.1007/978-3-642-38750-0_26
9. Hurrell, J., Holland, M., Gent, P., Ghan, S., Kay, J., Kushner, P., Lamarque, J.F., Large, W., Lawrence, D., Lindsay, K., Lipscomb, W., Long, M., Mahowald, N., Marsh, D., Neale, R., Rasch, P., Vavrus, S., Vertenstein, M., Bader, D., Collins, W., Hack, J., Kiehl, J., Marshall, S.: The community earth system model: a framework for collaborative research. Bull. Am. Meteorol. Soc. **94**, 1339–1360 (2013)
10. Islam, A., Pearlman, W.A.: Embedded and efficient low-complexity hierarchical image coder. In: Electronic Imaging'99, pp. 294–305. International Society for Optics and Photonics (1998)
11. Iverson, J., Kamath, C., Karypis, G.: Fast and effective lossy compression algorithms for scientific datasets. In: Kaklamanis, C., Papatheodorou, T., Spirakis, P.G. (eds.) Euro-Par 2012. LNCS, vol. 7484, pp. 843–856. Springer, Heidelberg (2012). doi:10.1007/978-3-642-32820-6_83
12. Kay, J., Deser, C., Phillips, A., Mai, A., Hannay, C., Strand, G., Arblaster, J., Bates, S., Danabasoglu, G., Edwards, J., Holland, M., Kushner, P., Lamarque, J.F., Lawrence, D., Lindsay, K., Middleton, A., Munoz, E., Neale, R., Oleson, K., Polvani, L., Vertenstein, M.: The Community Earth System Model (CESM) large ensemble project: A community resource for studying climate change in the presence of internal climate variability, vol. 96. Bulletin of the American Meteorological Society (2015)
13. Kowalik-Urbaniak, I., Brunet, D., Wang, J., Koff, D., Smolarski-Koff, N., Vrscay, E.R., Wallace, B., Wang, Z.: The quest for 'diagnostically lossless' medical image compression: a comparative study of objective quality metrics for compressed medical images. In: Medical Imaging 2014: Image Perception, Observer Performance, and Technology Assessment, Proceedings of SPIE. vol. 9037 (2014)
14. Lakshminarasimhan, S., Shah, N., Ethier, S., Klasky, S., Latham, R., Ross, R., Samatova, N.F.: Compressing the incompressible with ISABELA: in-situ reduction of spatio-temporal data. In: Jeannot, E., Namyst, R., Roman, J. (eds.) Euro-Par 2011. LNCS, vol. 6852, pp. 366–379. Springer, Heidelberg (2011). doi:10.1007/978-3-642-23400-2_34

15. Laney, D., Langer, S., Weber, C., Lindstrom, P., Wegener, A.: Assessing the effects of data compression in simulations using physically motivated metrics. In: Supercomputing (SC 2013) In: Proceedings of the International Conference on High Performance Computing, Networking, Storage and Analysis, SC 2013. pp. 76:1–76:12 (2013)
16. Li, S., Gruchalla, K., Potter, K., Clyne, J., Childs, H.: Evaluating the efficacy of wavelet configurations on turbulent-flow data. In: Proceedings of IEEE Symposium on Large Data Analysis and Visualization (LDAV), pp. 81–89, Chicago, IL, October 2015
17. Lindstrom, P.: Fixed-rate compressed floating-point arrays. IEEE Trans. Visual. Comput. Graph. **20**(12), 2674–2683 (2014)
18. Lindstrom, P., Isenburg, M.: Fast and efficient compression of floating-point data. IEEE Trans. Visual. Comput. Graph. **12**, 1245–1250 (2006)
19. Meehl, G., Moss, R., Taylor, K., Eyring, V., Stouffer, R., Bony, S., Stevens, B.: Climate model intercomparisons: preparing for the next phase. Eos, Trans. Am. Geophys. Union **95**(9), 77–78 (2014)
20. Paul, K., Mickelson, S., Xu, H., Dennis, J.M., Brown, D.: Light-weight parallel Python tools for earth system modeling workflows. In: IEEE International Conference on Big Data, pp. 1985–1994, October 2015
21. Sasaki, N., Sato, K., Endo, T., Matsuoka, S.: Exploration of lossy compression for application-level checkpoint/restart. In: Proceedings of the 2015 IEEE International Parallel and Distributed Processing Symposium, IPDPS 2015, pp. 914–922 (2015)
22. Small, R.J., Bacmeister, J., Bailey, D., Baker, A., Bishop, S., Bryan, F., Caron, J., Dennis, J., Gent, P., Hsu, H.m., Jochum, M., Lawrence, D., Muoz, E., diNezio, P., Scheitlin, T., Tomas, R., Tribbia, J., Tseng, Y.H., Vertenstein, M.: A new synoptic scale resolving global climate simulation using the community earth system model. J. Adv. Model. Earth Syst. **6**(4), 1065–1094 (2014)
23. Wang, Z., Bovik, A.C., Sheikh, H.R., Simoncelli, E.P.: Image quality assessment: from error visibility to structural similarity. IEEE Trans. Image Process. **13**(4), 600–612 (2004)
24. Wegener, A.: Compression of medical sensor data. IEEE Signal Process. Mag. **27**(4), 125–130 (2010)
25. Woodring, J., Mniszewski, S.M., Brislawn, C.M., DeMarle, D.E., Ahrens, J.P.: Revisiting wavelet compression for large-scale climate data using JPEG2000 and ensuring data precision. In: Rogers, D., Silva, C.T. (eds.) IEEE Symposium on Large Data Analysis and Visualization (LDAV), pp. 31–38. IEEE (2011)

Exploration of Pattern-Matching Techniques for Lossy Compression on Cosmology Simulation Data Sets

Dingwen Tao[1(✉)], Sheng Di[2], Zizhong Chen[1], and Franck Cappello[2,3]

[1] University of California, Riverside, CA, USA
{dtao001,chen}@cs.ucr.edu
[2] Argonne National Laboratory, Lemont, IL, USA
{sdi1,cappello}@anl.gov
[3] University of Illinois at Urbana-Champaign, Champaign, IL, USA

Abstract. Because of the vast volume of data being produced by today's scientific simulations, lossy compression allowing user-controlled information loss can significantly reduce the data size and the I/O burden. However, for large-scale cosmology simulation, such as the Hardware/Hybrid Accelerated Cosmology Code (HACC), where memory overhead constraints restrict compression to only one snapshot at a time, the lossy compression ratio is extremely limited because of the fairly low spatial coherence and high irregularity of the data. In this work, we propose a pattern-matching (similarity searching) technique to optimize the prediction accuracy and compression ratio of SZ lossy compressor on the HACC data sets. We evaluate our proposed method with different configurations and compare it with state-of-the-art lossy compressors. Experiments show that our proposed optimization approach can improve the prediction accuracy and reduce the compressed size of quantization codes compared with SZ. We present several lessons useful for future research involving pattern-matching techniques for lossy compression.

1 Introduction

Because of ever-increasing parallel execution scale, today's scientific simulations are producing volumes of data too large to be accommodated in storage systems. The limitation comes from the limited storage capacity and I/O bandwidth of parallel file systems in production facilities. Cosmology simulations such as the Hardware/Hybrid Accelerated Cosmology Code (HACC) [12] are typical examples of parallel executions facing this issue. HACC solves an N-body problem involving domain decomposition, a medium-/long-range force solver based on a particle-mesh method, and a short-range force solver based on a particle-particle/particle-mesh algorithm. According to cosmology researchers, the number of particles to simulate can be up to 3.5 trillion in today's simulations (and even more in the future), which leads to 60 PB of data to store; yet a system such as the Mira supercomputer has only 26 PB of file system storage. Currently, HACC users rely on decimation in time, storing only a fraction of the simulation

J.M. Kunkel et al. (Eds.): ISC High Performance Workshops 2017, LNCS 10524, pp. 43–54, 2017.
https://doi.org/10.1007/978-3-319-67630-2_4

snapshots, to reduce the pressure on the storage system. A reduction factor of 80% to 90% is commonly used. At exascale, temporal decimation will not be enough to address the limitations of the storage system: snapshots will be so large (each in the range of 5 PB) that the time to store each snapshot (83 min on a storage system offering a sustained bandwidth of 1 TB/s) will become a serious problem. HACC is not a special case. As indicated by [11], nearly 2.5 PB of data were produced by the Community Earth System Model for the Coupled Model Intercomparison Project (CMIP) 5, which further introduced 170 TB of postprocessing data submitted to the Earth System Grid [3]. Estimates of the raw data requirements for the CMIP6 project exceed 10 PB [2]. At exascale, storing each full snapshot in this case would also take too long, however, so that on-line/in situ compression of each snapshot is needed.

In this paper, we explore pattern-matching techniques for lossy compression, focusing on individual snapshots of the scientific data sets produced by cosmology simulations. Because of the constraints of memory consumption, we cannot leverage the smoothness of a particle's trajectory (such as smoothness along the time dimension) to reduce the data size; hence, we must perform compression on individual snapshots. Unlike the mesh data produced by conventional simulations, such as fluid dynamics, the data of particles in cosmology simulations, such as coordinate and velocity data, are stored in separate 1D arrays. In the HACC application, the indices of each 1D array are kept consistent for the same cosmology particle. Specifically, the HACC simulation data contains six 1D arrays: three coordinate fields (xx, yy, zz) and three velocity fields (vx, vy, vz). Because of the lack of correlation between adjacent particles in the HACC data set, state-of-the-art lossy compressors, such as FPZIP [16], ZFP [15] and SZ [9,20], reach relatively low compression ratios/factors (2 to 5 with the error bound set to 10^{-4}).

The rest of the paper is organized as follows. In Sect. 3, we formulate the data compression problem based on cosmology simulation data sets and the assessment of several state-of-the-art lossy compressors on the HACC data sets. In Sect. 4, we discuss the well-known dictionary-based lossless compression algorithm LZ77 and propose our pattern-matching-based optimization method for SZ lossy compression for low spatial coherence and highly irregular data, such as the velocity variables in the HACC data sets. In Sect. 5, we evaluate the compression ratios of our proposed optimization method and compare it with one variant of the SZ lossy compressor. We discuss related work in Sect. 2 and provide conclusions in Sect. 6.

2 Related Work

Data compression has been extensively studied for decades and can be split into two categories: lossless compression and lossy compression. The main limitation of the lossless compressors (such as GZIP [9]) is their fairly low compression ratio on scientific data sets composed of floating-point values, as confirmed by [10,20,22].

Fig. 1. Overview of SZ lossy compression algorithm.

Recently, many lossy compressors have been designed and implemented for scientific data. Most of them are designed for mesh data sets, which are expected to have strong coherence among the nearby data in the data set, but the quality of their compression declines on cosmology simulation data sets. For example, SZ [10,22] has five main steps including (1) data prediction for each point by its preceding neighbors in the multidimensional space, (2) error-controlled linear quantization, (3) customized Huffman coding [13] (i.e., variable-length encoding) to shrink the data size significantly, (4) unpredictable data compression, and (5) customized LZ77 coding (i.e., dictionary-based encoding). The compression framework of SZ is shown in Fig. 1. ZFP [16] splits the whole data set into many small blocks with an edge size of 4 along each dimension and compresses the data in each block separately by a series of carefully designed steps (including alignment of exponent, orthogonal transform, fixed-point integer conversion, and binary representation analysis with bit-plane encoding). FPZIP [17] adopts predictive coding and ignores insignificant bit planes in the mantissa based on the analysis of IEEE 754 binary representation [7]. SSEM [21] splits data into a high-frequency part and low-frequency part by wavelet transform [8] and then uses vector quantization and GZIP. ISABELA [15] sorts the data and then performs the data compression by B-spline interpolation; but it has to store an extra index array to record the original location for each point, and it suffers significantly from low compression ratio. Compression of particle simulation data sets has also been studied for years, but most of the methods proposed are based on smooth temporal trajectory of the same particles, which requires loading/keeping multiple snapshots during the compression/simulation [1,6,14,18,23]. Thus, they are not suitable for extremely large-scale simulation in which only one snapshot is allowed to be loaded into the memory. Omeltchenko et al. [19] proposed a lossy compression method (called CPC2000 in this paper) that does not rely on temporal coherence and relies on only a single snapshot. Its main steps involve reorganizing all particles in the space onto a zigzag-similar space-filling curve [5], sorting the particles based on the R-indices by a radix-similar sorting method in each block, and compressing the difference of the adjacent indices by adaptive variable-length coding.

3 Problem Formulation

Scientific data compression algorithms can be classified into two categories: lossless compression and lossy compression. The main limitation of lossless compressors is their limited data reduction capability, that is, up to 2:1 in general [20] and even lower on cosmology simulation simulation data sets. In this work, therefore, we focus on lossy compression methods for cosmology simulations.

Cosmology simulations generate multiple snapshots. Because of considerations of memory consumption, we focus on single-snapshot compression without using temporal coherence in this work. Such simulations contain many variables each representing one data field of particles. In the HACC simulation data considered in this study, the variables are stored in separate 1D arrays. Specifically, each snapshot of HACC simulation contains six single-precision floating-point variables: xx, yy, zz, vx, vy, and vz. The first three indicate coordinate information, and the other three indicate velocity along the three dimensions. The six variables are stored in separate floating-point arrays. Unlike regular multi-dimensional mesh data, the particle elements in each array are allowed to be reordered in the reconstructed data set, whereas the locations or indices of the elements with regard to the same particle must be consistent across arrays.

The main objective of our work is to optimize the single-snapshot lossy compression ratio for cosmology simulation data sets, provided that the compression errors are controlled within a user-specified bound for each data point. *Compression ratio* is the ratio of the original data size to the compressed data size. Table 1 shows the compression ratios of several state-of-the-art lossy compressors on the HACC data sets under the value-range-based relative error bound 10^{-4}, denoted by $eb_{rel} = 10^{-4}$. The version of the SZ lossy compressor we focus on in this work is "SZ-LV", which is based on the last-value prediction model. Note that for CPC2000, ZFP, and SZ, we use the absolute error bounds computed based on $eb_{rel} = 10^{-4}$ and the value range of each variable; for FPZIP, we set the number of retained bits to 21 as approximate $eb_{rel} = 10^{-4}$ for all the variables. The SZ lossy compressor has higher compression ratios on the coordinate variables (i.e., xx, yy, zz) than on the velocity variables (i.e., vx, vy, vz). Therefore, in this work we focus on optimizing the prediction accuracy and compression ratios based on SZ lossy compression for the velocity variables in the HACC data.

Table 1. Compression ratios of different variables with different compressors on HACC data sets under value-range-based relative error bound 10^{-4}.

Compressor	xx	yy	zz	vx	vy	vz
CPC2000	7.1	7.1	7.1	2.3	2.3	2.3
FPZIP	5.8	5.7	4.4	2.2	2.2	2.2
ZFP	2.3	2.3	2.2	2.3	2.3	2.3
SZ	8.2	8.3	5.9	4.0	4.0	4.0

4 Pattern-Matching Techniques for Lossy Compression

In this section, we first discuss the well-known dictionary-based lossless compression algorithm Lempel-Ziv 77 (LZ77). It can encode a sequence of symbols and compress the input source by using the information of recently frequent consecutive symbols. Inspired by LZ77's classic idea, we then propose our pattern-matching-based lossy compression method, called SZ-PM. Because of different input sources, we propose many tailored designs for dealing with lossy compression and floating-point scientific data.

4.1 LZ77: String Matching Based Lossless Compression

```
while look-ahead buffer is not empty do
    go backwards in search buffer to find longest match of the look-ahead
    buffer;
    if match found then
        output (offset, length, next symbol in look-ahead buffer);
        shift sliding window by length+1;
    else
        output (0, 0, first symbol in look-ahead buffer);
        shift sliding window by 1;
    end
end
```

Algorithm 1. Pseudo code of the LZ77 algorithm

The Lempel-Ziv 77 (LZ77) lossless compression algorithm is the first Lempel-Ziv compression algorithm. Unlike scientific data compression, LZ77 is designed for encoding a sequence of symbols byte by byte based on a dictionary constructed from a portion of the recently encoded sequence. Specifically, LZ77 encodes the input sequence through a sliding window composed of two buffers, a search buffer and a look-ahead buffer, as shown in Fig. 2. The search buffer contains the most recently compressed symbols, while the look-ahead buffer contains multiple uncompressed symbols. The algorithm searches the longest prefix of the look-ahead buffer that is also contained in the search buffer. The details of LZ77 are shown in Algorithm 1. The LZ77 algorithm searches all the consecutive symbols in the search buffer to identify whether these symbols match the consecutive symbols in the look-ahead buffer. The offset in the algorithm represents the distance of the longest match's first symbol (in the search buffer) from the look-ahead buffer, and length represents the length of the longest match. Therefore, the general idea of LZ77 is to save storage by using the information from the recent symbol sequences based on a string-matching approach. It inspires us to design a similar matching technique for lossy scientific data compression.

4.2 SZ-PM: Pattern-matching-based Lossy Compression

We propose a pattern-matching-based lossy compression method called SZ-PM. The idea of pattern matching is similar to the string matching idea used in LZ77. It is also designed to use the information of recent floating-point sequences with similar pattern in order to improve the prediction accuracy and compression

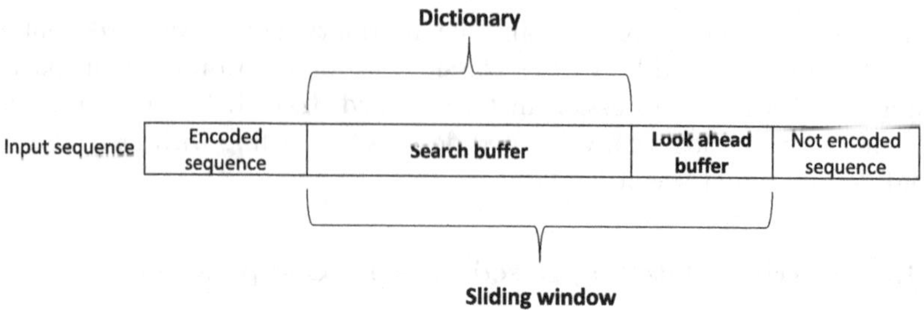

Fig. 2. Overview of LZ77 lossless compression algorithm.

ratio of SZ lossy compression for irregular data. Unlike the lossless compression algorithm for symbols (one byte per symbol), however, the lossy compression for scientific data is designed mainly for single/double floating-point data (4/8 bytes per value) and can tolerate compression errors within user-controlled error bounds. Therefore, we can design many tailored features for the pattern-matching method.

Let us first define necessary notations. Similar to LZ77, our algorithm also maintains two buffers in the sliding window during the compression: a search buffer and a look-ahead buffer. Let the search buffer size be m and the look-ahead buffer size be n. Here the buffer size represents the number of data points in the buffer. Let the m compressed data points in the search buffer be $\{s_1, s_2, ..., s_m\}$ and the n uncompressed data points in the look-ahead buffer be $\{l_1, l_2, ..., l_n\}$. Let the $m - n + 1$ sequences with length of n in the search buffer to be $X_1, X_2, ..., X_{m-n+1}$, where $X_1 = \{s_1, ..., s_n\}, X_2 = \{s_2, ..., s_{n+1}\}, ..., X_{m-n+1} = \{s_{m-n+1}, ..., s_m\}$. Let the one sequence with length of n in the search buffer be $Y = \{l_1, l_2, ..., l_n\}$.

We now describe our tailored designs of pattern matching for lossy compression and scientific data. For compression, (1) we fix the length of matching sequences to be the size of look-ahead buffer (i.e., n). In other words, we attempt to identify the most similar sequence in the search buffer for the whole look-ahead buffer with length n. (2) We sort the n data points in each sequence, including X_1, X_2, ..., X_{m-n+1} from the search buffer and Y from the look-ahead buffer. (3) For each sorted sequence, we subtract the mean value of the sequence from each value. In other words, we shift the sequence by its mean value as $X = (x_1 - \overline{X}, x_2 - \overline{X}, ..., x_n - \overline{X})$ and $Y = (y_1 - \overline{Y}, y_2 - \overline{Y}, ..., y_n - \overline{Y})$, where $\overline{X} = \frac{1}{n}\sum_{i=1}^{n} x_i$ and $\overline{Y} = \frac{1}{n}\sum_{i=1}^{n} y_i$. (4) We attempt to match the sequences from the search buffer for the look-ahead buffer, but we relax the "matching" condition. Specifically, the matching condition of LZ77 algorithm is that two symbol sequences are exactly the same; but in our algorithm we define two shifted floating-data sequences $X = (x_1, x_2, ..., x_n)$ and $Y = (y_1, y_2, ..., y_n)$ as "matched" if $(\sum_{i=1}^{n} |x_i - y_i|^p)^{1/p} < \theta$, where θ is a given threshold, X is one shifted sequence from the search buffer, and Y is the shifted sequence of the look-ahead buffer.

Note that the search buffer can have multiple matched sequences. (5) We pick the matched sequence X^* with the smallest distance from the multiple matched sequences as the most similar sequence for Y. We denote the values in X^* by $\{x_1^*, x_2^*, ..., x_n^*\}$. We name this matching process as "pattern matching" and the sequence X^* as the "pattern matched sequence" for Y. (6) We always shift the sliding window by length of n after we go over the $m - n + 1$ sequences in the search buffer. Unlike LZ77, we also shift the sliding window by length of n, even if we cannot find a matched sequence under the threshold θ. (7) We use X^* as the prediction sequence for Y, if the pattern matched sequence can be found. Specifically, we take $x_i^* - \overline{X^*}$ as the prediction value for $y_i - \overline{Y}$ of data point i. We use SZ's original prediction model proposed in [22] to generate the prediction values for Y, if no matched sequence exists in the search buffer. Therefore, we must use an extra bit, denoted by bit_{predmd}, to represent the prediction method of each sequence. For example, we use $bit_{predmd} = 0$ to indicate that the sequence is predicted by pattern-matching method and $bit_{predmd} = 1$ to indicate that the sequence is predicted by SZ's original prediction model. (8) Similar to LZ77, if the sequence is predicted by the pattern-matching method, we still have to store the offset; but we do not need to store the length due to the fixed length. We also have to store the mean value of Y in order to reconstruct the data during the decompression. (9) We use the linear quantization method and the customized Huffman coding proposed in [22] to encode the differences between prediction values and real values for Y and compress the quantization codes based on the user-set error bound. Because of space limitations, we do not describe them in detail here.

For decompression, we use the same decompression method proposed in [22] to construct the differences between prediction values and real values for each sequence. For example, in decompressing the sequence Y, we denote the difference of data point i in Y by y_i^{diff}. We then construct the prediction values of Y by its corresponding prediction method known from bit_{predmd}. If bit_{predmd} indicates Y is predicted by SZ's original prediction model during the compression, we construct its prediction values using the same process described in [22]; if bit_{predmd} indicates Y is predicted by the pattern-matching approach during the compression, we use the stored offset and mean value to construct the prediction values. Specifically, we can construct the prediction value of data point i by $y_i^{pred} = x_i^* - \overline{X^*} + \overline{Y}$, where X^* is the pattern-matched sequence that has already been decompressed. After constructing the prediction values for Y, we can reconstruct the value of data point i by $y_i^{decomp} = y_i^{pred} + y_i^{diff}$.

Algorithm 2 shows the pseudo code of our proposed pattern-matching-based lossy compression method. Figure 3 shows an example of two pattern-matched sequences transformed by sorting and shifting. We have several remarks here. (1) For our matching condition, we treat the two n-length floating-point sequences as two data points in the n-dimensional space and define them as "matched" if their distance in Lp norm is smaller than the threshold θ. According to [4], we set θ to 0.5 of the search buffer size. (2) From our initial study we find that $p > 1$ cannot reduce the size of the compressed quantization codes on the

HACC data; hence we set $p = 1/2$ in our algorithm and the following evaluation. (We will research the optimal p in the future.) (3) As a result of the sorting process, the reconstructed data is recorded in one sequence. But as described in Sect. 3, the particle elements in each 1D array are allowed to be reordered in the reconstructed data sets. Hence, we do not have to extra storage to record the initial index information. (4) We use extra memory space to sort and shift the sequences without any modifications of the original data. The reason for sorting and shifting is to increase the possibility of matching sequences due to the high irregularity of the data and the relatively large value range of the floating-point data.

```
while look-ahead buffer is not empty do
    sequence Y is composed of the n data points of the look-ahead buffer;
    search buffer contains m − n + 1 sequences {X_1, X_2, ..., X_{m−n+1}};
    sort each sequence including X_1, X_2, ..., X_{m−n+1} and Y;
    compare sorted Y with {X_1, X_2, ..., X_{m−n+1}} and find sequence X*
    with the smallest distance (in Lp norm) from Y, i.e., dist(X*, Y);
    if dist(X*, Y) < θ then
        bit_predmd = 0;
        store (offset, mean value Ȳ);
        prediction values of Y are calculated by y_i^pred = x_i* − X̄* + Ȳ;
    else
        bit_predmd = 1;
        use SZ's original prediction model to predict values of Y;
    end
    calculate differences between real value y_i and prediction value y_i^pred;
    encode differences using linear quantization method based on user-set
    error bound;
    compute and record decompressed value;
    shift sliding window by length of n;
end
compress linear quantization codes using Huffman coding;
compress unpredictable data by SZ's binary representation analysis;
```

Algorithm 2. Pseudo code of SZ-PM algorithm

5 Empirical Evaluation

In this section, we evaluate our proposed lossy compression method, SZ-PM, on the velocity variables in the HACC data sets, and we compare it with the SZ lossy compressor [22]. Note that the SZ lossy compressor we evaluate in this study is a variant of the original SZ. It first splits the original data into multiple segments. The segment size is consistent with the look-ahead buffer size. It then performs a sorting within each segment. After that, it conducts the original SZ compression on the transformed data. The reason of using this variant version

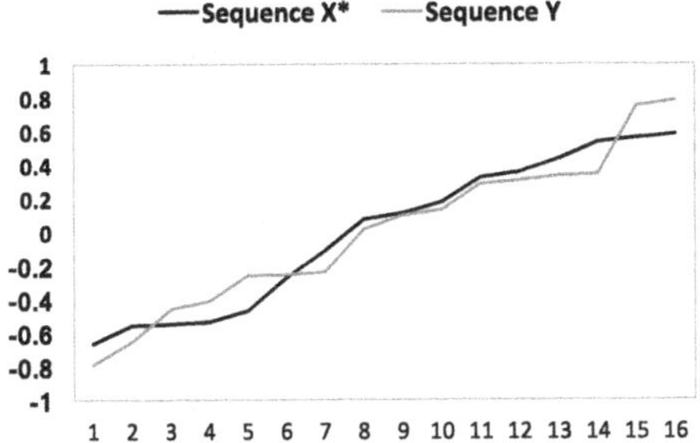

Fig. 3. Example of two pattern matched sequences after sorting and shifting.

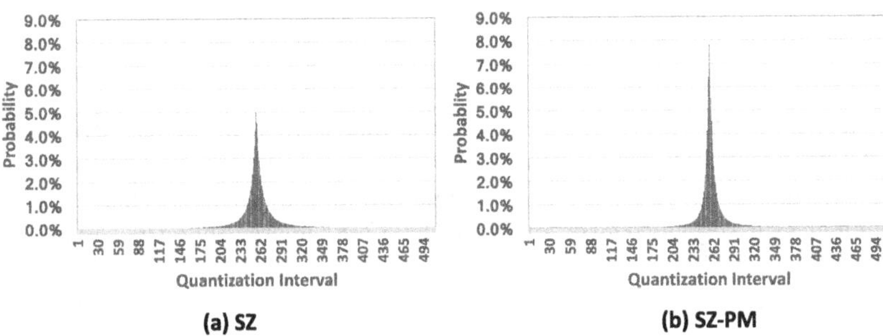

Fig. 4. Distribution produced by linear quantization encoder in (a) SZ and (b) SZ-PM on the velocity variable vx in the HACC data sets with 511 quantization intervals.

is that we want to evaluate the effects of the pattern-matching method without impact from the sorting technique and to compare SZ and SZ-PM in a fair level.

As described in [22], the distribution produced by linear quantization encoder can significantly affect the performance of Huffman coding [13]. Generally speaking, the more concentrated the distribution, the higher the compression ratio that the Huffman coding can achieve. Figure 4 shows the distributions produced by linear quantization encoder in the SZ and our proposed SZ-PM lossy compression method on the velocity variable vx in the HACC data sets. Note that we use a 10^{-4} value-range-based relative error bound and 511 quantization intervals. Based on our observation, 511 quantization intervals can cover more than 99.9% data points during the linear quantization in this case. The figure illustrates that our proposed SZ-PM can improve the prediction accuracy and make the distribution of quantization code more concentrated. (We will show the incremental results in detail later.)

Table 2 shows the experimental results of our evaluation for SZ-PM on the HACC data sets. In the experiments, we set the search buffer size to 1024; hence, we need to use 10 bits ($2^{10} = 1024$) to represent the offset value for each sequence that is predicted by the pattern-matching method during compression. We test SZ-PM with different configurations of three look-ahead buffer sizes: 8, 16, and 32. The size of each category presented in the table is the atomized

Table 2. Evaluation of our proposed SZ-PM on the velocity variable vx in the HACC data sets with different sizes of sorting/matching sequence.

	Size of quantization code (bits/value)	Size of bit_{predmd} (bits/value)	Ratio of PM sequence (%)	Size of offset (bits/value)	Size of mean value (bits/value)	Overall bit-rate (bits/value)	Compression ratio
CPC2000	/	/	/	/	/	13.9	2.30
SZ(8)	7.31	/	/	/	/	7.3	4.38
SZ-PM(8)	5.45	1/8	99.6%	1.25	3.98	10.5	2.96
SZ(16)	6.75	/	/	/	/	6.8	4.74
SZ-PM(16)	6.01	1/16	93.1%	0.58	1.86	8.5	3.76
SZ(32)	6.16	/	/	/	/	6.2	5.19
SZ-PM(32)	6.07	1/32	66.3%	0.04	0.66	6.8	4.71

size (i.e., bits per value). Note that the original data type of the HACC data is single floating-point (i.e., 32 bits per value); hence, the compression ratio can be calculated by $32/overall\_size$. The number in each bracket represents the segment size/sequence size; for example, SZ(8) means that the segment size used for sorting in SZ is 8, and SZ-PM(8) means that the length of sequence used in the pattern matching is 8. The column "Ratio of PM Sequence" means the ratio of the sequences predicted by the pattern matching during compression.

We make several observations from Table 2. (1) SZ-PM can improve the prediction accuracy and reduce the size of the compressed quantization codes. (2) The shorter the matching sequence is, the more accurately the SZ-PM can predict. (3) For SZ-PM, the shorter the matching sequence is, the smaller the compressed quantization codes will be; however, for SZ, on the contrary, the longer the segment is, the smaller the compressed quantization codes will be. (4) The longer the matching sequence is, the less the storage overhead that the offset and mean values will have. (5) The reduced size of the compressed quantization codes, achieved from the improvement of the prediction accuracy by SZ-PM, is counteracted by the incremental overhead of storing offset and mean values.

From these observations, we derive some useful lessons for future research with respect to the pattern-matching techniques in lossy compression as follows. (1) Our proposed pattern-matching technique can enhance the prediction accuracy and reduce the size of compressed quantization codes, but the improvement is not enough to cover the extra overhead introduced by storing offset and mean values. (2) We should further improve the prediction accuracy using a more advanced pattern-matching technique. (3) We should reduce/eliminate the extra overhead of offset and mean values, especially the mean values of floating-point data type. For example, we may shift the sequence by the value of the first element in the sequence; consequently, we do not need to store the mean values. (4) Currently, we consider reordering only one variable in the HACC data sets. In future research, we need to consider the impact of reordering one variable to the other variables, since we have to make all the variables consistent.

6 Conclusion

In this work, we explored pattern-matching techniques for lossy compression based on the SZ compressor. The experiments demonstrate that our proposed optimization method, SZ-PM, can improve the prediction accuracy and reduce the size of compressed quantization codes on the HACC velocity data, but the compression ratio cannot be improved because of storing extra information. We plan to explore ways to improve the prediction accuracy with the pattern-matching technique and to reduce the storage of extra information.

References

1. Ahmed, N., Natarajan, T., Rao, K.R.: Discrete cosine transform. IEEE Trans. Comput. **100**(1), 90–93 (1974)
2. Baker, A.H., Xu, H., Dennis, J.M., Levy, M.N., Nychka, D., Mickelson, S.A., Edwards, J., Vertenstein, M., Wegener, A.: A methodology for evaluating the impact of data compression on climate simulation data. In: HPDC 2014, pp. 203–214 (2014)
3. Bernholdt, D., Bharathi, S., Brown, D., Chanchio, K., Chen, M., Chervenak, A., Cinquini, L., Drach, B., Foster, I., Fox, P., et al.: The earth system grid: supporting the next generation of climate modeling research. Proc. IEEE **93**(3), 485–495 (2005)
4. Chan, K.P., Fu, A.W.C.: Efficient time series matching by wavelets. In: Proceedings of the 15th International Conference on Data Engineering, pp. 126–133. IEEE (1999)
5. Chanussot, J., Lambert, P.: Total ordering based on space filling curves for multivalued morphology. Comput. Imaging Vis. **12**, 51–58 (1998)
6. Chen, Z., Son, S.W., Hendrix, W., Agrawal, A., Liao, W., Choudhary, A.N.: NUMARCK: machine learning algorithm for resiliency and checkpointing. In: SC 2014, pp. 733–744 (2014)
7. Committee, I.S., et al.: 754–2008 IEEE standard for floating-point arithmetic. IEEE Comput. Soc. Std 2008 (2008)
8. Daubechies, I.: The wavelet transform, time-frequency localization and signal analysis. IEEE Trans. Inf. Theory **36**(5), 961–1005 (1990)
9. Deutsch, L.P.: GZIP file format specification version 4.3 (1996)
10. Di, S., Cappello, F.: Fast error-bounded lossy HPC data compression with SZ. In: 2016 IEEE International Parallel and Distributed Processing Symposium, IPDPS 2016, Chicago, IL, USA, 23–27 May 2016, pp. 730–739 (2016)
11. Gleckler, P.J., Durack, P.J., Stouffer, R.J., Johnson, G.C., Forest, C.E.: Industrial-era global ocean heat uptake doubles in recent decades. Nat. Clim. Chang. (2016)
12. Habib, S., Pope, A., Finkel, H., Frontiere, N., Heitmann, K., Daniel, D., Fasel, P., Morozov, V., Zagaris, G., Peterka, T., et al.: Hacc: simulating sky surveys on state-of-the-art supercomputing architectures. New Astron. **42**, 49–65 (2016)
13. Huffman, D.A., et al.: A method for the construction of minimum-redundancy codes. Proc. IRE **40**(9), 1098–1101 (1952)
14. Kumar, A., Zhu, X., Tu, Y.-C., Pandit, S.: Compression in molecular simulation datasets. In: Sun, C., Fang, F., Zhou, Z.-H., Yang, W., Liu, Z.-Y. (eds.) IScIDE 2013. LNCS, vol. 8261, pp. 22–29. Springer, Heidelberg (2013). doi:10.1007/978-3-642-42057-3_4

15. Lakshminarasimhan, S., Shah, N., Ethier, S., Ku, S., Chang, C., Klasky, S., Latham, R., Ross, R.B., Samatova, N.F.: ISABELA for effective in situ compression of scientific data. Concurr. Comput. Pract. Exp. **25**(4), 524–540 (2013)
16. Lindstrom, P.: Fixed-rate compressed floating-point arrays. IEEE Trans. Vis. Comput. Graph. **20**(12), 2674–2683 (2014)
17. Lindstrom, P., Isenburg, M.: Fast and efficient compression of floating-point data. TVCG **12**(5), 1245–1250 (2006)
18. Meyer, T., Ferrer-Costa, C., Pérez, A., Rueda, M., Bidon-Chanal, A., Luque, F.J., Laughton, C., Orozco, M.: Essential dynamics: a tool for efficient trajectory compression and management. J. Chem. Theory Comput. **2**(2), 251–258 (2006)
19. Omeltchenko, A., Campbell, T.J., Kalia, R.K., Liu, X., Nakano, A., Vashishta, P.: Scalable i/o of large-scale molecular dynamics simulations: A data-compression algorithm. Comput. Phys. Commun. **131**(1), 78–85 (2000)
20. Ratanaworabhan, P., Ke, J., Burtscher, M.: Fast lossless compression of scientific floating-point data. In: Proceedings of the Data Compression Conference, DCC 2006, pp. 133–142. IEEE (2006)
21. Sasaki, N., Sato, K., Endo, T., Matsuoka, S.: Exploration of lossy compression for application-level checkpoint/restart. In: 2015 IEEE International on Parallel and Distributed Processing Symposium (IPDPS), pp. 914–922. IEEE (2015)
22. Tao, D., Di, S., Chen, Z., Cappello, F.: Significantly improving lossy compression for scientific data sets based on multidimensional prediction and error-controlled quantization. In: 2017 IEEE International Parallel and Distributed Processing Symposium, IPDPS 2017, Orlando, Florida, USA, 29 May–2 June, 2017, pp. 1129–1139 (2017)
23. Yang, D.Y., Grama, A., Sarin, V.: Bounded-error compression of particle data from hierarchical approximate methods. In: Proceedings of the 1999 ACM/IEEE Conference on Supercomputing, SC 1999. ACM, New York, NY, USA (1999)

Third International Workshop on Communication Architectures for HPC, Big Data, Deep Learning and Clouds at Extreme Scale (ExaComm)

Design Space Exploration of the Dragonfly Topology

Min Yee Teh[1(✉)], Jeremiah J. Wilke[2], Keren Bergman[1], and Sébastien Rumley[1]

[1] Lightwave Research Laboratory, Columbia University, New York, NY 10027, USA
mt3126@columbia.edu
[2] Scalable Modeling and Analysis, Sandia National Labs, Livermore, CA 94551, USA

Abstract. We investigate possible options of creating a Dragonfly topology capable of accommodating a specified number of end-points. We first observe that any Dragonfly topology can be described with two main parameters, *imbalance* and *density*, dictating the distribution of routers in groups, and the inter-group connectivity, respectively. We then introduce an algorithm that generates a dragonfly topology by taking the desired number of end-points and these two parameters as input. We calculate a variety of metrics on the generated topologies resulting from a large set of parameter combinations. Based on these metrics, we isolate the subset of topologies that present the best economical and performance trade-off. We conclude by summarizing guidelines for Dragonfly topology design and dimensioning.

Keywords: Topologies · Dragonfly · Optical interconnects

1 Introduction

The Dragonfly topology, introduced by Kim et al. [1], is a direct topology, in which every router accommodates a set of *terminal* connections leading to end-points, and a set of *topological* connections leading to other routers. The Dragonfly concept fundamentally relies on the notion of *groups*. A collection of routers belonging to the same group are connected with *intra-group* connections, while router pairs belonging to different groups are connected with *inter-group* connections. In practical deployments, routers and associated end-points belonging to a group are assumed to be compactly colocated in a very limited number of chassis or cabinets. This permits connections between routers and terminals within a group to be implemented using short-distance, low-cost electrical transmission links. Meanwhile, *inter-group* connections are based on optical equipment capable of spanning inter-cabinet distances in the range of tens of meters.

Modularity is one of the main advantages provided by the dragonfly topology. Owing to the clear distinction between intra- and inter-group links, the wiring within a group is independent of the total number of groups in the topology.

J.M. Kunkel et al. (Eds.): ISC High Performance Workshops 2017, LNCS 10524, pp. 57–74, 2017.
https://doi.org/10.1007/978-3-319-67630-2_5

Vendors can therefore propose all-included, all-equipped cabinets corresponding to a group, while supercomputer operators are free to decide how many such groups/cabinets they want to acquire. For instance, the XC40 architecture proposed by Cray consists of 1 to 241 groups [3]. The fixed intra-group wiring also makes upgrading a dragonfly based supercomputer relatively straightforward from a hardware point-of-view, as only existing inter-group links may have to be reorganized. In some cases, incumbent inter-group links can even be kept in place, and simply complemented with additional inter-group links connecting the incumbent groups with several interconnected new groups.

A dragonfly topology also guarantees a large path diversity between end-points, enabling various flavors of adaptive, non-minimal routing schemes [1]. In the presence of congestion between two groups, traffic can first be deflected to third party groups, then forwarded to the correct destination. This feature allows the bandwidth available between two groups to be virtually multiplied by a factor of up to $g - 2$, where g is the number of groups.

Besides its modularity and capability to leverage non-minimal routing schemes, the Dragonfly topology also clearly distinguishes optical from electrical cables connecting the routers. Although the price gap is shrinking, optical links are still generally more expensive than their electrical counterpart, and thus represent a considerable fraction of an interconnect's total cost. There is therefore a motivation to allow fine-tuning of the expensive "optical bandwidth". A dragonfly cleanly separates the most expensive fraction of the bandwidth (optical) outside the cabinets while leaving the least expensive part (electrical) "hard-wired" inside the cabinets. As not all parallel applications require the same balance between bandwidth and computation, being able to adapt the bandwidth available at procurement time is an interesting feature. For instance, supercomputer operators interested in compute power and less concerned with bandwidth-intensive workloads can save on the "optical-bandwidth" and invest in additional cabinets.

All these interesting features make the Dragonfly topology the default choice for the whole XC series of Cray [4], and is thus widely adopted in the largest supercomputing platforms. The dragonfly concept also triggered sustained interest from the scientific community, with research papers addressing congestion in dragonflies [5] or optimizing throughput [6], and possible inclusion of optical switching [7].

One can note across literature, however, the varying ideas of what constitutes a Dragonfly. Here we aim to clarify the definition of the Dragonfly and then show what a Dragonfly can and cannot be. We first make the relatively trivial but important statement that a Dragonfly with fully-meshed intra-group connectivity can be assimilated into a *2-dimensional Flattened Butterfly* (2D-FB) [2], but with partial connectivity in one dimension (the one wired with optical cables). We then show that a Dragonfly topology can be described by a) the varying sizes of the two dimensions of the underlying 2D-FB, and b) the number of links in the optical dimension. Having reduced the shape of a Dragonfly topology to these two parameters, we perform a thorough exploration of the Dragonfly design space. We finally analyze the value of the identified designs by means of a cost model. Our analyses are related to the those reported by Camarero et al. [8], but with a focus on practical insights rather than graph theory.

2 Dragonfly Variants Description and Construction

2.1 Definitions

We begin by introducing a notation much inspired by the one originally given by Kim et al. [1]. We consider a Dragonfly as being made of g groups with a routers in each group, therefore with a total of $S = ag$ routers. Each router accommodates p *terminal* connections to end-points. Because we uniquely consider Dragonflies with fully-meshed intra-group connectivity in this paper, each router also accommodates $a - 1$ intra-group connections to the other $a - 1$ routers of the group. Finally, each router has h inter-group connections to routers located in other groups. We immediately remark that under these assumptions, each router must offer at least $radix = p + h + a - 1$ ports and that the topology can scale to $N = Sp = agp$ terminals. The topology is also made of $ga(a-1)/2$ bi-directional electrical links, and $gah/2$ optical ones.

We additionally introduce Δ as the global average distance in the Dragonfly graph, i.e. the average of the minimal number of hops separating every possible node pair (a node in the graph represents a router). We note that Δ is a function of the a, g and h parameters, nevertheless we privilege the Δ notation to $\Delta(a, g, h)$ for brevity. Next to the global average distance Δ, we also introduce δ_i as the minimal distance separating node i from another node on average, which relates to Δ as $\Delta = \frac{1}{S}\sum_{i=1}^{S}\delta_i$.

We set the *imbalance* coefficient $b \in [-1, 1]$ to represent the relative size mismatch between the optical and electrical dimensions, and the *density* coefficient $d \in [0, 1]$ to represent the degree of connectivity in the optical dimension. These two parameters will be further described in Sect. 2.4. Finally, because we are interested in comparing Dragonflies of similar scales, we introduce $S_{desired}$ as a parameter imposing a minimal number of routers (hence $S \geq S_{desired}$), and $N_{desired}$ to impose a minimal number of end-points ($N \geq N_{desired}$).

2.2 Dragonfly Construction

Six examples of Dragonflies all made of $S = S_{desired} = 42$ nodes are illustrated in Fig. 1. We call the case drawn in Fig. 1a the *canonical* design. We take this case as the starting point for our explorations. A Dragonfly is said to be *canonical* when $g = a + 1$ and $h = 1$. In that case, the number of *inter-group* connections associated to a group is $ha = g - 1$, i.e. a group is exactly connected once to every other group. This is in contrast with the case shown in Fig. 1b, which has the same g and a values as the *canonical* case but has $h = 6$ inter-group

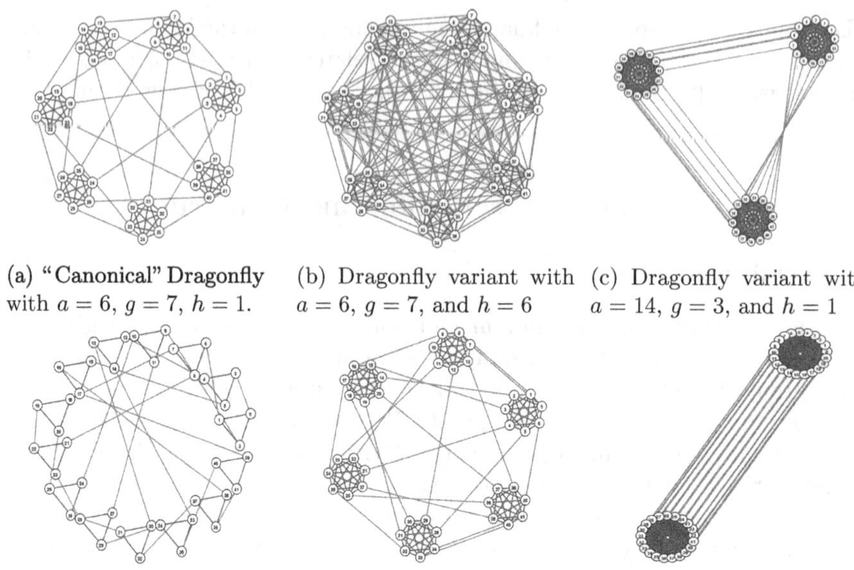

(a) "Canonical" Dragonfly with $a = 6$, $g = 7$, $h = 1$.
(b) Dragonfly variant with $a = 6$, $g = 7$, and $h = 6$
(c) Dragonfly variant with $a = 14$, $g = 3$, and $h = 1$
(d) Dragonfly variant with $a = 3$, $g = 14$, and $h = 1$
(e) Dragonfly variant with $a = 7$, $g = 6$, and $h = 1$
(f) Dragonfly variant with $a = 21$, $g = 2$, and $h = 1$

Fig. 1. Examples of $S_{\text{desired}} = 42$ Dragonfly variants parameterized using different combinations of a, g, and h. Purple links represent inter-group optical links, while blue links represent intra-group electrical links (Color figure online).

links per router. In this case, not only is every group connected to every other group, but every router is directly connected to every other group (as $h = g - 1$). As a result, the Dragonfly becomes effectively a 2D-FB with a maximal optical dimension. Through this example, we see that every router can be characterized by a point described by coordinate (x, y) in a 2D-lattice, with x giving the router's position in the electrical dimension (i.e. within a group) and y giving the group the router belongs to. We further remark that the size of the *electrical* dimension is a (as $x \in [0, a - 1]$), and the size of the *optical* dimension is g ($y \in [0, g - 1]$). The optical dimension is minimally populated when $h = 1$ and maximally populated with $h = g - 1$. We also note that the cases in Fig. 1a and b have similar sizes in both the optical and electrical dimensions, with Fig. 1b having maximal optical connections (note $h = g - 1 = 6$) while Fig. 1a has minimal optical connections (note $h = 1$). We can therefore describe the *canonical* dragonfly as a case with minimal optical wiring (since $h = 1$), in which routers are identically distributed across both electrical and optical dimensions. Note that this *canonical* construction still allows every group pair to be directly connected.

Figure 1c shows a case of great discrepancy between electrical and optical dimensions, with the electrical dimension ($a = 14$) much larger than the optical one ($g = 3$). We note that each group has $ah = 14$ inter-group links, the total number of inter-group links is $gah/2 = 21$, and that each pair of groups is connected through 7 connections. This means that exactly half of the routers in, say, group 0 are connected to group 1, and the other half to group 2.

Figure 1d shows an opposite case with a small electrical dimension ($a = 3$, $g = 14$). Since only one inter-group link is allocated to each router, the number of inter-group links leaving each group is only $ah = 3$, which does not permit full inter-group connectivity. Also note that it is not straightforward to pick which 3 among 13 other groups to form an inter-group connection with, since there are many such possible combinations. A similar problem of links/group-mismatching is faced in the example shown in Fig. 1e: each group has $ah = 7$ inter-group links at its disposal, whereas only $g - 1 = 5$ neighboring groups must be reached. To allocate inter-groups links in these "inharmonious" cases, a wiring algorithm is introduced in the next subsection. Finally, Fig. 1f shows a case of when $h = g-1$. Due to this equality, the resulting topology is a 2D-FB, and although $h = 1$, it is incidentally also equals to $g-1$, and thus cannot be scaled larger. Through these examples, we see that the design space for a Dragonfly with $S = 42$ is already quite wide, demonstrating the richness of designs when S scales to $1,000$ or higher.

2.3 Dragonfly Graph Wiring Algorithm

As discussed in the previous subsection, in order to explore the entire design space, we need to be able to generate a Dragonfly topology described by any arbitrary combination of a, g, and h parameters. Given this set of parameters, we would like to distribute the inter-group links between groups such that the diameter and global average distance Δ are minimized, while maintaining fairness by avoiding unevenly-connected nodes (indicated by high variance of δ_i).

The problem of distributing inter-group links is that to achieve optimal fairness, diameter or Δ (or a combination thereof) is NP-hard. Instead of targeting global optimality, the wiring algorithm we introduce is a greedy heuristic. The algorithm starts by considering every group as a vertex in a secondary graph $G = (V, E)$, and by allocating $a \times h$ links to each vertex $V_k \in V$, effectively creating an inter-group topology. The destination group V_i of each newly added link is chosen by considering the sum of two factors: (a) the total number of connections V_i has with every other vertex in G, and (b) the number of connections V_i has with the target group, V_k, specifically. To maintain wiring fairness and minimize diameter, the V_i that corresponds to the lowest sum of the aforementioned two factors is picked. As a result of this policy, the algorithm may select V_i even though one or more links have already been awarded to the (V_k, V_i) pair. Once the link has been allocated to said group pair, the algorithm then identifies the routers within groups k and i with the least number of connections so far, and connects these two routers.

When the graph G is sparsely occupied by edges, every group is equally likely to be picked to form a link with V_k, and inter-group link allocation resembles the *relative global link* arrangement as discussed in E. Hastings et al. [11]. As G becomes more saturated with edges, the algorithm tends to distribute links

Algorithm 1. Dragonfly Wiring Algorithm

define $G := (V, E)$, s.t V is set of all the Dragonfly groups and E is the set of inter-group links
initialize $\eta_{ij} := 0, \forall\, i, j \in V$
for $k \in V$ **do**
  for $d := 0, ..., a \times h$ **do**
    for $i \in V$ where $i \neq k$ **do**
      define $\mu_i := \eta_{ik} + \sum_{j \in V} \eta_{ij}, \forall\, i, j$ s.t $j \neq k$
      pick i s.t $\mu_i = \min_{i' \in V} \mu_{i'}$ and $\sum_{j \in V} \eta_{ij} < (a \times h)$
      $\eta_{ik} := \eta_{ik} + 1$
    end for
  end for
end for

in a fair way by selecting groups currently with the lowest number of formed connections, thus making inter-group link arrangement seem more random.

In the preceding pseudocode, η_{ij} is used to represent the total number of inter-group links connecting group i to group j. Since G is an undirected graph, symmetry dictates that $\eta_{ij} = \eta_{ji}$. μ_i denotes the "score" of the group i, which is used to account for the sum of both how many inter-group links the current target group k shares with destination group i (accounted for by η_{ik} term), and how many inter-group links destination group i currently shares with other groups (accounted for by $\sum \eta_{ij}$ term).

We evaluated the topologies obtained with our wiring algorithm in terms of global average distance Δ, diameter, and fairness. To measure wiring fairness, we consider two metrics: the first identifies δ_{min} and δ_{max} among all δ values, i.e. the average distances seen from the best and worst connected node, respectively, and calculate the greatest percentage difference, d, using $d = 100(\frac{\delta_{max} - \delta_{min}}{\delta_{min}})$. The second metric calculates the squared coefficient of variation across the δ_i set. Results for a set of topologies with at least $S_{desired} = 1000$ are displayed in Fig. 2. We observe that global average distances Δ generally decreases as more links are added to the optical dimension. In general, the larger the groups, g (thus smaller group sizes, a), the more reliant the Dragonfly is on optical

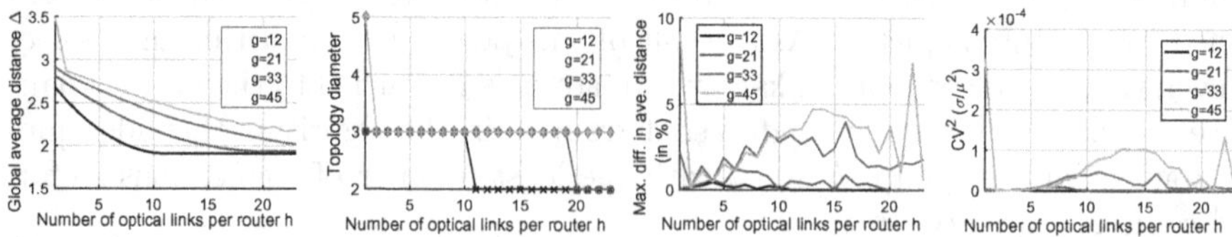

Fig. 2. (a) Global average distance Δ, (b) topology diameter, (c) maximum difference between smaller and larger node average distance δ_i, and (d) squared coefficient of variation of δ_i.

links to "reach" routers in other groups, as opposed to reaching them directly via the intra-group electrical links. This translates into larger Δ values for the same h. Note that ripples appear for $g = 45$, revealing some limitations in the wiring algorithm. More importantly, when $a \times h$ reaches or exceeds $g - 1$, both dimensions are fully populated, and we obtain a 2D-FB topology with diameter of 2. At this point, additional inter-group links are parallel to existing links, which does not affect Δ. In contrast, when $g = 45$, and $a = \lceil \frac{S_{\text{desired}}}{g} \rceil = 23$, the diameter is 5 for $h = 1$ as shown in Fig. 2b. Hence, with $ah = 23$ inter-group links per group, all-to-all group connectivity cannot be guaranteed anymore.

Figure 3 shows the sorted δ_i values for 16 datapoints of Fig. 2. The maximum difference d between δ_{min} and δ_{max} is also displayed. For $(g = 12, a = 84, h = 15)$, $(g = 21, a = 48, h = 15)$ and $(g = 21, a = 48, h = 10)$, the average distance δ_i is the same for all nodes and d is therefore null (ideal fairness). In the first case, h is larger than $g - 1$ leading to a saturation of the connectivity in the optical dimension thus to a 2D-FB topology. In the second case, each group has $a \times h = 48 \times 15 = 720$ inter-group links, which is a round multiple of $g - 1 = 20$. Every group pair is thus awarded $720/20 = 36$ links. The fact that these 36 links must be further allocated to the $a = 48$ routers composing each group is not causing unfairness, a fact that validates the viability of the wiring algorithm. The same situation occurs in the third case $(g = 21, a = 48, h = 10)$: there are 480 inter-group links per group, which is also a round multiple of 20.

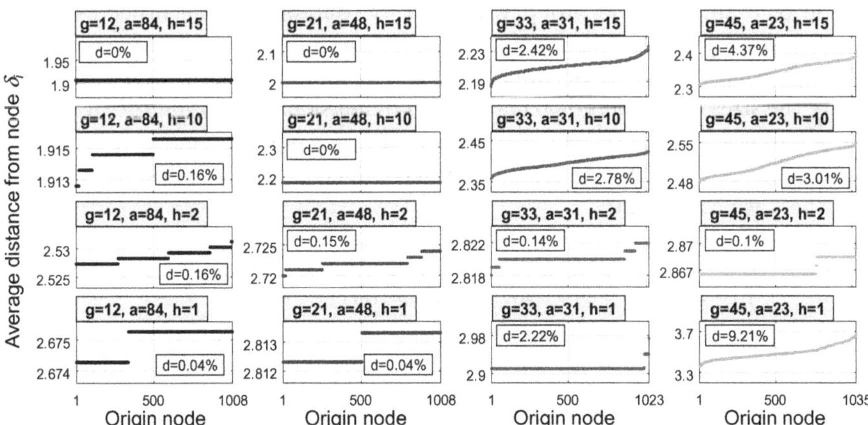

Fig. 3. Distributions of average distances of graph as viewed from each node. d in each plot denotes the percentage of greatest difference in average distance, δ_i

When $a \times h$ (the number of inter-group links per group) is not a multiple of $g - 1$, some group pairs receive extra links (the "remainder" links). These specific routers that are given the "remainder" links are consequently favored. Looking at the general behavior on Fig. 2(c-d), we observe that unfairness tend to grow with large h values, and with the number of groups g. In general, the more remainder links and group pairs, the harder it is to maintain fairness. Also note the bottom right cases on Fig. 3 ($h = 1$, $g = 33$ or 45): with less than one inter-group link per group pair on average, all-to-all inter-group connectivity is not maintained, causing the diameter to be 5. Such cases are also subject to increased unfairness.

2.4 Exploring the Dragonfly Using Imbalance and Density Parameters

As mentioned above, we introduce two parameters to control the shape of a Dragonfly topology. The *imbalance* coefficient $b \in [-1, 1]$ represents the relative size mismatch between the optical electrical dimensions, and the *density* coefficient $d \in [0, 1]$ represents to what extent the optical dimension is inter-connected. The density d parameter implicitly controls h through:

$$h = max(0, \lfloor 1 + d(g-2) \rfloor), \text{ where } 0 \leq d \leq 1 \text{ and g} > 1 \tag{1}$$

For $d = 0$, h is always equal to one (minimal inter-group connectivity). In contrast, for $d = 1$, $h = g - 1$, each router is connected to its counterpart in every other group, and the topology is thus a 2D-FB (maximal inter-group connectivity). For the imbalance parameter, $b = 0$ should reflect a situation as close to the *canonical* dragonfly as possible with $g = a - 1$. We define $b = -1$ as the case where the optical dimension is down-sized to $g = 1$, i.e. the topology is made of a single, large group with $a = S$ routers. On the other extreme, we define $b = 1$ to describe a topology with $g = S$ groups, each composed of a single router ($a = 1$). In order to control a and g using b, we first need to identify the sizes of the electrical and optical dimensions of a *canonical* Dragonfly corresponding to $S_{desired}$. Noting that $ag \geq S_{desired}$ and that $g = a + 1$, we can write $S_{desired} \geq a(a+1)$. Equality is achieved when $a_{canonical} = \frac{-1+\sqrt{1+4S_{desired}}}{2}$. From there we can define:

$$a = \begin{cases} \lceil a_{canonical} - b(S_{desired} - a_{canonical}) \rceil & \text{when } -1 \leq b < 0 \\ \lceil 1 + (1-b)(a_{canonical} - 1) \rceil & \text{when } 0 \leq b \leq 1 \end{cases} \tag{2}$$

$$g = \lceil S_{desired}/a \rceil \tag{3}$$

The above equations do permit us to obtain (i) $a = S_{desired}$ and $g = 1$ when $b = -1$; (ii) $a = 1$ and $g = S_{desired}$ when $b = 1$; and (iii) a construction close to one of the *canonical* dragonflies for $b = 0$. In the last case, taking for instance $S_{desired} = 2000$, we have $a_{canonical} \simeq 45.22$ thus $a = \lceil a_{canonical} \rceil = 46$ and $g = \lceil S_{desired}/a \rceil = 44$.

However, for negative b values, a linear control of a with b is ineffective. Hence, for $-1 < b < -0.5$, Eq. 2 returns $S_{desired} - 1 > a > S_{desired}/2$. When introduced into Eq. 3, these values all return $g = 2$. To avoid this pitfall, we use b to control g instead of a for negative b values. First, we similarly obtain $g_{canonical} = \frac{1+\sqrt{1+4S_{desired}}}{2}$. We then modify Eq. 3 into:

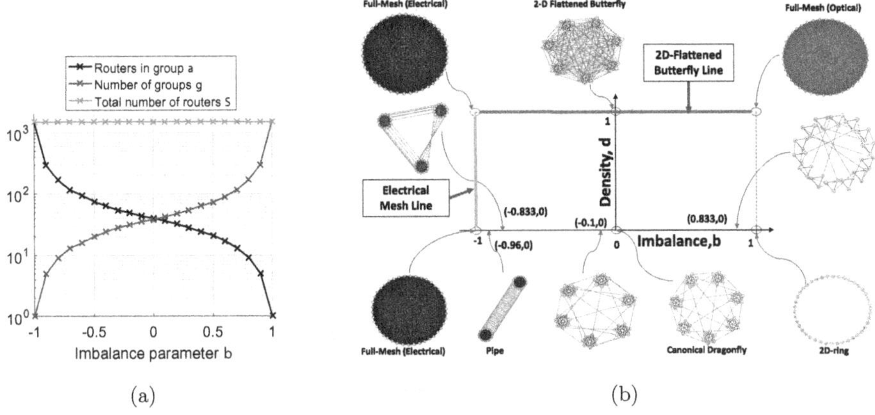

(a) (b)

Fig. 4. (a) Effect of imbalance parameter b on Dragonfly parameters. (b) Illustration of the Dragonfly design space. Each point within this space represents a unique Dragonfly variant.

$$g = \lceil 1 + (b+1)(g_{canonical} - 1) \rceil, a = \lceil S_{desired}/g \rceil \text{ when } -1 \leq b < 0 \tag{4}$$

$$a = \lceil 1 + (1-b)(a_{canonical} - 1) \rceil, g = \lceil S_{desired}/a \rceil \text{ when } 0 \leq b \leq 1 \tag{5}$$

Fig. 4a shows the obtained a, g and S values for $S_{desired} = 1500$ as a function of b. Defined this way, Eqs. 4 and 5 allow b to control a and g values while minimizing $ag - S_{desired}$.

Having introduced the mapping of (b, d) to (a, g, h), we can represent the Dragonfly design space as a rectangular space with $x \in [-1, 1]$ and $y \in [0, 1]$. The corner cases in the design space are drawn in Fig. 4b. Along the $b = -1$ line, the obtained topology is an electrical full-mesh. Since the optical dimension is non-existent, topologies along this line are not affected by density d. At coordinate $(1, 0)$ we find an optical ring. An optical full-mesh appears at coordinate $(1, 1)$. Finally, along the $d = 1$ line, we find all the 2D-FB constructs of size $S_{desired}$, except for $b = -1$ or $b = 1$ where either g or a, respectively, equals 1. We can also reverse-evaluate the *imbalance* and *density* coefficients of the designs shown in Fig. 1. In Fig. 1a, the canonical Dragonfly logically maps to $(0, 0)$ while the 2D-FB in Fig. 1b maps to $(0, 1)$. The other topologies of Fig. 1 are also reproduced in Fig. 4b along with their corrresponding coordinates in the design space.

Figure 5a and b depict how the ratio of optical links is affected by the two parameters b and d. As expected, when imbalance is $b = -1$ or $b = 1$ the topology has only one dimension, which is either fully electrical or optical. Figure 5c shows how the topology diameter is influenced by the density and imbalance. For $b = -1$, the topology is an electrical full-mesh of diameter 1. For $b = 1$ with densities $d = 0.5$ and $d = 0.8$, the resulting topologies are not 2D-FB, but the wiring density is large enough to always conserve one of the two 2-hop paths between each node pairs that a regular 2D-FB offers, resulting in diameter 2 topologies. When density $d = 0$ and $b = 1$, the topology becomes a ring with a diameter of 750. Figure 5d and e depict the impact of parameters on the global

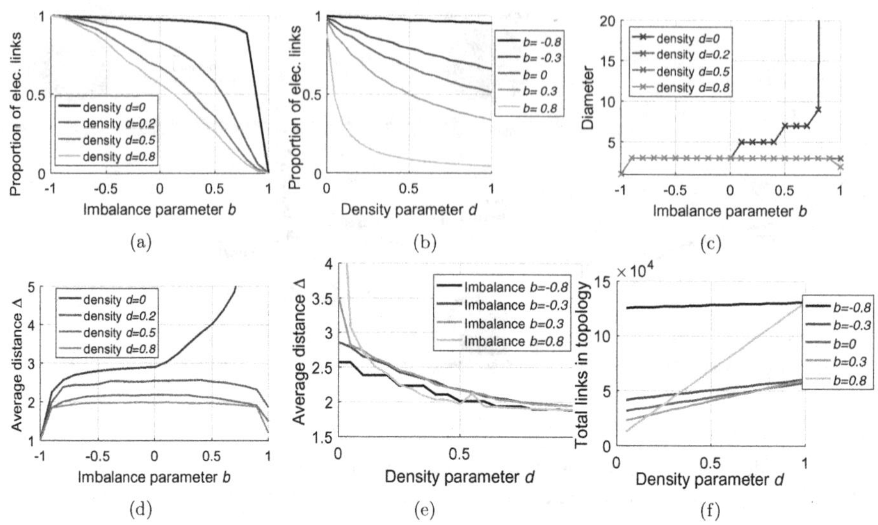

Fig. 5. Characteristics of Dragonfly topologies accommodating at least $S_{desired} = 1500$ routers.

average distance. As the imbalance leans toward negative values, Δ decreases, which is expected since more routers can be reached in 1 hop owing to the large intra-group electrical-mesh. Interestingly, positively imbalanced topologies also show lower Δ's than strictly balanced ones, provided enough *density* is given. This is mostly due to the high value that h can take when the number of groups g increases (as $h = \max(0, \lfloor 1 + d(g-2) \rfloor)$). Looking closer at the $b = 0.8$ case, we observe that the topology made from 167 groups translates into $h = 83$ when $d = 0.5$. The many inter-group links cause the vast majority of node pairs to be separated by two hops (electrical-optical, optical-electrical, and optical-optical). When $d = 1$ (2D-FB cases), graph diameter is at most 2, hence Δ converges to 1 as imbalance grows and the topology approaches a full-mesh.

These analyses highlight the diversity of Dragonfly designs, notably in terms of the proportion of optical links, average distance and diameter. However, this diversity also translates into a highly-varied total topological bandwidth (i.e. total number of links shown in Fig. 5f). Each topology thus possesses the ability to support different number of terminals (Fig. 5f) and corresponds to different implementation costs. In order to compare the diversely dense and balanced Dragonflies, we first show in the next section how to adapt our exploration space to exclusively identify topologies capable of accomodating a given number of terminals, $N_{desired}$. Then, in Sect. 4, we introduce a cost model to evaluate the cost of each design and elaborate on topologies supporting $N_{desired}$ terminals.

3 Constructing Dragonflies for a Minimal Number of End-Points

In our explorations so far, we have let the parameter p which denotes the number of terminals per router untouched. p is, however, a key factor in the Dragonfly construction, as it determines not only the final scalability of the topology, but also the required router radix. Moreover, we observe in Fig. 5f that the total number of links employed in the Dragonflies explored greatly varies with b and d, and consequently the available bandwidth of each topology also varies significantly. If a substantial amount of bandwidth is available within the topology, e.g. when the Dragonfly is heavily electrically-balanced ($b = -0.8$ as in Fig. 5f), we can populate the S routers with more terminals to ideally exploit the available bandwidth.

We can make the number of terminal attached to a router, p, proportional to the number of links attached to this same router $p \approx (a - 1 + h)$. This is the approach used in Kim et al. original Dragonfly proposal [1]. Since a Dragonfly is a diameter 3 topology, each transmitted bit is, in the worse case, forwarded twice onto a local link, once onto a global link, and once onto the destination's terminal link. This relationship gives us $p = \frac{a}{2} = h$. This approach, however, is too limited in our case, as our wiring algorithm may return topologies of variable diameter. Furthermore, for topologies strongly negatively-balanced (highly-negative b and large electrical groups), much of traffic remains within the groups, which contradicts the worst case assumption that every bit transits across groups.

To obtain a number of terminals p most suited to each of our designs, we start by remarking that the total traffic carried over a topology is proportional to the average path lengths (assuming no locality – every node pair have equal probability to exchange traffic). Thus, the total bandwidth made available by the topology should be proportional to Δ, and the number of traffic injectors should be inversely proportional to Δ. Since we cannot easily add bandwidth over the topology, we compensate Δ by changing p. This relationship can be expressed as follows:

$$p \approx \frac{S(a - 1 + h)}{\Delta} \tag{6}$$

In applying the methodology proposed by Rumley et al. [9], we can pick p such that the total traffic injected under uniform traffic must not exceed the total bandwidth installed, i.e. $N\Delta \leq S(a - 1 + h)$ which can be rewritten as:

$$p = \frac{N}{S} \leq \frac{(a - 1 + h)}{\Delta} \tag{7}$$

If we target an almost saturated topology under uniform traffic, $p_{selected} = \lfloor (a - 1 + h)/\Delta \rfloor$ terminals should be connected to every router. Note that the resulting network utilization (still under uniform traffic assumption) can be written as:

$$H = \frac{p_{selected}}{\left(\frac{(a-1+h)}{\Delta}\right)} \tag{8}$$

If equality is reached in Eq. 7, utilization is maximal (100%). In constrast, when equality in Eq. 7 is not met, $p_{selected}$ is smaller than $\frac{a-1+h}{\Delta}$ due to rounding, and utilization is consequently driven down.

Equation 7 is not entirely satisfying as it implies that the number of routers, S, best suited to support N terminals is already known – either dictated by a, g and h, or, when using our exploration mechanisms, given as a parameter alongside b and d. The resulting total number of terminals supported $N = pS$ might thus clearly differ from the original $N_{desired}$ goal. We can circumvent this limitation by iteratively testing a sequence of p values. As soon as p is fixed, $S_{desired}$ can be obtained as $S_{desired} = \lceil N_{desired}/p \rceil$, a Dragonfly topology of parameters b, d and S can be produced and its global average distance Δ subsequently obtained, which ultimately permits us to evaluate the bandwidth utilization (Eq. 8). The value $p_{selected}$ for which the utilization is the closest to 1 should be retained. To find $p_{selected}$, we note that the utilization necessarily grows with p. Hence, for very small p values, the number of routers S is large, which results greater number of links. As p is increases, the Dragonfly topology shrinks and so does its bandwidth. There is necessarily a p_{excess} for which utilization exceeds 1. Finding the p that maximizes the utilization can thus simply be achieved by considering incremental integer p values until reaching p_{excess}. This is computationally acceptable as p is typically smaller than 50 for most Dragonfly designs. One may also cap p by the limiting the router radix which equals $p+h+a-1$. Most modern routers available in the market today (year 2017) are limited to radices of ≈ 100. Meanwhile, Δ can be easily obtained as a side product of the wiring algorithm.

It is important to recognize the limitations of Eq. 7, as it only considers p such that the *total* bandwidth can support a uniform traffic, but does not guarantee that this bandwidth is available where the highest congestion occurs. For instance, Eq. 7 would not hold when the topology is one with two large groups connected by a single optical link, since the single optical link would need to support roughly half the traffic. Even with uniform traffic injection, the optical link would be subjected to extreme congestion, bottlenecking the network bandwidth at a lower bound than what the right-hand side of Eq. 7 provides. To prevent such situations, the utilization of each link could be individually evaluated and p selected in a way that would ensure that every link's utilization is below 1.

Figure 6 reports the properties of many Dragonflies generated with the technique described above, all of which capable of supporting at least $N_{desired} = 10,000$ terminals. We first observe how the value p corresponding to highest utilization, H, varies across designs (Fig. 6a). Through the $S = \lceil N_{desired}/p \rceil$ relationship, the number of routers S (Fig. 6b) is also affected and not stable as previously seen in Fig. 4a. Notice that the changing of S and density parameter also significantly affects the shape of the a and g curves of Fig. 6c.

We observe that the global average distances Δ in Fig. 6d is very much comparable to the constant $S_{desired}$ case depicted in Fig. 5d. This is because the average distance is mostly related to the structure of the topology, hence to b

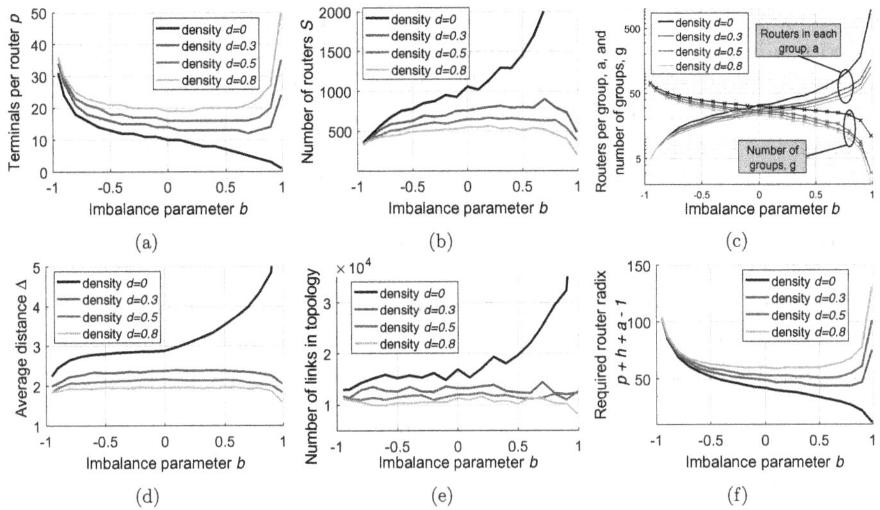

Fig. 6. Characteristics of Dragonfly topologies accommodating at least $N_{desired} = 10,000$.

and d, and only marginally related to its size. The shapes of the Δ curves propagates into the ones of p (Fig. 6a), as p is inversely proportional to Δ, and finally into the shapes of S. The number of links present in each topology (Fig. 6e) is also roughly proportional to Δ, and is overall less affected by the Dragonfly-"shaping" parameters b and d than previously when we explored topologies with a constant $S_{desired}$.

Figure 6f finally shows the impact of *imbalance* and *density* on the required radix. We note that when density is maximal, the radix requirements is minimized when topologies are balanced, which is a known property of Flattened-Butterflies. When density decreases, positively imbalanced topologies tend to favor low-radix routers. For minimal density $d = 0$, the required radix constantly decreases until the topology becomes a ring. It is interesting to note that designs with high b and low d becomes more favorable due to their low radix requirements. Figure 6b supports this as it shows that low router radices are required when there are more numerous routers in the Dragonfly. To clarify the value of these different option, we introduce in the next section a cost model for routers and links.

4 Design Selection via Cost Comparison

In this section we aim at estimating the cost a high-end HPC packet router switch of any radix. Based on pricing information available on ColfraxDirect [10], we considered a low-tier 24-port router currently priced at \$7095, and a high-tier 48-port router at \$10455, taken from the same supplier and both working at 100 Gb/s. These two data points are used to derive the following cost model.

We assume the marginal cost of adding a port to an existing router to be a U-shaped quadratic function with a minimum point at $radix = 36$. The rationales are the following: adding a port would benefit from economics of scale, but is also subject to technical complexity; the global minimum of the U-shaped curve correspond to the port count where the two effects negate each other. We place the minimum marginal cost in the middle of the low-tier and high-tier designs, assuming that with more resources, the supplier may incorporate a "mid-tier" 36-port router into its product line. Since this is not the case, two designs equally distant from the optimal cost will fulfill the market demands better. This causes the derivative of our cost model to be written as $\frac{d}{dr}cost(r) = c_1(r - 36)^2 + c_2$, where c_1 and c_2 are constants. Solving for the polynomial constants using the discussed price points, we arrive at the following cost model:

$$cost(r) = 0.0901r^3 - 9.73r^2 + 477r \tag{9}$$

where r is the radix/port count of the router, and cost(r) is in the units of \$'s. The resulting cost and it's derivative with respect to port-count for port counts between 0 and 128 are shown in Fig. 7a and b. We emphasize here that obtaining a model with a growing marginal cost per port is necessary to ensure that the router radix is not infinitely scalable. If the cost of a router is simply assumed a linear function of the number of ports, the cheapest topology becomes the one consisting of a single router with $N_{desired}$ ports. Provided that routers always have a radix multiple of 8 or 12, we then use this cost model to pinpoint the cost of routers with a range of radices. Logically, our model returns \$7095 and \$10,460 for 24-port and 48-port routers, respectively (\$296 and \$218 per port). A putative 64-port router is \$14,320 (\$228 per port). For 96 ports, this price grows to \$35,884 (\$374 per port).

For links, we consider a 100 Gb/s electrical link to be \$80 [10]. As we are interested in analyzing the impact the optical/electrical cost ratio has on the Dragonfly topology selection, we consider optical links to have cost comprised between \$80 (same as electrical) and \$800 (ten times more expensive). As of today (2017), optical links are about five times more expensive than their electrical counterparts.

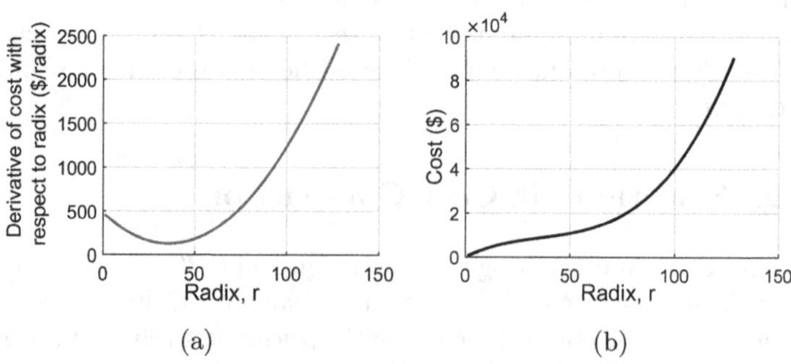

Fig. 7. Cost model for predicting router price as a function of radix/port count

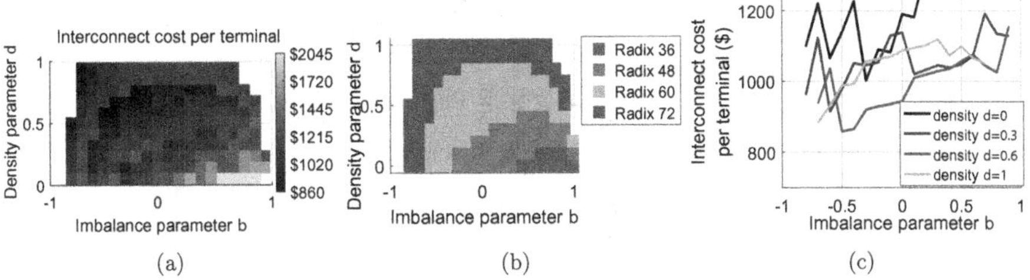

Fig. 8. Cost analysis of Dragonflies accomodating at least $N_{desired} = 10,000$ terminals

Results of the cost analysis are depicted in Fig. 8 for $N_{desired} = 10,000$, and considering radices of $[36, 48, 60, 72]$. Figure 8a shows how the cost evolves with the design space when considering \$400 for optical links. We note a correlation between Fig. 8a and b. The cheapest solutions are the ones that make the best use of the ports available. Figure 8c shows that the cheapest design found in our exploration is obtained for $b = -0.5$ and $d = 0.6$, which correspond to $g = 17$ groups of $a = 32$ routers, $p = 19$ terminals per router and $h = 10$ inter-group links per router. The proportion of electrical links to all links is 76%. We note that this cheapest design requires 60-port routers and dominates all designs requiring 72 ports. As expected, it is found in the negatively-balanced region that favors electrical links.

Figures 9a, b and c illustrate the cost per terminal by considering an optical link price of \$80, \$400 and \$800, respectively. We note that as the price of optics increases, negatively-balanced designs tend to become cheaper. Interestingly, in the presence of optical links that are equally expensive as electrical ones, six designs that achieve the cheapest cost are found at a cost of \$733.86 per terminal, with *densities* of 0.7 or 0.8, and *imbalance* spanning from -0.2 to 0.7. In the \$800 case, the cheapest design is a strongly imbalanced case ($b = -0.8$, $d = 0.5$) with only 10 groups made of 45 routers per group, and 23 terminals per router.

We complete our analysis by exploring designs supporting $N_{desired} = 25,000$ terminals (Fig. 9d). Here we assume radices of $[48, 64, 80]$ are available. We note first that the cost per terminal is slightly higher than that of the $N_{desired} = 10,000$ case, as the larger network scale incurs a cost premium. Even though we consider here \$400 for each optical link, it is still surprising to see the cheapest design being positively-balanced ($b = 0.2$). Our analyses show that for very large scale topologies, the positively-balanced designs emerge as among the cheapest options due to their lower radix requirements (as visible in Fig. 6f). In the $N_{desired} = 25,000$ case, the cheapest design found ($b = 0.2$ with a moderate density of $d = 0.3$) has 43 groups, 34 routers per group, $h = 13$ inter-group links per router, and $p = 18$ terminals per router. It still guarantees a high proportion of electrical links (72%), and requires routers with radix of 64.

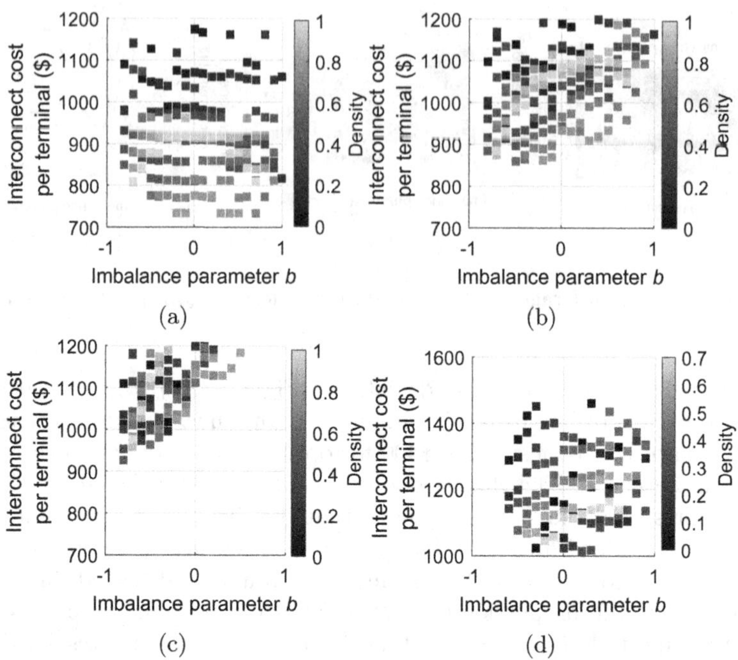

Fig. 9. Cost analysis for when optical links are set to (a) \$80, (b) \$400, (c) \$800 with $N_{desired} = 10,000$ and when optical links set to (d) \$400 when $N_{desired} = 25,000$

5 Conclusion

The Dragonfly topology, while having recently garnered much attention from the HPC community, have been subjected to different interpretations across literature. In this paper, we aim at formalizing the definition of a Dragonfly topology. To do so, we first state that any Dragonfly variant can be represented as 2D-Flattened Butterfly. In other words, a router can be represented in terms of its (x, y) coordinate in a 2-D lattice, where x (electrical dimension) represents the router's position in a group, and y (optical dimension) represents the group said router belongs to. Next, we introduce two Dragonfly-shaping parameters, namely: (a) the *imbalance* parameter, $b \in [-1, 1]$, which controls the relative sizes of the optical dimension to the electrical dimension, and (b) the *density* parameter, $d \in [0, 1]$, which controls a router's inter-group connectivity in the optical dimension. The space spanned by b and d creates the Dragonfly design space.

Using the wiring algorithm presented in Sect. 2.2, we generated various dragonflies in the design space, and subsequently identified several interesting designs. By studying dragonflies with 1500 routers, we found that as long as $d \neq 0$, the average global distance of the network remains fairly constant over the range of the *imbalances*, and only tending towards 1 when either the optical or electrical dimensions get downsized to 1. This is due to the topology approaching a full-mesh (when optical dimension is downsized to 1) or a flattened-butterfly (when electrical dimension is downsized to 1). In general, the number of links in the topology also increases as b becomes more negative due to the larger electrical dimension, in which more router pairs are directly-linked as a result of the larger full-mesh intra-group topology.

We found that topologies with a *density* of 0 exhibit poor network characteristics, since each router only has one inter-group link at its disposal. This minimal connectivity in the optical dimension incurs a higher global average distance on these topologies, an effect that is even more pronounced as the optical dimension expands (*imbalance* tending to more positive values). Our results in Sect. 4 indicate that if given access to routers with higher radices, it is generally worth maximizing the utilization of the allocated port counts to obtain interconnect designs of more optimal costs. This can be done either by (a) expanding bandwidth in the electrical dimension by opting for more nagatively-balanced Dragonflies or by (b) expanding bandwidth in the optical dimension by opting for Dragonflies with higher *densities*.

Finally, the effects of varying the cost of optical links relative to electronic links on cost-efficiency are explored on dragonflies supporting 10,000 terminals. Our results show that as the cost of optical links increases, negatively-balanced Dragonfly variants tend to be more cost-efficient due to their larger electrical dimension. A similar exploration done on topologies with 25,000 terminals, however, showed that positively-balanced Dragonfly offer more cost-efficient designs, despite considering optical links at 5× the cost of electrical links. These results unanimously indicate that *density* should generally be greater than 0 to yield cost-efficient designs with reasonable global average network distances. On the other hand, it is difficult to draw a conclusion on the range of *imbalance* that yields the most cost-optimal Dragonfly designs. We recognize that the regions in the design space corresponding to the most cost-optimal dragonflies vary significantly based on the targeted system scale (defined by number of terminals), the available router radix, and the cost of the network components (e.g. links and routers). However, the methodology employed to study cost-efficiency is valid, and we plan to investigate the ideal *imbalance* to scale relationship in the future by means of workload simulations.

References

1. Kim, J., Dally, W.J., Scott, S., Abts, D.: Technology-driven, highly-scalable dragonfly topology. In: 2008 International Symposium on Computer Architecture, pp. 77–88, June 2008
2. Kim, J., Dally, W., Abts, D.: Flattened butterfly: a cost-efficient topology for high-radix networks. In: Proceedings of the 34th Annual International Symposium on Computer Architecture, ISCA 2007, New York, NY, USA, pp. 126–137 (2007)
3. Alverson, B., Froese, E., Kaplan, L., Roweth, D.: Cray XC series network (2012), http://www.cray.com/sites/default/files/resources/CrayXcnetwork.pdf

4. Faanes, G., Bataineh, A., Roweth, D., Court, T., Froese, E., Alverson, B., Johnson, T., Kopnick, J., Higgins, M., Reinhard, J.: Cray cascade: a scalable HPC system based on a dragonfly network. In: Proceedings of the International Conference on High Performance Computing, Networking, Storage and Analysis, SC 2012, Los Alamitos, CA, USA, pp. 103:1–103:9. IEEE Computer Society Press (2012)
5. Bhatele, A., Jain, N., Livnat, Y., Pascucci, V., Bremer, P.T.: Analyzing network health and congestion in dragonfly-based supercomputers. In: 2016 IEEE International Parallel and Distributed Processing Symposium (IPDPS), pp. 93–102, May 2016
6. Jain, N., Bhatele, A., Ni, X., Wright, N.J., Kale, L.V.: Maximizing throughput on a dragonfly network. In: Proceedings of the International Conference for High Performance Computing, Networking, Storage and Analysis, SC 2014, Piscataway, NJ, USA, pp. 336–347. IEEE Press (2014)
7. Wen, K., Samadi, P., Rumley, S., Chen, C.P., Shen, Y., Bahadroi, M., Bergman, K., Wilke, J.: Flexfly: enabling a reconfigurable dragonfly through silicon photonics. In: Proceedings of the International Conference for High Performance Computing, Networking, Storage and Analysis, SC 2016, Piscataway, NJ, USA, pp. 15:1–15:12. IEEE Press (2016)
8. Camarero, C., Vallejo, E., Beivide, R.: Topological characterization of hamming and dragonfly networks and its implications on routing. ACM Trans. Archit. Code Optim. **11**, 39:1–39:25 (2014)
9. Rumley, S., Glick, M., Hammond, S.D., Rodrigues, A., Bergman, K.: Design methodology for optimizing optical interconnection networks in high performance systems. In: Kunkel, J.M., Ludwig, T. (eds.) ISC High Performance 2015. LNCS, vol. 9137, pp. 454–471. Springer, Cham (2015). doi:10.1007/978-3-319-20119-1_32
10. http://www.colfaxdirect.com/. Accessed 16 Apr 2017
11. Hastings, E., Rincon-Cruz, D., Spehlmann, M., Meyers, S., Bunde, D.P., Leung, V.J.: Comparing global link arrangements for dragonfly networks. In: 2015 IEEE International Conference on Cluster Computing, Chicago, IL, USA, pp. 361–370 (2015)

High-Throughput Sockets over RDMA for the Intel Xeon Phi Coprocessor

Aram Santogidis[1,2(✉)] and Spyros Lalis[3]

[1] Maynooth University, Maynooth, Ireland
aram.santogidis@cern.ch
[2] CERN, Geneva, Switzerland
[3] University of Thessaly, Volos, Greece
lalis@uth.gr

Abstract. In this paper we describe the design, implementation and performance of Trans4SCIF, a user-level socket-like transport library for the Intel Xeon Phi coprocessor. Trans4SCIF library is primarily intended for high-throughput applications. It uses RDMA transfers over the native SCIF support, in a way that is transparent for the application, which has the illusion of using conventional stream sockets. We also discuss the integration of Trans4SCIF with the ZeroMQ messaging library, used extensively by several applications running at CERN. We show that this can lead to a substantial, up to $3x$, increase of application throughput compared to the default TCP/IP transport option.

Keywords: RDMA · Fast data transfer · Stream sockets · Manycore processors · Intel Xeon Phi · ZeroMQ · High performance computing

1 Introduction

One of the systems used at CERN to process the data generated from the LHC experiments [12] is the O^2 online-offline distributed system, developed by the ALICE collaboration [1]. O^2 consists of over hundred different kinds of processes that perform data acquisition from the particle detectors, particle trajectory reconstruction, data compression and storage, as well as detector monitoring and calibration. They form a distributed data processing pipeline, interconnected via a message passing fabric based on the ZeroMQ [7] and NanoMSG [18] libraries.

With the introduction of the Intel Xeon Phi coprocessor [5], we started to investigate the possibility of taking advantage of this manycore architecture in order to increase the efficiency of O^2 workloads. Indeed, several O^2 computations could greatly profit from the high core count and high memory bandwidth of the Intel Xeon Phi coprocessor. However, our tests [17] have shown that the host-coprocessor communication throughput of ZeroMQ and NanoMSG over TCP/IP is up to $20x$ lower than what could be achieved using the RDMA support of the Symmetric Communication Interface (SCIF) [8], the native transport mechanism of the Intel Xeon Phi platform.

J.M. Kunkel et al. (Eds.): ISC High Performance Workshops 2017, LNCS 10524, pp. 75–86, 2017.
https://doi.org/10.1007/978-3-319-67630-2_6

For this reason, we decided to provide a high-throughput transport service over SCIF-RDMA, called Trans4SCIF, with two goals in mind. On the one hand, it should be straightforward to integrate this transport with the ZeroMQ messaging library, so that the O^2 stack can enjoy improved performance in a transparent way. On the other hand, this transport should be easy to use in other applications as well, offering the familiar abstraction of streaming sockets.

This paper describes the implementation of Trans4SCIF and discusses its integration with ZeroMQ. The main contributions are: (i) we present a socket-based RDMA-capable transport library with streaming semantics for the Intel Xeon Phi coprocessor; (ii) we introduce a novel synchronization algorithm for RDMA-based transport mechanisms; (iii) we discuss how the ZeroMQ library was extended with support for RDMA-based data transfers through Trans4SCIF (iv) we provide an evaluation showing that Trans4SCIF can lead to significant performance improvements vs. TCP/IP based data transfers for intra-node communication. We note that the developed support is also relevant for the second generation Intel Xeon Phi coprocessor (given that this was released in Q2 of 2017, after the paper was written, here we report results only for the first generation).

The rest of the paper is organized as follows. Section 2 describes the implementation of the Trans4SCIF library. Section 3 discusses the integration of Trans4SCIF with ZeroMQ. Section 4 provides a performance evaluation. Section 5 gives an overview of related work. Finally, Sect. 6 concludes the paper and points to some directions for future work.

2 The Trans4SCIF Library

We give an overview of the Symmetric Communication Interface of the Intel Xeon Phi coprocessor, and describe how Trans4SCIF was implemented on top of it. The code is available for download at *goo.gl/ynrmSL*.

2.1 The Symmetric Communication Interface (SCIF)

SCIF supports intra-node communication over the PCIe bus [8]. For small data transfers, it offers familiar POSIX-like *send()/recv()* operations. For bulk transfers, SCIF offers an RDMA interface that can fully utilize the capabilities of the PCIe bus. While this can lead to much higher throughput, it is harder to use due to the memory management and synchronization issues that must be handled by the programmer, in particular, registering the memory regions to be used for remote reading/writing, and detecting the completion of RDMA transfers. These issues also exist in other RDMA implementations [13].

Besides the classic RDMA *read/write* operations, SCIF offers the *scif_mmap()* function, which maps a pre-registered remote address region into the address space of the calling process. If successful it returns a pointer that can be used to transparently access that memory region of a remote process. This method enables a direct sharing of data structures between processes running on the coprocessor and the host. It also has the lowest communication latency [9], which makes it attractive for inter-process synchronization via shared state.

Data transfers via RDMA occur concurrently to normal program execution. One way to notify the program that the requested data transfers have been performed, is to use the *scif_fence_signal()* function. When called, it internally marks all transfers that have been scheduled so far, and upon their completion writes a given value into a specified local or remote memory location (or both). This is done asynchronously, and the program must check/read that memory location in an explicit way to determine whether the transfers have been completed.

2.2 Trans4SCIF API

To make SCIF-RDMA transport more accessible to application programmers, as well as to pave the way towards exploiting it through the messaging libraries of the O^2 stack, we have developed Trans4SCIF, a user-level library that uses the RDMA mechanism of SCIF and exposes an easy to use socket-like interface.

```
class Socket {
  {uint8_t*, size_t}  getSendBuffer(); // free region of internal send buffer
  size_t send(const uint8_t *data, size_t data_size); // non-blocking
  size_t recv(uint8_t *data, size_t data_size); // non-blocking
  void waitIn(long timeout); // block until there is data to receive
};
```

Fig. 1. Basic API of the Trans4SCIF library.

The basic primitives of the Trans4SCIF API are shown in Fig. 1 in simplified C++ syntax. In a nutshell, *send()* copies the data for transmission to an internal pre-registered buffer and schedules a corresponding RDMA-write operation. If the internal buffer is full, *send()* returns zero, indicating that the application should retry at a later point in time. To avoid data copying, the application can get a handle on the internal transport buffer via *getSendBuffer()*, and write data directly into it. Data reception is done via *recv()*, which immediately returns zero when no data is available. If desired, the application can block until data becomes available by calling *waitIn()*.

2.3 Trans4SCIF Implementation

We now turn to the implementation of the sending and receiving side of Trans4-SCIF, henceforth referred to as *sender* and *receiver*, respectively. Each side maintains its own pre-registered data buffer, the sender for the data that is written by the application, and the receiver for the data that is read by the application. Data copying between the two buffers is performed via RDMA-write. The synchronization between the sender and the receiver is done using two auxiliary data structures, the so-called *Buffer Records Table* (BRT) and *Write Records*

Table (WRT). These are shared between the two sides via *scif_mmap()*. The size of the data buffers can be set by the application at the initialization time; the size of the WRT and other parameters can be set at library compilation time.

The BRT resides in the memory of the sender, and is used to keep track of the free buffer space at the receiver. Each entry contains the starting and ending offset of a region in the remote receiver buffer that is available for writing over RDMA. For example, in Fig. 2, the sender checks the BRT and discovers that there are two regions available for RDMA writes, the first being [0x0..0x400] and the second [0xE00..0x1000]. Given that data chunks are written in the receiver buffer in the spirit of a circular buffer, there can be at most two regions available for write operations, thus the BRT only needs to have two entries.

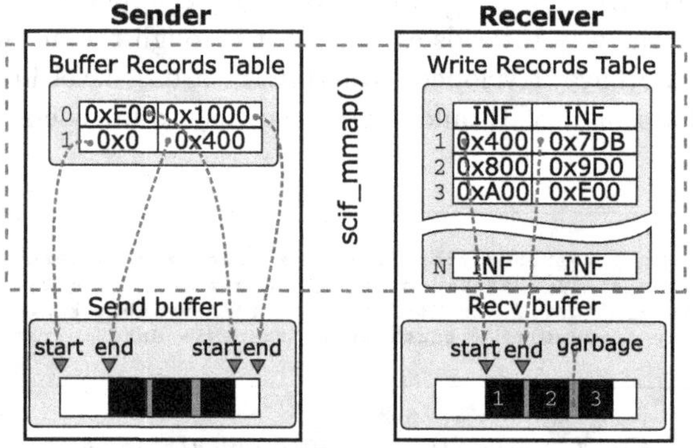

Fig. 2. Snapshot of the registered address spaces of a pair of Trans4SCIF endpoints. The sender's space contains the send buffer and the BRT, while the receiver's space contains the receive buffer and the WRT.

The WRT resides in the memory of the receiver, and is used to keep track of the RDMA writes performed by the sender in the receiver's data buffer. Similarly to a BRT entry, each WRT entry contains the start and end offset of a region in the receiver's data buffer. Taking a look at Fig. 2, the receiver knows that several writes have been performed in its data buffer, the first one in the region [0x400..0x7DB] followed by [0x800..0x9D0] and [0xA00..0xE00]. Note that a separate entry is needed for each individual data transfer. This is because although a write starts at a cache-aligned offset it may end at an arbitrary (non cache-aligned) offset. As a result the receiver's data buffer may have gaps that contain garbage, to be skipped when reading out data. Some WRT entries, like the first and last one in Fig. 2, can be empty (free to use by the sender to denote subsequent RDMA transfers), in which case the start and end fields have an invalid value (infinity). Like the receiver's actual data buffer, the WRT is filled by the sender and consumed by the receiver in the spirit of a circular buffer.

The pseudo-code in Algorithm 1 gives a high-level description of the sender and receiver logic. In a nutshell, the sender checks the BRT to see if there is available space in the receiver's data buffer, in which case it subsequently checks the next WRT entry to see if it is empty, and if so, proceeds with the data transfer and updates the BRT and WRT accordingly. Similarly, the receiver checks the next WRT entry to see if it is filled, in which case it reads out the corresponding region of its data buffer and updates the BRT and WRT. If the next WRT entry is empty the receiver knows no data is available.

Algorithm 1. High-level sender and receiver logic of Trans4SCIF

```
procedure SEND(data, data_size)
    if buf_space = 0 or free_WRT_slots = 0 then
        return 0
    sz ← min(buf_space, data_size, BUFSIZE/2)
    sz ← round_up(sz)                           ▷ to cacheline size boundary
    memcpy(send_buf, data, sz)                  ▷ destination, source, size
    rdma_write_to(recv_buf, send_buf, sz)       ▷ schedule asynchronous RDMA
    scif_fence_signal()                         ▷ commission update of WRT upon completion
    scif_send(token)                            ▷ send notification (blocking but fast)
    update(BRT)
    return sz + SEND(data + sz, data_size − sz)

procedure RECV(data, data_size)
    if pending_notifications > 0 then
        scif_recv(tokens)                       ▷ consume notifications (non-blocking)
    if buf_fill = 0 then                        ▷ buffer is empty
        return 0
    sz ← min(buf_fill, data_size)
    memcpy(data, recv_buf, sz)                  ▷ destination, source, size
    update(BRT); update(WRT)
    if WRT entry was consumed then
        pending_notifications++
    return sz + RECV(data + sz, data_size − sz)

procedure WAITIN(timeout)
    if pending_notifications > 0 then
        scif_recv(tokens)                       ▷ consume all notifications (blocking)
        pending_notifications ← 0
    scif_poll(timeout)(timeout)                 ▷ wait for notification (blocking)
```

The tail recursion in the *send* and *recv* procedures is merely for presentation purposes; in reality, this is implemented using a loop. At the sender, a repetition is performed when wrapping-around the sender's or the receiver's data buffer, in which case two distinct RDMA transfers are scheduled. At the receiver, a repetition is required when wrapping-around the local data buffer, leading to two distinct memory copy operations into the application buffer.

Since the BRT and WRT are directly shared via *scif_mmap()* they are transparently synchronized with the lowest possible latency. Special attention was paid to avoid race conditions, by eliminating concurrent writes on a single field. Importantly, when no data is available, the receiver only accesses a single entry of the (local) WRT. In a similar vein, when the receiver's data buffer is full, the sender only accesses the (local) BRT. Note that in principle it is possible for the receiver's data buffer to have free space and all WRT entries to be filled—in this case the sender cannot proceed with any further data transfers. This can happen if the sending program writes many small messages and the receiving program does not retrieve these messages fast enough. We consider this to be a marginal case given that Trans4SCIF is intended for large data transfers. Also, the application can avoid this by choosing a suitable size for the WRT.

Memory copies, local or remote, are faster when memory addresses are aligned to cacheline boundaries. This is even more crucial for DMA transfers over the PCIe bus [8]. Thus, to achieve good performance, the sender rounds up the amount of data to send to the cacheline boundary and communicates the actual data size to the receiver via the WRT entry. Moreover, the sender bounds the size of each data transfer up to the half of the buffer size. This way it becomes possible to pipeline consecutive data transfers, as the local data copy operation into the sender's buffer (of the next transfer) can be performed in parallel to the RDMA operation into the receiver's buffer (of the previous transfer); note that the asynchronous update of the WRT, when the scheduled transfer completes, is performed by SCIF outside the scope of the Trans4SCIF *send()* operation.

Finally, for each scheduled RDMA transfer the sender sends a notification message to the receiver. This allows the receiving side to block via *scif_poll()* (which in turn invokes the *poll()* system call) instead of busy-waiting until the next WRT entry becomes valid, in case the application wishes to wait until data arrives. Otherwise these notifications do not cause significant overhead since they are small and can be consumed by the receiver in lazy/non-blocking manner.

3 Integration of Trans4SCIF with ZeroMQ

ZeroMQ is a versatile and portable messaging technology for building distributed systems. Compared to other technologies, such as MPI, it provides higher-level communication abstractions that can lead to better programmer productivity. Many groups at CERN, including the ALICE collaboration, have chosen ZeroMQ as one of the main communication technologies for performance-critical distributed computing. The popularity of ZeroMQ at CERN as well as elsewhere [16,19] motivated us to extend it with support for SCIF in order to improve performance for programs running on the Intel Xeon Phi coprocessor. In the following, we give an overview of ZeroMQ, and describe how this was extended to support high-bandwidth data transfers via the Trans4SCIF transport.

3.1 Technical Overview of the ZeroMQ Messaging Library

The API of ZeroMQ is based on sockets, which can be configured to employ different lower-level transports, such as TCP/IP, UDP/IP and SCTP for communication over the network, Unix domain sockets for local inter-process communication, and shared memory between threads. Also, ZeroMQ sockets can be connected to several peers at the same time in order to form elaborate communication topologies. For instance, one can develop publish-subscribe schemes and processing pipelines with out-of-the-box load balancing and reconnection functionality. Another key feature of ZeroMQ is that it works in a direct peer-to-peer fashion, and does not require an intermediate messaging server/broker.

Once a connection is established between two ZeroMQ sockets, each socket instantiates a *session* object, which is used to keep the state of the connection. In turn, each session object is associated with an *engine* object, which is responsible for sending and receiving data over a lower-level transport service, e.g., TCP/IP or UDP/IP. Figure 3a depicts the relationship between theses objects. The transport engine provides two callback methods for sending and receiving data through the underlying transport. These callbacks are invoked by a so-called *poller* thread, which monitors a file descriptor for input/output readiness events (I/O events). The engine registers this file descriptor with the ZeroMQ runtime environment as part of the initialization procedure. To improve performance, the ZeroMQ runtime may be configured to keep a pool of poller threads, which are shared between the sockets created by the application.

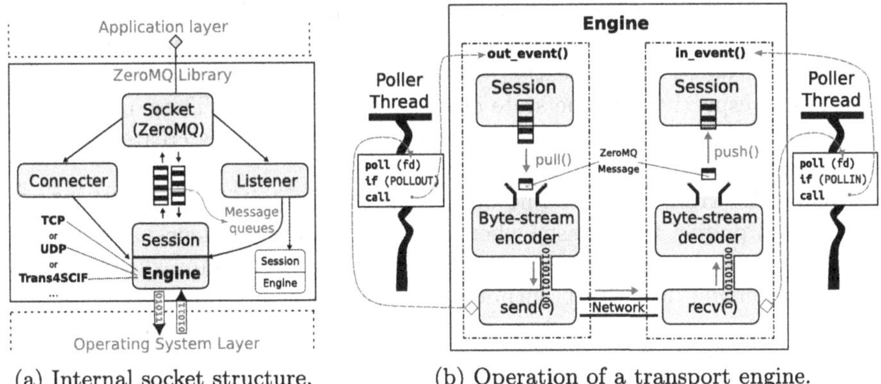

(a) Internal socket structure. (b) Operation of a transport engine.

Fig. 3. The ZeroMQ architecture.

Figure 3b illustrates the relationship between a poller thread and the engine's file descriptor and callback functions. The poller thread monitors the file descriptor using a suitable POSIX operation, such as *epoll()*, *kqueue()* or *select()*. When a POLLOUT event is raised, indicating that the file descriptor is ready for output, the *out_event()* callback of the engine is invoked. This pulls the next application message from the session's output queue, encodes it into a byte-blob according to the ZMTP protocol [7] of ZeroMQ, and sends it to the other side using the underlying transport service. Similarly, a POLLIN event leads to the invocation of the *in_event()* callback, which retrieves the raw byte-blob from the underlying transport, decodes it into a ZeroMQ message, and pushes it into the session's input queue.

3.2 The Trans4SCIF Engine for ZeroMQ

To enable the usage of SCIF-RDMA through ZeroMQ, we have developed a new ZeroMQ engine that uses Trans4SCIF as the underlying transport service, in the spirit of Fig. 3b. The application can select the Trans4SCIF engine for a ZeroMQ socket simply by prefixing the target address with `scif://` (e.g., instead of the prefix `tcp://` for TCP/IP). The API of the ZeroMQ library is left untouched and can be used in the same way as for all other transports.

When invoked by the ZeroMQ poller threads, the Trans4SCIF engine performs the data transmission and reception via the *send()* and *recv()* operations of the Trans4SCIF library. Recall that ZeroMQ requires the underlying transport to be accessible through a proper file descriptor that can be monitored through the standard POSIX polling mechanism. Fortunately, the SCIF API provides access to the underlying OS file descriptor that corresponds to a SCIF endpoint (and each Trans4SCIF socket is internally associated with such an endpoint). But note that the I/O readiness of this file descriptor depends on the state of SCIF's internal message buffers, and is not related to the actual RDMA transfers. At the receiver, POLLIN events are properly generated thanks to the arrival of the respective notification tokens that are issued by the sender for each RDMA transfer. This triggers the invocation of the *in_event()* callback which in turn calls the Trans4SCIF *recv()* function to retrieve the data from the local buffer. At the sender, the SCIF file descriptor is always ready for writing, and POLLOUT events lead to the invocation of *out_event()* and the Trans4SCIF *send()* operation, irrespectively of the state of the local data buffer. These invocations are needed to poll the BRT and determine when free space is created so as to proceed with the next transfer.

Finally, the Trans4SCIF engine unregisters the sender's file descriptor from the ZeroMQ polling mechanism when the session output queue has no more application messages. The file descriptor is registered back again when ZeroMQ informs the engine to restart output operation when an application message is added to the output queue. In a similar vein, the receiver's file descriptor is unregistered when the input message queue reaches its capacity, and is registered again as soon as ZeroMQ asks the engine to resume input operation.

4 Performance Tests

Our experimental testbed consists of two Intel Xeon Phi 7120 coprocessors with 61 cores clocked at 1.23 GHz and 16 GB GDDR memory. The host is a dual socket Intel Xeon E5-2690 server with 64 GB RAM. We run the Intel MPSS v3.8.1 on CentOS Linux kernel 3.10.0-514.2.2.el7.x86_64. For software building we have used the icc compiler v17.0.2 (gcc 6.2 compatibility) with optimizations enabled. Finally, we used ZeroMQ v4.2 and Trans4SCIF v2.4 for the experiments.

Figure 4a shows the results obtained when using the standalone Trans4SCIF library for host-to-coprocessor and coprocessor-to-host transfers. We transfer a total of 1 GB, in chunks ranging from 4 KB up to 256 MB. The benchmark is executed with varying internal buffer sizes, from 0.5 up to 128 MB.

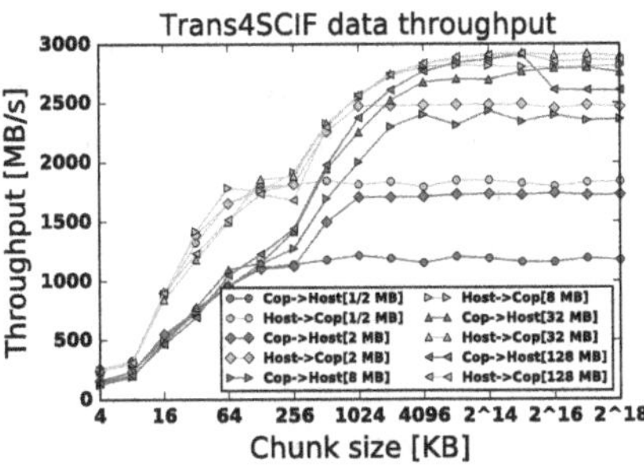

(a) The Trans4SCIF data throughput for different internal buffer sizes.

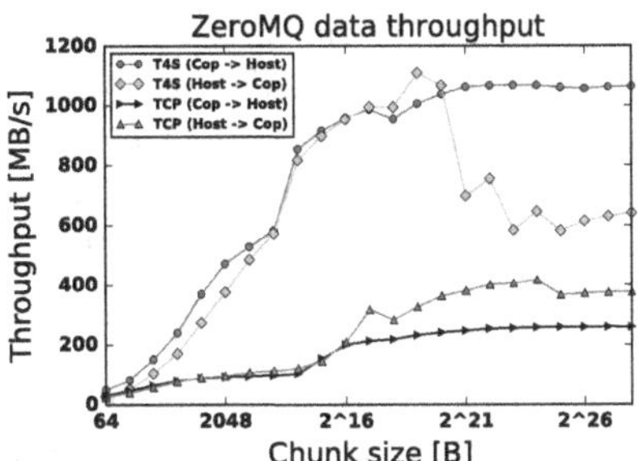

(b) The ZeroMQ data throughput with the TCP/IP and Trans4SCIF engines.

Fig. 4. Trans4SCIF and ZeroMQ throughput results.

The data points are the (arithmetic) mean values of 100 repetitions for each chunk size. As can be seen, throughput stabilizes at 2.5–3 GB/s for chunk sizes larger than 4 MB. Note that increasing the internal buffer size of Trans4SCIF above 32 MB does not improve performance. In previous work [17] we observed that the maximum throughput that could be achieved with zero-copy RDMA over SCIF was slightly over 6 GB/s on average. Although Trans4SCIF performs memory copies to/from intermediate buffers and needs to synchronize the sender and receiver in order to properly manage buffer occupancy, it still delivers over 40% of raw SCIF performance, which we consider quite acceptable. One also observes that coprocessor-to-host transfers are consistently slower than the ones in the reverse direction. This is attributed to the fact that the RDMA transfers scheduled by the coprocessor are slower than the ones scheduled by the host; this is in line with our previous observations [17].

Figure 4b shows the performance results obtained with ZeroMQ using the Trans4SCIF engine vs. the TCP/IP engine. In the same spirit as above, we transfer again a total of 1 GB, in chunks ranging from 64 B (one cacheline) up to 256 MB, with the internal data buffers of Trans4SCIF and TCP/IP set to 16 MB. It can be seen that ZeroMQ-Trans4SCIF transfers are 2-3x faster than ZeroMQ-TCP (but one has to keep in mind that the former is limited to communication over the PCIe bus whereas the latter can also be used for communication over a network). This is a significant improvement for the ZeroMQ-based applications targeting the Intel Xeon Phi platform. However, the throughput achieved by ZeroMQ-Trans4SCIF is only 50% of that of standalone Trans4SCIF. This heavy drop in performance can be explained considering that encoding and decoding of the data stream to ZeroMQ messages incurs non-trivial computational overhead. Moreover, the receiver makes one additional data copy from the Trans4SCIF buffer into the decoder's internal buffer, which further diminishes the performance (at the sender side, the encoder avoids an extra memory copy by writing directly into the internal Tans4SCIF buffer). We believe that this memory copy is also responsible for the sharp performance drop in host-to-coprocessor transfers with ZeroMQ-Trans4SCIF for chunk sizes larger than 2 MB. When chunk sizes are small, the RDMA transfers are pipelined to a certain extent with the memory copies performed by the decoder. However, as chunk sizes grow, RDMA transfers scale better than the respective memory copies, which in turn eliminates this pipelining effect. The coprocessor-to-host transfers are not severely affected due to the better single-core performance of the host CPU vs. the coprocessor. But even this highly non-optimal host-to-coprocessor throughput of ZeroMQ-Trans4SCIF at roughly 600 MB/s is still $3x$ faster than ZeroMQ-TCP at slightly over 200 MB/s.

We also measured the round-trip-times for the above transports. For chunk sizes up to 64 KB the RTT is stable at about 110 microseconds for Trans4SCIF and 1 millisecond for ZeroMQ-TCP and ZeroMQ-Trans4SCIF. We attribute this order of magnitude difference mainly to two reasons. First, ZeroMQ performs extra encoding/decoding on the application messages, whereas standalone Trans4SCIF leaves application data untouched. Secondly, ZeroMQ blocks for incoming data by waiting to receive an explicit (notification) message from the sending side, whereas standalone Trans4SCIF directly polls the WRT which is updated via the fast *scif_mmap()* method. Still, we do not expect this increased latency to have a notable effect on O^2 computations, which typically push large messages upstream along a uni-directional data-flow pipeline.

5 Related Work

Work on circumventing the limitations of TCP/IP on the Intel Xeon Phi coprocessor by exploiting SCIF-RDMA has also been done in [4,11], in the context of the ROOT software package [2]. However, the approach is more mission-specific, geared towards the parallel composition of output files, and also tightly coupled with the internal architecture of ROOT. In contrast, Trans4SCIF offers a general-purpose stream-based transport abstraction, which is also reused to enhance the performance of ZeroMQ.

Extensive research has been done to optimize MPI for the Intel Xeon Phi coprocessor. For instance, the implementation described in [14,15] employs a zero-copy rendezvous protocol over SCIF to achieve high data throughput for intra-node communication on the coprocessor MPI proxy. While the goal is similar to ours, such support is not easily reusable in the context of ZeroMQ, because the internal design of ZeroMQ does not support integration of RDMA-based transports. In particular, there is no consideration for memory registration and aligned allocations, which is a requirement not only for SCIF but also for numerous other RDMA-enabled interconnects.

An extension for the MVAPICH2 MPI library has been implemented to support transparent data movement between GPUs in a cluster environment with MPI primitives [20]. To hide the overhead of data movement over the PCIe bus, GPU-to-host memory copies are pipelined with node-to-node MPI RDMA transfers. We have adopted a similar approach in Trans4SCIF for the Xeon Phi coprocessor, by pipelining the memory copies to the internal buffer with the RDMA transfers. Also, our data transfer mechanism comes in the form of a standalone library which can be used for socket-oriented host-coprocessor communication. However, MVAPICH2-GPU also enables GPU-to-GPU communication over the network, while Trans4SCIF only works over the PCIe bus.

The work in [10] discusses the performance improvement of UNH-EXS library for data streaming over RDMA. A hybrid data transfer algorithm is presented, which under certain conditions switches to non-zero copy transfers by employing an intermediate circular receive buffer. Once data is copied out from this buffer, the receiver sends notifications back to the sender. Trans4SCIF differs from this approach by eliminating the receiver-to-sender notifications via explicit messaging. Instead, the desired synchronization on the sender side is achieved through shared data structures that are polled locally. However, Trans4SCIF does adopt an explicit notification approach in order to eliminate polling at the receiver side and avoid busywaiting when applications wait for data/messages to arrive.

The Rsockets protocol [6], a successor of the Sockets Direct Protocol (SDP) [3], aims at supporting TCP/IP-like streaming over RDMA by performing remote write operations into pre-exposed data buffers. As these buffers are consumed, new ones become available at the receiving end, for which the sender is notified via control messages. As mentioned, in Trans4SCIF the sender does not need to receive/handle such notifications. To avoid polling at the sender side, Trans4SCIF could be extended following a similar approach. However, the reception of notification messages at the sender would also complicate integration with ZeroMQ significantly.

6 Conclusions

In this paper we have described the design, implementation and performance of the Trans4SCIF library and its integration with the ZeroMQ library. We believe that the synchronization algorithm of Trans4SCIF is generic enough to be used with other RDMA-based transport protocols. Our performance tests show that standalone Trans4SCIF can achieve high data throughput over a second generation PCIe, even with relatively modest internal buffers of a few megabytes. Furthermore, when used through the ZeroMQ messaging library, Trans4SCIF yields a significant improvement over the TCP/IP transport option.

In the future we wish to extend Trans4SCIF to support zero-copy and blocking transfers on both the sender and receiver side, and to exploit these features through ZeroMQ. We will also investigate whether data encoding/decoding can be bypassed in the next versions of ZeroMQ-Trans4SCIF. Last but not least, we plan to port Trans4SCIF on the next generation of the Xeon Phi coprocessor and measure the performance enhancement on actual O^2 workloads.

Acknowledgments. Many thanks for the great support we received from Kristina Gunne, Omar Awile and Luca Atzori from CERN openlab and the CERN IT department.

References

1. ALICE Collaboration: Upgrade of the Online - Offline computing system (CERN-LHCC-2015-004; ALICE-TDR-019)
2. Antcheva, I., et al.: ROOT - A C++ framework for petabyte data storage, statistical analysis and visualization. Comput. Phys. Commun. **180**(12), 2499–2512 (2009)
3. Balaji, P., et al.: Sockets Direct Protocol over InfiniBand in clusters: is it beneficial? In: IEEE International Symposium on Performance Analysis of Systems and Software, pp. 28–35, IEEE (2004)
4. Farrell, S., Dotti, A., Asai, M., Calafiura, P., Monnard, R.: Multi-threaded Geant4 on the Xeon-Phi with complex high-energy physics geometry. In: IEEE Nuclear Science Symposium and Medical Imaging Conference, pp. 1–4 (2015)
5. George, C.: Intel Xeon Phi Coprocessor, the architecture. Intel Whitepaper (2014)
6. Hefty, S.: Rsocket, https://goo.gl/2uOsmZ
7. Hintjens, P.: ZeroMQ: Messaging for Many Applications. O'Reilly, Sebastopol (2013)
8. Intel Corporation: Symmetric Communications Interface (SCIF) For Intel Xeon Phi Product Family Users Guide , revision: 3.5 (2015)
9. Linux. https://www.kernel.org/doc/Documentation/mic/mic_overview.txt
10. MacArthur, P., Russell, R.D.: An efficient method for stream semantics over RDMA. In: IEEE International Parallel and Distributed Processing Symposium, pp. 841–851 (2014)
11. Monnard, R.: Concurrent I/O from Xeon Phi accelerator cards. Masters thesis, Haute Ecole Specialisee de Suisse Occidentale de Fribourg, Switzerland (2015)
12. Nowak, A., et al.: Does the Intel Xeon Phi processor fit HEP workloads?. J. Phys. Conf. Seri. 513(5) (2014). article no. 052024
13. Pfister, G.F.: An introduction to the infiniband architecture. High Perfor. Mass Storage and Parallel I/O **42**, 617–632 (2001)
14. Potluri, S., Hamidouche, K., Bureddy, D., Panda, D.K.: MVAPICH2-MIC: A high performance MPI library for Xeon Phi clusters with Infiniband. In: Extreme Scaling, Workshop, pp. 25–32 (2013)
15. Potluri, S., Venkatesh, A., Bureddy, D., Kandalla, K., Panda, D.K.: Efficient intra-node communication on Intel-MIC clusters. In: IEEE/ACM International Symposium on Cluster, Cloud and Grid Computing, pp. 128–135 (2013)
16. Radford, N.A., et al.: Valkyrie: NASA's first bipedal humanoid robot. J. Field Robot. **32**(3), 397–419 (2015)
17. Santogidis, A., Hirstius, A., Lalis, S.: Evaluating the transport layer of the ALFA framework for the Intel Xeon Phi Coprocessor. J. Phys. Conf. Ser. 664(9) (2015). article no. 092021
18. Sustrik, M.: NanoMSG. http://nanomsg.org/
19. Toshniwal, A., et al.: Storm@ twitter. In: ACM SIGMOD International Conference on Management of Data, pp. 147–156 (2014)
20. Wang, H., et al.: MVAPICH2-GPU: optimized GPU to GPU communication for InfiniBand clusters. In: Comput. Sci. Res. Dev. 26(3–4), p. 257 (2011)

Workshop on HPC Computing in a Post Moore's Law World (HCPM)

Workshop on Hpc Computing in a Post Moore's Law WorlD (HCPM) 2017

Co-chairs: George Michelogiannakis (LBNL) and Jeff Vetter (ORNL & Georgia Tech)

This year's HCPM is the first in the series held in conjunction with the international supercomputing conference (ISC). The workshop debated the forecoming challenges in digital computing after MOSFET scaling ends and with it Moore's law. This discussion included emerging technologies that promise to preserve Moore's law that can be new devices, memories, 3D stacking, specialization, and optics. The other half of the workshop debated neuromorphic computing and quantum computing. We discussed the challenges of adoption of these new technologies, their potential, and the possible kinds of problems they can solve.

The workshop attracted world-renounced experts of relevant fields. We had four high-quality paper submissions on various aspects of the topics covered by this workshop. We also had two 90-minute roundtable discussions after paper presentations and some short presentations by invited speakers. Finally, we had two keynotes from well-known speakers on digital computing and also quantum computing.

HCPM will continue next year and will debate important problems to prepare the HPC community for the end of traditional performance scaling. HCPM is not only relevant to experts in these fields but also the broader community and especially algorithm, runtime, and compiler designers so they can better prepare for future architectures.

In the next pages please find the four accepted papers of HCPM 2017.

Reconfigurable Silicon Photonic Interconnect for Many-Core Architecture

Hang Guan[1(✉)], Sébastien Rumley[1], Ke Wen[1], David Donofrio[2], John Shalf[2], and Keren Bergman[1]

[1] Department of Electrical Engineering, Columbia University, New York, NY 10027, USA
hg2388@columbia.edu
[2] Lawrence Berkeley Lab, Berkeley, CA 94720, USA

Abstract. In the context of declining Moore and Dennard Laws, efficient utilization of chip area and transistor is more than ever required. The portion of transistors devoted to compute operations can be maximized by off-loading as much as possible data-storage onto memory chips. This, however, requires wide off-chip IO bandwidth, and furthermore increases Network-on-chip (NoC) traffic. In this paper, we first present a concept of optically connected memory modules, delivering enough bandwidth to allow for cache reduction and memory externalization. Second, we show that connecting these memory modules in a reconfigurable interconnect permit to substantially offload NoC traffic.

Keywords: Silicon photonic · Multiprocessor interconnection

1 Introduction

Performance scalability of next generation computing systems is becoming increasingly constrained by limitations in memory access. From a programmer's perspective and performance point-of-view, computing resources (CPUs, GPUs, accelerators, etc.) would ideally hold all their memory needs locally. This approach, however, is uneconomical, as memory resources can be provided at a much lower cost on a dedicated chip fabricated in a memory specific semiconductor process. For this reason, local data storage units have been turned into caches of limited sizes, and IO logic blocks added to reach off-chip memory modules. The forecasted end of Moore's Law is expected to exacerbate this reliance on off-chip memories for data-storage. Hence, with transistors available in limited amounts on a single chip, there is an incentive to exploit them as much as possible for compute operations, therefore to further limit cache sizes [1].

Heavy reliance on off-chip memories implies that memory modules (1) are available in large enough quantities and (2) can be accessed with sufficiently ample bandwidths and low latencies. These requirements are, however, hard to meet with conventional means. First, the number of IO pins or bumps available to "escape" a chip is limited, both technologically (difficulty to fabricate pins or bumps of ever smaller sizes) and economically (fabrication and packaging costs balloon as bumps are miniaturized). Second, the volume immediately available around the chip is inherently

J.M. Kunkel et al. (Eds.): ISC High Performance Workshops 2017, LNCS 10524, pp. 89–97, 2017.
https://doi.org/10.1007/978-3-319-67630-2_7

limited. High data-rate signals are therefore required to overcome pin/bumps limitations, and to be routed over possibly long distances to reach the most distant memory modules. Meeting these requirements requires complex thus transistor and power avid IO blocks. If pushed too far, these IO blocks can reclaim the transistors made available by reducing caches, thereby negating the advantages of a heavily off-chip memory based approach.

The photonic solution has been considered to meet high bandwidth and longer communication distance requirements of modern memory systems at a lower transistor and area costs [2–5]. Chip integrated silicon photonics (SiP) optical modulator and receivers have been demonstrated. "Optical pins", i.e. fiber-chip optical couplers, to be disposed around the die, have similarly been shown. Processors and memory can be connected to the photonic IOs through monolithic integration [6], flip-chip bonding [7], and through-silicon via [8–10], as illustrated in Fig. 1. All combined, these technologies should enable IO blocks offering wide bandwidths over distance up to the meter. With ~600–800 Gb/s per "pin", i.e. per fiber [11, 12], and up to 100 fibers per chip, a total bandwidth of 10 TB/s (5 TB/s bi-directional) can be made available to the compute resources concentrated on a single chip. 5 TB/s bi-directional allows for instance a 10 TeraFLOPs many-core chips to received ~0.5 byte/FLOP, a desirable metric.

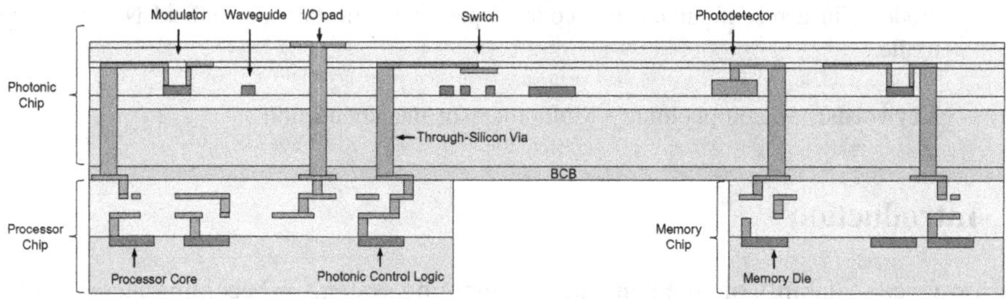

Fig. 1. Integration of photonic and electronic chips using through-silicon-via (TSVs).

In addition to providing the necessary bandwidth, optical interconnects can moreover offer an extra level of re-configurability to future memory system through optical switching [13, 14]. An optical switch, similarly integrated within a chip using silicon photonics, can be inserted between the compute chip optical IOs and the memory modules. In this paper, we investigate the benefits of such optically reconfigurable memory systems. We show how such an optical switch can be used to convey more effectively data from memory modules to the cores of a many-core chip.

2 Memory Traffic Induced Bottlenecks

We start by considering a system composed of multiple (i) cores and (ii) memory gateways interconnected with a Network-on-Chip NoC with a 2D mesh topology. Each memory gateway is assumed to lead to a unique memory module. Still from a programmer's perspective, the ideal case would consist in having all memory resources monolithically available in a single memory module, accessible over a unique gateway. However, despite recent drastic improvements, the bandwidth (byte/s) and storage capacity (bytes) of a single memory module are by far too limited to satisfy requirements of modern many-core processors. Second, such a "memory monolith" would lead to a major traffic imbalance once connected to a 2D-mesh organized NoC. Hence, all the data-traffic to and from this module would concentrate on a single spot of the NoC intersection, forcing one to over-dimension the NoC, or adopt an ad-hoc NoC topology. To provide adequate amounts of bandwidth and capacity to the cores, multiple modules are connected to the processor in parallel. For example, Intel "Knight Landing" Xeon Phi has no less than 10 distinct gateways leading to as many independent memory modules [15]. These multiple gateways can be disseminated across the NoC, which helps to more harmoniously inject or eject traffic.

Nevertheless, even with distributed traffic injection/ejection, the system remains potentially subject to severe memory traffic induced NoC bottlenecks. Two main types of bottleneck can be pinpointed: those arising when multiple cores need to communicate with one or more diametrically opposed gateways, and the bottlenecks caused by intensive exchanges between many cores and a unique "victim" gateway. In the first case, the data flows traversing the NoC may saturate the bisection bandwidth if they are too many (Fig. 2(a)). In the second case, the part of the NoC located around the victim gateway is saturated (Fig. 2(b)). In both cases, NoC bottlenecks prevent the "expensive" off-chip bandwidth to be fully utilized. Moreover, long journeys across the NoC (as depicted in either Fig. 2(a) or Fig. 2(b)) also increase latency of memory requests, which is also detrimental to performance.

Adversarial situations as depicted in Fig. 2 can be avoided or limited by means of shrewd allocation of memory addresses across the cores: as long as cores exclusively communicate with the nearest memory gateway, no excess traffic is injected onto the NoC. Realizing a precise and always coherent allocation of memory blocks is, however, a hard task, especially when processes may be shifted around by the OS over their lifetime. Of course, bottlenecks can also be solved by mean of NoC bandwidth over-provisioning. However, in relationship with the argument developed in the introduction, the number of transistors allocated to the NoC is to be minimized.

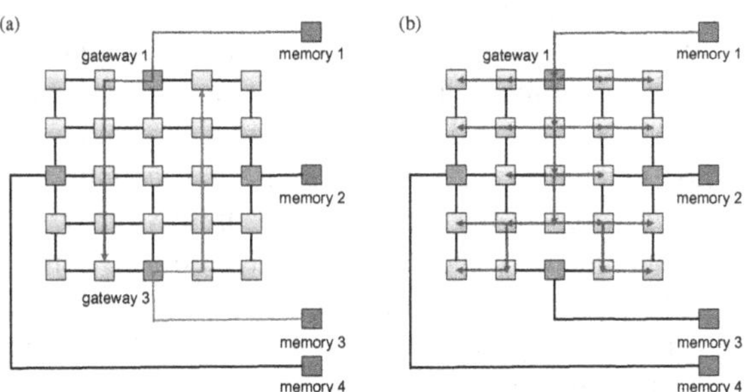

Fig. 2. (a) Multiple cores need to communicate with one or more diametrically opposed gateways (b) the part of the NoC located around the victim gateway is saturated.

To relieve the NoC from memory induced bottlenecks without bandwidth over-provisioning and without shifting the burden onto the programmer and/or compiler, an optical switch is inserted in between the gateways and the memory modules. The rationale of the concept can be described through a few examples: in situations where the memory storage available in a single module is actively solicited by numerous cores, the SiP switch can be used to shuffle the mapping between gateways and the heavily solicited module (Fig. 3). This module's gateway successively "appears" in proximity of every core, permitting to distribute the memory traffic over different sections of the NoC and thereby alleviating the bottlenecks.

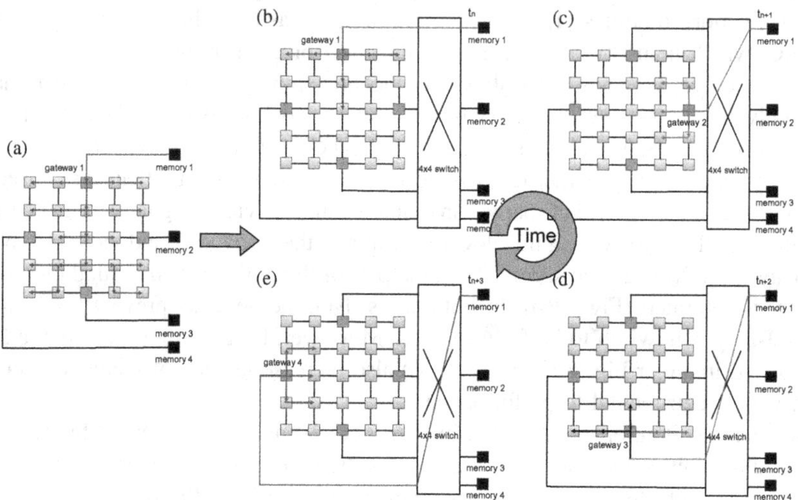

Fig. 3. (a) 21-core 4-memory system without photonic switch (b) At time t_n, traffic from memory 1 is directed to gateway 1, feeding the nearby processor cores, (c) at time t_{n+1}, the traffic from memory 1 is re-shuffled to gateway 2, (d) at time t_{n+2}, the traffic from memory 1 is re-shuffled to gateway 3, (e) at time t_{n+3}, the traffic from memory 1 is re-shuffled to gateway 4.

The SiP switch can also be leveraged to reduce the distance between cores and gateways, as shown in Fig. 4(a) and (b). The geometrical organization of many-core processors obliges requests to travel over a variable and potentially large number of NoC links. In architectures involving 4 memory gateways located in the edge middle, as depicted in Figs. 2 and 3, the hop distance between a core and a gateway can range from 1 (minimum hop counts) to 3/2n–1 (maximum hop counts) in an n-by-n mesh network, as shown in Fig. 4(c). In the worse-case the traffic scales with 1.5n. Figure 4 (c) also shows the average memory access hop count, across all cores, when each core uniquely accesses (i) its nearest memory interface (perfect locality – scaling as 0.31n), equally accesses all the memory interfaces (uniform access – scaling as 0.75n), or (iii) accesses its farthest memory interface (adversarial access – scaling with n). There is a wide gap between perfect locality and adversarial accesses. Asymptotically, adversarial memory traffic scales 3 times faster than perfectly local traffic, thus calls for

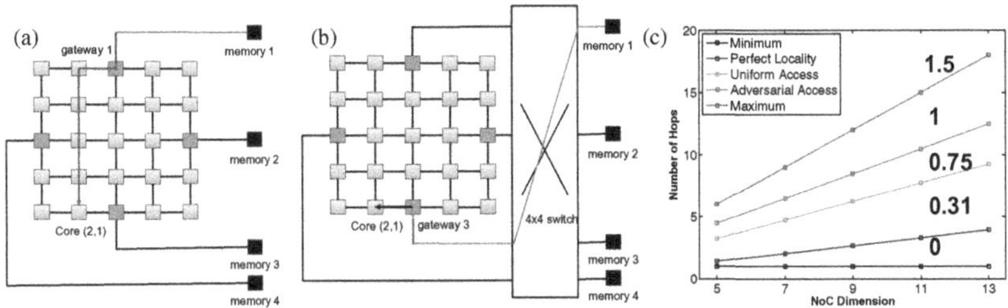

Fig. 4. (a) A many-core multi-memory architecture using electronic interconnects. Red path: 5 hop on NoC for memory 1 to reach core (2, 1), (b) a many-core multi-memory architecture using a 4×4 switch as reconfigurable memory fabric. Green path: 1 hop for memory 1 to reach core (2, 1), (c) number of average hops of all the cores vs. NoC dimension.

3 times larger NoC bandwidth to obtain the same congestion. Of course, inserting a SiP switch will not turn any adversarial situation into a perfectly local one, yet the room for progression is appreciable. Even the SIP switch reduces the hop count by a factor of 1.5x "only" (instead of 3x), the NoC bandwidth can be reduced by 1–1/1.5 = 33%.

Reducing the number of hops also participate to reduce the latency. Request latencies, however, are also negatively affected, as memory traffic is interrupted whenever the switch connectivity is adapted. To guarantee efficiency, the connectivity of the optical switch must be adapted with coarse time granularity rather than on a per-packet basis. However, if too coarse, the waiting time for the appropriate switch configuration (i.e. in Fig. 3, packets issued by memory 1 and destined to gateways 2, 3 and 4) starts to dominate the latency. The choice of the time separation switch adaptation is thus a fine trade-off, which we explore in the next section.

3 Simulation

3.1 Simulation Parameters and Benchmarks

We use Structural Simulation Toolkit (SST) [16] to evaluate the potential of our approach. We consider a simulation model consisting of 4 memory gateway models and 21 core models connected in a 5×5 mesh network (Fig. 5). Our simulation model is largely inspired by the Lightweight architecture model described in Voskuilen et al. [17], which itself seeks at mimicking an Intel Knights Landing Xeon Phi architecture.

A memory gateway (MG) tile consists of a router and a directory controller, which controls an external DRAM clocked at 300 MHz. A core tile consists of one SST Miranda lightweight processor, one router, 32 KB of L1 cache and 256 KB of L2 cache (private cache). The clock frequency of both cores and NoC is assumed to be 2.1 GHz. Considering, for instance, a width of 8 B for each direction, and a 25% NoC communication overhead (header, flow-control, etc.) this results in a bidirectional NoC link bandwidth of 12.6 GB/s (6B $\times$ 2.1 GHz). We assume only the read (from memory to the NoC) direction to use the SiP switching functionality, while the write direction still uses fixed connections. Miranda cores run a synthetic benchmark,

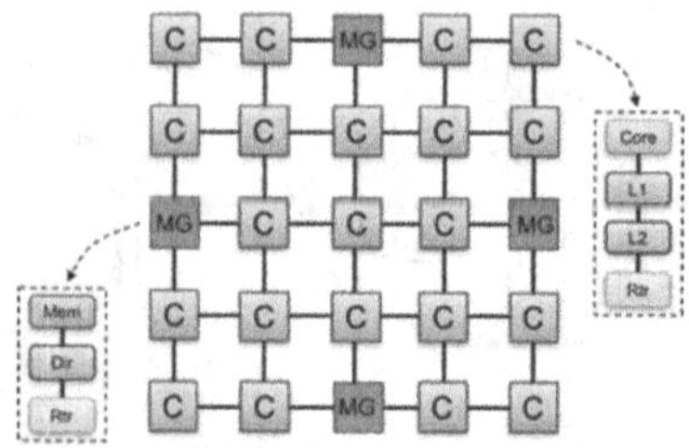

Fig. 5. Simulated 21-core 4-MG architecture.

STREAM, intended to measure sustainable memory bandwidth for simple vector kernels. To mimic a situation where a single DRAM module is heavily solicited by all cores, the address space to be accessed by the benchmark is set to reside in the first memory module exclusively.

Link re-configurability is modeled in a simplified way: the heavily accessed memory module is connected to the different gateways in a round-robin fashion. A change of gateway is triggered once a predefined number of memory responses M have been sent to the current gateway. The time the switch stays in the same configuration is therefore traffic dependent. For example, if M is fixed to 128, the switch remains at least for 1/300 MHz $\cdot$ 128 = 426 ns in the same state, which is long enough to amortize link unavailability times (resulting from the SiP reconfiguration) up to $\sim$100 ns. In general, the larger M, the longer the switch stays in the same configuration.

3.2 Simulation Results

The execution time of stream kernel with fixed memory injection point vs. TDM-switched injection point is shown in Fig. 6(a). We observe that the TDM-switched injection achieves lower execution time than the fixed injection when NoC bandwidth is available in limited amounts, i.e. inferior to 15.5 GB/s (equivalent to 10B width). This is expected: since the NoC traffic is linearly reduced by the reduced number of hops, the architecture tolerates more traffic before reaching the congestion point.

The insertion of an optical switch allows a substantial down-grading of the NoC bandwidth to reach the same performance level. For instance, in the ideal TDM = 0 ns case, the bandwidth required to execute the benchmark in less than 75us is 12 GB/s, whereas 22 GB/s are required to achieve the same performance in the fixed case (thereby enabling a 45% under-dimensioning). Figure 6(c)–(d) compare the cumulated load offered to the 25 routers during the simulation. The impact of the optical switch on the load distribution appears clearly. Figure 6(b) illustrates the performance impact of the M parameter, which dictates the frequency of switching occurrences. The NoC bandwidth is fixed to 12 GB/s. As expected, M is subject to a trade-off and should be selected taking the switch reconfiguration time into consideration.

Figure 7(a)–(d) show the execution time of stream benchmark when changing the NoC switching latency (input/output NoC latency) with a 6 GB/s, 12 GB/s, 18 GB/s, and 24 GB/s NoC bandwidth. The SiP switch permits to limit the number of hops, and thus makes the performance less affected by potentially high per-hop latencies.

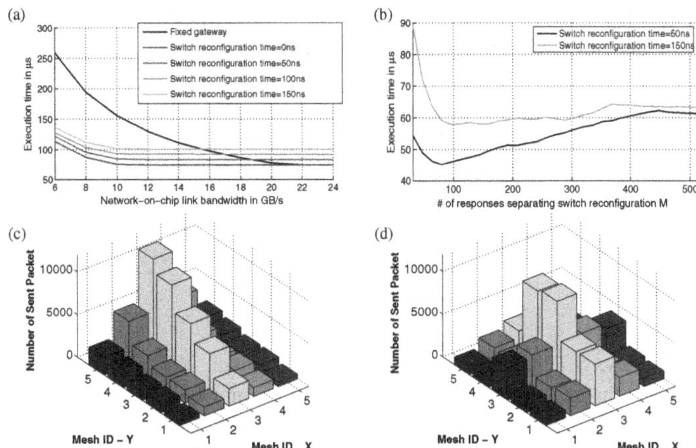

Fig. 6. (a) Execution time of stream benchmark under fixed or TDM-switched memory connections, (b) performance impact of the M parameter, (c) number of sent packet of 25 routers in mesh topology under fixed memory connection, and (d) under TDM-switched memory connection.

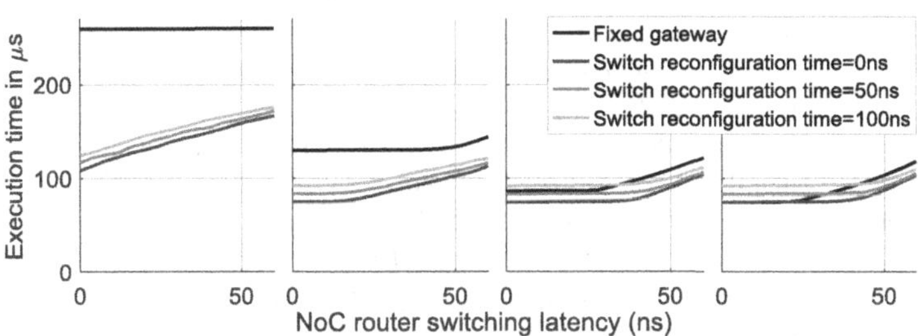

Fig. 7. (a–d) execution time of stream benchmark when changing the NoC switching latency (input/output NoC latency) with a 4 GB/s, 12 GB/s, 20 GB/s, and 24 GB/s NoC bandwidth.

In the 24 GB/s case, where bandwidth is abundant even for the fixed case, having variable injection points does not provide performance gains when the latency is hidden. In contrast, when NoC latency become significant, the reconfigurable architecture allows performance improvements, even with a relatively high switch reconfiguration time.

4 Conclusion

We showed that optical re-configurability, implemented with silicon photonic switches, can be used to offload network-on-chips from memory traffic. This enables a reduction of area and power budgets allocated to the network-on-chip, and guarantees an optimal utilization of off-chip memory links. These features are expected to mitigate the impact of declining Moore and Dennard's law in the near future.

Acknowledgments. This work was supported by the ASCR Office in the DOE Office of Science under contract number DE-AC02-05CH11231, and the DARPA Microsystems Technology Office (MTO) under the PERFECT (Power Efficiency Revolution for Embedded Computing Technologies) program.

References

1. Wen, K., Rumley, S., Samadi, P., Chen, C.P., Bergman, K.: Silicon photonics in post Moore's Law era: technological and architectural implications. In: Post-Moore's Era Supercomputing (PMES) Workshop, Salt Lake City. IEEE (2016)
2. Beamer, S., Sun, C., Kwon, Y.J., Joshi, A., Batten, C., Stojanović, V., Asanović, K.: Re-architecting DRAM memory systems with monolithically integrated silicon photonics. ACM SIGARCH Comput. Architect. News **38**(3), 129–140 (2010)
3. Loh, G.H.: 3D-stacked memory architectures for multi-core processors. In: 35th International Symposium on Computer Architecture (ISCA), pp. 453–464. IEEE (2008)
4. Sun, C., Wade, M.T., Lee, Y., Orcutt, J.S., Alloatti, L., Georgas, M.S., Waterman, A.S., Shainline, J.M., Avizienis, R.R., Lin, S., Moss, B.R.: Single-chip microprocessor that communicates directly using light. Nature **528**(7583), 534–538 (2015)
5. Wen, K., Guan, H., Calhoun, D.M., Donofrio, D., Shalf, J., Bergman, K.: Silicon photonic memory interconnect for many-core architectures. In: High Performance Extreme Computing Conference (HPEC), Waltham, pp. 1–7. IEEE, September 2016
6. Sun, C., Georgas, M., Orcutt, J., Moss, B., Chen, Y.H., Shainline, J., Wade, M., Mehta, K., Nammari, K., Timurdogan, E., Miller, D.: A monolithically-integrated chip-to-chip optical link in bulk CMOS. IEEE J. Solid-State Circ. **50**(4), 828–844 (2015)
7. Arakawa, Y., Nakamura, T., Urino, Y., Fujita, T.: Silicon photonics for next generation system integration platform. IEEE Commun. Mag. **51**(3), 72–77 (2013)
8. Kopp, C., Bernabe, S., Bakir, B.B., Fedeli, J.M., Orobtchouk, R., Schrank, F., Porte, H., Zimmermann, L., Tekin, T.: Silicon photonic circuits: on-CMOS integration, fiber optical coupling, and packaging. IEEE J. Sel. Top. Quantum Electron. **17**(3), 498–509 (2011)
9. Orcutt, J.S., Ram, R.J., Stojanović, V.: Integration of Silicon Photonics into Electronic Processes, p. 86290F. Society of Photo-Optical Instrumentation Engineers (SPIE) (2013)
10. Luo, X., Cheng, Y., Song, J., Liow, T.Y., Wang, Q.J., Yu, M.: Wafer-scale dies-transfer bonding technology for hybrid III/V-on-Silicon photonic integrated circuit application. IEEE J. Sel. Top. Quantum Electron. **22**(6), 443–454 (2016)
11. Bahadori, M., Rumley, S., Polster, R., Gazman, A., Traverso, M., Webster, M., Patel, K., Bergman, K.: Energy-performance optimized design of silicon photonic interconnection networks for high-performance computing. In: Design, Automation & Test in Europe Conference & Exhibition (DATE), Lausanne, pp. 326–331. IEEE (2017)
12. Bahadori, M., Rumley, S., Nikolova, D., Bergman, K.: Comprehensive design space exploration of silicon photonic interconnects. J. Lightwave Technol. **34**(12), 2975–2987 (2016)
13. Minkenberg, C., Rodriguez, G., Prisacari, B., Schares, L., Heidelberger, P., Chen, D., Stunkel, C.: Large-scale system partitioning using OCS. In: Photonics in Switching (PS), Florence. IEEE (2015)

14. Wen, K., Samadi, P., Rumley, S., Chen, C.P., Shen, Y., Bahadori, M., Wilke, J., Begman, K.: Flexfly: enabling a reconfigurable dragonfly through silicon photonics. In: International Conference for High Performance Computing, Networking, Storage and Analysis (SC), Salt Lake City. IEEE (2016)
15. Sodani, A., Gramunt, R., Corbal, J., Kim, H.S., Vinod, K., Chinthamani, S., Hutsell, S., Agarwal, R., Liu, Y.C.: Knights landing: second-generation intel xeon phi product. IEEE Micro **36**(2), 34–46 (2016)
16. Rodrigues, A.F., Hemmert, K.S., Barrett, B.W., Kersey, C., Oldfield, R., Weston, M., Risen, R., Cook, J., Rosenfeld, P., CooperBalls, E., Jacob, B.: The structural simulation toolkit. ACM SIGMETRICS Perform. Eval. Rev. **38**(4), 37–42 (2011)
17. Voskuilen, G.R., Frank, M.P., Hammond, S.D., Rodrigues, A.F.: Evaluating the Opportunities for Multi-Level Memory–An ASC 2016 L2 Milestone. Sandia Report (2016)

Instruction Set Architectures for Quantum Processing Units

Keith A. Britt(✉) and Travis S. Humble

Quantum Computing Institute, Oak Ridge National Laboratory,
Oak Ridge, TN 37830, USA
{brittka,humblets}@ornl.gov
http://quantum.ornl.gov

Abstract. Progress in quantum computing hardware raises questions about how these devices can be controlled, programmed, and integrated with existing computational workflows. We briefly describe several prominent quantum computational models, their associated quantum processing units (QPUs), and the adoption of these devices as accelerators within high-performance computing systems. Emphasizing the interface to the QPU, we analyze instruction set architectures based on reduced and complex instruction sets, i.e., RISC and CISC architectures. We clarify the role of conventional constraints on memory addressing and instruction widths within the quantum computing context. Finally, we examine existing quantum computing platforms, including the D-Wave 2000Q and IBM Quantum Experience, within the context of future ISA development and HPC needs.

Keywords: Quantum · Accelerator · Instruction set architecture · qubit

1 Quantum Processing Units

The realization of quantum processing units (QPUs) represents a milestone in computing. For decades theoretical computational complexity gains using QPUs have served as a lure to solving conventionally intractable problems. As an example, using two different models of quantum computing Grover's quantum search algorithm finds a marked item in an unordered database of size N in $O(\sqrt{N})$ whereas the best classical approach, a sequential search, requires $O(N)$ [1,2].

QPUs harness these gains in algorithmic efficiency by preparing quantum physical systems using superposition and entanglement. Superposition is a state

K.A. Britt—This contribution has been authored by UT-Battelle, LLC, under Contract No. DE-AC0500OR22725 with the U.S. Department of Energy. The United States Government retains and the publisher, by accepting the article for publication, acknowledges that the United States Government retains a non-exclusive, paid-up, irrevocable, world-wide license to publish or reproduce the published form of this manuscript, or allow others to do so, for the United States Government purposes. The Department of Energy will provide public access to these results of federally sponsored research in accordance with the DOE Public Access Plan.

J.M. Kunkel et al. (Eds.): ISC High Performance Workshops 2017, LNCS 10524, pp. 98–105, 2017.
https://doi.org/10.1007/978-3-319-67630-2_8

of a quantum mechanical particle storing mutually orthogonal values simultaneously within a single physical degree of freedom, e.g., position, spin, etc. Entanglement is the feature that the joint state of multiple particles may be correlated even in the absence of a physical communication channel between them. Using superposition and entanglement, QPUs initialize, store, and process quantum bits of information, i.e., *qubits*, by manipulating registers of quantum physical systems.

The gate model (or circuit model) of quantum computation closely matches the discrete set of operations found in conventional computing models. Sequences of one- and two-qubit gates represent the fundamental logic for transforming a quantum state. However, there are several unique features for quantum computing including the inability to copy, or clone, arbitrary quantum states. Thus the number of inputs into the circuit must be equivalent to the number of outputs [3].

Several small-scale QPUs based on gate model designs have been demonstrated and a few are available for use outside of laboratory settings. Notably, the IBM Quantum Experience is accessible via the internet and allows users to construct a circuit using 5 qubits and up to 80 gates per qubit [4]. This capacity for a QPU is still only useful in verifying not-to-scale quantum algorithms and empirical analysis of the reliability of the physical components. Interesting toy problems, like the half-adder depicted in Fig. 1 are also possible.

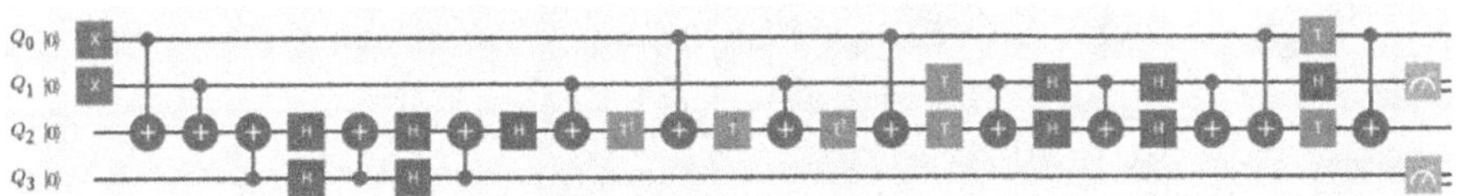

Fig. 1. This quantum circuit diagram describes the implementation of a half-adder using the gate model. This implementation was made using the QPU available from the IBM Quantum Experience [4]. The registers Q_0 and Q_1 are initialized to 1 using the X gate. Due to hardware constraints, not all qubits can serve as the target of a CNOT operation. Therefore, several *swap* operations are performed to facilitate interactions between qubits. The results of the half-adder, *Sum* and *Carry*, are output on qubits Q_3 and Q_1, respectively.

Another model of quantum computation is adiabatic quantum computation (AQC), which operates without discrete operations and no sequential constraints on the algorithmic steps [5]. In contrast to a discrete sequences of gates, the AQC model uses a continuous-time process during which the energetic interactions between register elements changes. Provided these changes are sufficiently slow, i.e., adiabatic, the evolution of the register can be well-defined relative to its energy eigenstates. In particular, if the register is initialized in an energetic ground state of the system Hamiltonian, it will remain in the energetic ground state under adiabatic evolution. The adiabatic model of computation is equivalent to the gate model in terms of computational power and the set of problems which can be efficiently solved. This equivalence arises through the influence of energetic changes on the computational state. Because the computational state is encoded by the energy eigenstates, changing these states is equivalent to performing a logical operation. The fidelity of this operation is controlled through the duration over which the energy changes.

AQC devices are also currently available from D-Wave Systems. These quantum annealing devices implement a selected subset of the AQC model that restricts the available problems to finding the energetic ground state of an Ising Hamiltonian. Notably, the Ising problem is NP-Hard in general and also equivalent to a Quantum Unconstrained Binary Optimization (QUBO) problem. The latest D-Wave 2000Q hardware system is composed of approximately 2000 physical qubits arranged in a topology called Chimera (see Fig. 2) [6,7]. This is a sufficient number of qubits to enable direct comparison with modest-sized domain-specific problems. There has yet to be any demonstration that the D-Wave hardware can outperform a best-in-class classical computing system for any particular problem type, but there have been demonstrations where the D-Wave outperforms with respect to specific problem instances. As a means to address the probability of erroneous computations, the current D-Wave QPU relies on statistical sampling over repeated runs of identical programs to boost the confidence of observing the correct solution.

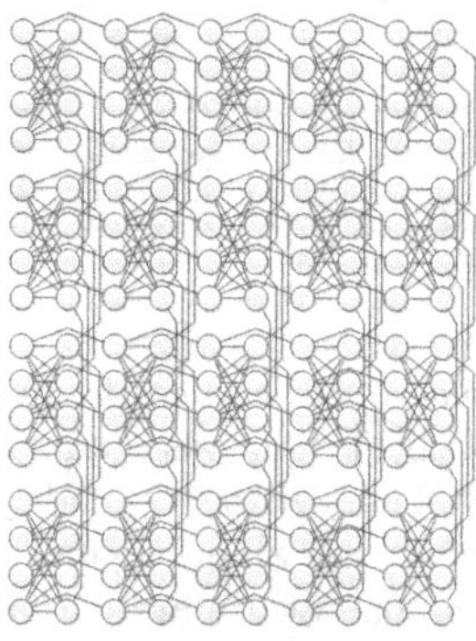

Fig. 2. The D-Wave Chimera graph in which each node represents a qubit and each edge represents a coupler. The D-Wave 2000Q, contains approximately 2000 qubits, expanding the grid of $K_{4,4}$ unit cells from 4×4 as shown here to 16×16.

Practical quantum processing is expected to require tens of thousands of qubits or more to solve problems with real world implications. The problem sizes for which quantum systems will surpass conventional computing system is still largely unknown due to the influence of engineering constraints on QPU performance. Nevertheless, a large QPU capacity is expected to be necessary. This requirement is underscored by additional technological realities. First, the degree of connectivity for any qubit is likely to be limited due to hardware fabrication constraints. This leads to the concept of virtualizing logical qubits using many physical qubits. Second, QPUs require very low noise environments to suppress erroneous computation. This typically implies working at cryogenic temperatures (below $1K$), but even then quantum registers are vulnerable to errors. Quantum error correction protocols are necessary to reach fault-tolerant operation, and this incurs a substantial overhead for redundantly encoding a logical qubit using many (virtualized) physical qubits. Finally, the large problem sizes at which performance crossovers occur are very likely to require a large number of intermediate variables in which the numerical representation of each variable requires many logical qubits.

Despite their potential, QPUs are not expected to act as stand alone devices but rather to require interactions with conventional central processing units (CPUs) and memory. Even though universal quantum computation is theoretically possible, near-term QPUs are most likely to be used as special-purpose processors. For example, the use of QPUs as accelerators for high performance computing (HPC) systems has already begun to mimic recent efforts with graphical processing units (GPUs) and today's leading scientific computing systems [8–10].

To date, the CPU-QPU interface for gate-model processors has largely focused on quantum assembly (QASM) instructions. Originally introduced as a visual modeling language, QASM operates as a sequential, ordered list of discrete instructions representing gates acting on qubits [11]. This language naturally enforces the view that quantum instructions are pre-processed and queued for execution on the quantum hardware, with all the operations in a given time slice being executed simultaneously, e.g., within the same clock cycle. Similarly, the special-purpose AQC device from D-Wave defines interactions between the CPU and QPU via quantum machine instructions (QMI), a language that describes the continuous-time change in state of the processor Hamiltonian. This means the device settings for all the interactions between qubits are applied and executed concurrently.

QASM and QMI are currently accepted by the quantum computing community as convenient methods for programming small-scale QPUs. Yet both approaches are unlikely to scale to larger processor sizes due to growth in the number of instructions and interactions defining a program and bottlenecks in processing these instructions concurrently. In particular, we note that there is a pending need to improve the message passing between CPU and QPU. This interface raises concerns about the number of qubits and gates as well as matching the clock between these different components. In this contribution, we address some of the considerations for designing new instruction set architectures that may be used to interface the CPU and QPU components, especially as these components become more tightly integrated. Our starting point is the recognition that while single and two-qubit gates may be easiest to implement within hardware, such fine grain description may not be compatible with efficient, large-scale quantum computing.

2 RISC and CISC

RISC architectures conform to a few main principals: segmentation of memory and computational operations, supporting a limited number of basic operations, instruction widths having a firm boundary, maximizing pipelining benefits, and minimizing pipelining penalties [12]. These principals give RISC architectures the advantage of standardization and instruction turnover efficiency, but they limit how well RISC architectures can optimize the processing of any particular or complex instruction sequence.

A fixed instruction width is what gives a RISC architecture the ability to pipeline instructions and gives RISC architectures an advantage when compared to CISC architectures for non-anticipated problem classes. As will be illustrated below however, adhering to this fixed instruction width will limit the total usable QPU register size.

Segmenting memory and computation is a given in AQC as the memory is the state of the qubits (and their association to one another) and the computation is the fluctuation of system energy (or alternatively, the passage of time). Segmenting memory and computation in a gate model QPU seems not to have a clear analogy. In the gate model, there is no loading or copying of values into registers between the beginning and ending of the algorithm. Quantum registers (qubits) are simply initialized to a beginning state and then gates are applied to the quantum registers. There are no memory operations other than initialization and reading the final collapsed classical value.

CISC architectures follow the principals of: limited memory registers, emphasizing efficiency improvements through instruction creation and modification, programmer ease, and non-standardized instruction widths [13]. CISC architectures become especially attractive in strict domain-oriented processing (like process controllers or vector processors).

In a quantum architecture, the line between memory and computation is inherently blurred as the computation is a process that happens to the memory registers (of which the values cannot be copied), much like as is seen in in-place or in-memory algorithms. However, the CISC concept of optimization through dedicated hardware resources is something that might fit well into a QPU architecture as the use of a QPU is based on a priori knowledge that CPU resources are theoretically inferior to the QPU in terms of processing time or resource efficiency. Thus, a specific set of predefined functions (error correction, quantum Fourier transform, etc.) operating on a specific set of qubits that can be cascaded across other non-preallocated qubits, may be a feature of value in a quantum ISA [14,15].

Limiting memory registers, for reasons outlined above, has no corollary in a QPU. Non-standardized instruction widths may serve some purpose if predefined functions are implemented in hardware, but the potential size of that library is not explored in this contribution and only the need for a gate set capable of universal quantum computation is described below. Given these considerations, QPUs and their interfaces to classical controls don't fit neatly into either a RISC or CISC silo as is true for most modern CPUs. However, both ISA models do hold principals that are important in guiding how a QPU ISA should operate.

3 QPU ISA Message Considerations

In contemplating an ISA for a theoretical gate model QPU (like the IBM Quantum Experience), we draw inspiration from the MIPS ISA J-type (RISC) instruction tuple of $\{opcode, address\}$. From this, we can imagine a similar ISA for quantum hardware of the form $\{opcode, qubit\}$. Taking into account that most circuits will require m qubit gates and that m qubit gates can be reduced to a series of 2-qubit and 1-qubit gates, we expand this quantum ISA to the form $\{opcode, target\_qubit, control\_qubit\}$ [3]. Assuming that the number of elemental 1-qubit and 2-qubit gate types does not exceed 16, our opcode width is then constrained to 2^4 [3]. Given a classical 64-bit computational and memory architecture, this leaves us 60 bits to specify our qubits. Assuming every qubit is able to participate in any operation as either the target or the control, the target qubit space must be the same width as the control qubit space. Thus, we have 30 bits to specify our target qubit and 30 bits to specify our control. This gives us a hard limit as to how many physical qubits can be used by our system, 2^{30} or approximately $1.0737 * 10^9$. Therefore, a 64-bit classical computing architecture limits us to a billion qubit system.

The most obvious solution to this ceiling would be to implement a 128-bit processing and memory ISA, which would expand our addressable qubits to 2^{62} or $4.6117 * 10^{18}$. However, as of 2017, Intel, AMD, and Arch all have publicly stated that there are no current plans to develop a 128-bit processor due to the lack of need. There are possibilities for solutions under the umbrella of a 64-bit architecture. Two qubit gates could be addressed via multiple ISA messages, allowing for 2^{60} qubits. This solution would require message management and correlation at the compiler (likely) or even the programmer level (less likely). In addition, this multiple message scheme might require the QPU to adhere to an Execute-Wait-Execute model that would likely reduce the coherence of the qubits in terms of number of gates before decoherence, limiting the depth (length) of quantum circuits.

Additionally, the concept of multiple classical controllers attached to a single QPU is a possibility, in essence dividing the QPU into several different sub-QPUs that could be bridged together when needed [9]. This scheme would seem to require synchronizing the controllers at the microsecond or even nanosecond level given today's quantum processing technology. In addition, it would seem to imply that there would be specific qubits that are special and exclusive in terms of their spatial relation to the adjoining sub-QPUs and this would complicate instruction compilation, possibly necessitating a need for programmer knowledge of the qubit hardware topology or artificially shrinking the size of quantum registers available for logical computation.

We can draw inspiration from the D-Wave 2000Q concept of QMI when contemplating an ISA for an adiabatic quantum computer. The structure of a

QMI instruction is $\{qubit, qubit, value\}$ where if the first and second *qubit* are equal, the *value* is the weight to assign to the *qubit* and if the first and second *qubit* are not equal, the *value* is the strength to assign to the coupler between the first *qubit* and second *qubit*. In addition to the QMI instructions is a header line specifying metadata about how many QMIs are being used. If we strip away the header line (which seems to be an unnecessary construct not at all vital to the adiabatic algorithm), we have what looks to be a very RISC-like architecture where the instruction widths are uniform and there is a strict segmentation of memory and computation operations. Issues of limited operations types and pipelining really don't fit into the adiabatic model as there is no segmentation of time or function within an adiabatic anneal.

While we don't explore how these instructions are currently passed to the quantum hardware, we theorize that the $\{qubit, qubit, value\}$ is contained in a single message. It has been demonstrated that the current bits of precision (BOP) available in tuning a qubit or coupler in the D-Wave architecture is 10 BOP, which gives us a width for *value* [16]. While hardware connectivity constraints don't allow any arbitrary physical qubit to interact with another arbitrary physical qubit, any qubit active in the D-Wave architecture can fill the role of the first or second *qubit*, thus we must assume that the remaining bits of the message are equally divided between the first and second *qubit*. Assuming a 64-bit architecture, each *qubit* would be allocated 27 bits of width, allowing for 2^{27} or $1.34217728 * 10^8$ qubits in the system which would allow a fully connected system of approximately 4096 logical qubits if the physical qubits had the same degree of inter-unit-cell connectivity and double the intra-unit-cell connectivity as available in the D-Wave 2000Q [7].

4 Conclusions

In examining how a QPU might fit into an HPC infrastructure and the necessary interface between classical instructions and quantum processing, we describe potential ISAs for both a gate model QPU and adiabatic model QPU. Our QPU ISAs used a fixed-width message size of 64-bits that if implemented as described would limit the addressable size of a gate model QPU to approximately 1 billion to 4.5 billion qubits and the addressable size of an AQC QPU to approximately 134 million qubits. Considerations for logical embedding due to multi-qubit variable types, physical qubit connectivity limitations, and error correction condense the logical qubit work-space in both models.

In trying to create an analogy to classical RISC and CISC architectural features, we find that gate model pipeline processing doesn't seem to fit and a fixed-width message size isn't essential, but might be advantageous in trying to maximize the coherence time of a quantum circuit. Also, issues of segmenting memory from computational tasks are far less of an issue as memory and computation are naturally conjoined (or disjoined depending on perspective) in both the gate model and AQC. The concept of allocating specific quantum register resources to predefined tasks may serve a useful purpose in the gate model (but not likely AQC) as it does in a classical CISC architecture.

Our recommendation is not to orient towards a RISC or CISC architecture when designing future QPU ISAs, but rather we suggest considering the long term consequences of the quantum-classical interface, in particular the message format, on small scale QPUs that might grow into large scale QPUs. Of particular importance is whether the QPU ISA will limit the addressable quantum register size and place an artificial ceiling on QPU scaling.

References

1. Grover, L.K.: A fast quantum mechanical algorithm for database search. In: STOC 1996, pp. 212–219 (1996)
2. Hen, I.: Realizable quantum adiabatic search [quant-ph] arXiv:1612.06012 (2016)
3. Nielsen, Michael A., Chuang, Isaac L.: Quantum Computation and Quantum Information: 10th Anniversary Edition. Cambridge University Press, New York (2011)
4. IBM Research Quantum Experience. http://www.research.ibm.com/quantum/
5. Farhi, E., Goldstone, J., Gutmann, S., Sipser, M.: Quantum computation by adiabatic evolution. Report MIT-CTP-2936, Massachusetts Institute of Technology (2000)
6. The D-Wave 2000Q^{TM}System. https://www.dwavesys.com/d-wave-two-system
7. Hamilton, K.E., Humble, T.S.: Identifying the Minor Set Cover of Dense Connected Bipartite Graphs via Random Matching Edge Sets (2016). arXiv:1612.07366
8. Top500.org: Global Supercomputing Capacity Creeps Up as Petascale Systems Blanket Top 100. Top500.org (2016)
9. Britt, K.A., Humble, T.S.: High-performance computing with quantum processing units. J. Emerg. Technol. Comput. Syst. **13**(3) (2017). Article 39
10. Fu, X., Riesebos, L., Lao, L., Almudever, C.G., Sebastiano, F., Versluis, R., Charbon, E., Bertels, K.: A heterogeneous quantum computer architecture. In: Proceedings of the ACM International Conference on Computing Frontiers (CF 2016), pp. 323–330. ACM, New York (2016)
11. Chuang, I.: qasm2circ. https://www.media.mit.edu/quanta/qasm2circ/
12. Patterson, David A.: Reduced instruction set computers. Commun. ACM **28**(1), 8–21 (1985)
13. George, A.D.: An overview of RISC vs. CISC. In: Proceedings of The Twenty-Second Southeastern Symposium on System Theory, pp. 436–438 (1990)
14. Calderbank, A.R., Shor, Peter W.: Good quantum error-correction codes exist. Phys. Rev. A **54**(2), 1098–1105 (1996)
15. Hales, L., Hallgren, S.: An improved quantum Fourier transform algorithm and applications. In: Proceedings 41st Annual Symposium on Foundations of Computer Science, pp. 5115–525 (2000)
16. Britt, K.A., Humble, T.S.: QUBO computational reliability via hamiltonian engineering. In: Adiabatic Quantum Computing Conference (2016)
17. Harrow, A.W., Hassidim, A., Lloyd, S.: Quantum algorithm for linear systems of equations. Phys. Rev. Lett. **15**(103), 150502 (2009)

Eliminating Dark Bandwidth: A Data-Centric View of Scalable, Efficient Performance, Post-Moore

Jonathan C. Beard(✉) and Joshua Randall

ARM Research, Austin, TX, USA
{jonathan.beard,joshua.randall}@arm.com

Abstract. Most of computing research has focused on the computing technologies themselves versus how full systems make use of them (e.g., memory fabric, interconnect, software, and compute elements combined). Technologists have largely failed to look at the compute system as a whole, instead optimizing subsystems mostly in isolation. The result, for example, is that systems are built where applications can only ask for a fixed multiple of data (e.g., 64-bytes from DRAM), even if what is required is far less. This is efficient from a hardware interface perspective, however, it results in consuming valuable bandwidth that is never utilized by the core; this hidden bandwidth is effectively dark to the system. The causes of dark bandwidth are systemic, built into the very core of our virtual memory abstractions and memory interfaces. Continued focus on newer, revolutionary memory technologies to improve surface performance characteristics without a systems focus on reducing data movement will simply push this problem off onto future systems. This paper examines the problem of dark bandwidth and offers a holistic approach to reduce overall data movement within future compute systems.

1 The Problem

Computation is typically not the bottleneck that it once was. Computing itself is faster and less hungry (in terms of energy [7]) than the memory and interconnect that supply the data for computation. Much computing research has focused on providing efficient compute, resulting in the compute cores found in today's CPU sockets. The aforementioned compute devices perform very well for SPEC [4] and LINPACK [3] workloads, however, the compute devices and accompanying subsystems optimized for these workloads do not necessarily perform well for the applications executed by many HPC [2] and big data systems [12]. Two things are clear: first, architecture researchers have produced a myriad of ways to compute things efficiently, and second, research into ways to feed compute has not kept up. The technical community has been working on a false thesis: that compute systems efficiently utilize the bandwidth provided to the core by the memory

J. Randall—Partially supported by U.S. DoE FastForward-2 Contract - Subcontract No. B609229.

J.M. Kunkel et al. (Eds.): ISC High Performance Workshops 2017, LNCS 10524, pp. 106–114, 2017.
https://doi.org/10.1007/978-3-319-67630-2_9

subsystem. Not only does research suggest that this is often not the case, it shows that many applications make use of only a small fraction of the data moved to the compute elements [10]. The trend towards heterogeneous accelerators only serves to exacerbate the problem as bus length and buffering increase. Recovering this lost bandwidth and reducing superfluous data movement gives the system more usable bandwidth for real computing. It is not just the size and speed of the memory technology that matters, it is how you use it that will enable future systems to utilize what is effectively dark or hidden memory bandwidth.

The type of compute elements today range from simple in-order cores to massively complex out-of-order ones. The compute elements within these go from small arithmetic units to heavyweight vector engines. General purpose CPUs are hobbled by the very fact that they must be general. For many applications the general purpose has given way to better adapted hardware [9]. The general purpose graphics processing unit (GPGPU) revolution was launched by the realization that vector units with many threads could operate on specific workloads very efficiently without the constraints of things like having to run an operating system. Many other accelerators have since become mainstream, including FPGAs. Data must still be delivered to the accelerator, just as it must be delivered to the CPU core itself. The main difference between the CPU, and accelerators like the GPU is that memory hand-off must be coordinated by an external agent: the CPU. No matter how efficient engineers and researchers make cores and accelerators, the model of paging in data from memory one DDR burst at a time [5], all coordinated by the general purpose core, limits the efficiency and scalability of all future systems intended for more sparse workloads.

Cache line utilization is one way of measuring the bandwidth utilization of a DRAM burst given that the burst and cache line granularity typically align (e.g., 64-bytes). On average, when measured with profiling tools (e.g., DynamoRio), HPC application utilization for the L1-D cache is between 20–80%, with spikes for kernels like *DGEMM* up to 100% during "hot" loops. The numbers for the L2 cache shift only slightly, with kernels like *DGEMM* exhibiting high reuse at this level as well. The worst offenders are applications like *GUPS* whose L1-D utilization stays at around 20%. Less bandwidth intensive applications like *LULESH* also have room for improvement as elements from a lattice must be gathered to contiguous memory and then scattered again. Simply increasing the available bandwidth, as many memory and interconnect focused technologies do, does nothing to address the critical problem of wasted data movement.

Even when a cache line is fully utilized, often it is quickly evicted and never used again because of high reuse distance. Reuse distance is the amount of relative time or number of bytes, depending on the metric used, between one use of a data element and another. Even when cached data are fully utilized, often the reuse distance is high. Most applications have varying phases where reuse can range from immediate (zero bytes between subsequent accesses), to kilobytes, all the way to infinity (perfectly streaming accesses). To make the most out of a modern hierarchy, it is critical that systems designers find a way to maximize the physical proximity of highly reused dense data to the best compute element possible, while providing the best bandwidth possible for the streaming data (high reuse distance). A cache hierarchy, which on a per component basis is generally static in size, is a poor structure for workloads where reuse distance scales with the data set size.

Sparse applications have both low utilization and high reuse distances. Irregular applications often share the aforementioned properties, but they also typically have unpredictable data access patterns (i.e., they are data dependent). Sparse and irregular applications are found both in HPC (e.g., lattice and geometric multigrid calculations) and big data analytics (e.g., MapReduce, databases). These applications often explore only a few data points within a data region (e.g., 4 KB page). In current systems, this often results in a page-sized region being loaded from network or nonvolatile memory into DRAM (through the main processor core) and then back to the core for computation. This results in a lot of data movement (e.g., from source, to CPU, to DRAM, and then back to core). This is very inefficient, however, the problem is worse. Performance-enhancing technology such as the hardware prefetch unit, as well as the DDR burst length itself, often inadvertently evict useful lines from the cache hierarchy, while allowing useless data to hitchhike into the cache, wasting scarce bandwidth. For off-chip accelerators (e.g., GPGPUs), additional hand-off and coordination of virtual pages must also be managed, adding even more overhead.

Memory technologies are proverbially five years out; that is they often perpetually remain science projects that fail to scale to production. Even when technologies do make it to production, more revolutionary technologies have a hard time competing with incremental improvements on a cost and performance basis. The time necessary to develop revolutionary technologies (e.g., MRAM) often makes possible for incremental improvements in legacy technologies to outpace the improvements that would come through adopting a newer, more revolutionary one. Even when new technologies come to market (dark bandwidth), they will inherit systemic flaws that result in wasted data movement. Ignoring the system deficiencies described in this section when bringing new technologies to market, only means pushing the data movement problem into the future rather than solving it.

2 Solutions

Data movement dominates computation at scale [1]. There are a few options to increase bandwidth utilization and reduce data movement. Some researchers suggest that byte-level addressing is the key to improving bandwidth utilization. While true, when faced with the harsh reality of engineering a system with addressing commands that equal the size of the data requested, at face value, this idea seems quite impractical. A creative solution that arrives at the same effect is in-/near-memory rearrangement [8], which effectively delivers byte-level addressing through bulk data requests. Processing in- or near-memory (PINM) is another solution quickly gaining traction with both academic and commercial researchers. The idea, however promising, is faced with many hurdles.

Increased proximity of memory cells and compute elements raise the risk of heat-induced memory leakage, decreasing efficiency. In modern systems, the virtual memory system is also an enemy of those wishing to reduce data movement. What engineers developed to protect systems, improve multiplexing, and ease system programmability, now hobbles scalability and performance.

2.1 Chopping Down Sparse Data

The efficiency of large, heavyweight compute units is extremely hard to beat. A wide vector unit can churn through packed-data computation extremely well. The issue with these is that data often does not come packed, so programmers often use gather-scatter instructions. These are used to pack data from multiple locations into a single vector register and then return it back to non-contiguous memory. In practice, gather-scatter instructions are not as efficient as they could be. The cache lines are still underutilized (only the register is packed) leading to corresponding unused memory bandwidth (see Fig. 1). The only way to reduce the data movement for applications in need of heavyweight compute (e.g., vector units) with middle (8 KB) to high (>128 KB) reuse distances and potentially low cache line utilization is through in-/near-memory or in-storage rearrangement (there are better techniques for workloads with less compute intensity) (Fig. 2).

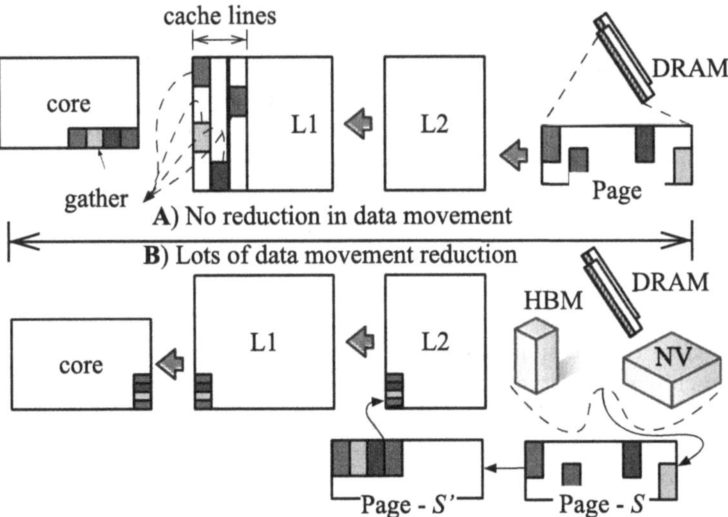

Fig. 1. Image **A** above shows the data movement pattern for a traditional gather instruction as implemented on many architectures. Cache lines are gathered into the cache hierarchy one-by-one, then offsets are accessed to pack data into a vector register. Image **B** shows the potential for in- or near-memory rearrangement, which requires relatively simple logic near memory to compact data from S before it reaches the cache hierarchy S'.

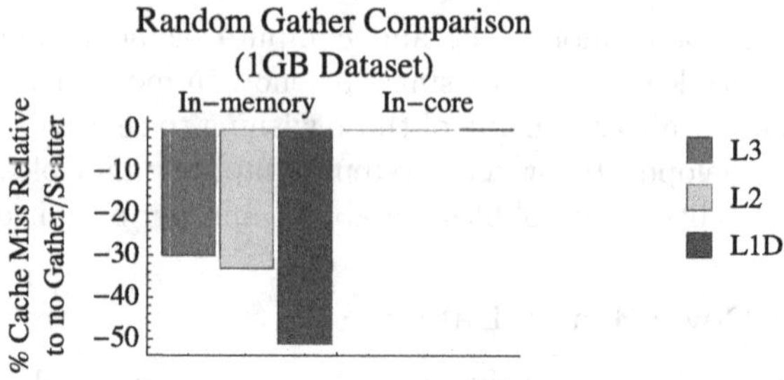

Fig. 2. Benchmark of a random gather across a 1 GB data set using a leading vector architecture's gather instruction to compare to an emulated near-memory rearrangement. Near-memory rearrangement results in a ~50% reduction in L1-D misses and a ~30% reduction in LLC misses compared to a standard gather instruction. Both results are normalized to the same code run without a gather instruction. In all cases, the hardware and software stacks are kept the same.

2.2 Processing In- or Near-Memory

For applications with middle to high reuse distances and/or low cache line utilization that can make do with less power hungry compute, PINM is a good option. As an example, if an architecture has a load width of 128b/cycle, the reuse distance of 8 KB gives 64-cycles to compute in cache. At a distance of 64 KB this grows to 512-cycles, which is more than enough for in-cache processing (assuming a reasonable access time for caches). Many big data applications fall into this category, as do database and string processing (e.g., genomics) workloads. The options for compute elements within a PINM system range from simple fixed-function state machines to putting heavyweight cores in- or near-memory. The line blurs between what is PINM and what is simply a processor with a shorter bus or giant cache made of high bandwidth memory. The definition that best fits is a processor closer to memory that is supplemental to a general purpose processing core (essentially an accelerator for sparse and irregular applications). There are two possible locations for PINM, on- or off-chip. The on-chip devices can be split into in-cache or in-system cache. The main advantage for on-chip is the potential availability of low-latency links to retrieve virtual to physical address translations. Off-chip devices fall into multiple categories as well, in-component devices (e.g., SSD), in-controller (e.g., external memory controller, interconnect), and in-memory devices (Fig. 3). A primary disadvantage for off-chip devices: high latency off-chip virtual memory translation.

Functional considerations for on-chip PINM devices are many, especially when coordinated from a general purpose core. Modern processors require things like out-of-order issue, exception handling, and for PINM outside of the coherence network (i.e., either on-chip or off-chip RAM) careful handling of virtual-to-physical address translation is required. Building a PINM in-cache is relatively simple, coordinating it as a system is quite difficult. With current virtual memory systems, off-chip PINM is hobbled by the fact that the software must be coordinated to know where the memory is located. This leads to several issues that must be considered outside of those listed for on-chip PINM. PINM with current virtual memory systems either must rely on the software to place pages statically in memory for the PINM device, restrict operation to huge pages, or rely on an input/output memory management unit (IOMMU). The IOMMU translation bottlenecks for GPGPU found in literature largely apply to PINM (e.g., 20x higher translation cost, 1–20 MPKI [6,11,12]), with some exceptions. For PINM, the ideal processor technology is not the heavyweight GPGPU type core, but many small simple cores. The access patterns are also different, instead of lock-step data parallelism, PINM targets very sparse memory access patterns. The usual solution of increasing page size (successful for GPGPU) typically fails for PINM (Fig. 4).

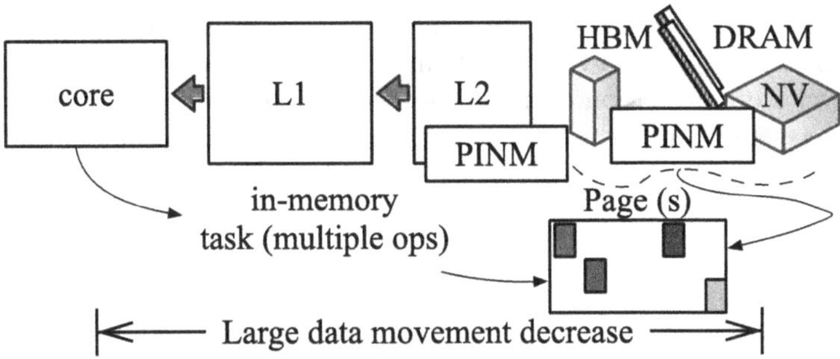

Fig. 3. PINM involves sending instructions closer to where the data rests within the memory device versus bringing the data to the core. Lightweight PINM cores could exist at multiple places in the memory hierarchy.

The simplest embodiment of PINM hands a single page at a time to each in-/near-memory processor (to reduce logic needed to handle contention), the use of huge pages in this scenario limits the number of cores that can be utilized without extra synchronization hardware, limiting the overall parallelism; ideally a smaller page size (e.g., 4 KB) would be used. Figure 4 demonstrates the inefficiencies of virtual memory for a PINM system using the preferred 4 KB page size. Removing the bottleneck of virtual memory would enable PINM technology to be more efficient. Without fixing the memory system, PINM technology will be forced to limit solutions to a select range of applications (e.g., in-memory databases) or force adoption of more restricted programming models (e.g., PGAS) to work around the fundamental limitations of page-based virtual memory. The same solution will likely enable faster, simpler, and easier implementation of a unified memory space for accelerators (including ease of handling pages in virtualized GPGPU clusters). The time is ripe for a rethink of virtual memory and a rethink for the relationship of the operating system, memory system, and runtime.

3 A Common Problem: Translation

The biggest hurdle to implementing the data movement reduction technologies described in the last section is page-based translation. The problem with page-based translation is, first and foremost, the fixed-size pages themselves (pages limit addressability and parallelism for tightly coupled accelerators and PINM devices). Secondly, the reliance on page table caches for non-general purpose compute elements becomes a bottleneck for all out-of-core accelerators [11]. As architectures vie for more efficiency, the trend of late is towards specialized accelerators. In order to maximize the utility of accelerators, something must change in the virtual memory system. Memory fabrics cannot continue to ignore the software co-design to optimize the extension of the virtual memory abstraction to all compute elements. Satisfactory solutions that would enable page-based virtual memory to extend outside of general purpose cores (e.g., accelerators) in a low overhead manner are yet to be found. The current state of the art results in ~1.5-cycles of translation overhead per cycle of compute for a PINM sparse compute accelerator device (see Fig. 4). Nothing short of a rethink of the virtual memory system will solve the problem.

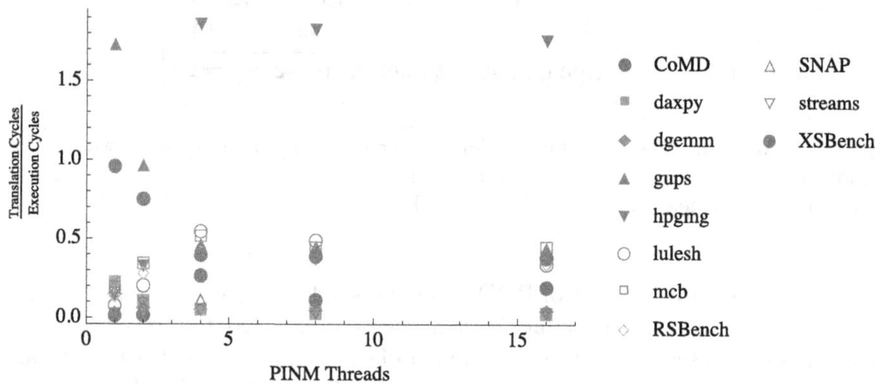

Fig. 4. Projected cycles used on translation versus execution, estimated by measuring actual application miss rates on a leading accelerator architecture (64-entry L1 TLB), assuming a 1 GHz clocked multi-core main processor, an average of 582-cycles per IOMMU page walk (times above estimated assuming a 60% IOMMU hit rate), PCIe ATS protocol, and 50-cycles PCIe latency round trip (optimistic). No latency is taken into account for page source (e.g., disk, RDMA), nor DRAM page open, making this graph optimistic. Execution time does not include time spent stalled.

Reliance on a set of fixed-size pages (even with an assortment of sizes) has the unfortunate characteristic that each page entry represents only N-bytes of memory and there can only be a set number of entries in the physical hardware. This results in the reach (range of addresses addressable by the translation look-aside buffer, TLB) being fixed by the number of entries in the TLB multiplied by the size of the largest page size supported. TLB size has grown (as well as number of entries and associativity), however, even the largest of TLBs can only address a small fraction of the available address space (e.g., 1TB). What happens when the memory space is a petabyte, then exabyte? It should be apparent that the lack of TLB reach is quickly becoming an issue for general purpose cores in addition to out-of-core devices. Any rethink of page-based virtual memory will clearly pay dividends for all compute elements, not just accelerators.

4 Conclusion: It's the System

Pulling the memory hierarchy into the compute system as a first class citizen, not only to feed cores but as an active participant, will enable extracting more performance from less revolutionary memory and compute technologies. Reducing overall system data movement will likely net system designers far more over the next decade than any revolutionary technology changes. Enabling small amounts of computation in- or near-memory along with fixing the virtual memory system could enable future systems to recapture dark bandwidth. Doing all of this, while not breaking all extant software is a huge, but not insurmountable, challenge. It's not just the memory technology or compute alone that should be the focus, it's how the compute system as a whole uses it.

References

1. Data Movement Dominates. https://goo.gl/rro35D. Accessed Mar 2017
2. Dongarra, J., Heroux, M.A.: Toward a new metric for ranking high performance computing systems. Sandia Report, SAND2013-4744 312 (2013)
3. Dongarra, J.J., Moler, C.B., Bunch, J.R., Stewart, G.W.: LINPACK Users' Guide. Society for Industrial and Applied Mathematics, Philadelphia (1979)
4. Henning, J.L.: SPEC CPU2006 benchmark descriptions. ACM SIGARCH Comput. Architect. News **34**(4), 1–17 (2006)
5. Jacob, B., Ng, S., Wang, D.: Memory Systems: Cache, DRAM, Disk. Morgan Kaufmann (2010)
6. Karakostas, V., Gandhi, J., Cristal, A., Hill, M.D., McKinley, K.S., Nemirovsky, M., Swift, M.M., Unsal, O.S.: Energy-efficient address translation. In: 2016 IEEE International Symposium on High Performance Computer Architecture (HPCA), pp. 631–643. IEEE (2016)
7. Kestor, G., Gioiosa, R., Kerbyson, D.J., Hoisie, A.: Quantifying the energy cost of data movement in scientific applications. In: 2013 IEEE International Symposium on Workload Characterization (IISWC) (2013)
8. Lloyd, S., Gokhale, M.: In-memory data rearrangement for irregular, data-intensive computing. Computer **48**(8), 18–25 (2015). doi:10.1109/MC.2015.230
9. Markov, I.L.: Limits on fundamental limits to computation. Nature **512**(7513), 147–154 (2014)
10. Srinivasan, J.R.: Improving cache utilisation. Technical report, University of Cambridge, Computer Laboratory (2011)

11. Vesely, J., Basu, A., Oskin, M., Loh, G.H., Bhattacharjee, A.: Observations and opportunities in architecting shared virtual memory for heterogeneous systems. In: 2016 IEEE International Symposium on Performance Analysis of Systems and Software (ISPASS), pp. 161–171. IEEE (2016)
12. Wang, L., Zhan, J., Luo, C., Zhu, Y., Yang, Q., He, Y., Gao, W., Jia, Z., Shi, Y., Zhang, S., et al.: Bigdatabench: a big data benchmark suite from internet services. In: 2014 IEEE 20th International Symposium on High Performance Computer Architecture (HPCA), pp. 488–499. IEEE (2014)

Towards an Integrated Strategy to Preserve Digital Computing Performance Scaling Using Emerging Technologies

Dilip Vasudevan(✉), Anastasiia Butko, George Michelogiannakis, David Donofrio, and John Shalf

Computer Science Department, Lawrence Berkeley National Lab, One Cyclotron Road, Berkeley, CA, USA
{dilipv,abutko,mihelog,ddonofrio,jshalf}@lbl.gov

Abstract. With the decline and eventual end of historical rates of lithographic scaling, we arrive at a crossroad where synergistic and holistic decisions are required to preserve Moore's law technology scaling. Numerous emerging technologies aim to extend digital electronics scaling of performance, energy efficiency, and computational power/density, ranging from devices (transistors), memories, 3D integration capabilities, specialized architectures, photonics, and others. The wide range of technology options creates the need for an integrated strategy to understand the impact of these emerging technologies on future large-scale digital systems for diverse application requirements and optimization metrics. In this paper, we argue for a comprehensive methodology that spans the different levels of abstraction – from materials, to devices, to complex digital systems and applications. Our approach integrates compact models of low-level characteristics of the emerging technologies to inform higher-level simulation models to evaluate their responsiveness to application requirements. The integrated framework can then automate the search for an optimal architecture using available emerging technologies to maximize a targeted optimization metric.

1 Introduction

Far from a physical law, Moore's law is a techno-economic observation on doubling the number of transistors per square inch of an integrated circuit. This led to Moore's subsequent observation that "shrinking the dimensions on an integrated structure makes it possible to operate the structure at higher speed for the same power per unit area" [8]. The expectation that early in the next decade 2D lithography will cease scaling, threatens the future of Moore's law. In response, a number of promising emerging technologies have been proposed. These alternative technologies appear throughout all levels of computing devices, ranging from transistors (devices), memory technologies and 3D integration to hybrid architectures, specialization, etc. [4]. While it is unlikely that a single technology will prevail to drive Moore's law, a combination of emerging technologies together with explicit understanding of application requirements is likely

J.M. Kunkel et al. (Eds.): ISC High Performance Workshops 2017, LNCS 10524, pp. 115–123, 2017.
https://doi.org/10.1007/978-3-319-67630-2_10

the solution [8]. This realization contradicts today's common practice of developing and evaluating each technology in isolation. Therefore, it is imperative to develop a comprehensive strategy to determine the optimal path forward to preserve digital computing performance scaling. To achieve this, we argue for a two-fold strategy that is composed of:

- an algorithmic methodology that takes into account each candidate technology's characteristics, and produces an optimal combination of emerging technologies for a given metric and application.
- a simulation and evaluation infrastructure across different levels (e.g., devices, circuits, architectures), that supports performance and cost models of emerging technologies.

2 Motivation and Background

Numerous emerging devices follow the traditional CMOS model but offer improved voltage–current characteristics. Devices such as tunnel FETs and carbon nanotube FETs have been demonstrated in practice, and initial studies discuss their impact to chip multiprocessors [1,7]. A recent influential study projected the future potential of several devices in terms of the energy–delay product to implement a 32-bit adder [5]. Similarly, new memory technologies offer attractive bandwidth, latency, and cost tradeoffs compared to traditional DRAM [6]. In fact, some memories such as resistive RAM are non-volatile and can be placed close to computational cores. Furthermore, 3D integration is growing capable of tens to hundreds of memory layers with fast and cheap inter-layer communication, and is projected to enable multiple logic layers as well in different interleaved patterns. Moreover, specialization is an attractive technique to remove performance and cost overhead of general-purpose architecture. Numerous other technologies are also promising candidates to preserve digital computing performance scaling, such as photonics and stochastic computing.

The heterogeneity of emerging technologies creates a challenge because different technologies are more suited for different applications and no clear winner is expected to emerge. In addition, a choice of one technology affects other choices when designing a complete chip or system. Finally, previous studies typically develop one solution in isolation and do not investigate any synergistic opportunities with other technologies. We propose a comprehensive strategy that paves the road forward for extending Moore's law using the entire range of emerging technologies.

3 Towards an Integrated Methodology for Comprehensive Evaluation of Optimal Architectures

Developing an integrated methodology to preserve Moore's law performance scaling by designing future architectures that use emerging technologies is made particularly challenging by the sheer number of options (technologies) available at each level, the dependencies between these options, and the increasing demands from the applications. Namely, some of these options are:

- Heterogeneous or homogeneous architectures. This includes the entire range from fully to partially and then to non-programmable fixed-function specialized hardware.
- Devices like TFET (Tunnel Field-Effect Transistor), CNFET (Carbon-Nanotube FET), NCFET (Negative Capacitance FET) and superconducting circuits like RSFQ (Rapid Single Flux Quantum) devices, and many others. There are to the order of a dozen emerging devices in today's literature in different stages of maturity [5].
- Future memory technologies like MRAM, STT-RAM etc., some of which are non-volatile and can be integrated close to computation cores. There are to the order of ten emerging memory technologies.
- 3D integration with memory such as conventional DRAM or HMC (Hybrid Memory Cube), as well as future capabilities of deep 3D integration with hundreds of interleaved logic and memory layers, and different inter-layer technologies.
- Implementation constraints like thermal equilibrium, area and power budgets and other factors like floating point versus fixed point representation, SIMD (Single Instruction Multiple Data), PIM (Processing In Memory) based architectures etc.

To illustrate the dependency between application demands for performance per watt and area and the several choices impacting architecture design, let us consider a sample set of applications: namely a climate modeling application code (MPES), a memory intensive graphics application, and the Fourier transform (FFT). These applications are power constrained, perform complex computations, but also demand high throughput of data from memory. Given these application constraints, as well as an optimization metric such as performance per watt, the globally optimal architecture using the most optimal technologies in each layer from the ones mentioned previously could be the one shown in Fig. 1. That architecture uses accelerators implemented with CNFETs to satisfy computational demands, HMC memory to satisfy high memory access bandwidth, high heterogeneity to optimize for power, and other choices in both architectures and other technologies such as devices and memories always to satisfy application demands and optimization metrics. Note that to truly be the globally optimal solution, it must consider how a choice of technology affects others and avoid locally optimal solutions.

Our goal is to design a comprehensive methodology to perform multi-objective optimization and systematically design a globally optimal architecture for a given metric and for a given set of application characteristics, using all available technology options from all the different layers previously explained. To achieve this we have to operate and optimize at various levels of the system architecture from devices, circuits, accelerators and others, but also to include potential modifications to programming languages, compilers, ISAs, and others.

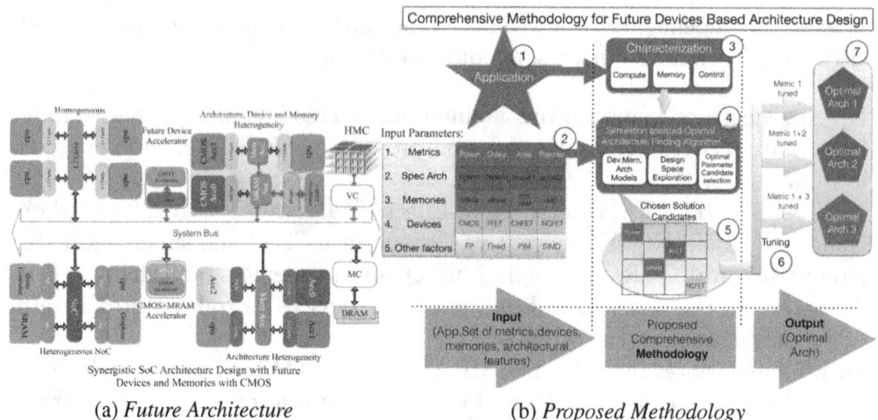

(a) *Future Architecture* (b) *Proposed Methodology*

Fig. 1. a. An example of a future architecture implemented with heterogeneous devices, b. Comprehensive and synergistic methodology for finding a global optimum by exploring the different levels of system design, including emerging devices and specialized architectures (only a subset of options is shown)

Methodology: Figures 1 and 2 shows our proposed methodology that involves seven constructive steps to be taken to arrive at a globally optimal architecture. The steps are:

1. Gathering any software engineering requirements of the application (functional and non-functional), such as any compiler and programming language requirements.
2. Secondly, this methodology requires comprehensive details and models of available emerging technologies in several levels of the system ranging from devices to architecture (logic design). In this step, a set of optimization metrics is also provided.
3. Next, characterization of the application code for compute, memory and control intensive instructions, to derive performance and other application requirements such as data movement, floating point computation, etc.
4. In the next step, the inputs generated from the previous three steps drive the optimal architecture finding algorithm. This step includes constraint optimization to make sure the solution is acceptable. This algorithm is further described below.
5. The fifth step produces a baseline architecture using the choices in technologies made by the algorithm in the previous step.
6. In this step, the architecture constructed is further tuned toward a subset of target optimization metrics.
7. Finally, a set of architectures and choice of emerging technologies targeting the given application will be generated. Each architecture will be a globally optimal solution for a choice of given metrics.

To formulate the inputs that step four (the algorithm) requires, we need a way to first identify and record the relevant characteristics and needs of applications, and then input those to our framework. This includes an array of factors such as data movement, memory access, floating point compute, and others shown as a row named "other factors" in Fig. 1. Each application's needs translate to different weights for each of these factors. Another input is the available technologies (step two). For those, we need to quantify the impact of each technology to application needs. Doing so requires reliable performance and cost models for each technology, which we describe in Sect. 4.

Algorithm: The algorithm itself (step four) will be formulated as a graph optimization problem with the design space represented as a graph with weighted vertices and edges. The algorithm is illustrated in Fig. 2. As shown, each vertex represents one computational unit, which is comprised of a choice of device technology (dev), memory technology (mem), logic design (logic), and as a result of these and other microarchitectural and emerging technology choices has a certain energy–delay (ED) product. Only four parameters are shown in this example. In other words, each vertex is just one of the possibly many computational units of the architecture. Edges, on the other hand, represent cost of communication in delay and energy between computational units. Using this notation, finding an optimal architecture (step six in the Figure) is a multi-objective graph optimization problem of finding a path in the graph where a given metric, such as performance over watt, is optimized. This path represents an architecture where the different components were chosen because their corresponding vertices were in the chosen path of the graph. This algorithm builds from obtaining and embedding into the feature vector of each vertex (step two in the Figure) simulation and energy–delay (ED) results for the various general-purpose cores, adders, multipliers, FFT accelerator blocks, and other computational blocks, for a given set of devices, memories, logic design, etc. From the chosen path, a new feature vector will be constructed for each computation block in the resulting architecture (step five in the Figure). In the example in Fig. 2, the feature vectors found in the enumerated red path will suggest a computational block with 2 adders, a multiplier, a FFT implemented using different devices and a 32KB MRAM for a constraint of low power for multiplier and a high memory density.

The outcome of this algorithm is an architecture with combination of technologies that reach a global maximum *for a specific metric and application.* From this, we can "average out" for a general-purpose solution and shape a general strategy to preserve digital computing scaling. Certainly, this output should consider the potential each technology has on top of its current state. Thus, for the example set of applications (MPES and FFT and graphics) introduced earlier in this section, the algorithm will find an optimal set of input parameters (technologies) while considering optimization metrics such as for power and memory bandwidth, and arrive at the selected parameters shown in step five in Fig. 1. After further tuning of the derived architecture using these metrics in step six will generate the required optimal architectures tuned for a specific set of metrics

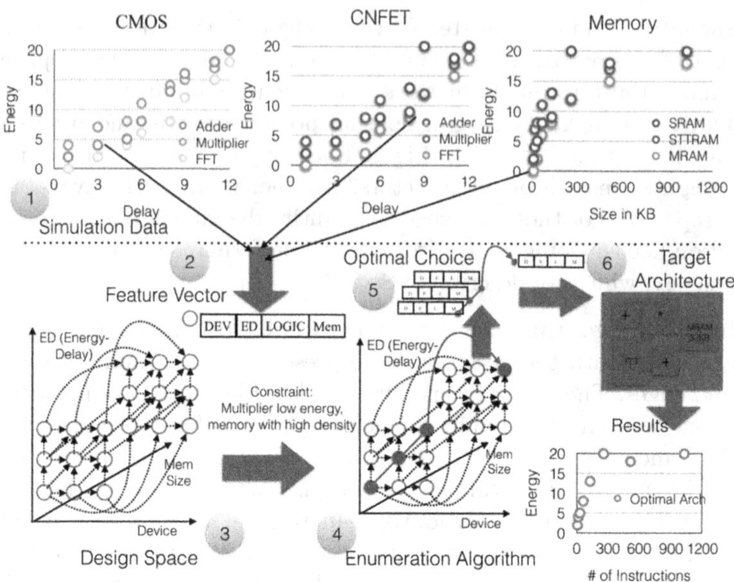

Fig. 2. Illustration of the algorithm for the optimal architecture selection. The energy–delay (ED) graphs are for illustration purposes only and not in scale.

shown as step seven in Fig. 1. Therefore, for our applications we will arrive at possibly at a different architecture per application.

4 Modeling Environment

4.1 Simulation Infrastructure

In order to generate the technology models necessary to conduct realistic experiments and therefore guide our methodology, we propose our simulation infrastructure as shown in Fig. 3. The proposed infrastructure consists of four main modeling levels: (i) device models, (ii) logic gates, (iii) logic and memory blocks and (iv) architecture. Each level contains three key components illustrated with colored blocks. Yellow blocks represent the *Target Modeling Unit*, which can be a device model, logic gate, accelerator, etc. depending on the modeling level. Blue blocks represent a set of *Evaluation tools* capable of providing target *Output metrics*. These output metrics are then used as *Input metrics* in the next modeling level. Here, we describe each modeling level in detail.

LEVEL 1: Device Models. In this level, we start from low-level device physics and generate current–voltage curves using Xyce, a open-source SPICE tool. In this step, detailed knowledge of device physics and operating conditions is required. Open-source Verilog-A models are already available for many of the emerging devices, but care must be exercised in verification of those models,

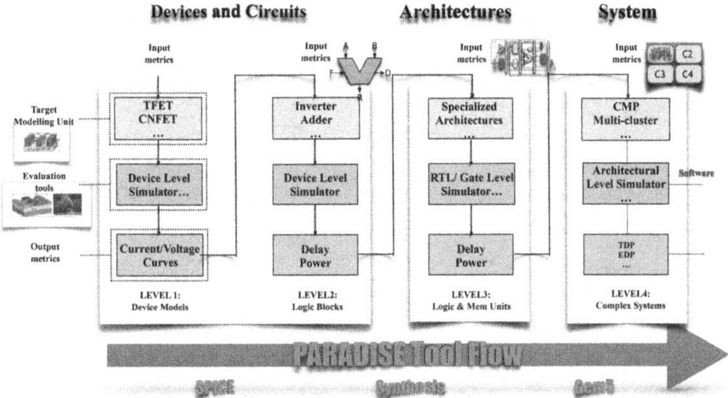

Fig. 3. Design space exploration flow. The example refers to results in Fig. 4. (Color figure online)

capturing the future potential of each device, and generating models for devices for which no models are available. Further metrics of interest such as error rates can also be captured in this step.

LEVEL 2: Logic Gates and Blocks. In this level, we use device models from the previous level to construct small functional blocks such as logic gates, adders, ring oscillators, and others. We do this by adding Verilog-A models from the previous emerging devices to Xyce, and describing the small functional blocks of this level in an Xyce netlist that uses emerging device models. From these experiments we extract delay and power for each block, and use that as inputs to the next higher level. Adders and multipliers result shown in Fig. 4-a and b are built using these logic gates.

LEVEL 3: Logic and Memory Blocks. In the logic and memory level, several new technologies can be modeled such as memories, 3D integration, and specialized architectures. Emerging memories have sometimes vastly different access times, energies, volatility, error rates, etc. In fact, memory access times for particular data may depend on the location of the data and the previous sequence of requests, which means that a careful study is required to investigate the level of accuracy that is sufficient versus the complexity of models. Furthermore, 3D integration affects distances and relevant performance-cost tradeoffs between any two points, especially when considering inter-layer communication technologies such as TSVs. 3D integration models need to include future capabilities such as deep integration with hundreds of layers, with multiple combinations of logic and memory. Finally, specialized architectures such as accelerators and fixed-function hardware have a range of different delays and energy costs to perform an operation. Non-programmable application specific hardware.

In order to rapidly model the technologies of this level, we can extend a modern HDL modeling tool such as Chisel [2] and use it to describe different

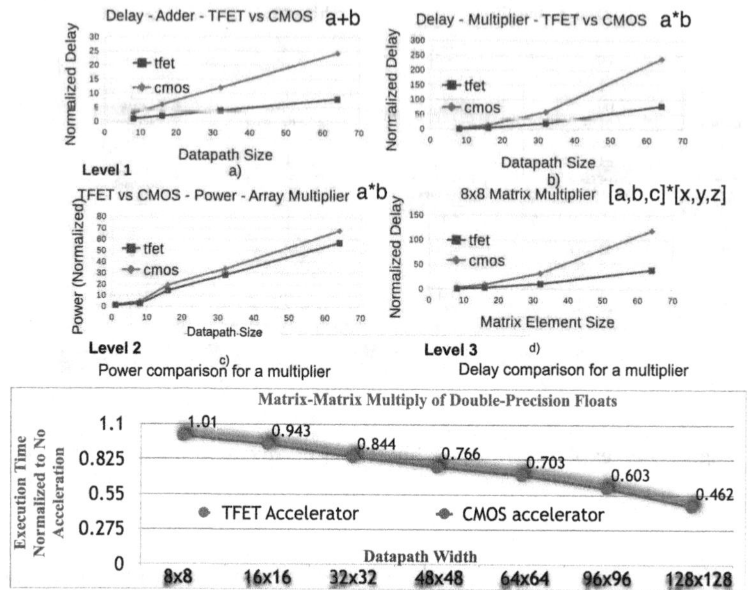

Fig. 4. a–d. Delay and Power comparison for adders and multipliers implemented with TFET and CMOS, e. Execution time impact for a matrix-matrix multiply code using an accelerator compared to a non-accelerated version. Results are for a single core co-located with the accelerator. While the CMOS accelerator is 3× slower resulting in two cycles instead of one for the TFET accelerator, the architectural-level impact is negligible.

logic and memory blocks. Chisel can be extended to capture and back annotate activity factors of logic gates and wires to models of emerging technologies from the previous two levels, and therefore generate the output metrics (delay, power, etc.) that are necessary for the next level. Figure 4-c and d show the delay comparison of adders and multipliers implemented using CMOS and TFET. Normalized delay and power shows that TFET based arithmetic units have higher performance and power benefit.

LEVEL 4: Architectural Level. To conduct high-level experiments, we use a software architectural-level simulator such as Gem5 [3]. A preliminary study of the impact of accelerators using TFET and CMOS devices is shown in Fig. 4-e. This shows that even though a TFET-based accelerator is 3× faster, the impact to the application is negligible. Still, this different can become substantial for large matrices, to which we are extending our study. This infrastructure will be capable of evaluating potentially vastly heterogeneous systems with all emerging technologies as options. This may require a parallel architecture simulator. In addition, we plan to extend high-level area and power models to include new devices.

5 Conclusion

Building systems using future devices and other technologies involves several levels of modeling with many factors to consider. The choice of components at each level impacts the choice in other levels and consequently the overall power and performance of future systems. Optimizing at only one level, such as solely focusing on new transistors/devices will lead only to a local optimal optimization point. However, a holistic approach to optimize the system at all levels for given optimization metrics and application needs will lead to a globally-optimal solution. In this paper, we present both a comprehensive methodology and a detailed modeling approach for emerging technologies capable of paving the path forward for preserving the performance scaling of digital computing.

References

1. Aly, M.M.S., Gao, M., Hills, G., Lee, C.S., Pitner, G., Shulaker, M.M., Wu, T.F., Asheghi, M., Bokor, J., Franchetti, F., Goodson, K.E., Kozyrakis, C., Markov, I., Olukotun, K., Pileggi, L., Pop, E., Rabaey, J., Rè, C., Wong, H.S.P., Mitra, S.: Energy-efficient abundant-data computing: the N3XT 1,000x. Computer **48**(12), 24–33 (2015)
2. Bachrach, J., Vo, H., Richards, B., Lee, Y., Waterman, A., Aviienis, R., Wawrzynek, J., Asanovi, K.: Chisel: constructing hardware in a scala embedded language. In: DAC Design Automation Conference 2012, pp. 1212–1221 (2012)
3. Binkert, N., Beckmann, B., Black, G., Reinhardt, S.K., Saidi, A., Basu, A., Hestness, J., Hower, D.R., Krishna, T., Sardashti, S., Sen, R., Sewell, K., Shoaib, M., Vaish, N., Hill, M.D., Wood, D.A.: The Gem5 simulator. SIGARCH Comput. Archit. News **39**(2), 1–7 (2011)
4. Cavin, R.K., Lugli, P., Zhirnov, V.V.: Science and engineering beyond Moore's law. In: Proceedings of the IEEE 100(Special Centennial Issue), pp. 1720–1749, May 2012
5. Esch, J.: Overview of beyond-CMOS devices and a uniform methodology for their benchmarking. Proc. IEEE **101**(12), 2495–2497 (2013)
6. Poremba, M., Mittal, S., Li, D., Vetter, J.S., Xie, Y.: DESTINY: a tool for modeling emerging 3d NVM and eDRAM caches. In: 2015 Design, Automation Test in Europe Conference Exhibition (DATE), pp. 1543–1546, March 2015
7. Saripalli, V., Mishra, A., Datta, S., Narayanan, V.: An energy-efficient heterogeneous CMP based on hybrid TFET-CMOS cores. In: 2011 48th ACM/EDAC/IEEE Design Automation Conference (DAC), pp. 729–734, June 2011
8. Shalf, J.M., Leland, R.: Computing beyond Moore's law. Computer **48**(12), 14–23 (2015)

5 Conclusion

HPC I/O in the Data Center (HPC-IODC)

HPC I/O in the Data Center Workshop (HPC-IODC)

Julian Kunkel[1,2,3](✉), Jay Lofstead[1,2,3], and Colin McMurtrie[1,2,3]

[1] Deutsches Klimarechenzentrum, Bundesstraße 45a, 20146 Hamburg, Germany
kunkel@dkrz.de

[2] Center for Computing Research, Sandia National Laboratories, Albuquerque, USA

[3] Swiss National Computing Center (CSCS), Lugano, Switzerland

1 Introduction

Many public and privately funded data centers host supercomputers for running large scale simulations and analyzing experimental and observational data. These supercomputers run usually tightly coupled parallel applications that require hardware components that deliver the best performance. In contrast, commercial data centers, such as Facebook and Google, execute loosely coupled workloads with a broad assumption of regular failures. The dimension of the data centers is enormous. A 2013 article summarizes commercial data centers' dimensions [1]. It estimates, for example, that Facebook hosts around 100 PB of storage and Google and Microsoft manage around 1 million servers each – although the hardware is split among several physical data centers – a modus operandi not suitable for HPC centers. With the hunger for information, the globally installed storage capacity increases exponentially and is expected to hit 7,235 Exabytes by 2017 [2]. This trend is visible in the sales reports of companies such as the disk drive manufacturer Seagate. Within 5 years, they shipped 1 billion HDDs, which means 700.000 units every day [3]. With state-of-the-art 8 TB disks, this would already account for 5.5 exabyte of capacity by day.

Management of the huge amount of data is vital for effective use of the contained information. However, with limited budgets, it is a daunting task for data center operators, especially as design and storage system required hardware depends heavily on the executed workloads. A co-factor of the increasing difficulty is the increase in complexity of the storage hierarchy with the adoption of SSD and memory class storage technology. The US Department of Energy recognizes the importance of data management, listing it among the top 10 research challenges for Exascale [4].

There are several initiatives, consortia and special tracks in conferences that target RD&E audiences. Examples are the Storage Networking Industry Association (SNIA) for enterprises, the Big Data and Extreme-Scale Computing (BDEC) initiative[1], the Exascale10 workgroup [5], the Parallel Data Storage Workshop/Data Intensive Scalable Computing Systems (PDSW-DISCS) and the HEC FSIO workshop [6].

[1] http://www.exascale.org/bdec/.

J.M. Kunkel et al. (Eds.): ISC High Performance Workshops 2017, LNCS 10524, pp. 127–131, 2017.
https://doi.org/10.1007/978-3-319-67630-2_11

There are many I/O workloads studies and performance analysis reports for parallel I/O available. Additionally, many surveys of enterprise technology usage include predictions of analysis for future storage technology and the storage market such as [7]. However, analysis conducted for HPC typically focuses on applications and not on the data center perspective. Information about data center operational aspects is usually described in file system specific user groups and meetings or described partially in research papers as part of the evaluation environment.

In this workshop, we bring together I/O experts from data centers and application workflows to share current practices for scientific workflows, issues and obstacles for both hardware and the software stack, and R&D to overcome these issues.

2 Organization of the Workshop

The workshop content consisted of three topics:

- **Research paper presentations** – authors needed to submit a paper regarding relevant research for I/O in the datacenter.
- **Talks from I/O experts** – authors needed to submit a rough outline for the talk related to the operational aspects of the data center.
- A moderated **discussion** to identify key issues and potential solutions in the community.

The CFP has been issued beginning of January. Important deadlines were:

- Submission deadline: 2017-04-12 AoE
- Author notification: 2017-04-25
- Workshop: 2017-06-22
- Camera-ready papers: 2017-07-22

From all submissions, the programm committee selected four talks from I/O experts and four research papers for presentation during the workshop.

2.1 Programm Committee

- Wolfgang Frings (*Jülich Supercomputing Center, Germany*)
- Javier Garcia Blas (*University Carlos III of Madrid, Spain*)
- Rob Ross (*Argonne National Laboratory, USA*)
- Carlos Maltzahn (*University of California, Santa Cruz, USA*)
- Thomas Boenisch (*HLRS, Stuttgart, Germany*)
- Sai Narasimhamurthy (*Seagate, United Kingdom*)
- Jean-Thomas Acquaviva (*DDN, France*)
- Julian Kunkel (*DKRZ, Germany*)
- Jay Lofstead (*Sandia National Laboratory, USA*)
- Colin McMurtrie (*CSCS, Switzerland*)

3 Workshop Summary

Throughout the day, on average 65 participants attended the workshop. We had a good mix of talks from I/O experts, data center relevant research followed by a short discussion. A short summary of the presentations is given in the following. The slides of the presentations are available on the workshop's webpage: http://wr.informatik.uni-hamburg.de/events/2017/iodc.

3.1 Research Papers

The research session covered 5 accepted papers from 6 submissions:

- In the first talk, Walker Haddock presented results of the efficiency for GPU offloaded erasure coding for Ceph. With a GPU plugin to support coding, a 1 GB/s full duplex performance is achievable for 100 shards.
- Eugen Betke introduced an online monitoring system for parallel I/O performance based on SIOX. The novelty of the approach is non-intrusive monitoring via an instrumented FUSE mountpoint allowing to cover `mmap()` operations.
- Jakob Lüttgau presented a simulator for hierarchical storage systems focusing on tape systems. Queuing systems are used to model I/O on the different storage tiers; the simulation allows to measure derived metrics in a fine-grained fashion for instance to analyzing waiting times (quality of service) and drive utilization.
- Jay Lofstead showed results for a large scale performance study for the IOR benchmark to identify performance variability and stragglers across the different OSTs. This demonstrated that for each measurement a small proportion of storage targets ($< 20\%$) are slower than the others but the performance of storage targets changes over time changing the assignment slow/fast targets.
- The last talk of the research papers by Pilar Gomez-Sanchez introduced a framework to recover the access pattern of MPI parallel applications on a high-level. The methodology characterizes I/O behavior for individual application phases and introduces several derived metrics. A process starts another phase when it invokes an instrumented MPI function.

3.2 Talks from Experts

The seven talks from experts included information about the site and typical application profiles but also contained information regarding I/O tools and strategies applied to mitigate pressing issues.

- In the first talk, Bryan Lawrence introduced the computation infrastructure in the UK with a focus on Earth-Science. He described the JASMIN infrastructure in detail which is managed and designed by STFC. A main distinction is that the infrastructure is continuously upgraded and the system architecture is developed by themself and not any vendor.

- Tiago Quintino shed light on the I/O challenges of ECMF. The center observes the need to adapt workflows to deal with paradigm shifts in technology. For example, to move from compute centric to a data centric paradigm minimizing data movement and shipping compute to data.
- Roland Laifer introduces the HPC systems at KIT. Highlights of his talk are results on using Lustre on a wide area Infiniband connection, their analysis approach by capturing I/O statistics, and the approach for disaster recovery.
- Yuichi Tsujita presented the K Computer and storage systems. He focused on obstacles due to large scale parallelism: the metadata server load, client eviction (loss of server connections), and cross node interference. Several strategies to mitigate these issues are presented.
- Sandra Mendez introduces the LRZ HPC systems and then focuses on monitoring of I/O patterns. The usage of deployed analysis tools PerSyst and Darshan are illustrated on several applications.
- Clemens Grelck introduced the cHiPSet project which is an community effort that fosters collaboration in the area of HPC and Big Data. The activity is still open and new researcher may join the project: http://www.chipset-cost.eu
- Rosemary Francis presented the tool Mistral that profiles I/O of large scale applications to identify bad I/O patterns, foster optimizing and load balancing. The monitoring tool allows to detect rogue applications based on policies such as limiting storage capacity or metadata. A case study shows the effectiveness to tame non well-formed I/O.

From the individual talks, it can be concluded that analyzing and understanding I/O behavior and achieving consistent performance is still the top priority for researchers and data centers.

3.3 Discussion Round

The major distinguishing feature for this workshop compared to other venues is the discussion rounds. The opportunity for themed, open discussions about issues both pressing and relevant to the data center community facilitates sharing experiences, solutions, and problems.

This year we focused on the community development of an IO-500 benchmark, see http://io500.org. The IO-500 benchmark consists of data and metadata benchmarks to identify performance boundaries for optimized and suboptimal applications. Each benchmark is run in an easy and hard mode to identify best-case performance for optimized applications and typical performance for applications with a suboptimal access pattern. Unlike other competitive benchmarks, "gaming" the system to get optimal results is encouraged because all configurations on how the performance results were achieved must be shared as part of any submission to the list. This transparency achieves three goals: (1) best practices for each different kind of storage on a platform are documented for users, (2) configurations and platform validation approaches can be better understood, and 3) a detailed catalog of storage options on various platforms over time with configurations for achieving specific performance is collected. The last of these will offer a long-term archive to understand the evolution of platform storage.

The Virtual Institute for I/O (VI4IO)[2] supports this activity and tracks comprehensive data from sites, supercomputers and storage on the high-performance storage list. This data allows for an in-depth analysis of system characteristics and fosters the understanding of I/O systems.

References

1. Blog, S.: Facts and stats of world's largest data centers, July 2013, https://storageservers.wordpress.com/2013/07/17/facts-and-stats-of-worlds-largest-data-centers/
2. International Data Corporation, http://www.businesswire.com/news/home/20131021005243/en/IDCs-Outlook-Data-Byte-Density-Globe-Big
3. Seagate: Storage Solutions Guide, http://www.seagate.com/files/www-content/product-content/_cross-product/en-us/docs/seagate-storage-and-application-guide-apac.pdf
4. Lucas, R., Committee members: Top ten exascale research challenges, February 2014, http://science.energy.gov/~/media/ascr/ascac/pdf/meetings/20140210/Top10reportFEB14.pdf
5. Brinkmann, A., Cortes, T., Falter, H., Kunkel, J., Narasimhamurthy, S.: E10 - Exascale IO, June 2014
6. Bancroft, M., Bent, J., Felix, E., Grider, G., Nunez, J., Poole, S., Ross, R., Salmon, E., Ward, L.: HEC FSIO 2008 workshop report. In: High End Computing Interagency Working Group (HECIWG), Sponsored File Systems and I/O Workshop HEC FSIO (2009)
7. IDC: Enterprise storage services survey, http://www.idc.com/getdoc.jsp?containerId=254468

[2] http://vi4io.org.

Simulation of Hierarchical Storage Systems for TCO and QoS

Jakob Luettgau(✉) and Julian Kunkel

Deutsches Klimarechenzentrum GmbH, Bundesstraße 45a, 20146 Hamburg, Germany
{luettgau,kunkel}@dkrz.de
http://www.dkrz.de/

Abstract. Due to the variety of storage technologies deep storage hierarchies turn out to be the most feasible choice to meet performance and cost requirements when handling vast amounts of data. Long-term archives employed by scientific users are mainly reliant on tape storage, as it remains the most cost-efficient option. Archival systems are often loosely integrated into the HPC storage infrastructure. In expectation of exascale systems and in situ analysis also burst buffers will require integration with the archive. Exploring new strategies and developing open software for tape systems is a hurdle due to the lack of affordable storage silos and availability outside of large organizations and due to increased wariness requirements when dealing with ultra-durable data. Lessening these problems by providing virtual storage silos should enable community-driven innovation and enable site operators to add features where they see fit while being able to verify strategies before deploying on production systems. Different models for the individual components in tape systems are developed. The models are then implemented in a prototype simulation using discrete event simulation. The work shows that the simulations can be used to approximate the behavior of tape systems deployed in the real world and to conduct experiments without requiring a physical tape system.

Keywords: Modeling · Simulation · Tape · Long-term archive · Hierarchical storage systems · Performance · Total cost of ownership

1 Introduction

With the increasing demand for long-term storage, automated tape libraries will likely remain an integral part of the storage hierarchy for many years to come. Tape as a storage medium has many attractive properties. It is fairly robust and provides high data densities, but the most important factor is that tape is very affordable in comparison to other storage technologies. Standardization efforts such as LTO make tape attractive and future proof, thus protecting investments. Despite tapes long history, the technology is still competitive [3,4], but incentives to turn technological improvements in capacity and performance In an effort to speed up innovation and to enable also newcomers and experts and without

J.M. Kunkel et al. (Eds.): ISC High Performance Workshops 2017, LNCS 10524, pp. 132–144, 2017.
https://doi.org/10.1007/978-3-319-67630-2_12

access to large scale tape systems to contribute, the objectives of this work were to develop a simulator, tools, and primarily appropriate models required to reproduce the dynamics of hierarchical storage systems and tape libraries. Modeling a complete tape system is a complex task, because many different components are involved. It was possible to identify a number of key components that are essential to any tape system. It was further possible to provide comprehensive models to describe the dynamics of many of these key components. In particular, models for hardware and software components were proposed and isolated in such a way that turning to more accurate models is possible.

2 Related Work

Efforts to improve tape storage systems often focus on advancing the technology that is used to read and write tape. This is mostly in the domain of vendors and not much of the research conducted is published to protect a business advantage. More openly discussed are strategies for data placement on tape [1,8,9] and the magnetic representation [2]. Such strategies maybe exploited by higher level algorithms, but tape drives and hardware generally do not expose fine-grained control to the users. Another form of placement which was researched but has not yet found its way into many production system is RAIT [4] or TapeRAID and combinations of RAID and tape [6]. Pure tape systems cease in relevance and hybrid and hierarchical storage systems promise to provide cost-efficient solutions with the best properties of multiple technologies. Dee et al. [2] stress the opportunities of automation, which enabled scalable solutions that seamlessly integrate into existing the storage hierarchy. Koltsidas et al. [5] focus especially on the integration of disk and tape. Zhang et al. [10] explore different object placement strategies within tape libraries to optimize tape switch, data seek and transfer times using a simulation. More recently, Mäsker et al. [7] use workload traces of the European Centre for Medium-Range Weather Forecasts (ECMWF) to simulate tape libraries, albeit not integrated into the hierarchical storage system of the data center.

3 Simulation Overview

To simulate tape libraries within hierarchical storage systems a huge variety of subsystems and software components can be modeled and implemented for simulation. Figure 1 provides an overview of some components that are of interest because they offer opportunities for optimization. In particular the simulator is designed to consider the following hardware components:

- Multiple clients or groups of clients that act together
- I/O Servers and server local disk/flash caches
- A global online based cache as is used with, e.g., HPSS
- Multiple libraries and the position of tapes and robots within the library
- Multiple drives and tape generations (e.g., LTO)

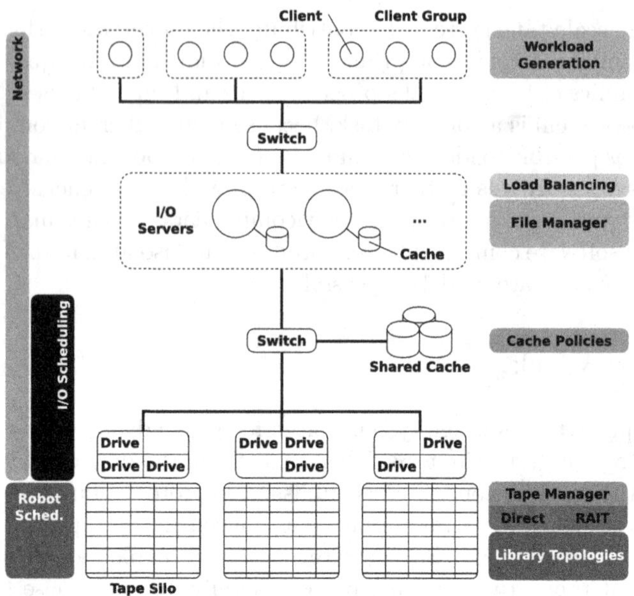

Fig. 1. An overview of different subsystems and software components that are relevant when simulating hierarchical storage systems and tape libraries.

More aspects about the network and library modeling are covered in Sect. 4 From the software side (see Sect. 5) the simulation has to implement the following components to drive the hardware:

- Various book-keeping and resource management components to keep track of files, tapes, free library slots and robots.
- Different I/O and network scheduling algorithms to grant resource allocation
- Cache displacement strategies for files in I/O node local or global caches
- (Potentially) load balancing mechanisms on different levels

Not all of these systems are implemented at this time. For example RAIT and easily exchangeable load balancing and caching policies are not supported. Besides functional components the simulator has to provide facilities to collect data that is relevant to compare different configurations of virtual systems. Different helpers to sanitize workload traces as well as R scripts to generate plots from the virtual monitoring data are provided.

4 Hardware Models

The problem with computer systems is the complexity that unfolds because of the large number of possible combinations for hardware and software. Modeling hardware is particular cumbersome because in the real world the system performance emerges as a result of the laws of physics, but for a virtual model the dynamics have to be understood and abstracted. For standardized components it is often relatively easy to find a model that is adequately applicable for the whole class of components. Composite components, such as the library topologies turn out to be harder to generalize in a simple way than expected. By mixing mostly 2D and graph-based topology approaches, good approximations of the library dynamics could be achieved. Another problem occurs with proprietary designs for which detailed information is hard to find. The same is true for benchmarks and a comprehensive catalog of performance parameters. The network is an integral part of hierarchical storage systems and can be used to model and simulate even low-level components (e.g., chip level) and communication.

4.1 Network Topology and Data Transfers

The network topology is represented using directed graphs. The approach is straight forward so that network devices such as compute nodes, I/O nodes and switches are represented by the vertices and edges are used for the individual links used to connect them. Each link may specify a latency and bandwidth. The network topology then is keeping track of available capacities. As data is moved between components, it is possible to allocate and release network allocations. This schema was used to reduce the number of events in comparison to a packet based network simulation. But the approach does not scale for large network topologies where determining the max-flow can become prohibitively expensive.

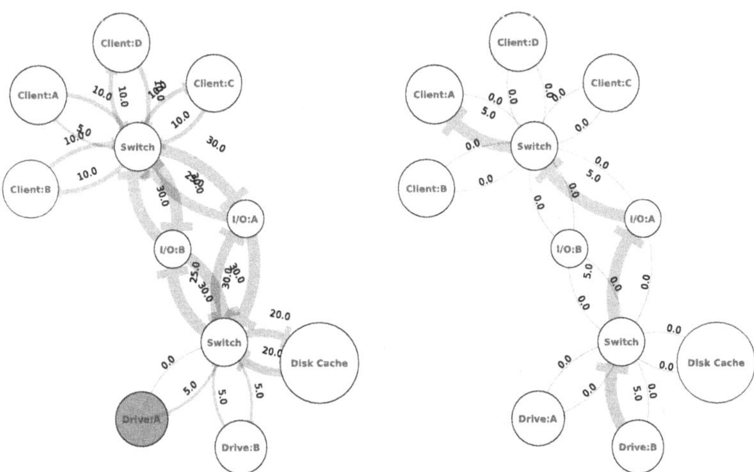

Fig. 2. Available capacities (left) and a flow from `Drive:B` to `Client:A` (right).

4.2 Library Topology

To model the library hardware we start with a coarse grained graph-based topology that connects individual components and combine it with detailed models where the graph-based model appears insufficient.

Graph-Based Topology Model: A coarse grained structure (e.g., the way multiple library units are connected to form library complexes including Pass-Through-Ports and elevators) is modeled using a graph that describe the paths a tape/a robot can travel. A vertex in the graph consequently is used for components and edges can be used to store distance or travel times from component to component. For each vertex or edge also callbacks can be registered, to allow individual components to use sophisticated models underneath (e.g., to account for their current state). In principle, the approach is very flexible and fairly accurate depending on the level of detail. For highly detailed models, the approach can be tedious to configure and will be more expensive to compute. When choosing low levels of detail, errors may accumulate rapidly. Figure 3 illustrates the concept, and in this case mixes distances and times; this is just one of many ways to interpret edges and nodes in a graph based topology. By using graphs modeling becomes intuitive and e.g., the task of serving a tape that sits in `Shelf-2` to `Drive-1` becomes the problem of finding the shortest path between the two. As we want to calculate the time penalty for the next event, for two vertexes v_i and v_j and edges e_{v_i,v_j} the time T_G to get from v_i to v_j calculates in principle as follows. v_{robot} is used to denote the maximum robot velocity:

$$\text{get\_time}(e_{v_i,v_j} \text{ or } v) := \begin{cases} t & \text{if } e_{v_i,v_j} \text{ or } v \text{ have time } t \text{ set} \\ \frac{\text{get\_distance}(v_i,v_j)}{v_{robot}} & \text{if } e \text{ but no time is set} \\ 0 & \text{otherwise} \end{cases}$$

$$T_G(v_a, v_b) = \sum_{v \in \text{shortest\_path}(v_a,v_b)} \text{get\_time}(v) + \text{get\_time}(e_{v,v+1})$$

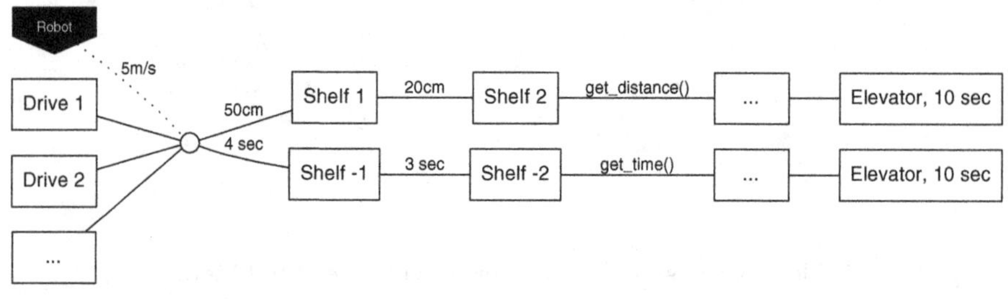

Fig. 3. The graph based topology for coarse grained relationships including library complexes, Pass-Through-Ports and Elevators connecting multiple rails.

2D Topology Model: Sometimes projecting complete robot libraries into a two-dimensional representation yields very good approximations. For the SL8500, this seems to be an efficient approach (see Fig. 4). The reasoning is that many significant movements that can be performed by the robots or the library are at most two-dimensional anyways. Finding a path within a 2D model then becomes calculating the *Euclidean-distance* between a number of points and a check if the robot is crossing a forbidden area or an obstacle, in which case additional measures have to be taken. Movements are usually decomposed of multiple linear movements, thus care must be taken when calculating distances and travel times. Logical components are resolved to coordinates by providing a mapping function for, e.g., slots and drives. Mounting a tape placed in `Slot-6,9` to `Drive 2` requires visiting multiple coordinates. May $T_{2D}(path)$ be the time it takes to traverse a $path \in \{(p_1, ..., p_n) \mid p_i \in (x, y); x, y \in \mathbb{R}\}$. Assuming different robot velocities v_x and v_y for each axis, the total travel time may be defined by the sum of the time traversing between two points $T_{2D}(p_i, p_j)$ and possibly occurring work and wait times $T_{wait/work}$:

$$T_{2D}(p_j, p_i) = max\left(\frac{|p_{ix} - p_{jx}|}{v_x}, \frac{|p_{iy} - p_{jy}|}{v_y}\right)$$

$$T_{2D}(path) = \sum_{p_i, p_j}^{path} T_{2D}(p_i, p_j) + T_{wait/work}$$

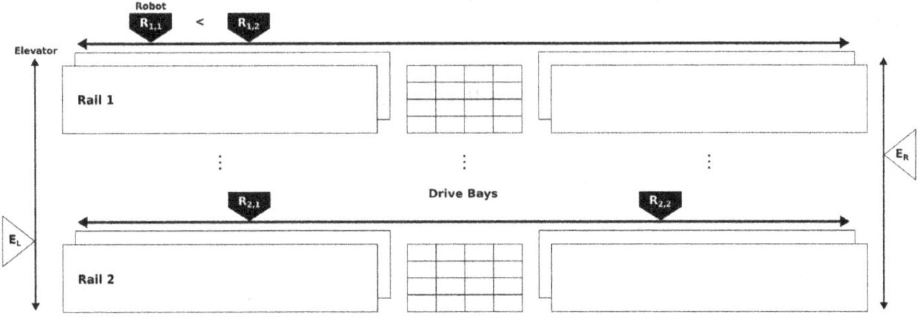

Fig. 4. The StorageTek SL8500 library in a two-dimensional model.

An easing function $e(|p_{id} - p_{jd}|, v_{max})$ can to be applied before taking the maximum, should gradual robot acceleration be taken into account. The exact times also depend on other robots, which reinforce the need for a component that guards the behavior of robots as was discussed for graph-based topologies. In general, we assume hybrid approaches that mix graph-based and 2D models to achieve good approximations at reasonable effort.

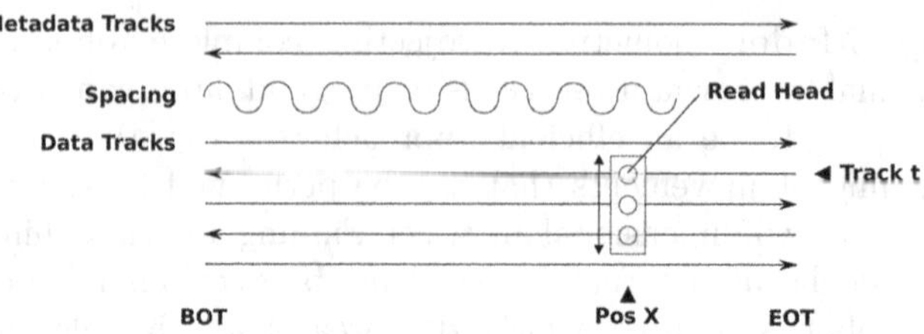

Fig. 5. Serpentine Tape Model

4.3 Tape-Seek- and Drive-Busy-Time Models

Commonly there are three layouts for writing data on tape (linear, linear-serpentine and helical-scan). We will consider only linear-serpentine tape as it appears to be the most relevant on modern systems. Figure 5 takes the perspective of the tape drive and illustrates how data is actually read or written on tape. An array of read/write heads can be positioned relative to the tape in two dimensions and imprint or read a magnetic signature as the tape passes underneath. When spooling to a specific position it is possible to move the tape quite fast, when reading or writing lower speeds yield the best results. By determining the following characteristics, it should become possible to approximate the time it takes to serve a request and how long a drive remains busy:

- $pos := (x, t)$: a tuple describing horizontal x and vertical (track) t displacements relative to the tape. pos_{BOT}, pos_{EOT} are used to reference the Begin-of-tape and End-of-tape. A single reel cartridge is mounted and unmounted with pos_{BOT}.
- T_{mount} and $T_{unmount}$: the time it takes to mount and unmount a tape
- v_{spool}, v_{head}: the speeds to reposition the tape and read-heads
- v_{read}, v_{write}: the speed in, e.g., *bytes/second* to read and write

The time to transition from a current position pos_i to target position pos_j is calculated as follows:

$$T_{seek}(pos_j, pos_i) = max\left(\frac{|pos_{ix} - pos_{jx}|}{v_{spool}}, \frac{|pos_{it} - pos_{jt}|}{v_{head}}\right)$$

The time $T_{read/write}$ to read or write from tape is calculated as follows:

$$T_{read/write}(bytes) = \frac{bytes}{v_{read/write}}$$

The time a tape drive remains busy T_{busy} would account for possibly multiple seek and reading phases, before it ejects the tape and becomes available again.

$$T_{busy} = T_{mount} + \left(\sum_{pos_i, pos_{i+1}}^{BOT,\ldots,BOT} T_{seek}(pos_i, pos_j) + T_{read/write}(bytes_i)\right) + T_{unmount}$$

5 Software Models

To stress the virtual tape library, a request object can be instantiated and submitted to the simulation. In addition to explicit submission, it possible to register event providers to the simulation which are polled for future events until they indicate they have been drained. A workload provider also could create requests on the fly according to a script, a probability distribution or a trace file. For a proof of concept it often seemed sufficient to turn to "naive" implementations.

Request Processing: A request is modeled by a process that waits for allocations to use a particular resource. Figures 6 and 7 illustrate the processing of a request. Writes occur in two-phases with the clients only waiting for the first phase. Tape I/O can be performed asynchronously for writes. Reads are handled based on their presence in the global disk cache.

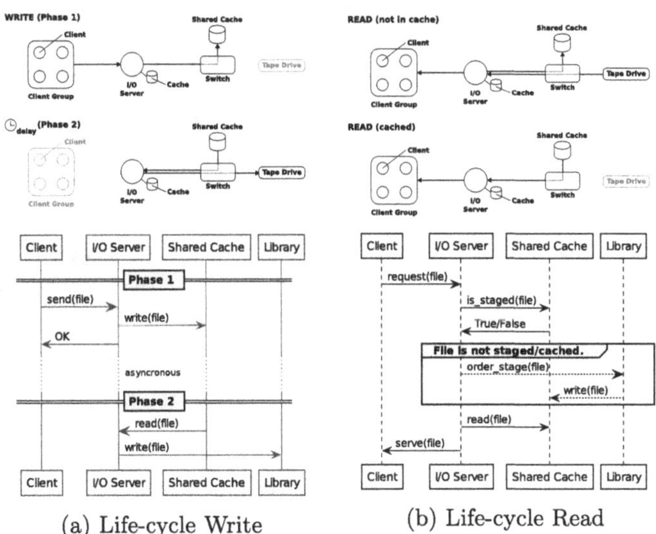

(a) Life-cycle Write

(b) Life-cycle Read

Fig. 6. Handling of read and write like requests for the HSM tape system.

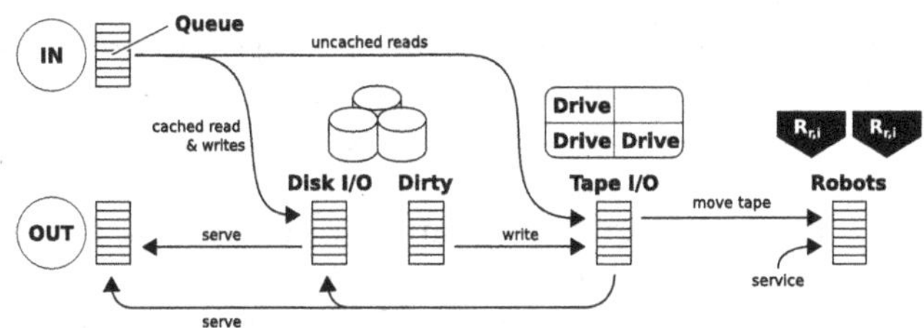

Fig. 7. Different resources and queues required to govern request handling.

6 Evaluation

This section outlines how the models are verified (see Sect. 6.1) and how simulation with alternative configurations can be used to minimize TCO. Two scenarios are discussed to show the potential.

6.1 Workload Trace Replay for Verification and Optimization

Workload Description: For verification and fine-tuning of the simulation HPSS request logs and monitoring records were used. Not all activities that occur in an actual tape system are included in these traces. As a result service workloads, and temporarily disabled drives are not accounted for. In addition, components in this simulation do not fail for the lack of reliable failure rates. The trace includes a week of scheduled downtime, which is interesting to compare the recovery of the virtual and the actual system. Figure 8 shows the distribution of file sizes and also the ratio of reads/writes that hit the system. Figure 9 shows the distribution of reads and writes over time. The following table provides a total count of requests as well as the number of involved files and clients:

Timeframe:	35 days	Requests:	213105
Files:	115856	Writes:	85961
Clients:	562	Reads:	127144

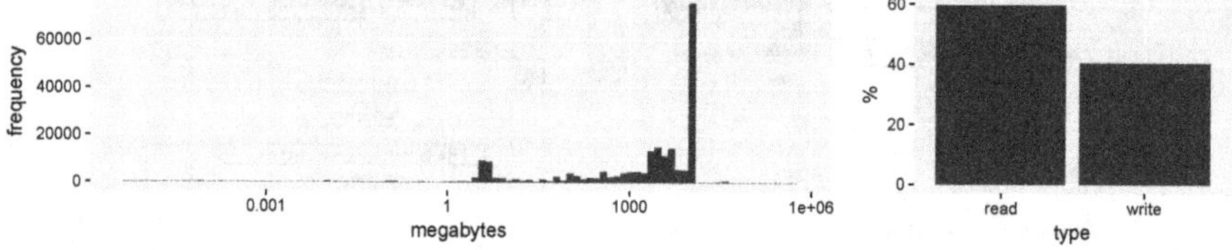

Fig. 8. Frequency of different request sizes. With a large peak for requests with a size of 10 GB, which is a result of the data centers pricing schema.

Staging Behavior and Wait-Times: To verify that the simulation can reproduce the run-time behavior from a virtual tape system two important factors are: (1) the number of busy drives and (2) the wait-times for requests over time. The number of busy drives is directly related to the number of stages, which is a metric provided by the HPSS monitoring. Figure 10 lists two plots each showing the number of FTP requests and the number of stages occurring as observed by (a) the HPSS monitoring and (b) the simulation. Figure 11 similarly plots the wait-times for queued requests, again (a) HPSS monitoring left and (b) the simulation result on the left. While there are differences in the perceived workloads, the peak times and magnitudes match in principle. The verification at this point also reveals that some components require further fine-tuning to more accurately approximate the original system. Yet, in comparison to conventional methods when procuring systems, the simulation allows taking site specific runtime behavior into account.

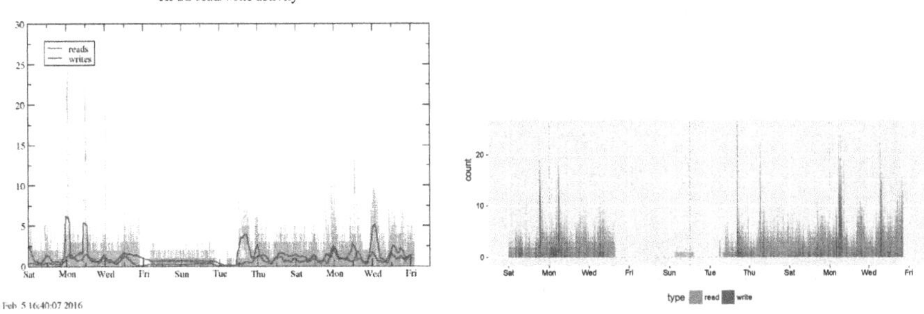

Fig. 9. Observed request types over time for a period of 3 weeks.

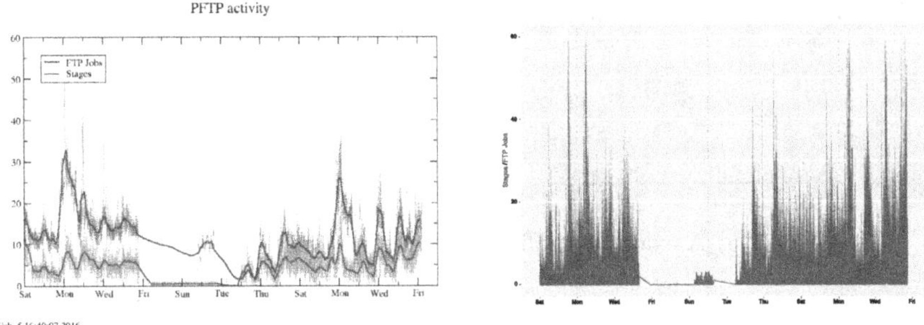

(a) FTP jobs and stage counts as reported by the monitoring.

(b) FTP Jobs as observed in the trace file and stages as occurred in the simulation.

Fig. 10. FTP activity for a period of three weeks. Validation of stage-counts by comparing the DKRZ monitoring (a) to the results of the simulation (b).

6.2 TCO and QoS Optimization Under Varying Drive Configuration

Among the most expensive components also being procured on a regular basis are tape drives. The reason for this is, that every 2–3 years a new LTO generation is released, usually doubling the capacity of tape cartridges in combination with modest improvements on read and write speeds. Depending on the use-case for a long-term archive in a data center different objectives may have priority, but common strategic decisions may relate to the following concerns:

- What is the lowest number of drives to meet a certain quality of service, e.g., serve every request to cold data within 10 min.
- What is the optimal placement for drives and tapes when considering library complexes, partitions and multiple service level agreements?
- When and how to switch to a new drive generation?
  - Under an expected change in workloads (e.g., additional users) when will the available resource fail to meet the requirements?
  - Tape media and drives become cheaper over time. What would be a good gradual transition strategy? Is it cheaper?

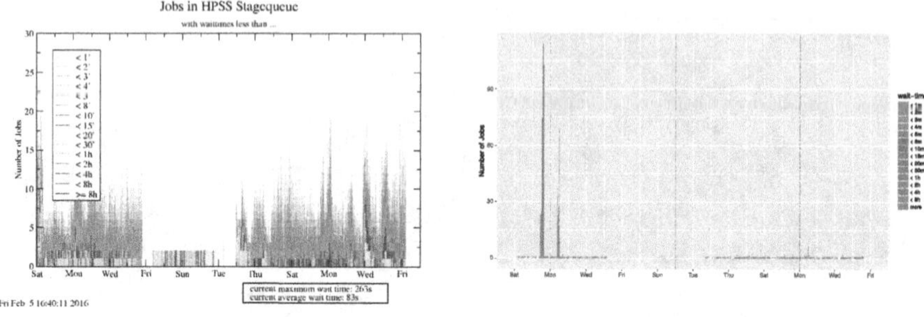

(a) Wait-time as observed in monitoring.

(b) Wait-time in simulation.

Fig. 11. The number of requests waiting in queue based on their wait-time.

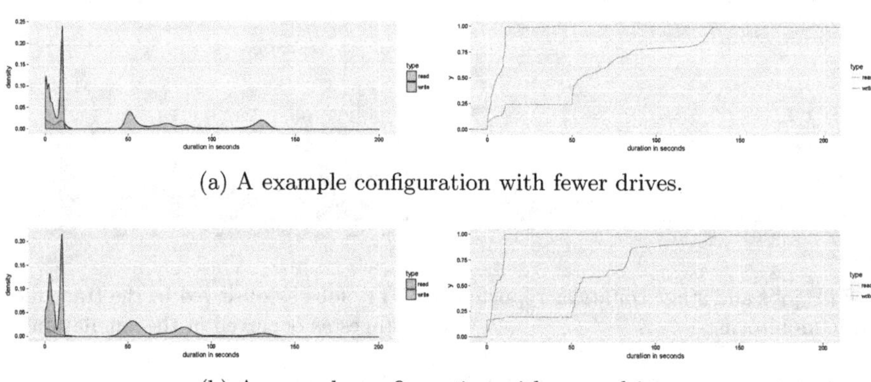

(a) A example configuration with fewer drives.

(b) A example configuration with more drives.

Fig. 12. Example comparison of request latency for different runs.

- Is it cheaper to run on a library with many slots and use more older drives? How would using RAIT effect this?

Figure 12 shows two configurations (a) fewer drives and (b) more drives. For each configuration the distribution of request latency is plotted. A second graph plots the same data using an empirical distribution functions to allow to easily determine, e.g., quality of service guarantees that can be made for a certain percentage of requests. In many cases these curves stabilize after handling a few thousand requests allowing to spin up only short simulations, and use similar or more advanced criteria for an optimization problem.

Power Consumption: Besides performance characteristics we can collect load statistics for individual components. One use for these statistics is the estimation of power consumption. Figure 13 shows a plot of the drive utilization over time. It is reasonable to assume that a busy drive consumes more energy than an idle drive. Thus, again only considering changes to the drive configuration, even

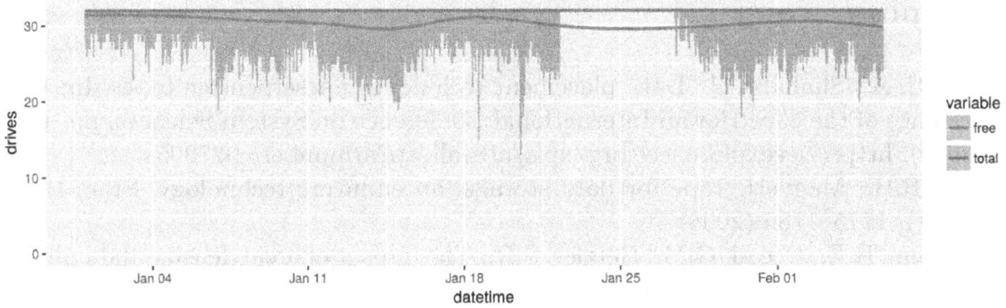

Fig. 13. Drive utilization as well as the total number of available drives over time. The trace in this case did not provide any data about enabled/disabled drives.

without concrete power consumption figures for a particular drive, it is possible to compare systems. For a more accurate estimate of power consumption, we can measure the power consumption for idle and busy phases of a tape drive and then aggregate busy and idle times to derive the estimate for a given configuration. This also allows to evaluate the switch to different power tariffs, e.g. a day/night tariff.

7 Summary

Equipped with comprehensive models and a simulator to approximate tape archives within hierarchical storage systems, it is possible to improve modern tape libraries without requiring a physical tape library for testing. Workflows to experiment and asses the performance directly influenced the design of the simulator, consequently the next step is to put it to use in experiments. Also, gradually turning the simulator into an open source tape library management solution for production systems could be an option. From a research perspective the interesting part of a simulation is to apply it to practical problems to learn and generate new insight. The next step is to carefully construct experiments with the current system and iteratively improve the tools required to conduct more experiments. In particular, this might include parameterized Monte-Carlo methods to optimize for budgets or quality of service. The foundation to perform these kinds of experiments is provided with this work. In addition, it would be useful to have a comprehensive database for benchmarks that collect the characteristics of tape drives, libraries and other devices. The database should also include component prices, though utilizing online price comparison APIs to fetch prices on demand may also be an option when provided with ways to apply a correction factor for discounts.

Acknowledgments. This work is part of the ESiWACE project which received funding from the European Union's Horizon 2020 research and innovation programme under grant agreement No 675191.

References

1. Dashti, A., Shahabi, C.: Data placement techniques for serpentine tapes. In: Proceedings of the 33rd Hawaii International Conference on System Sciences, pp. 1–10 (2000). http://ieeexplore.ieee.org/xpls/abs_all.jsp?arnumber=927005
2. Dee, R.H.: Magnetic tape for data storage: an enduring technology. Proc. IEEE **96**(11), 1775–1785 (2008)
3. Fontana, R.E., Decad, G.M., Hetzler, S.R.: The impact of areal density and millions of square inches (MSI) of produced memory on petabyte shipments of TAPE, NAND flash, and HDD storage class memories. In: 2013 IEEE 29th Symposium on Mass Storage Systems and Technologies (MSST), pp. 1–8. IEEE (2013). http://ieeexplore.ieee.org/xpls/abs_all.jsp?arnumber=6558421
4. Hughes, J., Fisher, D., Dehart, K., Wilbanks, B., Alt, J.: HPSS RAIT Architecture. White paper of the HPSS collaboration (2009). http://www.hpss-collaboration.org/documents/HPSS_RAIT_Architecture.pdf
5. Koltsidas, I., Sarafijanovic, S., Petermann, M., Haustein, N., Seipp, H.: Seamlessly Integrating Disk and Tape in a Multi-tiered Distributed File System, pp. 1328–1339 (2015)
6. Lingfang Zeng, D.F.: Hybrid RAID-Tape-Library Storage System for Backup. In: Second International Conference on Embedded Software and Systems (ICESS 2005), pp. 31–36 (2005). http://ieeexplore.ieee.org/lpdocs/epic03/wrapper.htm?arnumber=1609854
7. Mäsker, M., Nagel, L., Süß, T., Brinkmann, A., Sorth, L.: Simulation and Performance Analysis of the ECMWF Tape Library System. In: Proceedings of the International Conference for High Performance Computing, Networking, Storage and Analysis, pp. 22: 1–22: 12. SC 2016, IEEE Press, Piscataway (2016). http://dl.acm.org/citation.cfm?id=3014904.3014934
8. Pantazi, A., Furrer, S., Rothuizen, H.E., Cherubini, G., Jelitto, J., Lantz, M.A.: Nanoscale track-following for tape storage, pp. 2837–2843 (2015)
9. Pease, D., Amir, A., Villa Real, L., Biskeborn, B., Richmond, M., Abek, A.: The linear tape file system. In: 2010 IEEE 26th Symposium on Mass Storage Systems and Technologies, MSST2010 4 (2010)
10. Zhang, X., He, D., Du, D., Lu, Y.: Object placement in parallel tape storage systems. In: Proceedings of the 2006 International Conference on Parallel Processing (ICPP 2006), pp. 0–7 (2006). http://ieeexplore.ieee.org/xpls/abs_all.jsp?arnumber=1690610

GPU Erasure Coding for Campaign Storage

Walker Haddock[1(✉)], Matthew L. Curry[2], Purushotham V. Bangalore[1], and Anthony Skjellum[3]

[1] Department of Computer and Information Sciences, University of Alabama at Birmingham, Birmingham, USA
whaddock@uab.edu

[2] Center for Computing Research, Sandia National Laboratories, Albuquerque, USA

[3] Department of Computer Science and Engineering and McCrary Institute for Critical Infrastructure Protection and Cyber Systems, Auburn University, Auburn, USA

Abstract. High-performance computing (HPC) demands high bandwidth and low latency in I/O performance leading to the development of storage systems and I/O software components that strive to provide greater and greater performance. However, capital and energy budgets along with increasing storage capacity requirements have motivated the search for lower cost, large storage systems for HPC. With Burst Buffer technology increasing the bandwidth and reducing the latency for I/O between the compute and storage systems, the back-end storage bandwidth and latency requirements can be reduced, especially underneath an adequately sized modern parallel file system. Cloud computing has led to the development of large, low-cost storage solutions where design has focused on high capacity, availability, and low energy consumption at lowest cost. Cloud computing storage systems leverage duplicates and erasure coding technology to provide high availability at much lower cost than traditional HPC storage systems. Leveraging certain cloud storage infrastructure and concepts in HPC would be valuable economically in terms of cost-effective performance for certain storage tiers. To enable the use of cloud storage technologies for HPC we study the architecture for interfacing cloud storage between the HPC parallel file systems and the archive storage. In this paper, we report our comparison of two erasure coding implementations for the Ceph file system. We compare measurements of various degrees of sharding that are relevant for HPC applications. We show that the Gibraltar GPU Erasure coding library outperforms a CPU implementation of an erasure coding plugin for the Ceph object storage system, opening the potential for new ways to architect such storage systems based on Ceph.

1 Introduction

With the compute core density increasing per node in the past decade in high-performance computing (HPC), a trend that will likely continue for the next

A. Skjellum—Present affilation: SimCenter, University of Tennessee at Chattanooga.

J.M. Kunkel et al. (Eds.): ISC High Performance Workshops 2017, LNCS 10524, pp. 145–159, 2017.
https://doi.org/10.1007/978-3-319-67630-2_13

decade, I/O bandwidth requirements per node have also increased. This increase in computing power is applying pressure on the entire storage capacity and bandwidth for HPC systems. To minimize the time required for applications to complete I/O operations for initialization, checkpoint/restart (CR), and application result outputs, it is necessary to provide I/O bandwidth to the compute nodes that is much higher than today's petascale supercomputers. The stated requirements for the exascale initiative is for applications to run 50 times faster than they do on today's 20 PFLOP systems [21]. Los Alamos National Labs (LANL) is introducing Burst Buffers (BB) as an intermediate tier between the compute nodes and the Parallel File System (PFS) on Trinity. These BBs use Solid State Disks (SSDs) and Nonvolatile RAM (NVRAM) to provide high-speed storage to meet the faster IOPS and bandwidth requirements. BBs enable the applications to complete the IO operations in an acceptable time for CR or application recording task and get back to making forward progress on the application problem solution [10].

Both the BB and PFS file systems are expensive and, like registers and cache in the CPU memory hierarchy, are at the top of the storage pyramid, having minimal size but much greater performance [10]. Requirements also provide the constraints that the life time of the data in the compute node RAM is hours, the life time in the BBs is hours, and the life time in the PFS is weeks. The BBs are referred to as tier-1 in the storage pyramid and the PFSs are referred to as tier-2. Data that is needed to be kept for longer periods of time may be stored on lower tiers of the storage pyramid where lower latency and bandwidth requirements may be defined but with greater availability requirements due to the longer life of the data residence. The third layer of the storage stack, tier-3 storage is referred to as the "campaign" storage layer, a pre-archive, longer term, and higher capacity disk store [12]. This campaign storage layer is a strong candidate for lower-cost, cloud-type storage that provides availability with erasure coding and higher bandwidth than the fourth tier, the archive tier, which is magnetic tape [16] at LANL. The Campaign storage tier has been designed to store data for a period of time while the research project is actively computing so that it can be quickly moved to the PFS and BB when needed for computation or to the archive for longer term storage.

The key contribution of this paper is as follows. To enable the use of cloud storage technologies for HPC, we study the architecture for interfacing cloud storage between the HPC parallel file systems and the archive storage. In this paper we show that computing erasure coding for a high degree of sharding[1] on the Ceph Object File System [38] with GPUs outperforms a modern Intel CPU, opening the potential for new ways to architect such storage system based on Ceph. For use cases where data are moved to object storage systems via single points of mediation, such as the File Transfer Appliances (FTAs) in the LANL

[1] The literature uses the term "stripe" for a set of data that is protected by RAID or erasure coding implementation. The stripe is divided into k data chunks and protected by m parity or coding chunks. In this paper, the term "strip" and "shard" are used synonymously and refer to these chunks.

Trinity system, these mediators may be equipped with GPUs to perform erasure encoding and recovery at high speed and utilization. High degrees of sharding along with sufficient coding shards determined by the disk failure rate can result in lower capital costs and lower operating costs [13].

The remainder of this paper is organized as follows. We first discuss the architecture and performance of Ceph, a high performance distributed storage systems [38], particularly the plugin feature for erasure coding modules, review RAID and discuss the exascale campaign storage requirements for Trinity (see Sect. 2). We also discuss the Gibraltar GPU erasure coding and decoding library [4] there. In Sect. 3, we discuss our implementation of the Ceph erasure coding plugin using Gibraltar. We present our findings from our measurements of our experiments in Sect. 4. In Sect. 5 we discuss other research using GPU erasure coding for HPC storage followed by our conclusions in Sect. 6.

2 Background

We utilize Ceph as a platform for our work because of its convenient plugin architecture for erasure coding libraries. This structure enabled us to focus our work on the Gibraltar library and to follow the implementation of the Ceph plugin interfaces provided in its erasure code plugin classes. The existing erasure coding plugins in Ceph provide us with well know baselines against which to compare our results.

In previous work, we designed and reduced to practice a library that performs erasure coding on GPU hardware, Gibraltar [3,4]; this approach can further lower the price/performance for storage systems and provide opportunities for performing compute close to the data. One of the consequences of erasure coding in the design of high performance distributed file systems is the high computational and data transfer costs of reconstruction of a failed disk. By including GPUs in the architecture, we provide additional compute resources that can raise the achievable performance. As common disk drive storage capacities have increased from 750 GB in 2006 [9] to 10 TB in 2016 [34], this architecture performance enhancement will become even more important by off-loading computation for erasure coding to the GPU.

2.1 Ceph

Ceph is a distributed high performance file system that decouples metadata from data and provides a deterministic function for mapping metadata to data location, CRUSH – Controlled Replication Under Scalable Hashing [37]. It is an object storage system that uses peer-to-peer sharing of a compact hierarchical description of the cluster configuration and replication policy. This innovation distributes the computation to determine replica placement to any member of the cluster, including clients, thus eliminating the serialization that would otherwise result from determining data placement on a centralized metadata service. The CRUSH algorithm uses rule sets to define policies on data placement that result in evenly distributed storage of data across all of the Object Storage Devices (OSDs) in the cluster. These rules also enforce availability policies; for example, replicas must not be in the same rack or other defined failure domain in the data center. Ceph implements the data storage layer of file systems with the library *librados*, which exposes an interface to the Ceph object store. Traditional block based file systems can access the Ceph cluster object storage via the *RADOS Block Device*, a driver for Linux kernels based on *librbd* [39]. The Ceph POSIX file system (CephFS) uses the Metadata Service (MDS), which provides the POSIX compatible file name space features as well as the management of atomicity for operations (file creation, file deletion, file renaming, attribute changes, permissions, locks, etc.). CephFS consults the MDS to provide the client with the layout of a given file upon which operations are being performed.

In 2013, the Ceph community implemented a plugin framework to provide erasure coding features [8]. The Ceph development team used the framework to implement a concrete erasure coding capability using the Jerasure library [17]. The plugin includes an ErasureCode, ErasureCodeInterface, ErasureCodePlugin, and ErasureCodePluginRegistry classes. Implementers of concrete plugins can follow the example of the Jerasure plugin module in order to wrap their own erasure coding library into Ceph. The mechanism is activated by Ceph pools, which are configured to use replication or erasure coding with specific parameters. Erasure coding provides for various configuration selections based on the concrete implementation to include the algorithm, number of data shards, k, that object stripes will be divided into and the number of equally sized coding shards, m, that will be used to store the objects [7]. Choosing between replication or erasure coding for reliability trades space for computation. Choosing higher degrees of sharding distributes the object stripes over a greater number of disks, which reduces the time required to put or get the data on the disk by increasing parallelism. The disk read or write time for an object stripe is inversely proportional to the degree of sharding because the size of the shards are inversely proportional to the degree of sharding (k). Erasure coding can survive the loss of up to m shards. Where replication consumes raw storage at the rate of n times the size of the object where n is equal to the number of replicas + 1, the proportion of space used by m shards is usually about 20% of the size of the data (which can survive the loss of one shard out of five) [32,36].

2.2 RAID

Since the redundant array of inexpensive disks/devices (RAID) was introduced in 1988 by Patterson, Gibson and Katz [27] that provided an economical way for systems to be more resilient against data loss compared to other options such as pure mirroring, research has continued to provide more techniques for improving availability of data and improving performance. The principle methods for mitigating the loss of data resulting from media or system failure has been replication, RAID and erasure coding. The design choices between these methods must be balanced between the higher cost of storage for replication of

$n \times r$ where n is the size of the data and r is the number of replicas plus one versus the computational cost of parity generation for RAID and erasure coding.

Erasure coding provides a higher degree of durability in that the storage system can survive the loss of a greater number of disks while using less additional storage than replication [32,36]. The property that erasure coding can provide a higher order of redundancy by generating more than two parity disks has been heavily studied by James Plank [17,28–30]. Another consideration for data reliability is locality. Storage subsystems that replicate data or store parity on direct attached media can provide data storage services incurring a lower communications cost as compared to storage systems that distribute replicas or parity throughout a set of storage nodes that are connected over a high speed network. This particularly is the case of reconstructing parity for RAID-5, RAID-6 as compared to erasure coding where the minimum set of data or coding shards must be copied over the network and be assembled in a contiguous memory location for the erasure coding program to recompute the missing data or coding. After the data are reconstructed, the repaired shards must be copied back to their storage locations over the network. There is strong evidence that using erasure coding with commodity hardware for durability in high performance computing is more economical and faster than dedicated storage subsystems [31,33]. For instance, Microsoft has chosen to implement the storage systems in their Azure cloud service using erasure coding [15]. A thorough treatment of performance measurement for erasure coding is given in [14]. The power efficiency of erasure coding has been discussed previously by Greenan [11]. Lastly, DACO proposes a scheme where remote code is executed by disk drive controllers to update parity directly on the media saving on the data transfer costs that are usually associated with updates to erasure-coded stripes [20].

Storage services for high performance computing systems can be provided by storage area networks (SANs), which provide data resilience and high speed communications over specialized networks. Some high performance distributed file systems rely on these types of storage providers where the responsibility for data reliability is handled by the SAN [1,2]. These file systems can also be configured to provide availability in the event of the loss of data serving nodes by providing multi-path connections to the SAN storage. The SAN subsystems present storage volumes to the storage servers in the form of LUNs; these are logical volumes of media blocks formed by the SAN subsystem that have the resilience properties that have been specified by the administrator, otherwise providing the semantics of a local disk volume.

The Gibraltar project demonstrated that erasure codes could be efficiently generated and decoded with GPUs [3–6]. The Gibraltar library was designed to compute Reed-Solomon erasure codes for a wide range of k data shards and m coding shards. We have used this library to provide GPU-assisted erasure coding for Ceph through Ceph's Erasure Coding Plugin subsystem.

2.3 System Requirements

The Los Alamos National Laboratory (LANL) has presented requirements for a Campaign Storage System for the Trinity Super Computer [19]. The Campaign Storage should have about 25 PB capacity with future expansion capability. The bandwidth should be between 20 to 25 GB/s, which should increase with capacity. The files stored in the campaign storage system will not be updated in place. The system should use archive-grade hard disk drives, and gain performance through large scale parallel access. The system should use erasure coding for reliability. The system is not intended for high duty cycle workloads [19]. LANL expects to have 20 to 25 batch file transfer agents (FTAs) to move data between user home storage, Lustre PFS systems, archive storage and the campaign storage [19]. These requirements imply that the FTAs will be able to move about 1 GB/s each not including enough additional performance to provide fault tolerance.

LANL has also indicated the needed capability to store 1 PB sized checkpoints in the near future [19]. Baselining with archive storage disk drives with a capacity of 8 TB, it would require a minimum of 128 disk drives plus about 20% more for the erasure coding overhead to store 1 PB. Given this capacity requirement, a reasonable approach would be to use 128 data shards to distribute the 1 PB file over this number of disk drives. Choosing a ratio of one coding shard to five data shards would require another 25 disk drives. Using 8 TB disk drives, the 25 PB campaign storage system would therefore contain a minimum of 3,825 drives. The big advantage to this large degree of sharding is the lower bandwidth requirement to each of the target disk drives, 8 MB/s in this example where there are 128 shards and the FTA is delivering 1 GB/s to the storage system, Eq. (1). In this case, the bandwidth requirement at the leaf OSD can be met with a 100 Mb/s network and is well under the 150 MB/s peak performance for the current archive type 8 TB disks.

$$\left(\frac{\frac{1GB}{second}}{128 \times shards}\right) \tag{1}$$

3 Ceph Erasure Coding Plugin Implementation for Gibraltar

Ceph provides a well-defined interface for integrating erasure coding libraries into the product. This mechanism provides a means to incorporate new erasure coding libraries into the Ceph file system. The plugin architecture is modularized into two functional areas: registration of erasure coding profiles and the interface for the erasure coding/decoding services of the library [7]. Gibraltar can theoretically provide up to 256 data and coding shards in a stripe [4], although practical limits currently restrict $k + m$ to fewer total shards (see Sect. 4.2). Ceph erasure coded profiles can be constructed with many combinations of k and m.

The Ceph ErasureCodePlugin class is subclassed in our work in order to instantiate a Gibraltar instance; this instance is configured according to the parameters provided by the Ceph administrator command to create an erasure code profile. Gibraltar uses the NVIDIA® CUDA® library [25] to offload computation and retrieve results from the K40 GPU [24] in our system. The subclass ErasureCodePluginGibraltar calls the Gibraltar gib_cuda_driver function to initialize a CUDA context for the profile. The profile can then be used to create an erasure coded pool in Ceph.

The Ceph ErasureCode class is subclassed in our work to implement the Ceph ErasureCodeInterface functions for the Gibraltar library. We modified the Gibraltar erasure code library application programmer interface (API) to make it compatible with the Ceph architecture. Ceph uses a bufferlist data structure and aggregates $k + m$ shards for each erasure coded stripe where each shard is referenced by a pointer to the head of the list data structure for the shard. The call to Gibraltar has been modified to provide an array of these pointers and the logic copies each shard of data onto a contiguously allocated GPU memory block. The outputs of the coding or decoding are copied back to the Ceph bufferlist data structures in a similar way. In Fig. 1, we show how data is passed to the plugin. The plugin appends m coding shards onto the Bufferlist object and includes the pointers to these data structures in the array. New versions of the Gibraltar functions to encode and regenerate were created, whereas the original functions operated on a contiguous data block that was passed in the call. The original

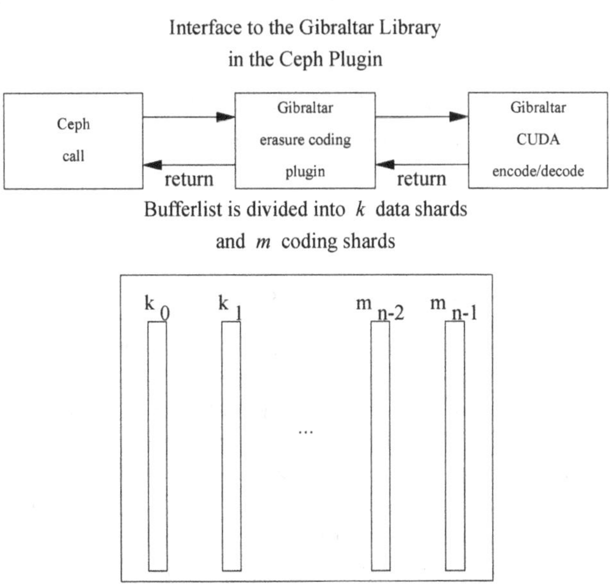

Fig. 1. Ceph calls the erasure coding module with a Bufferlist object containing the stripe to be written to the object. The Plugin divides the Bufferlist into k data shards and adds m coding shards. Gibraltar is called to perform the coding or recovery.

library interface for Gibraltar had proved sufficient for the target RAID system when originally designed, and was chosen to reduce register pressure in the GPU by reducing the number of variables [3].

4 Evaluation and Measurement

Here, we discuss the configuration of the system used to perform the experiments and then we show the results that we obtained.

4.1 System Description

We conducted the measurements on a Dell R730 server with a GPU. Table 1 lists the configuration of our test system.

Table 1. Dell R730 with GPU Configuration

CPUs	2x Xeon E5-2650 v3 @ 2.3 GHZ (HT-enabled: 40 threads)
RAM	128 GB 2133 MT/s RDIMM
Network	2 port Mellanox ConnectX-3 MCX354A-FCBS
	Intel X520 DP 10Gb DA/SFP+, I350 DP 1Gb Ethernet
GPU	NVIDIA® K40m GPU
System Drives	2x 300 GB 10K SAS 2
	2x 200 GB INTEL SSDSC2BG20 SATA
	2x 400 GB TOSHIBA PX02SMF040 SAS 3

4.2 Erasure Code Generation and Reconstruction Performance

Four experiments were conducted to understand the benefits of GPU erasure coding for the campaign storage application. The first two experiments were run using the ISA-L [35] erasure coding plugin included in Ceph v12.0.0 to provide a baseline for reference to our Gibraltar plugin performance. The Cauchy algorithm was selected for ISA-L because it was able to perform the encoding and decoding with the number of shards we needed to test while the ISA-L Vandermonde matrix implementation was limited to a maximum of 32 data shards in Ceph in order to guarantee an MDS codec (see ErasureCodeIsa.cc). The Reed-Solomon algorithm with the Vandermone matrix is well suited to computation on a GPU using a precomputed lookup table that has been implemented in the Gibraltar library. We selected a range of degrees of shardings between 20 and 128 based on experiments that are being conducted for Trinity campaign storage at LANL. Coding and decoding tests for 1 GB data size used degrees of sharding ranging between 50 and 128. Erasure decoding for Gibraltar is currently limited to 118 shards. We selected the number of coding shards for each data sharding choice to meet the one to five ratio. Test data set sizes of 512 MB and 1 GB were used for the experiments. We used the erasure coding benchmark tool included with v12.0.0 of Ceph to run the test cases. The benchmark tool instantiates an erasure coding profile as specified in our execution parameters and then runs a series of encoding generations and reconstructions over a set of data. We set the CPU core affinity to use a single core on the first CPU in the system because the NVIDIA® GPU is connected to the PCI bus of this CPU socket. In each experiment, the same CPU core was used for each erasure coding library. A set of 10 iteration runs were made totaling 10 GB of data for each run and the average reported. The results in Fig. 2 show that the Gibraltar library generates parity at five times the rate of ISA-L in the $50 + 10$ test and at seven times ISA-L performance for $128 + 24$ test. The ISA-L method was stable between the 512 MB and 1 GB data sizes but the Gibraltar method was 5% faster for the 1 GB data size with 128 shards than the corresponding 512 MB test.

In Figs. 3 and 4 we show the performance of reconstructing erasures for our second experiment. Times are shown for reconstructing one and four erasures in the configurations tested. At the 1 GB test data size, Gibraltar performance is 43% better than the ISA-L's performance with the $50 + 10$ test with one erasure but is only 84% as fast as the ISA-L's $118 + 24$ with one erasures. At the 1 GB test data size, Gibraltar performance is 3.77 times faster than the ISA-L performance for $50 + 10$ test with four erasures and is 2.98 times the performance of ISA-L with four erasures at the $118 + 24$ test data size.

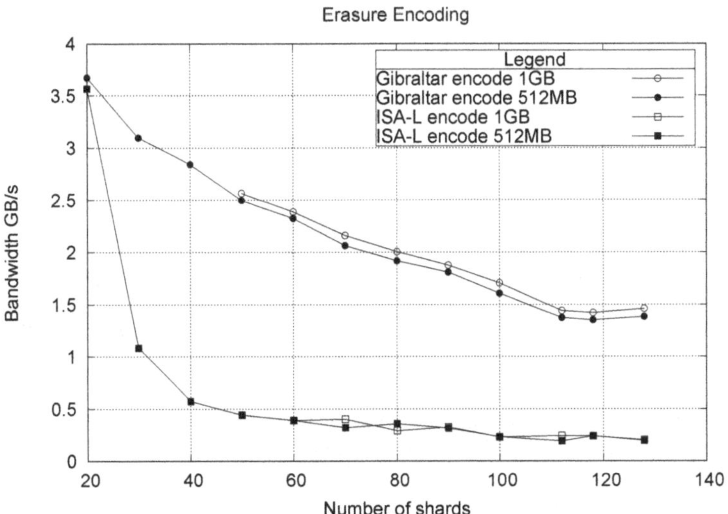

Fig. 2. Erasure coding bandwidth results with increasing number of shards. Coding shards are held to a ratio of one coding shard to five data shards.

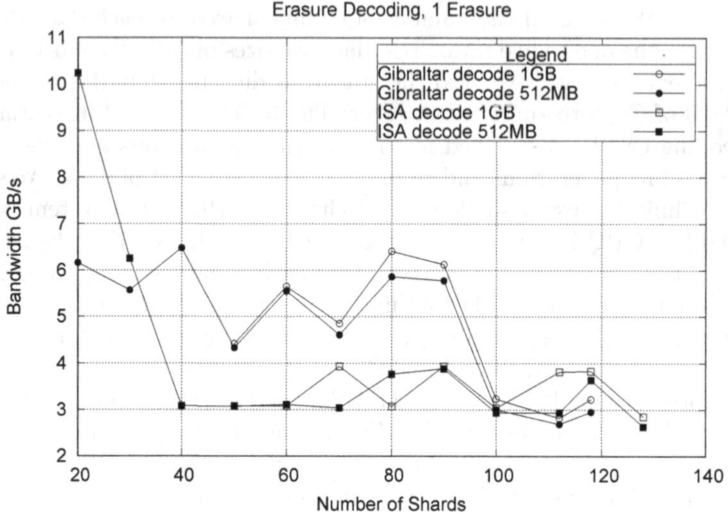

Fig. 3. Erasure recovery bandwidth results with increasing number of shards and one erasure. Coding shards are held to a ratio of one coding shard to five data shards.

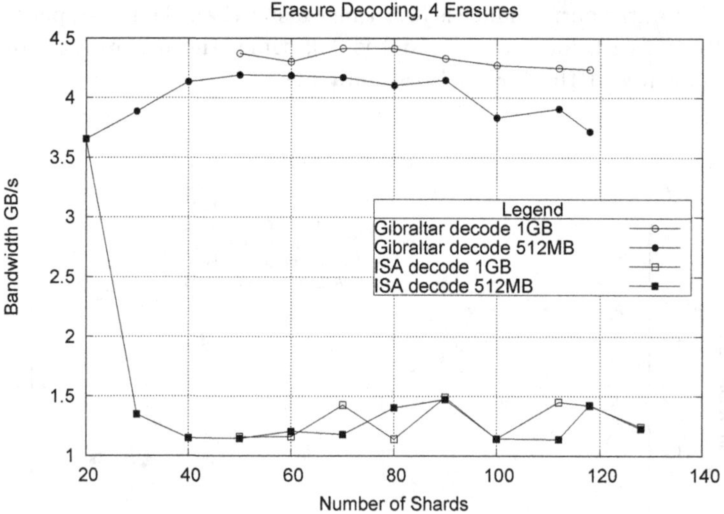

Fig. 4. Erasure recovery bandwidth results with increasing number of shards and four erasures. Coding shards are held to a ratio of one coding shard to five data shards.

Figure 5 shows the shard sizes for the 512 MB and 1 GB data sizes that we used in the experiments. A larger degree of sharding results in smaller chunks of the data, lowering the bandwidth requirements to copy the shard to the OSD.

The third experiment measured the Gibraltar encoding execution using the CUDA nvprof program. The same test configurations were used as in the first

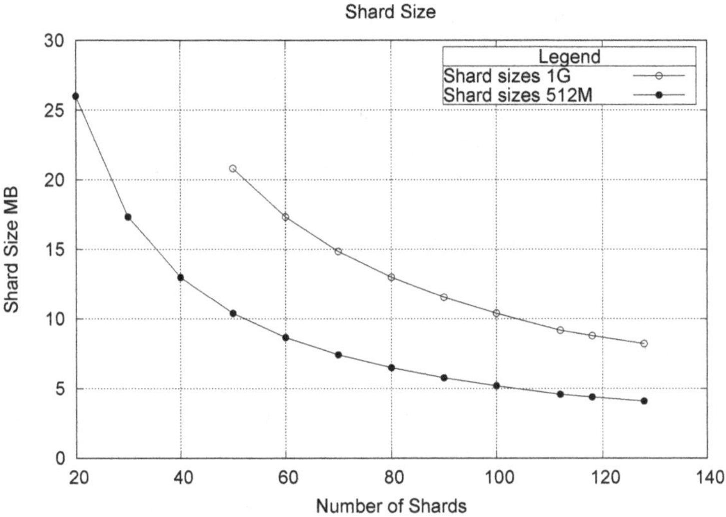

Fig. 5. Shard sizes used in the erasure coding and decoding measurements.

two experiments. We ran 10 iterations with 1 GB test data. For the $128 + 24$ configuration we measured 25% of the time was spent copying the data to the GPU memory, 70% of the time was spent generating the erasure coding shards and the remaining 5% of the time was spent copying the coded shards back to the host.

The fourth experiment measured the reconstruction using the $118 + 24$ configuration and four erasures. In the Gibraltar reconstruction, the Galois inversion matrix is computed on the host and copied to the GPU for the specific erasures that are present in the data. The Galois computation consumed 15% of the time. We measured 55% of the time was spent copying the data to the GPU memory, 23% of the time was spent reconstructing the data and parity, and 4% of the time was spent copying the four reconstructed data shards from the GPU memory to the host.

These experiments show that the Gibraltar GPU library can sustain a high bandwidth performance with larger degrees of sharding. For recovery, the Gibraltar GPU library can recover multiple erasures without loss of performance as compared to the ISA-L library. Using higher performance GPUs like the NVIDIA® Pascal [23] with NVLink® should provide even greater performance where more bandwidth is required.

5 Previous Work

Ceph provides an erasure coding plugin class as an extensible way for erasure coding libraries to be implemented in the product. Currently, in release 12.0.0, there are four erasure coding libraries implemented, namely: Jerasure [17], ISA-L [35], lrc [26] and Shingled Erasure Code (SHEC) [22]. Our study has shown that the Gibraltar library [5] can perform about half as well as these libraries for a sharding degree less than 40 while Gibraltar performs better than these for greater degrees of sharding. Khasymski et al., showed that GPU-assisted erasure coding and reconstruction can be performed on the Lustre file system. Their work required a software shim to integrate into Lustre, which has no defined interface for erasure coding libraries. Their work only implemented RAID-6, providing $m = 2$, but showed that the approach was feasible and can provide strong fault tolerance [18] without depending on RAID subsystems and failover mechanisms for availability.

6 Conclusion

We have implemented the Gibraltar GPU erasure coding library [4] as a plugin in the Ceph product and shown that it provides high bandwidth for large degrees of sharding. This capability can increase the value of cloud storage technologies in HPC by increasing the number of coding shards to provide extended availability and reducing the need for recovery of failed members. In these experiments, the Gibraltar library performance proved much greater than ISA-L [35] on the Intel E5-2650 v3 CPU. To achieve ISA-L performance measured here, it was necessary to dedicate a single core of the host computer whereas the Gibraltar library required 70% of the NVIDIA® K40 GPU's total capacity for generation and 23% of the NVIDIA® K40 GPU for reconstruction of four shards.

Our measurements show that the Ceph Gibraltar plugin can generate over 120 shards at nearly 1.5 GB/s while the ISA-L plugin has dropped to less than 250 MB/s. The Ceph Gibraltar plugin continues to reconstruct erasures at over 3 GB/s for one or four erasures with 118 shards while the ISA-L Ceph plugin drops from 3 GB/s for one erasure to 1.5 GB/s for four erasures. Ceph with the Gibraltar plugin can meet or exceed the current requirements for Trinity campaign storage with respect to erasure coding and reconstruction.

We have shown that erasure coding with ISA-L can be performed concurrently on multiple cores with linear speedup, which can increase bandwidth but does not improve latency of encoding or decoding data with the stripe sizes having large sharding degree as tested [13]. These results should inform the design of campaign storage systems to the selection of the most appropriate solution.

7 Future Work

The architecture for campaign storage at LANL moves all data between the campaign storage system and the other storage systems via File Transfer Appliances (FTAs) [19]. Generation of erasure codes requires data locality and is ideally performed on the file transfer appliance (FTA). The FTAs having GPU accelerator devices can generate coding and reconstruct shards efficiently where there is a high degree of sharding. Gibraltar can provide greater than $m = 2$ parity to support higher fault tolerance, which is needed for larger capacity disk drives. Using the FTAs to perform erasure coding and reconstruction in a Ceph implementation will require modification of the current interfaces and concepts for the Ceph erasure coding plugin architecture. The current implementation of erasure coding in Ceph only provides for OSDs to perform erasure coding and reconstruction.

A higher degree of sharding spreads the volume of data over a correspondingly large number of disk drives. The input bandwidth to the FTA is fanned out by the sharding degree resulting in the opportunity to use lower bandwidth communications for the Object Storage Nodes without reducing throughput performance of the FTA. This provides an opportunity for reducing the cost of campaign storage. We are currently studying the configuration options of campaign storage with regard to sharding degree, throughput, reliability and cost in greater depth.

Acknowledgments. This material is based upon work supported by the National Science Foundation under Grants Nos. ACI-1541310, CNS-0821497 and CNS-1229282. Any opinions, findings, and conclusions or recommendations expressed in this material are those of the authors and do not necessarily reflect the views of the National Science Foundation.

This material is based upon work supported by Sandia National Laboratories. Sandia National Laboratories is a multi-mission laboratory managed and operated by Sandia Corporation, a wholly owned subsidiary of Lockheed Martin Corporation, for the U.S. Department of Energy's National Nuclear Security Administration under contract DE-AC04-94AL85000.

References

1. Braam, P.J., Schwan, P.: Lustre: the intergalactic file system. In: Ottawa Linux Symposium, p. 50 (2002)
2. Corbett, P.F., Feitelson, D.G., Prost, J.P., Almasi, G.S., Baylor, S.J., Bolmarcich, A.S., Hsu, Y., Satran, J., Snir, M., Colao, R., Herr, B.D., Kavaky, J., Morgan, T.R., Zlotek, A.: Parallel file systems for the IBM SP computers. IBM Syst. J. **34**(2), 222–248 (1995), http://ieeexplore.ieee.org/lpdocs/epic03/wrapper.htm?arnumber=5387272
3. Curry, M.L., Skjellum, A., Lee Ward, H., Brightwell, R.: Accelerating reed-solomon coding in RAID systems with GPUs. In: Proceedings of the 2008 IEEE International Parallel & Distributed Processing Symposium, pp. 1–6. IEEE, Miami, April 2008, http://ieeexplore.ieee.org/lpdocs/epic03/wrapper.htm?arnumber=4536322
4. Curry, M.L., Skjellum, A., Lee Ward, H., Brightwell, R.: Gibraltar: a reed-solomon coding library for storage applications on programmable graphics processors. Concurrency Comput. Pract. Exp. **23**(18), 2477–2495, December 2011, http://doi.wiley.com/10.1002/cpe.1810
5. Curry, M.L., Ward, H.L., Skjellum, A., Brightwell, R.: A lightweight, GPU-based software RAID system. In: 2010 39th International Conference on Parallel Processing, pp. 565–572. IEEE, San Diego, September 2010, http://ieeexplore.ieee.org/lpdocs/epic03/wrapper.htm?arnumber=5599249
6. Curry, M.L.: A highly reliable GPU-based RAID system. Ph.D. thesis, University of Alabama at Birmingham (2010), http://contentdm.mhsl.uab.edu/cdm/ref/collection/etd/id/854

7. Dachary, L.: Ceph Replication vs Erasure Coding, July 2013, http://dachary.org/?p=2171
8. Dachary, L., Just, S.: Erasure Code, August 2013, https://github.com/dachary/ceph/blob/wip-4929/doc/dev/osd_internals/erasure-code.rst
9. Farrance, R.: Timeline: 50 Years of Hard Drives, September 2006, http://www.pcworld.com/article/127105/article.html
10. Grider, G.: HPC Storage and IO Trends and Workflows, April 2016, http://salishan.ahsc-nm.org/program.html
11. Greenan, K.: Reliability and Power-Efficiency in Erasure-Coded Storage Systems. Tech. Rep. UCSC-SSRC-09-08, University of California, Santa Cruz, December 2009
12. Grider, G.: MarFS, May 2015, http://storageconference.us/2015/Presentations/Grider.pdf
13. Haddock, W., Curry, M.L., Bangalore, P., Skjellum, A.: Using GPU erasure coding to lower HPC pre-archive storage costs. In: TBD (2017)
14. Hafner, J.L., Deenadhayalan, V., Kanungo, T., Rao, K.: Performance metrics for erasure codes in storage systems. IBM Res. Rep. RJ 10321 (2004)
15. Huang, C., Simitci, H., Xu, Y., Ogus, A., Calder, B., Gopalan, P., Li, J., Yekhanin, S.: Erasure coding in windows azure storage. In: Usenix Annual Technical Conference, pp. 15–26, Boston, MA (2012)
16. Inman, J., Grider, G., Chen, H.B.: Cost of tape versus disk for archival storage. In: 2014 IEEE 7th International Conference on Cloud Computing, pp. 208–215. IEEE, Anchorage, June 2014, http://ieeexplore.ieee.org/lpdocs/epic03/wrapper.htm?arnumber=6973743
17. Plank, J.S., Simmerman, S., Schuman, C.D.: Jerasure: A Library in C/C++ Facilitating Erasure Coding for Storage Applications. Tech. Rep. Technical Report CS-08-627, University of Tennessee, Knoxville, TN 37996 (2008), http://www.cs.utk.edu/plank/plank/papers/CS-08-627.html
18. Khasymski, A., Rafique, M.M., Butt, A.R., Vazhkudai, S.S., Nikolopoulos, D.S.: On the use of GPUs in realizing cost-effective distributed RAID. In: 2012 IEEE 20th International Symposium on Modeling, Analysis and Simulation of Computer and Telecommunication Systems, pp. 469–478, August 2012, http://ieeexplore.ieee.org/lpdocs/epic03/wrapper.htm?arnumber=6298207
19. Lamb, K.: Trinity Campaign Storage and Usage Model, August 2015, https://www.lanl.gov/projects/trinity/_assets/docs/trinity-usage-model-presentation.pdf
20. Li, M., Shu, J.: DACO: a high-performance disk architecture designed specially for large-scale erasure-coded storage systems. IEEE Trans. Comput. **59**(10), 1350–1362 (2010)
21. Messina, P.: A Path to Capable Exascale Computing, July 2016, http://press3.mcs.anl.gov/atpesc/files/2016/07/MessinaJul31.dinner.pdf
22. Miyamae, T., Nakao, T., Shiozawa, K.: Erasure code with shingled local parity groups for efficient recovery from multiple disk failures. In: 10th Workshop on Hot Topics in System Dependability (HotDep 2014). USENIX Association, Broomfield, CO, October 2014, https://www.usenix.org/conference/hotdep.14/workshop-program/presentation/miyamae
23. NVIDIA: NVIDIA Tesla P100, http://images.nvidia.com/content/pdf/tesla/whitepaper/pascal-architecture-whitepaper-v1.2.pdf
24. NVIDIA: Tesla K40 GPU Active Accelerator, November 2013, https://www.nvidia.com/content/PDF/kepler/Tesla-K40-Active-Board-Spec-BD-06949-001_v03.pdf
25. NVIDIA: CUDA Parallel Computing Platform, March 2017, http://www.nvidia.com/object/cuda_home_new.html

26. Papailiopoulos, D.S., Dimakis, A.G.: Locally repairable codes. IEEE Trans. Inf. Theory **60**(10), 5843–5855 (2014)
27. Patterson, D.A., Gibson, G., Katz, R.H.: A case for redundant arrays of inexpensive disks (RAID). In: Proceedings of the 1988 ACM SIGMOD International Conference on Management of Data, pp. 109–116. SIGMOD 1988, NY, USA (1988), http://doi.acm.org/10.1145/50202.50214
28. Plank, J.S.: A tutorial on reed-solomon coding for fault-tolerance in RAID-like systems. Softw. Pract. Exp. **27**(9), 995–1012 (1997)
29. Plank, J.S., Blaum, M., Hafner, J.L.: SD codes: erasure codes designed for how storage systems really fail. In: FAST, pp. 95–104. San Jose, CA, USA, February 2013
30. Plank, J.S., Thomason, M.G.: A practical analysis of low-density parity-check erasure codes for wide-area storage applications. In: 2004 International Conference on Dependable Systems and Networks, pp. 115–124. IEEE (2004)
31. Rashmi, K., Shah, N.B., Gu, D., Kuang, H., Borthakur, D., Ramchandran, K.: A "hitchhiker's" guide to fast and efficient data reconstruction in erasure-coded data centers. In: Proceedings of the 2014 ACM Conference on SIGCOMM, vol. 44, pp. 331–342. ACM Press, Chicago (2014), http://dl.acm.org/citation.cfm?doid=2619239.2626325
32. Rodrigues, R., Liskov, B.: High availability in DHTs: erasure coding vs. replication. In: Castro, M., van Renesse, R. (eds.) IPTPS 2005. LNCS, vol. 3640, pp. 226–239. Springer, Heidelberg (2005). doi:10.1007/11558989_21
33. Saito, Y., Frlund, S., Veitch, A., Merchant, A., Spence, S.: FAB: building distributed enterprise disk arrays from commodity components. In: Proceedings of the 11th International Conference on Architectural Support for Programming Languages and Operating Systems, ASPLOS XI, pp. 48–58. ACM Press, Boston (2004), http://portal.acm.org/citation.cfm?doid=1024393.1024400
34. Shilov, A.: Seagate Unveils 10 TB Helium filled Hard Disk Drive, January 2016, http://www.anandtech.com/show/9955/seagate-unveils-10-tb-heliumfilled-hard-disk-drive
35. Tucker, G.: ISA-L open source v2.14 API doc, April 2016, https://01.org/sites/default/files/documentation/isa-l_open_src_2.10.pdf
36. Weatherspoon, H., Kubiatowicz, J.D.: Erasure coding vs. replication: a quantitative comparison. In: Druschel, P., Kaashoek, F., Rowstron, A. (eds.) IPTPS 2002. LNCS, vol. 2429, pp. 328–337. Springer, Heidelberg (2002). doi:10.1007/3-540-45748-8_31
37. Weil, S., Brandt, S., Miller, E., Maltzahn, C.: CRUSH: controlled, scalable, decentralized placement of replicated data. In: Proceedings of the ACM/IEEE on SC 2006 Conference, pp. 31–31. IEEE, Tampa, November 2006, http://ieeexplore.ieee.org/lpdocs/epic03/wrapper.htm?arnumber=4090205
38. Weil, S.A., Brandt, S.A., Miller, E.L., Long, D.D., Maltzahn, C.: Ceph: A scalable, high-performance distributed file system. In: Proceedings of the 7th Symposium on Operating Systems Design and Implementation, pp. 307–320. USENIX Association (2006)
39. Weil, S.A., Leung, A.W., Brandt, S.A., Maltzahn, C.: RADOS: a scalable, reliable storage service for petabyte-scale storage clusters. In: Proceedings of the 2nd International Workshop on Petascale Data Storage: Held in Conjunction with Supercomputing 2007 (PDSW 2007), p. 35. ACM Press, Reno (2007), http://portal.acm.org/citation.cfm?doid=1374596.1374606

PIOM-PX: A Framework for Modeling the I/O Behavior of Parallel Scientific Applications

Pilar Gomez-Sanchez[1(✉)], Sandra Mendez[2], Dolores Rexachs[1], and Emilio Luque[1]

[1] Computer Architecture and Operating Systems Department, Universitat Autónoma de Barcelona, Campus UAB, Edifici Q, 08193 Bellaterra, Barcelona, Spain
{pilar.gomez,dolores.rexachs,emilio.luque}@uab.es

[2] High Performance Systems Division, Leibniz Supercomputing Centre (LRZ), 85748 Garching bei München, Germany
sandra.mendez@lrz.de

Abstract. Current parallel scientific applications generate a huge amount of data that must be managed efficiently for the HPC storage systems. However, the I/O performance depends on the application I/O behavior and the configuration of the underlying I/O system. To understand the I/O behavior in the software stack and its impact on the I/O operations defined in the application logic, we propose a design framework named PIOM-PX, which allows to define an I/O behavior model based on the I/O phases of HPC applications at POSIX-IO level. We validate our framework using the IOR benchmark for four I/O patterns and we analyze the I/O behavior of NAS BT-IO.

1 Introduction

Nowadays, parallel applications produce a huge amount of data that represents a challenge for modern I/O systems. The variability of the I/O patterns and diversity of storage architectures are other issues that make it difficult to take advantage of the I/O performance capacity of the HPC-IO systems. Depending on the I/O behavior of parallel applications and the processing performed in each layer of the I/O software stack, the performance obtained can differ significantly from the maximum performance expected.

Understanding I/O behavior is fundamental to evaluate the I/O performance of the HPC applications. Several works [1–5] have focused on the extraction of the I/O patterns to understand I/O behavior and to propose techniques to optimize I/O performance in different layers of the I/O software stack [6, 7]. Several tools exist to analyze the application's I/O behavior both for performance analysis and for I/O profiling such as Darshan [8] I/O profiling tool, SIOX [9] and Vampir [10] tool.

Due to the fact that most parallel applications are repetitive, and this repetitive behavior for I/O operations is observed as I/O bursts or I/O phases, we use

J.M. Kunkel et al. (Eds.): ISC High Performance Workshops 2017, LNCS 10524, pp. 160–173, 2017.
https://doi.org/10.1007/978-3-319-67630-2_14

the phase concept as the representation unit of the behavior of parallel applications. In this paper, we present a design framework named PIOM-PX, which allows us to obtain the main parameters at POSIX-IO to define an I/O behavior model.

We use PIOM-PX in order to evaluate the impact of the I/O phases on the I/O system and to replicate the application's I/O behavior in different HPC systems. The I/O phases are determined by identifying the global spatial and temporal pattern for each file opened during the execution of the parallel application. Our approach allows us to determine the I/O requirements of the application and to evaluate their impact on different I/O configurations.

This paper is organized as follows: Sect. 2 describes the proposed framework, Sect. 3 presents the validation of PIOM-PX and Sect. 4 explains the experimental results. Finally, in Sect. 5, we explain our conclusions and future work.

2 Proposed Framework

The I/O model of application is defined based on the I/O phase concept and the key characteristics, which are independent of the I/O system. We classify the application features as parameters for PIOM-PX into three levels: application, file, and phase. Table 1 summarizes the parameters for each level.

We define a design framework to obtain an I/O behavior model at POSIX-IO level named PIOM-PX. Figure 1 presents the steps of PIOM-PX structured in two main stages: tracing and post-processing.

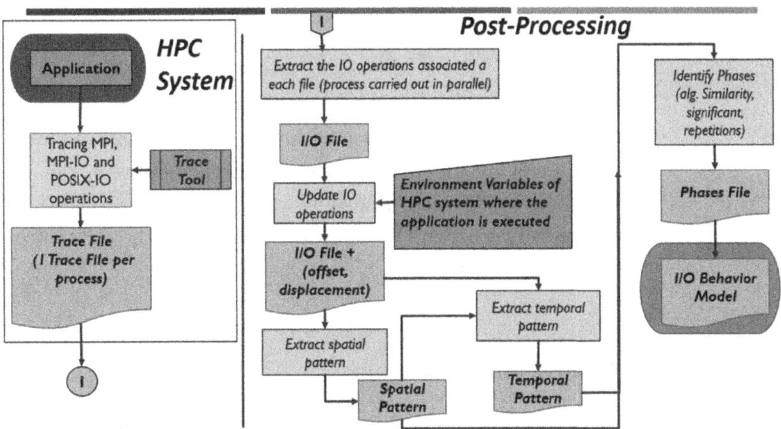

Fig. 1. Framework to extract the application's I/O behavior model based on identifying the I/O phases.

Table 1. PIOM-PX model parameters

Identifier	Application
app_np	Number of processes that the application needs to be executed
app_nfiles	Number of files used by the application
app_st	Storage capacity required by the application for the input files, temporal files and input/output files.
	File
file_id	File Identifier
file_name	File Name
file_size	File Size
file_np	Count of MPI processes that open the file *file_id*
file_accessmode	This can be sequential, strided or random
file_fileaccesstype	Read only(R), write only (W) or write and read (W/R)
file_accesstype	*file_np* processes can access to shared Files or 1 File per Process
file_nphase	Count of phases of the file.
	I/O Phase (PhIO)
Ph_id	Identifier of an I/O Phase
Ph_processid	Identifier of Process implied in the phase
Ph_np	Number of processes implied in the phase
Ph_weight	Transferred data volume during the phase. It is expressed in bytes
Ph_nrep	Number of repetitions per phase
Ph_niop	Number of I/O operations
IOP	Data access operation type, which can be write, read, or write/read
rs	Request size or size of an I/O operation
offset	Operation offset, which is a position in the file's logical view
disp	Displacement into file, which is the difference between the offset of two consecutive I/O operations
dist	Distance between two I/O operations, which is the difference between

2.1 Tracing I/O Operations

To obtain the information defined in Table 1, we have implemented a tracer to extract POSIX-IO events and to assign additional fields to detect I/O phases. This tracer was integrated with PIOM-MP (former PAS2P-IO), which allows us to trace I/O activities at MPI and POSIX-IO level.

Table 2 describes the fields included in a trace line (*TL*) of PIOM-PX. The events are traced between the `MPI_Init` and the `MPI_Finalize` operations and a trace file is generated for each MPI process. We trace the following operations:

```
POSIX-IO
open, open64, fopen64, close, fclose, write, fwrite, read, pread
pread64, pwrite, pwrite64,fread, fwrite, lseek, lseek64, fsync
creat, creat64, readv, writev, fseek, xstat, xstat64
```

```
Communication and MPI-IO
MPI_Send, MPI_Isend, MPI_Recv, MPI_Irecv, MPI_Wait, MPI_Allgather
MPI_Allreduce, MPI_Barrier, MPI_Bcast, MPI_Reduce, MPI_Sendrecv
MPI_Waitall, MPI_File_* // 51 I/O operations.
```

We define the tick concept to register the order of the MPI events and the subtick concept for POSIX-IO events. The tick is increased for each MPI event detected and the subtick is initialized after each MPI event and incremented for consecutive POSIX-IO events.

Table 2. PIOM-PX trace line

Identifier	Description
IdProcess	Identifier of Process
file_id	Identifier of File
TypeOperation	"MPI" or "POSIX"
NameOperation	Name of POSIX-IO event
offset	Operation offset, which is a position in the file's logical view
rs	Request size of for data access operations
	Metadata-line
file_name	File Name
FileAccessType	Open mode
	Added fields
Time	Logical time of the occurrence of a MPI or POSIX-IO event
Final_compute	Duration of the call of an MPI or POSIX-IO event
tick	Order of occurrence of the MPI events
subtick	Order of occurrence of the POSIX-IO events

In the *Extracting I/O operations* step, we extract the I/O operations per file opened by the application of each trace file into a new file. Therefore, from this step we obtain as many files as the application opens during its execution.

2.2 Updating I/O Operations

In this point, every file of I/O operations is reviewed to determine whether the offset and request size (rs) informed require evaluating another operation to obtain the real request or offset. For example, the case of the `write` and `read` operations, where the offset depends on `lseek` operation.

To modify the offset, we have to take into account the `whence` parameter of `lseek` operation: `SEEK_SET` (the file offset is set to `offset` bytes), `SEEK_CUR` (the file offset is set to its current location plus `offset` bytes) and `SEEK_END` (the file offset is set to the size of the file plus `offset` bytes).

We calculate the field displacement (*disp*), added in the TL structure, to identify the request size (rs) and how the displacement moves.

For Fortran program, the environment variable `FORT_BLOCKSIZE` is evaluated to determine the request size of a POSIX-IO event that the user actually wants to work with.

2.3 Extracting Spatial and Temporal Pattern

To extract the spatial pattern, for each I/O file, both for the write and read operation, we save the following fields: `NameOperation, file_id, file_name, offset and rs.`

Besides, we calculate the offset difference for all operations that have the same $file\_id$, $file\_name$ and rs. The offset difference is calculated between two consecutive operations (read-read or write-write) and the displacement (*disp*) is calculated between two write operations and read operations.

If the application uses a shared file, we identify the global spatial pattern based on I/O operations traced for each MPI process that opens the shared file.

To detect the Temporal pattern we establish the *tick* and *subtick* (See Fig. 2). The tick identifies the MPI and MPI-IO operations and the subtick identifies the POSIX-IO operations. `MPI_Sends` are interchanged between processes and

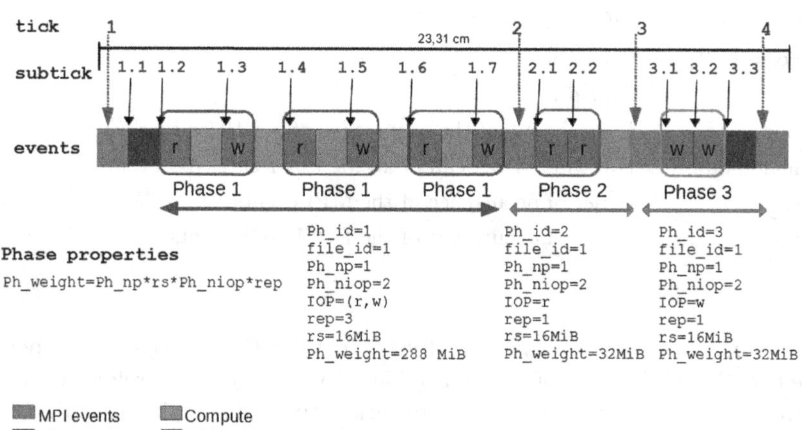

Fig. 2. Representation of the I/O phases of a parallel application. The view corresponds to an I/O process for an access type 1 file per process. Tick and subtick are used to obtain the order of occurrence of the application's events. An I/O phase is a consecutive sequence of similar I/O operations. Phase properties represent the transferred data volume during a phase and the I/O pattern.

the tick of `MPI_Sends` affects the operations of the processes that received this `MPI_Send`. If all processes write to one or more shared files, we must detect the relationship between all the operations carried out by all the processes to determine the actual logical order. This order helps us to detect dependencies among all processes and it is necessary to redefine the ticks and the subticks.

3 Experimental Validation

In this section, we validate the PIOM-PX functionality and its integration with PIOM-MP (former PAS2P-IO [4]). To do this, we define four experiments based on IOR [11] benchmark, which allows us to generate different I/O patterns for distinct I/O interfaces. We have executed IOR using intel and GNU compilers to analyze their influence on the operations detected. The MPI distribution utilized was Intel MPI 2017. Furthermore, to identify the impact of the parallel file system at the POSIX-IO level, PIOM-PX is evaluated in two HPC systems with IBM Spectrum Scale (former GPFS) and Lustre. Experiments were executed in SuperMUC (LRZ) and Finisterrae2 (CESGA) supercomputers, which are described in Table 3.

Table 3. HPC systems

Components	Finisterrae2	SuperMUC
Compute nodes	306	9216
CPU cores (per node)	24	16
RAM memory	128 GB	32 GB
Local Filesystem	ext4	ext3
Global Filesystem (GFS)	NFS	NFS
Capacity of GFS	1.1 TB	10×564×10TB
Global Filesystem (PFS)	Lustre	GPFS
Capacity of PFS	695 TB	12 PB
Data servers	4 OSS and 12 OSTs	80 NSD
Metadata servers	1	
Stripe size	1 MiB	8 MiB
Interconnection	IB FDR@56 Gbps	IB FDR10

3.1 Experimentation

Four experiments were designed to evaluate the I/O strategies `1 File per Process` and `1 Single Shared File`. Furthermore, we assess a nested strided pattern by using the collective buffering technique in "enable" and "automatic" mode. We executed the experiments for 16 MPI processes per compute node. Each experiment is described as follows:

(a) 1 File per Process using POSIX interface:
   - Objective: Detect the POSIX-IO operations for an application that only uses POSIX as I/O library.
   - Command Line:

```
IOR -a POSIX -s 1 -b 8m -t 1m -F
```

(b) 1 File per Process using MPI-IO interface:
   - Objective: Detect the POSIX-IO operations generated by an application that uses independent MPI-IO operations.
   - Command Line:

```
IOR -a MPIIO -s 1 -b 8m -t 1m -F
```

(c) A single shared file using collective buffering technique in `automatic` mode for a strided pattern:
   - Objective: Detect the POSIX-IO operations generated by an application that uses collective MPI-IO operations.
   - Command Line:

```
IOR -c -a MPIIO -s 16 -b 512k -t 512k
```

(d) A single shared file using collective buffering technique in `enable` mode for a strided pattern:
   - Objective: Detect the POSIX-IO operations generated by an application that uses collective operations with the collective buffering technique enabled.
   - Command Line:

```
romio_cb_read = enable
romio_cb_write = enable
IOR -c -a MPIIO -s 16 -b 512k -t 512k
```

Table 4 presents PIOM-PX model parameters for the four IOR experiments at application and file level.

To explain the I/O phases detected, we present snippets of trace files for each experiment, where lines with "##" present the selected field of a trace line. Furthermore, we detected two I/O phases for the four experiments because this depends on the IOR logic. For this reason, we only show a detailed figure of the I/O behavior for experiment (a). Each experiment is explained as follows:

(a) 1 File per Process using POSIX interface: IOR is configured to write 8 MiB per MPI process by using the POSIX interface for the I/O strategy 1 File per process. Each MPI process writes and reads in request size of 1 MiB ($rs = 1$ MiB). Figure 3 shows the I/O behavior for experiment (a). We detect two I/O phases per file composed of eight operations ($Ph\_niop = 8$) each. For each file, the first phase corresponds to 8 write operations and the second phase to 8 read operations. Sixteen files are accessed in parallel. IOR starts with a communication burst of 30 events between process 0 and the rest of the processes (See Fig. 3). Later, a write phase begins in tick 30. In the tick+subtick 50, an I/O Phase of read operations is generated.

Table 4. PIOM-PX Parameters for the IOR Benchmark

Identifier	(a)	(b)	(c)	(d)
app_np	16	16	16	16
app_nfiles	16	16	1	1
app_st	128 MiB	128 MiB	128 MiB	128 MiB
File				
file_name	testFile<IdProcess>	testFile<IdProcess>	testFile	testFile
file_size	8 MiB	8 MiB	128 MiB	128 MiB
file_accessmode	Seq	Seq	Strided	Strided
file_fileaccesstype	W/R	W/R	W/R	W/R
file_accesstype	1Fx1Proc	1Fx1Proc	Shared	Shared
file_nphase	2	2	2	2
file_np	1	1	16	16

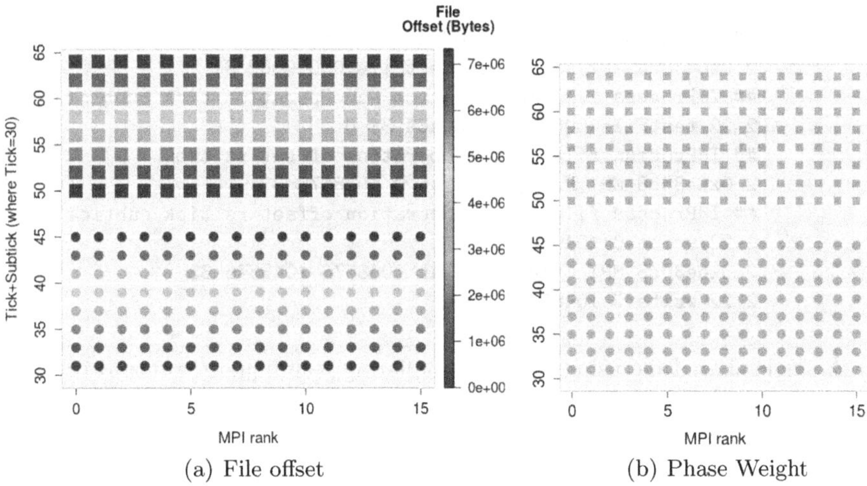

(a) File offset (b) Phase Weight

Fig. 3. IOR for POSIX interface configured for 16 MPI processes, 1 File per Process for a sequential pattern. Bullet (smaller circle) corresponds to write operations and the filled squares to read operations. Two I/O phases can be observed for each file. The Phase 1 is composed of 8 write operations and Phase 2 of 8 read operations. The color scale in (b) shows the weight, which is 1 MiB × *file_np* per subtick. The weight for both Phase 1 and Phase 2 is 8 MiB for each file per process. (Color figure online)

Snippet 1 presents part of the trace file of *IdProcess* 2, which shows part of the operations of Phase 1. We can observe that a `lseek64` operation is called before each `write` and this also occurs for `read` operations.

Snippet 1: Trace file of *IdProcess* 2

```
## IdProcess file_id file_name NameOperation  tick subtick
2 6 testFile.00000002 open64 30 0
## IdProcess file_id NameOperation offset tick subtick
2 6 lseek64 0 30 1
## IdProcess file_id NameOperation offset rs tick subtick
2 6 write 0 1048576 30 2
2 6 lseek64 1048576  30 3
2 6 write 0 1048576 30 4
...
```

(b) 1 File per Process using MPI-IO interface: the I/O phases for this case is similar to experiment (a) (See Fig. 3). In Snippet 2, a part of the *IdProcess* 2 trace file for this experiment can be seen. The number of I/O operations at POSIX-IO level changes, a `write` operation is called for each `MPI_File_write_at`. For read case, each `MPI_File_read_at` calls a `read` operation.

Snippet 2: Trace file of *IdProcess* 2

```
## IdProcess file_id NameOperation file_name tick
2 0x6e38b8 MPI_File_open testFile.00000002 31
## IdProcess file_id file_name NameOperation tick subtick
2 22 testFile.00000002 open64 31 0
## IdProcess file_id NameOperation offset rs tick
2 0x6e38b8 MPI_File_write_at 0 1048576 32
## IdProcess file_id NameOperation offset rs tick subtick
2 22 write 0 1048576 32 0
2 0x6e38b8 MPI_File_write_at 1048576 1048576 33
2 22 write 0 1048576 33 0
...
```

(c) A single shared file using collective buffering technique in `automatic` for a strided pattern:

Snippet 3: Trace file of *IdProcess* 0

```
## IdProcess file_id NameOperation file_name tick
0 0x2124fc8 MPI_File_open testFile3 31
## IdProcess file_id file_name NameOperation tick subtick
0 6 testFile3 open64 0 66 31 0
0 0x2124fc8 MPI_File_get_info 32
## IdProcess file_id NameOperation offset rs tick
0 0x2124fc8 MPI_File_write_at_all 0 524288 33
## IdProcess file_id NameOperation offset rs tick subtick
0 6 write 0 524288 33 0
0 0x2124fc8 MPI_File_write_at_all 8388608 524288 34
## IdProcess file_id NameOperation offset tick subtick
0 6 lseek64 8388608 34 0
0 6 write 0 524288 34 1
...
```

We define the strided pattern by setting the parameters blocksize (-b) and transfer size (-t) with the same value. Furthermore, to obtain a total I/O

equal to experiment (a) and (b), the segment count (-s) is set to 16. In total, each process writes and reads 8 MiB using a request size of 512 KiB.
In Snippet 3, we can observe a `lseek64` and `write` operation for each `MPI_File_write_at_all`, except for the first collective write. The displacement is equal to $file\_np \times rs = 8388608$ Bytes, where $file\_np = 16$ and $rs = t = 524288$ Bytes. In this case, each MPI process produces a similar trace file, with the exception of the offset, where the initial offset is equal to $IdProcess \times rs$ and $offset(i + 1) = offset(i) + rs \times file\_np \times (i - 1) + IdProcess \times rs$ with $i \in \{1..s\}$, where `s` is the number of segments set up for IOR benchmark.

(d) A single shared file using collective buffering technique enabled for a strided pattern:

Snippet 4: Trace file of IdProcess 0

```
## IdProcess file_id NameOperation file_name tick
0 0xac80f0 MPI_File_open testFile3 31
## IdProcess file_id file_name NameOperation  tick subtick
0 6 testFile3 open64 31 0
0 0xab9338 MPI_File_get_info 32
## IdProcess file_id NameOperation offset rs tick
0 0xab9338 MPI_File_write_at_all 0 524288 33
### IdProcess file_id NameOperation offset rs tick subtick
0 6 write 0 8388608 33
0 0xab9338 MPI_File_write_at_all 8388608 524288 34
## IdProcess file_id NameOperation offset tick subtick
0 6 lseek64 8388608 34 0
0 6 write 0 8388608 34 1
...
```

To trace the I/O operations for applications that use collective buffering enabled, we set up the ROMIO hints for this technique. The strided pattern discussed in experiment (c) is the same than we employed in this experiment. In Snippet 4, we can observe similar I/O operations to experiment (c), but the request size at POSIX level is different, in this case, it corresponds to $file\_np \times rs(MPI) = 8388608$ Bytes, where $rs(MPI)$ is the request size of the MPI-IO operations. This behavior is to be expected, because we select the IOR parameters to observe the collective behavior at POSIX-IO level.

3.2 Discussion

IOR benchmark allows us to reproduce more common I/O patterns of HPC applications. PIOM-PX detected the spatial and temporal pattern for POSIX-IO level and it represented them through I/O phases.

The results showed that the spatial pattern depends on the type of I/O operation and I/O method. We have selected the same amount of data, the number of MPI processes and similar I/O strategy, but the behavior is influenced by the I/O techniques and the I/O interface. We have detected that collective buffering technique was not working in `automatic` mode because all MPI processes were carrying out I/O and we only expected an I/O aggregator per compute node. As has been observed in experiments (c) and (d), MPI-IO operations are the same, but at POSIX level they depend on the hint values of the ROMIO library and the hints explicitly defined in the application. PIOM-PX considers this property to provide information to the user in order to help them understand what the I/O library is doing with the operations defined in the application logic.

4 Experimental Results

In this section, we analyze the BT-IO benchmark [12], which is part of the parallel benchmark suite NPB-MPI developed by the NASA Advanced Supercomputing Division. BT-IO presents a block-tridiagonal partitioning pattern on a three-dimensional array across a square number of processes.

Table 5. PIOM-PX parameters for the BT-IO benchmark subtype FULL

Identifier	Class A	Class B	Class C
app_np	16	16	36
app_nfiles	1	1	1
app_st	400 MiB	1.6 GiB	6.4 GiB
File			
file_name	btio.full.out	btio.full.out	btio.full.out
file_size	400 MiB	1.6 GiB	6.4 GiB
file_accessmode	Strided	Strided	Strided
file_fileaccesstype	W/R	W/R	W/R
file_accesstype	Shared	Shared	Shared
file_nphase	41	41	41
file_np at MPI-IO level	16	16	36
file_np at POSIX-IO level	1	1	3

We selected BT-IO to show the temporal pattern considering the tick and subtick concepts. Due to the fact that an I/O phase is identified depending on the communication events and compute part, BT-IO allows us to analyze a case with compute and communication events. BT-IO is implemented in Fortran, therefore we can evaluate the influence of Fortran I/O library in the request size at POSIX-IO level. We have selected the subtype FULL, which implements the I/O part with collective operations, derived data type, `MPI_File_view` and `MPI_Info` for enabled collective buffering in the application logic. We have executed BT-IO in SuperMUC and Finisterra2 supercomputers (See Table 3).

Figure 4 depicts the I/O phases at MPI-IO (Fig. 4(a)) and POSIX-IO (Fig. 4(b)) level. PIOM-PX parameters are described in Table 5 for Classes A, B

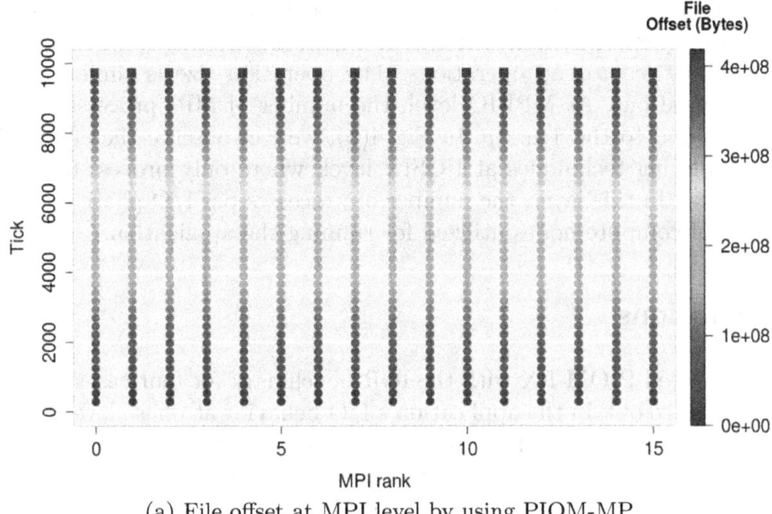

(a) File offset at MPI level by using PIOM-MP

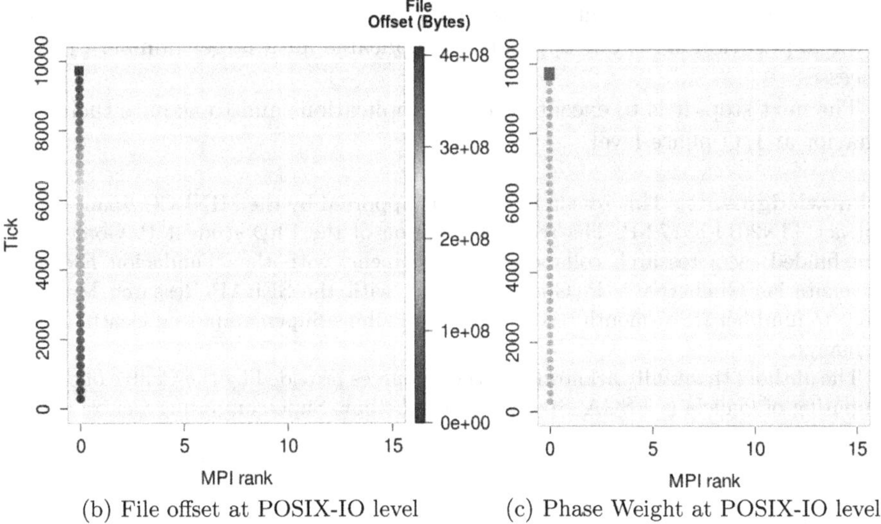

(b) File offset at POSIX-IO level (c) Phase Weight at POSIX-IO level

Fig. 4. BT-IO subtype FULL, Class A using 16 MPI processes for a strided pattern. The bullets (smaller circles) correspond to write operations and the shaded squares to read operations. Each first forty I/O phases (circles) are composed of 1 MPI write operation and Phase 41 of 40 read operations. At MPI-IO level, the weight of the Phase 1 to Phase 40 is 655360 Bytes × *file_np* for each one and for Phase 41 it is 10 MiB × np × 40. At POSIX-IO level, the colored scale in Fig. 4(c) shows the weight for Phase 1 to Phase 40, which is 10 MiB and the Phase 41 weight is 10 MiB ×40.

and C at application and file level. As can be observed in Table 5, 41 I/O phases are identified in a single shared file for a strided access mode.

In Fig. 4(a) each bullet line (y-axis) represents an I/O phase composed of *file_np* write operations. The red square represents Phase 41, which is composed of 40 × *file_np* read operations. The operation size is similar for read and write operations. At MPI-IO level, the number of MPI processes per I/O phase correspond to the *file_np*. In Fig. 4(b), we can observe the effect of the collective buffering techniques at POSIX level, where only process 0 performs I/O operations. In this layer, the number of processes per I/O phase is equal to the number of compute nodes utilized for running the application.

5 Conclusions

We have validated PIOM-PX with the IOR benchmark for four cases. Our approach allows us to obtain the application's I/O behavior at phase level. The I/O behavior helps to understand the relationship between the application and the I/O system. PIOM-PX is modular to facilitate the integration of more functionality or steps. Our framework makes it possible to have accurate information over the I/O phases. Despite the fact that number of MPI processes evaluated in validation and experimentation is small, as the I/O behavior model depends on the application logic, our approach is applicable for a larger number of MPI processes.

The next step, it is to execute the real applications and to acquire their I/O behavior at I/O phase level.

Acknowledgments. This research has been supported by the MINECO Spain under contract TIN2014-53172-P. The research position of the PhD student P. Gomez has been funded by a research collaboration agreement, with the "Fundación Escuelas Universitarias Gimbernat". P. Gomez awarded with the SEBAP Research Mobility Grant to fund her three-month research stay at Leibniz Supercomputing Centre (LRZ, Germany).

The authors thankfully acknowledge the resources provided by the Centre of Supercomputing of Galicia (CESGA, Spain) and the Leibniz Supercomputing Centre (LRZ, Germany).

References

1. Byna, S., Chen, Y., Sun, X.-H., Thakur, R., Gropp, W.: Parallel I/O prefetching using MPI file caching and I/O signatures. In: Proceedings of the 2008 ACM/IEEE Conference on Supercomputing, SC 2008, Piscataway, NJ, USA, pp. 44:1–44:12. IEEE Press, 2008. http://dl.acm.org/citation.cfm?id=1413370.1413415
2. He, J., Bent, J., Torres, A., Grider, G., Gibson, G., Maltzahn, C., Sun, X.-H.: I/O acceleration with pattern detection. In: Proceedings of the 22nd International Symposium on High-Performance Parallel and Distributed Computing, pp. 25–36. ACM (2013)

3. Kluge, M., Knüpfer, A., Müller, M., Nagel, W.E.: Pattern matching and I/O replay for POSIX I/O in parallel programs. In: Sips, H., Epema, D., Lin, H.-X. (eds.) Euro-Par 2009. LNCS, vol. 5704, pp. 45–56. Springer, Heidelberg (2009). doi:10.1007/978-3-642-03869-3_8
4. Méndez, S., Rexachs, D., Luque, E.: Modeling parallel scientific applications through their Input/Output phases. In: CLUSTER Workshops, vol. 12, pp. 7–15 (2012)
5. Carns, P., Harms, K., Allcock, W., Bacon, C., Lang, S., Latham, R., Ross, R.: Understanding and improving computational science storage access through continuous characterization. Trans. Storage **7**(3), 8:1–8:26 (2011). doi:10.1145/2027066.2027068
6. Behzad, B., Luu, H.V.T., Huchette, J., Byna, S., Prabhat, Aydt, R., Koziol, Q., Snir, M.: Taming parallel I/O complexity with auto-tuning. In: 2013 SC - International Conference for High Performance Computing, Networking, Storage and Analysis (SC), pp. 1–12, November 2013
7. Behzad, B., Byna, S., Prabhat, Snir, M.: Pattern-driven parallel I/O tuning. In: Proceedings of the 10th Parallel Data Storage Workshop, PDSW 2015, pp. 43–48. ACM, New York (2015). doi:10.1145/2834976.2834977
8. Carns, P., Latham, R., Ross, R., Iskra, K., Lang, S., Riley, K.: 24/7 Characterization of petascale I/O workloads. In: 2009 IEEE International Conference on Cluster Computing and Workshops, pp. 1–10. IEEE (2009)
9. Kunkel, J.M., Zimmer, M., Hübbe, N., Aguilera, A., Mickler, H., Wang, X., Chut, A., Bönisch, T., Lüttgau, J., Michel, R., Weging, J.: The SIOX architecture – coupling automatic monitoring and optimization of parallel I/O. In: Kunkel, J.M., Ludwig, T., Meuer, H.W. (eds.) ISC 2014. LNCS, vol. 8488, pp. 245–260. Springer, Cham (2014). doi:10.1007/978-3-319-07518-1_16
10. Knüpfer, A., et al.: The Vampir performance analysis tool-set. In: Resch, M., Keller, R., Himmler, V., Krammer, B., Schulz, A. (eds.) Tools for High Performance Computing, pp. 139–155. Springer, Heidelberg (2008). doi:10.1007/978-3-540-68564-7_9
11. Loewe, W., MacLarty, T., Morrone, C.: IOR Benchmark (2012). https://github.com/chaos/ior/blob/master/doc/USER_GUIDE. Accessed 14 May 2016
12. Wong, P., Wijngaart, R.F.V.D.: NAS parallel benchmarks i/o version 2.4, Computer Sciences Corporation, NASA Advanced Supercomputing (NAS) Division, Technical report (2003)

Real-Time I/O-Monitoring of HPC Applications with SIOX, Elasticsearch, Grafana and FUSE

Eugen Betke(✉) and Julian Kunkel(✉)

Deutsches Klimarechenzentrum, 20146 Hamburg, Germany
{betke,kunkel}@dkrz.de

Abstract. The starting point for our work was a demand for an overview of application's I/O behavior, that provides information about the usage of our HPC "Mistral". We suspect that some applications are running using inefficient I/O patterns, and probably, are wasting a significant amount of machine hours. To tackle the problem, we focus on detection of poor I/O performance, identification of these applications, and description of I/O behavior.

Instead of gathering I/O statistics from global system variables, like many other monitoring tools do, in our approach statistics come directly from I/O interfaces POSIX, MPI, HDF5 and NetCDF. For interception of I/O calls we use an instrumentation library that is dynamically linked with `LD_PRELOAD` at program startup.

The HPC on-line monitoring framework is built on top of open source software: Grafana, SIOX, Elasticsearch and FUSE. This framework collects I/O statistics from applications and mount points. The latter is used for non-intrusive monitoring of virtual memory allocated with mmap(), i.e., no code adaption is necessary. The framework is evaluated showing its effectiveness and critically discussed.

1 Introduction

The moderate progress of network and storage technologies, and comparatively fast increase of computational power over the last decades had a negative impact on the balance of many current HPC systems. Especially, increasing number of cores per node facilitates higher data processing rates that often exceed the capabilities of network or storage. In data-intensive research fields, like climate science, where data volumes are large and steadily increasing, I/O became an annoying bottleneck. Nowadays, the imbalance between computational power, network bandwidth and storage performance makes us re-think the usage of I/O resources. Researchers in the I/O field propose various directions for new HPC architectures (e.g. burst buffer), hardware solutions (e.g. SSDs), and non-intrusive software solutions (e.g. compression), that solve partially the problem. But in many cases, poor I/O performance is a result of inefficient I/O access patterns of applications. These applications could probably be fixed, but the difficulty is to detect these applications and to describe to what extend they are affected by the problem. An insight of how application uses the underlying I/O interface could be of great help.

J.M. Kunkel et al. (Eds.): ISC High Performance Workshops 2017, LNCS 10524, pp. 174–186, 2017.
https://doi.org/10.1007/978-3-319-67630-2_15

In data-intensive science, MPI-IO [11] is one of the most frequently used high I/O level interfaces. It was designed as a general purpose I/O interface, to facilitates parallel low level access to files. Most implementations contain a number of optimizations like Two-Phase I/O, Collective I/O, and Data Sieving, which purpose is to create from several I/O access, large and contiguous accesses, or other techniques like Non-Blocking I/O, which handle data asynchronously. HDF5 and NetCDF are high level, portable file formats, data models and libraries specialized to store large datasets. They also provide a set of tools for exploration and manipulation of data. The data size is not limited by the specifications (but limited by current implementations to 32 EiB). They run on a wide range of computational platforms, from laptops to large scale HPCs. Although, POSIX wasn't designed with parallel file access in mind and has some limitations when accessing shared file regions by multiple processes, it still remains one of the most important interfaces, especially because most of the back-ends of the high-level libraries use it to write data to storage.

Our long-term goals are the detection of poor performance and identification of problematic HPC applications. This work is an important step in this direction. Here, we present a user-friendly way for on-line visualization and description I/O of behavior of HPC applications. For that purpose, we build a monitoring framework on top of open source software: SIOX, Elasticsearch, Grafana, and FUSE. One of its features (and also our main contribution) is the novel approach for a non-intrusive instrumentation of virtual memory allocated by `mmap()` operation.

This paper has the following structure. Section 2 presents related work. Section 3 introduces the framework components. In Sect. 4 we show the design of our framework. In Sect. 5 we describe our experiments and evaluate the results in Sect. 6.

2 Related Work

In this section we introduce three monitoring tools: Darshan, Vampir, and SIOX. Unfortunately, it doesn't contain any related work about monitoring of `mmap()`, for the simple reason: even after a careful research, we didn't found any serios publication. This makes us think, our approach is a novelty.

Darshan. Darshan [1,6] is an analysis tool for characterization of I/O behavior of HPC systems. It was developed to capture accurate pictures of application behavior and properties, e.g., I/O access pattern on a file. For instrumentation Darshan uses a number of different wrappers. They intercept I/O operations of all files used by the application and produce output for each file. Instead of storing all the data in a trace file, like conventional tools do, Darshan creates statistics, that are reduced, compressed, and represented in a compact form. After analysis, the data is written to a log file. The data in these files describes the behavior of the entire application. This approach has a negligible overhead and requires a limited amount of memory.

For analysis of log file Darshan provides a number of command line tools. One of them is "darshan-job-summary". As the name indicates, it creates a summary of a log file. The Darshan instrumentation support different I/O interfaces. They have full support for the POSIX and MPI-IO interfaces. HDF5 and PNetCDF are supported partially. Darshan can be utilized in a broad spectrum of tasks, beginning with optimization of applications and ending with analysis of I/O behavior of entire HPC systems. The lightweight and efficient design of Darshan makes it possible to use it for load characterization on large systems, even on productive systems.

Darshan extended tracing (DXT) allows a more detailed profiling of I/O software stack. It contains two main components, the logging and the analysis tool. The former creates trace files while application runs and the latter can be used for the offline analysis and visualization of the data. The features work without any modification or recompilation of applications, provide a number of useful statistics and work with a negligible overhead.

Vampir. Vampir [3,9] is a graphical tool for performance analysis of parallel systems. It supports off-line analysis of parallel software (MPI, OpenMP, multi-threaded) and hardware accelerated (CUDA and OpenCL) applications. The analysis engine allows a scalable and efficient processing of large amounts of data. Vampir uses the infrastructure of Score-P [2] for instrumenting of applications. Score-P stores events in a file, that can be analysed by Vampir and converted to different views, e.g., events can be presented on a time-axis, or compressed to different statistics. Some views have elaborate filters and zoom functions, that can provide an overview, but can also show details. Effective usage of Vampir requires a deep understanding of parallel programming. Although, the program makes it possible to capture and to analyse sequences of POSIX I/O operations, it gives little or no information about the origin, or evaluation of I/O. The field of application of Vampir is restricted through the missing support of on-line analysis.

SIOX. SIOX [10] is a highly modular instrumentation, analysis and profiling framework. It contains an instrumentation tool *"siox-inst"*, a trace reader *"siox-trace-reader"*, and a set of plug-ins and wrappers.

Currently, there are wrappers for MPI, POSIX, NetCDF and HDF5 interfaces. They contain re-implementations of the original I/O functions. Inside a reimplemented function is a call to the original function or syscall, and instrumentation code, that generates an activity after each execution. Activities in SIOX are structures that contain various information about the calls. The wrappers can be dynamically linked to an application by using the `LD_PRELOAD` feature.

Extreme modular design is one of the key features of SIOX. The tools *siox-inst* and *siox-trace-reader* can be considered as pure plug-in infrastructures. In other words, there is no functionality inside until some plug-ins and wrappers are loaded. Usage of different sets of plug-ins and wrappers may result in "new" tools, that fits exactly the problem. There is no restriction on the number of wrappers and plug-ins can be loaded simultaneously, so that the functionality of SIOX can be easily extended, e.g., to perform complex tasks.

Other two important features of SIOX are the support of on-line and off-line analysis. On-line analysis can be done by *siox-inst*, by collecting activities from the wrappers and forwarding them to the registered plug-ins. Off-line analysis is based on both tools. In the first step *siox-inst* stores the activities in a file, by using the *activity-writer-plugin*. In the second step *siox-trace-reader* reads the activities from the file and forwards them to the loaded plug-ins. (The second step is the actual off-line analysis.)

Most of the SIOX plug-ins are using plug-in interfaces that are supported by *siox-inst* and *siox-trace-reader*, and consequentially these plug-ins can be used by both tools.

3 Components

This section contains a short description of components used in our online monitoring framework.

3.1 Elasticsearch

Elasticsearch [7] is a distributed, scalable, real-time search and analytics engine, published under the Apache 2 license. It is built on top of the Apache Lucene full-text search-engine library. The complexity of the library is hidden behind a RESTful API. The indexing of all fields allow very fast lookups, and makes it real-time capable. The library can be used on a broad range of devices. It is suitable for a single machine as well as for large-scaled super computers.

3.2 Grafana

Grafana [5] is a feature-rich, interactive visualization and dashboard software. For visualization, it provides different widgets, e.g., time series, tables, text fields for single metrics. It also supports a many data sources, e.g., Graphite, Elasticsearch, InfluxDB, OpenTSDB.

Especially remarkable is the wide range of available features. Quick range selection makes the navigation inside a time series precise and easy. It has zoom and auto refreshing functions, and a set of predefined, often used ranges. In most cases, a few mouse clicks are sufficient to visualize required range of data. Templating is one of the most powerful features of Grafana. Templates define arrays, which are dynamically filled with values, depending on the current data or state of Grafana. These array can be used on different places, e.g., in metric queries, panel titles, automatic dashboard generation. The latter means, that it is possible to generate for each value in the array a graph or other widget, e.g., suppose an array holds a list of node names, and performance graph was defined, then this graph can be created for each node name automatically. When a new node name appears in the array, the corresponding graph is automatically generated. Grafana support annotations. This feature is useful, when some event should be shown in the graph.

Grafana dashboards can be easily shared via URL. The URL is automatically updated on dashboard changes.

3.3 IOFS: A FUSE-Based File System

FUSE (Filesystem in Userspace) [8] is a kernel interface for file system drivers, which can be run in non-privileged mode. The FUSE project provides an implementation of this interface. It consists of two key components, the *fuse* kernel module and *libfuse* library. The latter can be linked against a program to establish a connection to the *fuse* kernel module.

Virtual file system (VFS) is an abstraction that hides real file systems. Applications see VFS only, and communicate with file systems only over VFS. Figure 1 shows how I/O requests to a FUSE file system are processed. VFS and FUSE modules act like switches. At VFS arriving I/O requests, which are addressed to a FUSE file system, are routed to the FUSE kernel module and then to the destination. The replies take the reverse route. How user level file system stores and retrieves the data, is left to the implementation.

IOFS is a user level file system that implements the FUSE interface. It was developed to be used as an auxiliary tool for instrumentation of mount points. IOFS mounts a folder from an existing file system on some mount point. It runs completely in user space and behaves like an ordinary application when started in foreground, i.e., SIOX wrappers can be dynamically linked using `LD_PRELOAD`. One important feature of IOFS is that it has neither caches nor buffers, i.e., all

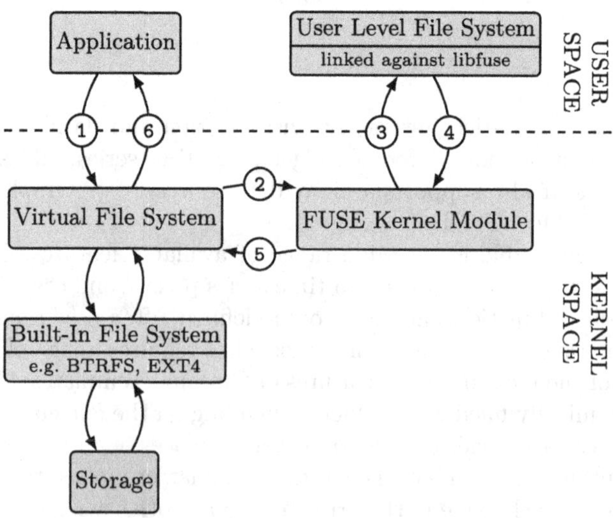

Fig. 1. FUSE I/O path.

I/O request are forwarded to VFS without delay. Furthermore, the implementation doesn't call `mmap()` function. All this makes it to a perfect candidate for instrumentation with SIOX.

3.4 SIOX + On-line Monitoring Plug-in

The SIOX-On-line-Monitoring plug-in captures data from SIOX activities, SLURM and system environment variables, and uses system clock for time stamp. The system clock is supposed to be synchronized. For performance reasons we don't collect all the data. Instead, in a defined time interval only relevant values are aggregated to statistics, and are sent to Elasticsearch in JSON format using the REST-API. This approach ensures a low data transfer rate and makes it independent from access pattern of applications. The data transfer rate increases only with number of files used in the application.

Statistics. A data point or statistics (Table 1) consist of metrics, tags, and a time stamp. The distinction is based on usage of the data in Grafana.

The current set of metrics consists of number of bytes (`*_bytes`), duration (`*_duration`), number of calls (`*_calls`), and number of bytes per call (`*_bytes_per_call`) for read and write operations. Number of bytes and duration are obtained directly from SIOX activities. Number of calls is a counter of occurred activities in a time interval. Derived metrics are calculated from more than two metrics. They must be created inside the plug-in, because Elasticsearch doesn't support arithmetic operations on data, and Grafana is limited to scaling with a constant value, e.g., `write_bytes_per_call` is derived from basic metrics.

Tags provide additional information to the metrics. The tags `username`, `hostname`, `procid`, `jobid` are obtained directly from SLURM environment variables. `hostname` is provided by the system. `filename` and `access` (access type: write, read, ...) are provided by SIOX activities. `layer` is a user defined tag and can take any value, e.g., we use different values for monitoring applications and mount points.

`timestamp` is playing a special role in data series. Currently, milliseconds are the highest possible resolution supported by Elasticsearch.

Categories of Operations. Some I/O interfaces contain different functions that do similar operations, e.g., POSIX offers `writev()`, `write()`, `pwrite()`, `pwrite64()`, `puts()`, and other functions, which can do a write operation. For our purposes it's not necessary to know function names, but operation names is fully sufficient. At the moment our prototype supports write and read operations. Further operations can be added with a minimal effort.

Visualization. For visualization of I/O behavior we use several Grafana dashboards. Generally, metrics are used on the y-axis and time stamp on the x-axis. The tags are used for filtering of data, e.g., we can choose a filename to show I/O behavior of a specific file. Several tags can be used simultaneously.

Table 1. Statistics

Name	Type	Value
`write_duration`	metric (basic)	time spent for writing
`write_bytes`	metric (basic)	bytes written
`write_calls`	metric (basic)	number of I/O operations
`write_bytes_per_call`	metric (derived)	`write_bytes`, `write_calls`
`read_duration`	metric (basic)	time spent for reading
`read_bytes`	metric (basic)	bytes read
`read_calls`	metric (basic)	number of I/O operations
`read_bytes_per_call`	metric (derived)	`read_bytes`, `read_calls`
`filename`	tag	filename
`access`	tag	access type (write, read, ...)
`username`	tag	SLURM_USER
`hostname`	tag	HOSTNAME
`procid`	tag	SLURM_PROCID
`jobid`	tag	SLURM_JOBID
`layer`	tag	user defined
`timestamp`	date	system clock

4 Monitoring Framework Design

On a properly configured system monitoring is enabled by starting an application with a SIOX wrapper. Virtually, one can think of SIOX as a function that takes an executable as argument. For this we use the notation: `SIOX(<exec>)`.

4.1 On-Line Monitoring of Applications

`SIOX(Application)` in Fig. 2 represents the instrumentation of an application. SIOX creates activities from I/O calls and builds an activity stream to the `Online-Monitoring-Plugin`. The plug-in aggregates the activities to statistics and sends them to Elasticsearch. Grafana uses data from Eleasticsearch for visualization.

Monitoring of `Virtual Memory` is not possible in this approach, because this component runs in kernel space, but it can produce application related I/O, e.g., when the application maps a part of a file to virtual memory by using the `mmap()` function and then accesses the content of the file through the memory.

4.2 On-Line Monitoring of Mount Points

The basic idea of this approach is to move I/O request produced by virtual memory from kernel space to user space. This can be easily achieved with a

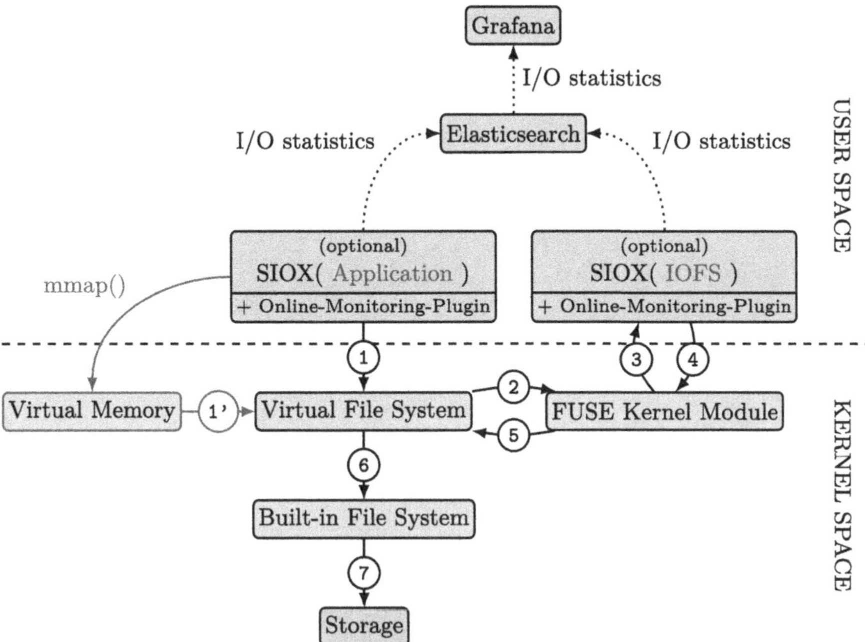

Fig. 2. Extended on-line monitoring

FUSE-based file system. In the first step IOFS mounts a folder, that contains required files, to some mount point. In the second step, we make sure, our application works on this directory. When the application applies the `mmap()` function to some file on this mount point, all I/O requests from virtual memory to this file will be forwarded to IOFS.

The monitoring works in the same way as `SIOX(Application)`, but this time we use `SIOX(IOFS)`.

Now, the monitoring is closer to the system than to the application. It provides information about real communication that takes place on a specific mount point. That means, in this way we can observe some thing that happens on system level, e.g., optimizations that are done by the operation system; changed access granularities or burst writes.

A nice side effect of this approach is the indirect instrumentation of POSIX `mmap` operations. Remember, that the direct instrumentation was a problem, because memory allocated by mmap is accessed directly without a syscall, and therefore, couldn't be instrumented by SIOX. In IOFS such accesses are transformed to common read/write POSIX operations, which in turn are supported by SIOX.

On-line monitoring of applications using this approach is possible only to a limited extent. Firstly, the I/O requests on this mount point cannot be tracked back to the application. There is an information loss. We must made an implicit

Fig. 3. Screenshot of the on-line monitoring dashboard

assumption, that we know which application works with the data and that all I/O requests belong to the same application. Secondly, on each node we can create only one mount point with the same name. This can be a disadvantage for multi-threaded applications, because there is no way to track I/O requests back the the threads. This information will also be lost, and there is no easy way to solve this issue. Thirdly, not all I/O operations are directed to the mount point. Typically, there is a number of files that are accessed outside the mount point. This information will also not be registered (Fig. 3).

5 Experiments

In the first experiment we measure how many metrics we can send to Elasticsearch. For that purpose Elasticsearch was installed on a system equipped with Intel i7-6700 CPU (Skylake) with 4 cores @ 3.40 GHz and 16 GB DDR3 RAM. The metrics were generated on Mistral by 10 nodes and 20 processes per nodes and sent over 1 GiB ethernet to Elasticsearch in JSON containers each containing 100 metrics.

In the second experiment, the measurement of overhead, we run a series of experiments on system equipped with Intel Core i5-660 (Clarkdale), 4M Cache, 3.33 GHz, 12 GB DDR3 RAM, 2 TB HDD (test disk), 1 GB/s network, 500 GB HDD (OS disk). The experiments were conducted with IOR and IOZone benchmarks. IOR was used to produce independent streams of POSIX operation calls and IOZone was started in mmap-mode. We varied the number of processes (NP) and request size and run the experiments several times for all four configurations.

The mean values of I/O performance of benchmarks without monitoring (NMON) were used as reference values. The same benchmarks were run with monitoring of application (APPIO), mount point (IOFS), and with both (BOTH). The experiments were repeated 10 times and the results are shown in Figs. 4 and 5.

6 Evaluation

The primary goal of the framework is to provide enough information to identify inefficient applications. Additionally, from the user perspective, the framework must be convenient to use and from the perspective of HPC systems, it must be scalable and perform well with low overhead. In this section we investigate both aspects.

6.1 Performance

In our test environment, Elasticsearch processes about 750,000 metrics per second, while the aggregated transfer rate stays below 10 MiB/s. Since our current plug-in implementation uses 16 metrics, this is sufficient to capture I/O statistics from about 46000 processes, simultaneously. The limiting factor is the CPU utilization induced by Elasticsearch, but this bottleneck can be relaxed by scaling up/out Elasticsearch.

6.2 Overhead

The Figs. 4 and 5 show relative overhead of monitoring (APPIO, IOFS, BOTH). To enhance comparability, it also contains benchmark results of test runs without monitoring (NMON). In these figures we can observe a negligible overhead for file I/O. For mmap I/O there is also a negligible overhead, but only for read operations. For write operations, the overhead is around 8% for file I/O and 3% for mmap I/O. In our case this was mostly the case. The outliers in Fig. 4a can be explained by a large number of function calls. For the outliers in Fig. 5b we have no explanation at the moment.

6.3 User Experience

We paid particular attention to user experience, because we are convinced, that software which is difficult to use or that doesn't work properly finds little or

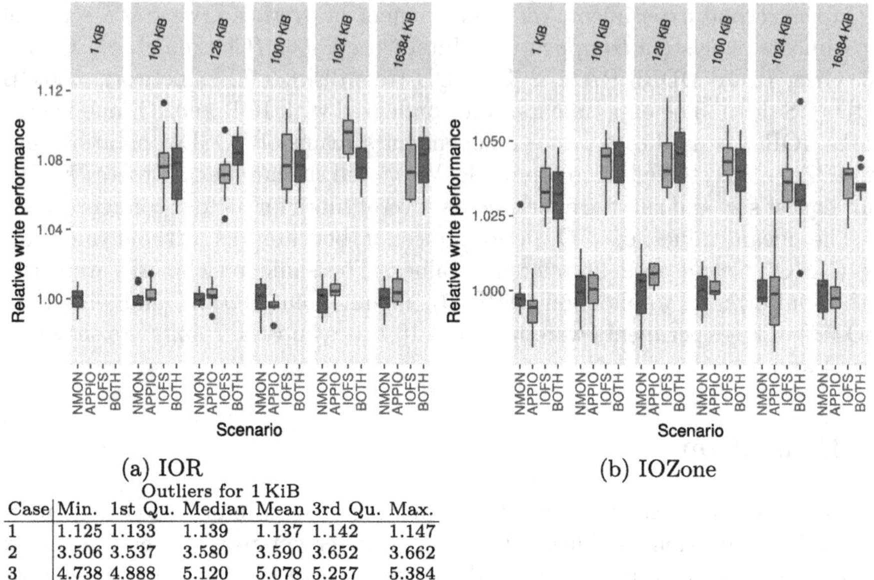

Outliers for 1 KiB

Case	Min.	1st Qu.	Median	Mean	3rd Qu.	Max.
1	1.125	1.133	1.139	1.137	1.142	1.147
2	3.506	3.537	3.580	3.590	3.652	3.662
3	4.738	4.888	5.120	5.078	5.257	5.384

Fig. 4. Write overhead. (NMON: no monitoring; APPIO: file I/O; IOFS: mmap I/O; BOTH: file and mmap I/O)

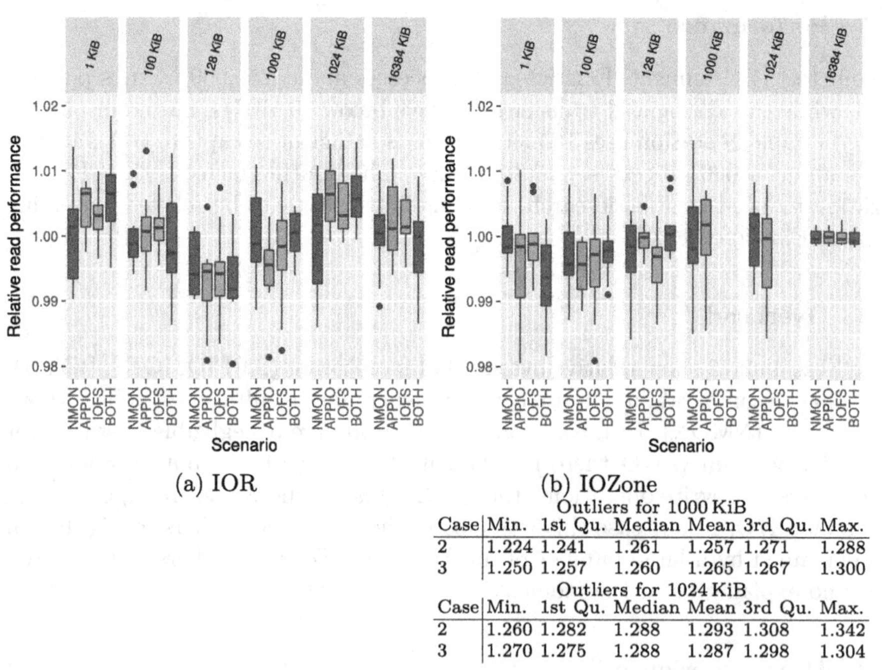

Outliers for 1000 KiB

Case	Min.	1st Qu.	Median	Mean	3rd Qu.	Max.
2	1.224	1.241	1.261	1.257	1.271	1.288
3	1.250	1.257	1.260	1.265	1.267	1.300

Outliers for 1024 KiB

Case	Min.	1st Qu.	Median	Mean	3rd Qu.	Max.
2	1.260	1.282	1.288	1.293	1.308	1.342
3	1.270	1.275	1.288	1.287	1.298	1.304

Fig. 5. Read overhead. (NMON: no monitoring; APPIO: file I/O; IOFS: mmap I/O; BOTH: file and mmap I/O)

no acceptance by users. Although, the most parts of the framework meet our expectations, after a closer look we found some limitations. The points below refer to Grafana 4.2.0.

Firstly, the update of information inside the drop-down lists is not sophisticated. Grafana provides two options: *update on dashboard load* and *update on time range change*. Under some conditions the drop-down list are not updated when new values are available in the database. Depending on the configuration, there are two workarounds to get the jobid appear. It can be done by leaving and entering the dashboard or by changing the time range. Both options are non-intuitive for users. In general, if entries doesn't appear in the drop-down lists, they can be entered manually, but it is also inconvenient, especially when several template values must be updated. A solution could be a third option (which is not implemented), that updates the information in the drop-down list automatically on each mouse-click.

Secondly, the zoom function doesn't provide an auto range function which shows all data for current template values or allows jumping to the beginning of the data.

Thirdly, neither Grafana nor Elasticsearch provide possibilities to compute new metrics from existing ones. This could be a problem for advanced users who need derived metrics. At the moment, derived metrics must be computed by SIOX and sent to Grafana, which means additional network overhead and more storage space consumption.

7 Summary

The paper proposes an on-line monitoring framework for HPC systems, which can help to detect and to describe the I/O behavior of parallel applications. It is built on top of open source software: the instrumentation framework "SIOX", database "Elasticsearch", visualization tool Grafana and a FUSE-based file system "IOFS".

SIOX is able to intercept the I/O requests from applications, and mount point, when used with IOFS. The latter method can be used as a novel approach for indirect interception of mmap I/O.

The performance of Elasticsearch on an office computer is sufficient to gather 750000 metrics per second. Since Elasticsearch is a distributed database this value can be easily increased. The preliminary experiments on an office computer showed that the overhead for file I/O is negligible in most cases. For mmap I/O the overhead is around 8% for file I/O and 3% for mmap I/O. We intend to run extended experiments on Mistral [4] as soon as the FUSE module is available, paying particular attention to the outliers.

References

1. Darshan HPC I/O Characterization Tool (2015). http://www.mcs.anl.gov/research/projects/darshan/
2. SCORE-P (2015). http://www.vi-hps.org/projects/score-p/
3. Vampir (2015). http://www.paratools.com/Vampir
4. Mistral (2016). https://www.dkrz.de/Nutzerportal-en/doku/mistral
5. Beautiful metric & analytic dashboards (2017). http://grafana.org/
6. Carns, P.: Darshan. In: High Performance Parallel I/O. Computational Science Series, pp. 309–315. Chapman & Hall/CRC (2015)
7. Gormley, C., Tong, Z.: Elasticsearch: The Definitive Guide, 1st edn. O'Reilly Media, Inc., Sebastopol (2015)
8. Kahanwal, B.: File System Design Approaches. CoRR abs/1403.5976 (2014). http://arxiv.org/abs/1403.5976
9. Knüpfer, A., Rössel, C., an Mey, D., Biersdorff, S., Diethelm, K., Eschweiler, D., Geimer, M., Gerndt, M., Lorenz, D., Malony, A., Nagel, W.E., Oleynik, Y., Philippen, P., Saviankou, P., Schmidl, D., Shende, S., Tschüter, R., Wagner, M., Wesarg, B., Wolf, F.: Score-P: a joint performance measurement run-time infrastructure for Periscope, Scalasca, TAU, and Vampir. In: Brunst, H., Müller, M., Nagel, W., Resch, M. (eds.) Tools for High Performance Computing, pp. 79–91. Springer, Heidelberg (2012). doi:10.1007/978-3-642-31476-6_7
10. Kunkel, J., Zimmer, M., Hübbe, N., Aguilera, A., Mickler, H., Xuan Wang, A.C., Thomas Bönisch, J.L., Michel, R., Weging, J.: The SIOX architecture – coupling automatic monitoring and optimization of parallel I/O (2014)
11. Thakur, R., Gropp, W., Lusk, E.: On implementing MPI-IO portably and with high performance. In: Proceedings of the Sixth Workshop on I/O in Parallel and Distributed Systems, IOPADS 1999, pp. 23–32. ACM, New York (1999). http://doi.acm.org/10.1145/301816.301826

Output Performance Study on a Production Petascale Filesystem

Bing Xie[1(✉)], Jeffrey S. Chase[1], David Dillow[2], Scott Klasky[3], Jay Lofstead[3], Sarp Oral[3], and Norbert Podhorszki[3]

[1] Department of Computer Science, Duke University, Durham, USA
bingxie@cs.duke.edu
[2] Oak Ridge National Laboratory, Oak Ridge, USA
dave@thedillows.org
[3] Center for Computing Research, Sandia National Laboratories, Albuquerque, USA

Abstract. This paper reports our observations from a top-tier supercomputer Titan and its Lustre parallel file stores under production load. In summary, we find that supercomputer file systems are highly variable across the machine at fine time scales. This variability has two major implications. First, stragglers lessen the benefit of coupled I/O parallelism (striping). Peak median output bandwidths are obtained with parallel writes to many independent files, with no striping or write-sharing of files across clients (compute nodes). I/O parallelism is most effective when the application—or its I/O middleware system—distributes the I/O load so that each client writes separate files on multiple targets, and each target stores files for multiple clients, in a balanced way. Second, our results suggest that the potential benefit of dynamic adaptation is limited. In particular, it is not fruitful to attempt to identify "good spots" in the machine or in the file system: component performance is driven by transient load conditions, and past performance is not a useful predictor of future performance. For example, we do not observe regular diurnal load patterns.

Keywords: Parallel I/O · Petascale filesystem · Output performance

1 Introduction

Output bandwidth is a precious resource in supercomputers. Trends suggest that this limitation is not likely to change. Therefore it is crucial for software to make efficient use of the bandwidth. In principle, large write bursts can stream effectively and achieve full bandwidth. In practice, delivered bandwidth is highly sensitive to the application's use of storage APIs and its data layout, placing an unwelcome burden on domain scientists to manage I/O performance tradeoffs at the application level.

In this paper, we summarize results from systematic I/O benchmarking—focusing on output bandwidth—of the production supercomputer Titan, the 4th

J.M. Kunkel et al. (Eds.): ISC High Performance Workshops 2017, LNCS 10524, pp. 187–200, 2017.
https://doi.org/10.1007/978-3-319-67630-2_16

fastest supercomputer in the world. We extended the methodology used to study the Jaguar supercomputer in [21], and designed a set of experiments to stress load on individual stages of Titan's multi-stage write path. These experiments yield distributions of performance behaviors on Titan over time and across the machine, enabling us to assess the impact of key configuration parameters and choices. By studying the results through sequences of such experiments, we can characterize the behaviors of individual stages in the write path over time.

The key contribution of our study is to enhance understanding of performance behaviors for a state-of-the-art parallel filesystem as currently deployed in a leadership-class production facility. The study is useful to understand the current Titan deployment and also to build models that predict output absorption time as a function of various parameter settings [22]. Although some factors may be unique to Lustre and/or Titan, we expect that many of our observations are representative of large-scale computing systems and their I/O performance behaviors. Here is a summary of the primary conclusions:

- We find that a small proportion of storage targets ($< 20\%$) are straggling at any given interval, but that stragglers are transient: over time, any target may appear as a straggler for some intervals. Stragglers throttle the write pipelines, limiting striping bandwidth and reducing the benefits of parallelism.
- As configured on Titan, the Lustre write pipelines do not allow a single client to obtain the full bandwidth of a storage target. The results suggest that in the ideal case each client writes to multiple files spread across multiple targets, with multiple clients per target.
- The I/O performance delivered on Titan is highly variable. Our study suggests that historical performance data and monitoring do not enable adaptive middleware to locate "good spots" in the supercomputer or in the file system. Local performance behavior is transient and unpredictable.
- Delivered aggregate output bandwidth is sensitive to location (density) of a job's compute nodes for large bursts, under a static node-to-router mapping policy adopted by Titan in its internal network configuration.

Our study offers insights that can inform design and deployment choices for exascale facilities and also technical choices for the ongoing development of integrated software stacks for parallel storage including parallel file systems and I/O middleware systems such as ADIOS [12]. ADIOS implements a variety of techniques to improve output performance, and many applications now use ADIOS, e.g., S3D [3], XGC [10] fusion codes, and M8 earthquake simulations [5]. For example, ADIOS enables applications to configure their output buffer size. It can issue writes to multiple independent files to avoid performance problems associated with write-shared files and striping, and it reorganizes output data for better read performance. The results in this study provide a foundation to understand and quantify the impacts of these techniques, and may expose new opportunities to manage I/O performance.

This paper summarizes some key aspects of our methodology and results. We are preparing a full-length paper to present the results in more detail.

2 Output Behavior on Titan

This section summarizes selected aspects of the burst absorption behavior of Titan and two of its Lustre file systems (see Table 1): Spider (Widow1) and Spider 2 (Atlas2). We design a sequence of experiments to stress the components and stages of the write pipeline using the methodology in [21]. Each experiment is a set of identical *runs*; each run varies one or more parameters across a sequence of values in each *round*. The experiments yield one instance (a sample point) in each round for each value of a varying parameter. Each instance reports output bandwidth delivered to a group of nodes writing a synchronized output burst from an IOR benchmark program. The runs occur at regular intervals over the measurement period. In this way, we profile Titan's write path statistically with multiple samples spread over time. We use several measures of output bandwidth:

- *Bandwidth* is measured as MB/s per client node.
- *Aggregate Bandwidth*, measured in MB/s, is bandwidth summed across all client nodes in an instance.
- *Effective Aggregate Bandwidth (EAB)* is aggregate bandwidth normalized to the peak bandwidth achievable from the number of targets written in an instance under a given set of parameters.

Table 1. File systems on Titan. A Lustre client (compute node) issues I/O operations to RAID targets (OSTs) attached to Object Storage Servers (OSSes). The I/O path traverses the internal interconnect to a selected I/O node, which acts as a router to forward I/O traffic between the internal interconnect and an external storage network. In Titan the mapping of compute nodes to I/O nodes is static ("fine-grained") when all I/O nodes are functioning normally [7].

File systems	Service time	Partitions	Routing policy	I/O nodes	OSSes	OSTs
Spider	Jan. 2008–Dec. 2013	4	Fine-grained	192	192	336 × 4
Spider 2	Nov. 2013–present	2	Fine-grained	432	288	1008 × 2

2.1 Pipeline Efficiency

We evaluated the efficiency of the write pipeline from a single client: a single process running on a single core to a single target (OST), as a function of burst size. The data is based on the measurements taken from March to July 2013 on Spider/Widow1. This experiment has 200 runs with 3 rounds each.

Figure 1 gives the results. Each boxplot displays a quantile distribution of samples for the corresponding parameter value on the x-axis, with "whiskers and dots" for the outliers. Each boxplot contains one point from each of the rounds—the result of the instance for the corresponding parameter value from that round. The upper and lower borders of each box are the 25th and 75th percentile values (lower quartile Q1 and upper quartile Q3). The band within

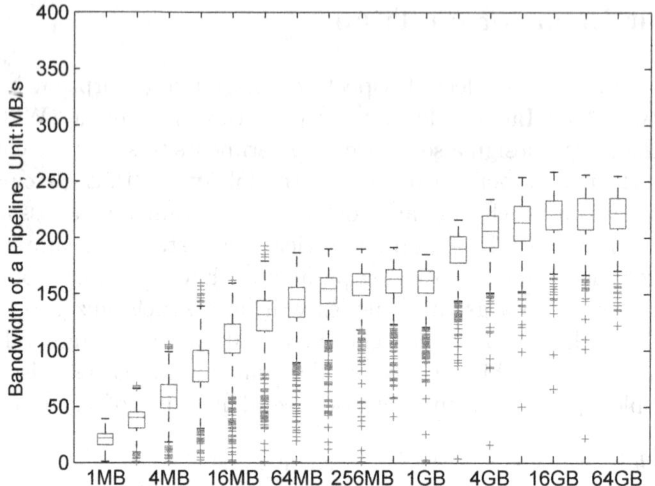

Fig. 1. Bandwidth of a single pipeline as a function of burst size. This graph shows results for a single process on a single core writing a single file on a single target. Other results (not shown) indicate that more client processes do not help: the configured write pipeline is not deep enough for one client to obtain full bandwidth from a target.

each box denotes the median value. The value Q3-Q1 is the interquartile range or IQR; thus 50% of the y-values reside within the box, and the IQR is the height of the box. The upper and lower whiskers cover the points outside of the box, except that the upper and lower bounds of the whisker do not extend beyond $Q3 + 1.5 * IQR$ and $Q1 - 1.5 * IQR$ respectively. All y-values outside of this whisker range are outliers and are plotted as individual points.

Figure 1 shows that single-pipeline bandwidth is sensitive to burst size, and that the write pipeline obtains its maximum overall bandwidth with a write burst of 2 GB or more. With these burst sizes the pipeline runs at full bandwidth for long enough to dominate the time to fill and drain the pipeline.

The results suggest that the conservative flow control configuration for output pipelines in Lustre (e.g., at most eight outstanding RPCs per client-target pair) prevents a single client from obtaining the full bandwidth of any target. This was true in the Jaguar study as well, and has continued to be true on the Titan Lustre deployment. One possible cause is that enhancements for asynchronous journaling (see [16]) may delay the RPC replies from the targets, requiring a larger number of outstanding RPCs for effective write streaming.

We determined from the multi-core experiment (not shown) that using multiple cores on a client does not help. In the multi-core experiment, each client runs multiple single-threaded IOR processes, each issuing a single output burst to a separate file on the single target, synchronized with MPI barriers. Using multiple cores from a client improves the delivered bandwidth by at most 5%.

Figure 1 also shows that many of the trials deliver low bandwidths. The results show substantial outliers on the low side (3% to 5% of all samples). Other experiments suggest that these are due to intermittent contention on the internal Titan interconnect.

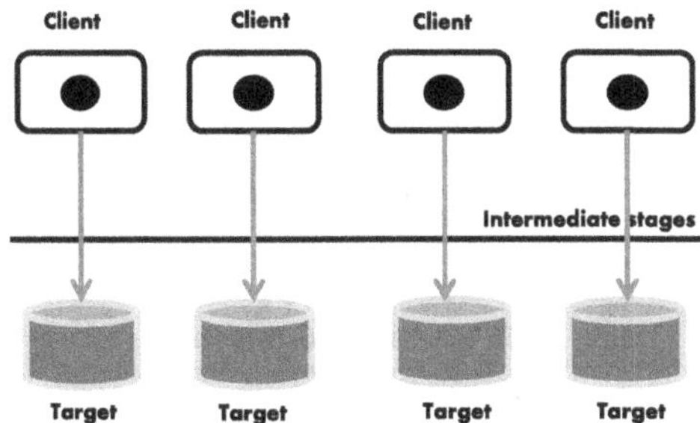

Fig. 2. Template for the many-pairs experiment. Each client node runs a single process that issues a 64 MB burst to an unstriped file on a selected target. Each client selects a different target. The bursts are synchronized. We vary the number of client-target pairs and measure aggregate bandwidth and the bandwidth (or completion time) for each client-target pair.

2.2 Many-Pairs Bandwidth and Stragglers

The "many pairs" experiment probe the aggregate I/O bandwidths achievable on Titan and the consistency of performance in different parts of the machine. The runs use equal numbers of clients and targets grouped in client-target pairs: each client runs a single process that writes a single file on a single target, following the template of Fig. 2. We ran this experiment from February to July 2013 on Spider/Widow1 and produced 200 runs with 3 rounds each. At the largest scale we use 336 compute nodes to write to all 336 targets in the Widow1 storage system on Titan. The results reported here use a fixed burst size of 64 MB for each node-target pair.

A key factor in this experiment is the variance in completion times for the pairs in each instance. The bursts for all pairs are synchronized, and the aggregate bandwidth (or EAB) is determined by the completion time of the slowest pair. Some pairs in each instance complete quickly while others are "stragglers" that limit the aggregate bandwidth.

To quantify the impact of stragglers, Fig. 3 plots the cumulative distributions of completion times across all client-target pairs for each instance of the experiment. In all cases, more than 95% of the synchronized bursts complete within 2 s, but almost every trial has a tail of stragglers, which cause other pairs in the instance to idle while waiting for the stragglers to finish. The impact of stragglers grows as we increase the number of pairs: both the number of stragglers and their completion times increase substantially.

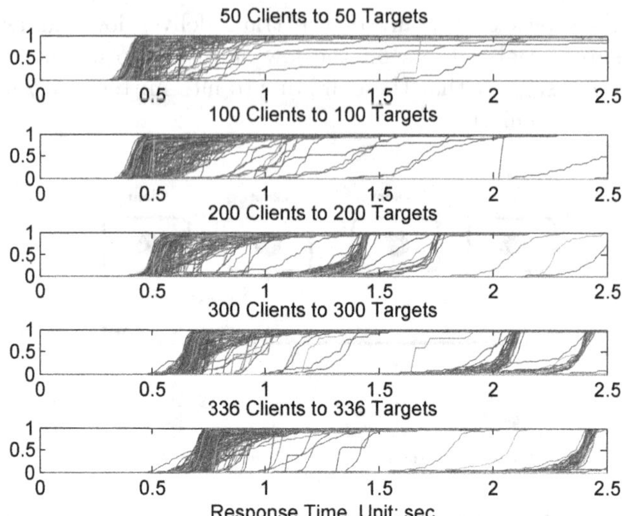

Fig. 3. CDFs of completion times for the instances of the many-pairs experiment. Each subgraph has 600 CDF lines, one for a trial of an instance. Each line shows the distribution of completion times for the pairs of one trial. Each line of the five types of instances has 50, 100, 200, 300 and 336 points (pairs) respectively. It is easy to see that almost every trial has good performance in some parts of the machine, as well as stragglers that limit the aggregate bandwidth.

Stragglers may be caused by bottlenecks in the interconnect, and not necessarily in the targets themselves. Using all 336 targets, the completion times of even the fastest pairs are noticeably higher, indicating that the run has triggered congestion in intermediate stages, uniformly affecting all pairs.

These stragglers are significant in part because of their impact on performance with striping. We found and reported in [21] that straggling targets gate the bandwidth of striped write operations. This situation improved when the Lustre client software was upgraded to improve internal concurrency using a pool of threads to handle RPC load in the client [19]. But the average write bandwidth with striping is still substantially lower than the bandwidth achievable using independent writes.

2.3 Performance Variability of Individual Components

To probe the stability of stragglers and further explore the opportunity to locate and avoid stragglers with adaptive I/O tools (e.g., ADIOS), we design a new experiment template to quantify the persistence of stragglers. It follows the template of the many-pairs experiment (Fig. 2): in each instance N synchronous processes from N clients write to a sequence of N OSTs. However, in this experiment each client is paired to one of the N-length OST sequence according to a round-robin policy across consecutive instances in a run. In each run, the group

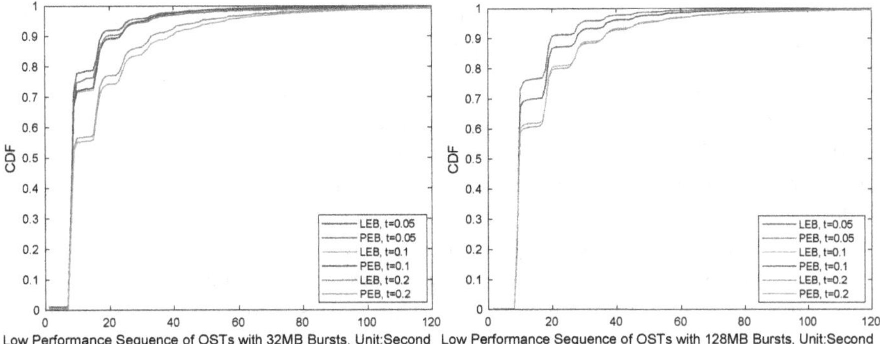

Fig. 4. CDFs of low behavior sequences of OSTs. From left to right, each subfigure shows the CDF of the time durations of the low-performance periods with 32 MB and 128 MB bursts respectively; in each subfigure, a line shows the CDF of the low-performance sequences determined by the quantile threshold t (defined in Sect. 2.3).

of clients, the candidate OSTs, and the burst size are all fixed. We conducted 8 such experiments on Titan/Atlas2 with 1008 OSTs (see Table 1) from January to February 2017: in each experiment 126 coordinated clients focus bursts on a different sequence of 126 OSTs with 32 MB and 128 MB bursts respectively. In this set of experiments, the time duration of a run ranges from 0.5–1.7 h; the time interval between two consecutive measures in a run ranges from 7–15 s.

To quantify the performance of individual components, we assign each node-target pair in an instance two relative measures: LEB (*Lag Effective Bandwidth*) and PEB (*Pair Effective Bandwidth*).

- The LEB score is the pair's bandwidth normalized to the fastest pair in its instance. The fastest pair ($LEB = 1$) gives a rough measure (a lower bound) of the performance achievable under the parameters and general system conditions for that instance.
- The PEB score is the pair's bandwidth normalized to the fastest pair measure within similar instances, which share identical parameter settings but run at different times. Such similar instances form *an equivalent instance set.* The fastest pair in a set ($PEB = 1$) gives a rough measure of the performance achievable for the set under ideal conditions: it is the best observed performance for any pair using those parameter settings.

We use these relative measures of component performance to compensate for the effect of general contention (e.g., in the interconnect) that affects a large share of the machine. We find that over 99.5% of the LEB/PEB scores of individual compute nodes and storage targets are within the range in 0.4—0.9 across experiments and burst sizes. These measures allowed us to identify targets that were persistent stragglers due to a load imbalance in an early Titan configuration; this problem has since been fixed.

We take a two-step approach to quantify the stability of performance behavior for individual components over time:

1. Label a LEB/PEB score of the component as *low* or *normal* performance according to a threshold: if the score of the component is below the threshold, it is considered a low performance measure; otherwise, it is a normal performance measure. We determine a threshold according to a chosen quantile (t) of LEB/PEB scores obtained from each equivalent instance set, i.e., of all instances with the same parameter setting.
2. Measure the lengths of consecutive sequences of low/normal performance measures for the component across its time series. Long sequences indicate that performance states are stable over time; short sequences suggest that they are not.

We focus on three quantiles: $t = 0.05$, $=0.1$, $=0.2$. Figure 4 shows the summary of low performance periods for storage targets. It suggests that for 32 MB (or 128 MB) bursts more than 96% (or 100%) of storage targets showing low performance return to normal within a minute (or 2 min). Similar analyses suggest that a node showing low performance tends to return to normal within 2 min, and any component showing normal performance tends to switch to low performance within 10 min.

Based on these system-wide measurements at small time scales, we conclude that local performance in Titan's I/O system is highly variable over time. This high variability suggests that it is not fruitful to identify "good spots" in the machine or in the file system for the purpose of improving I/O performance.

2.4 Performance Variability and Node Locality

This section probes performance variation across compute node locations. To this end, we examine the many-pairs experiment again (the template in Fig. 2) with 16 MB and 256 MB bursts from each of 1008 compute nodes to a different storage target. We also extend the methodology to group the runs into *sets* each comprising multiple identical runs with the same group of compute nodes, closely spaced in time. Different sets executed on different groups of compute nodes and at different times.

Our analysis is based on measurements taken from May to June 2015. We collected 95 sets with a total of 103 runs; a few sets have multiple runs. Each run comprises 15 rounds of instances with 16 MB and 256 MB bursts respectively.

To explore the set behaviors for different burst sizes, we estimate the node distribution of each set by measuring the average path length (L) between the nodes in all pairs of nodes drawn from the set. A smaller L indicates a more tightly packed (denser) node set; a larger L indicates a more widely scattered node set. To measure the distance for each node pair in a set, we choose a common metric, L_1 *routing distance*: the length of a path between two points in Titan's 3d torus. For a node pair at positions (x_1, y_1, z_1) and (x_2, y_2, z_2), the distance (d) of the pair is given by:

$$d = |x_1 - x_2| + |y_1 - y_2| + |z_1 - z_2| \tag{1}$$

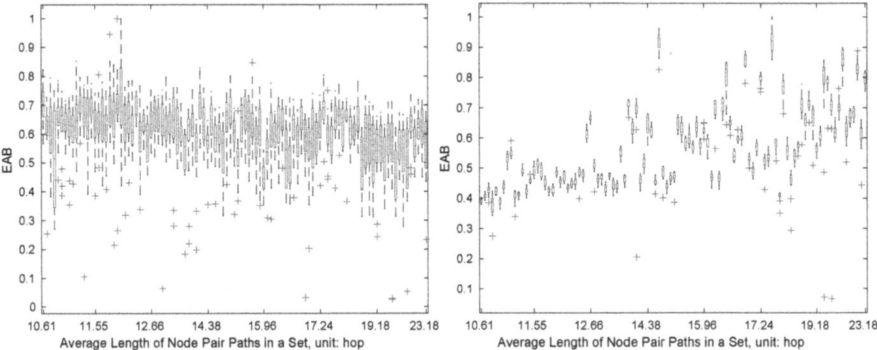

Fig. 5. EABs of the 95 sets with 16 MB and 256 MB bursts. From left to right, a subfigure reports the boxplots of the EABs of the 103 runs from the 95 sets with 16 MB and 256 MB bursts respectively. In each subfigure, the x-axis represents the 95 node sets sorted by L (defined in Sect. 2.4); the corresponding y values summarize the distribution of measured bandwidths (EABs) for that node set.

The L values of the 95 sets vary from 10.61 to 23.18 hops. To explore the correlation between output performance and set density, Fig. 5 plots their EABs ranked by density, for 16 MB and 256 MB bursts.

Figure 5 shows that for 16 MB bursts the EABs of all sets are distributed in a wide range and are only weakly correlated with density. Small bursts are sensitive to transient contention on the shared intermediate stages or on the storage servers/targets. However, for the 256 MB bursts, the sets with larger L are more likely to deliver higher aggregate bandwidths.

To quantify the behaviors of the sample-size bursts on various set densities, we further partition the 95 sets into three ranges of average hop distance: 10.61–15, 15.01–20 and 20.01–23.18. Figure 6 shows the output bandwidths (EABs) for the instances in each range. It suggests that, for 256 MB bursts, above 80% of the instances in the L range 1, range 2 and range 3 report ~0.4, ~0.52 and ~0.67 EABs respectively. For the larger bursts the sets with larger L tend to deliver higher aggregate bandwidths.

We conclude that while the bandwidth of small bursts is dominated by transient contention, the performance of large bursts is impaired by denser node sets. Of course, the job scheduler prefers dense node sets because a densely packed job experiences less cross-contention from other jobs on the internal interconnect. However, denser sets may experience self-contention on the internal interconnect and also are locked into using a smaller set of I/O routers, since the binding of nodes to routers is static and determined by node location (Table 1). More dispersed sets spread their loads across a larger portion of the interconnect and a larger number of I/O routers, and tend to show higher bandwidth accordingly.

Moreover, it is worth noting that for 16MB bursts, the results suggest slightly better performance for denser node sets. Even dense sets are free of self-contention for small bursts, and may benefit from the lack of cross-contention in

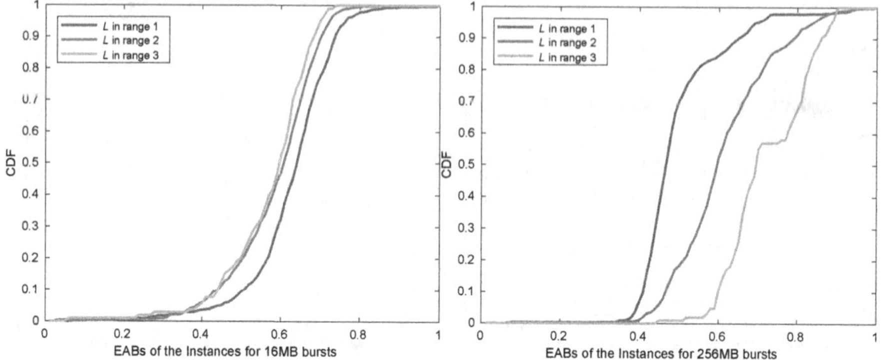

Fig. 6. CDFs of the instance EABs of the 95 sets with 16 MB bursts (left) and 256 MB bursts (right). In each subfigure, the lines (blue, red and yellow) depict the CDFs of the instances examined on the sets with L in three hop ranges respectively: 10.61–15 (720 instances), 15.01–20 (720 instances), and 20.01–23.18 (105 instances). (Color figure online)

the interconnect and I/O routers from other jobs on the machine. Even so, in a busy and highly contended system like Titan, the transient system conditions on the storage servers/targets dominates this effect. For longer bursts the transient hot spots in the storage system tend to cancel out, and the results are dominated by persistent self-contention in the interconnect and I/O routers. This suggests that the I/O routing policy could be improved to spread load for large burst. Moreover, in this scenario I/O adaptive tools (e.g., ADIOS) might be helpful to move and redistribute the load across the machine.

3 Related Work

Several studies benchmark HPC file systems by measuring their performance under real application workloads. Several influential studies were published in the 1990s [4,6,8,14,15]. A significant recent study installs continuous monitoring software on compute nodes to characterize the I/O requests of real application workloads in real time, modulating the data collected to keep overhead within acceptable limits [1,2,13].

Uselton et al. [20] propose a statistical method to collect and analyze I/O events to more fully characterize the I/O behavior of ensembles. They also observe the straggler phenomenon, suggesting that the straggler problem is a general issue in supercomputers. Their work focuses on improving the I/O performance of a given application in a given supercomputer system. Our goal is to characterize the multi-stage write pipeline in a petascale file system, locate write absorption bottlenecks, and capture component performance variability that influence on the design and configuration choices for adaptive middleware and HPC applications.

Other previous studies use an approach similar to ours: stress the file system with synthetic benchmarks. A number of HPC I/O benchmarks are designed to be sufficiently flexible to emulate the typical I/O behaviors in supercomputer environments, such as the FLASH I/O, IOR, and BTIO benchmarks. This flexibility enables users to configure the benchmark for a desired pattern approximating an observed application behavior. In our work, we take IOR as a generator and run different patterns and configurations to focus traffic on specific stages and elements of the write pipeline to gain a complete picture of output burst absorption in a production facility.

A recent study [11] uses a similar methodology to measure the performance of the Intrepid file system at the Argonne Leadership Computing Facility. The authors report the capacity of each I/O stage and measure the behavior of the entire subfile system for large-scale runs of a set of benchmarks. The measurements are taken on dedicated hardware before the supercomputer system was running in production mode. Our work explores the delivered bandwidth of the I/O stages in ongoing production use, reflects the impact of competing workloads under observed usage patterns in production, and shows how to filter noise from competing workloads to obtain insights into the behavior of the underlying hardware and software.

Earlier studies also use configurations of the IOR benchmark to analyze the behavior of HPC systems [17,18]. Kim et al. [9] collect I/O performance data from Titan's predecessor Jaguar. That study is complementary to ours: it reports monitoring data from the storage servers showing the combined workload on the machine. We focus on the end-to-end behavior observed by jobs running on the compute nodes, and the impact of write patterns and I/O configuration choices.

4 Conclusion

I/O bandwidth is a scarce resource on supercomputers. Output burst absorption can have a substantial impact on delivered performance, as demonstrated by a simple performance model. Observed output bandwidth is sensitive to various uses of the storage system APIs and different supercomputer I/O system conditions.

We apply a statistical benchmarking approach to probe Lustre filesystem output performance in Titan and its Spider and Spider 2 file stores. The measured distributions quantify the frequency and severity of contention (stragglers) and other transient system conditions. These imbalances lessen the benefit of coupled I/O parallelism (striping). This effect motivates structuring choices to loosen the coupling of parallel I/O. For example, on Titan's I/O system under typical conditions, the peak median output bandwidths are obtained with parallel writes to many independent files, with no write-sharing or striping, and with each target storing files for multiple clients, and each client writing files on multiple OSTs.

The prevalence of these imbalances motivates adaptive responses in the I/O middleware layer. To evaluate the potential of adaptation, we studied the behavior of individual components to expose temporal usage patterns, slow components and system-level performance variability that can lead to imbalances in the write path. Our results show that these performance stutters are difficult to predict, and that system changes state quickly and frequently, suggesting that dynamic adaptation to congestion is not a fruitful approach.

Under a static node-to-router mapping policy adopted by Titan in its network configuration, for large bursts output performance is sensitive to the density of a job's compute nodes, as measured by the mean pairwise routing path distance within the node group.

Acknowledgment. We thank Chris Zimmer from OLCF for his detailed explanation on the network configuration of Titan.

The work was supported by the U.S. Department of Energy, under FWP 16-018666, program manager Lucy Nowell.

This research used resources of the Oak Ridge Leadership Computing Facility, located in the National Center for Computational Sciences at the Oak Ridge National Laboratory, which is supported by the Office of Science of the Department of Energy under Contract DE-AC05-00OR22725.

Sandia National Laboratories is a multi-program laboratory managed and operated by Sandia Corporation, a wholly owned subsidiary of Lockheed Martin Corporation, for the U.S. Department of Energy's National Nuclear Security Administration under contract DE-AC04-94AL85000.

References

1. Carns, P., Harms, K., Allcock, W., Bacon, C., Lang, S., Latham, R., Ross, R.: Understanding and improving computational science storage access through continuous characterization. ACM Trans. Storage **7**(3), 8–26 (2011)
2. Carns, P., Latham, R., Ross, R., Iskra, K., Lang, S., Riley, K.: 24/7 characterization of petascale I/O workloads. In: Proceedings of the IEEE International Conference on Cluster Computing (CLUSTER 2009), pp. 1–10, New Orleans, LA (2009)
3. Chacón, L.: A non-staggered, conservative, finite-volume scheme for 3D implicit extended magnetohydrodynamics in curvilinear geometries. Comput. Phys. Commun. **163**(3), 143–171 (2004)
4. Crandall, P.E., Aydt, R.A., Chien, A.A., Reed, D.A.: Input/output characteristics of scalable parallel applications. In: Proceedings of the ACM/IEEE Conference on Supercomputing (SC 1995), pp. 59–89, San Diego, CA (1995)
5. Cui, Y., Olsen, K., Jordan, T., Lee, K., Zhou, J., Small, P., Roten, D., Ely, G., Panda, D., Chourasia, A., Levesque, J., Day, S., Maechling, P.: Scalable earthquake simulation on petascale supercomputers. In: Proceedings of the ACM/IEEE International Conference for High Performance Computing, Networking, Storage and Analysis (SC 2010), pp. 1–20, Washington, DC (2010)
6. Cypher, R., Ho, A., Konstantinidou, S., Messina, P.: Architectural requirements of parallel scientific applications with explicit communication. In: Proceedings of the 20th Annual International Symposium on Computer Architecture(ISCA 1993), pp. 2–13, San Diego, CA (1993)

7. Ezell, M., Dillow, D., Oral, S., Wang, F., Tiwari, D., Maxwell, D., Leverman, D., Hill, J.: I/O router placement and fine-grained routing on Titan to support Spider II. In: Proceedings of the Cray User Group Conference (CUG 2014), pp. 1–6, Lugano, Switzerland (2014)
8. Ganger, G.R.: Generating representative synthetic workloads: an unsolved problem. In: Proceedings of the Computer Measurement Group Conference (CMG 1995), pp. 1263–1269, Nashville, TN (1995)
9. Kim, Y., Gunasekaran, R., Shipman, G.M., Dillow, D.A., Zhang, Z., Settlemyer, B.W.: Workload characterization of a leadership class storage cluster. In: Proceedings of the 5th Petascale Data Storage Workshop (PDSW 2010), pp. 1–5, New Orleans, LA (2010)
10. Ku, S., Chang, C.S., Adams, M., Cummings, J., Hinton, F., Keyes, D., Klasky, S., Lee, W., Lin, Z., Parker, S.: The CPES team: Gyrokinetic particle simulation of neoclassical transport in the pedestal/scrape-off region of a Tokamak plasma. J. Phys. **46**(1), 87–91 (2006)
11. Lang, S., Carns, P., Latham, R., Ross, R., Harms, K., Allcock, W.: I/O performance challenges at leadership scale. In: Proceedings of the ACM/IEEE International Conference for High Performance Computing Networking, Storage and Analysis (SC 2009), pp. 40–52, Portland, OR (2009)
12. Lofstead, J., Zheng, F., Klasky, S., Schwan, K.: Adaptable, metadata-rich I/O methods for portable high performance I/O. In: Proceedings of the 23rd IEEE International Parallel & Distributed Processing Symposium (IPDPS 2009), pp. 1–10, Rome, Italy (2009)
13. Luu, H., Winslett, M., Gropp, W., Ross, R., Carns, P., Harms, K., Prabhat, M., Byna, S., Yao, Y.: A multiplatform study of I/O behavior on petascale supercomputers. In: Proceedings of the 24th International Symposium on High-Performance Parallel and Distributed Computing (HPDC 2015), pp. 33–44, Portland, OR (2015)
14. Narasimha Reddy, A.L., Banerjee, P.: A study of I/O behavior of perfect benchmarks on a multiprocessor. In: Proceedings of the 17th Annual International Symposium on Computer Architecture (ISCA 1990), pp. 312–321, Seattle, WA (1990)
15. Nieuwejaar, N., Kotz, D., Purakayastha, A., Ellis, C.S., Best, M.L.: File-access characteristics of parallel scientific workloads. IEEE Trans. Parallel Distrib. Syst. **7**(10), 1075–1089 (1996)
16. Oral, S., Wang, F., Dillow, D., Shipman, G., Miller, R., Drokin, O.: Efficient object storage journaling in a distributed parallel file system. In: Proceedings of the 8th USENIX Conference on File and Storage Technologies (FAST 2010), pp. 143–154, San Jose, CA (2010)
17. Shan, H., Antypas, K., Shalf, J.: Characterizing and predicting the I/O performance of HPC applications using a parameterized synthetic benchmark. In: Proceedings of the ACM/IEEE International Conference for High Performance Computing, Networking, Storage and Analysis (SC 2008), pp. 42–54, Austin, TX (2008)
18. Shan, H., Shalf, J.: Using IOR to analyze the I/O performance for HPC platforms. In: Proceedings of the Cray User Group Meeting (CUG 2007), pp. 1–15, Washington, DC (2007)
19. Shipman, G., Dillow, D., Fuller, D., Gunasekaran, R., Hill, J., Kim, Y., Oral, S., Reitz, D., Simmons, J., Wang, F.: A next-generation parallel file system environment for the OLCF. In: Proceedings of the Cray User Group Conference (CUG 2012), pp. 1–12, Stuttgart, Germany (2012)

20. Uselton, A., Howison, M., Wright, N.J., Skinner, D., Keen, N., Shalf, J., Karavanic, K.L., Oliker, L.: Parallel I/O performance: from events to ensembles. In: Proceedings of the 24th IEEE International Parallel & Distributed Processing Symposium(IPDPS 2010), pp. 1–11, Atlanta, GA (2010)
21. Xie, B., Chase, J., Dillow, D., Drokin, O., Klasky, S., Oral, S., Podhorszki, N.: Characterizing output bottlenecks in a supercomputer. In: Proceedings of the ACM/IEEE International Conference for High Performance Computing, Networking, Storage and Analysis (SC 2012), pp. 1–11, Salt Lake City, UT (2012)
22. Xie, B., Huang, Y., Chase, J.S., Choi, J.Y., Klasky, S., Lofstead, J., Oral, S.: Predicting output performance of a petascale supercomputer. In: Proceedings of the 26th International Symposium on High-Performance Parallel and Distributed Computing (HPDC 2017), pp. 1–12, Washington D.C. (2017)

Second International Workshop on OpenPOWER for HPC (IWOPH'17)

International Workshop on OpenPOWER for HPC 2017

Oscar Hernandez[1], M. Graham Lopez[1], Dirk Pleiter[2], and Jack Wells[1]

[1] Oak Ridge National Laboratory, Oak Ridge, TN 37831, USA
{oscar, lopezmg, wellsjc}@ornl.gov
[2] Forschungszentrum Jülich, JSC, 52425 Jülich, Germany
d.pleiter@fz-juelich.de

Abstract. The second edition of the International Workshop on OpenPOWER for HPC (IWOPH17) continued to establish itself as a forum for exchanging experience using technologies and architectures, which emerged from this new ecosystem. The goal was to bring together experts for applications and the different technologies as well as data centre professionals.

Keywords: OpenPOWER · High-performance computing · Big data · GPU acceleration · Power measurement · Containers · Programming tools

Four years have passed since the OpenPOWER Foundation was established as a non-profit consortium to give its members the ability to innovate on software and hardware solutions based on the POWER processor architecture. Meanwhile, various OpenPOWER solutions targeting scientific computing and big data workloads are proliferating. The goal of this workshop was to provide a venue for a broader community for sharing experience, to further understand OpenPOWER technologies, and to discuss how they can be harnessed to address science and engineering challenges.

The workshop took place on 22 June, 2017 co-loctated with the ISC conference in Frankfurt, Germany. After a welcome from the workshop organizers, a keynote address was offered by Mr. Christoph Hagleitner. Contributed talks followed for the majority of the day, and an hour long panel session closed the workshop with discussion between experts on the Minsky system and the workshop attendees. Contributed papers were chosen from a single-blind review process performed by reviewers from academia, industry, and research laboratories. Overall, nine contributions were submitted, and eight were selected for inclusion in the following workshop proceedings.

With IBM S822LC servers (also known as "Minsky") becoming available, clusters can be realised, which are first incarnations along a new HPC roadmap that soon will result in pre-exascale systems. An outstanding feature is the tight integration of IBM POWER processors and NVIDIA GPUs using the new NVLink technology. Several papers presented during this workshop provided an overview on experience using clusters of Minsky servers for a broader range of applications. V.G. Vergara Larrea et al. [7] reported on the acceptance of the Summitdev cluster and presented early results obtained from running CORAL benchmarks, different mini-applications and Oak Ridge Leadership Computing Facility (OLCF) applications. Hautreux et al. [2] explored the new architecture for a portfolio of applications that are representative for the French scientific community. A. Herten et al. [3] presented an in-depth analysis for a specific application, namely a particle-in-cell code.

The new Minsky server architecture is not only relevant for HPC applications, but also for applications from the area of big data with its increasing interest in exploiting accelerators. J. Peltenburg et al. [5] investigated the question whether software stacks running on top of a Java Virtual Machine can exploit the new capabilities for moving data between processor and accelerator.

Given the complexity of the heterogeneous Minsky node architecture and its extreme level of parallelism, programming tools are critical for supporting developers in parallelizing their applications and improving on productivity. M. Arenaz et al. [1] presented the roadmap of Parallware tools, which allow for identification of parallel design patterns and to aid parallization using the OpenMP or OpenACC programming model.

Recently, containers started to receive increasing attention for providing a portable environment, which is, e.g., of interest for complex software stacks. A. Kuity et al. [4] presented a container-based HPC ecosystem using Open-POWER and explored possible performance impacts.

With power consumption becoming more and more the limiting factor for pushing performance of future systems to higher levels, tools for managing and measuring power are becoming increasingly relevant. T. Rosedahl et al. [6] provided an update on design and implementation of the necessary measurement and management features found in OpenPOWER systems.

Within an overall view, the contributions reflect further adoption of Open-POWER technologies for addressing challenges in science and engineering. A concluding discussion session confirmed the need for providing opportunities for sharing experience and to contribute to building a user community for Open-POWER technologies both in the areas of HPC and big data.

References

1. Arenaz, M., Hernandez, O., Pleiter, D.: The technological roadmap of parallware and its alignment with the OpenPOWER ecosystem. In: Kunkel, J.M., et al. (eds.) ISC High Performance Workshops 2017. LNCS, vol. 10524, pp. 237–253. Springer International Publishing, Cham (2017)
2. Hautreux, G., et al.: Pre-exascale architectures: OpenPOWER performance and usability assessment for the French scientific community. In: Kunkel, J.M., et al. (eds.) ISC High Performance Workshops 2017. LNCS, vol. 10524, pp. 309–324. Springer International Publishing, Cham (2017)
3. Herten, A., Brömmel, D., Pleiter, D.: GPU-accelerated particle-in-cell code on Minsky. In: Kunkel, J.M., et al. (eds.) ISC High Performance Workshops 2017. LNCS, vol. 10524, pp. 205–219. Springer International Publishing, Cham (2017)
4. Kuity, A., Peddoju, S.K.: Performance evaluation of container-based high performance computing ecosystem using OpenPOWER. In: Kunkel, J.M., et al. (eds.) ISC High Performance Workshops 2017. LNCS, vol. 10524, pp. 290–308. Springer International Publishing, Cham (2017)

5. Peltenburg, J., Hesam, A., Al-Ars, Z.: Pushing Big Data into accelerators: can the JVM saturate our hardware? In: Kunkel, J.M., et al. (eds.) ISC High Performance Workshops 2017. LNCS, vol. 10524, pp. 220–236. Springer International Publishing, Cham (2017)
6. Rosedahl, T., Broyles, M., Lefurgy, C., Christensen, B., Feng, W.: Power/performance controlling techniques in openpower. In: Kunkel, J.M., et al. (eds.) ISC High Performance Workshops 2017. LNCS, vol. 10524, pp. 275–289. Springer International Publishing, Cham (2017)
7. Vergara Larrea, V.G., Joubert, W., Berrill, M., Boehm, S., Tharrington, A., Elwasif, W.R., Maxwell, D.: Experiences evaluating functionality and performance of IBM Power8+ systems. In: Kunkel, J.M., et al. (eds.) ISC High Performance Workshops 2017. LNCS, vol. 10524, pp. 254–274. Springer International Publishing, Cham (2017)

GPU-Accelerated Particle-in-Cell Code on Minsky

Andreas Herten(✉), Dirk Brömmel, and Dirk Pleiter

Forschungszentrum Jülich, JSC, 52425 Jülich, Germany
{a.herten,d.broemmel,d.pleiter}@fz-juelich.de

Abstract. Particle-in-cell (PIC) methods are widely used on today's supercomputers. In this paper we consider JuSPIC, an application for which good scaling properties could be demonstrated on a 6PFlop/s BlueGene/Q system. We report on efforts to port this application to emerging supercomputing architectures based on IBM POWER processors and NVIDIA graphics processing units.

Keywords: POWER8 · GPU acceleration · Performance analysis · Minsky · OpenPOWER · NVIDIA Tesla P100

1 Introduction

Numerical methods are key for investigating laser-plasma interactions due to the non-linear nature of the problem and the non-trivial geometries implied in the problem. Most commonly used is the particle-in-cell (PIC) method for simulating the motion of charged and neutral plasma particles. PIC codes solve Maxwell's equations on a grid using currents and charge densities calculated by weighting discrete particles onto the grid. In each update step, position and momentum of each particle are updated based on forces acting on them, which are obtained from self-consistently calculated fields. The development and use of this methods goes back into the 1950-60s [13].

Due to its intrinsic high level of parallelism, PIC applications simulating millions of particles are good candidates for massively-parallel computer architectures. In this contribution we focus on a special type of such architectures, which are based on IBM POWER processors and graphics processing units (GPU) from NVIDIA. Such solutions have become available only recently and the ecosystem for these is still emerging. In this paper we will explore the performance for JuSPIC, a PIC code developed at Jülich Supercomputing Centre, on IBM S822LC servers (also known as "Minsky"), which features novel tight integration of processor and GPU based on the new NVLink technology.
This paper makes the following contributions:

1. A port of JuSPIC to the Minsky platform and report of experiences for different porting strategies.

J.M. Kunkel et al. (Eds.): ISC High Performance Workshops 2017, LNCS 10524, pp. 205–219, 2017.
https://doi.org/10.1007/978-3-319-67630-2_17

2. Analysis of the performance as a function of different hardware settings employing a semi-empirical performance modelling approach.
3. Report on experience in optimisation for this new platform.

The paper is organised as follows: After the introductory Sect. 2 we introduce the architecture of the compute platform used in this paper in Sect. 3. We report in Sect. 4 on porting JuSPIC to GPUs, before presenting performance results in Sect. 5. After providing an overview on related work in Sect. 6 we summarise our results and present our conclusions in Sect. 7.

2 JuSPIC

JuSPIC [1,8], the Jülich Scalable Particle-in-Cell (PIC) code is used to simulate particles in electromagnetic fields. Like other PIC codes, it can be used as a numerical tool in the field of intense laser-plasma interaction, e.g. to simulate the generation of energetic electrons and ions with help of the radiation field of a laser to study approaches for table-top particle accelerators. The code is based on H. Ruhl's Plasma Simulation Code (PSC) [7] and further developed at the Jülich Supercomputing Centre (JSC) mainly for testing new HPC architectures and programming models. But it has also been used to support experimental investigations of relativistic, highly non-linear laser-plasma interaction acting as Terahertz light-source [12].

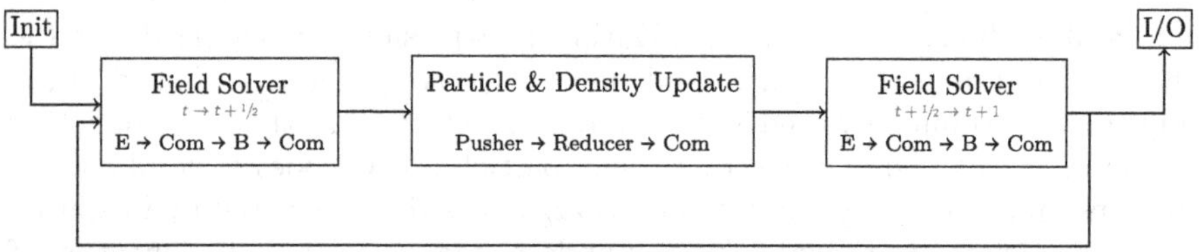

Fig. 1. Core steps of JuSPIC. After initializing (*Init*), the E and B fields are computed and communicated for a half-time step (*Field Solver*). Following this, the particle and density information is updated. The *Pusher* uses information from the grid to update particle information, the *Reducer* again takes this information to update the grid. A communication step ensues, before this iterations concludes with another invocation of the Field Solver. The algorithm is started again at the first Field Solver. Data can be written/output after one chain (*I/O*).

The interaction between fields and plasma is described by the relativistic Vlasov equation and Maxwell's equations. JuSPIC uses a regular mesh for the Maxwell fields and particle charge and current densities that are then integrated using the Finite-Difference-Time-Domain (FDTD) scheme. Plasma particles are modelled via distribution functions of quasi-particles with continuous coordinates within the mesh. Finite element approximations of the distribution functions are then used to integrate the Vlasov equation along the particle trajectories [6,15].

Omitting details about PIC codes in general, let us note that due to the required high particle numbers, the coupled system of Vlasov and Maxwell equations requires two very time-consuming steps: First, the particle update, computing new particle positions and velocities that requires the interpolation of the electromagnetic fields from their mesh coordinates to the position of the quasi-particles. We denote this part the *pusher*; it is the main focus of our GPU acceleration. The second step is the reduction of the continuous charge and particle densities of each quasi-particle onto the mesh (the *reducer*). This sparse reduction poses a special challenge since it happens irregularly on very large fields and is a non-local operation.

JuSPIC is written in modern Fortran and parallelised with MPI and OpenMP. The basic operation of the algorithm is outlined in Fig. 1. It is capable of scaling to the full JUQUEEN system, a 28-rack IBM BlueGene/Q using 1.8M hardware threads and listed in the High-Q Club [2]. JuSPIC is Open Source [3].

3 Compute Platform

The performance results shown in this paper have been obtained in large parts on **JURON**, a cluster based on IBM S822LC servers. Each server comprises 2 IBM POWER8 processors with 2 NVIDIA P100 GPUs each. One processor and 2 GPUs are interconnected in a ring topology using NVLink.

In this server, 4 out of 8 DMI channels per processor are used for attaching Centaur memory chips to which the DDR4 memory is attached. The GPUs use a new high-bandwidth memory technology called HBM2, which allows for significantly higher memory bandwidth but limited memory capacity. Due to the new NVLink connections, the bi-section bandwidth for data transport between processor and GPUs is similar to the processor-memory bandwidth.

Key hardware performance numbers are summarised in Table 1.
Additionally, two x86 systems are referenced in parts of this paper:

JUHYDRA. A testing system with 2 Intel Xeon E5-2650 CPUs (2 GHz) and 2 NVIDIA Tesla K20Xm and K40m GPUs, each, attached via PCIe.

JURECA. Jülich's large multi-purpose supercomputer with nodes with 2 Intel Xeon E5-2680 CPUs (2.5 GHz) and 2 PCIe-attached NVIDIA Tesla K80 GPUs (appearing as 2 GPU devices, each).

4 Acceleration for GPUs

For JuSPIC, a hybrid approach in acceleration for GPUs has been chosen. Parts of the code have been ported employing the OpenACC programming model, parts use CUDA Fortran.

Table 1. Selected (nominal) hardware parameters for the IBM S822LC servers.

IBM POWER8 processor	
Number of processors	2
Default clock frequency	3491 MHz
Total number of cores	20
Aggregate throughput of floating-point operations (DP)	559 GFlop/s
Aggregate memory read bandwidth	77 GByte/s
Aggregate memory write bandwidth	154 GByte/s
Aggregate memory capacity	256 GByte
NVIDIA P100 GPU	
Number of GPUs	4
Default clock frequency	1328 MHz
Total number of SMs	224
Aggregate throughput of floating-point operations (DP)	19038 GFlop/s
Aggregate memory bandwidth	2880 GByte/s
Aggregate memory capacity	128 GByte
Aggregate CPU-GPU bandwidth	160 GByte/s

4.1 OpenACC

In OpenACC, code to be accelerated is annotated with statements which are interpreted by a capable compiler to create programs for GPUs or other many-core systems. Since these compiler directives are usually in the form of comments in the code, portability across many different systems is achieved. Depending on the capabilities of the compiler, different accelerator architectures can be targeted from the same code base. For JuSPIC, the PGI compiler (version 16.10) is used. It features both support for OpenACC and CUDA Fortran.

OpenACC is used in JuSPIC to move data between the host and the device. Data regions are created to move data, partly asynchronously, to device or host memory depending on where the next part of the program operates. As an example, the first region is created by `!$acc enter data async copyin(e,b,ji)` which creates a copy of the matrices `e`, `b`, and `ji` on the GPU asynchronously. Data is transferred back, and also updated as-needed in subsequent steps of the algorithm. In the absence of any acceleration device, the compiler produces a version of the program in which the data regions are omitted.

OpenACC is used furthermore to port the time propagation of the electric and magnetic fields to the GPU. For each field, a three-fold nested loop updates three directions in space for different indexes. The `kernels` directive is used, giving the compiler the most freedom to accelerate the scope of the multiplication: `!$acc kernels loop collapse(3) present(e,b)`. The three loops are merged into a loop of one level by the `collapse` clause; the electro-magnetic fields are already on the device, since they have been copied asynchronously beforehand.

4.2 CUDA Fortran

By far the most compute-intensive part of JuSPIC is the update of particle velocities and momenta in the pusher. In an initial attempt, this part was also enabled for the GPU with OpenACC. Unfortunately, the structure of the code was yet to be supported by the compiler. Many structured data types (e.g. `particles(i)%x(0)`), operations on whole fields at once (`b=a*2`, where `a` and `b` are both fields), as well as the amount of operations on the data prevented efficient code generation by the compiler. The algorithm needed to be adapted vastly to make it more *recognisable* for the compiler. With those changes, the initially non-compiling OpenACC pusher did compile, but ran very slow. Only a version of the algorithm, which had each operation on a whole field replaced by operations on the individual elements of the field ran reasonably well. We decided to rather return to the original pusher algorithm and use CUDA Fortran to port it to the GPU. [14]

CUDA Fortran is a Fortran interface to NVIDIA's CUDA C/C++ programming model. It is developed by PGI and available in their Fortran compilers. It is modelled closely alongside CUDA C/C++ and additionally implements features of the Fortran programming language, like operations on whole fields.

Using CUDA Fortran, the pusher kernel is ported to the GPU. The original, serial code is taken, the `do` loop over the particles removed, and replaced with `threadIdx %x`-based indexing in typical CUDA . Compatibility to systems without GPUs or CUDA Fortran is ensured by wrapping the specialised GPU parts with pre-processor macros. This way, either the original pusher loop is called in the absence of CUDA Fortran, or the GPU kernel is called with `call gpupusher<<<dim3(nBlocks, 1, 1), dim3(nThreads, 1, 1)>>>`

Writing the pusher kernel in CUDA Fortran enables the evaluation of different strategies of handling the data of the particles. We study four cases:

1. All particles are stored in a single field, one particle after another, the field is copied to and from the GPU with CUDA Fortran (*Initial*).
2. As above, but data is copied using OpenACC `copy` statements (*Experiment One (Exp 1)*).
3. As above, data is copied with OpenACC statements, from pinned (zero-copy) host memory (*Experiment Two (Exp 2)*).
4. Instead of one field holding all data from all particles, spatial and momentum components for all particles are stored in separate fields (six fields in total); data is copied with CUDA Fortran statements (*Structure-of-Array Approach (SoA)*).

The results of the four cases are summarised in Table 2, averaged per invocation of the GPU pusher. Shown is JURON (with a P100 GPU) and, as a comparison, JUHYDRA (using a K40 GPU). In the table, *Kernel* denotes the

Table 2. Runtimes of the particle pusher of JuSPIC on the GPU for different methods of data handling. **Legend:** *Allocate* – Allocate host-side memory region; *LL2F* – Convert linked list data structure to field; *H2D* – Transfer data from host to device; *D2H* – Transfer data from device to host; *F2LL* – Copy data from field to linked list data structure.

in μs	$\sum$	Allocate	LL2F	H2D	Kernel	D2H	Others	F2LL
				JURON				
Initial	8039.71	–	567.27	81.86	83.71	61.70	350.19	6884.87
Exp 1	10434.51	–	353.08	80.39	81.82	91.48	379.87	9440.10
Exp 2	9695.39	563.50	526.69	79.19	82.57	72.38	107.87	7972.61
SoA	7810.95	0.94	843.69	65.74	76.57	53.03	376.25	6386.24
				JUHYDRA				
Initial	4955.59	–	907.63	267.11	229.27	207.62	735.92	2600.14
Exp 1	4687.25	–	763.99	231.58	228.51	197.59	804.41	2455.00
Exp 2	5328.37	576.97	1026.94	223.56	229.65	192.17	23.17	2651.33
SoA	4879.61	1.05	785.84	204.14	207.58	173.40	826.55	2673.97

runtime of the GPU pusher kernel itself. *H2D* and *D2H* shows the time spent for copying data to and from the GPU, respectively. *Others* incorporates the time the GPU is not processing or copying data – the device usually waits for instructions or synchronises. *Allocate* refers to the time needed to allocate a memory region on the host side (for pinned memory in case of *Exp 2* and for the individual SoA fields in case of *SoA*). *LL2F* and *F2LL* are pre-processing steps: The format in which JuSPIC stores particles is a linked list, with each particle including a pointer to the next. To enable coalesced loads on the GPU, data is copied from a linked list to a field before GPU kernel invocation and from a field back to a linked list after completion – *LL2F* and *F2LL*, respectively. The relatively high runtimes of these parts are analysed and discussed in Sect. 4.3.

Looking at each of the architectures, the runtimes of data copies and kernels in the SoA approach is in all cases the fastest. The data layout is not only beneficial for efficient execution but also for data movements. In case of preparing the data in the LL2F step, SoA is the slowest. The explicit filling of two three-vectors (position, momentum) to individual and distinct memory locations from one packed source particle seems to take more time then the simple copy from one memory position to another. For the post-processing F2LL step, the case appears to be inverted (see also Sect. 4.3). For Exp 2, where pinned memory is used, the overhead in form of waiting for data is the smallest. In this case, the CUDA runtime can omit safety measures and directly access the data. Unfortunately, the benefit in time is diminished by the overhead of allocating the pinned memory.

Comparing the two GPU (and also system) architectures shows that the P100 has, in nearly all cases, the lesser runtime (with F2LL being an important deviation, see Sect. 4.3). About a factor of 3 in performance gain can be obtained compared to using a K40m GPU.

Further potential optimization can be integrated combining the distinct benefits of the individual approaches. In the current implementation of Exp 2, pinned memory is allocated once before the pusher loop and deallocated afterwards. Moving the data region one level up would enable a more data-economical approach: Pinned memory can be allocated once at the beginning of the algorithm and only reallocated if the number of particles changes during the run of the algorithm. This is a strategy already employed by the SoA version. In the SoA version, though, pinned memory has not yet been tested. Since pinned memory leads to less overhead during the GPU pusher runtime, this could be a very rich modification.

In the current state of the algorithm, data transfers to and from the device take a significant fraction of time on the GPU. Our hope is that once the next part of the algorithm, the *reducer*, is ported to the GPU as well, most of the data transfers can be saved, since the majority of the data would stay on the GPU for different iterations. This is the case as well for the changes in data layout (linked list, fields). The Unified Memory feature of CUDA, which uses efficient page faults in CUDA 8.0 and on Pascal GPUs, promises to be a productive technique to reduce data migrations to a minimum.

4.3 Investigation of Slow Data Layout Conversion

Striking in the numbers of Table 2 are the times taken for copying data from fields to linked lists, F2LL. The runtimes of 6ms to 9ms for each invocation of the pusher are about 2.5× higher than on a x86 system.

In a benchmark study, we investigate the reason for this. We create linked lists for different numbers of particles, fill them, and destroy them again. We study different architectures: the two Intel-based architectures of JURECA and JUHYDRA and the POWER8NVL system of JURON. Additionally, different compilers are tested: the PGI Fortran compiler with and without an MPI wrapper[1]; the Fortran compiler from the GNU Compiler Collection (`gfortran`, *GCC*) with and without MPI; and the XL Fortran compiler, *XLF*, if available. The part of the benchmark code which fills the linked list – `add_one_to_list` – is implemented the following way:

```
allocate(list%tail%next)
nullify(list%tail%next%next)
list%tail%next%particle = particle
list%tail => list%tail%next
```

Using this scheme, each particle is added to the list iteratively.

Figure 2 displays the time spent for adding one particle to a linked list for different total list sizes and different compiler and system configurations. Systematically, on each system, GCC-compiled benchmarks take the least time for

[1] The compiler ships with its own compiled OpenMPI version.

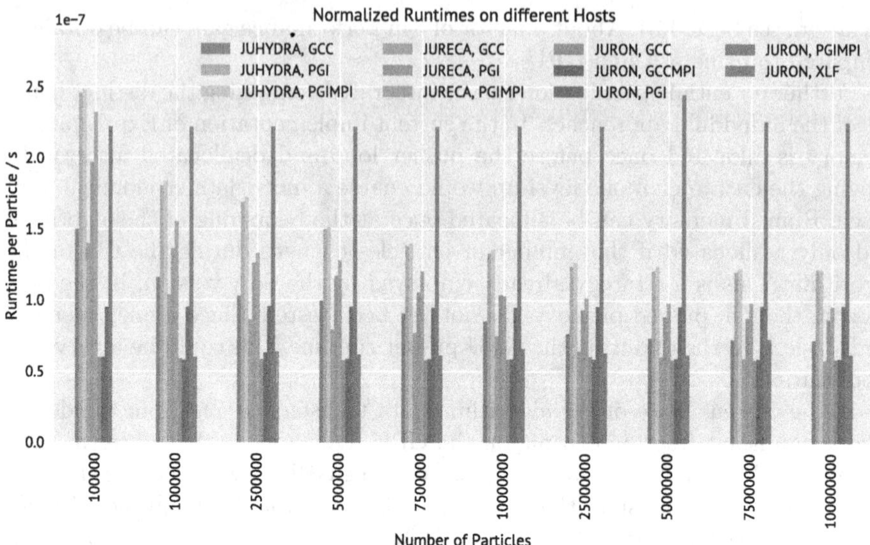

Fig. 2. Runtimes for adding a particle to a linked list vs. total number of added particles to the list for different compilers. Note: The data point of XLF for 100 000 particles is missing as the program reported no meaningful time in this case.

the operation. The PGI case is always 30% to 60% slower, compared to the respective runtime of a GCC-compiled program. On JURON, the XLF compiler produces code which is about as fast as the GCC version. The time spent for adding one particle to the list decreases with growing number of total particles for most of the versions tested on x86 – in these cases, there seems to be a undetermined overhead present which becomes more and more negligible[2].

The most important feature of the plot is the runtime of benchmarks compiled with MPI and underlying PGI compiler on JURON. The *PGIMPI* case is consistently at least 2× slower then the comparable PGI version. This is remarkable, since in both versions the same `pgfortran` compiler is used with identical compiler flags and resulting object code – just with an additional MPI wrapper in one case.

Using PAPI [17,18], we measure the number of instructions completed in the case of destroying a list in the benchmark. We choose destruction of a list over creation because this part of the code involves even fewer overhead. The performance counter measured with PAPI is `PAPI_TOT_INS`, which maps on JURON to `PM_INST_CMPL` and on JUHYDRA to `INSTRUCTION_RETIRED`. Table 3 summarises the measurements for different compilers. PGIMPI* in this case is a custom OpenMPI 2.0 version which is explicitly compiled for the benchmark test case. JuSPIC has yet to be run with this custom MPI version, as it is not officially

[2] Measurements show that the number of completed instructions is linear with the number of particles, so the overhead seems to come from the timing operation.

Table 3. Number of instructions of and time spent for clearing a linked list. The values are for a list of 10 million elements, but shown normalised per particle (pP). Time per particle is rounded to the nearest integer.

System	JURON					JUHYDRA		
Compiler	GCC	GCCMPI	PGI	PGIMPI	PGIMPI*	XLF	PGI	PGIMPI
Time pP/ns	36	37	46	154	–	41	32	32
Instructions pP	121	121	243	462	243	121	210	210

supported by the PGI compiler version. The version of GCC is 5.4.0, PGI is of version 16.10 on JURON and 16.3 on JUHYDRA. On JURON, GCCMPI uses OpenMPI 2.0.2 and PGIMPI uses OpenMPI 1.10.2 – the version shipped with the PGI compiler. The XLF version is 16.1.0. The MPI version used together with PGI on JUHYDRA is OpenMPI 1.8.1.

The results of runtimes already seen in Fig. 2 correlate with the number of completed instructions. The PGI compiler produces code which is slightly slower compared to the GCC version; in terms of instructions about twice as many are completed. The PGIMPI case doubles the number of instructions of the MPI-less PGI version further. At the same time, the number of instructions per cycle is reduced from about 2 to about 0.8.

The source code for creating and destroying linked lists is very simple. The only other operation apart from changing pointers is *allocation* and *deallocation*, respectively, see the code snippet at the beginning of Sect. 4.3. We suspect that the reason for the long runtimes lies in this allocation and deallocation.

When MPI is loaded on top PGI, a number of different libraries are linked additionally compared to the bare PGI case. We reckon that one of the libraries loaded replaces the memory allocation call with a particularly slow one in the JURON case. We test this assumption by using the linker's environment variable `LD_PRELOAD` to force loading of a specific `malloc` call when invoking JuSPIC– we use `LD_PRELOAD=/lib64/libc.so.6`. This indeed removes the instruction overhead compared to the bare PGI case entirely.

A second test replaces the PGI-shipped OpenMPI version with our own custom-compiled OpenMPI, PGIMPI*. Also in this case, the overhead is reduced to zero. The overhead hence seems to be tightly connected to the specific MPI version shipped with the PGI compiler on the POWER system[3].

While the strategies employed during investigation (`LD_PRELOAD`, custom OpenMPI) can be easily applied to the benchmark case, further in-detail studies are needed for the whole of JuSPIC to judge all ramifications and side-effects.

For the time being, we consider time spent for converting between linked lists and fields in the F2LL and LL2F regions an overhead, which is anomalously high in the system/compiler configuration at hand. The initial mitigation strategy in the future will be to test our custom OpenMPI version thoroughly with JuSPIC; a bug report with the vendor of the compiler has been filed. In a mid-range time

[3] True for both PGI 16.10 and PGI 17.1.

frame we hope to retire the linked list implementation of particles in JuSPIC in favour of a field approach globally, to better match the requirements of modern many-core architectures. Linked lists were chosen in the original design of JuSPIC because they were the fastest of the tested options to perform the sparse global reduction after the particle pusher in a multi-threaded approach [8].

5 Performance Modelling

To compare different GPU architectures and understand the behaviour of JuSPIC, we study the code in the scope of a simple performance model.

5.1 Determination of Effective Bandwidth

Our model incorporates the exchanged information of the kernel for a given amount of processed particles. It is a lower limit of the achieved bandwidth of the program. The model is parameterised by

$$t(N_{\text{part}}) = \alpha + I(N_{\text{part}})/\beta \ , \tag{1}$$

where α and β are fit parameters and I is the exchanged information, resulting in a kernel runtime of t. We call β the *effective bandwidth*. The tested version of the pusher kernel reads 572 Byte and stores 40 Byte per particle.

Figure 3 shows results of the performance model in Eq. 1 for different numbers of particles, leading to different amounts of exchanged information. Four different

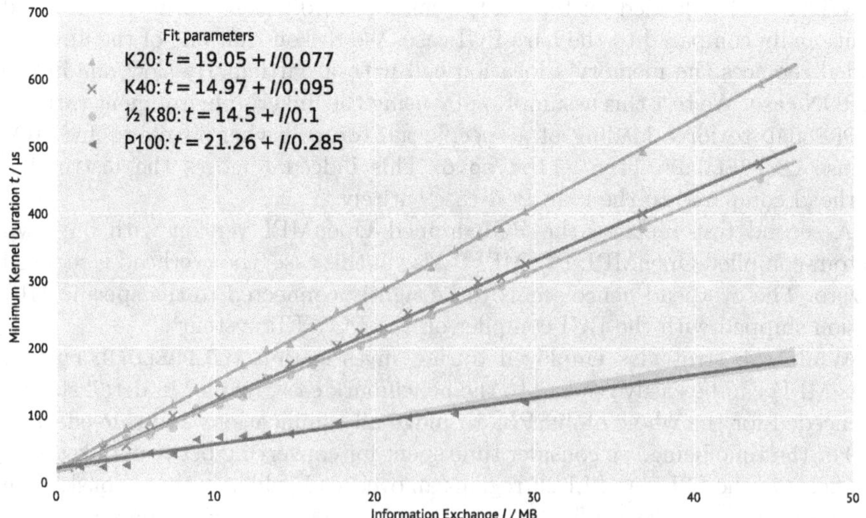

Fig. 3. GPU kernel duration as a function of exchanged information for four different GPUs: K20, K40, 1/2 K80, and P100. Shown in the legend are fit parameters to the performance model.

NVIDIA GPUs are studied: Tesla K20 and K40 devices (both on JUHYDRA), one part of a Tesla K80 GPU (1/2 K80; on JURECA), and the Pascal P100 on JURON. In all cases, the GPU boost feature, which automatically increases the graphics clock rate of the devices, has been disabled and the clock fixed to its default size.

From the linear regressions, which are superimposed in Fig. 3, the effective bandwidths as of the performance model can be deduced:

K20: 77 GB/s K40: 95 GB/s 1/2K80: 100 GB/s P100: 285 GB/s

The utilised bandwidth is higher for the K80 (42%) than for the K40 (33%), since the maximum available bandwidth is lower for the K80 (240 GB/s) than for the K40 (288 GB/s). The efficiency of JuSPIC on this device is higher. The same bandwidth utilization of the K80 is achieved for the P100 device: About 40% of the available 720 GB/s bandwidth is used.[4] The absolute value of utilised bandwidth is higher (285 GB/s), caused by the new Pascal architecture features: The higher bandwidth to the HBM2 memory offers more throughput of data, while the greater number of multiprocessors leads to more computations per time and more threads in flight. The occupancy of the GPU device is kept constant. The pusher kernel can be expected to be limited by memory access latencies. A larger number of active blocks could help hiding such latencies. However, such an increase of device-side parallelism is not possible as the large number of registers used by the kernel causes the number of available registers to become exhausted.

5.2 Clock Rates

Another parameter of GPU architectures are the clock rates with which the GPU operates. The P100 device on JURON can operate with graphics clocks between 544 MHz and 1480 MHz (the memory clock is fixed at 715 MHz); the K40 device operates between 666 MHz and 875 MHz at a memory frequency of 3004 MHz; the K80 can run with 562 MHz to 875 MHz at a slightly lower memory frequency, compared to the K40, of 2505 MHz.

Building upon the performance model of Eq. 1 the following relation can be formulated to model the effect of different GPU clock rates ($\mathcal{C}$) on effective bandwidths (β):

$$\beta(\mathcal{C}) = \gamma + \delta\mathcal{C} \tag{2}$$

As before, γ and δ are fit parameters.

To obtain δ and γ for one device, each effective bandwidth β for a possible clock rate is obtained per Eq. 1 – in each case the runtime of the GPU pusher kernel is measured for different amounts of exchanged information (*number of*

[4] Although the value of 720 GB/s is the design value of the P100, it might be different from a practical achievable bandwidth. Indeed, we measure a bandwidth of about 520 GB/s for the four mini-benchmarks of the STREAM benchmark. Using this as a reference value, the pusher kernel manages to use slightly more than 50% of this empirically determined bandwidth limit.

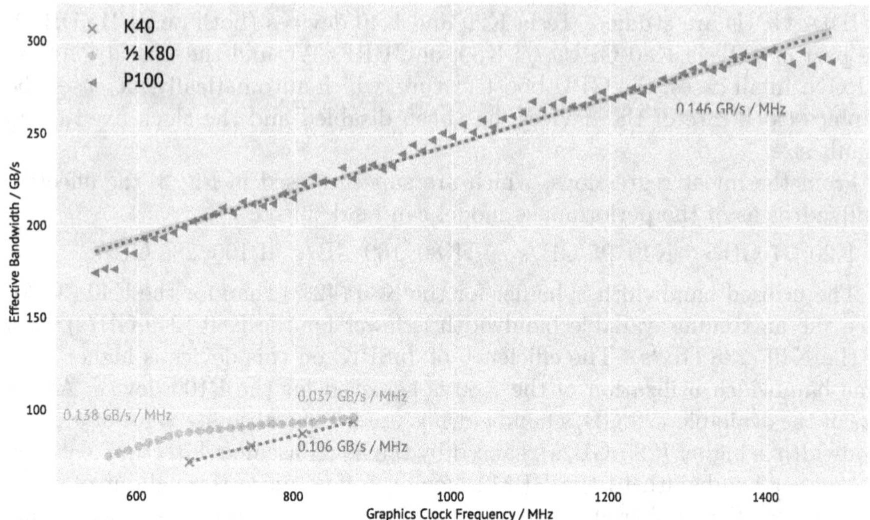

Fig. 4. Effective bandwidths from the performance model (see Eq. 1) for different graphics clock frequency. Shown are three GPU devices: K40, 1/2 K80, and P100. Superimposed are δ values of linear fits to the respective measurements using Eq. 2.

particles), and the slope of the linear fit noted. The resulting measurements are shown in Fig. 4 for the three GPUs.

The P100 covers a large range of possible clock rates, with the maximal values leading to bandwidths close to 300 GB/s. But also for frequencies below 875 MHz on which the K40 and K80 can operate on as well, the P100 surpasses the older devices vastly. As already determined in Sect. 5.1, the pusher benefits greatly from the increased memory bandwidth, and does so independently from the clock rate. Additionally, the Pascal architecture increases the number of multiprocessors over the previous Kepler systems; JuSPIC is capable of exploiting this as well. In total, the dependence of the bandwidth on the graphics clock is $\delta = 0.146\,(\text{GB/s})/(\text{MHz})$

The chips on K40 and on K80 are very similar, which can be seen in the values for the largest clock frequencies – they are close to identical. The performance is different for smaller clock rates: The bandwidth is reduced less for K80 devices. The chip seems to operate more efficiently. A distinct feature is visible for the K80: The distribution has two parts. For lower clock rates the effective bandwidth increases faster (0.138 (GB/s)/(MHz)) than for higher clock rates (0.037 (GB/s)/(MHz)). The kink in the curve marks the position where nearly the highest computing performance is reached – for further increase in clock rate only little performance is gained. The model parameter for the K40 is 0.106 (GB/s)/(MHz).

Judging from the δ parameters, it can be seen that the P100 device not only has the absolute best performance but also the largest increase in effective bandwidth with each step in clock frequency.

6 Related Work

Various PIC codes have been ported to GPU. The PSC code, on which JuSPIC is based, was later reimplemented in C and ported to GPUs [11]. More specifically, the code has been ported to the Titan supercomputer at Oak Ridge National Lab, a Cray XK7 system comprising just over 18 000 nodes with 1 GPU each. The same system was used to demonstrate extreme scalability of the PIConGPU, a PIC code specifically developed for GPU acceleration [9]. While PSC and PIConGPU are full production codes, other efforts for GPU porting have been performed using proof-of-concept codes [10,16,19].

As the Minksy platform is relatively new, not much work has been published exploring the performance of scientific applications on this platform. Various publications investigated the performance using the precursor platform where NVDIA K40 or K80 GPUs where attached to POWER8 processors via a PCIe GEN3 link. This included, e.g., evaluation of applications based on the Finite-Difference Time-Domain (FDTD) method [4], based on the Density Function Theory (DFT) method [5], or molecular dynamics simulations [20].

7 Summary and Conclusions

In this paper, we reported on our progress of accelerating the plasma physics PIC code JuSPIC with GPU devices.

A heterogeneous approach of employed programming models is chosen. We use OpenACC for data movement and simple kernels operating on three-dimensional fields. OpenACC offers the ability of creating portable and *backwards*-compatible code with only few annotating compiler directives.

For the most compute-intensive routine, the particle pusher, we use CUDA Fortran since earlier versions of PGI's OpenACC compiler were not able to generate efficient code for the original data structures. Compatibility to systems without GPUs is achieved by guarding the CUDA Fortran code with pre-processor directives. For the CUDA Fortran kernel, we evaluate different data layouts. The Structure-of-Array approach is fastest, providing best performance when moving data between host and device and smallest kernel runtime. In the future we want to implement pinned host data for this case, learning from the benefits of *Experiment 2*.

In the process of analysing the individual stages of the CUDA Fortran part we notice unexpected high runtimes for pre- and post-processing steps. In these steps the linked list of particles is copied to and from simple Fortran fields (to be processed on the GPU). Using a boiled-down benchmark we investigate this peculiarity and determine the performance issue to be a `malloc` call which is issued by the OpenMPI version shipped with the POWER version of the

PGI compiler. Although we find workarounds, a possible mitigation is yet to be applied to JuSPIC.

Moving on, we study the performance of the kernel of the pusher with different number of particles in the scope of a simple information exchange model. Four different GPU devices are investigated with the P100 of JURON providing by far the best performance. The GPU provides an effective bandwidth of 285 GB/s with its default clock setting. Subsequently, the performance model is adapted to incorporate different GPU clock frequencies. The P100 provides the most efficient scaling also in this case. An interesting additional investigation objective for the future is the incorporation of energy measurements – which device takes the least energy to come to a solution?

JuSPIC is a good fit for the new Pascal GPU architecture, benefiting well from the increased memory bandwidth. Currently, only the part of the pusher is ported to the GPU. We expect the performance gain from the GPU-accelerated version to be significant, once also the reducer is ported to the GPU. The data movements from and to the devices can be omitted in this case, reducing the overhead. Once the single-node version is accelerated, a next step will be Multi-GPU usage together with MPI. Currently, the OpenMP statements available in JuSPIC are ignored for the GPU version, to solely focus on this part of the acceleration and prevent race conditions. Once the GPU version is stable, we should ensure leveraging all possibilities of potential parallelism and enable OpenMP again.

Not only the GPU version of JuSPIC is currently developed, the code itself is progressing further. Different data layouts are being investigated to possibly remove storing particle data in linked lists, simplifying coalesced data handling. Effective load-balancing using space-filling curves is also currently studied.

Acknowledgements. This work has been carried out in the context of the *POWER Acceleration and Design Center*, a joined project between IBM, Forschungszentrum Jülich and NVIDIA, as well as the *NVIDIA Application Lab at Jülich*, a joined project between Forschungszentrum Jülich and NVIDIA. We acknowledge the support from Jiri Kraus (NVIDIA) and various helpful discussions with him. Research leading to these results has (in parts) been carried out on the Human Brain Project PCP Pilot Systems at the Juelich Supercomputing Centre, which received co-funding from the European Union (Grant Agreement no. 604102).

References

1. The Jülich Scalable Particle-in-Cell code, JuSPIC, http://www.fz-juelich.de/ias/jsc/juspic/
2. JuSPIC in the High-Q Club, http://www.fz-juelich.de/ias/jsc/EN/Expertise/High-Q-Club/JuSPIC/_node.html
3. JuSPIC Source Code Repository, https://trac.version.fz-juelich.de/juspic
4. Baumeister, P.F., Hater, T., Kraus, J., Pleiter, D., Wahl, P.: A performance model for GPU-accelerated FDTD applications. In: 2015 IEEE 22nd International Conference on High Performance Computing (HiPC), pp. 185–193, December 2015

5. Baumeister, P.F., Bornemann, M., Bühler, M., Hater, T., Krill, B., Pleiter, D., Zeller, R.: Addressing materials science challenges using GPU-accelerated POWER8 nodes. In: Dutot, P.-F., Trystram, D. (eds.) Euro-Par 2016. LNCS, vol. 9833, pp. 77–89. Springer, Cham (2016). doi:10.1007/978-3-319-43659-3_6
6. Birdsall, C.K., Langdon, A.B.: Plasma Physics via Computer Simulation. Series in Plasma Physics. Taylor & Francis, New York (2005)
7. Bonitz, M., Semkat, D. (eds.): Introduction to Computational Methods in Many Body Physics. Rinton Press, Princeton (2006)
8. Brömmel, D., Gibbon, P., Garcia, M., Lopez, V., Marjanovic, V., Labarta, J.: Experience with the MPI/STARSS programming model on a large production code. In: International Conference on Parallel Computing: Accelerating Computational Science and Engineering (CSE). Advances in Parallel Computing, vol. 25, pp. 357–366, Munich, Germany, 10–13 September 2013. IOS Press (2014)
9. Bussmann, M., Burau, H., Cowan, T.E., Debus, A., Huebl, A., Juckeland, G., Kluge, T., Nagel, W.E., Pausch, R., Schmitt, F., Schramm, U., Schuchart, J., Widera, R.: Radiative signature of the relativistic Kelvin-Helmholtz instability. In: 2013 SC - International Conference for High Performance Computing, Networking, Storage and Analysis (SC), pp. 1–12, November 2013
10. Decyk, V.K., Singh, T.V.: Adaptable particle-in-cell algorithms for graphical processing units. Comput. Phys. Commun. **182**(3), 641–648 (2011), http://www.sciencedirect.com/science/article/pii/S0010465510004558
11. Germaschewski, K., Fox, W., Abbott, S., Ahmadi, N., Maynard, K., Wang, L., Ruhl, H., Bhattacharjee, A.: The Plasma Simulation Code: A modern particle-in-cell code with load-balancing and GPU support. ArXiv e-prints, October 2013
12. Gopal, A., Herzer, S., Schmidt, A., Singh, P., Reinhard, A., Ziegler, W., Brömmel, D., Karmakar, A., Gibbon, P., Dillner, U., May, T., Meyer, H.G., Paulus, G.G.: Observation of gigawatt-class THz pulses from a compact laser-driven particle accelerator. Phys. Rev. Lett. **111**(7), 074802 (2013)
13. Harlow, F.H.: The particle-in-cell method for numerical solution of problems in fluid dynamics, March 1962, http://www.osti.gov/scitech/servlets/purl/4769185
14. Herten, A., Pleiter, D., Brömmel, D.: Accelerating Plasma Physics with GPUs (Poster). Tech. rep., GPU Technology Conference (2017)
15. Hockney, R.W., Eastwood, J.W.: Computer simulation using particles. Institute of Physics, Bristol (1988) (English)
16. Kong, X., Huang, M.C., Ren, C., Decyk, V.K.: Particle-in-cell simulations with charge-conserving current deposition on graphic processing units. J. Comput. Phys. **230**(4), 1676–1685 (2011), http://www.sciencedirect.com/science/article/pii/S0021999110006479
17. Mucci, P., ICL Team, T.: PAPI, the performance application programming interface, http://icl.utk.edu/papi/
18. Mucci, P.J., Browne, S., Deane, C., Ho, G.: PAPI: a portable interface to hardware performance counters. In. Proceedings of the Department of Defense HPCMP Users Group Conference, pp. 7–10 (1999)
19. Stantchev, G., Dorland, W., Gumerov, N.: Fast parallel particle-to-grid interpolation for plasma PIC simulations on the GPU. J. Parallel Distrib. Comput. **68**(10), 1339–1349 (2008), http://dx.doi.org/10.1016/j.jpdc.2008.05.009
20. Weber, V., Malossi, A.C.I., Tavernelli, I., Laino, T., Bekas, C., Modani, M., Wilner, N., Heller, T., Curioni, A.: First experiences with *ab initio* molecular dynamics on OpenPOWER: the case of CPMD. In: Taufer, M., Mohr, B., Kunkel, J.M. (eds.) ISC High Performance 2016. LNCS, vol. 9945, pp. 228–234. Springer, Cham (2016). doi:10.1007/978-3-319-46079-6_16

Pushing Big Data into Accelerators: Can the JVM Saturate Our Hardware?

Johan Peltenburg(✉), Ahmad Hesam, and Zaid Al-Ars

Computer Engineering Lab, Delft University of Technology, Delft, Netherlands
{j.w.peltenburg,z.al-ars}@tudelft.nl,a.s.hesam@student.tudelft.nl

Abstract. Advancements in the field of big data have led into an increasing interest in accelerator-based computing as a solution for computationally intensive problems. However, many prevalent big data frameworks are built and run on top of the Java Virtual Machine (JVM), which does not explicitly offer support for accelerated computing with e.g. GPGPU or FPGA. One major challenge in combining JVM-based big data frameworks with accelerators is transferring data from objects that reside in JVM managed memory to the accelerator. In this paper, a rigorous analysis of possible solutions is presented to address this challenge. Furthermore, a tool is presented which generates the required code for four alternative solutions and measures the attainable data transfer speed, given a specific object graph. This can give researchers and designers a fast insight about whether the interface between JVM and accelerator can saturate the computational resources of their accelerator. The benchmarking tool was run on a POWER8 system, for which results show that depending on the size of the objects and collections size, an approach based on the Java Native Interface can achieve between 0.9 and 12 GB/s, ByteBuffers can achieve between 0.7 and 3.3 GB/s, the Unsafe library can achieve between 0.8 and 16 GB/s and finally an approach access the data directly can achieve between 3 and 67 GB/s. From our measurements, we conclude that the HotSpot VM does not yet have standardized interfaces by design that can saturate common bandwidths to accelerators seen today or in the future, although one of the approaches presented in this paper can overcome this limitation.

1 Introduction

With the advance of the big data era, many different big data processing and storage frameworks have been developed. Many of these frameworks are written in languages that use a Java Virtual Machine (JVM) [10] as the underlying platform to execute compiled programs. This allows a cluster to easily scale out, adding nodes of any type of hardware, as long as they can run a JVM. A well known example is Apache Spark [18] which is written in Scala and is generally run on the OpenJDK HotSpot virtual machine.

Although the performance of programs run on the JVM can (in very specific situations) come close to the performance of native implementations, the added layers of abstraction still impose limits [8]. Speeding up JVM applications beyond

J.M. Kunkel et al. (Eds.): ISC High Performance Workshops 2017, LNCS 10524, pp. 220–236, 2017.
https://doi.org/10.1007/978-3-319-67630-2_18

Just-In-Time (JIT) compilation can be done using native libraries to squeeze out the last bits of performance that the underlying platform has to offer, sacrificing some of the portability of the application. While still a long way to go, the big data field is slowly catching up with the performance known from the high-performance computing (HPC) domain [1]. However, as the end of multicore scaling approaches, scaling up even native CPU performance will be troublesome in the near future [6].

Thus, as big data problems become bigger, there is a need to go even beyond the performance that traditional multicore systems can offer. For this reason, the research and industrial community is looking at other paradigms, such as combining accelerators or near-memory computing with big data platforms. In this paper, the focus is on accelerators.

GPGPU computing is currently the most popular method for accelerated computing. GPUs offer superior performance for tasks with a lot of thread-level parallelism and floating-point calculations. Effort is also put in the more power-efficient FPGA accelerators, suitable for deeply pipelined datapaths and other highly parallel algorithms. In either case, there is little explicit support for accelerated computing in specifications or implementations of major JVMs at the time of writing.

One of the major challenges during integration of JVM programs with accelerators is transferring the data represented as objects in the JVM memory to the accelerator. The interface between the data stored in objects managed by the JVM and an accelerator incurs a specific amount of overhead. If this overhead is higher than the performance gained from the accelerator, there is no point in investing effort to accelerate an algorithm.

Because we look at this matter within the context of big data frameworks, we assume that there is an application that would like to perform a transformation on a parallel collection of data items, represented as JVM objects. One example is a map transformation, which is a common operation for big data applications. The goal of this paper is now to give an overview of four different yet feasible approaches in transferring the object data from the JVM to the accelerator. Furthermore we attempt to quantify the overhead of this data transfer based on the layout of the object and the approach taken. This can help future development and integration of accelerators with JVM-based big data frameworks.

The contributions of this paper are:

- We give an overview of the most feasible approaches in transferring data between JVM and accelerator.
- We present a benchmarking tool that quantifies the parameters of the model for a given platform. This allows designers and researchers to get an estimation of the performance of their accelerated implementation, when JVM objects hold the source data. It will also give an indication on which approach will suit their performance requirements. The tool can also be used as a static analysis tool on custom object layouts.
- We measure the data transfer performance of each of the approaches on the OpenJDK HotSpot VM running on a POWER8 system.

The organization of the paper is as follows. Section 2 will discuss related work. In Sect. 3 a more thorough problem definition is given. In Sect. 4 we will give an overview of four feasible approaches. Section 5 comprises the experimental setup. In Sect. 6 the results are presented. A conclusion is given in Sect. 7.

2 Related Work

When accelerators are controlled by and attached to a host system, it is assumed that the accelerator interface partially consists of a native library. Therefore, the problem of transferring object data from JVM to accelerator is initially similar to the problem of native function access to JVM memory.

For this reason, the JVM implements the Java Native Interface (JNI). Many open-source projects exist (e.g. JNA [11], JavaCPP [2]) that mainly attempt to simplify integration of native libraries with Java programs through sugaring or abstraction of the JNI (which is normally used by writing C or C++ code). We will measure the best case performance of JNI without any of the overhead introduced by the frameworks.

Several researchers that attempt to integrate accelerators with JVM based big data frameworks note that the JNI interface causes a major performance bottleneck for their applications. In the work of [3,9], the massive latency that the JNI introduces is hidden by task pipelining, effectively overlapping JNI access with accelerator execution. Also, when a succession of transformations will take place on the accelerator, intermediate data is cached in local memory and can also be broadcast to other nodes as is.

Another interesting scheme is described in [7], which uses direct ByteBuffers for which the backing array is mapped to a region accessible through direct memory access by an FPGA. The authors use the Xilinx Zynq system, in which the host CPU shares the same physical memory as the FPGA. Such hardware setup enables easy access to the data from the accelerators, although it is not yet common in today's big data clusters.

In the Apache Spark project, with the introduction of the Tungsten engine, data items can be stored in off-heap memory using DataFrames and Datasets. At the time of writing, this is currently done mainly to prevent garbage collection overhead on the large collections of data. The community has been discussing the possibility of feeding data that is stored off-heap directly to native libraries, but any design, implementation or measurements have not yet been presented [16]. Furthermore, objects are serialized into the off-heap memory using serializers that in many cases will also introduce extra overhead by e.g. compressing the data [13].

More recently, with TensorFrames [5], integration of GPGPU accelerated computing in Spark using off-heap managed data is shown. However, internally the data is first deserialized back into the JVM and then JavaCPP is used (which is JNI based) to transfer the data row-wise through a native library to a GPGPU, which is rather inefficient. In the work on Spark-GPU [17], a similar approach is seen. Data items first have to be transferred to some off-heap memory region, before passing it to a GPGPU. In a specific case with string objects, the authors show that reading back this data from a GPU-friendly projection in an off-heap structure incurs significant overhead of between 10.5× to 18.3×.

Many of these previous works focus on accelerating a specific application, in which the interface between JVM and accelerator is not the main point of thorough investigation. In this work, we aim to give an overview and quantify *in detail* the properties of this interface, since it is one of the most critical components in such a system.

3 Problem Definition

In light of the advancing interest in accelerating JVM based big data applications and frameworks, the main question that this paper aims to address is as follows. *Which approaches exist to transfer data held by objects in a JVM to an accelerator, and how efficient are they?*

To scope the question, we assume that there is an application holding a collection of objects that contain data of interest to be used in a transformation. The transformation is implemented in an accelerator. This commonly means that each object in the collection will be transformed to some new object, or it will be reduced to some final result. We also assume the collection is parallel, thus the transformation may be applied to the objects in parallel as well, i.e. the objects within a collection do not refer to each other.

The fields of an object that represent its state and data, can be of the following types:

- A primitive (e.g. an integer, float or character).
- A reference to a child object or a child array object.

One exception is the array object type; it can hold multiple primitives or references, where each primitive or reference does not have a separate field identifier, merely an index. For the sake of simplicity we will assume that there are no loops in the reference graph of the object, i.e. all object reference graphs are trees.

The main problem within this scope is due to the fact that a programmer running applications on a JVM has no explicit control over the location or the layout of the objects in memory. In a system where one has control over both layout and location of objects, one may choose to lay out the data in such a way that it is convenient for an accelerator interface to access. This usually means that the data at least resides in a contiguous memory region.

Thus, to perform the transformation on one object of the collection, all primitives that reside in the object tree must first be obtained. This involves traversing the object tree, accessing all the primitives, whether they are in fields or in arrays. When this data is collected and saved in a contiguous memory region, this process is also known as *serialization*. Serialization is used to store the object to disk or to transfer it over a network, hence the object must usually be placed in a contiguous memory region so that it may fit in a file or a message. Later on,

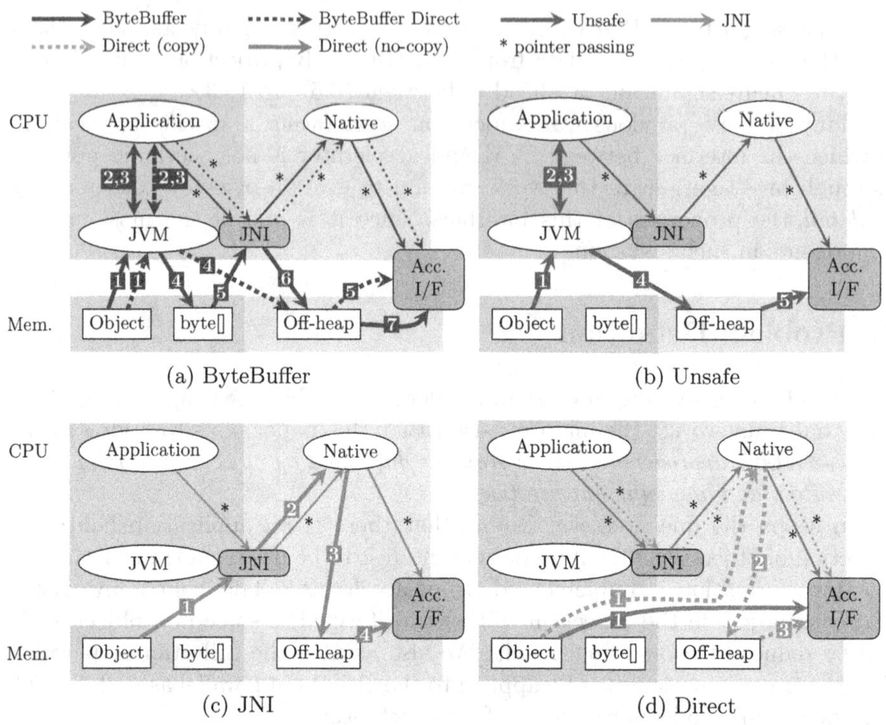

Fig. 1. Four different approaches of transferring the object data to the native environment. The thick lines represent the data path, and pointer/reference passing between different programs is shown with an asterisk. Label numbers indicate data flow order.

the serialized object is deserialized into the memory of another JVM. However, for a transformation to take place in an accelerator, the primitives must merely be transported to the accelerator's local memory; not necessarily reconstructing it in such a way that a JVM program can access it again.

Accelerators are often controlled by a host CPU. In most cases this CPU will also run the JVM. Controlling the accelerator from the application will therefore involve calling at least one, but possibly multiple native functions. In major JVM implementations, this can be done using the Java Native Interface (JNI). Therefore, there are two ways of where object traversal could take place; either by bytecode running on the JVM itself or by a native function invoked through the JNI.

To address the question posed at the beginning of this section, the next section will give an overview of four feasible approaches to obtain the primitives and transfer them to an accelerator.

Table 1. Summary of characteristics of different approaches

Approach	Traversal	Serialized	Copies	Portability	Support	Seen in
ByteBuffer	bytecode	yes	1-2	high	high	[13]
ByteBuffer (off-heap)	bytecode	yes	1	high	high	[7]
Unsafe	bytecode	yes	1	medium	low	[5][17]
JNI	native	yes	1-2	medium	high	[11][2][4]
Direct (copy)	native	yes	1	low	low	—
Direct (no-copy)	native	no	0	low	low	—

4 Overview of Data Transfer Approaches

This section first discusses the approaches of accessing a single JVM object using a single thread, and then how multiple objects can be accessed using multiple threads.

4.1 Single-Object, Single-Thread Approaches

There are four basic approaches by which the data of an object could be transferred to an accelerator (also shown in Fig. 1), namely:

(a) *ByteBuffer* approach — Using the JVM to traverse the object tree and write it into a byte array using the `java.nio.ByteBuffer` or its derivatives like `IntBuffer` or `FloatBuffer`. The byte array is then passed to the accelerator interface through the JNI.
(b) *Unsafe* approach — Using the JVM to traverse the object tree and write it directly to off-heap memory using the `sun.misc.Unsafe` library. The address of off-heap memory location of the object is then passed to the accelerator interface.
(c) JNI approach — The object reference is passed as an argument through the JNI to a native function. Then, the native function uses JNI functions such as Get<Primitive>Field or Get<Primitive>ArrayElements to obtain the primitives.
(d) *Direct* approach—Traversing the object tree directly while it resides inside the JVM memory. The accelerator interface may directly load the data or it may first be serialized in some off-heap memory location.

The following subsections will discuss each approach in more detail. A summary can be found in Table 1.

ByteBuffer approach: For this approach, the object tree is traversed using JVM bytecode. Primitives and primitive arrays are copied to a `ByteBuffer` using its `put` and `get` methods. ByteBuffers are objects that wrap around a byte array (called the *backing array*). They allow an easy interface to load and store primitives from and to the byte array. The reference to this byte array can be passed through the JNI to a native function that interfaces with the accelerator.

To obtain the actual array, the JNI function `Get<Primitive>ArrayElements` or `GetPrimitiveArrayCritical` can be used. This may[1] cause another copy (although less likely in the latter case) of the data, but in either case it makes the array accessible to the native function. A variant to this approach is where the ByteBuffers can also wrap around an off-heap byte array, if the byte array is allocated using the `allocateDirect` method. In this case, the data only has to be copied from VM memory to the byte array once. The address of the off-heap byte array can be obtained in the native code by using the JNI function `GetDirectBufferAddress`.

Unsafe approach: The Unsafe approach uses the `sun.misc.Unsafe` library. This library allows C-like memory operations such as allocation and freeing of off-heap memory. Within the Java programming paradigm it is considered 'unsafe' because usually memory management is not done explicitly by the programmer. The library is tightly coupled with the HotSpot VM, but its interface is not officially supported or standardized. Traversal of the tree is done using JVM bytecode. Primitives and primitive arrays are copied to an off-heap allocated memory location using `put` and `get` methods. This makes the Unsafe approach quite similar to the ByteBuffer Direct approach. To access the data, the memory address of the off-heap structure can be simply passed to a native function interfacing with the accelerator using the JNI.

JNI approach: The JNI approach is less straightforward, since traversing the object tree is done through JNI calls in the native code. First, the references to the classes of the objects in a tree must be obtained using `FindClass`. Then, the field IDs of the classes must be obtained using `GetFieldID`. Object references can be traversed using `GetObjectField`. Finally, with `Get<Primitive>Field`, primitive fields can be obtained. The functions `Get<Primitive>ArrayElements` or `GetPrimitiveArrayCritical` can be used to obtain array values, where both functions potentially copy the values into a newly allocated region that must be released afterwards. Because an accelerator cannot call JNI functions directly, it is assumed that when the JNI approach is used, the primitives are stored in some memory allocated by the native code, and thus the object is serialized. The serialized object is then passed to the accelerator interface.

Direct approach: The Direct approach involves traversing the object tree and obtaining the values from the JVM memory itself. Traversing the object tree is done through calculating pointers to the objects from JVM references directly. Fields are taken from offsets on the object pointers. This approach has low portability since the way in which references are represented and translated to virtual memory addresses is not standardized across implementations. For example, in the HotSpot VM, this depends on VM parameters and platform address size. References (called *ordinary object pointers* or OOPs) can be 32- or 64-bits, where the 64-bit representation is an actual native pointer, but the 32-bits representation might be a compressed OOP [12]. Also, the offsets or

[1] this depends on whether the representation of the array in the VM is the same as the native representation, and if the VM garbage collector supports "pinning".

implementation of field storage is not specified. Therefore, this approach is not straightforward and is extremely platform-dependent.

If the accelerator has an interface that allows to initiate loads/stores from/to the host application memory that is running the JVM (e.g. CAPI [15], or with CPU + FPGA SoCs where the acceleration fabric shares the data bus of the CPU [7], or with techniques such as NVIDIA's Unified Memory in CUDA), it is not required for the object to be serialized. Instead, the actual object traversal may take place on the accelerator itself. Therefore, the Direct approach allows serialized (copy) but also unserialized (no-copy) access to the object, which is unique to this approach.

We have not found an accelerator interface leveraging this technique published in literature. Note that for server-grade systems this technique seems yet unfeasible, since the latency of contemporary accelerator interfaces is still in the order of microseconds. When reference are traversed in large data structures with small objects, this will result in poor performance, because the ratio of requests to data is high.

It might appear that proper functioning of this approach can be endangered by the JVM garbage collection mechanism. However, when starting the Direct approach through a single JNI invocation that uses an object reference as a parameter, this reference is made a local reference. This means that as long as the JNI function has not yet returned, the garbage collector will not move the object of this reference, or its children. The reference could even be made global such that the object will not be garbage collected at all and can be passed between different JNI invocations or threads.

4.2 Parallel Access of Collections of Objects

When there is a collection of objects to be processed by an accelerator, and the objects of the collection do not refer to other objects in the collection, the collection may also be accessed in parallel. This can help to increase the throughput on multicore systems. In case of the Direct approach with load/store capable accelerators, loads for data of multiple objects could be pipelined.

To support parallel access for the ByteBuffer approaches, each thread gets its own ByteBuffer object with backing array in order to prevent race conditions. The backing arrays are obtained through the JNI and could be merged in the native code. They could also be sent to the accelerator interface in sequence, thus from the accelerator point of view, it will no longer be a single collection per se. This might introduce some overhead or require a slightly more complex control structure for the ByteBuffer approach.

For the Unsafe approach, the memory is allocated once, then each thread gets its own instance of `sun.misc.Unsafe`, again to prevent race conditions. Then, each thread operates on a different offset of the destination memory.

For the JNI approach, parallel access is more complicated. Because references to objects are only valid in the corresponding thread that obtained them through the JNI, the reference to the array holding the collection must first be made global before it is passed to each thread. New threads must also register with the JVM using the JNI function `AttachCurrentThread` before they may call other JNI functions. After accessing the values, the threads must detach and the global reference must be released to allow garbage collection to take place on the objects.

For the Direct approach, parallel access is straightforward. Multiple threads may have multiple outstanding accesses of JVM memory simultaneously, and store them on different offsets of off-heap memory.

5 Experimental Setup

To measure the access times of the different approaches, a benchmarking tool was implemented (see also Fig. 2). As an input to the tool, a layout of an object tree is first specified. From this specification, Scala sources and ultimately JVM bytecode is generated, containing the required object classes and an `Instantiator` class which contains methods to instantiate the object tree and fill it with random data. Furthermore, for each approach, in the top-level class, methods are generated to serialize the object to a byte array or to off-heap memory corresponding to the description of the ByteBuffer and Unsafe approach, respectively. These classes are then compiled to JVM bytecode. For the JNI and Direct approach, functions callable through the JNI are generated in C. They are then also compiled to a shared library, together with functions that access the data for the ByteBuffer and Unsafe approach. Finally, a second program (benchmark runner) can take the class files and library as an input and run measurements of object access time. The benchmarking tool is available as an open-source project [14]. Using this tool, it is possible to measure the access times of different types and

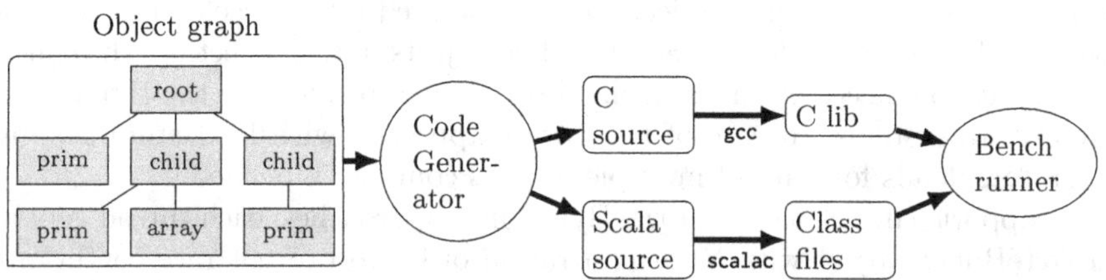

Fig. 2. General flow of the benchmarking tool

sizes of object trees. It is possible to generate two types of object layouts. One layout where the root object does not contain any references, except to primitive arrays (a *leaf* object). A leaf object contains only a variable amount of primitives and arrays of variable size. Another layout where the object has a specified width W and depth D, such that at the root level it contains W references to the second level, where each object contains $max(W-1, 1)$ references, until the level equals D. Only at the last level, the primitives and arrays are instantiated. This layout allows us to also make a linear object tree, by setting $W = 1$ and

$D > 1$. It is also possible to supply a custom class layout or object tree to the tool, such that it may be used as a static analysis tool for existing applications.

By varying the parameters of the aforementioned object tree layouts, it is possible to obtain the parameters of the model for a specific platform and JVM implementation. By varying the number of primitives in a leaf object, the average time to copy a primitive can be measured. By increasing the array size of a leaf object, the average array copy time per element can be measured. By varying the depth in a linear object tree, the average time to traverse a reference can be measured.

Parallel collection serialization and parallel access performance is also measured to get the peak performance for the platform. From the hardware point of view, when more cores and hardware threads run in parallel, we may assume that the internal memory infrastructure is at some point saturated, resulting in peak performance for that platform. Thus, besides specifying the object tree layout for a benchmark, it is also possible to generate a collection of N of these objects and specify with how many threads to access the objects. Furthermore, because run-time measurements on the JVM are very noisy, the experiments are repeated R times and averaged. These numbers are reported per experiment in Sect. 6.

The benchmarking system consists of two POWER8 CPUs running at 3.42 GHz on an IBM Power System S824L (8247-42L) with 256 GiB of total RAM. We confine our measurements to one of the two CPUs only. Primitives used are 32-bit integers. Attaching an actual accelerator is outside the scope of this paper, but by accumulating all serialized primitives into a single value on the CPUs we can validate the correctness of each approach and we can make a fair comparison for the Direct (no-copy) case. This is in theory the fastest approach, because it does not copy at all. Without any operations on the data it would otherwise only have to resolve all references without accessing the data itself. Native threads are controlled through OpenMP and JVM threads are statically managed.

In a real application, more dimensions to the problem are relevant, such as how to lay out the serialized objects in the memory such that its structure is convenient to process in a specific accelerator, how to retain references within the serialized format, how to deal with cyclic object graphs, how to deal with static fields of classes, and more detailed problems which are commonly seen in serialization. However, because we are primarily interested in the feasibility and best-case performance, these dimensions are also outside the scope of this work.

6 Results

6.1 Single Object

In Fig. 3a, the access time of a leaf object with an increasing number of primitive fields is shown. We found that the ByteBuffer, Unsafe and Direct approaches show a mainly linear increase in access time, while the JNI approach shows a significant quadratic increase when the number of fields increases in

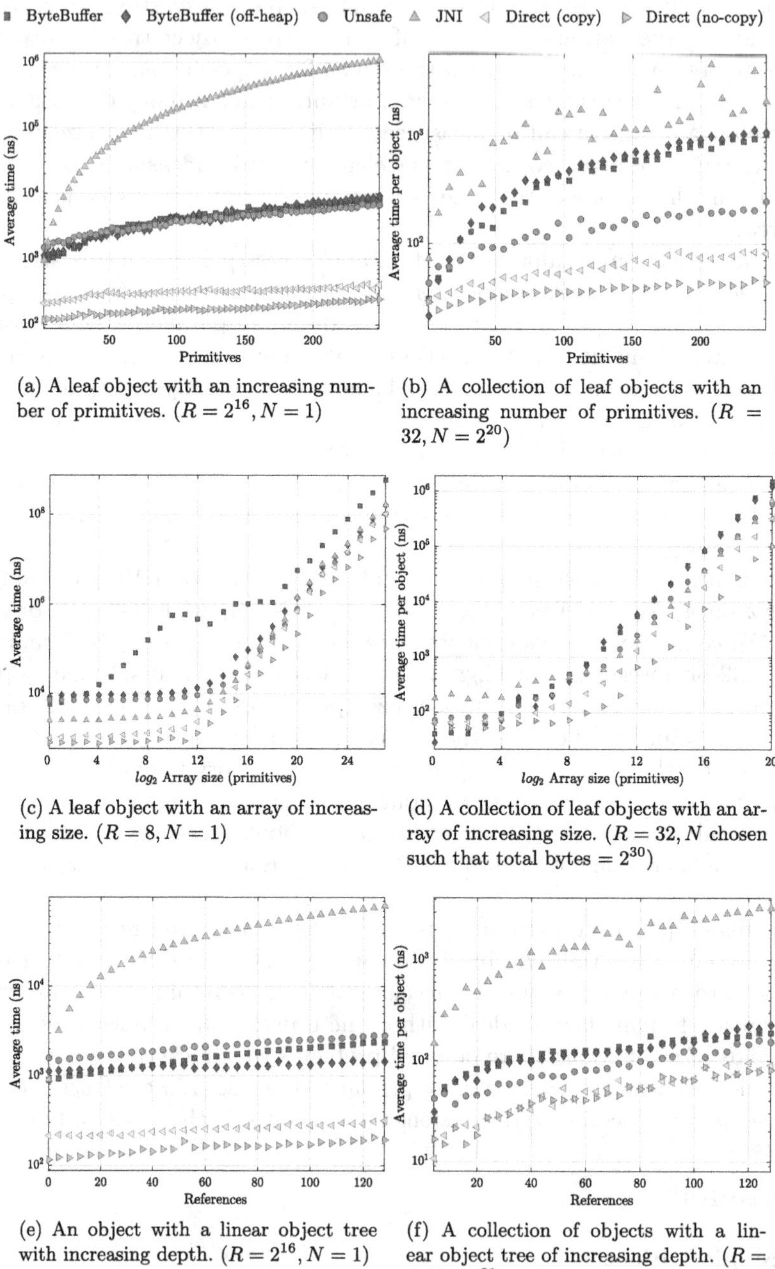

(a) A leaf object with an increasing number of primitives. ($R = 2^{16}, N = 1$)

(b) A collection of leaf objects with an increasing number of primitives. ($R = 32, N = 2^{20}$)

(c) A leaf object with an array of increasing size. ($R = 8, N = 1$)

(d) A collection of leaf objects with an array of increasing size. ($R = 32$, N chosen such that total bytes $= 2^{30}$)

(e) An object with a linear object tree with increasing depth. ($R = 2^{16}, N = 1$)

(f) A collection of objects with a linear object tree of increasing depth. ($R = 4, N = 2^{21}$)

Fig. 3. Average latency of accessing JVM objects.

a leaf object. This is due to the use of the JNI function `GetFieldID` for this particular experiment. This function looks up the field identifier string in the HotSpot symbol table. Suppose the number of primitives is p. We must search p symbols p times to access all primitives. Thus the time complexity to access a field by using `GetFieldID` is $O(p^2)$.

In Fig. 3c the access time of a leaf object containing only an array is shown. Accessing arrays of different sizes clearly shows the effect of the CPU cache hierarchy. The derivative of the access time with respect to the array size is small in regions where the array still fits in the cache. It becomes larger for array sizes that do not fit in the cache. Any initial overhead of the copies becomes relatively small. For each approach that has the same number of copies (see Table 1), for large arrays, their access times converge, because internally array copies are usually performed by highly optimized `memcpy` calls (although variants depending on the native platform exist, e.g. for the Unsafe and ByteBuffer approaches).

In Fig. 3e, the access time of a linear object tree is shown. We found that the access times increases in a mainly linear manner with respect to the number of references traversed.

6.2 Parallel Performance

In the case of a parallel collection, we first attempt to find a suitable number of threads. For each approach we measuring three cases; 1. small objects (2 primitives and an array with 16 primitives) 2. medium objects (8 primitives and an array of 1024 primitives) and 3. large objects (64 primitives and an array of 800×600 primitives. Reference traversal performance is included in these measurements since a collection consists of many references to all its objects. The collections are of such a size that their serialized representation is over several hundred MiB, to make sure each thread has enough work to justify the overhead from spawning it. The results of these three measurements are seen in Fig. 4.

From these measurements, we found that for all approaches except the Direct approaches, the scalability is rather poor. This is most likely due to race conditions on specific resources of the VM. These approaches scale very badly when the ratio of reference to data is high (small objects case). In the case of a high ratio of reference to data, the maximum number of threads even gives the best performance for the Direct approaches. In the medium and large object cases, the speedup increases all the way to the maximum number of threads only for the Direct (no-copy) case. This approach only performs a single load and accumulate on each data item. The gains from multi-threading are therefore more significant than in the case of the Direct (copy) approach, because the computation to communication ratio is three times higher. The Direct (copy) approach loads, stores and then loads again and accumulates the data. The Unsafe approach also scales rather well in the medium and large measurement, compared to the JNI approaches, which scales only well for the large case. The ByteBuffer approach does not scale very well beyond four threads. From these measurements we set a suitable number of threads for each approach as shown in Table 2.

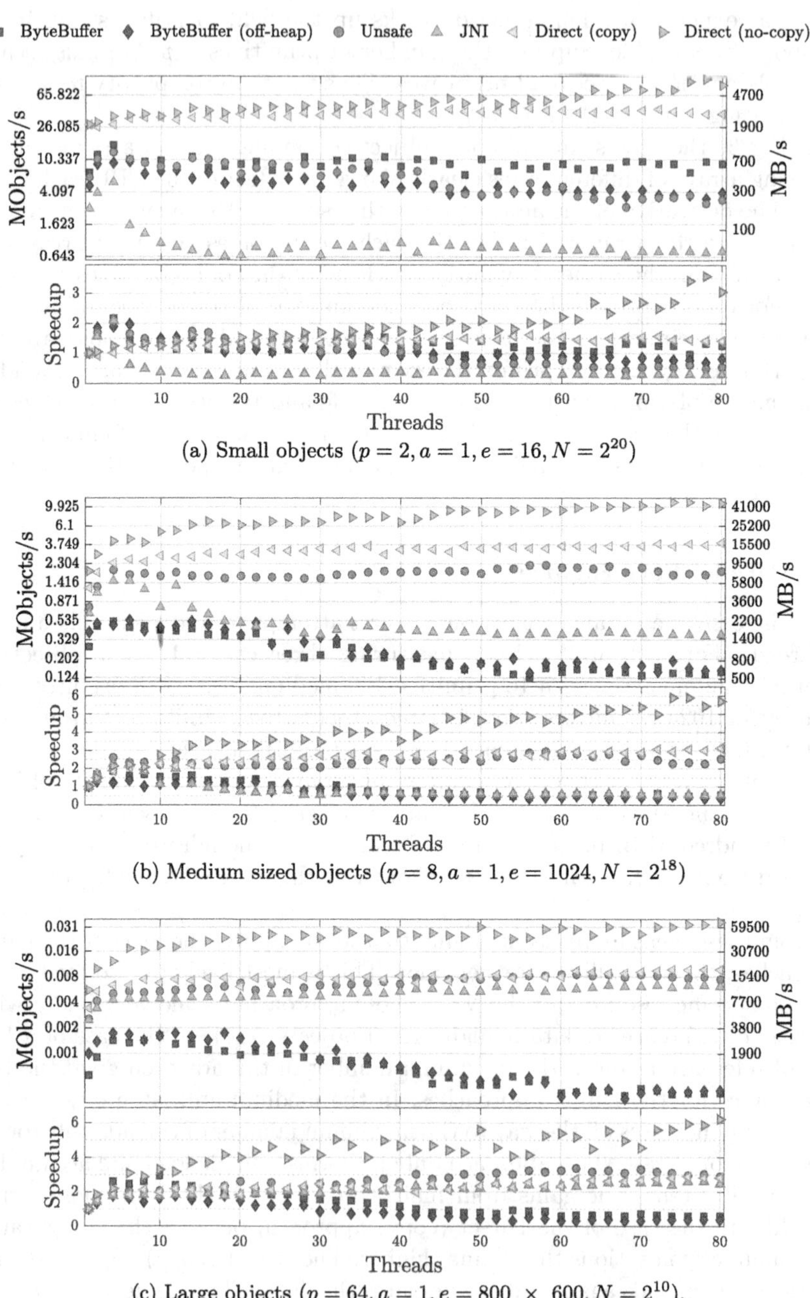

(a) Small objects ($p = 2, a = 1, e = 16, N = 2^{20}$)

(b) Medium sized objects ($p = 8, a = 1, e = 1024, N = 2^{18}$)

(c) Large objects ($p = 64, a = 1, e = 800 \times 600, N = 2^{10}$).

Fig. 4. Throughput and speedup of accessing collections of JVM objects.

Table 2. Maximum throughput and corresponding number of threads for the small, medium and large benchmark.

Approach	Small (threads)	MB/s	Medium (threads)	MB/s	Large (threads)	MB/s	Threads used for Fig. 3
ByteBuffer	4	1142	4	2159	10	3121	4
ByteBuffer (off-heap)	6	706	6	2231	4	3346	4
Unsafe	4	914	58	9080	62	16604	10
JNI	4	389	6	6094	78	12332	4
Direct (copy)	56	3232	80	16273	76	18788	80
Direct (no-copy)	78	7366	76	47064	80	67381	80

6.3 Collection

In the case of a parallel collection, the same types of measurements are performed as in the case for a single object, although on a collection of N of these objects. These measurements are shown in Fig. 3.

From measurements shown in Fig. 3b, we found that the quadratic increase in access time for the JNI approach is now relatively insignificant, because the field identifiers only have to be looked up once for the whole collection. However, the JNI approach is still slow, because for each field primitive, the function call `Get<Primitive>Field` JNI must still be made.

Figure 3d shows that after different initialization times, approaches with the same number of copies converge towards the same access latency as the arrays get larger, as was the case for the single-thread single-object measurements.

Lastly, for the measurement of reference traversal in a linear object graph (Fig. 3f), the direct approaches show similar access time, followed by the Unsafe and ByteBuffer approaches. Theoretically, there should not be much difference between the Unsafe and ByteBuffer approaches, because reference traversal is done in the JVM in the same way for both approaches. The difference in average time for the ByteBuffer approach is due to the overhead induced by spawning the threads and ByteBuffer objects. For the Unsafe approach, this overhead is much lower. Again, the JNI approach shows an order of magnitude worse performance.

6.4 Discussion

Contemporary commercially available accelerator cards are often connected via PCI-e GEN3 with peak bandwidths of almost 8 GB/s or 16 GB/s, depending on the configuration. One example includes the POWER8 system where the CAPI interface can be used over such a link. Even newer interfaces such as NVIDIA NVLink are expected to achieve up to 80 GB/s.

From the measurements presented in this section, it can be seen that the ByteBuffer approaches are generally unfavorable, because they cannot achieve near the bandwidths of the PCIe range easily. They are only faster than using the JNI approach in the case of accessing a collection of small objects. The JNI approach can be a feasible solution, but only when the ratio of references-to-data is low (e.g. when there are few but large arrays in the objects). At the same time, the Unsafe approach performs better in most cases and it is much easier to program, because traversal of the object graph can be written or generated in the JVM based source language. If it is necessary to saturate the link, with small objects (a high reference/data ratio) the only feasible solution is to take the Direct approach.

A major drawback of this approach is that it is highly platform dependent and it could even be considered more 'unsafe' than the Unsafe approach, since it accesses VM managed memory without some sort of interface that was designed into the VM. To mitigate this drawback, the VM could *by design* include some functionality to support fast object graph traversal, serialization and data transfer to accelerator interfaces, implemented with native code and tightly coupled with the VM as in the case of the Unsafe library.

7 Conclusion

In this paper, an overview is given for four different approaches for accelerator interfaces to obtain data from JVM managed objects; using ByteBuffers, the `sun.misc.Unsafe` library, the Java Native Interface (JNI) and to directly obtain the data from JVM managed memory (Direct).

A benchmarking tool was implemented that generates code to serialize the object or a collection of objects for use in an accelerator, using these four different approaches (where two approaches have two variants). By measuring the access times of single objects by a single thread, and access times of a parallel collection of objects by multiple threads, the performance of a POWER8 system with the HotSpot VM was measured. Furthermore, the throughput of a collection of small, medium and large objects was measurement with respect to the number of threads.

From the measurements we may conclude that the ByteBuffer approach does not perform well in most cases (it can achieve between 0.7 and 3.3 GB/s of throughput). Also, it does not scale well with the number of threads. The JNI approach can perform well in situations where the ratio of references to data is low, but also scales poorly with the number of threads (it can achieve between 0.9 and 12 GB/s of throughput). The Unsafe approach scales slightly better, up to the number of physical cores of CPU, and is also able to provide enough bandwidth to saturate common accelerator interfaces (it can achieve between 0.8 and 16 GB/s of throughput). The best approach in terms of performance is the Direct approach. It scales well and offers more than enough bandwidth for common accelerator interfaces, but its portability and ease of use is poor (it can achieve between 3 and 67 GB/s).

The measurements of the benchmarking tool can effectively be used to predict the interface speed of accelerators attached to a JVM. This may help researchers and developers to obtain a good estimation of the maximum speedup they may get by combining accelerators with JVM-based applications.

As new accelerator interfaces with higher bandwidths are introduced, the need for a faster interface that is integrated into the HotSpot VM *by design* is high. This is especially the case if users of big data frameworks based on the JVM want to make use of the computational power of accelerators.

Acknowledgment. The authors would like to thank Erik Vermij for his help using the POWER8 system and the Texas Advanced Computing Center and their partners for access to the hardware. This work was supported by the European Commission in the context of the ARTEMIS project ALMARVI (project #621439).

References

1. Anderson, M., Smith, S., Sundaram, N., Capota, M., Zhao, Z., Dulloor, S., Satish, N., Willke, T.L.: Bridging the gap between HPC and big data frameworks. Proc. VLDB Endow. **10**(8) (2017)
2. Bytedeco: JavaCPP, April 2017, https://github.com/bytedeco/javacpp
3. Chen, Y.T., Cong, J., Fang, Z., Lei, J., Wei, P.: When apache spark meets FPGAs: a case study for next-generation DNA sequencing acceleration. In: The 8th USENIX Workshop on Hot Topics in Cloud Computing (HotCloud 2016) (2016)
4. Chen, Z.N., Chen, K., Jiang, J.L., Zhang, L.F., Wu, S., Qi, Z.W., Hu, C.M., Wu, Y.W., Sun, Y.Z., Tang, H., et al.: Evolution of cloud operating system: from technology to ecosystem. J. Comput. Sci. Technol. **32**(2), 224–241 (2017)
5. Databricks: TensorFrames: Experimental tensorflow binding for Scala and Apache Spark, April 2017, https://github.com/databricks/tensorframes
6. Esmaeilzadeh, H., Blem, E., St Amant, R., Sankaralingam, K., Burger, D.: Dark silicon and the end of multicore scaling. In: ACM SIGARCH Computer Architecture News, vol. 39, pp. 365–376. ACM (2011)
7. Ghasemi, E., Chow, P.: Accelerating apache spark big data analysis with FPGAs. In: 2016 IEEE 24th Annual International Symposium on Field-Programmable Custom Computing Machines (FCCM), p. 94, May 2016
8. Gouy, I.: The computer language benchmarks game, 20 March (2017), http://benchmarksgame.alioth.debian.org/
9. Huang, M., Wu, D., Yu, C.H., Fang, Z., Interlandi, M., Condie, T., Cong, J.: Programming and runtime support to Blaze FPGA accelerator deployment at datacenter scale. In: Proceedings of the Seventh ACM Symposium on Cloud Computing, pp. 456–469. ACM (2016)
10. Lindholm, T., Yellin, F., Bracha, G., Buckley, A.: The Java Virtual Machine Specification, Java SE, 8th edn. Oracle (2015)
11. Open-source project: Java Native Access, April 2017, https://github.com/java-native-access/jna
12. Oracle: Java HotSpot virtual machine performance enhancements, April 2017, http://docs.oracle.com/javase/8/docs/technotes/guides/vm/performance-enhancements-7.html
13. Oracle: Object serialization stream protocol, April 2017, https://docs.oracle.com/javase/8/docs/platform/serialization/spec/serialTOC.html
14. Peltenburg, J.: JVM-to-Accelerator Benchmark Tool, https://github.com/johanpel/jvm2accbench

15. Stuecheli, J., Blaner, B., Johns, C., Siegel, M.: CAPI: a coherent accelerator processor interface. IBM J. Res. Dev. **59**(1), 1–7 (2015)
16. Weiss, P.: Off heap memory access for non-jvm libraries, March 2017, https://issues.apache.org/jira/browse/SPARK-10399
17. Yuan, Y., Salmi, M.F., Huai, Y., Wang, K., Lee, R., Zhang, X.: Spark-GPU: an accelerated in-memory data processing engine on clusters. In: 2016 IEEE International Conference on Big Data (Big Data), pp. 273–283, December 2016
18. Zaharia, M., Chowdhury, M., Das, T., Dave, A., Ma, J., McCauley, M., Franklin, M.J., Shenker, S., Stoica, I.: Resilient distributed datasets: a fault-tolerant abstraction for in-memory cluster computing. In: Proceedings of the 9th USENIX Conference on Networked Systems Design and Implementation, p. 2. USENIX Association (2012)

The Technological Roadmap of Parallware and Its Alignment with the OpenPOWER Ecosystem

Manuel Arenaz[1(✉)], Oscar Hernandez[2], and Dirk Pleiter[3]

[1] University of A Coruna and Appentra Solutions, A Coruña, Spain
manuel.arenaz@appentra.com
[2] Oak Ridge National Laboratory, Oak Ridge, TN, USA
oscar@ornl.gov
[3] Julich Supercomputing Center, Jülich, Germany
d.pleiter@fz-juelich.de

Abstract. Accelerated, heterogeneous systems are becoming the norm in High Performance Computing (HPC). The challenge is choosing the right parallel programming framework to maximize performance, efficiency and productivity. The design and implementation of benchmark codes is important in many activities carried out at HPC facilities. Well known examples are fair comparison of R+D results, acceptance tests for the procurement of HPC systems, and the creation of miniapps to better understand how to port real applications to current and future supercomputers. As a result of these efforts there is a variety of public benchmark suites available to the HPC community, e.g., Linpack, NAS Parallel Benchmarks (NPB), CORAL benchmarks, and Unified European Application Benchmark Suite. The upcoming next generation of supercomputers is now leading to create new miniapps to evaluate the potential performance of different programming models on mission critical applications, such as the XRayTrace miniapp under development at the Oak Ridge National Laboratory. This paper presents the technological roadmap of Parallware, a new suite of tools for high-productivity HPC education and training, that also facilitates the porting of HPC applications. This roadmap is driven by best practices used by HPC expert developers in the parallel scientific C/C++ codes found in CORAL, NPB, and XRayTrace. The paper reports preliminary results about the parallel design patterns used in such benchmark suites, which define features that need to be supported in upcoming realeases of Parallware tools. The paper also presents performance results using standards OpenMP 4.5 and OpenACC 2.5, compilers GNU and PGI, and devices CPU and GPU from IBM, Intel and NVIDIA.

Keywords: Hybrid heterogeneous programming models · OpenACC · OpenMP4 · Static analysis tools · LLVM · Performance portability · Use of parallware on minsky

J.M. Kunkel et al. (Eds.): ISC High Performance Workshops 2017, LNCS 10524, pp. 237–253, 2017.
https://doi.org/10.1007/978-3-319-67630-2_19

1 Introduction

Science, Technology, Engineering and Mathematics (STEM) plays a key role in the sustained growth and stability of the economy world-wide. There is a huge and urgent need in training STEM people in parallel programming, as well as in providing STEM people with better programming environments that help in porting scientific applications to modern supercomputers. It is key for code modernization, specially to exploit the computational power of new devices such as NVIDIA GPUs and Intel Xeon Phi.

The new specifications of directive-based parallel programming standards OpenMP 4.5 [24] and OpenACC 2.5 [23] are increasingly complex in order to support heterogeneous computing systems. There is some debate regarding the prescriptive nature of OpenMP 4.5 compared to the descriptive capabilities available in OpenACC. In addition, performance portability is not guaranteed by OpenMP 4.5 specification, and currently there is divergence in features supported by different vendors (e.g., PGI, Cray, IBM, Intel, GNU) in different devices (e.g., CPU, GPU, KNC/KNL). Overall, the responsibility falls on the developer to choose best practices that facilitate performance portability [18,20].

The new Parallware tools [2] aim at going one step forward towards supporting best practices for performance portability. It is useful to track the progress of new features in OpenMP 4.5 and OpenACC 2.5, as well as the availability and performance of their implementation in each available compiler and target device. We expect Parallware tools to be of interest for HPC facilities in the following use cases:

- Improvement of current HPC education and training environments in order to provide experiential learning to STEM people.
- Design and implementation of new miniapps to help porting HPC applications to next generation supercomputers.
- Creation of acceptance tests for HPC systems procurement.
- Port of HPC applications to upcoming (pre-)exascale supercomputers.

The rest of the paper is organized as follows. Section 2 discusses best practices from HPC expert developers in the parallel programming of CORAL Benchmarks [9], NAS Parallel Benchmarks [6] and XRayTrace miniapp [19]. The nomenclature of the *parallel design patterns* used internally in Parallware technology is introduced in order to compare the parallelization of the benchmark codes. Section 3 presents the new tool Parallware Trainer using as a guide the CORAL microbenchmark HACCmk. The technological challenges to be addressed in Parallware core technology in order to support modern HPC applications are described. It also introduces the foreseen tool Parallware Assistant oriented to development of HPC codes. Section 4 presents the current technological roadmap of Parallware tools. Finally, Sect. 6 presents conclusions and future work.

2 Analysis of Benchmarks: CORAL, NPB and XRayTrace

Benchmark suites are designed to test the performance of supercomputers at a hardware/software level, ranging from processor architecture, memory, interconnection network, I/O, file system, operating system, up to user applications that are mission critical for HPC facilities. In this study we analyze OpenMP and OpenACC parallel implementations of the compute-intensive C/C++ codes found in XRayTrace [19], CORAL [9] and NPB [6].

2.1 Parallel Design Patterns of Parallware

Several approaches try to divide programs into (parallel) algorithmic patterns and follow a pattern-based analysis of the code (see McCool et al. [22], Mattson et al. [21], Berkeley's dwarfs (or motifs) [5]). However, such patterns seem to be too difficult to apply in practice [25]. In contrast, we use the parallel design patterns detected by the Parallware technology [4], which have been successfully applied to real programs from the NAS Parallel Benchmarks [16], and from the fields computational electromagnetics [10], oil & gas [3] and computational astrophysics [12].

The pseudocodes presented in Fig. 1 describe three parallel design patterns detected by Parallware technology. The *Parallel Forall* of Listing 1.1 represents parallel computations without race conditions at run-time. In each iteration of `for_j`, a new value `A[j]` is computed. The value `T` is a loop temporary computed in each iteration of `for_j`, where `B[j]` denotes read-only values. The *Parallel Scalar Reduction* of Listing 1.2 represent a reduction operation whose result is a single value `A`, where `+` is a commutative, associative operator. The *Parallel Sparse Reduction* of Listing 1.3 represent a reduction operation whose result is a set of values. Each iteration of `for_j` updates a single value `A[B[j]]`, where the access pattern can only be determined at run-time and thus there may appear race conditions during the parallel execution.

Examples of parallel design patterns are presented in source code snippets of XRayTrace and HACCmk. In Listing 1.5, the loop `for_i` contains a parallel forall where the output is `vx1`, where `dx1` is a loop temporary and `fcoeff` is a read-only value. In Listing 1.6, the loop `for_j` contains a parallel scalar reduction whose output is `xi`, where `dxc` is a loop temporary and `fcxx1oeff` is a set of read-only values. Finally, Listing 1.4, the loop `for_it` contains parallel sparse reductions where the outputs `image` and `I_ang` have access patterns that are known at run-time only.

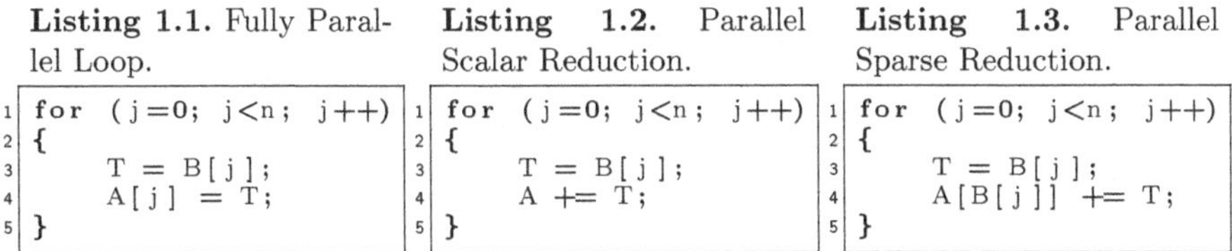

Listing 1.1. Fully Parallel Loop.

```
for (j=0; j<n; j++)
{
    T = B[j];
    A[j] = T;
}
```

Listing 1.2. Parallel Scalar Reduction.

```
for (j=0; j<n; j++)
{
    T = B[j];
    A += T;
}
```

Listing 1.3. Parallel Sparse Reduction.

```
for (j=0; j<n; j++)
{
    T = B[j];
    A[B[j]] += T;
}
```

Fig. 1. Pseudocodes of the *parallel design patterns* used in Parallware.

Listing 1.4. In XRayTrace version of routine *RayTraceImageLoop*

```
#define K_MAX 100 // Maximum number of frequencies
void RayTraceImageLoop(
    int N, int nx, int ny, int na, int nb, int nv,
    const double *x, const double *y, const double *a,
    const double *b, double dx, double dy, double dz,
    double da, double db, const double *dv,
    const RayTrace::ray_gain_struct *gain_in,
    const RayTrace::ray_seed_struct *seed_in,
    int method, const std::vector<ray_struct> &rays,
    double scale, double *image, double *I_ang,
    unsigned int &failure_code,
    std::vector<ray_struct> &failed_rays) {
    [...]
#pragma acc data copyin( x[0 : nx], y[0 : ny], a[0 : na],
     b[0 : nb], dv[0 : nv], rays2[0 :N_rays])
    deviceptr(gain, seed) copyout(image [0:nx * ny * nv],
     I_ang [0:na * nb]) {
// Initialize device images
#pragma acc parallel loop
        for (int i = 0; i < nx * ny * nv; ++i)
            image[i] = 0;
#pragma acc parallel loop
        for (int i = 0; i < na * nb; ++i)
            I_ang[i] = 0;
// Loop through y, x, b, a
#pragma acc parallel loop gang vector vector_length(32)
        for (int it = 0; it < N_rays; ++it) {
            const ray_struct ray = rays2[it];
            double Iv[K_MAX];
            ray_struct ray2;
            int error = RayTrace_calc_ray(
                ray, N, dz, gain, seed, nv, method, Iv,
                ray2);
            // Get the indices to the cells in image
            // and I_ang
            int i1, i2, i3, i4;
            int i1 = static_cast<int>(findfirstsingle(
                x, nx, ray2.x - 0.5 * dx));
 if (ray2.x < x[0] - 0.5 * dx ||
                ray2.x > x[nx - 1] + 0.5 * dx)
                i1 = -1; // The ray's z position is out
                         // of the range of image
            [...]
            // Copy I_out into image
            if (i1 >= 0 && i2 >= 0) {
                double *Iv2 =
                    &image[nv * (i1 + i2 * nx)];
                for (int iv = 0; iv < nv; iv++) {
#pragma acc atomic update
                    Iv2[iv] += Iv[iv] * scale;
                }
            }
            // Copy I_out into I_ang
            if (i3 >= 0 && i4 >= 0) {
                double tmp = 0.0;
                for (int iv = 0; iv < nv; iv++)
                    tmp += 2.0 * dv[iv] * Iv[iv];
#pragma acc atomic update
                I_ang[i3 + i4 * na] += tmp;
            }
        }
    } // pragma acc data region scope
}
```

Listing 1.5. CORAL microbenchmark HACCmk (file *main.c*).

```
#include <stdio.h>
#include <stdlib.h>
#include <omp.h>
#define N 15000
int main( int argc , char *argv[] )
{
  static float xx[N], yy[N], zz[N], mass[N], vx1[N], vy1[
      N], vz1[N];
  float fsrrmax2, mp_rsm2, fcoeff, dx1, dy1, dz1;
  int count = 327;
  ...
  for ( n = 400; n < N; n = n + 20 )
  {
    ...
    #pragma omp parallel for private( dx1, dy1, dz1 )
    for ( i = 0; i < count; ++i)
    {
      Step10_orig( n, xx[i], yy[i], zz[i], fsrrmax2,
          mp_rsm2, xx, yy, zz, mass, &dx1, &dy1, &dz1 );
      vx1[i] = vx1[i] + dx1 * fcoeff;
      vy1[i] = vy1[i] + dy1 * fcoeff;
      vz1[i] = vz1[i] + dz1 * fcoeff;
    }
    ...
  }
}
```

Listing 1.6. CORAL microbenchmark HACCmk (file *Step10_orig.c*).

```
#include <math.h>

void Step10_orig( int count1, float xxi, float yyi, float
      zzi, float fsrrmax2, float mp_rsm2, float *xx1,
    float *yy1, float *zz1, float *mass1, float *dxi,
    float *dyi, float *dzi )
{
    const float ma0 = 0.269327, ma1 = -0.0750978, ma2 =
        0.0114808, ma3 = -0.00109313, ma4 = 0.0000605491,
         ma5 = -0.00000147177;
    float dxc, dyc, dzc, m, r2, f, xi, yi, zi;
    int j;
    xi = 0.; yi = 0.; zi = 0.;
    for ( j = 0; j < count1; j++ )
    {
        dxc = xx1[j] - xxi;
        dyc = yy1[j] - yyi;
        dzc = zz1[j] - zzi;
        r2 = dxc * dxc + dyc * dyc + dzc * dzc;
        m = ( r2 < fsrrmax2 ) ? mass1[j] : 0.0f;
        f = pow( r2 + mp_rsm2, -1.5 ) - ( ma0 + r2*(ma1
            + r2*(ma2 + r2*(ma3 + r2*(ma4 + r2*ma5)))));
        f = ( r2 > 0.0f ) ? m * f : 0.0f;
        xi = xi + f * dxc;
        yi = yi + f * dyc;
        zi = zi + f * dzc;
    }
*dxi = xi;
    *dyi = yi;
    *dzi = zi;
}
```

The results in Table 1 reveal the usage of Parallware's parallel design patterns by HPC expert developers. The pattern *Parallel Forall* implementation *ParallelForLoopImpl* corresponds to a fully parallel loop implemented with pragmas *parallel for* in OpenMP and pragmas *parallel loop* in OpenACC. In contrast, the design patterns *Parallel Scalar Reduction* and *Parallel Sparse Reduction* add synchronization to guarantee correctness during parallel execution. Only three different implementations are used in the benchmarks: *AtomicImpl*, which prevents race conditions by adding pragmas *atomic* that guarantee atomic memory accesses to the reduction variable; *ReductionImpl*, which uses clause *reduction* to compute thread-local temporary results that are later reduced into the output reduction value; and *PrivateImpl*, which is a hand-made implementation of the clause *reduction* using clauses *private/shared* and pragma *critical*. The numbers show that *atomic* is not used for scalar reductions. In addition, *reduction* is not used for sparse reductions because the clause does not support arrays in OpenMP 3.1.

Table 1. Parallel design patterns used by HPC developers in the C/C++ implementation of NPB, CORAL and XRayTrace. (*) XRayTrace provides one OpenACC implementation; the remaining bechmark codes are OpenMP implementations only.

Benchmark	Parallel Design Pattern						
	Parallel Forall	Parallel Scalar Reduction			Parallel Sparse Reduction		
	Parallel ForLoop Impl	Atomic Impl	Reduction Impl	Private Impl	Atomic Impl	Reduction Impl	Private Impl
ORNL miniapp	0	0	0	0	2	0	0
XRayTrace					(*)2		
CORAL	24	0	1	1	0	0	4
lulesh	22						4
MILCmk	1		1	1			
HACCmk	1						
NPB	168	0	17	2	5	0	24
BT	25						14
CG	12		6				4
EP			2		1		
FT	7			1			
IS	5		1				
LU	28		3				2
MG	9		1	1			2
SP	32						2
UA	50		4		4		

2.2 Case Study: ORNL's Miniapp XRayTrace

Work in progress at ORNL is focused on creating the miniapp XRayTrace, a new benchmark that will be used to evaluate the performance of pre-exascale *Summit* supercomputer. The Listing 1.4 shows an excerpt of the GPU code implemented by the HPC expert using OpenACC 2.5. The miniapp also provides an OpenMP 3.1 version to run on multicore CPUs.

The routine `RayTraceImageLoop()` (see Listing 1.4, line 2) basically consists of a loop `for_it` that computes a parallel design pattern *Parallel Sparse Reduction* on variables `I_ang` and `image` using an *AtomicImpl* implementation (see `#pragma acc atomic`, lines 48 and 57). It is the best choice from the point of view of maintainability, as it provides a compact, easy-to-understand implementation. It is also applicable across standards and devices, all of which provide performant support for atomic operations. As shown in Table 1, it is noticeable that *AtomicImpl* was not the preferred implementation in NPB and CORAL, where *PrivateImpl* was largely the option of choice by HPC expert developers.

The OpenACC 2.5 implementation is optimized to reduce CPU-to/from-GPU data transfers, as this is a critical performance factor according to best practices for GPUs today [17]. The key issue here is to handle data scoping for scalar and array variables. The HPC expert developer has specified the array ranges in clauses `copyin` and `copyout` for arrays `x, y, a, b, dv, rays2, image, I_ang` (see Listing 1.4, line 14). In order to avoid unnecessary CPU-to/from-GPU data transfers, temporary array variables `gain` and `seed` have been allocated only in the device using the clause `deviceptr` and the API calls `copy_device()` and `free_device()`.

Finally, the C/C++ features used in the code[1] also pose technological challenges on the Parallware core technology. There are calls to the auxiliary functions `RayTrace_calc_ray()` and `findfirstsingle()` (see Listing 1.4, lines 29 and 35), aliases that temporarily point to the output array (see `double *Iv2` pointing to `double *image`, lines 45–46), as well as user-defined datatypes `ray_gain_struct`, `ray_seed_struct` and `ray_struct` (e.g. see lines 7, 8 and 9).

The execution times and speedups of Table 2 were measured on the *Juron* system at the Julich Supercomputing Centre (JSC). The hardware setup is a IBM S822LC with CPU 2x POWER8NVL, 10 cores each (8xSMT) and NVIDIA P100 GPUs (only 1 used for these runs). The tested setups are CPU-based sequential execution (*CPU Serial*), CPU-based parallel execution with OpenMP 3.1 (*CPU OMP3.1*) and GPU-based parallel execution with OpenACC 2.5 (*GPU ACC2.5*). The compiler flags for GCC 6.3 are `-fopenmp -O2` (thus, *CPU Serial* is measured as *CPU OMP3.1* with 1 thread). The flags for PGI 16.10 are `-mp -O2` for *CPU Serial* and *CPU OMP3.1*, and `-acc -O2 -ta=tesla` for *GPU ACC2.5*. Four increasing test sizes were considered: *Small ASE* (399000 rays, 3 lengths), *Medium ASE* (399000 rays, 8 lengths), *Small Seed* (7803000 rays, 3 lengths) and *Medium Seed* (7803000 rays, 8 lengths). The numbers show that GCC is

[1] The code also uses the C++ STL (`std::vector &failed_rays`). However, we do not consider it a key challenge because it has been commented out in the OpenACC code (the same may stand for OpenMP as well).

Table 2. Execution times (in seconds) and speedups of XRayTrace in Finisterrae (CPU Intel Xeon and NVIDIA GPU P100).

Test size	Original							
	Small ASE		Medium ASE		Small seed		Medium seed	
Compiler GCC 6.3								
CPU serial	4.42	–	10.69	–	46.21	–	94.33	–
CPU OMP3.1	0.14	31×	0.294	36×	1.579	29×	2.99	31×
Compiler PGI 16.10								
CPU serial	3.19	–	8.10	–	50.27	–	120.55	–
CPU OMP3.1	17.80	0.18×	49.07	0.08×	1126.21	0.04×	907.95	0.13×
GPU ACC2.5	0.04	79×	0.11	73×	0.73	68×	1.99	60×

the best choice for multi-threaded execution on the CPU (minimum speedup is 29× using 160 threads, with respect to *CPU Serial*). In contrast, PGI enables efficient execution on the GPU, which is 1.5 × −3.5× faster than *CPU OMP3.1* using GCC (minimum speedup is 60×, with respect to *CPU Serial*).

Finally, the execution times and speedups of Table 3 were measured on the *Finisterrae* system at the Supercomputing Centre of Galicia (CESGA). The test platform is a dual Intel Xeon E5-2680 v3 CPU, 12 cores each, running at 2.5 GHz (hyperthreading is disabled). The GPU accelerator for OpenACC computing is a Tesla K80. It is remarkable that, using the GCC compiler, *CPU OMP3.1* is significantly faster on Minsky nodes than on Intel-based nodes (minimum speedup is 29× on Juron, compared to 5.7× on Finisterrae). Regarding the PGI compiler, *CPU OMP3.1* does not perform well on Minsky nodes because the support of POWER ISA is very recent in PGI compilers, and more investigations on the correct usage of the PGI compiler are needed.

3 Parallware Trainer

Parallware Trainer [2] is a new interactive tool for high-productivity HPC education and training using OpenMP 4.5 and OpenACC 2.5. It allows experiential learning by providing an interactive, real-time GUI with editor capabilities to interact with the Parallware technology for source-to-source automatic parallelization of sequential codes.

Hereafter, the current strengths and weaknesses of Parallware Trainer binary release 0.4 (May 2017) are discussed using as a guide the CORAL microbenchmark HACCmk. Next, the suite of Parallware tools under development is presented, describing the key technological differences with respect to other tools available to the HPC community.

3.1 Case Study: CORAL Microbenchmark HACCmk

The Listings 1.5 and 1.6 show an excerpt of the source code of the CORAL microbenchmark HACCmk, written in C and parallelized using OpenMP 3.1 by an HPC expert developer. The main program consists of a loop that defines increasing tests sizes *n*, ranging from *400* up to *15000*. The HPC expert developer has used a parallel design pattern *Fully Parallel Loop*. For each test size, the pragma `#pragma omp parallel for` enables the conflict-free multi-threaded computation of the output arrays `vx1`, `vy1` and `vz1`.

Parallware Trainer 0.4 does not discover parallelism across calls to user-defined functions. It fails to find the fully parallel loop `for_i` in `main()` because of the call to `Step10_orig()` (see Listing 1.5, line 19). In contrast, Parallware succeeds to parallelize the loop `for_j` inside this routine (Listing 1.6, lines 10–22), and reports the following user messages:

```
Step10_orig.c:3:1: info: Analyzed function 'Step10_orig'
Step10_orig.c:10:5: info:
   Offloading to coprocessor device (use of target pragma)
   Parallel loop
   Dependencies due to temporary variables do not prevent parallelization:
      'dxc', 'm', 'r2', 'dzc', 'f', 'dyc'
   Parallel reduction on variable 'zi' with associative, commutative operator '+'
   Parallel reduction on variable 'yi' with associative, commutative operator '+'
   Parallel reduction on variable 'xi' with associative, commutative operator '+'
   Ranking of available parallelization strategies:
      #1 Use of the clause <reduction>   (*) selected
      #2 Use of pragma <atomic> (memory optimized)
   TODO list:
      * Complete access range for variables: xx1, yy1, zz1, mass1}
```

The code contains a parallel design pattern *Parallel Scalar Reduction* involving three scalar variables `xi`, `yi` and `zi`. It also displays the ranking of available implementations: `#1` being *ReductionImpl* and `#2` being *AtomicImpl* (see Table 1). Following best practices observed in CORAL and NPB, Parallware selects *ReductionImpl* as the option that minimizes synchronization during the execution of the parallel scalar reductions `xi`, `yi` and `zi`. The output source code produced by Parallware contains OpenMP 3.1, OpenACC 2.5 and OpenMP 4.5 pragmas annotated on loop `for_j` (see codes in Listings 1.7, 1.8 and 1.9).

Listing 1.7. In CORAL microbenchmark HACCmk, version of routine *Step10_orig* generated by Parallware Trainer using OpenMP 3.1.

```
    #pragma omp parallel default(none) shared(count1,
        fsrrmax2, mass1, mp_rsm2, xi, xx1, xxi, yi, yy1,
        yyi, zi, zz1, zzi)
    {
    #pragma omp for private(dxc, dyc, dzc, f, m, r2)
        reduction(+: zi) reduction(+: yi) reduction(+: xi
        ) schedule(auto)
    for ( j = 0; j < count1; j++ )
    {
...
        xi = xi + f * dxc;
        yi = yi + f * dyc;
        zi = zi + f * dzc;
    }
    } // end parallel
```

Listing 1.8. In CORAL microbenchmark HACCmk, version of routine *Step10_orig* generated by Parallware Trainer using OpenACC 2.5.

```
    #pragma acc data copy(xi, yi, zi) copyin(count1,
        fsrrmax2, mass1[], mp_rsm2, xx1[], xxi, yy1[],
        yyi, zz1[], zzi)
    {
    #pragma acc parallel
    {
    #pragma acc loop reduction(+: zi) reduction(+: yi)
        reduction(+: xi)
    for ( j = 0; j < count1; j++ )
    {
        ...
        xi = xi + f * dxc;
        yi = yi + f * dyc;
        zi = zi + f * dzc;
    }
    } // end parallel
    } // end data
```

Listing 1.9. In CORAL microbenchmark HACCmk, version of routine *Step10_orig* generated by Parallware Trainer using OpenMP 4.5.

```
    #pragma omp target map(to:xxi, fsrrmax2, mp_rsm2, xx1
        [], count1, yyi, zzi, yy1[], zz1[], mass1[]) map(
        tofrom:zi, yi, xi)
    {
    #pragma omp parallel default(none) shared(count1,
        fsrrmax2, mass1, mp_rsm2, xi, xx1, xxi, yi, yy1,
        yyi, zi, zz1, zzi)
    {
    #pragma omp for private(dxc, dyc, dzc, f, m, r2)
        reduction(+: zi) reduction(+: yi) reduction(+: xi
        ) schedule(auto)
    for ( j = 0; j < count1; j++ )
    {
        ...
        xi = xi + f * dxc;
        yi = yi + f * dyc;
        zi = zi + f * dzc;
    }
    } // end parallel
    } // end target
```

The OpenMP annotations manage data scoping explicitly both on the CPU version (Listing 1.7, lines 1–3, clauses `default`, `private`, `shared` and `reduction`) as well as on the accelerated version (Listing 1.9, line 1, clause `map`). Parallware also suggest a list of actions to be carried out by the user. For array variables `xx1`, `yy1`, `zz1` and `mass1`, the tool generates empty array ranges because it cannot determine the array elements to be transferred between the CPU and the accelerator (Listing 1.9, line 1, clause `map(to:...,xx1[])`). The development of more precise array range analysis is planned in Parallware's technological roadmap.

The execution times and speedups of Table 4 were measured on the *Juron* system at JSC (Table 5 shows similar numbers on the *Finisterrae* at CESGA). Running the OpenMP 3.1 version with 160 threads, we observe that HACCmk's original implementation runs faster than Parallware's automatically generated version (speedups 18× and 0.9×, respectively). The reason is that the HPC expert developer exploits coarser grain parallelism (number of parallel regions is 730 in Listing 1.5, line 13), while Parallware versions incur in high parallelization overhead because a parallel region is created/destroyed in each call to procedure `Step10_orig()` (number of parallel regions is $730 \times 327 = 238710$ in Listing 1.7). The PGI compiler provides worse performance for the original HACCmk (running time 9.14 versus 7.42 of GCC). However, the performance with Parallware version performs poorly, probably due to the fact that the PGI run-time incurs in higher overhead in creation/destruction of parallel regions. Work-in-progress aims at adding support for interprocedural detection of parallelism. By managing procedure calls that write only on scalar variables passed by reference (see Listing 1.5, line 19, parameters `&dx1`, `&dy1`, `&dz1`), Parallware will successfully detect and parallelize the fully parallel loop `for_i` (Listing 1.5, lines 17–23). By matching the HPC expert's parallel implementation, we expect Parallware to provide acceptable performance similar to the original version.

Finally, note that OpenACC-enabled version with PGI 16.10 does not accelerate CPU OMP3.1, probably because HACCmk requires many CPU-to/from-GPU data transfers of small size. However, it is remarkable that Parallware still achieves an speedup 4.8× with respect to the serial code. The numbers show that while thread creation/destruction is very expensive on the CPU, its overhead is not so critical on the GPU.

Overall, the experiments show that Parallware supports the parallel design pattern *Fully Parallel Loop*, but it needs improvements in inter-procedural analysis to exploit coarser-grain parallelism with OpenMP and OpenACC.

3.2 The Parallware Suite

Parallware technology [1,4] uses an approach for parallelism that does not rely on loop-level classical dependence analysis. The classical approach builds systems of mathematical equations whose solutions allow to identify pairs of memory references in the loop body that might lead to race conditions during the parallel execution of the loop. In contrast, Parallware uses a fast, extensible hierarchical classification scheme to address dependence analysis. It splits the code into

Table 3. Execution times (in seconds) and speedups of HACCmk in Finisterrae (CPU Intel Xeon and NVIDIA GPU Tesla K80).

Test size	Original							
	Small ASE		Medium ASE		Small seed		Medium seed	
Compiler GNU 4.8.2								
CPU Serial	3.57	–	8.82	–	41.23	–	90.42	–
CPU OMP3.1	0.47	7.6×	0.99	8.9×	7.27	5.7×	13.68	6.6×
Compiler PGI 16.10								
CPU Serial	3.24	–	8.09	–	41.36	–	96.87	–
CPU OMP3.1	1.17	2.8×	1.26	6.4×	33.74	1.2×	117.25	0.8×
GPU ACC2.5	0.24	13.5×	0.42	19.3×	2.91	14.2×	6.19	15.6×

a small domain-independent computational kernels (e.g. assignment, reduction, recurrence, etc.), combining multiple static analysis techniques including array access patterns, array access ranges, and alias analysis. Next, it checks contextual properties between the kernels in order to discover parallelism and to select the most appropriate paralleling strategy for the loop. Finally, Parallware adds the corresponding OpenMP/OpenACC directives and performs code transformations as needed (e.g. array privatization in parallel reductions, which is natively supported by OpenMP in Fortran but not in C). Parallware is also based on the production-grade LLVM compiler infrastructure.

Parallware Trainer [2] is a new interactive tool for high-productivity HPC education and training. It allows experiential learning by providing an interactive, real-time GUI with editor capabilities to assist in the design and implementation of parallel code. Powered by the hierarchical classification engine of Parallware technology, it discovers parallelism, provides a ranking of parallel design patterns, and implements those designs using standards OpenMP 4.5 and OpenACC 2.5 (see video tutorials *How to use Parallware Trainer* available at www.parallware.com). Overall, the main advantages of Parallware Trainer are high availability 24×7, reduction of costs, and broader audience of STEM people in far-away geographical locations.

Parallware Assistant, currently under development, will be the next tool of the suite. The Parallware Trainer is oriented to HPC education and training, so its GUI only shows the key information needed to understand why a code snippet can be parallelized (e.g., contains a scalar reduction with an associative, commutative sum operator), and how it can be executed in parallel safely (e.g., atomic update of the sum operator). In contrast, the Parallware Assistant will provide detailed information about every operator and every variable of the code, for instance, detailed data scoping and detailed array access ranges.

Table 4. Execution times (in seconds) and speedups of HACCmk in Juron (CPU IBM Power8 and NVIDIA GPU P100).

	Original		Parallware	
Compiler GCC 6.3				
CPU serial	137.99	–		
CPU OMP3.1	7.42	18×	157.68	0.9×
Compiler PGI 16.10				
CPU serial	92.91	–		
CPU OMP3.1	9.14	10.8×	268.07	0.35×
GPU ACC2.5	n/a	n/a	19.13	4.8×

Table 5. Execution times (in seconds) and speedups of HACCmk in Finisterrae (CPU Intel Xeon and NVIDIA GPU Tesla K80).

	Original		Parallware	
Compiler GCC 6.3				
CPU serial	126.26	–		
CPU OMP3.1	12.37	10.2×	708.44	0.18×
Compiler PGI 16.10				
CPU serial	104.21	–		
CPU OMP3.1	10.17	10.3×	236.64	0.44×
GPU ACC2.5	n/a	n/a	32.11	3.2×

4 The Technological Roadmap of Parallware

Following current startup business practices, we seek to attain the minimum viable product (MVP) as quickly as possible. At the same time we are doing the MVP work, we are testing the market from the business side. We are discussing the sales cycle, price sensitiveness and business value to the target customers. We are conducting an early access program for Parallware Trainer, our first product for high-productivity STEM education and training in parallel programming for undergraduate and PhD levels.

Parallware's technological roadmap is driven by the best practices observed in CORAL, NPB and XRayTrace. Our go-to-market strategy is based on engaging with world-class HPC facilities, working together to better understand how to help them with their mission-critical activities (e.g., technology scouting, creation of benchmark codes, porting of HPC applications). Thus, we are participating in strategic partnership programs (BSC, ORNL and TACC) and deploying Parallware Trainer in real production environments (BSC, ORNL, NERSC, LRZ).

As of writing, our priorities for the technological development of Parallware Trainer in the short and medium term are (in order of priority):

1. Improve the usability of the GUI to facilitate the analysis, compilation and execution of scientific programs. Analyze programs across multiple source code files that use MPI, OpenMP and OpenACC. Integrate the GUI with compilers from different vendors (e.g., IBM, PGI) in production-level supercomputers (e.g. *modules*, job queuing systems).
2. Improve the support for parallel design patterns *parallel scalar reduction* and *parallel sparse reduction*. As of writing, Parallware already supports the *AtomicImpl* and *ReductionImpl* implementations for OpenMP 4.5 and OpenACC 2.5, both for CPU and GPU devices. Work-in-progress aims at adding support for the *PrivateImpl* implementation as well.
3. Provide a ranking of parallel implementations, suggesting the "best" option for a given parallel programming standard, compiler and device. Mechanisms for the user to select the preferred implementation will be added.
4. Provide a list of suggestions for the user to improve the parallel implementation generated by the Parallware tools. Current work aims at improving data scoping support though advanced techniques for array range analysis and detection of temporary arrays. This information is useful to minimize CPU-to/from-GPU data transfers, for example by allocating temporary arrays directly on the GPU device.
5. Improve the Parallware core technology to discover parallelism across procedure calls. Inter-procedural analysis (IPA)[2] usually requires handling user-defined data structures (e.g. *struct*), auxiliary pointer variables that alias with output variables (*aliasing*), and C++ STL classes (e.g. `std::vector`).

Finally, our go-to-market strategy is aligned with world-class exhibitions ISC High Performance 2017 (ISC'17) and Supercomputing 2017 (SC17). During 2017, we plan to commercially launch Parallware Trainer, an interactive, real-time editor with GUI features to facilitate the learning, usage, and implementation of parallel programming. We also plan to test a prototype of Parallware Assistant, a new software tool that will offer a high-productivity programming environment to help HPC experts to manage the complexity of parallel programming. Example of technical features are detailed data scoping at the loop and functions levels, and visual browsing of the parallelism found in the code.

5 Related Work

Parallelization tools have been built in the past that discover parallelism in loops via symbolic equations, where the user can input ranges of values given a set of inputs. Some of these tools include SUIF [15], Polaris [7], Cetus [8], iPAT/OMP [11] and ParaWise [13] (CAPTools/CAPO). However, these tools are extremely hard to use with real applications, even for advanced application developers because they rely on research compilers with complex user interfaces and they take significant amount of time to complete their analysis. Some of

[2] Requirement for porting HPC applications, not for HPC education and training.

them are restricted to the older Fortran 77 standard or focus on loop level parallelism for simple array operations. In contrast, Parallware uses a fast, extensible hierarchical classification scheme to address dependence analysis. Based on the production-grade LLVM compiler infrastructure, Parallware is beginning to show success on the parallelization of C codes that defeat the other tools.

6 Conclusions and Future Work

Preliminary results suggest that the parallel design patterns used by HPC expert developers have not changed significantly across NPB, CORAL and new bechmarks such as XRayTrace. The latest updates in OpenMP 4.5 and OpenACC 2.5 improve support for reductions and atomic operations. This is expected to simplify implementations, leading to better productivity and maintainability.

Writing performance portable code is a challenge and a responsability for the programmer. Parallware tools are a step forward to help in this regard by supporting best practices for OpenMP 4.5 and OpenACC 2.5 across different compilers and devices. The parallel design patterns used in Parallware technology have been shown to be an effective approach to discover the parallelism available in the benchmark NPB, CORAL and XRayTrace.

As future work, we plan to finish this study with NPB, CORAL, XRayTrace and other well-known benchmark suites such as SPECaccel. We are aware of the importance of Fortran, and we are working to support it as soon as the new Fortran front-end is available for LLVM [14].

Acknowledgements. The authors gratefully acknowledge the access to the HPB PCP Pilot Systems at Julich Supercomputing Centre, which have been partially funded by the European Union Seventh Framework Programme (FP7/2007-2013) under grant agreement no. 604102 (HPB). Also thanks to the Supercomputing Centre of Galicia (CESGA) for providing access to the FinisTerrae supercomputer.

References

1. Andión, J., Arenaz, M., Rodríguez, G., Touriño, J.: A novel compiler support for automatic parallelization on multicore systems. Parallel Comput. **39**(9), 442–460 (2013)
2. Appentra: Parallware Trainer, April 2017. http://www.parallware.com/
3. Arenaz, M., Domínguez, J., Crespo, A.: Democratization of HPC in the oil & gas industry through automatic parallelization with parallware. In: 2015 Rice Oil and Gas HPC Workshop, March 2015
4. Arenaz, M., Touriño, J., Doallo, R.: XARK: an extensible framework for automatic recognition of computational kernels. ACM Trans. Program. Lang. Syst. (TOPLAS) **30**(6), 32:1–32:56 (2008)
5. Asanovic, K., Bodik, R., Catanzaro, B.C., Gebis, J.J., Husbands, P., Keutzer, K., Patterson, D.A., Plishker, W.L., Shalf, J., Williams, S.W., Yelick, K.A.: The landscape of parallel computing research: a view from Berkeley. Technical report, UC Berkeley (2006)

6. Bailey, D., Barszcz, E., Barton, J., Browning, D., Carter, R., Dagum, L., Fatoohi, R., Frederickson, P., Lasinski, T., Schreiber, R., Simon, H., Venkatakrishnan, V., Weeratunga, S.: The NAS parallel benchmarks - summary and preliminary results. In Proceedings of the 1991 ACM/IEEE Conference on Supercomputing, Supercomputing 1991, pp. 158–165. ACM (1991)
7. Blume, W., Doallo, R., Eigenmann, R., Grout, J., Hoeflinger, J., Lawrence, T., Lee, J., Padua, D., Paek, Y., Pottenger, B., Rauchwerger, L., Tu, P.: Parallel programming with Polaris. Computer **29**(12), 78–82 (1996)
8. Dave, C., Bae, H., Min, S.-J., Lee, S., Eigenmann, R., Midkiff, S.: Cetus: a source-to-source compiler infrastructure for multicores. IEEE Micro **42**(12), 36–42 (2009)
9. Department of Energy (DoE): CORAL Benchmark Codes (2014). https://asc.llnl.gov/CORAL-benchmarks/
10. Gómez-Sousa, H., Arenaz, M., Rubiños-López, O., Martínez-Lorenzo, J.: Novel source-to-source compiler approach for the automatic parallelization of codes based on the method of moments. In: Proceedings of the 9th European Conference on Antenas and Propagation, EuCap 2015, April 2015
11. Ishihara, M., Honda, H., Sato, M.: Development and implementation of an interactive parallelization assistance tool for OpenMP: iPat/OMP. IEICE Trans. Inf. Syst. **89–D**(2), 399–407 (2006)
12. Jiang, Q., Lee, Y.C., Zomaya, A., Arenaz, M., Leslie, L.: Optimizing scientific workflows in the cloud: a montage example. In: Proceedings of the 2014 IEEE/ACM 7th International Conference on Utility and Cloud Computing (UCC), pp. 517–522. IEEE, December 2014
13. Johnson, S., Evans, E., Jin, H., Ierotheou, C.: The ParaWise expert assistant – widening accessibility to efficient and scalable tool generated OpenMP code. In: Chapman, B.M. (ed.) WOMPAT 2004. LNCS, vol. 3349, pp. 67–82. Springer, Heidelberg (2005). doi:10.1007/978-3-540-31832-3_7
14. Lawrence Livermore National Laboratory: Open-Source Fortran Compiler Technology for LLVM (2015). https://www.llnl.gov/news/nnsa-national-labs-team-nvidia-develop-open-source-fortran-compiler-technology
15. Liao, S.-W., Diwan, A., Bosch Jr., R.P., Ghuloum, A., Lam, M.S.: SUIF explorer: an interactive and interprocedural parallelizer. In: Proceedings of the 7th ACM SIGPLAN Symposium on Principles and Practice of Parallel Programming, PPopp 1999, pp. 37–48. ACM Press, New York (1999)
16. Lobeiras, J., Arenaz, M.: a success case using parallware: the NAS parallel benchmark EP. In: Proceedings of the OpenMPCon Developers Conference (2015)
17. Lobeiras, J., Arenaz, M., Hernández, O.: Experiences in extending parallware to support OpenACC. In: Chandrasekaran, S., Foertter, F. (eds.) Proceedings of the Second Workshop on Accelerator Programming using Directives, WACCPD 2015, Austin, Texas, USA, 15 November 2015, pp. 4:1–4:12. ACM (2015)
18. Lopez, M.G., Larrea, V.V., Joubert, W., Hernandez, O., Haidar, A., Tomov, S., Dongarra, J.: Towards achieving performance portability using directives for accelerators. In: Proceedings of the Third International Workshop on Accelerator Programming Using Directives, WACCPD 2016, pp. 13–24. IEEE Press, Piscataway (2016)
19. Berril, M.: XRayTrace miniapp (2017). https://code.ornl.gov/mbt/RayTrace-miniapp
20. Martineau, M., Price, J., McIntosh-Smith, S., Gaudin, W.: Pragmatic performance portability with OpenMP 4.x. In: Maruyama, N., de Supinski, B.R., Wahib, M. (eds.) IWOMP 2016. LNCS, vol. 9903, pp. 253–267. Springer, Cham (2016). doi:10.1007/978-3-319-45550-1_18

21. Mattson, T., Sanders, B., Massingill, B.: Patterns for Parallel Programming, 1st edn. Addison-Wesley Professional (2004)
22. McCool, M., Reinders, J., Robison, A.: Structured Parallel Programming: Patterns for Efficient Computation, 1st edn. Morgan Kaufmann Publishers Inc., San Francisco (2012)
23. OpenACC Architecture Review Board: The OpenACC Application Programming Interface, Version 2.5, October 2015. http://www.openacc.org
24. OpenMP Architecture Review Board: OpenMP Application Program Interface, Version 4.5, November 2015. http://www.openmp.org
25. Wienke, S., Miller, J., Schulz, M., Müller, M.S.: Development effort estimation in HPC. In: Proceedings of the International Conference for High Performance Computing, Networking, Storage and Analysis, SC 2016, pp. 10:1–10:12. IEEE Press, Piscataway (2016)

Experiences Evaluating Functionality and Performance of IBM POWER8+ Systems

Verónica G. Vergara Larrea(✉), Wayne Joubert, Mark Berrill, Swen Boehm, Arnold Tharrington, Wael R. Elwasif, and Don Maxwell

Oak Ridge National Laboratory, Oak Ridge, TN, USA
{vergaravg,joubert,berrillma,boehms,arnoldt,elwasifwr,maxwellde}@ornl.gov

Abstract. In preparation for Summit, Oak Ridge National Laboratory's next generation supercomputer, two IBM Power-based systems were deployed in late 2016 at the Oak Ridge Leadership Computing Facility (OLCF). This paper presents a detailed description of the acceptance of the first IBM Power-based early access systems installed at the OLCF. The two systems, Summitdev and Tundra, contain IBM POWER8+ processors with NVIDIA Pascal GPUs and were acquired to provide researchers with a platform to optimize codes for the Power architecture. In addition, this paper presents early functional and performance results obtained on Summitdev with the latest software stack available.

1 Introduction

The Collaboration of Oak Ridge, Argonne, and Livermore (CORAL) was launched in 2014 by the U.S. Department of Energy (DOE) [14]. The CORAL collaboration is led by Office of Science and National Nuclear Security Administration (NNSA) facilities which include the Oak Ridge Leadership Computing Facility (OLCF) at Oak Ridge National Laboratory (ORNL), the Argonne Leadership Computing Facility (ALCF) at Argonne National Laboratory (ANL), and Lawrence Livermore National Laboratory (LLNL). This joint effort between three DOE national laboratories aims to build high performance computing (HPC) technologies to support DOE's mission and procure next generation large-scale systems for each participating laboratory. Two distinct architectures were selected for CORAL, one based on Intel's manycore processors, and another based on IBM Power processors with NVIDIA Volta accelerators. As a result of

J.M. Kunkel et al. (Eds.): ISC High Performance Workshops 2017, LNCS 10524, pp. 254–274, 2017.
https://doi.org/10.1007/978-3-319-67630-2_20

CORAL three new systems will be deployed in the 2018 timeframe: Aurora at ANL, Summit at ORNL, and Sierra at LLNL. Aurora will be based on Intel's third generation Xeon Phi manycore architecture and is expected to have over 50,000 compute nodes and provide 180 PFLOPS [1]. Summit is ORNL's next generation supercomputer and will be based on IBM's POWER9 architecture with multiple NVIDIA Volta GPUs per node interconnected via NVLink. Summit is expected to have approximately 3,400 compute nodes and to deliver more than 5 times the performance of Titan, ORNL's flagship supercomputer today [11]. Sierra will also be based on IBM's POWER9 processors and NVIDIA Volta GPUs and is expected to have 4–6 times the performance of Sequoia, LLNL's production supercomputer [9].

In preparation for the arrival of Summit, the OLCF procured two early access (EA) systems, Summitdev and Tundra, which are one generation removed from Summit's architecture. The goal of the EA systems is to give researchers an opportunity to optimize their applications for the Power architecture and to use multiple GPUs per node. Summitdev is the main system supporting the Center for Accelerated Application Readiness (CAAR) efforts [2]. In addition, Summitdev will be used by several researchers as part of the Exascale Computing Project [5]. Tundra, on the other hand, will be used as an internal system to test new software and gain a better understanding of the IBM ecosystem.

The EA systems were installed in November of 2016. In order to ensure that each system would be able to fulfill its main purpose, the OLCF developed an acceptance test plan that focused on functionality and reflected the needs of the CAAR applications. Acceptance of the EA systems was completed in December 2016. Both Summitdev and Tundra were officially released to users in January 2017.

This paper describes the novel features of the hardware and software stack, the test plan and procedures used to accept the system, and early results obtained from running real-world applications and benchmarks on this new architecture. Section 2 describes the system configuration, followed by a high-level description of the acceptance test plan in Sect. 3. Sections 4–8 describe the benchmarks and applications used, why they were chosen, and present individual results. Section 9 discusses several challenges and lessons learned from accepting the EA systems. Finally, Sect. 10 presents initial conclusions based on the experience the ORNL team gained from using the IBM Power architecture.

2 System Configuration

Summitdev and Tundra are the two POWER8+ early access (EA) systems deployed at the OLCF in late 2016. The main building block for the EA systems is the IBM Power System S822LC server, which is the first IBM Power-based system to provide NVIDIA NVLink Technology. Summitdev is comprised of 54 IBM POWER8 S822LC compute nodes. It has access to an NFS file system that provides home directories, as well as two high performance parallel file systems: the OLCF's center-wide Lustre parallel file system, Spider 2 [24], and a dedicated

GPFS file system, Leto. The Tundra system is based on the same server offering as Summitdev but contains 18 compute nodes. Tundra has access to a separate NFS file system that provides home directories as well as project workspaces.

Hardware. Each compute node has two IBM POWER8 processors running at 2.860 GHz in normal operation and at 3.492 GHz in turbo mode. Each processor has 10 cores, each capable of up to 8-way simultaneous multithreading (SMT), i.e., each core supports up to 8 hardware threads. Each CPU is connected to two NVIDIA Tesla P100 Pascal GPUs via NVIDIA NVLink Technology which provides a bandwidth of 80 GB/s from the CPU to the GPUs and between GPUs. Each NVIDIA Tesla P100 GPU is capable of delivering 5.3 TFLOPS of double precision, 10.6 TFLOPS of single precision, and 21.2 TFLOPS of half precision floating point performance. Furthermore, the P100 GPU is the first accelerator to use High Bandwidth Memory 2 (HBM2) and includes four vertical stacks of four memory dies totaling 16 GB of HBM2 memory and providing 732 GB/s peak memory bandwidth [7]. The compute node also has 256 GB of DDR4 memory capable of 340 GB/s peak memory bandwidth as well as one 1.6 TB Non-Volatile Memory (NVMe) device [12,20]. All compute nodes are interconnected via Mellanox EDR InfiniBand in a full fat-tree network that provides two links each with 100 Gbps bandwidth between compute nodes. Figure 1 shows the high-level structure of the compute node architecture used in Summitdev and Tundra.

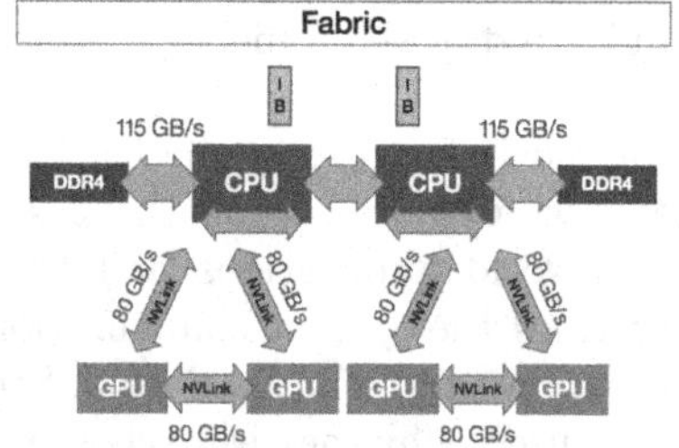

Fig. 1. IBM POWER8 S822LC compute node obtained from [20].

Software Stack. IBM provides a specialized software stack that targets their HPC offerings. The products included in IBM's HPC software stack as well as IBM's partners, NVIDIA and PGI, are described in Table 1. After Summitdev and Tundra were accepted and IBM's HPC software stack was officially released, both systems were upgraded to use the generally available (GA) software. The versions used in production are listed under the "GA" column in Table 1. Since then, the software stack has continued to mature, and the systems now have newer pre-release versions of certain components. The current versions available on the EA systems are listed under the "Production" column.

Table 1. EA systems software stack

Feature	Product	Acceptance	GA	Production	Vendor
Batch scheduler	Spectrum LSF	10.1.0[a]	10.1.0.1	10.1.0.1	IBM
MPI library	Spectrum MPI	10.1.0.2[b]	10.1.0.2	10.1.0.2	IBM
Math libraries	ESSL	5.5[b]	5.5	5.5	IBM
Compilers	XL C/C++	13.1.5[b]	13.1.5	14.1.0[b]	IBM
	XL Fortran	15.1.5[b]	15.1.5	16.1.0[b]	IBM
	PGI	16.10[a]	17.1	17.3	PGI
	clang (LLVM C/C++)	3.8.0[b]	3.8.0[b]	3.8.0[b]	IBM
	xlflang (LLVM Fortran)	4.0.0[b]	4.0.0[b]	4.0.0[b]	IBM
	GCC	4.8.5	4.8.5	4.8.5	RedHat
CUDA support	CUDA Toolkit	8.0.44 – 1[b]	8.0.54	8.0.54	NVIDIA
	CUDA Driver	361.103	361.107	375.51	NVIDIA
Parallel file system	Spectrum Scale (GPFS)	4.2.1.2	4.2.1.2	4.2.3	IBM

[a] Patched version.
[b] Beta version.

3 Acceptance Test

The OLCF developed a comprehensive acceptance test (AT) plan to verify the functionality of the EA systems. The AT plan contains three test phases: a hardware test (HWT), an I/O test (IOT), and a functionality test (FT). The AT on the EA systems took approximately three days to complete.

Hardware Test (HWT). The HWT is designed to ensure that all the hardware components are functioning correctly. This is accomplished by running vendor-provided hardware diagnostics as well as the HPL High Performance Linpack benchmark both to identify slow nodes and to ensure that each node meets or exceeds expected performance levels. The HWT also includes system administration tasks that are commonly needed in production. First, the full system is rebooted twice to ensure that it can be put back into production in a reasonable amount of time. Then, an MPI application is used to start multi-node jobs across the system and a node failure is simulated. The test is considered successful if the node failure only impacts the job that was allocated on that node. If all tests in the HWT phase succeed, the IOT is started.

I/O Test (IOT). As previously mentioned, Summitdev has access to a small GPFS file system called Leto and to the Spider 2 Lustre file system. For the IOT, only Leto was tested given that the OLCF will have a center-wide GPFS file system in the Summit timeframe. The IOT basic functionality tests include measuring metadata performance with the *mdtest* benchmark, measuring I/O bandwidth of POSIX, HDF5, and MPI-IO using the *IOR* benchmark, and creating a 10 TB file in the file system. If no issues are observed during the IOT, the FT starts.

Functionality Test (FT). The FT phase includes tests to evaluate the functionality of compilers, math and I/O libraries, MPI implementation, and tools. To accomplish this a set of miniapps, benchmarks, and real-world applications is used. These were selected to ensure high coverage of features commonly used by scientific application developers. Table 2 summarizes the codes used during the FT phase and each code's test objectives.

Table 2. FT benchmarks, miniapps, and applications

Test	Purpose
Intel MPI Benchmarks	MPI bandwidth and latency
OpenMP 3.1 verification and validation suite	OpenMP 3.1 specification
CUDA & GPU Direct tests	CUDA, CUDA Fortran CUDA MPS, and GPU Direct
NVLink Tests	CPU↔GPU, GPU↔GPU bandwidth
SPEC OMP2012	OpenMP 3.1 functionality and performance
SPEC ACCEL ACC suite	OpenACC 1.0 functionality and performance
SPEC ACCEL OMP suite (pre-release)	OpenMP 4.5 functionality and performance
ScaLAPACK tests	Parallel dense linear algebra (DLA) operations
Minisweep	Radiation transport miniapp with OpenMP 3.1 and CUDA support
NUCCOR kernels	Nuclear physics miniapp; DLA operations using: LAPACK, OpenBLAS, ESSL; programming models: OpenMP 3.1, OpenMP 4.5, OpenACC
XRayTrace	Ray propagation miniapp; uses: C++11 threads, OpenMP, OpenACC, CUDA
Nekbone	CORAL benchmark; simulates Nek5000
HACCmk	CORAL benchmark; simulates HACC
QBOX	CORAL benchmark; first-principles molecular dynamics application
GTC	Gyrokinetic 3D particle-in-cell application

During the FT phase, each code is compiled with each target compiler. Then, a single job for each test is submitted. Once each test has completed successfully at least once, the entire set of tests is launched continuously for a period of at least 8 h. During that period, any job failure is investigated and classified.

The test phase is considered complete if there are no job failures, or in the event that there are failures, if the root cause for each failure has been identified and a remediation or a fix exists.

4 Benchmarks

Several benchmarks and standard tests were used to evaluate the functionality of the EA systems. A set of performance tests was also used to verify that the hardware met vendor specifications; this set included bandwidth intra-node tests (i.e., between node components) and inter-node tests (i.e., between compute nodes).

GPU Specific Tests. A set of tests (i.e., CUDA tests) was created to ensure correct functionality of the NVIDIA CUDA driver, the NVIDIA CUDA Toolkit, and the P100 GPUs. The set includes modified versions of the NVIDIA CUDA Toolkit code samples [4], in particular the "Simple References" examples.

Specific tests were also developed to evaluate GPUDirect capabilities (i.e., GPU_Direct tests), NVLink Technology (i.e., NVLink tests), and Unified Virtual Addressing (NVLink UVA tests). Three simple GPUDirect codes were created: *PingPong*, *Stencil*, and *Collective*. Variations of each code were also created to test CUDA MPS, CUDA Fortran, and managed memory. Tests with 1, 4, and 25 compute nodes were created for each code, and each was built with XL, PGI, GCC, and LLVM. Three additional tests were created to measure the host-device and device-device bandwidths as well as ensure proper functionality of each device. These tests are based on the *bandwidthTest*, *deviceQuery*, and *topologyQuery* code samples provided in the "Utilities" section of the CUDA SDK examples. The *bandwidthTest* example was also extended to include support for unified memory. The bandwidth values measured using the NVLink tests are shown in Fig. 2.

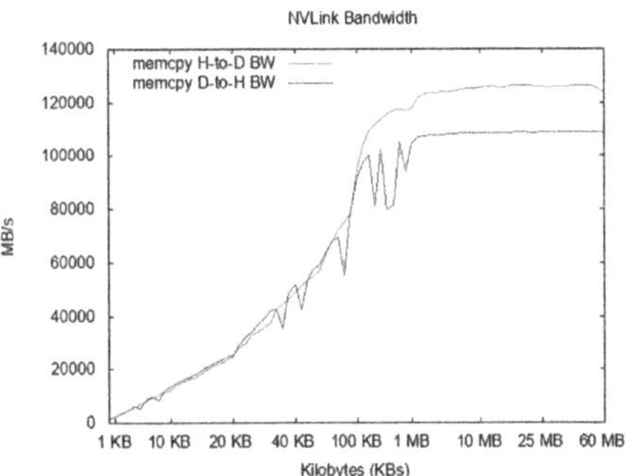

Fig. 2. NVLink host-device and device-host bandwidth using memcpy and unified memory.

During Summitdev's acceptance, the CUDA, GPU_Direct, and NVLink tests were able to identify several issues on the system. The Collective CUDA Fortran tests triggered a bug in the CUDA driver that caused the GPU to hang instead of returning an appropriate error. The Collective OpenACC test was able to identify an issue in how a pre-release version of Spectrum MPI was launching OpenACC code. The NVLink tests identified a performance regression between CUDA drivers as well as find two Summitdev compute nodes in which peer-to-peer access between GPUs 2 and 3 was not functioning correctly.

MPI Tests. The Intel MPI Benchmarks suite (IMB) [6] provides a set of tests of MPI capabilities and performance on parallel platforms. The test suite was run on Summitdev to thoroughly check functionality and evaluate target performance measurements of MPI over the EDR InfiniBand network.

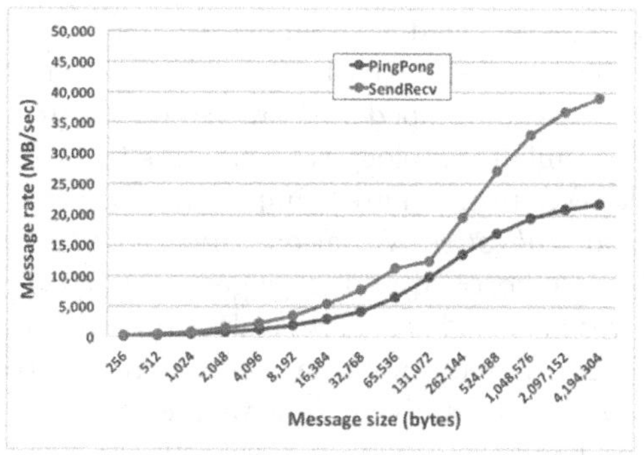

Fig. 3. MPI point-to-point bandwidth

Figure 3 shows point-to-point communication results. Maximum bandwidths attained were 21.793 unidirectional (resp. 39.062 bidirectional) GB/sec, comparing favorably to theoretical peak values of 25 (resp. 50) GB/sec; measured latencies were 1.29 (resp. 1.43) µs. This test was performed using 2 MPI ranks on 2 nodes without any special action to specify node placement.

5 Compiler Tests

The following test suites were selected to evaluate the different compiler implementations available on Summitdev. The test suites were chosen both to evaluate the implementation against the corresponding programming model specification and also to evaluate the functionality and performance of each compiler.

OpenMP Verification and Validation Suite. The OpenMP 3.1 Validation Testsuite [29] is a portable and robust validation test suite execution environment to validate the OpenMP implementation in several compilers. This test suite targets version 3.1 of the OpenMP specification, which does not support offloading to accelerators. OpenMP offloading was tested using the pre-release SPEC ACCEL suite for OpenMP. We used the version of the test suite that is included in the ongoing work to incorporate OpenMP offloading support into Clang and LLVM [18].

Table 3. OpenMP validation suite results

NTHREADS	C				Fortran		
	GNU	PGI	XL	CLANG	GNU	PGI	XL
2	94.3%	94.3%	94.3%	93.5%	88.5%	85.4%	88.5%
8	95.9%	95.9%	95.9%	95.1%	88.5%	85.4%	88.5%
16	95.9%	94.3%	95.9%	93.5%	88.5%	85.4%	87.5%
64	95.9%	94.3%	95.1%	93.5%	88.5%	85.4%	86.5%

The test suite included a total of 219 tests (123 tests for C and 96 for Fortran) that cover 115 OpenMP constructs (62 C constructs and 53 using Fortran). The test suite framework includes four varieties of tests for a target OpenMP directive; *normal tests* check that the directive (or clause) is implemented correctly, *cross tests* checks the impact of removing the target construct from the code. More details can be found in [29].

The test suite was exercised using different numbers of OpenMP threads for each of the available compilers. No special binding and mapping controls were used. Table 3 shows the percentage of successful tests for the combination of compilers, languages, and number of threads. Only GA versions of the compilers as listed in Table 1 were used. For GCC, the *gomp-4_0-branch* branch of the GCC 6.3 compiler suite was used.

The test suite results show better support for OpenMP C bindings among all tested compilers than for Fortran binding. The testing matrix for all OpenMP constructs across all compilers and using different number of threads helps identify issues with the compiler implementation (or in some cases, with the testing suite itself). For this evaluation, a total of 15 tests (2 C tests and 13 Fortran tests) failed for all combinations of compilers and number of threads, possibly indicating a problem in the tests themselves. Some tests show a different failure behavior as the number of threads change. In such cases, comparing the failure pattern with results for the same tests from other compilers may help identify if the failure is due to compiler implementation bug or an issue with the test itself that makes it invalid for certain thread counts.

SPEC ACCEL and SPEC OMP2012. The Standard Performance Evaluation Corporation (SPEC) releases a variety of realistic and standardized benchmarks to evaluate the performance of computer systems. For acceptance, two SPEC benchmark suites were used to evaluate the different compilers available for the EA systems. The benchmarks used were SPEC OMP2012 and SPEC ACCEL. The SPEC OMP2012 benchmark measures the performance of OpenMP-based applications. It includes 14 applications and is focused on OpenMP 3.1. SPEC ACCEL is a benchmark suite of computationally intensive applications and measures the performance of accelerator based systems. SPEC ACCEL supports OpenCL and OpenACC. Support for OpenMP 4.5 is currently in development and is expected to be released this year. In this work, a pre-release version of SPEC ACCEL with OpenMP 4.5 support was used to evaluate offloading capabilities of the available compilers.

For the evaluation, "base" runs were produced following SPEC rules. All benchmarks were built using common optimization flags, and were run with the test and train problem sizes, and 3 iterations of the benchmarks with the reference problem sizes. All of the metrics presented in this section are *measured estimates*. To build the benchmarks the "Production" compilers listed in Table 1 were used with the exception of the GCC compilers. For GCC, the development version of GCC 6.3.1 built from the *gomp-4_0-branch* branch was used because it provides partial support for OpenACC.

All SPEC OMP2012 runs are executed on a dedicated node for each benchmark run. For these tests 160 OpenMP threads were used to fully utilize the hardware threads available on the Power architecture. SPEC ACCEL benchmarks are also executed on a dedicated node for each benchmark run. While 4 P100 GPUs are available on the compute node, only one is used for the execution of the benchmarks.

PGI is the only production compiler that delivers successful results for SPEC OMP2012 and SPEC ACCEL for OpenACC. The measured estimates for the SPEC OMP2012 and SPEC ACCEL compute performance metrics can be seen

Table 4. Overview of execution of the SPEC OMP2012 suite.

	Benchmark													
	350.md	351.bwaves	352.nab	357.bt331	358.botsalgn	359.botsspar	360.ilbdc	362.fma3d	363.swim	367.imagick	370.mgrid331	371.applu331	372.smithwa	376.kdtree
XL	✓	✓	✓	✓	✓	✓	✓	✓	✓	✓	✓	✓	✓	✓
PGI	✓	✓	✓	✓	✓*	✓	✓	✓	✓	✓	✓	✓	✓	✓
GNU	✓	✓	✓	✓	✓	✓	✓	✓	✓	✓	✓	✓	✓	✓
LLVM	✗[a]	✓	✓	✗[a]	✓*	✓	✓	✗[a]	✗[a]	✓	✗[a]	✗[a]	✓	✓

[a] Compile Error.

Table 5. Overview of execution of the SPEC ACCEL OpenACC suite.

	Benchmark														
	303.ostencil	304.olbm	314.omriq	350.md	351.palm	352.ep	353.clvrleaf	354.cg	355.seismic	356.sp	357.csp	359.miniGhost	360.ilbdc	363.swim	370.bt
PGI	✓	✓	✓	✓	✓	✓	✓	✓	✓	✓	✓	✓	✓	✓	✓
GNU	✓	✓											✓		

Table 6. Overview of execution the SPEC ACCEL OpenMP suite.

	Benchmark														
	503.postencil	504.polbm	514.pomriq	550.pmd	551.ppalm	552.pep	553.pclvrleaf	554.pcg	555.pseismic	556.psp	557.pcsp	559.pminiGhost	560.pilbdc	563.pswim	570.pbt
XL	✓	✓	✗[b]	✗[b]	✗[a]	✗[b]	✗[b]	✗[b]	✗[b]	✗[b]	✗[a]	✗[b]	✓	✗[c]	✗[a]
LLVM	✓	✓	✗[b]	✗[a]	✗[a]	✓	✗[a]	✗[b]	✓	–[d]	✗[a]	✗[a]	✗[c]	✗[a]	✓

[a] Compile Error.
[b] Runtime Error.
[c] Verification Error.
[d] *556.psp* is a mixed C and Fortran code, and cannot be compiled. clang and xlflang cannot be used together.

in Tables 7 and 8. The compute performance metric (labeled as "Overall") is the geometric mean of the normalized ratios of all the benchmarks in a particular SPEC benchmark suite.

The measured estimates for OMP2012 with the IBM XL compiler can be found in Table 7. ACCEL estimates for OpenMP with the XL compiler are not presented here because the compiler does not provide full support for OpenMP 4.5 yet. The current status of ACCEL for OpenMP with the XL compiler is summarized in Table 6. While most of the benchmarks successfully compile, only 3 pass the verification. All other benchmarks currently either do not compile or link correctly, experience runtime errors, or do not pass the verification.

Measured estimates for OMP2012 using the GCC compilers can be found in Table 7. The GCC compiler provides partial support for OpenACC offloading, and because it does not yet support *acc kernels* only three benchmarks in ACCEL OpenACC, as shown in Table 5, are parallelized. GCC does not currently provide OpenMP 4.0 offloading for GPU targets, therefore ACCEL OpenMP was not included. For GCC, measured estimates obtained with the reference problem size are reported.

Table 7. Measured estimates of the SPEC OMP2012 suite (higher is better).

	XL	PGI	GNU
350.md	6.38	6.88	1.41
351.bwaves	0.898	10.90	2.14
352.nab	3.98	4.49	5.93
357.bt331	10.20	7.50	9.95
358.botsalgn	3.78	3.30	3.74
359.botsspar	2.97	3.39	3.42
360.ilbdc	8.93	8.84	0.132
362.fma3d	4.30	4.19	6.17
363.swim	10.8	9.85	11.20
367.imagick	8.63	9.15	7.71
370.mgrid331	8.52	7.67	8.75
371.applu331	11.10	8.99	12.20
372.smithwa	7.40	8.26	12.60
376.kdtree	3.78	4.46	13.50
Overall	5.53	6.50	4.74

Table 8. Measured estimates of the SPEC ACCEL for OpeACC (higher is better).

	PGI	GNU
303.ostencil	7.66	3.26
304.olbm	11.10	8.86
314.omriq	8.86	
350.md	13.70	
351.palm	2.98	
352.ep	8.47	
353.clvrleaf	8.43	
354.cg	7.18	
355.seismic	8.16	
356.sp	8.21	
357.csp	8.94	
359.miniGhost	6.67	
360.ilbdc	9.33	4.39
363.swim	5.61	
370.bt	18.70	
Overall	8.31	

The *358.botsalgn* benchmark in the OMP2012 suite does not successfully run for the test and train problem sizes when compiled with the PGI and the GCC compilers. Running the benchmarks with the "ref" problem size, however, produces valid runs. The benchmarks are marked with a * in Table 4 since they will currently not produce a reportable run according to the SPEC reporting rules [10].

6 CORAL Benchmarks

The CORAL Benchmark codes are a suite of benchmarks and mini-applications designed to represent the workloads of the laboratories involved in the CORAL collaboration and will be used to evaluate the systems when deployed. More information about the CORAL Benchmark codes and unmodified versions of the applications can be found in [3].

Nekbone. Nekbone is a CORAL benchmark used to capture the basic structure and user interface of the Nek5000 software. Nek5000 is a high order, incompressible Navier-Stokes solver based on the spectral element method. Nekbone solves a standard Poisson equation using a conjugate gradient iteration with a simple preconditioner on a block or linear geometry. The benchmark is highly scalable and can accommodate a wide range of problem sizes. The benchmark is intrinsically well load balanced, with each process having the same number of spectral elements and point-to-point communication with up to 26 surrounding neighbors.

For the purposes of acceptance, a modified version of Nekbone to utilize the GPUs based on CUDA using the XL compiler was used. A single node was used to run a small problem and verify the correct output using the accelerated version of the application.

HACCmk. The Hardware Accelerated Cosmology Code (HACC) framework uses N-body techniques to simulate the formation of structure in collisionless fluids under the influence of gravity in an expanding universe. The HACC framework was designed with great flexibility making it easily portable between different platforms. HACC uses MPI and OpenMP and depends on an external FFT library.

For acceptance, a modified version of the HACC microkernel to utilize the GPUs based on CUDA using the XL compiler. A small problem utilizing 2 nodes and 8 processes (1 process/GPU) was used to verify the correct output using the accelerated version of the application. Detailed performance data was not collected, and a comparison of runtime across different node counts, problem sizes, and CPU vs. GPU was not performed.

QBOX. QBOX is a scalable first-principles molecular dynamics (FPMD) application used to compute properties of materials. QBOX is written in C++ and uses MPI [8,26].

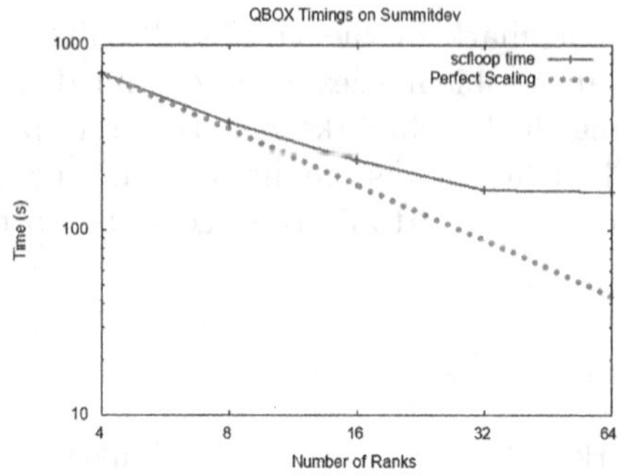

Fig. 4. QBOX results for a 640-atom bcc magnesium oxide system.

For the Summitdev acceptance, a single test case was run using 4 MPI ranks with 4 OpenMP threads per rank on a single node. To better understand the scalability of the code, four additional cases were created with 8, 16, 32, and 64 MPI ranks. Figure 4 shows the results obtained when running the standard GPU-enabled QBOX benchmark which simulates a large bcc magnesium oxide system with 640 atoms. The results show that the case does not scale well beyond 2 nodes. Further investigation is needed to better understand the scalability of QBOX.

7 Mini-applications

ScaLAPACK Tests. ScaLAPACK [21] is a Fortran library for performing dense linear algebra operations on distributed CPU-based systems using MPI. It is required by some OLCF applications including one of the thirteen Summit early readiness applications targeted by the ORNL CAAR program. For this test case, the `xsgsep` code is executed, a symmetric eigensolver test from the ScaLAPACK test suite. The test executes with four MPI ranks on one Summitdev node.

ScaLAPACK must be built against a version of the LAPACK [17] library. For this we tested two options: use of the standard LAPACK distribution, or use of the optimized LAPACK functionality found in ESSL [15]. For the latter, since ESSL is missing some required routines of the standard LAPACK version needed by ScaLAPACK, the code build's linker step was set up to use standard LAPACK as a backing library to satisfy any unsatisfied references, and repeated references to LAPACK routines were ignored. Also, the ScaLAPACK version included in the standard release of the PGI compiler was tested.

Cases run are shown in Table 9. All cases were successful except for those involving LLVM. The LLVM xlflang compiler used is an early beta version still in development. It is expected that robustness will improve as the compiler becomes more mature.

Table 9. ScaLAPACK cases tested

Compiler	LAPACK version	ScaLAPACK version	Status
GCC	Standard	Standard	Passed
GCC	ESSL	Standard	Passed
PGI	Standard	Standard	Passed
PGI	ESSL	Standard	Passed
PGI	Standard	PGI	Passed
LLVM	Standard	Standard	Failed
LLVM	ESSL	Standard	Failed
XL	Standard	Standard	Passed
XL	ESSL	Standard	Passed

Though not attempted here, ScaLAPACK use cases employing ESSL can in principle be modified to use the CPU-threaded or the CUDA-enabled version of ESSL to accelerate the performance of ScaLAPACK on Summitdev.

Minisweep. Minisweep is a miniapp designed to mimic the behavior of the sweep operation of the Denovo S_n radiation transport code [16]. It can be built with OpenMP 3.1 or CUDA support under multiple compilers in single processor or MPI mode.

Figure 5 shows the results obtained from running Minisweep using 8 MPI ranks on 2 compute nodes under the three different configurations: MPI-only, MPI with 2 OpenMP threads per rank, and MPI with CUDA. Minisweep built with the XL compiler shows a smaller performance improvement when OpenMP threads are enabled. This will require further investigation to understand how thread pinning and placement will impact performance.

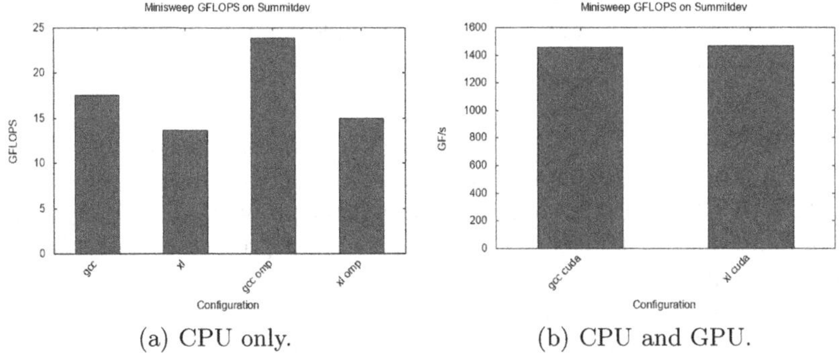

(a) CPU only. (b) CPU and GPU.

Fig. 5. Minisweep results using the XL and GCC production compilers.

	GNU, F	GNU, F, OMP3	GNU, C	GNU, C, OMP3	LLVM, F	LLVM, F, OMP3	LLVM, C	LLVM, C, OMP3	PGI, F	PGI, F, OMP3	PGI, C	PGI, C, OMP3	XL, F	XL, F, OMP3	XL, C	XL, C, OMP3
ESSL																
ESSL/SMP		N/A		N/A												
ESSL/SMPCUDA		N/A		N/A												
LAPACK																
PGI LAPACK	N/A	N/A	N/A	N/A	N/A	N/A	N/A	N/A					N/A	N/A	N/A	N/A
OpenBLAS																
MAGMA																
OpenMP 4	N/A	N/A	N/A	N/A					N/A	N/A	N/A	N/A				
OpenACC+cuBLAS	N/A	N/A	N/A	N/A	N/A	N/A	N/A	N/A					N/A	N/A	N/A	N/A

Fig. 6. NUCCOR kernels: configuration combinations tested

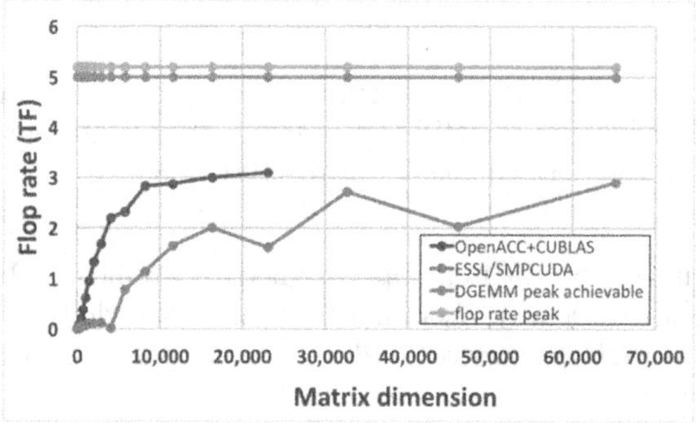

Fig. 7. NUCCOR kernels: timings for matrix products including transfers

During acceptance, the distributed version of Minisweep that uses CUDA and is compiled with GCC resulted in the highest performance. Building Minisweep with CUDA enabled with the PGI compiler resulted in build errors, and so did the OpenMP and CUDA versions of the miniapp when built with the LLVM compiler. The Minisweep test ran during acceptance was a small case to test functionality only.

NUCCOR Kernels. The NUCCOR kernels code is designed to model the performance of a significant computation of the NUCCOR nuclear physics application [23]. NUCCOR kernels computes the matrix product $C = A_1^T A_2 A_3$ for a series of dense matrix triples (A_1, A_2, A_3) of sizes representative of cases from NUCCOR workloads.

NUCCOR kernels tests multiple combinations of compiler family, source language, library and threading model. In practice, not all combinations of options are allowed, and not all allowed combinations are tested. The purpose of the test is to verify correctness for many supported combinations expected to be required by users of Summitdev rather than test all combinations.

Figure 6 shows the combinations tested. The designator "OMP3" denotes that the host code included OpenMP 3.1 constructs as a test for compatibility. In each LAPACK case, the library was entirely built by the respective host compiler. PGI LAPACK is a custom CPU-only build of LAPACK provided by PGI. OpenMP 4 cases use offload constructs and hand-coded DGEMM loops. The OpenACC/cuBLAS case uses OpenACC directives for offloading and cuBLAS for the DGEMM. The designated LLVM tests used an early OpenMP 4 implementation [13] Every case tested ran successfully and gave correct results, even though many of these combinations are very new, including XL/OpenMP 4, PGI/POWER, LLVM/Fortran and LLVM/OpenMP 4. The capability of these components to perform efficiently and interoperate correctly will be important to our users going forward.

Figure 7 shows timings for selected cases using square matrices for a range of sizes on a single GPU. The PGI Fortran compiler is used in both cases. Timings include data transfers to and from the GPU. The OpenACC+cuBLAS case benefits from less transfer due to the ability to keep an intermediate matrix on the GPU. The reasons for performance irregularities for the ESSL/SMPCUDA case, particularly for the $n = 4,081$ case, are unknown. For both cases, DGEMM performance is a significant fraction of peak attainable. We expect performance to improve as the software stack matures.

XRayTrace. The XRayTrace miniapp represents the primary computational component for a 3D coupled atomic-physics/ray-propagation code used to simulate ASE (Amplified Spontaneous Emission) and seeded X-ray lasers [16,19]. XRayTrace consists in solving many independent rays in parallel, aggregating the results to form an image that is used to couple the atomic physics in the full application.

Most C++ standard compilers are supported, and multiple programming models are tested including C++11 threads, OpenMP, OpenACC, and CUDA. No external libraries are required and all programming models are optional.

For acceptance, XRayTrace was used to test the C++ compiler support for the different programming models and to compare the relative performance of the available compilers. All GPU tests used a single GPU only, while CPU tests used all CPU cores. The timings listed in seconds only include the cost of the kernel or work performed for one iteration within the main application. Table 10 shows the results of the ASE/seeded problems for two common problem sizes. For all cases, all compilers/parallel models produced the correct output. In general, all compilers had similar timing results, CUDA showing the largest speedup. OpenACC with PGI had similar performance to CUDA. An unknown issue occurs when running OpenMP with PGI that causes a significant slowdown that was not seen with other compilers, which will require more investigation. In all cases, optimized flags for each compiler were chosen.

Table 10. XRayTrace timing results shown in seconds.

Problem	Compiler	Serial	Threads	OpenMP	OpenAcc	CUDA
ASE (small)	GCC	3.902	0.178	0.278	—	0.035
	PGI	3.296	0.197	12.082	0.038	—
	XL	2.766	0.150	0.314	—	0.056
	LLVM	3.898	0.197	0.409	—	0.059
ASE (medium)	GCC	9.377	0.376	0.611	—	0.073
	PGI	7.923	0.396	12.711	0.085	—
	XL	7.177	0.308	0.637	—	0.071
	LLVM	9.501	0.351	0.790	—	0.073
Seeded (small)	GCC	49.759	1.734	1.950	—	0.472
	PGI	49.996	1.969	619.476	0.453	—
	XL	32.519	1.481	4.609	—	0.463
	LLVM	51.546	1.776	3.991	—	0.456
Seeded (medium)	GCC	103.923	3.281	6.266	—	0.678
	PGI	117.806	4.326	371.055	0.734	—
	XL	78.791	3.017	7.189	—	0.670
	LLVM	111.715	3.558	6.529	—	0.666

8 OLCF Applications

To ensure that the system can support realistic workloads, a set of applications commonly used at OLCF were selected for acceptance of the EA systems including GTC [27], NAMD [25], and LSMS [22]. For this work, the GTC test cases were extended and its results are presented in this section.

GTC. GTC [27] is a 3D particle-in-cell code developed by the Princeton Plasma Physics Laboratory and the University of California at Irvine to study microturbulence in magnetically confined fusion plasmas. [27]. It is scalable to hundreds of thousands of processor cores and has been used previously for acceptance testing of OLCF systems [28]. The version of GTC used here is an older mature version based on MPI and OpenMP 3.1. Two cases are run, at 2 and 26 nodes with 10 MPI ranks per node and 2 OpenMP threads per rank. The cases represent 10 simulation steps with 769 radial and 3,072 poloidal gridcells with two electrons and two ions per gridcell.

After acceptance, additional cases using 4, 8, 16, and 32 nodes were added in order to better understand GTC's scaling on the Power architecture. Results obtained from running GTC with OpenMP enabled are shown in Fig. 8(a). In addition, Fig. 8(b) shows a strong scaling plot of GTC when running on Summitdev. GTC was compiled using GCC.

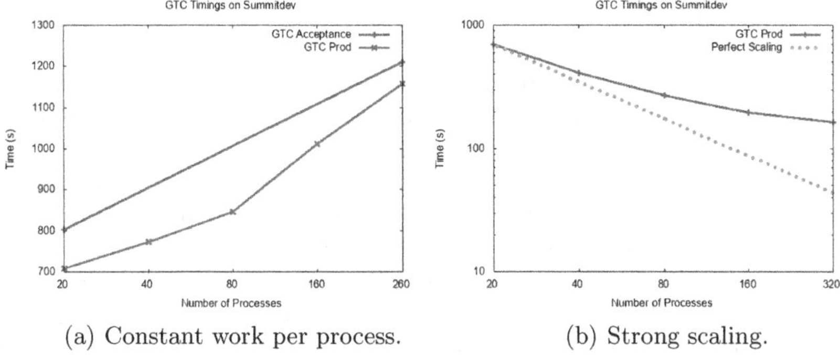

(a) Constant work per process. (b) Strong scaling.

Fig. 8. GTC timing results. (a) Problem size is doubled with the number of processes to keep the amount of work per process approximately constant. (b) Problem size is kept constant and the number of MPI ranks is doubled with each experiment.

9 Lessons Learned

Several considerations are necessary when porting codes to the IBM Power architecture. First, on Power, *char*s are by default *unsigned* whereas on x86 the default is *signed*. This is an important consideration as it can result in incorrect results. This was observed when running the SPEC OMP2012 benchmarks, which required the addition of *-qchars=signed*, and *-fsigned-char* for the XL and GCC compilers, respectively. Another difference to be aware of is that *long double*s on Power are by default 128-bits. It is also important to understand the different optimization levels provided by each compiler. The XL compilers, unlike GCC and PGI, provide up to optimization level *-O5* so careful consideration must be given to selection of optimization flags that match the compiler. For example, the Minisweep OpenMP tests built the XL compiler required *-O4 -qsmp=omp* in order to achieve performance improvements when compared to the MPI-only version of the code.

Looking at support for the different programming models, results showed varied levels of support. OpenMP 3.1 is well supported by the four compilers tested, however, some of the tests executed showed little or no performance improvements as with Minisweep, while others showed lower performance as was the case with Nekbone when built with PGI. This can be partially attributed to the fact that by default in the Power environment, threads are not pinned. This will require further investigation. As far as OpenMP 4.5 is concerned, two compilers are scheduled to provide support: XL and LLVM. While XL provides partial support OpenMP 4.5 offloading to the GPU, the implementation is still maturing as shown by the SPEC ACCEL OMP results. Similarly, OpenMP 4.5 support in LLVM is currently in active development. OpenACC support on Power is currently provided by the PGI compiler, which, as results of SPEC ACCEL ACC show, is a mature implementation. Partial support for OpenACC in GCC is currently provided in GCC 6.3 and is expected to be fully supported in the GCC 7 release.

10 Conclusions

At roughly 1 PF of peak performance and only 54 nodes, Summitdev is a very powerful system. The step-up in performance of the Summitdev nodes compared to Titan nodes is immediately felt by applications.

As expected with a new system, some replacements of problematic hardware were required shortly after delivery. Careful testing with multiple diagnostic benchmark codes was valuable for uncovering these problems.

Programming the node is a more complex process, ostensibly due to the presence of multiple GPUs per node, but also from other factors such as simultaneous multithreading (SMT) modes and the need to coordinate use of GPUs and CPU threads across multiple NUMA domains. The interplay of LSF and mpirun with respect to node execution configuration and the interaction of these with OpenMP and CUDA environment variables, MPS, host code threading and device selection must also be managed. This will most likely become more tractable through time and experience.

Relationships between different compiler versions, supported features and libraries have become complex and will require careful build configuration management by users. Newly developed compiler features, in some cases still in beta, are expected to mature and harden over time. Vendors are aggressively working to improve these products and respond to reported bugs.

We anticipate Summitdev to be an effective resource for preparing applications for Summit, and it has already begun to bear fruit in this regard.

Acknowledgements. The authors would like to thank the entire Summitdev Acceptance Test team for the development of tests for each phase. In addition to the authors, the team also includes: Adam Simpson, Mike Brim, Dustin Leverman, Oscar Hernandez, Chris Zimmer, Sarp Oral, Scott Atchley, and Matt Ezell.

This research used resources of the Oak Ridge Leadership Computing Facility at the Oak Ridge National Laboratory, which is supported by the Office of Science of the U.S. Department of Energy under Contract No. DE-AC05-00OR22725.

References

1. Aurora. http://aurora.alcf.anl.gov/
2. Center for Accelerated Application Readiness (CAAR). https://www.olcf.ornl.gov/caar
3. CORAL Benchmark Codes. https://asc.llnl.gov/CORAL-benchmarks
4. CUDA Samples. http://docs.nvidia.com/cuda/cuda-samples/index.html#samples-reference
5. Exascale Computing Project. https://exascaleproject.org/
6. Intel MPI Benchmarks User Guide. https://software.intel.com/en-us/imb-user-guide
7. NVIDIA TESLA P100 GPU Accelerator. https://images.nvidia.com/content/tesla/pdf/nvidia-tesla-p100-datasheet.pdf
8. Qbox: First-Principles Molecular Dynamics. http://qboxcode.org/
9. Sierra. https://asc.llnl.gov/coral-info

10. SPEC ACCEL Run and Reporting Rules. https://www.spec.org/accel/docs/runrules.html
11. Summit: Scale New Heights Discover New Solutions. https://www.olcf.ornl.gov/summit/
12. Summitdev Quickstart. https://www.olcf.ornl.gov/kb_articles/summitdev-quickstart
13. Using OpenMP 4.5 in the CLANG/LLVM compiler toolchain. https://www.olcf.ornl.gov/wp-content/uploads/2017/01/SummitDev_Using-OpenMP-4.5-in-the-CLANGLLVM-compiler-toolchain.pdf. Accessed 12 Apr 2017
14. Fact Sheet: Collaboration of Oak Ridge, Argonne, and Livermore (CORAL). Technical report, Department of Energy (2014). https://energy.gov/sites/prod/files/2014/12/f19/CORAL%20Fact%20Sheet__FINAL%20AS%20ISSUED_UPDATED.pdf
15. ESSL Guide and Reference (2016). https://publib.boulder.ibm.com/epubs/pdf/a2322688.pdf
16. Miniapps derived from production HPC applications using multiple programing models. Int. J. High Perform. Comput. Appl. 1094342016668241 (2016). doi:10.1177/1094342016668241
17. Anderson, E., Bai, Z., Dongarra, J., Greenbaum, A., McKenney, A., Du Croz, J., Hammerling, S., Demmel, J., Bischof, C., Sorensen, D.: LAPACK: a portable linear algebra library for high-performance computers. In: Proceedings of the 1990 ACM/IEEE Conference on Supercomputing, Supercomputing 1990, CA, USA, pp. 2–11 (1990). http://dl.acm.org/citation.cfm?id=110382.110385
18. Antao, S.F., Bataev, A., Jacob, A.C., Bercea, G.T., Eichenberger, A.E., Rokos, G., Martineau, M., Jin, T., Ozen, G., Sura, Z., Chen, T., Sung, H., Bertolli, C., O'Brien, K.: Offloading Support for OpenMP in Clang and LLVM. In: Proceedings of the Third Workshop on LLVM Compiler Infrastructure in HPC, LLVM-HPC 2016, pp. 1–11. IEEE Press, Piscataway (2016). doi:10.1109/LLVM-HPC.2016.6
19. Berrill, M.: Modeling of laser-created plasmas and soft x-ray lasers. Ph.D. thesis, Colorado State University (2010)
20. Caldeira, A., Haug, V., Vetter, S.: IBM Power Systems S822LC for High Performance Computing: Technical Overview and Introduction. Technical report, IBM, September 2016
21. Choi, J., Dongarra, J.J., Pozo, R., Walker, D.W.: ScaLAPACK: a scalable linear algebra library for distributed memory concurrent computers. In: 1992, Fourth Symposium on the Frontiers of Massively Parallel Computation, pp. 120–127. IEEE (1992). http://ieeexplore.ieee.org/document/234898/. Accessed 11 Oct 2016
22. Eisenbach, M., Zhou, C., Nicholson, D.M., Brown, G., Larkin, J., Schulthess, T.C.: Thermodynamics of magnetic systems from first principles: WL-LSMS
23. Hagen, G., Jansen, G.R., Papenbrock, T.: Structure of ^{78}Ni from first-principles computations. Phys. Rev. Lett. **117**, 172501 (2016). https://link.aps.org/doi/10.1103/PhysRevLett.117.172501
24. Oral, S., Dillow, D.A., Fuller, D., Hill, J., Leverman, D., Vazhkudai, S.S., Wang, F., Kim, Y., Rogers, J., Simmons, J., et al.: OLCFs 1 TB/s. Next-Generation Lustre File System
25. Phillips, J.C., Braun, R., Wang, W., Gumbart, J., Tajkhorshid, E., Villa, E., Chipot, C., Skeel, R.D., Kalé, L., Schulten, K.: Scalable molecular dynamics with NAMD. J. Comput. Chem. **26**(16), 1781–1802 (2005). doi:10.1002/jcc.20289
26. Schlipf, M., Gygi, F.: Optimization algorithm for the generation of ONCV pseudopotentials. Comput. Phys. Commun. **196**, 36–44 (2015). http://www.sciencedirect.com/science/article/pii/S0010465515001897

27. Tang, W., Wang, B., Ethier, S., Lin, Z.: Performance portability of HPC discovery science software: fusion energy turbulence simulations at extreme scale. Supercomputing Front. Innovations **4**(1), 83–97 (2017)
28. Tharrington, A., Hai Ah Nam, W.J., Brown, W.M., Anantharaj, V.G.: Early applications experience on the cray XK6 at the Oak Ridge leadership computing facility. In: Cray User Group Meeting CUG (2012)
29. Wang, C., Chandrasekaran, S., Chapman, B.: An OpenMP 3.1 validation testsuite. In: Chapman, B.M., Massaioli, F., Müller, M.S., Rorro, M. (eds.) IWOMP 2012. LNCS, vol. 7312, pp. 237–249. Springer, Heidelberg (2012). doi:10.1007/978-3-642-30961-8_18

Power/Performance Controlling Techniques in OpenPOWER

Todd Rosedahl[1], Martha Broyles[1], Charles Lefurgy[1], Bjorn Christensen[1(✉)], and Wu Feng[2]

[1] IBM Corporation, Rochester, USA
{rosedahl,mbroyles,lefurgy,bjornc}@us.ibm.com
[2] Virginia Tech University, Blacksburg, USA
wfeng@vt.edu

Abstract. This paper presents the design and implementation of new power measurement and management features found in OpenPOWER systems, along with new techniques for increasing system performance in power constrained environments. The firmware and its ecosystem are open source to allow the community to extend the current capabilities.

Keywords: Energy · Measurement · Management · Performance · OpenPOWER · Firmware · POWER8 · POWER9

1 Overview

The balance between power consumption and performance in a modern computer system requires detailed measurements and sophisticated control techniques. This paper describes the hardware and software infrastructure on OpenPOWER systems, which in turn, provides the basis for the measurement and management of power, energy, and performance. Existing techniques, which are available now on P8 servers, are described and new techniques, which will be delivered soon for P9 are discussed. Additionally, measurement abilities are presented and discussed and, with the emergence of the GPU as major computing platform to artificial intelligence (AI) and machine learning, we explore methods to maximize system performance with GPUs in power-constrained environments.

To enable research to advance the state of the art in power and performance management, most of the firmware that enables such management has been released to the open-source community as a part of the OpenPOWER initiative. As such, this paper seeks to address the challenges and to present the techniques used to control power and performance in OpenPOWER systems.

2 Power/Thermal Management/Measurement Infrastructure Overview

The heart of the power/performance measurement and management is the On Chip Controller (OCC) [1]. The OCC is designed to measure and manage performance and energy consumption and to provide access to detailed chip temperature, power, and

J.M. Kunkel et al. (Eds.): ISC High Performance Workshops 2017, LNCS 10524, pp. 275–289, 2017.
https://doi.org/10.1007/978-3-319-67630-2_21

utilization data. It has complete control of processor frequency and memory bandwidth which enables customization for performance and energy management, or for maintaining system reliability and availability.

The OCC is a PowerPC 405 processor that is embedded directly on the POWER processor chip along with the main POWER processor cores. It has its own dedicated 512 K SRAM, access to main memory, and 2 dedicated General Purpose off-load Engines (GPEs). Figure 1 shows how the OCC interacts with other hardware and firmware in Power8. The main OCC firmware runs a 250 μs loop that utilizes the GPEs to continuously collect system power data by domain, processor temperatures, memory temperatures, and processor utilization data. The firmware communicates with the open source OpenPOWER Abstraction Layer (OPAL) stack via main memory. In conjunction with the operating system, it uses the data collected to determine the proper processor frequency and memory bandwidth to enable the following functions described in Sect. 2.1,

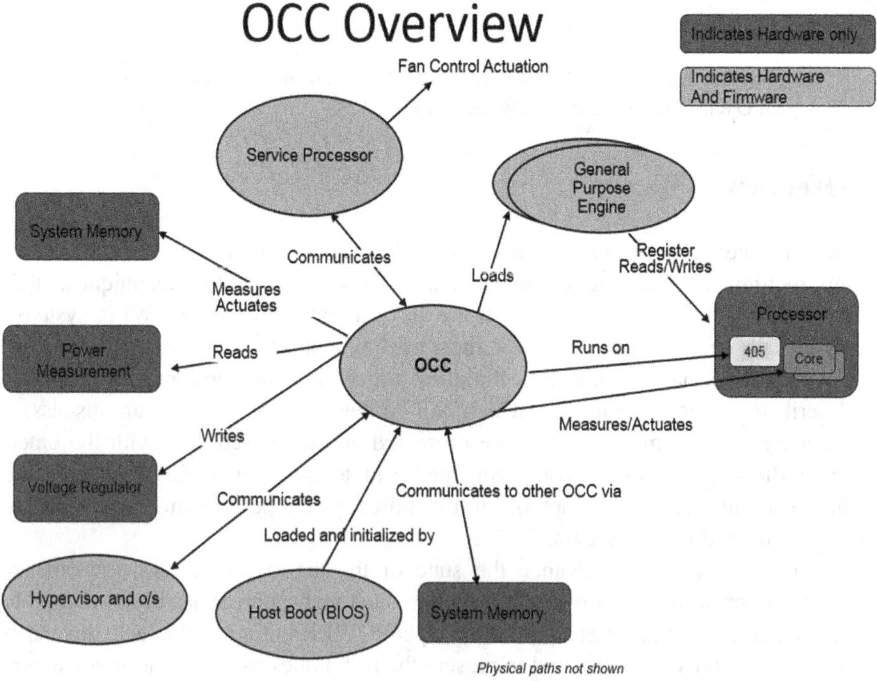

Fig. 1. On-chip controller overview

2.1 Functional Overview

This section provides a brief overview of the measurement and management capabilities of the POWER processor [5].

Performance Boost. The POWER processors can be set to frequencies above the nominal frequency. The OCC monitors the system and controls the processor frequency and memory bandwidth to keep the system thermally safe and within acceptable power limits.

Power Capping. A system power limit can be set. The OCC continually monitors the power consumption and will reduce the allowed processor frequency to maintain that power limit.

Energy Saving. When the system utilization is low, the OCC infrastructure can be used to put the system into a low power state to save energy. This function can be used to comply with various government idle power regulations and standards.

System Availability. OCC supports a "Quick Power Drop" signal that can be used to respond to power supply failures or other system events that require a rapid power reduction. This function enables systems to run through component or data center power and thermal failures without crashing.

System Reliability. The OCC can be used to keep component temperatures within reliability limits, extending device lifetime and limiting service costs.

Performance per Watt tuning. As the system utilization varies, the OCC can provide monitoring information and frequency control that maximizes system performance per watt metrics.

Data Collection. At a high level, Fig. 2 shows several approaches to collect sensor data from the system. These approaches can be categorized as (1) in-band measurement and (2) out-of-band measurement. In-band measurement reads sensor data via the OS, and thus, can affect performance; while out-of-band measurement reads sensor data via dedicated hardware so as to not affect system performance. Such sensor data may include power readings from various power rails within the system as well as processor and memory temperatures.

The IPMI Tool: The intelligent platform management interface (IPMI) [6–10] provides a message-based interface for out-of-band management of computing resources. IPMI also provides a serial-over-LAN communication, where console output can be viewed remotely. However, the IPMI interface suffers from limited scalability due to fixed commands and well-known security vulnerabilities, where an attacker can use IPMI to gain physical access to the system and bypass the operating system to reboot the system, install a new operating system, or compromise data. As a consequence, a new standard called Redfish has been proposed.

The Redfish Specification: Similar to the IPMI interface, the Redfish API [11] is used for scalable platforms management performs out-of-band system management, but it does so via a RESTful interface [12]. It is suitable for single-node systems or multi-node systems and scales up to large-scale systems, e.g., cloud or supercomputing environments. The Redfish API provides a way to standardize across vendors and can facilitate a simpler and modern system-management software stack. In our case, we realized the Redfish API specification as part of OpenBMC, short for Open Baseboard Management Controller. As a RESTful-based API, all resources are accessed via a

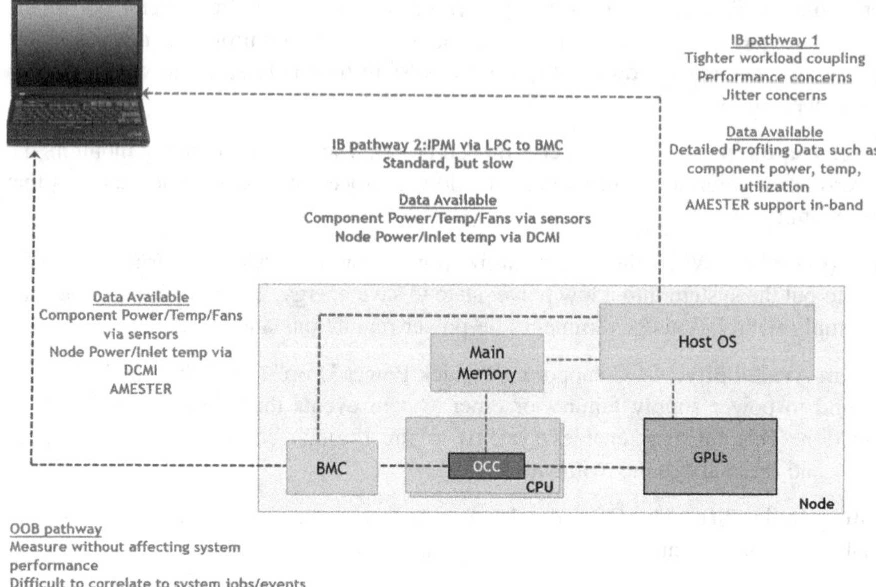

Fig. 2. Telemetry data

uniform resource identifier (URI) using the hypertext transfer protocol (http) and are dynamically discoverable. In addition, the Redfish schema specifies the component URI, allowable actions, and detailed messages in case an error happens. The above features facilitate easier and more scalable platforms management and enable automated management in a large-scale setting, e.g., datacenter.

AMESTER Tool: AMESTER [2, 3], now available both in and out of band, is a tool for detailed monitoring power consumption, temperatures and performance counters as discussed further in Sect. 5.

OCC-to-OPAL Interface: A new OCC-to-OPAL interface provides data in-band via standard Linux utilities as discussed in Sect. 4.

2.2 OCC Details

The OCC works in conjunction with the operating system to provide customized energy management solutions. The standard Linux governors allow users to select power management modes that made specific performance and power consumption trade-offs. For example, the "on demand" governor adjusts core clock frequency to maintain a high level of core utilization for the running workload. The role of OCC is to keep the system within specified power and thermal limits. It does this by running power and thermal control loops that monitor the following: node power, socket powers, DIMM temperature, processor core temperatures. When the operating system requests a frequency, this gets translated to a PSTATE by OPAL using data presented by the OCC via a shared main memory. If the PSTATE selected by the OS will cause the system to exceed a power or thermal limit, the OCC complex will clip the frequency and only allow the PSTATE in the "maximum PSTATE" register to be realized in the hardware. See Sects. 6 and 7 below for more information on new techniques to select the maximum PSTATE and boost performance.

3 Hardware Infrastructure Overview

In order to understand the power and performance trade-offs internal to a computer system, one must understand the underlying hardware structure. For POWER9, the processor will be split into "Quads" with each Quad consisting of four (4) cores and two (2) L2 Caches. Each Quad has its own voltage and frequency for power management purposes along with the ability to turn off various pieces of the chip for idle power management and performance boost. There are two temperatures sensors per core, one for each cache, and three for the nest. Averaging is done on each of these sensors in order to provide an overall chip temperature. Another interesting note is that much of the hardware that provides functions such as frequency and voltage scaling as well as core on/off has been replaced by Power Processing Engines (PPEs) that have firmware associated with them in order to provide flexibility for future enhancements. These are represented by the dark orange boxes in Fig. 3.

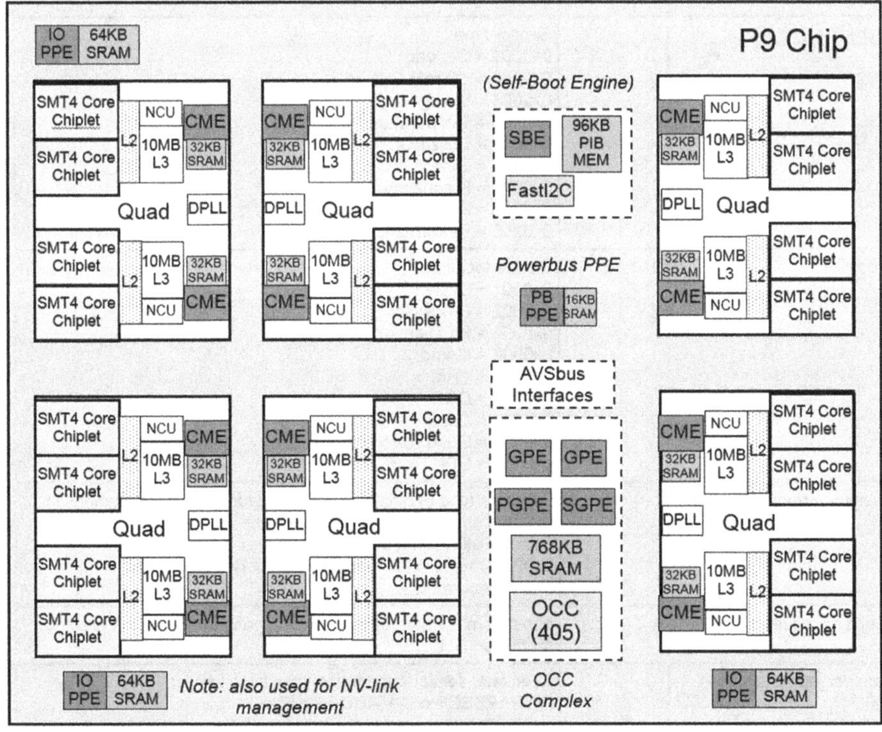

Fig. 3. Hardware infrastructure

4 Data Measurement – OPAL Interface for Power, Thermal, Performance Measurements

The OCC, in conjunction with open-source OpenPOWER Abstraction Layer (OPAL) stack provides a new interface that delivers telemetry data in-band to the Linux operating system (OS). The OCC will push data up to main memory continually such that all sensor data will be updated within 100 ms. In all, data from over 400 sensors can be obtained for power, thermal, and performance metrics on processors and memory. Each sensor reading will be timestamped with the same system timestamp used by the operating system to provide time correlation. OPAL will grab this data and present it to the user via standard Linux interfaces (lm_sensor). Each sensor will have associated static metadata that describes the sensor and shows information such as

FIELD	SIZE (BYTES)	DESCRIPTION
name	16	Sensor name
units	4	Sensor units of measurement
gsid	2	Global sensor ID – assigned by its constructor
freq	4	Update frequency
scale_factor	4	Scaling factor
type	2	Sensor type: 0x0001 = Generic 0x0002 = Current 0x0004 = Voltage 0x0008 = Temperature 0x0010 = Utilization 0x0020 = Time 0x0040 = Frequency 0x0080 = Power 0x0200 = Performance
location	2	Sensor location: 0x0001 = System 0x0002 = Processor 0x0004 = Partition 0x0008 = Memory 0x0010 = VRM 0x0020 = OCC 0x0040 = Core 0x0080 = Quad (Cache) 0x0100 = GPU
sensor_structure_version	1	Indicates type of data structure used for the sensor readings in the ping and pong buffers for this sensor 0x01 = Full reading structure (min/max fields supported) 0x02 = Counter structure (this sensor is a counter no min/max/current)
reading_offset	4	offset from the start of the ping and pong buffers to the readings for this sensor
sensor_specific_info1	1	Additional sensor information specific to sensor. PWRAPSSCHxx --> ADC func ID:

Fig. 4. Sensor metadata

update frequency and units. Note that sensor min/max values can be cleared to provide job-level min/max measurement granularity. Also, the accumulator and update tag provide the ability to read accumulated values (such as power over time) without requiring a clear of any value. See the red path in Fig. 2 for the system path used to collect this data. See Fig. 4 for a description of the sensor metadata. See Fig. 5 for the sensor structure.

FIELD	SIZE (BYTES)	DESCRIPTION
gsid	2	Global sensor ID – assigned by its constructor
timestamp	8	64bit time base counter in the core. Resolution is 512MHz
sample	2	Latest sample of this sensor
sample_min	2	Minimum value since last OCC reset
sample_max	2	Maximum value since last OCC reset
CSM_sample_min	2	Minimum value since last reset request by CSM
CSM_sample_max	2	Maximum value since last reset request by CSM
profiler_sample_min	2	Minimum value since last reset request by profiler
profiler_sample_max	2	Maximum value since last reset request by profiler
job_s_sample_min	2	Minimum value since last reset by job scheduler
job_s_sample_max	2	Maximum value since last reset by job scheduler
accumulator	8	Accumulator register for this sensor
update_tag	4	Count of the number of 'ticks' that have passed between updates to this sensor – used for time-derived sensors

Fig. 5. Sensor structure

5 Measurement AMESTER – Detailed Profiling Tool

This section gives a brief overview of AMESTER (Automated Measurement of Systems for Temperature and Energy Reporting). AMESTER is a tool for monitoring power consumption and performance metrics in IBM systems. It has proven to be valuable for visualizing power measurements and prototyping new power management policies. AMESTER is now an open-source project to make it broadly available to the OpenPOWER community.

AMESTER provides both a GUI for interactive use and a non-interactive mode for unattended data collection. AMESTER is written completely in Tcl/Tk. Users can write scripts for AMESTER in Tcl to direct its operation. Additionally, scripts may load dynamically linked libraries that are written in other languages, such as C. Every aspect of AMESTER may be modified and controlled from a script. This is useful for building rapid prototypes of power management policies and custom visual demonstrations based on AMESTER's graphing capability.

5.1 Operation

AMESTER has traditionally been run on a laptop and connected remotely over the Internet to the server that is to be measured. AMESTER conncets to OpenPOWER servers through the BMC using the IPMI protocol or now on some POWER9 systems via a new RESTful interface. The BMC routes AMESTER commands to OCCs without having to understand the command details. Each OCC processes the command and responds with a buffer of data that represents system telemetry as requested by the user.

5.2 Sensors

The principal function of AMESTER is to collect power and performance metrics from the firmware. The user specifies a list of sensors for AMESTER to gather in the background as quickly as possible. As sensors arrive, the GUI is updated and user provided callbacks are processed. Figure 6 shows a screenshot of data collection.

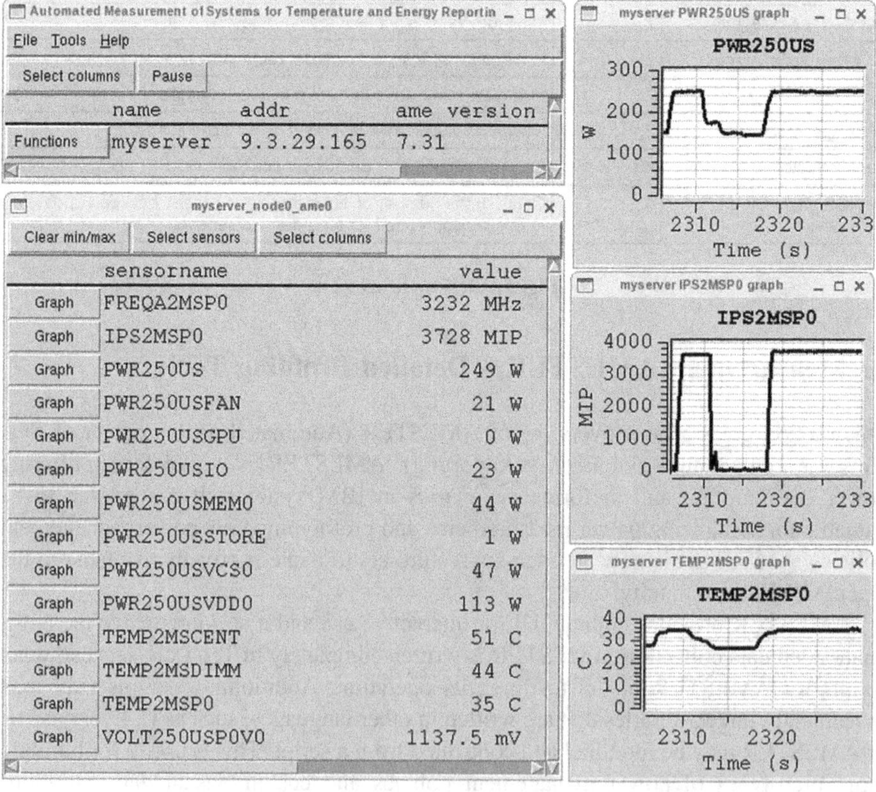

Fig. 6. Screenshot of sensor data collection

5.3 Trace Buffers

The AMESTER trace buffer interface makes it possible to study system behavior at small timescales. Since the sensor interface can take 100 s of milliseconds to poll sensor values, it is not sufficient for studying and debugging OCC control loops which often operate at a sub-millisecond granularity. The trace buffers are implemented by reserving some of the OCC SRAM memory to capture runs of sensor values. Every sensor value change can be captured until the buffer fills.

5.4 In Band AMESTER

In POWER9, a new interface will be enabled that will allow direct access from Linux to the OCC SRAM. In this way, AMESTER can be run in the o/s and this will provide rapid data analysis that can be tightly coupled with jobs or portions of jobs. Additionally, this will eliminate the lengthy delays in data collection caused by the network and BMC processing time.

6 Workload Optimized Frequency (WOF)

Prior to POWER8, systems were shipped with a maximum processor frequency called "Turbo" that was achievable at lower ambient temperatures and all reasonable workloads. The result was a higher maximum frequency, but still there was a significant frequency boost potential left untapped when the system was running workloads that used less than the maximum amount of power. Starting in POWER8 Minsky servers, a new function called Workload Optimized Frequency (WOF) was introduced. With WOF, the OCC is continually measuring the power consumption of the socket and, if there is power and frequency headroom, the OCC will raise the frequency ceiling to allow the Linux governor to select a higher frequency – up to what is called "Ultra Turbo". Note that in order to avoid part to part variation and non-deterministic performance, the OCC must use only the active switching (herein referred to as AC) portion of the power for this calculation, which is abstracted as an effective switching capacitance, or Ceff. The leakage (herein referred to as DC) power, containing both voltage and temperature driven leakage, must be subtracted off so that only the power consumed by the active workload is factored in. In addition to taking advantage of lower power workloads, the OCC also factors in cores that are turned off to allow an even greater performance boost on the remaining active cores. The actual frequency increase gained is dependent on system type, thermal environment, and workload, but gains of over 10% can be realized and will be consistently produced system to system and run to run given the same system configuration and workload for any thermal environment within the system's Thermal Design Point (TDP) operating range.

Figure 7 is a graphical sketch intended to show design methodology, not actual results. It graphically shows the intended results similar to what is shown in the 10-core WOF boost table (Fig. 8). Processor sorts vary in core count, frequency, and power (TDP), thus each sort has different base and boost frequency points. The WOF benefit range depicts where lighter workloads may boost beyond the target base frequency.

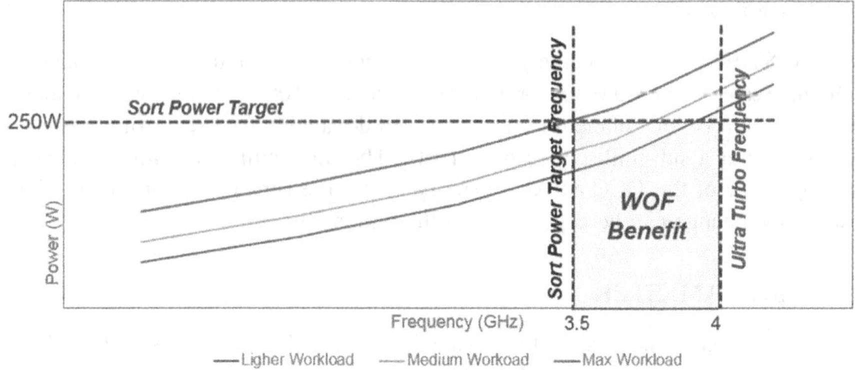

Fig. 7. WOF frequency boost for an example processor sort

Figure 8 shows an example WOF frequency uplift table. Note that the Ceff Ratio column should be thought of as the AC component of the workload. So a 0% Ceff would be an idle workload and a 100% Ceff would be a TDP workload. The columns are the numbers of cores that are active. Note that if all cores are active and the workload is maximum, the frequency result is the same as the "Turbo" point. As the workload or active core count decreases, the frequency potential increases.

	8 Core		10 Core			
CEFF RATIO	1 to 7	8	1 to 7	8	9	10
0%	4024	4024	4024	4024	4024	4024
5%	4024	4024	4024	4024	4024	4024
10%	4024	4024	4024	4024	4024	4024
15%	4024	4024	4024	4024	4024	4024
20%	4024	4024	4024	4024	4024	4024
25%	4024	4024	4024	4024	4024	4024
30%	4024	4024	4024	4024	4024	4024
35%	4024	4024	4024	4024	4024	4024
40%	4024	4024	4024	4024	4024	4024
45%	4024	4024	4024	4024	4024	4024
50%	4024	4024	4024	4024	4024	4009
55%	4024	4024	4024	4024	4024	3963
60%	4024	4024	4024	4024	4024	3907
65%	4024	4024	4024	4024	4000	3847
70%	4024	4024	4024	4024	3956	3787
75%	4024	4024	4024	4024	3905	3730
80%	4024	4014	4024	4014	3852	3677
85%	4024	3978	4024	3978	3799	3628
90%	4024	3941	4024	3936	3748	3581
95%	4024	3900	4024	3891	3700	3535
100%	4024	3857	4024	3845	3655	3492

Fig. 8. WOF uplift table

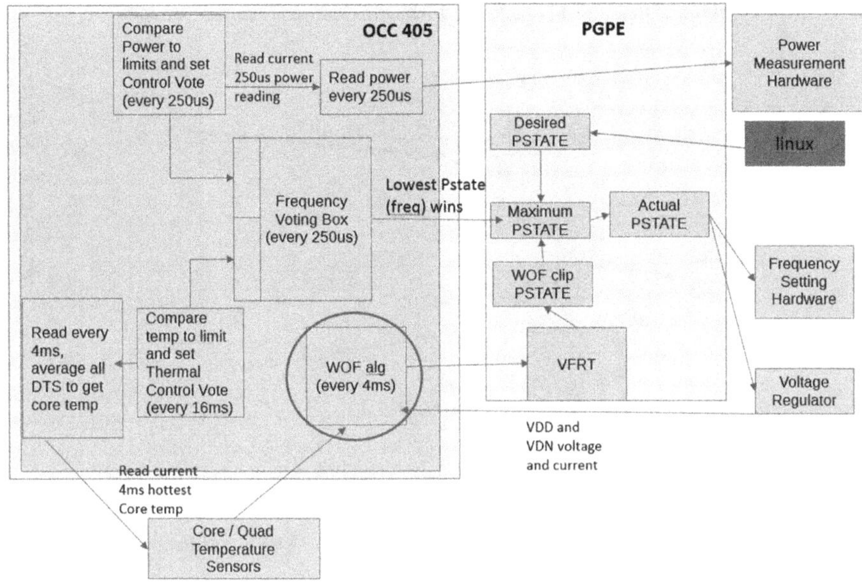

Fig. 9. OCC control algorithms

Figure 9 below shows how the WOF algorithm plays in with the existing OCC power and thermal control loops as well as with the Linux governor. Note that since the OCC continues to run all power and thermal control loops, all power and thermal limits will be maintained separately from any performance boost that could be realized from WOF.

6.1 WOF Experimental Results

Figure 10 shows the frequency boosts obtained using WOF [4] with a variety of workloads in a POWER8 Minsky server. A brief description of the workloads in this example is shown in Fig. 11. In Fig. 10, the frequency boost is denoted as a percentage of the "Turbo" frequency and it shows that when the CPU is idle, the WOF boost potential is high. However, the Linux "On Demand" governor sees the low utilization and lowers the actual frequency accordingly to save energy. If the "Maximum Performance" governor would be used for idle, the potential WOF benefit shown would be realized. Also, as expected, with the maximum workload no WOF benefit is seen. The CPU_GPU and MEMBW workloads show the WOF benefit since they utilize the CPU enough for the "On Demand" governor to select the maximum frequency, but are not so power intensive that the WOF benefit is negated.

Workload Optimized Frequency with OnDemand Governor 10-core

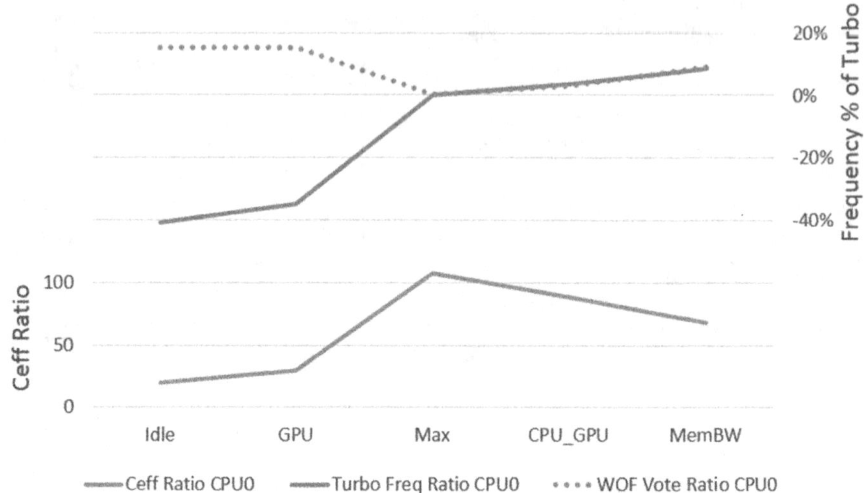

Fig. 10. WOF frequency boost and Ceff Ratio

Workload	CPU Utilization	GPU Utilization
Idle	Low	Low
GPU	Low	High
Max	High	Low
CPU_GPU	Med-high	Med
MemBW	Med	Low

Fig. 11. WOF sample workload descriptions

7 Core/Quad Power on/off

In POWER7 and POWER8 processors, processor cores can be turned off when idle in order to reduce socket power consumption. In POWER8 Minsky servers, as described above in the WOF section, cores that are turned off can have the added benefit of allowing active cores to run at higher frequencies. New to this space for POWER9 is the concept of turning off entire quads. In Fig. 12 below, all cores in a quad are shown to be powered off. At this point, the entire quad, with both L2 and L3 cache, can be powered off to reduce the power consumption of the socket. The OCC then can take

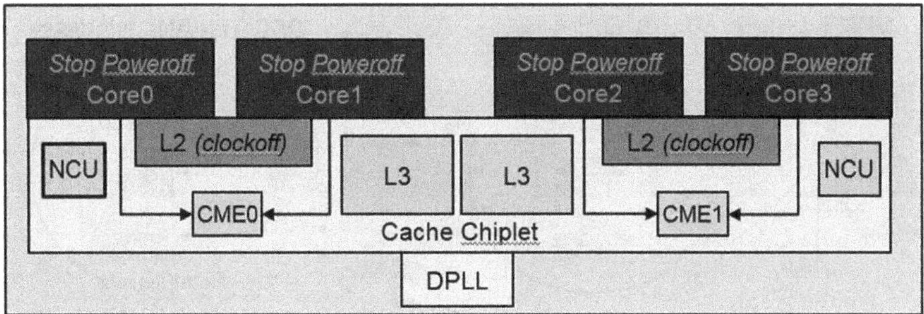

Fig. 12. Core stop states

advantage of this reduced power consumption and allow the Linux governor to increase the frequency of the cores in the other quads.

A power/performance decision has to be made when allocating work to a new core. Take the case where 3 cores are actively running a workload and are all allocated on 1 quad. All other quads are powered off and the WOF algorithm running on the OCC has set the maximum frequency high due to the available power. When a new workload needs to run, there is a core placement decision that has to be made. If the fourth remaining core on the active quad is activated, the additional power consumption will be low which will result in a minimal impact to the maximum frequency. However, the overall performance may be lower because the new core will now have to share the L2 cache. Activating the core on a new quad will result in higher power consumption and possibly lower maximum frequency, but also higher performance since it owns the entire cache. This is an area that requires further study in order to determine the best active core placement.

8 Power Capping and Shifting for GPUs

GPUs now represent a large portion of system power – far more than the processors that drive them. In order to provide GPU power management for P9, a new OCC to GPU interface has been enabled in OpenPOWER systems for NVlink attached GPUs. On this interface, GPU data will be collected, power capping will be done and a new power shifting algorithm will be implemented. A block diagram of a typical OpenPOWER system is shown in Fig. 13 with the new GPU interface circled.

A new power shifting algorithm is shown in Fig. 14. Consider the case where a system power limit has been reached. The CPU, memory, and GPU all have levers that the OCC can pull in order to reduce the overall system power to an acceptable limit. The GPU is the slowest to respond, taking on the order of 100 ms to react to a new cap. The OCC will first take the power away from the processors, adjust the GPU power cap accordingly, and then restore the CPU power to a higher level based on a pre-determined “Power Shifting Ratio” (PSR). Note that setting this PSR correctly is an area of future study and deeper discussions on this topic are left to another paper.

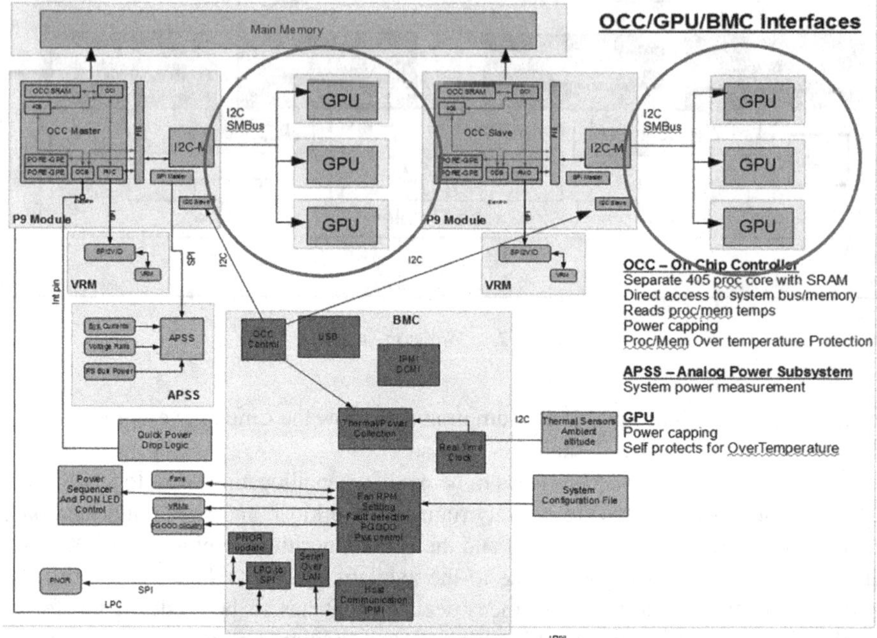

Fig. 13. OCC to GPU interface

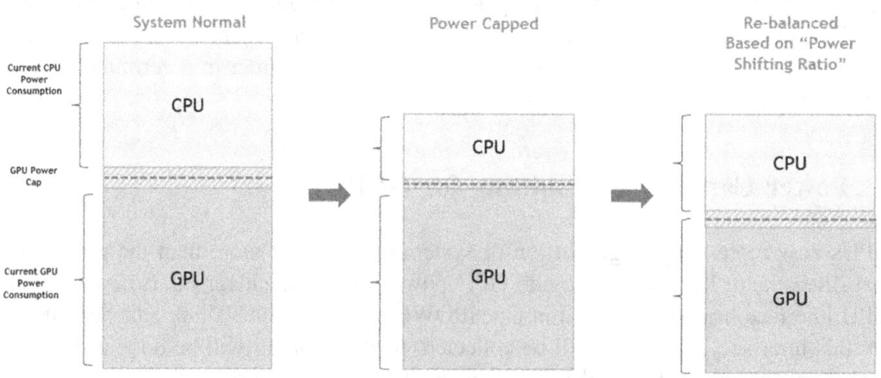

Fig. 14. CPU and GPU power shifting

9 Conclusion

OpenPOWER systems have rich data collection mechanisms and power/performance balancing features that improve system energy efficiency, performance, and reliability. New Linux facilities for data measurement, in-band AMESTER, GPU data collection, and Workload Optimized Frequency provide the OpenPOWER community with a strong foundation for maximizing system performance and for prototyping new power management capabilities.

References

1. OpenPOWER OCC. https://github.com/open-power/occ
2. AMESTER. https://github.com/open-power/amester
3. El-Essawy, W.: IPMItoolRaw Command Interface to OpenPOWER POWER8 On Chip Controller: Sensor reading commands, Version 0.4 (2016). https://github.com/open-power/docs/blob/master/occ/OCC_ipmitool_sensors.pdf
4. Zyuban, V., et al.: IBM POWER8 circuit design and energy optimization. IBM JR&D **59**(1), 1–16 (2015)
5. Broyles, M., et al.: IBM EnergyScale for POWER8 processor-based systems, white paper, November 2015. http://public.dhe.ibm.com/common/ssi/ecm/po/en/pow03125usen/POW03125USEN.PDF
6. Intel, Hewlett-Packard, NEC, and Dell, IPMI - Intelligent Platform Management Interface Specification Second Generation v2.0, Rev. 1.1, E7 Markup, 21 April 2015
7. NXP, I^2C-bus specification and user manual, Rev. 6, 4 April 2014
8. Intel, Intel Intelligent Power Node Manager 3.0 External Interface Specification Using IPMI, Document Number 332200-001US, March 2015
9. System Management Interface Forum, PMBus Power System Management Protocol Specification Part II – Command Language, Rev. 1.2, 6 September 2010
10. Intel, DCMI – Data Center Manageability Interface Specification, Ver. 1.5, Rev. 1.0, 23 August 2011
11. Distributed Management Task Force, Redfish Scalable Platforms Management API Specification, Ver. 1.1.0, January 2017
12. Fielding, R.: Architectural styles and the design of network-based software architectures, University of California – Irvine, Ph.D. thesis (2000)

Performance Evaluation of Container-Based High Performance Computing Ecosystem Using OpenPOWER

Animesh Kuity(✉) and Sateesh Kumar Peddoju

High Performance Computing Lab, Department of Computer Science and Engineering, Indian Institute of Technology, Roorkee 247667, India
anics.dcs2015@iitr.ac.in

Abstract. Container-based High Performance Computing (HPC) has started gaining popularity due to its almost negligible performance penalty compared to the BareMetal hardware. Although HPC hardware architectures and programming models are continuously evolving, the platform models are suffering from the HPC community's awareness. Power-awareness, hardware and application-aware co-design along with security related concerns have attracted the most in recent time to empower the platform models. Otherside, the OpenPOWER ecosystems have stepped into our life to fulfill the thirst of exploiting the last drop of a performance benefit from our invested system. It has Power8 compliant processor with a larger cache, big fat instructions and data path accompanied by the popular coherent accelerator. In this paper, we have proposed a container-based HPC ecosystem established using OpenPOWER machine. The performance of the designed and developed ecosystem is evaluated stressing on different subcomponents of the system such as processor, memory, IO, and interconnect. Finally, the results are compared with the performance of the equivalent environments made of virtual machines and BareMetal hardware.

Keywords: High Performance Computing · OpenPOWER · Container · Benchmark · HPCC · Performance evaluation · Virtual Machine · BareMetal · Ecosystem · Cloud

1 Introduction

High Performance Computing (HPC) [2] remains a challenge to the majority of researchers in scientific computing community due to its significantly high cost in the system and environment setup, extremely complex software stack and its dependencies, and limited access to a group of community members.

The cloud computing service providers are trying to provide HPC as a service on a Virtual Machine (VM) based cluster. But the hypervisor-based VMs incur high start-up times, performance overheads, inter-communication latencies, network overheads, IO overheads along with complex patching and life

J.M. Kunkel et al. (Eds.): ISC High Performance Workshops 2017, LNCS 10524, pp. 290–308, 2017.
https://doi.org/10.1007/978-3-319-67630-2_22

cycle management compared to the BareMetal hardware. Hence, it leads to the poor performance. So the VMs assisted HPC solution in the cloud remains a big research challenge to the scientific computing community.

The main challenge here is to provide an abstract dynamic environment for small and medium scale scientific computing users so that they can concentrate on their computations without compromising on the performance and worrying about the underlying nasty environmental details. The problem is interesting because it can offer several benefits including:

- it will increase the resource utilization of the underlying environment.
- it can fulfill the variable user platform requirements in term of physical resources, software stack, and their dependencies.
- it will decrease the environment management effort, and
- reproducibility of the previously created environment.

Linux container Technology [3] is a light-weight operating system virtualization mechanism that has attracted the attention of HPC community in recent time due to its numerous advantages over hypervisor assisted VM technology. The Linux container provides an isolated and portable environment for a group of processes using namespaces[1] and cgroups[2]. The immensely popular Docker[3] uses Linux namespace features that are brought into mainstream kernel after Docker employed it as its core. The container following the trend "doing more with less" introduced much less overhead compared to hypervisor based virtualization technology as depicted in Fig. 1 [8,27]. The scientific community is forced to use gigantic software stacks for their application needs. These stacks are difficult to install, port, and managed by system administrators. To address these problems, *users can bring their own runtime images produced at home environment* to set up the chain-rooted container environment of choice to carry out their experiments efficiently.

In this paper, we have established a container-based HPC ecosystem using OpenPOWER to address these challenges and an analysis is performed using HPC Challenge and IO related benchmarks. To the best of our knowledge, this is the first work which presents

- *a Container-based HPC ecosystem using OpenPOWER.*
- *a performance evaluation of Container-based HPC ecosystem using OpenPOWER.*
- *comparison of the proposed ecosystem performance with the HPC clusters developed on VMs and BareMetal servers.*

The rest of this paper is organized as follows: Sect. 2 reviews existing research work related to HPC deployments on the virtualized environments using VM-based and Container-based approach. Section 3 describes our proposed model on

[1] https://lwn.net/Articles/531114/.
[2] https://www.kernel.org/doc/Documentation/cgroup-v1/cgroups.txt.
[3] https://docs.docker.com/.

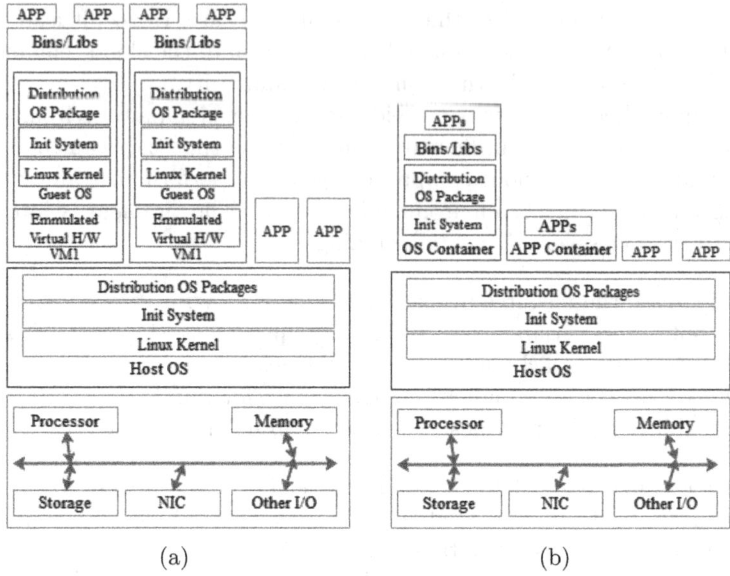

Fig. 1. (a) Hypervisor based VM. (b) Container.

Container-based HPC ecosystem that uses OpenPOWER machine during experiments and Sect. 4 presents the methodology of implementing it on OpenPOWER systems. In Sect. 5, we present a detailed experimental setup; and the performance analysis results of different benchmark applications on developed ecosystems with containers, BareMetal, and VMs are presented in Sect. 6. Section 7 draws conclusions and outline for future work.

2 Related Work

HPC is a highly matured technology which is treated to be a domain of experts using the overpriced proprietary system. HPC environment's requirement for computational scientists is detailed in [5,21]. They focus only on timely executing and maximizing scientific output of the computational workload with allocated resources by optimizing the performance benefit. This approach leverages numerous advantages including portability, manageability, reproducibility, accessibility, reliability, high security, productability, integration, and availability apart from maximizing utilization.

Several existing solutions such as [24,34] are proposed for HPC environment in the cloud using VM-based approach. The performance of migrated HPC application to the cloud is evaluated and analysed in [15–17] using benchmark applications [7,11,30]. But it was never considered as a feasible solution due to virtualization overhead, memory wall, IO overhead, poor network interconnect and heterogeneous nature of systems. Gupta *et al.* [14] with exhaustive benchmarking analysis confirmed that only small and medium scale HPC users want to take advantage of massive parallelism and cloud-bursting in addition to the cost-effective economic model that can leverage the cloud for their HPC environment. The hurdles of existing public cloud environments are that they are not optimized enough to overcome the challenges arisen due to poor inter-process communication over a slow network connection and the advanced multi-core processing technology.

To examine the untapped potential of HPC in the cloud, David *et al.* [4] conducted the benchmarking experiments to study the feasibility of container-based HPC environment that shows its near native performance against its competitor hypervisor-based solution on KVM. By considering CPU performance metric and holding the same standpoint, Felter *et al.* [12] also confirmed that both techniques need better tuning to support IO intensive workload in HPC. Migual *et al.* [32] also agreed on using container-based virtualization for HPC. They investigated an in-depth performance comparison among different Container-based virtualization technologies such as Linux Container, OpenVZ and Linux Vserver along with hypervisor representative Xen. They have considered several performance overheads including Compute, Memory, Disk, Network, and Isolation [23]. They have claimed that LXC gives the superior performance in most of the cases except isolation where hypervisor based solution dominates. Scheepers *et al.* [26] also supported the statements based on macro benchmark performance comparison using application and inter-VM communication benchmark. Single Root IO Virtualization (SR-IOV)[4] alleviates the significantly high IO overhead problem of hypervisor-based virtualization that usually occurs in IO intensive HPC workloads. But container-based solutions outperforms VM-based solutions [35] in terms of start-up latency, inter-process communication, low network latency, and higher bandwidth. However, hypervisor-based VM's are stronger in isolation features.

Undoubtedly popular container manager, called Docker, has received a lot of attention to be used in HPC. This is due to their attractive features like light-weight deployment, fast and transparent nature, application encapsulation and cloud mobility, application lifecycle management, consistency, repeatability, and compliance with its strong potential for resource guaranteedness, and performance isolation using Linux kernel features. Most importantly, it uses Advance Multi-Layered Unification File system for image handling [1,20,22]. But Docker runtime was not designed keeping HPC in mind. It does not address security concerns related to the multi-user shared HPC environment. It does not support resource manager plug-in integration, one of the essential components of HPC environment to run a task in an optimized way when multiple nodes are used. Although Docker Swarn can be used to run on multiple nodes, it is not suitable for HPC environment as the infiniband, GPU, and MPI support can not be provided natively without some modification of Docker. Yu *et al.* [33] presented virtual HPC cluster using Docker container technology to resolve software dependency issues by reducing the burden on system administrators. Charles *et al.* [36]

[4] https://pubs.vmware.com/vsphere-51/index.jsp?topic=%2Fcom.vmware.vsphere.networking.doc%2FGUID-CC021803-30EA-444D-BCBE-618E0D836B9F.html.

have also given a light on the similar issue of providing workflow-aware environment by managing container in a shared manner. This solution provides only manual auto scaling feature. Skyport [13] provides a container-based scientific workflow execution environment using Docker and Shock [29]. But it only uses Docker inherent resource utilization policy and does not consider any suitable container placement strategy. Zheng *et al.* [28] addressed the problem with an outline on a scientific execution environment by detecting failure, performance bottleneck, optimized placement and runtime migration of a container. But it lacks precise design considerations. Weidner *et al.* [31] presented a symmetric and application-centric HPC platform considering the physical state of application processes and environmental awareness. This approach uses subscription-based demands and associated notification control. But it lacks dynamic requirement and power-awareness features.

Ali *et al.* [19] presented a Kubernetes managed highly available container cluster that can be used for HPC. The drawback of the system is that Kubernetes master takes a longer time to realize container engine failure. Whereas, Ubercloud[5], also based on enhanced Docker container, provides a computational environment for engineering and scientific applications by removing the roadblock of application runtime environment but it suffers from unpredictable performance benefits of the provided ecosystem. It didn't consider the hardware features and performance metrics of the underlying environment which was later attempted by Shifter [6,18]. In this system, containers for HPC rely on popular Docker ecosystem with the extended run-time engine. They have enhanced security policies with setuid-incapable and bind-mounted image path wherever required, improved user defined image creation and distribution along with workload manager integration for dealing with heterogeneous technical and scientific application domains.

Although few authors such as [4,12,25,32] evaluated and analyzed the performance impact of container-based HPC solutions, however, there are few gaps.

- (i) They compared the container-based solutions with either virtual machines or BareMetal machines alone, but not both.
- (ii) They did not use HPC sub-components (including CPU, Memory, IO, and Interconnect) all together in their evaluations. Particularly, it is not the case with considering all container, VM, and BareMetal.
- (iii) All reported works on the container used either LXC on a virtual machine or Docker or Linux Vserver or OpenVZ. The workload manager plug-in integration is not readily available in these environments for HPC.
- (iv) Most importantly, so far no work is reported on container-based HPC ecosystems that are developed on OpenPOWER machines.

In this paper, we have attempted to design and develop a Container-based ecosystem for HPC using OpenPOWER and a performance analysis is done on sub-components like computing, memory, interconnect, and IO to assess the system with popular benchmark applications. The container based solutions are compared with, both, VM and BareMetal machine solutions.

[5] https://www.theubercloud.com/.

3 Container-Based HPC Ecosystem on OpenPOWER

Traditional HPC environments are highly optimized for specific scientific and technical computing workloads using specially designed OS, parallel file systems, super-fast interconnects and enhanced MPI library. They fail to deal with a daunting set of requirements due to the dynamic nature of almost insatiable appetite for high application performance. HPC users want their ecosystem to be comprehensive, coherent and highly performed on their application meeting the requirements of elastic growth of their environmental resources, heterogeneous workloads with sophisticated software stack, heterogeneous processing elements, power-awareness, and reliability of the scale [9]. Keeping several weaknesses of traditional systems in mind and research potential in adapting containers in HPC, this paper aims to design and develop a Container-based ecosystem for HPC as shown in Fig. 2 using OpenPOWER machines.

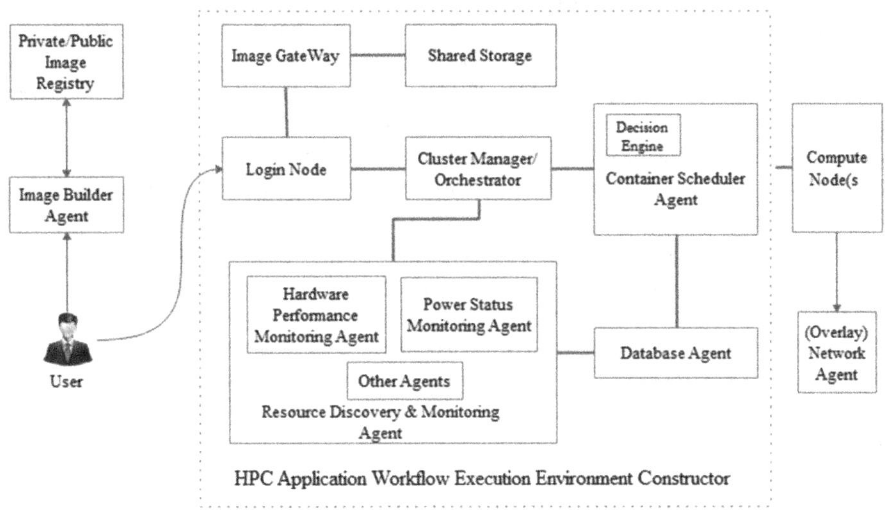

Fig. 2. High-level prototype for Container-based HPC ecosystem on OpenPOWER

In the proposed model, initially, a user prepares an image to setup the container runtime on OpenPOWER according to the execution environment requirement of a particular application workflow. Any Image builder agent can be employed to build the image in their home environment. It primarily uses layered image approach to maintain information about each layer to facilitate easy, light-weight, and flexible container deployment. The user can publish the image to the private or public repository, preferably Docker registry, that can be accessed later to pull the required image and store it to a shared location of the ecosystem with mandate authentication credentials. The user can login through the LoginNode with appropriate authentication credentials and submit the scientific application workflow to cluster manager by providing the required execution environmental parameters along with the image(s) to be used. Cluster Manager/Orchestrator queues the submitted application workflow maintaining priorities according to the Quality of Service (QoS) requirements. It analyses and splits the application workflow into subtasks that can be executed on individual containers. The queue of application workflows is handed over to cluster manager core. Subsequently, the cluster manager core invokes the other agents such as databases, Resource Discovery & Monitoring (RDM) agent, Container scheduler and network. It dispatches the subtasks to selected containers deployed on OpenPOWER machine. Database agent stores and processes the information collected by RDM agent using key-value store mechanism. RDM agent communicates with the client discovery agent to collect the information about currently alive OpenPOWER compute nodes. It monitors the application performance at run-time and invokes the scheduler agent if necessary and gathers the information regarding hardware performance and power status of compute node(s) running on OpenPOWER, and triggers the scheduler to take appropriate action.

Container scheduler agent is the primary component to facilitate HPC run-time environment for application workflows. It selects the appropriate OpenPOWER compute node(s) to deploy the subtasks of application workflow using several metrics received including computing node list, collected hardware performance parameters and power status information along with QoS parameters. It also runs the load-balancing and fault tolerance mini-agent to dynamically react and change environment whenever required. Image Gateway pulls the requested image and makes it available to the Shared Storage to be utilized by container run-time. It also publishes the image endpoint and preserves the integrity. The container runtime on OpenPOWER Compute node(s) creates the containers on which subtasks of a specific task are executed. The OpenPOWER node runs the slave agents to discover, application performance monitoring, hardware, and power status monitoring to push the related information to the RDM agent. Network agent creates the dynamic network among the containers deployed on OpenPOWER machines for different application workflows.

The proposed ecosystem, finally, will have several containers running on OpenPOWER nodes that are communicating as per the need of the application within the system (intra-hosts) or across the systems (inter-hosts).

4 Implementation

The proposed ecosystem aims to provide a user perspective application environment over the container to deal with sophisticated software dependencies and related system-wide configurations. The proposed model is inspired by Shifter [6], an open-source HPC environment provisioning project, developed by NERSC[6].

The ecosystem is built with Image Gateway running on OpenPOWER node developed in Python and an executable binary, Container-based HPC runtime (CHPCE) along with site specific optimization modules. The workflow of the

[6] http://www.nersc.gov/.

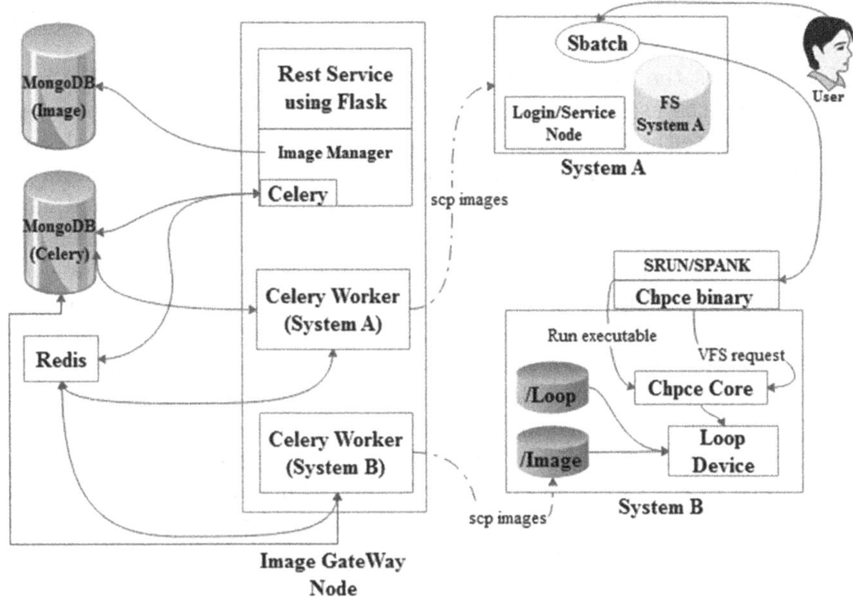

Fig. 3. Workflow of Image Gateway and Chpce core

image gateway and Container-based HPC core is presented in Fig. 3. The *chpceimg* (command line tool implemented in C to interact with image gateway) starts parsing the configuration file and command line options related to image gateway. It gets the requests to pull the required image to run the user specified tasks. The image gateway query URL constructed consists of selected gateway URL, query mode, image type, and tag along with requesting system information using *libcurl* easy handle object.

HTTP post request is sent using *libcurl* easy handle object with munge encrypted authentication credential to the target Image Gateway which receives the request using *Flask* implementation of REST API. The Image Gateway creates a new session with requested authentication credentials using *munge* and system information for subsequent operations. It then constructs the image query object using session info, system info, image type, tag, and status depending on the user requested mode for the image. If the requested mode is either list or lookup and the request is authorized then the Image Gateway responds with the corresponding record from the *Mongo* database. If it is an image pull request and the record corresponding to the pull request is not present in the database or has expired, then inserts the new pull record to the database along with its current state. The Image Manager queues the image pull request in the *RabbitMQ* message queue and starts the celery workers to pull the layers of the images parallel using public or private image registry API such as Docker registry V2 protocol. The pulled layers are saved and integrity is checked before extraction into a specific location. Later, the pulled image is converted to the user requested format and transfers it to the shared location along with the meta data if not present already.

User requests the Container-based HPC ecosystem runtime (implemented in C) to set up the user defined image environment on OpenPOWER compute node(s) to execute the jobs. The *chpce* runtime parses its configuration files and command line options to find information about the requested image from the predefined shared location. It sets working directory, mount point, and entry point appropriately after ensuring user's authorization. Then it checks whether the user is authorized to get root access to set up user defined image, and the requested image is not already loaded on the target system. It unshares the filesystem namespace after obtaining the root privileges to create an empty root under the specified mount point. The suitable mount device is selected depending on the requested image format. If loop device is needed for the requested image format, the image is mounted on the requested mount point using loop device driver with *suid* incapable and read-only mode. The loopback-mounted image is bind-mounted to the target for constructing user defined runtime environment. The *chroot jail* is applied on the apparent root directory of the newly created user defined image environment and the current working directory is changed. Finally, the job is executed on that user define chrooted environment running on OpenPOWER machine and results are returned to the user.

5 Experimental Testbed

In this section, we outline our experimental testbed in terms of the ecosystems made of containers, virtual machines, and BareMetal Servers running on OpenPOWER machine. KVM hypervisor is chosen as VMM solution due to its widespread popularity and superior performance benefit.

Our experimental setup consists of OpenPOWER Server with one socket IBM Turismo SCM 3.857 GHz POWER8 processor having 8 cores/socket (capable of running 8 hardware threads/core), 64k L1 data cache & 32k L1 instruction cache, 512k L2 cache, 8 MB L3 shared cache, 128 GB of RAM and 10GbE LAN Mezz Card. All nodes are interconnected by smart managed 10-Gigabit switch. The CentOS Linux release 7.3.1611 (AltArch) having kernel 3.10.0-514.10.2.el7 was installed on the OpenPOWER Server and the default configurations were maintained except the packages that were built from source to make it work on OpenPOWER server. We haven't imposed any kind of optimizations during our experiments. Hence, experimental environments made of BareMetal(s), Container(s) and VM(s) were tried to keep unchanged during the runtime for all experiments to achieve performance that can be utilized for fair comparison purpose. HPC Challenge benchmark (HPCC) [10] which stresses all the subcomponents of the system such as processor, memory, and interconnect are used to evaluate the performance of the ecosystems made of containers, virtual machines, and BareMetals. It consists of seven benchmarks: HPL, STREAM, RandomAccess, PTRANS, FFTE, DGEMM, and b_eff Latency/Bandwidth. HPCC-1.5.0 package is used with mpich-2.15 and OpenBLAS to compile and run benchmark programs. To cope with standard benchmark evaluations, our constructed ecosystems maintains the largest problem size fitting into 70% (i.e. approximately 90 GB) of the total memory for all experiments. The problem size is of 100000 and block size is of 100 are tested. Flat process grid ratios 2:16, 3:16, and 4:14 are used as input because of our employed simple Ethernet network. All experiments are repeated 20 times, and median values are taken to plot the graphs. We observe a clear peak at median values in all cases.

6 Performance of OpenPOWER on HPC Ecosystems

This section critically analyses the results achieved due to experiments conducted on proposed container-based HPC ecosystem that is deployed on OpenPOWER system. It is important to understand the performance of subsystems of OpenPOWER machine like Compute, Memory, Interconnect, and Disk on running the benchmark HPC applications. We did a comparative analysis of the proposed ecosystem functionality on OpenPOWER using different deployment methods like containers, VMs, and BareMetal hardware. The following subsections detail the impact of OpenPOWER system parameters on HPC ecosystem.

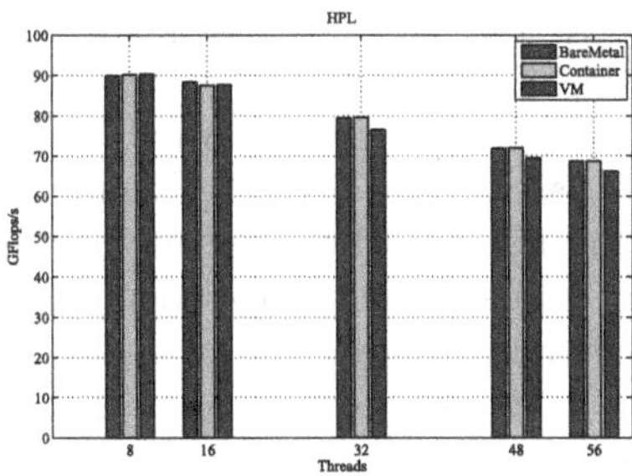

Fig. 4. Performance of HPL on BareMetal, Container, and VM based Ecosystem

6.1 Compute Performance

We used High Performance LINPACK (HPL) TPP benchmark of HPCC to evaluate the compute performance of our constructed ecosystems. It solves a dense linear system of equations using LU factorization with partial row pivoting method. This reports the estimated performance of the system with the help of local matrix multiplication operations. To achieve optimal performance of our ecosystems made of BareMetal, Container, and VM, we executed the LINPACK benchmark for matrices of order 100000 and block size of 100 with process grid ratios as 2:16, 3:16, and 4:14. In Fig. 4, we have shown the performance of the G-HPL benchmark for each of the three ecosystems. The Container-based ecosystem obtained the performance result slightly greater than BareMetal based ecosystem whereas VM based ecosystem shows degraded performance with an overhead of 3% compared to BareMetal. Overall, all the three ecosystems have shown almost similar performance on compute intensive G-HPL benchmark. This is due to the fact that G-HPL spends most of its time running highly optimized kernels that near optimally handle cache hierarchies, TLB misses, inter-process communications. And it introduces very little overhead due to the abstraction provided by the container at OS level and virtualization overhead by KVM.

The DGEMM, a simple multi-threaded dense matrix *multiply* benchmark, is used to investigate the sustained floating-point computational rate of double precision real matrix-matrix multiplication of a single node. It measures the achievable double-precision FLOPS of a single node. The computation kernel used in the DGEMM benchmark is

$$C = \alpha AB + \beta C; \tag{1}$$

where A, B, and C are with the dimensions $M \times K, K \times N$, and $M \times N$ respectively. In our experiments, we evaluated the performance for the matrices with the size of $10205 \times 10205, 8332 \times 8332$, and 7714×7714 to fit them into the available caches to reduce the bandwidth requirement. In Fig. 5, the performance of the DGEMM benchmark is shown for each of the three ecosystems. In SingleDGEMM case, initially container based ecosystem shows slightly better performance, but as the number of threads is increased, the performance of Container-based ecosystem begins to drop proportionally compared to BareMetal. But, we observed that the performance of the VM based ecosystem drops rapidly. In the case of StarDGEMM, container shows better performance initially, but as the number of threads is increased, VM shows better performance. The reason behind this is not evident to us. In all the cases the performance degrades gradually, due to the fact that as we increase the total number of threads, the effective memory bandwidth available for each thread reduces. We need to choose tile dimensions used in DGEMM benchmark carefully, keeping the architecture in mind because it may degrade the performance due to cache associative conflict and TLB pressure.

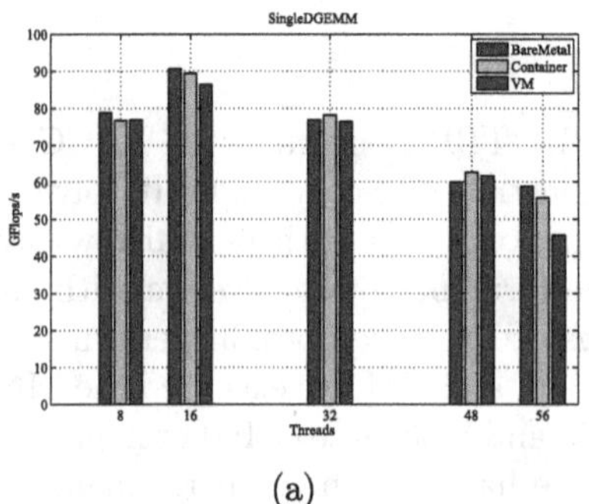

(a)

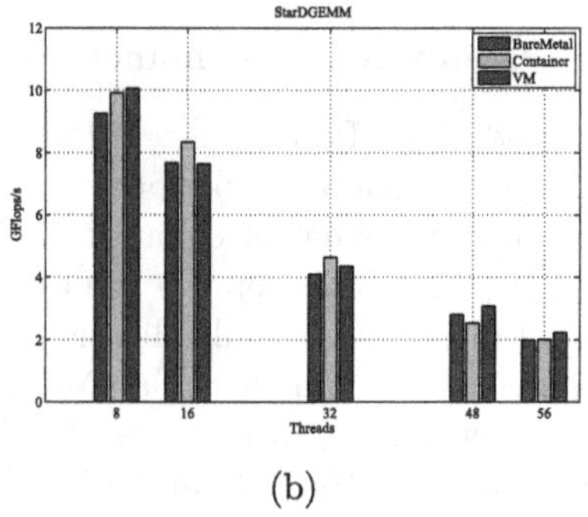

(b)

Fig. 5. Performance of (a) SingleDGEMM. (b) StarDGEMM.

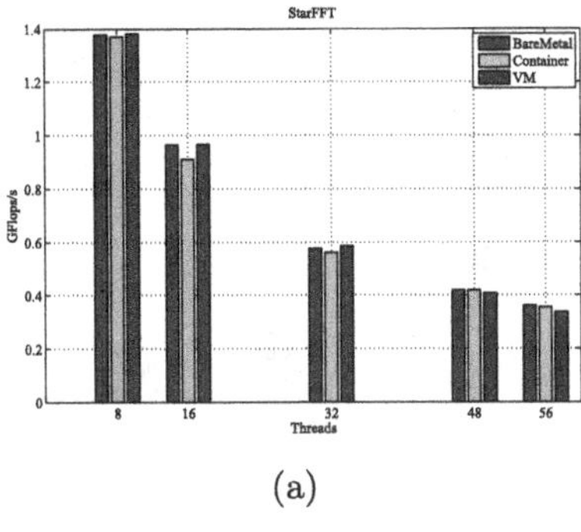

(a)

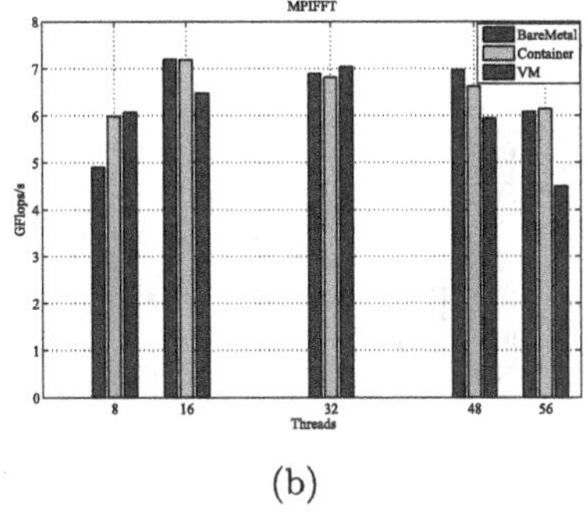

(b)

Fig. 6. Performance of (a) StarFFT. (b) MPIFFT.

The FFT benchmark is used to measure floating point rate of execution of double precision complex one-dimensional discrete Fourier transform (DFT) of size m. It stresses on the inter-process communication using large messages. In Fig. 6, we plotted the performance of the FFT benchmark for each of the three ecosystems. The StarFFT shows superior performance than G-FFT due to the low latency and higher bandwidth availability of intra-node communication. The Performance of the FFT benchmark degrades as we increase the number of the threads.

6.2 Memory Performance

We used a simple synthetic benchmark program, STREAM, to evaluate the sustainable memory bandwidth of the constructed ecosystems. It measures computation rate using four simple vector kernels.

$$\begin{aligned} COPY &: c = a \\ SCALE &: b = \alpha c \\ ADD &: c = a + b \\ TRIAD &: a = b + \alpha c \end{aligned} \quad (2)$$

where a,b, c are vectors and α is a scalar.

The used array size for STREAM benchmark experiment as 104166666 which require a total memory of size 2.3283 GiB, that is greater than 2x the size of 8 MB L3 cache of our OpenPOWER system. In Fig. 7, we have shown memory bandwidth using an EP-STREAM benchmark for each of the three ecosystems. The average measured memory bandwidth is 1.00 GB/s, 1.01 GB/s, and 0.998 GB/s for BareMetal, container, and VM based ecosystem respectively. In the case of SingleSTREAM, only a single thread performs the computations and uses the available memory bandwidth, so it shows nearly same behavior in all threads case, because at any time the total available bandwidth will be shared among active threads. VM based ecosystem shows a slightly degraded performance; this

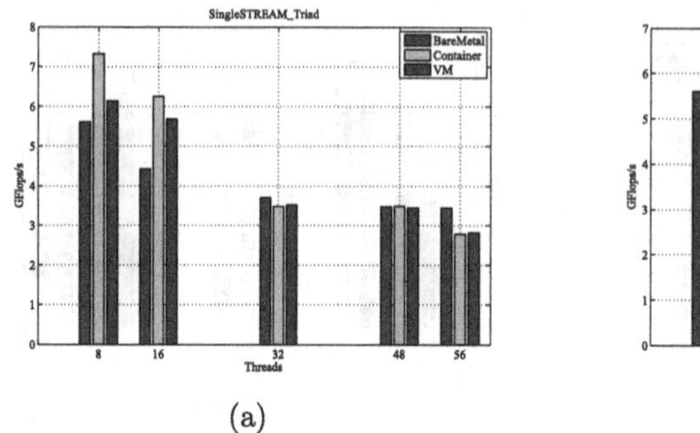

(a)

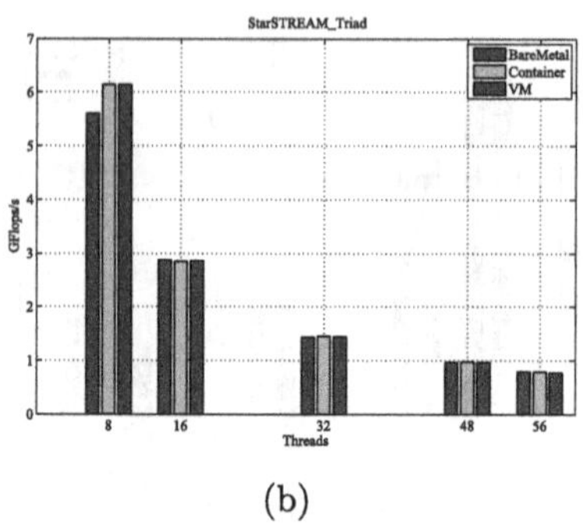

(b)

Fig. 7. Performance of (a) SingleSTREAM_Triad. (b) StarSTREAM_Triad.

is due to the address translation overhead and also double caching problem in virtualization layer. The measured bandwidth is close to the theoretical value for the systems. In the case of StartSTREAM, all the threads perform computation and share L3 cache along with the available memory bandwidth among them, so it shows degraded performance as we increase threads due to memory contention. We can conclude that a high number of threads execution and poor choice of a memory location can present negative impact on memory performance.

The RandomAccess benchmark is used to evaluate peak capacity of the memory subsystem while updating the random locations of the system memory. The benchmark works on a large distributed table of size 2^p, occupying approximately half of system memory and profiles the memory architecture of the system. In the case of MPIRandomAccess, total main table of size $8589934592(2^{33})$ words is used in all tests. The PE main table of size 2^{28}, $(2^{33})/48$, and $(2^{33})/56$ words are used respectively for 32, 48, and 56 threads in case of both MPIRandomAccess and StarRandomAccess. The number of performed updates is four times the table size. Figure 8 shows the performance of RandomAccess benchmark for each of the three ecosystems. It can be observed that benchmark scales well. Similar performance is observed from the StarRandomAccess benchmark in all the three cases. In the case of MPIRandomAccess, initially, BareMetal gives slightly better performance than the container. But, it gradually converges as the number of threads is increased. VM based ecosystem presents 52.6% and 37.5% overhead compared to BareMetal in 32 and 48 threads cases, due to its high pressure on TLB and handling of a very large number of short messages between the processor in virtualized environment. Performance degrades gradually as the number of threads is increased. This is due to the fact that the threads of non-power 2 introduce overhead by integer division operation to figure out the location of the memory operation. The multi-thread mapping mode and error tolerance incur negative impact.

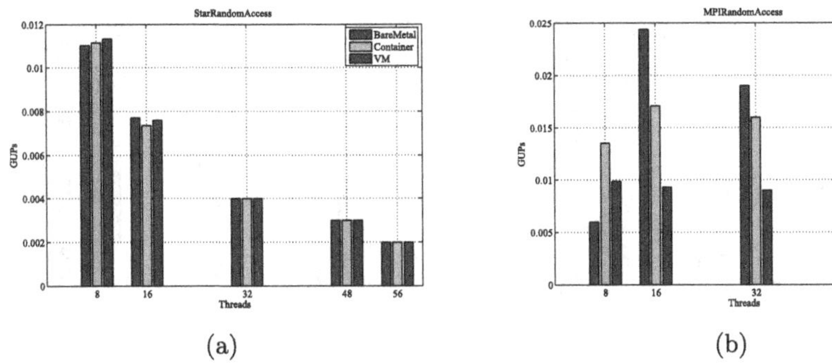

(a) (b)

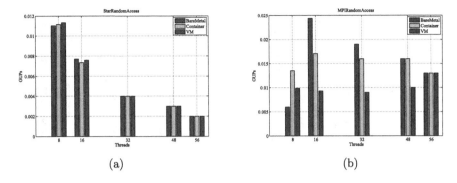

Fig. 8. Performance of (a) StarRandomAccess. (b) MPIRandomAccess.

6.3 Interconnect Performance

PTRANS (Parallel Matrix transpose) is used to investigate communication, where pairs of processors communicate with each other using large messages simultaneously. It is used to test total communication capacity of the system interconnect. We input a matrix of size 50000×50000 processes and process grid of size 2×16, 3×16, and 4×13. Figure 9 depicts the performance of the PTRANS benchmark for each of the three ecosystems. The result shown is for the configuration that produces the optimal result. The VM based ecosystem presents the lowest performance among the three ecosystems. The benchmark stresses the global network and shows the degraded performance when we increase the number of threads, this is due to the involvement of communication interconnects.

The *b_eff* benchmark is utilized to measure effective bandwidth and latency on interconnect of the constructed ecosystems. It exchanges 8 bytes and 2,000,000 bytes of messages respectively using simple MPI point-point routines for measuring latency and bandwidth of communication interconnects. In ring communication, all the communicating processes are arranged in a ring, and each process sends and receives messages to its neighbor in parallel. The ring communication

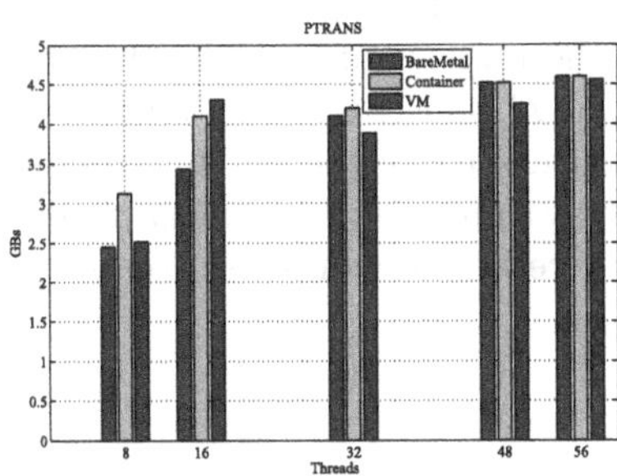

Fig. 9. Performance of PTRANS on BareMetal, Container, and VM based ecosystem

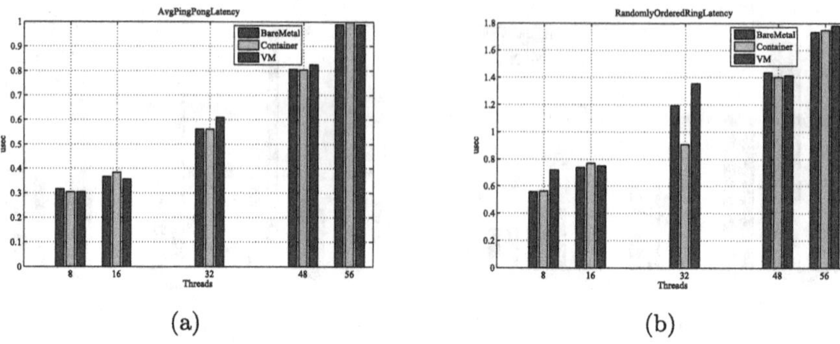

Fig. 10. Performance of (a) AvgPingPongLatency. (b) RandomlyOrderedRingLatency.

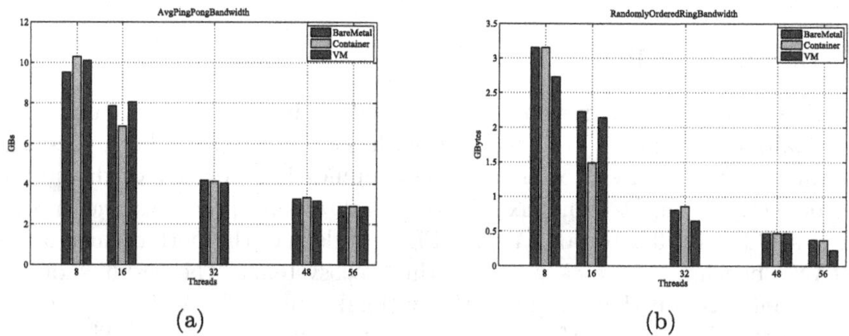

Fig. 11. Performance of (a) AvgPingPongBandwidth. (b) RandomlyOrderedRing-Bandwidth.

was conducted on 32, 48, and 56 processes. The Ping Pong communication was operated on 992(32*(32-1)), 2256, and 3080 pairs of processes for latency and bandwidth benchmarking. In Fig. 10, avgPingPong and random-order ring latency are presented for each of the three ecosystems. The BareMetal and Container-based ecosystem report the same latency behavior. But VM-based ecosystem presents a higher latency. This is due to the network virtualization overhead. In all cases, latency increases gradually as we increase the number of threads. As we increase the number of threads, the processes need to traverse a number of stages. Figure 11 shows the avgPingPong and random-order ring bandwidth for each of the three ecosystems. The BareMetal and container based ecosystems depict the nearly same bandwidth. Again, all cases show a rapid drop in performance once we increase the number of communicating processes due to traversal of multiple stages.

6.4 Disk Performance

The well-known IOzone[7] benchmark is used to evaluate the disk performance of our build ecosystems. This benchmark generates and measures a variety of file operations such as *read, writes, re-read, re-write, read backwards, read strided, fread, fwrite, random read/write, pread/pwrite variants, aio_read, aio_write, mmap* to examine file IO operation of the ecosystems. The benchmark is run with maximum file size of 15 GB and record size of 16 MB. Figure 12 evaluates the performance of the IOzone benchmark related to different read and write operations for each of the three ecosystems. We observe very little performance penalty related to different IO operation in Container-based ecosystem compared to native performance. But, a significant performance penalty is encountered in VM based ecosystem due to its high overhead related to IO operations, mainly write inside the virtualized environment. A noticeable difference is seen in VM case as we increase file size due to the inefficiency of virtualization driver to handle large file size. The Container-based ecosystem shows proportional degradation in IO performance as we increase the file size. This is due to the fact that, container scheduler tries to reorder IO aggressively to avoid starvation as much as possible.

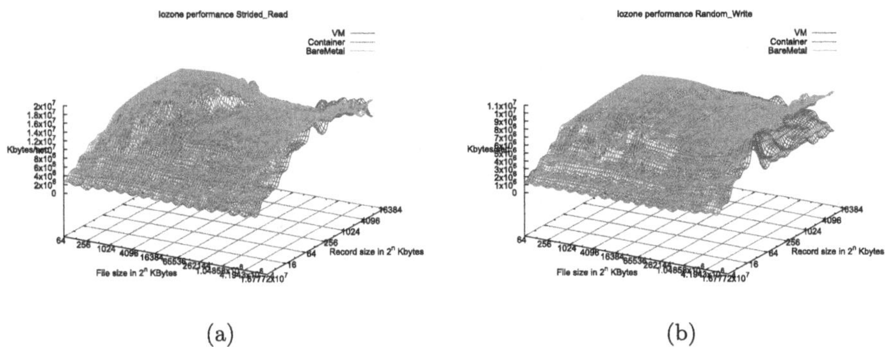

(a) (b)

Fig. 12. Performance of IOzone (a) Strided_Read. (b) Random_write.

7 Conclusion and Future Work

In this study, the performance analysis of the Container-based HPC ecosystem using OpenPOWER is presented. The suitability of the container based HPC ecosystem running on OpenPOWER is evaluated stressing on the different subcomponents of the HPC environment using different benchmarks, HPCC and IOzone. With the help of these benchmarks, it can be observed that the Container-based HPC ecosystem with OpenPOWER combination shows very

[7] http://www.iozone.org/.

little performance penalty in all aspects compared to native performance. Our experiments show that the VM based HPC solution is not optimized enough to be used with workloads on supercomputing facilities. One primary observation is that there is no work reported implementing Containers on OpenPOWER systems. But the experimental results indicate that the Container-based HPC solution implemented on OpenPOWER can be treated as the most viable solution to fulfill the user's customized environment requirements in shared HPC cluster without compromising the raw performance of the systems. In some cases, it is noticed that the Container-based solution outperforms the native environment; it might be due to less interference by other running processes and optimized library used in a container environment.

In future, an attempt will be made to compare the Container-based HPC ecosystem run on OpenPOWER with that of x86 systems. Also, the system aware and the environment specific tuning can be accomplished in our current benchmark experiment.

References

1. Adufu, T., Choi, J., Kim, Y.: Is container-based technology a winner for high performance scientific applications? In: 17th Asia-Pacific Network Operations and Management Symposium: Managing a Very Connected World, APNOMS 2015, pp. 507–510 (2015)
2. Basili, V.R., Carver, J., Cruzes, D.S., Hochstein, L., Hollingsworth, J.K., Shull, F., Zelkowitz, M.V.: Understanding the high performance computing community: a software engineer's perspective. IEEE Softw. **25**(4), 29–36 (2008)
3. Bernstein, D.: Containers and cloud: from LXC to Docker to kubernetes. IEEE Cloud Comput. **1**, 81–84 (2014)
4. Beserra, D., Moreno, E.D., Endo, P.T., Barreto, J., Sadok, D., Fernandes, S.: Performance analysis of LXC for HPC environments. In: Proceedings - 2015 9th International Conference on Complex, Intelligent, and Software Intensive Systems, CISIS 2015, pp. 358–363 (2015)
5. Brief, S.: Dell solutions for high performance computing. Technical report, June 2015
6. Canon, R.S., Jacobsen, D.: Shifter: containers for HPC. In: Cray Users Group Conference (CUG 2016) (2016)
7. Carter, J., Oliker, L., Shalf, J.: Performance evaluation of scientific applications on modern parallel vector systems. In: Daydé, M., Palma, J.M.L.M., Coutinho, Á.L.G.A., Pacitti, E., Lopes, J.C. (eds.) VECPAR 2006. LNCS, vol. 4395, pp. 490–503. Springer, Heidelberg (2007). doi:10.1007/978-3-540-71351-7_38
8. Cisco; Red Hat: Linux Containers: Why They're in Your Future and What Has to Happen First Application Delivery: Today's Challenges. Technical report (2014)
9. Conway, S., Joseph, E.C., Sorensen, B.: An Approach for Designing HPC Systems with Better Balance and Performance, vol. (1), pp. 1–7 (2016)
10. Dongarra, J.J., Luszczek, P.: Overview of the HPC challenge benchmark suite. In: Proceeding of SPEC Benchmark Workshop. Citeseer (2006)
11. Dunigan, T.H., Vetter, J.S., White, J.B., Worley, P.H.: Performance evaluation of the cray X1 distributed shared-memory architecture. IEEE Micro **25**, 30–40 (2005)

12. Felter, W., Ferreira, A., Rajamony, R., Rubio, J.: An updated performance comparison of virtual machines and Linux containers. In: 2015 IEEE International Symposium on Performance Analysis of Systems and Software (ISPASS), pp. 171–172 (2015)
13. Gerlach, W., Tang, W., Keegan, K., Harrison, T., Wilke, A., Bischof, J., Dsouza, M., Devoid, S., Murphy-Olson, D., Desai, N., Meyer, F.: Skyport - container-based execution environment management for multi-cloud scientific workflows. In: Proceedings of DataCloud 2014: 5th International Workshop on Data Intensive Computing in the Clouds - Held in Conjunction with SC 2014: The International Conference for High Performance Computing, Networking, Storage and Analysis, pp. 25–32 (2015)
14. Gupta, A., Kale, L.V., Gioachin, F., March, V., Suen, C.H., Lee, B.S., Faraboschi, P., Kaufmann, R., Milojicic, D.: The Who, What, Why, and How of high performance computing in the cloud. In: 2013 IEEE 5th International Conference on Cloud Computing Technology and Science, pp. 306–314 (2013)
15. Gupta, A., Kalé, L.V., Milojicic, D.S., Faraboschi, P., Kaufmann, R., March, V., Gioachin, F., Suen, C.H., Lee, B.S.: Exploring the performance and mapping of HPC applications to platforms in the cloud. In: Proceedings of the 21st International Symposium on High-Performance Parallel and Distributed Computing - HPDC 2012, pp. 121–122 (2012)
16. He, Q., Zhou, S., Kobler, B., Duffy, D., Mcglynn, T.: Case study for running HPC applications in public clouds. In: Proceedings of the 19th ACM International Symposium on High Performance Distributed Computing - HPDC 2010, pp. 395–401 (2010)
17. Jackson, K., Ramakrishnan, L., Muriki, K., Canon, S., Cholia, S., Shalf, J., Wasserman, H., Wright, N.: Performance analysis of high performance computing applications on the amazon web services cloud. In: 2010 IEEE Second International Conference on Cloud Computing Technology and Science (CloudCom) (2010)
18. Jacobsen, D.M., Canon, R.S.: Contain this, unleashing Docker for HPC. In: Cray User Group 2015 (2015)
19. Kanso, A., Huang, H., Gherbi, A.: Can Linux containers clustering solutions offer high availability? In: Second Workshop on Containers (WoC) - Colocated with IC2E 2016 (2016)
20. Liu, D., Zhao, L.: The research and implementation of cloud computing platform based on Docker. In: 2014 11th International Computer Conference on Wavelet Active Media Technology and Information Processing (ICCWAMTIP), pp. 475–478 (2014)
21. Lu, K., Chi, W., Liu, Y., Tang, H.: HPVZ: a high performance virtual computing environment for super computers. Technical report 111072 (2009)
22. Mancini, M., Aloisio, G.: How advanced cloud technologies can impact and change HPC environments for simulation. In: Proceedings of the 2015 International Conference on High Performance Computing and Simulation, HPCS 2015, No. Cmcc, pp. 667–668 (2015)
23. Matthews, J.N., Hu, W., Hapuarachchi, M., Deshane, T., Dimatos, D., Hamilton, G., McCabe, M., Owens, J.: Quantifying the performance isolation properties of virtualization systems. In: Proceedings of the 2007 Workshop on Experimental Computer Science (ExpCS 2007), p. 6 (2007)

24. Ruiu, P., Terzo, O., Carlino, G., Prandi, R., Falzone, A., Maggi, P., Torterolo, L., Usai, E., Perego, G.: HPC CloudPills: on-demand deployment and execution of HPC application in cloud environments. In: Proceedings - 2014 9th International Conference on P2P, Parallel, Grid, Cloud and Internet Computing, 3PGCIC 2014, pp. 82–88 (2015)
25. Ruiz, C., Jeanvoine, E., Nussbaum, L.: Performance evaluation of containers for HPC. In: Hunold, S., Costan, A., Giménez, D., Iosup, A., Ricci, L., Gómez Requena, M.E., Scarano, V., Varbanescu, A.L., Scott, S.L., Lankes, S., Weidendorfer, J., Alexander, M. (eds.) Euro-Par 2015. LNCS, vol. 9523, pp. 813–824. Springer, Cham (2015). doi:10.1007/978-3-319-27308-2_65
26. Scheepers, M.J.: Virtualization and containerization of application infrastructure: a comparison. In: 21st Twente Student Conference on IT, pp. 1–7 (2014)
27. Soltesz, S., Pötzl, H., Fiuczynski, M.E., Bavier, A., Peterson, L.: Container-based operating system virtualization: a scalable, high-performance alternative to hypervisors. ACM SIGOPS Operating Syst. Rev. **41**(3), 275–287 (2007)
28. Stankovski, V., Taherizadeh, S., Taylor, I., Jones, A., Mastroianni, C., Becker, B., Suhartanto, H.: Towards an environment supporting resilience, high-availability, reproducibility and reliability for cloud applications. In: 2015 IEEE/ACM 8th International Conference on Utility and Cloud Computing (UCC), pp. 383–386 (2015)
29. Tang, W., Wilkening, J., Desai, N., Gerlach, W., Wilke, A., Meyer, F., Bischof, J., Gerlach, W., Wilke, A., Desai, N., Meyer, F.: A scalable data analysis platform for metagenomics. In: 2013 IEEE International Conference on Big Data, pp. 21–26 (2013)
30. Varghese, B., Subba, L.T., Thai, L., Barker, A.: Container-based cloud virtual machine benchmarking. In: 2016 IEEE International Conference on Cloud Engineering (IC2E), pp. 192–201 (2016)
31. Weidner, O., Atkinson, M., Barker, A., Vicente, R.F.: Rethinking high performance computing platforms: challenges, opportunities and recommendations, pp. 19–26 (2016)
32. Xavier, M., Neves, M., Rossi, F., Ferreto, T., Lange, T., De Rose, C.: Performance evaluation of container-based virtualization for high performance computing environments, pp. 233–240 (2013)
33. Yu, H.e., Huang, W.: Building a virtual HPC cluster with auto scaling by the Docker. In: Computing Research Repository, vol. abs/1509.0, p. 4 (2015)
34. Zhang, J., Lu, X., Arnold, M., Panda, D.K.: MVAPICH2 over OpenStack with SR-IOV: an efficient approach to build HPC clouds. In: Proceedings - 2015 IEEE/ACM 15th International Symposium on Cluster, Cloud, and Grid Computing, CCGrid 2015, pp. 71–80 (2015)
35. Zhang, J., Lu, X., Panda, D.K.: Performance characterization of hypervisor-and container-based virtualization for HPC on SR-IOV enabled InfiniBand clusters. In: 2016 IEEE International Parallel and Distributed Processing Symposium Workshops (IPDPSW), pp. 1777–1784 (2016)
36. Zheng, C., Thain, D.: Integrating containers into workflows. In: Proceedings of the 8th International Workshop on Virtualization Technologies in Distributed Computing - VTDC 2015, vol. 2, pp. 31–38 (2015)

Pre-exascale Architectures: OpenPOWER Performance and Usability Assessment for French Scientific Community

Gabriel Hautreux[1(✉)], Alfredo Buttari[7], Arnaud Beck[11], Victor Cameo[9], Dimitri Lecas[9], Dominique Aubert[9], Emeric Brun[10], Eric Boyer[1], Fausto Malvagi[10], Gabriel Staffelbach[4], Isabelle d'Ast[4], Joeffrey Legaux[4], Ghislain Lartigue[5], Gilles Grasseau[11], Guillaume Latu[2], Juan Escobar[2], Julien Bigot[2], Julien Derouillat[2], Matthieu Haefele[2], Nicolas Renon[8], Philippe Parnaudeau[1], Philippe Wautelet[1], Pierre-Francois Lavallee[1], Pierre Kestener[1], Remi Lacroix[1], Stephane Requena[1], Anthony Scemama[3], Vincent Moureau[5], Jean-Matthieu Etancelin[6], and Yann Meurdesoif[6]

[1] GENCI, Paris, France
gabriel.hautreux@genci.fr
[2] Maison de la Simulation, CEA, CNRS, Univ. Paris-Sud, UVSQ, Université Paris-Saclay, 91191 Gif-sur-Yvette, France
[3] Laboratoire de Chimie et Physique Quantiques, Université de Toulouse, CNRS, UPS, Toulouse, France
[4] CERFACS, Toulouse, France
[5] CORIA, CNRS UMR6614, Normandie Université, Saint-Etienne-du-Rouvray, France
[6] CReSTIC EA3804, ROMEO HPC Center, University of Reims Champagne-Ardenne, Reims, France
[7] IRIT, CNRS UMR5505, Université de Toulouse, Toulouse, France
[8] CALMIP, Université de Toulouse, Université Paul Sabatier, CNRS, UMS3667, Toulouse, France
[9] Observatoire Astronomique de Strasbourg, UMR 7550 Universite de Strasbourg - CNRS, Strasbourg, France
[10] Den-Service d'Études des Réacteurs et de Mathématiques Appliquées (SERMA), CEA, Université Paris-Saclay, 91191 Gif-sur-Yvette, France
[11] Leprince-Ringuet Laboratory (LLR), CNRS/IN2P3, Ecole Polytechnique, Palaiseau, France

Abstract. Exascale implies a major pre-requisite in terms of energy efficiency, as an improvement of an order of magnitude must be reached in order to stay within an acceptable envelope of 20 MW. To address this objective and to continue to sustain performance, HPC architectures have to become denser, embedding many-core processors (to several hundreds of computing cores) and/or become heterogeneous, that is, using graphic processors or FPGAs. These energy-saving constraints will also affect the underlying hardware architectures (e.g., memory and storage hierarchies, networks) as well as system software (runtime, resource managers, file systems, etc.) and programming models. While some of these architectures, such as hybrid machines, have existed for a number of years

J.M. Kunkel et al. (Eds.): ISC High Performance Workshops 2017, LNCS 10524, pp. 309–324, 2017.
https://doi.org/10.1007/978-3-319-67630-2_23

and occupy noticeable ranks in the TOP 500 list, they are still limited to a small number of scientific domains and, moreover, require significant porting effort. However, recent developments of new paradigms (especially around OpenMP and OpenACC) make these architectures much more accessible to programmers. In order to make the most of these breakthrough upcoming technologies, GENCI and its partners have set up a technology watch group and lead collaborations with vendors, relying on HPC experts and early adopted HPC solutions. The two main objectives are providing guidance and prepare the scientific communities to challenges of exascale architectures.

The work performed on the OpenPOWER platform, one of the targeted platform for exascale, is described in this paper.

Keywords: OpenPOWER assessment · Technological watch · OpenMP · OpenACC · Benchmarks · Usability · Programmability

1 Introduction: Technological Watch Group Environment

1.1 Partners and Goals

The technological watch group, lead by GENCI, is gathering 20 experts from the French HPC community including: CEA, CNRS, Inria, Maison de la Simulation, Groupe Calcul and the national computing centers (CINES, IDRIS, TGCC) The main goal of this activity is to assess the usability of standard programming paradigms in order to port/optimize scientific applications and tools on multiple heterogeneous novel HPC platforms. As many efforts have been done during the past to port applications using standards like OpenMP, it has been defined as the main pre-requisite for our assessment.

On top of that, the collaboration initiated with IBM and NVidia within this project helped us to enable the application thanks to multiple workshops performed since the beginning of 2016.

1.2 Platform and Environment Available

One of the key platform assessed by GENCI and its partners is the Ouessant OpenPOWER system, hosted at IDRIS, Orsay, integrated by IBM with the following characteristics:

- 12 IBM System S822LC "Minsky" nodes with for each:
  - 2 IBM POWER8 10-core processors clocked at 4.2 GHZ and 128 GB of main memory;
  - 2 NVidia P100 GPUs per socket;
  - each socket is connected to the 2 GPUs via NVLink 1.0;
- all the nodes are federated through a Mellanox EDR Infiniband interconnect
- and access to a high bandwidth filesystem (IBM Spectrum Scale, formerly known as GPFS)

This platform is installed using a Linux distribution (RedHat7) and has a variety in its compilation/execution environment. PGI, IBM and LLVM compilers were used on the platform to assess the applications. The main difficulty is that, at the moment, those compilers all have pros and cons. As LLVM had (beginning of 2016) difficulties to compile Fortran applications for the POWER8 architecture, most of the users compiled using either PGI or IBM compilers.

The compilers are evolving very frequently (almost every other week). Hence, the results presented in this paper are a snapshot of the work performed at the end of March 2017.

1.3 Applications

To assess the platform, we first used the following portfolio of 15 representative "real" applications, running daily in production, with the involvement of their respective developers:

- **AVBP** [1]**:** a parallel CFD code that solves the three-dimensional compressible Navier-Stokes equations on unstructured and hybrid grids.
- **CMS-MEM** [2]**:** a Matrix Element Method for High Energy Physics (HEP)
- **Dynamico:** a new dynamical core for LMD-Z, the atmospheric general circulation model (GCM) part of IPSL-CM Earth System Model
- **EMMA** [3]**:** an adaptive mesh refinement cosmological simulation code with radiative transfer.
- **GPS** [4]**:** Gross Pitaevskii Simulator: modeling of Bose-Einstein Condensates, quantum turbulence, or ultracold quantum gases in optical lattices
- **Gysela:** models the electrostatic branch of the Ion Temperature Gradient turbulence in tokamak plasmas
- **Hydro** [5]**:** a mini-application which implements a simplified version of RAMSES, a code developed to study large scale structure and galaxy formation
- **Meso-NH** [6]**:** the non-hydrostatic mesoscale atmospheric model of the French research community
- **Metalwalls:** a French molecular dynamic application
- **PATMOS** [7]**:** a Monte Carlo transport application
- **QMC=Chem:** a Quantum Monte Carlo code applied to chemistry
- **qr_mumps:** a direct solver for sparse linear systems
- **RAMSES:** CFD applications for astrophysics
- **SPECFEM3D_GLOBE:** simulates global and regional (continental-scale) seismic wave propagation
- **YALES2** [8]**:** parallel CFD for two-phase combustion in complex geometries, solving 3D low-Mach number Navier-Stokes equations on unstructured grids.

This portfolio of applications has been chosen as it represents a wide range of domains and the close collaboration we have with the developers helped us to define significant (scientifically speaking) test cases.

1.4 Performance Indicators

The aime of this project is to provide guidance for the future HPC users of such architecture. First workshops have demonstrated that porting an application to the POWER8 architecture is completely straightforward (compile and run), at least since the end of 2016.

However, the OpenPOWER platform involving its 4 NVidia GPUs enables the nodes to provide such a huge computational capacity that the POWER8 processor alone can not be the target for an application.

Hence, the relevant results obtained on Ouessant aim to define:

- Baselines in terms of performance (time to solution) for a given field of application ported on a full Minsky node
- the GPU porting effort for different paradigms (CUDA, OpenMP, OpenACC, ...)
- the maturity of the software stack for code offloading to GPUs

The results obtained will help the scientific communities and GENCI to define if OpenPOWER is a suitable architecture for their simulations on top of providing guidance for the upcoming HPC procurements for French national computing centers.

2 Work Performed on Each Application

The contributions in this section are mainly provided by the users. Hence, some of the applications listed earlier are not described as the worked performed on the platform is not sufficient in order to get relevant results.

2.1 AVBP

AVBP is an explicit compressible code for fluid mechanics and reactive applications used by both research and industry groups[1]. It has a hybrid, parallel MPI + OpenMP implementation. The domain is partitioned over the MPI tasks. For each MPI task, the local domain is partitioned into groups of cells.

The main computational section of the code is constituted by an external loop over the groups of cells. The internal routine `scheme` includes 50% of the code with internal vectorized loops over the cells. The data implementation is structured in FORTRAN modules and globally shared over the routines. AVBP is based on a coarse grain OpenMP approach with the parallel static loop over the groups of cells. In order to remove memory bottlenecks, variables and arrays are declared with OpenMP Private clause and Threadprivate directive in the modules. The contributions of every thread are store independently in the arrays passed in parameter and indexed in the latest dimension over the groups, as illustrated below with the arrays `avis`.

[1] http://cerfacs.fr/logiciels-de-simulation-pour-la-mecanique-des-fluides/.

```
!$OMP PARALLEL DO SHARED(nvert,avis,...) &
PRIVATE(kgroup,itype,ng1,...)
DO kgroup=1,ngroup
   call scheme(nglen, nvert(kgroup),kgroup,ng1,itype,...,&
      volc(ng1), factor(ng5), avis(kgroup),  .. avis2(kgroup),&
      avis4_tpf(kgroup),dw_spec_c_nv_buf(:,:,:,kgroup),&
      dw_fic_c_nv_buf(:,:,:,kgroup),...)
```

The first GPU implementation has been performed using OpenACC programing model; a switch to OpenMP 4.5 will be eventually studied in a second step. The choice of OpenACC over OpenMP 4.5 has been motivated by the existence of the Unified Memory feature, even though in the very first implementation of the code, the data transfers have been manually managed using explicit directives. The GPU implementation uses the same scheme as the current OpenMP implementation, with an offload of the entire `scheme` function to the GPU. The OpenMP directive controlling the main loop over the groups has been substituted by an OpenACC directive to generate OpenACC gang or CUDA block. The internal, vectorized loops are parallelized over OpenACC vectors and threads, to ensure a good GPU occupancy. Compared to the current, pure-CPU implementation, the following evolutions are required to manage the GPU offload:

- Data from modules used within the `scheme` routine has to be allocated on the GPU using the OpenACC `declare create` directive in the corresponding module, bound with enter and exit data directives, and copied or updated to/from the GPU using OpenACC `copy/update_device/update_host` directives before and after the main loop.
- Private variables and arrays in the threads with OpenMP Threadprivate directive was declared in the private clause of the OpenACC loop over the gang.
- All the routines and function potentially offloaded to the GPU have been declared with OpenACC `seq/vector` directives. These directives direct the compiler to generate both CPU and GPU paths.

2.2 EMMA

EMMA is an MPI + CUDA code which was already running on GPUs before the beginning of the project. The porting effort was very small, a simple compilation and then a run enabled to get first results on the platform. At the moment, around 50% of the code is running on GPUs. The goal is to reach 80% of the code by the end of 2017. However, first results on the platform are available for this application.

The CUDA kernel results are summarized in Table 1 while the full application is presented in Table 2.

We see a huge decrease in terms of performance for running the entire application, this is clearly explained as the full application has not been ported to CUDA.

Table 1. EMMA single Kernel on OpenPOWER

Node	SMT Mode	Processes/Node	Tasks/GPU	Time	Speed-up
P8	1	4	0	5.75	1.0
P8+4P100	1	4	1	0.21	27.4

Table 2. EMMA full application on OpenPOWER

Node	SMT Mode	Processes/Node	Tasks/GPU	Time	Speed-up
P8	1	4	0	14.6	1.0
P8+4P100	1	4	1	5.8	2.5

2.3 GPS

GPS is an application developed in MPI and relying heavily on Fast Fourier Transforms.

Approximately 100% of the code used by the test case is offloaded using OpenACC.

The performance of this OpenACC implementation suffers from the absence of the GPU-Direct feature, which is set to be made available in 2018 with the next generation of systems based on POWER9. This leads to a significant performance penalty when using the Managed Memory feature in OpenACC.

In order to evaluate the expected performance gain from GPU acceleration once the GPU-Direct feature will be released, the code has been tested without MPI; numerical results will not be valid, but the same amount of computation is performed. In this configuration (with no specific optimization), the execution is approximately twice faster when using 4 GPU versus 16 POWER8 cores.

2.4 GYSELA

The first target was to evaluate the potential of the performance boost which could be provided through GPU acceleration, and thus confirm that the OpenPOWER platform was a valid architecture for the GYSELA exploitation.

In the context of this preliminary validation phase, the work was conducted:

- On a subset of the full application: the 2D-Advection Kernel.
- Through a CUDA implementation, in order to bypass the potential current limitations of the compilation environment with respect to directive-based programming models (OpenACC or OpenMP).

The performance results achieved at the end of this first step are available in Table 3.

These performance levels fully validate the capacity to benefit from a significant performance boost thanks to GPU acceleration. Based on this first outcome, the second phase started in Q2 2017, which will shift:

Table 3. GYSELA 2D-Advection Kernel performance on OpenPOWER

Node	Processes/Node	MCells/s	Speed-up
P8	1	9.0	1.0
P8+1P100	1	56.9	6.3

- From the single 2D-Advection Kernel to the whole application.
- From a CUDA-based implementation to an OpenACC-based implementation.

2.5 Hydro

Hydro is a MPI + OpenMP code widely used by IDRIS in their workshops as a tutorial to learn MPI and OpenMP. This application is not involving deep optimization and tries to mimic what a common developer could implement in its application. The idea with Hydro is therefore to develop an OpenACC and an OpenMP implementation that could make the most of the P100 with a limited effort of development. This code could also become a good porting example for the community.

However, a CUDA implementation has been developed as a first step, in order to evaluate the performance gain the GPU acceleration can offer. The performance level achieved through the CUDA implementation will constitute a reference target for the directive-based implementations.

The following performance results have been obtained on a 8192×8192 grid (0.5 GB memory usage) using the CUDA implementation (Table 4):

Table 4. HYDRO performance on OpenPOWER

Node	Time (s)	Speed-up
OpenPOWER, POWER8, SMT4	29	1.0
OpenPOWER, POWER8 + 1P100	1.9	15.5

The development of an OpenACC implementation has already started. The performance of this implementation currently suffers from the absence of the GPU-Direct feature, which is set to be made available in 2018 with the next generation of systems based on POWER9.

2.6 Meso-NH

Meso-NH is a code developed in MPI and OpenACC.

A part of the code was already ported in OpenACC before the beginning of the project. There is an ongoing development and the team aims to port a huge part of the application before the end of 2017.

Table 5. Meso-NH single Kernel performance on OpenPOWER

Node	Processes/Node	Tasks/GPU	Speedup
P8	16	0	1.0
P8+2K80	16	8	2.6
P8+4P100	16	4	5.6

First results on one node are already available for a given kernel in Table 5.

For this particular kernel, we see a speedup of 5.6 for using 4 GPUs on top of the POWER8 processor. We also can see a speedup of 2.2 using 4 P100 compared to 2 K80.

Those results are pretty good, however if we run the full application, the speedups, in Table 6 are not as good.

Table 6. Meso-NH whole application performance on OpenPOWER

Node	Processes/Node	Tasks/GPU	Speedup
P8	16	0	1.0
P8+2K80	16	8	1.3
P8+4P100	16	4	1.5

At the moment, the developer have troubles to port a significant part of the application on GPU. The solver involved is not as easy to port as the one previously ported. A porting effort of 2 years is envisioned in order to obtain a speed-up of 5 on the full application.

2.7 Metalwalls

Metalwalls is a full MPI application for molecular dynamics. The code is written in Fortran 90 and has 20.000 lines of codes. The time loop (computational part) is 3.500 lines long and represents almost 100% of the time spent in the application. The strategy chosen by the development team was to port this application using OpenACC as it seemed, in their opinion, to be the most reliable technology available. 75% (of loop time) of the application is now ported to OpenACC, it took them 1 month to carry out this work. The estimated time for porting the full application is one other month.

The first results are in Table 7.

Those results, after only one month of work are pretty good. However the work now has to be focused on running multiple GPUs and porting the remaining part of the code(the speed-up for 1 GPU is 3.8, while 4GPUs is 4.9, which means that the scalability on multiple GPUs is not good at the moment).

Table 7. Metalwalls performance on OpenPOWER

Test case	Nodes	SMT Mode	Tasks/Node	Tasks/GPU	Time	Speed-up
Small	1	4	80	0	5.9	1.0
Small	1	1	4	1	2.0	3.0
Large	1	4	80	0	364.7	1.00
Large	1	1	1	1	96.7	3.8
Large	1	1	4	1	74.6	4.9

However, as only a bit more than 75% of the code has been ported, that means the theoretical speed-up they can achieve is around 4.0 (Amdahl's law). That's the reason why we can consider that porting this application on the OpenPOWER architecture is a success for them at the moment.

2.8 PATMOS

PATMOS is developed in C++11/14 with an hybrid parallelism based on MPI + OpenMP. A CUDA version of the application was also available in a prior release and the main work performed by the development team was to include those CUDA kernels into the main branch of the application. This work has been done during the project and now 5% of the code (in lines, but representing 75% of the CPU time) is available in CUDA. The target is to port another 5% in order to almost cover the whole application.

The results in Tables 8 and 9 are obtained using 1 MPI process per node, OpenMP threads are then used for the in-node parallelism. The results obtained on multiple nodes are almost as good as the ones obtained on the single node, which shows that the scalability of the application on this platform is very good.

Unfortunately, no test has been done using OpenMP for offloading to GPUs, but still we hope that we could run an OpenMP version on the platform in order to compare the performances we reach in CUDA and the performances

Table 8. PATMOS single node result

Test case	Nodes	SMT Mode	Threads/Node	GPU used	Time	Speed-up
Small	1	4	80	0	24.0	1.0
Small	1	4	80	4	6.0	4.0

Table 9. PATMOS multiple node result

Test case	Nodes	SMT Mode	Threads/Node	GPU used	Time	Speed-up
Large	8	4	80	0	582.1	1.0
Large	8	4	80	4	152.2	3.8

we can reach using OpenMP. This part is ongoing and we expect to have good performances using OpenMP as well.

2.9 QMC=Chem

QMC=Chem is a quantum chemistry code which applies the quantum Monte Carlo (QMC) method to molecules to solve the Schrödinger equation. [9] Due to the embarrassingly parallel nature of the algorithm, its parallel scaling is almost ideal, and single-core optimization is crucial to improve the performance. Hence, QMC=Chem was specifically optimized for Intel Xeon processors, used in combination with the Intel Fortran compiler.

In this study, we have used QMC=Chem as a benchmark to test the performance obtained with the Power8 CPU combined with the XL compiler toolchain. We compare the results obtained on one node of the Ouessant cluster with those obtained on one node of the Occigen cluster, namely a dual-socket Intel Xeon CPU E5-2690v3 @ 2.6 GHz (Haswell). We used two test cases, one small and one large, for which the hot spots are different kernels, both very representative of the usual production runs. For the two test cases, we have counted, with the Intel Software Development Emulator, [10] the total number of single precision (SP) and double precision (DP) floating point instructions using an SSE2 executable. This information combined with the elapsed time of the benchmarks allows us to give an estimate of the performance in GFlops/s. Using the ratios of single and double precision instructions (86% SP, 14% DP for the small case, and 4% SP, 96% DP for the large case), we can also give an estimate of the percent of the peak performance that was reached. The results are given in Table 10.

To reduce the bias due to the compiler we have first used the GNU Fortran compiler on both architectures. On the small benchmark, the performance is higher on the Power8 than on the Haswell, probably due to its larger L3 cache. On the large benchmark, the performance is higher on the Haswell node, and the multi-threading on the Power8 is really crucial to approach the performance of the Xeon. Then, we have run the benchmarks compiled with vendor compilers. Using the Intel compiler gives a $\times 2.1$ acceleration on the Haswell node for the small test case, and a $\times 1.5$ acceleration of the large test case. Such a large difference is due to the heavy use of Intel compiler directives in the hottest loops. Going from the GNU to the IBM XL compiler, only a $\times 1.05$ acceleration is gained on the small test case, and the large test case becomes less efficient by a factor of $\times 0.86$.

These results show that, without any particular tuning, QMC=Chem is able to reach 22.8% of the peak performance of the Power8 node on small cases, and 17.9% on large cases. This is a good start, and as there is no performance gain using the XL compiler, we expect that a substantial performance increase could be obtained with the XL compiler if some parts of the code are rewritten in a more Power8-friendly fashion.

Table 10. Single node performance in GFlops/s. Percent of the peak (mixed single and double precision) is given in parenthesis.

Compiler	CPU	Number of threads	Small		Large	
			GFlops/s	% Peak	GFlops/s	% Peak
GNU	Haswell	1	6.8		7.1	
		24	134.5	*(7.2%)*	145.0	*(13.9%)*
		48	158.5	*(8.5%)*	136.9	*(13.2%)*
GNU	Power8	1	10.2		2.1	
		20	182.5	*(15.5%)*	39.3	*(5.9%)*
		40	230.1	*(19.2%)*	68.4	*(10.2%)*
		160	258.2	*(21.6%)*	119.7	*(17.9%)*
Intel	Haswell	1	18.3		10.9	
		24	332.9	*(17.9%)*	219.1	*(21.1%)*
		48	346.6	*(18.7%)*	183.4	*(17.8%)*
IBM XL	Power8	1	12.1		3.5	
		20	218.3	*(18.3%)*	64.4	*(9.6%)*
		40	272.2	*(22.8%)*	96.4	*(14.4%)*
		160	244.2	*(20.4%)*	103.0	*(15.4%)*

2.10 qr_mumps

qr_mumps is a direct solver for sparse linear systems based on the multifrontal QR factorization. It currently supports single nodes with multiple cores and one GPU. The parallelization is achieved through the StarPU runtime system. The problem data is decomposed into blocks and the computations are arranged into tasks whose dependencies are expressed by a Directed Acyclic Graph. StarPU takes care of launching the execution of tasks when the related dependencies are satisfied and when computational units are available [11]. In qr_mumps a dynamic and hierarchical data partitioning is used in order to have a good mix of large grain tasks, which are executed on the GPU, and fine grain tasks which are executed on the CPU cores. Moreover, when a GPU is available, a dedicated scheduling policy is used which aims at maximizing the efficiency of tasks by assigning each to the unit which is best suited for its execution. These techniques allow for an effective use of all the computational resources available on the node [12].

The porting on the OpenPOWER platform was relatively easy and needed only minor code fixes due the strict compliance to the Fortran standards enforced by IBM compilers. The graph below reports the strong scalability of the qr_mumps solver on a number of problems from the University of Florida Sparse Matrix Collection.

On the largest problem (matrix TF18) a performance of 407 Gflop/s was achieved using 20 cores, which corresponds to a remarkable 73% of the peak, with a very good scalability.

Using one GPU with the 20 cores, the performance of 1.2 Tflop/s was reached (see Table 11, meaning of speed-up of 3 between one P8 node and one P8 node + one P100.

Table 11. qr_mumps: Performance in Tflop/s

Nodes	Processes/Node	GPUs	Performance	Speed-up
1	80	0	0.4	1.0
1	80	1	1.2	3.0

The main problem at the moment is that the code does not use multiple GPUs on a single node as this functionality has not been implemented. qr_mumps will soon be integrated in a larger code which will enable this feature. The multi-GPU results are expected to be very good as well.

2.11 RAMSES

RAMSES-GPU is developed since 2009 in CUDA/C++ for astrophysics applications on regular grid. The code is 70 k lines long (out of which about 16 k are written in CUDA).

The main goal of the project was to make the code more portable. In order to achieve this goal, the developer decided to use Kokkos [13]. The first result using this paradigm is very interesting.

On average Pascal P100 is 2.8 to 4.0 faster than Kepler K80 (single GPU) with no special optimization, only using rebuild architecture flags in the CUDA implementation.

On top of that, Pascal P100 is about 10 times faster than Power8 (with 8 threads per core), still with CUDA. This result is illustrated in Table 12.

Table 12. RAMSES cell-update per second on POWER8, K80 and P100

Test Case	POWER8	K80	P100	Speed-up P100 vs POWER8
"P1"	6.7	32.8	83.5	12.5
"P2"	2.1	4.7	19.5	9.3
"P3"	0.7	X	7.5	10.7
"P4"	0.27	0.83	2.7	10.0

On the Kokkos part, the 2nd-order MUSCL (2D/3D) performance are 2% to 5% slower compared to hand-written CUDA kernels in RamsesGPU, which is an impressive result for a less intrusive implementation.

2.12 SPECFEM3D_GLOBE

Specfem3D is widely known code developed in MPI, OpenMP and CUDA. The two test cases tested here are those available in the git repository (*test small bench very simple earth* and *test small bench more complex earth*).

The code is running well on one node, with a speed-up up to 27 using a GPU versus a single P8 core. The constraint with Specfem3D is that the test case defines a number of MPI processes (which corresponds to the mesh partitioning). Moreover, we tried using the NVIDIA MPS (Multi-Process Service) for the P100 which would enable to run multiple CUDA kernels sent by different MPI processes on the same GPU. This lead to huge slow-down caused by memory copy to the GPU. This constraint has to be addressed in order to improve performance.

The code is generated with the PGI compiler, CUDA gencode60 and IBM Spectrum MPI. Results for a single node workload are available in Table 13.

Table 13. Specfem3D: test small bench more complex earth

Nodes	Processes/Node	GPUs	Time	Speed-up
1	24	0	707.27	1.00
1	24	2	52.66	13.43
1	24	4	37.83	18.69

Results are good as we have a 18.69× speed-up between P8 node and P8 node + 4 GPUs. However, as we had a 13.43× using only 2 GPUs, we could have expected at least a speed-up of 20 for using the 4 of them. A deeper analysis on this point has to be done. On top of that, a scalability test on multiple nodes using a bigger test case has to be considered.

2.13 YALES2

The main flow solver of YALES2 relies on hybrid MPI+OpenMP parallelism and on object-oriented Fortran. The project of the development team was to assess the usability of the GPUs by porting one of the most time consuming kernel (the conjugate gradient algorithm for the solving of the Poisson equation) to CUDA and by running a realistic test case. This work consisted in (i) changing the conjugate gradient iteration to exhibit data parallelism, (ii) writing a generic C to Fortran interface so that CUDA can access to the data structures of the code, (iii) integrating the kernel in the full application. A work is ongoing for porting all the kernels to GPUs, this task is starting and may take a few months/years before it is completed.

The performances for the simulation of the flow around a 3D cylinder with 3.9 million cells are given in Table 14. The speed-up is measured only for the conjugate gradient (CG) step. Interestingly, running with a single process and

Table 14. Yales2 simulation of the flow around a 3D cylinder performances on OpenPOWER

Node	Code	SMT Mode	Processes/Node	Tasks/GPU	Speed-up
P8	Standard	1	4	0	1.00
P8+1P100	CUDA	1	1	1	1.16
P8+4P100	CUDA	1	4	1	3.63

a single GPU is faster than using 4 processes. The changes in the CG step, to exhibit data parallelism, slow down the code by approximately 20% but this is largely compensated by the speed-up of the GPU. Running with 1 GPU per process lead to a speed-up close to 4.

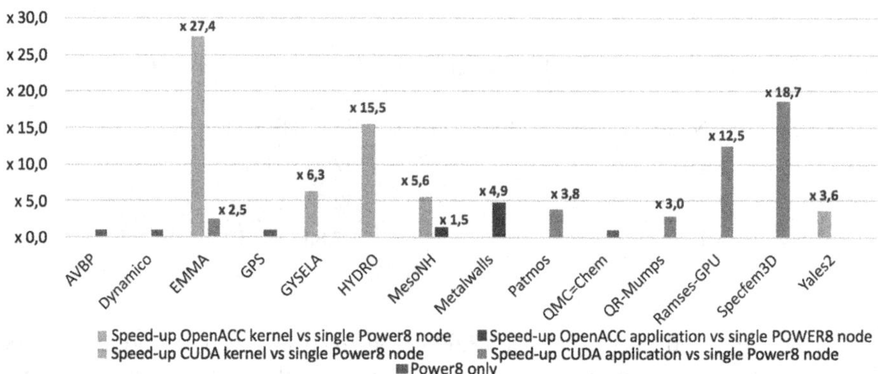

Fig. 1. First results obtained on Ouessant

3 Conclusion and Future Work

First of all, the POWER8 processor has to be defined as a very easy to use processor. We clearly have seen over the last year an improvement in the compilation environment which helped all of our users to port their application on the machine very easily. Unfortunately, for now, the goal that we want to achieve (i.e. porting all our applications to GPUs using OpenMP) is still a bit far from us. Indeed, the main difficulty for the users on this platform is to understand the GPU and how to adapt their application to it. While all of the users managed to port their application on the POWER8, only a few applications were run on the GPUs with a relevant level of performance. The platform can achieve very high performances while using CUDA kernels, the IBM XL compiler is mainly used for the code using CUDA kernels and provides a good level of performances. First results on OpenACC show that we can also get good performances using this paradigm but the time to achieve the performance is not in days, but in weeks (and even sometimes months or years). However, we have seen over the past year that the PGI compiler really adapted to the POWER8 architecture and can achieve very high performance. The first results obtained on the platform are available in Fig. 1.

OpenMP remains our main goal for legacy and portability of our applications, but we do have troubles at the moment using this paradigm on the platform. Indeed, the few tests we performed on the platform didn't give us good performances for GPU offloading, that's one of the reason why none of our users ported their application using OpenMP. On top of that, as the project started at the beginning of 2016, the OpenMP functionality were not available and that did not help the community to choose this paradigm. However, we still expect that this platform will manage to run OpenMP for GPUs and get the same level of performances than OpenACC. Those features should be implemented in the IBM compiler by the end of the year. We also expect that modifying the code from OpenACC to write OpenMP kernel will not be too much time consuming.

The opening of the platform, since April 2017, to the full French scientific community will be a new opportunity for us to push for OpenMP and to continue working using this paradigm at the national level. On top of that, we will assess the scalability of the platform, using even larger test cases. The results obtained with PATMOS (having an almost perfect scalability up to 8 nodes) make us believe that this particular point should not be an issue.

Despite some porting troubles, the first results on the platform are very promising and we are looking forward to the next generation of OpenPOWER nodes.

Besides, we now have a focus on deep learning applications and the number of project that applies for the Ouessant platform using PowerAI is increasing. The first results are impressive and we are sure that this platform will help the artificial intelligence community to address new challenges.

Acknowledgments. GENCI thanks all its partners within the project for their support as well as IBM and nVIDIA experts and all the developers that contributed to the work performed on this platform.

References

1. Gourdain, N., Gicquel, L., Montagnac, M., Vermorel, O., Gazaix, M., Staffelbach, G., Garcia, M., Boussuge, J.F., Poinsot, T.: High performance parallel computing of flows in complex geometries - part 1: methods. Comput. Sci. Disc. **2**, 015003 (2009)
2. Grasseau, G., Chamont, D., Beaudette, F., Bianchini, L., Davignon, O., Mastrolorenzo, L., Ochando, C., Paganini, P., Strebler, T.: Matrix element method for high performance computing platforms. In: Journal of Physics: Conference Series, vol. 664, Bristol, Institute of Physics Publishing (2015). 092009
3. Aubert, D., Deparis, N., Ocvirk, P.: EMMA: an adaptive mesh refinement cosmological simulation code with radiative transfer. MNRAS **454**, 1012–1037 (2015)

4. Parnaudeau, P., Suzuki, A., Sac-Epee, J.M.: GPS: an efficient & spectrally accurate code for computing gross-pitaevskii equation. In: Research Posters Session, ISC-2015, Germany, 12–16 July 2015
5. Lavallée, P.-F., de Verdière, G.C., Wautelet, P., Lecas, D., Dupays, J.-M.: Porting and optimizing hydro to new platforms and programming paradigms - lessons learnt
6. http://mesonh.aero.obs-mip.fr/mesonh53/MesoNHReferences
7. Brun, E., Chauveau, S., Malvagi, F.: Patmos: a prototype Monte Carlo transport code to test high performance architectures. In: M&C 2017 - International Conference on Mathematics & Computational Methods Applied to Nuclear Science & Engineering, Jeju, Korea, 16–20 April 2017
8. Moureau, V., Domingo, P., Vervisch, L.: Design of a massively parallel CFD code for complex geometries. Comptes Rendus Mcanique **339**(2), 141–148 (2011)
9. Scemama, A., Caffarel, M., Oseret, E., Jalby, W.: Quantum Monte Carlo for large chemical systems: Implementing efficient strategies for petascale platforms and beyond. J. Comput. Chem. **34**(11), 938–951 (2013)
10. Intel software development emulator. https://software.intel.com/en-us/articles/intel-software-development-emulator. Accessed 26 Apr 2017
11. Agullo, E., Buttari, A., Guermouche, A., Lopez, F.: Implementing multifrontal sparse solvers for multicore architectures with sequential task flow runtime systems. ACM Trans. Math. Softw. **43**(2), 13:1–13:22 (2016)
12. Agullo, E., Buttari, A., Guermouche, A., Lopez, F.: Task-based multifrontal QR solver for GPU-accelerated multicore architectures. In: HiPC, pp. 54–63. IEEE Computer Society (2015)
13. https://github.com/kokkos

Experiences on Intel Knights Landing at the One-Year Mark (IXPUG)

IXPUG: Experiences on Intel Knights Landing at the One Year Mark

Estela Suarez[1(✉)], Michael Lysaght[2], Simon J. Pennycook[3], and Richard A. Gerber[4]

[1] Jülich Supercomputing Centre (JSC), Forschungszentrum Jülich GmbH, Leo Brandt Strasse, 52428 Jülich, Germany
e.suarez@fz-juelich.de
[2] Irish Centre for High End Computing (ICHEC), Trinity Technology and Enterprise Campus, Grand Canal Quay, Dublin 2 D02 HP83, Ireland
[3] Intel Corporation, Santa Clara, USA
[4] National Energy Research Scientific Computing Center (NERSC), Lawrence Berkeley National Laboratory (LBL), Berkeley, USA

Abstract. One year on since the launch of the 2nd generation Knights Landing (KNL) Intel Xeon Phi platform, a significant amount of application experience has been gathered by the user community. This provided IXPUG (the Intel Xeon Phi User Group) a timely opportunity to share insights on how to best exploit this new many-core processor, and in particular, on how to achieve high performance on current and upcoming large-scale KNL-based systems.

Keywords: Intel Xeon Phi · KNL · Many-core · Performance · Benchmark · Optimisation · IXPUG

1 IXPUG: The Intel Xeon Phi User Group

The Intel Xeon Phi User's Group (IXPUG) is an independent users group whose mission is to provide a forum for the free exchange of information that enhances the usability and efficiency of scientific and technical applications running on large High Performance Computing (HPC) systems using the Intel® Xeon Phi™processor[1]. IXPUG is administered by representatives of member sites that operate large Intel Xeon Phi-based HPC systems.

IXPUG holds meetings and other activities as determined by its members to further its mission. Participation in IXPUG meetings and other activities is open to anyone interested in using the Intel Xeon Phi for large-scale scientific or technical computing. Current participants include staff from member sites, users of member sites' facilities, Intel staff, and others with an interest in using the Intel Xeon Phi for scientific computing on large HPC systems.

[1] Referred to as Intel Xeon Phi, without explicit registration and trademark superscripts, throughout the rest of this document.

J.M. Kunkel et al. (Eds.): ISC High Performance Workshops 2017, LNCS 10524, pp. 327–333, 2017.
https://doi.org/10.1007/978-3-319-67630-2_24

A Steering Committee (see Sect. 1.2) manages the overall direction of IXPUG, planning meetings and activities and working with members and sponsors to determine the most effective way to serve the HPC community.

IXPUG provides an effective conduit for application developers to interact directly with Intel engineers and other experts. As part of its community activities, IXPUG regularly organizes workshops and BoFs at the main supercomputing conferences, plus longer self-hosted user meetings distributed over the year and world-wide geography. The IXPUG workshop at ISC 2017 is already the third of a workshop series initiated at ISC 2015, which have been very positively taken up by the community. Slides and training materials presented at IXPUG events are accessible through the group website [1].

IXPUG workshops cover topics in application performance and scalability challenges at all levels - from single processors to moderately-scaled clusters, up to large HPC configurations with many Xeon Phi devices. The next IXPUG event is the *2017 IXPUG US Annual Meeting*, which will take place at the Texas Advanced Computing Center (TACC) in Austin, USA, in September 26–28, 2017. Further information can be found under: http://www.ixpug.org/events.

1.1 Discussion Forum and Working Groups

Additional to the workshops and face-to-face meetings, the IXPUG has set-up a number of online/remote platforms to facilitate the interaction between members of the user community and with experts in the use of Intel Xeon Phi. The two most important ones are the IXPUG forum and the IXPUG working groups.

The IXPUG online forum (https://www.ixpug.org/discussion) enables all users to ask questions, share experience, and get support from the rest of the community and also from Intel experts.

The working groups have been created to foster greater collaboration and knowledge-sharing related to specific topics of particular interest. The working groups provide virtual means to meet more regularly with other IXPUG members between yearly face-to-face meetings, and are a great way to get involved in the IXPUG community.

Working groups are open to anybody that wishes to join. Inclusion in the mailing list of a working group is achieved by contacting the group organizer. Contact data of the organizers and instructions to dial into individual meetings are given under https://www.ixpug.org/working-groups.

Currently, IXPUG holds following working groups:

- **General Optimization and Tuning:** focused on sharing general results and techniques, troubleshooting optimization issues, and facilitating collaboration between community members and Intel engineers.
- **Vectorization:** focused on identifying frequent patterns and challenges encountered in using compiler-assisted (auto-) vectorization, to generate feedback for compilers and language standards (e.g. OpenMP).

- **MPI:** focused on sharing knowledge of methods for using MPI generally and of Intel-oriented exploitation of MPI (e.g. Intel fabric, MPI library and profilers).

New working groups are created when a significant amount of interest in a specific topic is given, which gives sufficient momentum to sustain it.

1.2 Steering Committee

The IXPUG Steering Committee is currently composed of the following members, which cover a wide range of supercomputing institutions and regions:

- Taisuke Boku, University of Tsukuba (Japan)
- Doug Doerfler, NERSC - National Energy Research Scientific Computing Center/Berkeley Lab Supercomputing Center (USA)
- Richard Gerber, NERSC - National Energy Research Scientific Computing Center/LBL - Lawrence Berkeley National Laboratory (USA)
- Clay Hughes, Sandia National Laboratory (USA)
- Juha Jaykka, The University of Cambridge (UK)
- David Keyes, KAUST - King Abdullah University of Science & Technology (Saudi Arabia)
- Kent Milfeld, Texas Advanced Computing Center (USA)
- Hai Ah Nam, Los Alamos National Laboratory (USA)
- John Pennycook, Intel Corporation (USA)
- Thomas Steinke, Zuse Institute Berlin (Germany)
- Vit Vondrak, VSB - Technical University of Ostrava (Czech Republic)

The steering board is chaired by a leadership board. Its current members are:

- **President:** David Martin, Argonne National Laboratory (USA)
- **Vice-President:** Estela Suarez, Jülich Supercomputing Center, Forschungszentrum Jülich GmbH (Germany)
- **Secretary:** Melyssa Fratkin, Texas Advanced Computing Center, The University of Texas at Austin (USA)

2 Workshop Overview

The one full-day IXPUG workshop *Experiences on Intel Knights Landing at the one year mark* at ISC 2017 brought together about 50 members of a world-wide community of application developers and technology experts working on Intel Xeon Phi platforms.

The workshop was organized as an open forum with application programmers, software developers, system administrators, Intel Xeon Phi architecture designers, and compiler and tool experts. Application performance and scalability challenges at all levels were covered, focusing on application tuning on large

HPC systems with many KNL devices. Participants shared ideas, implementations, and experiences that help other users taking advantage of new Intel Xeon Phi features, such as AVX512 and high-bandwidth MCDRAM memory, as well as relevant high-performance system fabrics on large-scale KNL-based systems (e.g. OmniPath).

By sharing knowledge on how to best exploit the major advances in vectorization, memory, and communication featured on the 2nd generation Intel Xeon Phi platform, the workshop also had the wider aim of boosting the adoption of many-core architectures in HPC and beyond.

The workshop consisted of three parts: a keynote presentation, talks on the accepted papers, and a final panel session.

- The keynote, held by Richard Gerber, described success stories with high-impact on science, coming out of the applications running on NERSC's Cori.
- The submitted talks covered optimization in real-world HPC applications, e.g. data layouts and code restructuring for efficient SIMD operation, thread management, use of different memory modes, etc.
- The panel session was a lively discussion in which participants took the opportunity to discuss optimization strategies for Intel Xeon Phi, provide feedback to the toolchain developers, and get insight from Intel experts on what is expected from its future evolution.

3 Call for Papers

The call for papers to the IXPUG workshop at ISC 2017 was made public on February 1, 2017. IXPUG welcomed paper submissions on innovative work from KNL users in academia, industry and government labs, describing original discoveries and experiences that will promote and prescribe efficient use of many-core and multicore systems. Authors were requested to submit papers not published in or being in preparation for other conferences, workshops or journals.

Topics of interest include (but are not limited to):

- **Vectorization:** Data layout in cache for efficient SIMD operations, SIMD directives and operations, and 2-core tiling with 2D interconnected mesh.
- **Memory:** Data layout in memory for efficient access (data preconditioning), access latency concerns (prefetch, streams, costs for HBM), partitioning of DDR and HBM for applications (memory policies).
- **Communication:** Inter-node network communication, including early experiences with OmniPath.
- **Thread and Process Management:** Process and thread affinity issues, SMT (simultaneous multi-threading, in core), balancing processes and threads.

- **Multi-node Application Experience:** Results obtained running codes across several KNL nodes, specially on large-scale KNL systems.
- **Programming Models:** OpenMP 4.x, hStreams, using MPI 3 on Xeon Phi, hybrid programming (MPI/OpenMP, others)
- **Algorithms and Methods:** Numerical solutions, including scalable and vectorizable algorithms
- **Software Environments and Tools**
- **Benchmarking and Profiling Tools**
- **Visualization**

Following this call, the organising committee received a total of nineteen submissions, all of which were peer-reviewed by the Programm Committee (see Sect. 6) applying a standard single-blind review process. The evaluation of the submissions was based on the quality of the results, originality and new insights, technical strength, and correctness. The overall quality was high and the nine best submissions were selected (acceptance rate 47%) for a presentation at the workshop, and to publish their papers in the ISC 2017 Workshop proceedings volume within the Springer LNCS series.

4 Best Paper Award

For the first time in an IXPUG event, the Organisation Committee decided to acknowledge the authors of the best submission with a *Best Paper Award.*

The two papers that received the best evaluation after the peer-review process were identified as possible candidates for the award. All members of the Programme Committee were requested to read the two submissions and vote for the best one. The outcome of this vote was a tie, with exactly the same amount of votes for the two candidates. Both were qualified as excellent contributions, and no arguments were found to favour one against the other. Therefore the Program Committee finally decided to award both submissions.

The two recipients of the *Best Paper Award* at the IXPUG workshop at ISC 2017 are:

- *Performance Evaluation of NWChem Ab-Initio Molecular Dynamics (AIMD) Simulations on the Intel Xeon Phi Processor*
  Eric Bylaska (PNNL), Mathias Jacquelin (LBL), Bert de Jong (LBL), Jeff Hammond (Intel), and Michael Klemm (Intel Deutschland GmbH).
- *KART - A Runtime Compilation Library for Improving HPC Application Performance*
  Matthias Noack (ZIB), Florian Wende (ZIB), Georg Zitzlsberger (Intel Deutschland GmbH), Michael Klemm (Intel Deutschland GmbH), and Thomas Steinke (ZIB)

5 Workshop Agenda

Time	Title	Authors (Speaker*)
09:00	Opening	David Martin
09:15	Keynote: High-Impact Science on NERSC's Cori: A KNL success story	Richard Gerber*
10:00	**Best Paper Award:** KART - A Runtime Compilation Library for Improving HPC Application Performance	Matthias Noack*, Florian Wende, Georg Zitzlsberger, Michael Klemm and Thomas Steinke
10:30	**Best Paper Award:** Performance Evaluation of NWChem Ab-Initio Molecular Dynamics (AIMD) Simulations on the Intel Xeon Phi Processor	Eric Bylaska, Mathias Jacquelin, Bert de Jong, Jeff Hammond and Michael Klemm*
11:00	*Coffee Break*	
11:30	Porting Tissue-scale Cardiac Simulations to the Knights Landing Plattform	Johannes Langguth*, Chad Jarvis and Xing Cai
12:00	Analyzing Performance of Selected NESAP Applications on the Cori HPC System	Thorsten Kurth*, William Arndt, Taylor Barnes, Brandon Cook, Jack Deslippe, Doug Doerfler, Brian Friesen, Helen He, Tuomas Koskela, Mathieu Lobet, Tareq Malas, Leonid Oliker, Andrey Ovsyannikov, Samuel Williams, Woo-Sun Yang and Zhengji Zhao
12:30	amask: A tool for Evaluating Affinity Masks in Large Systems	Kent Milfeld*
13:00	*Coffee Break*	
14:00	On the mitigation of cache hostile memory access patterns on many-core CPU architectures	Tom Deakin*, Wayne Gaudin and Simon Mcintosh-Smith
14:30	Optimizing fusion PIC code performance at scale on Cori Phase 2	Tuomas Koskela* and Jack Deslippe
15:00	Performance variability on Xeon Phi	Brandon Cook*, Thorsten Kurth, Samuel Williams, Jack Deslippe and Brian Austin
15:30	From Knights Corner to Landing: a Case Study Based on a Hodgkin-Huxley Neuron Simulator	George Chatzikonstantis, Diego Jimenez, Esteban Meneses, Christos Strydis, Harry Sidiropoulos* and Dimitrios Soudris
16:00	*Coffee Break*	
16:30	Panel Discussion	Richard Gerber, Matthias Noack, Michael Klemm, Joe Curley, Thomas Steinke
17:50	Closing	David Martin

6 Program Committee

Damian Alvarez	Jülich Supercomputing Centre (JSC)
Carlo Cavazzoni	INECA
Gilles Civario	DELL
Doug Doerfler	Lawrence Berkeley National Lab (LBL)
Richard Gerber	LBL/NERSC
Clayton Hughes	Sandia National Laboratories
Balint Joo	Thomas Jefferson National Accelerator Facility (Jefferson-Lab)
Rakesh Krishnaiyer	Intel Corporation
Michael Lysaght	Ireland's High-Performance Computing Centre (ICHEC)
Simon McIntosh-Smith	University of Bristol
Andrew Mallinson	Intel Corporation
David E. Martin	Argonne National Laboratory
Hideki Saito	Intel Corporation
Thomas Steinke	Zuse Institute Berlin (ZIB)
Estela Suarez	Jülich Supercomputing Centre (JSC)
Zhengji Zhao	Lawrence Berkeley National Lab (LBL)

7 Workshop Organisers

Estela Suarez	Jülich Supercomputing Centre (JSC)
Michael Lysaght	Ireland's High-Performance Computing Centre (ICHEC)
Simon J. Pennycook	Intel Corporation
Richard Gerber	LBL/NERSC

References

1. IXPUG: Intel Xeon Phi User Group, http://www.ixpug.org

Analyzing Performance of Selected NESAP Applications on the Cori HPC System

Thorsten Kurth[1(✉)], William Arndt[1], Taylor Barnes[1], Brandon Cook[1], Jack Deslippe[1], Doug Doerfler[1], Brian Friesen[1], Yun (Helen) He[1], Tuomas Koskela[1], Mathieu Lobet[1], Tareq Malas[1], Leonid Oliker[2], Andrey Ovsyannikov[1], Samuel Williams[2], Woo-Sun Yang[1], and Zhengji Zhao[1]

[1] National Energy Research Scientific Computing Center, Berkeley, CA, USA
tkurth@lbl.gov

[2] Computational Research Division, Lawrence Berkeley National Lab, Berkeley, CA, USA

Abstract. NERSC has partnered with over 20 representative application developer teams to evaluate and optimize their workloads on the Intel® Xeon Phi™Knights Landing processor. In this paper, we present a summary of this two year effort and will present the lessons we learned in that process. We analyze the overall performance improvements of these codes quantifying impacts of both Xeon Phi™architectural features as well as code optimization on application performance. We show that the architectural advantage, i.e. the average speedup of optimized code on KNL vs. optimized code on Haswell is about 1.1×. The average speedup obtained through application optimization, i.e. comparing optimized vs. original codes on KNL, is about 5×.

1 Introduction

The National Energy Research Scientific Computing Center (NERSC) [10] is the production HPC facility of the U.S. DOE Office of Science. It's mission is to enable and accelerate scientific discoveries through high performance computing and data analysis. The center supports over 6,000 users with more than 700 applications which cover a wide variety of science domains [7]. Therefore, HPC systems deployed at NERSC should not only support a diverse workload from a broad user base but also satisfy the increasing demand of computing cycles required to fulfill scientific goals. At the same time, power constraints for exascale computing are forcing major HPC and data centers to transition to more energy efficient-architectures.

At NERSC the transition to an energy-efficient pathway to exascale was realized via the procurement of the Cori system: a Cray XC40 powered by more than 9600 Intel® Xeon Phi™7250 (*Knights Landing*, KNL) based nodes which were added to an existing Cori phase I system powered by 1900+ Xeon™E5-2698 (*Haswell*) CPUs. The Xeon Phi™7250 is a self-hosted x86-64 compatible CPU. As such, in principal, all current NERSC users can immediately run their application without modification. In order to leverage the full capability of

J.M. Kunkel et al. (Eds.): ISC High Performance Workshops 2017, LNCS 10524, pp. 334–347, 2017.
https://doi.org/10.1007/978-3-319-67630-2_25

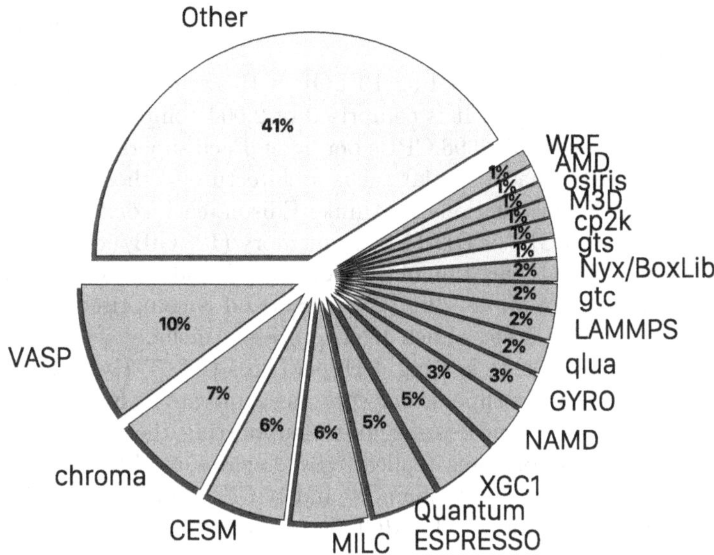

Fig. 1. Breakdown of NERSC workload in fractions of overall compute hour budget for 2015. NESAP applications are colored blue (note that the *Other* chunk includes four other NESAP apps). (Color figure online)

the Knights Landing architecture however, scientific applications often require some non-trivial optimization. In order to facilitate this transition, NERSC has established the NERSC Exascale Science Application Program (NESAP) — a collaboration of NERSC staff along with experts at Cray and Intel, as well as the scientific application developers — with the goal of optimizing selected applications for the Xeon Phi™ architecture [8]. As shown by the blue regions of Fig. 1, the NESAP codes constitute about 60% of the overall NERSC workload.

In this paper, we present the results of the NESAP effort by discussing achieved speedups, lessons learned, and multi-node specific challenges developers might face when they aim at running their applications on KNL-based Cray XC40 systems at scale.

2 HPC Systems at NERSC

We will briefly describe the three major HPC systems at NERSC as well as compare the performance of (un-)optimized NESAP codes on all three systems later on. We consider the following systems:

- **Edison** is a Cray XC30 supercomputer with peak performance of about 2.57 PFLOP/s. It is comprised of 5,586 compute nodes with two 12-core Intel® Xeon™ E5-4603 CPUs per node. Each of the 12 superscalar out-of-order cores runs at 2.4 GHz and is capable of hosting 2 threads per core. Each cores supports the AVX instruction set and includes a 32 KB L1 and 256 KB

L2 cache, and each socket includes a shared 30 MiB L3 cache and 32 GiB of DDR3 memory (64 GiB/node).
- **Cori-Haswell** represents the 1.92 PFLOP/s Haswell partition of the Cori Cray XC40 supercomputer. It is comprised of 2,004 compute nodes with two 16-core Intel® Xeon™E5-2698 CPUs per node. Each superscalar out-of-order core runs at 2.3 GHz, has a similar cache architecture to those in Edison, but supports the AVX2 instruction set. Unlike Edison, each socket has a 40 MiB L3 cache and has 64 GiB of DDR4 main memory (128 GiB/node).
- **Cori-KNL** is the KNL partition of the Cori Cray XC40 supercomputer. It has a peak performance of about 29.1 PFLOPS/s and is comprised of 9,688 self-hosted KNL compute nodes. Each KNL processor includes 68 cores running at 1.3 GHz and capable of hosting 4 HyperThreads (272 HyperThreads per node). Each out-of-order superscalar core has a private 32 KiB L1 cache and two 512-bit wide vector processing units (supporting the AVX-512 instruction set[1]). Each pair of cores (called "tile") shares a 1 MiB L2 cache and each node has 96 GiB of DDR4 memory and 16 GiB of on-package high bandwidth (MCDRAM) memory. The MCDRAM memory can be configured into different modes, where the most interesting being *cache* mode in which the MCDRAM acts as a 16 GiB L3 cache for DRAM. Additionally, MCDRAM can be configured in *flat* mode in which the user can address the MCDRAM as a second NUMA node. The on-chip directory can be configured into a number of modes, but in this publication we only consider *quad* mode, i.e. in *quad-cache* mode where all cores are in a single NUMA domain with MCDRAM acting as a *cache* for DDR, and in *quad-flat* mode where MCDRAM acts as a separate, *flat* memory domain.

All three systems feature the Cray Aries low-latency, high-bandwidth interconnect utilizing the dragonfly topology.

There are a number of challenges associated with optimizing codes for Xeon Phi™. Perhaps the most obvious is that new sources of parallelism must be identified. This is not limited to only thread parallelism, but also includes vectorization opportunities. The latter imposes restrictions on data layouts (i.e. data should be preferably contiguous and 64-bit aligned) and data dependencies between loop iterations should be avoided. Furthermore, maximizing cache locality is more important as there is no on-chip L3 cache to capture misses. Finally, and this is important for multi-node scalability, a single Xeon Phi™core can not saturate the injection rate of the Aries interconnect. Therefore, multiple cores (multiple threads or multiple MPI ranks per node) should be employed in order to achieve good performance. The detailed analysis of this is beyond the scope of this paper and can be found in another reference [20].

3 NESAP Results Overview

In this paper, we present the results from a variety of NESAP codes or their proxies. Table 1 displays an overview of these codes along with categorizations

[1] This includes the subsets F, CD, ER, PF but not VL, BW, DQ, IFMA, VBMI.

of their scientific field and, if applicable, the application they act as proxy for. The table further shows the most performance-critical kernels. Many of these kernels are representative for kernels in modern scientific codes used on a variety of HPC systems worldwide. The selection of codes further encompasses a broad variety of communication patterns (nearest neighbor exchanges or other point-to-point patterns, global reductions, all-to-all exchange, etc...) representative of those found in a wide range of applications.

Table 1. Overview of NESAP applications discussed in this paper including important references. The specified kernels represent the hot spots at the beginning of the NESAP effort. Due to optimization efforts, their importance relative to the rest of the code has decreased in general, but they still consume a significant fraction of the overall wall time.

Name	Scientific field	Description	Kernels	Proxy
BerkeleyGW [1,19]	Materials Science	MBPT	FFT, Linear Algebra	
CESM [2,28]	Climate Modeling	Grid	Stencil(Multiple), Linear Algebra	WRF
Chombo-Crunch [42–44]	Multiple	AMR EB	EB Stencil(3D), Solver(AMG)	
Chroma [23,29,30]	Nuclear Physics	Lattice QCD	Stencil(4D), Solver(BiCGStab)	qlua
DWF	HEP	Lattice QCD	FFT, Stencil(5D), Solver(BiCGStab)	qlua
EMGeo [38,39]	Geophysics	Grid	SpMM, Solver(IDR)	
GROMACS [4,40]	Materials Science	Molecular Dynamics	Force Calculation	LAMMPS, NAMD
HISQ	HEP	Lattice QCD	Stencil(4D), Solver(BiCGStab)	
HMMER [5,22]	Bioinformatics	Gene Annotation	Dynamic Programming(2D), Byteword Arithmetics	
MFDN [18,34–36]	Nuclear Physics	Many Body	SpMM, Eigensolver(lanczos)	
MILC [6,17]	HEP	Lattice QCD	Stencil(4D), Solver(BiCGStab)	qlua
MPAS-O [37,41]	Climate Modeling	Unstructured Grid	Gather, Solver(RK4)	WRF
Nyx/BoxLib [14,24,33]	Multiple	AMR	Stencil(3D), Solver(GMG)	
Qbox [11,26]	Materials Science	PW DFT	FFT, Linear Algebra, Eigensolver(lanczos)	cp2k
Quantum ESPRESSO [16,25]	Materials Science	PW DFT	FFT, Linear Algebra, Eigensolver(lanczos)	
VASP [31]	Materials Science	PW DFT	FFT, Eigensolver(multiple)	
WARP [12,45]	Accelerator Physics	PIC	Gather, Sort, FFT, Solver	osiris
XGC1 [13,27,32]	Fusion Research	PIC	Gather, Sort	gtc, gts, GYRO

3.1 Optimizations Summary

Historically, when a user is presented with a new architecture, they must often weigh the relative costs of porting and optimization effort against potential performance benefits. This is especially the case for Intel Xeon Phi™as most x86-64 applications can run natively without modification. In the following sections we summarize the optimizations undertaken by the NESAP teams and quantify the performance benefits not only to KNL but also on traditional Xeons (Haswell, Ivy Bridge). We found the following techniques had the largest impact on a wide range of NESAP applications:

- *identifying and exploiting parallelism/creating more work for individual threads*: This maybe the most important thing to consider when switching from multi-core to many-core architectures. Small OpenMP sections that do not contain enough work for multiple threads will hurt performance significantly due to implicit barriers at the end of these sessions. Profiling usually highlights this as large `omp` or `kmp` sync/barrier overheads. Where possible, loop nests should be collapsed to maximize parallelism. Whereas perfect rectangular loop nests can be collapsed using the OpenMP 4 `collapse` clause, more complicated loop structures often require more manual transformations including data structure rearrangements such as extending array dimensions to allow for batched processing. We found the latter to be especially beneficial for batched node-local Fast Fourier Transforms (FFT).
- *loop tiling*: Cache blocking to achieve cache locality of heavily used arrays can be realized by reordering and tiling inner loops. This advice is not new as it is in general a good practice to optimize code for L1/L2 accesses. On Xeon Phi™this is even more important as there is no L3 cache to mitigate the impact of L2 misses on application performance. Unfortunately, as this is a manual code transformation rather than a directive, code can become less readable and more brittle. Nevertheless, this technique benefits application performance on most architectures. In terms of loop tile sizes, we found that blocking to shared L2, i.e. 512 KiB/core, performs best for most applications.
- *short loop unrolling*: Short loops do not provide sufficient work for either threads or the wide vector registers. Instead it is beneficial to unroll them using compiler directives or manual unrolling.
- *ensuring efficient vectorization*: This may sound obvious but can often result in a major challenge as it may entail loop reordering, loop restructuring, and/or data layout transformations. It is nevertheless desirable not only because there is a potential 16× loss in performance from not vectorizing (vs. 4× on Ivy Bridge), but it also affects memory and cache bandwidth as single element loads and stores are inefficient. Further compounding this challenge on scientific codes, efficient mathematical function implementations for square roots, exponentials, etc. are only available as vectorized variants. Where the compiler is deficient in auto-vectorizing parallel loops, compiler hints and the OpenMP 4 `simd` pragmas were found to be particularly useful.
- *using optimized mathematical functions*: This is related to the previous point that vectorization enables the compiler to utilize efficient implementations of

expensive functions. Unfortunately, their generation may only be enabled by instructing the compiler to use a relaxed floating-point model. Under the same restrictions, compilers may not be able to factor a divide by a loop constant out of an inner loop. We found that manually factoring out the divide (by multiplying by the inverse of the loop-carried constant) could significantly improve performance.

This list is not meant to be a complete guide, and we recommend reviewing some of our NESAP case studies which discuss some of these topics [9] and a previous overview of the NESAP program results [15]. Nevertheless, this list can serve as a guideline for developers who aim at getting their current codes ready for Xeon Phi™.

3.2 Optimized vs. Original

We will first compare the speedup achieved by optimizing the code for Xeon Phi™on the three different systems. The current state of this effort is displayed in Fig. 2. It shows the speedup of optimized vs. original codes on all HPC systems at NERSC for a typical production partition size. Single node results represent capacity workloads with ideal weak scaling. The plot shows several important results: speedups of up to 17× (on KNL) to about 6× (on Haswell) could be achieved. The diagram shows that optimizations targeting Xeon Phi™can significantly benefit multi-core architectures as well. The main reason for that is that the optimized applications feature improved cache locality, contiguous aligned data access which facilitates vectorization and offers better thread-level parallelism. The improvements for some applications have an even bigger effect on Cori-Haswell. For example, this can happen if chunks of data are accessed in a random fashion but those chunks fit into the big L3 cache of the two multi-core architectures but not into L2 on Xeon Phi™. These problems are usually memory latency bound and MCDRAM does not offer a significant advantage over conventional DRAM. An example for this is Chombo, which utilizes comparably large lookup tables in order to retrieve memory locations of the next relevant chunk of data. Another more obvious reason is that serial sections or sections with insufficient vectorization are hurting Xeon Phi™performance more than conventional multi-core architectures. The median speedup achieved on Xeon Phi™is 2.8×, which generated a median speedup of about 1.7× and 1.4× on Edison and Cori-Haswell respectively.

3.3 Manycore vs. Multicore

Perhaps one of the most fundamental questions is to quantify the performance advantage provided by manycore architectures like KNL compared to traditional multicore architectures like Ivy Bridge and Haswell. Figure 3 shows the speedup of the optimized codes on Cori-KNL with respect to Cori-Haswell and Edison. It shows that almost all applications on Xeon Phi™exceed Edison's performance (node for node) by at least 30% with similar power-requirements per node.

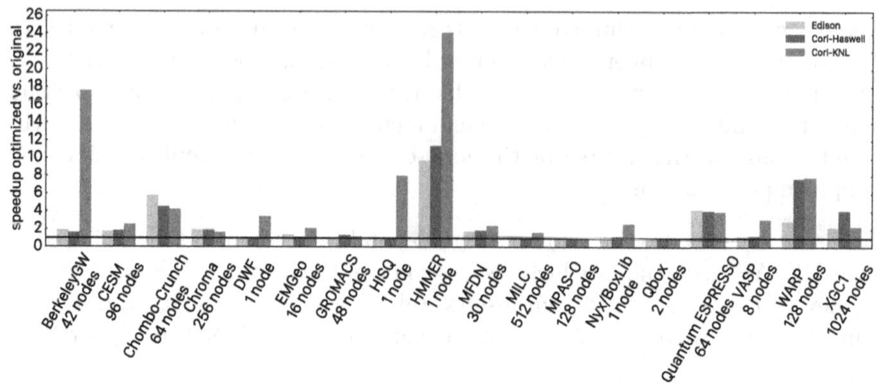

Fig. 2. Performance of optimized vs. original codes on the three major HPC systems/partitions at NERSC. The number of nodes mentioned below the application name are representative for a typical production run on the Cori-KNL system. The single node numbers represent embarrassingly parallel capacity workloads.

We should mention that almost all original versions of NESAP applications, except for some heavily memory bound applications such as EMGeo, were initially significantly slower on Xeon Phi^{TM}than on Haswell and some even compared to Edison.

Compared to Cori-Haswell (a contemporaneous architecture), in many cases, the performance difference is not that significant. MFDn for example shows a huge speedup on Cori-KNL compared to Edison, but not to Cori-Haswell. This might look surprising as the architectural differences between Edison and Cori-Haswell are not very big, but there are three significant differences which can cause this behavior. MFDn constructs a huge sparse matrix at first. In this construction, vector instruction gather and broadcast routines are available on Haswell (AVX2) and, in an improved version on Xeon Phi^{TM}(AVX-512), that offer a significant advantage over individual loads and stores that might be used on Edison. Furthermore, the construction step used bitwise comparisons (XOR) that can be accelerated with AVX2(Haswell) and AVX-512(KNL), and the linear algebra part benefits from the fused multiply-add instructions also only available in AVX2 and AVX-512. The combination of all three effects can cause a significant architectural benefit for Haswell and Xeon Phi^{TM}over Ivy Bridge (Edison).

For the other applications the picture looks more consistent, where some applications favor Haswell over Xeon Phi^{TM}. Quantum ESPRESSO for example is very similar to BerkeleyGW and VASP but performs worse on Xeon Phi^{TM}than on Haswell. This is mainly due to inefficiencies in the eigenvalue solver: Quantum ESPRESSO can utilize SCALAPACK and ELPA but both libraries seem to have insufficient support for threading and/or vectorization. Other parts of the code, for example sections which heavily employ FFT and dense linear algebra, perform much better on Xeon Phi^{TM}than on Haswell.

The median overall speedups over Edison and Cori-Haswell are 1.8× and 1.1× respectively when running code optimized for the target machine.

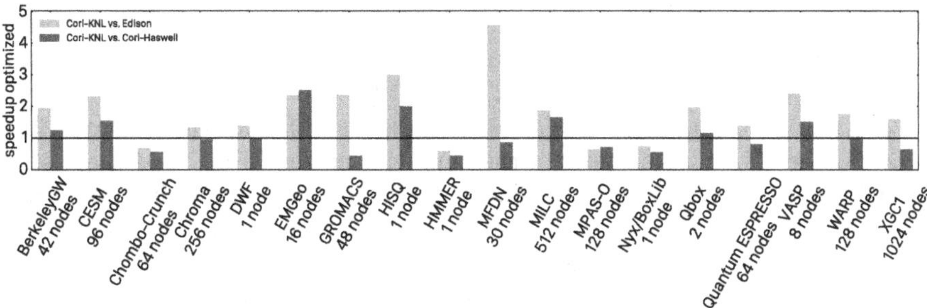

Fig. 3. Speedups of optimized NESAP codes on Cori-KNL vs. Cori-Haswell and Edison.

3.4 Value of Wider Vectors (AVX-512)

Another question we asked is whether AVX-512 offers a significant advantage over AVX2. Theoretically, the former offers a potential 2× speedup (ignoring bandwidth) because the vector units are twice as wide. However, it forces the developer to restructure for longer unit-stride access with no data dependencies and thus might restrict the application design in undesirable ways. Figure 4 shows the speedups achieved by running the application on Xeon Phi^{TM}with either AVX-512 or AVX2 enabled. That is, for the same code, architecture, and compiler, what is the value of doubling the vector length. For applications that depend on libraries, we ensure the appropriate libraries were linked or environment variables were set (e.g. for selecting the instruction set in Intel MKL). In case of Chroma and MILC, which utilize QPhiX [29] which in turn uses a domain specific language to generate architecture dependent code [30], we made sure that the instruction level support was consistent. Figure 4 shows that the value of doubling the vector length varies significantly (naively, a 100% speed is expected because the vector lanes are twice as wide). Benefits lower than 100% can be attributed to multiple factors. The simplest reason for this speedup is that the code suffers from a low degree of vectorization. Another explanation is that code is memory bandwidth bound and thus cannot benefit fully from vectorization. However, it turns out that even bandwidth-bound codes such as MFDn or EMGeo or MILC can be significantly accelerated by using AVX-512. Although applying the Roofline Model [21,46,47] to such codes suggests there should be little gain, the reality is that AVX-512 instructions reduce contention in the pipeline and inject more parallelism into the memory subsystem thereby allowing for higher bandwidth. Codes such as DWF and EMGeo that observe more than 2× might benefit from advanced AVX-512 features such as masking. This allows AVX-512 compilers to vectorize loops with certain types of conditionals which otherwise would not vectorize under AVX2. EMGeo vectorizes the solver over multiple right hand sides and relies on this masking for removing converged right hand sides from the solve. Additionally, AVX-512 provides 32 registers and thus twice as many as AVX2. For some codes, these extra registers likely mitigate register spill performance penalties. Finally, there are other advanced features such as optimized mathematical functions and broadcast operations which can give a gain exceeding the expected gain. Chroma is a special case as the performance for AVX-512 or AVX2 seems to be the same. At the time of writing, we could not find a satisfying explanation for that behavior but we have to note that about 90% of the time is spent in QPhiX and the rest in plain Chroma. The Chroma part utilizes LLVM with JIT and we had to disable AVX-512 JIT-support in because of an LLVM compiler bug. This means that this part of the code actually uses AVX2 in both cases. However, the time dominating part of the code should be sensitive to the instruction set and we cannot explain the differences here.

Ultimately, the median speedup achieved by using AVX-512 in lieu of AVX2 is approximately 1.2×.

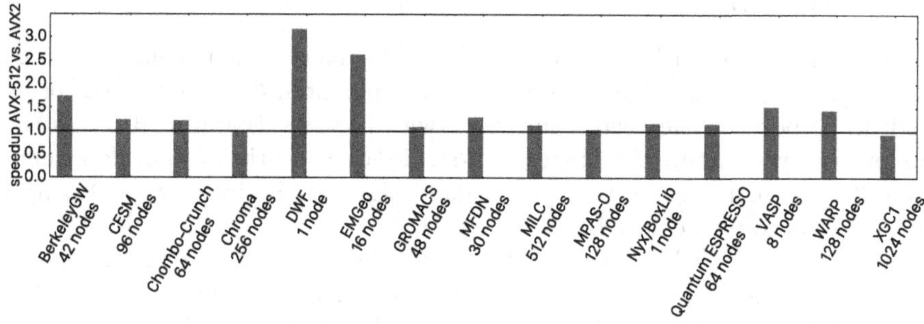

Fig. 4. Speedup from AVX-512 over AVX2 for optimized NESAP codes on Cori-KNL.

3.5 Flat and Cache Memory Mode Comparison

No memory technology simultaneously provides high capacity, high bandwidth, and energy efficiency. Thus, KNL instantiates two distinct memories — an energy-efficient, high-capacity DDR, and a high-bandwidth MCDRAM. The KNL architecture can be configured to present these memories to the user as either two distinct memories (*flat mode*) or can be configured to treat the MCDRAM as a cache for DDR (*cache mode*). In this section we quantify the performance differences of using either cache or flat mode or not using MCDRAM at all; we do not consider hybrid modes as we have not identified any suitable use cases thus far.

Figure 5 shows the speedup attained with flat mode over the simpler cache mode as well as the benefit of MCDRAM over pure DDR. The figure clearly exhibits that MCDRAM should be used in any case as the performance was never worse than running from DDR for our selected applications. Furthermore, the use of MCDRAM can significantly speed up heavily memory bandwidth limited codes. For cache vs. flat the story is more complicated: we observe that the best performance gains for our codes are 15–20%. The codes that perform equally well in either mode have local problem sizes which fit into MCDRAM and thus suffer no MCDRAM cache capacity misses. Codes that show a significant performance penalty in flat mode (ChomboCrunch, DWF, and Qbox) feature local problem sizes that cannot entirely fit into MCDRAM. Instead of utilizing AutoHBW or compiler directives for selectively placing *hot* arrays into MCDRAM, they use `numactl -p 1` to prefer memory allocation in MCDRAM[2]. Unfortunately, this only places the first $\mathcal{O}(16\,\text{GiB})$ of allocated data in MCDRAM and the rest will be allocated in DDR. With that approach, a speedup can only be achieved if all *hot* arrays are allocated at the beginning and if they fit into MCDRAM. Nevertheless, codes that use pool allocators such as e.g. HISQ and Chroma can safely use this procedure. For all other codes we conclude that cache mode should be favored if one wishes minimal code modification.

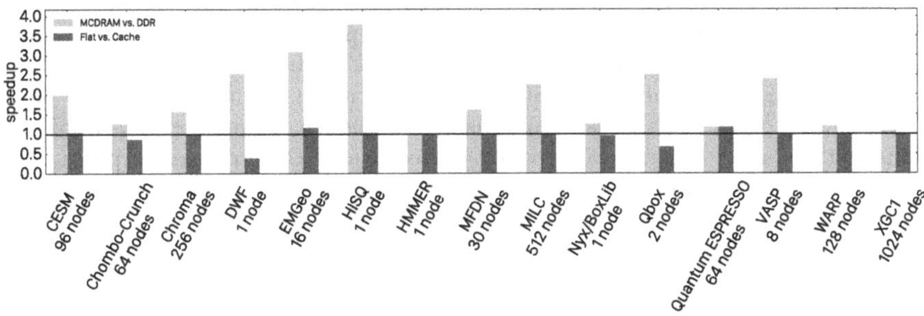

Fig. 5. Speedups of optimized NESAP codes achieved by running from MCDRAM vs. DDR and in flat vs. cache mode on Cori-KNL.

3.6 Total Savings in CPU Hours

We can now estimate the overall savings in units of CPU hours for the NERSC workload due to optimized applications and KNL architectural features. We assume that the CPU time fractions for the individual codes will be the same on Cori-KNL as those on Edison in 2015, and that the speedups are representative for the overall workload, the problem sizes are representative for the typical use of the specific application at NERSC, and users actually use the KNL-optimized versions. Based on these assumptions we can combine the data from Fig. 1 with the speedups achieved in Fig. 2. This yields an expected saving of ~1.8 B CPU hours by using the optimized code instead of the original code on Cori-KNL. This is about 23% of total available CPU hours. Since NERSC charges by the node-hour, the savings are real and can be used by the application teams to tackle more complicated science problems.

[2] `numactl -p 1` mimics the behavior of `numactl -m 1` but it is safer as it will not abort execution if there is no remaining free space in MCDRAM.

4 Conclusions

We have presented overall and relative performance improvements of selected NESAP applications and discussed specifics of Xeon Phi™that have to be considered when applications are optimized for this architecture. We further showed that improvements targeting Xeon Phi™will usually benefit conventional multi-core architectures. Thus, it can be beneficial for developers to start adapting their codes to many-core systems even if they are still primarily targeting multi-core architectures. Those improvements mainly target memory locality by applying cache blocking to L2, and loop and data layout restructuring to exploit parallelism and facilitate vectorization. Using a combination of these techniques is essential if one is to outperform traditional multi-core architectures.

Acknowledgement. Research used resources of NERSC, a DOE Office of Science User Facility supported by the Office of Science of the U.S. DOE under Contract No. DE-AC02-05CH11231. This article has been authored at Lawrence Berkeley National Lab under Contract No. DE-AC02-05CH11231 and UT-Battelle, LLC under Contract No. DE-AC05-00OR22725 with the United States Department of Energy. The United States Government retains and the publisher, by accepting the article for publication, acknowledges that the United States Government retains a non-exclusive, paid-up, irrevocable, worldwide license to publish or reproduce the published form of this manuscript, or allow others to do so, for United States Government purposes. The Department of Energy will provide public access to these results of federally sponsored research in accordance with the DOE Public Access Plan [3].

References

1. BerkeleyGW Website. http://www.berkeleygw.org
2. CESM Web Site. http://www.cesm.ucar.edu
3. DOE Public Access Plan. https://energy.gov/downloads/doe-public-access-plan
4. GROMACS Web Site. http://www.gromacs.org
5. HMMER Web Site. http://hmmer.org/
6. MILC Website. http://physics.indiana.edu/~sg/milc.html
7. NERSC and DOE Requirements Reviews Series. http://www.nersc.gov/science/hpc-requirements-reviews/
8. NERSC NESAP applications. http://www.nersc.gov/users/computational-systems/cori/nesap/nesap-projects/
9. NERSC NESAP case studies. http://www.nersc.gov/users/computational-systems/cori/application-porting-and-performance/application-case-studies/
10. NERSC Web Site. http://www.nersc.gov
11. QBox Web Site. http://qboxcode.org
12. Warp Web Site. http://warp.lbl.gov
13. XGC1 Web Site. http://epsi.pppl.gov/computing/xgc-1
14. Almgren, A.S., Bell, J.B., Lijewski, M.J., Lukić, Z., Van Andel, E.: Nyx: a massively parallel AMR code for computational cosmology. Astrophys. J. **765**, 39 (2013)

15. Barnes, T., Cook, B., Deslippe, J., Doerfler, D., Friesen, B., He, Y.H., Kurth, T., Koskela, T., Lobet, M., Malas, T., Oliker, L., Ovsyannikov, A., Sarje, A., Vay, J.L., Vincenti, H., Williams, S., Carrier, P., Wichmann, N., Wagner, M., Kent, P., Kerr, C., Dennis, J.: Evaluating and optimizing the NERSC workload on knights landing. In: Proceedings of the 7th International Workshop on Performance Modeling, Benchmarking and Simulation of High Performance Computing Systems, PMBS 2016, pp. 43–53. IEEE Press (2016)
16. Barnes, T.A., Kurth, T., Carrier, P., Wichmann, N., Prendergast, D., Kent, P.R., Deslippe, J.: Improved treatment of exact exchange in quantum espresso. Comput. Phys. Commun. **214**, 52–58 (2017)
17. Bauer, B., Gottlieb, S., Hoefler, T.: Performance modeling and comparative analysis of the MILC Lattice QCD application su3_rmd. In: Proceedings of CCGRID 2012: IEEE/ACM International Symposium on Cluster, Cloud, and Grid Computing (2012)
18. Binder, S., Calci, A., Epelbaum, E., Furnstahl, R.J., Golak, J., Hebeler, K., Kamada, H., Krebs, H., Langhammer, J., Liebig, S., Maris, P., Meißner, U.G., Minossi, D., Nogga, A., Potter, H., Roth, R., Skinińki, R., Topolnicki, K., Vary, J.P., Witała, H.: Few-nucleon systems with state-of-the-art chiral nucleon-nucleon forces. Phys. Rev. C **93**(4), 044002 (2016)
19. Deslippe, J., Samsonidze, G., Strubbe, D.A., Jain, M., Cohen, M.L., Louie, S.G.: Berkeleygw: a massively parallel computer package for the calculation of the quasiparticle and optical properties of materials and nanostructures. Comput. Phys. Commun. **183**(6), 1269–1289 (2012). http://www.sciencedirect.com/science/article/pii/S0010465511003912
20. Doerfler, D., Austin, B., Cook, B., Deslippe, J., Kandalla, K., Mendygral, P.: Evaluating the networking characteristics of the cray XC-40 intel knights landing based cori supercomputer at NERSC. In: Cray User Group Meeting (CUG), May 2017
21. Doerfler, D., Deslippe, J., Williams, S., Oliker, L., Cook, B., Kurth, T., Lobet, M., Malas, T., Vay, J.-L., Vincenti, H.: Applying the Roofline Performance Model to the Intel Xeon Phi Knights Landing Processor. In: Taufer, M., Mohr, B., Kunkel, J.M. (eds.) ISC High Performance 2016. LNCS, vol. 9945, pp. 339–353. Springer, Cham (2016). doi:10.1007/978-3-319-46079-6_24
22. Eddy, S.R.: Accelerated profile hmm searches. PLOS Comput. Biol. **7**(10), 1–16 (2011). https://doi.org/10.1371/journal.pcbi.1002195
23. Edwards, R.G., Joo, B.: The Chroma software system for lattice QCD. Nucl. Phys. Proc. Suppl. **140**, 832 (2005)
24. Friesen, B., Almgren, A., Lukić, Z., Weber, G., Morozov, D., Beckner, V., Day, M.: In situ and in-transit analysis of cosmological simulations. Comput. Astrophys. Cosmol. **3**, 4 (2016)
25. Giannozzi, P., Baroni, S., Bonini, N., Calandra, M., Car, R., Cavazzoni, C., Ceresoli, D., Chiarotti, G.L., Cococcioni, M., Dabo, I., Corso, A.D., de Gironcoli, S., Fabris, S., Fratesi, G., Gebauer, R., Gerstmann, U., Gougoussis, C., Kokalj, A., Lazzeri, M., Martin-Samos, L., Marzari, N., Mauri, F., Mazzarello, R., Paolini, S., Pasquarello, A., Paulatto, L., Sbraccia, C., Scandolo, S., Sclauzero, G., Seitsonen, A.P., Smogunov, A., Umari, P., Wentzcovitch, R.M.: Quantum espresso: a modular and open-source software project for quantum simulations of materials. J. Phys. Condens. Matter **21**(39), 395502 (2009). http://stacks.iop.org/0953-8984/21/i=39/a=395502
26. Gygi, F.: Architecture of Qbox: a scalable first-principles molecular dynamics code. IBM J. Res. Dev. **52**(1/2), 137–144 (2008). http://dl.acm.org/citation.cfm?id=1375990.1376003

27. Hager, R., Yoon, E., Ku, S., D'Azevedo, E., Worley, P., Chang, C.: A fully non-linear multi-species fokkerplancklandau collision operator for simulation of fusion plasma. J. Comput. Phys. **315**, 644–660 (2016). http://www.sciencedirect.com/science/article/pii/S0021999116300298
28. Hurrell, J., Holland, M., Gent, P., Ghan, S., Kay, J., Kushner, P., Lamarque, J.F., Large, W., Lawrence, D., Lindsay, K., Lipscomb, W., Long, M., Mahowald, N., Marsh, D., Neale, R., Rasch, P., Vavrus, S., Vertenstein, M., Bader, D., Collins, W., Hack, J., Kiehl, J., Marshall, S.: The community earth system model: a framework for collaborative research. Bull. Am. Meteorol. Soc. **94**, 1339–1360 (2013)
29. Joó, B.: `qphix` package web page. http://jeffersonlab.github.io/qphix
30. Joó, B.: `qphix-codegen` package web page. http://jeffersonlab.github.io/qphix-codegen
31. Kresse, G., Furthmueller, J.: Efficiency of ab-initio total energy calculations for metals and semiconductors using a plane-wave basis set. Comput. Mater. Sci. **6**(1), 15–50 (1996). http://www.sciencedirect.com/science/article/pii/0927025696000080
32. Ku, S., Chang, C., Diamond, P.: Full-f gyrokinetic particle simulation of centrally heated global itg turbulence from magnetic axis to edge pedestal top in a realistic tokamak geometry. Nucl. Fusion **49**(11), 115021 (2009)
33. Lukić, Z., Stark, C.W., Nugent, P., White, M., Meiksin, A.A., Almgren, A.: The Lyman α forest in optically thin hydrodynamical simulations. Mon. Not. R. Astron. Soc. **446**, 3697–3724 (2015)
34. Maris, P., Caprio, M.A., Vary, J.P.: Emergence of rotational bands in ab initio no-core configuration interaction calculations of the Be isotopes. Phys. Rev. C **91**(1), 014310 (2015)
35. Maris, P., Vary, J.P., Navratil, P., Ormand, W.E., Nam, H., Dean, D.J.: Origin of the anomalous long lifetime of ^{14}C. Phys. Rev. Lett. **106**(20), 202502 (2011)
36. Maris, P., Vary, J.P., Gandolfi, S., Carlson, J., Pieper, S.C.: Properties of trapped neutrons interacting with realistic nuclear Hamiltonians. Phys. Rev. C **87**(5), 054318 (2013)
37. Petersen, M.R., Jacobsen, D.W., Ringler, T.D., Hecht, M.W., Maltrud, M.E.: Evaluation of the arbitrary lagrangian-eulerian vertical coordinate method in the MPAS-ocean model. Ocean Modell. **86**, 93–113 (2015). http://www.sciencedirect.com/science/article/pii/S1463500314001796
38. Petrov, P.V., Newman, G.A.: Three-dimensional inverse modelling of damped elastic wave propagation in the fourier domain. Geophys. J. Int. **198**(3), 1599–1617 (2014)
39. Petrov, P.V., Newman, G.A.: 3D finite-difference modeling of elastic wave propagation in the laplace-fourier domain. GEOPHYSICS **77**(4), T137–T155 (2012). http://dx.doi.org/10.1190/geo2011-0238.1
40. Pronk, S., Pll, S., Schulz, R., Larsson, P., Bjelkmar, P., Apostolov, R., Shirts, M.R., Smith, J.C., Kasson, P.M., van der Spoel, D., Hess, B., Lindahl, E.: Gromacs 4.5: a high-throughput and highly parallel open source molecular simulation toolkit. Bioinformatics **29**(7), 845 (2013). http://dx.doi.org/10.1093/bioinformatics/btt055
41. Ringler, T., Petersen, M., Higdon, R.L., Jacobsen, D., Jones, P.W., Maltrud, M.: A multi-resolution approach to global ocean modeling. Ocean Model. **69**, 211–232 (2013). http://www.sciencedirect.com/science/article/pii/S1463500313000760

42. Straalen, B.V., Trebotich, D., Ovsyannikov, A., Graves, D.T.: Scalable structured adaptive mesh refinement with complex geometry. In: Exascale Scientific Applications: Programming Approaches for Scalability Performance and Portability. CRC Press (in press)
43. Trebotich, D., Adams, M.F., Molins, S., Steefel, C.I., Chaopeng, S.: High-resolution simulation of pore-scale reactive transport processes associated with carbon sequestration. Comput. Sci. Eng. **16**(6), 22–31 (2014)
44. Trebotich, D., Graves, D.: An adaptive finite volume method for the incompressible Navier-Stokes equations in complex geometries. Commun. Appl. Math. Comput. Sci. **10**(1), 43–82 (2015)
45. Vincenti, H., Lobet, M., Lehe, R., Sasanka, R., Vay, J.L.: An efficient and portable SIMD algorithm for charge/current deposition in particle-in-cell codes. Comput. Phys. Commun. **210**, 145–154 (2017). http://www.sciencedirect.com/science/article/pii/S0010465516302764
46. Williams, S., Waterman, A., Patterson, D.: Roofline: an insightful visual performance model for multicore architectures. Commun. ACM **52**(4), 65–76 (2009). http://doi.acm.org/10.1145/1498765.1498785
47. Williams, S.W.: Auto-tuning Performance on Multicore Computers. Ph.D. thesis, EECS Department, University of California, Berkeley, December 2008. http://www2.eecs.berkeley.edu/Pubs/TechRpts/2008/EECS-2008-164.html

On the Mitigation of Cache Hostile Memory Access Patterns on Many-Core CPU Architectures

Tom Deakin[1(✉)], Wayne Gaudin[2], and Simon McIntosh-Smith[1]

[1] Department of Computer Science, University of Bristol, Bristol, UK
tom.deakin@bristol.ac.uk
[2] UK Atomic Weapons Establishment, Aldermaston, UK

Abstract. Kernels with low arithmetic intensity with memory footprint exceeding cache sizes are typically categorised as memory bandwidth bound. Kernels of this class are typically limited by hardware memory bandwidth. In this work we contribute a simple memory access pattern, derived from a widely-used upwinded stencil-style benchmark, which presents significant challenges for cache-based architectures. The problem appears to grow worse as CPU core counts increase, and the pattern in its initial form shows no benefit from the new high-bandwidth memory now appearing on the Intel Xeon Phi (Knights Landing) family of processors. We describe the memory access scenarios which appear to be causing lower than expected cache performance, before presenting optimisations to mitigate the problem. These optimisations result in useful effective memory bandwidth and runtime improvements by up to 4X on cache based architectures. Results are presented on the Intel Xeon (Broadwell) and Xeon Phi (Knights Landing) processors.

1 Introduction

For kernels (computational routines) with low arithmetic intensity, the Roofline model typically shows that memory bandwidth becomes the performance limiter [9]. Examples of such kernels can be seen in the STREAM [8] and GPU-STREAM [3] benchmarks, where in the later we have explored the achievable memory bandwidth of a highly diverse range of computer architectures. However for some memory bandwidth bound codes, an increase in the available memory bandwidth does not necessarily yield a proportionate improvement in performance, as the performance of such an application may depend on the degree to which it has been optimised—specifically, the degree to which its implementation is *actually* bandwidth bound (as opposed to *theoretically* bandwidth bound). Once such application is the SNAP performance proxy for modern deterministic transport codes from Los Alamos National Laboratory [5,10].

We have previously optimised SNAP to perform well on GPUs [2] and explored its scaling characteristics on large supercomputers [1]. GPU architectures are typically optimised for greater memory bandwidth relative to

J.M. Kunkel et al. (Eds.): ISC High Performance Workshops 2017, LNCS 10524, pp. 348–362, 2017.
https://doi.org/10.1007/978-3-319-67630-2_26

traditional CPU architectures. For SNAP we are able to demonstrate significant performance improvements, with the time to solution halved using NVIDIA K20X GPUs compared to Intel Xeon (Haswell) CPUs at scale. The Intel Xeon Phi (Knights Landing) processor also offers a memory bandwidth increase relative to traditional multi-core CPUs, due to its on-package MCDRAM. For a bandwidth bound code therefore, assuming efficient vectorisation and memory access pattern optimisations have already been applied (as is the case with SNAP), running on the Knights Landing architecture utilising MCDRAM should provide a performance improvement utilising the extra memory bandwidth available. However, initial results for SNAP show that one Knights Landing achieves comparable performance to dual-socket Intel Xeon processors, which have around a quarter of the memory bandwidth relative to Knights Landing's MCDRAM [5]. We had also previously observed that the performance on Intel Xeon Phi (Knights Corner) co-processors was low, attaining only a small fraction of achievable memory bandwidth [2]. It is therefore the case that the SNAP application is not actually memory bandwidth bound on the Xeon Phi architecture; instead, some other bound is in place. There is however little tangible or actionable evidence as to what the limiting factor is (for the SNAP mini-app); the profiling tools suggest a good ratio of cycles per instruction, good vectorisation efficiency and stride-one data access patterns. As such, a 'glass ceiling' exists beneath the memory bandwidth limit in the Roofline model for this kernel. In this paper we present some intuition around the reasons for this limit to exist in this style of application; namely an upwind stencil. We then provide some solutions allowing a benchmark application to break through the ceiling and reach the memory bandwidth bounds as predicted under the Roofline model; this also comes with a significant improvement in the runtime of the benchmark.

2 Stencil Patterns

A stencil access pattern describes the neighbouring data requirements for the solution of each cell in the mesh. For a typical 5-point stencil, each cell (i, j) requires values from cells $(i \pm 1, j \pm 1)$, and for a structured mesh this can be visualised as in Fig. 1a. The values in the centre of each cell are used in the solution of the cell centred value of the cell in question, a pattern typical of many computational fluid dynamic codes, such as in the Lattice-Boltzmann method.

The 5-point stencil however is applied differently in other fields, and we consider a particularly interesting and important variant in this paper. At first glance this application looks very similar to a standard 5-point stencil, with the cell centred solution of a particular cell using values from neighbouring cells. However the values from neighbouring cells are *edge* centred rather than cell centred as shown in Fig. 1b. The edge centred solutions are calculated using a simple finite difference relation given the cell centred value. Also, only data from half the edges are used for the solution, with the other edge solutions shared to downwind neighbouring cells; note the change in direction of the arrows in the figure. Specifically, for the sweep direction shown and an origin at the bottom left of

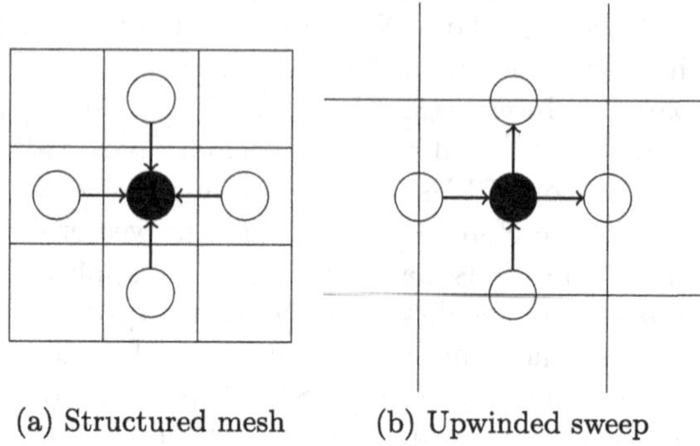

(a) Structured mesh (b) Upwinded sweep

Fig. 1. Applications of a typical 5-point stencil

the diagram, cell (i,j) requires values originally calculated in cells $(i-1,j)$ and $(i,j-1)$, and the edge centred solutions in cell (i,j) are required by cells $(i+1,j)$ and $(i,j+1)$.

The data dependency is formed by *upwinding* whilst discretizing a partial differential equation in the spatial domain. It results in a *wavefront sweep*, an important programming pattern which appears in a variety of applications such as dynamic programming, LU factorisation and deterministic transport [7,10].

The available parallelism is also different compared to a standard application of the stencil. The cells must now be computed in the order defined by the sweep; this is in contrast to the mesh in Fig. 1a where the cells can be computed concurrently as long as a copy of cell centred values is stored. Solution on a large distributed system also uses a standard halo exchange communication pattern for the standard approach, whereas outgoing edge data is sent to downwind neighbours as it becomes available here. The focus of this paper is the on node performance and so communication differences will not be discussed further.

Because the edge centred values are temporary, and only half are required to share between neighbouring cells, it is typical to optimise the memory footprint and store the incoming and outgoing edge values in the same memory location. This reduces the memory footprint and also encourages reuse of array elements.

The descriptions in the 2D case are analogous in three dimensions using a seven-point stencil, and it is the 3D case that we investigate in this paper.

3 Memory Access Patterns

The generalised memory access pattern of the upwinded stencil may be described as follows. Multiple values are calculated per cell, which are operated on in parallel through vectorisation, and are hence stored contiguously as the inner most dimension within the mesh array to allow for simple stride 1 memory access patterns.

The cell centred solution computation is somewhat similar to a STREAM Triad operation [8] and is calculated based on its previous value along with weighted contributions from the upwind neighbour cells' edge centred solutions.

Simple floating point arithmetic (typically fused multiply add) is used to combine the terms. This computation is clearly memory bandwidth bound as the computational intensity is very low, with a ratio of arithmetic to memory locations accessed of close to 1.0. Specifically the computational intensity in double precision, with eight bytes per element, is 1/8. Subsequent calculation of the edge centred values is also similar to STREAM Triad, and is just a simple finite difference operation requiring a single fused multiply add. Finally, a within cell SIMD reduction of the cell centred values is calculated and stored for each cell.

Unlike STREAM operations, the arrays containing the data are of different sizes. The cell centred values are stored in a mesh sized array and are therefore large in size. The weights used are in very small arrays, and there is one weight for each cell centred value which are the same in every cell and are therefore shared and independent of the mesh size. The arrays containing the edge centred values are allocated on Cartesian planes in the mesh, and are therefore smaller than the total mesh size, existing in one less dimension than the mesh; this is a memory footprint optimisation as incoming values are overwritten in this array by the outgoing equivalent. The threads operate on disparate slices of the arrays via a final outer dimension so as to avoid false sharing. All data access is stride 1.

In summary, there are three operations we consider within the kernel:

1. Calculate cell centred values with low computational intensity, streaming through the large array.
2. Calculate outgoing edge centred solutions.
3. Reduce cell centred values within each cell.

4 Cache Based Architectures

The memory hierarchy of CPU style architectures typically consists of a set of data caches between the execution units and the main memory. Using the Intel Xeon (Broadwell) CPU as an exemplar, its hierarchy consists of three levels of cache and main DDR memory. Level 1 (L1) and Level 2 (L2) caches are available to each core independently and are 32 KB (for data) and 256 KB in size respectively. Level 3 (L3) cache is 55 MB for the high end E5-2699 v4 model, and is shared between all cores on the socket.

The Intel Xeon Phi (Knights Landing) Processor has a different memory hierarchy, although there are many similarities. Level 1 caches are available per core with a capacity of 32 KB. A 1 MB L2 cache is shared between pairs of cores, which are organised on tiles, with the entire device consisting of some number of tiles. High bandwidth MCDRAM and standard DDR are also available, and their position in the hierarchy depends on the mode the processor is booted into. The MCDRAM is available either as a directly mapped cache for DDR, or else as a separate memory space; it is this latter mode that we consider here where all data is resident in the high bandwidth memory.

For both processors, when a load instruction is encountered the cache hierarchy is always checked. Data not present in the caches is moved down through the hierarchy, with data being evicted according to the cache policy. For a store instruction, both processors operate a "read for ownership" policy, whereby the data is first loaded into cache before being written. Both processors also support non-temporal store instructions which bypasses this mechanism, writing directly to the highest level in the memory hierarchy (MCDRAM or DDR).

Hardware (and software) prefetchers also operate in the background to assist the movement of memory through the cache hierarchy. If a data access pattern is detected, the prefetcher will move data down the hierarchy in advance of when the memory is predicted to be used. Therefore the required data will hopefully be in a fast, low level cache in time and hence increase the throughput of the processor as it need not stall waiting for the data to arrive.

5 Investigation into Memory Bandwidth Issues

In order to practically investigate the performance issues of this style of stencil operation a small benchmark code was written. This code, named *mega-stream*, was distilled from the SNAP mini-app which encounters the previously described performance issues on cache based architectures. The simple computational kernel is shown in Listing 1.1. We display the Fortran version in print as it allows for compact representation of the multi-dimensional array accesses; the C version is similar and we ensure that the memory layout matches that of the loop nest in both cases to ensure stride 1 access for the innermost loop. The kernel consists of five nested loops with the three operations from Sect. 3; the cell centred computation on line 6, the outgoing edge centred solutions on lines 7–9, and the reduction over the innermost dimension on line 10. OpenMP work-sharing threads are employed on the outermost loop (`Nm`) and compiler auto-vectorisation via the OpenMP `simd` clause is employed on the innermost loop (`Ni`).

```
DO m = 1, Nm
  DO l = 1, Nl
    DO k = 1, Nk
      DO j = 1, Nj
        DO i = 1, Ni
          r(i,j,k,l,m) = q(i,j,k,l,m) + a(i)*x(i,j,k,m) +
↪ b(i)*y(i,j,l,m) + c(i)*z(i,k,l,m)
          x(i,j,k,m) = 0.2*r(i,j,k,l,m) - x(i,j,k,m)
          y(i,j,l,m) = 0.2*r(i,j,k,l,m) - y(i,j,l,m)
          z(i,k,l,m) = 0.2*r(i,j,k,l,m) - z(i,k,l,m)
          total(j,k,l,m) = total(j,k,l,m) + r(i,j,k,l,m)
        END DO
      END DO
    END DO
  END DO
END DO
```

Listing 1.1: The mega-stream kernel

The data reuse of the `x`, `y` and `z` arrays are of some interest. Note that each of these arrays is missing one of the three middle indices; `x` is missing the `l` index, `y` is missing the `k` index, and `z` is missing the `j` index. All three arrays have the innermost index `i`. Using the `z` array as an example, the subsection of the array used is the same for all `j`, and as such one would hope that for a given `k` and `l` the associated `Ni` values remain in cache for the duration of the `Nj` loop. Note that none of the writes can be hoisted above loops as the updated values of one iteration are used in line 6. This pattern can be visualised with Fig. 1b whereby this array carries data in the j-axis (in jkl-space) between adjacent cells. There is no reuse of the `r` array.

A model for the memory bandwidth of the routine in Listing 1.1 can be constructed by simply counting the number of bytes moved under some basic assumptions. We assume that a write counts as a single memory movement; in particular, read for ownership is not required. Indeed, this is an architecture specific design decision and in theory the computation does not require this. We also assume that once we have read a memory location, further reads and writes are free. Specifically, once we read a location in the `x`, `y` or `z` arrays, these are cached and the update is free. It is typical that such assumptions are made on memory bandwidth models since they represent the best-case behaviour and form an upper-bound for performance. The model is therefore the total of all reads and writes under these assumptions: `r` is written to once per element, `q` is read once per element, `x`, `y` and `z` are read and written once per element (assuming future updates are free), `a`, `b` and `c` are read once per element, and `total` is read and written once per element. The data are double precision floating point elements which are of size 8 bytes. Therefore the estimated (modelled) amount of data moved is:

$$\begin{aligned}(N_i * N_j * N_k * N_l * N_m + N_i * N_j * N_k * N_l * N_m +\\ 2 * N_i * N_j * N_k * N_m + 2 * N_i * N_j * N_l * N_m + 2 * N_i * N_k * N_l * N_m +\\ N_i + N_i + N_i + 2 * N_j * N_k * N_l * N_m) * 8 \text{ bytes}\end{aligned} \quad (1)$$

The estimated memory bandwidth is therefore the data moved divided by the runtime of the kernel. The benchmark runs the kernel 100 times and takes the minimum kernel time to calculate the bandwidth.

5.1 List of Experimental Platforms

The Intel Xeon Phi (Knights Landing) used for our experiments is a 7210 64-core at 1.30 GHz. The processor was configured in Flat/Quadrant mode, and has 16 GB MCDRAM with 96 GB DDR (unused). The mesh is clocked at 1.6 GHz resulting in a rate of 6.4 GT/s for MCDRAM. Transparent huge pages were enabled on the system. The code was compiled with the Intel Compiler 17 update 2 specifying the `-O3 -xMIC-AVX512` flags. We ran from MCDRAM using the `numactl` tool with one OpenMP thread per physical core, pinned using the `OMP_PROC_BIND` environmental variable. The STREAM Triad benchmark achieves 448 GB/s on this system.

We also use an Intel Xeon E5-2699 v4 (Broadwell) 22-core dual-socket node from a Cray XC40 supercomputer. This processor is clocked at 2.2 GHz and has 128 GB DDR. The code was compiled with the Intel Compiler 17 update 1 specifying the `-O3 -xCORE-AVX2` flags. We ran with one OpenMP thread per physical core, pinned using the `OMP_PROC_BIND` environmental variable and the `aprun` command. The STREAM Triad benchmark achieves 128 GB/s on this system.

The default problem size sets `Ni` = 128, `Nj` = `Nk` = `Nl` = 16, and `Nm` = 64. The `q` and `r` arrays are therefore sized 256 MiB, `x`, `y` and `z` are 16 MiB, and `a`, `b` and `c` are 1 KiB each. The model predicts moving 612 MiB to/from main memory for each kernel execution for the default problem size.

5.2 Baseline Performance

Throughout this investigation we will quote results for the default inputs unless specified otherwise. The initial estimated memory bandwidth as a percentage of STREAM Triad is shown in Fig. 2 labelled "Baseline". The performance on Knights Landing, or lack thereof, is rather striking and certainly highlights the need for an investigation; note that this kernel, which has stride 1 access patterns very reminiscent of STREAM, only achieves 16.4% of STREAM bandwidth (74 GB/s) when running solely out of the MCDRAM. On Xeon the achieved memory bandwidth is, at 65.1% of STREAM, perhaps on the low side for a stride 1 access code. While this is not necessarily low enough to cause concern, it is clear there is scope for improvement on CPUs too. The important corollary is that these observations are similar to the measurements we make with the SNAP application itself. Note too that the runtime of the kernel is similar on both architectures, whereas if it was memory bandwidth bound the advantages of MCDRAM on the Knights Landing should result in a speedup of around 3.5X (the ratio of their achieved bandwidth on STREAM).

We aligned all the arrays to 2 MB page boundaries (matching the page size of Knights Landing) to minimise any latency of unaligned loads and stores. This is a common optimisation step for memory bandwidth bound codes when examining vectorisation, and was performed as part of due diligence in the early stages of development. The alignment is performed at allocation via the C11 `aligned_alloc` library call. Alignment in this fashion also means that peel loops are not required (even though they would have been generated by the compiler).

Whilst the bandwidth reported by the application is estimated, it is possible to compare to a measured memory bandwidth obtained through hardware counters via a tool such as Intel vTune Amplifier XE. For the Knights Landing run, the tool was reporting near peak memory bandwidth use to MCDRAM, indicating that more memory must be moving than our model predicts, and as such this movement is considered wasteful by the model. This observation also hints at the underlying problem that is resulting in lower effective bandwidth. The Roofline analysis in the Intel Advisor tool initially shows that the innermost `Ni` loop lies on the MCDRAM bandwidth line, and this could be interpreted that the application is indeed memory bandwidth bound as expected, however in

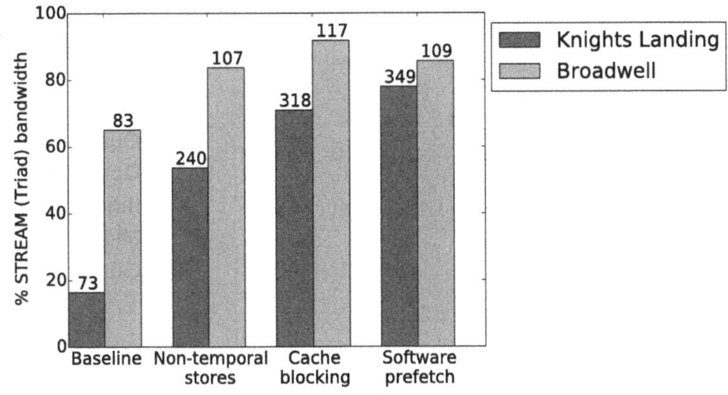

Fig. 2. Estimated memory bandwidth of the default problem size shown as a percentage of STREAM (Triad) memory bandwidth on Xeon and Xeon Phi as optimisations are applied (inclusively). Achieved memory bandwidth numbers are shown above each bar.

this paper we should optimisations which improve the runtime by 4X. However, analysis of the entire kernel as a whole is not shown in current versions of this tool and so inference from the analysis should be used with care.

Figure 3 shows the estimated memory bandwidth of the baseline code with dashed lines for a variety of problem sizes, and explores the ranges of the different loops, leaving the others fixed at the default size. The "inner" line varies the `Ni` range, the "middle" varies the `Nj`, `Nk` and `Nl` ranges identically, and the "outer" line varies the `Nm` range. As such the three dashed lines represent an exploration of the problem space spanned by the set of nested loops. For example, setting the middle loops to 8 yields the following configuration: `Ni` = 128, `Nj` = `Nk` = `Nl` = 8, `Nm` = 64. Varying the number of iterations each thread performs by increasing `Nm` alone shows little change in the achieved bandwidth from the default case, as shown by the outer dashed red line. The other dashed lines show the loop extents of the four innermost loops have a more dramatic effect. It is clear in the figure that there is a large variation in bandwidth, up to 145% (excluding the first data point of the "middle" dashed green line), with bandwidths of 49.9–122.3 GB/s depending on the input size. Where the iteration space of the middle jkl loops are set to 4 (leftmost point of the "middle" dashed green line) the baseline performance for this input exceeds the memory bandwidth available from MCDRAM, and as such must already be taking advantage of the cache hierarchy; indeed, the total problem is only 179 KiB per core, so can be fully resident in L2 cache.

It is usual to run the STREAM benchmark with one thread per physical core, and the results presented throughout the paper for the mega-stream benchmark also assume one thread per physical core. However, higher memory bandwidth is achieved for the baseline code by using the hyperthreads on Knights Landing and increasing `Nm` to match the number of hyperthreads, so that each thread performs the same amount of work. Using 2 and 4 hyperthreads per physical core increases

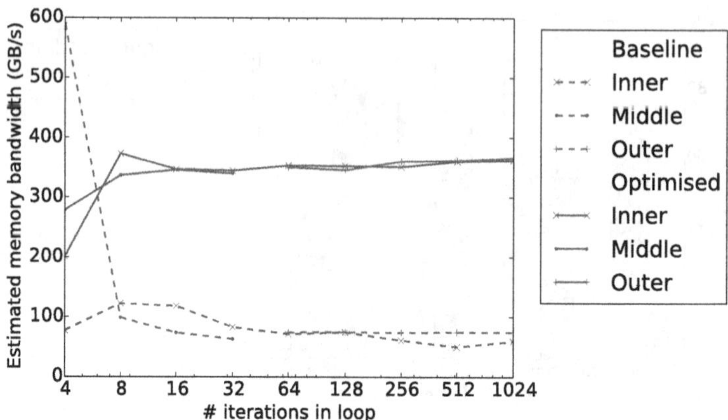

Fig. 3. Estimated bandwidth for a range of inputs by varying one dimension. The dashed lines show the baseline performance with the solid lines showing the performance the optimisations applied. (Color figure online)

the bandwidth to 138 and 114 GB/s respectively, an increase from the initial 73 GB/s attained from 1 thread per physical core. These results are still much lower than the expected memory bandwidth limits of this processor, however using the hyperthreads for the baseline may allow for some memory latency hiding thus increasing the estimated memory bandwidth. However, we have had to increase the problem size in order to take advantage of the hyperthreads which may not be applicable to all applications.

5.3 Improving the Performance

In order to improve the performance, we seek to minimise the wasteful data movement observed above and ensure that data is only moved the minimum number of times, something which is captured by our model. We take an incremental approach of three steps:

1. Ensure data which *is not* re-used *is not* in cache.
2. Ensure data which *is* re-used *is* in cache.
3. Ensure data is in the cache in time for use.

Whilst these optimisations sound obvious it is critical to observe that the code itself already has "good" memory access patterns; it is stride 1 access, should be very predictable for a cache lookahead engine, and we have confirmed that the code is vectorised well by the compiler. Indeed, the STREAM kernels are typically optimised though the first and last of these steps, however there is no data reuse. Note too that the STREAM benchmark kernels require little user intervention as the compiler performs this optimisations on our behalf; for mega-stream the programmer had to intervene. There are few mechanisms for explicitly controlling what is present in a CPU's cache hierarchy, as the memory subsystem is managed automatically by the processor itself, primarily based on data locality. As such, controlling what data is in the cache is more a result of side effects of the instruction stream rather than from any explicit description of the memory location. This is somewhat similar to programs being NUMA-aware in the sense that they, for example, ensure data is allocated and used on a core within a NUMA region, however this is achieved without any form of annotation or mechanism to explicitly state that this was the intended effect. GPU architectures tend to be very different in this regard, as they provide a scratchpad memory whose contents are explicitly controlled by the programmer.

Non-temporal Stores. The `r` array is large in size, there is no data-reuse within the kernel and it is only written to, so the previous value is not required. Therefore there is little use in the `r` array consuming cache space, or worse, evicting data that would benefit from caching.

The Streaming SIMD Extensions (SSE) instruction set introduced the notion of non-temporal stores with the `MOVNTQ` instruction. This instruction hinted that the cache hierarchy should be avoided and the data should be stored directly in main memory [4]. Additionally this avoids the "read for ownership" policy and it is no longer necessary to read `r` before writing to it, thus saving the unnecessary read of this entire array; previously every element was read before being written and therefore writing to this array caused 512 MiB of data movement (for the default problem size) instead of 256 MiB (its total size).

We can encourage the Intel compiler to generate such instructions for the target architecture via compiler directives, specifically by decorating the inner loop with the directive `#pragma vector nontemporal(r)`. Note however that this is not a portable solution as this is a directive specific to the Intel compiler; at the time of writing the authors have been unable to find similar directives for other compiler vendors. Intel architectures require non-temporal instructions to occur on aligned memory locations. The improvement is shown in Fig. 2, where the achieved memory bandwidth is much better, with 3X faster runtime than the baseline on Knights Landing, a significant improvement. However, the percentage of STREAM bandwidth that mega-stream achieves on Knights Landing is still relatively low, and therefore further improvements are required.

On Broadwell we see a comparatively small 1.3X improvement in runtime from non-temporal stores. We interpret this as the larger caches per core mitigating the effects on Broadwell relative to Knights Landing. Broadwell's 55 MB L3 cache is shared between all 22 cores on a socket, which results in around 2.5 MB of L3 cache per core; significantly more in this last level of cache than the 512 KB per core in last level (L2) cache on Knights Landing. As such, the effects of reducing the cache pollution from the `r` array are less pronounced. Indeed, the CrayPat profiler reports that, on Broadwell, the baseline is achieving 76.1% L1 cache hits, with non-temporal stores increasing this to 85.6%. However, the L2 cache hit rate has reduced; on Broadwell the baseline achieved 7.3% misses, whereas adding the non-temporal directive increased this to 40.1%. This increase is likely down to highlighting cache miss behaviour of other data arrays rather than obtaining a high hit rate for the `r` array as a side effect of cache pollution.

Cache Blocking. There is reuse of the `x`, `y` and `z` arrays, although the reuse pattern is somewhat complex for the middle three jkl loops. We want to ensure that data remains in cache whilst there is some temporal locality of the elements of these arrays. For the default problem size on Knights Landing, each core is accessing a 256 KiB contiguous portion of each of these three arrays. Each pair of cores share a 1 MB L2 cache, and assuming there is no sharing of data each core has approximately 512 KB of L2 cache available. The combined total of the local portion of these arrays (768 KiB) therefore exceeds the capacity of its available L2 cache, and therefore the data will at some point be evicted from this level of cache; as there is no L3 cache on Knights Landing the data will fall back to MCDRAM. Therefore the data will need to be read from main memory multiple times, whereas our bandwidth estimate assumes that the data remains resident in cache, as it should, and as the programmer might expect, due to the temporal locality and predictable access patterns.

As discussed above, there are no explicit mechanisms for controlling what is in a CPU cache, and therefore we must use other techniques to ensure that only the appropriate data remains resident in the cache. We therefore implement a *cache blocking* scheme, alternatively known as tiling, with the aim of decreasing the amount of data required in cache at any given time. By controlling which tiles are in use at any one time, we can also prevent cacheable data evicting other data that we want to retain in the caches. In many applications this is done by tiling the spatial dimension in one or more dimensions, however in this benchmark we have multiple values per spatial cell and so in contrast we tile in this extra dimension. We shall use one core's portion of the `x` array as an example; by default this is 256 KiB in size. Each `x(:,j,k)` element is accessed `Nl` times, once for each iteration of the `l` loop. By breaking the first index of the array into blocks, where each block is the size of a cache line, we can reduce the amount of memory kept in cache for the duration of the `l` loop; we can then ensure that all of these accesses are made from cache. An extra loop over the blocks is inserted between lines 1 and 2 in Listing 1.1; we also modify the inner loop in line 5 to index within a block. The arrays are allocated and initialised with an extra dimension, again keeping the order of the extents matching the loop nesting. By splitting the `Ni` dimension into blocks of eight, which corresponds to eight double precision elements forming a 64 byte cache line, the portion of the `x` array to be kept in cache for reuse drops from 256 KiB to just 16 KiB. The reduction in size is the same for the `y` and `z` arrays, and therefore the portion of *all* three arrays which is reused totals 48 KiB, which can certainly remain inside the 512 KB cache. The performance improvements from blocking are shown in Fig. 2, where the optimisations are applied inclusively. On Knights Landing this is a good improvement in memory bandwidth and a 1.3X runtime improvement over applying non-temporal stores alone; achieving 71.0% of STREAM bandwidth (318 GB/s) once we apply both cache blocking and non-temporal stores, compared to 53.6% for the non-temporal stores alone. The variation in performance between different problem sizes has also vanished, and all inputs now achieve similar results (not shown for brevity).

The Broadwell architecture again improves a little with this optimisation, but not significantly; the fraction of STREAM bandwidth we have achieved increases from 83.7% to 91.8%. We believe this is down to the large caches holding the `x`, `y`, `z` arrays entirely in L3 cache and avoiding going to main memory entirely, but improvements can be seen at lower levels of the cache hierarchy. Profiler output from the CrayPat tool shows that L1 cache misses have fallen from 14.4% to 7.1%, a significant saving. Additionally L2 cache misses have reduced from 40.1% to 15.5%. What is clear though, is that the cache hit rates are generally high on Broadwell throughout these optimisation stages, and as such the impact on runtime is minimal. The Intel vTune profiler was not available on the platform so we are unable to provide L3 cache statistics.

This cache blocking technique applied in isolation does improve the performance of the baseline by around 1.7X on Knights Landing, however 4X over the baseline is demonstrated with both non-temporal stores and cache blocking combined.

Software Prefetching. Finally a small improvement is available by ensuring that the prefetching of data is suitably early to hide the associated latency of memory movement. On profiling the cache blocked version, it can be seen that there are L2 cache misses for the read of the `q` array, indicating that the data is not there in time to be read when it is required. Therefore we can use Intel software prefetch intrinsics to generate prefetch instructions earlier in the instruction stream. We found that prefetching with a depth of 32 vector instructions was sufficient, and the intrinsic was inserted inside the `j` loop; software prefetching typically requires some experimentation in determining a suitable prefetch distance. This experimentation was done by firstly enabling automatic software prefetching in the compiler via the `-qopt-prefetch=3` flag, with the distance reported by the compiler used as the starting value for the prefetch distance. This results in a 10% boost in performance on Knights Landing, taking us up to 77.9% of STREAM bandwidth (349 GB/s).

Interestingly on the Broadwell architecture the use of the same software prefetch actually reduces the performance, from 91.8% to 85.6%. We could not find a suitable value for the prefetch distance which did not reduce performance from that achieved via cache blocking and non-temporal stores alone. Using software prefetchers may cause conflicts with the compiler automatically inserting these instructions, however no improvements could be found by turning off compiler prefetching. Note too that hardware prefetching will not function on the data stream if manual prefetching instructions are issued; therefore on the Broadwell architecture the hardware prefetchers alone seem sufficient for this benchmark; after all the benchmark was achieving over 90% of STREAM Triad bandwidth after the cache blocking optimisation.

Summary. Listing 1.2 shows the code changes described above applied to the kernel originally shown in Listing 1.1. Again we show the Fortran kernel for brevity; note the inclusion of the compiler directive for non-temporal stores, the software prefetch intrinsic, and the additional loop and corresponding index.

```
DO m = 1, Nm
  DO n = 1, Ni/8
    DO l = 1, Nl
      DO k = 1, Nk
        DO j = 1, Nj
          CALL MM_PREFETCH(q(1+32*8,j,k,l,n,m), 1)
          !DIR$ VECTOR NONTEMPORAL(r)
          DO i = 1, 8
            r(i,j,k,l,n,m) = q(i,j,k,l,n,m) +
↪ a(i,h)*x(i,j,k,n,m) + b(i,n)*y(i,j,l,n,m) +
↪ c(i,n)*z(i,k,l,n,m)
            x(i,j,k,n,m) = 0.2*r(i,j,k,l,n,m) - x(i,j,k,n,m)
            y(i,j,l,n,m) = 0.2*r(i,j,k,l,n,m) - y(i,j,l,n,m)
            z(i,k,l,n,m) = 0.2*r(i,j,k,l,n,m) - z(i,k,l,n,m)
            total(j,k,l,m) = total(j,k,l,m) + r(i,j,k,l,n,m)
          END DO
        END DO
      END DO
    END DO
  END DO
END DO
```

Listing 1.2: The optimised mega-stream kernel

With these optimisations in place, the mega-stream benchmark is obtaining close to 80% of STREAM bandwidth on Knights Landing MCDRAM, a significant increase over the initial 16.4% we observed. The mega-stream benchmark has one large read data stream and one large write data stream, and therefore we would not expect to reach close to Triad bandwidth which has two read and one write stream. The Knights Landing MCDRAM has separate channels for read and write and therefore we will not maximise the memory bandwidth available with a single read stream [6]. The Scale kernel in the STREAM benchmark is more similar to the read and write balance here, which achieves 400 GB/s on Knights Landing and 100 GB/s on Broadwell. Based on Scale as an achievable peak instead of Triad, mega-stream is now achieving 87.3% of the available memory bandwidth on Knights Landing, a significant improvement over the baseline. On Broadwell it achieves well over 100% of the memory bandwidth according to our model, indicating good cache usage—the model over-estimates the number of bytes loaded into cache from memory through the assumption that all future reads after the first are not counted. The STREAM kernels are simple and so we not expect to achieve parity with this more complex benchmark.

The solid lines in Fig. 3 show the final estimated memory bandwidth after the optimisations. Remember that this figure explores the variation in achieved memory bandwidth over different problem sizes with the baseline performance for the various input sizes shown with dashed lines. Firstly note that the results are more consistent with each other, generally within 6% (excluding the first points), compared to 145% initially. As such, the effective utilisation of the available memory bandwidth is no longer as dependent on the problem size. With the "middle" iterations set to four (leftmost point of the "middle" dashed green line), the optimised code actually realises an *increased* runtime for this input; this problem size is fully cache resident and hence non-temporal stores moving the memory out of cache to MCDRAM are a hindrance.

Running the optimised mega-stream utilising the hyperthreads on the Knights Landing results in reduced bandwidth. Using 2 and 4 hyperthreads per physical core with `Nm` set to 128 and 256 as before, the bandwidth is estimated as 300 and 245 GB/s respectively; recall running 1 thread per physical core achieves 349 GB/s. This behaviour is in-line with running memory bandwidth bound kernels such as those in the STREAM benchmark.

The Roofline analysis in the Intel Advisor tool shows that for the optimised code the `Nj` loop is limited by L2 cache bandwidth, however again does not show results for the kernel as a whole.

6 Conclusions

A simple benchmark code with sensible, stride 1 memory access patterns and vectorisation is shown which initially does not take full advantage of available memory bandwidth; yet the code should be memory bandwidth bound due to its low computational intensity. The code follows a pattern which may be present in a wide range of important codes: a stencil style access where cell edge values contribute to neighbouring cells. The results we present in this paper could therefore help identify many more cases where performance on Knights Landing could be significantly improved. We have presented a series of three optimisations which improve the runtime of our simple benchmark code by 4X on the Intel Xeon Phi (Knights Landing) processor, and thus allow it to take advantage of the improved memory bandwidth on this architecture. The optimisations also helped on Intel Xeon processors with close to a 1.5X speedup, however due to the large cache sizes on these processors the improvement is much smaller than on Knights Landing.

We are planning on examining the performance of mega-stream on other cache based CPU architectures as well as a GPU port; focusing on uncovering the fundamental reasons why the GPU port of SNAP achieves good performance. We will also apply the techniques and optimisations discussed to SNAP itself.

Acknowledgement. We would like to thank John Pennycook and Andrew Mallinson of Intel Corporation for their assistance with this work. The mega-stream code is made available from the UK Mini-App Consortium on GitHub at https://github.com/UK-MAC/mega-stream. The University of Bristol is an Intel Parallel Computing

Center, and the authors would like to thank Intel Corporation for the provision of the Intel Xeon Phi (Knights Landing) Processor. The authors would like to thank Cray Inc. for providing access to the Cray XC40 supercomputer, "Swan".

References

1. Deakin, T., McIntosh-Smith, S., Gaudin, W.: Many-core acceleration of a discrete ordinates transport mini-app at extreme scale. In: Kunkel, J.M., Balaji, P., Dongarra, J. (eds.) ISC High Performance 2016. LNCS, vol. 9697, pp. 429–448. Springer, Cham (2016). doi:10.1007/978-3-319-41321-1_22
2. Deakin, T., McIntosh-Smith, S., Martineau, M., Gaudin, W.: An improved parallelism scheme for deterministic discrete ordinates transport. Int. J. High Perform. Comput. Appl. http://hpc.sagepub.com/cgi/doi/10.1177/1094342016668978
3. Deakin, T., Price, J., Martineau, M., McIntosh-Smith, S.: GPU-STREAM v2.0: benchmarking the achievable memory bandwidth of many-core processors across diverse parallel programming models. In: Taufer, M., Mohr, B., Kunkel, J.M. (eds.) ISC High Performance 2016. LNCS, vol. 9945, pp. 489–507. Springer, Cham (2016). doi:10.1007/978-3-319-46079-6_34
4. Intel: Programming with Intel Streaming SIMD Extensions, Intel 64 and IA-32 Architectures Software Developer's Manual, chap. 10, vol. 1. Intel Corporation, December 2016
5. Jeffers, J., Reinders, J., Sodani, A.: Trinity workloads. In: Intel Xeon Phi Processor High Performance Programming, chap. 25, pp. 549–579. Morgan Kaufmann, Boston (2016). http://www.sciencedirect.com/science/article/pii/B9780128091944000259
6. Jeffers, J., Reinders, J., Sodani, A.: Quantum chromodynamics. In: Intel Xeon Phi Processor High Performance Programming, pp. 581–598. Elsevier (2016). http://linkinghub.elsevier.com/retrieve/pii/B9780128091944000260
7. Lamport, L.: The parallel execution of DO loops. CACM - Commun. ACM **17**(2), 83–93 (1974)
8. McCalpin, J.D.: Memory bandwidth and machine balance in current high performance computers. In: IEEE Computer Society Technical Committee on Computer Architecture (TCCA) Newsletter, pp. 19–25, December 1995
9. Williams, S., Waterman, A., Patterson, D.: Roofline: an insightful visual performance model for multicore architectures. Commun. ACM **52**, 65–76 (2009)
10. Zerr, R.J., Baker, R.S.: SNAP: SN (discrete ordinates) application proxy - proxy description. Tech. report, LA-UR-13-21070, Los Alamos National Laboratory (2013)

From Knights Corner to Landing: A Case Study Based on a Hodgkin-Huxley Neuron Simulator

George Chatzikonstantis[1(✉)], Diego Jiménez[2], Esteban Meneses[2,3], Christos Strydis[4], Harry Sidiropoulos[1], and Dimitrios Soudris[1]

[1] Microprocessors and Digital Systems Lab, National Technical University of Athens, Athens, Greece
{georgec,harry,dsoudris}@microlab.ntua.gr

[2] Advanced Computing Laboratory, Costa Rica National High Technology Center, San José, Costa Rica
{djimenez,emeneses}@cenat.ac.cr

[3] School of Computing, Costa Rica Institute of Technology, Cartago, Costa Rica

[4] Neuroscience Department, Erasmus Medical Center Rotterdam, Rotterdam, Netherlands
c.strydis@erasmusmc.nl

Abstract. Brain modeling has been presenting significant challenges to the world of high-performance computing (HPC) over the years. The field of computational neuroscience has been developing a demand for physiologically plausible neuron models, that feature increased complexity and thus, require greater computational power. We explore Intel's newest generation of Xeon Phi computing platforms, named Knights Landing (KNL), as a way to match the need for processing power and as an upgrade over the previous generation of Xeon Phi models, the Knights Corner (KNC). Our neuron simulator of choice features a Hodgkin-Huxley-based (HH) model which has been ported on both generations of Xeon Phi platforms and aggressively draws on both platforms' computational assets. The application uses the OpenMP interface for efficient parallelization and the Xeon Phi's vectorization buffers for Single-Instruction Multiple Data (SIMD) processing. In this study we offer insight into the efficiency with which the application utilizes the assets of the two Xeon Phi generations and we evaluate the merits of utilizing the KNL over its predecessor. In our case, an out-of-the-box transition on Knights Landing, offers on average 2.4× speed up while consuming 48% less energy than KNC.

Keywords: Intel Xeon Phi · Knights landing · Computational neuroscience

1 Introduction

In recent years neuroscientists have been gradually revealing details of neuron operation. Using this knowledge, there is a wide research interest in studying the

J.M. Kunkel et al. (Eds.): ISC High Performance Workshops 2017, LNCS 10524, pp. 363–375, 2017.
https://doi.org/10.1007/978-3-319-67630-2_27

behaviour of single-neuron, a network of neurons and eventually study brain-wide populations of neurons. Simulating these neuronal networks on various platforms is an active field of research [3,19].

A major challenge is the sheer computational complexity that many of these neuron models entail. Even the less complex types have significant demands as the studied neuronal network increases in size both in terms of computation and data transfer or storage. Traditionally in the domain of neuroscience, the most common methods for simulating neuron models and studying their behaviour were either through widely-known mathematical software suites such as MATLAB [24] or through specific neuromodeling tools like NEURON [13] and Brian [12]. It has become clear that these methods are not suitable for simulating neuronal networks of realistic sizes and high detail within a reasonable timeframe for brain research. High-Performance Computing (HPC) has been recently recognized as a viable domain for providing a variety of solutions to cope with this limitation [2,5,11,18,22,25].

In our current case study we feature a simulator for biophysically plausible neuron models, targeting a part of the human brain named the Inferior Olivary Nucleus, which specializes in the coordination and learning of motor function [9]. The modeling accuracy is at the cell conductance level (Hodgkin and Huxley models [14]), belonging at an analytical and complicated class of models which allow us to expose fine details of the neuron's mechanisms. This workload is an excellent candidate for parallelization on HPC architectures, such as the Intel Xeon Phi system [10], due to the large inherent parallelism of the models. Additionally, it constitutes a realistic worst-case scenario in terms of model complexity, hence a benchmark for neuron modeling workloads.

In order to explore whether Intel's newest generation of the Xeon Phi computing platform, named Knights Landing (KNL), is a suitable platform for neuroscientific workloads, in the current paper we evaluate its performance and energy consumption compared to the previous version, Knights Corner (KNC). We utilize the aforementioned Inferior Olivary Nucleus simulator, named InfOli, which was developed for the KNC generation of Xeon Phi [6]. This comparison will highlight how the evolution of Intel's Xeon Phi architecture can improve the performance of a challenging application in the field of computational neuroscience. Since the application is fine-tuned to the previous version of Xeon Phi processors, we will, accordingly, explore the behaviour of an "out-of-the-box" application on the KNL.

In this paper, we shall first discuss the nature and parallelization method of our simulator. We will then briefly present the architecture of the two generations of Xeon Phi HPC architectures and highlight their significant differences in hardware. Furthermore, we will present the methodology of our experimentation and evaluate their results. Finally, we will conclude with remarks on the merits and shortcomings of each platform.

2 System Design

2.1 Software

The InfOli simulator, depicted in Fig. 1, is a transient simulator; brain activity is calculated in simulation steps, with each step set to represent 50us of activity in a fixed manner. The steps are calculated sequentially, until the entirety of the requested brain activity is computed.

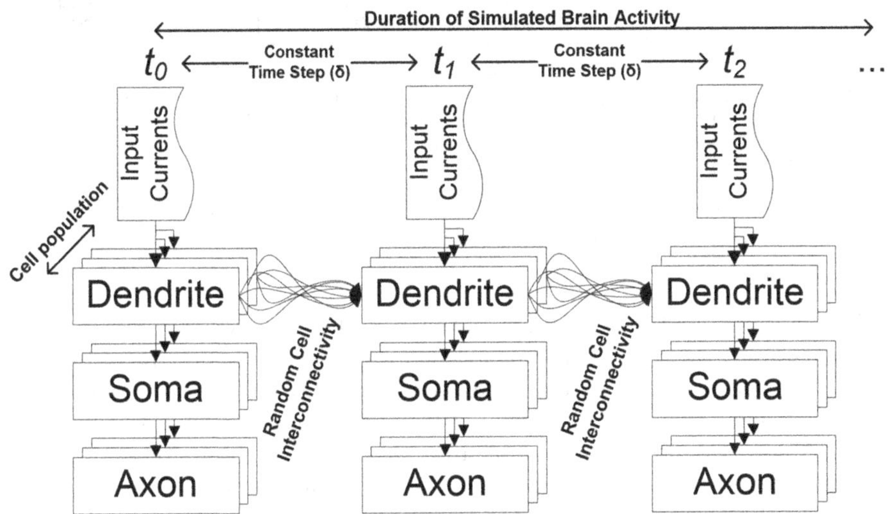

Fig. 1. The InfOli simulator [6]

In each simulation step, the simulator has the task of updating the status of each neuron in a pre-defined network. The neurons are based on an elaborate, realistic model of the human neuron, derived from the work of Hodgkin and Huxley [14]. As such, they are comprised of 3 compartments, each modelling a different part of the neuron. The dendritic compartment holds the important task of communicating with the rest of the network; it forms connections with other neurons in the network, modelled as electrical synapses named Gap Junctions (GJ) [8]. The somatic compartment is the main body of the neuron, where most calculations for the neuron's inner state take place. Finally, the axonal compartment acts as the output port of the neuron (specifically, in our application, of the Inferior Olivary neuron) to other parts of the brain (such as, the cerebellum). In each step, the simulator processes the current flow in the GJs of the network and then, re-calculates the states of the three compartments of each neuron. This is achieved by solving the Ordinary Differential Equations (ODE) governing the model via the Euler forward method [20]. Each neuron may also receive an external stimulus by its environment, in each step of the simulation.

In order to boost simulation speed, OpenMP [7] has been employed to parallelize the application. Figure 2 relays how the simulator utilizes OpenMP threads.

The network is divided in equal parts and assigned to different OpenMP threads, ensuring a balanced distribution of workload.

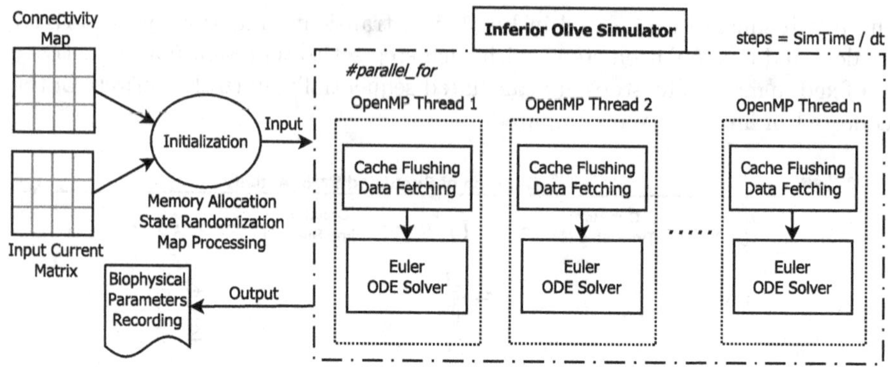

Fig. 2. OpenMP implementation of the InfOli simulator

In each step, the threads read from the Xeon Phi's shared memory in order to calculate the state of their assigned neurons' GJs. This task requires that each thread accesses other threads' data concerning the dendritic compartments of their assigned neurons; these shared memory accesses enforce the flushing of cache lines that hold invalid data from previous simulation steps. After all relevant dendritic data is refreshed, the state of each neuron can be calculated independently from the rest of the network. When the simulation step is completed, biological data that needs to be tracked, such as the voltage levels of the somatic membrane, is collected from each thread and recorded in the simulation's output file.

The simulator has been ported and tested primarily on the Intel KNC. An analytic methodology has been followed to boost vectorization processing unit (VPU) usage, in order to optimally utilize the platform's asset [6]. Data transformations (struct to arrays), aligning data to cache lines and loop transformations have been tested on the KNC, with the help of Intel's profiling tools (Intel VTune Amplifier). As such, the simulator is not expected to be optimal for the second generation of Xeon Phi, the KNL. However, due to their similar architectural design, the application is a good candidate for porting on both platforms.

2.2 Hardware

The first commercial generation of Xeon Phi products is named Knights Corner. This version of Xeon Phi is an Intel accelerator platform arranged in a host-and-coprocessor fashion and features up to 61 cores, each with four instruction streams [15]. It supports traditional parallel-programming paradigms, such as MPI [23] and OpenMP [7], in contrast to Graphics Processing Units (GPU) requiring platform-specific programming paradigms [1]. After the Xeon host boots a KNC-specific software stack on the Phi, named Intel Manycore Platform Software Stack (MPSS), the latter may be used independently, for native workload execution. The KNC accelerator features vectorization processing units (VPU) [15], which can parallelize multiple floating-point (FP) operations.

Intel's second generation of Xeon Phi processors introduced several architectural differences with respect to its predecessor. KNL is a standard Intel Many-Integrated Core (MIC) Architecture standalone processor that can boot stock operating systems and connect to a network directly via common interconnects such as Infiniband, Ethernet, etc. This is a significant differentiation over Knights Corner, which is a PCIe-connected device and, therefore, could only be used when connected to a separate host processor. In KNL, cores are integrated in couples into structures named tiles in which they share a 1 MB L2 cache. Each core is connected to two vector processing units as opposed to the single VPU unit per core present in KNC models, making vectorization a key aspect in this platform's computational power. KNL processors can have up to 36 tiles for a total of 72 cores, each capable of hyperthreading with up to 4 threads per core, and 144 VPUs. Communication between those 36 tiles is achieved through a cache-coherent 2D mesh interconnect which replaces the bidirectional ring bus used on the KNC coprocessor. This on-die interconnect allows for different clustering modes of operation which offer various degrees of address affinity to improve performance in HPC applications.

In addition to these features, KNL introduced a new memory architecture to provide both large memory capacity as well as high memory bandwidth. To do so, traditional DDR memory is complemented with what Intel named MultiChannel Dynamic Random Access Memory (MCDRAM). This on-package memory does not achieve higher single data access performance than main memory but supports a higher bandwidth [16]. As with the mesh clustering modes, MCDRAM can be configured in different memory modes: (i) to serve as cache for the DDR memory (cache mode), (ii) to be mapped as regular memory into the system's address space (flat mode) or, (iii) to work as hybrid memory where part of the MCDRAM acts as cache and the rest is allocated to the address space (hybrid mode). KNL's characteristics and its high degree of customization make it a suitable platform for high performance computing applications like the Inferior Olive simulator.

3 Evaluation

3.1 Experimental Setup

The measurements presented in this section have been carried out using two different generations of Intel Xeon Phi. The Knights Corner co-processor's model is 3120P, featuring 57 cores at 1.1 GHz, each supporting up to 4 threads running concurrently via multithreading technology. Cores run at 300 W thermal design power (TDP). The application is designed to run natively on the co-processor, thus excluding any impact from its Intel Xeon host on its measured performance.

Specifically, after compiling and transferring via Secure Copy Protocol (scp) all necessary binaries to the co-processor, the host remains idle throughout the experiment.

The Knights Landing processor's model is 7210, with 64 cores at 1.3 GHz and similar multithreading capacities. Its TDP is noticeably lower at 215W. MCDRAM for the KNL was set to cache mode as this setting is completely transparent to software and allows for "out-of-the-box" codes like the neuron simulator being tested, to take advantage of the high-bandwidth-memory technology. As for the clustering mode, quadrant configuration was chosen based on recognition that the cache-quadrant combination offers performance gain to HPC applications [16,21].

Finally, in order to get a better grasp on the performance offered by the two generations of accelerator platforms, we include performance curves from an Intel Xeon E5-2609-v2, a 4-core server-grade processor utilizing 4 threads concurrently. The processor's simulation speed acts as a baseline, with the added benefit that codebases developed for Xeon Phi accelerators are compatible with Xeon (or any generic x86) processors.

For the power measurements in this section, different methodologies have been followed for the two platforms. For the Knights Landing processor, the processor's power consumption was sampled via Intelligent Platform Management Interface (IPMI) [17] via a script running concurrently with each experiment's execution. Polling frequency was set to approximately 1 Hz. Energy consumption for each experiment was then calculated by integrating the power samples over the simulation's duration. On the other hand, power measurements on the Knights Corner co-processor is achieved by accessing the host's logs of information and errors regarding the co-processor. These logs are attained via a built-in tool named micrasd which can track the KNC's power in intervals of 5 milliseconds. The reports are generated from the beginning of the simulation and by summation of each report until the end of the experiment, an accurate estimation of total energy consumption can be attained.

In each experiment, a network of neurons connecting to each other via the Gap Junction mechanism, explained in Subsect. 2, is generated. The neuron connections are generated randomly, with each pair of neurons given a chance to form a bond regardless of their position on the neuronal grid. This chance is calculated based on the amount of connections each neuron is designed to have for each experiment, as well as the total neuronal network size; a division of the two variables calculates the network's average connection density, which, in turn, directly leads to the chance of a pair of neurons forming a bond.

Compilation for the KNC has been carried out using Intel's compiler icc version 16.0.1, whereas on the KNL, icc Version 17.0.0.098 has been used. On both platforms, the options used for vectorized code are `-O3` for the best available compiler optimizations, `-vec-report6` for a detailed analysis of vectorized code generated, `-opt-subscript-in-range` to inform the compiler that no integer in the main loop is calculated exceeding the value of 2^{31}, allowing more loop transformations and `-lm` to access math libraries needed throughout the model's calculations. For measurements that use unvectorized code, the options `-no-vec -no-simd -no-qopenmp-simd` have been utilized to ensure the compiler avoids all SIMD commands.

3.2 Experimental Results

In Fig. 3, we can observe obtained simulation speed of each platform for networks of varying connectivity density. The measurements explore varying network sizes, where each neuron has a fixed average amount of connections to the rest of the network.

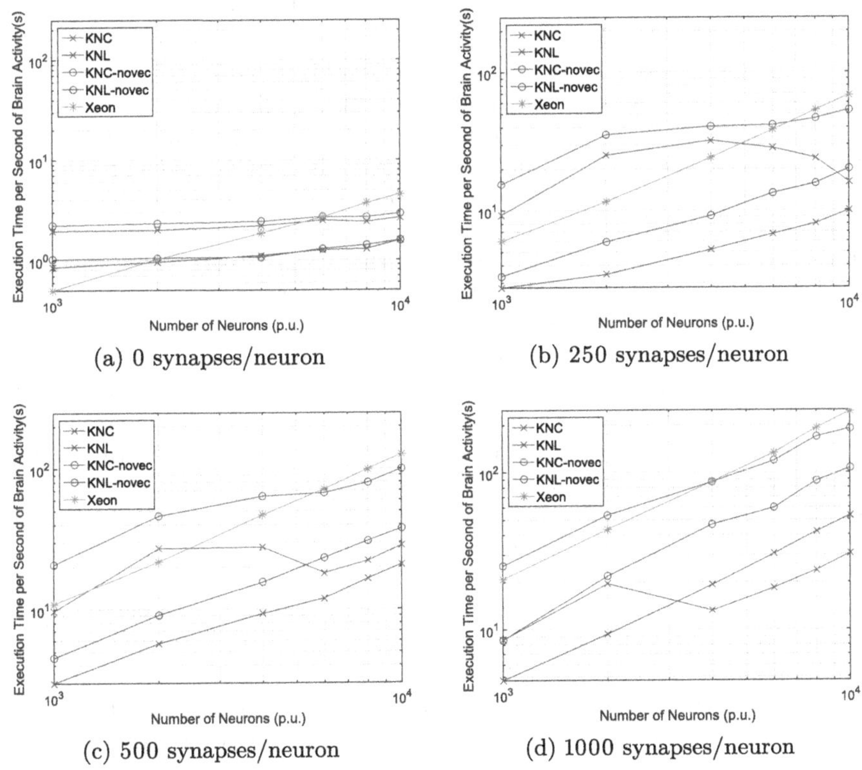

(a) 0 synapses/neuron
(b) 250 synapses/neuron
(c) 500 synapses/neuron
(d) 1000 synapses/neuron

Fig. 3. Execution Time per second of simulated brain activity, comparison between Knights Corner (KNC) and Knights Landing (KNL) on different Simulator configurations. Performance on Xeon processor (4 threads) added as a baseline.

All experiments in Fig. 3 have been carried out using approximately the maximum amount of threads available to each platform. For the KNC, we used 220 threads, whereas the KNL offered 256 threads. On average the KNL platform outperforms the KNC platform by 2.4× in terms of execution time. The maximum speed-up is 6×, while in some cases the KNC comes in front with up to

1.6× speed up over the KNL. More specifically, we can observe that, in the cases of low connectivity density, which translates to a low amounts of workload per thread, the KNL shows a superior performance to the KNC.

In cases of small workloads, the efficiency in usage of parallelization assets is diminished, thus single-threaded performance becomes much more important for overall simulation speed. The KNL demonstrates a considerably stronger single-threaded processing power and overtakes the KNC by a fair margin. For both the KNL and the KNC, we can observe that the difference between vectorized and unvectorized code is minimal when connectivity density is low; Gap Junctions represent a significant portion of the total workload and thus, when they are few or completely absent, vectorization fails to boost application performance. We can also observe that the Xeon processor, which excels at handling mostly serial code, may even surpass the KNC accelerator for small-scale simulations.

On the other hand, as the computational workload assigned to each thread increases for denser networks, the KNC performs significantly better. The performance gap between the two platforms lessens as the KNC can use its assets with increasing efficiency, since the application has been optimized with the KNC architecture in mind. The gap between vectorized and unvectorized code widens significantly for the KNC, whereas there is a more stable difference in the case of the KNL. Better usage of VPUs leads to the KNC outperforming the KNL; indeed, for workloads of more than 4,000 neurons, each forming approximately 1,000 synapses, the KNL is surpassed by the KNC. As expected, both platforms perform significantly better than the baseline Xeon processor; the KNL and the KNC simulate networks of 10,000 neurons, each with 1,000 synapses, approximately 4.6× and 8.1× faster than the server-grade processor, respectively.

It should be noted that, in terms of performance predictability, the KNL is heavily favoured. Its performance is linear and very predictable. On the contrary, the KNC's performance is harder to anticipate, when operating with vectorization options enabled. The platform's capability to take advantage of its computational resources (threads, VPUs) increases with the supplied workload. Because of this behaviour, it forms a "plateau", during which simulation time for larger networks remains stable, or even lessens, due to better usage of the SIMD commands generated by compiler directives.

Beyond a certain point in network sizes, which differs based on how dense the network is, the aforementioned "plateau" ceases to exist and KNC's performance curve resumes its linear nature. The existence of such "plateaus" impacts the performance predictability of the KNC, whereas the KNL does not exhibit similar behaviour. This can be attributed to the less efficient usage of vectorized code in the KNL's case. For both platforms, unvectorized code, which omits the usage of VPUs, displays a very predictable behaviour.

In Fig. 4, we present information regarding the energy required by each computing fabric in order to simulate a second of brain activity, measured in mWh. The Figure is directly linked to Fig. 3, since energy consumption is dependent on execution time needed for simulation of each second of brain activity. As such, we can observe similar patterns between the two Figures. On average we have

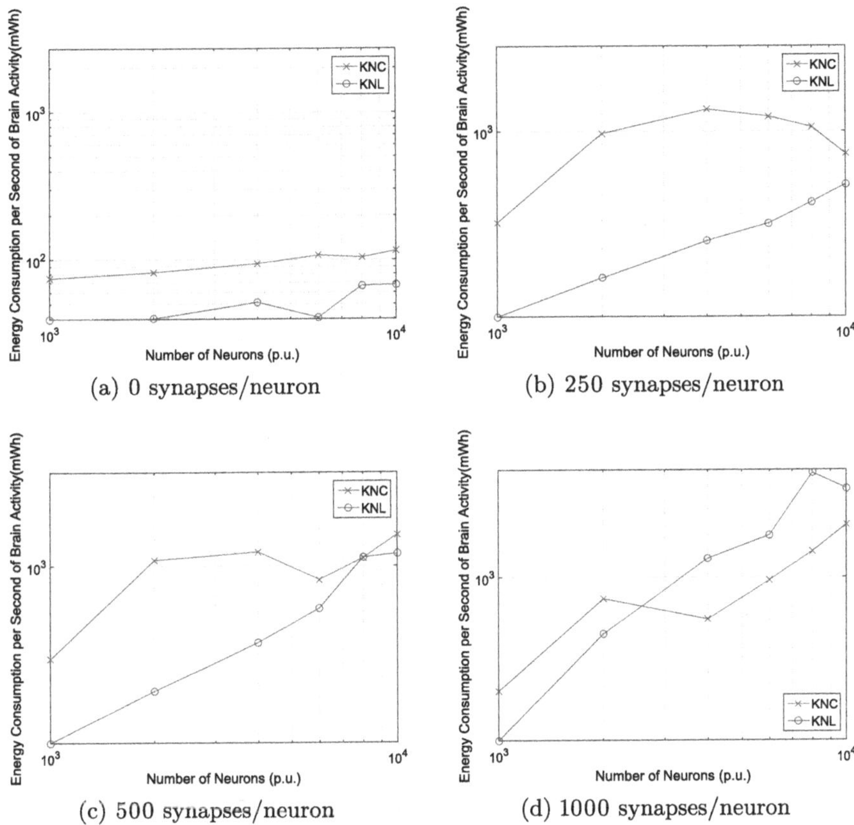

(a) 0 synapses/neuron

(b) 250 synapses/neuron

(c) 500 synapses/neuron

(d) 1000 synapses/neuron

Fig. 4. Energy Consumption per second of simulated brain activity, comparison between Knights Corner (KNC) and Knights Landing (KNL) on different Simulator configurations

to note that the KNL consumes 48% less energy than the KNC. Because of the KNL's lower TDP and better performance for light workloads, there is a significant reduction in energy consumption when computing for small networks. To put this claim into perspective, whereas the simulation of one second of brain activity in a network of 4000 neurons, with a density of 250 synapses per neuron, requires over 1200 mWh for the KNC, the KNL consumes under 300 mWh for the same workload, improving on energy efficiency by a factor of 4×.

On the contrary, due to the KNC's smaller execution times for larger, denser networks, it is preferable from a power consumption standpoint to the KNL for such workloads. A network of 10,000 neurons, each forming 1,000 synapses with the rest of the network, requires 27% less energy on the KNC (1600 mWh per second of simulated time) than on the KNL (2200 mWh for the same amount of activity).

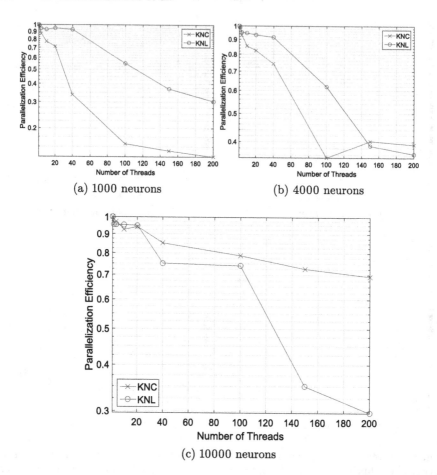

(a) 1000 neurons

(b) 4000 neurons

(c) 10000 neurons

Fig. 5. Threading Efficiency on the Knights Corner (KNC) and Knights Landing (KNL), for different Simulator configurations

In Fig. 5, information regarding the efficiency with which each platform manages its OpenMP threads is displayed. In HPC, the efficiency with which an application utilizes the underlying platform's resources can be calculated as the speedup yielded by employing said resources, compared to a single-threaded performance, divided by the amount of resources used, such as the number of processors used to run the application, or the number of threads spawned by the application. In our case, we calculated the efficiency metric by dividing execution speedup with the number of OpenMP threads spawned, with a range of OpenMP threads utilized from 1 to 200, on both platforms. In each subfigure, network density has been set to 1,000 synapses per neuron and we explore networks of different size.

For the KNL, we can observe that the efficiency of utilizing up to approximately 50 threads remains at satisfactory levels. In these cases, each core spawns either one or two threads (due to the selected balanced thread affinity) and, in contrast to the KNC, the KNL's cores operate significantly better when operating with only one thread [16]. The KNL maintains a reliable efficiency for low degrees of threading regardless of the simulated network's size, whereas the KNC's efficiency suffers for small workloads, such as for networks of 4000 neurons.

Larger networks, however, offer better opportunities for the KNC to utilize its computational assets efficiently, maintaining a speedup-to-threads ratio above 70% even for 200 threads. The KNL's threading efficiency sharply declines when employing massive degrees of parallelism, dropping below 40% when using more than 140 threads. The application's inability to utilize the entirety of KNL's assets efficiently to tackle demanding simulations explains the performance gap between the two platforms for larger workloads. This inability is mostly attributed to the fact that the simulator has been fine-tuned to the KNC environment and has been tested "out-of-the-box" on the KNL.

4 Conclusion and Outlook

In this paper, a computationally demanding application from the field of computational neuroscience that had previously been extensively developed and optimized for the Intel KNC, has been tested "out-of-the-box" for the second generation of Xeon Phi, the KNL. The InfOli biophysically-accurate simulator's performance was tested using a range of workloads, from small, unconnected neuronal populations to larger, dense networks. The results were evaluated from both a simulation-speed and a power-efficiency standpoint. On average KNL offers a speed up of 2.4× while consuming 48% less energy. Smaller workloads, by taking advantage of the KNL's superior single-threaded performance, exhibit very significant gains in both speed and, even more so, energy consumption, with specific experiments demanding 75% less Wh of energy per second of simulated brain activity on the KNL. On the other hand, without further fine-tuning of the application to the architectural details of the KNL, OpenMP-thread efficiency suffers when running on the KNL, causing the simulator to handle more demanding networks poorly, relatively to the optimized KNC version. Furthermore, throughout the whole range of experiments, it has been shown that the KNL offers a more robust, dependable performance curve with little variability.

These findings are promising enough to warrant further optimization of the simulator for the new generation of the Xeon Phi. As future work, we would suggest using an optimized version of the simulator on a cluster of KNL processors, in order to simulate neuronal networks of much larger sizes and take advantage of Intel's OmniPath technology for inter-node communication [4].

Acknowledgments. This work is partially supported by European Commission project H2020–687628–VINEYARD.

References

1. CUDA C Programming Guide. Technical report, NVIDIA Corporation
2. Bhuiyan, M., Nallamuthu, A., Smith, M., Pallipuram, V.: Optimization and performance study of large-scale biological networks for reconfigurable computing. In: Fourth International Workshop on High-Performance Reconfigurable Computing Technology and Applications (HPRCTA), pp. 1–9, November 2010
3. Bhuiyan, M., et al.: Acceleration of spiking neural networks in emerging multi-core and GPU architectures. In: IPDPSW (2010)
4. Birrittella, M.S., Debbage, M., Huggahalli, R., Kunz, J., Lovett, T., Rimmer, T., Underwood, K.D., Zak, R.C.: Intel® omni-path architecture: enabling scalable, high performance fabrics. In: 2015 IEEE 23rd Annual Symposium on High-Performance Interconnects (HOTI), pp. 1–9. IEEE (2015)
5. Chatzikonstantis, G., Rodopoulos, D., Nomikou, S., Strydis, C., De Zeeuw, C.I., Soudris, D.: First impressions from detailed brain model simulations on a Xeon/Xeon-Phi Node. In: Proceedings of the ACM International Conference on Computing Frontiers, CF 2016, NY, USA, pp. 361–364 (2016). doi:10.1145/2903150.2903477
6. Chatzikonstantis, G., Rodopoulos, D., Strydis, C., De Zeeuw, C.I., Soudris, D.: Optimizing extended Hodgkin-Huxley neuron model simulations for a Xeon/Xeon Phi node. IEEE Trans. Parallel Distrib. Syst. (2017)
7. Dagum, L., Enon, R.: OpenMP: an industry standard API for shared-memory programming. IEEE CSE **5**(1), 46–55 (1998)
8. De Zeeuw, C.I., Hoebeek, F.E., Bosman, L.W., Schonewille, M., Witter, L., Koekkoek, S.K.: Spatiotemporal firing patterns in the cerebellum. Nat. Rev. Neurosci. **12**(6), 327–344 (2011)
9. De Zeeuw, C.I., et al.: Microcircuitry and function of the inferior olive. Trends Neurosci. **21**(9), 391–400 (1998)
10. Fang, J., et al.: Test-driving Intel Xeon Phi. In: ICPE (2014)
11. Glackin, B., Wall, J.A., McGinnity, T.M., Maguire, L.P., McDaid, L.: A spiking neural network model of the medial superior olive using spike timing dependent plasticity for sound localization. Front. Comput. Neurosci. **4**(18) (2010)
12. Goodman, D.F., Brette, R.: The brian simulator. Front. Neurosci. **3**, 26 (2009)
13. Hines, M.L., Carnevale, N.T.: The NEURON simulation environment. Neural Comput. **9**(6), 1245–1249 (1997)
14. Hodgkin, A.L., Huxley, A.F.: Propagation of electrical signals along giant nerve fibres. Proc. R. Soc. Lond. Ser. B Biol. Sci. **140**(899), 177–183 (1952)
15. Jeffers, J., Reinders, J.: Intel Xeon Phi Coprocessor High-Performance Programming. Elsevier, Waltham (2013)
16. Jeffers, J., Reinders, J., Sodani, A.: Intel Xeon Phi Processor High Performance Programming: Knights Landing Edition. Morgan Kaufmann, Boston (2016)
17. Kaufman, G.J., et al.: System and method for application programming interface for extended intelligent platform management. US Patent 7,966,389, 21 Jun 2011
18. Nguyen, H.D., Al-Ars, Z., Smaragdos, G., Strydis, C.: Accelerating complex brain-model simulations on GPU platforms. In: Design, Automation, and Test in Europe, DATE 2015, March 2015
19. Du Nguyen, H.A., et al.: Accelerating complex brain-model simulations on GPU platforms. In: DATE, pp. 974–979 (2015)
20. Press, W.H., Teukolsky, S.A., Vetterling, W.T., Flannery, B.P.: Numerical Recipes in C, vol. 2. Cambridge University Press, Cambridge (1996)

21. Rosales, C., James, D., Gómez-Iglesias, A., Cazes, J., Huang, L., Liu, H., Liu, S., Barth, W.: TACC Technical Report TR-16-03 KNL Utilization Guidelines. Technical report, University of Texas at Austin, Texas Advanced Computing Center, November 2016. https://portal.tacc.utexas.edu/documents/10157/1334612/KNL+Utilization+Guidelines/95cc0f23-1755-424d-8d29-64a91a09cf33
22. Smaragdos, G., Isaza, S., Eijk, M.V., Sourdis, I., Strydis, C.: FPGA-based biophysically-meaningful modeling of olivocerebellar neurons. In: 22nd ACM/SIGDA International Symposium on Field-Programmable Gate Arrays (FPGA), February 2014
23. Snir, M.: MPI-the Complete Reference: The MPI Core. MIT, Cambridge (1998)
24. Wallisch, P., Lusignan, M.E., Benayoun, M.D., Baker, T.I., Dickey, A.S., Hatsopoulos, N.G.: MATLAB for Neuroscientists: An Introduction to Scientific Computing in MATLAB. Academic Press, San Diego (2014)
25. Yamazaki, T., Igarashi, J.: Realtime cerebellum: a large-scale spiking network model of the cerebellum that runs in realtime using a graphics processing unit. Neural Netw. **47**, 103–111 (2013). http://www.sciencedirect.com/science/article/pii/S0893608013000348. Computation in the Cerebellum

Porting Tissue-Scale Cardiac Simulations to the Knights Landing Platform

Johannes Langguth[1(✉)], Chad Jarvis[1], and Xing Cai[1,2]

[1] Simula Research Laboratory, 1364 Fornebu, Norway
{langguth,chad,xingca}@simula.no
[2] Department of Informatics, University of Oslo, 0316 Oslo, Norway

Abstract. To study the performance difference between the two generations of Xeon Phi, as well as the respective programming techniques, we port and optimize a simulation code for 3D tissues of the human cardiac ventricle to the new Knights Landing (KNL) platform. The amount of computation arises from a large number of cardiac cells and a physiologically realistic model adopted for each cell, which is resolved as having 10^4 calcium release units and controlled by 10^6 stochastically changing ryanodine receptors and 1.5×10^5 L-type calcium channels. The programming challenge arises from the fact that the involved computational tasks have various levels of arithmetic intensity and control complexity, requiring in some cases hardware-specific manual optimizations. We also study how the new memory system of KNL can be properly used to allow larger simulations beyond the capacity of the 16 GB MCDRAM. The combined advancements in hardware and software result in an almost ninefold increase in performance on the KNL over the previous generation.

1 Introduction

The second generation of the Intel Xeon Phi manycore processor, which is generally referred to as Knights Landing (KNL), constitutes a significant change from the previous Knights Corner (KNC) model. Thus, a natural subject to study is the performance improvement that can be derived from migrating KNC codes to the new KNL devices. This paper investigates this subject in the context of a real-world simulation code of computational cardiology.

Realistic simulations of calcium handling and action potential formation are essential for understanding the causative and preventive mechanisms of arrhythmogenesis, which originates from the local nanoscopic level of channel and dyadic dysfunction and develops into the subcellular and cellular levels of membrane potential abnormalities. For physiological fidelity, it is important to adopt sophisticated cell models of electrophysiology and calcium handling, because these models incorporate the discrete nature of subcellular stochastic calcium release processes [5,12,14,16]. The study of arrhythmias, which occur at the tissue and organ scales, therefore requires detailed simulations at such scales. Due to the

J.M. Kunkel et al. (Eds.): ISC High Performance Workshops 2017, LNCS 10524, pp. 376–388, 2017.
https://doi.org/10.1007/978-3-319-67630-2_28

massive computations on independent cells, such simulations are well suited for manycore systems.

In our previous work, we presented an MPI+OpenMP implementation of a tissue-scale cardiac simulator for the study of cardiac arrhythmias, using clusters of Xeon CPUs [9] and KNC coprocessors [11]. The code was later used to run large-scale experiments on the *Tianhe-2* [15] supercomputer [10]. Our ultimate goal is to enable massive simulations on the next generation of KNL based supercomputers. We will thus discuss the code transitions that are necessary to obtain high performance on the new device, report our experiences and the performance achieved, and give recommendations for future implementations.

2 Target Hardware

Although the number of cores increases only slightly from KNC to KNL, a higher clock frequency and a doubling of the vector processing units (VPU) lead to about a threefold increase in peak floating point performance[1]. In addition, a new core architecture capable of out-of-order execution makes it easier for applications to reach a higher fraction of that peak on KNL. The 8 GB device memory of the KNC has been replaced by 16 GB of on-chip memory called MCDRAM, with roughly three times the memory bandwidth [3]. In addition, the KNL can be equipped with up to 384 GB of DDR4 memory with a bandwidth of up to 90 GB/s. Unlike the KNC coprocessor, which is usually installed in compute nodes together with multicore CPUs and other KNCs, the KNL can have the same role as a CPU. Thus, in modern KNL-based supercomputers, a compute node consists of a single KNL device.

Both KNL and KNC use a 512-bit wide SIMD instruction set. KNL's implementation is called AVX-512 and KNC's implementation is called Initial Many Core Instructions (IMCI). IMCI is the predecessor to AVX-512 and it is not binary compatible with AVX-512. It offers many of the same features of AVX-512 but there are important differences, some of which will be discussed in later sections.

3 Tissue-Scale Simulation

3.1 Multiscale Tissue and Cell Modeling

In pursuit of physiological fidelity, a multiscale modeling strategy is adopted. First, a slab of cardiac tissue is mathematically represented by a 3D uniform grid of cells, where the inter-cell coupling is described by the well-known monodomain model in form of a reaction-diffusion equation. Here, each cell possesses a membrane potential and a cell-wide ionic current. The latter is the sum of various ionic currents determined by an underlying multiscale cell model of detailed calcium handling.

[1] The exact values vary for the different models. See [8] for the technical specifications.

Second, the per-cell model incorporates detailed stochastic calcium handling as described in [5], in combination with the O'Hara-Rudy model [13] of electrophysiological current formulation for a healthy human cardiac ventricular action potential. More specifically, each cardiac cell is assumed to have 10,000 calcium release units, also termed as dyads, which form an internal $100 \times 10 \times 10$ grid. Each dyad then consists of five calcium compartments: myoplasm Ca_{myo}, submembrane space Ca_{ss}, network sarcoplasmic reticulum Ca_{NSR}, junctional sarcoplasmic reticulum Ca_{JSR}, and dyadic space Ca_{ds}. The five local calcium concentrations are modeled by an intricate system of ordinary and partial differential equations, where intra-cell diffusion (between the dyads) applies to Ca_{myo}, Ca_{ss} and Ca_{NSR}. An overview of this composition is shown in Fig. 1.

Third, the dyadic space is modeled with additional details, where each dyad contains 100 ryanodine receptors (RyRs) and 15 L-type calcium channels. At any given time, each RyR is in one of four possible states each having two possible transition paths (see Fig. 1), whereas each L-type channel is either open or closed. The stochastic transitions between the states follow a Markov model with probabilities that are related to the local calcium concentrations.

We refer readers to [5] and its supplementary information for details about the multiscale stochastic calcium handling model of the cardiac ventricular myocyte.

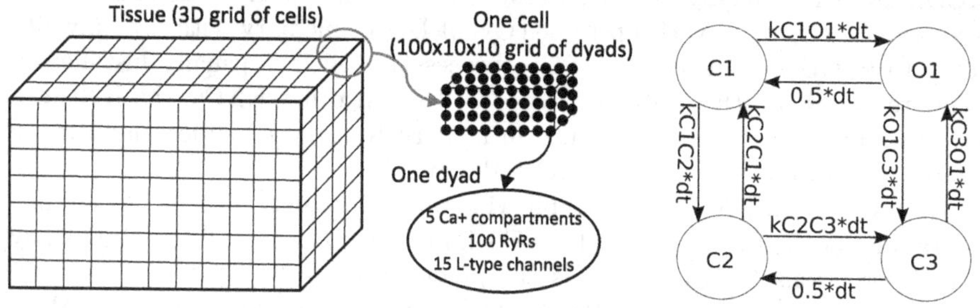

Fig. 1. Left: An overview of the computational composition of the cardiac tissue. Right: The four possible states of a dyad and the eight possible transition paths, with the corresponding transition probabilities.

3.2 Numerical Strategy

The overall numerical strategy is formulated as a time-stepping procedure, for which a rather small time step size has to be used due to the intricate dynamics of intra-cell calcium handling. The advantage of using a small time step is that straightforward explicit numerical schemes can be used to solve the various differential equations, at both cell and dyad levels.

During each time step, for every dyad, we sample eight times from a binomial distribution corresponding to the eight possible transition paths between the four different RyR states (see Fig. 1). This suffices for updating the numbers of RyRs in the four states (always totalling 100 per dyad), instead of individually simulating the stochastic transition of each of the 100 RyRs. Similarly, two samples from a binomial distribution per time step are sufficient for updating the numbers of open and closed L-type calcium channels per dyad. Additionally, the five local calcium concentrations per dyad are updated per time step, using a forward Euler scheme to solve the involved ordinary differential equations. When all the 10,000 dyads per cell have updated their local calcium concentrations, intra-cell diffusion of Ca_{myo}, Ca_{ss} and Ca_{NSR}, between the dyads, are computed by explicit finite differencing. At the end of each time step, when all the cells have finished their intra-cell computation, the monodomain equation is solved by explicit finite differencing between the cells.

4 Implementation

4.1 Parallelization Strategy

The tissue-scale simulator works on a cuboid domain consisting of an arbitrary integral number of cuboid subdomains in each dimension, which are again composed of an arbitrary integral number of cells in each dimension. Each subdomain is assigned to a single KNL device, and the KNLs communicate via MPI. As the inter-subdomain communication is only needed for the monodomain equation between the cells, which incurs negligible overhead relative to the entire computation, for this paper we focus only on the computation on a single device where we use an OpenMP *parallel for* loop with static scheduling to divide the cells among the threads. For load balance reasons, the number of cells will always be a multiple of the number of available hardware threads (272 for the 7250 model) in our experiments. Since every cell takes approximately the same time to compute, there is no need to use dynamic scheduling (which induces extra overhead). It is possible to use nested OpenMP regions to reduce this granularity. For example, it would be possible to assign one cell per core, and divide the cell computation among 4 threads. However, since our ultimate goal is to perform organ scale simulations involving more than a billion cells, the benefit of this technique is marginal and does not justify the increased complexity.

As a consequence, all computations performed for one cell remain on a single core. Alternatively, it would be possible to split the computations for each cell's $10,000$ dyads over multiple cores, because the dyad computations can also be performed independently. This would allow for better load balancing when the number of cells is small. However, previous experiments revealed that this decreased performance significantly, which implies that for large enough subdomains, our cell-level work division approach is preferable.

We use the SIMD vector units to process eight dyads in parallel on each core. This vectorization is crucial for performance. Due to the complexity of the code, we employ both automatic vectorization via the Intel C++ compiler and manual vectorization using intrinsics. To do so, we split the computations performed for each of the $10,000$ dyads into *arithmetic* and *conditional* sections.

In our simulations, *arithmetic* sections involve determining the probabilities for the opening of L-type channels or RyR state transitions, computing the calcium concentrations, and performing the diffusion among the dyads.

They contain expensive computations, but have a trivial control flow and can be vectorized automatically to yield the full eightfold speedup, although some sections are memory bandwidth bound, which limits their scalability.

The *conditional* sections concern sampling from binomial distributions in order to determine the number of state transitions, since this requires *while* loops or equivalent structures to be efficient. The compiler does not vectorize these on its own, but can be instructed to do so using the *simd* pragma. However, manual vectorization using intrinsics yielded significantly better results.

Mixing automatic and manual vectorization sections makes it necessary to split a large computational loop into several smaller loops, one for each section. As each of these iterates over 10, 000 dyads, intermediate results (such as probabilities for state transitions) must be written to memory and retrieved later, which generates additional memory traffic. Some of this traffic can be avoided by manually vectorizing small *arithmetic* sections and merging them with *conditional* sections in order to reduce the temporary variables that need to be stored and read from memory. Doing so for the L-type channel computation provided a small but noticeable performance gain.

4.2 Vectorized Binomial Sampling

We vectorize the *conditional* sections manually using the AVX-512 intrinsics provided by Intel. The vectorization of sampling from a binomial distribution on the KNC was described in [11]. While some intrinsics had to be adapted to render the code compatible with KNL, the basic algorithm is unchanged. The key to vectorizing code containing conditional statements lies in the powerful `mask` instructions. They allow the SIMD units to apply vector instructions only on some elements of the vector, which are determined by a bit mask. The AVX-512F instruction set of the KNL also allows us to use 32-bit integers rather than doubles to store the number of RyR channels in different states. Once architectures with the upcoming AVX-512VL instructions become available, this could be improved further by using 8-bit integers.

The sampling algorithm iteratively builds the cumulative distribution function of the binomial distribution. This requires computing a power function, and up to 100 iterations (the number of RyRs per dyad) of a short loop that includes a division. For the KNC code, this constituted the main computational cost, as KNC does not have a floating point division instruction. However, it does have a fast reciprocal instruction. A single iteration of Newton's method, which can be implemented with two FMA operations, can greatly improve the precision of the fast reciprocal operation. With the default floating point model (*fp-model fast = 1*) the Intel C++ compiler generates about 40 instructions with the *_mm512_div_pd* intrinsic. With the looser floating point model (*fp-model fast = 2*) it generates about half the instructions. In both cases it implements division using the reciprocal instructions.

KNL does have floating point division instructions, which provided a major increase in performance without any code changes. It also has fast reciprocal instructions which are about 4–5 times faster than the division, but getting the same precision requires the addition of at least two FMA operations and a multiplication, which mostly counteracts the gain. We did not observe a noticeable speedup from using this technique and removed it from the final code.

Due to the improvements in the division, the power function became the main bottleneck of the sampling code. One possibility of accelerating it is to use special instructions, since the $pow(x, y) = x^y$ function can be implemented using $pow(x, y) = exp(log(x) * y)$. KNC has fast single precision exponential and logarithm instructions but no double precision versions. KNL has single and double exponential instructions but strangely no logarithm instructions. The double precision exponential instructions suffer from a large loss in precision and unlike the fast reciprocal instructions there is no simple method to improve the precision. Because of this the Intel C++ compiler will not generate these instructions automatically unless special options (e.g. *-fimf-domain-exclusion = 1 -fimf-accuracy-bits = 22*) are used. Thus, instead of relying on special instructions, we exploit the fact that all exponents will be small integers. A generic $pow(double, integer) = x^n$ function can be implemented using repeated squaring. For example $y = x^9$ can be implemented as $t1 = x * x, t2 = t1 * t1, y = x * t2 * t2$. This algorithm has $O(log(n))$ time complexity. Since $n \leq 100$ in our code this means at most seven iterations are needed to implement x^n.

4.3 Random Number Generation

In order to generate the random numbers required by the binomial samplings, we use the `vdRngUniform` function provided by the Intel MKL library [7] at the beginning of every time step. Since `vdRngUniform` is a predefined library function, we can perform no further optimizations on it. Due to the 8 possible state transitions for the RyRs and 2 transitions for the L-type channels, up to 10 random numbers per dyad are used in every time step. To ensure reproducibility of the computed results, random numbers are generated at the beginning of every time step and stored until they are used. Generating the random numbers takes about 32% of the total compute time and is by far the most expensive part of the code. Thus, its relative share has increased compared to KNC [11], which means that potentially a faster random number generation on the KNL should be used.

In addition, reading the random numbers from memory slows down the binomial sampling. A more efficient way is to generate smaller batches of random numbers within the *conditional* sections and then use them immediately. In this manner, we can keep them in cache and avoid storing them in memory altogether. We found that batches of 640 random numbers yielded the best performance for this. Generating smaller batches with `vdRngUniform` tends to be less efficient. However, except for specifically testing this method, we do not use it in our other experiments since it spoils reproducibility and can introduce additional variance in the computation time. It should be used for actual simulations though.

5 Experimental Setup

We run all our experiments on an Intel Xeon Phi 7250 system with 68 cores and 4 hardware threads per core with a base frequency of 1.4 GHz[2]. Codes are compiled with the Intel C++ compiler version 17.0.0. We use OpenMP for shared memory parallelism over all cores, placing 272 threads on the device. For load balancing reasons, the number of cells in all experiments is a multiple of 272. Threads are allocated using the *balanced* affinity. As the cores share essentially no data, different affinities do not change our results when using 272 threads. For scalability experiments, we also test the *compact* affinity.

By default, we configure the Xeon Phi in *quadrant* clustering mode and in *flat* memory mode. We use *numactl –preferred 1* to automatically place as much data as possible in MCDRAM. We also test the *cache* mode. In cache mode, the MCDRAM works as a hardware controlled L3 cache that is shared by all cores. Note that the KNL also possesses a hybrid mode which combines features from cache and flat modes. While this is useful to run multiple codes that are optimized for different modes, for a single code it is unlikely to be faster than the two alternatives, so we omit it in our experiments. Furthermore, since the code is not designed NUMA environments, using the *SNC4* sub-NUMA clustering mode resulted in severe performance degradation. Also, it is not possible to use *numactl –preferred 1* in the sub-NUMA clustering modes. However, it would be possible to use this mode efficiently with multiple MPI processes per KNL.

For most experiments, we run 10,000 time steps which amount to simulating one cardiac beat of 500 ms. The cells are stimulated at $t = 50$ ms. However, there is very little difference in performance between stimulated and resting cells. Due to the large number of dyads, each cell requires approximately 2.78 MB of memory, which limits the number of cells that fit into MCDRAM to about 5000. However, using the DDR4 memory allows for much larger subdomains, at the cost of performance. Thus, for the large instance experiments, we only run 100 time steps. Over 100 executions, the running time of the simulation varied by a maximum of 3%.

To make running times comparable between different simulation durations, we report performance in cell computations per second (CC/s). The total number of cell computations performed in a simulation is simply the number of cells in the experiment times the number of time steps. A single cell computation includes about 6.4 million floating point operations. As observed in [10], the performance of this code is almost completely independent of inter-node communication performance. Thus, it is expected that the speedups measured on a single device in our experiments will also apply to larger clusters.

We compare the KNL with two KNC models, the 57-core Xeon Phi 31S1P running at nonstandard 0.8 GHz, and the 60-core 5110P model running at 1.05 GHz [11]. In addition, we use dual Intel Xeon E5-2692v2 Ivy Bridge CPUs,

[2] Our code generally runs at 1.5 GHz due to the built-in turbo functionality.

each of which has 12 cores (with deactivated Hyperthreading) running at 2.2 GHz for comparison. Both the 31S1P and the Ivy Bridge CPUs are part of the Tianhe-2 supercomputer [10].

6 Performance Experiments

6.1 Code Optimization

In our first set of experiments, we establish the performance baseline and measure the incremental effect of our code optimizations. Since the KNC code is not compatible with the KNL, we use the unmodified CPU code as a baseline. We run a small experiment (272 cells, i.e. one per thread), using high-bandwidth memory only and compare the results with KNC and CPU performance. Results in Fig. 2 show that the KNL doubles the performance w.r.t. the dual CPUs and triples it w.r.t. the KNC.

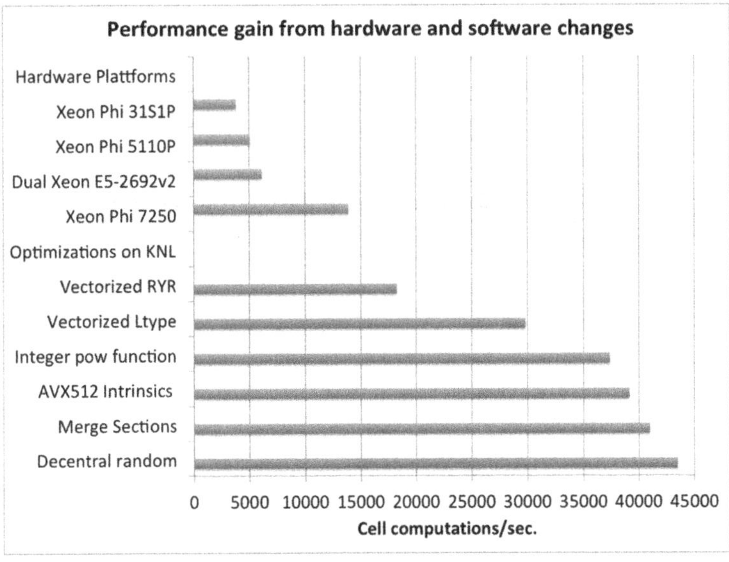

Fig. 2. The blue bars show previously reported performance on the KNC and CPU, and KNL baseline performance using the same CPU code. The red bars show improvements due to the different code optimizations on the Xeon Phi 7250. Performance is given in cell computations per second. The code optimizations are incremental. (Color figure online)

Our next step is to adapt the manually vectorized sampling from the binomial distributions that were originally written for KNC to the KNL. This requires changing a small number of intrinsics. We then apply this code to the opening of RyRs and then L-type channels. The latter provides a greater increase in performance, even though the number of L-type channels is smaller. The reason for this was the inefficient implementation of the power function for the RyR channels. After improving the function as discussed in Sect. 4.2, we observe another significant gain in performance. In addition, the new AVX-512 intrinsics using 32-bit integers rather than doubles to store the number of RyR channels in different states improves performance again slightly. In total, using the correct vectorization tripled the performance over the KNL baseline value.

Small additional improvements are obtained by merging the L-type channel opening probability computation with their binomial distribution sampling, and by merging the intracellular diffusion and reduction operations. Finally, by generating the random numbers used for cell computations in small batches that are stored in cache, we save some additional memory bandwidth, thereby increasing the performance further.

6.2 Strong Scalability

We test the strong scaling properties of the code on the KNL platform, showing performance per core as a function of the number of threads and cores used in Fig. 3. When using a single thread per core, performance increases by a factor of 60 when going from 1 to 68 cores, indicating very good strong scaling behaviour.

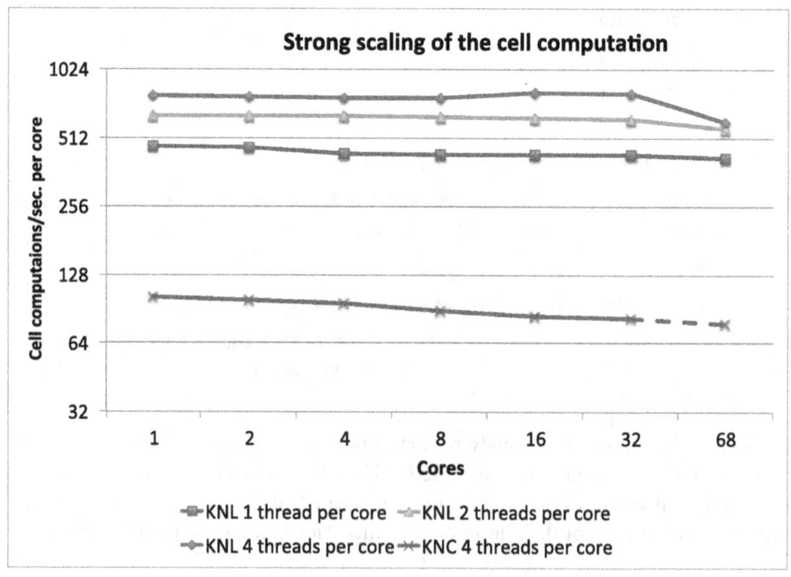

Fig. 3. Strong scaling of the code using a variable number of threads per core. Performance is shown per core. KNC performance is given for comparison. Note that due to numbers of available cores, the KNC value for 68 cores is based on measurements for 118 and 236 threads (marked by a dashed line).

As the KNL supports simultaneous multithreading, the number of hardware threads can exceed the number of available cores. When using 2 threads per core, performance increases by about 40%. For 4 cores, this number is 66%, making it worthwhile to use this feature as long as there are enough cells to balance the load. However, at 68 cores, this is reduced to 44%. When using all cores, the code becomes increasingly memory bound, which implies that the improvement due to multithreading is limited, as it can only hide latency. Still, the overall gain in performance is substantial. For the 5110P KNC, the behavior was similar, but at a much lower level of performance. While in practice there is no reason to use fewer than all available threads, these results imply that on future architectures, this code will mostly benefit from increased memory bandwidth.

6.3 Memory Optimization for Large Instances

So far, we have only considered small instances where the entire problem fits inside the 16 GB MCDRAM. However, when increasing the number of cells further, we can easily exceed this limit. For the KNC, the 8 GB device memory constituted a hard limit. Since our code has little reuse of data within a time step, swapping data from CPU memory into KNC device memory and back via the PCIe bus is generally too slow. The same is true for accelerators such as GPUs using that connection. The KNL on the other hand can access a large amount of DDR4 memory at high speeds (about 90 GB/s of sustained bandwidth). However, the overall performance is substantially lower when using the DDR4 memory alone, as shown in Fig. 4. The difference is about a factor of 4, which is close to the difference in bandwidth between the two memory types. Thus, it is imperative to use the MCDRAM as much as possible.

There are three ways of doing this. The easiest is to configure the KNL to cache mode. In flat mode, data can be placed in MCDRAM automatically by using *numactl –preferred 1*. This provides slightly better performance than cache mode. It also offers 16 GB of additional RAM, since data from DDR4 memory is not duplicated in MCDRAM. For the largest instance in Fig. 4, the lack of memory caused disk swapping in cache mode, severely limiting performance.

The third way is to use the *hbw_malloc* command from the *memkind* library in flat mode, which allows the programmer to decide the objects that should be placed in MCDRAM. We performed the manual placement for an instance consisting of 17,408 cells, i.e. 64 cells per thread, which occupy approximately 50 GB of memory. Since each cell has 10,000 dyads, storing one double value for each dyad takes about 1.4 GB which means that 11 (out of a total of 35) such arrays can be placed in MCDRAM using the *memkind* library. In Fig. 4, we see that for the intended size and beyond, the manual placement delivers the same performance as the automatic placement. For smaller instances however, parts of the MCDRAM are not used, resulting in suboptimal performance.

Selectively placing objects in MCDRAM using the *memkind* library did not increase performance in our experiments, although other codes might benefit from this technique. However, in many typical scientific applications, almost all memory is reserved at the beginning of the program. Thus, a similar placement

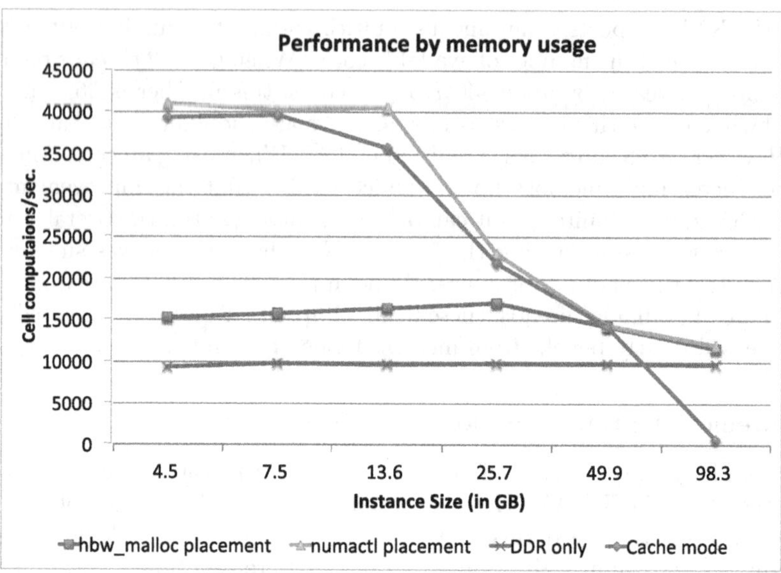

Fig. 4. Performance for different instance sizes under the different MCDRAM usage strategies. *hbw_malloc* placement is optimized for the 49.9 GB instance only. Cache mode starts swapping on the 98.3 GB instance.

can also be obtained by selecting the order in which objects are allocated, since *numactl -preferred 1* places objects in MCDRAM consecutively as long as it is available. The advantage of the latter technique beyond its simplicity is that it automatically adapts to the instance size. In Fig. 4, for the smaller instances, this technique placed a larger fraction of the data in MCDRAM, thereby increasing performance beyond that of the manual placement.

For optimal performance on large instances, one would have to select the optimal combination of memory objects to be placed in MCDRAM. However, even with autotuning, this might be infeasible for codes with a large number of arrays since one would have to test a large number of placement combinations. A more practical approach might be to count accesses to different memory objects and then decide on the placement based on that information. A tool for counting accesses already exists [2], but designing a system for fully automatic placement is beyond the scope of this paper. Thus, for our experiments, we simply selected the variables that are accessed in the most compute expensive kernels for placement in MCDRAM.

7 Conclusion

The KNL generation constitutes a major redesign of the original Xeon Phi, introducing several new features. Our experiments show that for complex scientific codes such as our tissue-scale simulator, these changes pay off. Even without any changes to the code, the KNL outperformed both the KNC Xeon Phi and dual Ivy Bridge Xeon processors by a significant margin. Preliminary experiments showed that this is still true for a dual-socket Xeon E5-2697A v4 Broadwell system. With code optimizations, it ran seven times faster than on the dual Xeon CPUs, at approximately the same efficiency (i.e. ratio of attained vs. peak theoretical FLOPS). Compared with the KNC, we saw roughly a ninefold increase in actual performance. As the theoretical peak performance of the KNL is about three times that of the KNC, the combined changes in hardware and software yielded a threefold increase in efficiency. Our observations are in line with other studies, such as [4,6], which also report good results on the KNL.

While programming the KNL has become significantly easier than the KNC, performance still depends on good parallel programming practices. A proper domain decomposition, vectorization, and memory access optimization are certainly necessary. As of now, the compiler cannot take over this job entirely, even though auto vectorization was very helpful for some of the pure arithmetic sections of the code. Correct use of nontrivial OpenMP parallelization also plays a major role in obtaining high performance.

Furthermore, since the available memory per device constitutes a principal limitation on the size of the simulation, the increased memory per KNL is another welcome addition, as it will eventually make organ-level simulations at very high detail possible. Such simulations would require about 6 PB of memory. Currently the NERSC Cori supercomputer is equipped with 96 + 16 GB of memory per KNL. With 9,688 such devices, this is not enough to simulate a whole heart. The upcoming Aurora supercomputer from the CORAL initiative [1] with more than 50,000 such nodes would be sufficient. Thus, running calcium handling simulations at organ scale will be within reach in the near future.

In parallel to this work, we performed experiments using NVIDIA Kepler K20X GPUs, which yielded more than 20,000 cell computations per second. Since the device has about half the peak memory bandwidth of the KNL, it attains a similarly high level of bandwidth utilization as the KNL. It remains to be seen whether the Pascal and Volta generations of GPUs can match this level of performance. However, even if that is the case, we believe that for memory intensive simulations, the KNL still has the advantage of having fast access to a relatively large amount of DDR4 memory.

References

1. Brueckner, R.: A closer look at Intel's Coral supercomputers coming to Argonne (2015). http://insidehpc.com/2015/04/intel-build-coral-supercomputers-argonne-200-procurement/
2. Cicotti, P., Carrington, L.: ADAMANT: tools to capture, analyze, and manage data movement. Procedia Comput. Sci. **80**, 450–460 (2016)
3. Doerfler, D., Deslippe, J., Williams, S., Oliker, L., Cook, B., Kurth, T., Lobet, M., Malas, T., Vay, J.-L., Vincenti, H.: Applying the roofline performance model to the Intel Xeon Phi Knights landing processor. In: Taufer, M., Mohr, B., Kunkel, J.M. (eds.) ISC High Performance Workshops 2016. LNCS, vol. 9945, pp. 339–353. Springer, Cham (2016). doi:10.1007/978-3-319-46079-6_24

4. Farrell, S., Calafiura, P., Leggett, C., Tsulaia, V., Dotti, A.: Multi-threaded ATLAS simulation on Intel Knights landing processors. Technical report ATL-SOFT-PROC-2017-017, CERN, Geneva, January 2017. http://cds.cern.ch/record/2242857
5. Gaur, N., Rudy, Y.: Multiscale modeling of calcium cycling in cardiac ventricular myocyte: macroscopic consequences of microscopic dyadic function. Biophys. J. **100**(12), 2904–2912 (2011)
6. Heinecke, A., Breuer, A., Bader, M., Dubey, P.: High order seismic simulations on the Intel Xeon Phi processor (Knights landing). In: Kunkel, J.M., Balaji, P., Dongarra, J. (eds.) ISC High Performance 2016. LNCS, vol. 9697, pp. 343–362. Springer, Cham (2016). doi:10.1007/978-3-319-41321-1_18
7. Intel Math Kernel Library – Documentation (2015). https://software.intel.com/en-us/articles/intel-math-kernel-library-documentation
8. Intel Corporation (2017). http://www.intel.com/content/www/us/en/products/compare-products.html?productIds=94033,94034,94035,95830
9. Lan, Q., Gaur, N., Langguth, J., Cai, X.: Towards detailed tissue-scale 3D simulations of electrical activity and calcium handling in the human cardiac ventricle. In: Wang, G., Zomaya, A., Perez, G.M., Li, K. (eds.) ICA3PP 2015, Part III. LNCS, vol. 9530, pp. 79–92. Springer, Cham (2015). doi:10.1007/978-3-319-27137-8_7
10. Langguth, J., Lan, Q., Gaur, N., Cai, X., Wen, M., Zhang, C.Y.: Enabling tissue-scale cardiac simulations using heterogeneous computing on Tianhe-2. In: 2016 IEEE 22nd International Conference on Parallel and Distributed Systems (ICPADS), pp. 843–852, December 2016
11. Langguth, J., Lan, Q., Gaur, N., Cai, X.: Accelerating detailed tissue-scale 3D cardiac simulations using heterogeneous CPU-Xeon Phi computing. Int. J. Parallel Program. **45**(5), 1236–1258 (2016)
12. Nivala, M., de Lange, E., Rovetti, R., Qu, Z.: Computational modeling and numerical methods for spatiotemporal calcium cycling in ventricular myocytes. Front. Physiol. **3**, 114 (2012)
13. O'Hara, T., Virág, L., Varró, A., Rudy, Y.: Simulation of the undiseased human cardiac ventricular action potential: model formulation and experimental validation. PLoS Comput. Biol. **7**(5), e1002061 (2011)
14. Restrepo, J.G., Weiss, J.N., Karma, A.: Calsequestrin-mediated mechanism for cellular calcium transient alternans. Biophys. J. **95**(8), 3767–3789 (2008)
15. Tianhe-2 (Milky Way-2) Supercomputer. http://www.tianhe2.org
16. Williams, G.S., Chikando, A.C., Tuan, H.T.M., Sobie, E.A., Lederer, W., Jafri, M.S.: Dynamics of calcium sparks and calcium leak in the heart. Biophys. J. **101**(6), 1287–1296 (2011)

KART – A Runtime Compilation Library for Improving HPC Application Performance

Matthias Noack[1(✉)], Florian Wende[1], Georg Zitzlsberger[2], Michael Klemm[2], and Thomas Steinke[1]

[1] Zuse Institute Berlin, Berlin, Germany
{noack,wende,steinke}@zib.de
[2] Intel Deutschland GmbH, Feldkirchen, Germany
georg@zitzlsberger.com, michael.klemm@intel.com

Abstract. The effectiveness of ahead-of-time compiler optimization heavily depends on the amount of available information at compile time. Input-specific information that is only available at runtime cannot be used, although it often determines loop counts, branching predicates and paths, as well as memory-access patterns. It can also be crucial for generating efficient SIMD-vectorized code. This is especially relevant for the many-core architectures paving the way to exascale computing, which are more sensitive to code-optimization. We explore the design-space for using input-specific information at compile-time and present KART, a C++ library solution that allows developers to compile, link, and execute code (e.g., C, C++, Fortran) at application runtime. Besides mere runtime compilation of performance-critical code, KART can be used to instantiate the same code multiple times using different inputs, compilers, and options. Other techniques like auto-tuning and code-generation can be integrated into a KART-enabled application instead of being scripted around it. We evaluate runtimes and compilation costs for different synthetic kernels, and show the effectiveness for two real-world applications, HEOM and a WSM6 proxy.

1 Introduction

Many C, C++, and Fortran HPC applications are generalized solutions for their respective domains. They typically implement a wide range of algorithms that are meant to be applicable for many different workloads or combinations of input sets. Whilst the applications grow with adding more methods and features there is also a growing demand for applying a subset of methods to restricted workloads. Such use cases do not require the full complexity and flexibility of the original implementations. Hence users strive for optimizing their (limited) workloads by tuning the implementations. This starts with algorithmic optimizations, delivering different implementations of the original algorithm, such as reducing dimensions or replacing algorithms that work better for smaller problem sizes. To give a few examples, for the WSM6 proxy code [7], the authors provided constants at compile time and achieved a more than 40% performance gain on the

J.M. Kunkel et al. (Eds.): ISC High Performance Workshops 2017, LNCS 10524, pp. 389–403, 2017.
https://doi.org/10.1007/978-3-319-67630-2_29

Intel® Xeon Phi™ coprocessor (former codename "Knights Corner", KNC). For the DL_MESO code it was recently demonstrated [19] that if increasingly more source code constants are known at compile time a performance improvement of more than five times can be achieved by enabling better SIMD optimizations for the compiler's auto-vectorizer.

At some point in this process, implementations in source code are specific enough to be further optimized by compilers. Compilers typically do not apply algorithmic optimizations that change the semantics, but they have a rich set of optimizations to enhance code generation. However, compiler optimizations for C, C++, and Fortran can only be applied for the provided algorithms in the application code. They need to be general and adhere to the specification of the programming language. Knowledge about the runtime context of a unit of code would allow to optimize for specific memory access strides, eliminate conditional code, or apply workload-dependent loop transformations.

A typical approach to remedy this is to apply multi-versioning, that is, generating multiple specialized instantiations of the same function, loop, or code fragment. This can be achieved by a programmer using dedicated implementations, like C++ template specializations, or preprocessor macros, for example. Compilers can also emit versioned code to handle aligned versus unaligned data, to create different code paths for different instructions sets (e.g., Streaming SIMD Extensions and Advanced Vector Extensions), or to avoid SIMD vectorization for too small loop trip counts, to just name a few. Because multi-versioning can dramatically increase the code size, compilers usually only generate a few code versions and provide a general code path as fallback. For the large combinatorial space spanned by the potential inputs of an HPC application, multi-versioning becomes ineffective.

Programmers can try to help the compiler by adding compilation hints (e.g., pragmas/directives or attributes) to limit the amount of code versions. But even if a programmer provides different implementations there are limits. Optimizations can only be applied for a small set of categories of workloads, and also lead to code size increase which can make an implementation harder to maintain. While it is quite simple to provide different optimizations for different dimensionality of input data sets, it is much harder to do so for different memory access patterns, access strides, or loop trip counts. There are far too many different goals to optimize for, and grouping them into categories for directed optimization is hard.

The main contributions of this work are the exploration of the design space for exploiting runtime data for compiler optimization, a light-weight, flexible runtime-compilation framework (KART), and its evaluation. Our solution is to recompile algorithms (kernels) during the runtime of an application, thereby optimizing within the current context of kernel execution. This especially allows to optimize for values that manifest as constants during runtime but were not known at compile time. KART is general enough to benefit a wide range of applications without being limited to a certain back-end. The approach is particularly relevant for many-core architectures like the Intel Xeon Phi (co)processor, whose microarchitecture is more sensitive to code-optimizations.

For frequently used kernels, we show that the improved optimization outweighs the runtime compilation overhead. We also regard this approach as a solution for OpenMP* [16] applications to benefit from the same dynamic recompilation advantages that OpenCL* [9] and CUDA* [12] provide.

2 Related Work

Here, we exclude work which is focused on just-in-time compilation for interpreter or scripting languages (e.g., Python, Perl, Lua). We are aware that Java and Microsoft's .NET Framework rely on JIT compilation for high-speed code execution, but both have still a small representation in the HPC domain.

The LLVM compiler infrastructure [11] includes a JIT code generation system which supports various CPU architectures, and provides a foundation for just-in-time compilation projects. For the QCD application domain, the QDP-JIT/LLVM approach [8], which extends the ideas of QDP-JIT/PTX [20], uses C++ expression templates to implement LLVM IR code generators that emit executable code via the LLVM JIT component. In Julia, the language design is combined with the high-performance LLVM-based JIT compiler [3,4]. This enables code generation that comes close to the performance of a C implementation.

The LIBXSMM library [5] for small dense matrix-matrix multiplications enables static and JIT code generation for Intel® Xeon® processors and Intel Xeon Phi (co)processors. While the basic ideas of LIBXSMM are similar to our proposal in that it specifically compiles kernels for a particular target architecture, it only supports *sgemm* and *dgemm* with restricted *alpha* and *beta* inputs.

In the context of MPI communication, Schneider et al. [18] demonstrate that through runtime compilation of (un)pack functions for non-contiguous data in MPI an order of magnitude better performance can be achieved over the interpretation scheme found in today's MPI implementations. In contrast to the specialized solutions above, our approach is more general, as it applies to arbitrary code, whole source files or just subsets, and supports different C, C++, and Fortran compilers that are common in the HPC domain. Additional changes to code and external dependencies are kept flat thanks to KART being lightweight and easy to use.

3 Design Space

Recompile Everything. The most straight-forward approach to using input-specific data as compile-time constants would be to simply recompile the whole application for each set of input data. It completely avoids the complexity of additional compilation at runtime and enables the compiler to apply cross-module optimization techniques like whole-program optimization. However, large parts of the code are typically not performance critical and recompiling them would introduce a prohibitive compilation overhead that grows with the size of the code base and optimization levels. For large codes with compile times in the range of hours, this is a significant impact on time-to-solution and renders quality assurance procedures less feasible. An important question for this approach is: How to acquire the needed data from the input at build time? Typically, reading and parsing of input data is done at runtime during the initialization phase. So some application code has to be executed to get the data required for building the application. To break this circular dependency, an input parser would be required to analyse the input data and to provide the necessary constant values before the build process can be started. A concern for some developers, e.g., of commercial codes, might also be that binary releases of applications (or libraries) would still require to contain the runtime-compiled code sections as source.

Pre-instantiate Code for All Cases. A different approach would be to prepare for a potential and classified set of inputs. Performance critical functions would be instantiated or specialized multiple times with different classes of compile-time constants when compiling the application. This is similar to what some compilers already do when generating multiple versions of functions or loops, e.g. to provide both a scalar and a vectorized version. Such multi-versioning is bound by combinatorial effects of the parameter space and for all input variables their numerical domain needs to be known at compile time. One manual implementation approach is to use C++ templates with desired constants as template parameters, i.e. classification of values. Those can be explicitly instantiated to collect the resulting function pointers in a map with their classification as the key. Additionally, a fall-back implementation without compile-time constants but a set of additional parameters could be provided. At runtime, the calling code uses actual values from the input to select the appropriate function template specialization, or a fall-back if no suitable instantiation was found. For dimensions of domains this might be applicable as those are typically limited. However, optimizing for different sizes becomes infeasible if their values cannot be restricted to a small amount of classes to define the different specializations.

Call a Compiler Library at Runtime. Another solution that is already commonly used and inspired this work is OpenCL that aims for portability across heterogeneous compute devices, such as CPUs, GPGPUs, Intel Xeon Phi (co)processors, or FPGAs. It divides the application into host code for a host processor and device code that runs on a compute device and is compiled at runtime. This enables portability, but can also be used for passing runtime-data from the host program into the compilation of the device code. Previous work has shown that there can be a performance benefit when compile-time constants are known to the OpenCL compiler [6]. Since recently, Nvidia's CUDA GPGPU framework provides similar means [15]. Porting an existing (HPC) application to OpenCL is a major effort and requires rewriting code using OpenCL's kernel language, explicitly managing kernel invocations and memory transfers between host and compute device.

OpenMP supports heterogeneity but is limited to one code version and does not provide runtime compilation. C, C++, or Fortran compilers do not expose a library API that could be used in an OpenCL-like fashion. LLVM with its modular architecture would be a viable basis to implement such a mechanism. The major drawback of an LLVM-based solution is the limitation to mere LLVM optimization abilities. OpenMP support of LLVM is still not complete, although catching up fast [1,2].

Call Arbitrary Compilers at Runtime. A more abstract and flexible solution is to provide an API to use any installed command-line compiler from within the application and then incorporate the resulting object code into the running program. Being close to the OpenCL model, it yields the highest flexibility, as any compiler, even for different languages, can be used. It can defer the compilation of performance critical-code sections until execution time and apply the best-optimizing compiler for a specific code fragment and target architecture, or to multi-version a kernel using different compilers and apply auto-tuning. Also different (hand-written) implementations of the same kernel can be used. As such, optimization is not only defined by compiler capabilities and varying compile-time constants, but also by the user at algorithmic level. Kernels can be supplied in languages different from the one chosen for the host application, which increases the flexibility, e.g., by using C SIMD intrinsics within a Fortran application. This is the approach we have chosen for the solution presented in this paper.

4 The KART Library

4.1 Design and Implementation

KART provides application developers with the means to compile and use pieces of code at runtime with minimal overhead and maximal flexibility. KART resembles a simple build system with a library interface. It offers a slim API to compile a code fragment given either as a text string or a source file, and to call the result after compiling the code. KART is implemented in C++ using several Boost libraries [17] and provides APIs for C, C++, and Fortran, so far. The intended flexibility to use any compiler requires the invocation of command-line compilers and linkers in a separate process at runtime to create a shared library from a given source. Subsequently, the resulting library is linked to the running program via `dlopen()`, and the contained functions can be accessed and executed using their (symbolic) name. Constants can be integrated into the runtime-compiled code by either generating the corresponding lines before passing the code to KART, or can be specified using compiler command line options (e.g., `-DNAME=VALUE`). Figure 1 illustrates the working principle of KART.

A *toolset* abstraction encapsulates the specification of a compiler and linker command, as well as different sets of options. Toolsets are defined in small configuration files. A default toolset file can be set via an environment variable. Once a toolset object is created, additional options can be specified.

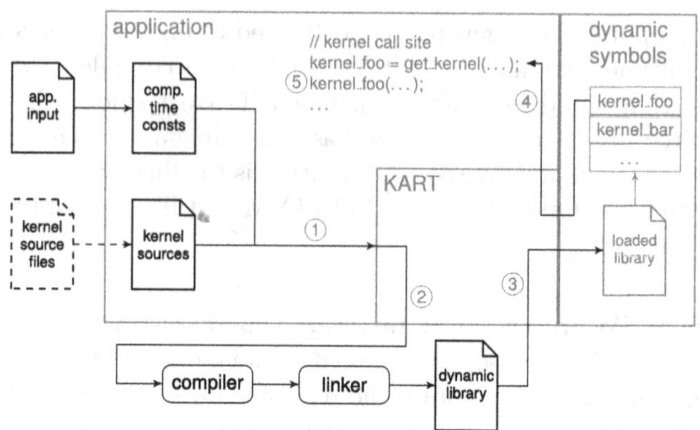

Fig. 1. Schematic of KART: (1) Compile-time constants derived from the input, and kernel source code are passed to KART. (2) KART starts a system compiler and linker to create a dynamically linked library. (3) The library is dynamically linked into the application. (4) The application queries KART using the kernel's function name to get a callable function pointer. (5) The kernel is invoked.

The second main abstraction is the *program*, which is constructed from either a string or a file containing the source code. The program is then built using a toolset. Once built, callable function pointers can be acquired by specifying a name, and optionally a signature to ensure type-safety in C++. Already built programs can be rebuild with a different toolset. This is more efficient than creating new program objects from the same source. This allows applying many configurations to the same code, e.g. for benchmarking or auto-tuning codes, or in cases when compiled-in data changes, like loop trip counts or sizes of data structures after a load-balancing step.

In order to cover the most relevant languages for HPC applications, there is also an API for C and Fortran. The C API is a wrapper around the C++ implementation that uses opaque handles and functions, instead of objects and methods. The Fortran interface is a set of bindings for the C API using the Fortran 2003 `BIND` attribute and `iso_c_binding` intrinsic module.

Internally, KART uses the POSIX calls `dlopen()`, `dlsym()`, and `dlclose()` for interfacing with the generated shared libraries. This allows the use of different compilers and even languages within the same application—as long as the resulting libraries are binary compatible. The application, as well as the runtime-compile code can be still statically linked. There are some ABI-based constraints, especially when combining compilers of different major versions, but we have not found any issues when combining the typical GNU, Intel, and LLVM/clang compilers for C, C++, and Fortran. Whereas C and C++ have a fixed ABI on Linux, it can be problematic to mix different Fortran compilers. It is recommended to use the Fortran ISO-C bindings to have a common ABI.

GNU-compiled C/C++ applications can use the most recent Intel® C++ Compiler to generate performance-critical code using its vectorization capabili-

```
#include "kart/kart.hpp"

// signature type
using my_kernel_t = double(*)(double, double);
const char my_kernel_src[] = R"kart_src(
extern "C" {

// original function
double my_kernel(double a, double b)
{ return a * b * CONST; }

})kart_src"; // close raw string literal

int main(int argc, char** argv)
{
  // create program
  kart::program my_prog(my_kernel_src);
  // create default toolset
  kart::toolset ts;
  // append a constant definiton (runtime value)
  ts.append_compiler_options(" -DCONST=5.0");
  // build program using toolset
  my_prog.build(ts)
  // get the kernel
  auto my_kernel =
       my_prog.get_kernel<my_kernel_t>("my_kernel");

  /* ... application code ... */

  // call the kernel as usual
  double res = my_kernel(3.0, 5.0);

  /* ... application code ...  */
}
```

Fig. 2. This example shows how to embed a kernel as source code, and compile it at runtime using KART. The highlighted lines show what is needed to introduce KART. Raw string literals, as provided by C++11 can be used to embed source code without having to escape some characters.

ties in addition to the input-specific compile-time constants. Fortran codes could use a C/C++ compiler to facilitate manual vectorization for kernels via C SIMD intrinsics. A benchmark or auto-tuning code could use KART to automatically evaluate different compilers and sets of options, e.g., for different optimization levels, pre-fetching settings, or numerical precision levels.

4.2 Usage

KART was designed with ease of use in mind. Figure 2 shows a simple example, where the function `my_kernel` is compiled at runtime. For a single function, wrapping the original code into a raw string literal, as shown in the example above, is sufficient. Using an `extern "C"` block makes sure the kernel's name does not get mangled by the compiler and can be used directly. However, if the needed source code already is a separate compilation unit or gets larger, it is more convenient to use source files instead of embedded strings.

There are two ways to specify dependencies and other compile/link options: toolset configuration-files, intended for the compiler and the host-specific part (often non-portable), and methods called at runtime for the application-specific part. This way, the source code remains portable.

For existing code, the most convenient way of integrating runtime compilation would be a directive-based approach, where code is simply annotated as runtime compilation target. A mechanism like the one provided by KART could become part of a widely accepted and standardized programming model like OpenMP in a future version. However, this would mean giving up the flexibility to use any compiler and the library-only implementation.

Adapting Existing Code. When adapting a code, the best method is identifying hotspots whose index computations, memory access patterns, loop counts, and branching predicates depend on input data. Once identified, it can be recompiled using compile-time constants for a few inputs to estimate the potential gain before restructuring the code. The runtime gain determines an upper bound for the acceptable compilation overhead. The process is very similar to adapting an application for offloading to an accelerator—without the need to rewrite kernels in another language and optimize them for the accelerator's architecture. The intrusiveness of incorporating runtime kernel compilation into an existing code base depends on the current code structure, as the build-time and run-time compiled source needs to be separated. For a well-structured code base, this means identifying the compilation units and adding the KART API calls into the application's initialization phase. For the Hexciton benchmark, 23 new lines of code were added and the interface of the benchmarking function was modified.

Most build systems provide a verbose mode that prints out the compile and link commands used. That is the natural starting point to generate a toolset specification for KART that includes necessary flags and dependencies. In a second step, the dependencies can be minimized, and compile flags further optimized to improve compilation and runtime of the kernel, respectively.

We successfully tested KART within the restricted compute-node software-environment of a Cray XC40 supercomputer. The following sections describe how KART can be used in different HPC application patterns.

Coprocessors. Applications for the Intel Xeon Phi coprocessor often use an offload programming model like OpenMP or Intel's LEO (Language Extensions for Offload). In such a setting, KART can be called prior to the offload to cross-compile the coprocessor code leveraging the better single-thread performance of the host CPU. Within a more flexible offloading framework, like HAM Offload [14], a reverse offload from a native coprocessor application to the host can be used to offload the compilation, even remotely over a fabric.

OpenMP. OpenMP can be used within KART-compiled kernels or higher up in the calling tree. We have successfully tested both. Code that is built at runtime using KART is and behaves like a shared library. So as with other libraries that make use of OpenMP, the developer has to make sure that there is no conflict between the OpenMP implementation used in the application code and the one used inside the library. Other than that, there are no known limitations.

MPI. For large distributed jobs, solely using KART on the node level is the easiest way, but not always the best. It is beneficial in cases where every node uses different constants, for example if loop counts for local partitions of an irregular grid are used. In cases where every node does the same work, there is potential for optimization. The situation can be used for an auto-tuning step, where different compilation options or kernel variants are built and timed, followed by an exchange of the timings and the best-performing kernels. Ranks can exchange their compilation results via a distributed file system or by transferring the generated binaries as messages. KART can also use wrapper compilers if the runtime-compiled code uses MPI directly. A problem with commercial compilers is the limited number of licenses and their management. It is either impossible, or at least not desirable, to check out thousands of licenses. For these cases, compilation needs to be limited to a few ranks, or be performed using a prologuẽjob.

Auto-tuning. KART can be used to easily implement auto-tuning and also to complement it orthogonally. Within an application, the use-cases are slightly different: KART can address given runtime-values, not subject to tuning, by making them a compile-time known value enabling better optimization. Where auto-tuning typically generates multiple versions for a wide variety of options/inputs with later run-time selection, KART can also generate the code for just the current scenario at runtime. Beside the described HPC-relevant patterns and use cases, the availability of a general runtime compilation mechanism can be exploited in more sophisticated ways. There is no fixed pattern. For instance, instead of just using compile-time constants or different compilers, languages, and options for existing code, KART can be used as a back-end for code generators and domain-specific languages.

5 Evaluation

We exemplify the potential of runtime kernel compilation with two simple and synthetic benchmarks, and demonstrate the achieved speed-ups for two real world applications. The benchmark systems are an Intel Xeon Phi 7210 (Knights Landing/KNL), and a dual socket Intel Xeon E5-2630 v3 (Haswell/HSW) node. The used software versions are: Intel OpenCL Runtime 16.1.1, Intel C++ Compiler 17.0.2, GCC 6.3.0, and Clang 4.0.0.

Runtime Compilation. Runtime compilation introduces overhead and it is important to understand the trade-off between this overhead and kernel speed-up first. The overhead introduced by KART is largely determined by the runtime of the invoked compiler and linker. The speed-up of the runtime-compiled kernel (without the compile time) over the reference kernel is $s_b = t_{\text{ref}}/t_{\text{kart}}$, with $s_b > 1$ for $t_{\text{ref}} > t_{\text{kart}}$. It is an upper bound for the actual speed-up that includes the compile time, which is $s = \frac{n \cdot t_{\text{ref}}}{n \cdot t_{\text{kart}} + t_{\text{compile}}}$ with n being the number of kernel calls. Numerator and denominator are two linear functions for the respective overall runtime cost of the reference and KART-compiled kernel. For given run and compile times, there is an n_c where both functions cross and $s = 1$. For every $n > n_c$, there is an actual application speed-up, asymptotically approaching s_b. Runtime compilation techniques pay off when the accumulated runtime savings of all kernel calls exceed the runtime compilation cost.

Figure 3 shows the compilation cost using Intel OpenCL as a reference and KART with different compilers. These are roughly the same timings as measured when executing the command lines for compiling and linking generated by KART by manually typing them into a console terminal—the cost of the KART API itself is negligible. The linking step took roughly two thirds of the time. The timings for the empty kernels show that there is a large constant cost coming with the command line compilers. This includes starting processes and lots of file operations when handling dependencies like a large set of header and library files, all not present in OpenCL. A library interface to existing compilers together with a set of small headers and libraries specifically optimized for compilation time could improve the situation. For commercial compilers, additional time is lost for fetching licenses from a file system or network. Caching the compilation results between application runs could mitigate these costs if the actual reuse is high.

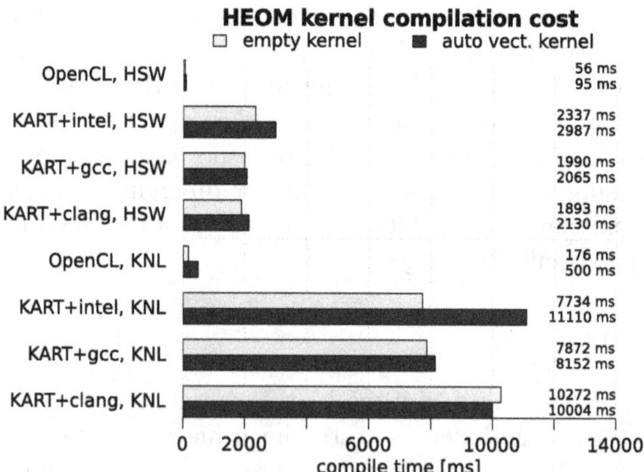

Fig. 3. Runtime compilation overhead for the HEOM Hexciton and an empty kernel. There is a high constant cost for any compilation regardless of the code size. Only the Intel compiler adds significant cost to the empty kernel, but also generates the fastest auto vectorized code. OpenCL's compiler is two orders of magnitude faster, due to the library ABI and less indirectly included headers. The Xeon Phi (KNL) values suffer from the lower single thread performance.

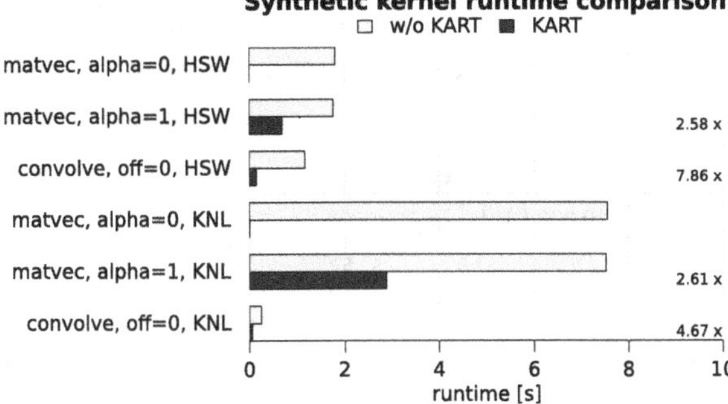

Fig. 4. Speed-ups for two synthetic kernels *matvec* (single threaded) and *convolve* (OpenMP). The speed-ups do not include the compilation overhead, as it this would require defining a somehow "realistic" number of kernel calls. A compile-time known *alpha=0* entirely removed the computation loops. The average compilation times for each kernel ranges from 0.87 to 0.93 s on the Xeon (HSW) and 3.43 to 3.54 s on the Xeon Phi processor (KNL).

For all use-cases that only need a single runtime build per kernel during initialization, a few seconds are tolerable, given that the kernel runtimes for computational hotspots can easily add up to many minutes or even hours during large production runs. For more dynamic use cases, where kernels are regularly rebuilt as values of compile-time constants need to be adapted, we recommend profiling the performance gain per kernel invocation, the compilation cost, and the frequency of recompilation. The large constant cost of each compiler invocation can be distributed among multiple kernels by using a single program object that aggregates all sources.

Synthetic Kernels. The potential of runtime kernel compilation highly depends on the kernel itself and the context it is invoked in. It also depends on the used compiler, compiler options, and processor architecture. We have selected two simple kernels to highlight the principal usefulness of runtime compilation for HPC kernels: (a) a one-dimensional linear convolution with an offset into the input vector (for different threads), and (b) a matrix vector multiplication with scaling (*alpha*). To give the compiler's optimizer some optimization headroom, we assume the scaling to be 0.0 or 1.0, and matrix a to have just one column. This simulates cases where the compiler can remove invariant statements and/or loops. Both kernels have been compiled via KART and as ordinary C functions with all parameters as arguments (e.g., *alpha*, *rows*, and *cols* for kernel *matvec*). Figure 4 shows the results. For the *matvec* kernel the compiler was able to entirely eliminate the loops for *alpha=0* and even showed a 2.6× kernel speed-up for *alpha=1* where the inner-most loop was removed since there is only one column of matrix a. For the *convolve* kernel, having *offset*, *input size*, and *kernel size* known by the compiler could improve kernel runtimes by 7.9×.

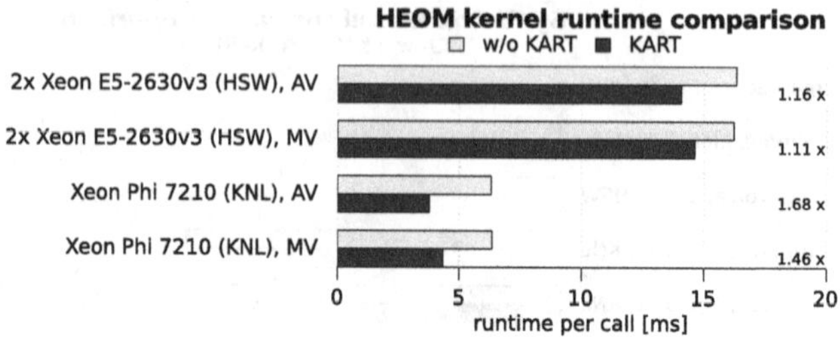

Fig. 5. Runtimes and speed-ups achieved by using KART for the OpenMP version of the HEOM benchmark. Matrix size and number of matrices read from the input are used as compile-time constants during runtime compilation. AV is automatic and MV is manual vectorization. Amortization of compile time requires 1321 and 15117 calls on Xeon (HSW) and Xeon Phi (KNL), respectively. Typical application runs need 10^3 to 10^6 calls.

HEOM. HEOM is a short for Hierarchical Equations of Motion, which is a mathematical approach to solving open quantum system models of, e.g., photoactive molecular complexes. For the GPU HEOM OpenCL implementation [10], a detailed case study [13] including a benchmark is publicly available. It compares a variety of implementations of the Hexciton kernel. We integrated KART into the OpenMP version of the benchmark to build the different kernel variants at runtime and enable the use of input-specific constants at kernel compile time. Two constants, the matrix dimension and the number of matrices of the central HEOM data-structure, are most relevant for the memory access pattern and the loop counts. Figure 5 shows the results. The plotted values are from the best-performing kernel variants using the Intel C++ Compiler. The highest speed-up of 2.6× was observed for Clang on the Xeon CPU with the manually vectorized kernel, but the absolute runtime was still slower than that of the code emitted by the Intel C++ Compiler. The Intel Xeon Phi (co)processor benefits much more from the compiler optimizations. Its light-weight cores and the missing L3 cache require better optimized code than the Haswell architecture. The compile-time overhead is not relevant as production runs typically take several hours.

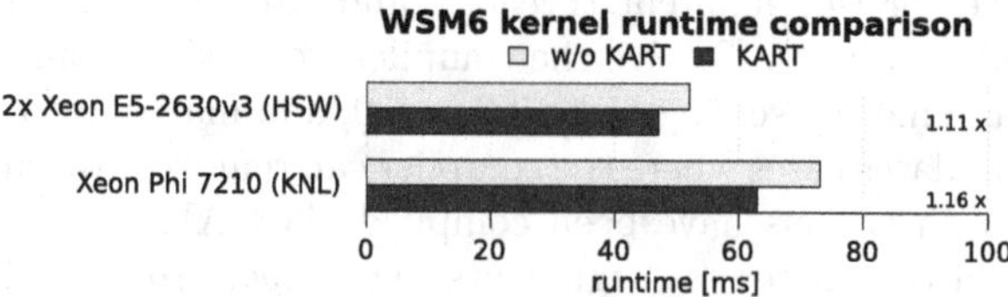

Fig. 6. Runtime comparison and speed-ups for using runtime compilation with the WSM6 Kernel on the Xeon (HSW) and Xeon Phi (KNL). Average compilation times are 3.24 s on the Xeon (HSW) and 20.13 s on the Xeon Phi processor (KNL).

WSM6 Proxy Code. We integrated KART into the WSM6 proxy code [7] written in Fortran. WSM6—the WRF Single Moment 6-class Microphysics schema—is part of the Weather Research and Forecast (WRF) model, widely used for weather prediction. The original benchmark uses the C preprocessor and a set of Perl scripts to modify the source code to generate a version with compile time constants for every run. This is no longer necessary when using KART. Our modified Kernel uses the preprocessor only to simplify the build process at runtime. For the WSM6 proxy code, KART achieved a speed-up of 1.16× for the slightly modified kernel (see Fig. 6).

6 Conclusion and Outlook

Studies on the optimization of HPC workloads for many-core CPUs demonstrate the impact of available constants on the optimization capabilities during the compilation step. The more parameters affecting the data layouts and loop/branching structures can be provided, the better the compiler is able to optimize. Thus, compiling kernels at run-time for the context of their invocation can yield shorter time-to-solutions.

We have presented KART, a flexible and easy to use framework that allows runtime compilation with a variety of C, C++, and Fortran command line compilers. It supports dynamic re-compilation during program execution if kernel parameters such as data sizes are changed, e.g., after load-balancing steps between nodes or to adjust for different input data sets. For applications with irregularly distributed data across the compute nodes, our approach can support individually optimized kernels for each node.

We have demonstrated the effectiveness of our solution for synthetic and real-world kernels. The approach is particularly effective on the Intel Xeon Phi (co)processor, which represents a many-core architecture whose successors are a likely technology for exascale systems. The convenience and efficiency of runtime compilation could be further improved if it were integrated into a programming model like OpenMP or if compiler vendors were providing an—ideally standardized—API to their tools. KART is under continued development and available on GitHub (https://github.com/noma/kart). We appreciate feedback.

Acknowledgments. This work is partially supported by Intel Corporation within the "Research Center for Many-core High-Performance Computing" (Intel PCC) at ZIB. We thank the "The North-German Supercomputing Alliance - HLRN" for providing us access to the HLRN-III production system 'Konrad' and the Cray TDS system with Intel KNL nodes.

consult other information and performance tests to assist you in fully evaluating your contemplated purchases, including the performance of that product when combined with other products. For more information go to http://www.intel.com/performance.

Intel's compilers may or may not optimize to the same degree for non-Intel microprocessors for optimizations that are not unique to Intel microprocessors. These optimizations include SSE2, SSE3, and SSSE3 instruction sets and other optimizations. Intel does not guarantee the availability, functionality, or effectiveness of any optimization on microprocessors not manufactured by Intel. Microprocessor-dependent optimizations in this product are intended for use with Intel microprocessors. Certain optimizations not specific to Intel microarchitecture are reserved for Intel microprocessors. Please refer to the applicable product User and Reference Guides for more information regarding the specific instruction sets covered by this notice.

References

1. OpenMP Compilers, September 2016. http://openmp.org/wp/openmp-compilers/
2. OpenMP®: Support for the OpenMP language, April 2016. http://openmp.llvm.org/
3. Bezanson, J., Edelman, A., Karpinski, S., Shah, V.B.: Julia: a fresh approach to numerical computing, November 2014
4. Bezanson, J., Karpinski, S., Shah, V.B., Edelman, A.: Julia: a fast dynamic language for technical computing. http://julialang.org
5. Heinecke, A., Henry, G., Hutchinson, M., Pabst, H.: LIBXSMM: accelerating small matrix multiplications by runtime code generation. In: Proceedings of the International Conference for High Performance Computing, Networking, Storage and Analysis, pp. 84:1–84:11, SC 2016. IEEE Press, Piscataway (2016). http://dl.acm.org/citation.cfm?id=3014904.3015017
6. Heinecke, A., Klemm, M., Pflüger, D., Bode, A., Bungartz, H.J.: Extending a highly parallel data mining algorithm to the Intel® many integrated core architecture. In: Alexander, M., et al. (eds.) Parallel Processing Workshops, Euro-Par 2011. LNCS, vol. 7156. Springer, Heidelberg (2011)
7. Henderson, T., Michalakes, J., Gokhale, I., Jha, A.: Chapter 2 - Numerical weather prediction optimization. In: Reinders, J., Jeffers, J. (eds.) High Performance Parallelism Pearls, pp. 7–23. Morgan Kaufmann, Boston (2015)
8. Joó, B.: LLVM and QDP-JIT. In: iXPUG Workshop, Berkeley (2015). https://www.ixpug.org/events/ixpug-annual-meeting-2015
9. Khronos OpenCL Working Group: The OpenCL Specification, Version 2.2. https://www.khronos.org/registry/cl/specs/opencl-2.2.pdf
10. Kreisbeck, C., Kramer, T., Aspuru-Guzik, A.: Scalable high-performance algorithm for the simulation of exciton dynamics. Application to the light-harvesting Complex II in the presence of resonant vibrational modes. J. Chem. Theory Comput. **10**(9), 4045–4054 (2014). pMID: 26588548. http://dx.doi.org/10.1021/ct500629s
11. Lattner, C., Adve, V.: LLVM: a compilation framework for lifelong program analysis and transformation. In: CGO, pp. 75–88, San Jose, CA, USA, March 2004. llvm.org
12. Nickolls, J., Buck, I., Garland, M., Skadron, K.: Scalable parallel programming with CUDA. Queue **6**(2), 40–53 (2008). http://doi.acm.org/10.1145/1365490.1365500
13. Noack, M., Wende, F., Oertel, K.D.: Chapter 19 - OpenCL: there and back again. In: Reinders, J., Jeffers, J. (eds.) High Performance Parallelism Pearls, pp. 355–378. Morgan Kaufmann, Boston (2015)

14. Noack, M., Wende, F., Steinke, T., Cordes, F.: A unified programming model for intra- and inter-node offloading on xeon phi clusters. In: International Conference for High Performance Computing, Networking, Storage and Analysis, SC 2014, New Orleans, LA, USA, 16–21 November 2014, pp. 203–214 (2014). http://dx.doi.org/10.1109/SC.2014.22
15. NVIDIA: NVRTC - CUDA Runtime Compilation User Guide. http://docs.nvidia.com/cuda/pdf/NVRTC_User_Guide.pdf
16. OpenMP Architecture Review Board: OpenMP Application Program Interface, Version 4.5 (2015). http://www.openmp.org/
17. Schling, B.: The Boost C++ Libraries. XML Press, Fort Collins (2011)
18. Schneider, T., Kjolstad, F., Hoefler, T.: MPI datatype processing using runtime compilation. In: Proceedings of the 20th European MPI Users' Group Meeting, pp. 19–24. ACM, September 2013
19. Siso, S.: DL_MESO Code Modernization. Intel Xeon Phi Users Group (IXPUG). IXPUG Workshop, Ostrava, March 2016
20. Winter, F.T., Clark, M.A., Edwards, R.G., Joó, B.: A framework for lattice QCD calculations on GPUs. In: Proceedings of the 2014 IEEE 28th International Parallel and Distributed Processing Symposium, pp. 1073–1082, IPDPS 2014 (2014). http://dx.doi.org/10.1109/IPDPS.2014.112

Performance Evaluation of NWChem Ab-Initio Molecular Dynamics (AIMD) Simulations on the Intel® Xeon Phi™ Processor

Eric J. Bylaska[1](✉), Mathias Jacquelin[2], Wibe A. de Jong[2], Jeff R. Hammond[3], and Michael Klemm[4]

[1] Environmental Molecular Sciences Laboratory, Pacific Northwest National Laboratory, Richland, WA, USA
eric.bylaska@pnnl.gov
[2] Computational Research Division, Lawrence Berkeley National Laboratory, Berkeley, CA, USA
{mjacquelin,wadejong}@lbl.gov
[3] Data Center Group, Intel Corporation, Portland, OR, USA
jeff.r.hammond@intel.com
[4] Software and Services Group, Intel Deutschland GmbH, Feldkirchen, Germany
michael.klemm@intel.com

Abstract. Ab-initio Molecular Dynamics (AIMD) methods are an important class of algorithms, as they enable scientists to understand the chemistry and dynamics of molecular and condensed phase systems while retaining a first-principles-based description of their interactions. Many-core architectures such as the Intel® Xeon Phi™ processor are an interesting and promising target for these algorithms, as they can provide the computational power that is needed to solve interesting problems in chemistry. In this paper, we describe the efforts of refactoring the existing AIMD plane-wave method of NWChem from an MPI-only implementation to a scalable, hybrid code that employs MPI and OpenMP to exploit the capabilities of current and future many-core architectures. We describe the optimizations required to get close to optimal performance for the multiplication of the tall-and-skinny matrices that form the core of the computational algorithm. We present strong scaling results on the complete AIMD simulation for a test case that simulates 256 water molecules and that strong-scales well on a cluster of 1024 nodes of Intel Xeon Phi processors. We compare the performance obtained with a cluster of dual-socket Intel® Xeon® E5–2698v3 processors.

Keywords: Xeon Phi · Many-core · Chemistry · AIMD · Ab-initio · Molecular dynamics

1 Introduction

One of the more computationally demanding scientific simulations used extensively on today's large-scale parallel computers is Ab-initio Molecular Dynamics

J.M. Kunkel et al. (Eds.): ISC High Performance Workshops 2017, LNCS 10524, pp. 404–418, 2017.
https://doi.org/10.1007/978-3-319-67630-2_30

(AIMD) [4,5,7,9,10,13,14,20,25,28]. In this type of simulation the motions of the atoms are simulated using Newton's laws in which the forces on the atoms are calculated directly from the electronic Schrödinger equation, or more specifically in this work, the Kohn-Sham Density Functional Theory (DFT) equations [18,24]. These simulations are computationally expensive because the DFT equations, which are already expensive in their own right for systems beyond a few atoms, are solved at every time integration step in the simulation.

For an AIMD simulation to be viable for the scientist, each step in the full DFT calculation must take the order of a second or less [5] to complete. The need for such fast DFT calculations is driven primarily by the fact that the time step of a conventional AIMD simulation can be quite small (~ 0.2 femtoseconds $= 2 \times 10^{-16}$ s) along with the fact that the length of the simulation will need be at least 10 picoseconds. For many chemical processes of interest, the simulations will need to run on the order of nanoseconds (10^{-9} s and larger). A scientific simulation of about 10 picoseconds requires solving 500,000 DFT calculations in sequence, which takes about 5.8 days assuming that a single DFT calculation (time-step) completes within one second, about 50.8 days with a 10-second time step, and about 1/2 year with a 30 second time step. Compared to merely optimizing a molecule or crystal, which require at most a few 100 evaluations, this is extremely expensive.

It should be noted that, for carrying out geometry optimizations only, the need for extremely fast DFT calculations is not as important as calculating larger numbers of atoms. As a consequence the focus of HPC DFT algorithm development has almost exclusively been on weak parallel scaling algorithms that maintain parallel efficiency as the system size grows. In contrast, the focus of HPC AIMD algorithm development has focused on truly strong parallel scaling algorithms, rather than weak parallel scaling, since the time per step needs to be as small as possible.

With the advent of new HPC systems with multiple levels of parallelism composed of many-core CPUs, e. g., the second generation Intel® Xeon Phi™ processor (code-named "Knights Landing", KNL) [29], and connected by high-speed networking, such as the Cray* Aries* network, algorithms can now be developed that take advantage of fast data movement and fast synchronization between threads on the CPUs. These new systems have the potential for improved strong parallel scaling, however, new algorithms need to be developed that can make use of these massively parallel processor architectures [15].

Although the MPI (or MPI-only) model can be used on many of today's architectures with large numbers of cores [16], and in principle can take advantage of the fact that memory is shared, this programming model has several drawbacks. Performance hits can happen using this programming model because of its lack of ability to control memory at the node resulting in a lack of memory coherency, higher latencies, and slower synchronizations. A more suitable approach for developing strong scaling algorithms on large core architectures is to use a hybrid execution model [27], where data movement between nodes is handled by MPI and the data movement and execution within a node is handled by a multi-threading model such as OpenMP* [11,12,23]. The advantages of this model are that synchronizing between threads is faster, extra data movements can be avoided, and the memory footprint is potentially smaller since particular data structures may not need to be duplicated among threads.

In this paper, recent developments of adding thread-level parallelism to the plane-wave density functional theory (DFT) methodology in NWChem are presented [2,4,6,10]. In our current development, thread-level parallelism is integrated into a MPI-only code using OpenMP constructs and threaded mathematical libraries, such as the Intel® Math Kernel Library. Similar efforts are underway with other codes [1], however, to our knowledge our development is at present unique in that the focus is on having ab-initio molecular dynamics simulations AIMD with very fast iteration times (i. e., very small times per AIMD step). The target platform for our work is the NERSC-8 supercomputer "Cori", which employs a mix of Intel® Xeon® and Intel Xeon Phi processors that are connected through the Cray Aries fabric.

2 Prior Work

There are three key kernels in AIMD that need be efficiently parallelized: 3D FFTs, non-local pseudopotential, and Lagrange multiplier kernels that are used for maintaining orthogonality of Kohn-Sham orbitals [4,7,14,22,32].

In the MPI-only parallel AIMD code in NWChem, the parallel efficiency of the 3D FFT is by far the worst performing kernel, and the best algorithms are only able to use N MPI tasks for a 3D FFT of an $N \times N \times N$ grid. The lack of parallel performance of 3D FFTs is well-known [3,8] and is related to the presence of global all-to-all operations. To overcome this bottleneck, algorithms have been developed that distribute the Kohn-Sham orbitals in addition to partitioning the simulated space [5,7,14,32]. This results in a 2D processor geometry of $Np = Np_i \cdot Np_j$ processors or MPI ranks (see Fig. 1).

The drawback of this strategy is that the Lagrange multiplier kernel becomes less efficient as Np_j becomes larger. In general, increasing Np_j significantly improves the efficiency of the 3D FFT and the non-local pseudopotential kernels, while increasing Np_i favors the Lagrange multiplier kernel. Hence, the best parallel performance is found by balancing the individual performance of the three kernels with respect to Np_i and Np_j. It should be noted that clusters of Xeon Phi processors have the potential to improve strong parallel scaling of the 3D FFT, and as a consequence the overall scaling of AIMD, due to improved memory performance of the high-bandwidth and on-package memory. Using multi-threading instead of MPI primitives, synchronization times of the large numbers of threads within the node can be reduced to increase execution efficiency of the kernels.

Recently, we have reported results from adding thread-level parallelism to the AIMD code in NWChem [15]. The work focused on single-node performance and showed promising results for the multi-threaded implementation of the key kernels in the AIMD calculation. It was shown that through careful optimizations of tall-and-skinny matrix products, which are at the heart of the Lagrange

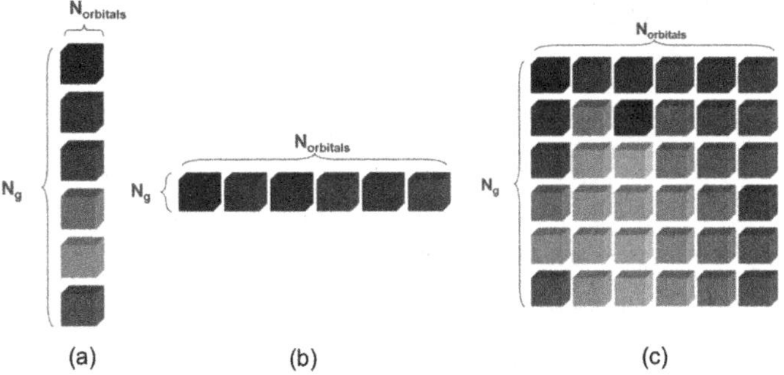

Fig. 1. Possible types of parallel distributions of the Kohn-Sham orbitals in plane-wave DFT software. (a) Each of the Kohn-Sham orbitals is identically spatially decomposed. (b) Each Kohn-Sham orbital is located on different MPI tasks. (c) The 2D-parallel distribution suggested by Gygi et al. [14], where the total Kohn-Sham orbital set are block decomposed.

multiplier and non-local pseudopotential kernels, as well as other optimizations for 3D FFTs, our OpenMP implementation delivered excellent strong scaling for the 68 cores of the Xeon Phi Knights Landing processor. Moreover, it was shown that the straightforward and naive approach of calling a multi-threaded BLAS library from a serial (MPI) rank does not yield a satisfactory level of performance for the Lagrange multiplier and non-local pseudopotential kernels. A roofline model analysis [33] of the Lagrange multiplier verified that our implementation was close to the roofline model of the execution platform for various problem sizes.

3 AIMD Implementation for the Intel Xeon Phi Processor

The bulk of the computational work in AIMD revolves around the solution of N_e eigenvalue equations, $H\psi_i = \epsilon_i \psi_i$, for the electron orbitals ψ_i, appearing as a result of the DFT approximation to the Schrödinger equation.

These eigenvalue equations are subject to orthogonality constraints

$$\int_{\Omega} \psi_i(\boldsymbol{r})\psi_j(\boldsymbol{r})d\boldsymbol{r} = \delta_{i,j} \tag{1}$$

Most standard AIMD algorithms use non-local pseudopotentials and plane-wave basis sets to perform the DFT calculations and are typically solved using a conjugate gradient algorithm or a Car-Parrinello algorithm [4,20]. For DFT, the Hamiltonian operator H may be written as

$$H\psi_i = \begin{pmatrix} -\frac{1}{2}\nabla^2 + V_l + V_{NL} + V_H[\rho] \\ +V_x c[\rho] \end{pmatrix} \psi_i \tag{2}$$

$$(-1/2)\nabla^2\Psi + V_{ext}\Psi + V_H\Psi + V_{xc}\Psi = E\Psi$$

$$\langle \Psi_i | \Psi_j \rangle = \delta_{ij}$$

$(-1/2)\nabla^2\Psi$ :: N_eN_{pack}

$V_{ext}\Psi$ :: $(N_aN_{pack} + N_gLogN_{pack} + N_eN_{pack}) + N_aN_eN_{pack}$

$V_H\Psi$ :: $N_eN_gLogN_g + N_eN_g + 2N_gLogN_g + N_g + N_eN_g$

$V_{xc}\Psi$ :: $N_eN_gLogN_g + N_eN_g$

$\langle \Psi_i | \Psi_j \rangle$ :: $N_e^2N_{pack} + N_e^3$

N_a - number of atoms, N_e - number of electrons
N_g – size of FFT grid, N_{pack}- size of reciprocal space

Fig. 2. Operation count of $H\psi_i$ in a plane-wave DFT simulation.

where the one-electron density is given by

$$\rho(\boldsymbol{r}) = \sum |\psi_i(\boldsymbol{r})|^2 \tag{3}$$

The local and non-local pseudpotentials, V_l and V_{NL}, represent the electron-ion interaction. The Hartree potential V_H is given by

$$\nabla^2 V_H = -4\pi\rho \tag{4}$$

and the exchange and correlation potential is V_xc. The algorithmic cost to evaluate $H\psi$ and maintain orthogonality are shown in Fig. 2.

Due to their computational complexity, the electron gradient $H\psi_i$ and orthogonalization need to be calculated as efficiently as possible. The main parameters that determine the cost of a calculation are N_g, N_e, N_a, and N_{proj}, where N_g is the size of the three-dimensional FFT grid, N_e is the number of occupied orbitals, N_a is the number of atoms, N_{proj} is the number of projectors per atom, and N_{pack} is the size of the reciprocal space. Detailed estimates for the scalability of these calculations in terms of the AIMD parameters can be derived and fit in terms of a finite set of rates and bandwidths that are machine dependent (e.g., see Bylaska et al. [5]). Fitting the machine dependent parameters was not performed in this initial parallel benchmark study, because a large number of calculations is needed for accurate fitting.

As shown in Fig. 2, the evaluation of the electron gradient (and orthogonality) contains three major computational pieces:

- *applying* V_H and V_{xc}, involving the calculation of $2N_e$ 3D FFTs;
- *the non-local pseudopotential*, V_{NL}, dominated by the cost of the matrix multiplications $W = P^TY$, and $Y_2 = PW$, where P is an $N_{pack} \times (N_{proj} \cdot N_a)$ matrix, Y and Y_2 are $N_{pack} \times N_e$ matrices, and W is an $(N_{proj}N_a) \times N_e$ matrix;
- *enforcing orthogonality*, where the most expensive matrix multiplications are $S = Y^TY$ and $Y_2 = YS$, where Y and Y_2 are $N_{pack} \times N_e$ matrices, and S is an $N_e \times N_e$ matrix.

In the next subsections, we focus on the main components of an AIMD step that need to be parallelized both at the shared-memory and the distributed-memory levels to achieve good parallel performance. All invocations of MPI primitives in NWChem are done from within an OpenMP `master` region, requiring the `MPI_THREAD_FUNNELLED` threading level to be used [21]. This keeps messages size larger and all threads then work on the same data block that was send once, instead of having each thread communicate a smaller block.

3.1 3D FFTs

For each iteration of an AIMD simulation, N_e Kohn-Sham orbitals, $\psi(G, 1 : N_e)$, are converted from reciprocal space to real space and N_e orbital gradients are transformed from real space to reciprocal space. This corresponds to computing N_e reverse 3D FFTs and N_e forward 3D FFTs. In reciprocal space, only a sphere of radius E_{cut} (or hemisphere for a Γ-point code), and contained within the 3D FFT block, is needed and saved in the program.

Each 3D FFT consists of six distinct steps, each of which is executed for each of the N_e Kohn-Sham orbitals in a pipelined fashion as illustrated in Fig. 3. For the forward 3D FFT, the steps are (in reverse order for backward FFTs):

1. Unpack the reciprocal space sphere into a 3D cube, where the leading dimension of the cube is in the z-direction, second dimension is the x-direction, and the third dimension is the y-direction.
2. Perform $nx \times ny$ FFTs along the z-direction. Note that only the arrays that intersect the sphere need to be computed.
3. Rotate the cube so that the first dimension is the y-direction, $z, x, y \rightarrow y, z, x$.
4. Perform $nz \times nx$ 1D FFTs along the y-direction.
5. Rotate the cube so that the first dimension is the x-direction, $y, z, x \rightarrow x, y, z$.
6. Perform $ny \times nz$ 1D FFTs along the x-direction.

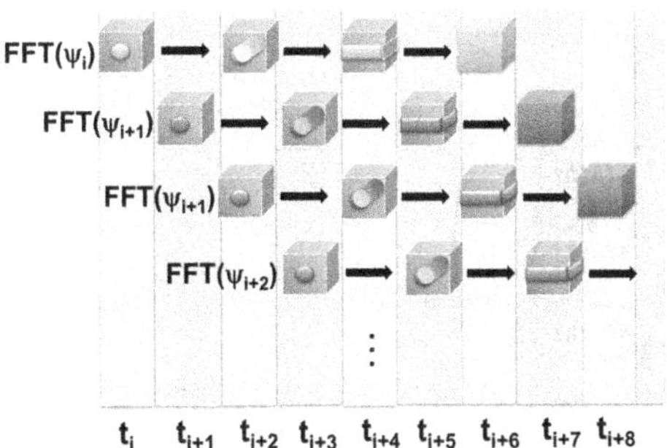

Fig. 3. Illustration of the pipelined 3D FFT algorithm used in the NWChem AIMD code.

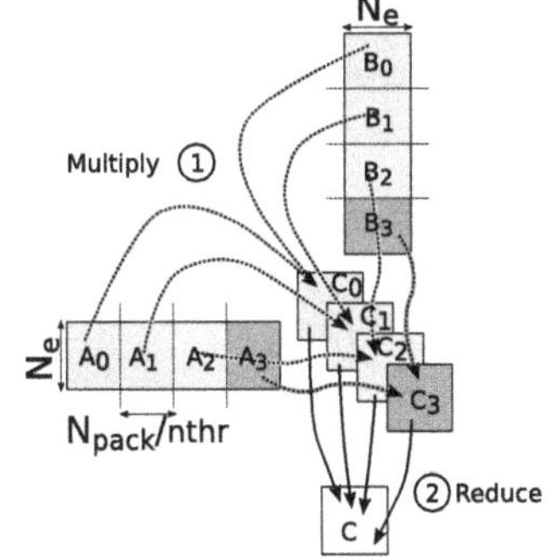

Fig. 4. Multithreading scheme of the ***FFM*** operation.

The 3D FFTs used in this paper were implemented by modifying the existing parallel 3D FFTs contained in the NWChem plane-wave module (called NWPW). More details on the implementation of these FFTs can be found in prior work by Bylaska et al. [5,6,16].

In the initial parallel FFT code, the 3D cube is distributed along the 2nd and 3rd dimension. This distribution is block-mapped using a two-dimensional Hilbert curve spanning the grid of the second and third dimensions (see [6]). This two-dimensional Hilbert parallel FFT was built using a 1D FFT and a parallel block rotation. The FFTPACK library [30] is used to perform the 1D FFTs, and the parallel block rotation was implemented using non-blocking MPI primitives.

We generalized the FFTs to a hybrid MPI-OpenMP model by making the following changes. The planes of 1D FFTs in steps 2, 4, and 6 execute on multiple threads through an OpenMP `DO` directive so that a single 1D FFT is carried out on one thread. The data rearrangement in steps 1, 3, and 5 is threaded using a `DO` directive on the loops that perform the data-copying on the node.

3.2 Lagrange Multipliers and Non-local Pseudopotentials on 1D and 2D Processor Grids

At each step of an AIMD simulation, wave functions need to be orthogonalized. This is the purpose of the Lagrange multiplier method. Details on the algorithm itself can be found in [4,20,26]. The Lagrange multiplier method solves several matrix Riccatti equations [19] at every step. We have introduced a highly scalable multi-threaded implementation of the Lagrange multiplier for the Xeon Phi processor in [15]. In the following, we go through the different steps that were required to derived a scalable hybrid MPI-OpenMP implementation for a distributed memory many-core cluster.

The Lagrange multiplier algorithm can be described as a sequence of matrix-matrix products of different sizes. In [15], we have introduced the following formalism. The letter **F** refers to an $N_{pack} \times N_e$ or an $N_e \times N_{pack}$ matrix, and **M**

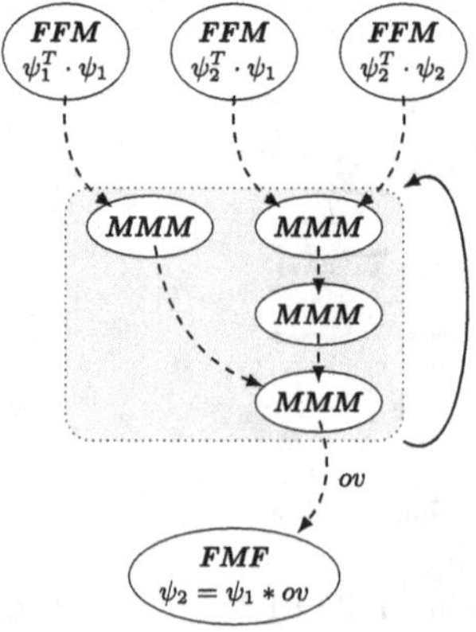

Fig. 5. Dependencies between operations of the Lagrange multiplier algorithm.

refers to an $N_e \times N_e$ matrix. A matrix product $C = AB$ can then be described by a sequence of three letters, the first referring to matrix A, the second to matrix B, and the last one to matrix C. In general, $N_{pack} >> N_e$, thus, **F** matrices or their transpose are *tall-and-skinny* matrices.

The Lagrange multipliers method requires three types of matrix product to be computed: ***MMM***, ***FMF***, and ***FFM***. The dependencies between these operations is depicted in Fig. 5.

The ***FFM*** type of matrix product is the most expensive part of the Lagrange multiplier method. For this particular matrix shape, multi-threaded implementations available in vendor libraries do not scale well. In [15], we have introduced an OpenMP algorithm that scales better than vendor solutions and that blends well with the outer-level parallelism of an active OpenMP `parallel` region. The parallelization scheme used in this approach is depicted in Fig. 4.

In order to exploit distributed memory processor grids (cf. Sect. 2), we have implemented a version of the Scalable Universal Matrix Multiplication Algorithm (SUMMA) [31]. The rationale behind SUMMA is to leverage the efficiency of MPI collective communications. When computing $C = AB$ on a $Np_i \times Np_j$ 2D process grid, SUMMA broadcasts the current block of matrix A within row of processes and the current block of B across a column a processes. The product between these two blocks is then added to the local block of C. These local contributions are computed using the OpenMP multi-threaded algorithm introduced in [15]. In the case of the ***FFM*** operation, matrix A is of size $N_e \times N_{pack}$, and is distributed over a $Np_j \times Np_i$ grid of MPI ranks. The C matrix is $N_e \times N_e$ and is replicated over $Np = Np_i \cdot Np_j$ copies. SUMMA is applied followed by a global reduction of C to produce replicated matrices.

As part of the non-local pseudopotentials computation, a sequence of ***FFM***, ***MMM***, and ***FMF*** matrix products also need to be computed. This is similar to the Lagrange multipliers method except that **M** refers to a $(N_a N_{proj}) \times N_e$ matrix and **F** refers to either a $N_{pack} \times N_e$ or $N_{pack} \times (N_a N_{proj})$ matrix, where N_a is the number of atoms and N_{proj} is the average number of projectors per atoms. For most systems, N_e is approximately $N_a N_{proj}$. Note that the matrix operations for non-local pseudopotentials (and Projector Augmented Wave projectors) are separable across atoms (and, for some pseudopotentials, separable across projectors), that is, C is block diagonal between atoms, and can be evaluated atom by atom, although blocking is usually done to improve the efficiency.

4 Performance Evaluation

Our evaluation of the plane-wave DFT AIMD method has been performed on the "Cori" system at NERSC. We use both partitions of the system to compare the performance of the new code on both Intel Xeon processors (codename "Haswell") and Intel Xeon Phi processors (codename "Knights Landing" or KNL for short).

The "Haswell" partition is a Cray XC40 system and consists of 2388 dual-socket nodes with Intel Xeon E5-2698v3 processors running 16 cores per socket.

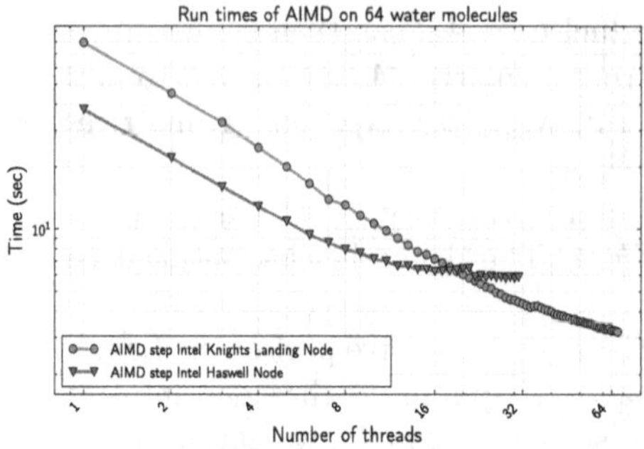

Fig. 6. Scalability of the multi-threaded NWPW code within a single Xeon and Xeon Phi node for 64 water molecules.

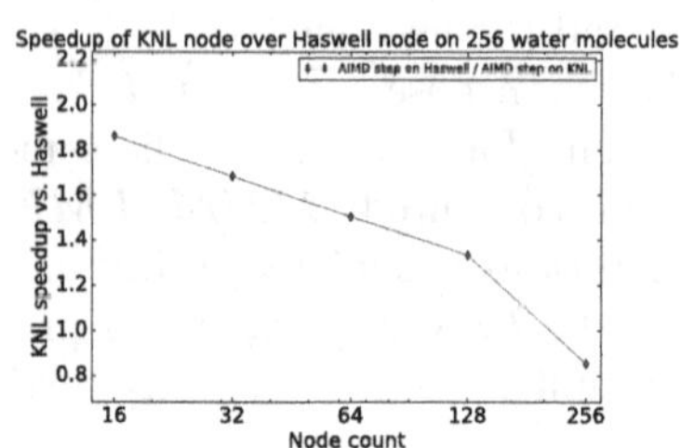

Fig. 7. Speedups of the Xeon Phi processors over the Xeon processors the "water256" benchmark at different numbers of nodes.

The nodes are configured without Hyper-Threading, run at frequency of 2.3 GHz, and are equipped with 128 GB of DDR4 memory with 2133 MHz. The nodes are connected through the Cray Aries interconnect with Dragonfly topology [17].

The "Knights Landing" partition is also a Cray XC40 system with 9688 single-socket nodes with Intel Xeon Phi 7250 processors. Each processor features 68 cores with four hardware threads per core. The cores are running at a frequency of 1.4 GHz. Each node contains 96 GB of DDR4 memory running at 2400 MHz. For our evaluation, the 16 GB on-package high-bandwidth memory has been configured to run in quadrant mode and is used in cache mode [29]. Similarly to the Xeon partition, the Xeon Phi partition uses the Cray Aries interconnect with the Dragonfly topology.

In order to compare the performance of a node of the Xeon partition of Cori to that of a node of the Xeon Phi partition, we conducted an intra-node strong scaling study with a benchmark that simulates 64 water molecules ("water64"). The pertinent dimensions for this system are $N_e = 512$, $N_g = 1,259,712$ (108^3) and $N_{pack} = 106,456$. To assess cluster performance, we use a larger input deck that simulates 256 water molecules ("water256"). The matrix dimensions for this system are $N_e = 2056$, $N_g = 5,832,000$ (180^3) and $N_{pack} = 437,600$. We run the "water256" benchmark on up to 256 nodes of the Xeon partition to establish the baseline performance and to compare it with the Xeon Phi nodes. We then scale the benchmark to up to 1024 nodes of the Xeon Phi partition to show the feasibility of the AIMD plane-wave algorithm at a large-scale many-core system.

The first set of experiments aims at comparing the single-node performance of the processors. This gives insight into the relative speed-up of the Xeon Phi processor over the Xeon processor without the effects of the interconnect fabric. Increasing number of threads from one to the maximum available physical cores, we observe that a Xeon Phi node achieves a 1.8x speedup over a Xeon node when used at full capacity (see Fig. 6). The Haswell processor shows a flat performance profile at about 16 threads, as it reaches its memory-bandwidth limits, whereas

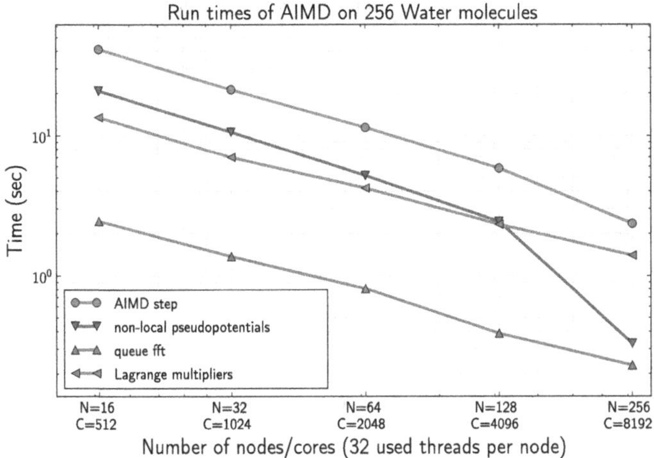

Fig. 8. Scalability of major components of an AIMD step on the Xeon partition for "water256".

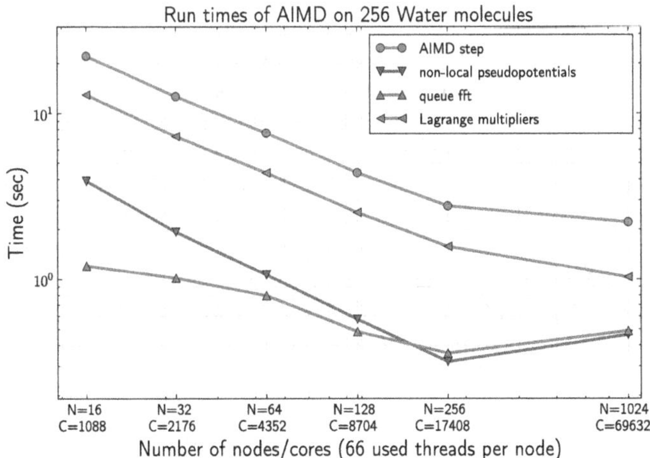

Fig. 9. Scalability of major components of an AIMD step on the Xeon Phi partition for "water256".

the Knights Landing processor still provides a speed-up with all physical cores utilized due to the high-bandwidth on-package memory.

Next, we compare results obtained of the "water256" benchmark on 16, 32, 64, 128, and 256 nodes of each partition. We use 32 threads per Xeon node and 66 threads per Xeon Phi node. Leaving two cores of the Xeon Phi processor for the operating system is best for performance. The Xeon Phi partition achieves a speedup of 1.86x, 1.68x, 1.5x, and 1.3x over the Xeon partition on 16, 32, 64, and 128 nodes (see Fig. 7), showing that NWChem is able to exploit the additional

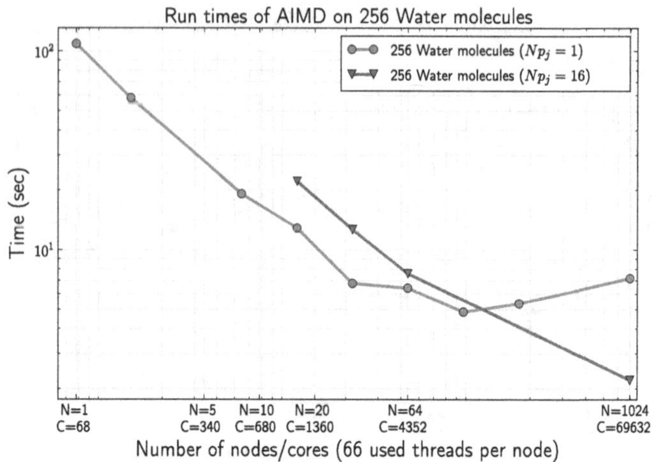

Fig. 10. Scalability of AIMD on 256 water molecules ($Np_j = 1$ and $Np_j = 16$).

computing power of Xeon Phi nodes. It is important to note that as the number of nodes grows, the local amount of work per node is reduced while the impact of the interconnect and communication increases. This explains why the speedup of KNL nodes over Xeon nodes decreases when the number of nodes increases. Ultimately, the local work per node becomes too small to occupy the network fully and thus the performance advantage of the Xeon Phi processor vanishes. When using 256 nodes, Xeon nodes become faster than Xeon Phi nodes in this latency-limited regime due to the 2x higher clock frequency, 0.5x flops/cycle, and 0.25x bytes/sec of the Xeon nodes. Figure 8 and Fig. 9 illustrate the scalability of the most expensive components of the AIMD simulation, which are the calculation of the FFTs, the Lagrange multipliers method, and the non-local pseudopotentials computation. The results show that all components scale well on both Xeon and Xeon Phi nodes. However, it is interesting to note that due to the differences in the underlying processor architectures, the relative cost of each component is different on Xeon and Xeon Phi. The computation of non-local pseudopotentials and Lagrange both dominate the cost on Xeon, while the Lagrange multiplier is the dominating kernel on Xeon Phi. Computing the non-local pseudopotentials is a similar process as the Lagrange multiplier, with fewer intermediate steps between the ***FFM*** operations. As the Xeon Phi nodes use more threads than the Xeon nodes, the N_{pack} dimension is split in smaller blocks. Therefore, each thread receives a smaller amount of work. For the Lagrange multipliers method, the dependencies between the ***FFM*** operations and the ***MMM*** operations are such that the effect of this trend is less visible (see Fig. 5).

Figure 10 shows the effect of changing the processor grid by increasing the Np_j dimension, as briefly described in Sect. 2. As can be seen from Fig. 10, the scalability of the computation can be improved from 128 to 1024 nodes by balancing Np_i and Np_j to favor the calculation of 3D FFTs and non-local pseudopotentials. For the sake of brevity, we did not fully explore the full parameter space of node counts and the shape of the $(Np_i \times Np_j)$-grid distribution. We plan to conduct such an analysis as a future work.

5 Conclusion and Future Work

The parallelism available on machines with many-core processors requires to revisit the implementation of their programs to efficiently use the available resources. In this paper, we have demonstrated that rewriting key kernels in NWChem's plane-wave AIMD module to use a hybrid MPI-OpenMP that provides good scalability on a many-core cluster based on the Intel Xeon Phi Processor. However, to achieve this level of performance for large AIMD simulations the parallelism within a node must be implemented at a very fine grain level and needs careful orchestration of MPI-level parallelism and OpenMP threading.

The unique implementations of key kernels used in AIMD such as sphere to cube 3D FFTs and the matrix multiplication of tall-skinny matrices require special attention and are not well for suited standard computational math libraries. For example, due to the shape the matrices, standard BLAS libraries such as Intel Math Kernel Library have a hard time to provide close-to-optimal performance on a many-core system. However, by rewriting these kernels from scratch using the hybrid MPI-OpenMP model at a required very fine grain level we were able to obtain good performance.

For this paper, we simulated up to 256 water molecules, a standard benchmark for AIMD, to test our implementation. The experiments showed strong scaling up to 1024 KNL nodes (69632 cores) for 256 water molecules. The timings of the major kernels, the pipelined 3D FFTs, non-local pseudopotential, and Lagrange multiplier kernels all displayed significant speedups. Further, comparisons between the KNL and Haswell nodes showed that that Xeon Phi partition was able to attain more than 1.5x speedup over the Xeon partition.

As future work, we plan to implement hybrid MPI-OpenMP algorithms for exact exchange kernels needed for hybrid DFT calculations, as well as propagate our current developments into the band structure code in NWChem. We also plan to explore the parameter space in more detail and determine the best setting of Np_i and Np_j for various node counts. Lastly, we are planning to carry out runs at scale of a multiple of thousands of many-core cluster nodes to simulate a problem that is of interest to the chemistry and geochemistry communities.

Acknowledgment. This work was supported by the NWChem project in the William R. Wiley Environmental Molecular Sciences Laboratory (EMSL), the U.S. Department of Energy, Office of Science, Advanced Scientific Computing Research ECP program (NWChemEx project), and E.J.B was also supported by the the U.S. Department of Energy, Office of Science, Office of Basic Energy Sciences, Chemical Sciences, Geosciences, and Biosciences Division at PNNL, DE-AC06-76RLO 1830. EMSL operations are supported by the DOE's Office of Biological and Environmental Research. M.J. and W.A.D. were partially supported by the Scientific Discovery through Advanced Computing (SciDAC) program funded by U.S. Department of Energy, Office of Science,

Advanced Scientific Computing Research and Basic Energy Sciences. In particular, M.J. was supported by the FASTMath SciDAC institute. We wish to thank the Scientific Computing Staff, Office of Energy Research, and the U. S. Department of Energy for support through the NERSC NESAP program the National Energy Research Scientific Computing Center (Berkeley, CA). This work was also supported by Intel as part of its Intel Parallel Computing Centers effort. This research used resources of the National Energy Research Scientific Computing Center, a DOE Office of Science User Facility supported by the Office of Science of the U.S. Department of Energy under Contract No. DE-AC02-05CH11231.

References

1. Measuring arithmetic intensity, http://www.nersc.gov/users/application-performance/measuring-arithmetic-intensity/. Accessed 22 Oct 2016
2. Aprà, E., Bylaska, E.J., Dean, D.J., Fortunelli, A., Gao, F., Krstić, P.S., Wells, J.C., Windus, T.L.: NWChem for materials science. Comput. Mater. Sci. **28**(2), 209–221 (2003)
3. Ayala, O., Wang, L.P.: Parallel implementation and scalability analysis of 3D fast fourier transform using 2D domain decomposition. Parallel Comput. **39**(1), 58–77 (2013). http://www.sciencedirect.com/science/article/pii/S0167819112000932
4. Bylaska, E., Tsemekhman, K., Govind, N., Valiev, M.: Large-scale plane-wave-based density functional theory: formalism, parallelization, and applications. In: Computational Methods for Large Systems: Electronic Structure Approaches for Biotechnology and Nanotechnology, pp. 77–116 (2011)
5. Bylaska, E.J., Glass, K., Baxter, D., Baden, S.B., Weare, J.H.: Hard scaling challenges for ab initio molecular dynamics capabilities in nwchem: using 100,000 CPUs per second. In: Journal of Physics: Conference Series, vol. 180, p. 012028. IOP Publishing (2009)

6. Bylaska, E.J., Valiev, M., Kawai, R., Weare, J.H.: Parallel implementation of the projector augmented plane wave method for charged systems. Comput. Phys. Commun. **143**(1), 11–28 (2002)
7. Canning, A., Raczkowski, D.: Scaling first-principles plane-wave codes to thousands of processors. Comput. Phys. Commun. **169**(1), 449–453 (2005)
8. Canning, A., Shalf, J., Wang, L.W., Wasserman, H., Gajbe, M.: A comparison of different communication structures for scalable parallel three dimensional FFTs in first principle codes. In: Chapman, B., Desprez, F., Joubert, G.R., et al. (eds.), pp. 107–116 (2010)
9. Car, R., Parrinello, M.: Unified approach for molecular dynamics and density-functional theory. Phys. Rev. Lett. **55**(22), 2471 (1985)
10. Chen, Y., Bylaska, E., Weare, J.: First principles estimation of geochemically important transition metal oxide properties. In: Molecular Modeling of Geochemical Reactions: An Introduction, p. 107 (2016)
11. Cramer, T., Schmidl, D., Klemm, M., an Mey, D.: OpenMP programming on Intel Xeon Phi Coprocessors: an early performance comparison. In: Proceedings of Many Core Applications Research Community (MARC) Symposium, pp. 38–44 (2012)
12. Dagum, L., Menon, R.: OpenMP: an industry standard API for shared-memory programming. IEEE Computat. Sci. Eng. **5**(1), 46–55 (1998)
13. Fattebert, J.L., Osei-Kuffuor, D., Draeger, E.W., Ogitsu, T., Krauss, W.D.: Modeling dilute solutions using first-principles molecular dynamics: computing more than a million atoms with over a million cores. In: International Conference for High Performance Computing, Networking, Storage and Analysis, SC 2016, pp. 12–22. IEEE (2016)
14. Gygi, F.: Architecture of Qbox: A scalable first-principles molecular dynamics code. IBM J. Res. Develop. **52**(1.2), 137–144 (2008)
15. Jacquelin, M., De Jong, W., Bylaska, E.: Towards highly scalable Ab initio molecular dynamics (AIMD) simulations on the Intel knights landing manycore processor. In: 31st IEEE International Parallel & Distributed Processing Symposium. IEEE Computer Society (2017, Accepted)
16. de Jong, W.A., Bylaska, E., Govind, N., Janssen, C.L., Kowalski, K., Müller, T., Nielsen, I.M., van Dam, H.J., Veryazov, V., Lindh, R.: Utilizing high performance computing for chemistry: parallel computational chemistry. Phys. Chem. Chem. Phys. **12**(26), 6896–6920 (2010)
17. Kim, J., Dally, W.J., Scott, S., Abts, D.: Technology-driven, highly-scalable dragonfly topology. SIGARCH Comput. Archit. News **36**(3), 77–88 (2008). http://doi.acm.org/10.1145/1394608.1382129
18. Kohn, W., Sham, L.J.: Self-consistent equations including exchange and correlation effects. Phys. Rev. **140**(4A), A1133 (1965)
19. Lancaster, P., Rodman, L.: Algebraic Riccati Equations. Clarendon Press, Oxford (1995)
20. Marx, D., Hutter, J.: Modern methods and algorithms of quantum chemistry. Grotendorst, J. (ed.), pp. 301–449 (2000)
21. MPI Forum: MPI: A Message-passing Interface Standard. Tech. rep., June 2015
22. Nelson, J., Plimpton, S., Sears, M.: Plane-wave electronic-structure calculations on a parallel supercomputer. Phys. Rev. B **47**(4), 1765 (1993)
23. OpenMP Architecture Review Board: OpenMP Application Program Interface, Version 4.5, November 2015. http://www.openmp.org/

24. Parr, R.G.: Density functional theory of atoms and molecules. In: Fukui, K., Pullman, B. (eds.) Horizons of Quantum Chemistry. Académie Internationale Des Sciences Moléculaires Quantiques/International Academy of Quantum Molecular Science, vol. 3, pp. 5–15. Springer, Dordrecht (1980). doi:10.1007/978-94-009-9027-2_2
25. Payne, M.C., Teter, M.P., Allan, D.C., Arias, T., Joannopoulos, J.: Iterative minimization techniques for ab initio total-energy calculations: molecular dynamics and conjugate gradients. Rev. Mod. Phys. **64**(4), 1045 (1992)
26. Polian, A., Loubeyre, P., Boccara, N.: Simple molecular systems at very high density. In: NATO Advanced Science Institutes (ASI) Series B, vol. 186 (1989)
27. Rabenseifner, R., Hager, G., Jost, G.: Hybrid MPI/OpenMP parallel programming on clusters of multi-core SMP nodes. In: 2009 17th Euromicro International Conference on Parallel, Distributed and Network-based Processing, pp. 427–436. IEEE (2009)
28. Remler, D.K., Madden, P.A.: Molecular dynamics without effective potentials via the car-parrinello approach. Mol. Phys. **70**(6), 921–966 (1990)
29. Sodani, A.: Knights landing (KNL): 2nd Generation Intel® Xeon Phi Processor. In: Presentation at Hot Chips: A Symposium on High Performance Chips, August 2015
30. Swarztrauber, P.: Fftpack: a package of fortran subprograms for the fast fourier transform of periodic and other symmetric sequences. Obtainable by e-mail or by ftp from nctlib@ornl.gov (1985)
31. Van De Geijn, R.A., Watts, J.: Summa: scalable universal matrix multiplication algorithm. Concurrency-Pract. Exp. **9**(4), 255–274 (1997)
32. Wiggs, J., Jonsson, H.: A hybrid decomposition parallel implementation of the car-parrinello method. Comput. Phys. Commun. **87**(3), 319–340 (1995)
33. Williams, S., Waterman, A., Patterson, D.: Roofline: an insightful visual performance model for multicore architectures. Commun. ACM **52**(4), 65–76 (2009). http://doi.acm.org/10.1145/1498765.1498785

Performance Variability on Xeon Phi

Brandon Cook(✉), Thorsten Kurth, Brian Austin, Samuel Williams, and Jack Deslippe

Lawrence Berkeley National Laboratory, Berkeley, CA 94720, USA
{bgcook,tkurth}@lbl.gov

Abstract. An understanding of sources of performance variability is important for high performance application developers and users. In this paper we discuss non-I/O sources of application performance variability on Cori, a Cray XC40 at NERSC with 9600+ Xeon Phi nodes connecting to an Aries high speed network with a Dragonfly topology. Our survey covers variability due to on-node effects from MCDRAM configured as cache and clock frequency scaling as well as off-node effects due to the network. For each source of variability we quantify the variability through micro-benchmarks and mini-applications, discuss potential mitigation strategies and analyze the impact on applications.

Keywords: Cori · NERSC · Aries · Dragonfly · Performance variability

1 Introduction

High performance computing platforms harbor many potential sources of performance variability, including features of the on-node architecture, network, and I/O subsystem. Quantifying and understanding the various sources of variability is essential to application developers and performance engineers who want to analyze and measure application performance and for scientists to make efficient and informed use of resource allocations. In this paper we focus on non-I/O sources of variability on the Intel Xeon Phi many integrated core architecture.

In Sect. 2, we describe the target architecture. In Sect. 3, we describe applications that will be used to demonstrate the effects on variability on real-applications. Sections 4, 5 and 6 discuss different on-node and off-node sources of variability: MCDRAM configured as direct map cache, dynamic voltage-frequency scaling, and job placement. For each section, the mechanism of variability is introduced, mitigation and identification methodologies are discussed and illustrated with microbenchmarks. Finally, the impact on of variability on the performance of real applications is presented.

2 System Architecture

The Cori supercomputer at the National Energy Research Scientific Computing Center (NERSC) is a Cray XC40 based supercomputer currently ranked 5th on

J.M. Kunkel et al. (Eds.): ISC High Performance Workshops 2017, LNCS 10524, pp. 419–429, 2017.
https://doi.org/10.1007/978-3-319-67630-2_31

the Top 500 list. Cori is unique in that it contains both Xeon and Xeon Phi nodes with a common scheduler, I/O subsystem and high speed network (HSN). Cori is configured with the following components; our analysis focuses on Cori's Xeon Phi partition.

- 2000+ compute nodes with 128 GB DDR4@2133 MHz per node and two 16-core 2.3 GHz Intel Haswell processors
- 9600+ compute nodes with 96 GB DDR4@2400 MHz per node, 16 GB on-package MCDRAM and one 68-core 1.4 GHz Intel Xeon Phi processor
- 1 PB aggregate memory
- 30 PB scratch filesystem with over 700 GB/s peak bandwidth
- Cray Aries network with Dragonfly topology and 45 TB/s bi-directional global bandwidth.

3 Applications

We use the following applications to illustrate several sources of variability and to discuss their impact on realistic workloads.

The HPGMG-FV benchmark [4,5] is highly instrumented, thus providing an immediate and detailed timing breakdown, and it is heavily optimized for threaded environments. Moreover, as it implements a variable-coefficient, fourth-order Laplacian on a structured grid, it is moderately compute intensive and thus sensitive to frequency variations.

The deep learning framework IntelCaffe [1] features highly optimized compute kernels for Intel® Xeon Phi as well as Intel Machine Learning Scalability Library (MLSL) [2] which provides communication primitives optimized for deep learning applications. The computational kernels are mostly SGEMM-like and are thus very compute intensive. The communication pattern is very well-defined as IntelCaffe uses only non-blocking allreduce operations. This communication pattern is very demanding because allreduces of large messages can put pressure on the network.

The lattice QCD application Chroma [3], together with the QPhiX Wilson operator and solver package [6,7], uses a hybrid OpenMP and MPI approach to parallel programming. It makes heavy use of JIT compilation, AVX512 intrinsics and employs pool allocators in order to improve memory allocation performance on Xeon Phi. Chroma's performance is limited by memory bandwidth and is sensitive to communication latency at large scale. The primary communication pattern nearest neighbor boundary exchange in the Wilson operator (4D stencil) and the BiCGStab solver additionally issues small allreduce operations.

MiniFE mimics the key operations of many finite-element applications that rely on implicit solvers. MiniFE uses a simple, non-preconditioned conjugate-gradient solver that consists mainly of sparse matrix-vector products and vector-vector operations that are memory bandwidth sensitive.

4 MCDRAM Cache

4.1 Introduction

Cache conflict misses are a well-known phenomenon arising from memory references aliasing to the same cache line in a limited associativity cache and resulting in superfluous data movement. Users often mitigate this by padding array sizes so that the (virtual) addresses of concurrently accessed array elements no longer alias. Such techniques work well on virtually-addressed caches or in cases where the padding is smaller than a page. Unfortunately, for cache architectures with very large numbers of sets (e.g. the MCDRAM cache on KNL), it is possible for multiple pages within or across processes to map to the same cache set despite having distinct (virtual) address bits (the TLB hides the true aliasing from users). This is an artifact of, upon a `malloc/sbrk`, the system (perhaps agnostic of the cache architecture) allocating two physical (and aliased pages) from the free page list to disjoint virtual addresses. On a system like KNL where the cache is direct mapped (no associativity), such accesses can result in MCDRAM cache thrashing and degraded performance.

4.2 Mitigations/Solutions

For a freshly booted node, the page list is initially "well ordered" in the sense that the first pages allocated from the heap do not conflict with each other. Over time, as various processes allocate and free memory, the entropy of the free page list increases, the probability of being allocated conflicting pages increases, and performance decreases.

One might consider rebooting nodes before each job to eliminate this source of performance variation, but lengthy reboot times make this suggestion untenable. To help avoid cache conflict misses without rebooting, Intel developed the so-called "Zone-Sort" kernel module, which performs on-demand sorting of Linux's free page list. The overhead for running Zone-Sort is small enough (<1 s) that it can be run before each job. On Cori, we have modified the Slurm prologue to call Zone-Sort immediately before each application launch. (This can be optionally disabled by adding `--zonesort=off` option to either of the sbatch or srun commands.)

4.3 Microbenchmarks

KNL's vulnerability to cache thrashing is illustrated in Fig. 1(left), which shows the average performance of 128 single-node runs of the MiniFE application in KNL's *quad,cache* mode. The first iteration scans a series of problem sizes, ranging from 4 to 50 GB, and achieves good performance up to the MCDRAM cache size of 16 GB, but decreases rapidly for larger problems as the number of capacity cache misses increases. The second iteration scans the same series, but has significantly worse performance for problems that fit into MCDRAM cache. Figure 1(right) repeats the scan of MiniFE problems, but calls Zone-Sort before each run. The two scans now generate the same performance for all problem sizes, which confirms that the poor performance observed in Fig. 1(left)-2nd run was due to cache thrashing, and demonstrates the effectiveness of Zone-Sort for MiniFE. However, the extent of the performance degradation depends on the state of the free page list, which varies across nodes, but also on the susceptibility of an application's memory access pattern to cache conflicts; other applications might not show the same sensitivity or improvement.

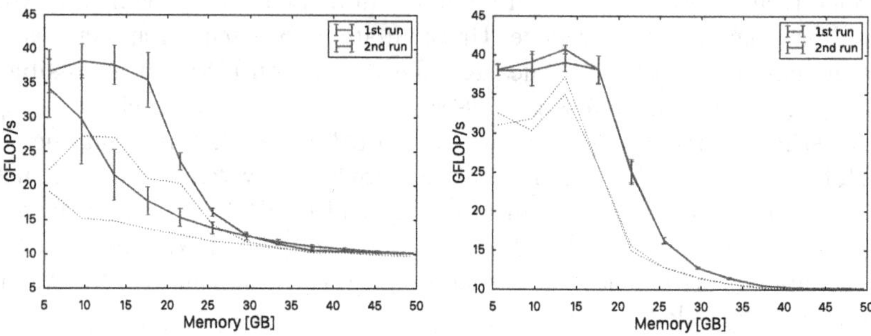

Fig. 1. MiniFE performance without (left) and with (right) the Zone-Sort kernel module. Each curve shows the average, standard deviation and minimum performance for 128 single-node runs.

4.4 Impact on Applications

Figure 2 presents the run time for HPGMG's smooth operator on the finest multigrid level for a problem size of 256^3 per process under either cache mode (*quad, cache*) or flat mode (*quad,flat* with `numactl -m 1`). Without Zone-Sort or rebooting for several weeks, the time per process for this ideally load balanced computation is far from uniform in cache mode (the Linux kernel on each node behaves independently based on its unique history). Conversely, in flat mode, there is only a 5% variation in performance. For bulk synchronous or frequently synchronizing applications like HPGMG, this node-to-node variability induced load imbalance manifests as increased `MPI_Wait` times, reduced performance (limited by slowest node), and reduced scalability (as one scales to higher concurrencies, the probability of being allocated a 'slow' node increases). With `#SBATCH --zonesort=on` and a more frequent reboot schedule, the discrepancy between flat and cache mode is diminished. As a result, overall performance and scalability are improved.

5 Dynamic Voltage and Frequency Scaling (DVFS)

5.1 Introduction

In response to thermal limits, power limitations and instruction modern architectures can dynamically adjust processor clock frequency. On Cori the default

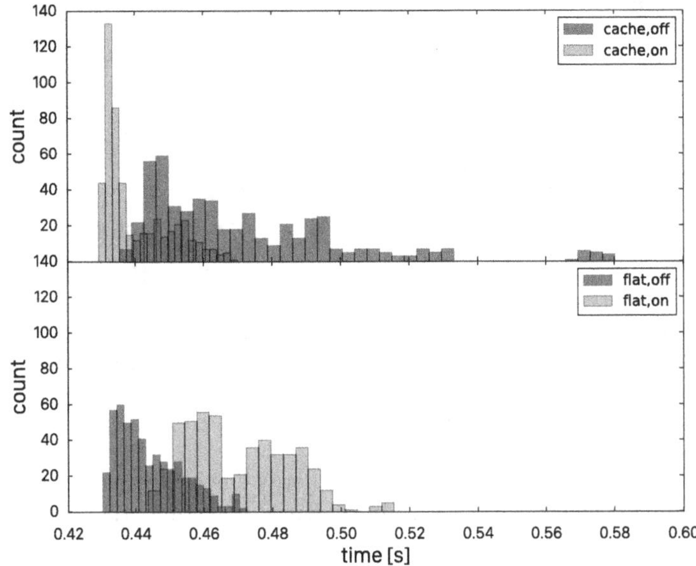

Fig. 2. MCDRAM Cache aliasing induced load imbalance on HPGMG. There are 512 processes spread over 64 nodes. Each count represents the nominally load-balanced smooth time for that process averaged over 60 s.

cpufreq driver is "acpi-cpufreq" and the minimum and maximum scaling frequencies are 1000000 kHz and 1401000 kHz. The default governor is "performance" which will attempt to run the CPU at the maximum possible frequency. However, this is an upper bound and the processor can always run at a lower frequency than that requested by the operating system. For example, when executing AVX-intensive blocks of code, the cores on a node will downclock to 1.2 GHz.

Cori users can select non-default frequency scaling through SLURM's `--cpu-freq=P1` option, which will set the target(upper) frequency (in KHz) a job can nominally run at. These can be used either on a job-wide (#SBATCH) or run step (srun) basis.

5.2 Microbenchmarks

One of the most widely used BLAS operations is `DGEMM`. Figure 3 shows histograms of DGEMM performance collected with $n = m = k = 2048$, $\alpha = 1$ and $\beta = 1$ with Intel MKL distributed with Intel compilers 2017.1.132. The processor was in *quad,flat* mode and the benchmark was run using pure OpenMP with `numactl -m 1` to bind memory to the MCDRAM. For each frequency, 500 calls to `DGEMM` were made and the first call was excluded.

Increasing the number of threads greatly increases the variability, as shown by the wide spread with 64 threads in Fig. 3. However, reducing the clock frequency increases the sharpness of the variability at the cost of reducing the peak

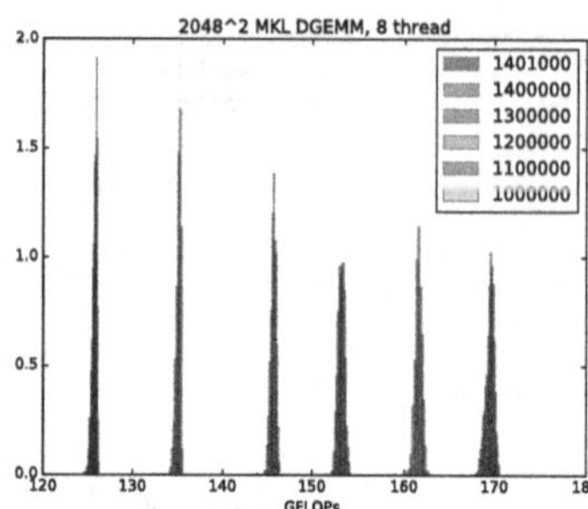

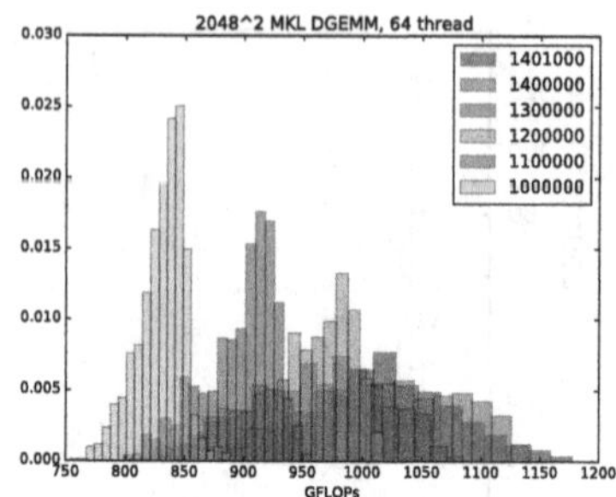

Fig. 3. Normalized histograms of 1000 DGEMM's with $n = m = k = 2048$ with 8 and 64 threads for different frequencies (kHz). All measurements were done on the same node using a single process at a time.

performance. In some cases this may be an energy efficiency optimization or just a tool for reducing the impact of variability when analyzing other potential code modifications.

5.3 Impact on Applications

Figure 4 presents on-node variability for HPGMG as a function of frequency (e.g. `--cpu-freq=1200000`). In affect, reducing the frequency makes the application more compute-limited and sensitive to slightly different code execution paths. In all cases, we used 64 nodes running in *quad,flat* with either 8 threads per process (512 processes) or 64 threads per process (64 processes). Figure 4(left) shows substantial variation in smoother (on-node computation) performance at low frequencies with 8 processes per node. This is quite surprising as all processes perform exactly the same computation (perfect load balance). As one increases frequency, one approaches the lower bound imposed by the memory limit and thus reduces variability. Close examination shows the 8 processes on each node deliver similar performance while processes on different nodes can deliver substantially different performance. Conversely, Fig. 4(right), which is configured to use one 64-thread process per node, shows neither variability between processes nor variability between nodes. At high frequencies, 64 threads deliver nearly the same on-node performance as 8 processes of 8 threads (memory bandwidth wall). Unfortunately, at low frequency run time is now consistently at the upper bound of variability.

Although this routine is perfectly load balanced on-node computation, the prior routines (filling ghost zones with MPI data or with a boundary condition) will vary from process to process. This suggests that these routines can artificially warm up the caches or pollute the TLBs such that the effects are seen in the subsequent (plotted) smooth routine. At high thread concurrencies, threads walk all over memory to affect the boundary condition or to fill in ghost zones, and are thus unlikely to have warmed up the caches for the smoother stencil.

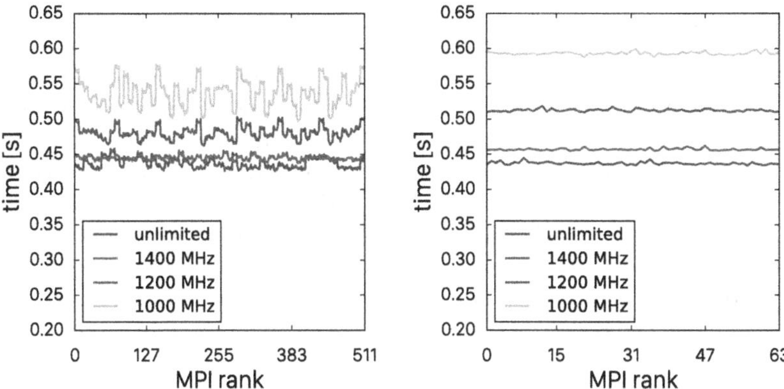

Fig. 4. Effects of frequency scaling on HPGMG's on-node smoother (averaged over 60s) at 64 nodes in *quad,flat* mode. Observe, there is far more variability in the 512 process ×8 thread configuration (left) while the 64 × 64 configuration (right) generally runs slower at low frequencies.

6 Job Placement

6.1 Introduction

A "Dragonfly" topology consists of groups of locally connected routers with groups connected to each other by high-speed global links. Within the Cray's Aries implementation of the dragonfly topology, local groups consists of a two-cabinet pair and contains a total of six chassis. A chassis houses sixteen blades, and each blade has four slots (or nodes) and a (shared) Aries router. This leads to a total of 384 slots in each Aries two-cabinet group. However, burst buffer nodes and other system service nodes may displace compute nodes, reducing the number of compute nodes per group to as few as ~355. All blades in a chassis are wired in an all-to-all fashion called rank-1 network or *green* links. The rank-2 network (*black* links) connect each blade in a chassis with each of its peers in other chassis of the same group. The latency and all-to-all bandwidths for rank-1 and rank-2 connections are similar. Finally, the rank-3 network (optical *blue* links) connects each Aries group with every other group. Adaptive routing is enabled on Cori, which allows packages to take routes which are not considered as shortest routes in terms of number of hops. This feature mitigates network congestion problems by rerouting packages through different chassis and cabinets. However, this can also lead to interference with applications running in other cabinets. Applications that span multiple nodes are expected to be more vulnerable than applications which only run on few nodes. Applications that span multiple chassis and cabinets are likely be more affected than jobs that are placed in a compact manner. In this section, we will investigate the performance variability dependent on job placement.

6.2 Mitigations/Solutions

SLURM provides control over job placement topology through the switches option to sbatch. The syntax is `--switches=N@HH:MM:SS`, where N is number of Dragonfly groups and HH:MM:SS is the maximum time to delay the start of the job until an allocation satisfying the requested number of switches is found. If the time elapses then the job will take the next available allocation which may not satisfy the requested number of switches. From the application side, hugepages can be used to mitigate Aries TLB thrashes. For that purpose, the code has to be recompiled with cray-hugepages module enabled and at runtime a page size has to be set.

6.3 Impact on Applications

We first tested if adaptive routing has the potential to interfere with applications running at very small scale and compact job placement. For that purpose, we ran IntelCaffe on 4 and 8 nodes on Cori ensuring that the 4 node jobs are contained within a single blade and the 8 node jobs span two adjacent blades. In both cases, we employed 66 OpenMP threads where each thread is bound to one physical core and dedicated additional 2 cores to the operating system by using the core specialization feature of SLURM (i.e. by specifying `-S 2` in the submit script). We are used 2MiB hugepages and RDMA accelerated collectives through DMAPP by enabling `MPICH_NETWORK_BUFFER_COLL_OPT`, `MPICH_RMA_OVER_DMAPP` and `MPICH_USE_DMAPP_COLL`. Our experiments were carried out on *quad,cache* configured nodes. Since all node-local data fits fully into MCDRAM, we did not see any difference from *quad,flat* mode. For comparison, we also ran the eight node job on our TDS system Gerty, using the same binary, same setup and system configuration. Gerty is a small-scale, lightly used test and development system with a comparably quiet network and thus much less prone to network noise. The neural network used was a 5 layer convolutional neural network (CNN) with small fully connected layer and $224 \times 224 \times 3$-sized input images that could be fully cached in memory. We measured the execution speed of forward, backward and update steps averaged over 10 iterations. The backward pass issues non-blocking allreduce operations that are concluded by a wait command in the subsequent update step of the corresponding layer. Therefore, only the latter should be affected by communication variability. The results from this test are displayed in Fig. 5, which shows that the computationally heavy forward and backward passes do not show any variability for any system and node count. The update step however shows severe performance variations. We further notice that variability on Cori depends on job compactness, i.e. jobs contained within a blade show much less variability than jobs spanning multiple blades. The same code executed on eight Gerty nodes shows very little performance variation with a somewhat periodic pattern[1]. The performance variation on Cori is less regular

[1] We observed spikes in the execution time about once every 20 iterations; averaging over 10 iterations gave rise to the figure's zig-zag pattern.

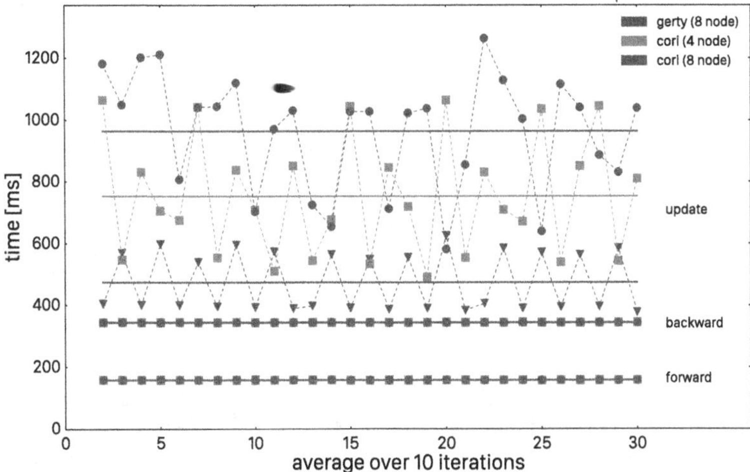

Fig. 5. Timings for forward, backward and update steps of a 5 layer CNN in IntelCaffe on different systems and for different node counts. The timings are averaged over 10 subsequent iterations. Solid lines represent mean timings for the respective steps.

and suggests that those runs were potentially impacted by other applications running on the same machine.

To further investigate the job placement dependence of performance variability, we performed medium scale runs with Chroma. Since this code is mostly doing nearest neighbor message exchanges, it is not as sensitive to network congestion from concurrently running applications as IntelCaffe. For this experiment, we employ 4 MPI ranks per node and 256 nodes in total. We further utilize 32 threads per rank and allocate 3.5 GiB of memory pool data and use 2 MiB hugepages. We run the Chroma Hybrid Molecular Dynamics (HMC) trajectory benchmark over several trajectories on a global $64^3 \cdot 128$ lattice (local size $16^2 \cdot 8 \cdot 16$) and measure the performance of each call to the BiCGStab solver. Comparing performance variation with in a job to its distribution of nodes across the network can provide a qualitative understanding of the impact of node placement on Chroma's performance. Figure 6(a) shows the performance histories for three selected jobs as well as their placements Fig. 6(b), (c) and (d). The later three depict the compactness of the job: they each show 4 cabinets of the Cori system along with worker nodes (open rectangles), service nodes (solid black rectangles) and the nodes occupied by the respective job (solid red rectangles). Rows and columns of the images can be directly mapped to physical rows and columns of the system. We observed that job 3724518 showed low performance variability and was also placed inside one cabinet in a contiguous fashion. Job 3731220 is contiguous to a certain extent, but spans two cabinets and has "holes" in between; the performance of this job is significantly less reliable. Finally, job 3828179 was scattered across four cabinets and shows huge variation over the duration of the run. Job 3731220 features some severe downward spikes at the

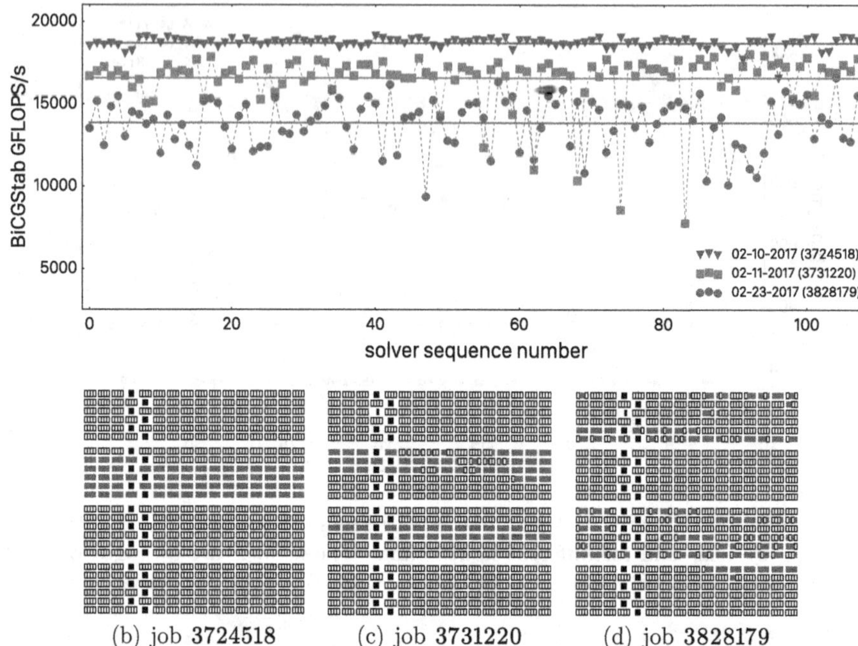

Fig. 6. Performance histories of Chroma HMC runs (a) with three different job placements: compact and contiguous (b), contiguous with holes (c) and scattered (d). The solid lines in (a) represent the corresponding mean flop rates. Solid red rectangles in (b, c, d) represent nodes occupied by the given job, black rectangles are service nodes and open rectangles are other worker nodes which might run other jobs at the same time (not shown). (Color figure online)

end of its lifetime that have not yet been fully explained. Given the approximate periodicity of the spikes, they may be related to heavy I/O operations by another job on the system. The root cause is still under active investigation.

7 Conclusions

In this paper we have highlighted three non-IO sources of performance variability on the Cori machine at NERSC. Effects of cache conflicts when MCDRAM is configured as a cache are one of the most prominent potential sources of performance variability on Xeon Phi, and the use of the Zone-Sort kernel module was found to be very beneficial in recovering lost performance. Variability stemming from DVFS does not show the same clear, well-defined signal and is highly application dependent, particularly when MKL is used. However, by running applications and benchmarks at different nominal clock frequencies this source of variability can be probed potentially at the cost of absolute performance, but of benefit to developers benchmarking code changes. Job placement in a large-scale production environment is a difficult problem, particularly when adaptive routing is in use and applications which are communication intensive should take job placement and interference effects into consideration when analyzing performance. The identification of sources of performance variability will continue to be important as processor architecture becomes more complex and system size increases.

Acknowledgments. This research used resources of the National Energy Research Scientific Computing Center (NERSC), a DOE Office of Science User Facility supported by the Office of Science of the U.S. Department of Energy under Contract No. DE-AC02-05CH11231.

References

1. Intel® distribution of Caffe* (2017). https://github.com/intel/caffe
2. Intel® Machine Learning Scaling Library for Linux* OS (2017). https://github.com/01org/MLSL
3. Edwards, R.G., Joo, B.: The Chroma software system for lattice QCD. Nucl. Phys. Proc. Suppl. **140**, 832 (2005)
4. http://crd.lbl.gov/departments/computer-science/PAR/research/hpgmg
5. https://bitbucket.org/hpgmg/hpgmg
6. Joó, B.: `qphix` package web page. http://jeffersonlab.github.io/qphix
7. Joó, B.: `qphix-codegen` package web page. http://jeffersonlab.github.io/qphix-codegen

Optimizing Fusion PIC Code Performance at Scale on Cori Phase Two

Tuomas Koskela(✉) and Jack Deslippe

National Energy Research Scientific Computing Center, Bekeley, CA, USA
tkoskela@lbl.gov

Abstract. In this paper we present the results of optimizing the performance of the gyrokinetic full-f fusion PIC code XGC1 on the Cori Phase Two Knights Landing system. The code has undergone substantial development to enable the use of vector instructions in its most expensive kernels within the NERSC Exascale Science Applications Program. We study the single-node performance of the code on an absolute scale using the roofline methodology to guide optimization efforts. We have obtained 2× speedups in single node performance due to enabling vectorization and performing memory layout optimizations. On multiple nodes, the code is shown to scale well up to 4000 nodes, near half the size of the machine. We discuss some communication bottlenecks that were identified and resolved during the work.

Keywords: Fusion · Applications · Performance · Optimization · Particle in cell

1 Introduction

Magnetic confinement devices are at present the most promising path towards controlled nuclear fusion for sustainable energy production [1]. The most successful design is the tokamak, a toroidal device where a burning hydrogen plasma is confined by a combination of magnetic field coils and an externally induced plasma current [2]. The ITER project [3], currently in construction phase in southern France, aims at demonstrating the feasibility of a tokamak fusion power plant in the 2030's. To ensure the success of ITER, and to pave the path towards commercial fusion power plants, self-consistent simulations of the turbulent fusion plasma at exascale are urgently needed to understand and control the complex plasma phenomena that are born from the interplay of electromagnetic fields and charged particles.

Since directly computing the N^2 number of infinite-range particle-particle interactions in a plasma is impractical, the Particle-In-Cell (PIC) method is a powerful tool for plasma physics simulations in laboratory, space, and fusion plasmas [4–6]. A PIC code solves the kinetic evolution of the particle distribution function and the evolution of electromagnetic fields self-consistently. Typically PIC codes consist of four steps that are iterated in a time-stepping loop: (1)

J.M. Kunkel et al. (Eds.): ISC High Performance Workshops 2017, LNCS 10524, pp. 430–440, 2017.
https://doi.org/10.1007/978-3-319-67630-2_32

field solve, (2) field gather, (3) particle push, and (4) charge deposition. In fusion applications that deal with collisional plasmas, a collision step is normally added to collectively treat small-angle scattering. A particle shift step is introduced when the algorithm is parallelized to handle communication between processes due to the motion of particles between computational domains. Steps (1), (3) and the collision step are computation intensive, involving linear algebra and numerical integration. Steps (2) and (4) are mapping steps between the particles and the mesh that are dominated by memory access.

The vast majority of fusion PIC applications use the *gyrokinetic* theory [7] to reduce the dimensionality of the kinetic problem and, therefore, achieve large savings in computation time. However, the gyrokinetic equation of motion contains higher order derivatives in steps (2) and (3) that set them apart from PIC codes in other fields. Typically the compute time in gyrokinetic PIC codes is dominated by the electron push cycle. Electrons move at a much higher speed than ions and therefore need to be advanced with a much shorter time step. Many codes employ an electron sub-cycling loop where electron-scale field fluctuations are neglected and the electrons are pushed for O(10) time steps for each ion time step. The electron sub-cycling loop is a prime candidate for performance optimization since it's trivially parallelizable and has a high arithmetic intensity. The main obstacle for high performance is random memory access due to the complex motion of the electrons across the grid.

Cori is the first large-scale supercomputer that is leveraging the Intel Knights Landing (KNL) architecture [8]. It is installed at the National Energy Research Scientific Computing Center (NERSC) at Lawrence Berkeley Laboratory (LBL) in Berkeley, CA. At present it has 9688 KNL nodes and 2004 Haswell nodes, making it the world's 5th fastest supercomputer on the top 500 list. However, getting good code performance on KNL is not always trivial due to various features of the KNL architecture; large number of relatively slow processors, high-bandwidth memory and wide vector processing units. In order to enable key scientific applications to run on Cori, NERSC started the NERSC Exascale Science Applications Program (NESAP) in 2014 [9]. One of the outcomes of NESAP is the development a new methodology for optimizing application performance on KNL [10]. The XGC1 code [12] is the only fusion PIC application accepted to NESAP and serves as a test case for other fusion PIC codes that aspire to run on Cori KNL and future Intel Xeon Phi systems. The unique feature of XGC1 is that it uses real-space coordinates and an unstructured mesh for the field solution making it capable of simulating the full tokamak volume simultaneously.

2 Roofline Baseline Performance Measurement and Main Bottlenecks

We use the roofline methodology [13,14] in our performance measurements to discuss performance on an absolute scale. The roofline model is a visual performance model that can be applied to both applications and computing

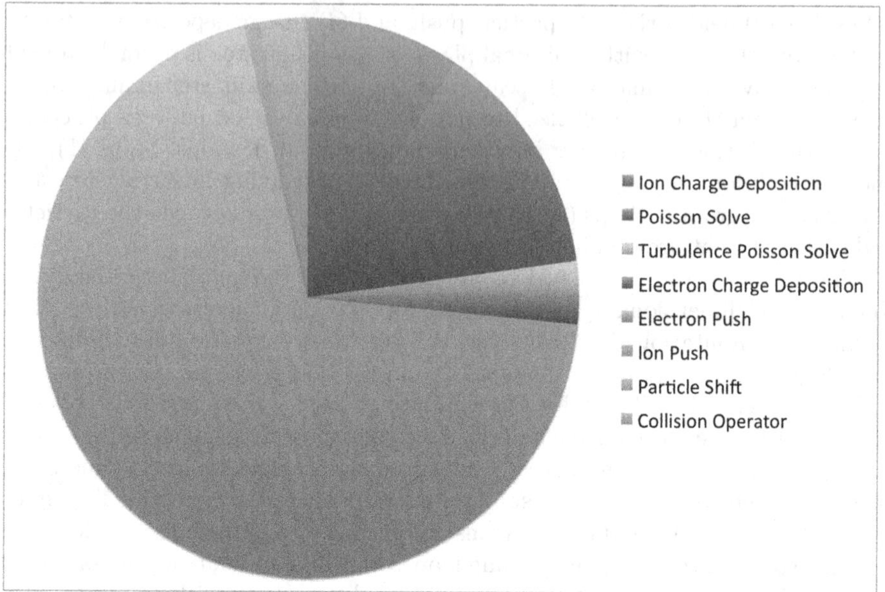

Fig. 1. Relative contributions to the XGC1 runtime of main kernels. Electron push contributes roughly 75% of the runtime in typical jobs.

architectures. It describes performance in terms of flops per second (FLOPS) as a function of Arithmetic Intensity (AI), the ratio of the FLOPS executed vs. the bytes read from some level of the cache memory hierarchy. A computing architecture will set roofs of achievable performance that are bound by the compute capability and the memory bandwidth. Placing an application's hot kernels on the roofline chart will give information on attainable performance, current performance bounds, and most promising optimization directions [10].

The main kernels of XGC1 are the particle push, particle shift, the Poisson solver, charge deposition and the collision operator. The field gather routine is so closely tied to the particle push kernel that it is impossible to treat it separately. Furthermore, the particle kernels can be divided into ion and electron kernels that contain slightly different physics approximations and, in the case of the push kernel, are called with a different frequency. The contributions of the main kernels on the runtime of XGC1 are plotted in Fig. 1, showing that most of the computation time is spent in the electron push kernel, as was suggested in the previous section. In this paper we mostly focus on optimizations to the electron push kernel, and only touch on the communication intensive kernels in Sect. 4. Extensive optimization work has also been performed on the collision kernel [11] which scales with N^2 where N is the number of particle species. Most XGC1 simulations currently use $N = 2$ but multi-ion species runs are forecast for the future.

The main kernels of XGC1 lie in very different regions of the roofline chart. The electron push kernel is compute intensive and has a relatively high AI, since multiple floating point operations are performed on the field data that is read from memory to calculate the equation of motion at each time step. The roofline chart does not immediately give the performance bound of the kernel, i.e. it is not memory bandwidth bound, yet it does not reach any of the peak compute performance roofs. In Fig. 2 we show the results of a more detailed analysis of the electron push kernel on the roofline chart. We can identify three main classes of loops that spend significant fractions of the computing time.

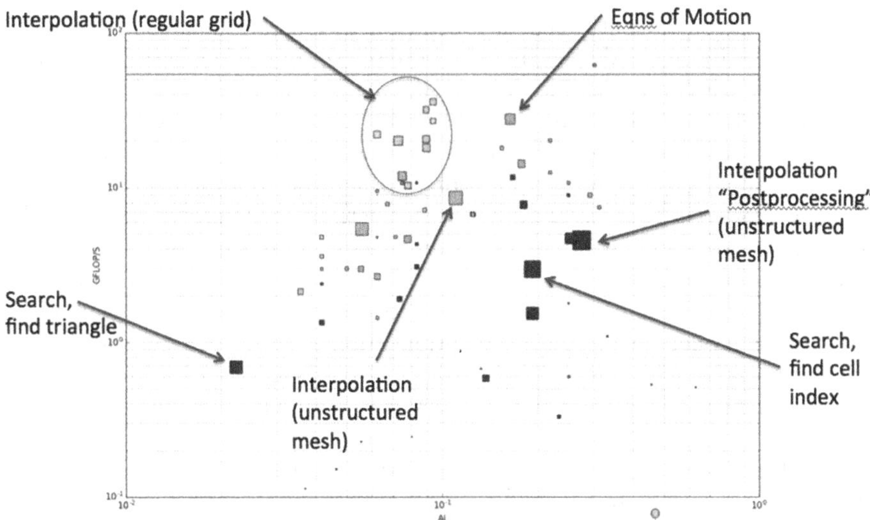

Fig. 2. A breakdown of the performance of loops in the electron push kernel as a function of Arithmetic Intensity based on the cache-aware roofline model.

1. Field gather loops. A field gather operation is made before each time step. The field gather kernel locates the nearest grid nodes, accesses field vector data stored at them, and performs an interpolation to the particle position. The algorithm fundamentally requires indirect memory access to field data due to the "random" motion of the particles across the grid. Furthermore, the innermost loops of the algorithm have short trip counts, making automatic compiler optimization ineffective.
2. Force calculation loops. The forces acting on the particle are calculated from gradients and cross and dot products of the gathered field variables to advance the equations of motion [12] forward in time. The field data is stored in fortran derived data types and the equations of motion require several strided memory accesses to the field vectors and the Jacobian matrix. It is also non-ideal for cache reuse.

3. Search loops. The unstructured mesh that is used in XGC1 to store the electric field solution introduces an additional search step after each particle push to locate the mesh element the particle was pushed into. In addition to suffering from indirect memory access to the coordinates stored at grid nodes, search algorithms are difficult for the compiler auto-vectorization due to irregular exit conditions once the search has finished.

3 Optimizations and Performance Improvements

3.1 Vectorization of Electron Push

Since we have established that the electron push kernel is not memory bandwidth bound due to its high AI, the most reasonable optimization path is enabling vectorization wherever possible. The XGC1 code has a complex hierarchy of subroutine calls from the main program down to the computation kernels that operated on scalar arguments. The main routine loops over particles and passes them one by one down to the computation routines that contain no loops or loops with very short trip counts. To enable vectorization, blocking was added to the main particle loop and the inner loop over blocks of particles was moved down to the innermost computation subroutines. The interpolation and computation subroutines were then restructured to vectorize over the particle loop, while letting the compiler decide the best optimization strategy for the short outer loops over nearby grid points. With this strategy, good vectorization efficiency was achieved in the field interpolation loops and the equation of motion compute loop.

Particle sorting by grid element was added to improve the cache reuse in the interpolation loop. Due to the field-aligned grid that is elongated in the parallel direction, particles in XGC1 move across grid cells relatively rarely, less than 1% of time steps end in a different cell than where they started. Therefore, if the particle array is sorted at the beginning of the electron sub-cycling loop, it remains in reasonably good order for the duration of the sub-cycling. The aim is to group particles in the same cell at the beginning of the sub-cycling close together in memory so that all access to a set of grid points can be performed consecutively. To reach this goal, the order of the time step loop and the outer particle loop was changed in the electron push kernel so that a block of particles is pushed through the sub-cycling continuously before moving on to the next block.

While it is not possible to completely eliminate gather/scatter instructions in the vectorized algorithm, we can optimize the memory alignment of the data to minimize the number of expensive gathers. Generally vector codes favor an Structure-of-Arrays (SoA) data layout because it allows contiguous access to individual structures. However, we find that variables stored on the 3D mesh that are gathered from scattered locations in memory an Array-of-Structures (AoS) layout yields better performance. The improvement comes from reducing the number of expensive gather/scatter instructions. A particle is connected to six grid points on the unstructured mesh (eight on a regular mesh). When data from all nearby grid points is read for an interpolation, they can be accessed on a single cache line with a vector gather instruction in an AoS layout. For the particle data, an SoA layout yields better performance, as expected.

The search algorithm can theoretically benefit from all the optimizations that have been discussed above and applied to the interpolation and computation algorithms. However, a search algorithm can not know how many iterations it has to search through before completing, which is not a feature that is easy to vectorize. Because the trip count of the search loop is unknown at each time that it is entered it is impossible for the compiler to vectorize over particles. However, we can use the fact that a new search is necessary only when a particle enters a new grid cell to bring down the cost of the search routine. A pre-check was added to determine if a new search is needed and the serial search is executed only when necessary, bringing down the search cost.

The optimizations are summarized, on the roofline chart, in Fig. 3. The total speedup in the kernel is close to 3× from the baseline code. In this figure, the kernel is measured as a whole, using the bytes moved from DRAM as the arithmetic intensity. We have assumed the amount of flops computed does not significantly change during optimizations. The data and the roofs are measured for a single KNL thread. We see a significant increase of DRAM AI (equivalent to improved cache reuse) from the particle loop blocking optimization. However, we are unable to reach either the compute or memory bandwidth peaks of the hardware. We conclude the code is now limited by memory latency due to the irregular memory access patterns in the interpolation and search routines.

3.2 Threading of Charge Deposition

Charge deposition in XGC1 is performed after every ion time step for both ions and electrons. Each MPI rank deposits charge on the whole grid, dividing the work among its OpenMP threads. The ion charge is deposited in a 3-D array with the dimensions [number of grid nodes per toroidal plane, number of velocity space grid points, number of adjacent toroidal planes]. The number of adjacent toroidal planes is always 2. The velocity grid is required for the gyro-averaging routine and usually has 4 or 8 points. The total size of this array is therefore 2 × 8× the size of the unstructured mesh, usually 100k–1M, totaling 1.6M–16M elements. The electron charge is deposited without using a velocity space grid, which reduces the size of the array by 8–16×.

In the initial implementation, a separate copy of the charge density array was allocated for each thread. Each thread would initialize it to 0 and deposit charge from a subset of particles to its own copy of the array. In the end a sum over all copies of the array would be stored on the master thread, but the reduction sum was done manually with a loop written in the code. We found two problems in large-scale runs on Cori KNL: (1) The initialization of 16M elements per thread avx512_memset function became extremely slow and (2) the manual reduction was not well optimized. To solve (1) and (2) we eliminated the allocation and initialization of separate copies for each thread. However, when all threads write to the same array, we have to take care of not to create

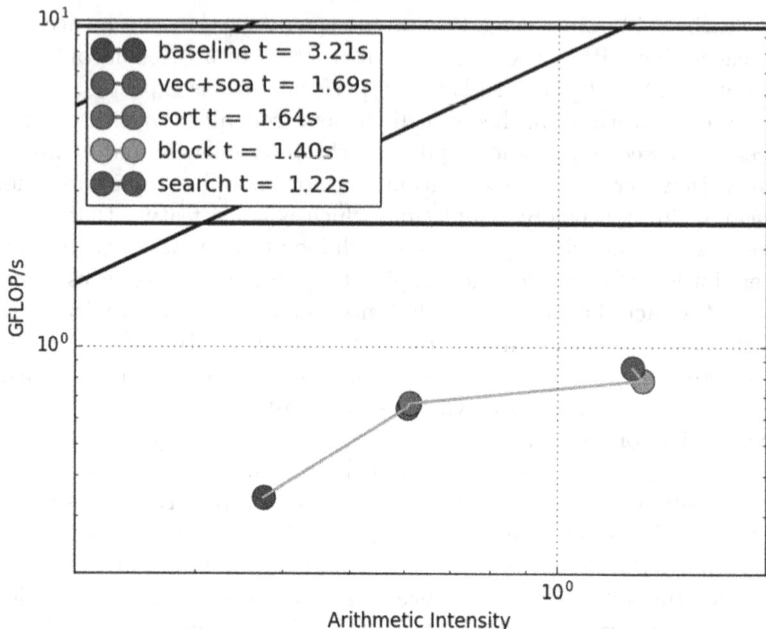

Fig. 3. Optimization steps of electron push on the roofline chart. Both roofs and application measurements are for a single thread on KNL. The lower horizontal roof is the scalar add peak and the upper roof is the vector add peak.

race conditions. We developed two solutions: I: Declare the charge density array with `omp reduction(+:)`. This imitates what the code was doing before but the OpenMP runtime provides a much better optimized implementation. II: Declare the charge density array `omp shared` and declare all updates to the array `omp atomic`.

The performance of optimizations I and II depend on the size of the problem, especially the size of the unstructured mesh and the number of particles per thread. The OpenMP reduction operation incurs an overhead from creating private copies of the array at the beginning of the parallel region and calculating the sum over all threads at the end of the parallel region. This overhead depends on the size of the unstructured mesh. The OpenMP atomic update operation on the other hand incurs an overhead whenever two threads try to update the same memory location and the other thread has to wait, and potentially retrieve the value from the cache of another core before updating it. This overhead is fairly constant per particle (i.e., a certain fraction of particles will cause a wait, regardless of the total number of particles), therefore increasing the number of particles increases the total overhead.

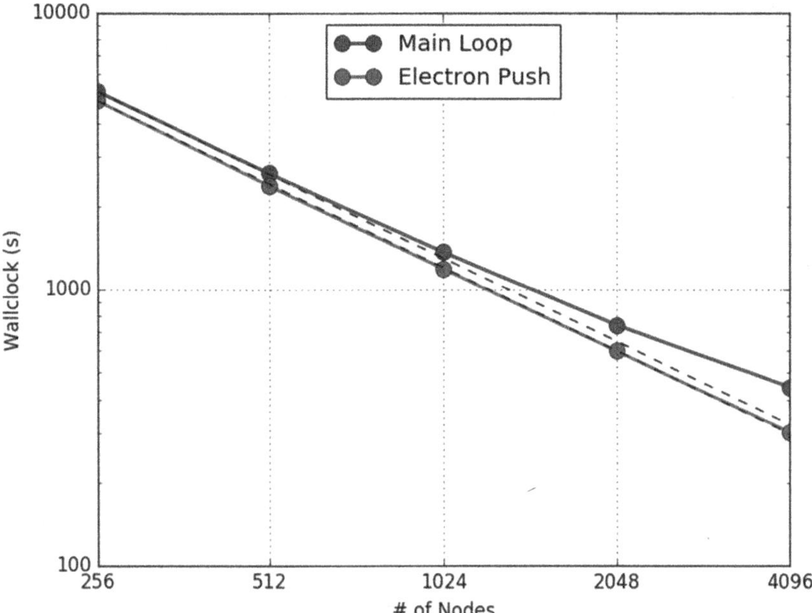

Fig. 4. Strong scaling of the main loop of the full XGC1 application and the electron push kernel. The electron push follows ideal scaling almost exactly, while the main loop deviates from the ideal scaling at high concurrency, reaching roughly 30% at 4092 nodes.

4 Scaling Results on Cori

XGC1 has been using the Titan and Mira systems at near their maximal capabilities for production runs. However, the Cori system presents different challenges with its many-core Knights Landing architecture that allows up to 272 threads per node. Here we will present the first results of strong and weak scaling of the full XGC1 production code up to half machine size on Cori Phase Two.

Strong scaling is important to make better use of emerging exascale systems for faster turn-around time of "routine" simulations of present tokamaks. In this strong scaling study, we have used an unstructured mesh of 56 000 nodes per toroidal plane and 32 toroidal planes. The particle array has a total of 25 billion ions and 25 billion electrons. We run the code for ten ion time steps and three collision steps and measure the time spent in the main time step loop. The results are shown in Fig. 4 for up to 4096 nodes on the Cori KNL partition. We find near perfect strong scaling in electron push routine, within 2% of ideal scaling and good strong scaling in whole main loop, within 30% of ideal scaling at half machine size. The slowdown comes communication in the Poisson solver and charge deposition.

We consider two variations of weak scaling, a weak scaling in total particle number for a fixed grid size and a more complete weak scaling in both total

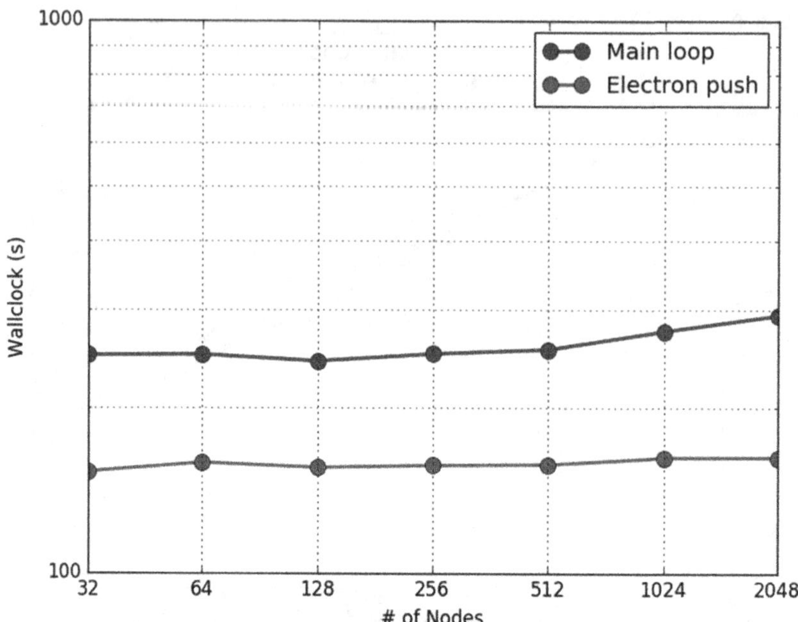

Fig. 5. Weak scaling in particle number. The number of particles per thread is fixed at 12 500 and grid size is kept fixed at 56 000 grid nodes. The scaling behaviour is qualitatively similar to the strong scaling behaviour.

particle number and the grid size. Both have merit, as increasing the number of particles on a fixed grid size allows better statistics and noise reduction in the full-f method where marker particles represent the entire distribution function, instead of a perturbation around an analytic equilibrium distribution. Increasing both the grid and particles in proportion allows scaling up to simulations of large fusion devices on larger machines, which is the main goal in the project for exascale. The weak scaling of XGC1 on Cori in particle number is shown in Fig. 5 where flat horizontal lines represent ideal weak scaling. We used the same unstructured mesh as in the strong scaling study and 3.2 million particles per node, up to 2048 nodes on the Cori KNL partition. We find the scaling of the electron push routine to be again very good, which is to be expected based on the strong scaling results. For this grid size the main loop also shows reasonable weak scaling, although some degradation begins to occur when scaling up to 1024 nodes and above. This degradation is attributed mostly to the Poisson solver and work is ongoing to address it. Finally, the weak scaling in both total particle number and grid size is shown in Fig. 6. We are still using 3.2 million particles per node but now the grid size is scaled with the problem size, using 235 grid nodes per compute node up to 1 million total grid nodes at 4096 compute nodes. We find that the performance is degraded more rapidly when simulation size reaches 1024 nodes and 240 000 grid nodes. We have separated the scaling

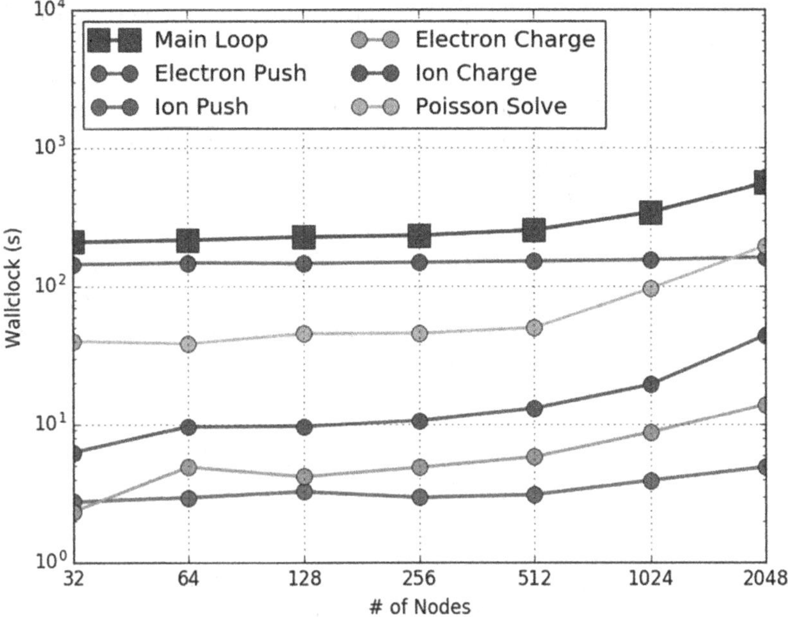

Fig. 6. Weak scaling in particle number and grid size

of the main kernels in the main loop in Fig. 6 and it is shown that most of the performance degradation originates from the Poisson solver. The optimization of the Poisson solver is outside the scope of this paper, since it mostly relies on calls to the PETSc library. We have however identified a scalar code bottleneck, outside of the PETSc calls. We expect to improve the scaling significantly once it is parallelized.

5 Summary and Discussion

In this paper, we have discussed the performance and the optimizations performed on the XGC1 code within the NESAP project in preparation for running with good performance on the Cori Phase Two Knights Landing system and future exascale CPU systems. We have identified the hot kernels of the code, and using the roofline methodology developed strategies to optimize the performance. The key item for XGC1 is enabling vectorization in the electron push sub-cycling. In order to achieve good vectorization efficiency, a number of loop nest restructuring and data layout optimizations were performed. The Particle-in-Cell algorithm fundamentally contains a large number of random indirect memory accesses, that do not perform well in vectorized code. We have developed techniques to reduce those accesses as much as possible by data reuse and sorting. However, the remaining gather/scatters inherent to the algorithm incur memory latency that limits the performance below the theoretical FLOP or bandwidth limits.

The XGC1 code scales very well up to 4000 nodes, and beyond, for a typical present-day problem size as has been shown by our scaling tests. Good strong allows for faster turn-around times of present-day problems on larger computing systems. Weak scaling is, however, more complicated and great care must be taken in studying it. A PIC code has kernels, such as the particle push and shift, that scale with the number of particles per thread. These are relatively easy to scale and show good scaling in XGC1. Weak scaling the particle kernels has merit by itself, since it allows going to higher resolution in the full particle distribution function for a given problem size. There are also kernels that scale with the size of the grid, such as the field solver, and both the number of particles and the size of the grid, such as the charge deposition. Great care must be taken in adjusting the aggregated size of the problem to ensure representative weak scaling. This is an interesting problem that is still a work in progress. We hope to be able to provide valuable insights into how different parts of codes like XGC1 weak scale on Cori in the near future.

Acknowledgements. The authors wish to thank Drs. S. Abbot, E. D'Azavedo, E. Yoon, S. Ku, R. Hager and C.S. Chang for their help in understanding the XGC1 code and many helpful ideas during the optimization efforts. This research used resources of the National Energy Research Scientific Computing Center (NERSC), a DOE Office of Science User Facility supported by the Office of Science of the U.S. Department of Energy under Contract No. DE-AC02-05CH11231.

References

1. International Atomic Energy Agency: Fusion Physics, chap. 1. IAEA, Vienna (2012)
2. Artsimovich, L.A.: Nucl. Fusion **12**(2), 215 (1972)
3. http://www.iter.org
4. Ethier, S., Tang, W.M., Lin, Z.: J. Phys. Conf. Ser. **16**(1). IOP Publishing (2005)
5. http://warp.lbl.gov
6. Markidis, S., Rizwan-uddin, Lapenta, G.: Math. Comput. Simul. **80**(7), 1509–1519 (2010)
7. Brizard, A.J., Hahm, T.S.: Rev. Mod. Phys. **79**(2), 412–468 (2007)
8. http://www.nersc.gov/users/computational-systems/cori/
9. Barnes, T., et al.: Supercomputing Conference, 7th International Workshop on Performance Modeling, Benchmarking and Simulation of High Performance Computer Systems, pp. 43–53 (2016)
10. Doerfler, D., et al.: International Conference on High Performance Computing, pp. 339–353 (2016)
11. Hager, R., et al.: J. Comput. Phys. **315**, 644–660 (2016)
12. Ku, S., et al.: Nucl. Fusion **49**(11) (2009). Article 115021
13. Williams, S., et al.: CACM **52**(4), 65–76 (2009)
14. Ilic, A., et al.: IEEE Comput. Archit. Lett. **12**(1), 21–24 (2013)
15. Kurth, T., et al.: Submitted to the International Supercomputing Conference IXPUG Workshop (2017)

amask: A Tool for Evaluating Affinity Masks in Many-Core Processors

Kent Milfeld(✉)

Texas Advanced Computing Center, Austin, TX, USA
milfeld@tacc.utexas.edu

Abstract. Today's multi- and many-core systems have NUMA nodes, sockets, tiles, cores, and Symmetric Multi-Threading (SMT) which may require complicated affinity settings to optimally map processes to processors. In many-core systems with hundreds of processors, evaluating the affinity of a single process by surveying a list of processor numbers is time consuming and error prone. Comparing two or more process affinities is even more troublesome. The **amask** tool displays all process affinities as an easy-to-read matrix of processor-ids versus ranks and/or thread-ids, allowing researchers to quickly confirm default settings and the effect of manipulating affinity, either before or during a parallel execution (through a stand-alone executable or API, respectively).

Keywords: Affinity mask · Tool · KNL

1 Introduction

In the early days of HPC clusters there were only nodes with single cores, and only time-slicing, rather than process locality, was an important concern. Now, with multiple and many-core processors in a single node, placement of processes through affinity has become more important. *Process* is used in a general sense throughout, and includes threads.

There are a number of ways to set the affinity for a process: inside an executable (with an API), at execution launch time through MPI [9] or OpenMP environment variables [3] or direct affinity control (with `numactl`), and even as a Unix command targeting a process id (with `taskset` or `numactl`).

The diversity of processor layouts, BIOS configurations, Simultaneous MultiThreading (SMT) and Non-Uniform Memory Access (NUMA) nodes makes it difficult to obtain an optimal process placement even for the seemingly inconsequential situation of having a process on every processor.

While the runtimes for multi-processing (MPI, OpenMP, etc.) may set reasonable affinity defaults, users now want to understand and control the affinity for their application to achieve higher performance and make them portable.

This paper does not focus on the achievement of higher performance through affinity, per se; rather, it presents a tool, **amask**, for determining the affinity mask for the user's application in a parallel environment– for a pure MPI, pure

J.M. Kunkel et al. (Eds.): ISC High Performance Workshops 2017, LNCS 10524, pp. 441–451, 2017.
https://doi.org/10.1007/978-3-319-67630-2_33

OpenMP, or Hybrid [6] execution. Acquiring the actual masks of a run in a multi-processing environment is the first step, and often the stumbling block, in the quest to strategically bind or affinitize processes for higher performance.

Version 1.0 of the **amask** tool suite provides executables and an API for quickly reporting affinity masks of each process in a parallel run. The matrix format for the masks, as opposed to a list of process-ids for each process mask, provides a clear visual for comparing of all masks, and an easy determination of the processor-ids (the core-id or the hardware thread-id for SMT). When dealing with hundreds of processors and processes the organization and the clarity makes an affinity analysis much easier.

In Sect. 2 the basics of an affinity bit map are reviewed, and a discussion of MPI and OpenMP affinities follows. The basics of affinity bit maps are related to a need for a comprehensive, high-level approach for visualizing affinity. Next, **amask** features and tool operations are presented in Sect. 3. Section 4 illustrates use cases for **amask**. Finally, a summary is presented, and is followed by a Future Work Section.

2 Affinity Masks

An affinity mask is a list of processor-ids (proc-ids) that a process can run on. As already introduced, we use process in the general sense as an MPI process or an OpenMP thread; and a processor, identified by a proc-id, is a logical computing unit (generally a hardware thread for SMT, and a core otherwise).

To be efficient, the kernel uses a bit mask to hold this list. If there are N processors on the system, the mask will have N bits, the bit number corresponding to a proc-id. When a bit is set (to 1), then the process owning the map is allowed to execute on the processor corresponding to the set bit. In essence, the process becomes bound to the processor. When multiple bits are set, the process is allowed to execute on any one of the processors, and the process may migrate to any other processor with a set bit. That is, for the latter case the process can float (is affinitized) among a set of processors. Specifically, bits 0 through N-1 represent proc-ids 0 to N-1; where the proc-id is the "processor" number assigned in the /proc/cpuinfo file (on Linux clusters).

For Intel MPI (IMPI), the mask for each process is printed for the application when the I_MPI_DEBUG environment variable is set to 4 or above. When the number of processors and/or processes is small it is easy to extract mask information from the listing; however, for a many-core system like an Intel Knights Landing (KNL) [7], just determining the number of set bits might be difficult, let alone determining the union or intersection of two masks. Masks for IMPI-compiled executables can be set through environment variables. Intel affinity features hierarchy semantics for mapping processes onto a hardware hierarchy (without using explicit proc-ids). Explicitly setting affinity can be complicated, and often a report of the masks from I_MPI_DEBUG is employed to confirm expectations of an affinity setting. The report is just a list of numbers for each process, and a list for one process is difficult to relate to another process's list when there are hundreds of proc-ids to deal with.

Unlike IMPI, MVAPICH2 (MV2) MPI does not have an interface for extracting affinity masks for MPI processes. MV2 binds an MPI process to a single processor, with exclusive ownership. This may be turned off through the MV2_ENABLE_AFFINITY variable to allow the MPI launcher to use `numactl` to control the process placement. The MPI launcher (`ibrun`) at the Texas Advanced Computing Center (TACC) allows users to turn off MV2 affinity and subscribe to the `tacc_affinity` wrapper script to determine and set an optimal machine-specific affinity for a specified number of tasks per node (with the syntax: `ibrun tacc_affinity ./a.out`).

There are other affinity tools that show masks, such as the Cray **xthi** program. These are quite useful for observing affinities within a parallel environment, too; nevertheless, **amask** was designed for easy comparisons of the masks, and has a rich feature set (not discussed here).

Only since OpenMP 4.0 has the standard addressed setting thread affinity; and only lately has it been working on an API to display thread masks. For now there is no direct way to extract affinities for each thread. However, by setting the OMP_DISPLAY_ENV variable, the OpenMP runtime will display the affinity requested in the OMP_PLACES and OMP_PROC_BIND environment variables, or defaults if the content of either variable is not understood or the variable is not defined.

OpenMP Affinity is described here because the semantics for contiguous sequences, repetitions and striding provides a concise expression for complicated masks, and yet it is simple for setting a single bit or contiguous bit fields in a mask. The variable OMP_PROC_BIND specifies a distribution policy, such as SPREAD and CLOSE. For the list of places in OMP_PLACES, thread id j is assigned to the proc-id in the $j+1$ place. Each place may contain multiple entries (proc-ids) for a thread to float. Before OpenMP 4.0 non-standard environment variables, such as the GNU GOMP_CPU_AFFINITY and the Intel KMP_AFFINITY variables, were used to explicitly modify the default affinity.

No matter if the application runs in hybrid, pure MPI, or pure OpenMP mode, acquiring a map listing is important for validating what the user would expect from the default parallel environment or a tailored affinity setting.

3 Acquiring Process Maps in a Parallel Environment

The **amask** tool suite contains three executables for displaying the process maps for parallel environments: `amask_omp`, `amask_mpi`, and `amask_hybrid`. These can be executed alone or immediately before a parallel application is run to display the process maps the user's application will run with (provided the application does not change the affinity internally). Typical example scenarios are given in Listing 1.1.

Listing 1.1. amask executables for displaying process maps

```
$ # Pure OpenMP Execution
$    export OMP_NUM_THREADS=68
$    amask_omp                          # amask executable
$    my_ompapp
$
$ # Pure MPI Execution
$    mpirun -np 4  amask_mpi
$    mpirun -np 4  my_mpiapp            # amask executable
$
$ # Hybrid Execution
$    export OMP_NUM_THREADS=17
$    mpirun -np 4 amask_hybrid          # amask executable
$    mpirun -np 4 my_mpiompapp
```

The **amask** tool suite also contains a single library of three no-argument routines. These C/C++/F90 callable routines allow users to display the process masks inside an MPI and/or OpenMP parallel region. The typical uses are shown in Listing 1.2.

Listing 1.2. amaks API calls for displaying process maps

```
// Pure OpenMP Code
   #pragma omp parallel
      amask_omp();          // amask API
      ...

// Pure MPI Code
   MPI_Init(NULL,NULL);
      amask_mpi();          // amask API
      ...
   MPI_Finalize();

// Hybrid Code
   MPI_Init(NULL,NULL);
   ...
     #pragma omp parallel
      {
         amask_hybrid();   // amask API
         ...
      }
   ...
   MPI_Finalize();
```

amask was created with large processor-count and SMT nodes in mind–specifically, for the TACC's Lonestar5 [1,5] 24-core Hyper-Threaded nodes and the Stampede2 KNL [8] nodes, as shown in Listings 1.6–1.9 below. A matrix map listing can be quite useful when exploring affinity settings when a subset of the SMTs in a core are to be used. Often 24 or fewer processes are launched on the 48 hardware-thread Lonestar5 nodes. Likewise, **amask** is quite useful when exploring MPI process placement on the 68-core Stampede2 KNL system. For instance, with a matrix list format it is easy to discover if core-sharing by two MPI processes occurs for MPI-process counts that do not divide 68 evenly.

amask is available on github [4]. The present version of the **amask** tool was written for the TACC systems (Centos/SuSE). However, it is written in a portable context (no vendor-specific features in the MPI, OpenMP and Unix utils coding). We are open-sourcing the code for community support to make it portable to other platforms.

4 Use Cases

The next three Listings illustrate how to use the **amask** `amask_mpi` executable to discover the affinity masks that would be applied to any MPI application for three different parallel environments. The system is a 2-socket, 8-core/socket non Hyper-Threaded node (Stampede1 system at TACC). Proc-ids 0–7 are assigned to cores on socket0 by the BIOS, and 8–15 are assigned to socket1. For simplicity only 2 MPI tasks are launched.

In Listing 1.3 the parallel environment is for an executable compiled with the MVAPICH2 MPI library and no explicit affinity settings. The `amask_mpi` binary is executed, as an application would be executed, to obtain the affinity (masks) for the environment (see `mpirun` statement). The final two lines in the output are the masks for the two MPI processes. They consist of labels for their ranks, 0000 and 0001, followed by 16 characters representing the 16 proc-ids of the mask. A dash (-) means that the corresponding bit is not set, and a single digit means that the bit is set. The proc-id for a set bit is determined by adding the single digit in the mask (row) with the group number in the header. For instance, the rank 0000 process is bound to proc-id 0, as determined by adding the "0" to the group number "0" in the header line. Likewise, the rank 0001 process is bound to proc-id 1, as determined by adding 1 to the group number 0 in the header. This is explained in the first two lines of the output. A set bit is represented as a single digit (character) to provide room for a terminal to display masks with hundreds of proc-ids.

In Listing 1.4 the `tacc_affinity` wrapper is used to modify the affinity of each MPI process. Here too, the `amask_mpi` executable is launched (in lieu of the application executable) to determine the affinities the application processes would have. In this case the rank 0000 process has bits 0–7 set, corresponding to proc-ids 0–7. The rank 0001 process has bits 8–15 set, as determined by adding group number 0 to the digit 8 and 9, and adding the group number 10 to the digits 0, 1, 2, 3, 4, and 5. This is an appropriate MPI mask for running a hybrid application: since an OpenMP thread team inherits the mask of its MPI process, rank 0000 will allow threads to execute on proc-ids 0–7, while rank 0001 will allow its threads to execute on proc-ids 8–15. For a hybrid execution in the environment of Listing 1.3 the threads would be confined to only two proc-ids (cores)! To see the masks for a hybrid execution, simply set the OMP_NUM_THREADS environment variable, and use the `amask_hybrid` executable instead of `amask_mpi`.

Listing 1.5 shows the process maps for an Intel environment (application and amask suite built with an Intel compiler and the Intel IMPI libraries). In the IMPI environment, the default affinity setting is the same as the `tacc_affinity` environment of Listing 1.4 except that the sockets have been switched. The IMPI mapping algorithm was designed to automatically put rank0 on the closest socket to the InfiniBand adapter (socket1) for efficient collective communication through rank0 as root. The `tacc_affinity` environment has rank0 closest to the local disk interfaces on socket0.

From these three examples it becomes evident that the affinity should be checked in any new parallel environment. The **amask** executables allow researchers to easily determine affinities without resorting to vendor or site documentation.

Listing 1.3. amask Listings: MV2 Environment, 2 MPI tasks on 2×8 cores

```
$# compiled and run in MVAPICH2 environment

$ mpirun -np 2 amask_mpi
          Each row of matrix is an Affinity mask.
          A set mask bit = matrix digit + column group # in |...|
rank |    0    |    10     |
0000 0---------------
0001 -1--------------
```

Listing 1.4. amask Listings: `tacc_affinity` Environment, 2 MPI tasks on 2×8 cores

```
$# compiled and run in MVAPICH2 environment
$ mpirun -np 2  tacc_affinity amask_mpi

          Each row of matrix is an Affinity mask.
          A set mask bit = matrix digit + column group # in |...|
rank |    0    |    10     |
0000 01234567--------
0001 --------89012345
```

Listing 1.5. amask Listings: IMPI Environment, 2 MPI tasks on 2×8 cores

```
$# compiled and run in IMPI environment
$ mpirun -np 2 amask_mpi

          Each row of matrix is an Affinity mask.
          A set mask bit = matrix digit + column group # in |...|
rank |    0    |    10     |
0000 --------89012345
0001 01234567--------
```

Affinity masks are not too helpful without an understanding of the proc-id assignments to the cores, tiles, sockets and NUMA nodes. These details can be extracted from `/proc/cpuinfo`, `lscpu`, and `lstopo` (`hwloc`[2]), and are invaluable for customizing affinity for an application. If **amask** discovers that a platform has SMT turned on, it displays a core-centric list rather than a pure proc-id mask list. **amask** uses `lscpu` to determine if the system has SMT turned on. Listing 1.6 shows the pure mask and core-centric forms. Either form can be specified by an option on the command line: `-lc` for core format and `-ls` for the pure mask (SMT) format. The core-centric form presents a new line for each hardware thread. Core ids are determined by adding the single digits in the row to the group number. The proc-ids can be obtained by adding a factor of the total number of cores for each additional row of hardware threads. Unfortunately, obtaining proc-ids in the core format is not simple.

The (Lonestar5) node used for Listing 1.6 has 2 sockets, each with 12 Hyper-Threaded cores (48 proc-ids). Proc-ids 0–11 are on socket0 and the following proc-ids 12–23 are on socket1; all have hardware-thread ids of 0. Proc-ids 24–35 are on socket0, subsequently 36–47 are on socket1 (in a round-robin manner); all have hardware-thread ids of 1. The pure mask display shows that rank0 and rank1 can float on 12 hardware threads of socket0. Likewise for rank2 and rank3 on socket1. The core-centric (default for a SMT system) listing readily shows that the processes are not allowed to float on the second hardware thread of each core.

In Listing 1.6 the proc-ids of the second-line entries are obtained by adding 24 (number of cores) to the number derived by adding the single-digit row value to the header group value.

Listing 1.6. amask Listing for Hyper-Threaded system: pure vs core-centric mask

```
$ mpirun -np 4 amask_mpi   -ls
     Each row of matrix is an Affinity mask.
     A set mask bit = matrix digit + column group # in |...|
rank |    0    |    10    |    20    |    30    |    40    |
0000 012345678901------------------------------------
0001 012345678901------------------------------------
0002 ------------234567890123------------------------
0003 ------------234567890123------------------------

########################################################

$ mpirun -np 4 amask_mpi

     Each row of matrix is a CORE mask for a HW-thread.
     core id = matrix digit + column group # in |...|
     mask bit = core id + add 24 to each additional row
rank |    0    |    10    |    20    |
0000 012345678901============        HW-thread 0
     ------------------------        HW-thread 1
0001 012345678901============
     ------------------------
0002 ============234567890123
     ------------------------
0003 ============234567890123
     ------------------------
```

Listing 1.7 shows the process mask for execution with 24 OpenMP threads on the same Hyper-Threaded (Lonestar5) system above, under 3 different OpenMP affinity settings. The first two listings for OpenMP executions readily illustrate that the OMP_PROC_BIND SPREAD and CLOSE distributions are working across cores. A thread is not assigned to a single proc-id (hardware-thread) but can float on the core. These affinity characteristics might be difficult to discover from the documentation. The listing for the third run, without any OpenMP affinity, shows the implementation default: any thread can run on any hardware-thread.

Listing 1.7. amask Listing for Hyper-Threads system: OpenMP Affinity Policies

```
$ export OMP_NUM_THREADS=12
$ export OMP_PROC_BIND=spread
$ amask_omp

     Cores
thrd |    0    |   10    |   20    |
0000 0=======================
     0-----------------------
0001 ==2=====================
     --2---------------------
0002 ====4===================
     ----4-------------------
...

0009 ==================8=====
     ------------------8-----
0010 ====================0===
     --------------------0---
0011 ======================2=
     ----------------------2-

$ export OMP_NUM_THREADS=12
$ export OMP_PROC_BIND=close
$ amask_omp

     Cores
thrd |    0    |   10    |   20    |
0000 0=======================
     0-----------------------
0001 =1======================
     -1----------------------
0002 ==2=====================
     --2---------------------
...

0009 =========9==============
     ---------9--------------
0010 ==========0=============
     ----------0-------------
0011 ===========1============
     -----------1------------

$ export OMP_NUM_THREADS=12
$ unset OMP_PROC_BIND
$ amask_omp

     Cores
thrd |    0    |   10    |   20    |
0000 012345678901234567890123
     012345678901234567890123
0001 012345678901234567890123
     012345678901234567890123
...

0010 012345678901234567890123
     012345678901234567890123
0011 012345678901234567890123
     012345678901234567890123
```

Much of the discussion up to this point developed a representation and consistent perspective for quickly assessing all affinity masks through a matrix format, for systems with a large processor count. **amask** was designed to give users a view of affinities that will help in efforts to optimize process affinities for different NUMA node settings in KNL systems, and for all the different combinations of MPI task counts, OpenMP thread counts and process layouts. The following listing demonstrates the power of **amask**. Listing 1.8 readily shows a situation where two MPI processes share a core, when one might expect them not to. On a Stampede2 68-core KNL node a 16-process MPI execution shows rank0 and rank1 masks overlapping core-wise on core4. Similar pairs of overlaps are seen to occur throughout the listing. In a hybrid calculation with 16 MPI tasks and 17 threads per task (all hardware threads active), it may not be desirable to have two different MPI tasks sharing a core. Likewise, in other situations avoiding tile or NUMA node sharing might enhance performance. For comparison, a second run with 17 MPI processes in Listing 1.9 shows no core sharing.

Listing 1.8. Core sharing in a KNL system

```
 $ #IMPI on 68-core KNL, default environment
 $ mpirun -np 16 amask_mpi
        Cores
rank |    0    |    10   |    20   |    30   |    40   |    50   |    60   |
0000 01234===============================================================
     0123----------------------------------------------------------------
     0123----------------------------------------------------------------
     0123----------------------------------------------------------------
0001 =====5678===========================================================
     ----45678-----------------------------------------------------------
     ----4567------------------------------------------------------------
     ----4567------------------------------------------------------------
0002 =========9012=======================================================
     ---------9012-------------------------------------------------------
     --------89012-------------------------------------------------------
     --------8901--------------------------------------------------------
0003 =============3456===================================================
     -------------3456---------------------------------------------------
     -------------3456---------------------------------------------------
     ------------23456---------------------------------------------------

0013 ========================================================6789========
     -------------------------------------------------------56789--------
     -------------------------------------------------------5678---------
     -------------------------------------------------------5678---------
0014 ============================================================0123====
     ------------------------------------------------------------0123----
     -----------------------------------------------------------90123----
     -----------------------------------------------------------9012-----
0015 ================================================================4567
     ----------------------------------------------------------------4567
     ----------------------------------------------------------------4567
     ---------------------------------------------------------------34567
```

Listing 1.9. Non-shared cores in a KNL system

```
 $ #IMPI on 68-core KNL, default environment
 $ mpirun -np 17 amask_mpi
          Cores
rank |    0    |    10   |    20   |    30   |    40   |    50   |    60   |
0000 0123================================================================
     0123----------------------------------------------------------------
     0123----------------------------------------------------------------
     0123----------------------------------------------------------------
0001 ====4567============================================================
     ----4567------------------------------------------------------------
     ----4567------------------------------------------------------------
     ----4567------------------------------------------------------------
0002 ========8901========================================================
     --------8901--------------------------------------------------------
     --------8901--------------------------------------------------------
     --------8901--------------------------------------------------------
...
0016 ================================================================4567
     ----------------------------------------------------------------4567
     ----------------------------------------------------------------4567
     ----------------------------------------------------------------4567
```

5 Summary

The **amask** tool suite provides a convenient way to display process masks in a matrix format for the environment in which an application runs. Also, through the **amask** API a developer can readily instrument an application to display all of its process masks. This tool can be a valuable resource for confirming affinity configurations whenever developers and users explore the optimal proc-id space for process execution on diverse platforms in the HPC world.

6 Future Work

The following list contains a short description of the features users might want to see in **amask**: (1) Adapt code for a more diverse set of operating systems and hardware platforms. (2) Extract more hardware configuration details and encode this information into the proc-ids (e.g. by color coding proc-ids according to NUMA nodes and/or sockets) (3) Report anomalous affinity conditions that inherently create an imbalance in memory access or processor overloading. (4) Employ an XML protocol to export affinity data– to encourage the development of a GUI.

Acknowledgments. The author would like to acknowledge the support and cooperation of the HPC Group at TACC (Texas Advanced Computing Center) in the perparation of this paper. Thanks to Antonio Gomez and Roberto Garza for reviewing this document. Financial support for this work was provided by the National Science Foundation.

References

1. Lonestar5 Second Petascale System Deployed at TACC (2017). https://www.tacc.utexas.edu/systems/lonestar
2. Broquedis, F., Clet-Ortega, J., Moreaud, S., Furmento, N., Goglin, B., Mercier, G., Thibault, S., Namyst, R.: hwloc: A generic framework for managing hardware affinities in HPC applications. In: 2010 18th Euromicro International Conference on Parallel, Distributed and Network-Based Processing (PDP), pp. 180–186. IEEE (2010)
3. Eichenberger, A.E., Terboven, C., Wong, M., an Mey, D.: The design of OpenMP thread affinity. In: Chapman, B.M., Massaioli, F., Müller, M.S., Rorro, M. (eds.) IWOMP 2012. LNCS, vol. 7312, pp. 15–28. Springer, Heidelberg (2012). doi:10.1007/978-3-642-30961-8_2
4. Milfeld, K.: amask, reports affinity masks of parallel processes (2017). https://github.com/tacc/amask
5. Proctor, C., Gignac, D., McLay, R., Liu, S., James, D., Minyard, T., Stanzione, D.: Lonestar 5: Customizing the cray xc40 software environment
6. Rabenseifner, R., Hager, G., Jost, G.: Hybrid MPI/OpenMP parallel programming on clusters of multi-core SMP nodes. In: 2009 17th Euromicro International Conference on Parallel, Distributed and Network-based Processing, pp. 427–436. IEEE (2009)
7. Sodani, A., Gramunt, R., Corbal, J., Kim, H.S., Vinod, K., Chinthamani, S., Hutsell, S., Agarwal, R., Liu, Y.C.: Knights landing: second-generation Intel Xeon Phi product. IEEE Micro **36**(2), 34–46 (2016)
8. Stanzione, D., Barth, B., Gaffney, N., Gaither, K., Hempel, C., Minyard, T., Mehringer, S., Werner, E., Tuffo, H., Panda, D.K., Teller, P.: Stampede2: the Evolution of an XSEDE Supercomputer. In: PEARC, Practice and Experience in Advanced Research Computing, New Orleans (2017, to appear)
9. Zhang, C., Yuan, X., Srinivasan, A.: Processor affinity and MPI performance on SMP-CMP clusters. In: 2010 IEEE International Symposium on Parallel and Distributed Processing, Workshops and Phd Forum (IPDPSW), pp. 1–8. IEEE (2010)

Second International Workshop on Performance Portable Programming Models for Accelerators (P^3MA)

Second International Workshop on Performance Portable Programming Models for Accelerators (P^3MA)

http://www.csm.ornl.gov/workshops/p3ma2017/
June 22, 2017 co-located with ISC 2017

Workshop Organizers

Sunita Chandrasekaran	University of Delaware, USA
Graham Lopez	ORNL, USA

Summary of the Workshop's CFP Process

The Second International Workshop on Performance Portable Programming Models for Accelerators (P^3MA) co-located with ISC 2017 was held at Frankfurt, Germany on June 22. The workshop solicited papers on topics covering feature sets of programming models (including but not limited to directives-based programming models), their implementations, and experiences with their deployment in HPC applications on multiple architectures, performance modeling and evaluation tools, asynchronous task and event-driven execution/scheduling. We received 7 submissions in total. All submitted manuscripts were peer reviewed. The review process was not double blind, i.e., authors were known to reviewers. Submissions were judged on correctness, originality, technical strength, and significance, quality of presentation, and interest and relevance to the conference scope. We chose 6 papers to be published in the workshop proceedings, Springer-Verlag Lecture Notes in Computer Science (LNCS) volumes.

Workshop Summary

The workshop was held on June 22 at ISC and brought together researchers, vendors, users and developers to brainstorm aspects of heterogeneous computing and its various tools and techniques. Around 50 attendees were present to see Prof. David Keyes from KAUST, Saudi Arabia, give a keynote on Algorithmic and Programming Model Pillars for Emerging Architectures.

All of the 6 accepted papers were presented at the workshop with topics ranging from using low-level to high-level programming models for heterogeneous systems, experiences porting legacy code to accelerators, addressing memory requirements, and creating translations from one standard to the other.

Prof. Eric Stahlberg, Frederick National Laboratory for Cancer Research, gave an invited talk on Abstraction and Portability – Accelerating Predictive Oncology discussing HPC workflows required for exploring cancer dataset.

NVIDIA generously offered to sponsor the 'Best Paper Award' with NVIDIA's TITANX. This award was presented to Anne Kusters, Sandra Wienke and Lukas Arnold for their work on "Performance Portability Analysis for Real-Time Simulations of Smoke Propagation using OpenACC". The award was determined by the Technical Program Committee and the Program Chairs from viewpoints of the technical and scientific merits, impact on the science and engineering of the research work and the clarity of presentation of the research contents in the paper.

Organizing Committee

Steering Committee

Matthias Muller	RWTH Aachen University, Germany
Barbara Chapman	Stony Brook University, USA
Oscar Hernandez	ORNL, USA
Duncan Poole	OpenACC, USA
Torsten Hoefler	ETH, Zurich
Michael Wong	OpenMP, Canada
Mitsuhisa Sato	University of Tsukuba, Japan
Michael Klemm	OpenMP
Kuan-Ching Li	Providence University, Taiwan

Program Committee

Samuel Thibault	Inria, University of Bordeaux, France
James Beyer	NVIDIA, USA
Wei Ding	AMD, USA
Saber Feki	King Abdullah University, Saudi Arabia
Robert Henschel	Indiana University, USA
Michael Klemm	Intel, USA
Eric Stotzer	Texas Instruments, USA
Amit Amritkar	University of Houston, USA
Guido Juckeland	HZDR, Germany
Will Sawyer	ETH, Zurich
Sameer Shende	University of Oregon, USA
Costas Bekas	IBM, Zurich
Toni Collis	University of Edinburgh, Scotland
Adrian Jackson	University of Edinburgh, Scotland
Henri Jin	NASA, USA
Andreas Knuepfer	TU Dresden, Germany
Steven Olivier	Sandia National Laboratory, USA

Suraj Prabhakaran	TU Darmstadt, Germany
Bora Ucar	ENS De Lyon, France
Manisha Gajbe	Intel, USA
Daniel Tian	PGI, USA

Analyzing Offloading Inefficiencies in Scalable Heterogeneous Applications

Robert Dietrich[1(✉)], Ronny Tschüter[1], Guido Juckeland[2], and Andreas Knüpfer[1]

[1] Center for Information Services and High Performance Computing, Technische Universität Dresden, 01062 Dresden, Germany
{robert.dietrich,ronny.tschueter,andreas.knuepfer}@tu-dresden.de
[2] Department of Information Service and Computing, Helmholz-Zentrum Dresden-Rossendorf, Bautzner Landstr. 400, 01328 Dresden, Germany
g.juckeland@hzdr.de

Abstract. With the rise of accelerators in high performance computing, programming models for the development of heterogeneous applications have evolved and are continuously being improved to increase program performance and programmer productivity. The concept of computation offloading to massively parallel compute devices has established itself as a new layer of parallelism in scientific applications, next to message passing and multi-threading. To optimize the execution of a respective parallel heterogeneous program for a specific platform, performance analysis is crucial. This work abstracts from specific offloading APIs such as available with CUDA, OpenCL, OpenACC, and OpenMP and summarizes common inefficiencies for offloading. Based on the definition of inefficiency patterns, the offloading concept can be included in generic analysis techniques such as critical-path and root-cause analysis. We implemented the detection and evaluation of inefficiency patterns as a post-mortem trace analysis, which finally highlights program activities with a high potential to reduce the total program runtime.

1 Introduction

Programming models for the fast evolving parallel heterogeneous systems are subject to a similar rapid evolution and development. A major challenge for open programming standards with offloading support, such as OpenCL, OpenACC, and OpenMP, is performance portability between different devices. The abstraction from hardware-specific APIs enables access to numerous compute devices, ranging from CPUs over GPUs to FPGAs and DSPs. An important aspect that influences the program performance is that there is a certain freedom in implementing the specification of the standard, which may result in unexpected behavior. Although offloading APIs share common functionality, they also provide individual means to express computation offloading.

J.M. Kunkel et al. (Eds.): ISC High Performance Workshops 2017, LNCS 10524, pp. 457–476, 2017.
https://doi.org/10.1007/978-3-319-67630-2_34

Programming approaches for computation offloading as provided with CUDA, OpenCL, OpenACC, and the OpenMP target construct are host-directed. This means that the host manages the device, triggers device initialization, synchronization, and finalization as well as device tasks, e.g. data movement and kernel execution. Initiating a device task is called launch (CUDA), queue (OpenCL), or enqueue (OpenACC) depending on the wording of the respective offloading API specification. Different terms for device execution queues on the offloading device are CUDA stream, OpenCL command queue, OpenACC asynchronous queue. A device for computation offloading is called device (CUDA and OpenCL), target device (OpenMP), or accelerator (OpenACC) depending on the offloading API.

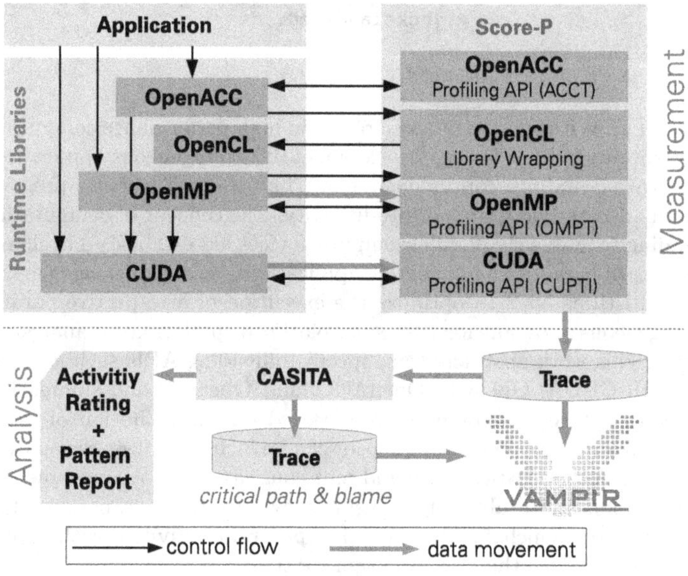

Fig. 1. Performance analysis workflow: Score-P collects performance data using profiling interfaces and library wrapping. CASITA analyzes program traces for execution inefficiencies.

With computation offloading as additional parallel execution layer, next to message passing and multi-threading, performance analysis is getting increasingly important to optimize the execution of a parallel heterogeneous program. This paper abstracts from specific offloading APIs and defines common inefficiencies which can be used for performance analysis. We describe their detection and evaluation as basis for an automatic analysis which identifies wait states, their causal activities, and the critical path. Furthermore, we extended the trace analyzer CASITA [17] to generate a summary on the occurrence of inefficiency patterns in MPI, OpenMP, and offloading models, which enables developers to easily spot the most runtime-relevant inefficiencies.

Figure 1 provides an overview on the interaction of application, runtime libraries, measurement, and analysis tools, which are used in this work. Section 2 depicts related work. Performance measurement and respective requirements for our analysis are presented in Sect. 3. In Sect. 4 we define execution patterns for offloading inefficiencies as well as their detection and evaluation. Section 5 describes the integration of the pattern-based offloading analysis into OpenMP and MPI analysis. We demonstrate our analysis on two benchmarks codes and a real-world application in Sect. 6 and finally conclude our work in Sect. 7.

2 Related Work

Inefficiency patterns for MPI, OpenMP, and SHMEM have already been defined by Wolf et al. [18]. The Scalasca trace analyzer [12] automatically detects such patterns and generates a call-path profile. It scales similar to the original application by replaying the MPI communication that has been recorded in a program trace. Böhme et al. developed a scalable approach to detect the critical-path, wait states, and their root-cause in MPI programs [5,6], which has also been implemented in Scalasca.

HPCToolkit [2] uses a technique called blame shifting. It blames busy threads for causing idleness on other threads in multi-threaded applications. Besides support for lock contention and barriers, Chabbi et al. [7] introduced CPU-GPU blame shifting which follows the same principle by blaming the non-idle resource. Blame shifting in multi-threaded and GPU programs is performed during the application execution.

The CASITA trace analyzer [17] automatically detects inefficiencies in scalable heterogeneous applications. Based on critical-path analysis and blame shifting it determines the optimization relevance of program activities. Schmitt et al. [16] defined respective inefficiency patterns for the CUDA programming model and developed a scalable critical-path analysis for hybrid MPI-CUDA applications. Automatic detection of inefficiencies in OpenMP 4.0 offloading programs has been investigated in [9]. Similar to Scalasca, CASITA performs a post-mortem analysis on traces that are generated by Score-P [4] and applies the MPI communication replay technique to scale with the number of MPI ranks.

This work extends the CASITA trace analyzer to detect the offloading inefficiency patterns that are defined in Sect. 4. A pattern summary is printed as textual output. Device idle time events are added to the output trace. To enable the CASITA analysis for offloading with OpenCL, respective attributes for dependency tracking have been implemented in Score-P. We use the Vampir [15] trace visualization to investigate arbitrary intervals in a program trace and validate the CASITA analysis results.

3 Performance Measurement

To detect and analyze offloading inefficiencies, a minimum set of events and correlation information is required. We use event traces to preserve the required information for a post-mortem analysis. This allows to apply time-consuming analyses such as critical-path and cause-effect analysis, which cannot be applied at runtime.

As shown in Fig. 1, different data acquisition sources are used for distinct offloading APIs. Score-P implements so called adapters to acquire runtime information from CUDA, OpenCL, OpenACC, and OpenMP. It provides a tracing back-end that writes OTF2 traces. In the context of this work, we extended Score-P to record additional attributes, which are needed to detect offloading inefficiencies in OpenCL and OpenMP. For the offloading analysis, the following information is required:

- begin of task launch operations, including the device queue where the task will be executed
- begin and end of blocking device synchronization
- begin and end of operations that test for the completion status of operations on the device and their results
- begin and end of device tasks
- dependencies between device tasks

3.1 CUPTI for CUDA Targets

The CUDA Profiling Tools Interface (CUPTI) provides—among others—the activity and the callbacks API, which are used in Score-P to collect the required information. The CUPTI activity API enables tools to collect traces of device tasks, while the CUPTI callbacks API allows tools to register callbacks for CUDA API routines. The callbacks cover begin and end of launch, synchronization, and test routines as well as the function arguments.

A correlation ID is used to associate a device task with its launch operation. It is passed to each CUDA API callback and available in each device record. This correlation information is not a requirement for the offloading analysis. As device tasks are executed in its launch order on CUDA streams, it is sufficient to store the CUDA stream ID with each launch operation.

3.2 OpenCL Library Wrapping

As OpenCL does not provide a tools interface, we intercept calls to the OpenCL library to inject time measurement for both, the OpenCL API routines and device tasks. This method and its integration into Score-P has been presented in [10]. Library wrapping enables the wrapper library to access and modify the values of function arguments. This is used to collect the device queue in OpenCL *enqueue**-routines and *clFinish()*. The latter is a blocking wait operation for a given OpenCL command queue. Data movement is blocking, if the respective argument in the buffer read or write enqueue call is set to true. This information has to be recorded to detect offloading inefficiencies. OpenCL events are retained or added in enqueue operations to enable the collection of OpenCL device tasks. Currently, the approach does not support out-of-order command queues. Hence, it is sufficient to store the device queue with *enqueue**-routines and *clFinish()*.

3.3 OpenACC Profiling Interface

The profiling interface that has been introduced in OpenACC 2.5 specifies an API for event-based performance measurement. A tool can register callbacks for event types, which are defined in the interface. There are three groups of events: kernel launch, data, and other events. According to the group different information is available in the event-specific callback argument. The implementation of the OpenACC profiling interface into Score-P has been presented in [8].

The OpenACC runtime events cover begin and end of enqueue and wait operations. There are no events specified for the begin and end of OpenACC runtime library routines such as *acc_async_test** and *acc_memcpy_**. Hence, device test operations and blocking data movement cannot be recorded based on the interface. Events that occur on the accelerator are also not covered. If no information from low-level APIs such as CUDA or OpenCL is available, the runtime of device activities can only be estimated using the enqueue and wait events. Section 4 describes the impact on the inefficiency detection and evaluation.

3.4 OpenMP Tools Interface

The OpenMP Tools (OMPT) interface has been developed for instrumentation-based and sampling-based performance tools. It is part of the first preview on OpenMP 5.0 which has been published as technical report 4 [3]. A tool can register callbacks for events that are specified in OMPT. In this work, only the events for offloading to target devices are considered. This includes the begin and end of *target*, *target data*, *target enter data*, *target exit data*, *target update*, and *taskwait* regions. Begin and end of *omp_target_**-routines are not covered in OMPT. However, these events are relevant for the detection of offloading inefficiencies, because *omp_target_memcpy**, *omp_target_alloc*, and *omp_target_free* are blocking the host execution and synchronize with the device.

OpenMP extended the concept of tasks for computation offloading. A *target* region is executed as a target task on the encountering host thread. Events on task scheduling are covered in OMPT. Instead of device execution queues, OpenMP supports the more expressive task dependencies for target tasks (since OpenMP 4.5), which can also be recorded with OMPT callback events.

OMPT also specifies a monitoring interface for device activities, which allows to determine when an offloading device is executing communication and computation tasks. To correlate host and device operations an OpenMP runtime dispatches the callback *ompt_callback_target_submit_t* for target regions and the callback *ompt_callback_target_data_op* for target data operations. Both callbacks and respective target records contain the *target id*, which identifies the target region on the host, and the *host op id*, which identifies the host operation.

4 Inefficiency Patterns in Offloading Models

Typical symptoms of inefficient parallelization are idle resources or wait states. In the case of computation offloading, inefficiency occurs when the host is waiting for the device or the offloading device is idle waiting for work.

Device tasks can run concurrently to operations on the host. To ensure data consistency, it is necessary to synchronize with the offloading device, which potentially results in a wait state on the host. Host-device synchronization can be either blocking or non-blocking. A comprehensive list of inefficiency patterns that might occur in offloading scenarios is given in Table 1. The severity specifies the start and end of the inefficiency, which is used to generate the optimization rating.

Table 1. Offloading inefficiencies and their severity

Pattern	Accounting
Early wait for device	Time between synchronization start and offloading task end
Early test for completion	Execution time of unsuccessful tests
Idle offloading device	Time when no offloading kernel is active (sum)
Synchronous kernel offloading	Kernel execution time
Synchronous data transfer	Transfer time
Late data transfer	Transfer time
Multiple consecutive data transfers	Product of the overhead of one transfer and the number of excessive transfers

Furthermore, there are inefficiencies that cannot be avoided. For example, data has to be copied to the offloading device before it can start computation and a final synchronization between host and device is also necessary. Nevertheless, the goal of performance tuning is to minimize the severity of all inefficiency patterns. An improved load balancing, double buffering to enable overlapping of computation and communication, or combined data transfers are typical optimization approaches. This work supports program developers by detecting performance inefficiencies and evaluating their severity.

4.1 Early Wait for Device

Early blocking synchronization is reasonable, if data from the offloading device are required before the host thread can continue execution. Programs that do not balance the computational load between host and offloading device, often start to wait early for a device to complete its tasks, because there is nothing else to process. Table 2 gives an overview on device synchronization possibilities that block the host execution for different offloading APIs.

Pattern Description: A host thread starts waiting for a device before it completes execution. It can wait for all activities or events, a queue, an event, or a task on the device. A device task is associated to a host wait operation, if it is a

Table 2. Host-blocking synchronization: The host waits until the completion of all device tasks, all tasks in a device queue, or a single device task. Depending on the offloading API there are routines and directives dedicated to wait for device tasks, which induces an *explicit* host-device synchronization. In addition, there are operations such as synchronous data transfers or OpenMP target directives without the nowait clause. Although, synchronization is not the primary task of these operations, they are *implicitly* synchronizing.

	Device	Stream/Queue	Event/Task
CUDA	explicit & implicit	explicit & implicit	explicit
OpenCL		explicit & implicit	explicit
OpenACC	explicit & implicit	explicit	explicit
OpenMP	implicit		explicit & implicit

device global synchronization, if the task is executed on the synchronized queue, or if the task is directly executed before the synchronized event.

Figure 2 illustrates early blocking synchronization with task *t2*, which is triggered asynchronously. The host synchronizes with a device queue before *t2* is completed, which results in a wait state on the host and therewith wasted computing resources.

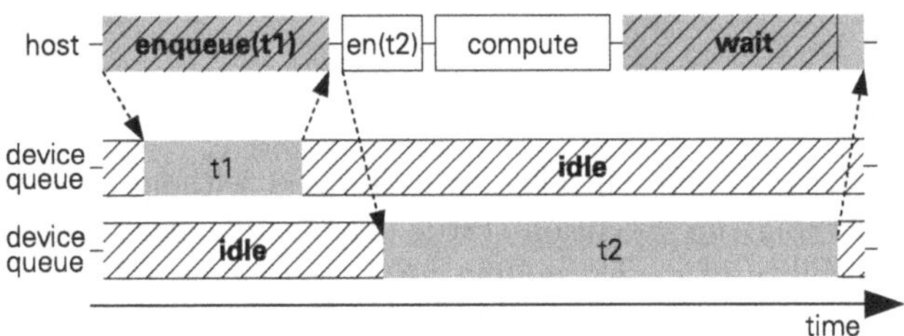

Fig. 2. Synchronous offloading (task *t1*), early wait for device (wait for task *t2*), and idle offloading device. Hatched areas denote waiting or idle time. The dashed arrows represent dependencies between events.

Synchronous kernel offloading and synchronous data transfer are the worst cases of early blocking synchronization. The inefficiency occurs because the host is waiting during the execution of the device task. In Fig. 2 task *t1* is launched with a blocking enqueue operation (kernel or data transfer). There is some offloading overhead before the task starts and after its execution, which is not accounted to the inefficiency.

Detection and Evaluation: The end event of the wait operation on the host triggers the detection. A synchronization interval forms between two wait operations for the same set of associated device queues. Device tasks that are associated to the wait operation and complete during the wait as well as their direct predecessors in the synchronization interval are blamed for causing the wait state on the host. Blame is assigned proportional to the runtime of the device tasks that keep the host waiting. Direct predecessors tasks execute instantaneously before another task and delay their execution. The time between the start of the wait and the end of the last overlapping device task is marked as wait state in the host wait operation.

The critical path detection starts at the last event on the host, moving backwards in time. It changes the execution stream at the end event of the wait operation, if it is marked as a wait state. The critical path continues on the last ending task that is associated to the wait operation and follows its direct predecessors and indirect predecessors. An indirect predecessor task executes on a different device queue and delays the associated task due to a dependency. Finally, the critical path changes to the enqueue begin event of the temporally first predecessor.

Table 3. Query routines for the device execution status

	Device	Stream/Queue	Event/Task
CUDA		cuStreamQuery	cuEvenQuery
OpenCL			clGetEventInfo
OpenACC	acc_async_test_all	acc_async_test	acc_async_test

4.2 Early Test for Completion

Host-device synchronization can also be performed without blocking the host execution by querying the execution status of a device operation. Table 3 summarizes the possibility of device polling for CUDA, OpenCL, and OpenACC. Although a single call to the query routine should return fast, many calls might introduce a significant overhead that should be avoided. This pattern is an optimization of early blocking synchronization, if the host is not continuously polling.

Pattern Description: A host thread queries a device, a device stream, an event, or a task on the device until *completed* status is returned. The query that returns *completed* status finishes the synchronization. All queries for the same device object but the last one that returns *completed* status are redundant or unnecessary.

Figure 3 depicts the respective inefficiency pattern. The first two queries for the task execution status introduce waiting time as the task is still running. The third query completes the synchronization by returning the *completed* status.

Detection and Evaluation: The analysis is triggered by the end event of a successful test for completion. Prior unsuccessful tests for the same synchronization object are identified and assigned with waiting time. The accumulated waiting time is assigned as blame to all affected device tasks proportional to their runtime. Affected devices tasks are determined as described in the early

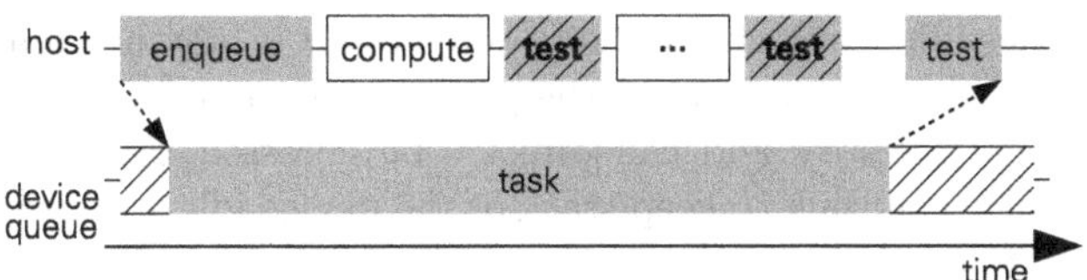

Fig. 3. Early test for completion: The execution status of the task is queried periodically without blocking the host execution. The dashed arrows show event dependencies

blocking synchronization pattern. As no wait states occur in this pattern, the critical path does not change the execution stream and stays on the host thread.

The detection of this pattern requires at least two successive queries for the same device object without other synchronization in between, where the last query returns the *completed* status. Furthermore, it is assumed that the the purpose of the status query is synchronization.

As OpenMP does not provide a mechanism to query the execution status of an offloading device, the early test for completion pattern cannot be detected for OpenMP offloading.

4.3 Idle Offloading Device

As the concept of offloading is often used to accelerate only portions of the code, it might be tolerable that the offloading device is idle some of the time. The application developer has to decide whether a device idle phase is tolerable or not. An example is the startup and shutdown phase of a parallel program, when no device task can be executed. Device initialization and shutdown as well as memory allocation and deallocation on the device are typically not considered as device tasks. Such device idle states cannot be avoided.

Pattern Description: The offloading device is idle when it does not execute any task on any device queue. In Fig. 2 the device is idle before task *t1*, between task *t1* and *t2*, and after task *t2*. The device is considered *compute idle*, when it does not execute any compute kernel. This metric is useful as data movement is parallelization overhead and does not process data.

Detection and Evaluation: The detection of the device idle state from a program trace has one major limitation. The system might allow to access a single device from multiple concurrently executed programs, e.g. with time slicing. In this case, device idle can only be detected from the perspective of the program's event trace. To detect the global device idle state, it is possible to request the device state with periodical sampling, e.g. with the NVIDIA management library, which provides an interface to request the device utilization. However, this requires to gather additional information at program runtime and it does not consider data movements between host and device as device tasks.

On HPC systems, compute resources, such as offloading devices, are usually exclusively allocated for a single program. In case of one offloading device per process, the device idle state can be easily detected. It is only necessary to examine all device queues that are local to the process. Hence, the device task events are stored in local memory and can directly be accessed. An implementation might use reference counting to keep track of the device idle state when multiple device queues are used.

The software stack and the capabilities of the offloading device may allow multiple processes to utilize the same device, e.g. with NVIDIA's Multi Process Service (MPS)[1] and the Hyper-Q[2] technology. If the detection runs on a single process, all required events can be accessed from local memory, which enables efficient implementations, e.g. via reference counting. Scalable analysis approaches, such as Böhme's MPI communication replay [5], have to exchange information on the device idle state. As this is only possible at global collectives, the additionally required memory for buffering the device idle intervals and the communication overhead might be infeasible.

The compute idle time of an offloading device represents the time a device does not perform any productive work, hence it does not execute a compute kernel. Although this metric does not show how efficient an offloading device is utilized, it is of relevance for a typical top-down performance analysis.

4.4 Inefficient Data Movement

Optimizing the communication is a common goal in most programming models that involve data movement. It is often the key to major performance improvements. In case of offloading the importance of optimizing data movement increases when host and device do not share the same physical memory. One of the following three criteria has identifies an inefficient data movement.

Pattern Description: (1) Data movement is considered inefficient in offloading scenarios, if it blocks the host execution. Hence, synchronous data transfers are inefficient as they delay the execution on both, host and device. They are already handled in the *early blocking synchronization* pattern.

(2) A data movement task is considered inefficient, if it delays the execution of a device kernel and does not fully overlap with a device kernel.

(3) Two consecutive data movements are inefficient, if the following conditions are true:

- they are tasks on the same device
- they are not overlapping
- neither is overlapping with a compute task on the same device
- no compute task on the same device is executed between them
- no communication of any other paradigm is initiated or ends between the trigger of the offloading data movements

[1] https://docs.nvidia.com/deploy/pdf/CUDA_Multi_Process_Service_Overview.pdf, vR352, May 2015.

[2] https://docs.nvidia.com/cuda/kepler-tuning-guide/index.html#hyper-q, DA-06288-001_v8.0, January 2017.

Detection and Evaluation: (1) Synchronous data transfers can be easily detected by function names in CUDA. In OpenCL, the function arguments of *clEnqueueReadBuffer** and *clEnqueueWriteBuffer** have to be evaluated and the respective information stored in the trace. The OpenACC profiling interface provides the *async* field for data events, which allows to identify blocking data movement. OpenMP uses the *map* clause on *target*, *target data*, *target enter data*, and *target exit data* constructs to trigger data movement. The *nowait* clause can be applied on *target*, *target update*, *target enter data*, and *target exit data*, which allows an OpenMP implementation to use asynchronous data movement. In this case, a target directive is executed as deferred task, which can return the execution control before the result of the task is available. The OpenMP API routines *omp_target_memcpy* and *omp_target_memcpy_rect* perform a blocking data movement between host and target device. A synchronous data movement can always be replaced with an asynchronous equivalent and a respective synchronization mechanism if needed.

(2) Immediately successive and overlapping tasks can be detected by searching for respective tasks events on local device streams. The costs of the detection depend on the data structures which are used to store the task events from device streams. Using lists, successive tasks should be detected with constant complexity O(1), whereas overlapping tasks might be detected based on a binary search with logarithmic complexity O(log n). The part of a delaying data movement task that is not overlapping with device computation can be exposed as inefficiency.

(3) It is reasonable to combine multiple consecutive data transfers as each transfer induces a certain overhead [11]. All but the first data movement operation in a series of consecutive data movements can be marked as inefficient, although the advantage of a large data transfers over multiple small ones in terms of latency and bandwidth cannot be reliably determined from an execution trace. The respective transfer enqueue operations on the host are marked as inefficient according to their execution time. Multiple consecutive data movements is a common inefficiency in directive-based approaches, because variables or arrays that are referenced in an offloading region and do not appear in a copy or map clause are implicitly copied or mapped. This can result in many consecutive data movement operations, as the programmer does not need to explicitly specify each data movement and may not be aware of the resulting deficiency.

4.5 Analysis Limitations for OpenACC

To detect inefficient host-device synchronization and an idle offloading device, a minimum set of runtime events are required. This includes the begin and end of wait and test operations as well as begin and end of device tasks. The enqueue operations for device tasks are required for the critical path analysis.

The OpenACC 2.5 profiling interface specifies events which reflect the behavior of an OpenACC runtime. It does not cover events on device tasks, which however can be collected with APIs such as CUPTI for CUDA targets. Without device events, it is only possible to determine the maximum runtime of device tasks based on the begin and end events for wait and enqueue operations. A device task cannot start before its enqueue begin event and has to be completed before the end event of the wait operation. When multiple device tasks are enqueued and synchronized, these tasks can only be handled as a group, which means that the group is blamed for causing waiting time and the group is on the critical path. Due to the missing device events, it is also not possible to reliably detect device idle. Blame and critical path time for device tasks can be assigned to names and source code locations. Enqueue kernel events carry the kernel name. Enqueue upload and download events provide information on the transferred data, such as the variable name and its size.

The OpenACC profiling events do not cover test operations, which are triggered by *acc_async_test* or *acc_async_test_all*. Hence, an early test for completion cannot be detected. Library wrapping could be used to gather begin and end events of all OpenACC runtime library routines.

5 Integrating Offloading Patterns into MPI and OpenMP Analysis

Sophisticated performance tools enable the analysis of execution inefficiencies in parallel programs. Parallelization inefficiencies, e.g. suboptimal load balancing, provide a high optimization potential without the need for fine-tuning of code regions. On the other hand, program regions that are not on the critical path do not contribute to the total program runtime and are no valuable optimization targets. To guide the application developer in the program tuning process, it is reasonable to detect the critical path and the cause of waiting time. Both require the prior identification of wait states. In computation offloading models, wait states can be detected based on the inefficiency patterns that have been described in Sect. 4.

Available tools that are based on inefficiency pattern detection support only an offloading paradigm (e.g. NVIDIA Visual Profiler) or only MPI and OpenMP (e.g. Scalasca). We contribute by integrating the analysis of offloading inefficiencies into available pattern analysis for MPI and OpenMP.

5.1 MPI with OpenMP or Offloading

For parallel programs that scale across multiple processes, a respective analysis has to scale as well. In HPC, MPI is typically used for inter-process communication and OpenMP for multithreading. Offloading is another parallel layer which can be orthogonally applied. The offloading analysis cannot be applied orthogonally to MPI and OpenMP analyses. Figure 4 shows two scenarios of MPI and offloading cooperation. *MPI over offloading* is the common case. MPI provides the skeleton, offloading is used between MPI communication or synchronization operations. The offloading device is idle during MPI operations. *Offloading over*

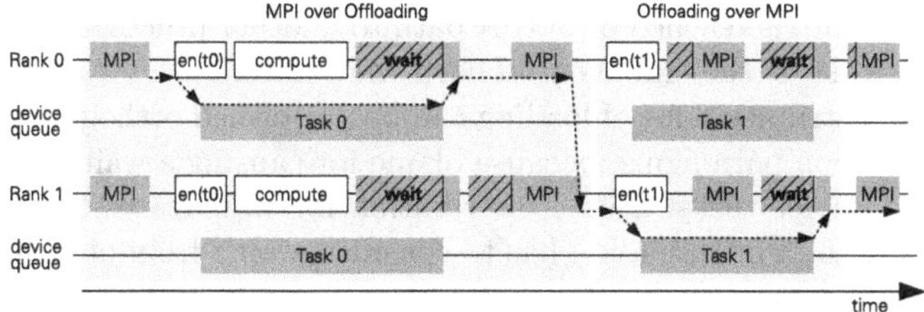

Fig. 4. Offloading is most often used between MPI communication. The vice versa usage could increase the utilization of the offloading device.

MPI is a rarity in applications. MPI operations are concurrently executed to offloaded tasks, which can strongly reduce the idle time of an offloading device.

Another aspect is the critical path, which cannot be detected separately for MPI and offloading. Schmitt et al. [16] perform the MPI analysis at first to split the execution into segments, which are analyzed in parallel. Although this approach works well for applications that use *MPI over Offloading*, it fails in the *Offloading over MPI* cases, which is illustrated in Fig. 4. When an offloaded task is on the critical path, the concurrently executed MPI operation does not affect the critical path. Nevertheless, the replay of MPI communication [5] is a reasonable approach for a parallel performance analysis. In case of a hybrid MPI program the node-local parallelization with multithreading and offloading has to be considered in the critical path analysis.

Multithreading with OpenMP is similar to offloading most often used between MPI communication or MPI synchronization. If an algorithm allows it, it might be also reasonable to hide MPI communication by concurrently executing threads. Hence, OpenMP analysis can neither be applied orthogonally to MPI analysis.

5.2 Multithreading and Offloading

To balance the workload between CPU cores and offloading devices, multithreading and offloading can act concurrently. The usual approach portions the work into an offloading and a CPU part and triggers the offloaded execution before starting to spread the CPU workload across threads. When the CPU finishes parallel execution, it synchronizes with the device. This fits well to current node architectures, where one CPU is often assembled with one offloading device. However, multiple threads can also offload work to one or multiple devices within a multithreaded region. This allows to hide the offloading overhead and the device synchronization behind other threads' computations.

The critical path changes the execution stream whenever it encounters a wait state independent of the originating paradigm. It does not need to distinguish between a wait state in the offloading or threading model. A respective analysis has to consider both paradigms in a combined analysis run, as it is not known whether a wait state is reached or not. A path to another process-local execution stream has to exist at the end event of each wait state.

The blame distribution for offloading can be performed orthogonally to other other parallelization paradigms, because blame for causing a wait state can only be assigned to device tasks. Blame distribution for wait states that arise from locks or barriers in multithreading has to consider events from other paradigms.

As multithreading and offloading are used in the context of a process, e.g. an MPI process, performance data are gathered locally and can also be analyzed on local shared memory without the need for inter-process communication.

6 Application Studies

To evaluate the usefulness of the pattern analysis for computation offloading we investigated the two known benchmarks Lulesh [14] and CloverLeaf [13] as well as the molecular dynamic package Gromacs without any knowledge about the codes. As a manual analysis of these patterns is infeasible, even with powerful visualization tools such as Vampir, we implemented it in the trace analyzer CASITA, which has been extended with a pattern summary output for inefficiency patterns in MPI, OpenMP, and computation offloading models.

MPI patterns include late sender, late receiver, early MPI_Waitall as well as wait in MPI_Sendrecv, and MPI collectives. Currently, there is only one OpenMP pattern implemented which quantifies wait states in OpenMP barriers. Offloading patterns expose the overall device idle time, the compute idle time of the device, early wait-for-device operations, early test for completion of device tasks, blocking host-device data movement, and consecutive data movement.

Our test system was the GPU partition of TU Dresden's Taurus. We ran the benchmark codes Lulesh and CloverLeaf on nodes equipped with two Intel Xeon E5-2450 CPUs at 2.10 GHz and two NVIDIA Kepler K20X (6 GB RAM) GPUs. The Gromacs experiments were executed on nodes equipped with two Intel Xeon E5-2680v3 CPUs at 2.50 GHz and four NVIDIA Tesla K80 (12 GB RAM) GPUs. We use the Intel compiler 16.0.2 with CUDA 8.0 for the CUDA benchmarks and the Gromacs experiments, and the PGI compiler 17.1 with CUDA 8.0 for the OpenACC benchmarks.

6.1 Mini-Apps with CUDA and OpenACC

We ran a couple of experiments with the CUDA and the OpenACC version of CloverLeaf and Lulesh. Neither of the benchmarks balances workload between GPU and CPU, which is still often the case for simulation codes that have been ported to GPUs. Hence, we expect and also confirm in our experiments a decreasing device idle time and an increasing host waiting time when the workload is increasing.

Lulesh represents some aspects of hydrodynamics codes. It solves a simple Sedov blast problem. In our benchmarks we ran a fixed number of 20 iterations with variable problem sizes from 30 to 135 in steps of 15. The cubic of the problem size determines the number of volumetric elements. For the OpenACC version 135 was the maximum problem size that could be executed per GPU. Increasing the iteration number increases the runtime, but it does not change the offloading behavior, which is why there is no need to run longer experiments.

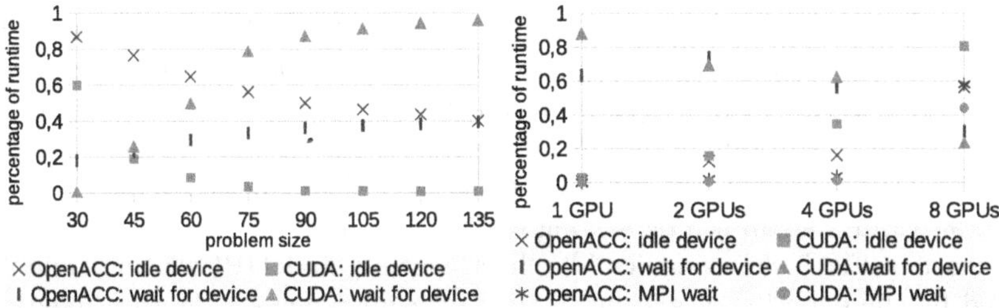

Fig. 5. Lulesh with different problem sizes (left) and CloverLeaf strong scaling (right)

The left chart in Fig. 5 shows the device idle and the host waiting time for an increasing problem size of Lulesh CUDA and OpenACC. The CUDA version shows the expected results. With increasing workload the GPU idle time approximates 1% of the program runtime, while the host waiting time reaches about 96% of the program runtime. The OpenACC version is less efficient. At the largest executable problem size (135) the GPU is still about 40% idle. As the waiting time for the GPU is below 40% of the program runtime, there has to be a serial part within the benchmark phase. The critical path analysis reveals several functions on the host (*Calc*ConstraintsForElems*) which take about 15% of the program runtime (problem size 135) and do not overlap with GPU tasks.

The total duration of data movements can be determined from the device idle and the device compute idle time. In the OpenACC version, device compute idle is about 1% more than device idle at the problem size 30. The gap increases up to 5% data movement until the problem size 90 and stays constant at larger problem sizes. The benchmark phase in the CUDA version does not contain host-device data movement, but 29 consecutive data movements are performed beforehand. In the OpenACC version, the consecutive data movements are below 0.5% of the program runtime and therefore negligible. Nevertheless, with larger problem sizes their number is increasing (from 83 to 181).

For all tested problem sizes, the most runtime dominating device kernel also dominates the critical path. It is *CalcFBHourglassForceForElems* in the OpenACC runs and *CalcKinematicsAndMonotonicQGradient_kernel* in the CUDA version.

CloverLeaf solves the compressible Euler equations on a Cartesian grid with an explicit, second-order accurate method. In our experiments we doubled the grid size, starting with 960^2 for the smallest workload up to a grid size of 3840^2 for the largest workload. As expected we get similar results as in our Lulesh experiments considering the device idle and host wait time. The latter doubles by doubling the problem size in both, the CUDA and the OpenACC version. With an increasing problem size the device idle time approximates 1% of the program runtime for the CUDA version and 5% for the OpenACC version. For similar problem sizes the OpenACC experiments take more time, which also results in longer waiting times for the device.

The data movement is between 2.5% and 3% of the program execution time in the OpenACC version, whereas it is negligible in the CUDA experiments. The number of consecutive data movements (241 to 766) and their total execution time (1.1% to 2.6% of the program runtime) is increasing with the problem size in the OpenACC version. In the CUDA version the number of consecutive data movements is constantly 270 and their total execution time negligible.

We also ran a small strong scaling experiment with up to eight GPUs. The right chart in Fig. 5 shows device idle, host waiting, and MPI waiting time normalized by the experiment execution time over all processes. With a fixed grid size of 3840^2 the code scales well with two and four GPUs. By scaling up to eight GPUs, the runtime got much slower with a dramatic increase in MPI waiting time. Scaling up to more GPUs continues to increase the runtime. We also determined the time between the kernel launch enter event and the kernel start event (kernel startup delay), which increased dramatically to about 0.6ms/kernel from only a few microseconds. The runtime share of data movements is between 2.5% and 5% in the OpenACC version and about 1% in the CUDA version.

6.2 Gromacs with OpenCL

Gromacs [1] is a versatile molecular dynamics (MD) software package. It is widely used to simulate interactions of biochemical molecules like proteins, lipids and nucleic acids. Our Gromacs experiment setup was inspired by the tutorial of Justin A. Lemkul[3]. We used Gromacs in version 2016.2 and generated input data based on the hen egg white lysozyme protein structure file, the all-atom OPLS force field, and a cubic box filled with water and ions. This input data was used to investigate the run of a 1-ns MD simulation.

We executed the experiment with one, two, and eight processes (weak scaling), each process using two OpenMP threads and one OpenCL device (NVIDIA K80 GPU). Table 4 shows the results of the pattern summary for our experiments. Even in the experiment with the most workload per GPU (one process, two threads), its idle time is about 49%. The host is waiting only a very short amount of time for roughly a fifth of the executed OpenCL kernels, which means that probably more load could be put on the GPU, without introducing host-device imbalances. There is a major increase of MPI and OpenMP waiting time when moving from two to eight processes (4 to 16 threads). As the workload per GPU is getting smaller in this case, its idle time increases. The total waiting time is four times larger than the actual program runtime, which is obviously not efficient.

[3] http://www.bevanlab.biochem.vt.edu/Pages/Personal/justin/gmx-tutorials/lysozyme/index.html.

Table 4. Inefficiency pattern summary for Gromacs (MPI, OpenMP, OpenCL), same workload in each experiment

	1 Pr., 2 Thrds, 1 GPU	2 Pr., 4 Thrds, 2 GPUs	8 Pr., 16 Thrds, 8 GPUs
Total program runtime	33.289 s	28.86 s	20.25 s
Total waiting time	1.387 s	7.047 s	**79.954 s**
MPI wait patterns		63 618 (1.681 s)	**670 985 (55.837 s)**
- Late Sender		2 (0.000 s)	8 813 (0.208 s)
- MPI_Sendrecv		50 760 (1.034 s)	480 367 (14.1208 s)
- (Early) MPI_Waitall			57 878 (4.247 s)
- MPI collective		12 852 (0.645 s)	123 465 (37.260 s)
OpenMP barrier wait	168 296 (0.729 s)	400 620 (2.405 s)	**1 649 924 (12.652 s)**
Offloading			
- Idle device	**13.590 (48.80%)**	**25.916 s (56.40%)**	**105.042 s (83.94%)**
- Compute idle device	14.151 (50.81%)	26.674 s (58.05%)	106.563 s (85.15%)
- Early blocking wait	**574 (0.492 s)**	**8 509 (2.519 s)**	**8 225 (3.288 s)**
- Consecutive transfers	6 108 (0.327 s)	22 426 (0.581 s)	57 317 (0.537 s)
- Avg. kernel startup	0.072 ms	0.473 ms	0.297 ms

For the experiments with one and two MPI processes CASITA's activity rating reveals the OpenCL kernel *nbnxn_kernel_ElecEwTwinCut_VdwLJCombGeom_F_opencl* as the most important candidate for optimization. While the application runs 33.29 s (one process) resp. 28.86 s (two processes) this function has an overall exclusive runtime of 12.48 s resp. 6.10 s. For the experiment with two processes a hot spot analysis based on the exclusive runtime pin points on the OpenCL kernel *nbnxn_kernel_ElecEw_VdwLJCombGeom_F_opencl* with a total exclusive runtime of 21.87 s. The host spends more time in waiting for the first mentioned kernel, which is also more time on the critical path.

Figure 6 shows the Vampir timeline visualization of the enriched trace file. Gromacs is one of the rare codes that uses MPI collectives within OpenMP parallel regions. Furthermore, OpenCL kernels are concurrently executed to MPI operations, which hides communication between processes behind device computation.

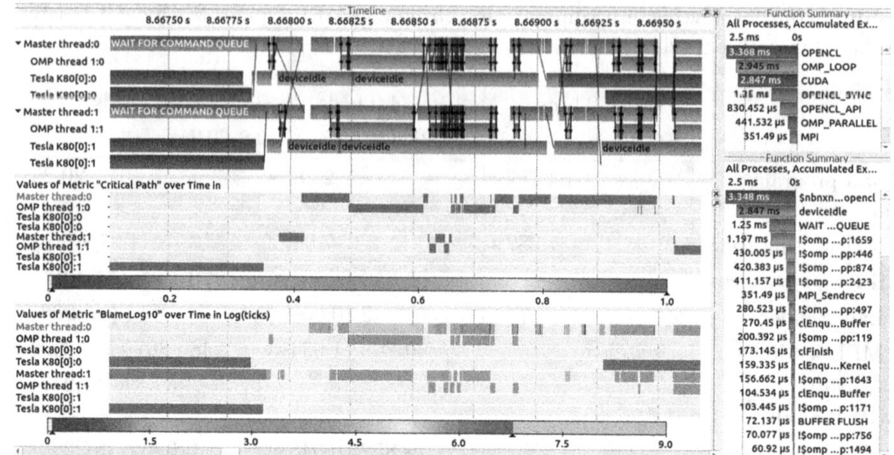

Fig. 6. Gromacs with MPI, OpenMP, and OpenCL on two MPI processes, each using two OpenMP threads and one OpenCL device (Nvidia Tesla K80 GPU). A large share of workload is assigned to the CPU leading to GPU device idle times (gray *deviceIdle* bars in the top display). Thus, the critical path is detected on CPU processes and threads except for the beginning of the depicted time interval (center timeline display). Blame is attributed to both, CPU and GPU activities (bottom timeline display).

6.3 Pattern Evaluation

In our application studies the most relevant offloading inefficiencies are the early wait-for-device operations and the device idle time, which can be used to adjust the workloads on host and device. The critical path supplements these metrics by exposing critical regions on the host during device idle. It also pinpoints on device regions with impact on the program runtime. Consecutive data transfers have a negligible or very small runtime impact in our experiments. The MPI scaling runs showed that it is important to cover all parallel layers for a reasonable evaluation of the program execution. For example, the wait for device time is decreasing even for eight GPUs in our CloverLeaf strong scaling, but the MPI waiting time exposes the bottleneck.

The analysis of the benchmarks showed that the pattern analysis is not needed in all cases. However, it is more accurate than estimations from a function profile and provides more information such as the device idle, device compute idle, and consecutive data movements. The pattern analysis of our OpenACC experiments exposed heavier inefficiencies than for the CUDA experiments. This probably results from the fact that the compiler implicitly generates device operations, which are required and have not been explicitly specified by the programmer, e.g. implicit data copies of small data portions.

7 Conclusion

This paper defines common inefficiency patterns for computation offloading models such as CUDA, OpenCL, OpenACC, and OpenMP target. We describe the detection and evaluation of such patterns and their usage for performance analysis. The patterns are the basis to identify wait states, to quantify the cause of wait states, and to detect program regions on the critical path. Together with already defined inefficiencies for MPI, OpenMP, and SHMEM, most HPC applications can be extensively analyzed. We also described possibilities and challenges in the efficient and cooperative use of MPI, OpenMP, and computation offloading.

A summary about the occurrences and wasted execution time in individual inefficiency patterns provides the analyst with additional means to evaluate a program run. It allows developers to focus optimizations on patterns which caused the most significant waiting times. Together with program regions that have a large share of the critical path and cause wait states, our top-down performance analysis can identify the most relevant optimization targets.

The application studies demonstrated our pattern-based analysis. The wait-for-device time, the device idle time, and the critical path time are the most important metrics for program performance evaluation. As future work we will further extend CASITA's features for performance evaluation of heterogeneous programs.

References

1. Abraham, M.J., Murtola, T., Schulz, R., Pll, S., Smith, J.C., Hess, B., Lindahl, E.: Gromacs: high performance molecular simulations through multi-level parallelism from laptops to supercomputers. SoftwareX **1–2**, 19–25 (2015). doi:10.1016/j.softx.2015.06.001
2. Adhianto, L., Banerjee, S., Fagan, M., Krentel, M., Marin, G., Mellor-Crummey, J., Tallent, N.R.: HPCTOOLKIT: tools for performance analysis of optimized parallel programs. Concurrency Comput. Pract. Exp. **22**(6), 685–701 (2010)
3. All members of the OpenMP Language Working Group: OpenMP Technical report 4: Version 5.0 Preview 1. OpenMP Architecture Review Board (2016)
4. An Mey, D., et al.: Score-P: a unified performance measurement system for petascale applications. In: Bischof, C., Hegering, H.G., Nagel, W.E., Wittum, G. (eds.) Competence in High Performance Computing 2010, pp. 85–97. Springer, Heidelberg (2012). doi:10.1007/978-3-642-24025-6_8
5. Böhme, D., Geimer, M., Wolf, F., Arnold, L.: Identifying the root causes of wait states in large-scale parallel applications. In: 39th International Conference on Parallel Processing, ICPP, pp. 90–100. IEEE (2010)
6. Böhme, D., Wolf, F., de Supinski, B.R., Schulz, M., Geimer, M.: Scalable critical-path based performance analysis. In: 26th International Parallel Distributed Processing Symposium, IPDPS, pp. 1330–1340. IEEE (2012)
7. Chabbi, M., Murthy, K., Fagan, M., Mellor-Crummey, J.: Effective sampling-driven performance tools for GPU-accelerated supercomputers. In: International Conference on High Performance Computing, Networking, Storage and Analysis, SC 2013, pp. 43:1–43:12. ACM (2013)

8. Dietrich, R., Juckeland, G., Wolfe, M.: OpenACC programs examined: a performance analysis approach. In: 44th International Conference on Parallel Processing, ICPP. IEEE (2015)
9. Dietrich, R., Schmitt, F., Grund, A., Stolle, J.: Critical-blame analysis for OpenMP 4.0 offloading on Intel Xeon Phi. J. Syst. Softw. **125**, 381–388 (2016). doi:10.1016/j.jss.2015.12.050
10. Dietrich, R., Tschüter, R.: A generic infrastructure for opencl performance analysis. In: 8th International Conference on Intelligent Data Acquisition and Advanced Computing Systems, Technology and Applications. IEEE (2015)
11. Eschweiler, D., Becker, D., Wolf, F.: Patterns of inefficient performance behavior in GPU applications. In: 19th International Euromicro Conference on Parallel, Distributed and Network-Based Processing, PDP 2011, pp. 262–266. IEEE Computer Society (2011)
12. Geimer, M., Wolf, F., Wylie, B.J.N., Erika Abraham, D.B., Mohr, B.: The scalasca performance toolset architecture. Concurrency Comput. Pract. Exp. **22**(6), 702–719 (2010)
13. Herdman, J.A., et al.: Accelerating hydrocodes with OpenACC, OpenCL and CUDA. In: SC Companion: High Performance Computing, Networking Storage and Analysis, pp. 465–471 (2012)
14. Karlin, I., Keasler, J., Neely, R.: Lulesh 2.0 updates and changes. Technical report LLNL-TR-641973 (2013)
15. Knüpfer, A., et al.: The Vampir performance analysis tool-set. In: Resch, M., Keller, R., Himmler, V., Krammer, B., Schulz, A. (eds.) Tools for High Performance Computing, pp. 139–155. Springer, Heidelberg (2008). doi:10.1007/978-3-540-68564-7_9
16. Schmitt, F., Dietrich, R., Juckeland, G.: Scalable critical-path analysis and optimization guidance for hybrid MPI-CUDA applications. Int. J. High Perform. Comput. Appl. (2016)
17. Schmitt, F., Stolle, J., Dietrich, R.: CASITA: a tool for identifying critical optimization targets in distributed heterogeneous applications. In: 43rd International Conference on Parallel Processing Workshops, ICPPW. IEEE (2014)
18. Wolf, F., Mohr, B., Dongarra, J., Moore, S.: Automatic analysis of inefficiency patterns in parallel applications. Concurrency Comput. Pract. Exp. **19**(11), 1481–1496 (2007)

Performance Portability Analysis for Real-Time Simulations of Smoke Propagation Using OpenACC

Anne Küsters[1(✉)], Sandra Wienke[2,3], and Lukas Arnold[1]

[1] JSC, Forschungszentrum Jülich GmbH, Wilhelm-Johnen-Straße, 52428 Jülich, Germany
a.kuesters@fz-juelich.de
[2] IT Center, RWTH Aachen University, Seffenter Weg 23, 52074 Aachen, Germany
[3] JARA-HPC, 52074 Aachen, Germany

Abstract. Real-time simulations of smoke propagation during fires in complex geometries challenge engineers, physicists, mathematicians and computer scientists due to the complexity of fluid dynamics and the large number of involved physical and chemical processes. Recently, several application scenarios emerged that require real-time predictions during an incident to support the rescue teams. Therefore, we develop the CFD-based simulation software JuROr aiming to run in real-time by leveraging parallel computer architectures like CPUs and GPUs. For that, we parallelize the code with OpenACC directives that promise maintenance of a single source base by delegating some architecture-agnostic optimizations to the compiler. We investigate the performance portability of JuROr using PGI's OpenACC implementation across four Intel CPUs and three NVIDIA GPUs. We present the achieved performance shares as part of a roofline model where we focus on traditionally-computed arithmetic code intensities, as well as on a measurement approach based on performance counters.

Keywords: Parallel CFD applications · Fire safety engineering · GPU computing · OpenACC · Performance portability · Roofline model

1 Introduction

In almost all underground stations in Germany, the equipment for smoke extraction remains rare to find. To support effective firefighting measures and tactics, the long-term goal is to develop a decision making tool for firefighters in cases of complex geometries where air and smoke flows are both complex and hard

The original version of this chapter was revised: The ORCIDs of second and third authors have been corrected. The erratum to this chapter is available at https://doi.org/10.1007/978-3-319-67630-2_54

J.M. Kunkel et al. (Eds.): ISC High Performance Workshops 2017, LNCS 10524, pp. 477–495, 2017.
https://doi.org/10.1007/978-3-319-67630-2_35

to predict. Therefore, concepts must adapt to the current situation dynamically and scenario-based.

During the last decade, computational fluid dynamics (CFD) has gained much attention in fire safety engineering by simulating smoke propagation. However, currently, users of commercial or open source smoke simulation tools widely apply these methods to simplified geometries that do not fit the regulatory prescription of the Pattern Building Code (e.g. enabling escape, rescue and effective fire fighting measures). Thus, these complex geometries need individual evaluation. Furthermore, it remains a challenge for them to meet the crucial constraint of simulating the smoke propagation in real time or less.

To simulate smoke propagation in complex 3D geometries, we develop a C++-based CFD solver, called 'JuROr' (Jülich's Real-Time Simulation within Orpheus). The goal of the Orpheus project funded by the 'Federal Ministry of Education and Research' (BMBF) is the improvement of personal safety in underground stations in case of fire. Further information can be found in [1].

We parallelize the CPU-based solver JuROr using the directive-based programming model OpenACC and leverage the compute power of CPUs and GPUs to enable real-time simulations. One advantage of using OpenACC over a low-level accelerator model is the delegation of the responsibility of producing performance-portable code to the compiler. Here, we investigate the performance portability of PGI's OpenACC implementation across various hardware architectures: NVIDIA Kepler and Pascal GPUs, and Intel Xeon Sandy Bridge, Ivy Bridge, Haswell and Broadwell CPUs (using PGI's multicore target). For that, we build roofline models [2] for the different architectures, i.e., we model performance limiters such as Flop/s and memory bandwidth on base of the application's arithmetic intensity. Then, we present performance portability of the real-world code JuROr as percentage of sustainable peak performance.

Thus, our main contributions are:

- A CFD solver and its parallelization with OpenACC to enable the prediction of smoke propagation in complex rooms
- Analysis of its performance portability using the roofline model based on manually-computed arithmetic intensity vs. measured intensity, and hardware performance counters
- Investigation of various hardware architectures: three NVIDIA GPUs, four Intel CPUs

The paper is structured as follows: Sect. 2 presents related work regarding CFD solvers utilizing GPUs as well as performance portability analysis of OpenACC codes. We introduce JuROr's CFD methods solving weakly compressible Navier-Stokes equations for a turbulent flow in Sect. 3 and its parallelization using OpenACC in Sect. 4. In Sect. 5, we describe our approach for modeling and measuring performance. We present our results on performance portability in Sect. 6. Finally, we conclude and give a short outlook in Sect. 7.

2 Related Work

So far, no possible solutions exist in the field of flow simulations for smoke propagation in real-time using CFD and covering complex rooms while taking sensor data into account. Yet, interest in producing real-time predictions, like those investigated in the *FireGrid* project [3], already exists. However, the utilized fire simulation model in FireGrid is a zone model, which splits the domain of interest into very few zones (cf. [4]). Properties like temperature or smoke density are computed via a set of coupled ordinary differential equations (ODEs) and thus only allow for very crude approximations and applications on simple geometries.

Instead of using a zone model, Glimberg et al. studied the governing mathematical models of CFD which describe the smoke propagation sufficiently (cf. [5]). In their work, GPUs were employed to solve the governing equations in highly simplified geometries using a fractional step method. This approach resulted in a solution within less than a minute of runtime for ten seconds simulation time. For comparison, the simulation took more than one hour on a CPU. However, this approach did not include the coupling of sensor data.

On the basis of sensor data, Daniel and Rein implemented *The Fire Navigator* forecasting the spread of building fires (cf. [6]). Using the techniques of a cellular automata building fire model (instead of CFD), they employed sensor data assimilation, inverse modeling and genetic algorithm techniques. With this approach the governing parameters of a fire, such as the flame spread rate, the smoke ceiling jet velocity and the outbreak location and time, can be indirectly uncovered and then used to produce real-time as well as forecast maps of the flame spread and smoke propagation. Therewith, the *Fire Navigator* achieves positive lead times of several minutes meaning the predictions are actually forecasts (without the usage of GPUs). Nonetheless, cellular automata simulations simplify the problem and do not produce results as accurate as computational fluid dynamics.

Instead, in JuROr we aim to predict smoke propagation in complex geometries deploying computational fluid dynamics and taking sensor data into account in future works.

By leveraging parallel processing power of GPUs and CPUs, JuROr tackles the real-time constraints for complex geometries. Its OpenACC parallelization shall enable good performance across various kinds of clients' hardware architectures. Although the architecture-specific assembler optimization by OpenACC compilers ease the maintenance of a single code base (e.g. over using OpenCL [7]), the performance portability of OpenACC implementations have been scarcely studied so far. While OpenACC performance comparisons across different architectures have been targeted in research, they have mostly been conducted by taking absolute numbers such as the application's runtime, floating point operations per second or speedup over CPU runs.

For example, Lopez et al. [8] show memory bandwidth or speedup numbers for a Jacobi and n-body kernel for different OpenACC implementations (PGI, Cray) on NVIDIA Kepler GPUs. They failed on using OpenACC on multicore CPUs. Sabne et al. [9] evaluated the performance by showing speedup numbers based on OpenARC's OpenACC implementation on NVIDIA GPUs, AMD GPUs and Intel Xeon Phi coprocessors using 12 kernels. The hydrodynamic mini-app CloverLeaf [10] has been tested on NVIDIA GPUs, Intel Xeon Phi Coprocessors, one AMD APP and different CPUs using the vendor OpenACC implementations from CAPS, PGI and Cray. For real-world codes, Nicolini et al. [11] present runtimes of an aeroacoustic simulation software package using PGI's OpenACC implementation for NVIDIA Kepler GPUs and Intel CPUs. Calore et al. [12] investigate a lattice Boltzmann application also using PGI's OpenACC implementation on NVIDIA GPUs, AMD GPU and Intel CPU.

However, performance portability investigations should not only consider absolute numbers, but need to account for the hardware's and application's characteristics. For that, some studies [9,10,12] compare their gained OpenACC performance to hand-tuned low-level implementations written in CUDA or OpenCL, or to libraries like MKL or CUBLAS. As a percentage of peak performance, Lopez et al. [8] present their DAXPY and DGEMV kernels. For two non-trivial kernels, Calore et al. [12] show an OpenACC efficiency of 54% to 70% of peak across different architectures for memory-bound code, while compute-bound code achieves 14% to 24% efficiency.

Modeling OpenACC performance using a roofline model has only been conducted by Wang et al. [13] who base their model on STREAM and Flop/s measurements and apply CAPS' OpenACC implementation to NVIDIA GPUs and Intel Xeon Phi coprocessors. However, they only examine basic kernels from the EPCC OpenACC Benchmark Suite. There, they get up to 82% of sustained performance while most kernels achieve about 10%. In contrast, we do not only focus on absolute performance, but especially apply the roofline model to the real-world code JuROr.

Nomenclature

C_S	Smagorinsky constant	β	thermal extension coefficient
$\mathbf{f}$	force ($\frac{kg \cdot m}{s^2}$)	κ	thermal conductivity ($\frac{W}{m \cdot K}$)
$\mathbf{g}$	gravitational force ($\frac{kg \cdot m}{s^2}$)	μ	dynamic viscosity ($\frac{kg}{m \cdot s}$)
N_x	number of cells in x-direction	ν	kinematic viscosity ($\frac{m^2}{s}$)
N_y	number of cells in y-direction		
p	pressure ($\frac{kg}{m \cdot s^2}$)	ρ	density($\frac{kg}{m^3}$)
S	stress tensor	$\overline{(\cdot)}$	filtered quantity
S_T	source term ($\frac{kg \cdot m}{s^2}$)	$(\cdot)_{eff}$	effective quantity
T	temperature (K)	Δ_f	filter width
T_0	ambient temperature (K)	$(\cdot)_{mol}$	molecular quantity
t	time (s)	$(\cdot)_t$	turbulent quantity
$\mathbf{u}$	velocity ($\frac{m}{s}$)	Δt	size of time step (s)
$\mathbf{u}_0$	velocity at time $t = 0$ ($\frac{m}{s}$)	Δx	grid size in x-direction (m)
$\mathbf{x}$	point in space $(x, y)^\top (m)$	Δy	grid size in y-direction (m)

3 Numerical Methods of JuROr

To simulate the transport of hot smoke, we first introduce the governing equations which mathematically describe the physics of smoke propagating. Then, we describe the numerical methods approximating the solution of those equations.

3.1 Governing Equations

Smoke propagation can be described with the weakly compressible Navier-Stokes equations (1) and (2) for a turbulent gas with velocity $\mathbf{u}$, pressure p and temperature T as well as no-slip boundary conditions ($\mathbf{u} = \mathbf{0}, \nabla p = 0$) at the walls

$$\partial_t \mathbf{u} + (\mathbf{u} \cdot \nabla)\, \mathbf{u} - \nu \nabla^2 \mathbf{u} + \frac{1}{\rho} \nabla p = \mathbf{f}(T) \tag{1}$$

$$\nabla \cdot \mathbf{u} = 0 \tag{2}$$

$$\partial_t T + (\mathbf{u} \cdot \nabla)\, T - \kappa \nabla^2 T = S_T. \tag{3}$$

Here, weakly compressible means that the density is dependent on the temperature $\rho = \rho(T)$ wherefore the energy equation (3) has to be solved. The force density is described by $\mathbf{f}(T) = -\beta(T - T_0)\mathbf{g}$, where β represents the thermal extension coefficient, T_0 is the ambient temperature and $\mathbf{g}$ is the gravitational force.

For the sake of computing time, we neglect pyrolysis, combustion, and heating/ cooling of surrounding walls and therefore, we focus only on the transport of hot smoke. For this case, we only take the fire far field into account and therefore, we simply consider pyrolysis and combustion by prescribing a mass and heat source.

3.2 Numerical Approach

To solve the governing equations, we take a finite difference (FD) approach on a regular grid. In space, we use central finite differences of 2nd order and in time backwards differencing of 1st order.

Therewith, we implement a fractional step method which follows the scheme outlined in Glimberg's work [5]:

$$\partial_t \mathbf{u}_1 = -\left(\mathbf{u}_1 \cdot \nabla\right) \mathbf{u}_1 \tag{4}$$

$$\partial_t \mathbf{u}_2 = \nu \nabla^2 \mathbf{u}_2 \tag{5}$$

$$\partial_t \mathbf{u}_3 = \mathbf{f}(T) \tag{6}$$

$$\partial_t \mathbf{u}_4 = -\tfrac{1}{\rho} \nabla p. \tag{7}$$

Advection via a Semi-Lagrangian Approach. The idea is to trace back velocities in time to find the current velocities since they do not change along streamlines according to the method of characteristics. Thus, we calculate the starting point from the current position (back tracing) $\mathbf{x}_d = \mathbf{x} - \Delta t \mathbf{u}_0$ to calculate the current velocity in (4) with bilinear interpolation $\mathbf{u}_1 = \mathbf{u}_0(\mathbf{x}_d(-\Delta t, \mathbf{x}))$. This method is stable in time since it is true that $\max(|\mathbf{u}_1|) \leq \max(|\mathbf{u}_0|)$ holds for all times.

Diffusion with an Implicit Jacobi Method. After applying backwards differencing in time to (5)

$$\frac{\mathbf{u}_2 - \mathbf{u}_1}{\Delta t} = \nu \nabla^2 \mathbf{u}_2,$$

we get a linear system of equations $\left(\mathbf{I} - \Delta t \nu \nabla^2\right) \mathbf{u}_2 = \mathbf{u}_1$ which is solved with Jacobi's method

$$x_i^{(k+1)} = \frac{1}{a_{ii}} \left(b_i - \sum_{j \neq i} a_{ij} x_j^{(k)} \right)$$

for $\mathbf{A} = \left(\mathbf{I} - \Delta t \nu \nabla^2\right)$, $\mathbf{x} = \mathbf{u}_2$ and $\mathbf{b} = \mathbf{u}_1$.

External Forces via Euler Scheme. With an explicit Euler scheme in time, we get a discretized version of Eq. (6) $\mathbf{u}_3 = \mathbf{u}_2 + \Delta t \mathbf{f}$. In order to update the temperature T, we need to additionally solve the energy equation

$$\partial_t T + (\mathbf{u} \cdot \nabla) T - \kappa \nabla^2 T = S_T,$$

where κ characterizes the thermal diffusion coefficient and S_T a temperature source term. Since the energy equation again describes advection and diffusion with a source term, all of the above methods can be applied here.

Pressure Equation with a Geometric Multigrid Method. After backwards differencing the Laplace equation (7) in time to get $\mathbf{u}_4 = \mathbf{u}_3 - \frac{\Delta t}{\rho} \nabla p$, we deploy the incompressibility of $\mathbf{u}_4$ yielding

$$0 = \nabla \cdot \mathbf{u}_4 = \nabla \cdot \mathbf{u}_3 - \frac{\Delta t}{\rho} \nabla^2 p.$$

Now, we solve the pressure-poisson equation $\nabla^2 p = \nabla \cdot \mathbf{u}_3$ with the multigrid method reusing the Jacobian method in the relaxation phases.

Incompressibility Through Projection. We establish incompressibility through orthogonal projection using the Helmholtz-Hodge decomposition by Chorin [14]. Therefore, we define a linear orthogonal projection of $\mathbf{u}$ onto P via $P(\mathbf{u}_3) = \mathbf{u}_4$ such that $\mathbf{u}_3 = P(\mathbf{u}_3) + \nabla p$ with $P(\nabla p) = 0$ to get $\mathbf{u}_4 = \mathbf{u}_3 - \nabla p$.

Turbulence with an Implicit, Constant Smagorinsky-Lilly Large Eddy Simulation (LES). We are solving the LES equations for the spatially filtered velocity $\bar{\mathbf{u}}$ and temperature $\bar{T}$ with filter width $\Delta_f = (\Delta x \Delta y)^{\frac{1}{2}}$ and an effective viscosity of

$$\nu_{eff} = \frac{\mu_{eff}}{\bar{\rho}} = \frac{\mu_{mol} + \mu_t}{\bar{\rho}},$$

where $\mu_t = \bar{\rho} C_S^2 \Delta_f^2 |\bar{S}|$ with Smagorinsky constant C_S [15] (commonly set to $C_S = 0.2$) and the norm of the filtered stress tensor $|\bar{S}| = \sqrt{2\bar{S}_{ij}\bar{S}_{ij}}$, where $\bar{S}_{ij} = \frac{1}{2}\left(\partial_{x_j}\bar{u}_i + \partial_{x_i}\bar{u}_j\right)$.

4 Parallelization with OpenACC

The OpenACC parallelization of the JuROr software is based on a serial runtime profile that can be seen in Fig. 1. The diffusion and pressure methods (depicted in blue) take 50% to 65% (in sum) of the runtime on an Intel Sandy Bridge CPU. The shares for diffusion and pressure highly depend on the problem size, i.e. we get 65% for $N_x = N_y = 512$ and 50% for $N_x = N_y = 2048$. Within the two methods of diffusion and pressure, the 5-point Jacobian stencil operation takes 20% to 80% of the serial runtime when measured by Intel VTune's hotspot analysis. Thus, the Jacobian stencil describes the hotspot of the CPU code and has been parallelized first using OpenACC's `kernels` and `data` regions.

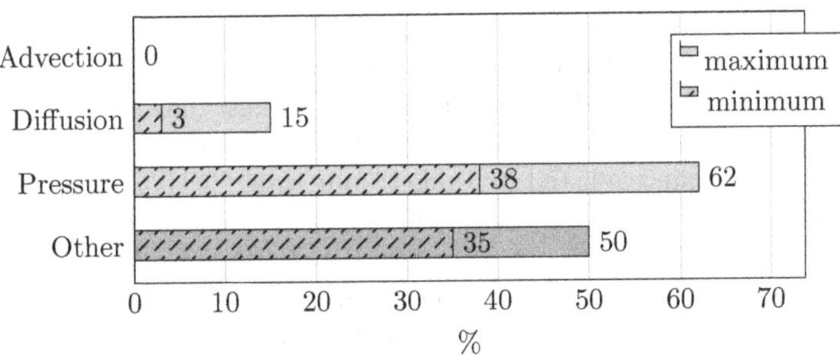

Fig. 1. Share of runtime for different JuROr kernels on one Intel Sandy Bridge core with $N_x = N_y \in \{512, \ldots, 4096\}$ (Color figure online)

After parallelizing the hotspot, all outstanding parallelizable methods (e.g., advection, pressure, boundary conditions) were also ported to the GPU. While we marked all applicable loop nests as parallelizable `independent loops`, we did not specify a certain loop schedule in order to leave it up to the compiler to choose an appropriate loop schedule for the corresponding target architecture. This is an important step in reaching performance portability. Furthermore, we maximized the parallelism across loops by merging smaller loops into one kernel. To reduce the kernel launch latency, we enabled pipelining by `async`hronous kernel launching from the CPU. Data management optimizations include the minimization of data transfers. For example, the access to C++ member attributes in parallelized subroutines caused unnecessary CPU-to-GPU and GPU-to-CPU transfers which were avoided by introducing local variables. In the OpenACC CPU versions, all data transfers are automatically ignored by the compiler so that we can use the same code base for GPU and CPU execution.

For all performance measurements, we run a benchmark test case of JuROr in double precision. This test case describes a $2D$ Navier-Stokes equation comprising advection, diffusion and pressure (without turbulence or external forces) in a $[0, 2\pi]^2$ cube, which are solved using the methods in Sect. 3. The underlying uniform grid varies from being coarse (with 8×8 cells) to very fine (with 4096×4096 cells), where each single cell stores the local values of the variables $\mathbf{u}$ and p. Additionally, we introduced ghost cells (two in each direction) to handle the boundary conditions properly. Thus, the memory size of one matrix of our biggest data set comprises roughly $4098 \times 4098 \times 8 \approx 135$ MB. While this data set fits into our CPU main memory and GPU global memory, it exceeds the CPU and GPU cache sizes.

5 Roofline Model

To investigate the performance portability of our JuROr parallelization using the PGI compiler, we setup a roofline performance model that allows comparison of achieved performance as percentage share of (sustainable) peak performance.

The roofline model [2] builds upon peak floating point performance and sustainable memory bandwidth. It assumes that computation and communication can be completely overlapped and takes only the slowest data path into account. Based on this assumptions, we build our roofline model for seven different hardware architectures that are listed in Table 1: four Intel CPUs and three NVIDIA GPUs. It is noteworthy that we use either one CPU socket or one GPU chip of the given hardware, and do not consider GPU-CPU hybrid computations for now. Correspondingly, we only model performance bounds for either the CPU or GPU chip, even though the host of a GPU-based system actually adds theoretical peak performance to the GPU performance limiters. The latter would also require a corresponding two-device roofline model with inclusion of data transfers which is out of the scope of this paper. Further, we compute the theoretical arithmetic intensity (A.I.) of JuROr and compare it to the measured value by using performance counters. We present the corresponding approaches in the following subsections.

For clarification, we will use the following terminology for our performance numbers:

- *theoretical*: values defined in or computed from technical hardware specifications or from manual code investigations
- *sustainable*: upper performance values that might be obtained in real world usually using benchmarks
- *measured/ achieved*: actual measured performance values with real codes on real hardware.

5.1 Peak Floating-Point Performance and Sustainable Memory Bandwidth

To get the architectural performance limiters, we compute the peak double-precision floating-point performance and measure the bandwidth using (micro) benchmarks.

Calculating Flop/s numbers, we need to consider that most architectures nowadays provide boosting capabilities of the clock frequency that are applied if thermal processor conditions allow it. Since this is difficult to track, we disable auto boosting where possible and base our Flop/s computations on the base operational frequency of the CPU or GPU given in Table 1. This approach is in line with the reporting rules of the *Rpeak* value of the Top 500 list [17].

Regarding the memory bandwidth measurement, it holds that achievable memory bandwidth can be significantly lower than the theoretical peak bandwidth. This is especially true for systems that employ error correcting code (ECC) such as our given architectures do. Therefore, we use benchmarks to obtain the sustainable memory bandwidth. For the GPU systems, we take the CUDA version of the GPU-STREAM benchmark [19,20] and evaluate the bandwidth of the triad kernel. We verify our measurements using the SHOC benchmark [21] as well as comparing them with the published results on the GPU-STREAM website (where possible). For the CPU systems, we take the triad results of McCalpin's OpenMP STREAM benchmark [18] using the Intel Compiler with the flag `-qopt-streaming-stores=always`. We verify these results using Intel VTune's memory access analysis that automatically evaluates the local DRAM single-package bandwidth using a (not further specified) micro benchmark. This micro benchmark delivers slightly higher bandwidth numbers

Table 1. Used hardware architectures and compilers

Name	Hardware	Used	Compiler and Flags
BDW	2-socket Intel Xeon Broadwell E5-2650 v4 @2.20 GHz, 2×12 cores	1 socket	PGI 16.10 -ta=multicore
HSW	2-socket Intel Xeon Haswell E5-2680 v3 @2.50 GHz, 2×12 cores	1 socket	PGI 16.1 -ta=multicore
SNB	2-socket Intel Xeon Sandy Bridge E5-2650 0 @2.00 GHz, 2×8 cores	1 socket	PGI 16.1 -ta=multicore
IVB	2-socket Intel Xeon Ivy Bridge E5-2640 v2 @2.00 GHz, 2×8 cores	1 socket	PGI 16.1 -ta=multicore
P100	NVIDIA Pascal P100 SMX2 GPU, 1328 MHz, 16 GB, autoboost off, ECC on, BDW host	1 GPU	PGI 16.10 -ta=tesla:cc60
K80	NVIDIA Kepler K80 with 2 GPUs, 562 MHz, 2×12 GB, autoboost off, ECC on, HSW host	1 GPU	PGI 16.1 -ta=tesla:cc35
K40	NVIDIA Kepler K40 GPU, 745 MHz, 12 GB, autoboost N/A, ECC on, SNB host	1 GPU	PGI 16.1 -ta=tesla:cc35

Table 2. Floating-point performance and memory bandwidth (BW) of the hardware architectures under investigation

Machine	Peak GFlop/s	Peak BW [GB/s]	STREAM BW [GB/s]	VTune BW [GB/s]
BDW	422.40	76.80	60.71	68.00
HSW	240.00	68.00	55.76	61.00
SNB	128.00	51.20	35.88	43.00
IVB	128.00	51.20	40.43	43.00
P100	4759.55	720.00	550.35	N/A
K80	935.17	240.00	149.70	N/A
K40	1430.40	288.00	191.20	N/A

why we base our CPU performance portability investigations on these values. All results can be found in Table 2.

5.2 Arithmetic Intensity

To evaluate which performance boundary is hit by our JuROr code, we take a look at its arithmetic intensity in Flop per Byte [Flop/B]. Since the concept of arithmetic intensity does only make sense for individual kernels, we focus on JuROr's hotspot – the Jacobian stencil. While it takes up to 80% of the runtime in serial execution, its parallelized version still takes up to 50% of the runtime on a K40 for a 2D test case with $N_x = N_y = 4096$ grid cells in each direction. Thus, again it describes the hotspot and we can apply (8) to compute its sustainable performance with respect to its performance limiters:

$$\begin{aligned}\text{sustainable performance } [GFlop/s] \\ &= \min(\text{sustainable BW } [GB/s] \cdot \text{A.I. } [Flop/B], \\ &\qquad \text{peak Flop/s performance } [GFlop/s])\,. \end{aligned} \tag{8}$$

In a second step, we will use performance counters to measure the achievable performance and compute its percentage share from sustainable peak:

$$\text{performance share } [\%] = \frac{\text{measured performance of hotspot } [GFlop/s]}{\text{sustainable performance of hotspot } [GFlop/s]}. \tag{9}$$

For determining the arithmetic intensity of the Jacobian stencil kernel, we differentiate between theoretical arithmetic intensity and measured arithmetic intensity. Here, *theoretical* arithmetic intensity refers to the traditional approach of investigating the kernel's source code and manually counting (double) floating-point operations and transferred words. While this approach works well for small regular kernels, it is very challenging for real-world codes that also employ special built-in function calls or complex data access patterns. For example, a call of the `pow` or `sin` function does not deliver an intuitive Flop per Byte ratio and, thus, is little predictable. Therefore, we also examine a *measured* arithmetic intensity of the JuROr's hotspot which is based on performance counters.

Theoretical Arithmetic Intensity. Besides counting floating-point operations, we only take the slowest data path into account, i.e., access to main memory (CPU) or global memory (GPU). For that, we evaluate the cache reuse with layer conditions to exclude corresponding data accesses. Furthermore, we verify that non-temporal stores are used on the CPU systems. Overall, for JuROr's hotspot we have:

$$\text{A.I.} = \frac{\text{floating-point operations}}{\text{data movement}} = \frac{12\,\text{Flops}}{(2\,\text{reads} + 1\,\text{write}) \cdot 8\,\text{Bytes}} = 0.500\,\frac{Flop}{B}.$$

Measured Arithmetic Intensity. The approach of measured arithmetic intensity has the advantage of being applicable for any kind of code. However, it might not reflect the best possible arithmetic intensity, since it also tracks unnecessary data transfers or occurring macho-Flop/s. To get the measured arithmetic intensity, we run the code with performance counters for double-precision floating-point operations and the transferred bytes. Since no common performance counter interface is available across the selected machines, we manually track the counters using different tools: NVIDIA's nvprof 7.5 on the NVIDIA GPU systems and Intel's VTune Amplifier 2016/2017 on the Intel CPU systems. It must be noted that a direct mapping from memory access counter values to our hotspot function is not possible since they are based on uncore events. Therefore, we use VTune's filter capabilities to track our hotspot function within the timeline view and read values from that timeline. To ease our calculations, we directly use VTune's calculated bandwidth numbers. A summary of the applied setups can be found in Tables 3 and 4.

Due to known hardware restrictions on the Intel Haswell machine [16], we are not able to use Flop performance counters on this architecture. Nevertheless, we are able to run parts of the code with the Intel Advisor tool that shall be able to measure arithmetic intensities for roofline models automatically. From the intermediate result (before crashing), we take the achieved GFlop/s number on the Haswell system. Unfortunately, the Intel Advisor is not capable of running our real-world code successfully on all architectures due to crashes. Thus, we rely on our own performance counter measurements as described above for the other architectures.

Given the counters in Tables 3 and 4, we can compute the measured arithmetic intensity as follows:

$$\begin{aligned}\text{A.I.}_{\text{CPU}} &= \frac{\text{X87} + \text{SCALAR} + \text{SSE\_PACKED} \cdot 2 + \text{256\_PACKED} \cdot 4}{(\text{RD} + \text{WR}) \cdot 64\,\text{Bytes}} \\ &= \frac{\text{X87} + \text{SCALAR} + \text{SSE\_PACKED} \cdot 2 + \text{256\_PACKED} \cdot 4}{\text{BW} \cdot \text{runtime}_{\text{hotspot}}}\end{aligned}$$

as well as

$$\text{A.I.}_{\text{GPU}} = \frac{\text{flop\_count\_dp}}{(\text{read} + \text{write}) \cdot 32\,[\text{threads per warp}]},$$

Table 3. Performance counters: Flops counters

Machine	Flops counter	Tool
BDW	FP_ARITH_INST_RETIRED.SCALAR_DOUBLE, FP_ARITH_INST_RETIRED.128B_PACKED_DOUBLE, FP_ARITH_INST_RETIRED.256B_PACKED_DOUBLE, INST_RETIRED.X87	VTune
HSW	N/A	N/A
SNB	FP_COMP_OPS_EXE.SSE_SCALAR_DOUBLE, FP_COMP_OPS_EXE.SSE_PACKED_DOUBLE, SIMD_FP_256.PACKED_DOUBLE, FP_COMP_OPS_EXE.X87	VTune
IVB	FP_COMP_OPS_EXE.SSE_SCALAR_DOUBLE, FP_COMP_OPS_EXE.SSE_PACKED_DOUBLE, SIMD_FP_256.PACKED_DOUBLE, FP_COMP_OPS_EXE.X87	VTune
P100	flop_count_dp	nvprof
K80	flop_count_dp	nvprof
K40	flop_count_dp	nvprof

Table 4. Performance counters: Bytes counters

Machine	Bytes counter	Tool
BDW	UNC_M_CAS_COUNT:RD, UNC_M_CAS_COUNT:WR	VTune
HSW	UNC_M_CAS_COUNT:RD, UNC_M_CAS_COUNT:WR	VTune
SNB	UNC_M_CAS_COUNT:RD, UNC_M_CAS_COUNT:WR	VTune
IVB	UNC_M_CAS_COUNT:RD, UNC_M_CAS_COUNT:WR	VTune
P100	dram_read_transactions, dram_write_transactions	nvprof
K80	dram_read_transactions, dram_write_transactions	nvprof
K40	dram_read_transactions, dram_write_transactions	nvprof

where

$$\text{read} + \text{write} = \text{dram\_read\_transactions} + \text{dram\_write\_transactions}.$$

Following those two approaches – of theoretical vs. measured arithmetic intensity – we present our results in the following section.

6 Results

Following the methodology introduced in Sect. 5, we present performance portability results with respect to the theoretical and measured arithmetic intensity.

6.1 Measurement Setup

In addition to the hardware setups given in Table 1, we compile all code versions with -fast -O3. We run all performance and counter measurements three times and take the corresponding average value while runtime deviations are below 0.6%. Furthermore, all measurements are executed on machines with exclusive access. For OpenACC runs on our CPU systems, we also enable thread binding to ensure good data affinity: ACC_NUM_CORES=<#cores> ACC_BIND=yes MP_BIND=yes MP_BLIST=0,1,<...#cores-1>.

Since selecting OpenACC loop schedules is left to the compiler, Table 5 gives an overview on the PGI compiler's choice for the Jacobian stencil on different hardware setups. For our CPUs, the outer loop of the Jacobian loop nest gets distributed across gangs (i.e. CPU cores), while the compiler attempts to vectorize the inner loop. Contrarily, the compiler choses a two-dimensional work distribution on the GPUs: Each dimension gets distributed across the GPU's multiprocessors (gangs) and the double-precision logic units (vector). While the overall thread tile size is the same across all GPUs, i.e., 128 threads per block, the compiler selects different distributions within the tiles for Kepler and Pascal GPUs.

Table 5. Loop schedules for loop nests of Jacobian stencil kernel chosen and reported by the PGI compiler

Machine	Outer loop	Inner loop
BDW	gang	vector sse + prefetching
HSW	gang	vector sse + prefetching
SNB	gang	vector sse + prefetching
IVB	gang	vector sse + prefetching
P100	gang vector(32)	gang vector(4)
K80	gang vector(4)	gang vector(32)
K40	gang vector(4)	gang vector(32)

6.2 Theoretical and Measured Arithmetic Intensity

Results for the theoretical and measured arithmetic intensity of the Jacobian stencil are presented in Table 6. Values of the measured arithmetic intensity show only little deviation with values in the range of 0.332 to 0.498 Flop/B across all architectures. In addition, they are roughly in line with the theoretical arithmetic intensities of 0.500 since the Jacobian stencil does not exhibit any special built-in functions or macho-Flop/s.

Table 6. Theoretical and measured A.I. of the Jacobian stencil kernel

Machine	Theoretical A.I. $[\frac{Flop}{B}]$	Measured A.I. $[\frac{Flop}{B}]$	Performance limiter
BDW	0.500	0.340	Memory bandwidth
HSW	0.500	0.332	Memory bandwidth
SNB	0.500	0.386	Memory bandwidth
IVB	0.500	0.354	Memory bandwidth
P100	0.500	0.498	Memory bandwidth
K80	0.500	0.416	Memory bandwidth
K40	0.500	0.418	Memory bandwidth

6.3 Performance Portability

As an overview, two exemplary roofline models for JuROr running on the Broadwell CPU in Fig. 2 and the Pascal GPU in Fig. 3 illustrate the theoretical intensity (vertically dashed line) and measured arithmetic intensity (circle marker) while also visualizing the performance limiters as rooflines. This representation also shows the achieved performance (circle marker) in comparison to the sustainable memory bandwidth.

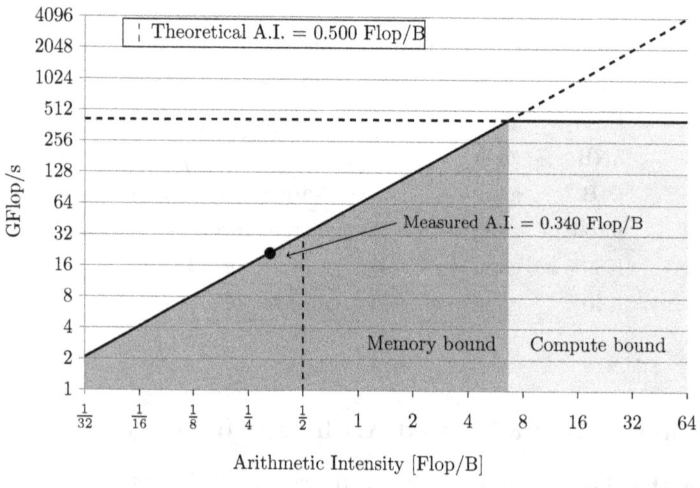

Fig. 2. Roofline of BDW based on data set size of $N_x = N_y = 4096$

For our detailed analysis, we list the absolute performance numbers in Table 7 that are derived by our performance counter measurements running the JuROr code. All these numbers, i.e., GFlop/s, GB/s and runtime in seconds, highly differ across the architectures giving the impression of having non-portable code with respect to performance.

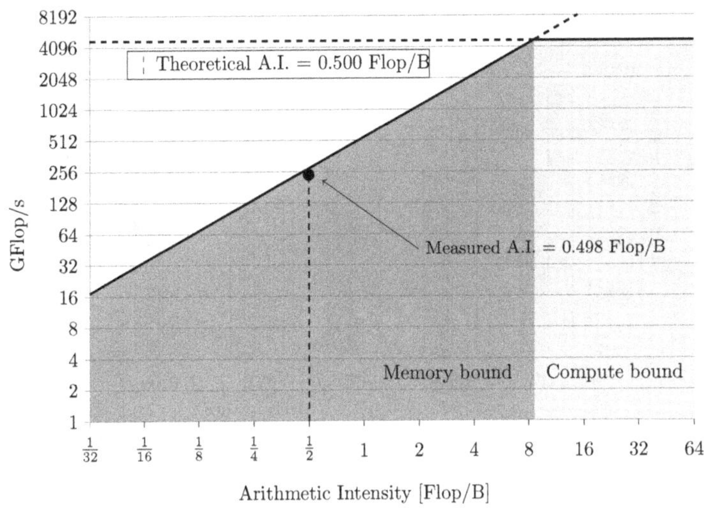

Fig. 3. Roofline of P100 based on data set size of $N_x = N_y = 4096$

Table 7. Flop/s, memory bandwidth and runtime measurement for Jacobian stencil kernel. Bandwidths given in brackets are based on ECC overhead.

Machine	Measured GFlop/s	Measured BW [GB/s]	Kernel runtime [s]
BDW	21.66	63.71	4.97
HSW	19.81	59.59	5.29
SNB	14.93	38.65	8.54
IVB	14.90	42.04	7.70
P100	251.77	505.14	0.47
K80	71.17	170.91 (−29.08)	1.65
K40	91.47	218.79 (−36.30)	1.29

However, in the following, we express performance portability as performance share to sustainable peak by applying our definition in (9). These results are illustrated in Fig. 4.

Looking at the theoretical arithmetic intensities, the Jacobian stencil achieves 64% to 69% of sustainable memory bandwidth (given by Intel VTune's micro benchmarks) across the CPUs. For the GPU systems, it achieves higher performance shares that range from 91% to 96% with respect to the GPU-STREAM results. Since the measured arithmetic intensities are slightly below the theoretical values, they also assume a lower sustainable peak performance in GFlop/s (exemplary illustrated in Fig. 2). Therefore, we see higher performance shares for the measured arithmetic intensities ranging from 90% to 98% on the CPUs with respect to Intel VTune's bandwidth micro benchmark and from 104% to 108% with respect to the OpenMP STREAM benchmark results. Thus, our

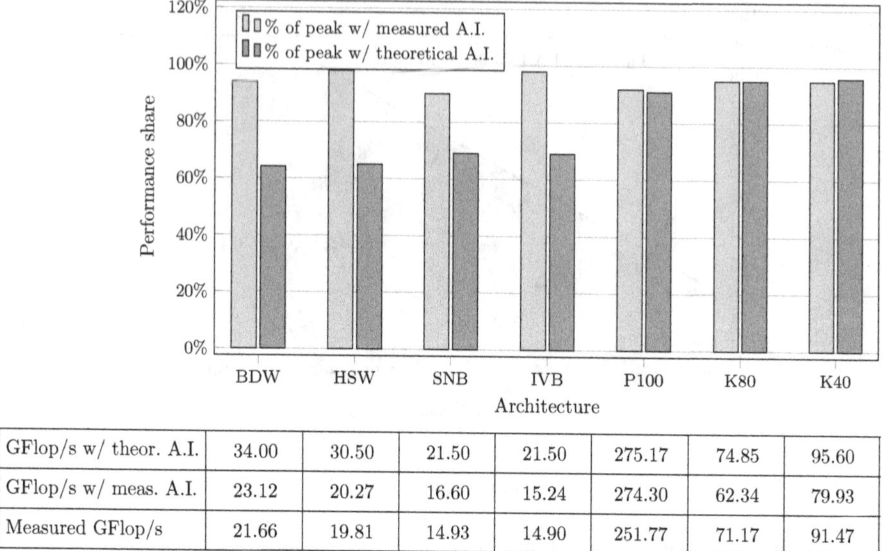

GFlop/s w/ theor. A.I.	34.00	30.50	21.50	21.50	275.17	74.85	95.60
GFlop/s w/ meas. A.I.	23.12	20.27	16.60	15.24	274.30	62.34	79.93
Measured GFlop/s	21.66	19.81	14.93	14.90	251.77	71.17	91.47

Fig. 4. Performance share of all considered architectures for $N_x = N_y = 4096$

hotspot delivers higher bandwidth measurements than the STREAM benchmark which may be due to additional transferred bytes for prefetching. For the GPU performance shares, initially, we see a similar behavior with values from 92% to 114%. When investigating the appearance of the GPU performance shares above 100% further, i.e., for the two Kepler architectures K80 and K40, we find that NVIDIA's device memory performance counters also track transactions caused by ECC overhead (cf. Table 7). Since these extra ECC bytes do not contribute to the bandwidth achieved by the application, we subtract corresponding values (counters `ecc_transactions/ ecc_throughput`) from the measured bandwidth of the Jacobian stencil. In contrast, the Pascal architecture supports ECC natively and, hence, does not show ECC effects on bandwidth. With that, we get more realistic performance shares for JuROr of 92% to 95% across the GPUs.

Overall, although absolute performance numbers suggest otherwise, the results that are based on the specific hardware and software characteristics show that for our real-world OpenACC code the PGI compiler is capable in producing performance portable code across different target architectures with a single source code base.

7 Conclusion and Outlook

In the context of the OpenACC-parallel real-world C++-code JuROr that simulates smoke propagation based on computational fluid dynamics, we investigated the performance portability of its memory-bound hotspot using PGI's OpenACC across four Intel CPUs and three NVIDIA GPUs.

For our analysis of performance portability, we setup roofline models for all architectures and computed the arithmetic intensity of the code's hotspot – the Jacobian stencil. We examined this theoretical arithmetic intensity, as well as measured arithmetic intensities that were obtained using performance counters for floating-point operations and memory transfers. Our measured arithmetic intensities are in the range of 0.332 to 0.498 Flop/B for all architectures and, thereby, roughly in line with the theoretical arithmetic intensity of 0.500 Flop/B.

Using the theoretical arithmetic intensity, we obtained 64% to 69% of sustainable bandwidth on the CPUs and 91% to 96% on the GPUs. Regarding the measured arithmetic intensities, the performance shares increased to 90% to 98% on the CPUs and remained roughly constant with 92% to 95% on the GPUs referring to the according STREAM bandwidths, respectively. Our investigations show that it is important to account for ECC overhead in memory bandwidth on Kepler GPUs when using NVIDIA's device memory performance counters. Pascal GPUs lift this problem by natively supporting ECC in hardware.

Due to the similar performance shares across architectures, our OpenACC parallelization of JuROr shows good performance portability relying on the PGI compiler. While hand-tuned or low-level code might generally achieve higher performance, our OpenACC approach gives us the possibility to maintain one source code base for different architectures while still delivering good performance.

In future, to achieve further parallelization and acceleration, we will constantly optimize the code for both, CPU and GPU usage and model the data transfer for the roofline. Moreover, we will investigate OpenACC performance on AMD GPUs. While we could already show that our OpenACC code is runnable on AMD Tahiti GPUs, problems with the measurement infrastructure hindered us in presenting portability results in this paper. Currently, we are working on a 3D code to handle 3D geometries, where we will further include handling of inner boundaries to expand the code to complex 3D geometries. Complex 3D geometries (e.g., several rooms) will then be used for the validation of the OpenACC code.

Acknowledgements. This study was performed within the project ORPHEUS funded by the Federal Ministry of Education and Research (BMBF) Program on 'Research for Civil Security - Protection and Rescue in complex Disaster Situations' (funding code 13N13266). Some simulations were performed with computing resources granted by RWTH Aachen University under project rwth0207.

References

1. BMBF funded research project, Optimierung der Rauchableitung und Personenführung in U-Bahnhöfen: Experimente und Simulationen (ORPHEUS) - Teilvorhaben: Brand- und Personenstromsimulationen in unterirdischen Verkehrsstationen (2015–2018). http://www.orpheus-projekt.de

2. Williams, S., Waterman, A., Patterson, D.: Roofline: an insightful visual performance model for multicore architectures. Commun. ACM **52**(4), 65–76 (2009)
3. Han, L., et al.: FireGrid: an e-infrastructure for next-generation emergency response support. J. Parallel Distrib. Comput. **70**(11), 1128–1141 (2010)
4. Koo, S.-H.: Forecasting fire development with sensor-linked simulation, Dissertation, University of Edinburgh (2010)
5. Glimberg, S.L., Erleben, K., Bennetsen, J.: Smoke simulation for fire engineering using a multigrid method on graphics hardware. In: VRIPHYS, pp. 11–20. Eurographics Association (2009)
6. Daniel, N., Rein, G.: The Fire Navigator: forecasting the spread of building fires on the basis of sensor data, FPE Extra Issue 3, March 2016. http://www.sfpe.org/general/custom.asp?page=FPEExtraIssue3
7. Pennycook, S.J., Hammond, S.D., Wright, S.A., Herdman, J.A., Miller, I., Jarvis, S.A.: An investigation of the performance portability of OpenCL. J. Parallel Distrib. Comput. **73**(11), 1439–1450 (2013)
8. Lopez, M.G., Larrea, V.V., Joubert, W., Hernandez, O., Haidar, A., Tomov, S., Dongarra, J.: Towards achieving performance portability using directives for accelerators. In: Third Workshop on Accelerator Programming Using Directives (WACCPD), pp. 13–24 (2016)
9. Sabne, A., Sakdhnagool, P., Lee, S., Vetter, J.S.: Evaluating performance portability of OpenACC. In: Brodman, J., Tu, P. (eds.) LCPC 2014. LNCS, vol. 8967, pp. 51–66. Springer, Cham (2015). doi:10.1007/978-3-319-17473-0_4
10. Herdman, J.A., Gaudin, W.P., Perks, O., Beckingsale, D.A., Mallinson, A.C., Jarvis, S.A.: Achieving portability and performance through OpenACC. In: First Workshop on Accelerator Programming using Directives, pp. 19–26. IEEE Press (2014)
11. Nicolini, M., Miller, J., Wienke, S., Schlottke-Lakemper, M., Meinke, M., Müller, M.S.: Software cost analysis of GPU-accelerated aeroacoustics simulations in C++ with OpenACC. In: Taufer, M., Mohr, B., Kunkel, J.M. (eds.) ISC High Performance 2016. LNCS, vol. 9945, pp. 524–543. Springer, Cham (2016). doi:10.1007/978-3-319-46079-6_36
12. Calore, E., Gabbana, A., Kraus, J., Schifano, S.F., Tripiccione, R.: Performance and portability of accelerated lattice Boltzmann applications with OpenACC. Concurr. Comput. Pract. Exper. **28**(12), 3485–3502 (2016)
13. Wang, Y., Qin, Q., See, S.C.W., Lin, J.: Performance portability evaluation for OpenACC on Intel Knights Corner and Nvidia Kepler. In: HPC China (2013)
14. Chorin, A.: Numerical solution of the Navier-Stokes equations. Math. Comput. **22**, 745–762 (1968)
15. Smagorinsky, J.: General circulation experiments with the primitive equations. Mon. Weather Rev. **91**(3), 99–164 (1963)
16. JURECA, Jülich Research on Exascale Cluster Architectures. http://www.fz-juelich.de/ias/jsc/EN/Expertise/Supercomputers/JURECA/JURECA_node.html
17. Top500.org, Top500 List, November 2016. https://www.top500.org/list/2016/11/
18. McCalpin, J.D.: Memory bandwidth and machine balance in current high performance computers. IEEE Comput. Soc. Techn. Committee Comput. Archit. (TCCA) Newsl. 19–25 (1995). https://www.cs.virginia.edu/stream/
19. Deakin, T., McIntosh-Smith, S.: GPU-STREAM v1.0/ v3.1. https://github.com/UoB-HPC/GPU-STREAM

20. Deakin, T., Price, J., Martineau, M., McIntosh-Smith, S.: GPU-STREAM v2.0: benchmarking the achievable memory bandwidth of many-core processors across diverse parallel programming models. In: Taufer, M., Mohr, B., Kunkel, J.M. (eds.) ISC High Performance 2016. LNCS, vol. 9945, pp. 489–507. Springer, Cham (2016). doi:10.1007/978-3-319-46079-6_34
21. Danalis, A., Marin, G., McCurdy, C., Meredith, J., Roth, P., Spafford, K., Tipparaju, V., Vetter, J.: The scalable heterogeneous computing (SHOC) benchmark suite. In: Proceedings of the Third Workshop on General-Purpose Computation on Graphics Processors (GPGPU 2010), pp. 63–74 (2010)

Tuning and Optimization for a Variety of Many-Core Architectures Without Changing a Single Line of Implementation Code Using the Alpaka Library

Alexander Matthes[1,2(✉)], René Widera[1], Erik Zenker[3], Benjamin Worpitz[3], Axel Huebl[1,2], and Michael Bussmann[1]

[1] Helmholtz-Zentrum Dresden – Rossendorf, Dresden, Germany
{a.matthes,m.bussmann}@hzdr.de
[2] Technische Universität Dresden, Dresden, Germany
[3] LogMeIn, Inc., Boston, USA

Abstract. We present an analysis on optimizing performance of a single C++11 source code using the Alpaka hardware abstraction library. For this we use the general matrix multiplication (GEMM) algorithm in order to show that compilers can optimize Alpaka code effectively when tuning key parameters of the algorithm. We do not intend to rival existing, highly optimized DGEMM versions, but merely choose this example to prove that Alpaka allows for platform-specific tuning with a single source code. In addition we analyze the optimization potential available with vendor-specific compilers when confronted with the heavily templated abstractions of Alpaka. We specifically test the code for bleeding edge architectures such as Nvidia's Tesla P100, Intel's Knights Landing (KNL) and Haswell architecture as well as IBM's Power8 system. On some of these we are able to reach almost 50% of the peak floating point operation performance using the aforementioned means. When adding compiler-specific `#pragmas` we are able to reach 5 TFLOPs/s on a P100 and over 1 TFLOPs/s on a KNL system.

This project has received funding from the European Unions Horizon 2020 research and innovation programme under grant agreement No 654220. This project received funding within the MEPHISTO project (BMBF-Förderkennzeichen 01IH16006C). Research leading to these results has in parts been carried out on the Human Brain Project PCP Pilot System JURON at the Juelich Supercomputing Centre, which received co-funding from the European Union (Grant Agreement no. 604102). We thank for the access to and support for the HPC cluster Taurus at the Centre for Information Services and High Performance Computing (ZIH), Technical University Dresden, as well as the cluster Hypnos at the Helmholtz-Zentrum Dresden – Rossendorf.

J.M. Kunkel et al. (Eds.): ISC High Performance Workshops 2017, LNCS 10524, pp. 496–514, 2017.
https://doi.org/10.1007/978-3-319-67630-2_36

1 Introduction

1.1 Motivation

We have developed Alpaka [28] due to our own need in programming highly efficient algorithms for simulations [27] and data analysis on modern hardware in a portable manner. The aim of our approach is to have a single C++ source code in which we can express all levels of parallelism available on modern compute hardware, using a parallel redundant hierarchy model similar to that found in CUDA or OpenCL. Taking a look at the recent top ten high performance computing (HPC) systems [16], it becomes clear that many-core architectures and heterogeneous systems are dominating the landscape and will continue to do so.

The main design goal of Alpaka is to describe all levels of parallelization available on modern heterogeneous hardware. It neither makes assumptions on the memory layout or access patterns, nor does it handle the underlaying resource and event management of the whole application, nor does it abstract the internode communication.

Our open-source projects PIConGPU [2,3] and HaseOnGPU [5] both use Alpaka for the kernel abstraction for various many-core hardware [27,28], but different libraries for the mentioned topics not handled by Alpaka, like Graybat [26] for the network communication, mallocMC for the memory management or libPMacc for containers and asynchronous event handling. Alpaka is not meant as a full grown solution for developing or porting whole HPC applications, but as a single-purpose library that can easily be included into the individual software of an exiting HPC project. We have chosen to provide a lightweight, yet powerful C++ meta programming library for coherently expressing parallelism for a large variety of many-core platforms.

Modern C++11 template programming enables us to implement an abstraction layer between the application and the various, often vendor-specific programming models available for programming many-core hardware. With modern compilers the abstraction layer is completely resolved during compilation, leaving only efficient code in the binary.

While performance portability and close-to-zero overhead of Alpaka code could be shown in previous work [28] we will here concentrate on a subject important for high performance computing, namely optimization of code for various hardware platforms by means of tuning and vendor-specific compiler optimizations while maintaining a single-source, portable code. The presence of architecture independent parameters outside the algorithm implementation itself may also enable auto-tuning in a later step.

We will show that indeed parameter tuning and compiler optimization generate highly efficient code on various platforms. However, we will discuss some pitfalls of this approach that arise due to limiting tuning parameters to a small number and due to the lack of full support for C++11 in some vendor compilers.

1.2 Alpaka

Alpaka allows for a multidimensional, hierarchical abstraction of computation hardware as seen in Fig. 1. Kernels are written and run as threads executed in a task parallel manner. Threads are organized in *blocks*, which themselves are organized in *grids*. Every thread inside a block is assumed to run in parallel to the other threads in the same block, enabling intra-block synchronization. Blocks on the other hand may run concurrently or sequentially inside a grid. Every execution layer has a corresponding memory hierarchy level. In addition to task-parallel execution Alpaka introduces an element layer inside the thread level for data-parallel execution, where the same instruction or program is executed for multiple data. This latter level is usually used for expressing vectorization.

For any given hardware, these layers are mapped onto the hardware using a suitable back end. As such, Alpaka does not implement any functionality beyond this mapping and the underlying optimizations come from the back end and mapping chosen for a specific hardware.

Alpaka currently supports Nvidia's CUDA [23], OpenMP [4] 2 and 4, Boost Fibers and C++Threads as back ends. Furthermore, we have started to add OpenACC [24] and Thread Building Blocks [11] (TBB) support, while support for AMD HIP [1] is foreseen for the near future. Alpaka has two accelerators using OpenMP 2: One is running blocks in a grid concurrently, the other one threads inside a block. For the first one only one thread per block is allowed. With the same constraint it is possible to run the code sequentially with Alpaka.

In the scope of this paper we will restrict ourselves to the OpenMP 2 Blocks and Nvidia CUDA back ends so that we are able to compare our new results to our previous work. Although OpenCL [7] is widely supported, it is not suitable as an Alpaka back end, as it is not single source C++. SYCL [13,25] has the goal to close this gap and will probably be considered in the future. C++ AMP [17] looks similarly promising, but fails in support of current HPC architectures.

Alpaka leaves performance enhancements due to data layout to the user or another, independent library. Memory in Alpaka thus is always represented by a plain pointer. This strategy leaves room for optimization, but currently requires more development effort by the user.

Optimized memory access patterns are as important for achieving performance as expression of algorithmic parallelism and we have carefully chosen the example GEMM algorithm as it seems simple enough to go without memory abstraction. However, optimizing memory access and memory copies is outside the scope of Alpaka, which distinguishes our approach from the design goals of libraries such as Kokkos [6] or RAJA [10] that aim for providing a full software environment for portable programming of many-core architectures. A separate memory access abstraction library is planned, but will be an independent, orthogonal part of the already mentioned software stack.

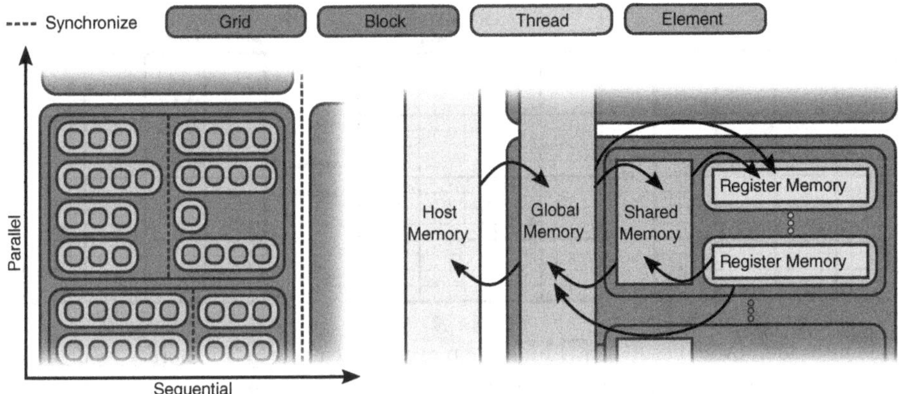

Fig. 1. Systematic view of the abstract redundant parallel hierarchy model of Alpaka taken from [28]. A compute device works on a grid, inside this grid are blocks. Every block has the same amount of threads, which are defined by the user as kernels. Explicit looping over elements inside the kernel enables autovectorization but also gives a better utilization for simple kernels. For each computation layer Alpaka introduces an appropriate memory layer. The copies between those are explicit (depicted as arrows).

2 The Alpaka General Matrix Multiplication Implementation

Similar to [28] we use a general matrix multiplication (GEMM) example

$$C = \alpha \cdot A \cdot B + \beta \cdot C \tag{1}$$

for performance tuning, as it allows for tiling without the need for changing the memory representation of the matrices.

For the sake of simplicity we choose A, B and C to be quadratic matrices with N rows and columns each. The total number of floating point operations then follows as

$$\mathrm{O}(N) = 3N^2 + 2N^3 \approx 2N^3 \ . \tag{2}$$

The number of elements per thread e and threads per block t result in the number of blocks in the grid

$$\mathrm{B}(e,t) = \frac{N}{t \cdot e} \ , \tag{3}$$

where $t = 1$ for the OpenMP 2 Blocks and the sequential accelerator.

We measure the time t in seconds for executing the algorithm without copy operations to device memory, keeping the maximum over ten runs, which proved sufficient to suppress any statistical fluctuations. With this we calculate the performance P in $^{\mathrm{GFLOPs}}/_{\mathrm{s}}$ as

$$\mathrm{P}(N,t) = \frac{\mathrm{O}(N)}{t} \cdot 10^{-9} = \frac{2N^3}{t} \cdot 10^{-9} \ . \tag{4}$$

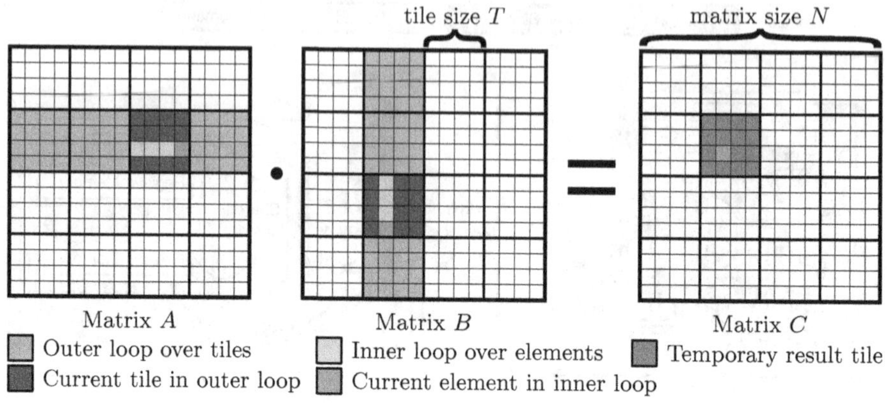

Fig. 2. Performance critical $A \cdot B$ part of the GEMM using a tiling strategy. A thread iterates over smaller sub matrices (tiles) in A and B (purple), performs the matrix multiplication per tile using the element layer (green) for vectorization, and adds it to a temporary thread local C tile (orange). The remaining part of the GEMM algorithm using the temporary C tile needs to load and write the C matrix only once (streaming), thus it doesn't need to be cached.

2.1 Tiled GEMM Algorithm

There exist many highly optimized GEMM implementations, reaching up to 90% [14] of the theoretical peak performance. The solution depicted here is not intended to compete with these algorithms. Instead, it serves as a code example reasonably designed to exploit parallelism on many-core hardware. As such, it already achieves 20% of the peak performance without tuning, which is a value regularly found in applications. In the following, we aim to show that Alpaka allows for platform specific tuning by parameter tuning without specializing the implementation. As long as the tiles of the two matrices A, B fit completely in the cache memory, increasing the tile size will usually result in better performance. Based on the size S in bytes of the data type used (single or double precision) the required cache size K is

$$\mathrm{K}(S,T) = 2T^2S \ . \tag{5}$$

The tiling matrix multiplication has $N_{\text{blocks}} = {}^{N}/_{T}$ tiles in each matrix dimension. For every tile of C N_{blocks} tiles of A and B need to be loaded (see Fig. 2). Furthermore the C tile itself needs to be loaded, leading to a total number of

$$\mathrm{M}(N,T) = N_{\text{blocks}}^2(2T^2N_{\text{blocks}} + T^2) = 2\frac{N^3}{T} + N^2 = N^2\left(2\frac{N}{T} + 1\right) \tag{6}$$

memory operations, which gives us the ratio of compute to memory operations as

$$\mathrm{R}(N,T) = \frac{\mathrm{O}(N)}{\mathrm{M}(N,T)} = \frac{2N^3}{N^2(2\frac{N}{T}+1)} = \frac{2N}{(2\frac{N}{T}+1)} = \frac{2N}{\frac{2N+T}{T}} = \frac{2NT}{2N+T} \tag{7}$$

with $\lim\limits_{N\to\infty} \mathrm{R}(N,T) = T$, showing again that larger tile sizes are preferable.

With cache hierarchies present in most modern architectures, it is not trivially predictable for which cache T should be optimized. We thus chose to calculate one tile of the matrix C per Alpaka block. Every element in the block calculates one entry in the C tile. We use a two dimensional indexing for the parallelization levels. Every element stores the partial result of $\alpha \cdot A \cdot B$ in element local memory. Depending on the architecture, we can increase the number of elements per block by increasing the number of threads per block, which makes sense for GPUs, or the number of elements per thread, which should enable autovectorization for CPUs.

```
// Class for optimal tile size depending on the Accelerator type
template< typename T_Acc >
struct OptimalVectorSize {
    using type = alpaka::dim::DimInt<1u>;
};
// Number of elements per tiles predefined, but changeable as compiler option
#ifndef GPU_ELEM_NUM
    #define GPU_ELEM_NUM 2u
#endif
#ifndef OMP_ELEM_NUM
    #define OMP_ELEM_NUM 256u
#endif
// Specialization of the tile size type for CUDA, steered by GPU_ELEM_NUM
#ifdef ALPAKA_ACC_GPU_CUDA_ENABLED
    template< typename... T_Args >
    struct OptimalVectorSize< alpaka::acc::AccGpuCudaRt< T_Args... > > {
        using type = alpaka::dim::DimInt<GPU_ELEM_NUM>;
    };
#endif
// Specialization for OpenMP Blocks, steered by OMP_ELEM_NUM
#ifdef ALPAKA_ACC_CPU_B_OMP2_T_SEQ_ENABLED
    template< typename... T_Args >
    struct OptimalVectorSize< alpaka::acc::AccCpuOmp2Blocks< T_Args... > > {
        using type = alpaka::dim::DimInt<OMP_ELEM_NUM>;
    };
#endif
// Easily extensible macro for every independent loop
#define VECTOR_PRAGMA \
    _Pragma ("ivdep") \
    _Pragma ("GCC ivdep")
```

Listing 1.1. Settings for the tiled matrix multiplication. `OptimalVectorSize::type::value` represents the tile size T. The parameters and the loop `#pragmas` can directly be used inside the kernel.

We implement the tile size T as an accelerator dependent class as seen in Listing 1.1, thus avoiding mixing tuning and kernel parameters. It is set via `#define`, thus making tuning easier. The matrix sizes N are passed as kernel parameters (not shown).

2.2 Architectures

We test Nvidia K80 and P100 GPUs. The K80 and the PCIe version of the P100 are hosted in the cluster Hypnos at the Helmholtz-Zentrum Dresden – Rossendorf whereas an nvlink using version of the P100 is part of the OpenPower pilot system JURON at the Jülich Supercomputing Center. All GPU architectures considered in this paper are listed in Table 1.

Table 1. Single (SP) and double (DP) precision peak performances and other characteristic variables of GPUs considered in this paper. Notice that the P100 connected via nvlink has a higher frequency and thus a higher theoretical peak performance. The K80 has two GPU chips on one board of which we use only one. The cores of GPUs are grouped in Streaming Multiprocessors (SMs) similar to CPU sockets.

Vendor		Nvidia		
Architecture		K80	P100	
Interconnect to host		PCIe	nvlink	PCIe
Number of SMs		13 [21]	56 [22]	
Cores per SM	SP	192 [21]	64 [22]	
	DP	64 [21]	32 [22]	
Shared memory per SM		112 KB [21]	48 KB [22]	
Registers per SM (32 Bit)		131,072 [21] [22]		
Clock frequency		0.88 Ghz (Boost clock)	1.48 Ghz	1.39 Ghz
Theoretical peak performance	SP	4.37 TFLOPs/s [19]	10.6 TFLOPs/s [20]	9.3 TFLOPs/s [20]
	DP	1.46 TFLOPs/s [19]	5.3 TFLOPs/s [20]	4.7 TFLOPs/s [20]
Release date		Q4/2014	Q4/2016	

As modern GPUs can directly access host CPU memory, we test both manual offloading and Nvidia unified memory. For the first case we do not measure the time for explicit memory transfer between CPU and GPU. Be aware that memory handling is not part of Alpaka and native vendor code is used when necessary. We thus focus on measuring algorithmic performance while disregarding analysis of e.g. efficient latency hiding when offloading code to an accelerator.

Intel Xeon E5-2680 v3 (Haswell) and Xeon Phi Knights Landing (KNL) architectures are hosted on the HPC cluster Taurus located at Technical University Dresden whereas the Power8 processor is also part of the HPC pilot system JURON. The CPU architectures considered in this paper are listed in Table 2.

Clock frequency f, FLOP per cycle and core o, and number of cores n give the theoretical peak performance

$$\mathrm{P}(f, o, n) = f \cdot o \cdot n \ . \tag{8}$$

The Haswell CPU does not have hyperthreading activated and has two AVX units per core, which allows for instruction level parallelism and thus up to 64 single precision floating point operations (FLOPs) per cycle and clock. For measurements we use 2 sockets resulting in a total amount of 24 cores. The KNL architecture allows for up to 128 single precision floating point operations per cycle and core. With hyperthreading activated this architecture can be used similar to a multi-core CPU with 256 independent threads. The IBM Power8 processor has a uniquely high CPU frequency of 4 Ghz, but the lowest peak performance of all tested systems. However, with 8 hardware threads per core,

Table 2. Single (SP) and double (DP) precision theoretical peak performances (see Eq. 8) and other characteristic variables of CPUs considered in this paper. Performance gains come mostly from vector operations and fused multiply adds, especially for Intel CPUs, and higher clock frequencies when running on Power8.

Vendor and architecture		Intel Xeon E5-2680 v3 (Haswell)	Intel Xeon Phi^{TM} CPU 7210 (KNL)	IBM Power8
Used sockets		2	1	2
Total number of cores n		24	64	20
Hardware threads per core		1	4	8
Clock frequency f		2.1 Ghz (AVX base frequency [18])	1.3 Ghz	4.02 Ghz
FLOP per cycle and core o	SP	64 (2·AVX,FMA)	128 (2·AVX-512,FMA)	16 [9]
	DP	32 (2·AVX,FMA)	64 (2·AVX-512,FMA)	8 [9]
Theoretical peak performance (8)	SP	1.61 TFLOPs/s	5.33 TFLOPs/s	1.29 TFLOPs/s
	DP	0.81 TFLOPs/s	2.66 TFLOPs/s	0.64 TFLOPs/s
Cache sizes reducing the memory latency	L1	64 KB (core)		
	L2	256 KB (core)	1 MB (2 cores)	512 KB (core)
	L3	30 MB (socket)	–	80 MB (socket)
Release date		Q3/2014	Q2/2016	Q2/2014

160 independent tasks can be executed without a context switch, allowing for high levels of parallelism.

We test a variety of compilers for most architectures, see Table 3. The GNU compiler is used as a reference available for all architectures and for GPUs to compile the steering host code.

2.3 Single Source Code File vs. Optimization

As pointer alignment and dependencies cannot be known at compile time, autovectorization needs some hints from developer side. As pointed out, applications or additional libraries can provide additional information on data types that fosters autovectorization when using Alpaka. We thus are forced to add compiler dependent `#pragmas`, namely `#pragma ivdep` and `#pragma GCC ivdep` for the Intel and GNU C++ compilers, respectively, in order to declare pointers inside loops as independent and executable in parallel. Furthermore, all memory is aligned to a multiplier of 64 with `__declspec(align(64))` (Intel) and `__attribute__ ((aligned (64)))` (GNU compiler), which makes it faster to load whole chunks of memory to vector registers on some architectures. As one cannot pass this information via function parameters, we also explicitly tell the compilers about this in the most time critical loop over the A and B tiles with `__assume_aligned` (Intel) and `__builtin_assume_aligned` (GNU).

Table 3. Compilers, compiler options, and compiler versions considered for every architecture in this paper. Every binary is compiled on the same system it is executed on later, allowing for architecture- and system-aware compiler optimization.

	Intel Compiler	CUDA	XL Compiler	GNU Compiler
Haswell	`-Ofast -xHost` (Version: 17.0.0)	–	–	`-Ofast -mtune=native -march=native` (Version: 6.2)
KNL	`-Ofast -xHost` (Version: 17.0.0)	–	–	`-Ofast -mtune=native -march=native` (Version: 6.2)
Tesla P100	–	`--use_fast_math` (Version: 8.0.44)	–	`-mtune=native -march=native` (Version: 5.3, only host)
Tesla K80	–	`--use_fast_math` (Version: 8.0.44)	–	`-mtune=native -march=native` (Version: 5.3, only host)
Power8	–	–	`-O5` (Version: 14.01) **(Only for C!)**	`-Ofast -mtune=native -mcpu=native -mveclibabi=mass` (Version: 6.3)

XL C++ Work Around. Alpaka is a very demanding C++ code and most compilers fully support C++11, with the exception of the IBM XL compiler. For this reason we move the most performance critical code, the matrix multiplication of tiles in A and B, to an extra C file for every XL test and compile all C code with the XL compiler, while the C++ code including all Alpaka abstractions is compiled with the GNU C++ compiler. This means that we are not testing XL's OpenMP implementation. With full C++11 support by the IBM compiler we expect similar to better performance than we see with this approach. This workaround currently breaks our single source goal and prevents code optimizations like code inlining, but still helps to improve performance compared to using just the GNU compiler.

KNL Specific Parameter Settings. The Intel KNL is programmable similarly to a CPU, but like an offloading acceleration device it brings its own dedicated memory called MCDRAM. Compared to the global RAM the latency is almost the same, but the bandwidth around five times higher with over 450 GB/s ([12], p. 20). The Intel KNL supports three modes of accessing the MCDRAM: As a cache for RAM, directly accessed (flat memory) or a hybrid mode, where a part is used as cache and another part as flat memory. The first two modes are compared in performance, as they form opposite cases. The Intel KNL can furthermore be operated in different cluster modes, which may improve the cache latency. In this paper we restrict ourselves to using quadrant mode only.

Multidimensional Parameter Tuning. We choose T and the number of hardware threads as tuning parameters before running scaling tests for different matrix sizes N. Tuning is performed for a fixed $N = 10240$ as a good compromise between runtime and problem size and further for an arbitrary $N = 7168$, thus avoiding effects only occurring at some certain combinations of parameters. After finding optimal parameter sets scaling tests with matrix sizes from $N = 1024$ up to $N = 20480$ with an increment of $\Delta N = 1024$ are performed. We repeat every measurement first 5 than 10 times, which in all cases yields the same maximum result. This shows that any effects visible are not due to statistics, and we thus refrain from averaging over more measurements.

3 Parameter Tuning

As hyperthreading is deactivated for the Haswell CPU and as we have found an efficient number of threads $e = 16^2$ for Nvidia GPUs in previous work, only the tile size T is used for tuning for these architectures, see Fig. 3. An obvious observation for Haswell is that doubling the tile size often also doubles the achieved performance, while $T = 4$ seems to be optimal for current GPU generations.

Tuning for KNL and Power8 adds the number of hardware threads as a second parameter, see Fig. 4 for KNL. We see that optimal parameter combinations highly depend on the chosen precision and compiler. The double precision binary created by the Intel compiler using a single hardware thread results in best performance of 510 GFLOPs/s. We also perform a measurement for the KNL in flat memory mode directly using the MCDRAM instead of the caching mechanism. Except for a slightly better performance ($\sim 2\%$), the results are the same.

For Power8 we test from $T = 16$ up to $T = 512$ and from one to eight hardware threads always using only powers of two as parameters similar to KNL (not shown). Contrary to KNL, optimization for the Power8 architecture delivers similar performance results for a variety of parameters even when using the IBM

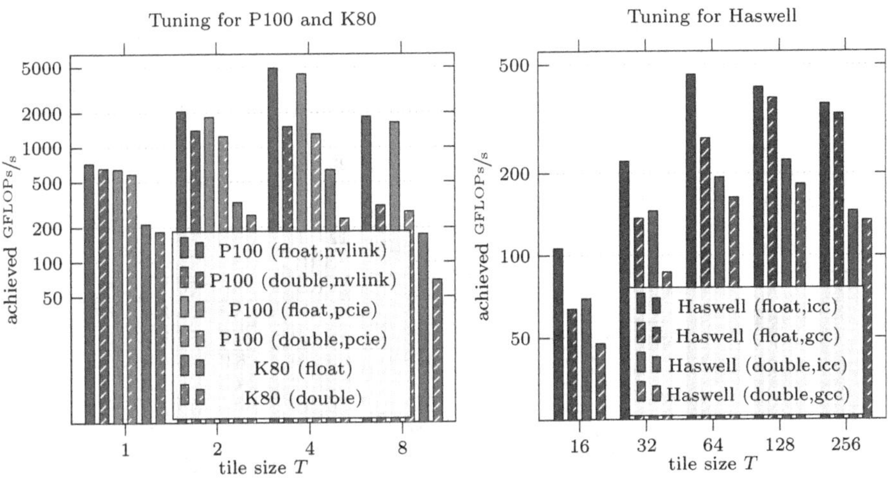

Fig. 3. Achievable GFLOPs/s for Nvidia K80 and P100, and for Intel Haswell depending on the compiler, the floating point precision and the chosen tile size of the GEMM algorithm. As there are not lesser cores than hardware threads, all of them are used.

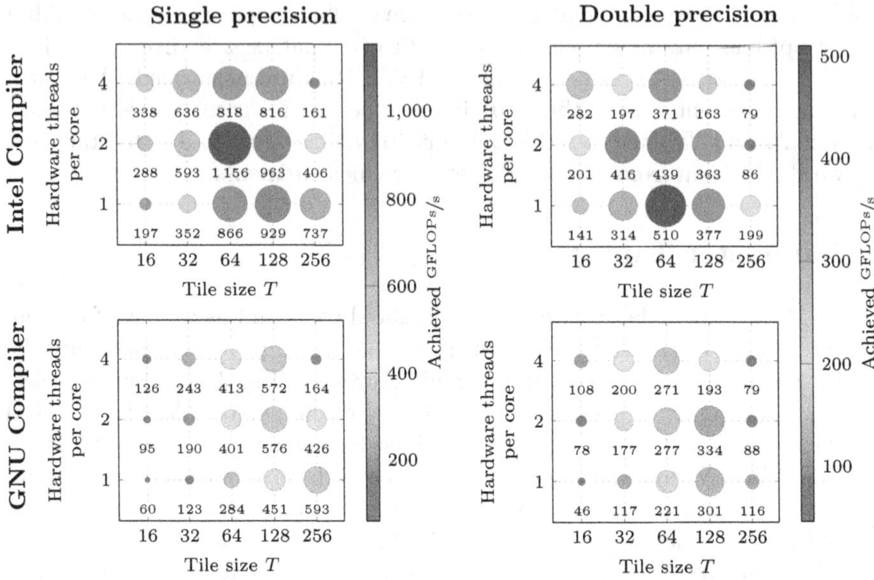

Fig. 4. Achievable GFLOPs/s for Intel Xeon Phi Knights Landing (KNL) depending on the compiler, the floating point precision, the chosen tile size of the tiled matrix multiplication algorithm and the used hardware threads per core. The bigger the mark size the higher the achieved GFLOPs/s. The mark radius is calculated with (achieved GFLOPs/s)$^{5/7}$ as this has been shown a good value for human perception [8]. GNU compiler 6.2 and Intel compiler 17 are used. For compiler options see Table 3.

Table 4. Estimated optimal tile size T and number of hardware (HW) threads. Memory for A and B tiles $\mathrm{K}(S,T)$ (Eq. 5) and the available cache per HW thread and cache level are listed in addition. The first cache level that can hold a complete tile is marked.

Architecture	Compiler	Precision	HW Threads	Optimized tile size T	$\mathrm{K}(S,T)$ (see (5))	Cache per HW thread L1	L2	L3
P100 (nvlink)	CUDA	single	–	4	128 B	–	–	–
		double		4	256 B			
P100 (pci)		single		4	128 B			
		double		4	256 B			
K80		single		4	128 B			
		double		2	64 B			
Haswell	Intel	single	1	64	32 KB	64 KB	256 KB	2.5 MB
		double		128	256 KB	64 KB	256 KB	2.5 MB
	GNU	single		128	128 KB	64 KB	256 KB	2.5 MB
		double		128	256 KB	64 KB	256 KB	2.5 MB
KNL	Intel	single	2	64	32 KB	32 KB	256 KB	–
		double	1	64	64 KB	64 KB	512 KB	
	GNU	single	1	256	512 KB	64 KB	512 KB	
		double	2	128	256 KB	32 KB	256 KB	
Power8	XL	single	2	512	2 MB	32 KB	256 KB	4 MB
		double	2	512	4 MB	32 KB	256 KB	4 MB
	GNU	single	8	256	512 KB	8 KB	64 KB	1 MB
		double	4	256	1 MB	16 KB	128 KB	1 MB

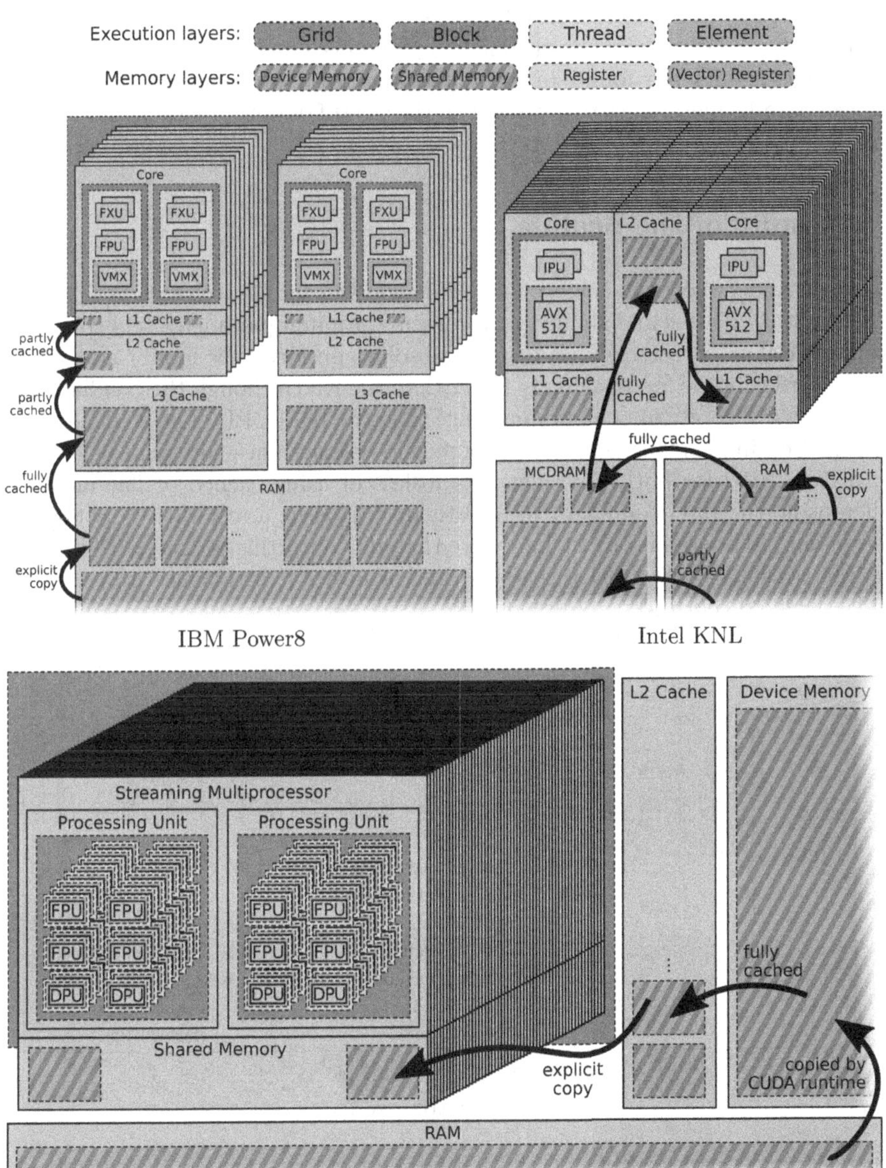

Fig. 5. Alpaka mappings for IBM's Power8, Intel's KNL, and Nvidia's Tesla P100. Every mapping uses the optimal parameters of the parameter tuning for double precision and the vendor compiler from Table 4. The CPU mappings use the OpenMP2 Block back end. The GPU mapping uses the CUDA back end and unified memory.

XL compiler. We don't see large deviations from our tuning results for the control case $N = 7168$ (not shown) on all architectures. Although bigger matrix sizes improve the GFLOPs/s slightly, optimum parameters remain the same.

Tuning results are found in Table 4, while the corresponding mapping of Alpaka parallel hierarchies to hardware in the case of double precision and vendor compilers selected is presented in Fig. 5.

4 Results of the Scaling

Figures 6 and 7 show the achieved GEMM GFLOPs/s for all architectures considered, for both double and single precision and optimum parameter sets [15]. The Nvidia P100 as expected shows the best absolute performance in all cases, while the Power8 runtime is surprisingly faster than the K80 although the Nvidia GPU has a higher theoretical peak performance than the IBM CPU. The KNL shows a drastic drop in peak performance every second or fourth measurement beginning with $N = 8192$ for both precisions, regardless of using cached or flat memory when using the Intel compiler. To investigate this issue a test with $N = 8192$ is run in double precision but 91 hardware threads. With this we get 490 GFLOPs/s instead of 303 GFLOPs/s (64 threads), which is only 7% less than for $N = 7168$ and $N = 9216$ (both 527 GFLOPs/s).

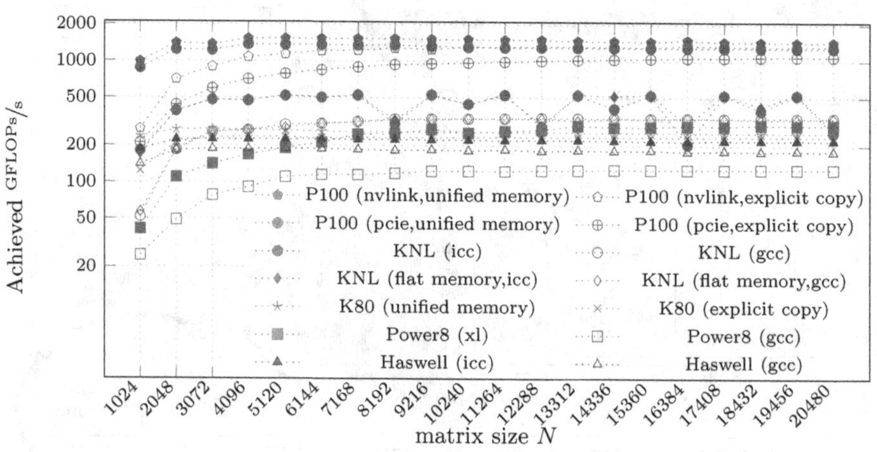

Fig. 6. Achievable GFLOPs/s for all considered architectures for double precision depending on the matrix size and the compiler.

Most architectures show an increase in the performance for higher N, with the exception of Intel Haswell which for single precision shows best peak performance (665 GFLOPs/s) for $N = 2048$ and afterwards decreases reaching a plateau at 400 GFLOPs/s. In contrast to our expectations, all GPUs show a better performance when using unified memory instead of device memory, especially for small N.

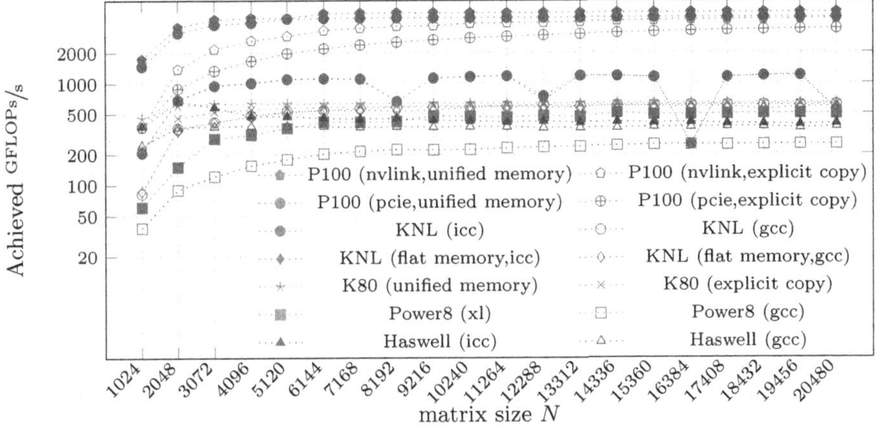

Fig. 7. Achievable GFLOPs/s for all considered architectures for single precision depending on the matrix size and the compiler.

In order to compare results Fig. 8 shows the relative peak performance for the best parameter combinations for every architecture and single and double precision. For architectures investigated in 2016 [28], we find similar or only slightly better performance. But whereas the last paper has stated a general performance around 20% the most recent systems are now capable to reach almost 50% of the peak performance using Alpaka.

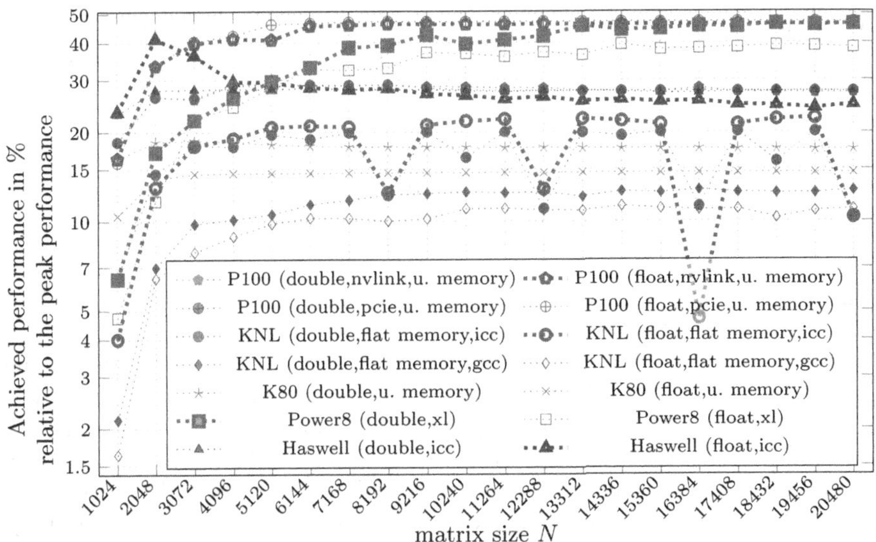

Fig. 8. Achieved performances relative to the peak performance for the fastest parameter combinations of every architecture for single and double precision. Some scalings of particular interest are highlighted.

```
for( TSize j(0); j < numElements; ++j )
{
        lineC[j] += a * lineB[j];
  422a5e: 62 a2 ed 40 b8 0c 18    vfmadd231pd (%rax,%r11,1),%zmm18,%zmm17
  422a65: 62 a2 ed 40 b8 44 18    vfmadd231pd 0x40(%rax,%r11,1),%zmm18,%zmm16
  422a6c: 01
  422a6d: 62 32 ed 40 b8 7c 18    vfmadd231pd 0x80(%rax,%r11,1),%zmm18,%zmm15
  422a74: 02
  422a75: 62 32 ed 40 b8 74 18    vfmadd231pd 0xc0(%rax,%r11,1),%zmm18,%zmm14
  422a7c: 03
  422a7d: 62 32 ed 40 b8 6c 18    vfmadd231pd 0x100(%rax,%r11,1),%zmm18,%zmm13
  422a84: 04
  422a85: 62 32 ed 40 b8 64 18    vfmadd231pd 0x140(%rax,%r11,1),%zmm18,%zmm12
  422a8c: 05
  422a8d: 62 b2 ed 40 b8 64 18    vfmadd231pd 0x180(%rax,%r11,1),%zmm18,%zmm4
  422a94: 06
  422a95: 62 b2 ed 40 b8 5c 18    vfmadd231pd 0x1c0(%rax,%r11,1),%zmm18,%zmm3
  422a9c: 07
```


Listing 1.2. Dissambled output of `objdump -DSC` for the most inner and performance critical loop of the tile matrix multiplication kernel. It shows that loop unrolling, vectorization and fused multiply add are realized by the compiler.

5 Analysis

Autovectorization. Listing 1.2 shows the dissembled KNL binary built by the Intel compiler for the most inner and performance critical loop of the tiling matrix multiplication kernel. C++ code is marked blue, assembler code red. With `vfmadd231pd` being the fused multiply add vector function working on AVX-512 vectors 0 and loop unrolling we find that the Intel compiler is capable of optimizing the inner loop despite the heavy templated Alpaka code.

Parameter Tuning. We assume that tuning for KNL resulted in best FP performance using one hardware thread (see Fig. 4) because larger tiles then fit best into the L2 cache of 512 KB, which otherwise would have to be shared between threads. This is supported by the fact that using double precision often requires smaller tile sizes than single precision. Figure 3 shows the element layer with $T = 4$ causing performance gain, especially for the P100, as it has more shared memory and registers available per thread than the K80.

Scaling. Most architectures show poor performance for small matrix sizes $N \leq 2048$ which at first glance could be blamed on under-utilization, although at closer look is questionable e.g. in case of the KNL which performs 2×10^9 floating point operations that clearly dominate over memory operations following Eq. 7.

We found the KNL in flat memory mode to be only about $\sim 2\%$ faster than in cached memory mode, except for very small N, which can be explained by the fact that the same memory is needed very often, but needs to be copied from RAM to MCDRAM only once. In all cases, using RAM only is much slower than using MCDRAM. We see performance degradation on KNL for (almost) every second N (DP) and for every fourth N (SP) starting with $N = 8192$, except for $N = 14336$ (flat memory, DP). When choosing an uneven number of 91 hardware threads, performance improves for $N = 8192$ (DP). As the issue always appears on very even numbers we assume that the KNL has performance issues if many hardware threads access the very same memory location at the same time. As this issue does not occur for the GNU compiler, we suspect Intel's optimized OpenMP implementation to cause this.

The K80's relative peak performance is only around 15% for single precision (SP) and around 18% for double precision (DP) whereas the P100 reaches 46% (SP) and 28% (DP). As loading to shared memory is not optimally realized, we attribute this difference to the P100 having more registers per thread and more shared memory than the K80, thus more blocks can run concurrently which better hides memory latencies. Although SP values need half the space of DP the K80 has three times more SP units than DP, thus the SP version needs to load more memory for all scheduled blocks, which leads to performance degradation, which is not the case for the P100 with only two times more SP than DP units. Another problem of the algorithmic implementation (but not of Alpaka) is that the index arithmetics lead to a unfavorable ratio of integer to floating point operations, thus degrading FPU utilization. We emphasize that platform-dependent memory access optimizations are within the responsibility of the user code when using Alpaka.

The Haswell architecture shows a different behavior than all other systems for SP where the peak performance has its peak at $N = 2048$ and then slowly decreases. For $N = 2048$ matrices A and B use only 32 MB which fits into the L3 cache of one Haswell CPU (see Table 3 2), thus accelerating memory access.

6 Conclusion

Within the scope of this work we have shown that portable single-source C++11 code using Alpaka can run on current many-core architectures without changing any line inside the algorithmic relevant part of the source code, seeing good floating point performance for the most recent systems when reasonably designing the code for exploiting many-core parallelism. We find that optimizing the number of hardware threads and the tile size for a simple GEMM algorithm leads to considerable increase in performance that can be well explained by the architectural characteristics and is independent of the Alpaka abstractions.

This becomes evident when analyzing the effects of vendor-specific compiler optimization. These do not only show that expected optimizations such as autovectorization, loop unrolling and the use of fused multiply adds are performed using Alpaka but that for bleeding edge hardware like Intel KNL, Nvidia P100 and IBM Power8 using vendor compilers gives a significant boost in performance.

When using vendor-specific compilers with appropriate optimization flags and `#pragma` statements we are able to come close to 50% of the expected peak floating point performance on the Nvidia P100 and IBM Power8 architectures, and in addition could increase the performance on well known architectures like Haswell by about five percentage points. We can thus conclude that the abstract parallel redundant hierarchy interface introduced by Alpaka does not prevent compiler optimization and tuning. However, we also find that the performance gains observed heavily depend on the target architecture and software environment available. We express our hope that the implementation of modern C++ support in compilers relevant for high performance computing will foster the approach we take to performance portability with Alpaka.

Our analysis shows that for some architectures such as Intel's KNL more tuning parameters have to be included in order to achieve optimum results for certain problem sizes when optimizing with vendor-specific compilers. For future applications this potentially increases the time it takes for tuning a code, making tuning itself a compute- and memory-intensive task.

We clearly find that most modern vendor-specific compilers, with the prominent exception of IBM's XL compiler, are able to create highly optimized code for their target architecture from the Alpaka GEMM implementation. This shows that with Alpaka writing abstract, single-source C++ code with close-to-zero overhead is possible on todays high performance many-core architectures, demonstrating that code abstraction for sake of portability and architecture-specific tuning do not contradict each other.

References

1. AMD: HIP DATA SHEET - It's HIP to be Open, November 2015, https://gpuopen.com/wp-content/uploads/2016/01/7637_HIP_Datasheet_V1_7_PrintReady_US_WE.pdf. Accessed 11 April 2017
2. Burau, H., Widera, R., Honig, W., Juckeland, G., Debus, A., Kluge, T., Schramm, U., Cowan, T.E., Sauerbrey, R., Bussmann, M.: Picongpu: a fully relativistic particle-in-cell code for a gpu cluster. IEEE Trans. Plasma Sci. **38**(10), 2831–2839 (2010)
3. Bussmann, M., Burau, H., Cowan, T.E., Debus, A., Huebl, A., Juckeland, G., Kluge, T., Nagel, W.E., Pausch, R., Schmitt, F., Schramm, U., Schuchart, J., Widera, R.: Radiative signatures of the relativistic kelvin-helmholtz instability. In: Proceedings of the International Conference on High Performance Computing, Networking, Storage and Analysis, SC 2013, NY, USA, pp. 5:1–5:12 (2013), http://doi.acm.org/10.1145/2503210.2504564
4. Dagum, L., Menon, R.: Openmp: an industry standard API for shared-memory programming. IEEE Comput. Sci. Eng. **5**(1), 46–55 (1998)
5. Eckert, C., Zenker, E., Bussmann, M., Albach, D.: Haseongpu - an adaptive, load-balanced mpi/gpu-code for calculating the amplified spontaneous emission in high power laser media. Comput. Phys. Commun. **207**, 362–374 (2016)
6. Edwards, H.C., Trott, C.R.: Kokkos: enabling performance portability across manycore architectures. In: 2013 Extreme Scaling Workshop (XSW 2013), pp. 18–24. IEEE (2013)
7. Khronos Group: The opencl specification - Version 2.1, 11 November 2015, https://www.khronos.org/registry/cl/specs/opencl-2.1.pdf. Accessed 23 March 2017
8. Gumhold, S.: Lecture "Scientific Visualization" (2011)
9. Hernandez, O.: Overview of the Power8 Architecture (2016), https://indico-jsc.fz-juelich.de/event/24/session/24/contribution/0/material/slides/. Accessed 24 March 2017

10. Hornung, R., Keasler, J., et al.: The Raja Portability Layer: Overview and Status. Lawrence Livermore National Laboratory, Livermore (2014)
11. Intel Corporation: Intel Threading Building Blocks, https://www.threadingbuildingblocks.org/. Accessed 12 April 2017
12. Jeffers, J., Reinders, J., Sodani, A.: Intel Xeon Phi Processor High Performance Programming Knights Landing Edition. Morgan Kaufmann, 1 July 2016
13. Khronos OpenCL Working Group SYCL subgroup: Sycl specification - Version 1.2., 8 May 2015, https://www.khronos.org/registry/sycl/specs/sycl-1.2.pdf. Accessed 23 March 2017
14. Li, J., Li, X., Tan, G., Chen, M., Sun, N.: An optimized large-scale hybrid DGEMM design for CPUs and ATI GPUs. In: Proceedings of the 26th ACM International Conference on Supercomputing, pp. 377–386. ACM (2012)
15. Matthes, A., Widera, R., Zenker, E., Worpitz, B., Hübl, A., Bussmann, M.: Matrix multiplication software and results bundle for paper Tuning and optimization for a variety of many-core architectures without changing a single line of implementation code using the Alpaka library for P^3MA submission, April 2017, https://doi.org/10.5281/zenodo.439528
16. Meuer, H.W., Strohmaier, E., Dongarra, J., Simon, H., Meuer, M.: November 2016 — TOP500 Supercomputer Sites, November 2016
17. Microsoft Corporation: C++ amp : language and programming model - Version 1.2, December 2013, http://download.microsoft.com/download/2/2/9/22972859-15c2-4d96-97ae-93344241d56c/cppampopenspecificationv12.pdf. Accessed 23 March 2017
18. Newman, B.: Intel Xeon E5–2600 v3 "Haswell" Processor Review — Microway, 8 September 2014, https://www.microway.com/hpc-tech-tips/intel-xeon-e5-2600-v3-haswell-processor-review/. Accessed 24 March 2017
19. Nvidia: Tesla K80 HPC and Machine Learning Accelerator (2014), https://www.nvidia.com/object/tesla-k80.html. Accessed 23 March 2017
20. Nvidia: Tesla P100 Most Advanced Data Center Accelerator (2016), https://www.nvidia.com/object/tesla-p100.html. Accessed 23 March 2017
21. Nvidia Corporation: NVIDIAs Next Generation - CUDA Compute Architecture: Kepler GK110/210. Whitepaper (2014)
22. Nvidia Corporation: NVIDIA Tesla P100 - The Most Advanced Datacenter Accelerator Ever Built. WP-08019-001_v01.1., May 2016
23. Nvidia Corporation: NVIDIA CUDA C Programming Guide Version 8.0., January 2017, http://docs.nvidia.com/cuda/pdf/CUDA_C_Programming_Guide.pdf. Accessed 23 March 2017
24. OpenACC-Standard.org: The OpenACC Application Programming Interface - Version 2.5, October 2015, http://www.openacc.org/sites/default/files/OpenACC_2pt5.pdf, Accessed 23 March 2017
25. Wong, M., Andrew, R., Rovatsou, M., Reyes, R.: Khronos's OpenCL SYCL to support Heterogeneous Devices for C++, 12 February 2016, http://www.open-std.org/jtc1/sc22/wg21/docs/papers/2016/p0236r0.pdf. Accessed 23 March 2017
26. Zenker, E.: Graybat - Graph Approach for Highly Generic Communication Schemes Based on Adaptive Topologies, 5 March 2016, https://github.com/ComputationalRadiationPhysics/graybat
27. Zenker, E., Widera, R., Huebl, A., Juckeland, G., Knüpfer, A., Nagel, W.E., Bussmann, M.: Performance-portable many-core plasma simulations: porting PIConGPU to OpenPower and beyond. In: Taufer, M., Mohr, B., Kunkel, J.M. (eds.) ISC High Performance 2016. LNCS, vol. 9945, pp. 293–301. Springer, Cham (2016). doi:10.1007/978-3-319-46079-6_21

28. Zenker, E., Worpitz, B., Widera, R., Huebl, A., Juckeland, G., Knüpfer, A., Nagel, W.E., Bussmann, M.: Alpaka-an abstraction library for parallel kernel acceleration. In: 2016 IEEE International Parallel and Distributed Processing Symposium Workshops, pp. 631–640. IEEE (2016)

An Embedded Domain Specific Language for General Purpose Vectorization

Przemysław Karpiński[1,2(✉)] and John McDonald[2]

[1] CERN, The European Organization for Nuclear Research, 1211 Geneva 23, Switzerland
przemyslaw.karpinski@cern.ch

[2] Maynooth University, Maynooth, Co Kildare, Ireland

Abstract. Portable SIMD code generation is an open problem in modern High Performance Computing systems. Performance portability can already be achieved, however it might fail when user-framework interaction is required.

Of all portable vectorization techniques, explicit vectorization, using wrapper-class libraries, is proven to achieve the fastest performance, however it does not exploit optimization opportunities outside the simplest algebraic primitives. A more advanced language is therefore required, but the design of a new independent language is not feasible due to its high costs.

This work describes an Embedded Domain Specific Language for solving generalized 1-D vectorization problems. The language is implemented using C++ as a host language and published as a lightweight library. By decoupling expression creation from evaluation a wider range of problems can be solved, without sacrificing runtime efficiency.

In this paper we discuss design patterns necessary, but not limited, to efficient EDSL implementation. We also study specific scenarios in which a language-based interface can surpass procedural interfaces in both efficiency, portability and ease of use. In particular we demonstrate higher performance when compared with equivalent BLAS Level 1 routines.

Keywords: Vectorization · SIMD · EDSL · Performance · Portability · Programmability

1 Introduction

In this paper we present an Embedded Domain Specific Language (EDSL) for explicit vectorization. This work extends Unified Multi/Many-Core Environment (UME) [13] framework with the expression template based mechanism to provide an additional level of abstraction over different SIMD and SIMT architectures.

We start our discussion with an overview of current state-of-art, focusing on selected techniques and their usage. We also discuss problems arising from routine-based vectorization interfaces.

J.M. Kunkel et al. (Eds.): ISC High Performance Workshops 2017, LNCS 10524, pp. 515–537, 2017.
https://doi.org/10.1007/978-3-319-67630-2_37

Next we present our abstract vector language and show how this type of abstraction can reduce overall code complexity, as well as improve code readability and make it easier to comprehend.

Then we discuss how such a language can be implemented for CPU-based computations, without the need for a costly, custom compilation toolchain. We also discuss specific problems of portable SIMD code generation.

The discussion is continued with a presentation of selected C++ techniques useful for solving issues of performance bottlenecks arising between frameworks and application codes. Specifically we present a technique for compile-time coalescence between user, and framework defined kernels.

We then present a concept of custom evaluation schemes, capable of handling more complex statement classes. This concept is necessary for providing high language expressibility without losses in performance.

The discussions described above are followed by a performance comparison of vector code kernels and their equivalent implementation using an EDSL approach.

Finally we discuss scenarios in which this approach might fail, as well as some of practical limitations flowing from the current C++ specification and compliant compilers.

The main contribution of this paper is a concept of decoupling expression graph creation and machine code generation scheme. We show that more than one evaluator class is required in order to handle arbitrary vector statements. We also present selected evaluation schemes for handling non-trivial expressions. A secondary contribution is a discussion of design patterns useful for both evaluator creation and for interaction between framework and end-user code. In particular we show that user defined expressions can be coalesced with external solvers thus improving machine code quality. We also investigate scenarios in which expression-based vector processing can be more efficient than routine based approaches, with simultaneous improvement in code readability and portability. All our considerations are demonstrated by UME::VECTOR, an open source library that provides an existing implementation of the vector language [11].

1.1 Prior Work

Evaluation of SIMD programming models performed by [17] showed that explicit vectorization gives the best performance when compared to compiler auto-vectorization. We presented a design for this approach [13] that makes the concept of an abstract SIMD vector more portable, and using masking as a primary mechanism for control flow. As we discuss further this approach for SIMD code generation has multiple drawbacks. In this paper, we explain how to overcome these difficulties, with minimal losses in expressibility.

The approach presented here is strongly based on the *expression templates* (ET) technique [18,20]. Work presented by Härdtlein et. al. [7] demonstrated an approach in which the expression templates can be either made easier to implement or faster in terms of runtime performance. In this work we simplify this idea by implementing an ET generator which allows us to propagate design changes in ET without the need for manual code changes. This approach allows simplifications in ET design, without relying on complex template-metaprogramming techniques needed otherwise, and exploited by libraries such as boost::proto [15] and NT2 [2].

Creating *Embedded Domain Specific Languages* has been explained already in [8] but without considerations for performance. In [2] the authors deal with parallelization schemes for ET graphs, but the topic of efficient SIMD code generation is not explained there in detail. We discuss this topic and show what trade-offs are required between expressibility and ease of use when fine granularity of code generation is required.

Using expression templates for EDSL design for linear algebra package design, has been already demonstrated multiple times for instance in [6,21]. They both explore in detail the topic of user-interface for matrix-based computations but focus only on matrix computations, with more object-oriented approach for data storage and compute flow. We present a generic set of vector primitives suited to a wider class of array processing problems and discuss further situations where this programming model can improve portability and performance, and reduce software efforts.

1.2 Selected Problems

A basic motivation for this work comes from a practical situation that we observed in GeantV, a particle detector simulator developed at CERN [1]. The main goals of the project are to improve performance of simulations by exploiting multi-threading and vectorization capabilities of modern HPC systems. Since the High Energy Physics(HEP) community is largely fragmented in terms of the type of computational resources available, the framework has to retain very high portability. As a framework it is also expected to provide components that can be re-used for wide variety of fields including HEP, medical imaging, aeronautics and others, meaning that the interface flexibility is an important design issue.

For the GeantV project, a decision was made to use an explicit SIMD library for efficient machine code generation. The feasibility of this approach was already discussed in [13,17]. A problem arising from this solution is, that the framework code has to implement the iterative structure around the data sets, as presented in Listing 1.1. In the simplest case, the framework developers need to write both SIMD and scalar versions of the same kernel. An alternative for loop peeling is to only use data buffers of lengths that are multiples of hardware supported SIMD strides. Both approaches require additional effort from developers to either duplicate the functionality by providing both scalar and SIMD versions of the same kernel, or to make sure that data sets are padded properly, so that only the SIMD version of the kernel is required. As we explained before in [13] the problem of code duplication can be solved by extending the scalar typeset with support for a vector interface, where certain vector operations become identities for 1-element vectors. Code Listing 1.2 shows both a peel loop and a remainder loop implemented using a templated version of such a kernel. Thanks to compiler optimizations, the codes generated by compilers are the same in both situations, with the latter one requiring only a single framework kernel implementation.

Listing 1.1. Loop peeling for correct explicit SIMD-ization. Peel loop and remainder loop require different kernels.

```
template<int SIMD_LENGTH>
void framework_func(float *input0,*input1, float *output, int LENGTH){
 int REMAINDER_OFF = (LENGTH/SIMD_LENGTH)*SIMD_LENGTH;

 for(int i=0;i<LENGTH; i+=SIMD_LENGTH) {
     SIMD_kernel<SIMD_LENGTH>(&input0[i],&input1[i],&output[i]); // Execute peel loop
 }
 for(int i=REMAINDER_OFF; i<LENGTH; i++) {
     scalar_kernel(input0[i], input1[i],&output[i]); // Execute remainder loop
 }
}
```

Listing 1.2. Loop peeling with SIMD-1. Both peel and remainder loops use the same kernel definition.

```
template<int SIMD_LENGTH>
void framework_func(float *input0,*input1, float *output, int LENGTH)
{
 int REMAINDER_OFF=(LENGTH/SIMD_LENGTH)*SIMD_LENGTH;

 for(int i=0;i<LENGTH; i+=SIMD_LENGTH) {
     // Execute peel loop
     SIMD_kernel<SIMD_LENGTH>(&input0[i],&input1[i],&output[i]);
 }
 for(int i=REMAINDER_OFF; i<LENGTH; i++) {
     // Execute remainder loop
     SIMD_kernel<1>(input0[i], input1[i],&output[i]);
 }
}
```

Even with the scheme described above, the framework has to provide a set of **SIMD_kernel** implementations, as well as as set of wrapper functions **framework_func** to expose a SIMD-agnostic interface to the end user. The user code would then make a series of invocations similar to one presented at Listing 1.3. In this kind of a situation, the user requests execution of specific fast kernels, developed as part of a domain specific framework. A potential performance problems arise in this situation. If the data buffers are big enough to exceed the cache size, the temporary data resulting from call to **framework_func_1** might be pushed out from cache towards slower memory, before a call to **framework_func_2** happens. In that case, data locality is not preserved, and therefore computational resources might not be utilised efficiently.

Listing 1.3. User and framework code interaction.

```
void user_func(float *input0, *input1, *input2, float *output, int LENGTH){
  float* tmp = new float[LENGTH]; // allocate a temporary buffer for intermediate

  framework_func_1(input0, intput1, tmp,LENGTH);
  framework_func_2(tmp, input2, output,LENGTH);

  delete[] tmp;
}
```

Similar scenarios can lead either to significant performance losses or to users developing custom kernels of code and effectively replicating work already performed by framework developers. In very optimistic scenarios, framework developers can design custom functions for instance to merge the functionality of functions **framework_func_1** and **framework_func_2**. Unfortunately this will only happen when there is enough direct feedback from users to framework developers, when there is an existing business need to do so, and if it doesn't explode the size of framework code. In most situations such an approach cannot be used.

Listing 1.4. Scalar solver for 4-th order Runge-Kutta method.

```
// User-defined function to be passed
// to RK-4 method as the 'func' parameter
float user_func_scalar(float x, float y){
    return 5.0f*x*x/exp(x+y);
}
//...
float framework_RK4_solver_scalar(float x, float y, float dx, USER_FUNC &func){
  float halfdx=dx*0.5f;
  float k1=dx*func(x,y);
  float k2=dx*func(x+halfdx,y+k1*halfdx);
  float k3=dx*func(x+halfdx,y+k2*halfdx);
  float k4=dx*func(x+dx,y+k3*dx);
  return y+(1.0f/6.0f)*(k1+2.0f*k2+2.0f*k3+k4);
}
```

Another kind of problem can be visualised by an example shown in Listing 1.4. In this example, the framework implements a domain specific algorithm for calculating Runge-Kutta method. The problem that we can identify quickly, is that the user defined function **func** is not known at the time of framework development. For this reason the framework cannot assure the users that this function will be properly inlined to avoid excessive function calls, nor that it will be properly SIMD-ized, as the function defined by the user might not be subject to vectorization. An alternative would be to force the users to write their functions using an explicit SIMD library already exploited by the framework. An example of such interaction is presented in Listing 1.5. In this example the users need to be fully aware of the concept of SIMD computations. The direct benefit of this approach is that there is no performance penalty from SIMD under-utilisation, however the function might still not be inlined properly. In addition to that, the users still might need to implement a scalar duplicate of their function, to be used with the rest of their code. Also there is no guarantee that current explicit SIMD approaches will retain their portability over future SIMD hardware, forcing the users to write possibly less-portable code.

Listing 1.5. Explicit SIMD solver for 4-th order Runge-Kutta method.

```
// User-defined function to be passed to RK-4 method as the 'func' parameter
SIMD<float,8> user_func_SIMD(SIMD<float,8> &x, SIMD<float,8> &y){
  return 5.0f*x*x / (x+y).exp();
}
...
SIMD<float,8> framework_RK4_solver_scalar(SIMD<float,8> &x, SIMD<float,8> &y,
          float dx, USER_FUNC &func){
  SIMD<float,8> dx_vec(dx);
  SIMD<float,8> halfdx_vec(dx*0.5f);
  SIMD<float,8> k1=dx*func(x,y);
  SIMD<float,8> k2=dx*func(x+halfdx,y+k1*halfdx);
  SIMD<float,8> k3=dx*func(x+halfdx,y+k2*halfdx);
  SIMD<float,8> k4=dx*func(x+dx,y+k3*dx);
  return y+(1.0f/6.0f)*(k1+2.0f*k2+2.0f*k3+k4);
}
```

2 Vector EDSL Overview

Given the issues detailed in the previous section we would argue that there is a clear need for a more expressive way to communicate between user and framework codes. We could imagine such communication happening by a user expressing an intent for a more complex aggregation of framework primitives (routines), and by frameworks making decisions as late as possible about the final machine code to be executed. This concept of *Lazy evaluation* is already being explored for higher level parallelism, for example in [10], however it cannot be applied for efficient code generation at instruction level. The main problem is the requirement for the higher-level code to be presented in a form that is *statically deductible*. That is, the decision about the specific instruction to be generated, must be made at the compile time. Hence, this *lazy code generation* applies currently at the level of low-level programming languages and is handled by compilers.

Development of a new language, and a corresponding compiler, is not a feasible solution for a lazy SIMD code generation, as it would require replication of work already done at the level of compiler toolchains and core libraries. An equivalent effort put into extension of C++ language and compliant compilers could bring more benefits, than re-designing a new language just to exploit this specific hardware feature. Recent developments in C++ language standard made it more feasible to use Expression Templates as a way to provide a library with compiler-like capabilities [19]. Specific meta-programming features, such as automatic type deduction, variadic templates, move semantics and constant expressions allow providing more static (compile-time) information to the compiler, enabling it to generate more efficient machine code. By operator overloading expression templates also allow creation of more intuitive interfaces.

In this paper we present UME::VECTOR which provides a C++ based implementation of EDSL dedicated for handling 1-dimensional vectors, focusing on efficient SIMD code generation. The language provides a set of types representing scalars and vectors of scalar elements, and a set of basic operations applicable to these types.

2.1 Typeset

Listing 1.6 shows basic declarations for terminal types. The basic requirement is made that the size of a vector needs to be passed at the latest moment of vector declaration. The rationale behind this requirement is, that the operations between vectors are possible only if specific requirements on vector lengths are correct in terms of the arithmetic operations to be executed. The fundamental type of packed elements is passed as a template parameter. This requirement is in line with standard C++ conventions, and it is driven by static deductibility requirement.

In the given example, vectors **a** and **b** are initialized using external memory locations owned and managed by user code. By *binding* the memory region to vector primitives it is possible to decrease both the memory footprint and execution time. Since the vector primitive does not own any memory location, no additional allocations have to be performed. If such an allocation would have to be handled, the data from the original location would still have to be copied to new location, requiring significant amount of time if a specific computational kernel has to be executed repetitively.

In some cases the user might want to have a dedicated memory region, used for the storage of vectors, e.g. for temporaries. It is possible for the user to pass a specific allocator type to be used to handle specific memory region allocations. Since the language cannot make extensive assumptions about specific execution environment and target platform, the possibility to allocate memory in the specific memory regions, such as high bandwidth memory, is required. Since the method of allocation, or specific external tools required might differ depending on the user platform, it is up to the user to choose a proper allocator. The information about specific vector storage locations can be used by an *expression evaluator* to perform additional memory-based optimizations. At the same time a default allocation mechanism is provided to facilitate ease of use in the simplest scenarios.

Listing 1.6. Declaration of terminals.

```
float raw_a[1000];
int   raw_b[123];
bool  raw_mask[1000];

UME::VECTOR::Vector<float> a(1000, raw_a);
UME::VECTOR::Vector<int> b(123, raw_b);
UME::VECTOR::Vector<float, userAllocator> c(1000);
                               //Vector is responsible for memory management.
UME::VECTOR::Scalar<float> pi(3.14);
UME::VECTOR::Mask mask(1000, raw_mask);
```

Listing 1.6 presents also a declaration of a **Scalar<float>** type. Since C++ already provides a mechanism, for scalar declarations, the standard scalar types can be used in user defined formulas instead. Any C++ scalar variable and constant will be automatically converted to a corresponding **Scalar<>** type when used in such a formula. The main reason behind this wrapping of scalar types is that different semantic rules apply for C++ fundamental and non-fundamental types. Creating a scalar wrapper allows more uniform handling of 1-D vectors and scalars within a language implementation. The second reason is, that a wrapped scalar type is derived from the same interface as the *Vector* types and composite expressions. As a result the same invocation conventions and interfaces can be used to handle both scalar variables and vector variables within the library implementation. Awareness of the Scalar type might be important for handling some minor corner-cases in user code, and is critical for the situations when a custom, user-defined evaluator is developed. We will discuss the topic of evaluators in Sect. 3.

The last type in Listing 1.6 is a *Mask* type. A mask, or a predicate vector, is a vector of elements responsible for conditional evaluation of an expression. The concept has been already discussed in [13,14] with the rationale of masks already being an integral part of existing instruction sets [9,16]. The vector EDSL does not provide any block level control flow, such as **if-else** or **for** statements. The only way of providing an efficient handling of conditional executions is by the means of mask types. For the purpose of C++ compatibility, a mask vector should be considered as a vector of packed boolean variables used for selective execution of specified operations.

2.2 Syntax

The most natural way of providing language extensions in C++ can be done using the operator overloading mechanism. Overloaded operators offer the capability of changing the default meaning of supported unary and binary operators, and provide a custom evaluation scheme for a new operation. There are couple of issues that have to be overcome when dealing with operator overloading in terms of performance and expressibility.

First of all, an operator is essentially a function. For efficiency reasons, excessive function calls have to be avoided. In the case of the vector language each overloaded function relates roughly to a single CPU instruction, therefore function calls have to be completely avoided. C++ offers the **inline** keyword to inform the compiler that a given function (or an operator) should not generate a corresponding stack frame, however due to the fact that **inline** is only a hint, there is no guarantee on compiler behaviour. Luckily most of the compilers, including open-sourced GNU GCC and Clang++, support additional function attribute to force inlining. We use this non-standard keyword wrapped as a portable macro to pass our stronger intent to compilers.

The second problem is, that at the moment C++ only permits a limited number of operators to be overloaded. As we already pointed out in [13] the number of available operators is not sufficient for expressive SIMD vectorization. There is also no possibility to overload the ternary operator (*<mask >? <true-exp >: <false-exp >*), required for binary operations using the optional mask operand. This made it necessary to develop an alternative interface. We therefore use a *Member Function Interface* (MFI) to provide the user with a mechanism to express all operations with a uniform interface. At the same time, we also allow users to use the classical operator form to facilitate easier expressibility for operations for which it is possible. Listing 1.7 shows few examples of how the user can write down specific expressions. In case of MFI operations, the operand on the left of **.** operator is treated as an implicit operand.

As can be observed, some of the operations do not have a corresponding C++ operator. MFI offers a wider and more uniform interface. As we pointed out already in [13], the MFI function calls can be easily mapped to C-like functions without further losses in portability and performance. We reserve this type of language syntax for future library releases.

Listing 1.7. Syntactic conventions of vector language.

```
\\ Operator syntax
a=b+c;
\\ Masked syntax with MFI
a=b.add(mask,c);
\\ Ternary operation with MFI
a=b.fmuladd(c,d);
\\ Binary destructive addition (+=)
a.adda(b);
\\ Operations can be nested if necessary
c=b.add(a > 0, d * e);
```

Element-Wise Operations. The set of *arithmetic operations* consists of the ones already defined by the C++ standard but generalized for vectors of packed scalars. As already mentioned most of the arithmetic operations accept required **Vector** and arithmetic expression operands, and return an arithmetic expression or, in case of comparison operations, a logical expression. Similarly all *logical operations* accept **Mask** and logical expressions and return a logical expression. Except for comparison instructions, all arithmetic operations accept an optional mask operand.

A subset of arithmetic operations called *destructive* operations allow the operation to modify one of the operands. A C++ equivalent of such operations would be to use assignment operators, such as '+=' or '\='. Since use of an assignment operator with a left hand vector is considered to be an *evaluation trigger*, that is an operation forcing expression evaluation, its use would prohibit nesting of destructive operations within expressions. From the performance perspective however, nesting these operation within composite expressions allow us to improve data locality. Therefore destructive operations need to be accessed using MFI interface, if they are meant to be used as parts of an expression. An example can be reviewed in Listing 1.8. In the second case of that listing, the destructive operation is performed on operand 'c' before its value is passed for evaluation of the rest of the expression. Since a destructive operation can only be applied to a proper l-value, a compile-time error will occur when the operation is applied on a r-value type.

Listing 1.8. Using destructive operations.

```
\\ basic destructive operation (/=)
a/=b;
\\ Nested destructive operation (+=)
\\ Both'a' and'c' are modified.
a = b + c.adda(d);
```

Control Flow. As mentioned before, masking is the only way to perform control flow in this language. An example of a masking operation has already been presented in Listing 1.7. For MFI functions, the optional mask operator is always the first parameter.

A mask can be either loaded by the user in the process of binding with a **bool** array, or obtained as a result of one of the arithmetic comparison instructions. The comparison operations can be expressed using either one of the relational operators, or an equivalent MFI function. The class of logical expressions does not accept an optional mask parameter, as it accepts and returns a mask parameter only. Masking of a logical operation can therefore be performed using an additional **.land** (Logical AND, or &&) operation.

When a masked operation is executed, its effect is applied only for the elements where the mask value was equivalent to 'true'. We don't specify how an implementation should treat the masks within an expression, as such assumptions might impact the performance on specific platforms. We only make a requirement on the final persistent result of the operation. In that sense, a masked operation has to operate 'as if' it was propagated towards the evaluation destination (left hand side of the"="operator) and through specific destructive operations. This soft requirement offers optimization opportunities for platform specific evaluators' implementations.

Reduction Operations. A set of operations converting a vector type into a fundamental-castable type is called *a reduction operation.* At the same time applying a reduction operation on a **Scalar<T>** will be considered an identity operation. Reductions are an important class of basic problems, as they already have their reflection in existing instruction sets. On the other hand, reduction operations are not as trivial to parallelize as element-wise operations. Since a reduction operation requires traversal of all elements of a vector, or evaluation of sub-expression forming such vector, it might create a performance bottleneck. For that reason reductions might require a specialized implementation. A classical way of providing a serial reduction operation in C/C++ consists of iterating over an array of elements, and performing a partial reduction in each iteration. Implemented as such, reductions might require a small number of additional lines of code to be expressed.

By making basic reduction operations accessible using the MFI interface, it is possible to make the user code more compact, and easier to read. At the same time writing more complex reduction operations can be implemented using existing horizontal operations, and basic reduction operations. Listing 1.9 shows the example implementation of an infinity norm applied between two vectors.

A complete list of operations available as part of the language is subject to frequent changes, therefore we refer the reader to the implementation website [11] for further reading.

Listing 1.9. Using max-reduction to calculate infinity norm between two vectors.

```
// Inifinity norm calculation using vector EDSL:
err = ((a-b).abs()).hmax();
...
// The same intent expressed using scalar C++ code:
err = 0.0f;
for(int i=0;i<LEN; i++) {
  float diff=abs(a[i]-b[i]);
  if(diff>err) err=diff;
}
```

3 EDSL Implementation

While we don't limit the possibility of implementing our vectorization EDSL to any type of interpreted or compiled languages, it was designed primarily to be implemented using a library approach. As the implementation required has to be able to reach very high performance without sacrificing usability, we find it important to discuss specific design patterns and techniques used. Most of these techniques can be adopted to user codes to reach more flexible and efficient designs.

We find two existing design patterns to be critical for our design: *Expression Templates* (ET) and *Curiously Recurring Template Pattern* (CRTP). Both patterns are already well established and can be referred to in [18]. In our case

ET pattern is important, as it gives the ability to construct expression graphs with minimal overhead, and handle them using a lazy evaluation approach. The CRTP technique is used as a basis not only for ET creation, but also as a core technique for advanced patterns and for expression evaluator creation. Its biggest advantage is that it allows generation of machine codes specialized for specific expressions.

3.1 Additional Design Patterns

We would like to present few additional design patterns that show flexibility of the embedded language, and its compiler-like nature. We discuss these patterns on simple examples, however we would like to point out that the their applicability is not limited to such.

Static Expression Visitor Pattern. A visitor pattern, such as described in [4] is useful for recursive traversal of a tree-like graph. The visitor pattern has the advantage of being separate from the graph structure definition and allows both introspection and modification of graphs. Since the ET pattern creates a static graph, there is no need for virtual function dispatch. Instead, the visitor class takes the form of a template class with the type of expression treated as a specialization parameter. Such a functor might still need to perform certain operations at runtime as some information, such as exact memory locations, is not available at compilation time. Because the graph traversal order is known at compile time **visit** methods can be inlined, possibly decreasing the runtime overhead.

Listing 1.10 shows an example of *Static Expression Visitor* pattern with the purpose of printing a specific instance of an expression. We found this technique particularly useful when debugging EDSL code, as mangled names for nested types are difficult to analyse.

Static Transformation Pattern. The Static Expression Visitor pattern, can be further used to implement *Static Transformations* of expressions. We don't provide a detailed exploration of the requirements here, or an effective complex implementation of this pattern, but only show that a basic variation can be constructed and applied easily.

In the example given in Listing 1.11, an expression **A*B** is being transformed into an expression **A+B**. As the traversal happens using type recursion, it is possible to apply this pattern for a complex expressions, to replace all occurrences of a given expression structure with a different one. The transformation happens at compilation time so no runtime overhead is introduced.

Listing 1.10. Expression printing is a simple way to debug ET code.

```
template<typename EXP>
class ExpressionPrinter{
public:
  // Construct the visitor from
  // specific expression instance
  ExpressionPrinter(EXP exp){ visit(exp); }
  ...
  // Visit a terminal
  template<typename SCALAR_T>
  FORCE_INLINE void visit(FloatVector<SCALAR_T> exp){
    std::cout<<"Vector("<<exp::LENGTH()<<")"<<&exp.elements[0]<<"\n";
  }
  ...
  // Recursively print ADD expression
  template<typename SCALAR_T, typename E1, typename E2>
  FORCE_INLINE void visit(ArithmeticADDExpression<SCALAR_T,E1,E2> exp){
    std::cout <<"ADD:\n";
    visit(exp._e1); // Visit children
    visit(exp._e2);
  }
  ...
};
...
// Print expression
ExpressionPrinter printer(myExpression);
...
```

Listing 1.11. An example on how to transform one expression into another.

```
//Replace a MUL(E1,E2) node
//with an ADD(E1,E2) node
template< typename SCALAR_TYPE, typename E1, typename E2>
FORCE_INLINE ArithmeticADDExpression<SCALAR_TYPE,E1,E2>
  transform(ArithmeticMULExpression<SCALAR_TYPE,E1,E2> exp)
{
  // Construct a replacement expression using sub-expression nodes of 'exp'
  return ArithmeticADDExpression<SCALAR_TYPE,E1,E2>(exp._e1, exp._e2);
}
...
// Call transformation on
float a[10],b[10];
Vector<float> A(10,a), B(10,b);
auto t0=A*B;
auto t1=transform(t0); // t1 is now 'A+B'
...
```

Static Expression Coalescence Pattern. Certain scenarios of interaction between user and framework codes such as Runge-Kutta method described in Sect. 1.2 can now be solved effectively using vector EDSL. By using the *Static Expression Coalescence* pattern, a generic solver provided by a framework can be specialized for a specific user defined function.

In Listing 1.12 we show an implementation together with an invocation of a RK-4 solver. The **auto** keyword used on input parameters of the solver makes it possible to pass either specific scalar or vector expression types. In the case of the former, the behaviour would be the same as if the solver was defined using scalar code similar to one from Listing 1.4.

If the parameters passed as **x**, **y** are of the EDSL types then instead of carrying in-place computations, such as calls to the function **func**, a static graph is created. This graph treats the user function as a structure to be merged into a full computational graph, meaning that both the framework code, and user code become *coalesced* into a single vector EDSL expression. As the language can then apply lazy code generation for the fully coalesced expression, the resulting code can be vectorized and inlined more effectively.

Two minor drawbacks of this design pattern exist at present. First of all, the constructions used require *generalized return type deduction* features available as of C++14. This might delay the introduction of this design pattern into popular frameworks relying on older language standards. Second, a contractual agreement needs to exist between framework and user code to use vector EDSL, or its specific dialect. While this can be easily achieved for framework codes, additional user education might be required.

Listing 1.12. Static Expression Coalescence pattern merges user function written using Vector EDSL with framework-defined solver.

```
template<typename USER_FUNC_T>
void rk4_framework_solver(auto & result, auto x, auto y, float dx,
                          USER_FUNC_T& func) {
  float halfdx=dx*0.5f;
  auto k1=dx*func(x,y);
  auto k2=dx*func(x+halfdx,y+k1*halfdx);
  auto k3=dx*func(x+halfdx,y+k2*halfdx);
  auto k4=dx*func(x+dx,y+k3*dx);
  result=y+(1.0f/6.0f)*(k1+2.0f*k2+2.0f*k3+k4);
                                        // Evaluation starts with this statement
}
...
// User defined function has to be defined using the same Vector EDSL dialect.
auto userFunction=[](auto X, auto Y){
  return X.sin()*Y.exp();
};
...
// User passes her function to solver
rk4_framework_solver(result_vec, x_exp, y_exp, timestep, userFunction);
...
```

An obvious benefit of this approach is that it greatly simplifies complexity of both user and framework code. A specific solver is described as a hardware-agnostic kernel which can be treated differently by the language depending on target architecture. The same observation applies for user codes as the user is no longer required to write architecture specific SIMD code, using for instance an explicit vectorization approach. The same user-defined function can be used for graph coalescing, as well as directly within the user code, meaning that no unnecessary code replication happens.

3.2 Evaluators

As we have explained, the vector EDSL is used to construct a static graph of vector operations. This graph stores the relation between nodes representing specific vector operations, and vector terminals. The construction of a graph is a process taking place at compile-time. At the same time we want to create a kernel of code, preferably using SIMD instructions, and responsible for evaluation of a given expression depending on specific run-time terminals. For performance reasons, construction of such kernel should follow the lazy code generation principle, and for that reason has to be also carried at a compile-time.

Default Evaluators. We described previously, that the evaluation of a specific expression is triggered when an assignment operator = is used with a LHS expression being either of **Vector** or **Scalar** type, and with RHS being a valid vector EDSL expression. We call this evaluation method a *default evaluator*. The default evaluator is an integral part of current implementation and is provided together with ET classes. The evaluation is triggered by **Vector::operator=** implementation, as presented in Listing 1.13. This scheme splits the execution of a vector expression into two loops similar to ones from Listing 1.1. In each loop a recursive evaluation of the expression, for a given dataset offset is triggered, and the result is written to the data array representing LHS vector.

Each expression class defines **evaluate_SIMD** method (Listing 1.14), responsible for generating instructions corresponding to the specific expression semantics. The evaluation method is forced to be inlined as, in most cases, the actual code is limited to only a few machine instructions. Depending on the number of arguments of the expression and its additional semantic meaning, the method calls evaluation methods of sub-expressions.

Listing 1.13. Default evaluator uses very straightforward evaluation scheme. Instead of traversing a vector in the data direction (horizontally), depth-first (vertical) traversal of the full expression is performed. The 'elements' pointer refers to the memory location represented by an instance of 'FloatVector' type.

```
template<typename E>
UME_FORCE_INLINE FloatVector<SCALAR_TYPE>&
                              operator= (ArithmeticExpression<SCALAR_TYPE,E>& vec){
  E & reinterpret_vec=static_cast<E&>(vec);

  // SIMD_STRIDE - a target specific library macro
  for(int i=0;i<LOOP_PEEL_OFFSET(); i+=SIMD_STRIDE){
    auto t0=reinterpret_vec.evaluate_SIMD<SIMD_STRIDE>(i);
    t0.store(&this->elements[i]);
                              // t0 needs to be a type respecting UME::SIMD interface.
  }
  for(int i=LOOP_PEEL_OFFSET(); i<mLength; i++){
    auto t1=reinterpret_vec.evaluate_SIMD<1>(i);
                              // Evaluate remainder part using SIMD-1 (scalar) mode.
    t1.store(&this->elements[i]);
  }
  return *this;
}
```

Listing 1.14. Evaluation method can use a depth-first approach to calculate dependencies.

```
template<int SIMD_STRIDE>
UME_FORCE_INLINE SIMDVec<SCALAR_T,SIMD_STRIDE> evaluate_SIMD(int index){
  SIMDVec<SCALAR_T,SIMD_STRIDE> t0=_e1.evaluate_SIMD(index);
                                                  // Evaluate subexpressions
  SIMDVec<SCALAR_T,SIMD_STRIDE> t1=_e2.evaluate_SIMD(index);
  return t0.add(t1); // Evaluate current expression node
}
```

Custom Evaluators. The scheme just described is useful only in basic cases, when the left-hand destination is an explicit terminal. When the destination is an implicit operand, for instance when the last operation is a destructive operation, an alternative trigger mechanism must be provided. The **operator** = trigger can be generalized by providing an external class with a specific evaluation scheme, dedicated to handling a specific statement form. Because of that there is no explicit LHS operand to be used to trigger the evaluation. A similar situation will also happen when the last operation is a reduction operation.

Listing 1.15. Monadic evaluator definition. Stores are removed, as they will be carried as side-effects of **evaluate_SIMD** calls.

```
class MonadicEvaluator {
  ...
  // Evaluate expression with an implicit destination
  template<typename SCALAR_TYPE, typename EXP_T>
  FORCE_INLINE MonadicEvaluator(ArithmeticExpression<SCALAR_TYPE,EXP_T>& exp){
    EXP_T& r_exp=static_cast<EXP_T&>(exp);

    for(int i=0;i<r_exp.LOOP_PEEL_OFFSET(); i+=SIMD_STRIDE){
      r_exp.evaluate_SIMD<SIMD_STRIDE>(i); // implicit operand is updated automatically
    }
    for(int i=r_exp.LOOP_PEEL_OFFSET();i<r_exp.LENGTH(); i++) {
      r_exp.evaluate_SIMD<1>(i);
    }
  }
  ...
};
...
// user code uses destructive operation:
auto t0=a.adda(b);
// user triggers evaluation manually
MonadicEvaluator eval(t0);
```

The example of a *generalized monadic evaluator* is presented in Listing 1.15. A monadic evaluator is responsible for evaluating an expression with only one, possibly implicit, destination operand. In the scheme presented, no explicit **store** operations occur, as they are carried out as a side-effect of the destructive operation evaluation.

Listing 1.16. Expression divergence happens when two expressions share a common sub-expression. This problem can cause memory locality issues, but can be solved with a very simple evaluation scheme.

```
auto t0=A+B;
auto t1=C+D;
auto t2=t0*t1;
E=t2*F;
G=t2*H;
```

Listing 1.17. Dyadic evaluator calculates both expressions before updating destination values. This way data hazards are avoided.

```
class DyadicEvaluator {
public:
  ...
  // Evaluate a pair of expressions simultaneously
  template<typename SCALAR_T_1,typename DST_T_1,typename EXP_T_1,
           typename SCALAR_T_2,typename DST_T_2,typename EXP_T_2>
  DyadicEvaluator(
    DST_T_1& dst1, ArithmeticExpression<SCALAR_T_1,EXP_T_1>& exp1,
    DST_T_2& dst2, ArithmeticExpression<SCALAR_T_2,EXP_T_2>& exp2)
  {
    EXP_T_1& r_exp1=static_cast<EXP_T_1&>(exp1);
    EXP_T_2& r_exp2=static_cast<EXP_T_2&>(exp2);

    for(int i=0;i<dst1.LOOP_PEEL_OFFSET(); i+=SIMD_STRIDE){
      auto t0= r_exp1.evaluate_SIMD<SIMD_STRIDE>(i);
                                      // evaluate multiple results at a time
      auto t1= r_exp2.evaluate_SIMD<SIMD_STRIDE>(i);
      dst1.update_SIMD(t0, i);
      dst2.update_SIMD(t1, i);
    }
    for(int i=dst1.LOOP_PEEL_OFFSET();i<dst1.LENGTH();i++){
      auto t0= r_exp1.evaluate_SIMD<1>(i); // evaluate single result at a time
      auto t1= r_exp2.evaluate_SIMD<1>(i);
      dst1.update_scalar(t0, i);
      dst2.update_scalar(t1, i);
    }
  }
};
...
auto t0=A+B;
auto t1=C+D;
auto t2=t0*t1;

DyadicEvaluator eval(E,t2*F,G,t2*H); // Evaluation trigger
```

Non-monadic Evaluators. A more complicated scenario, when the default evaluator cannot be used is when *expression divergence* occurs. In the example in Listing 1.16 the sub-expression **t2** is calculated twice: once for statement **E=t2*F** and once for statement **F=t2*H**. In both cases both sub-expressions **t0** and **t1** require accessing all data fields of **A**, **B**, **C** and **D**. This might have a serious performance impact when operating on long vectors, as data locality will not be preserved.

Listing 1.18. Main loop of DyadicEvaluator generated by Clang++. The assembly code is very close to expected.

```
.LBB019:
  vmovups ymm0,ymmword ptr[rbx+4*rdx]        # A
  vaddps  ymm0,ymm0,ymmword ptr[rsi+4*rdx]   # t0=A+B
  vmovups ymm1,ymmword ptr[rdi+4*rdx]        # C
  vaddps  ymm1,ymm1,ymmword ptr[rcx+4*rdx]   # t1=C+D
  vmulps  ymm0,ymm0,ymm1                     # t2=t0*t1
  vmulps  ymm1,ymm0,ymmword ptr[r14+4*rdx]   # t3=t2*E
  vmulps  ymm0,ymm0,ymmword ptr[r12+4*rdx]   # t4=t2*F
  vmovups ymmword ptr[rbp+4*rdx],ymm1        # G=t3
  vmovups ymmword ptr[r15+4*rdx],ymm0        # H=t4
  add rdx,8
  cmp rdx,rax
  jl  .LBB019
```

By defining a *Dyadic Evaluator*, such as presented in Listing 1.17, we can improve the data locality of such divergent expressions by a mechanism that triggers evaluation of both of them simultaneously. With such an evaluation scheme, any data reads on input vectors are local, as the expression evaluation is carrying the same index localization to both expressions. In addition a capable compiler, such as Clang, is able to remove recursive function calls, and reorder operations in such a way that common dependencies are executed only once. Listing 1.18 shows the optimized loop for the dyadic evaluator compiled for an AVX2 instruction set. Because a specific instance of evaluator is specialized for a specific expression, generated code can be highly specialized.

3.3 Language Extensibility

As with every language, there are certain limitations for both expressibility and performance. By its nature, a DSL should offer users the ability to adopt it for specific scenarios required within the computational domain.

By making the language embedded, it is possible to extend it with user defined operations, without the need to re-design the language from scratch. The process of extension can be achieved in two ways. The first approach is to design a functor composed with basic operations and provide more compact notation for the user code. An example can be viewed in Listing 1.19. This mode of extension is the advised mode, as it is similar to already known paradigms of functional programming and, except for a few syntactic differences, is as easy to work with, as regular C++ functions. The second method of extending the functionality of the EDSL is to provide custom expressions and specific evaluation schemes for these expressions. The drawback of this method is that it might require modifications to all evaluators used by the user code. A most obvious benefit of this solution is that the user can express precisely the meaning of such scheme and reach potentially higher performance for specific usage scenarios.

Listing 1.19. Infinity L_∞ norm functor.

```
auto inf_norm(auto a, auto b) {
    return ((a-b).abs()).hmax();
}
...
auto c = inf_norm(a, b);
```

The default evaluation scheme works only for platforms that can be supported under the UME::SIMD typeset. For other targets, a separate implementation would have to be provided to carry out computations using specific language extensions or techniques. Providing additional evaluators does not require modification to either EDSL-based expressions, nor to the expression-based code. The only modification required might be the evaluation trigger invocation.

At the same time a number of particular cases, which cannot be predicted at the moment of language design, might appear for specific domains or even expression groups. The users are given the ability to design additional evaluation schemes that might accelerate the evaluation of their codes, without the need to re-write user or framework based algorithms.

4 Performance Evaluation

Performance evaluation of vectorization techniques poses multiple issues. Various compiler optimizations such as auto-vectorization, inlining and constant folding/propagation can affect the results obtained. As compilers evolve, we can also expect performance improvements on the same benchmarking target and configuration. Selection of compiler flags can also affect the results, as some unsafe optimizations, such as *fast-math* [3] offer significant speedups with the cost of decreased accuracy. As different compilers offer different sets of compiler flags, improper selection of flag configuration might result in an unfair comparison.

At the same time incorrect benchmarking methodology can lead to results which do not reflect the actual computational problem. A simple, yet not uncommon, example is when the results of computation is not used in any way within the benchmarking application. In such case compilers can generate code that carries incorrect or incomplete computations.

Each computational kernel might depend on specific compile-time and runtime parameters, as well as on data with or without specific distribution. Different algorithms/implementations can perform differently based on given parametrization. It is therefore required to verify specific implementations for a whole range of input parameter values.

4.1 Benchmarking Methodology

To follow the spirit of scientific method, we developed a set of benchmarks that allow easier comparison of different approaches in both the performance, and expressibility. All benchmarks are available as a part of the UME framework and can be accessed online [12]. Due to large number of possible combinations, we only present a few selected benchmarks here, and discuss both qualitative and quantitative aspects of the EDSL approach. As it is difficult to find universal metrics to assess expressibility of a language, we reserve additional space for discussion of why an EDSL approach is easier to operate with the context of such benchmarks.

We limit the discussion to a single platform (Intel Xeon E3-1280v3, Haswell architecture, 16GB of DDRAM, running SLC6 operating system), as the qualitative differences would only be an effect of the different system software stack and the underlying explicit SIMD implementation. The platform we used is dedicated for benchmarking purposes and was not used for any other purpose during each benchmarks' execution. We used linux *top* command to determine least used core and pinned each benchmark execution to that core using the *taskset* command.

We built each benchmark using selected toolchains and equivalent compile-time configuration (−O2, AVX2 enabled, no fast-math). In each execution of a benchmark, we ran each implementation of the benchmark multiple times, calculating average of all runs. We also ran each benchmarking application multiple times, averaging results from each run. The reason for this approach is that interlacing of different implementation executions distributes noise uniformly over all configurations. The specific number of repetitions is defined separately for each benchmark, as the memory and execution time requirements vary.

Each benchmarking code is written carefully, so that compilers couldn't remove or reorder measurement-sensitive fragments of the code. A specific technique we used was to place fragments of benchmarked code within a function marked with the **never-inline** attribute (actual mapping varies for different compilers). Such a function is placed between two calls to a stopwatch using *std::chrono*. The time is measured with nanosecond precision.

For all benchmarks, a mandatory verification step is performed which serves two purposes. Firstly, the numerical correctness of an implementation is verified. We don't impose any limit on how accurate a specific implementation should be, but we rather treat this as a measure of performance orthogonal to execution time. Secondly, the verification steps disallow compilers to generate code carrying incorrect computations and possibly generating fake time measurements.

4.2 Runge-Kutta Solver

In each case the user function is available as a lambda function, defined within the benchmarked routine as: $x^2 + y$. The solver is defined outside the benchmarking code, as a templated function with the approach defined previously.

Results of the Runge-Kutta benchmark can be reviewed in Table 1. All values are shown as speedup versus scalar code compiled with GCC. Numbers separated with '/' are for single and double floating point precision, respectively. There are two important points to note here. Firstly, out of the three compilers used, only Clang was able to auto-vectorize the code efficiently. This suggests that this code could be, but is not, auto-vectorized by other compilers. For Clang the performance obtained with an explicit SIMD approach is almost the same as for the scalar code. Secondly, for all configurations the majority of the best results, are reached using vector EDSL, with the explicit approach being second-best. Furthermore, the best performance obtained with GCC and ICPC is, in general, higher than for Clang.

Table 1. Speedup of different implementations of RK4 solver vs. reference. Values given for single/double precision. Only Clang gives comparable results with auto-vectorization. Highest performance obtained with explicit SIMD and EDSL in all cases.

Problem size	1	10	10^2	10^3	10^4	10^5	10^6	10^7	Geomean
GCC 5.2									
Scalar	1.00/1.00	1.00/1.00	1.00/1.00	1.00/1.00	1.00/1.00	1.00/1.00	1.00/1.00	1.00/1.00	1.00/1.00
UME::SIMD	0.97/0.98	2.66/2.43	5.72/3.72	7.33/3.09	6.39/3.26	6.13/3.17	6.12/2.68	5.78/2.99	4.43/2.63
UME:: VECTOR	0.96/0.98	2.75/3.50	6.37/4.47	7.39/3.44	7.38/3.76	7.27/3.61	7.01/2.93	6.43/3.34	**4.84/3.02**
ICPC 17.0									
Scalar	1.29/1.78	1.58/1.98	1.58/1.53	1.58/1.77	1.65/1.76	1.65/1.76	1.66/1.90	1.63/1.60	1.57/1.75
UME::SIMD	1.17/1.60	2.85/3.61	8.27/5.74	10.89/4.67	8.85/5.04	8.73/4.80	8.68/3.84	7.07/3.69	5.88/3.9
UME:: VECTOR	1.56/2.16	2.70/4.17	8.21/6.11	9.56/4.66	8.95/4.94	8.77/4.72	8.66/3.66	6.87/3.60	**5.94/4.1**
Clang 3.9									
Scalar	1.01/1.21	2.66/2.54	6.01/2.66	7.40/1.92	6.83/3.20	6.76/3.25	6.55/3.78	6.18/3.32	4.66/2.6
UME::SIMD	0.97/1.19	2.69/2.63	6.06/4.40	7.18/2.58	6.88/3.15	6.68/3.22	6.53/3.52	5.89/3.06	4.6/2.81
UME:: VECTOR	0.98/1.15	2.76/3.15	6.13/4.41	7.21/2.88	7.15/3.20	6.90/3.29	6.70/3.28	5.86/3.09	**4.68/2.89**

4.3 BLAS Kernels

We will now present a comparison of three selected BLAS-based kernels, with a very straightforward implementations obtained using vector EDSL. As the nature of the EDSL presented is to operate on vector primitives and not matrices, we only compare vector-vector operations.

Some works such as Eigen [5] show comparison for kernels consisting of a single invocation of a BLAS primitive. A similar comparison for BLAS AXPY kernel performance is presented in Fig. 1 (a) & (b). Performance of vector EDSL is similar to that of the BLAS implementation, and compiler-optimized scalar code.

Rarely a single kernel is all we need to execute in a complex algorithm. We therefore defined a second benchmark, which consists of a chained execution of 10 AXPY kernels, with each of them being dependant on results of the previous one. Results for this variant are presented in Fig. 1 (c) & (d). The second variant shows an interesting property of kernel-based computations: operation atomicity breaks potential for data-locality based optimization. For high problem sizes UME configurations are up to 2x faster than the BLAS implementation. At the same time this potential does not seem to be exploited by the compilers when dealing with scalar codes. This performance gap can be only exploited with an expression-based interface, as it requires information about a broader computational context.

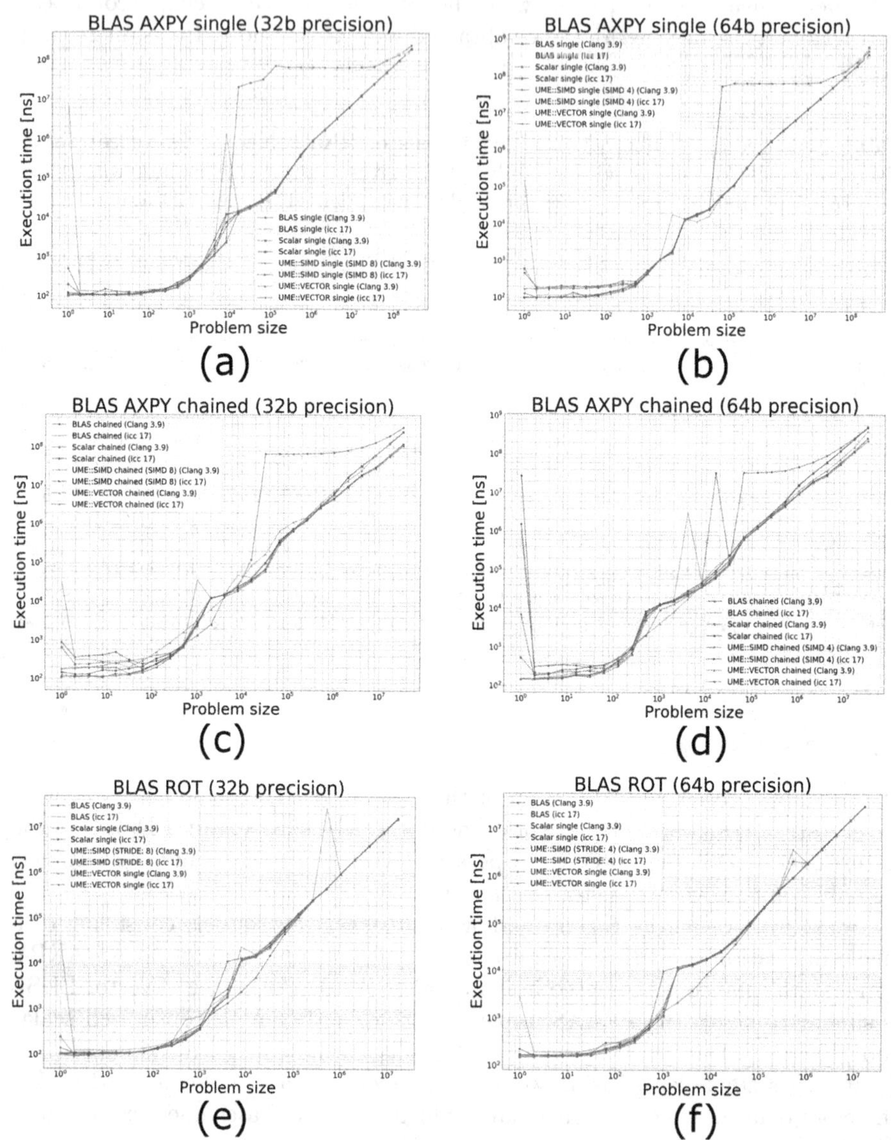

Fig. 1. Blas comparison benchmarks. Clang configuration uses OpenBlas, ICC uses MKL. (a) and (b) show results of a single AXPY kernel execution for 32b and 64b precision. Vector EDSL (UME::VECTOR) does not differ significantly from current technologies. (c) and (d) show that both UME::SIMD and EDSL are faster when solving complicated vector expressions. In (e) and (f) we show that there is no performance penalty when evaluating multi-statement expressions.

Given that AXPY is a very straightforward kernel and might put into doubt the actual expressibility of the language, we also present results for BLAS ROT kernel (Fig. 1 (e) & (f)). In this kernel a pair of variables is updated simultaneously, and depend on previous values of each variable. This makes it impossible to evaluate such a scheme as a single expression. It is also not possible to serialize both expressions, as the results would be invalid. We therefore construct two expressions and then use a dyadic evaluator to perform simultaneous evaluation. Results show that there is no performance degradation and no losses in language expressibility.

5 Practical Limitations

While we already showed, that with modern C++ techniques EDSLs can be a very powerful mechanism however, we would like to briefly point at certain limitations of this technique. Identification of these limitations is necessary for future developments of both EDSL, and its host language.

One of the most important limitations is the fact, that type-based expressions cannot be manipulated during program runtime. This limitation comes from the fact that usual machine code generation cannot happen at runtime.

Another limitation is the possibility of inefficient code generation in cases when a specific vector is used more than once in expression evaluation. Pointer aliasing might not be recognized and as a result some amount of repetition of code might appear, leading to suboptimal performance.

Last but not least, an optimal evaluator for a given class of statements might be difficult to create. The same expression can have more than one optimal evaluation scheme, depending on specific runtime-data and target platforms. This limitation might prohibit creation of very complex expressions and in turn lead users to revert to non-portable coding techniques.

6 Conclusions and Future Work

We have presented an EDSL for explicit vectorization. The language allows high-performance operations to be carried on 1-D vectors and scalars. We have shown that the SIMD programming model can be simplified, compared to an explicit SIMD approach, without a need for any compiler toolchain extensions. Furthermore we showed that in certain situations an expression-based approach can make better use of memory locality, leading to performance improvements over kernel-based interfaces such as BLAS.

The construction of an EDSL can be difficult, especially when performance is of highest importance. We presented a study of specific design patterns required for an effective EDSL implementation, as well as discussion of selected problems related to user-code. We presented a concept of separation between expression graph creation and evaluation, which allows solving more general classes of computational problems.

For future work we predict two directions: investigation of possible performance improvements for matrix expressions, and generalization of the concept of evaluators, so that arbitrary classes of vector statements could be handled. We hope to also investigate the possibility of JIT compilation given that it might allow building a dynamic language representation, further improving performance of expression evaluators.

References

1. Apostolakis, J., Bandieremonte, M., Bitzes, G., Brun, R., Canal, P., Carminati, F., Cosmo, G., De Fine Licht, J.C., Duchem, L., Elviera, V., Gheatea, A., Jun, S.Y., Lima, G., Nikitina, T., Novak, M., Sehgal, R., Shadura, O., Wenzel, S.: Towards a high performance geometry library for particle-detector simulations. J. Phys. Conf. Ser. 608(1) (2015). IOP Publishing
2. Falcou, J., Sérot, J., Pech, L., Lapresté, J.-T.: Meta-programming applied to automatic SMP parallelization of linear algebra code. In: Luque, E., Margalef, T., Benítez, D. (eds.) Euro-Par 2008. LNCS, vol. 5168, pp. 729–738. Springer, Heidelberg (2008). doi:10.1007/978-3-540-85451-7_78
3. Free Software Foundation: GNU GCC reference: Semantics of Floating Point Math in GCC. https://gcc.gnu.org/wiki/FloatingPointMath. Accessed 27 Mar 2016
4. Gamma, E., Helm, R., Johnson, R., Vlissides, J.: Design Patterns: Elements of Reusable Object-Oriented Software. Addison-Wesley Longman, Reading (1995). ISBN:0-201-63361-2
5. Gunnabaus, G., Jacob, B., et al.: Eigen benchmarks website: http://eigen.tuxfamily.org/index.php?title=Benchmark. Accessed 27 Mar 2016
6. Gunnabaus, G., Jacob, B., et al.: Eigen v3. http://eigen.tuxfamily.org. Accessed 27 Mar 2016
7. Härdtlein, J., Pflaum, C., Linke, A., Wolters, C.H.: Advanced expression templates programming. Comput. Vis. Sci. **13**, 59–68 (2010). ISBN:1432-9360
8. Hudak, P.: Building Domain-Specific Embedded Languages. ACM Comput. Surv. 28 (1996)
9. Intel Corporation: Intel®64 and IA-32 Architectures Software Developer's Manual. https://software.intel.com/sites/default/files/managed/39/c5/325462-sdm-vol-1-2abcd-3abcd.pdf. Accessed 27 Mar 2016
10. Kaiser, H., et al.: HPX V0.9.99: A general purpose C++ runtime system for parallel and distributed applications of any scale, July 2016. https://zenodo.org/record/58027
11. Karpiński, P.: UME:: VECTOR: Vectorization EDSL library. https://github.com/edanor/umevector. Accessed 27 Mar 2016
12. Karpiński, P.: UME: Unified Multi/Many-Core Environment. https://github.com/edanor/ume. Accessed 27 Mar 2016
13. Karpinski, P., McDonald, J.: A high-performance portable abstract interface for explicit SIMD vectorization. In: PMAM 2017 (2017). ISBN: 978-1-4503-4883-6
14. Kretz, M., Lindenstruth, V.: VC: A C++ library for explicit vectorization. Softw. Pract. Experience **42**(11), 1409–1430 (2012). Wiley
15. Niebler, E.: Proto: A compiler Construction Toolkit for DSELs. In: LCSD 2007. ACM, October 2007. ISBN 978-1-60558-086-9
16. Petrogalli, F.: A sneak peak into SVE and VLA programming. https://developer.arm.com/hpc/a-sneak-peek-into-sve-and-vla-programming. Accessed 27 Mar 2016

17. Pohl, A., Cosenza, B., Mesa, M., Chi, C., Juurlink, B.: An evaluation of current SIMD programming models for C++. In: WPMVP 2016. ACM, March 2016. ISBN 978-1-4503-4060-1
18. Vandevoorde, D., Josuttis, N.: C++ Templates: The Complete Guide. Addison-Wesley, Boston (2002). ISBN:0-201-73484-2
19. Veldhuizen, T.: Blitz++: The library that thinks it is a compiler. In: Langtangen, H.P., Bruaset, A.M., Quak, E. (eds.) Advances in Software Tools for Scientific Computing. Lecture Notes in Computational Science and Engineering, vol. 10, pp. 57–87. Springer, Heidelberg (2000)
20. Veldhuizen, T.: Expression Templates. C++ Mag., June 1995. ISSN:1040–6042
21. Veldhuizen, T., Ponnambalam, K.: Linear algebra with C++ template metaprograms. Dr. Dobb's J. Softw. Tools (1996)

Exploiting Auto-tuning to Analyze and Improve Performance Portability on Many-Core Architectures

James Price(✉) and Simon McIntosh-Smith

Department of Computer Science, University of Bristol, Bristol, UK
j.price@bristol.ac.uk

Abstract. Performance portability has rapidly become one of the key concerns for application developers targeting modern computer architectures. Although there are various programming models that can offer functional portability when moving application code between different devices, it remains an open research question as to whether it is possible to guarantee some degree of performance portability in these situations. Automatic performance tuning approaches have been shown to be effective tools for removing the burden of code optimization from the developer, but somewhat sidestep the issue of performance portability by enabling an environment where code is repeatedly optimized for each architecture individually.

In this work, we present an in-depth analysis of the performance portability of code that has been highly optimized for specific devices via auto-tuning. We perform this analysis across a wide range of modern, many-core architectures from multiple hardware vendors, examining performance portability both across different vendors and between devices from the same vendor. We then demonstrate how the auto-tuning process can be modified to bring performance portability into the equation, in order to automatically generate a single implementation that achieves high efficiency across many different devices.

1 Introduction

Modern computer architectures are becoming increasingly complex. Hardware vendors are continually finding new ways to improve performance whilst meeting strict power and thermal budgets. The resulting processors exhibit complex performance characteristics that can be difficult to predict or explain for real-world application codes, which leads to a demand for highly skilled developers to spend significant effort in optimizing codes for these architectures. The diversity of devices available to developers further exacerbates this problem. Developers are increasingly using GPUs and other accelerators in order to deliver even greater application performance.

One of the key concerns facing the developers tasked with producing codes that can make use of all of these architectures is that of performance portability. Whilst standardized, portable programming models such as OpenMP and

J.M. Kunkel et al. (Eds.): ISC High Performance Workshops 2017, LNCS 10524, pp. 538–556, 2017.
https://doi.org/10.1007/978-3-319-67630-2_38

OpenCL make it possible to write code that can function on multiple different devices with few or no changes, there are no guarantees about the performance of such codes. In the worst case, developers would need to optimize their codes separately for each architecture they wish to target, significantly increasing the development and maintenance efforts required.

Automatic performance tuning (auto-tuning) has been shown to be an effective tool for optimizing code for modern processors. Some of the earliest examples involved tuning the performance of linear algebra libraries for CPUs with varying memory microarchitectures [4,6]. More recently, auto-tuning has also proven extremely useful for automatically optimizing various codes for GPUs and other accelerators [10,11,18,19]. Auto-tuning frameworks often employ machine learning techniques in order to reduce the number of different implementations to empirically evaluate on the target device [9,24].

Although auto-tuning can ease the burden of manual code optimization from developers, the issue of performance portability is avoided rather than directly addressed, by producing individually optimized codes for each target device. In some situations this may be perfectly acceptable, however it may also be desirable to produce a single implementation that achieves reasonable performance on multiple devices at once. Developers may wish for their applications to run efficiently on new architectures for which they have not yet been specifically optimized, or there may simply be too many different platform configurations to ship a separate implementation for each one. If a single implementation of the code could achieve reasonable performance on every architecture it might need to run on, even if some efficiency is lost when compared to device-specific implementations, then this may represent an attractive trade-off with respect to development and maintenance effort.

In this work, we analyze the performance portability of a highly tunable Jacobi solver across a wide range of CPU and GPU devices from multiple hardware vendors. We utilize runtime code generation in order to expose a large number of different implementation decisions that may affect performance on modern, many-core architectures. We exploit the black-box nature of stochastic auto-tuning processes in order to examine the implementation decisions that have the greatest impact on performance and performance portability when moving between different devices. We then demonstrate a simple yet effective technique that can be used to greatly improve the performance portability of code generated during the auto-tuning process when targeting multiple architectures at once.

2 Tunable Jacobi Solver

The benchmark we use in this paper is an implementation of the Jacobi method [12]. Although some of the analyses we perform are specific to this algorithm, many of the approaches we use for analyzing and improving performance portability are general enough to be applied to other application areas.

2.1 The Jacobi Method

The Jacobi method is an iterative algorithm for solving systems of linear equations. Given a known, diagonally dominant matrix A and a known vector $\mathbf{b}$, we aim to find the vector $\mathbf{x}$ that satisfies the following equation:

$$A\mathbf{x} = \mathbf{b}. \tag{1}$$

We first split the matrix A into the diagonal D and the remainder R:

$$(D + R)\mathbf{x} = \mathbf{b}, \tag{2}$$

and then rearrange to form an iterative solution:

$$\mathbf{x}_{i+1} = D^{-1}(\mathbf{b} - R \cdot \mathbf{x}_i), \tag{3}$$

where $\mathbf{x}_i$ is the 'guess' for the value of $\mathbf{x}$ produced by iteration i of the solver. We seed the solver with an arbitrary initial guess for $\mathbf{x}_0$, often by setting each element to 0. We then repeatedly run the equation given in (3) (henceforth referred to as the *kernel*) until the solver has converged on a solution within an acceptable tolerance. A sequential implementation of this kernel is shown in Fig. 1.

```
for row from 1 to N do
    sum ← 0
    for col from 1 to N do
        if col ≠ row then
            sum ← sum + A[col, row] · xold[col]
        end if
    end for
    xnew[row] ← (b[row] − sum) / A[row, row]
end for
```

Fig. 1. A sequential implementation of the main Jacobi kernel. A is a square matrix of order N, and b, $xold$, and $xnew$ are vectors of length N.

Although the Jacobi kernel is relatively simple, it still exposes many different implementation decisions that can drastically affect performance on modern architectures, such as how to map the available parallelism onto the hardware, or how to lay the matrix data out in memory. This makes it an ideal candidate for exploring performance portability across many different architectures.

2.2 Implementation

In order to perform a detailed analysis of performance portability across a wide range of different architectures, we chose to implement the Jacobi solver using OpenCL [16], which both enables portability and gives the programmer a great deal of control over how their algorithm is mapped onto the hardware. This allows us to explore a broad landscape of different implementations of the Jacobi solver kernel from within a single programming model, and compare these different kernels across various architectures from different hardware vendors.

OpenCL applications typically rely on runtime compilation of their OpenCL kernels in order to achieve portability; the target architecture is only known at runtime, and so this is the earliest point at which native binaries can be generated. We further exploit the just-in-time compilation nature of OpenCL by also *generating* the kernels at runtime. Given a set of parameters that describe how the kernel should be implemented, we construct the OpenCL C kernel strings dynamically, before passing them on to the OpenCL platform driver to be compiled. This gives us greater flexibility in how the kernels can be tuned, beyond that which is provided by simple conditional statements and preprocessor macros.

To simplify the process of generating kernel strings and managing the OpenCL devices, we implemented our Jacobi solver in Python, using the PyOpenCL bindings [17]. The runtime of the solver is entirely encapsulated in the kernel execution; there is no interference to the performance from the Python code itself. The kernel tuning options are specified via a JSON configuration file, which is simple to generate and manipulate from an auto-tuning framework. The source code for our tunable Jacobi solver is available on GitHub[1].

2.3 Tuning Options

There are thirteen different implementation options that can be tuned, which are described below.

Work-group size. A two-element tuple that specifies the OpenCL work-group size to use when launching the kernel, which also describes how the computation should be mapped onto the hardware. Given a work-group size of (X, Y), a square matrix of order N is processed by $\frac{N}{Y}$ work-groups. Each work-group operates on Y rows of the matrix, with each row being cooperatively processed by X work-items. Figure 2 demonstrates this mapping of work-groups onto the matrix. If X is larger than 1, this requires a work-group reduction in order to produce the final result for each row. For a detailed description of work-items and work-groups in OpenCL, refer to [16].

Memory layout. A string option that specifies the memory layout of the matrix data. The valid values are `"row-major"` and `"col-major"`.

Column access pattern. A boolean option that controls how work-items should access entries in the matrix row that they are assigned. This specifies whether a given work-item should process a contiguous set of columns, or whether their

[1] https://github.com/jrprice/jacobi-ocl.

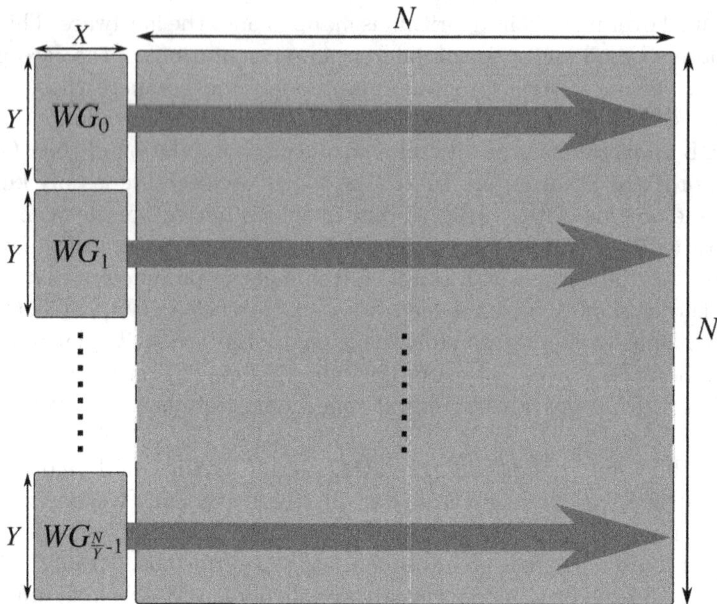

Fig. 2. Mapping of OpenCL work-groups onto the matrix in the main Jacobi kernel. The work-group size is (X, Y), and the matrix is order N.

columns should be strided by the work-group width such that adjacent work-items access adjacent columns. This parameter only has an effect when more than one work-item processes each row.

Loop unroll factor. An integer value that specifies how many times to unroll the loop over columns in the Jacobi kernel (line 3 in Fig. 1). This value must exactly divide the number of matrix columns processed by each work-item.

Multiply-accumulate. A string option that specifies how the expression `(a*b + c)` should be formed (line 5 in Fig. 1). Some devices may have native hardware support for efficiently approximating a multiply-accumulate, or for performing an IEEE 754 compliant fused multiply-add operation.

`"op"`	`(a*b + c)`	regular C operators
`"mad"`	`mad(a, b, c)`	approx. multiply-accumulate
`"fma"`	`fma(a, b, c)`	fused multiply-add

Conditional. A string option that specifies how to execute a conditional accumulation (lines 4 and 5 in Fig. 1).

`"branch"`	`if (condition) acc += x;`
`"mask"`	`acc += x * (condition ? 1 : 0);`

Division by diagonal. A string option that specifies how to perform a division by the matrix diagonal (line 8 in Fig. 1). The `"normal"` option simply loads the diagonal and performs a division using the `/` operator. The `"precompute-global"` and `"precompute-constant"` options run a kernel at the beginning of the solve to generate the reciprocals of each element in the diagonal, and stores them in the `global` or `constant` address spaces respectively. The main kernel then loads this reciprocal and multiplies by it, instead of performing a division.

Use mad24. A boolean option that specifies whether to use the `mad24()` builtin function for indexing. As the two-dimensional matrix data is necessarily flattened into a one-dimensional array, indexes into this array have the form `x + y*N`. Some architectures may have native support for efficiently computing such expressions using just the lower 24-bits of `x` and `y`.

Integer signedness. A boolean option that specifies whether integers used for indexing should be signed (`int`) or unsigned (`uint`).

Address space of b vector. A string option that specifies the address space that should be used for the `b` vector. The valid values are `"global"` and `"constant"`.

Address space of xold vector. A string option that specifies the address space that should be used for the `xold` vector. The valid values are `"global"` and `"constant"`.

Compile-time constant matrix size. A boolean option that specifies whether the size of the matrix should be embedded in the kernel as a compile-time constant, instead of being passed as a kernel argument.

Compile-time constant work-group size. A boolean option that specifies whether the work-group size should be embedded in the kernel as a compile-time constant, instead of being queried via the `get_local_size()` built-in kernel function.

These implementation options yield a search space of size $\mathcal{O}(10^6)$, assuming we limit work-group sizes and loop unrolling factors to be powers of two.

3 Performance Portability Analysis

3.1 Approach

To obtain the optimal kernel implementation for each device, we perform an extensive round of auto-tuning that empirically tests several thousand kernel variants. The auto-tuning process utilizes OpenTuner [1], an open source Python framework for writing bespoke application auto-tuners. We use a simple genetic algorithm [13] with uniform crossover and mutation to stochastically search through the set of possible kernel implementations. Genetic algorithms have previously been shown to be effective search tools for automatic performance tuning [3,5]. The auto-tuning process is run for 24 hours on each device, and logs the performance of every set of implementation options that is tested. The Jacobi solver is set to process a matrix of size 4096×4096, using 32-bit floating point data. We fix the iteration count to 5000 and disable convergence checking to focus purely on the performance of the main computational kernel, whose performance characteristics are not affected by the number of iterations performed.

Once we have obtained optimal kernel implementations for each device individually, we then measure the performance that each of these implementations achieves when run on every other device in our test set. We define the efficiency of an arbitrary implementation I running on device d relative to the best performing implementation for that device B_d as:

$$Efficiency(I, d) = \frac{Runtime(B_d, d)}{Runtime(I, d)} . \tag{4}$$

This provides a normalized metric with respect to a known achievable peak performance, giving values in the range $(0, 1]$ which can suitably be represented as percentages. We then define the worst-case efficiency of an implementation I across all devices in the set D as:

$$WCE(I) = \min_{d \in D}(Efficiency(I, d)) . \tag{5}$$

This allows us to describe an implementation of the kernel with a single numeric value which captures its performance portability across multiple devices. These metrics are similarly described by Tzannes in [27]. While it may be possible to outperform the peak performance achieved by any given B_d (for example, with handwritten assembly code), we believe that this represents a suitable proxy for the achievable peak performance that enables a thorough performance portability analysis.

3.2 Devices

We select ten devices spanning a range of GPUs from NVIDIA, AMD, and Intel, as well as two different Intel CPUs. We focus on devices from the consumer market as this provides us with the broadest range of architectures to experiment with. The devices, and the driver versions used, are listed in Table 1. Aside from the drivers, the devices were all housed in workstations with identical software stacks, running CentOS 7.2 and Linux kernel 3.10.

3.3 Results

Figure 3 shows a heatmap of the efficiencies achieved when running each of the tuned Jacobi kernels across all of the devices. Each row of the heatmap corresponds to a single implementation of the kernel tuned for a specific device. An entry marked as X indicates that the kernel was unable to run on the target device at all. These cases are caused by the work-group size exceeding the maximum allowed on certain devices. Table 2 lists the best parameters selected for each device.

Table 1. Devices used for evaluating performance portability.

Vendor	Product	Architecture	Compute units	Driver version
NVIDIA	GeForce GTX 580	Fermi (GF110)	16	367.27
	GeForce GTX 680	Kepler (GK104)	8	
	GeForce GTX 780 Ti	Kepler (GK110)	15	
	GeForce GTX 980 Ti	Maxwell (GM200)	22	
AMD	Radeon HD 7970	Tahiti XT	32	fglrx 15.302.2001
	Radeon R9 290X	Hawaii XT	44	
	Radeon R9 Fury X	Fiji XT	64	
Intel	HD Graphics 2500	Ivy Bridge GT1	6	Beignet 1.1.2
	Core i5-3550	Ivy Bridge	4	Intel OpenCL 16.1
	Core i5-4590	Haswell	4	

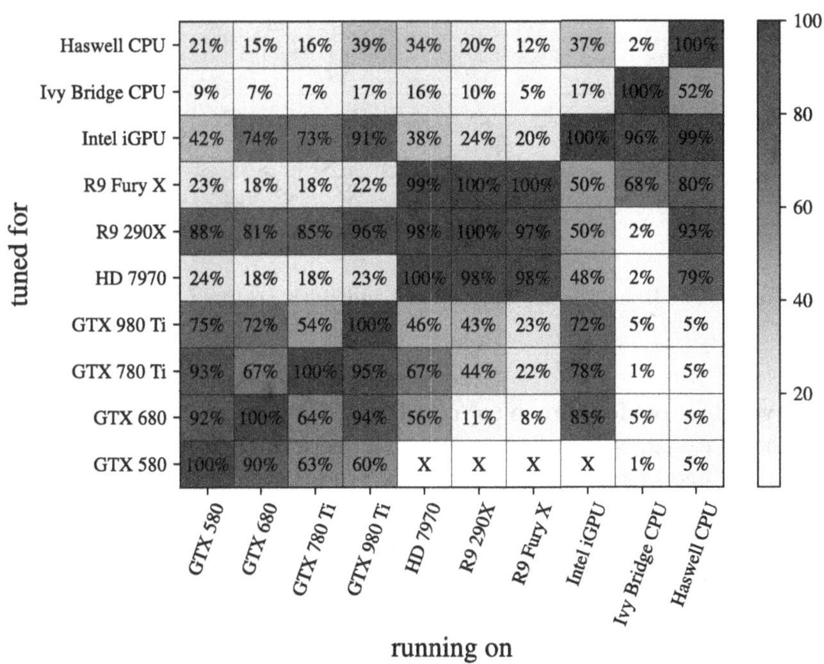

Fig. 3. Efficiencies of a set of tuned Jacobi kernels across a range of devices.

To ensure that these tuned kernels are actually performing well in absolute terms, we compute the bandwidth that they achieve and compare against the `dot` kernel from the BabelStream benchmark [7] (see Fig. 4). In all but one case the achieved bandwidth comes very close to the bandwidth given by the `dot` benchmark, in some cases exceeding them as the BabelStream kernels are not extensively tuned for individual devices. We attribute the lower fraction on the Intel iGPU to the open-source Beignet drivers being much less mature.

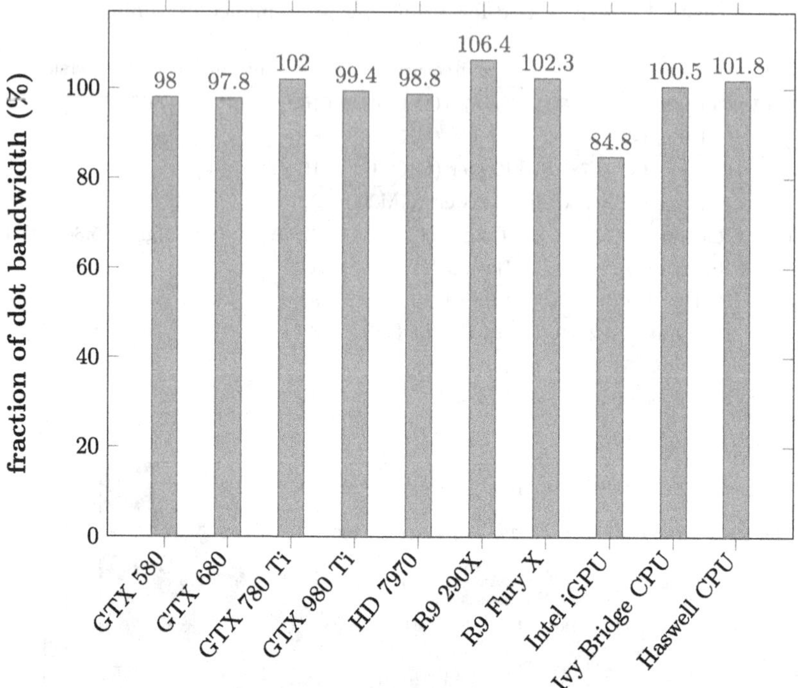

Fig. 4. Fraction of BabelStream `dot` kernel bandwidth achieved by best performing kernel for each device.

Single vendor performance portability. By looking at specific regions within the heatmap, we can first examine the performance portability achieved when moving between devices from a single vendor.

The lower-left section of the heatmap shows us how kernels tuned for NVIDIA GPUs faired when run on other NVIDIA architectures. For each of the four implementations, the worst-case efficiency across the other NVIDIA GPUs was <70%. These performance losses were most often caused by inefficient work-group sizes: the two older GPUs preferred large work-group sizes whereas the newer GPUs were capable of achieving high utilization with much smaller work-groups, needing more of them to saturate the increased number of compute units. The lowest worst-case efficiency was observed with the kernel tuned for the Maxwell architecture (GTX 980 Ti), which achieved just 54% efficiency on the Kepler-based GTX 780 Ti device. In this case, the work-group size of 2×16 selected for Maxwell was too small for the GTX 780 Ti, which needed at least 64 work-items to keep its processing elements busy. Even when moving between the two variations of the Kepler architecture (GTX 680 and GTX 780 Ti), one third of the performance was sacrificed by using a highly-tuned device-specific kernel. Although work-group size played a part in this, there were also significant performance differences when simultaneously changing the address space of the `xold` vector (the GTX 680 preferred to use the `constant` address space) and the mapping of matrix elements to work-items (the GTX 780 Ti preferred to coalesce columns across work-items). The GTX 680 also required the use of the `mad24` builtin when using signed integers, which indicates that it has a lower integer instruction throughout.

In contrast, the center of the heatmap shows that the performance portability when moving between three generations of AMD GPUs is exceptionally high. Each of the three implementations achieved close to 100% efficiency when running on each of the other AMD devices. Unlike the NVIDIA GPUs, the AMD devices all preferred exactly the same work-group size of 256×1, which played a big role in achieving high performance portability. The AMD GPUs also unanimously chose values for other parameters that had significant impacts on these devices, such as using masking instead of branches, embedding the work-group size as a compile-time constant, and using similar loop unrolling factors.

The Intel devices encompass two CPUs and an integrated GPU (iGPU), so perhaps offer the biggest difference in architectures from a single vendor. The implementation tuned for the iGPU does very well on both of the CPUs, achieving close to 100% efficiency. The converse is not true however, with the two implementations tuned for the CPUs achieving 17% and 37% efficiency when running on the iGPU. This performance drop is due to several different implementation decisions, with the iGPU preferring the `xold` vector to be in the constant address space, more aggressive loop unrolling, and taking a significant performance hit from conditional execution when masking techniques are not used. The work-group sizes offered by the CPU implementations were also far too small to fully utilize the iGPU's execution units. The Haswell-tuned kernel performs extremely poorly on the Ivy Bridge CPU, at just 2% efficiency. This is due to it making use of the `fma()` builtin function, which maps onto a native hardware implementation of FMA available in Haswell's AVX2 instruction set. Since the Ivy Bridge architecture doesn't have a hardware implementation of FMA, this will likely be emulated in software instead, which causes a significant performance drop. The Ivy Bridge kernel loses almost 50% efficiency on the Haswell CPU since it uses a work-group size of 4×1, which will not fully utilize the AVX2 units that can process eight FP32 values at once. Despite the Ivy Bridge AVX units also being 8-wide, for this device the Intel OpenCL compiler chooses a vector width of four for the Jacobi kernel as it is integer-heavy.

Multi-vendor performance portability. The remaining regions of the heatmap allow us to analyze the performance portability when running code that was tuned for a device from one vendor on hardware from another vendor.

The performance portability achieved when moving tuned implementations between NVIDIA and AMD GPUs is generally quite poor. The implementations tuned for the Tahiti (HD 7970) and Fiji (R9 Fury X) architectures from AMD achieve around 20% efficiency on each of the NVIDIA devices, although the kernel tuned for Hawaii (R9 290X) does reasonably well. Similarly, the implementations tuned for the NVIDIA architectures perform fairly poorly on the AMD devices, worst of all on the Fiji GPU. These issues are largely due to differences in thread-data mapping and memory layout. The AMD devices all prefer having each work-group cooperatively process a single row, with the matrix stored row-major in order to facilitate coalesced accesses between adjacent work-items when vectorizing horizontally across the work-group. Conversely, the NVIDIA implementations process multiple rows per work-group with the matrix stored column-major, and only one or two work-items process each row.

The total number of work-groups launched by any kernel is equal to the matrix order divided by the work-group height. For kernels that process many rows per work-group, this limits the total number of work-groups in flight at any time, potentially under-utilizing devices which have many compute units to fill. The AMD GPUs have many more compute units than the NVIDIA GPUs, hence they perform poorly with the kernels tuned for NVIDIA which launch much smaller numbers of work-groups. The NVIDIA GPUs are capable of executing kernels with row-major layout and horizontal vectorization reasonably efficiently as demonstrated with the R9 290X implementation, however they perform very poorly if the `xold` vector is placed in the `constant` address space as is done by the other AMD kernels. This is due to the fact that each compute unit can only fetch a single 32-bit value from the constant data cache each cycle on NVIDIA GPUs; non-uniform accesses to constant memory within a half-warp are serialized.

The Intel iGPU suffers a 15–30% performance penalty when executing the kernels tuned for NVIDIA GPUs as a result of the thread-data mapping, memory layout, and use of arithmetic operators instead of the `mad`/`fma` builtins. It achieves around 50% efficiency with the AMD kernels, purely as a result of an excessively large work-group size. Similarly, the implementation tuned specifically for the Intel iGPU performs poorly on the AMD devices due to the smaller work-group size as well as producing more integer operations when certain parameters are not embedded into the kernel as constants. The NVIDIA GPUs executed the Intel iGPU kernel reasonably well, with some performance loss due to memory layout and thread-data mapping, which was particularly noticeable on the GTX 580.

The achieved performance portability is even worse when moving between CPU and GPU architectures. The NVIDIA-tuned implementations all achieve $\leq$5% efficiency on both CPUs. This is because of the column-major memory layout, which will result in vector gather operations with the horizontal work-item vectorization performed by the Intel OpenCL compiler. The AMD-tuned implementations perform reasonably well on the Haswell CPU as they also prefer a row-major memory layout, but two of them perform poorly on Ivy Bridge due to their use of the `fma()` builtin as discussed in Sect. 3.3. From the other direction, both implementations tuned for the CPUs perform very poorly on all GPUs from NVIDIA and AMD. For NVIDIA this can be largely attributed to the insufficiently large work-group size, with the differences in memory layout and thread-data mapping contributing too. For the AMD devices, performance was lost through a combination of small work-group sizes, excessive control flow due to insufficient loop unrolling, and other parameters that resulted in lower throughput of integer indexing operations.

When considering all of the devices together, no single implementation achieved high efficiency for every architecture. In all cases, there was at least one device which achieved $\leq$20% efficiency, and in many cases the worst-case efficiencies were much lower. This highlights the potential for a black-box auto-tuner to reduce performance portability by over-optimizing code for one particular architecture.

4 Multi-objective Auto-tuning

4.1 Approach

In order to improve the performance portability of the code that is generated by the auto-tuning process, we modify the tuning framework to allow it tune for more than one device at the same time. Whenever a new kernel implementation is generated, it is tested on every device in the target set, and these performance results are reduced into a single number that indicates the overall 'fitness' of that implementation. This constitutes a form of multi-objective or multi-criteria optimization [25]. There are many available choices for the fitness function, but in this work we simply use the worst-case efficiency as defined by Eq. 5 in Sect. 3.1, which requires that we have obtained the peak performance figures for each individual device prior to performing this multi-objective tuning process. This simple fitness function will direct the auto-tuner to improve the worst-case efficiency at any cost, potentially at the expense of reducing the performance on devices that are already doing quite well.

From a practical standpoint, this multi-objective tuning approach requires that all of the target devices are accessible from the machine that is running the auto-tuning process. In our experimental set-up, all of the target devices are available across several nodes in a single Linux cluster, sharing a network filesystem. This allows our tuning framework to generate a kernel implementation and then invoke the benchmark remotely on all devices via SSH. To reduce the time needed to collect performance results, we configure the framework to launch the benchmarking code asynchronously across devices that are in distinct nodes, whilst only serializing benchmarking between devices in the same node in order to avoid timing interference.

To further improve the efficacy of our multi-objective auto-tuning approach, we seed the initial population of the genetic algorithm with each of the best device-specific kernels generated during the first round of auto-tuning which targeted devices individually. This provides the stochastic search with a set of implementations that are known to have high performance for certain devices, and enables it to combine and mutate these implementations to try and find effective compromises that work well everywhere, rather than starting from scratch. This is potentially an important short-cut to apply since the complexity of the search space when optimizing for several different objectives may be greatly increased over the single-device case.

4.2 Results

Figure 5 shows the efficiency achieved for every device by a single kernel implementation generated with our multi-objective tuning approach. This implementation achieves a worst-case efficiency of almost 80% across all of the devices, and in many cases exceeds 90% efficiency. This is a significant improvement over the worst-case efficiencies of ≤20% achieved by any of the device specific kernels discussed in Sect. 3.3. The final row in Table 2 shows the parameters selected with this approach.

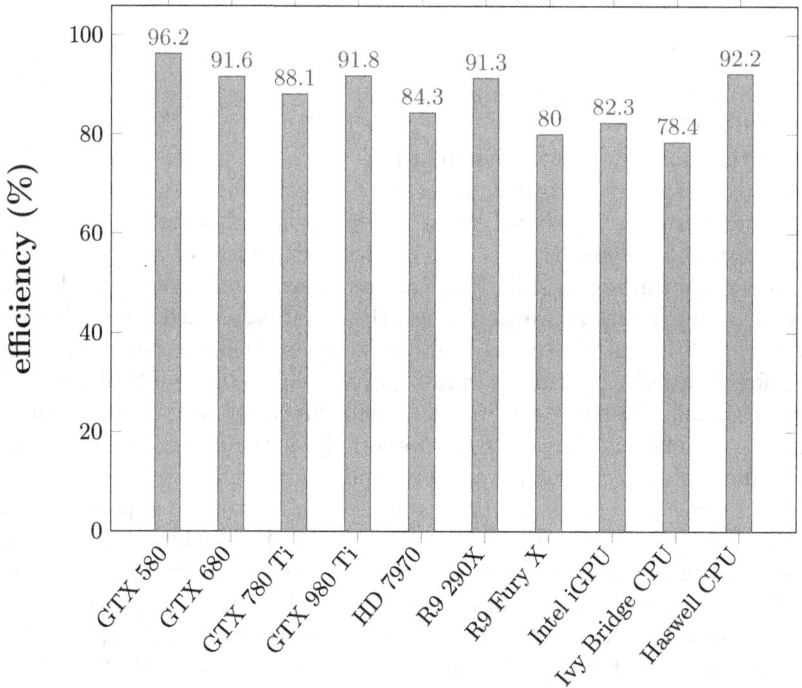

Fig. 5. Normalized efficiency achieved by a single implementation tuned for all devices simultaneously.

The implementation generated with this approach elected to use a row-major memory layout with a work-group size of 64×2, which suits devices that prefer horizontal work-item vectorization with a minimal performance penalty on the NVIDIA GPUs. The `fma()` builtin was avoided to satisfy the Ivy Bridge CPU, with `mad()` being used instead as needed by the Intel iGPU. The best loop unroll factor was determined to be 32, which is an effective compromise between the devices that prefer either smaller or larger values. Several parameter values were unanimously selected where they helped significantly on one or more devices whilst making no different to the others, such as replacing conditional

Table 2. Best parameters selected for each device.

Device	Work-group size	Mem. layout	Coalesce columns	Unroll factor	FMAD	Condition	Division by diagonal	mad24	Integer	Address space of b	Address space of xold	Const. matrix size	Const. work-group size
GTX 580	(2,256)	Column major	Yes	512	fma	Mask	Precomp. in constant	Yes	Signed	Global	Constant	No	Yes
GTX 680	(1,256)	Column major	No	64	mad	Mask	Precomp. in global	Yes	Signed	Global	Constant	Yes	Yes
GTX 780 Ti	(2,32)	Column major	Yes	64	fma	Mask	Precomp. in constant	No	Signed	Global	Global	Yes	Yes
GTX 980 Ti	(2,16)	Column major	Yes	64	op	Mask	Precomp. in constant	No	Signed	Global	Constant	Yes	Yes
HD 7970	(256,1)	Row major	Yes	4	fma	Mask	Precomp. in constant	No	Signed	Global	Constant	Yes	Yes
R9 290X	(256,1)	Row major	Yes	16	fma	Mask	Normal Division	No	Unsigned	Global	Global	No	Yes
Fury X	(256,1)	Row major	Yes	16	mad	Mask	Precomp. in constant	Yes	Signed	Global	Constant	Yes	Yes
Intel iGPU	(16,4)	Row major	Yes	64	mad	Mask	Precomp. in constant	No	Unsigned	Constant	Constant	Yes	No
Ivy Bridge CPU	(4,1)	Row major	Yes	2	mad	Mask	Normal division	No	Unsigned	Global	Constant	No	No
Haswell CPU	(8,1)	Row major	Yes	16	fma	Mask	Normal division	No	Unsigned	Global	Global	Yes	No
Multi-objective	(64,2)	Row major	Yes	32	mad	Mask	Normal division	No	Signed	Global	Global	No	No

branches with masks, keeping the `xold` vector in the `global` address space, and avoiding the use of `mad24()`. Some of the other parameters that affected performance when optimizing for certain individual devices were found to be relatively insignificant when focusing on worst-case efficiency across many devices, such as embedding the work-group size or matrix order into the kernel as a compile-time constant, integer signedness, or precomputing the diagonal reciprocals.

We can also use this multi-objective tuning technique to improve performance portability when targeting smaller sets of devices, such as a range of architectures from a single vendor. We applied this technique to generate a single kernel that was performance portable across the four NVIDIA devices in our test set, and were able to produce an implementation that achieved >93% efficiency on each device - a significant improvement over the worst-case efficiency of <70% achieved by the device-specific kernels. Interestingly, each of the implementations that achieved the highest worst-case efficiencies across all of the NVIDIA GPUs used a row-major memory layout, with the work-group sizes similarly transposed to 32×4. Despite each individual device strongly preferring the column-major layout, it seems that there is no compromise for the other parameters that leads to acceptable performance portability with this approach.

5 Related Work

Zhang et al. analyze the performance of a few OpenCL benchmarks for three devices from NVIDIA, AMD and Intel [28]. They identify several implementation decisions that can significantly impact performance, some of which we also examine in this work. They then manually tune the benchmarks for one of the architectures, and quantify the performance gap between the portable baseline implementation and their highly tuned version. Our work eliminates the need for expensive manual tuning, which in turn enables a much broader study of performance portability. We also look specifically at how code aggressively tuned for one architecture performs on many others in order to draw out the key performance portability issues, whereas the authors above start with an untuned benchmark.

In [8], Dolbeau et al. investigate the performance portability of OpenCL code generated by an OpenACC compiler for a non-trivial mini-application executing on three accelerators from NVIDIA, AMD and Intel. They tune the work-group sizes used for each kernel and examine the efficiency for each architecture compared to the best achieved performance. The authors observe that by carefully selecting a single work-group size they can minimize the efficiency loss across all three architectures, thus improving performance portability. Their work strongly motivates the need for auto-tuning techniques to analyze performance portability when faced with many implementation decisions, which we present in this work.

Stratton et al. investigate the performance of GPU optimized OpenCL kernels when moving to CPU architectures [26]. They identify programming conventions that can be used to express a kernel's performance properties which can efficiently map onto both GPU and CPU devices. The authors assert that in order for performance portability to be achieved, each implementor of a programming model must conform to the same set of programming guidelines. They demonstrate improved performance portability by changing the implementation of the programming model itself, rather than that of the application. This is an attractive solution for applications developers, as it shifts the burden of performance portability onto the implementors, however the increasingly diverse and fast evolving landscape of many-core architectures makes this a unstable target, and solutions at the application or middleware level are still desirable.

McIntosh-Smith et al. demonstrate codes achieving performance portability from a single codebase for structured grid [21] and molecular drug docking [22] applications. In these works, performance portability is judged based on the fraction of peak bandwidth and peak FLOP/s achieved, respectively. These theoretical peak figures provide a simple proxy for an application's performance upper bound, but potentially fail to capture any factors inherent to the architecture, compiler, or runtime implementation that may further limit a code's performance on a particular device. In this work, we instead determine the maximum achievable performance on a given architecture *empirically*, using auto-tuning as a means to arrive at this implementation. While this is still an imperfect upper bound, we believe that this provides a metric of implementation efficiency that is much more useful when analyzing the performance portability of a specific implementation of the code.

Multi-objective optimization techniques have previously been explored for generating code that demonstrates acceptable compromises between two or more distinct constraints. Balaprakash et al. present a multi-objective auto-tuning approach for exploring tradeoffs between performance and other metrics such as power or energy [2]. In [15], Jordan et al. investigate the use of multi-objective auto-tuning for simultaneously optimizing for both performance and parallel efficiency. Hoste et al. apply automated multi-objective techniques to a compiler framework in order to optimize for both code execution time and compilation time [14]. Lokuciejewski et al. use evolutionary multi-objective search algorithms in an adaptive compiler that considers both average-case execution time and worst-case execution time when generating code for real-time systems [20].

In [23], Muralidharan et al. present a system that automatically generates a model for selecting code variants for a given architecture based on training data collected offline. A multi-task learning algorithm is used to combine empirical results collected for each code variant from two or more source architectures into a variant selection model. This model allows the runtime to select an appropriate code variant for a previously unseen target architecture, using only a simple set of device characteristics extracted at a one-off cost. Their work considers a relatively small number of code variants (<10) at a coarse-grained level: each variant is an entire implementation. In contrast, we explore a much more vast search space comprising several independent implementation decisions. In addition, their techniques are only evaluated for NVIDIA GPUs, whereas this work covers a much more diverse set of architectures.

6 Conclusion

In this work, we have a presented an approach for analyzing performance portability across many-core architectures that exploits the black-box nature of automatic performance tuning techniques. We have performed a detailed analysis of performance portability both between devices from a single vendor and across many different architectures from multiple hardware vendors. Our analysis has highlighted the potential for over-optimization, either manual or automatic, to produce code that exhibits low performance portability. We then demonstrated a simple, multi-objective auto-tuning technique that can deliver much greater performance portability across a diverse range of modern computer architectures.

In the future, we aim to assess the effectiveness of our multi-objective auto-tuning approach for a variety of other codes from different application areas. We believe that these techniques could also help improve performance portability within a single architecture when varying other parameters such as input data sizes. We plan to compare various reduction functions for quantifying the overall fitness of an implementation when tuning for performance portability across multiple objectives. We also intend to explore techniques that will allow us to remove the requirement to have predetermined the peak performance of each device before beginning the multi-objective auto-tuning process.

Acknowledgment. We would like to thank Imagination Technologies for providing funding for this work. We also give thanks to Tom Deakin from the University of Bristol for providing valuable feedback on this paper.

References

1. Ansel, J., O'Reilly, U.M.: OpenTuner: an extensible framework for program autotuning. MIT CSAIL Technical report MIT-CSAIL-TR-2013-026 (2013)
2. Balaprakash, P., Tiwari, A., Wild, S.M.: Multi objective optimization of HPC kernels for performance, power, and energy. In: Jarvis, S.A., Wright, S.A., Hammond, S.D. (eds.) PMBS 2013. LNCS, vol. 8551, pp. 239–260. Springer, Cham (2014). doi:10.1007/978-3-319-10214-6_12
3. Balaprakash, P., Wild, S.M., Hovland, P.D.: Can search algorithms save large-scale automatic performance tuning? Procedia Comput. Sci. **4**, 2136–2145 (2011). Proceedings of the International Conference on Computational Science ICCS 2011
4. Bilmes, J., Asanovic, K.C.: Optimizing matrix multiply using PHiPAC: a portable, high-performance, ANSI C coding methodology. In: International Conference on Supercomputing, pp. 340–347 (1997)
5. Bolme, D.S., Beveridge, J.R., Draper, B.A., Phillips, P.J., Lui, Y.M.: Automatically searching for optimal parameter settings using a genetic algorithm. In: Crowley, J.L., Draper, B.A., Thonnat, M. (eds.) ICVS 2011. LNCS, vol. 6962, pp. 213–222. Springer, Heidelberg (2011). doi:10.1007/978-3-642-23968-7_22
6. Clint Whaley, R., Petitet, A., Dongarra, J.J.: Automated empirical optimizations of software and the ATLAS project. Parallel Comput. **27**(1–2), 3–35 (2001)
7. Deakin, T., Price, J., Martineau, M., McIntosh-Smith, S.: Evaluating attainable memory bandwidth of parallel programming models via BabelStream (2017, in press)

8. Dolbeau, R., Bodin, F., de Verdire, G.C.: One OpenCL to rule them all? In: 2013 IEEE 6th International Workshop on Multi-/Many-core Computing Systems (MuCoCoS), pp. 1–6, September 2013
9. Falch, T.L., Elster, A.C.: Machine learning based auto-tuning for enhanced OpenCL performance portability. CoRR abs/1506.00842 (2015). http://arxiv.org/abs/1506.00842
10. Fang, J., Varbanescu, A.L., Sips, H.: An auto-tuning solution to data streams clustering in OpenCL. In: Proceedings of the 14th IEEE International Conference on Computational Science and Engineering, CSE 2011 and 11th International Symposium on Pervasive Systems, Algorithms, and Networks, I-SPA 2011 and 10th IEEE International Conference on IUCC 2011, pp. 587–594 (2011)
11. Garvey, J.D., Abdelrahman, T.S.: Automatic performance tuning of stencil computations on GPUs. In: 2015 44th International Conference on Parallel Processing (ICPP), pp. 300–309, September 2015
12. Goldstine, H.H., Murray, F.J., von Neumann, J.: The Jacobi method for real symmetric matrices. J. ACM **6**(1), 59–96 (1959). doi:10.1145/320954.320960
13. Holland, J.H.: Adaptation in Natural and Artificial Systems. The University of Michigan Press, Ann Arbor (1975). http://www.citeulike.org/group/664/article/400721
14. Hoste, K., Eeckhout, L.: Cole: Compiler optimization level exploration. In: Proceedings of the 6th Annual IEEE/ACM International Symposium on Code Generation and Optimization, CGO 2008, NY, USA, pp. 165–174 (2008). doi:10.1145/1356058.1356080
15. Jordan, H., Thoman, P., Durillo, J.J., Pellegrini, S., Gschwandtner, P., Fahringer, T., Moritsch, H.: A multi-objective auto-tuning framework for parallel codes. In: Proceedings of the International Conference on High Performance Computing, Networking, Storage and Analysis, SC 2012, CA, USA, pp. 10:1–10:12 (2012). http://dl.acm.org/citation.cfm?id=2388996.2389010
16. Khronos OpenCL Working Group: The OpenCL Specification, Version 1.2 (2012). https://www.khronos.org/registry/cl/specs/opencl-1.2.pdf
17. Klöckner, A.: PyOpenCL. https://mathema.tician.de/software/pyopencl/
18. Li, Y., Zhang, Y.Q., Liu, Y.Q., Long, G.P., Jia, H.P.: MPFFT: an auto-tuning FFT library for OpenCL GPUs. J. Comput. Sci. Technol. **28**, 90–105 (2013)
19. Li, Y., Dongarra, J., Tomov, S.: A note on auto-tuning GEMM for GPUs. In: Allen, G., Nabrzyski, J., Seidel, E., van Albada, G.D., Dongarra, J., Sloot, P.M.A. (eds.) ICCS 2009. LNCS, vol. 5544, pp. 884–892. Springer, Heidelberg (2009). doi:10.1007/978-3-642-01970-8_89
20. Lokuciejewski, P., Plazar, S., Falk, H., Marwedel, P., Thiele, L.: Multi-objective exploration of compiler optimizations for real-time systems. In: 2010 13th IEEE International Symposium on Object/Component/Service-Oriented Real-Time Distributed Computing, pp. 115–122, May 2010
21. McIntosh-Smith, S., Boulton, M., Curran, D., Price, J.: On the performance portability of structured grid codes on many-core computer architectures. In: Kunkel, J.M., Ludwig, T., Meuer, H.W. (eds.) ISC 2014. LNCS, vol. 8488, pp. 53–75. Springer, Cham (2014). doi:10.1007/978-3-319-07518-1_4
22. McIntosh-Smith, S., Price, J., Sessions, R.B., Ibarra, A.A.: High performance in silico virtual drug screening on many-core processors. Int. J. High Perform. Comput. Appl. **29**(2), 119–134 (2015). http://hpc.sagepub.com/content/29/2/119.abstract

23. Muralidharan, S., Roy, A., Hall, M., Garland, M., Rai, P.: Architecture-adaptive code variant tuning. In: Proceedings of the Twenty-First International Conference on Architectural Support for Programming Languages and Operating Systems, ASPLOS 2016, NY, USA, pp. 325–338 (2016). doi:10.1145/2872362.2872411
24. Price, J., McIntosh-Smith, S.: Improving auto-tuning convergence times with dynamically generated predictive performance models. In: 2015 IEEE 9th International Symposium on Embedded Multicore/Many-core Systems-on-Chip (MCSoC), pp. 211–218, September 2015
25. Steuer, R.: Multiple Criteria Optimization: Theory, Computation, and Application. Wiley Series in Probability and Mathematical Statistics. Wiley, New York (1986). https://books.google.co.uk/books?id=0H9jQgAACAAJ
26. Stratton, J.A., Kim, H.S., Jablin, T.B., Hwu, W.M.W.: Performance portability in accelerated parallel kernels. Technical report IMPACT-13-01, University of Illinois at Urbana-Champaign, Urbana, May 2013
27. Tzannes, A.: Enhancing Productivity and Performance Portability of General-purpose Parallel Programming. Ph.D. thesis, College Park, MD, USA (2012). aAI3543143
28. Zhang, Y., Sinclair, M., Chien, A.A.: Improving performance portability in OpenCL programs. In: Kunkel, J.M., Ludwig, T., Meuer, H.W. (eds.) ISC 2013. LNCS, vol. 7905, pp. 136–150. Springer, Heidelberg (2013). doi:10.1007/978-3-642-38750-0_11

OpenACC 2.5 Validation Testsuite Targeting Multiple Architectures

Kyle Friedline[1(✉)], Sunita Chandrasekaran[1], M. Graham Lopez[2], and Oscar Hernandez[2]

[1] University of Delaware, Newark, DE, USA
{utimatu,schandra}@udel.edu
[2] Oak Ridge National Lab, Oak Ridge, TN, USA
{lopezmg,oscar}@ornl.gov

Abstract. Heterogeneous computing has emerged as a promising fit for scientific domains such as molecular dynamics simulations, bioinformatics, weather prediction. Such a computing paradigm includes x86 processors coupled with GPUs, FPGAs, DSPs or a coprocessor paradigm that takes advantage of all the cores and caches on a single die such as the Knights Landing. OpenACC, a high-level directive-based parallel programming model has emerged as a programming paradigm that can tackle the intensity of heterogeneity in architectures. Data-driven large scientific codes are increasingly using OpenACC, which makes it essential to analyze the accuracy of OpenACC compilers while they port code to various types of platforms. In response, we have been creating a validation suite to validate and verify the implementations of OpenACC features in conformance with the specification. The validation suite also provides a tool to compiler developers as a standard for the compiler to be tested against and to users and compiler developers alike in clarifying the OpenACC specification. This testsuite has been integrated into the harness infrastructure of the TITAN and Summitdev systems at Oak Ridge National Lab and is being used for production.

Keywords: Programming models · Testsuite · Hardware · Validation

---

J.M. Kunkel et al. (Eds.): ISC High Performance Workshops 2017, LNCS 10524, pp. 557–575, 2017.
https://doi.org/10.1007/978-3-319-67630-2_39

1 Introduction

Hardware continues to evolve very rapidly expecting programmers to quickly deploy or redeploy scientific codes in order to exploit the rich feature set of these hardware platforms. These platforms are also becoming increasingly heterogeneous thus creating programming challenges and maintenance of single code bases. At the same time there is a constant demand for improved performance. Currently these heterogeneous platforms can be programmed using a variety of languages or models such as OpenACC [17], OpenMP [19], CUDA [15], OpenCL [18], NVIDA Thrust [3], Kokkos [8]. This paper focuses on OpenACC, which is an emerging directive-based programming model for traditional X86, accelerators such as GPUs, IBM Power processors, and, with OpenACC research compilers, FPGAs [4]. Since OpenACC can target more than just one or two platforms, it allows the programmers to maintain a single code base. Commercial compilers include support from PGI, Sunway Taihulight and Cray. Currently only PGI and GCC support OpenACC 2.5 (the version of the specification we are testing), though GCC has only partial support for the 2.5 feature set. Cray and Sunway provides support for OpenACC only until 2.0 features.

Open Source compilers include GNU Compiler Collection (GCC) with initial support for OpenACC 2.5. Academic compilers include Omni Compiler from Riken, OpenARC from ORNL, OpenUH from SBU and UH, RoseACC from LLNL, UDEL. More information on existing compilers can be found on the OpenACC webpage[1].

The model has been gaining wide adoption among the scientific community and is being used to accelerate scientific codes such as molecular dynamics, computational fluid dynamics, weather modeling to an accelerator. Instead of writing explicit code to offload or parallelize a given region of code, the programmer simply inserts compiler hints or directives into a C11, C++14 or a Fortran code, and the compiler offloads compute intensive portions of the code to an accelerator which could be multiple CPU cores and/or GPUs. As the OpenACC specification evolves and it's feature set is expanded, it is critical to ensure that the implementations of the features are conforming to the specifications and consistent with the definition of the features. It is quite common for different implementors to interpret the specifications differently. As a result there may be differing implementations of a particular feature defined in the specifications. Our previous publication on this effort [24] captured these discrepancies. The specifications has since evolved and there have been some major updates including providing support for both shared and discrete memory machines. So most, if not all, tests which this paper discusses are new and have been written to adhere to the current specifications.

This project creates a validation and verification testsuite where we construct a number of functional test cases to test several constructs such as the `parallel` or `kernel` constructs, clauses such as `async` or `reduction`, or combinations of occurrences of clauses on constructs. The testsuite is built to check

[1] https://www.openacc.org/tools.

for correctness and conformance of features to the OpenACC specifications. We will also demonstrate the results of the testsuite on multiple compilers/versions to compare implementations' adherence to the OpenACC specifications. This testsuite will enable the compiler implementors to improve the quality of their tools and ensure compliance of their implementations with the specifications of the language.

OpenACC has been adopted for large-scale scientific applications on accelerator-based supercomputers such as Titan at the Oak Ridge Leadership Facility (OLCF). These applications include: ACME Land Model and CAM/SE [21,22], One-Way Based Methods OWBM (Oil and Gas), Dalton [6], Maestro [14] (Astro-physics), GTC-p [5,9], and many are part of funded user programs such as INCITE [2] and CAAR [1]. These show that OpenACC has already afforded applications early successes at scale on heterogeneous machines such as Titan. Such large scale applications demand updates to OpenACC data clauses to allow deep copy. This feature is needed to handle complex data structures and how they are mapped to the limited memory capacity of discrete accelerators with disjoint memory address spaces. The OpenACC organization put together a technical report (TR-16-1) discussing challenges to support deep copy and also propose probable solutions [16]. Secondly, the increasing complexity of upcoming architectures means that OpenACC needs to be improved to handle and optimize for deeper node-level memory hierarchies; currently, the `acc cache` directive provides insufficient optimization and limits performance where memory capacity and bandwidth trade-offs are critical. Finally, the ability to better handle multiple accelerators per node will be critical to exploiting upcoming machines.

A comprehensive and community-driven OpenACC validation suite is an essential tool for computing facilities that must procure and evaluate both large production and experimental systems. As multiple compiler implementations are adapted to new architectures and updated to support evolving specifications, OpenACC consumers benefit greatly from having a way to evaluate each implementation's coverage of a given specification on each architecture where OpenACC-enabled applications are used. By having a community-driven validation suite that can be used in common by any vendor as well as the end users, application developers have a way to evaluate and push for consistency in functionality across implementations.

Since the tests are in a more matured state than it was earlier, we plan to release the testsuite by July 2017, just in time for the camera ready version of this paper. This testsuite will be released under a dual license scheme and we welcome contributions. One license will preserve the license used by the contributor, the second OpenACC license will ensure consistency in code version, and the running and reporting of results. Currently all OpenACC members can use and contribute to the testsuite.

The paper makes the following contributions:

- Develop test cases that can test on both shared and discrete memory models
- Identify and report compiler bugs and runtime errors

- Evaluate different compilers' implementations for its conformance to the OpenACC specifications
- Delivered initial release of OpenACC 2.5 Testsuite[2]

2 Overview of the Programming Model

The underlying goal of OpenACC is to deliver an API for parallelizing code targeting a generic heterogeneous architecture. With three layers of parallelism as well as a compute construct designated for compiler targeting of generic architectures, the model aims to abstract the architecture with minimal adjustments to the logic of the code thus allowing maintenance of a single code base. With often only minor adjustments to memory management near parallelized compute regions, the model accommodates both shared and discrete memory or any combination of the two across any number of devices.

The basic functionality of the model deals with specifying the compute intensive regions of code that needs to run on an accelerator as well as manage data on multiple devices. A great deal of this is managed by creating scopes with certain descriptors. `Parallel` or `kernels` directives need to be added to the code region that needs to be offloaded to the accelerator.

Since the last time this topic has been discussed (see [24]), the OpenACC specifications have undergone two major changes. OpenACC 2.0 version was released with features for queuing and resynchronization of asynchronous compute regions via the `wait` clause (see Code 1); dynamic data lifetimes via the `enter data` and `exit data` directives (see Code 2); asynchronous synchronizing of queues via the `async` clause on a `wait` directive (see Code 3); and function calls from compute regions via the `routine` directive (see Code 4).

Code 1. Resynchronization of Queues

```
#pragma acc parallel loop present(a[0:n], \
  b[0:n], c[0:n]) async(1)
for (int x = 0; x < n; ++x){
  c[x] = a[x] + b[x];
}
#pragma acc parallel loop present(d[0:n], \
  e[0:n], f[0:n]) async(2)
for (int x = 0; x < n; ++x){
  f[x] = d[x] + e[x];
}
#pragma acc parallel loop present(c[0:n], \
  f[0:n], g[0:n]) async(3) wait(1, 2)
for (int x = 0; x < n; ++x){
  g[x] = c[x] + f[x];
}
```

[2] https://github.com/OpenACCUserGroup/OpenACCV-V.

Code 2. Executable Data Directives

```
#pragma acc enter data copyin(data[0:n])
#pragma acc parallel loop present(a[0:n]) reduction(+:total)
     for (int x = 0; x < n; ++x){
  a[x] = a[x] * 2;
  total += a[x];
}
if (total < n){
  \\Conditionally updates data
  #pragma acc exit data copyout(data[0:n])
}
else {
  #pragma acc exit data delete(data[0:n])
}
```

Code 3. Asynchronous Synchronization of Queues

```
#pragma acc parallel loop present(a[0:n], \
  b[0:n], c[0:n]) async(1)
for (int x = 0; x < n; ++x){
  c[x] = a[x] + b[x];
}
#pragma acc parallel loop present(d[0:n], \
  e[0:n], f[0:n]) async(2)
for (int x = 0; x < n; ++x){
  f[x] = d[x] + e[x];
}
#pragma acc wait(1, 2) async(3)
#pragma acc parallel loop present(c[0:n], \
  f[0:n], g[0:n]) async(3)
for (int x = 0; x < n; ++x){
  g[x] = c[x] + f[x];
}
```

OpenACC 2.5, released in 2015, had a major update on the data management. In previous versions, data was managed by `copy`, `copyin`, `copyout`, and `create` data clauses as well as their respective counterparts, `present_or_copy`, `present_or_copyin`, `present_or_create`, `present_or_copyout`, that would check their presence on the device and allocate/copy as necessary. However, with version 2.5 data control was simplified by merging the data clauses and only supporting the functionality that tests for data's presence on device. Along with this, reference counting and conditional data updates with the `if_present` clause were added in version 2.5 to further simplify data management.

Code 4. Routine

```
int pow(int base, int exponent){
  returned = 1;
  for (int x = 0; x < exponent - 1; ++x){
    returned = returned * base;
  }
  return returned;
}
#pragma acc routine(pow) seq
#pragma acc parallel loop present(a[0:n])
for (int x = 0; x < n; ++x){
  a[x] = pow(a[x], 2);
}
```

To briefly discuss reference counting, this is managed by the compiler runtime libraries. Every time a variable is either used in an `enter data` directive or at the entrance to a data region, the variable's reference count is incremented. At either an `exit data` or at the exit of a data region, it is decremented. If before incrementation, the count is zero, the data clause is executed, either copying the data in or allocating the data on device. And if after decrementing, the count is zero, the data clause is again executed, either copying out the data or deallocating it on device.

One of the issues with this functionality is that it still leaves data validity very hard to determine due to data clauses potentially only altering reference counts instead of updating data. Also with the 2.5 version, the clause `if_present` for the `update` directive allows the update to be dependent on the presence of the data on device. This, in conjunction with the updated data management directives/clauses the user is able to exploit much finer control over the data environment.

3 Methodology

As mentioned in Sect. 1, we develop tests that target platforms with discrete or unified memory, or a combination of the two. This means that when a test is executed, the parallel regions of the code could be operating on a device with direct access to the host-processes memory. We also develop tests that address the dynamic execution order. The nature of parallel programming creates race conditions and difficulty with ordering and flow control. These, among other complications, pose difficulties to creating platform-agnostic tests. Furthermore, the desire of these tests is to find flaws in the compilation of the program and to do so we try to design tests in such a way that they can strain the limits of what the specifications dictate.

The constraints with the model often limit our ability to make the test as discerning as we might want. Although there are hundreds of test case scenarios, in this section we will illustrate these constraints using the example of testing the `create` clause.

According to the language specifications, the `create` clause only allocates the memory on the device; it does not copy the host's values for the data to the device. When testing this aspect of the language, there are some vague aspects of the execution of the clause. First, the code could be run on either a shared memory device, or a discrete memory device. This means that at the `create` call, if the application is running on a shared memory device, the data will already be present and the data clause will be ignored. On a discrete memory device, at the call to the `create` clause, the memory will be allocated on the separate memory device. The data is not copied and will be uninitialized in the device memory.

With these potentialities for possible execution methods, how does one test that the creation happened without the copy? To demonstrate the complications in writing tests that satisfy these requirements, let's look at an example for testing this clause on an `enter data` directive. The specifications state that when an array is in a create clause, that the data is allocated, but not copied. If we wanted to test this functionality, we might create something such as what is in Code 5.

Code 5. Enter Data Create V.1

```
double * a = (double *)malloc(n * sizeof(double));
double * a_copy = (double *)malloc(n * sizeof(double));
for (int x = 0; x < n; ++x){
  a[x] = rand();
  a_copy[x] = a[x];
}
#pragma acc enter data create(a[0:n])
#pragma acc exit data copyout(a[0:n])
int err = 1; //Failing
for (int x = 0; x < n; ++x){
  if (fabs(a[x] - a_copy[x]) > PRECISION){
    err = 0; //Passing
  }
}
```

In this test, we initialize the data to be random values and make a copy of the data for verification. We then create the one set of data on the device. This would initialize the data over garbage data on the device. On the following line, we copyout the data, which would copy out the garbage data on the device. After this, we iterate over the data and make sure that it is different from the copy of the initial data. If it is different, it demonstrates that the allocation happened without the copy of data.

Now, while this test is well designed to test that the data was not copied, the test fails to consider the possibility that the test could be operating on a shared memory device. If this test was running on a machine with a shared memory device, at line 7, when the data is copied in, the memory would not be allocated and any device operations would occur on the data that is also available to the host. The `exit data` on the following line would again do nothing. During the loop on lines 10–14, the loop would operate again on the data as it was initially and would fail the conditional statement within every iteration, resulting in a failing test. However, this problem could be worked around as shown in Code 6.

Code 6. Enter Data Create V.2

```
double * a = (double *)malloc(n * sizeof(double));
double * a_copy = (double *)malloc(n * sizeof(double));
int devtest = 1;
int err = 0;
#pragma acc enter data copyin(devtest)
#pragma acc parallel present(devtest)
{
  devtest = 0;
}
for (int x = 0; x < n; ++x){
  a[x] = rand();
  a_copy[x] = a[x];
}
if (devtest == 1){
  #pragma acc enter data create(a[0:n])
  #pragma acc exit data copyout(a[0:n])
  err = 1; //Failing
  for (int x = 0; x < n; ++x){
    if (fabs(a[x] - a_copy[x]) > PRECISION){
      err = 0; //Passing
    }
  }
}
```

Here, we create a new variable, ‘devtest’, as an `int` that is meant to test the presence of a separate memory device before entering into separate memory dependent code. We initiate the variable to a passing condition and copy it into the device memory. If the device memory is separate, the data transfer occurs and its value on device is subsequently updated to a failing condition. However, at the exit of the `parallel` region, since the scalar was explicitly copied in, there is no implicit copy back to the host data. Thus, the host version of the devtest variable is still in the passing condition. However in the case of a shared memory system, we have the same issue as the previous version of the test. The `parallel` region updates the host version, causing the devtest variable to be in the failing condition. This allows the test to bypass the test conditionally on the presence of a device. The new functionality of conditionally skipping separate memory dependent testing is also dependent on proper data management, which increases the chances of misdiagnosing issues.

Code 7. Enter Data Create V.3

```
double * a = (double *)malloc(n * sizeof(double));
double * a_copy = (double *)malloc(n * sizeof(double));
int * devtest = (int *)malloc(sizeof(int));
int err = 0;
devtest[0] = 1;
#pragma acc enter data copyin(devtest[0:1])
#pragma acc parallel present(devtest[0:1])
{
  devtest[0] = 0;
}
for (int x = 0; x < n; ++x){
  a[x] = rand();
  a_copy[x] = a[x];
}
if (devtest[0] == 1){
  #pragma acc enter data create(a[0:n])
  #pragma acc exit data copyout(a[0:n])
  err = 1; //Failing
  for (int x = 0; x < n; ++x){
    if (fabs(a[x] - a_copy[x]) > PRECISION){
      err = 0 //Passing
    }
  }
}
```

While Code 7 is almost exactly the same, we change the type of the devtest variable to be a `int *`. A strict reading of the specifications describes the data transfer protocols for scalar variables in parallel regions as being treated as if it appeared in a firstprivate clause for the region if the scalar has not already appeared in another data clause or in a surrounding data region, in which case, the operation is that of the explicit data clause. This means that partial implementations could potentially implement the implicit data transfer without allowing them to be overridden by other data clauses. Instead, by using a pointer to the data, it gets treated as a non-scalar, avoiding any potential issues with implicit data transfer and getting incorrect results with regards to the presence of a separate memory device.

There is yet another issue with this test. The test, which creates the data and copies it back to host, relies on the assumption that the data on device will be allocated over garbage data that has different values than that of the host version of the data. While relatively unlikely, this allows for mixed results that, if users are testing for only strict adherence of the language, may be unwelcome. Instead of removing a test over a minor risk or keeping a code that may give unreliable results, we instead move it to a conditional region dependent on configuration settings of the test-suite as seen in Code 8 on line 16.

Code 8. Enter Data Create V.4

```
double * a = (double *)malloc(n * sizeof(double));
double * b = (double *)malloc(n * sizeof(double));
double * a_copy = (double *)malloc(n *sizeof(double));
int * devtest = (int *)malloc(sizeof(int));
int err = 0;
devtest[0] = 1;
#pragma acc enter data copyin(devtest[0:1])
#pragma acc parallel present(devtest[0:1])
{
  devtest[0] = 0;
}
for (int x = 0; x < n; ++x){
  a[x] = rand();
  a_copy[x] = a[x];
}
if (devtest[0] == 1 && run_probabilistic == 1){
  #pragma acc enter data create(a[0:n])
  #pragma acc exit data copyout(a[0:n])
  err = 1; \\Failing
  for (int x = 0; x < n; ++x){
    if (fabs(a[x] - a_copy[x]) > PRECISION){
      err = 0;
    }
  }
}
for (int x = 0; x < n; ++x){
  a[x] = rand();
  b[x] = 0.0;
}
#pragma acc enter data copyin(a[0:n]) create(b[0:n])
#pragma acc parallel present(a[0:n], b[0:n])
{
  for (int x = 0; x < n; ++x){
    b[x] = a[x];
  }
}
#pragma acc exit data copyout(b[0:n]) delete(a[0:n])
for (int x = 0; x < n; ++x){
  if (fabs(a[x] - b[x]) > PRECISION){
    err += 1;
    break;
  }
}
```

In order to add at least some minimal testing for systems that either have shared memory or are being run without probabilistic tests, we also include a test that is written to be completely independent of device type or garbage data. On lines 30–43 we test the `create` clause, but instead of testing the lack of data transfer, we only test that the data was allocated and available for use. While this severely limits this test, it does provide proof of the dependability of the clause for any standard code that doesn't depend on any non-deterministic structures.

This example demonstrates some of the difficulties that come with varying memory models. While these are not inherent to a parallel programming model, many devices that run these codes depend on separate memory while other technologies, such as Knight's Landing, focus on reunifying the memory to minimize the startup cost to parallelization. There are other issues to protect the tests against in terms of the non-sequential processing model which is inherent to any parallelization.

In the case of testing the `reduction` clause on a `loop` directive with a multiply operator, one of the problems that can be run into with this sort of reduction is overflowing the reduction variable. In order to sanitize the data to avoid this, it might be tempting to keep a rolling multiplied total when initializing the data and limiting the randomization to a range that will not allow for overflow. When processing sequentially, there would be no problems with this solution. However, since the reduction does not execute sequentially, all the largest of the numbers could, by chance be multiplied together before any of the lower ones, which could cause undefined values before the completion of the reduction.

4 Setup, Compilation Flags and Infrastructure

For our tests, we ran the suite on three different systems. The first system is University of Delaware's (UD) Community Cluster, Farber,[3] where our compute node consists of Intel Xeon CPU E5-2670 v2 processor (20 cores) of Ivy Bridge architecture and a single NVIDIA Tesla K80 GPU. The second system is Titan[4] housed at ORNL where each compute node contains 1 AMD Interlagos 6274 processor (16 cores) of the Bulldozer architecture and a single NVIDIA Tesla K20 GPU. The third system is Summitdev consisting of IBM Power8+ processor CPUs (20 cores) with 4 NVIDIA Tesla P100 GPUs. We were also able to test on a machine running on an Intel Knights Landing chip, the Xeon Phi 7230.

With the first two systems, we were able to use PGI 16.10, which is also the version for the community edition (at the time of writing this paper). For the first system - UD's Farber, we use 17.3 (the latest version of the compiler at the time of writing this paper). On the third system and the Knights Landing system, we use PGI 17.1 due to the lack of availability of the 16.10 version on that system. We also used the GNU 6.3-20170303 compiler version on the second system, Titan. Between these various environments, we were able to test all supported

[3] http://docs.hpc.udel.edu/clusters/farber/start#farber.

[4] https://www.olcf.ornl.gov/titan/.

platforms for both PGI and GNU except for little-endian PowerPC systems for GNU. In all, we ran the testsuite 13 times as shown in Table 1 with variations of compiler vendor, compiler version, platform type, and platform version to ensure we do not spot any flaky tests.

Table 1. Compiler versions and platforms

Run	Compiler	Platform
1	PGI 16.10	Ivy Bridge Multicore
2	PGI 16.10	K80
3	PGI 17.3	Ivy Bridge Multicore
4	PGI 17.3	K80
5	PGI 16.10	Bulldozer Multicore
6	PGI 16.10	K20
7	PGI 17.1	Power8+ Multicore
8	PGI 17.1	P100
9	PGI 17.1	Knights Landing
10	GNU 6.3-20170303	Bulldozer Multicore
11	GNU 6.3-20170303	K20
12	GNU 6.0.0-20160415	Ivy Bridge Multicore
13	GNU 6.0.0-20160415	K80

The compilation uses various flags. For instance with the PGI compiler, to target the CPUs either the -ta=multicore or -ta=host flags is used (multicore for multithreading and host for single threaded execution). For the GPUs, the target accelerator flag is set to -ta=tesla for the Kepler cards or -ta=tesla:cc60 when targeting the P100 cards. With the GNU compiler, targeting is not handled at compile time. Instead, both host and device versions of the code are built. In order to run the host version (There is no multicore option for GNU as of yet), the internal control variable has to be set with ACC_DEVICE_TYPE=host, or, in order to force device operation, ACC_DEVICE_TYPE=nvidia.

With the GNU compiler, compilation failure due to linking issues were sometimes resolved by adding the -lm flag. If the issues were still not resolved, adding the -foffload=-lm would occasionally fix the compilation error as well. With fortran codes, due the strict adherence of GNU to fortran specifications, the -ffree-line-length-none could be used when lines were longer than 72 characters.

5 Results

(Note: We have used 16.10 wherever possible as at the time of writing this paper PGI's Community Edition supports 16.10[5]). In executing the testsuite on

[5] https://www.pgroup.com/products/community.htm.

the assortment of platforms discussed in Sect. 4, we can statistically verify the integrity of these tests. We developed 177 tests and out of the 177 tests, 89.3% passed in all runs with the PGI compiler and 51.7% passed in all runs with PGI and GNU compilers. In addition, no test failed all runs. The overall success rate for the tests is 90.6% across 2301 individual test-runs (includes the combination of compiler versions on the variety of hardware architectures).

5.1 Comparison of PGI Compiler Targeting Various Architectures

Between the systems we had access to, we were able to test seven separate architectures. As far as accelerators are concerned, we were able to run the testsuite on NVIDIA's K20 architecture, K80 architecture, and the P100 architecture. Of these, on the P100 we were not able to use PGI's 16.10 compiler version; instead we used PGI's 17.1 compiler version available on that system. However, targeting these accelerators was very uniform, having a total pass rate of 525/531 or 98.9%. Across all platforms, tests for the `tile` clause on a `parallel loop` in C and the test for the `firstprivate` clause on a `parallel` region in Fortran failed. However, the test for the `tile` clause is not a surprising failure. The test takes the lack of a range of valid values for the arguments in the specifications to test that all values should work. As an optimization clause, even if the tiling arguments are out of bounds for the loops, it should not change the results of the test. On other versions of the test that did not do this, the `tile` clause did execute properly.

Targeting multicore processors/shared memory devices had much more varied results. We were able to run the testsuite on the Intel Ivy Bridge architecture, the AMD Bulldozer architecture (TITAN), the IBM Power8+ architecture (Summitdev), and the Intel Knights Landing (KNL) architecture (though KNL is not yet officially supported by PGI). We used PGI's 16.10 version on the Ivy Bridge and Bulldozer architectures, and PGI's 17.1 version on Power8+ and Knights Landing. The average pass rate for these architectures was lower than that of the discrete graphics cards tested. Instead of 98.9% pass rate, these tests averaged a 95.3% pass rate or 675/708 passing over total, though this is not surprising, due to PGI's relatively recent support of OpenACC targeting multicore on x86 and Power processors.

Across all multicore architectures, the test for the `firstprivate` clause on a `parallel` construct in C and the test of a multiplication `reduction` in a `parallel` region in C were the only consistent failures. Others were also very close to across the board failure, such as the Fortran versions of each of these tests, which failed all but the Ivy Bridge architecture, and the test of an *AND* `reduction` on a `parallel loop` with a scalar that has been privatized in a surrounding loop in C, which failed on all but Power8+. The test of the `tile` clause on a `parallel loop` in C failed on all architectures but Bulldozer. Both the test of the *AND* `reduction` on a `parallel loop` in C and the test of the *OR* `reduction` on a `parallel loop` in C also failed for both Ivy Bridge and Knights Landing. In particular, though, the Power8+ architecture had a good amount of additional failures that should be noted. The Power8+ architecture failed a simple test having multiple loops inside of a `parallel` construct in both C and Fortran as well as many of the tests that utilized the `create` clause. The tests associated with the `create` clause that failed were the tests that used the functionality of removing the lower bound on the data clause to have it default to zero on a `data` construct in both C and Fortran and on an `enter data` directive in Fortran and the use of a `create` clause on a `parallel` construct in both C and Fortran.

The performance of these various platforms can be seen in Table 2.

Table 2. Performance of PGI architecture targeting

Architecture	Pass rate	Percent passed
K20	175/177	98.9%
K80	175/177	98.3%
P100	175/177	98.9%
Ivy Bridge	171/177	96.6%
Bulldozer	172/177	97.2%
Power8+	165/177	93.3%
Knights landing	167/177	94.4%

5.2 Comparison of Various PGI Compiler Versions

We were also able to test a series of PGI's compilers using a NVIDIA K80 as shown in Table 3 The first version that we were able to test was 14.10 (at the time of this version, PGI did not support the 2.5 specifications). Thus, there is quite a

Table 3. Comparison of K80 targeting across PGI versions

Compiler version	Fortran pass rate	C pass rate	Fortran percent passed	C percent passed
14.10	60/86	67/91	69.8%	73.6%
15.1	64/86	80/91	74.4%	87.9%
15.5	65/86	80/91	75.6%	87.9%
15.10	68/86	84/91	79.1%	92.3%
16.1	69/86	84/91	80.2%	92.3%
16.4	82/86	84/91	95.3%	92.3%
16.7	85/86	90/91	98.8%	98.9%
16.10	85/86	90/91	98.8%	98.9%
17.1	85/86	90/91	98.8%	98.9%
17.3	85/86	90/91	98.8%	98.9%

noticeable improvement across 14.10 to 15.1, causing issues with about nineteen of the tests. In the 15.5 version, the `tile` clause was added, fixing the errors associated with the Fortran version of the test of the `tile` clause, though the C version continues to have errors even now due to its inability to handle abnormal arguments for the `tile` clause. With the 15.10 version, PGI added support for the `num_gangs`, `num_workers`, and `vector_length` for the `kernels` construct, resolving compilation errors caused by the use of these clauses. Also, until the 16.4 version, having variables copied into the device multiple times would cause errors in Fortran. This situation appears in another fourteen of the tests. With 16.7, reference counting was added (including the finalize clause), fixing another five tests. Also with 16.7, the `num_gangs`, `num_workers`, and `vector_length` clauses were added to the `kernels` construct in the C language, fixing another three tests. The remaining issues have been reported to PGI in order to be fixed.

5.3 Comparison of PGI 16.10 and PGI 17.3 Multicore Support

In our runs on the UD Farber machine, we were able to compare results between the 16.10 (community edition) and the 17.3 (latest edition) of the PGI compiler on both Ivy Bridge multicore and NVIDIA K80. Overall the success rate of the 16.10 version was 346/354 between both platforms. Of the seven failures on the 16.10 version targeting the Ivy Bridge multicore, four were failures during testing the reduction clause in the C language. However, in the 17.3 version, all but one of these is resolved. Also, when targeting K80, there are no such failures. There also seem to be issues working with the `firstprivate` clause. With both version, Ivy Bridge failed the test of the `firstprivate` clause in the C language while on K80, both versions failed the Fortran version. Also, both versions exhibited some shortcomings in dealing with `async` clauses on `parallel` regions when targeting K80. The last issue is with the `tile` clause. While the operation seems to be proper in many cases, there seems to be an issue with properly tiling when the tiling arguments fall beyond the bound of the iterations in the nested loops. For these specific platforms, we only see an improvement with the multicore targeting when using the `reduction` clause, bringing the 17.3 version's success rate to 349/354. It is possible, though, that testing in a similar fashion on other platforms would show a greater/other improvements that are not evident here.

5.4 The GNU Compiler's Accuracy to the OpenACC Specifications

We also were able to use the GNU compiler on the Farber system and Titan. While it is far from competitive with the PGI results, GNU also does not, at this point, support the features that were added in the 2.5 version of the OpenACC specifications. Notably among these new features are reference counting and the new ways memory is managed. Instead of using `pcopy` or `copy`, now the functionality of `copy` has been completely removed in favor of treating all `copy` clauses as `pcopy`. This drastically changes the way the tests are interpreted by the compiler. Many of the tests use some form of multiple references in order to test proper data management and thus the GNU compiler is, by supporting the

2.0 version, predestined to fail. On the Farber machine, 38 of the tests failures were memory related runtime errors. While we cannot guarantee that these errors would be fixed with support for 2.5, many most likely would pass. Results for GNU in Table 4 indicate ACC_DEVICE_TYPE is set to host; single-threaded host-fallback execution, in a shared-memory mode. An in-depth evaluation of GCC OpenACC implementation on Cray systems is discussed in[6]. However these discussions are based on an older version of the testsuite.

Table 4. GNU vs. PGI pass rates

Architecture	PGI pass rate	GNU pass rate
K20	175/177	112/177
K80	175/177	113/177
Ivy Bridge	171/177	154/177
Bulldozer	172/177	157/177

6 Discussion

With this testsuite, we have shown both the status of the compilers and their ability to target various architectures. We also had the opportunity to run the suite on Cray compiler. However, due to the compiler's adherence to an outdated version of the OpenACC specifications, and lack of demand from users to use Cray OpenACC compiler we have not summarized our test results on the compiler. Also, since we plan to release the testsuite, anyone interested to validate Cray OpenACC implementations is welcome to use our testsuite to validate Cray's OpenACC implementation.

When using the `firstprivate` clause in the Fortran language using the PGI compiler, due to it's potential for causing errors we recommend starting debugging there. One potential solution to if it will not work is to replace the `firstprivate` clause with a `private` clause and initialize the data in a gang redundant loop. Though this will take it's toll on performance, it could solve incorrect calculations or runtime errors.

Our testsuite has helped validate OpenACC compilers on the Titan supercomputer and the pre-exascale machine Summitdev at Oak Ridge National Laboratory (ORNL). Our tests have already been integrated to the official harness testsuite of Titan.

There are multiple types of users with quite different requirements for a comprehensive validation suite, the accessibility and usability features need to be flexible. End users need an easy way to run all of the tests in the suite and see a useful summary of the results to know how much coverage their software stack and architecture supports. However, when using for QA purposes,

[6] https://cug.org/proceedings/cug2017_proceedings/includes/files/pap174s2-file1.pdf.

an implementer needs to be able to easily run and debug at the single-test level of granularity. These different types of requirements require a robust testsuite infrastructure that is currently not in place but under discussion. This infrastructure needs to be simple so that anybody can contribute new tests or fix bugs by only needing to understand the host language and OpenACC, not the details of the test harness. Only by minimizing the effort for new contributions will the test be widely adopted and expanded by the community.

7 Related Work

Our first paper on this effort [24] covers the specifications through version 1.0 of the OpenACC specifications. A closely related work to this effort is the OpenMP Validation Suite [20] that also validates and verifies the features of OpenMP compiler implementations. In 2003, an OpenMP validation suite was developed [12] to validate OpenMP implementations for OpenMP 2.0. This work was extended [13] to build test cases to validate implementations of OpenMP 2.5 features. This work was further extended [23] to develop a more robust OpenMP validation suite and provided up-to-date test cases covering all the features until OpenMP 3.1.

Other related efforts to building and using a testsuite include Csmith [25], a comprehensive, well-cited work where the authors perform a randomized test-case generator exposing compiler bugs using differential testing. Such an approach is quite effective to detecting compiler bugs but does not quite serve our purpose since it is hard to automatically map a randomly generated failed test to a bug that actually caused it. Thus we could say that our approach is complimentary to that of Csmith's approach.

LLVM has a testing infrastructure [10] that contains regression tests and whole programs. The regression tests are expected to always pass and should be run before every commit. These are a large number of small tests that tests various features of LLVM. The whole programs tests are referred to as the "LLVM test suite" (or "test-suite"). The tests itself are driven by *lit* testing tool, which is part of LLVM.

The parallel testsuite [7] chooses a set of routines to test the strength of a computer system (compiler, run-time system, and hardware) in a variety of disciplines with one of the goals being compare the ability of different Fortran compilers to automatically parallelize various loops. The Parallel Loops test suite is modeled after the Livermore Fortran kernels [11].

8 Conclusion and Future Work

This project develops test cases to validate and verify compilers' implementations of OpenACC features as of Version 2.5. As the features of the programming model have evolved, so has the testsuite. The tests have enabled identification of compiler bugs that have been or are being fixed in subsequent compiler versions, thus improving the quality of the compilers. In addition to testing the platforms and compilers with the testsuite as shown in the results, the variety of compiler environments and hardware platforms have evaluated the tests to verify that they properly conform to OpenACC specification.

We aim to build a comprehensive OpenACC testsuite for conformance of the language features in the OpenACC specification. To that end, we are adding tests to cover corner cases that may otherwise be not possible via simple unit tests. We will also add tests to cover features as they are added to the specification. We will also build interpreters to generate for each test a variety of variations on that test to test fringe cases and feature limitations such as testing each numeric type for each operator in a given parallelized region or testing limitations on optimization variables. To make the testsuite easily usable, we will create forward and backward references for the testsuite with the specification such that each test in the open-source GitHub repository can be related to a definition in the specification and definitions in the specification can be tagged to a test in the repository.[7]

Acknowledgments. We are very grateful to OpenACC and NVIDIA for supporting this project. Special thanks to Mathew Colgrove, Duncan Poole, Christophe Harle, Jeff Larkin, Michael Wolfe, James Beyer, Pat Brooks, Doug Holt, Wael Elwasif, Thomas Swinge, Cesar Philippidis, Randy Allen and Alex Rech.

This material is based upon work supported by the U.S. Department of Energy, Office of science, and this research used resources of the Oak Ridge Leadership Computing Facility at the Oak Ridge National Laboratory, which is supported by the Office of Science of the U.S. Department of Energy under Contract No. DE-AC05-00OR22725.

References

1. CAAR center for accelerated application readiness. https://www.olcf.ornl.gov/caar/
2. INCITE program. http://www.doeleadershipcomputing.org/incite-program/
3. NVIDIA Thrust. https://developer.nvidia.com/thrust. Accessed 03 Feb 2017
4. OpenACC
5. Adams, M.F., Ethier, S., Wichmann, N.: Performance of particle in cell methods on highly concurrent computational architectures. J. Phys. Conf. Ser. **78**(1), 012001 (2007)
6. Aidas, K., Angeli, C., Bak, K.L., et al.: The dalton quantum chemistry program system. Wiley Interdiscip. Rev. Comput. Mol. Sci. **4**(3), 269–284 (2014)
7. Dongarra, J., Furtney, M., Reinhardt, S., Russell, J.: Parallel loops–a test suite for parallelizing compilers: description and example results. Parallel Comput. **17**(10–11), 1247–1255 (1991)
8. Edwards, H.C., Trott, C.R., Sunderland, D.: Kokkos: enabling manycore performance portability through polymorphic memory access patterns. J. Parallel Distrib. Comput. **74**(12), 3202–3216 (2014)
9. Ethier, S., Tang, W.M., Walkup, R., Oliker, L.: Large-scale gyrokinetic particle simulation of microturbulence in magnetically confined fusion plasmas. IBM J. Res. Dev. **52**(1.2), 105–115 (2008)

[7] For more detailed explanation and example, see https://github.com/OpenACCUserGroup/OpenACCV-V/blob/master/README.md.

10. LLVM. Llvm Testing Infrastructure Guide. http://www.llvm.org/pre-releases/4.0.0/rc2/docs/TestingGuide.html#test-suite
11. McMahon, F.H.: The livermore fortran kernels: a computer test of the numerical performance range. Technical report, Lawrence Livermore National Lab, CA, USA (1986)
12. Müller, M., Neytchev, P.: An openMP validation suite. In: Fifth European Workshop on OpenMP, Aachen University, Germany (2003)
13. Müller, M., Niethammer, C., Chapman, B., Wen, Y., Liu, Z.: Validating openMP 2.5 for fortran and C/C. In: Sixth European Workshop on OpenMP, KTH Royal Institute of Technology. Citeseer (2004)
14. Nonaka, A., Almgren, A.S., Bell, J.B., Lijewski, M.J., Malone, C.M., Zingale, M.: MAESTRO: an adaptive low mach number hydrodynamics algorithm for stellar flows. Astrophys. J. Suppl. Ser. **188**(2), 358 (2010)
15. NVIDIA. CUDA SDK Code Samples. http://developer.nvidia.com/cuda-cc-sdk-code-samples. Accessed 03 Feb 2017
16. OpenACC. Deep Copy Attach and Detach. http://www.openacc.org/sites/default/files/TR-16-1.pdf
17. OpenACC. OpenACC, Directives for Accelerators. http://www.openacc.org/
18. OpenCL. OpenCL. https://www.khronos.org/
19. OpenMP. OpenMP 4.5 specification. http://www.openmp.org/wp-content/uploads/openmp-4.5.pdf
20. OpenMP Validation and Verification Suite. OpenMP 3.1 Specification. https://github.com/sunitachandra/omp-validation
21. Taylor, M.A., Edwards, J., Cyr, A.S.: Petascale atmospheric models for the community climate system model: new developments and evaluation of scalable dynamical cores. J. Phys. Conf. Ser. **125**(1), 012023 (2008)
22. Taylor, M.A., Edwards, J., Thomas, S., Nair, R.: A mass and energy conserving spectral element atmospheric dynamical core on the cubed-sphere grid. J. Phys. Conf. Ser. **78**(1), 012074 (2007)
23. Wang, C., Chandrasekaran, S., Chapman, B.: An OpenMP 3.1 validation testsuite. In: Chapman, B.M., Massaioli, F., Müller, M.S., Rorro, M. (eds.) IWOMP 2012. LNCS, vol. 7312, pp. 237–249. Springer, Heidelberg (2012). doi:10.1007/978-3-642-30961-8_18
24. Wang, C., Xu, R., Chandrasekaran, S., Chapman, B., Hernandez, O.: A validation testsuite for OpenACC 1.0. In: 2014 IEEE International Parallel and Distributed Processing Symposium Workshops (IPDPSW), pp. 1407–1416. IEEE (2014)
25. Yang, X., Chen, Y., Eide, E., Regehr, J.: Finding and understanding bugs in C compilers. In: ACM SIGPLAN Notices, vol. 46, pp. 283–294. ACM (2011)

12th Workshop on Virtualization in High-Performance Cloud Computing (VHPC'17)

A Survey of Fast Packet I/O Technologies for Network Function Virtualization

Giuseppe Lettieri(✉), Vincenzo Maffione(✉), and Luigi Rizzo(✉)

Dipartimento di Ingegneria dell'Informazione, Università di Pisa, Pisa, Italy
{giuseppe.lettieri,vincenzo.maffione,luigi.rizzo}@unipi.it

Abstract. Network Function Virtualization (NFV) aims at bringing the benefits of virtualization to network middleboxes (routers, firewalls, Intrusion Detection Systems, ...). In the last few years the NFV use-case, initially hampered by the poor performance of traditional virtualized-I/O and network stacks, has prompted the design of several frameworks, all trying to provide a fast network for VMs and/or containers. These solutions share many common ideas, but also differ in performance, flexibility, portability, amount of specialized hardware required and/or software to be rewritten, attention to energy consumption issues, and so on. In this survey we focus on the NFV data-path, as opposed to the orthogonal control-path. We define a set of desirable features for NFV data-paths and use them to compare a selection of the most promising and/or widely used NFV frameworks. No single solution is optimal for all the features, so our survey may prompt for further research in this area.

1 Introduction

The advent of NFV [1,2] has led to the introduction of several frameworks and tools that can deal with the pressing network I/O requirements of NFV deployments. Some of these frameworks were also introduced independently of NFV, as a solution to overcome the performance limitations of traditional OS and hypervisor networking capabilities. Traditional in-kernel network stacks are known to be unable to bear the high traffic loads that are expected on large server machines with high VM density and high-end 10–100Gbit NICs, severely limiting the maximum packet rate that can be achieved between the different components in the system. In any case, different solutions have been proposed, each one coming with its own degree of flexibility, features, performance limitations, so that there are several aspects that an user should take into consideration when making a choice. As an example, some solutions require hardware NIC drivers to be installed in the VMs, while other do not; some solutions provide a *virtual switch* to connect VMs on the same physical machine, while others explicitly provide a faster "virtual link" abstraction. As a result it is often hard for the users to choose the right option. A comprehensive comparison and classification w.r.t. different practical aspects is needed to let the user choose wisely, according to their needs in terms of performance, flexibility, reusability, NIC support, etc.

J.M. Kunkel et al. (Eds.): ISC High Performance Workshops 2017, LNCS 10524, pp. 579–590, 2017.
https://doi.org/10.1007/978-3-319-67630-2_40

In this paper we conduct a comparative survey of fast network I/O solutions for NFV, describing and comparing the options selected as the most promising and/or in-use at time of writing. Our study is limited to the *data-plane* capabilities, and therefore does not consider issues related to *control-plane*, being these problems completely orthogonal. Other NFV surveys exist, but they either touch only lightly on existing data path solutions ([3,4]) or they focus on other aspects like resource allocation [5] or security [6].

We focus primarily on how VMs running on the same host can be connected between each other and/or with the external network, and how flexible and fast these connection are. For space reasons we leave out other, non VM-based technologies (e.g. *containers*).

The solutions that we analyze are the hardware-based ones (PCI passthrough with SR-IOV) and some software-based ones, i.e. Open vSwitch (enhanced with DPDK), NetVM, netmap and Snabb.

2 Overview of Existing Solutions

Here we provide a short overview of the selected data-path solutions. In the following, the term *host* refers to the physical machine hosting the VMs that make up the NFV chain and it includes the VM hypervisor.

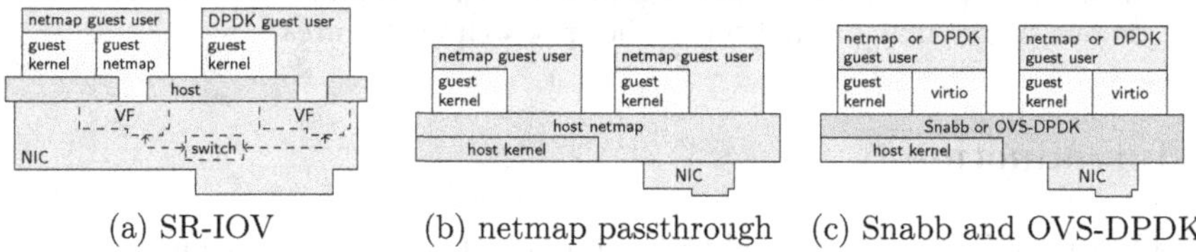

(a) SR-IOV (b) netmap passthrough (c) Snabb and OVS-DPDK

Fig. 1. The data-path solutions surveyed in the paper. Different colors denote different protection domains. (Color figure online)

SR-IOV. PCI-passthrough is a widely used technique [7,8] to passthrough a host PCI device inside a VM (a NIC in this case). On its (emulated) PCI bus, the VM OS sees a PCI device belonging to the *same NIC model*, and uses its specific driver. The IOMMU [9] is used to provide those memory protection and address translation functionalities that are necessary to let the VM access a host device. The main advantage of SN is that the performance is normally the same as bare-metal. However, the host PCI bus can become a bottleneck as it is shared by all the NICs, and the low number of NICs that can be physically attached to a machine clearly limits the per-host VM density. SR-IOV [10,11] is a standard for hardware-based network I/O sharing, that tries to overcome this density limitations. SR-IOV extends NIC capabilities allowing a device to expose to the OS multiple instances of itself, known as *virtual functions* (VFs). The OS sees each VF as a separate PCI NIC (with a separate MAC), which it can passthrough to a VM. A VF is a *lightweight* version of a fully featured NIC, equipped with its own private TX/RX ring descriptors (data transfer capabilities), while all the other parts of the hardware (configuration capabilities) are shared with the other VFs. According to the standard, a SR-IOV-capable NIC can create up to 256 VFs, although the real limit can be lower (e.g. 64), because of the need for private hardware resources and the negative performance impact of sharing internal data-path components. SR-IOV largely removes the VM density bottleneck, since a host can support as many VMs as the total number of VFs available in its NICs, as shown in Fig. 1a. The inter-VM packet switching between two VFs belonging to the same physical NIC happens inside the NIC hardware, by means of an internal Ethernet bridge. The switching flexibility is somewhat limited, as it is usually based on L2 addresses only. If VFs belong to different physical NICs, external switching is necessary.

DPDK-accelerated Open vSwitch (OVS-DPDK). Open vSwitch (OVS) [12] is a distributed multilayer virtual switch with extensive support for programmability. Due to the wide range of supported features, it is commonly used as software bridge to connect together VMs and NICs, where the data-path can be implemented in software (kernel-space or user-space). The most interesting capability of OVS w.r.t. NFV is the possibility to attach VMs to the switch through DPDK-capable ports, which leverages the *vhost-user* hypervisor technology [13,14] to exchange packets with the VM through the VirtIO paravirtualized network device. DPDK-capable OVS ports (including NIC ports) are served by user-space OVS threads and traffic flowing between them is forwarded through the high performance DPDK framework [15], as shown in Fig. 1c. DPDK forwards packets using fast user-space networking techniques, i.e. batch packet processing, preallocated packet buffers, etc.

NetVM. NetVM [16] is a framework specifically designed for NFV, that builds on DPDK [15] to provide high-level abstractions for developing, deploying and managing chains of VNFs. NetVM relies on DPDK for high-speed NIC I/O and augments it with a shared memory mechanism that allows applications running in trusted VMs (or trusted containers in the more recent OpenNetVM [17]) to exchange packets among them and with the NICs without any data copy. The NetVM threads let NICs DMA data into the hugepages-backed shared memory area and then use lockless queues (rings) to move buffer grants (descriptors) across the chains of VMs, while the data itself is not moved. In addition to zero-copy, NetVM focuses on NUMA-awareness (forcing socket locality) and busy-waiting to completely avoid interrupts and other types of notifications (same as DPDK does). Applications must be written in terms of callbacks (similar to Linux netfilter hooks), using a NetVM-specific library. The callbacks instruct NetVM about the packet's fate, e.g., drop, forward to other VM, transmit to NIC.

Netmap. Netmap [18] is a framework for fast user-space I/O that provides an hardware-independent API for raw I/O on physical NICs and other types of software interfaces. Similarly to DPDK, Netmap achieves high performance by means of OS bypass techniques (batch operation, buffer preallocation, memory mapping in the application, etc.). Several extensions have been introduced to support network I/O for VMs and containers: the VALE software switch [19,20] can connect together NICs and VMs (through virtual ports); Netmap pipes implement fast point-to-point links between two processes; Netmap passthrough [21,22] allows any host netmap port to be directly seen by the VM using a standard paravirtualized driver. All the types of netmap port (NIC, virtual port, pipe, passthrough port, ...) can be accessed with the same Netmap API, so that applications can run unmodified everywhere. Some Netmap features specifically target NFV scenarios: pipes supports VM-to-VM virtual links in NFV chains; VALE provides a way to attach many VMs to a physical network; Netmap passthrough is then used to make VALE ports and pipes available inside the VM without the overhead of a *virtual NIC emulation layer.*

Snabb. Snabb [23,24] is a flexible networking toolkit that allows the programmer to build a custom software packet processing network by connecting together reusable functional blocks, known as *Apps.* Apps can be very simple (mux/demux, repeaters, splitters, etc.) or more complex (learning bridge, IPSec, etc.). A packet processing system is modeled as directed graph of Apps, known as the *AppEngine*, which runs in the context of the single-threaded Snabb engine process. Multiple independent engines can be used if needed. See Fig. 1c. Snabb supports NFV in the following way: (i) the *VhostUser* App allows for fast data exchange with VMs, using the same *vhost-user* technology used by OVS-DPDK; and (ii) some Apps (e.g. Intel10G) are available to access NIC hardware, implementing user-space drivers with OS bypass techniques similar to DPDK and Netmap.

Other related work. ClickOS [25] uses Netmap VALE as a fast Xen hypervisor switch, and a specialized passthrough technique to let the VM map VALE ports in its address space, which is analogous to the current Netmap passthrough; for the purposes of this paper, ClickOS is just an application of Netmap. SoftNIC [26] focuses on an hybrid software/hardware DPDK-based approach to augment NIC features to provide flexible packet processing pipelines (similar to Click), where each stage implements a low-level NIC feature (e.g. checksum, TSO, ...); the pipeline performs in software those operations that the hardware can't do. SoftNIC can be used as a virtual switch for NFV, as it uses OS-bypass and passthrough techniques to map the pipeline address space into user-space applications running in the host or in a VM. NetBricks [27] is an NFV architecture that enforces isolation by requiring all functions to be written in a memory safe language (rust); since we are limiting this survey to VM-based solutions, we have to leave it out.

3 Comparing Architectures and Features

We compare the solutions described in Sect. 2 against various aspects that we deem important to meet the NFV I/O requirements. NFV aims at replacing hardware-based network appliances with software-based Virtual Functions to achieve several benefits: reduce cost, remove vendor lock-in, increase flexibility, while still achieving good performance [2]. Criteria (a), (b) and (c) below evaluate some barriers to vendor lock-in removal; criteria (d), (e) and (f) explore aspects related to performance and cost, while criteria (g), (h) and (i) focus on flexibility.

(a) Network backends and portability of VM images. To enhance flexibility, it is desirable that VMs can run unmodified everywhere, independently on the host hardware. It is then important to minimize the amount of software required in the VM image to be *portable*. Both OVS-DPDK, Netmap and Snabb are very portable, as they require only a standard driver to access the virtual interface: *ptnet* [22] for Netmap, *virtio-net* [28,29] for the other two. The network backend for OVS-DPDK and Snabb is a vhost-user port of a software switch, where NICs and other software ports can be attached. The backend of a Netmap ptnet interface can be any host Netmap port, i.e. NIC, pipe, VALE port, monitor, etc. Also NetVM applications are fully portable to any NetVM deployment, as they are written in terms of callbacks and don't see the virtual interface; under the hood, NetVM uses a custom PCI device to access the backend rings. In contrast, SR-IOV is backed by physical NICs (or Virtual Functions) and require the VM to contain a driver for any NIC model that may be passed-through as the image is deployed across the ever-moving virtualization infrastructure.

(b) Dependency on specific NIC models. One of the main concerns of NFV is the possibility to deploy applications anywhere, independently on the specific network hardware of the host where they run. While traditional virtualization technologies are usually able to provide this decoupling, the solutions in Sect. 2 may add some constraint, as they may only support a limited range of NICs. Being a PCI passthrough technique, SR-IOV reuses the standard kernel-space drivers shipped with the OS, which are available for virtually any NIC model on the market. On the contrary, the other solutions are required to provide explicit driver support for each NIC to be used. Performance of traditional kernel drivers, even for high-end NICs, is limited by the legacy OS interfaces, which hinder important optimizations like the use pre-allocated packet buffers and batch I/O (e.g. [18])[1]. As a consequence, NIC drivers need to be rewritten or modified for optimized performance. DPDK-based framework (OVS-DPDK and NetVM) and Snabb rely on user-space drivers rewritten from scratch. DPDK supports 1–40 Gbit NICs from many hardware vendors (Amazon, Broadcom, Cavium, Chelsio, Cesnet, Cisco, Emulex, Intel, Mellanox, Netronome, QLogic, ...) and software devices (virtio-net, Xen, vmxnet3, ...), while Snabb only supports Intel 10Gbit NICs and virtio-net. Netmap only supports Intel 1–40Gbit NICs, Chelsio 10Gbit NICs, and virtio-net, veth and ptnet software devices.

(c) Effort required to support more NICs. While SR-IOV reuses standard drivers, the other network I/O frameworks need specialized drivers. It is therefore important to evaluate the development effort needed to add a support for future (or yet unsupported) NIC models. DPDK-based solutions and Snabb need a

[1] Although also traditional OSes are slowly evolving, e.g. Linux recently introduced support for batch transmission.

whole driver to be rewritten from scratch. Being written in lua, Snabb drivers are quite compact (1–2 Klocs), while DPDK drivers typically require 5–40 Klocs. In contrast, Netmap only needs to apply a relatively small patch (~600 locs) to the standard kernel driver; the patch mainly implements the *bypass* I/O routines. It is worth nothing that both Netmap, Snabb and DPDK are able to work with unmodified kernel drivers, at reduced performance. This is very useful in practice, although not interesting for our study, as we target maximum performance.

(d) Provisioning of VM-to-VM virtual links. NFV setups are often described in terms of chained VNFs, logically connected by *p2p* (point-to-point) links. This contrasts with the use of traditional *virtual switches* where many VMs/containers are attached, together with the NIC(s). Clearly, one ore more p2p links can be implemented with a single virtual switch, but in practice a true p2p mechanism can reach better performance than any virtual switch, because there is no central bottleneck and its task is simpler. Snabb is flexible enough that its Apps (e.g. two VhostUser ones) can be connected in a p2p fashion. NetVM explicitly creates chains using dedicated threads to move packets between a stage to the next one. Netmap provides *pipes* and netmap-accelerated *veth* devices that implement fast p2p links between two VNFs. OVS-DPDK is less flexible as it does not provide p2p links: packets must flow through the OVS instance that can be configured with static OpenFlow [30] rules to forward packets between pairs of ports. This comparison item does not apply to SR-IOV, where inter-VM switching is done by the NIC hardware.

(e) Synchronization and CPU utilization. Many frameworks for high-speed network I/O (DPDK-based solutions and Snabb among our selection) heavily rely on busy-wait polling to maximize throughput and minimize latency. The rationale behind this are (i) the assumption that the system is always under high load; and (ii) the research for best possible performance irrespectively of the CPU utilization and protection of NIC hardware. This is achieved by completely avoiding NIC interrupts and system calls and dedicating CPU cores to NIC queues (physical or VirtIO). However, if the system is not always under high load, or there are mismatches in the processing pipeline, most of the CPU time is wasted on busy waiting. This problem becomes even worse if busy-waiting is also used inside the VM (e.g. DPDK application on the virtio-net interface), in addition to being used in the host. In contrast, Netmap uses NIC interrupts and standard kernel synchronization mechanisms (e.g. `poll()`) to block on empty or full NIC queues. This allows the system to be efficient under low load, at the cost of reduced performance under high load. The performance gap may be small because (i) the cost of system calls and interrupts is usually amortized over very large batch of packets (e.g. 512); and (ii) the per-packet cost due to application processing is often at least an order of magnitude higher than the per-packet I/O cost, so that differences in the per-packet I/O cost are hidden.

(f) Zerocopy capabilities. If the VMs/containers of an NFV chain mutually trust each other, avoid copying data among them saves many CPU cycles. On the other hand, if the VMs are not trusted, the copy is necessary to ensure memory isolation. OVS-DPDK and Snabb use the VirtIO interface to isolate

VMs among each other (packet buffers are allocated by the VMs), and need to copy packet data between VM memory and host memory. Instead, NetVM and Netmap (using pipes) support zerocopy using a shared memory area to store packets, while only small *packet descriptors* are copied across the chain. While NetVM only provides zerocopy, Netmap also allows multiple shared memory areas, so that when two VMs use different areas, a copy is necessary and isolation is guaranteed; this is possible with both VALE ports and pipes.

(g) Threading model. Since the number of host CPUs cores or hyperthreads is limited and many solutions rely on busy-waiting, it is important to evaluate how many threads are needed to properly run an NFV chain. SR-IOV is neutral on this aspect, as it doesn't impose a threading model; DPDK or Netmap are often used on the passed-through interfaces for high speed I/O. Snabb runs as a single-threaded process: the Apps in the AppEngine network are *passive* objects, and the thread continuously scans them all to move the data between input and output ports. The user can run multiple independent AppEngines, but data exchange between them is not supported. OVS-DPDK requires a pool of threads that busy-wait on the switch ports (*vhost-user* or NIC); the number of threads and their mapping to ports is configurable; moreover, at least one thread runs in the VM to process packets, typically busy-waiting on the virtio-net interfaces. Netmap passthrough currently requires a host thread for each RX or TX queue of the passed-through ports; however, threads can sleep when there is no work to do. Similarly to OVS-DPDK, Netmap is often used in the VM to access the passed-through port. In NetVM each NF needs a dedicated host TX thread to move packet descriptors towards the next element in the chain; an RX thread is used for each NIC queue to poll for new packets and move them to a VM; finally, a thread is used to run the NF processing.

(h) Support for virtual switch programmability. In addition to performance and portability, NFV also greatly benefits from flexible programmability of the inter-VMs (or container) switch [31]. This aspect is important because it allows for easy reconfiguration of the NFV chains and fine-grained and/or dynamic control of the forwarding rules. With SR-IOV the switching flexibility is quite limited, as it happens in the NIC hardware only using L2 MAC addresses. Snabb allows for custom switching logic by means of composition, as VhostUser Apps can be connected through an arbitrary network of Apps. In the Netmap VALE switch the user can override the forwarding function (L2 learning by default), but this requires working at OS-kernel level. NetVM allows for more sophisticated switching based on SDN controller and load balancing on queues statistics. OVS-DPDK uses a standard (and more reusable) approach since the switch can be programmed with OpenFlow rules.

(i) Support for live migration. The ability to migrate applications from one physical host to another, while minimizing downtime, is very important for load balancing and hardware maintenance [32]. VMs enable migration by encapsulating into the guest memory almost all the state that has to be moved. Moreover, if the guest only uses virtual devices, the migration can also be kept transparent (i.e., no support is needed on the guest part) and flexible (moving to hosts with different hardware). Passthrough solutions are generally at odds with migration, as they create tight dependencies with the host and keep state out of the VM memory. Live migration of PCI passthrough solutions like SR-IOV is typically not transparent (the guest sees the NIC temporarily disappearing), and limited to hosts with similar hardware. Currently, complete solutions are only available for some combinations of hypervisor and guest [33]. Netmap passthrough is potentially more flexible (VM only accesses the hardware through Netmap API), but it would require migration of state stored in the Netmap module in the host; this is not currently supported and may be hard to implement. On the contrary, both Snabb and OVS-DPDK fully support transparent live migration, thanks to the isolation provided by VirtIO.

Table 1. Summary of the qualitative analysis. Letters refers to the qualitative criteria of Sect. 3.

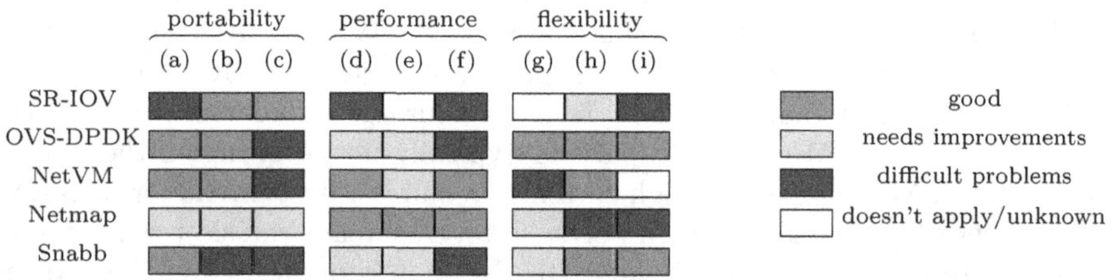

Table 1 summarizes the results of our qualitative analysis, with colors denoting how the solution fares w.r.t. the corresponding criteria. White boxes denote that the corresponding criteria does not apply or cannot be evaluated, for lack of data. It is clear from the Table that no perfect solution emerges from the comparison.

4 Experimental Evaluation

We now complete the qualitative analysis presented in Sect. 3 with a performance comparison addressing throughput and CPU utilization. Even if an exhaustive performance analysis could not be included in this paper for space reasons, we are able to numerically show the impact of the different architectures adopted. We did not evaluate NetVM as its source code is not publicly available. Figure 2 reports the measured throughput (on the left chart) and CPU utilization (on the right chart) for our experiments on the various configurations.

vm2vm experiment. Two VMs have a network interface each, with the two interfaces directly connected to each other by means of a non-zero-copy p2p link (VMs don't trust each other). A VM sends 64-bytes packets at maximum speed, while the other VM measures the received packet rate. The Netmap `pkt-gen` application is used as a sender/receiver, as it can run in all our deployments and it is not a bottleneck. The purpose of this experiment is to evaluate how

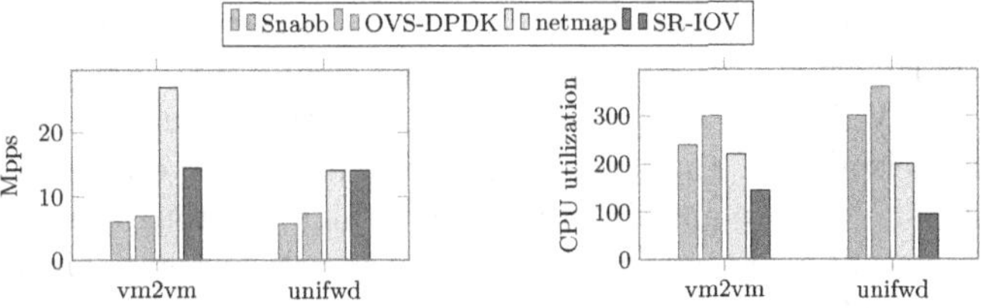

Fig. 2. On the left the measured packet-rate throughput for vm-to-vm and forwarding experiments with 64 bytes packets, across the various NFV solutions. On the right the corresponding total CPU utilization on the host machine.

memory-isolated p2p links provided by the various solutions behave under the most stressful conditions, i.e. high packet-rate with short packets. For SR-IOV two VFs are passed-through to the guests. For Netmap, two passed-through VALE ports are used to ensure memory isolation. For OVS-DPDK and Snabb two vhost-user ports are used, connected to each other by static OpenFlow rules (OVS-DPDK) or AppEngine configuration (Snabb).

unifwd experiment. A VM with two network interfaces, each one connected to a different host 10G NIC. The VM runs the Netmap `bridge` program to zero-copy forward the packets between two interfaces (packets content is never accessed). An external machine transmits 64-bytes packets at line rate (14.88 Mpps) to one of the NICs and measures the packet-rate received from the other NIC. This experiment assesses how the different solution allow the VMs to access the host physical network under the most stressful conditions. For Netmap two NICs are passed-through to the guest, while two VFs from different NICs are passed-through for SR-IOV. For OVS-DPDK and Snabb two switch instances are used to connect each VM vhost-user port to a different host NIC, and each switch is served by a CPU.

Testbed description. Our test machine has an Intel Core i7-4790K CPU at 4.00 GHz (4 cores, 2 hyperthreads per-core), 16 GB DD3 RAM at 1.867 GHz, and it runs Linux 4.10.8. We use a recent version of all the involved software: QEMU (git master, April 2017), Snabb (git master, April 2017), OVS 2.7.0, DPDK 16.11, Netmap (git master, April 2017). The NICs are configured with an interrupt moderation interval or 40 μs, which is reasonable for throughput experiments, and we let `pkt-gen` and `bridge` work with interrupts rather than busy-wait. The machine is configured to maximize the reproducibility of results, by disabling frequency scaling, sleeping C-states, Turbo mode, KVM halt polling [34] and pinning processes to different cores. We did not disable hyperthreading as we did not observe instabilities related to that.

Throughput analysis. The most evident fact in the throughput chart in Fig. 2 is that Snabb/OVS-DPDK achieve a lower performance than the other three passthrough solutions. This was expected, as Snabb/OVS-DPDK use VirtIO, which introduces an additional level on indirection (very useful to support live migration) which is not present in the other solutions: each packet sent or received by the VM needs to go through the VirtIO queues before getting to the network backend (i.e. the software switch), and these queues are a bottleneck. In contrast, Netmap and SR-IOV achieve higher throughput as they allow for direct (or loosely mediated) access to the network backend. Their bottleneck for *unifwd* is the 10G line rate, since the network backend is a host 10G NIC. For *vm2vm*, SR-IOV is still limited by the internal switch, while Netmap can reach a peak of 27 Mpps as it is only limited by the memory bandwidth. Finally, while Snabb/OVS-DPDK are similar solutions, OVS-DPDK performance is slightly higher for both experiments; we believe this happens because OVS-DPDK software is more mature, and Snabb performance depends on the ability of the Lua JIT compiler in this specific AppEngines.

CPU utilization analysis. The most evident fact in the CPU utilization chart in Fig. 2 is that SR-IOV achieves lower CPU utilizations than the other solutions, as the packet transport is performed by the NIC hardware for both experiments. Within *unifwd* only one CPU is necessary (for the VM to run `bridge`) while Netmap needs an additional CPU to perform the packet transport in software and achieve the same throughput; Snabb/OVS-DPDK need two more CPUs since they busy-wait on two switches, and they offer lower throughput as they spend more CPU cycles per packet. A similar analysis also holds for *vm2vm*. SR-IOV only needs to spend ~1.5 CPUs to run the `pkt-gen` transmitter and receiver; Netmap needs 60% more CPU to move packets across the link but it is able to achieve higher throughput because CPU can do copies faster than NIC can transmit/receive packets; Snabb/OVS-DPDK need even more CPU cycles because of the additional indirection layer. Differences between Snabb and OVS-DPDK are also due to different interrupts regimes, that disappear if `bridge/pkt-gen` work in busy-wait mode (not shown here).

5 Conclusions

In this paper we have carried out a qualitative and quantitative analysis of different NFV data-path solutions. There is no clear winner: VirtIO eases portability and live migration at the cost of performance, while passthrough makes migration harder but offers higher rates. PCI-passthrough technologies use less CPU but they are less portable and their throughput is limited by the NIC rate and PCI bus. Netmap offers good throughput with lower CPU utilization than the other software-based solutions, but it needs to improve on several qualitative criteria. We plan to extend our analysis to upcoming NFV data-paths and deeper performance comparisons involving latency, scaling and more.

Acknowledgements. This paper has received funding from the European Union's Horizon 2020 research and innovation programme 2014-2018 under grant agreement No. 644866. This paper reflects only the authors' views and the European Commission is not responsible for any use that may be made of the information it contains.

References

1. Network Functions Virtualisation: Architectural Framework (2012). http://www.etsi.org/deliver/etsi_gs/nfv/001_099/002/01.01.01_60/gs_nfv002v010101p.pdf
2. Network function virtualisation introductory white paper (2012). https://portal.etsi.org/nfv/nfv_white_paper.pdf
3. Jain, R., Paul, S.: Network virtualization and software defined networking for cloud computing: a survey. IEEE Commun. Mag. **51**(11), 24–31 (2013)
4. Li, Y., Chen, M.: Software-defined network function virtualization: a survey. IEEE Access **3**, 2542–2553 (2015)
5. Herrera, J.G., Botero, J.F.: Resource allocation in NFV: a comprehensive survey. IEEE Trans. Netw. Serv. Manag. **13**(3), 518–532 (2016)
6. Yang, W., Fung, C.: A survey on security in network functions virtualization. In: 2016 IEEE NetSoft Conference and Workshops (NetSoft), pp. 15–19. IEEE (2016)
7. Jones, T.: Linux virtualization and PCI passthrough (2009). http://www.ibm.com/developerworks/linux/library/l-pci-passthrough/
8. VFIO linux kernel documentation. https://www.kernel.org/doc/Documentation/vfio.txt
9. Ben-Yehuda, M., et al.: Utilizing IOMMUs for virtualization in Linux and Xen. In: Proceedings of the Linux Symposium (2006)
10. Dong, Y., Yang, X., Li, X., Li, J., Tian, K., Guan, H.: High performance network virtualization with SR-IOV. In: HPCA - 16 2010 The Sixteenth International Symposium on High-Performance Computer Architecture, pp. 1–10, January 2010
11. Intel, PCI-SIG SR-IOV primer (2011). http://www.intel.com/content/dam/doc/application-note/pci-sig-sr-iov-primer-sr-iov-technology-paper.pdf
12. Pfaff, B., Pettit, J., Koponen, T., Jackson, E., Zhou, A., Rajahalme, J., Gross, J., Wang, A., Stringer, J., Shelar, P., Amidon, K., Casado, M.: The design and implementation of Open vSwitch. In: 12th USENIX Symposium on Networked Systems Design and Implementation (NSDI 2015), Oakland, CA, pp. 117–130. USENIX Association (2015)
13. QEMU documentation, vhost-user protocol. http://git.qemu.org/?p=qemu.git;a=blob_plain;f=docs/specs/vhost-user.txt;hb=HEAD
14. OVS documentation, DPDK vhost-user ports. http://docs.openvswitch.org/en/latest/topics/dpdk/vhost-user/
15. Data plane development kit. http://www.dpdk.org
16. Hwang, J., Ramakrishnan, K.K., Wood, T.: NetVM: high performance and flexible networking using virtualization on commodity platforms. In: 11th USENIX Symposium on Networked Systems Design and Implementation (NSDI 2014), pp. 445–458 (2014)
17. Zhang, W., Liu, G., Zhang, W., Shah, N., Lopreiato, P., Todeschi, G., Ramakrishnan, K., Wood, T.: OpenNetVM: a platform for high performance network service chains. In: Proceedings of the 2016 Workshop on Hot Topics in Middleboxes and Network Function Virtualization, HotMIddlebox 2016, pp. 26–31. ACM, New York (2016)
18. Rizzo, L.: netmap: a novel framework for fast packet I/O. In: USENIX ATC 2012. USENIX Association, Boston (2012)
19. Rizzo, L., Lettieri, G.: VALE, a switched ethernet for virtual machines. In: ACM CoNEXT (2012)
20. Honda, M., Huici, F., Lettieri, G., Rizzo, L.: mSwitch: a highly-scalable, modular software switch. In: Proceedings of the 1st ACM SIGCOMM Symposium on Software Defined Networking Research. ACM (2015)

21. Garzarella, S., Lettieri, G., Rizzo, L.: Virtual device passthrough for high speed VM networking. In: Proceedings of ACM/IEEE ANCS 2015, pp. 99–110 (2015)
22. Maffione, V., Rizzo, L., Lettieri, G.: Flexible virtual machine networking using netmap passthrough. In: IEEE LANMAN 2016 (2016)
23. Paolino, M., Nikolaev, N., Fanguede, J., Raho, D.: Snabbswitch user space virtual switch benchmark and performance optimization for NFV. In: 2015 IEEE Conference on Network Function Virtualization and Software Defined Network (NFV-SDN), pp. 86–92, November 2015
24. The Snabb reference manual. http://snabbco.github.io/
25. Martins, J., Ahmed, M., Raiciu, C., Olteanu, V., Honda, M., Bifulco, R., Huici, F.: ClickOS and the art of network function virtualization. In: Proceedings of the 11th USENIX Conference on Networked Systems Design and Implementation, NSDI 2014, Berkeley, CA, USA, pp. 459–473. USENIX Association (2014)
26. Han, S., Jang, K., Panda, A., Palkar, S., Han, D., Ratnasamy, S.: SoftNIC: a software NIC to augment hardware, Technical report UCB/EECS-2015-155, EECS Department, University of California, Berkeley, May 2015
27. Panda, A., Han, S., Jang, K., Walls, M., Ratnasamy, S., Shenker, S.: Netbricks: taking the V out of NFV. In: 12th USENIX Symposium on Operating Systems Design and Implementation (OSDI 2016), GA, pp. 203–216. USENIX Association (2016)
28. Russell, R.: Virtio: towards a de-facto standard for virtual I/O devices. ACM SIGOPS Operating Syst. Rev. **42**(5), 95–103 (2008)
29. Russel, R., Tsirkin, M., Huck, C.: The VirtIO specification. http://docs.oasis-open.org/virtio/virtio/v1.0/virtio-v1.0.html
30. McKeown, N., Anderson, T., Balakrishnan, H., Parulkar, G., Peterson, L., Rexford, J., Shenker, S., Turner, J.: OpenFlow: enabling innovation in campus networks. SIGCOMM Comput. Commun. Rev. **38**, 69–74 (2008)
31. Kreutz, D., Ramos, F.M.V., Verssimo, P.E., Rothenberg, C.E., Azodolmolky, S., Uhlig, S.: Software-defined networking: a comprehensive survey. Proc. IEEE **103**, 14–76 (2015)
32. Clark, C., Fraser, K., Hand, S., Hansen, J.G., Jul, E., Limpach, C., Pratt, I., Warfield, A.: Live migration of virtual machines. In: Proceedings of the 2nd Conference on Symposium on Networked Systems Design & Implementation, NSDI 2005, vol. 2, Berkeley, CA, USA, pp. 273–286. USENIX Association (2005)
33. Live migrate guests w/PCI pass-through devices. https://www.fujitsu.com/jp/documents/products/software/os/linux/catalog/LinuxConJapan2015-Izumi.pdf
34. KVM halt-poll optimization. https://lkml.org/lkml/2015/2/6/319

Machine Learning Using Virtualized GPUs in Cloud Environments

Uday Kurkure(✉), Hari Sivaraman, and Lan Vu

VMware, Palo Alto, CA 94304, USA
{ukurkure,hsivaraman,lanv}@vmware.com

Abstract. Using graphic processing units (GPU) to accelerate machine learning applications has become a focus of high performance computing (HPC) in recent years. In cloud environments, many different cloud-based GPU solutions have been introduced to seamlessly and securely use GPU resources without sacrificing their performance benefits. Among them are two main approaches: using direct pass-through technologies available on hypervisors and using virtual GPU technologies introduced by GPU vendors. In this paper, we present a performance study of these two GPU virtualization solutions for machine learning in the cloud. We evaluate the advantages and disadvantages of each solution and introduce new findings of their performance impact on machine learning applications in different real-world use-case scenarios. We also examine the benefits of virtual GPUs for machine learning alone and for machine learning applications running together with other GPU-based applications like 3D-graphics on the same server with multiple GPUs to better leverage computing resources. Based on our experimental results benchmarking machine learning applications developed with TensorFlow, we discuss the scaling from one to multiple GPUs and compare the performance between two virtual GPU solutions. Finally, we show that mixing machine learning and other GPU-based workloads can help to reduce combined execution time as compared to running these workloads sequentially.

Keywords: Machine learning · Virtualization · GPU · High performance computing · Cloud computing · DirectPath I/O · GRID vGPU

1 Introduction

Machine Learning (ML) has recently made significant progress in research and development and has become a growing workload in the cloud [1, 2]. The emergence of Deep Learning and the computing power enhancement of accelerators like GPU, TPU [3], and FPGA have enabled adoption of machine learning applications in a broader and deeper aspect of our lives in many areas like health science, finance, data center monitoring and intelligent systems [4]. For virtualized cloud environments, either direct pass-through (e.g. DirectPath I/O for VMware vSphere [5]) and virtual GPU technologies (e.g. Nvidia GRID vGPU and AMD MxGPU technologies [6, 7]) can be applied to deploy a machine learning workload that uses these accelerators. While the pass-through solution is widely adopted in HPC, virtual GPUs have not yet

J.M. Kunkel et al. (Eds.): ISC High Performance Workshops 2017, LNCS 10524, pp. 591–604, 2017.
https://doi.org/10.1007/978-3-319-67630-2_41

been fully investigated and applied because these techniques have only recently been introduced. In our study, we provide better understanding of performance characteristics of GPU-based workloads, especially machine learning ones, in the cloud. To the best of our knowledge, it is the first study that explores the general-purpose computing capability of the GRID vGPU solution [6] which has potential to give better consolidation for GPU-based workloads compared to the traditional pass-through I/O solution. In this paper, we present our new findings using these virtual GPU solutions for machine learning on VMware vSphere; currently the most widely used hypervisor in private cloud environments [8]. The main contributions of our research include:

- Providing a performance study of different virtual GPU solutions for machine learning workloads on VMware vSphere. We analyze the performance impact of virtual GPU from multiple aspects: scalability, overhead, and performance comparisons. We show in our study that this overhead, one of the biggest concerns in virtualization adoption, is very low for GPU-based workloads like machine learning ones.
- Analyzing the benefits and performance of GRID vGPU, the technology which is used for GPGPU applications including machine learning. We illustrate that the performance of machine learning workloads running on vSphere using either VMware DirectPath I/O or vGPU is comparable to the performance of these workloads running natively on bare metal servers.
- Presenting the analysis of mixing different types of GPU-based workloads, including machine learning and 3D-graphics workloads on the same virtualized server. We show that mixing workloads can improve the resource utilization and total execution time of all workloads while introducing minimal performance overhead when choosing the right virtual GPU profile for the workloads.

2 GPU Virtualization for Machine Learning in the Cloud

2.1 Machine Learning

Machine learning is an area of study aimed at building intelligent systems using knowledge automatically learned from data. Many machine learning methods have been introduced like Neural Networks (e.g., ANN, FNN, CNN, RNN), Support Vector Machines, Genetic Algorithms, Hidden Markov Models, etc., and are applied in artificial intelligence (AI) applications as well as data analysis applications [9]. Deep Learning is a subcategory of machine learning and has been increasingly used because it improves prediction accuracy. Some application areas of machine learning include facial recognition, medical diagnosis in MRIs, robotics, automobile safety, and text and speech recognition [4]. For cloud systems, it can be used for hardware failure prediction or root cause analysis. In our study, we choose well-known machine learning applications which are typical workloads on the cloud. These include handwriting recognition, object recognition and language modeling. These applications are implemented with TensorFlow [13–15, 17, 18], a machine learning framework developed by Google. The use of machine learning in intelligent applications usually includes two main stages: building models using ML algorithms, which is known as training stage, and then applying the models for intelligent tasks like recognition, prediction or classification, which is known as the inference stage.

Most machine learning methods are very computationally intensive. The training time for building prediction models can take hours, days or even weeks for large datasets and fast inference time is a critical requirement in many real-world applications. Hence, applying HPC techniques to accelerate the process of machine learning has become an essential need. Among available HPC solutions, machine learning acceleration using GPUs is currently the most widely adopted because of the massively parallel computing capabilities of GPU devices. We can use CUDA and its cuDNN library for developing ML applications for Nvidia's GPUs or OpenCL for applications running on AMD's GPUs.

2.2 GPU Virtualization for Machine Learning

For cloud environments, server virtualization with hypervisors (e.g., vSphere, KVM, Hyper-V, Xen) is used as the security and resource management layer and virtual machines (VM) are used to isolate the workloads among different applications and users. Currently, 80% of workloads running on x86 architecture have been virtualized [8]. Even with the use of container technologies, a hypervisor with VMs can be still needed for security requirements of the cloud and the overhead of Docker containers running inside VMs is small in many use cases [10]. For hypervisors like VMware ESXi, we can either use direct pass-through or virtual GPU technologies to assign GPUs to VMs on which machine learning workloads are run. We chose VMware DirectPath I/O and Nvidia GRID vGPU for our performance study of machine learning applications on VMware vSphere.

VMware DirectPath I/O. This technology gives a guest operating system (OS) on a VM direct access to the physical PCI or PCIe hardware devices of the server on which the vSphere hypervisor runs. Each VM can be assigned one or more physical PCI devices, including GPUs [5]. Because the guest OS bypasses the virtualization layer to access the PCI devices, the overhead of using this pass-through technology is low (i.e., less than 5% overhead in most use cases [11]). For GPU-based general purpose applications like machine learning, also known as GPGPU, we can add GPUs to the VMs using DirectPath I/O and install the generic GPU driver on the guest OS. In addition to the benefits of low overhead, DirectPath I/O supports a large set of GPU devices including those from AMD and Nvidia, and this gives us a wide choice of devices in a virtualized environment. Figure 1-a depicts the use of GPU with pass-through (i.e., DirectPath I/O for vSphere).

Nvidia GRID vGPU. This solution works via a virtualization management layer installed in the hypervisor and a custom GPU driver in the guest OS. Nvidia GRID creates virtual GPUs, known as vGPUs, and allows multiple vGPUs sharing a single physical GPU by using time slicing execution model [6, 7]. The memory of physical GPU is divided into equal chunks whose size is specified by vGPU profiles. The type of vGPU profile used by a VM will decide the maximum number of vGPUs per single physical GPU. Figure 1-b illustrates the Nvidia GRID GPU virtualization solution.

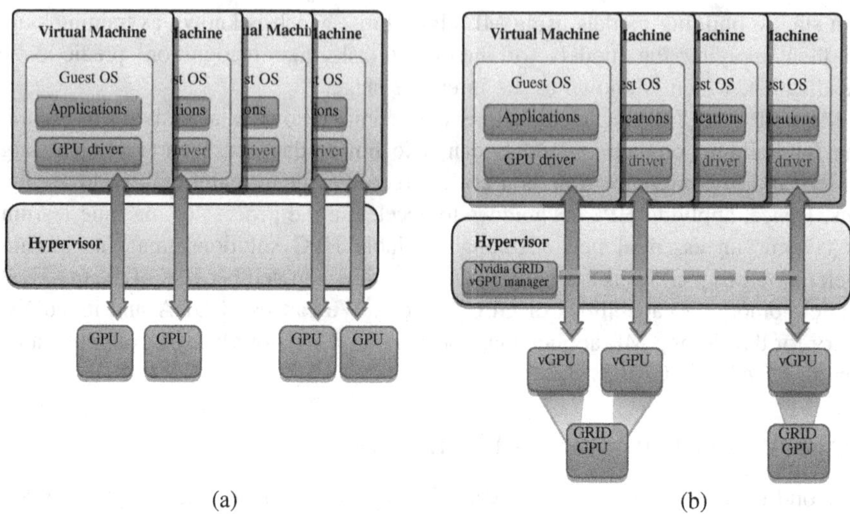

Fig. 1. GPUs in VMs using (a) VMware DirectPath I/O and (b) vGPUs in VMs using Nvidia vGRID.

This technology is currently enabled on following the GPU cards: K1, K2, M60, M6, and M10 [6]. While sharing the GPU is currently enabled for 3D graphics and H.264 encode/decode capabilities of GRID vGPUs, this feature is not yet supported for GPGPU applications. Hence, using vGPU for ML applications requires using the highest vGPU profile which maps one vGPU to one physical GPU. This use case makes the vGPU behave similarly to pass-through mode with DirectPath I/O. However, there are still benefits to using GRID as compared to pass-through including, (1) the capability to flexibly mix and switch among machine learning, 3D graphics and video encoding/decoding workloads to make efficient use of the hardware resources, and (2) reducing the time and the complexity of administering and maintaining the GPUs. For AMD GPUs, the MxGPU technology is the virtualization solution for sharing GPU and GPGPU devices [7] which will be explored in our future work.

Both VMware DirectPath I/O and Nvidia GRID vGPU have their own advantages and disadvantages, which makes each of them suitable for a subset of use cases for machine learning jobs. While DirectPath I/O is widely used for GPGPU applications on vSphere, the use of Nvidia GRID vGPU for machine learning is currently not widespread because of the relatively recent introduction of this technology. In our research, we explore the benefits of the two GPU virtualization solutions to provide an understanding of both approaches and to give recommendations to best leverage both technologies. We also present performance studies that demonstrate the benefits of using GPUs in a virtualized environment and analyze the pros and cons of these two GPU virtualization approaches in Sect. 3.

3 Performance and Scalability of Virtualized GPU for Machine Learning

3.1 Machine Learning with Virtualized GPUs

Performance is one of the biggest concerns that keep HPC users from choosing virtualization as the solution for deploying HPC applications despite its benefits such as reduced administration costs, resource utilization efficiency, energy saving, security, etc. However, with the constant evolution of virtualization technologies, the performance gaps between bare metal and virtualization have almost disappeared and in some real use cases, applications running virtualized can give better performance than running on bare metal because of the intelligent and highly optimized resource utilization of hypervisors. For example, a prior study [12] shows support vector machine applications running on a virtualized cluster of 10 servers having a better execution time than running on bare metal.

Virtual GPU vs. physical GPU. To understand the performance impact of machine learning with GPUs using virtualization, we used a complex language modeling application—predicting next words given a history of previous words using a recurrent neural network (RNN) with 1500 Long Short Term Memory (LSTM) units per layer, on the Penn Treebank dataset (PTB) [13, 14]. We tested three cases: (1) a native physical GPU installed on bare metal, (2) a DirectPath I/O GPU inside a VM on vSphere 6, (3) a GRID vGPU (i.e., an M60-8Q vGPU profile with 8 GB memory) inside a VM on vSphere 6, and (4) a VM with 12 virtual CPUs (vCPUs), 60 GB RAM, and 96 GB SSD storage. The benchmark was implemented using Tensorflow [15]. Tensorflow was also used for the implementation of the other ML benchmarks in our experiments. We used CUDA 7.5, cuDNN 5.1, and CentOS 7.2 for both native and guest OSs. These test cases were run on a Dell PowerEdge R730 server with dual 12-core Intel Xeon CPU E5-2680 v3, 2.50 GHz sockets (24 physical core, 48 logical with hyperthreading enabled), 768 GB memory, and an SSD (1.5 TB). This server also has two Nvidia Tesla M60 cards (each has two GPUs) for a total of 4 GPUs where each has 2048 CUDA cores, 8 GB memory, 36 x H.264 video 1080p30 streams, and can support 1-32 GRID vGPUs whose memory profiles range from 512 MB to 8 GB. This experimental setup was used for all tests presented in this section.

The results in Fig. 2 show the relative execution times of DirectPath I/O and GRID vGPU compared to native GPU. Virtualization introduces a 4% overhead—the performance of DirectPath I/O and GRID vGPU are similar. These results are consistent with prior studies of virtual GPU performance with pass-through where overheads in most cases are less than 5% [11, 16].

GPU vs. CPU in a virtualization environment. One important benefit of using GPU is the shortening of the long training times of machine learning tasks, which has boosted the fruitful results of AI research and developments in recent years. In many cases, it helps to reduce execution times from weeks/days to hours/minutes. We illustrate this benefit in Fig. 3, which shows the training time with and without vGPU for two applications: RNN with PTB described earlier and CNN with MNIST, a handwriting recognizer that uses a convolution neural network (CNN) on the MNIST dataset [17].

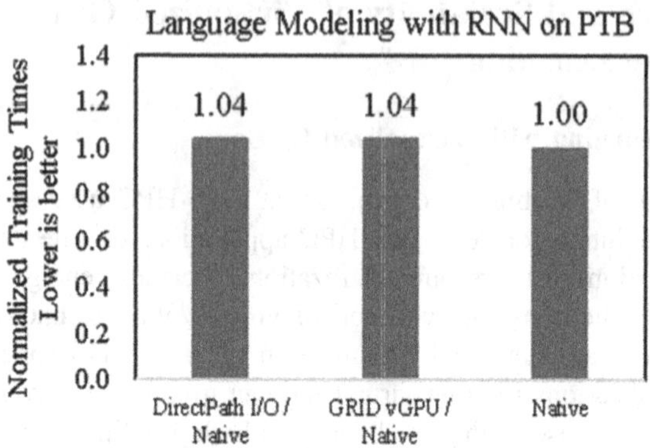

Fig. 2. DirectPath I/O and Nvidia GRID vs. native GPU.

From the results, we see that the training time for RNN on PTB with CPU was 7.9X times higher than with vGPU training time (Fig. 3-a) The training time for CNN on MNIST with CPU was 10.X times higher than with the vGPU training time (Fig. 3-b). The VM used in this test has 1 vGPU, 12 vCPUs, 60 GB memory, 96 GB of SSD storage and the test setup is similar to that of the above experiment.

3.2 Comparison of DirectPath I/O and GRID VGPU

We evaluate the performance, scalability and other benefits of DirectPath I/O and GRID vGPU whose features have been presented in Sect. 2. We also provide some recommendations of the best use cases for each virtual GPU solutions.

Performance. To compare the performance of DirectPath I/O and GRID vGPU, we benchmarked them with RNN on PTB, and CNN on MNIST and CIFAR-10. CIFAR-10 is an object classification application that categorizes RGB images of 32 × 32 pixels into 10 categories: airplane, automobile, bird, cat, deer, dog, frog, horse, ship, and truck [18]. MNIST is a handwriting recognition application. Both

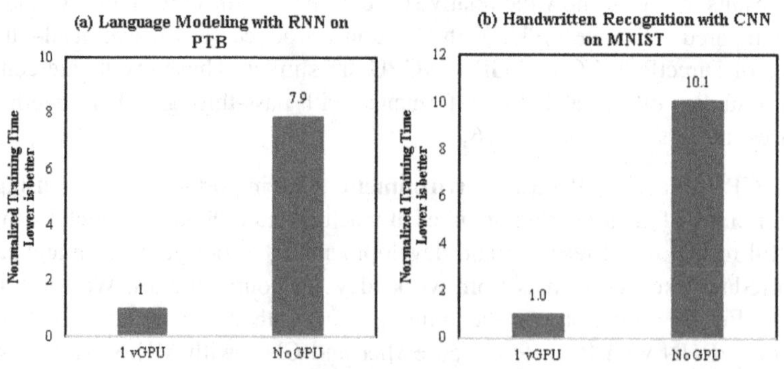

Fig. 3. Normalized training time of PTB, MNIST with and without vGPU.

CIFAR-10 and MNIST use a convolutional neural network. The language model used to predict words based on history used Recurrent Neural Network. The dataset used is The Penn Tree Bank (PTB).

The results in Fig. 4 show the comparative performance of the two virtualization solutions in which DirectPath I/O gives slightly better performance than GRID vGPU. This improvement is due to the pass-through mechanism of DirectPath I/O adding minimal overhead to GPU-based workloads running inside a VM. In Fig. 4-a, DirectPath I/O is about 5% faster than GRID vGPU for MNIST and they have the same performance with PTB. For CIFAR-10, DirectPath I/O can process about 13% more images/second than GRID vGPU. We use images per second for CIFAR-10 because it is a frequently used metric for this dataset. The VM in this experiment has 12 vCPU, 60 GB VRAM and one GPU (either DirectPath I/O or GRID vGPU).

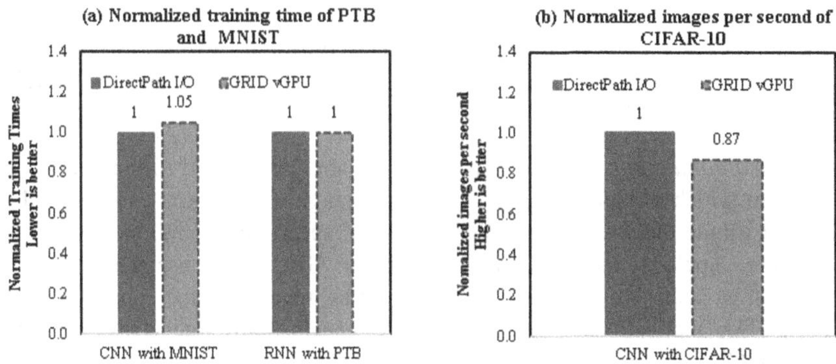

Fig. 4. Performance comparison of DirectPath I/O and GRID vGPU.

Scalability. We look at two types of scalability: user and workload.

User scalability. In a cloud environment, multiple users can share physical servers, which helps to better utilize resources and save cost. Our test server with 4 GPUs can allow up to 4 users needing a gpu. Alternatively, a single user can have four VMs with a vGPU. The number of virtual machines run per machine in a cloud environment is typically high to increase utilization and lower costs [19]. Machine learning workloads are typically much more resource intensive and using our four-GPU test systems for up to only four users reflects this.

Figure 5 presents the scalability of users on CIFAR-10 from 1 to 4 where each uses a VM with one GPU, and we normalize images per second to the of DirectPath I/O - 1 VM case (Fig. 5-a). Similar to the previous comparison, DirectPath I/O and GRID vGPU show comparable performance as the number of VMs with GPUs scale. Specifically, the performance difference between them is 6%–10% for images/sec and 0%–1.5% for CPU utilization. This difference is not significant when weighed against the benefits that vGPU brings. Because of its flexibility and elasticity, it is a good option for ML workloads. The results also show that the two solutions scale linearly

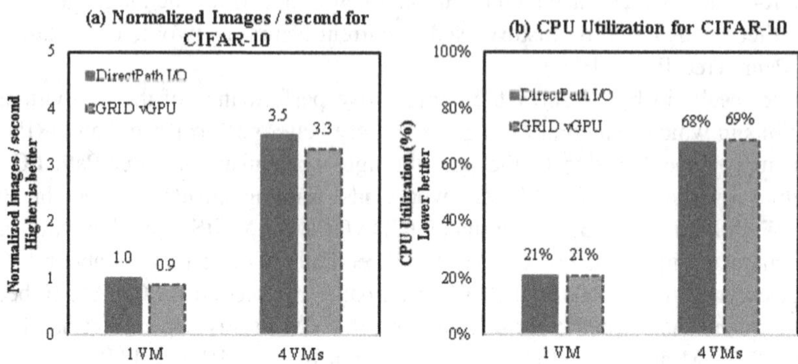

Fig. 5. Scaling the number of VMs with vGPU on CIFAR-10.

with the number of VMs both in terms of execution time and CPU resource utilization. The VMs used in this experiment have 12 vCPUs, 16 GB memory, and 1 GPU (either DirectPath I/O or GRID vGPU).

Workload scalability. For machine learning applications that need to build very large models or in which the datasets cannot fit into a single GPU, users can use multiple GPUs to distribute the workloads among them and speed up the training task further. On vSphere, applications that require multiple GPUs can use DirectPath I/O pass-through to configure VMs with as many GPUs required. This capability is limited for CUDA applications using GRID vGPU because only one vGPU per VM is allowed for CUDA computations. We demonstrate the efficiency of using multiple GPUs on vSphere by benchmarking the CIFAR-10 workload and using the metric of images per second (images/sec) to compare the performance of CIFAR-10 on a VM with different number of GPUs scaling from 1 to 4 GPUs. From the results in Fig. 6, we found that the images processed per second improves almost linearly with the number of GPUs on the host (Fig. 6-a). At the same time, their CPU utilization also increases linearly (Fig. 6-b). This result shows that machine learning workloads scale well on the vSphere platform. In the case of ML applications that require more GPUs than the physical server can support, we can use the distributed computing model with multiple distributed processes using GPUs running on a cluster of physical servers. This will be explored in our future work. With this approach, both DirectPath I/O and GRID vGPU can be used to enhance scalability with very large number of GPUs.

How to choose between DirectPath I/O and GRID vGPU.
For DirectPath I/O. From the above results, we can see that DirectPath I/O and GRID vGPU have comparable performance and low overhead compared to the performance of native GPU, which makes both good choices for machine learning applications in virtualized cloud environments. For applications that require low short training times and use multiple GPUs to speed up ML tasks, DirectPath I/O is a suitable option because this solution supports multiple GPUs per VM. In addition, DirectPath I/O

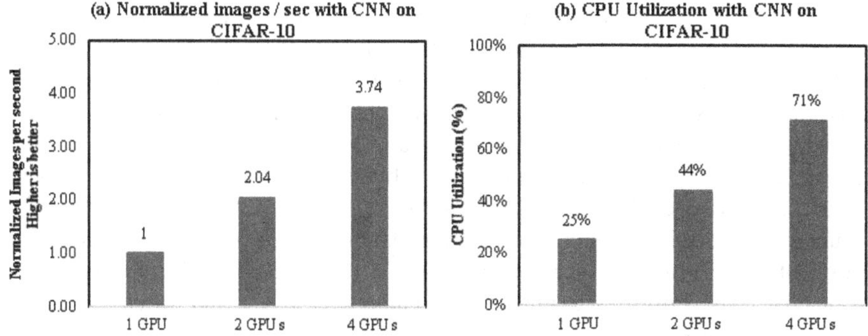

Fig. 6. Scaling the number of GPUs per VM on CIFAR-10.

which supports a wider range of GPU devices, can provide a more flexible choice of GPU for users.

For GRID vGPU. When each user needs a single GPU, GRID vGPU can be a good choice. This configuration provides a higher consolidation of virtual machines and leverages the benefits of virtualization including: (1) GRID vGPU allows the flexible use of the device because vGPU supports both shared GPU (multiple users per physical machine) and dedicated GPU (one user per physical GPU), mixing and switching among machine learning, 3D graphics and video encoding/decoding workloads using GPUs is much easier and allows for more efficient use of the hardware resource. Using GRID solutions for machine learning and 3D graphics allows cloud-based services to multiplex the GPUs among more concurrent users than the number of physical GPUs in the system as illustrated in Sect. 4. This contrasts with DirectPath I/O, which is the dedicated GPU solution, where the number of concurrent users are limited to the number of physical GPUs. (2) GRID vGPU reduces administration cost because its deployment and maintenance does not require server reboot, so no down time is required for end users. For example, changing the vGPU profile of a virtual machine does not require a server reboot. Any changes to DirectIO configuration requires a server reboot. GRID vGPU's ease of management reduces the time and the complexity of administering and maintaining the GPUs. This benefit is particularly important in a cloud environment where the number of managed servers would be very large.

4 Mixing GPU-Based Workloads on Virtualized Server

Many users of GPUs on vSphere run 3D CAD workloads. The traditional approach to run 3D CAD and machine learning workloads is by scheduling their execution times to be nonoverlapped, which is inflexible, or to have separate infrastructures for each type of workload, which increases cost. GRID vGPU helps to solve this problem by allowing both 3D graphics and machine learning workloads to be co-located on a same server to maximize consolidation. In this use case, users can choose their guest OS platforms to deploy their applications. For example, in our test, we mixed two types of workloads: Windows and Linux. This is critical in cloud environments.

In addition, for GPGPU applications, a large portion of their computation is shifted from CPU to GPU, and this can lead to the underutilization of host CPUs. Running 3D CAD applications on the same server as ML applications achieves higher resource utilization than running them separately. Figure 7 shows that off-loading ML workloads to GPU can help reduce CPU utilization by 26X for RNN on PTB (from 78% to 3% in Fig. 7-a) and 5.3X for CNN on MNIST (from 43% to 8% in Fig. 7-b). Reducing CPU load can help more workloads share the same server, increase the consolidation of VMs and increase efficiency of resource usage. In this section, we characterize the performance impact of running 3D CAD and machine learning workloads concurrently.

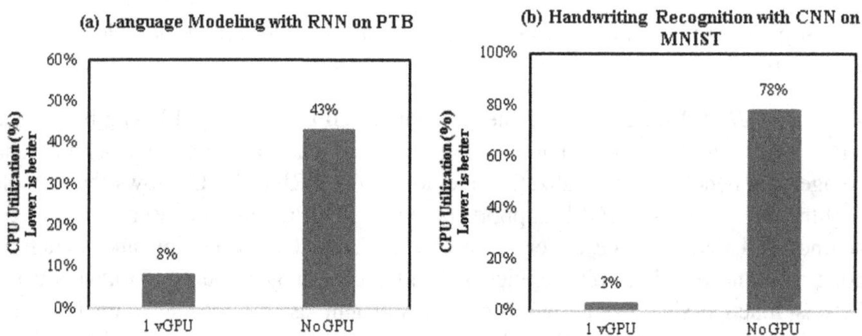

Fig. 7. CPU utilization of PTB, MNIST with and without vGPU.

4.1 Configuration and Methodology

Two benchmarks were used in our experiment. We chose the SPECapc using Autodesk 3ds Max 2015 benchmark [20] as a representative for 3D CAD workloads. We did not comply with the benchmark reporting rules, nor do we use or make comparisons to the official SPECapc metrics. We chose MNIST as a representative for machine learning workloads. The performance metric in this comparison is the run time, as measured by a wall-clock, for the benchmark. As described earlier, each physical GPU can support several different types of virtual GPUs. M60-1Q, M60-2Q, M60-4Q and M60-8Q are vGPU profile names for different type of virtual GPUS supported by the physical GPU on Tesla M60 card. With M60-1Q, M60-2Q or M60-4Q, more than one vGPUs share a same physical GPU. M60-8Q vGPU type does not share a physical GPU and has the entire GPU for itself. The 3D CAD benchmark was installed in a 64-bit Windows 7 (SP1) VM with 4 vCPUs, 16 GB RAM and 1 vGPU whose profile was configured as M60-1Q, M60-2Q, M60-4Q, or M60-8Q for different runs (Table 1). We used this VM as the golden master from which we made clones so that we could run the 3D CAD benchmark at scale with 1, 2, 4, …, 24 VMs running 3D CAD simultaneously. The software configurations used for the 3D CAD workload are shown in Table 1.

Table 1. Software configuration used to run the 3D CAD benchmark.

vGPU profile used for 3D CAD VMs	Size of vGPU VRAM	# of VMs running 3D CAD
M60-8Q	8 GB	3
M60-4Q	4 GB	6
M60-2Q	2 GB	12
M60-1Q	1 GB	24

Our experiments included three sets of runs. In the first set, we ran only the 3D CAD benchmark for each of the four configurations listed in Table 1 and measured the run time, CPU utilization, and GPU utilization. Once this set of runs was completed, we did a second set in which we ran the 3D CAD benchmark concurrently with the MNIST benchmark. The VM for MNIST has CUDA 7.5, cuDNN 4.0, and CentOS 7.2 and was configured with 1 vGPU, using a M60-8Q profile. For the runs in this second set we used the configurations shown in Table 2. The server configuration used in our experiments is a Dell PowerEdge R730 server with dual 14-core Intel Xeon CPU E5-2680 v3, 2.40 GHz sockets (28 physical core, 56 logical with hyperthreading enabled), 768 GB memory, SSD (1.5 TB). This server also has two Nvidia Tesla M60 cards with a total of 4 GPUs as described in Sect. 3. The third set had runs with only MNIST on the server.

Table 2. Software configuration used to run the mixed workloads.

vGPU profile used for 3D CAD VMs	# of VMs running 3D CAD	# of VMs running MNIST	Total # concurrent VMs
M60-8Q	3	1	4
M60-4Q	6	1	7
M60-2Q	12	1	13
M60-1Q	24	1	25

4.2 Performance Results

We measured the run times of three sets of runs and computed the percentage increase in the run time for 3D CAD when it shared the server with MNIST (second set) compared to when it ran without MNIST (first set). We also computed the percentage increase in run time for MNIST when running concurrently with 3D CAD (second set) compared to MNIST run in isolation (third set). Our results in Fig. 8 show that the performance impact on the 3D CAD workload due to sharing the server and GPUs with the machine learning workload is below 5% for the M60-2Q, M60-4Q, and M60-8Q profiles when compared to running only the 3D CAD workload on the same hardware. Correspondingly, the performance impact on the machine learning workload when sharing the hardware resources with the 3D CAD workload compared to running all by itself is under 15% in the M60-2Q, M60-4Q, and M60-8Q profiles. In other words, the run time for the 3D CAD benchmark increases by less than 5% when sharing the hardware with the machine learning workload when compared to when it does not share the hardware. The increase in run time for machine learning was under 15% when sharing compared to not sharing the hardware. Only the M60-1Q profile, which can support up to 24 VMs running 3D CAD and one VM running MNIST, shows any significant performance penalty due to sharing. Note that if the workloads were run sequentially, the total time to complete the tasks would be the sum of the run time for 3D CAD and the machine learning workloads.

A comparison of the total run time for ML and 3D CAD workloads is shown in Fig. 8. From the results, we can see that the total time to completion of the workloads is always less when run concurrently as opposed to when run sequentially.

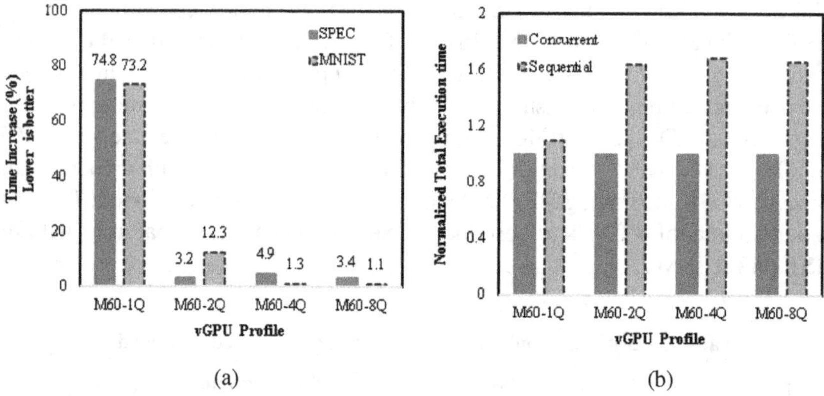

Fig. 8. Percentage increase of time (a) and total run time (b) for SPEC and for MNIST running concurrently compared to running in isolation.

Further, running the workloads concurrently results in higher server utilization, which could result in higher revenues for a cloud service provider. The CPU utilization on the server for the M60-8Q, M60-4Q, M60-2Q, and M60-1Q profiles with only 3D CAD (3D) and with 3D CAD plus machine learning (3D + ML) are shown in Fig. 9. Offloading compute to GPUs results in CPU underutilization. This enabled scaling from 4 VMs using M60-8Q profiles to 25 VMs comprising of 24 VMs using M60-1Q profile for graphics workloads and 1 VM using M60-8Q for GPGPU machine learning workload.

In summary, running 3D CAD and ML workloads simultaneously results in a reduction in total time to completion with M60-2Q, M60-4Q, and M60-8Q profiles as compared to running the workloads sequentially. It also significantly increases server utilization. GRID vGPU, which supports sharing GPUs, can bring better consolidation of VMs per server which can result in higher revenues for a cloud service provider.

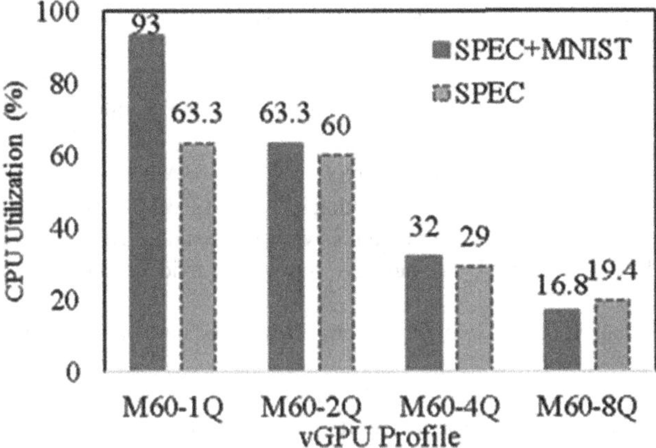

Fig. 9. CPU Utilization on server for mixed workload configuration and for 3D graphics only.

5 Conclusion

We conducted and presented a comprehensive study of performance of different virtual GPU solutions in a cloud environment. This study presents new findings that help us understand the performance impacts and benefits of using virtual GPU resources on machine learning applications as well as on mixing these applications with other GPU-based workloads like 3D graphics. This also gives cloud providers and users useful information in choosing the right virtual GPU solutions that works best for their cloud. For example, DirectPath I/O and GRID vGPU have comparable performance, where DirectPath I/O is slightly better. Cloud users who care about high performance and low latency of applications can choose DirectPath I/O to deploy their workloads on multiple GPUs. For those who care more about the flexibility of datacenter deployment and do not require multiple GPUs for each VM, GRID vGPU is a better option. This solution also allows flexibly mixing machine learning with other types of workloads to save costs and increasing resource utilization. In the future, we plan to extend our study to investigate the performance of AMD MxGPUs and ML applications with the cluster scale of multiple GPU nodes and the performance of 3D CAD and ML workloads with different remote display protocols and/or with containers.

Acknowledgements. The authors would like to thank Josh Simons, Na Zhang, Julie Brodeur, Aravind Bappanadu, and Bruce Herndon for their support for this project.

References

1. Díaz, M., Martín, C., Rubio, B.: State-of-the-art, challenges, and open issues in the integration of internet of things and cloud computing. J. Netw. Comput. Appl. **67**, 99–117 (2016). doi:10.1016/j.jnca.2016.01.010

2. Canny, J., Zhao, H.: Big Data analytics with small footprint—squaring the cloud. In: Proceedings of the 19th ACM SIGKDD International Conference on Knowledge Discovery and Data Mining, pp. 95–103 (2013)
3. Jouppi, N., et al.: Datacenter performance analysis of a tensor processing unit. In: Proceedings of 44th International Symposium on Computer Architecture, Toronto, Canada (June 26, 2017)
4. Qiu, J., Wu, Q., Ding, G., Xu, Y., Feng,S.: A Survey of Machine Learning for Big Data Processing. J. Adv. Sig. Process. (2016). doi:10.1186/s13634-016-0355-x
5. VMware Directpath I/O, https://communities.vmware.com/docs/DOC-11089
6. NVIDIA GRID virtual GPU technology, http://www.nvidia.com/object/grid-technology.html
7. AMD Virtualization Solution, http://www.amd.com/en-us/solutions/professional/virtualization
8. Bittman, T., Dawson, P., Warrilow, M.: Magic Quadrant for x86 Server Virtualization Infrastructure. In: Gartner Research Report, 3 August (2016)
9. Hastie, T., Tibshirani, R., Friedman, J.: The Elements of Statistical Learning. Data Mining, Inference, and Prediction, 2nd edn. Springer, New York (2009)
10. Docker Containers Performance in VMware vSphere, https://blogs.vmware.com/performance/2014/10/docker-containers-performance-vmware-vsphere.html
11. Vu, L., Sivaraman, H., Bidarkar, R.: GPU Virtualization for High Performance General Purpose Computing on the ESX hypervisor. In: Proceedings of the 22nd High Performance Computing Symposium (2014)
12. Big Data Performance on vSphere 6, http://www.vmware.com/content/dam/digitalmarketing/vmware/en/pdf/techpaper/bigdata-perf-vsphere6.pdf
13. Zaremba, W., Sutskever, I., Vinyals, O.: Recurrent Neural Network Regularization. arXiv:1409.2329 (2014)
14. Taylor, A., Marcus, M., Santorini, B.: The penn treebank: an overview. In: Abeille, A. (ed.) Treebanks: the State of the Art in Syntactically Annotated Corpora. Kluwer (2003)
15. Tensorflow Homepage, https://www.tensorflow.org
16. Walters, J.P., Younge, A.J., Kang, D.I., Yao, K.T., Kang, M., Crago, S.P., Fox, G.C.: GPU passthrough performance: a comparison of KVM, Xen, VMWare ESXi, and LXC for CUDA and OpenCL Applications. In: Proceedings of 2014 IEEE 7th International Conference on Cloud Computing (2014)
17. LeCun, Y., Bottou, L., Bengio, Y., Haffner, P.: Gradient-based learning applied to document recognition. Proc. IEEE **86**(11), 2278–2324 (1998)
18. Multiple Layers of Features from Tiny Images, https://www.cs.toronto.edu/~kriz/cifar.html
19. Pandey, A., Vu, L., Puthiyaveettil, V., Sivaraman, H., Kurkure, U., Bappanadu, A.: An automation framework for benchmarking and optimizing performance of remote desktops in the cloud. In: To appear in Proceedings of the 2017 International Conference on High Performance Computing & Simulation (2017)
20. SPECapc for 3ds Max (2015), https://www.spec.org/gwpg/apc.static/max2015info.html

A Locality-Aware Communication Layer for Virtualized Clusters

Simon Pickartz(✉), Jonas Baude, Stefan Lankes, and Antonello Monti

Institute for Automation of Complex Power Systems,
E.ON Energy Research Center, RWTH Aachen University, Aachen, Germany
{spickartz,jbaude,slankes,amonti}@eonerc.rwth-aachen.de

Abstract. Locality-aware HPC communication stacks have been around with the emergence of SMP systems since the early 2000s. Common MPI implementations provide communication paths optimized for the underlying transport mechanism, i.e., two processes residing on the same SMP node should leverage local shared-memory communication while inter-node communication should be realized by means of HPC interconnects. As virtualization gains more and more importance in the area of HPC, locality-awareness becomes relevant again. Commonly, HPC systems lack support for efficient communication among co-located VMs, i.e., they harness the local InfiniBand adapter as opposed to the shared physical memory on the host system. This results in important performance penalties, especially for communication intensive applications. With IVShmem there exist means for the exploitation of the local memory as communication medium. In this paper we present a locality-aware MPI layer leveraging this technology for efficient intra-host inter-VM communication. We evaluate our implementation by drawing a comparison to a non-locality-aware communication layer in virtualized clusters.

Keywords: Locality-awareness · Virtualization · IVShmem · MPI

1 Introduction

Virtualization plays an important role in a variety of application fields of computing. These range from a simplified application deployment enabled by virtualized instruction sets for mobile computing to the flexible assignment of resources in data centers. Even in the field of High-Performance Computing (HPC), virtualization starts to become more and more important [21]. The strong level of isolation provides for the flexibility of a user-defined software environment which is currently not possible in common compute centers. Thereby, the efficient deployment of complex HPC software stacks including all their dependencies is facilitated. Furthermore, the migration of applications across the cluster allows the system administrators for eased maintenances and the implementation of load balancing strategies.

J.M. Kunkel et al. (Eds.): ISC High Performance Workshops 2017, LNCS 10524, pp. 605–616, 2017.
https://doi.org/10.1007/978-3-319-67630-2_42

However, the additional virtualization layer results in a disguise of locality information that is necessary for efficient communication. Locality-awareness in HPC systems came up in the early 2000s with the emergence of Symmetric Multiprocessing (SMP) [16]. Communication layers should be capable of taking the locality information of the processes into account, i.e., on the intra-node level best performance can be obtained by leveraging the shared memory between the co-residing processes while the communication across nodes is usually realized by means of high performance interconnects. Although this field of research has been investigated extensively in the past [8,15], it becomes relevant in the context of virtualization again. Processes residing within Virtual Machine (VMs) should be capable of determining whether a communication peer is co-located within another VM on the same physical node. In the former case, the two processes should leverage the shared physical memory for communication as opposed to a communication link over a local high-speed network adapter.

As of today, most Message Passing Interface (MPI) implementations lack according support for virtualized clusters, i.e., usually they leverage the local InfiniBand (IB) adapter for intra-node communication if available at all. Furthermore, the dynamic behavior of according systems is not taken into account, i.e., the communication library should adapt to migrations by an adjustment of the communication paths between the affected processes. In this paper we present a locality-aware MPI library that provides support for dynamically changing topologies arising from migrations. Therefore, it leverages Nahanni, a mechanism for Inter-VM Shared-Memory (IVShmem) communication for co-located VMs. Our communication layer reduces the point-to-point latency by 67% compared to communication over the local IB adapter while providing throughputs comparable to those obtained via shared memory natively on the host. In summary, we make the following key contributions:

- Support for intra-host inter-VM communication within a fully MPI-3 compliant MPI library,
- a comprehensive performance evaluation of the IVShmem support for co-located VMs, and
- the investigation of the performance benefits in case of dynamically changing process topologies due to VM migrations.

This paper is structured as follows: the next section provides relevant background information on virtualization and IVShmem. Sections 3 and 4 present the design and evaluation of our locality-aware MPI layer. Before concluding the paper in Sect. 6, we discuss related work in Sect. 5.

2 Background

This section provides basic knowledge on virtualization and the communication layer we used for our work. In doing so, it starts with a discussion on system-level virtualization and obstacles that appear in the context of I/O virtualization.

2.1 System-Level Virtualization

We focus on system VMs in our work. These realize a virtualization on the hardware-level, i.e., a process on the host system is started representing a complete substitute for a computer system. We leverage the hypervisor Kernel-based Virtual Machine (KVM) for the management of multiple guests which is part of the Linux vanilla kernel since version 2.6.30 in 2007 [9]. It relies on hardware support for the full-virtualization of the x86 based on Intel's VT-x extensions [17]. From the hypervisor's point of view, a VM acts as and an ordinary process and can be treated like any other process running on the host system. KVM only implements the facilities that are necessary for the virtualization of the CPU and the memory subsystem. The remaining parts of the computer system, e.g., network devices or hard drives, have to be emulated in software by the user-space emulator QEMU [4].

2.2 I/O Virtualization

System-level virtualization based on hypervisors has envolved in the past years enabling nearly native CPU performance [12,19]. However, the efficient virtualization of I/O devices is still a challenge which is circumvented by device pass-through techniques such as Intel VT-d [2]. On the one hand, this gives the VM direct control over the device's hardware registers while avoiding expensive guest-to-host transitions. On the other hand, the device may directly write to/read from the guest-physical memory without host involvements.

This solution requires the same amount of physical devices as the number of guests running on the system. As a result, a single I/O device may only be used by one guest at a time. Hence, if multiple guests are co-located on the same physical system, just as many physical devices were necessary. To overcome this issue, the Peripheral Component Interconnect Special Interest Group (PCI-SIG) introduced the Single Root I/O Virtualization (SR-IOV) [6] specification as part of the PCIe standard. This allows for the native sharing of a single physical I/O device concurrently by multiple VMs while providing nearly native I/O performance [14].

2.3 Nahanni

Although, SR-IOV-enabled clusters allow for communication at low latencies and high data rates within VMs, there is still a major performance gap concerning the intra-node communication. In previous works we could observe performance penalties of up to 26% for communication-bound applications executed within multiple co-located VMs [13].

Nahanni [7] is an alternate mechanism for the communication between co-located VMs over shared memory, i.e., IVShmem. It comprises three parts: (1) a shared-memory region on the host, (2) an extension of QEMU's virtual hardware support by means of a new virtual device called *ivshmem*, and (3) a guest driver representing the memory region as PCI device. The shared-memory region is

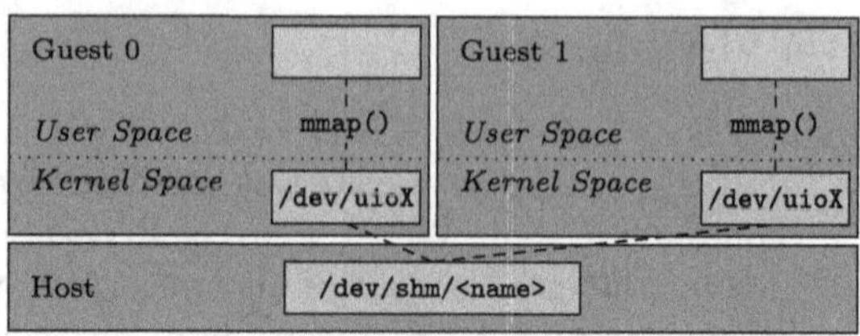

Fig. 1. Overview of Nahanni for the sharing of a memory region on the host between two guests. Once mapped into the virtual adresspace, applications can access the device's memory region just as normal regions allocated via malloc().

created by the host or hypervisor using the POSIX API, and therefore no further modifications to the host Operating System (OS) are required. Furthermore, the QEMU modifications are included in the upstream sources since version 0.13 in 2010 and allow for the automatic creation of the memory region on the startup of a VM. The guest driver is build upon the User-Space I/O (UIO) framework and can be used by the guests for the configuration of the ivshmem device. This appears as common PCI device and supports synchronization over shared-memory, e.g., via spinlocks. Since we focused on the shared-memory offered by Nahanni in the scope of this work, we omit a detailed discussion of the other mechanisms at this point.

The guests see the ivshmem device as /dev/uioX (cf. Fig. 1). Here, X is an integer assigned by the guest kernel consecutively to all UIO devices. Using the open() and mmap() system calls, the device can be mapped into the processes' virtual address space and subsequently be used for data exchange between co-located VMs.

2.4 The Pscom Library

The pscom library is a low-level communication library especially designed for the employment in HPC systems. Although its main objective is to serve as the low-level communication substrate of ParaStation MPI [5], it can also be used as a light-weight standalone communication library. ParaStation MPI is a fully MPI-3 compliant, MPICH-based MPI implementation. The pscom library already ships with support for a variety of interconnects and interfaces commonly used in the HPC domain. In doing so, it provides a flexible software architecture that can be extended by means of *plugins* for the accommodation of new technologies. These are loaded and selected at runtime of the library based on priorities, i.e., those plugins promising fast communication are favored. The pscom comes with two special plugins which are tightly integrated into the library's sources. First, the TCP-plugin serves as lowest common denominator, i.e., it is assumed that the cluster nodes are always able to communicate via socket-based TCP/IP connections. Second, the shared-memory plugin with the highest priority provides high efficient communication among processes residing on the same compute node by implementing true zero-copy data transfers.

The session management of the pscom library is based on the Berkeley Socket API. This allows the processes to perform the initial connection establishment via the TCP-plugin by means of the common connect/accept scheme. In a second step, the processes determine the actual plugin that is used for further communication via a pre-defined handshake procedure. ParaStation MPI leverages the pscom for the establishment of a fully connected MPI session in the default case. This approach may result in a potential waste of resources as usually only a fraction of the $n \cdot \frac{n-1}{2}$ possible connections is required. Therefore, the pscom library provides a so-called *ondemand* mechanism promising a better resource utilization by implementing a lazy connect approach. In doing so, the actual connection setup is postponed to the first write attempt on the respective connection.

3 Design

For compliance with the architectural design of ParaStation MPI, we integrate the support for IVShmem communication as plugin into the pscom library. This bases on the original plugin for shared-memory communication and divides into two parts (cf. Fig. 2): (1) the upper pscom layer providing the interface to the hardware-independent part of the pscom library and (2) the lower device layer for the management of the IVShmem device provided by Nahanni. The pscom layer implements the handshake mechanism that is required for every pscom plugin. This mainly comprises the detection of the locality information as discussed below. The device layer's main task is the management of the shared memory region. It implements the synchronization among the processes residing on the same physical host for the allocation of the send and receive buffers realizing the communication channels.

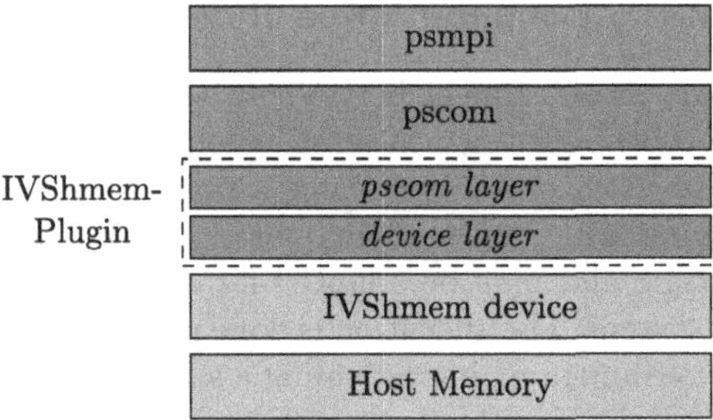

Fig. 2. The integration of the IVShmem plugin into the ParaStation MPI communication stack. The upper pscom layer implements the interface defined for pscom plugins to the hardware-agnostic part of the library and the lower device layer takes over the management of the shared-memory region provided by Nahanni.

3.1 Detection of Locality Information

First, the plugin has to determine whether the VM is equipped with an IVShmem device. Therefore, the pscom layer instructs the device layer to map the shared-memory region of the respective PCI device into the process' virtual address space.

Afterwards, the communication peers need to assess whether this region is located on the same physical host. Therefore, we use a UUID of 16 Byte at a pre-defined offset within this memory region. In accordance with pscom's handshake mechanism, the two processes exchange their local UUIDs. If these match, the processes can assume to be co-located and establish a communication channel via IVShmem. Otherwise, the handshake aborts and the pscom library proceeds with the next plugin. For the assessment of the locality information via the UUID, we assume that the IVShmem device is initially filled with zeros. Otherwise, the processes were not able to determine whether the device has already been initialized or not. This should be valid in most cases, as memory gets usually zeroed on page-faults by the operating system. However, the mechanism still works on other systems if the hypervisor is involved in this first synchronization step, e.g., on startup of the VMs.

In the initialization phase of the plugin, the first byte of the shared-memory segment is polled by an atomic test-and-set operation. This byte indicates the initialization of the segment and concomitant the initialization of the UUID which is performed by the first process (of *all* processes running within potentially different VMs on that host) entering the critical section. Furthermore, this process creates a POSIX spinlock that is used for the synchronization of future memory allocations within the memory region. All other processes initializing their plugin will detect the UUID that can be exchanged via the handshake procedure subsequently.

3.2 Allocation of the Communication Buffers

The actual connection establishment between two processes is conducted by an allocation of local receive buffers which serve as send buffers for the communication peer. In doing so, each process allocates a portion of the IVShmem region with a fixed size serving for a dedicated amount of buffers. These parameters are defined at compile time and may be adapted for a tuning of the plugin to the underlying memory system. The allocation is done in accordance with the *first-fit* strategy within the IVShmem region providing a simple and efficient mechanism for the memory allocation. This should be sufficient for the allocation of the communication buffers in case of static topologies. Here, one can assume that their lifetime lasts from the beginning of the MPI session—or the first write attempt on that connection in case of the ondemand mechanism—to its end introduced by the MPI_Finalize() call. However, in case of frequent migrations during the processes' lifetime, more sophisticated allocation schemes would be desirable.

3.3 Migration Within Virtualized Clusters

We build upon our previous works realizing migration support for MPI applications [10,11]. These extend the pscom library by the implementation of our Shutdown/Reconnect(S/R) protocol that ensures data integrity for so-called *non-migratable* connections, e.g., an IB connection relies on location-dependent resources such as the Queue Pair Number(QPNs) which are determined by the local IB adapter. At the same time, the protocol allows for a dynamic change of the underlying transport after the migration since we rely on the pscom ondemand mechanism for the connection re-establishment.

The combination of both mechanisms—IVShmem and migration support—enables an adaption of the communication paths in accordance with the process topology as we show in the following section. After a consolidation of two VMs, e.g., the processes may communicate via IVShmem although they used IB beforehand.

4 Evaluation

All benchmarks were run on a two-node research cluster equipped with Intel IvyBridge CPUs (E5-2650 v2) being clocked at 2.6 GHz. Each CPU possesses eight physical cores with support for two Hardware Thread Context (HTC) per core, resulting in a total of 32 HTCs per node. The nodes are connected by a Mellanox IB fabric using ConnectX-3 VPI two-port adapters implementing the PCIe 3.0 standard. These provide a theoretical peak throughput of 56 G bit/s in accordance with the FDR signaling rate. Furthermore, the adapters offer support for the SR-IOV standard. The hosts and guest systems employ a 4.9.0 Linux kernel compiled by using the upstream sources. All systems use the OFED Stack in version 4.0-1.0.1 provided by Mellanox. Our virtulization stack bases on KVM in conjuction with QEMU version 2.6.0. As interface to the hypervisor we use libvirt[1] version 3.2.0 which comes with hot-plug support for IVShmem devices. Furthermore, we have made the source code of our implementation available via GitHub [2].

Throughput and latency constitute the basic key figures of a communication library. Therefore, we performed a microbenchmark analysis for the determination thereof by using a self-written MPI benchmark[3] executing a PingPong pattern [1]. In doing so, we investigated the following communication scenarios:

Native-SHM shared-memory on the host
Native-IB the local IB adapter on the host
VM-IB the local IB adapter shared between co-located VMs using SR-IOV
VM-IVShmem the IVShmem plugin used by MPI processes in co-located VMs

[1] https://libvirt.org.
[2] https://github.com/rwth-os/pscom.
[3] https://github.com/rwth-os/mpi-benchmarks.

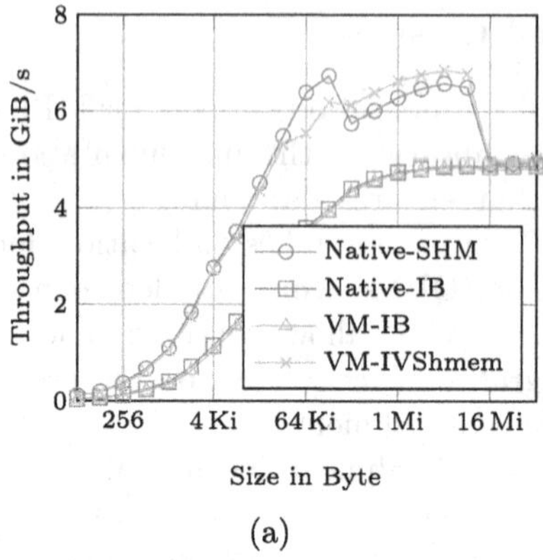

(a)

Mode	Ø	σ
Native-SHM	0.33	0.07
Native-IB	0.88	0.08
VM-IB	1.13	0.32
VM-IVShmem	0.34	0.14

(b)

Fig. 3. The figures present (a) a throughput and (b) a latency analysis of the pscom IVShmem plugin showing the average (Ø) and the standard deviation (σ). The results were obtained by using a benchmark performing a PingPong pattern between two processes within distinct VMs running on the same host. The latencies are given in µs and are averaged over 10 million runs.

The throughput results for VM-IVShmem reveal a performance comparable to that of Native-SHM (cf. Fig. 3a). The curves were captured by averaging over 1000 individual PingPong exchanges. Messages smaller than the L2 cache experience a little overhead whereas messages that fit into the last-level cache can be transmitted slightly faster over IVShmem than over the original shared-memory plugin. We can only assume that cache effects and differences in the respective implementation of both plugins are the reason for this behavior. However, more research is necessary for a validation of these assumptions. However, the performance deviations are negligible small and essentially, the new IVShmem plugin boosts the throughput performance by up to 40% compared to the communication over SR-IOV (VM-IB) which is the common case for most MPI librarys as of today. The latencies draw a similar picture (cf. Fig. 3b) revealing a reduction of the latency by almost 70% when using VM-IVShmem instead of VM-IB. Although the variance slightly increases compared to Native-SHM, it is only at 44% of the variance that can be observed for VM-IB.

To get an impression how real-world applications benefit from the IVShmem communication channel, we compared the execution of the NAS Parallel Benchmarks (NPB) [3] using VM-IB and VM-IVShmem (cf. Fig. 4). We started the kernels by using problem class C on a single cluster node with 16 processes, i.e. one process per available CPU core, in a row for 30 min respectively. This yield stable average runtimes. This test was repeated for different VM counts such that the process-to-core pinning has been preserved. The results are normalized to the execution within a single VM to avoid a distortion caused by the virtualization itself. However, to get an impression of the performance compared to Native-SHM, we included this case as well, i.e., 0 VMs. The light bars represent the measurements obtainted by using standard VM-IB mode while the opaque bars represent the VM-IVShmem results.

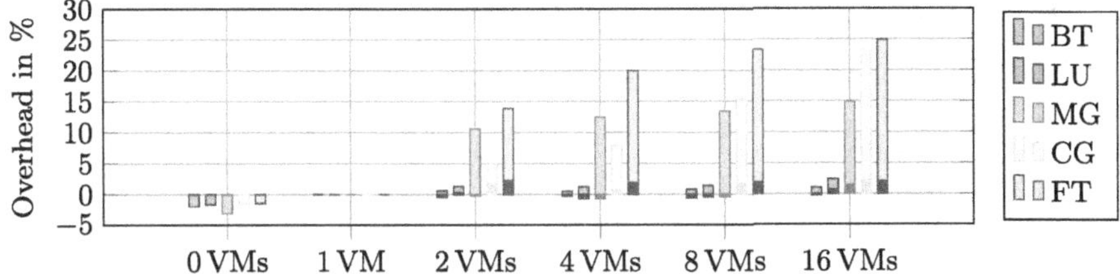

Fig. 4. Overhead when running the NPB across multiple VM compared to the execution within one VM: for VM-IB (light bars) and VM-IVShmem (opaque bars).

In all cases we can observe an overhead when executing the benchmarks within multiple VMs if the processes leverage the local IB adapter as communication link, i.e., VM-IB. Especially, communication intensive applications such as CG and FT suffer extremely from the execution within multiple VMs, i.e., runtime overheads of up to 25% are the result. In contrast, the results for VM-IVShmem do not reveal a dependency of the applications' performance to the amount of VMs. The overhead with respect to the execution within a single VM ranges from −1% to 2%, and is therefore within the range of measurement noise.

The previous experiments showed that locality-awareness is an important attribute for communication systems for their deployment in virtualized environments. However, for the full exploitation of the benefits that come with virtualization, e.g., the migration of applications across the cluster, the support for dynamically changing communication relations is indispensible. Figure 5 gives an impression of the consequences thereof for point-to-point latencies. We ran an MPI session with two processes distributed across two VMs on distinct compute nodes. They exchanged 1000 messages in accordance with the PingPong pattern every 500 ms. The curves represent the average latency that could be achieved for each meter point, i.e., the average latency for every burst of 1000 message exchanges. After around 30 s, we issued a migration request of one VM to the host of the second VM. This demands for the temporary shutdown of the connection via IB and the later re-establishment. This, in turn, is now possible via the pscom IVShmem plugin as the two VMs are now co-located on the same host. Thereby, the average latency could be improved by about 17% compared to its original value. In contrast, the same scenario executed with disabled pscom IVShmem plugin results in an average latency of 1.558 µs which is more than four times as much, i.e., around 72% of its original value.

5 Related Work

Locality-awareness in the context of virtualized HPC clusters has rarely been studied in the past. Diakhaté et al. present a virtual device designed the sharing of memory between co-located VM. Although they leverage a minimal MPI implementation for their evaluation only providing basic point-to-point communication primitives, the focus of their work is put on the device implementation.

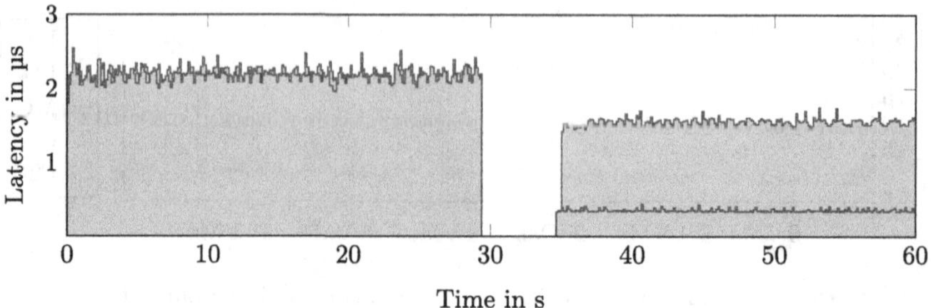

Fig. 5. PingPong latency during a consolidation of two VMs onto the same physical host: without IVShmem support (red curve) and with IVShmem support (blue curve). (Color figure online)

In contrast to Nahanni, the solution relies on the *fork()* system call for the creation of VMs which only allows for uniformly configured guests. Furthermore, VM migrations are exacerbated since their solution does not support a varying number of VMs.

Zhang et al. present a locality-aware MPI implementation [20] leveraging IVShmem for intra-host inter- VM communication. Based thereon, they propose Slurm-V [21], a framework for virtualized HPC clouds, which uses the SLURM [18] resource manager. The framework supports different execution models such as exclusive allocations and sharing of nodes for concurrent jobs. However, until now their solution lacks migration support within virtualized clusters which would enable load balancing or an improvement of the fault tolerance.

6 Conclusion

This paper investigates the viability of IVShmem mechanisms for virtualized HPC clusters. Therefore, we present a locality-aware MPI layer that dynamically detects co-located processes within distinct VMs on the same node. In contrast to existing approaches, we make use of the fact that synchronization primitives such as atomic operations can be used on IVShmem memory regions just as with normal shared-memory segments. Therefore, a single UUID is sufficient for the detection of the locality information.

Furthermore, we integrate the implementation into our MPI library providing support for application migration. In doing so, the MPI processes may detect dynamically changing communication relations during runtime and react accordingly. In a migration scenario we could show that this approach results in a reduction of the point-to-point latency by a factor of four compared to the communication over the local IB adapter. For future work we plan to extend our library by support for dynamic topology-awareness optimizing collective operations with respect to dynamically changing process topologies.

Acknowledgment. This research and development was supported by the Federal Ministry of Education and Research (BMBF) under Grant 01IH16010C (Project ENVELOPE).

References

1. Intel MPI benchmarks. Technical report Intel Corporation (2014)
2. Intel virtualization technology for directed I/O. Technical report, Intel Corporation (2014)
3. Bailey, D., Barszcz, E., Barton, J., Browning, D., Carter, R., Dagum, L., Fatoohi, R., Frederickson, P., Lasinski, T., Schreiber, R., Simon, H., Venkatakrishnan, V., Weeratunga, S.: The NAS parallel benchmarks. Int. J. Supercomput. Appl. **5**(3), 63–73 (1991)
4. Bellard, F.: QEMU, a fast and portable dynamic translator. In: USENIX Annual Technical Conference, FREENIX Track, pp. 41–46 (2005)
5. Clauss, C., Moschny, T., Eicker, N.: Dynamic process management with allocation-internal co-scheduling towards interactive supercomputing. In: Trinitis, C., Weidendorfer, J. (eds.) Proceedings of the 1st COSH Workshop on Co-scheduling of HPC Applications, p. 13, January 2016
6. Intel LAN Access Division: PCI-SIG SR-IOV primer. Technical report 2.5, Intel Corporation, January 2011
7. Macdonell, A.C.: Shared-memory optimizations for virtual machines. Ph.D. thesis, University of Alberta (2011)
8. Mamidala, A.R., Chai, L., Jin, H.W., Panda, D.K.: Efficient SMP-aware MPI-level broadcast over InfiniBand's hardware multicast. In: Proceedings of 20th IEEE International Parallel Distributed Processing Symposium, p. 8, April 2006
9. Nussbaum, L., Anhalt, F., Mornard, O., Gelas, J.P.: Linux-based virtualization for HPC clusters. In: Montreal Linux Symposium, Montreal, Canada, July 2009
10. Pickartz, S., Clauss, C., Lankes, S., Krempel, S., Moschny, T., Monti, A.: Non-intrusive migration of MPI processes in OS-bypass networks. In: 2016 IEEE International Parallel and Distributed Processing Symposium Workshops (IPDPSW), pp. 1728–1735, May 2016
11. Pickartz, S., Lankes, S., Monti, A., Clauss, C., Breitbart, J.: Application migration in HPC?–A driver of the exascale era? In: 2016 International Conference on High Performance Computing Simulation (HPCS), pp. 318–325, July 2016
12. Pickartz, S., Breitbart, J., Clauss, C., Lankes, S., Monti, A.: Co-scheduling of HPC applications. In: Virtualization in HPC - An Enabler for Adaptive Co-scheduling? IOS Press, January 2017
13. Pickartz, S., Breitbart, J., Lankes, S.: Implications of process-migration in virtualized environments. In: Proceedings of the 1st COSH Workshop on Co-Scheduling of HPC Applications, p. 6, January 2016
14. Pickartz, S., Gad, R., Lankes, S., Nagel, L., Süß, T., Brinkmann, A., Krempel, S.: Migration techniques in HPC environments. In: Lopes, L., Žilinskas, J., Costan, A., Cascella, R.G., Kecskemeti, G., Jeannot, E., Cannataro, M., Ricci, L., Benkner, S., Petit, S., Scarano, V., Gracia, J., Hunold, S., Scott, S.L., Lankes, S., Lengauer, C., Carretero, J., Breitbart, J., Alexander, M. (eds.) Euro-Par 2014. LNCS, vol. 8806, pp. 486–497. Springer, Cham (2014). doi:10.1007/978-3-319-14313-2_41
15. Träff, J.L.: SMP-aware message passing programming. In: Eighth International Workshop on High-Level Parallel Programming Models and Supportive Environments, Proceedings, pp. 56–65, April 2003

16. Träff, J.L.: Improved MPI all-to-all communication on a Giganet SMP cluster. In: Kranzlmüller, D., Volkert, J., Kacsuk, P., Dongarra, J. (eds.) EuroPVM/MPI 2002. LNCS, vol. 2474, pp. 392–400. Springer, Heidelberg (2002). doi:10.1007/3-540-45825-5_57
17. Uhlig, R., Neiger, G., Rodgers, D., Santoni, A.L., Martins, F.C.M., Anderson, A.V., Bennett, S.M., Kagi, A., Leung, F.H., Smith, L.: Intel virtualization technology. Computer **38**(5), 48–56 (2005)
18. Yoo, A.B., Jette, M.A., Grondona, M.: SLURM: simple Linux utility for resource management. In: Feitelson, D., Rudolph, L., Schwiegelshohn, U. (eds.) JSSPP 2003. LNCS, vol. 2862, pp. 44–60. Springer, Heidelberg (2003). doi:10.1007/10968987_3
19. Younge, A.J., Henschel, R., Brown, J.T., von Laszewski, G., Qiu, J., Fox, G.C.: Analysis of virtualization technologies for high performance computing environments. In: 2011 IEEE International Conference on Cloud Computing (CLOUD), pp. 9–16. IEEE (2011)
20. Zhang, J., Lu, X., Jose, J., Li, M., Shi, R., Panda, D.: High performance MPI library over SR-IOV enabled infiniband clusters. In: 2014 21st International Conference on High Performance Computing (HiPC), pp. 1–10, December 2014
21. Zhang, J., Lu, X., Chakraborty, S., Panda, D.K.: SLURM-V: extending SLURM for building efficient HPC cloud with SR-IOV and IVShmem. In: Dutot, P.-F., Trystram, D. (eds.) Euro-Par 2016. LNCS, vol. 9833, pp. 349–362. Springer, Cham (2016). doi:10.1007/978-3-319-43659-3_26

YASMIN: Efficient Intra-node Communication Using Generic Sockets

Michalis Rozis(✉), Stefanos Gerangelos, and Nectarios Koziris

Computing Systems Laboratory, National Technical University of Athens, Athens, Greece
{mrozis,sgerag,nkoziris}@cslab.ece.ntua.gr

Abstract. Nowadays, virtual machines are becoming widely used and their range of applications include a large number of scientific fields. From HPC to IaaS, communication between co-located VMs is a critical factor of efficiency. In our paper, we examine communication methods between VMs located in the same physical node, optimizing communication cost without sacrificing upper-layer API compatibility. We present *YASMIN (Yet Another Shared Memory Implementation for Intra-Node)*, a generic socket-compliant framework for intra-node communication in the Xen hypervisor. We build on the concept of Vchan, a Xen library for intra-node communication between different VMs and we use Xen granting and signaling mechanisms to provide an efficient communication framework. The key of our design is the transport layer which runs underneath the `AF_VSOCK` protocol family, implemented as a dynamically inserted module. We are able to achieve 4.4x higher bandwidth rate and 65% lower latency without the need of application binary recompilation.

Keywords: Intra-node · Virtualization · Sockets · Xen · Networking · Shared-memory

1 Introduction

The advent of High Performance Computing (HPC) systems and the increasing needs for better control, isolation and resource management have made Virtual Machines (VMs) a significant part of modern data centers, HPC scientific applications and enterprise service platforms [1–3]. The key reason that make VMs such a critical factor of modern computing systems is the ability to execute intense applications and services providing a secure, isolated environment of execution, improving system utilization and communication cost between applications [4]. Today, power consumption is becoming an important topic for data center providers [5]. Virtual machines provide the capability of more efficient system utilization which results in energy cost reduction [6]. For these reasons, investing in virtualization technologies is a major trend for different applications and service providers.

Due to the benefits that virtualization provides to infrastructure providers, the same concept is also exploited in network facilities. With the exploding data

J.M. Kunkel et al. (Eds.): ISC High Performance Workshops 2017, LNCS 10524, pp. 617–628, 2017.
https://doi.org/10.1007/978-3-319-67630-2_43

traffic through vast network infrastructures, middleboxes, i.e. hardware network devices, are a fundamental part of today's networks. Although there are many advantages in using hardware middleboxes, there are also many reasons for shifting to *virtualized network functions* (VNFs), such as IP Routing, firewall, intrusion detection etc. [7,8]. VNFs are part of modern *network function virtualization* infrastructures (NFV) where VMs run on top of hardware network infrastructure and take responsibility for providing network services [9]. In addition to the above topics, virtual machines are also used in distributed execution environments, such as Hadoop MapReduce [10]. This framework is widely used in applications that require intensive data computations [11]. Virtual machines have become an attractive entity for hosting MapReduce workloads, which require fast communication between parallel tasks. For example, cloud-based services, such as Amazon's EC2, rely on VMs to process large amounts of data by spawning tasks on different VMs.

Thus, recent virtualization techniques have given rise to a major set of new capabilities, but also to a number of limitations that researchers try to overcome. The field of improving virtualized computing environments is of great interest and refers to a large number of topics, from hypervisor scheduler optimization [12] to virtual machine reconfiguration [13,14].

In addition to these aspects, one important limitation that arise in both HPC applications but also in Cloud Computing applications is the communication cost between VMs. Virtual machines can reside in the same physical node or in different nodes. Proper placement or migration of VMs is a basic factor for providing low-latency and high-bandwidth communication for the reason that VMs hosting HPC or cloud applications can exploit their physical locality to increase performance. For instance, VNFs running in co-located VMs (such as routing, load balancing, firewall) may intensively exchange traffic, hence, taking advantage of proper VM placement and optimizing intra-node communication can offer significant overall performance gain. We focus on Xen [15] hypervisor and explore communication mechanisms in VMs located in the same physical node to achieve improvement in both latency costs and bandwidth rates.

We introduce YASMIN, a generic socket-compliant, efficient intra-node communication framework for co-located VMs in the Xen hypervisor. Although our implementation is built on Xen mechanisms, the basic concept can be applied to other hypervisors as well. YASMIN exploits the Xen's *grant table* and *event channel* mechanisms and provides page sharing between co-located VMs to simplify the data path in the network stack without sacrificing transparency. We achieve this by creating a communication channel between VMs that are aware of their location, bypassing the TCP/IP stack. We evaluate YASMIN using generic micro-benchmarks and compare it to conventional communication paths and bare-metal memory bandwidth (Sect. 4). We can observe that our framework outperforms the conventional methods both in terms of throughput as well as latency.

2 Background

2.1 Overview of Xen Architecture

Xen is a bare-metal hypervisor (Virtual Machine Monitor - VMM) which enables virtualization in paravirtualized mode. This means that the kernel of the guest VMs (domains) is modified in order to allow them to communicate with the privileged guest VM (Dom0). Basic operations for paravirtualized guests (disk, networking, GPU, etc.) are serviced through requests to the control domain which is responsible for communication with the hardware. Xen also exposes a set of hypercalls to guests. Hypercalls are privileged requests to the hypervisor which include granting page access to foreign domain, transferring and copying pages between domains and setting up an interrupt mechanism between domains.

2.2 Xen Default Networking

An overview of Xen's default network data path is shown in Fig. 1. Networking is based upon the split-driver model; control domain is responsible for the coordination between the two communication ends. One end (domainX) forwards packets through the network stack (*TCP/IP*) to a virtual ethernet driver (*netfront*). The driver then copies the requests to a memory area mapped to the control domain. The driver in the control domain (*netback*) reads the requests from a ring buffer and copies the data in a proper kernel structure of the other end's *netfront* memory and delivers a signal. The other end (domainY) can now accept the new packet and forward it to the network stack (TCP/IP). The main limitation of this method is that all networking has to pass through the control domain which is a huge bottleneck for scaling to either a large number of processes between the same pair of VMs or a large number of processes between different pairs of VMs in the same physical node.

3 Design and Implementation

3.1 Design Overview

We decide to implement YASMIN design on top of the Xen hypervisor 4.4 using Linux 3.16 as guest OS. We build on Vchan [16], a Xen library which invokes system calls (`open()`, `ioctl()`, `mmap()`) to Xen's exported devices (`xen_gntdev`, `xen_gntalloc`) in order to initialize a channel between co-located domains and exchange data. We take this idea further and implement a transport layer for *vSockets* [17], i.e. a generic sockets API similar to the POSIX interface which supports fast and efficient communication between guest virtual machines. vSockets API introduces a new address family (`AF_VSOCK`) and refers to the common socket-layer calls (`socket()`, `bind()`, `connect()`, etc.). A socket connection between two guest VMs can be established by using their domain ID numbers and a remote port. YASMIN consists of a loadable kernel module and a shared library to intercept system calls. The shared library intercepts IPv4 socket calls

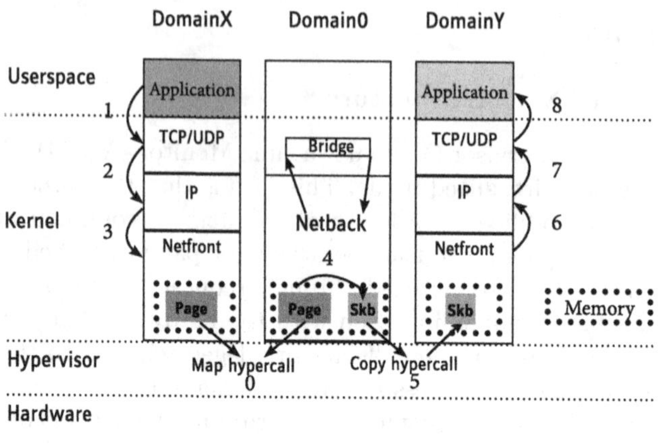

Fig. 1. The default inter-domain communication path in the Xen hypervisor. Numbers correspond to steps involved in the data path. Page is mapped before any exchange of data (step 0). Packet traverses the TCP/IP stack (steps 1-2), to the page shared between domX and dom0 (step 3). The packet is copied to a temporary buffer in dom0 (step 4) and then it is copied to the receiver's frontend (step 5) and back to the receiver's userspace (steps 6-8).

and translate them to vSockets socket calls, by using a 1-1 mapping between intra-node IP addresses and local domain IDs. An overview of YASMIN design is shown in Fig. 2.

3.2 Implementation Details

YASMIN implementation is based on Xen's primitive hypercalls, i.e. granting page access to foreign VMs through grant-table mechanism, mapping pages using grant table's index number and invoking interrupts through the event channel mechanism. We exploit the producer-consumer shared ring technique, which does not require any locking mechanisms between the reader and the writer. Contrary to common approaches which do not take transparency into account thus resulting in efficient but not binary-compatible code, we decide to design not only an efficient but also a transparent framework. In order to achieve this, we bypass the TCP/IP protocol stack which introduces an extra overhead to each packet transmission, and we utilize the vSockets socket protocol layer. It is part of Linux kernel release and currently designed to support VMCI [18] as well as VIRTIO [19] transport layers. We extend this work and build a new transport layer for vSockets by adapting to Xen mechanisms. In this way, not only we avoid building a new network protocol from scratch but we also provide users with the capability of choosing the transport layer on the fly. To provide an architectural overview, we briefly describe how the operations are realized in each layer, from top to bottom:

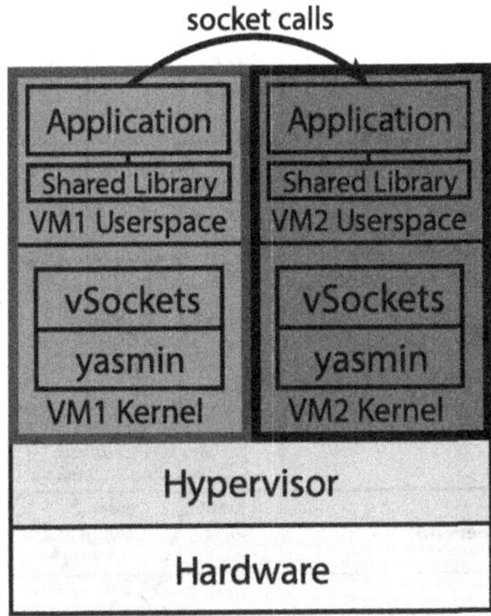

Fig. 2. YASMIN design overview

Application layer: One of the most important aspects of our design is the API compatibility with the generic socket interface. Specifically, we aspire to provide a low-overhead socket communication framework to applications running in co-located VMs without the need to refactor, reimplement or even recompile them. We implement a shared library which intercepts all system calls, filters out socket-API system calls (`bind()`, `listen()`, `accept()` etc.) and replaces them as follows: Our library queries a file which consists of entries of *domain_id-to-IP-addresses* mappings of all running guest domains in the same physical node. If the socket-call's target IPv4 address is matched, then the respective structures are initialized and the system call is forwarded to the kernel as a vSockets socket call (i.e. `AF_VSOCK`). Otherwise, the remote application is not located in the same node and the default data path is followed.

Transport layer - Link layer: Each socket call invoked by userspace that corresponds to `AF_VSOCK` is serviced by vSockets protocol. This protocol is responsible for data fragmentation and packet delivery to the transport layer. The transport layer is the core of our implementation and is capable of creating a communication channel between co-located VMs, deliver messages and notify the remote domain for new packets. It is implemented as a kernel module and dynamically inserted to the kernelspace of each guest VM. Link layer is embedded in this module as a producer - consumer ring buffer in memory mapped between communicating VMs.

As mentioned earlier, Xen provides the *grant table* mechanism which enables page sharing between VMs; one domain (granter) allocates a new page, grants access to the foreign domain by invoking a hypercall and refers to that page using its index in the grant-entry table. The other-end domain (grantee) allocates a new page and maps this page to the granter's page (also by invoking a hypercall) using the same grant-entry table index. The shared producer-consumer ring is part of the communication channel and is implemented as a set of pages shared by

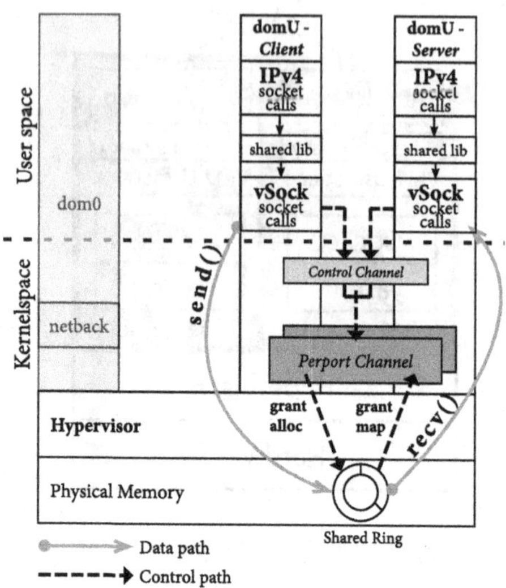

Fig. 3. YASMIN implementation overview. Each new socket connection is established through the *control channel* (control path arrows). For every connected pair of sockets, a new *perport channel* with its own shared ring is created, where data are exchanged (data path arrows)

the two ends using the previous mechanism. Xen also introduces a simple signal passing mechanism between VMs, the *event-channel*, so as to inform the other end for packet delivery. The first domain (*allocator*) creates a new connection with the remote domain (*binder*) by invoking a hypercall which returns a local channel port number. *Allocator* then registers a new interrupt handler to this port. *Binder* can now "bind" to the port by invoking a hypercall, which in turn returns a local channel port number. *Binder* then registers a new interrupt handler to its local port. Each end can then invoke a hypercall and raise a virtual interrupt to notify the other end that data are available in the ring buffer and the respective interrupt handler will be invoked. We can now describe the path for a successful client-server message transmission between two co-located VMs. The overview of our design is presented in Fig. 3.

- The inserted module, exports a XenStore path which will be monitored for incoming connection requests. When the client invokes a `connect()` socket call, our transport checks if previous requests to the specified remote domain have been made. If not, it creates a new intra-node communication channel between the domains and caches channel's parameters for future communication requests. Channel's parameters[1] are transmitted to remote domain via its XenStore path. This channel (*control channel*) is used only for transmission of control messages between domains (e.g. *new socket connection request, socket release*). After the establishment of the control channel between a pair

[1] grant-entry index and event-channel port number.

of guest VMs, a single-page queue is realized, which is used for sending new socket connections requests. These packets consist of the packet header, the grant-table's indices and event channel ports which will be used by the remote domain for mapping and registering respectively.

Next, it creates a new *persocket channel* and sends a new connection request to the remote application using the *control channel*. The new connection request specifies a remote domain ID and a remote port to connect to, similarly to IPv4 requests to a remote IP and a remote port. This channel is used for packet transmission between connected sockets. When the remote domain successfully registers the *persocket channel*, a reference to this channel is stored and vSockets `connect()` returns successfully. Each connection request to a new socket between the communicating VMs will create a new *persocket channel* but the *control channel* is unique for each pair of communicating VMs and will be teared-down only if guests shutdown or migrate.
- Server-side applications can call `socket()`, `bind()`, and `listen()` to wait for incoming connections similarly to corresponding IPv4 socket calls. When the new connection request is made by the client-side application through the *control channel*, a virtual interrupt is triggered and the server-side's interrupt handler is invoked causing proper packet processing and enqueuing in listener's accept queue. This packet contains the grant references and event-channel ports of the *persocket channel*. The server-side will map the shared pages and bind the event-channel.
- A call to `accept()` by the server-side will dequeue the new connection request and send a *Connection OK* message to the client.
- `send()` socket call will cause a memory copy from userspace to the shared ring located in kernelspace and the update of the producer index.
- Similarly, `recv()` will cause a memory copy from the shared ring to userspace and the update of the consumer index.

Finally, to retain compatibility and transparency with `AF_INET` applications, we wrap around socket calls a library that re-issues all IPv4 calls with `AF_VSOCK` family.

4 Performance Evaluation

We setup a host machine with 2x Xeon E5335, 8GB RAM and single core guest VMs in order to evaluate the performance of our implementation in comparison to the default *netback/netfront* data path. We perform two microbenchmark experiments to test throughput and latency as well as scaling. We compare our results with the performance of bare-metal Unix Domain Sockets and also with the system's bare-metal memory bandwidth. We use NetPIPE [20] to test latency and scaling, Iperf [21] to test throughput, netperf [22] to measure Unix Domain Sockets throughput and STREAM benchmark [23] to compare to bare-metal memory bandwidth.

4.1 Microbenchmark Evaluation

As shown in Figs. 4 and 5, YASMIN outperforms the *netback/netfront* model in comparison to latency as well as throughput.

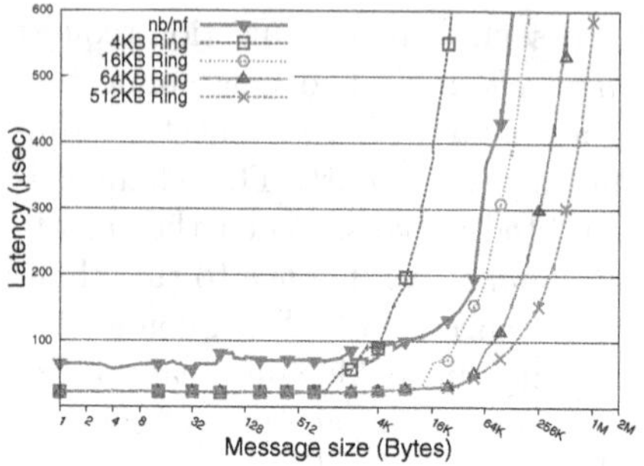

Fig. 4. Latency–to–message–size performance plot. "nb/nf" refers to the default netback/netfront data path.

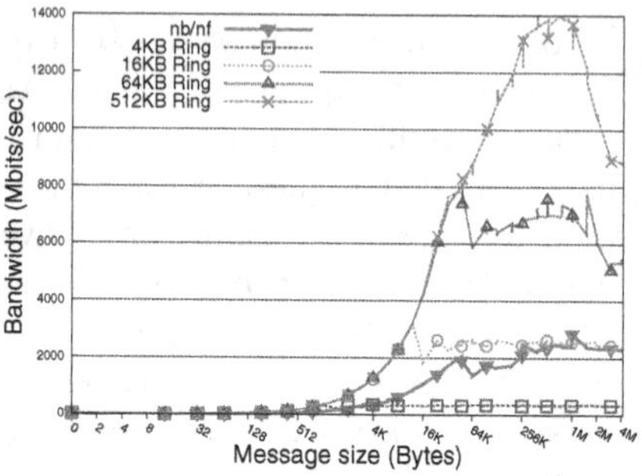

Fig. 5. Throughput performance for different ring sizes in comparison to the *netback/netfront* (nb/nf line).

However, ring size is an important variable of performance. In Fig. 4 we can observe the effect of ring size on latency and in Fig. 5 the effect on throughput. For low message sizes (up to 1 Kb), latency is not affected by the increase in ring size. We also observe that bandwidth is increasing for message sizes up to 2 MB. However, there is a decrease in performance for messages up to 4 MB, as depicted in Fig. 5. We are certain that this is caused due to increased contention on the memory bus. We plan to perform a detailed break-down analysis to validate our assumption.

In addition, throughput increases proportionally to the increase in ring size, as shown in Fig. 6. Throughput performance for ring size of 2 MB reaches 76% of throughput performance of Unix Domain Sockets on the bare-metal system, as shown in Fig. 6.

Nonetheless, we choose to implement a ring size of 512 kB (128 pages) trading-off throughput and lower kernel memory consumption. For this ring size, latency is reduced by 65%[2] compared to *netback/netfront* and average throughput is increased by a factor of 4.4, as measured by *Iperf*. Compared to the system's bare-metal memory bandwidth, YASMIN can perform at 16 Gbps (2048 MBytes/sec) while memory bus performance is measured at 2813 MBytes/sec for 1 executing thread and 3784 MBytes/sec for 8 executing threads, and Unix Domain Sockets performance is measured at 3250 MB/s.

4.2 Scaling Evaluation

Finally, in order to test YASMIN scaling performance, we setup in parallel up to 8 single core VMs which exchange messages in pairs (VM1 to VM2, VM3 to

[2] This value refers to a 1 Byte message.

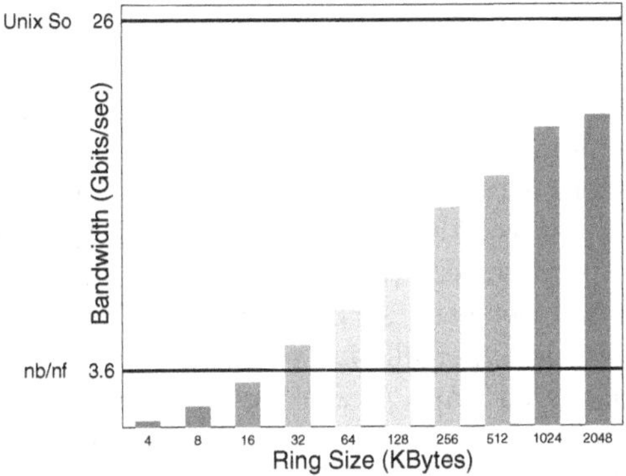

Fig. 6. Ring size effect on throughput. The line labeled "nb/nf" refers to throughput performance of the netback/netfront model and the line labeled "Unix So" to bare-metal Unix Domain Sockets throughput.

VM4, and so on...). Each VM is pinned to a CPU core and communicating VMs share a 4 MB L2 cache memory. For example, when VM1 and VM2 are exchanging data, VM1 is pinned to CPU0 and VM2 to CPU1, where CPU0 is sharing a L2 cache with CPU1. The results of this experiment are depicted in Fig. 7. We can observe that the aggregate throughput increases proportionally to the number of communicating VMs. For instance, two VMs are exchanging a 512 KB message at 13.2 Gbps, while 8 VMs achieve 4x aggregate throughput for the same message size (53 Gbps or 6625 MBytes/s). In comparison to the above result, we point out that bare-metal memory bus throughput for 8 threads of execution is measured at 3784 Mbytes/s.

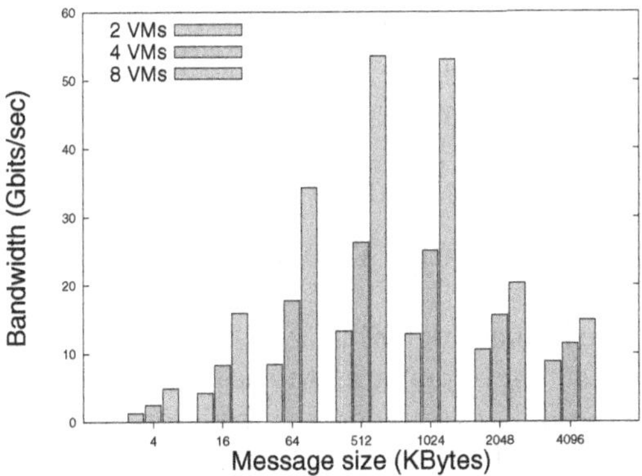

Fig. 7. Scaling performance

5 Related Work

Due to the significance of optimizing intra-node communication, literature in this field include a large number of proposals. A common proposed concept involves shared memory buffers between communicating VMs. Diakhate et al. [24] use shared memory techniques on the KVM hypervisor [25] by modifying QEMU [26] instances. IVC [27] proposes creating a one-way channel by using shared-page techniques and a new userspace API. XenSocket [28] also uses shared pages through Xen grant table hypercalls in order to create an one-way channel, by modifying BSD Sockets API and presenting a new address family. In addition to these, a paravirtualized protocol for POSIX syscalls, best suitable for Linux containers, is implemented as a split driver in PV Calls [29]. Although these techniques can achieve better latency and bandwidth performance compared to the default model, transparency and compatibility are sacrificed. Applications need to be aware of running in co-located VMs and source code needs to be refactored and recompiled. XenLoop [30] creates a full-duplex channel between co-located VMs without sacrificing transparency by intercepting outgoing packets from the network layer and establishing a fast communication channel between these VMs. A kernel module is responsible for analysing the packet destination MAC address and forwarding it in the established channel. A software bridge is responsible for keeping records of co-located MAC addresses. Although this technique can perform better in terms of throughput, there is not significant reduction in latency. Another approach in intra-domain communication is proposed by V4VSockets [31], a generic socket-applicant framework which performs better in terms of bandwidth as well as latency. The key idea of this implementation is based on copies made by the hypervisor to the receiver via the V4V mechanism, which resides in the Xen hypervisor. However, in this approach, the hypervisor is modified and the data path consists of three copies between the sender and the receiver.

In our implementation we combine the best parts of each of these techniques by bypassing both the control domain and the TCP/IP network stack. We also provide transparency and avoid binary recompilation as well as hypervisor-intrusive techniques.

6 Conclusion and Future Work

YASMIN is a complete framework for intra-node communication which optimizes both throughput and latency compared to the default *netback/netfront* model. The data path includes only two copies, the first from sender's userspace to the kernelspace shared ring and the second from the shared ring to the receiver's userspace. Moreover, our implementation can successfully respond to scaling challenges, as shown in Fig. 7. In addition to these, YASMIN optimizes communication between co-located VMs without the need to recompile binaries.

We conclude that in a large field of applications where communication is a critical factor of performance, placement of VMs in the same physical node is crucial for performance due to the fact that optimization techniques can be exploited. For these reasons, YASMIN can provide benefits to applications running in virtualized context.

We plan to improve YASMIN by upgrading the *hosts* file query process. Currently, the hosts file, which is queried by guest VMs to determine if a remote IP is co-located in the same node, is maintained by the node administrator. Therefore, in order to resolve VM migration issues, we plan to build a control domain backend driver or a guest VM daemon which will be responsible for monitoring any changes due to migration of virtual machines.

Moreover, we plan to test YASMIN in comparison to the related proposals, in order to validate further the facts that make our framework a better approach on intra-node communication.

Finally, we plan to test our framework in NFV environments, where different VNFs can run on top of YASMIN transport layer. Suitable for testing are network functions such as routers, firewalls, load balancers, because they require fast packet processing and low latency response time.

YASMIN is an open-source framework and can be found at https://github.com/mrozis/YASMIN.git

References

1. Huang, W., Liu, J., Abali, B., Panda, D.K.: A case for high performance computing with virtual machines. In: ICS 2006, Cairns, Queensland, Australia, 28–30 June (2006)
2. Reuther, A., Michaleas, P., Prout, A., Kepner, J.: HPC-VMs: virtual machines in high performance computing systems. In: IEEE High Performance Extreme Computing (HPEC) Conference, Waltham, MA, 10–12 September (2012)
3. Tikotekar, A., Ong, H., Alam, S., Vallee, G., Naughton, T., Engelmann, C., Scott, S.L.: Performance comparison of two virtual machine scenarios using an HPC application. a case study using molecular dynamics simulations. In: HPCVirt 2009 Proceedings of the 3rd ACM Workshop on System-level Virtualization for High Performance Computing, Nuremburg, Germany, 31 March (2009)
4. Strazdins, P., Alexander, R., Barr, D.: Performance enhancement of SMP clusters with multiple network interfaces using virtualization. In: Min, G., Di Martino, B., Yang, L.T., Guo, M., Rünger, G. (eds.) ISPA 2006. LNCS, vol. 4331, pp. 452–463. Springer, Heidelberg (2006). doi:10.1007/11942634_47
5. Shehabi, A., Smith, S.J., Horner, N., Azevedo, I., Brown, R., Koomey, J., Masanet, E., Sartor, D., Herrlin, M., Lintner, W.: United States Data Center Energy Usage Report. Lawrence Berkeley National Laboratory, Berkeley, California. LBNL-1005775 (2016)
6. Yang, C.-T., Tseng, C.-H., Chou, K.-Y., Tsaur, S.-C., Hsu, C.-H., Chen, S.-C.: A xen-based paravirtualization system toward efficient high performance computing environments. In: Hsu, C.-H., Malyshkin, V. (eds.) MTPP 2010. LNCS, vol. 6083, pp. 126–135. Springer, Heidelberg (2010). doi:10.1007/978-3-642-14822-4_14
7. Network Functions Virtualisation, An Introduction, Benefits, Enablers, Challenges & Call for Action, https://portal.etsi.org/nfv/nfv_white_paper.pdf

8. DiGiglio, J., Ricci, D.: High Performance, Open Standard Virtualization with NFV and SDN, A Joint Hardware and Software Platform for Next-Generation NFV and SDN Deployments
9. Network Function Virtualisation (FV); Use Cases, ETSI GS NFV 001, http://www.etsi.org/deliver/etsi_gs/NFV/001_099/001/01.01.01_60/gs_NFV001v010101p.pdf
10. Apache Hadoop, https://wiki.apache.org/hadoop
11. List of institutions that are using Apache Hadoop for educational or production uses, https://wiki.apache.org/hadoop/PoweredBy, https://wiki.apache.org/hadoop/Distributions
12. Kang, H., Chen, Y., Wong, J., Sion, R., Jason, W.: Enhancement of Xen's scheduler for MapReduce workloads. In: HPDC 2011, San Jose, California, USA, 8–11 June (2011)
13. Park, J., Lee, D., Kim, B., Huh, J., Maeng, S.: Locality-aware dynamic VM reconfiguration on MapReduce clouds. In: HPDC 2012, Delft, The Netherlands, 18–22 June (2012)
14. Ibrahim, S., Jin, H., Lu, L., He, B., Wu, S.: Adaptive Disk I/O Scheduling for MapReduce in Virtualized Environment. In: 2011 International Conference on Parallel Processing (2011)
15. Xen Project Hypervisor, https://wiki.xen.org/wiki/Xen
16. Vchan Xen Library, https://github.com/mirage/xen/tree/master/tools/libvchan
17. VMware vSockets, https://pubs.vmware.com/vsphere-65/index.jsp#com.vmware.vmci.pg.doc/vsockAbout.3.2.html#1023121
18. Virtual Machine Communication Interface, https://pubs.vmware.com/vmci-sdk/
19. Virtio - IO Virtualization in KVM, http://www.linux-kvm.org/page/Virtio
20. NetPIPE - Network Protocol Independent Performance Evaluator, https://linux.die.net/man/1/netpipe
21. iPerf Benchmark, https://iperf.fr/
22. netperf - a network performance benchmark, https://linux.die.net/man/1/netperf
23. McCalpin, J.D.: Memory bandwidth and machine balance in current high performance computers. In: IEEE Computer Society Technical Committee on Computer Architecture (TCCA) Newsletter, December 1995
24. Diakhaté, F., Pérache, M., Namyst, R., Jourdren, H.: Efficient shared memory message passing for inter-VM communications (2008)
25. Kernel Virtual Machine, https://www.linux-kvm.org/page/Main
26. QEMU, http://www.qemu.org/
27. Huang, W., Koop, M.J., Gao, Q., Panda, D.K.: Virtual machine aware communication libraries for high performance computing. In: SC 2007: Proceedings of the 2007 ACM/IEEE Conference on Supercomputing, NY, USA (2007)
28. Zhang, X., McIntosh, S., Rohatgi, P., Griffin, J.L.: XenSocket: a high-throughput interdomain transport for virtual machines. In: Cerqueira, R., Campbell, R.H. (eds.) Middleware 2007. LNCS, vol. 4834, pp. 184–203. Springer, Heidelberg (2007). doi:10.1007/978-3-540-76778-7_10
29. PV Calls: A new paravirtualized protocol for POSIX syscalls
30. Wang, J., Wright, K.-L., Gopalan, K.: XenLoop: a transparent high performance inter-vm network loopback. In: HPDC 2008: Proceedings of the 17th International Symposium on High Performance Distributed Computing (2008)
31. Nanos, A., Gerangelos, S., Alifieraki, I., Koziris, N.: V4VSockets: low-overhead intra-node communication in Xen. In: CloudDP 2015, Bordeaux, France, 21–24 April (2015)

Dynamic Paging Method Switching - An Implementation for KVM

Yu Zhang(✉), Peter Tröger, and Matthias Werner

Operating Systems Group, Technische Universität Chemnitz, Chemnitz, Germany
zhayu@hrz.tu-chemnitz.de,
{peter.troeger,matthias.werner}@informatik.tu-chemnitz.de

Abstract. The increasing adoption of virtualization in high-performance computing domain makes it necessary to reduce the performance loss due to virtualization for the workloads. In a single computing node, the loss is mainly incurred by memory virtualization. To take the advantages of virtual memory, page tables are commonly adopted for the mapping from virtual to physical address in operating systems. To take the advantages of system virtualization, page tables are also adopted for the mapping from guest virtual to host physical address. The two standard approaches are *shadow* and *nested page tables*. As each of them has its strengths and weaknesses, neither can simply be replaced by the other. An optimal practice is to exploit these strengths as the workload is always changing. However, the current hypervisors cannot do this due to the static way of configuring the paging method. This paper proposes and realizes DPMS - a variant of the idea "dynamic page method switching" in the context of KVM. DPMS is able to detect the workload type and adjust the page method accordingly. Benchmark results show that DPMS yields the best performance compared with the *shadow* and *nested paging* for almost all the tested workloads.

1 Introduction

Virtualization is an increasingly relevant topic in the area of high-performance computing (HPC). It adds an indirection layer of abstraction below the operating system, so that whole machine installations can be dynamically instantiated and migrated on the available physical resources. The constantly increasing support for virtualization in modern physical hardware (processor, memory management unit, I/O controllers) lowers the performance loss down to such a level that these solutions are starting to be incorporated by default in HPC environments.

The currently standard approaches for memory virtualization in hypervisors are *shadow paging* and *nested paging*. SPT (shadow page tables) are controlled by the hypervisor and interpreted by the MMU (memory management unit) of the physical processor. SPT maps the virtual addresses in the guest to physical addresses in the host with a single step. This makes the approach very efficient, especially for memory-intensive computational applications. A major downside is the need to temporarily suspend the guest execution (called a *vmexit*), when

J.M. Kunkel et al. (Eds.): ISC High Performance Workshops 2017, LNCS 10524, pp. 629–641, 2017.
https://doi.org/10.1007/978-3-319-67630-2_44

SPT must be updated. This occurs each time the guest decides to modify its own page tables. The frequency of such events depends on the application workload.

The *nested paging* scheme adopts a two-step translation strategy, under which the mapping is first performed by using the guest page tables, from guest virtual to guest physical address, then by using nested page tables (NPT) further to host physical address[1]. Under *nested paging*, the guest operating system is permitted to handle all the page faults by itself, without forcing a *vmexit* due to the need of maintaining any host paging structure. Unlike SPTs, NPTs are maintained by the physical processor, thus saves the effort to force an expensive *vmexit* at this moment and eliminates the performance loss suffered by shadow paging.

The downside of *nested paging* is incurred by the extension of the page table walk length (second-dimension). A two-dimensional paging walk with four-level in both guest and nested page tables has five times more page entry references than a four-level native page walk [1]. Although this can be mitigated by using the translation look-aside buffer (TLB), the benefit of TLB depends mainly on how well the cached results of the recent translations can be reused. Therefore, workloads with better memory locality make better use of the TLB and suffer less overhead. This explains why the ability to use TLB is critical for the performance of a workload under *nested paging*. The same view is also found in [1,2].

Figure 1(a) and (c) show the normalized performances of PARSEC-3.0 [3] yielded by the KVM guests with 4-KB and 1-GB page tables, respectively. A few workloads suffer higher performance losses. In the cases with single thread, such examples includes: `fft` (10.03%), `lu_ncb` (9.61%), and `radix` (10.65%). It may become more apparent as the number of thread increases. By using the 1-GB large pages, performance for these workloads is generally improved (`fft` (102.19%), `lu_ncb` (99.97%), and `radix` (96.27%)). Nevertheless, this may also lead to more degradation for some other workloads (`dedup` (−7.56%), `barnes` (−3.87%), `volrend` (−2.48%)) against with 4-KB pages. As a reference, Fig. 1(b) and (d) compare the performances of the same benchmark for *shadow* and *nested paging*, with 4-KB, 1-GB page tables, respectively. What they show is that a single paging method, either *shadow* or *nested paging*, does not yield equally well performance for all workload. While for most of the workloads, *nested paging* outperforms *shadow paging*, the opposite is true for some others. And this is also the case even when 1-GB large page is used. Large page size may really improve the performance for many workloads, but exhibits the same nature regarding the strengths and weaknesses of a paging method.

These reflects the limitation to treat the diverse HPC workloads with a single way of paging, and justifies a combined use of *shadow paging* and *nested paging* on demand of the workload. The drawback of using a single paging method is that hypervisor cannot get feedback from the workload thus cannot treat it in its favorite way for paging. Within the current framework of memory virtualization, this paper explores the feasibility of applying the two paging methods during a single-shot run of the guest or even of an application, to avoid higher overhead.

[1] More precisely, this approach involves three steps, but the second step (guest physical to host virtual) and third (host virtual to host physical) are typically combined.

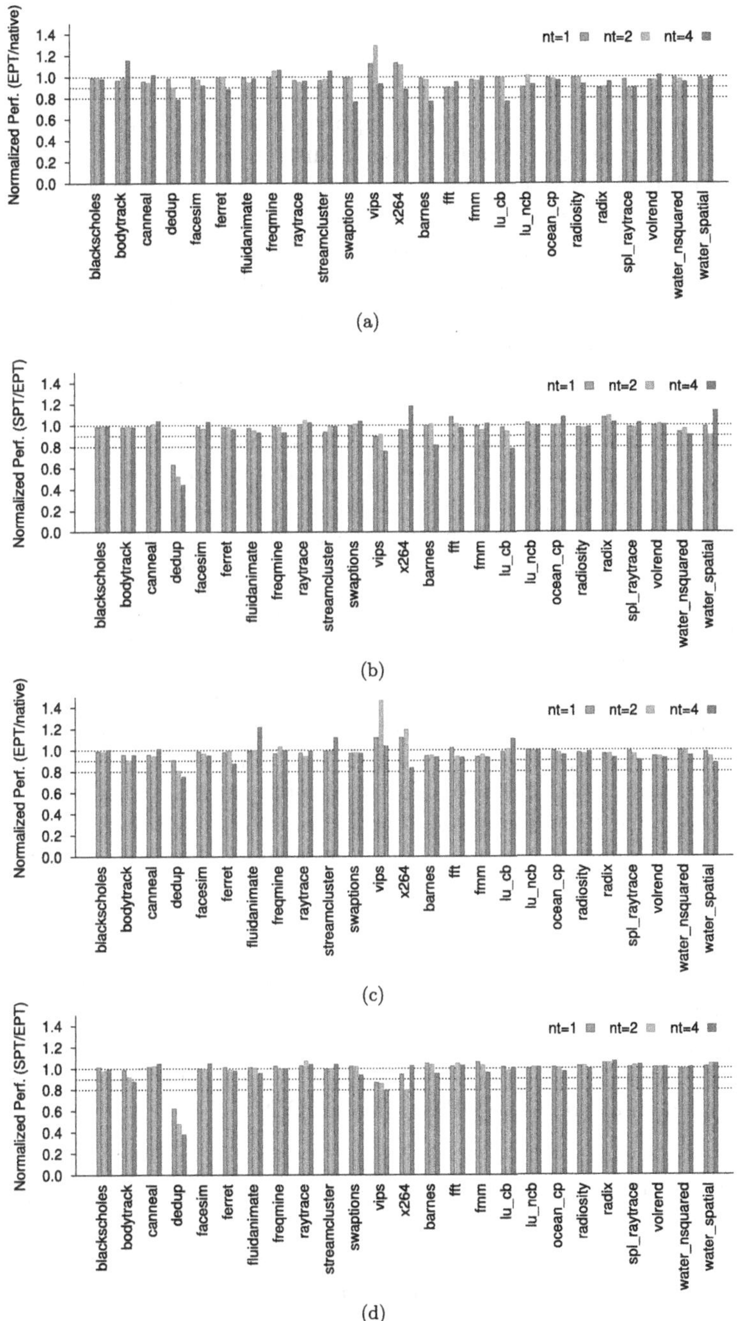

Fig. 1. Comparison of (a) EPT(4 KB)/native(4 KB), (b) SPT(4 KB)/EPT(4 KB), (c) EPT(1 GB)/native(4 KB), (d) SPT(1 GB)/EPT(1 GB)

2 Related Work

Dynamic switching of paging methods for running workloads is not a new idea. The first appearance seems to be in [4]. The authors argued that the nested paging is better for database-oriented applications since it eliminates a large number of `vmexit` events. Shadow paging, instead, is better for computation-intensive workloads that incur limited activities in the guest kernel space. The authors pointed out that the type of workload could be automatically detected by QEMU-KVM at run-time. Two according implementations are worked out in [5,6], based on Xen and Palacios, respectively. Although different hypervisors, policies and mechanisms are applied in their implementations, each of them has showed that the dynamic switching of paging methods is able to yield on-par or higher performance than the best one yielded by shadow and nested paging. The early-stage of our work on this idea can be found in [7], which describes part of the implementation for QEMU-KVM. It mainly relates to performance data sampling and a coarse-grain paging method switching details.

A recent further development for dynamic switching is contributed by [8], which views shadow and nested paging as two extreme cases for guest memory virtualization. Based on the observation that the frequency for updating varies greatly at different levels of page tables, the authors propose *agile paging*, which is capable of switching between the two paging methods dynamically for a single address translation process. According to the benchmark results, it outperforms the best of shadow and nested paging. *agile paging* requires a slight modification not only to the hypervisor software, but also to the current processor hardware.

A few other attempts for improving the performance of guest memory virtualization are discussed in [9,10]. The former proposes a hashed page table as the paging scheme for walking the second dimension page tables. The latter, based on the feasibility of mapping the large memory chunks in a process's virtual address space by means of segmentation rather than paging, and only the remained small regions by paging, proposed the shift from paging to segmentation for the guest memory virtualization, leading to near-zero translation and better-than-native performance. While both of them sound reasonable, they lack true hardware support, thus not practicable with the current available hardware.

Contributions of this paper are: (1) study of performance impact delivered by large page size, (2) design of new strategies for paging method switching, and (3) the implementation of the DPMS idea in KVM.

3 Design of the Dynamic Paging Method Switching

The DPMS consists of four functional units, namely, (1) Sampling of performance data, (2) Processing of performance data, (3) Decision making, and (4) Switching.

By making decisions based on the real-time performance statistics, *dynamic paging method switching* can react to the ever-changing behavior of the running workload by instructing an immediate change of the current paging method to

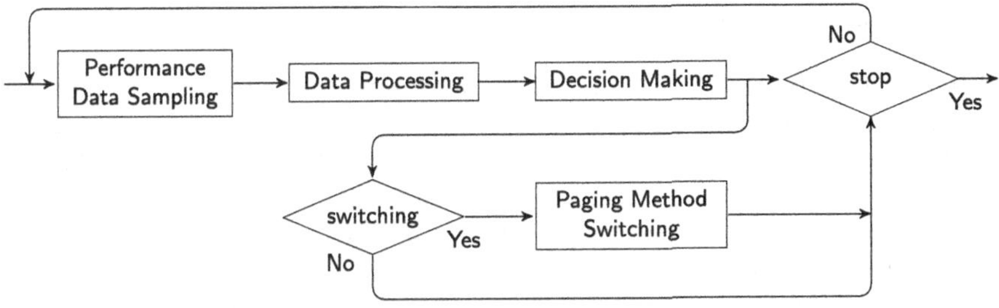

Fig. 2. Design of DPMS

the more suitable one for the running workload, and eventually this leads to a self-adaptive system inside the hypervisor, as Fig. 2 depicts.

3.1 Performance Data Sampling and Processing

Modern processors have special hardware facility, the Performance Monitor Unit (PMU), to collect specific events related with the operation of processor [11]. A PMU typically consists of a Performance Monitor Counter (PMC) and an event selector. DPMS makes use of them for collecting the necessary data about the run-time memory-access behavior of the given workload.

Considering that the *vmexit* incurred by guest page faults are critical for the performance under *shadow paging*, and that the TLB miss rate is critical for that under *nested paging*, the following indicators become relevant: (1) *vmexit* events due to guest page faults, (2) *vmexit* events due to any reason, (3) TLB miss events, both for data and instructions, (4) Retired instructions, and (5) Clock cycles.

The first two are monitored directly in the context of the hypervisor therefore can be obtained internally. The other three indicators are hardware-related and must be obtained through PMCs.

For *Decision Making*, these indicators are only raw data, and used to calculate the more related performance metrics, which includes the PFR (page fault rate), TMR (TLB miss rate), and IPC (instruction per cycle). By their definitions, the calculation of these performance metrics is fairly straightforward. The more important duty for data-processing is to yield the statistics which can be directly used by decision-making. As this part tends to be a more concrete aspect closely related with the decision-making phase, it is better to defer the discussion to the implementation with more details. At this stage, what can be determined is the basic process for *Decision Making*. Several previous values of the concerned metrics need to be stored to compared with the corresponding current values in a certain form. A circular array (ring buffer) can be used for this purpose. Data in an array can be the metric value itself, or a comparison result. Each time the stalest data will be replaced by the current one. The decision will be influenced by the comparison between the mean of previous values with the current value.

3.2 Decision Making

The central task for decision-making is to determine the criterion, or conditions under which the paging method should be launched. But the performance can be influenced by many factors. It is non-trivial to identify these influence-factors. Figure 3 shows the result of such an investigation for shadow paging. Workloads with the heaviest performance loss are `dedup` (36.94%) and `vips` (10.87%). PF and *vmexit* exhibited by these two are at least one order of magnitude higher than other workloads do. No other metric indicate stronger connections with the high performance loss under *shadow paging*. For this reason, the PF and *vmexit*, rather than PFR are taken as the conditions for the switching from *shadow* to *nested paging*. The figure shows that `fft`, `radix` also exhibit similar behaviors but proved *shadow paging*-inclined. These are only platform-specific exceptions.

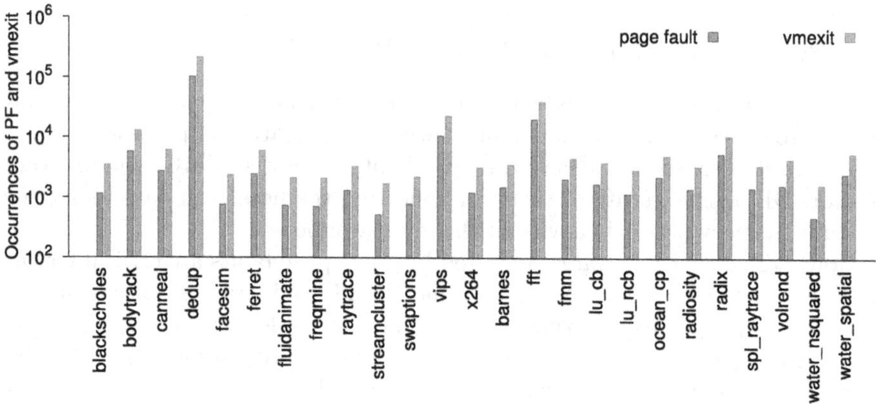

Fig. 3. Comparison of PF (page fault) and `vmexit` for *shadow paging*

On the other hand, conditions for switching from the opposite direction is also investigated. Table 1 displays the majority of possible indicators, which includes the global mean occurrences of iTLB miss, dTLB miss, PF/s, *vmexit*/s, PFR, TMR and IPC for 25 workloads in PARSEC-3.0. Comparison reveals that the occurrences of iTLB and dTLB really connect with high performance loss under nested paging, but the rule does not always hold true. For this reason, TMR is examined, whose result indicates that workloads which exhibit a TMR below 10^{-5} suffer nearly no visible performance loss for *nested paging*, otherwise, further conditions are needed for the final decision.

Meanwhile, workloads suffer heavily under *nested paging* exhibit nearly negligible PF and *vmexit* than those suffer less. Therefore, TMR, together with PF and *vmexit* are taken as the conditions for the switching from *nested* to *shadow paging*. Another observation is that the occurrence of IPC does not necessarily indicate heavy performance loss for either *shadow* or *nested paging*, thus is not considered for decision-making.

Table 1. Statistics of PARSEC-3.0 for *nested paging*.

workload	iTLBM	dTLBM	TMR	PF/s	vmexit/s	IPC	PFR
blackscholes	3097.14	3227.50	0.000027365	0.38	911.38	1.9309	0.0004
bodytrack	13516.93	7507.07	0.000338611	14.38	1413.81	0.9063	0.0102
canneal	2043.63	1138.65	0.000080206	11.56	844.48	1.5812	0.0137
dedup	4301.13	7634.83	0.000208871	82.31	1427.80	1.1261	0.0577
facesim	8069.18	3095.81	0.000244451	13.27	964.16	0.2271	0.0138
ferret	26428.27	21702.62	0.000014441	16.20	1177.99	1.3346	0.0137
fluidanimate	2369.36	293.61	0.000106478	76.84	900.10	2.0261	0.0854
freqmine	5673.26	66952.09	0.000011414	12.23	846.67	1.7229	0.0145
raytrace	2516.07	5157.16	0.000141858	11.58	1274.26	0.2749	0.0091
streamcluster	1308.22	1574.71	0.000003803	0.01	1415.04	0.7949	0.0000
swaptions	673.58	456.70	0.000031505	0.12	1418.63	1.9764	0.0001
vips	19986.51	37846.63	0.000402917	52.68	1177.81	0.9843	0.0447
x264	29353.84	7946.45	0.000263719	0.43	1239.54	0.8887	0.0003
barnes	1763.70	788.61	0.000061923	0.32	26.56	0.3828	0.0121
fft	13232.65	6744437.91	0.001055395	0.09	22.42	1.8127	0.0041
fmm	5965.21	2845.51	0.000266594	0.47	51.40	0.3718	0.0091
lu_cb	1236.32	500.42	0.000057584	0.04	16.97	0.4338	0.0022
lu_ncb	1162.77	499.47	0.000052648	0.01	25.52	0.6798	0.0002
ocean_cp	5931.80	2866.20	0.001096807	0.00	36.01	0.6756	0.0000
radiosity	1111.16	484.60	0.000043282	0.03	15.38	0.3818	0.0020
radix	7564.72	3189.60	0.000407778	0.09	75.77	1.3580	0.0012
spl_raytrace	1845.39	764.98	0.000070307	0.37	19.95	0.4681	0.0185
volrend	41151.24	14288.29	0.000010477	0.49	64.14	1.4947	0.0077
water_nsquared	13815.92	3437.95	0.000002209	0.00	12.77	2.0934	0.0000
water_spatial	2385.17	5795.79	0.000007623	0.14	240.51	0.8953	0.0006

3.3 Switching

As the central part of DPMS, the design of the switching mechanism deals with two basic questions: (1) What needs to be performed for the switching operation at hardware and hypervisor level; and (2) In which part of hypervisor's context should the switching occur.

Regarding to the first question, Fig. 4 depicts the minimal set of operations for switching in the context of a hypervisor and the hardware. Two key aspects for switching are: how to handle with the *shadow page tables* when switching to *nested paging*, and how to handle with the *nested page tables* when switching to *shadow paging*. The answers depend on the nature of the two different kinds of page tables. Researches [5,7,8] pointed out that *shadow page tables* are by nature more volatile in their content than *nested page tables*. While the latter is also changing during the execution of guest system, the pace is potentially much slower than that of the former. Furthermore, the former must still be constantly synchronized even under *nested paging* for reuse after *shadow paging* is resumed, which adds extra burden to the performance. For this reason, the strategy is to retain the *nested page tables* before switching and restore them after being back, but to abandon the *shadow page tables* before switching, and rebuild them after being back. A problem arises if the guest is started initially with *shadow paging* and is switching to *nested paging*. In this case, *nested page tables* must be rebuilt at first. Figures 4(a) and (b) highlight this difference.

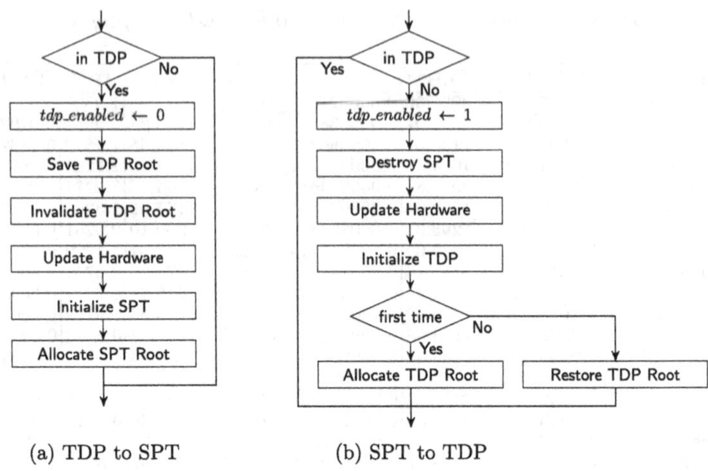

(a) TDP to SPT (b) SPT to TDP

Fig. 4. Minimal set of operations for switching the paging method

The answer to the second challenge is deeply related with the implementation of the hypervisor, therefore is left when the concrete implementation is discussed.

4 Implementation in QEMU-KVM for x86-64

The first functional unit of this implementation is the gathering of performance data. For the x86-64 processor family, PMCs are well documented in the system programming manuals [12,13]. Its configuration for DPMS is illustrated in Table 2.

The software-related events are directly gathered from the internal KVM data structures. The structure - `vcpu->stat` contains statistics regarding the status of the VCPUs, including `pf_fixed` and `exits`, serving as counters for the events - *fixed guest page faults* and *vmexits*, respectively. `pf_fixed` counts the number of fixed shadow page table entry (PTE) maps – not exactly the event occurs to the guest page tables. However, as the shadow page tables update is incurred by

Table 2. Configuration of PMC MSRs on x86-64 platform

Event	Selector address	Counter address	Event Code	Mask
i-TLB miss	0x186	0xc1	0x85	(0x01ull << 8) |(0x03ull << 16)
d-TLB miss	0x187	0xc2	0x49	(0x01ull << 8) |(0x03ull << 16)
clock cycle	0x188	0xc3	0x3c	(0x00ull << 8) |(0x03ull << 16)
retired instructions	0x189	0xc4	0xc0	(0x01ull << 8) |(0x03ull << 16)

updating in the guest page tables, `pf_fixed` serves as an approximate indicator to the number of fixed page faults in the guest page tables.

For managing the DPMS, a newly-defined data structure `pmc_val_t` is introduced to keep all performance data, the calculation results, as well as a number of the heuristic data in the context of the hypervisor for each guest.

In this prototype of the implementation, spikes of PF and *vmexit* events for longer time periods are encountered under *shadow paging*. For this reason, a few cyclic arrays (ring-buffers) are used – not for saving the values of metrics, but for saving the comparison results between them and their corresponding thresholds. Each time, a current value is compared with the corresponding thresholds. It scores 1 if the result is *greater than* or *equal to*, or else 0. The ring-buffers keep the records of these comparisons, with the aim of detecting whether the PF and *vmexit* for current workload are spiking to higher levels.

Upon decision making, the mean of all elements stored in a cyclic array are to be compared with a proportion of the top values ($1 \times$ length of the ring buffer). The percentage is also an empirical value (for example, 60%), to ensure that the majority of the recent PF and *vmexit* values are higher than the pre-determined thresholds, meanwhile leaving a certain degree of freedom for the sequence of occurrence (the occurrence order is unimportant). Under *nested paging*, similar procedure is followed, with the comparison result of TMR as the major condition. In addition, as TMR also has a bit ambiguity for heavy performance loss, PF and *vmexit* are also monitored and compared, but with the bottom thresholds to guard against some falsified cases (high TMR, but little performance loss).

Figure 5 depicts the major part of the control flow in the QEMU-KVM hypervisor. `qemu_kvm_cpu_thread_fn` is the routine of a function in QEMU's context that creates the needed number of VCPUs. It initiates and then begins to execute these VCPUs. Both the "kick-off" and interaction with VCPUs are implemented by sending commands from the KVM "device" (`/dev/kvm`) via a sequence of the device-specific function - `ioctl`. Guest code enters into execution after a `vmentry` instruction by the physical processor, until a certain event is encountered in the guest, which can not be handled by the guest but needs hypervisor's cooperation in the host (kernel or even user) space. Switching occurs in `vcpu_enter_guest` and takes the advantage of each *vmexit* in the inner loop. Switching is signaled by setting a request for MMU-reloading in function "`kvm_x86_ops->run`". The bitmap "`requests`" will be checked in `vcpu_enter_guest` and actions in Fig. 4 will be taken if necessary.

The major aspects of the implementation are described above; besides, a few other aspects closely related with the implementation also need to be covered, which may include: (1) Repetitive mechanism that ensures periodical output of performance data needed by the *paging method switching*; (2) Integration of the performance monitoring mechanism into the QEMU-KVM context.

In Linux kernel, a bunch of APIs were created for repetitive work deferral and periodic timer scheduling. Among them, a critical thing is timing. DPMS uses a standard timer in the Linux kernel defined by `timer_list` structure, which contains a pointer to a list of timers, the value for expiration, a user-

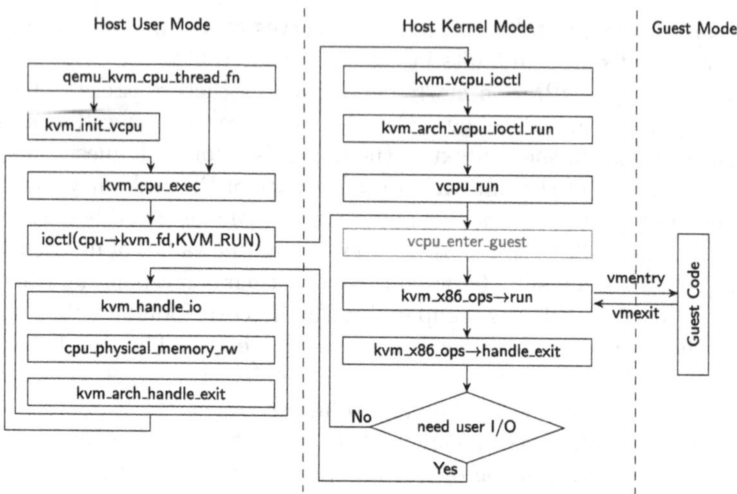

Fig. 5. Control flow in QEMU-KVM

definable callback function, a pointer to a region as the callback parameters, and a few optional variables for other uses. To create, initialize, renew, and delete the timer, the following APIs are provides by Linux kernel: (1) `init_timer`; (2) `setup_timer`; (3) `mod_timer`; (4) `del_timer`. To minimize the modification on the original code, the `timer_list` instance is in `kvm_arch` - the place where `pmc_val_t`'s instance is. `pmc_start` and `pmc_stop` are defined for controlling the PMCs. The former is used to start the PMCs on a specific core (known as the "leader"), and do initialization work necessary for performance data sampling as soon as the guest is booted up, such as creating the timer and initializing the `pmc` instance. The latter, conversely, removes the timer and stops the PMCs when the guest is about to go down. The most interesting part - data sampling function, is fulfilled by the callback routine of the timer. Furthermore, *Data Processing, Decision Making*, and "timer renewal" are all encapsulated in this function. The APIs defined for PMC controlling also form a call chain, as depicted in Fig. 6(a, b, c).

For an automatic control of the PMCs by the guest, it is necessary to integrate the PMC-related functions into the QEMU-KVM context. The purpose is that the PMCs can start immediately as the guest enters into execution, sample data afterwards, and stop as the guest is shutdown. After an in-depth examination of the source code and testing, `pmc_start` and `pmc_stop` find their places in the execution path of the KVM. Figure 7 depicts this scenario, and the cascading call chains after the two PMC-related functions are joined to the original paths. Similar with other parts of Linux kernel, KVM adopts callback feature when dealing with the file system operations. `pmc_start` and `pmc_stop` can be executed as soon as the corresponding execution paths are triggered by these callbacks.

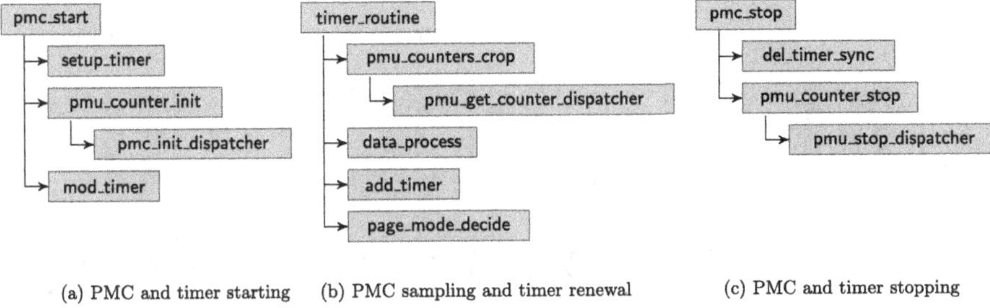

(a) PMC and timer starting (b) PMC sampling and timer renewal (c) PMC and timer stopping

Fig. 6. Call chains formed by the APIs for PMCs control

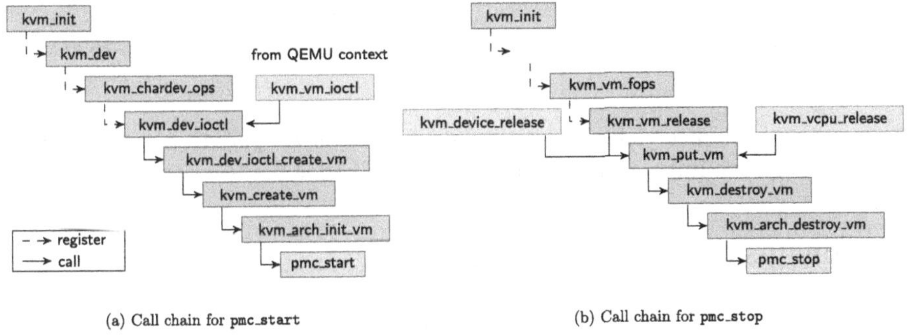

(a) Call chain for `pmc_start` (b) Call chain for `pmc_stop`

Fig. 7. The position for the integration of PMC mechanism

5 Benchmark Results

The prototype of DPMS implementation has been tested on three platforms, two with Intel processors, and one with AMD processor. The results show that all functional units of DPMS work as expected on the two Intel platforms. On the AMD platform, however, the switching operation causes immediately a reboot of the guest, rather than a recovery or rebuilding of the desired page tables. An assumption is that the AMD NPT is implemented a little different from the Intel EPT, thus may treat the switching as a kind of failure, and passes the control flow simply to the exception-handler which in turn triggers a reboot of the guest.

The two Intel platforms are also bothered with some corruption of the MMIO region in the guest memory due to paging method switching. The problem is caused more and more likely with the accumulated number of switching operations. A temporary solution is to slow down the tempo for switching. For the sake of performance, this may both eliminate many unnecessary switching and reduce the chance of guest crash. All these problems are flaws in the prototype and will be further examined and debugged.

Figure 8 illustrates the benchmark results of DPMS on an Intel platform. All workloads are executed sequentially in a batch to test the performance and stability. The results show that DPMS can improved the performance of `dedup` by 20.95%, `vips` by 9.09%, `barnes` by 1.03%, and `fft` by 0.03%, compared with

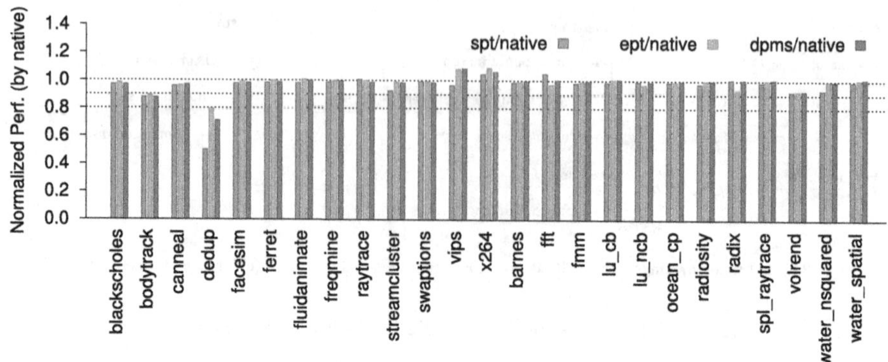

Fig. 8. Performance of DPMS, SPT and EPT on Platform with Xeon e5-1620-v2

the worst performance yielded by either *shadow* or *nested paging*, and meanwhile has little negative impact on the performance of other non-sensitive workloads.

6 Conclusion and Future Work

The dynamic switching of paging methods has the potential to improve the performance of workloads which are sensitive to the chosen paging method for guest memory paging. The idea is feasible and implementable. Some hypervisor-specific problems must be solved for a practicably useful solution. However, to outperform the best of current solutions, hardware modification is still needed. The patch for DPMS in KVM is to be found at https://github.com/zhayu.

References

1. Bhargave, R., Serebin, B., Spadini, F., Manne, S.: Accelerating Two-Dimensional Page Walks for Virtualized Systems. Advanced Micro Devices, March 2008
2. Barr, T.W., Cox, A.L., Rixner, S.: Translation Caching: Skip, Don't Walk (the Page Table). Houston, TX, June 2010
3. Bienia, C., Kumar, S., Singh, J.P., Li, K.: The PARSEC benchmark suite: characterization and architectural implications. In: PACT 2008, Ontario, Canada (2008)
4. Arcangeli, A., Kivity, A.: Using Linux as Hypervisor with KVM. Qumranet Inc., CERN, Geneve, September 2008
5. Wang, X., Zang, J., Wang, Z., Luo, Y., Li, X.: Selective hardware/software memory virtualization. In: VEE 2011, California, USA, March 2011
6. Bae, C.S., Lange, J.R., Dinda, P.A.: Enhancing virtualized application performance through dynamic adaptive paging mode selection. In: ICAC 2011. Northwestern University and University of Pittsburgh, June 2011
7. Zhang, Y., Oertel, R., Rehm, W.: Paging method switching for QEMU-KVM guest machine. In: BigDataScience 2014. Proceedings of the 2014 International Conference on Big Data Science and Computing, Article No. 22, August 2014

8. Gandhi, J., Hill, M.D., Swift, M.M., Paging, A.: Exceeding the best of nested and shadow paging. In: ISCA 2016. Proceedings of the 43rd International Symposium on Computer Architecture, pp. 707–718, June 2016
9. Hoang, G., Bae, C., Lange, J., Zhang, L., Dinda, P., Joseph, R.: A case for alternative nested paging models for virtualized systems. Comput. Archit. Lett. **9**, 17–20 (2010). University of Michigan
10. Gandhi, J., Basu, A., Hill, M.D., Swift, M.M.: Efficient Memory Virtualization. University of Wisconsin-Madison and AMD Research, October 2014
11. Liang, Q.: Performance Monitor Counter data analysis using Counter Analyzer. IBM developerWorks, February 2009
12. Intel Inc.: Intel 64 and IA-32 Architectures Software Developer's Manual, vol. 3B 18-3. Intel Corporation, June 2016
13. Advanced Micro Devices Inc.: AMD64 Architecture Programmer's Manual Volume 2: System Programming, p. 80. Advanced Micro Devices, May 2015

Aggregating and Managing Memory Across Computing Nodes in Cloud Environments

Luis A. Garrido(✉) and Paul Carpenter

Barcelona Supercomputing Center, C/Jordi Girona. 31, 08034 Barcelona, Spain
{luis.garrido,paul.carpenter}@bsc.es
http://www.bsc.es

Abstract. Managing memory capacity in cloud environments is a challenging problem, mainly due to the variability in virtual machine (VM) memory demand that sometimes can't be met by the memory of one node. New architectures have introduced hardware support for a shared global address space that, together with fast interconnects, enables resource sharing among multiple nodes. Thus, more memory is globally available to a computing node avoiding the costly swaps or migrations. This paper presents a solution to aggregate the memory capacity of multiple nodes in a virtualized cloud computing infrastructure. It is based on the Transcendent Memory (Tmem) abstraction and uses a user-space process to manage the memory available to a node, and distribute the aggregated memory across the computing infrastructure. We evaluate our solution using CloudSuite 3.0 benchmarks on Linux and Xen.

Keywords: Virtualization · Simulation, modeling and visualization

1 Introduction

Current data centres use large numbers of servers provisioned with their own computing resources. These servers share none of their resources, and they communicate over an Ethernet (or similar) network. Newer system architectures try to improve over this resource isolation approach, allowing servers to share their resources through the memory hierarchy. These systems provide a shared global physical address space, accessing memory at low latency using very fast interconnects. These systems are composed of *coherence islands* (*nodes*), with cache coherency enforced within an island, with no global hardware coherence.

Each node's physical memory capacity is distributed by the hypervisor among one or more Virtual Machines (VMs). The demand for memory resources generated by the VMs varies due to the different workloads that execute over time. To improve utilization of the memory capacity of the node, physical memory is often overcommitted, which causes a VM to have less memory than the amount it was configured with at boot time. The physical memory given to a VM is usually adjusted using memory ballooning and/or memory hotplug. Xen's Transcendent Memory (Tmem) [1] is another way to make memory capacity available to the VMs, through a paravirtualized put–get interface.

J.M. Kunkel et al. (Eds.): ISC High Performance Workshops 2017, LNCS 10524, pp. 642–652, 2017.
https://doi.org/10.1007/978-3-319-67630-2_45

This paper presents a mechanism, called GV-Tmem (Globally Visible Tmem), that extends the hypervisor to share the memory capacity of the nodes across the computing infrastructure. GV-Tmem introduces minimal changes to the hypervisor, keeping it small, secure and self-contained. Most of the complexity is in a user-space memory manager process running in the privileged domain that supports memory management policies, inter-node communication and dynamic addition and isolation of nodes. Our main contributions are:

1. A software architecture to aggregate memory across nodes using Tmem.
2. A two-tier mechanism for allocation and management of aggregated memory.

This paper is organized as follows. Section 2 gives the necessary background on virtualization, Tmem and coherence islands. Section 3 explains GV-Tmem. Section 4 describes the experimental methodology and Sect. 5 shows our results. Section 6 compares with related work and Sect. 7 concludes the paper and outlines future work.

2 Background

2.1 Virtualization in IaaS Clouds

Cloud computing provides on-demand access to an apparently unlimited pool of computing resources. There are multiple cloud computing service models, but the most fundamental is Infrastructure-as-a-Service (IaaS). IaaS shares the underlying hardware memory resources among customers using virtualization software known as a hypervisor.

Virtualization and Memory Management. The hypervisor virtualizes the physical resources, including memory, of the node. It creates and manages Virtual Machines (VMs), each of which runs its own (guest) Operating System (OS). When a VM is created, the hypervisor allocates to it a portion of the physical memory capacity. If a VM later requires more memory (*memory underprovisioning*) it will generate accesses to its (virtual) disk device, even if some of the node's memory is unassigned or sits idle in a VM that does not need it. When a VM has more memory than needed (*memory overprovisioning*), then the memory is underutilized and will be used for disk caches. In both cases, it is beneficial to re-allocate memory, making it available to the VM that needs it.

There are solutions for dynamically re-allocating memory among VMs, including memory ballooning and memory hotplug, both implemented in the Xen and Linux. These mechanisms have been widely deployed in current data centres, with significant performance benefits in terms of higher memory utilization. However, they do not provide adequate interfaces to aggregate memory capacity across multiple nodes.

State-of-the-Art Transcendent Memory. Transcendent memory (Tmem) [1] is another memory management mechanism that pools the idle or unassigned physical pages. Tmem is abstracted as a key–value store in which pages are accessed through a put–get interface, a put operation to write a page in the store that becomes mapped to the VM that issued it, and a get operation to read pages back. The Tmem interface supports also flush-page and flush-object operations, which return pages to the Tmem pool. In order to enable Tmem, the VMs need to have a Tmem kernel module (TKM) which handles all accesses to the Tmem pages on behalf of the VM by issuing hypercalls to the hypervisor.

2.2 Hardware Support for Coherence Islands

In systems such as Venice [2] and EUROSERVER [3] (based on ARM), the processors in each node are connected in clusters via a local cache-coherent interconnect to local resources. In particular, the Euroserver architecture implements the UNIMEM (*Unified Memory*) model [3].

In UNIMEM, remote memory is visible through the global physical address space, and communication across nodes is achieved through an *inter-node interface* and *global interconnect*. Systems that implement UNIMEM usually consist of 4 to 8 nodes. There are other architectures that also implement a global physical address space using different memory models, such as dRedBox [4] and Beehive [5]. The essential characteristics of these architectures are:

- Each node executes its own hypervisor and OSs.
- Global physical memory address space with low-latency access.
- Routing is based on the global physical address (e.g. high-order bits).
- Fast communication is provided across the nodes of the system, bypassing traditional network protocols (e.g. TCP/IP).

3 GV-Tmem Design

GV-Tmem consists of three software components:

- Extended Xen Hypervisor (Sect. 3.1)
- Tmem Kernel Module in the kernel of all domains (Sect. 3.2)
- Memory Manager (MM) in user space in Dom0 (Sect. 3.3)

3.1 Xen Hypervisor with Extensions

The hypervisor extensions for GV-Tmem are minimum and localized in the Tmem subsystem. First, the hypervisor enforces the memory allocation constraints determined by the MM. Second, it allocates and deallocates physical pages and passes ownership of blocks of pages in and out of the hypervisor. Third, it collects information of Tmem utilization that it sends to the MM.

Enforcing Local per-VM Memory Constraints: The hypervisor constrains the Tmem consumption of its VMs, based on the allocation determined by the MM. The MM specifies the maximum number of pages a VM can use.

Page Allocation and Transfer of Ownership: GV-Tmem ensures that each physical page is *owned* by at most one hypervisor. Tmem pages owned by a hypervisor are allocated using a zoned Buddy allocator, with a zone for each node from which it has ownership of at least one page.

A Tmem put operation allocates the closest free page from the allocators. A Tmem flush operation causes a page to be returned to the corresponding Buddy allocator. A Grant hypercall is used when the MM receives ownership of a list of blocks (each an appropriately-aligned power-of-two number of pages). These are added as free blocks to the appropriate Buddy allocator. In contrast, a Request hypercall is used to release ownership of pages on behalf of another node.

Memory Statistics: The hypervisor collects information about the Tmem utilization of the VMs. More specifically, the hypervisor monitors:

- Number of active VMs
- Amount of total Tmem capacity available to the hypervisor
- Amount of Tmem capacity in use by each VM
- Number of put, get and flush operations of each VM
- Number of failed put operations of each VM

The information gathered needs to be minimum to avoid communication overhead from the hypervisor to the MM. The hypervisor sends this information to the MM approximately every second by issuing a custom virtual interrupt request (VIRQ) to the privileged domain. The TKM (Sect. 3.2) captures the interrupt and forwards the information to the MM.

3.2 Tmem Kernel Module (TKM)

Interfacing to the Tmem client interface requires a kernel module in each VM, but the kernel module in the privileged domain (Dom0) acts only as an interface between the hypervisor and the node's MM (using netlink sockets).

3.3 Dom0 User-space Memory Manager (MM)

Each node has a user-space Memory Manager (MM) in Dom0. The MMs perform most of the work of GV-Tmem by cooperating to:

1. Distribute memory owned by each node among its guests
2. Distribute global memory capacity among nodes
3. Implement the flow of page ownership among nodes
4. Enable nodes to join and leave, and handle failures

Joining the GV-Tmem System: There is one MM Master (MM–M) that controls the system and distributes the global memory capacity. The messages passed among the MMs are listed in Table 1. A node requires a configuration file, which provides the network addresses of all nodes, their mappings to a node ID and credentials to establish secure connections. When a node R wishes to

Table 1. MM message types. *SL: slave, MT: master, I: Inactive, A: Active, R: Recovery, L: Leaving*

Command	Direction	Description	Slave state
Distribution of global memory capacity			
Statistics(S)	SL→MT	Send node statistics S to Master	A
Grant-Any(n, x)	SL→MT	Request grant of n pages to slave x	A
Grant-Fwd(n, x)	MT→SL	Forward request of n pages to y from x	A
Force-Return(x)	MT→SL	Return pages located at x and disable it	A
Mem-Limit(n)	MT→SL	Limit allocated pages to store local data	A
Flow of page ownership			
Grant($b, \cdots$)	SL/MT→SL	Transfer ownership of blocks of pages	A
Node state changes			
Register	SL→MT	Register a new node	$I \rightarrow A$
Leave-Req	SL→MT	Node requests to leave or shutdown	$A \rightarrow L$
Leave-Notify	MT→SL	MM–M notifies that the recipient has left	$L \rightarrow I$
Enable-Node(x, e)	MT→SL	Accept ($e = 1$) or reject ($e = 0$) pages at x	A

join the GV-Tmem system, it sends Register to the MM–M (see Table 1). The MM–M sets R's state to Active. Then it sends a Enable-Node(R,1) message to all registered nodes. Every node maintains a bitmap of the active nodes.

Distributing Memory Owned by a Node Among Guests: The local MM determines the maximum number of pages for each VM. This is done using a policy that determines this maximum based on the statistics sent from the hypervisor. This is the first tier of the memory management strategy. Pages are distributed subject to a memory consumption limit, set by the MM–M using the Mem-Limit hypercall. The MM detects when a VM is running out of memory and starts generating disk accesses in a specific period of time.

Distributing Global Memory Capacity Among Nodes: Nodes in the Active state, regularly send Statistics messages to the MM–M. These messages consist of the statistics gathered by the hypervisor of each node and information regarding the utilization and requests for remote memory of the node. In this way, the MM–M has a general view of the status of each node.

Based on these statistics and the global memory policy, the MM–M redistributes the memory among nodes when it receives a new Grant-Any message, which is a request to transfer ownership of a number of free physical pages to a node that requested memory. The MM–M can forward the request to another node by sending a Grant-Fwd message or give some of its pages to the requesting node. This is the second tier of the memory management strategy.

Implementing Flow of Page Ownership: The MM–M rebalances memory capacity, without knowing the physical addresses. Ownership of physical addresses is transferred in a peer-to-peer way using Grant messages, which passes a list of blocks, each an appropriately-aligned power-of-two number of addresses of physical pages.

Once a node is granted ownership of remote pages, it has exclusive access to them, and it is free to allocate these pages to store data on behalf of its VMs. The other nodes in the system, including the donor node, will not perform any reads or writes to those pages, since a page can be owned by only one node at a time. Thus, there is no need to order writes among multiple nodes.

With this way of distributing memory, the OS inside VMs is oblivious to the amount and location of the Tmem pages, only the hypervisor has a clear view of these details. The VMs are able to store any data that its VMs attempt to swap to disk, without any constraints regarding the nature of the data.

Leaving the GV-Tmem System. To cleanly shutdown a node R that is in GV-Tmem, the following procedure must be followed.

1. Node R sends a Leave-Req message to the MM–M.
2. Upon receiving the Leave-Req, the MM–M sets the node to Leaving state and sends Force-Return(R) to all nodes. The nodes return the pages at R that they own and will reject any pages received in future Grant messages.
3. Node R frees all pages used by Tmem and returns ownership of all remote pages to their home nodes.
4. Periodically, each node sends Grant messages to node R to return ownership of the pages that it had borrowed.
5. Once the MM–M has received Statistics messages from all nodes indicating that R is disabled and that it owns no pages at R, the MM–M moves R to Inactive and sends Leave-Notify to R.
6. At this point, the node R may shutdown.

Hardware Support for Memory Aggregation. GV-Tmem is suitable for UNIMEM-based architectures such as Euroserver [3]. GV-Tmem requires the underlying hardware to provide the following features:

1. A fast interconnect, providing a synchronous interface across the system.
2. Direct memory access from the hypervisor to all the memory available. Memory accesses from the hypervisor could be either through load/store instructions or RDMA, bypassing TCP/IP or similar protocols.
3. Remote access to a node's pages is disabled on hardware boot. Access is enabled only when the node joins GV-Tmem by sending the Register message.
4. Given a physical address, it must be possible to extract the Node ID.

4 Experimental Methodology

We tested GV-Tmem in a platform consisting of three nodes, which is consistent with UNIMEM-based architectures that currently have 4 to 8 nodes, with 6 to 8 processor cores per node [3]. Every VM runs Ubuntu 14.04 with Linux kernel 3.19.0+ as the OS, and Xen 4.5. The MMs in the nodes communicate using Ethernet TCP/IP sockets. Node 2 acts as the Master node and executes no VMs. Table 2 summarizes the hardware properties of the nodes.

Table 2. Hardware characteristics

Node	CPU	Frequency	Memory
Node 1	AMD FX Quad-Core	1.4 GHz	6 GB
Node 2	Intel Core i7	2.10 GHz	8 GB
Node 3	Intel Xeon	2.262 GHz	64 GB

Table 3. List of scenarios used for benchmarking

Scns.	VM Parameters	Description
Scn. 1	VM1, VM2: 768MB RAM, 1 CPU; VM3: 1GB RAM, 1 CPU	All VMs execute in-memory-analytics, sleep 5 seconds and then execute it again. The data set used is from [7].
Scn. 2	VM1, VM2, VM3: 512MB RAM, 1 CPU	VM1 and VM2 execute *usemem*, and VM3 starts when VM1 allocates 640MB.
Scn. 3	VM1, VM2: 512MB RAM, 1 CPU	Every VM executes graph-analytics once. They use the dataset provided by [8–10].

The shared global address space was emulated using the node's local memory. Remote access emulation was the best choice in order to offer the possibilty to analyze the impact of the latency of the interconnect on the memory aggregation and management mechanisms. However, the analysis of the impact of latency and non-uniform latencies is out of the scope of this work. We modified Xen to start up using a portion of the physical memory capacity, equalling the emulated memory capacity of the node. The rest of the node's memory capacity was reserved to emulate remote data storage. Whenever the hypervisor performs an "emulated" remote access after remote memory becomes available, we add a delay in the hypervisor lasting 50 µs to model hardware latency.

We evaluate GV-Tmem using CloudSuite 3.0 [6]. We also designed a microbenchmark called *usemem*, which allocates a varying amount of memory, starting with 128 MB. Every time it allocates memory, it performs a series of write/read operations while checking the correctness of the values read in the allocated memory. We execute at most three DomUs simultaneously, and refer to each set of DomUs as a *scenario* (or *Scn*). Table 3 shows the scenarios used. For Scns. 1 and 3, all nodes have 1 GB of Tmem capacity. For Scn. 2, Node 2 has 1 GB of Tmem, while Nodes 1 and 3 have 384 MB.

This paper uses three memory management policies:

- **greedy-local**: Default policy used in Tmem with only local memory, which gives memory away on demand. No maximum values are set to limit the amount of memory taken by a VM.
- **greedy-remote**: An extended version of greedy-local using remote memory.
- **TTM**: A two-tier memory management strategy that allocates memory locally for each VM (first-tier) depending on the node's statistics, and issues requests for remote memory (second-tier) depending on the perceived memory pressure.

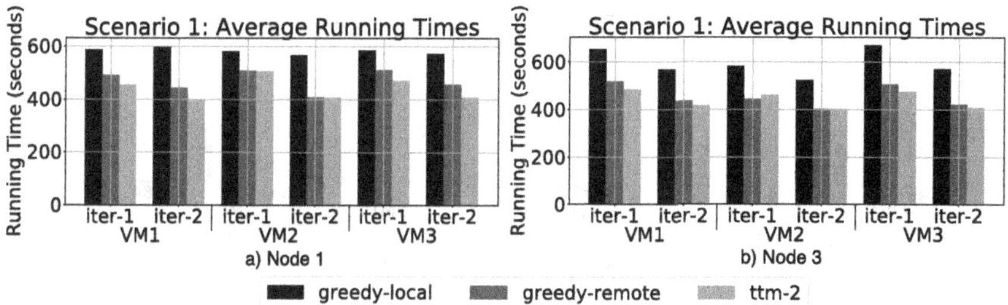

Fig. 1. Running time for Scn. 1 in nodes 1 and 3. Time is in seconds (less is better).

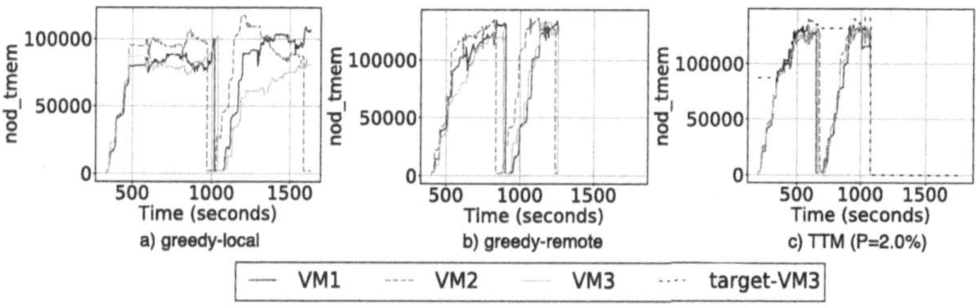

Fig. 2. Tmem capacity (nod-tmem) obtained by every VM in node 3 for Scn. 1. The label *target-VM3* refers to the target allocation of VM3.

The pages allocated and deallocated to a VM are increased by a percentage $\%P$ of the pages owned by the node (local or remote).

5 Results

Results for Scenario 1. Figure 1 shows the average running times of each VM for Scn. 1. The running time improves by an average of 19.4% and 23.5% in nodes 1 and 3, respectively, when going from greedy-local to greedy-remote. When implementing TTM with $P = 2.0\%$, there is further improvement of 6.0% and 4.0% over greedy-remote, demonstrating the need to implement memory management policies when there is significant memory pressure.

Figure 2 shows the amount of Tmem capacity that each VM is able to use for the three policies mentioned in node 3. With greedy-local (Fig. 2(a)), VM3 in both iterations cannot obtain a fair share of the available Tmem capacity. With greedy-remote (Fig. 2(b)), the VMs are able to get more total Tmem, but because of the lack of memory management policies, some VMs are unable to obtain a fair share of Tmem. With TTM (Fig. 2(c)), every VM is ensured a fair amount of the available Tmem, demonstrating that TTM is able to ensure fairness regarding the VMs' allocation of Tmem, improving the running times.

Results for Scenario 2: the Usemem Scenario. The average running times for Scn. 2 are shown in Fig. 3. When enabling greedy-remote, VM3, VM2 and VM1 reach an average performance improvement of 63%, 20% and 13% respec-

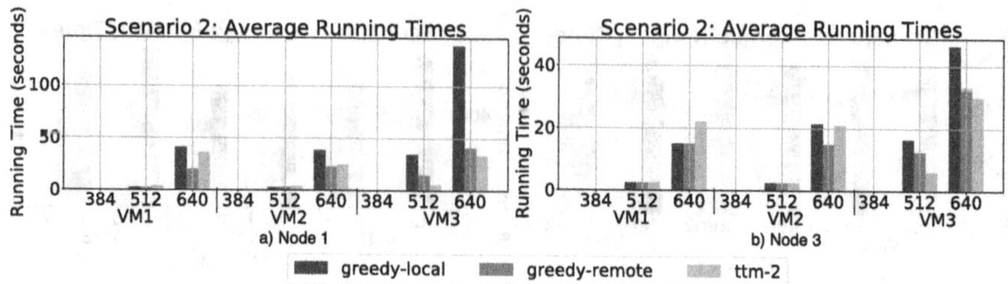

Fig. 3. Running time for Scn. 2 for nodes 1 and 3.

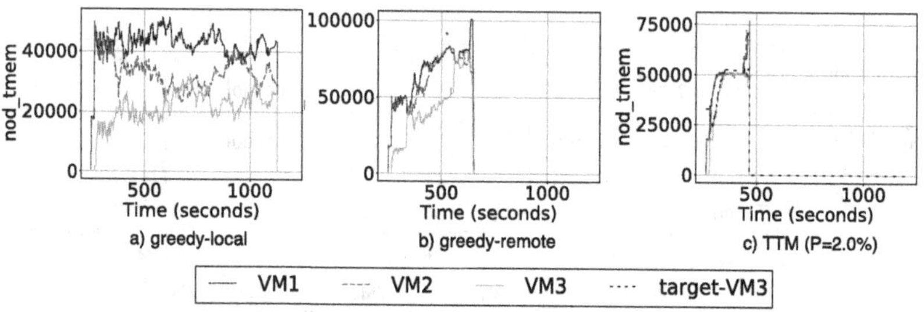

Fig. 4. Tmem capacity (nod-tmem) obtained by every VM in node 3 for Scn. 2.

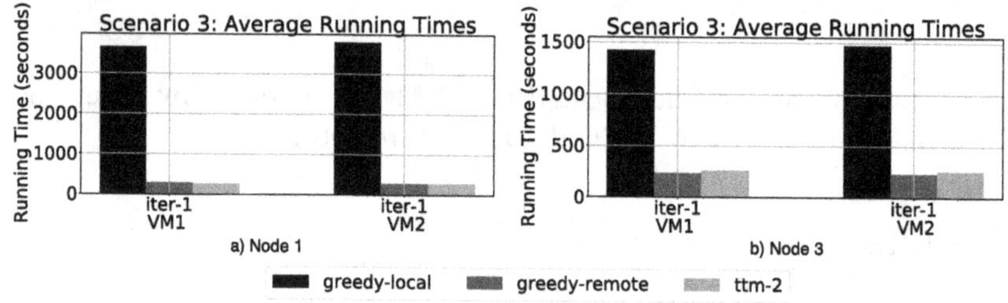

Fig. 5. Running time for Scn. 3 for nodes 1 and 3.

tively. When TTM is enabled, VM3 shows a maximum and minimum improvement of 27% and 5.5% in node 1, respectively, and a maximum and minimum improvement of 51% and 9.3%, respectively, in node 3. However, VM1 and VM2 both experience a performance reduction.

Figure 4 shows the remote memory capacity that each VM is using for the three policies. Figure 4(a) shows that VM3 struggles to obtain memory pages using *greedy-remote*. This is similar to the case in Fig. 2(a), in which the VM3 was unable to reach its fair share of Tmem. With TTM, VM3 obtains a larger amount of Tmem, improving its performace. Here, VM3's improvement comes at the expense of VM1 and VM2, balancing the Tmem pages every VM can have.

Results for Scenario 3. The average running times for Scn. 3 are shown in Fig. 5. In this case, node 1 improves by a maximum and a minimum of 92.3%

and 92.1%, respectively, when comparing greedy-local to greedy-remote. When enabling TTM, it improves by a maximum and a minimum of 6.0% and 0.9%.

In node 3, there's a maximum and mininum improvement of 84.4% and 83.1% when comparing greedy-local to greedy-remote. However, performance degrades by 10% with TTM compared to greedy-remote. When enabling TTM, the VMs require more memory but TTM enforces limits, although flexible, on the memory they can take, similar to what occurs in Scn. 2 for VM1 and VM2. When disabling TTM, the VMs take memory unrestrained thus performing slightly better than TTM. This highlights the need for more adaptive memory management policies.

6 Related Work

Zcache [11] is a backend that provides a compressed cache for swap and clean filesystem pages. *RAMster* [11] is an extension of zcache that uses kernel sockets to store pages in the RAM of remote nodes. In contrast, our approach grants and releases blocks of pages at greater granularity, reducing the amount of software communication between nodes, since we exploit the shared global address space. RAMster is implemented in the kernel whereas our approach uses a user-space process in a privileged VM, providing greater flexibility for memory management. RAMCloud [12] is a POSIX-like filesystem in which all data is stored in DRAM across nodes, placing the data in one or more nodes, introducing issues of global coherency and exclusivity of access. Our solution aggregates memory exploiting a global shared address space, without requirements for global coherency. Hecatonchire [13] achieves resource aggregation by decoupling virtual resource management from physical resources. It uses a mediation layer that arbitrates how applications access resources. We differ from [13] by making memory available to the hypervisor through a user-space process.

7 Conclusions and Future Work

This paper introduces GV-Tmem, a method that exploits Tmem to share memory capacity across multiple nodes. We evaluated GV-Tmem using CloudSuite, obtaining up to 51% performance improvement using simple memory management policies. The results demonstrate the effectiveness of GV-Tmem, and the need for two-tier memory management strategies within and across nodes.

Future work will investigate how to integrate GV-Tmem with other resource management mechanisms of other cloud software. It is also necessary to develop more sophisticated two-tier global memory management policies, in order to improve adaptivity and responsiveness to changes in memory demand. Aspects of resiliency fault tolerance also need to be addressed, as well as scalable non-centralized memory aggregation approaches that do not require a MM–M.

Acknowledgements. This research has received funding from the European Union's 7th Framework Programme (FP7/2007-2013) under grant agreement number 610456

(Euroserver). The research was also supported by the Ministry of Economy and Competitiveness of Spain under the contract TIN2012-34557, HiPEAC-3 Network of Excellence (ICT- 287759), and the FI-DGR Grant Program (file number 2016FI_B 00947) of the Government of Catalonia.

References

1. Magenheimer, D., Mason, C., McCracken, D., Hackel, K.: Transcendent memory and Linux. In: Proceedings of the Linux Symposium, pp. 191–200. Citeseer (2009)
2. Dong, J., Hou, R., Huang, M., Jiang, T., Zhao, B., Mckee, S., Wang, H., Cui, X., Zhang, L.: Venice: exploring server architectures for effective resource sharing. In: IEEE International Symposium on High-Performance Computer Architecture (HPCA) (2016)
3. Durand, Y., Carpenter, P., Adami, S., Bilas, A., Dutoit, D., Farcy, A., Gaydadjiev, G., Goodacre, J., Katevenis, M., Marazakis, M., Matus, E., Mavroidis, I., Thomson, J.: Euroserver: energy efficient node for european micro-servers. In: 17th Euromicro Conference on Digital System Design (DSD), pp. 206–2013. IEEE (2014)
4. Katrinis, K., Syrivelis, D., Pnevmatikatos, D., Zervas, G., Theodoropoulos, D., Koutsopoulos, I., Hasharoni, K., Raho, D., Pinto, C., Espina, F., Lopez-Buedo, S., Chen, Q., Nemirovsky, M., Roca, D., Klosx, H., Berends, T.: Rack-scale disaggregated cloud data centers: the dReDBox project vision. In: Design, Automation & Test in Europe Conference & Exhibition (DATE). IEEE (2016)
5. Thacker, C.: Beehive: a many-core computer for FPGAs. In: MSR, Silicon Valley (2010)
6. Ferdman, M., Adileh, A., Kocberber, O., Volos, S., Alisafaee, M., Jevdjic, D., Kaynak, C., Popescu, A.D., Ailamaki, A., Falsafi, B.: Clearing the clouds: a study of emerging scale-out workloads on modern hardware. In: Proceedings of the 17th International Conference on Architectural Support for Programming Languages and Operating Systems, pp. 37–48. ACM (2012)
7. Harper, F.M., Konstan, J.A.: The MovieLens datasets: history and context. In: ACM Transactions on Interactive Intelligent Systems, pp. 19:1–19:19. ACM (2015)
8. Rossi, R.A., Ahmed, N.K.: SOC-twitter-follows - Social Networks. http://networkrepository.com/soc-twitter-follows.php
9. Ross, R.A., Ahmed, N.K.: The network data repository with interactive graph analytics and visualization. In: Proceedings of the 29th AAAI Conference on AI (2015)
10. Ross, R.A., Ahmed, N.K.: An interactive data repository with visual analytics. SIGKDD Explor. **17**(2), 37–41 (2016)
11. Magenheimer, D.: Zcache and RAMster (oh, and frontswap too) overview and some benchmarking (2012). https://oss.oracle.com/projects/tmem/dist/documentation/presentations/LSFMM12-zcache-final.pdf
12. Ousterhout, J., Agrawal, P., Erickson, D., Kozyrakis, C., Leverich, K., Mazières, D., Mitra, S., Narayanan, A., Parulkar, G., Rosenblum, M., Rumble, S., Stratmann, E., Stutsman, R.: The case for RAMClouds: scalable high-performance storage entirely in DRAM. In: SIGOPS Operating Systems Review, vol. 43, pp. 92–105. ACM (2010)
13. Svärd, P., Hudzia, B., Tordsson, J., Elmroth, E.: Hecatonchire: towards multi-host virtual machines by server disaggregation. In: Lopes, L., et al. (eds.) Euro-Par 2014. LNCS, vol. 8806, pp. 519–529. Springer, Cham (2014). doi:10.1007/978-3-319-14313-2_44

Visualization at Scale: Deployment Case Studies and Experience Reports

In-situ Visualization for Computation Workflows

Alejandro Ribes[1(✉)], Ovidiu Mircescu[1], Anthony Geay[1], and Yvan Fournier[2]

[1] EDF Lab Paris-Saclay, 91120 Palaiseau, France
alejandro.ribes@edf.fr
[2] EDF Lab Chatou, 78400 Chatou, France

Abstract. The open-source numerical simulation platform SALOME provides a set of services to create simulation workflows that connect different computation units. These computation units can be different solvers that communicate to create a complex multi-physics simulation. The SALOME platform can execute such a workflow on a distributed network of computers or on a supercomputer. This article presents the integration of in-situ visualization using Catalyst into the computation workflows module of the SALOME platform. This integration allows complex simulations to easily use in-situ visualization and requires no development efforts.

Keywords: In-situ visualization · Large numerical simulations · Computation workflows

1 Introduction

1.1 An Industrial Context

In the past, studies and improvements in scientific simulation have been mainly focused on the solver, due to being the most cycle-consuming part in the simulation process. Thus, visualization has been traditionally run sequentially on a smaller computer and at the very end of the solver computation. At the time, this was easily explained by the small need for both memory and computation resources in most of the visualization cases. Nevertheless, with the increase of our computational capabilities, we tend to use and generate much more data than what we were used to. Thus, as the scale of industrial simulation problems is getting larger, specific issues are emerging related to input/output efficiency. In particular, data generated during the solver computation and used for the visualization are the source of a worrisome overhead. Even worse, some researchers are starting to spend more time for writing and reading data than for running solvers and visualizations (Ross et al. 2008). Storage volume, even short-lived, can also be an issue. This trend is pushing us to design new I/O strategies and consider visualization as a part of our high-performance simulation systems.

Electricité de France (EDF), being one of the biggest electricity producer in Europe, extensively uses numerical simulation and has developed, for the past 25 years, several solvers. Examples of these solvers are: *code_aster* (solid mechanics finite elements

J.M. Kunkel et al. (Eds.): ISC High Performance Workshops 2017, LNCS 10524, pp. 655–661, 2017.
https://doi.org/10.1007/978-3-319-67630-2_46

solver [http://code-aster.org/]), *Telemac-2D* (Hervouet 2000) (shallow water equations solver [http://opentelemac.org/]), *Code_Saturne* (navier-stokes solver [http://code-saturne.org]), SYRTHES (thermodynamics solver) or *Code_Carmel* (electromagnetic solver [http://code-carmel.univ-lille1.fr/]). EDF has several supercomputers that regularly run these code in order to perform analysis involving large amounts of data. In this context, the post-processing and visualization of data becomes a critical step.

EDF also develops (in collaboration with OpenCascade and the *French Center of Atomic Research*, CEA) an open-source numerical simulation platform called SALOME, [http://www.salome-platform.org/]. This platform provides generic methods for Pre- and Post-Processing of numerical simulations. It is based on an architecture made of reusable components. Among others, these components deal with: computer aided design, meshing, HPC execution management, multi-physics coupling, data post-processing and visualization. ParaView is currently integrated in this platform as a visualization module.

1.2 A Catalyst Adaptor for *Code_Saturne*

In 2012 (five years before writing the current article), we successfully integrated Catalyst into *Code_Saturne*:

- Catalyst is an in-situ visualization library developed by Kitware to help reduce the data post-treatment overhead.
- *Code_Saturne* is a computational fluid dynamics software designed to solve the Navier-Stokes equations in the cases of 2D, 2D axisymmetric or 3D flows.

Both Catalyst (Fabian et al. 2011) and *Code_Saturne* (Archambeau et al. 2004) are Open Source software and can be download, used or tested freely. At the time the implementation was performed and after testing the prototype in our former corporate supercomputer Ivanoe, we found Catalyst to be a relevant solution to provide in-situ visualization. Catalyst proved to allow a simple and fast implementation of an adaptor; 51 M and a 204 M elements mesh where tested, which was above the average size case used by EDF engineers in our industrial environment at that time. A detailed report of this work can be found in (Ribés et al. 2015).

1.3 In-situ Visualization for Computation Workflows

Nowadays, several solvers of the SALOME eco-system at EDF are implementing in-situ services. This is a consequence of the positive experience using Catalyst on *Code_Saturne*. In this context, the choice of Catalyst is not questioned but we worry about the generalization of this approach. Indeed, EDF has designed numerous (at least 20) solvers during the last 25 years and in-situ services are in increasing demand from the physicists and engineers. Thus, are we going to build a Catalyst adapter in every single solver? If this is the case, can we ease this integration? Or maybe there exists a more general solution to this problem?

In this article, we present an ongoing effort to generalize the use of in-situ visualization in the SALOME platform. This is performed by using the *computation workflows* of this platform. The idea is to integrate Catalyst in a node of a workflow which will allow a twofold positive effect:

1. Solvers already implementing SALOME interfaces for using computation workflows can perform in-situ or in-transit visualization without any development effort.
2. Existing or future workflows, for instance multi-physics simulations, can be enriched with several in-situ or in-transit visualization outputs.

2 Computation Workflows in SALOME

2.1 SALOME

The SALOME platform is an open source software framework for the integration of numerical solvers in various scientific domains. CEA (*French Center of Atomic Research*) and EDF (*Electricité de France*) are using SALOME to perform a wide range of simulations, which are typically related to industrial equipment in power plants (nuclear power plants, wind turbines, dams…). Among primary concerns are the design of new-generation reactor types, nuclear fuel management and transport, material ageing for the life-cycle management of equipment, and the reliability and safety of the nuclear facilities.

In order to accurately simulate complex industrial systems, scientists and engineers need to integrate most fields of physics such as material science, solid mechanics, structural dynamics, fluid physics, thermo-hydraulics, nuclear physics, radiations or electromagnetism. The SALOME platform gathers all these fields in one single simulation environment.

The main features of the SALOME are:

- Design of the geometric representation for physical systems (CAD modelling) and its associated discretized model (meshing functions for finite elements or finite volumes solvers).
- Ability to integrate domain specific solvers into normalized software components with standard interface to facilitate the coupling of different physical domains.
- Supervision of computation workflows defined as graphs of distributed software components, including CAD modelling, domain specific solvers and data processing components.
- Analysis of simulation output, in particular using visualizations of physical fields resulting from computation workflows in 3D views using ParaView.

In this context, one of the key points of the platform is the usage of standardized data models to describe physical concepts for numerical analysis, and to ensure interoperability between software components. For instance, the MED data model is used for meshes and fields descriptions. Figure 1 depicts the main parts of the SALOME platform.

The SALOME platform is available under LGPL license and can be downloaded from its web site [http://www.salome-platform.org/] for several Linux distributions and

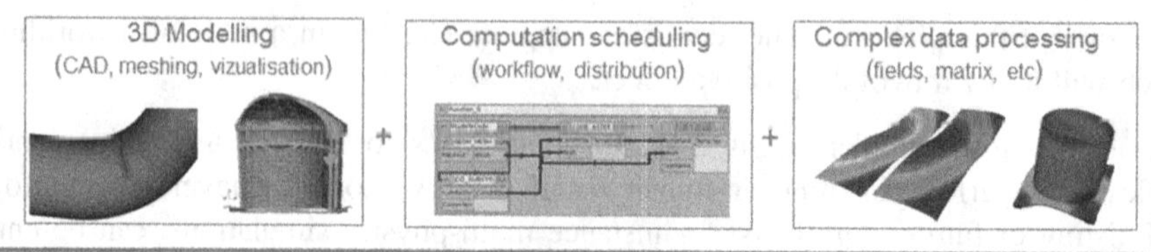

Fig. 1. Depiction of the three main steps when performing a simulation on the SALOME platform.

for Windows. The site provides tutorials, a forum section and gives access to the user documentation and the source code.

2.2 Supervision of Computation Workflows

There is an increasing need for multidisciplinary simulations in various research and engineering domains. Fluid-structure interaction and thermal coupling are two examples. The software strategy in many contexts of simulation (at least at EDF) is to develop numerical solvers dedicated to their own domain, and then to execute multi-domains simulation by coupling these specific solvers.

SALOME provides a set of services to create a simulation workflow that connects different computation units. Then it executes this workflow on a distributed network of computers or HPC resources. The main features are:

The possibility to integrate domain specific solvers as normalized components with standard interfaces to ease the coupling of different physical domains. These SALOME components can be used as the computational units of a simulation process. Some tools are provided to automatize this integration for standard configurations (integration of executable programs, functions of a library or python scripts).

The supervision of a computation workflow defined as a graph of connected SALOME components, including CAD modelling, meshing, domain specific solvers and data processing components. The graph can be edited using a graphical user interface (GUI) or the Python Text User Interface (TUI). A GUI snapshot of a multi-physics simulation for a nuclear safety study is shown in Fig. 2.

The distribution on HPC resources. SALOME contains a job manager that can be used to define a computation job (including either a simple SALOME component or a complete workflow) and to drive the submission of the job to a distributed set of computers or HPC resources. The job manager can handle many batch systems like PBS, LSF, SGE, LOADLEVELER or SLURM through a normalized generic interface. A GUI, a C++ interface or a Python interface can be used (or combined) to create simple scripts or domain specific tools.

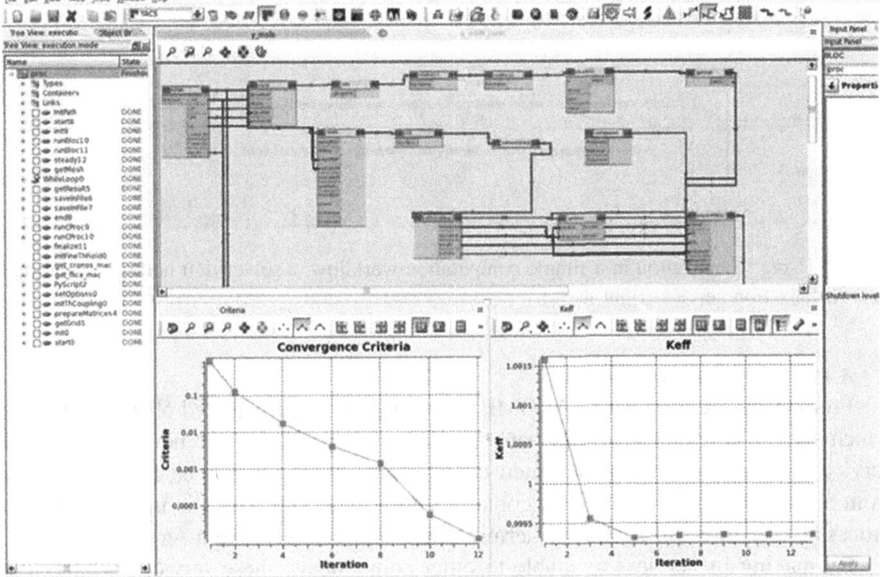

Fig. 2. Example of a multi-physics simulation involving the coupling of a neutronics model with a thermal-hydraulics model for a nuclear safety study (study performed at the CEA/DEN).

3 Inserting Visualization in Computation Workflows

3.1 Visualization as a Graph Node

The main idea we have implemented is dealing with visualization as another node in the graph representing a computation workflow. This is illustrated in Fig. 3 where we can see a simple graph representing a simulations: the node of the left side encapsulates a solver while the node on the right side encapsulates the visualization. Thus, by inserting a "visualization node" in a graph like the one shown in Fig. 2 a user can run a multi-physics simulation with in-situ or in-transit visualization services. This involves no programming efforts.

3.2 Some Implementation Details

The aim of the work described in this document is to propose, in the SALOME workflows, an "in-situ" visualization service usable by various solvers. A first constraint that emerges from this objective is to use a standard data format for the representation of the data to be visualized. The standard format that SALOME uses for exchange in its computation workflows is MED. Indeed, MED serves mainly for the representation of meshes and fields and this format is implemented in the MEDCoupling library. As part of the integration into SALOME, the visualization services must accept data in the MED format, however Catalyst only deals with VTK. An adaptor was then implemented, inside the visualization service, in order to perform this conversion. Figure 4 schematically represents this process.

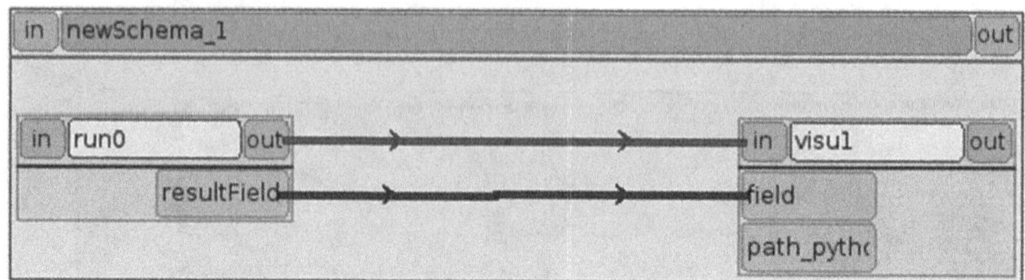

Fig. 3. Using visualization in a simple computation workflow, a solver (left node) is connected to a visualization service (right node).

A new workflow component

From the point of view of SALOME, a component is a distributed object (CORBA) which has an internal state and can provide services. Thus, our new visualization service is a component. A distributed object is an object that can be called remotely from a, for example, the CORBA communication bus. The object is instantiated in a process ("container" in SALOME terminology) and behaves like a server.

By making its services available to other components, these services behave like black boxes that generate output data from input data. The SALOME computation workflow' terminology uses the concept of "port" to refer to the input and output data of a service. On the other hand, services are the processes represented in the nodes of the computation workflow; the creation of such a computation workflow is to connect the ports of the different nodes involved in the calculation. In Fig. 3 we can see how arrows graphically connect the ports of two nodes.

The data exchanges in the computation workflows are done by serialization and transfer through a CORBA communication bus. This data is transmitted from a CORBA object to another. The processes described in the calculation nodes are executed in "containers". A container is a process launched by the computation workflow on a computing resource (a machine that has a version of SALOME installed and registered in the resource catalog). Each node of the workflow must be associated with a container, but a container can execute several nodes. If several nodes run in the same container, it means that they are executed on the same machine and in the same process.

It is also possible to have MPI containers, which gather processes run by an MPI session. MPI containers can host MPI components that dispatch components over every MPI process available. From the workflow point of view simply one node, one component and one container are seen. When a service of an MPI component is called, the request is relayed to the components of every MPI process in order to provide MPI parallelism. MPI components can deal with distributed data, as input or output, which are a group of CORBA objects distributed over MPI processes. From this angle, CORBA objects are just used as a broker choosing the best way to perform the data transfer; no copy using the CORBA channel is performed.

In conclusion, in the context of in-situ techniques the data exchange is performed by a memory pointer and no copy is needed. Indeed, the visualization component automatically detects if the two components (solver and visualization) are in the same

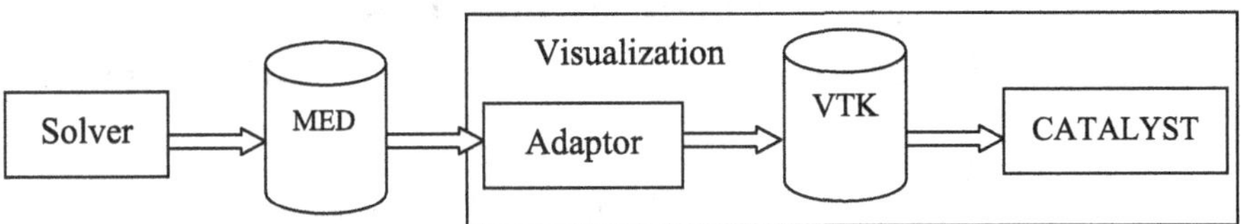

Fig. 4. Using visualization in a simple computation workflow, a solver (left node) is connected to a visualization service (right node).

container. If this is the case (for instance in the same node of a supercomputer) then the visualization service just reads a memory pointer and an in-situ execution is performed. In the other case, a copy is made and send over the network to the visualization service thus implementing an in-transit visualization system.

4 Conclusion

We have presented our ongoing effort to generalize the use of in-situ visualization in the SALOME platform. This is performed by using the *computation workflows* of this platform. We have successfully integrated Catalyst as a node of a workflow which allows a solvers already implementing SALOME interfaces for using computation workflows (MED format) to perform in-situ or in-transit visualization without any development effort. Thus, multi-physics simulations, can be enriched with several in-situ or in-transit visualization outputs.

We used *Code_Saturne* and a turbulent fluid dynamics numerical simulation to validate our visualization services in the SALOME workflows. Our preliminary tests are satisfactory but large scale HPC testing is still required before using this new component into industrial multi-physics simulations.

References

Archambeau, F., Mechitoua, N., Sakiz, M.: Code_Saturne: a finite volume code for the computation of turbulent incompressible flows. Industrial applications. Int. J. Finite **1**, 1–62 (2004)

Fabian, N., Moreland, K., Thompson, D., Bauer, A.C., Marion, P., Geveci, B., Rasquin, M., Jansen, K.E.: The paraview coprocessing library: a scalable, general purpose in situ visualization library. In: IEEE Symposium on Large Data Analysis and Visualization (LDAV), pp. 89–96 (2011)

Ribés, A., Lorendeau, B., Jomier, J., Fournier, Y.: In-situ visualization in computational fluid dynamics using open-source tools: integration of catalyst into *Code_Saturne*. In: Bennett, J., Vivodtzev, F., Pascucci, V. (eds.) Topological and Statistical Methods for Complex Data. MV, pp. 21–37. Springer, Heidelberg (2015). doi:10.1007/978-3-662-44900-4_2

Ross, R.B., Peterka, T., Shen, H.-W., Hong, Y., Ma, K.-L., Yu, H., Moreland, K.: Visualization and parallel i/o at extreme scale. J. Phys: Conf. Ser. **125**(1), 012099 (2008)

Hervouet, J.-M.: TELEMAC modelling system: an overview. Hydrol. Process. **14**(13), 2209–2210 (2000)

From Big Data to Big Displays High-Performance Visualization at Blue Brain

Stefan Eilemann(✉), Marwan Abdellah, Nicolas Antille, Ahmet Bilgili, Grigory Chevtchenko, Raphael Dumusc, Cyrille Favreau, Juan Hernando, Daniel Nachbaur, Pawel Podhajski, Jafet Villafranca, and Felix Schürmann

Blue Brain Project, Ecole Polytechnique Federale de Lausanne, Lausanne, Switzerland
{stefan.eilemann,marwan.abdellah,nicolas.antille,ahmet.bilgili, grigory.chevtchenko,raphael.dumusc,cyrille.favreau,juan.hernando, daniel.nachbaur,pawel.podhajski,jafet.villafranca, felix.schurmann}@epfl.ch

Abstract. Blue Brain has pushed high-performance visualization (HPV) to complement its HPC strategy since its inception in 2007. In 2011, this strategy has been accelerated to develop innovative visualization solutions through increased funding and strategic partnerships with other research institutions.

We present the key elements of this HPV ecosystem, which integrates C++ visualization applications with novel collaborative display systems. We motivate how our strategy of transforming visualization engines into services enables a variety of use cases, not only for the integration with high-fidelity displays, but also to build service oriented architectures, to link into web applications and to provide remote services to Python applications.

1 Motivation

The Blue Brain Project (BBP) uses simulation-based research to analyze and reverse engineer cortical neuron circuits. The simulated models go beyond using detailed models of individual neurons or large-scale network models of simplified neurons, they model in the order of hundreds of thousands of detailed neurons in a fully connected circuit. The project generates a multitude of data for the model building and during the simulation of these models. This data ranges from terabyte-sized image stacks for data extraction to detailed in-silico circuit models of large geometric complexity and terabyte-size simulation reports.

Visualization supports the BBP along all parts of the project to understand and debug model data, building and simulation algorithms as well as validating and discovering new insight from the in-silico experiments. Our strategy to support this mission is based on components linked through network protocols: High-fidelity display systems to see more detail in complex data, a set of standard rendering engines (rasterization, out-of-core volume rendering, interactive

J.M. Kunkel et al. (Eds.): ISC High Performance Workshops 2017, LNCS 10524, pp. 662–675, 2017.
https://doi.org/10.1007/978-3-319-67630-2_47

raytracing), and decoupled, light-weight applications using these components remotely. In the following we will present these components along with a few use cases.

2 High-Fidelity Displays

High-fidelity display systems are the integration point of the Blue Brain visualization capabilities. They are the evolution of existing visualization systems, enabling high resolution, immersion and team collaboration. Compared to current single-user or single-presenter systems, collaborative display systems allow real team work through a combination of size, resolution and user friendly implementation. Compared to immersive visualization systems like the CAVE, they provide a more approachable environment for high-fidelity visualization. For all use cases, the increased display size and resolution allows better data exploration for 2D and 3D content, facilitating large data exploration.

2.1 Tiled Multitouch Display Walls

The core of the Blue Brain visualization infrastructure are multiple high-resolution tiled display walls driven by our Tide software [1]. All walls are equipped with a multitouch user interface and can be remote controlled from any web browser. The walls are built using thin-bezel, 55 inch, Full HD LCD panels with a hardened glass sheet. We use 4×3 and 3×3 configurations for a total of 24 and 18 Megapixel resolution, respectively. The display size of over five meter diagonally (four meter for 3×3) allows team-size collaboration (up to ten people) or project-wide presentations (up to a hundred people). Figure 1 shows one wall during a project-wide presentation with multiple interactive applications running remotely on the wall.

2.2 Tide

Tide (Tiled Interactive Display Environment) is the software driving the Blue Brain tiled display walls. It provides multi-window, multi-user touch interaction on large surfaces — think of a giant collaborative wall-mounted tablet. Tide is a distributed application that can run on multiple machines to power display walls or projection systems of any size. Its user interface is designed to offer an intuitive experience on touch walls. It works just as well on non touch-capable installations by using its web interface from any web browser. Figure 1 shows Tide on a 4×3 display wall and Fig. 2 shows the Tide web interface in a browser.

While there is substantial research on tiled display wall software [3,4,6,11,12,14], we found that most solutions were not ready for production use in a 24×7 unattended environment. For this reason, we started with the TACC DisplayCluster open source software [12], which we incrementally refactored and improved to the current TIDE implementation. On the other hand, the hardware has been commoditized to make these type of installations affordable to

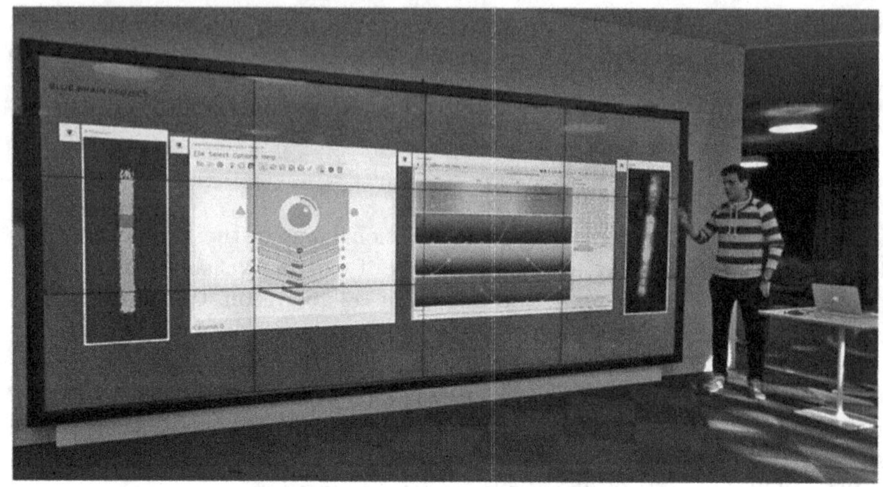

Fig. 1. Blue Brain 4 × 3 tiled display wall

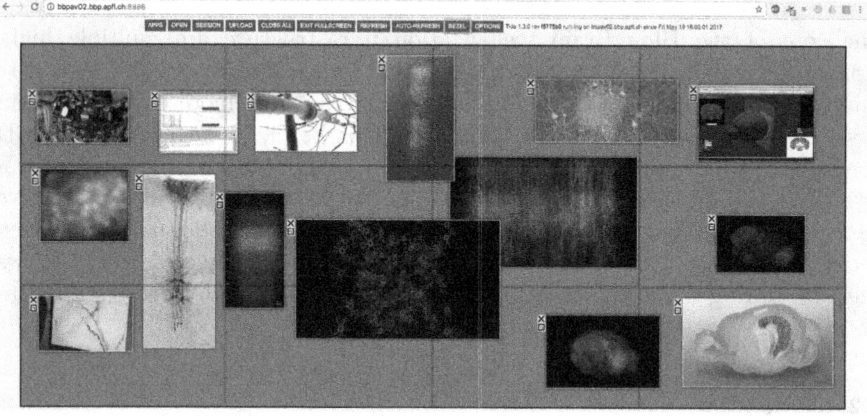

Fig. 2. Tide web interface

medium-sized institutions which allowed us to build the software integration for a reasonable startup cost. We have focused on the multitouch user interface, which implements a low entry barrier for new users, a unique capability of our solution.

Tide supports three types of content: files (high-resolution images, movies, pdfs), built-in applications (web browser, whiteboard) and remote applications using the Deflect library (DesktopStreamer, Equalizer-based applications, Brayns). The multitouch user interface can handle multiple users manipulating different windows and their content simultaneously.

2.3 Deflect

Deflect is the client library for Tide. It provides an API for pixel streaming to Tide and for receiving events from Tide. The pixel streaming allows synchronized parallel streaming from parallel rendering application as well as monoscopic and stereoscopic streams. Various events allow the application to react to multi-touch input from the wall.

Deflect is integrated into the Equalizer parallel rendering framework [5], enabling transparent usage of Equalizer applications on Tide walls. Furthermore, the DesktopStreamer application mirrors the desktop of other machines onto a wall window and allows interaction with the remote desktop. Other rendering applications, such as our interactive raytracing engine Brayns [2] are easily integrated with Deflect and Tide.

2.4 OpenDeck

OpenDeck is our next-generation visualization system, aiming to integrate the success of tiled display walls with a seamless transition to fully immersive environments. We are currently in the process of installing a system which consists of a semi-cylindrical back-projection screen with 41 Megapixel usable resolution on a 36 m^2 surface (Fig. 3). Like the display walls, it is equipped with multitouch capabilities which makes it usable as a monoscopic collaboration system from the first day of installation. Unlike tiled display walls, it is active stereo capable and equipped with a 3D tracking system for immersive rendering. For increased immersion, a lower resolution front projection system fills in the floor area. OpenDeck will run TIDE and our immersive applications based on Equalizer [5] once the system is installed.

OpenDeck will provide a unique environment for the research and development of new visualization techniques. It will open a set of questions along

Fig. 3. OpenDeck concept rendering

immersive touch user interfaces, transitions and mixing of monoscopic to immersive usage, the combination of tracked and touch devices, multi-user immersion, latency reduction for remote immersive rendering as well as multi-site collaboration.

3 Rendering Applications

The rendering applications form the backbone of our ecosystem. They cover a wide range of established rendering algorithms to serve a broad set of use cases for visual debugging, scientific illustrations and communication.

3.1 Brayns: Interactive Raytracing

Advances in computer hardware and software have brought raytracing to the point where it replaces classical rasterization for virtually all use cases in scientific visualization. On one hand, OpenGL-like local illumination for typical data sets used with rasterization (up to hundred million triangles) can be done at similar framerates to OpenGL [16]. For small datasets, OpenGL performs better, but for larger data sets raytracing outperforms OpenGL. This is due to a better scalability with respect to the data set size ($O(\log N)$ vs $O(n)$). Furthermore, CPU-based raytracing allows the rendering of larger data sets without any level-of-detail algorithms due to the larger memory size. Last, but not least, advanced rendering algorithms such as shadowing, reflections and global illumination (Fig. 4, left) are significantly easier to implement in a raytracer. The only area where rasterization provides a benefit is for rendering at very high frame rates, needed for example for immersive visualization, or very high resolutions.

It is for these reasons that interactive raytracing is the future technology for interactive and offline rendering at Blue Brain. We have developed a first open source implementation of a visualization engine with different backends:

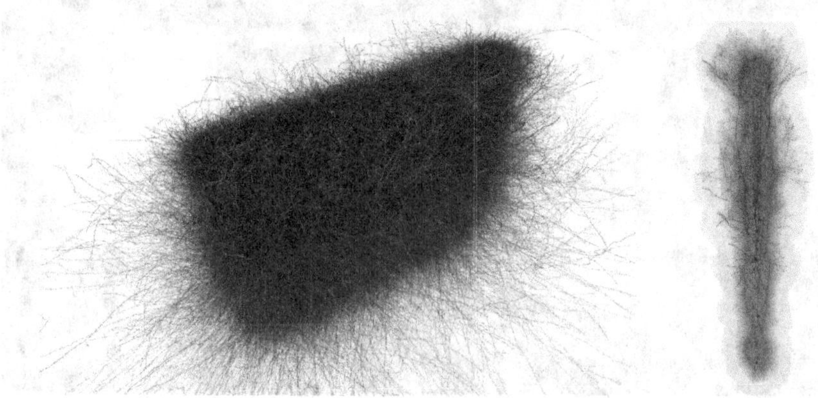

Fig. 4. Interactive raytracing for neuroscience

OSPRay [16] for CPU-based raytracing and OptiX [15] for GPU-based raytracing. This application called Brayns can load and visualize our data sets in a variety of modes and integrates with our messaging solution to be accessible from Python. We are currently integrating the key algorithms from Livre for out-of-core volume rendering in Brayns, which will also facilitate mixing polygonal with large volumetric data in a single scene (Fig. 4, right).

3.2 RTNeuron: OpenGL Parallel Rendering

RTNeuron [10] is the oldest of our interactive visualization tools. Originally conceived as a standalone application for visualizing simulation results, it has evolved into a rasterization-based rendering engine library implemented in C++ with a Python wrapping. The power of RTNeuron lies in a domain specific API designed for the visualization of detailed neuronal circuit models, this API allows for building custom applications tailored for specific use cases. It provides features to visualize static circuit data and some simulation results. Static data visualization includes different visual representations for neurons, synapses, selective pruning of neuronal trees, clipping planes and others. The simulation results that can be displayed are the spiking activity of the neurons and scalar variables from the cable models mapped to the neuron surface. The color maps for displaying these data are highly configurable, allowing to apply different color maps to different cell subsets.

Neurons can be displayed with different levels of detail ranging from simple spheres, cylinder-like geometric models and detailed polygonal meshes. Advanced rendering techniques included are several types of parallel rendering algorithms (such as sort-first and sort-last) and several algorithms for transparency rendering that enable efficient and correct rendering of scenes with great geometrical complexity and high depth complexity. Transparency is particularly suitable for masking and highlighting features of interest on the circuit. Ongoing work is a more scalable parallel rendering algorithm specially suited for transparency. Tiled rendering is also possible, which allows very high resolution renderings suitable for printing at sizes larger than A0 (the original of Fig. 5 left is a 36640 × 26000 pixel image).

The core engine is implemented in C++ using Equalizer and OpenSceneGraph and leverages part of our messaging framework to allow coupling with other applications. The 3D view can be embedded inside Qt applications (Fig. 5, right), in particular in Python with PyQt and QML for overlaying GUI elements. Several use case specific applications have been built this way.

3.3 Livre: Out-of-Core Volume Rendering

Livre is an interactive volume rendering engine available under a permissive open source license. Our main contributions are: a state-of-the-art implementation of an octree-based level-of-detail (LOD) selection, a task parallel rendering

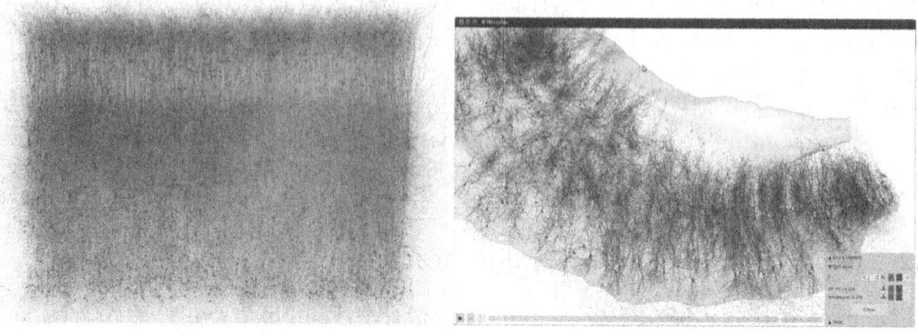

Fig. 5. RTNeuron rendering the simulated membrane potential of a fraction of the simulation (left) and a circuit visualization application for hippocampus model validation (right)

pipeline, a multi-GPU parallel rendering engine, and an easily extensible renderer through the use of plugin data sources. Our system brings together state-of-the art algorithms to create a volume rendering engine capable of handling extremely high-resolution volumes using a high degree of parallelism, both on a single system and in a distributed cluster. We employ a GPU-based ray casting algorithm to compute the radiance absorption of the given volumetric data. The computation is executed per pixel on the pixel shader hardware of the GPU.

In our out-of-core data access layer, multi-resolution data is represented as an octree data structure. This representation accelerates the selection of the proper level-of-detail and to track the status of the LODs (in CPU memory, in GPU memory, not loaded). While rendering, view-based LOD selection is performed using the screen-space-error (SSE) [9] technique. Figure 6 shows the rendering of a MicroCT dataset with an illustration of the selected LOD levels.

The creation of volume bricks, their upload to the GPU and the rendering are executed in separate tasks. These tasks run asynchronously, that is, rendering is decoupled from data loading. Livre uses a plugin mechanism to access the volume data, where data sources are implemented as shared libraries and are

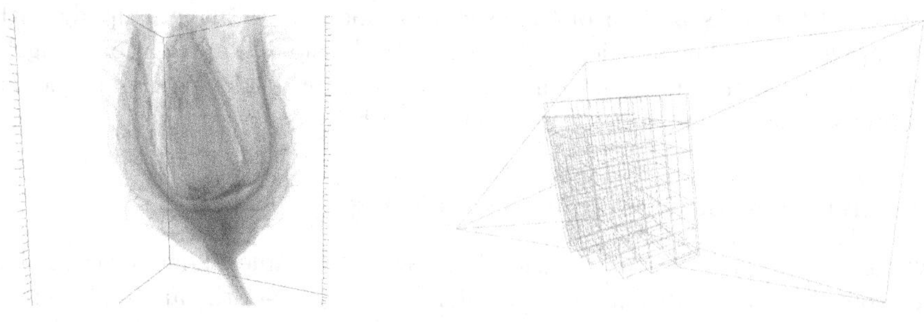

Fig. 6. Livre rendering a MicroCT dataset (left) and the selected LODs (right)

loaded on application startup based on the URI of the input data. Data sources only have to provide the requested volume bricks, that is, there is no defined file format or even requirement to read the input data from a file system. This flexibility of the plugin approach lead to novel volume rendering use cases, where volume representations are created on the fly from different input data sets, for example from simulation data.

4 Messaging and Service Architecture

All Blue Brain applications integrate messaging libraries which allow them to be used as services in a variety of use cases. For example, the Tide web server providing the user interface shown in Fig. 2, is based on this messaging solution. Other use cases are remote python APIs, JavaScript user interfaces and service architectures combining multiple visualization applications with data providers such as HPC simulations (Fig. 7).

The base communication layer ZeroEQ utilizes ZeroMQ as the transport layer, the ZeroConf protocol for discovery, and our novel ZeroBuf serialization library for high-performance messaging. A fully integrated HTTP server provides a bridge to JavaScript, Python and similar environments by implementing REST APIs with JSON payload. Figure 8 shows a class diagram of our messaging solution.

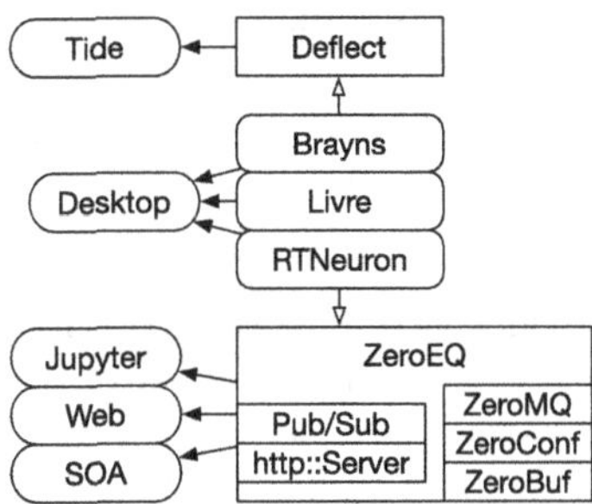

Fig. 7. Messaging-enabled use cases

4.1 ZeroEQ

ZeroEQ is our C++ messaging library, wrapping up existing technologies into an API which is convenient to use and easy to integrate into C++ code. It

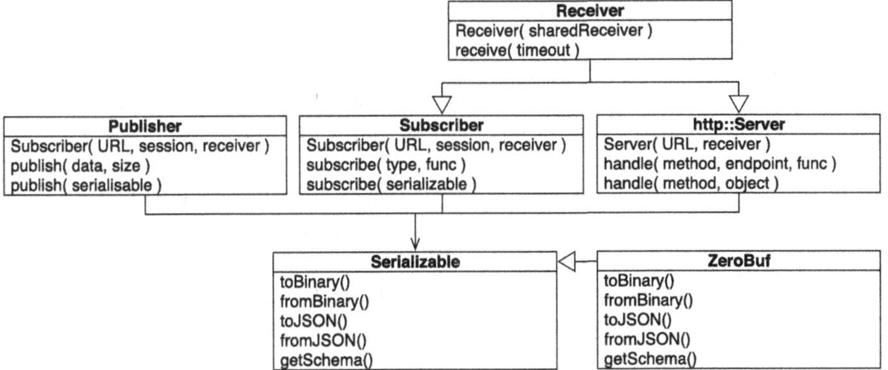

Fig. 8. UML Diagram of the main messaging classes

```
zerobuf::render::Camera camera;
zeroeq::Publisher publisher;
zeroeq::Subscriber subscriber;

subscriber.subscribe( camera );

while( rendering )
{
    if( updateCamera( camera )) // had user event
        publisher.publish( camera );
    else // poll subscription
        subscriber.receive( 0 /*ms*/ );
    renderFrame( camera );
}
```

Listing 1.1. Publish-Subscribe Example

```
zeroeq::URI uri("tcp://localhost");
zeroeq::Publisher publisher( uri, zeroeq::NULL_SESSION );
                                          // deactivate zeroconf
zeroeq::Subscriber subscriber( publisher.getURI( ));
                                          // use concrete port
```

Listing 1.2. Explicit Addressing

provides two messaging services: publish-subscribe and HTTP. For binary and JSON encodings it relies on a simple Serializable interface, for which ZeroBuf provides a sample implementation. To facilitate the simple use case of linking a few applications, ZeroEQ uses the zeroconf protocol to discover and connect to related applications. For more complex scenarios, explicit connections are supported.

Publish-Subscribe. The publish-subscribe service is implemented in a Publisher and Subscriber class. It provides event-based messaging, based on a 128-bit message type with arbitrary payload. The message type is used for message subscription, filtering and routing. The payload is expected to be uniquely identified by the message type, that is, all applications agree for the decoding and semantics of any given message type. ZeroBuf provides a sample implementation for this. The underlying transport uses ZeroMQ pub-sub sockets.

The pub-sub service is stateless, that is, applications have no expectation of when messages are received or who receives published messages. This communication pattern naturally leads to robust services, since there is no possibility for deadlocks or undefined behaviour. The pub-sub API is provided in two flavors: a simple *pointer & size* memory buffer, and a higher level object-based abstraction. The object-based API is syntactic sugar for the low-level API, and allows automatic publish and update of objects with a few lines of code. It uses the toBinary() and fromBinary() methods of the Serializable interface to call the low-level API.

The example in Listing 1.1 shows the integration of camera synchronization in a visualization application. This example relies on the built in zeroconf proto-

```
zeroeq::Subscriber local( zeroeq::URI("localhost:29387"));
zeroeq::Subscriber global( local );

local.subscribe( colorMap );
global.subscribe( camera );

while( true )
    local.receive(); // updates colorMap and camera
```

Listing 1.3. Subscriber Sharing

col to connect application instances. Subscribers only subscribe to events from publishers within the same session. The default session name is the user name, and can be customized using an environment variable or non-default constructor. Similarly, the subscriber can subscribe by session or address. Listing 1.2 illustrates an explicitly addressed subscription. Notice that the subscriber uses the publisher URI, which will contain the concrete port chosen for the publisher.

Subscribers are derived from a (Receiver) base class, which is shared with the http server. All receivers can share their receive() operation at construction time, that is, the blocking receive operation applies to all receivers in the shared group. Listing 1.3 shows an example of selectively receiving different updates on different input sockets.

HTTP Server. The http server is built using cppnetlib [8] for the transport and http protocol handling. It supports all standard http verbs (GET, POST, PUT, PATCH, DELETE). It is a zeroeq::Receiver, that is, it can share its receive() update operation with other subscribers and http servers. Unlike a subscriber, the http server follows the HTTP request-reply semantics, that is, a request received by a server has to be followed directly by its reply. To allow asynchronous request processing, the return value from the request handler is a std::future which is retrieved from an internal thread, thus allowing the application to continue operations.

The data served by the http server is introspectable, it allows querying the available endpoints (objects) and the JSON schema [13] for each endpoint. Listing 1.4 shows an excerpt of the Tide registry, and Listing 1.5 an excerpt of the schema for one of the exposed objects. This REST API is used by the Tide web interface from Javascript and to generate remote python APIs.

```
> GET /registry HTTP/1.0
{
[...]
  "tide/open": ["PUT"],
  "tide/options": ["GET","PUT"],
  "tide/resize-window": ["PUT"],
[...]
}
```

Listing 1.4. HTTP Server Registry

```
> GET /tide/options/schema HTTP/1.0
{
[...]
   "properties": {
       "alphaBlending": {
           "type":"boolean"
       },
[...]
}
```

Listing 1.5. Object JSON Schema

4.2 ZeroBuf

ZeroBuf is a sample implementation of serialization for ZeroEQ. Based on a grammar closely related to Flatbuffers schemas [7], it generates C++ classes with random set/get access. All data is stored internally in one continuous memory buffer, which can be used for the ZeroEQ binary serialization without any copy. The conversion to and from a JSON representation involves a copy using a std::string. ZeroBuf can store:

- (u)int[8,16,32,64,128]_t, float, double and string members
- fixed size arrays and dynamic vectors of static-sized elements (intrinsic members or composite types)
- static and dynamic sub-classes (composite types of the above)

Figure 9 shows two simple ZeroBuf schemas together with example usage of the generated code in C++ and their memory layout. The static example shows

FBS Schema

```
namespace zerobuf.render;

table Vector3f
{
  x: float;
  y: float;
  z: float;
}

table Camera
{
  origin: Vector3f = 0, 0, 1;
  lookAt: Vector3f;
  up: Vector3f = 0, 1, 0;
}
```

C++ Code

```
namespace render = zerobuf::render;

render::Camera camera;
camera.getOrigin() = render::Vector3f(0, 0, 1);
```

Memory Layout

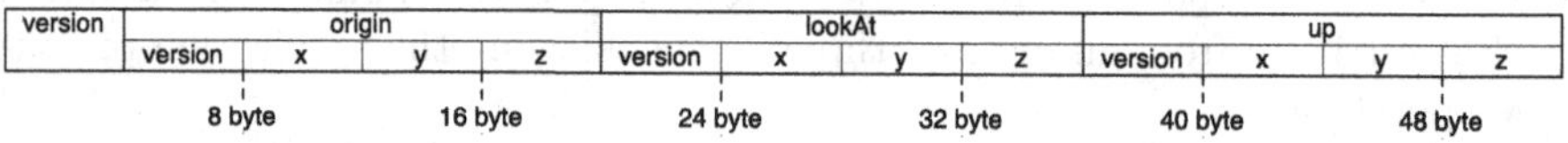

version | origin (version, x, y, z) | lookAt (version, x, y, z) | up (version, x, y, z)

8 byte, 16 byte, 24 byte, 32 byte, 40 byte, 48 byte

FBS Schema

```
namespace zerobuf.render;

table ImageJPEG
{
  data:[ubyte];
}
```

C++ Code

```
namespace render = zerobuf::render;

render::ImageJPEG imageJPEG;
glReadPixels( … );
tjCompress2( …, ptr, size );
imageJPEG.setData( ptr, size );
```

Memory Layout

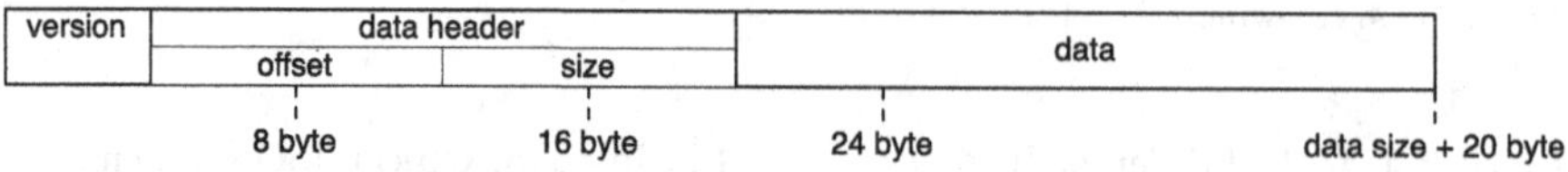

version | data header (offset, size) | data

8 byte, 16 byte, 24 byte, data size + 20 byte

Fig. 9. ZeroBuf Examples for static (top) and dynamic (bottom) sized objects

nested ZeroBuf classes for the camera used in Listing 1.1, and the dynamic example shows how raw data access is used to prepare a JPEG image for publishing.

4.3 Remote Python API

The remote python API provides easy to use access to remote applications using the http server. It integrates two features: generic code generation for the REST API exposed by the application, and automatic resource allocation and application launch.

The generic code generation is implemented in a pure python module, which has no dependency to the interfaced C++ application. It queries the http server and generates a python API for all exposed objects. This API can then be conveniently used in python to remote control the application.

Access to the application is established either through an explicit connection of a pre-launched application, or via a resource allocator. The allocator hides the details of allocating a resource, e.g. using a scheduling system like slurm, launching and connecting to the launched application from the python programmer.

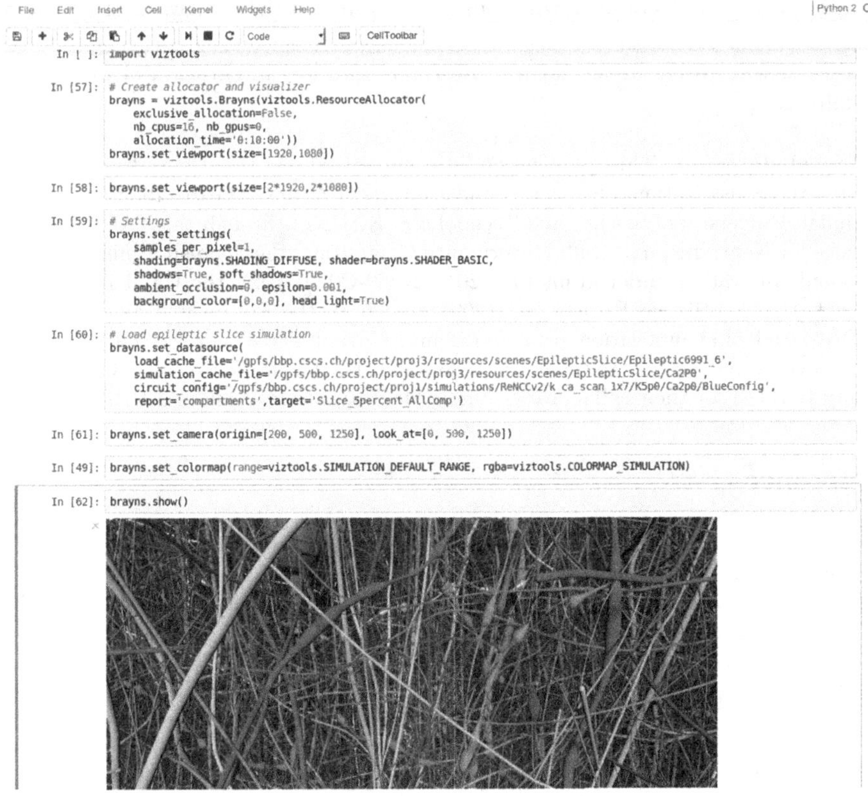

Fig. 10. Example Jupyter notebook session using Brayns

Figure 10 shows an example session of using this Python API from a Jupyter notebook, allocating and launching a Brayns instance, setting relevant rendering parameters and retrieving an image. Note that the whole notebook runs in a light-weight VM with no GPU and interacts with a Brayns instance launched on a bare-metal visualization cluster node.

5 Discussion and Conclusion

We presented a modular visualization architecture for large data visualization over a wide range of use cases, glued together by a modern and easy to use messaging infrastructure. This ecosystem allows us to flexibly support novel use cases, while pushing novel visualization capabilities, providing Blue Brain with a competitive visualization infrastructure. Messaging and remote APIs not only surprised us in their versatility and ease of integration with other ecosystems, but also have a significant potential for future exploration in classical visualization software. Interactive raytracing is the future rendering algorithm for us, and Brayns is becoming the integration point for our domain-specific visual applications and algorithms. Tiled display walls are affordable for a large set of institutions, and coupled with our open source TIDE software create new ways of truely collaborative work. TIDE, together with cheaper visualization hardware, will evolve in the future towards a seamless integration of immersive visualization.

Acknowledgments. This publication was supported by the Blue Brain Project (BBP), the Swiss National Science Foundation under Grant 200020-129525, the King Abdullah University of Science and Technology (KAUST) through the KAUST-EPFL alliance for Neuro-Inspired High Performance Computing, the Spanish Ministry of Science and Innovation under grant (TIN2010-21289-C02-01/02), the Cajal Blue Brain Project, Hasler Stiftung Projekt Nr. 12097, and from the European Unions Horizon 2020 research and innovation programme under grant agreement No 720270 (HBP SGA1). We would also like to thank the people from GMRV at the Rey Juan Carlos University (URJC) for their collaboration under the Cajal Blue Brain and HBP projects.

References

1. Blue Brain Project. Tide: Tiled Interactive Display Environment (2016). https://github.com/BlueBrain/Tide
2. Blue Brain Project. Brayns: Interactive raytracing of neuroscience data (2017). https://github.com/BlueBrain/Brayns
3. DeFanti, T.A., Leigh, J., Renambot, L., Jeong, B., Verlo, A., Long, L., Brown, M., Sandin, D.J., Vishwanath, V., Liu, Q., Katz, M.J., Papadopoulos, P., Keefe, J.P., Hidley, G.R., Dawe, G.L., Kaufman, I., Glogowski, B., Doerr, K.-U., Singh, R., Girado, J., Schulze, J.P., Kuester, F., Smarr, L.: The optiportal, a scalable visualization, storage, and computing interface device for the optiputer. Future Gener. Comput. Syst. **25**(2), 114–123 (2009)

4. Doerr, K.-U., Kuester, F.: CGLX: a scalable, high-performance visualization framework for networked display environments. IEEE Trans. Vis. Comput. Graph. **17**(2), 320–332 (2011)
5. Eilemann, S., Makhinya, M., Pajarola, R.: Equalizer: a scalable parallel rendering framework. IEEE Trans. Vis. Comput. Graph. **15**(3), 436–452 (2009)
6. Febretti, A., Nishimoto, A., Mateevitsi, V., Renambot, L., Johnson, A., Leigh, J.: Omegalib: a multi-view application framework for hybrid reality display environments. In: 2014 IEEE Virtual Reality (VR), pp. 9–14, March 2014
7. Google, Inc., Cross Platform Serialization Library (2017). http://google.github.io/flatbuffers/
8. D.M.B.G.M. Google, Inc., The C++ Network Library Project (2017). http://cpp-netlib.org/
9. Guthe, S., Strasser, W.: Advanced techniques for high-quality multi-resolution volume rendering. Comput. Graph. **28**(1), 51–58 (2004)
10. Hernando, J.B., Biddiscombe, J., Bohara, B., Eilemann, S., Schürmann, F.: Practical parallel rendering of detailed neuron simulations. In: Proceedings of the 13th Eurographics Symposium on Parallel Graphics and Visualization, EGPGV, Aire-la-Ville, Switzerland, pp. 49–56. Eurographics Association (2013)
11. Johnson, A., Leigh, J., Morin, P., Van Keken, P.: GeoWall: stereoscopic visualization for geoscience research and education. IEEE Comput. Graph. Appl. **26**(6), 10–14 (2006)
12. Johnson, G.P., Abram, G.D., Westing, B., Navr'til, P., Gaither, K.: DisplayCluster: an interactive visualization environment for tiled displays. In: 2012 IEEE International Conference on Cluster Computing, pp. 239–247, September 2012
13. JSON Schema. JSON Schema (2017). http://json-schema.org/
14. Marrinan, T., Aurisano, J., Nishimoto, A., Bharadwaj, K., Mateevitsi, V., Renambot, L., Long, L., Johnson, A., Leigh, J.: SAGE2: a new approach for data intensive collaboration using scalable resolution shared displays. In: Collaborative Computing: Networking, Applications and Worksharing, pp. 177–186 (2014)
15. Parker, S.G., Bigler, J., Dietrich, A., Friedrich, H., Hoberock, J., Luebke, D., McAllister, D., McGuire, M., Morley, K., Robison, A., Stich, M.: OptiX: a general purpose ray tracing engine. ACM Trans. Graph. **29**, 66:1–66:13 (2010)
16. Wald, I., Johnson, G., Amstutz, J., Brownlee, C., Knoll, A., Jeffers, J., Gnther, J., Navratil, P.: OSPRay - a CPU ray tracing framework for scientific visualization. IEEE Trans. Vis. Comput. Graph. **23**(1), 931–940 (2017)

Workshop on Performance and Scalability of Storage Systems (WOPSSS)

Workshop on Performance and Scalability of Storage Systems

Jean-Thomas Acquaviva[1] and Jalil Boukhobza[2]

[1] DDN, Meudon la Forêt 92360, France
jacquaviva@ddn.com
[2] UBO, Brest 29200, France

Summary of 2017 Edition

In our pre-Exacale era, profound changes are on-going in storage architectures. New storage media technologies are revisiting the traditional relation between latency and bandwidth. Consequently novel designs are blossoming in the community. WOPSSS intends to be an opportunity for members of the storage community to analyze on these emerging technologies with a specific focus on performance evaluation.

This year Michele Weilland from EPCC has presented a comprehensive utilization of these new storage devices in the frame of the NextGenIO European project. Fol-lowing her keynote, two papers were proposing performance evaluation of new stor-age systems. George Markomanolis from KAUST presented an in-depth study of the impact of burst buffers on scientific applications. The second paper from Julian Kun-kel, DKRZ, has detailed the performance impact of proxy I/O nodes based on DRAM. The corpus of applications analyzed was centered on MPI. These two research papers focused on performance analysis are illustrating the general motivation of the WOPSSS workshop.

The second powerful trend in the redesign on the storage architectures is coming from disruptive usages, namely the Cloud. In this field the scalability is specifically challenged. An invited talk of Gabriele Paciucci from INTEL detailed DAOS a new object storage architecture proposing to bring scalability to new heights. Then Georgios Bitzes, from CERN, tackled the key bottleneck in file system scalability: the names-pace. A second paper form CERN, authored by Jakob Blomer, was centered on the Large Hadrons Collider storage stack.

Michael Kuhn from the University of Hamburg addressed a convergence of these two trends, novel architectures plus new functionalities requested by users. He advo-cated for more flexibility in storage stack with the ability to provide plug-in extension at the opposite of dominant monolith approaches. The last presentation was from Georgios Koloventzos, BSC, where he proposed to harness the diversity of possible storage back-end technologies in a unified, yet heterogeneous file system.

The workshop was concluded by a discussion panel about both the results present-ed and the general scientific orientations in the storage community. Overall, revisiting the legacy software stack and re-think current architectures is a daunting task which needs a considerable effort from our community. Such a long and probably painful journey cannot be envisioned without insights. At it modest scale WOPSSS is trying to contribute to this effort.

An MPI-IO In-Memory Driver for Non-volatile Pooled Memory of the Kove XPD

Julian Kunkel(✉) and Eugen Betke(✉)

German Climate Computing Center (DKRZ), Hamburg, Germany
kunkel@dkrz.de, betke@dkrz.de

Abstract. Many scientific applications are limited by the performance offered by parallel file systems. SSD based burst buffers provide significant better performance than HDD backed storage but at the expense of capacity. Clearly, achieving wire-speed of the interconnect and predictable low latency I/O is the holy grail of storage. In-memory storage promises to provide optimal performance exceeding SSD based solutions. Kove®'s XPD® offers pooled memory for cluster systems. This remote memory is asynchronously backed up to storage devices of the XPDs and considered to be non-volatile. Albeit the system offers various APIs to access this memory such as treating it as a block device, it does not allow to expose it as file system that offers POSIX or MPI-IO semantics.

In this paper, we (1) describe the XPD-MPIIO-driver which supports the scale-out architecture of the XPDs. This MPI-agnostic driver enables high-level libraries to utilize the XPD's memory as storage. (2) A thorough performance evaluation of the XPD is conducted. This includes scale-out testing of the infrastructure and "metadata" operations but also performance variability.

We show that the driver and storage architecture is able to nearly saturate wire-speed of Infiniband (60+ GiB/s with 14FDR links) while providing low latency and little performance variability.

Keywords: MPI-IO · Evaluation · In-memory storage

1 Introduction

In an alternative storage architecture, a burst buffer [1,2] is placed between compute nodes and the storage. Acting as an intermediate storage tier, it's goal is to catch the I/O peaks from the compute nodes. Therefore, it provides a low latency and high bandwidth to the compute nodes, but also utilizes the backend storage by streaming data constantly at a lower bandwidth.

In-memory systems, like the Kove® XPD® [3], provide better latency, endurance and availability as flash chips. Theoretically, the address space of the XPD could be used to deploy a parallel file system, but performance would be limited by the POSIX semantics. The relaxed MPI-IO semantics would enable lock-free access. Since many of the current MPI-IO implementation are optimized for the conventional storage, we believe a in-memory MPI-IO driver for pooled memory deserves a thorough analysis.

J.M. Kunkel et al. (Eds.): ISC High Performance Workshops 2017, LNCS 10524, pp. 679–690, 2017.
https://doi.org/10.1007/978-3-319-67630-2_48

Our **contributions** are: (1) we provide an MPI-IO implementation for the pooled memory of the XPD (2) we investigate the performance of the developed MPI-IO driver. While the large and scale-out storage provided by the XPD is valuable by itself, the driver can be considered as an intermediate step towards a burst buffer solution.

This paper is structured as follows: Sect. 2 discusses related work, then Sects. 3 and 4 describe the used API and MPI-IO implementation, Sects. 5 and 6 show the test setup and performance results. Finally, the paper is summarized in Sect. 7.

2 Related Work

Relevant state-of-the-art can be grouped into performance optimization, burst buffers to speedup I/O and in-memory storage solutions.

Optimization and tuning of file systems and I/O libraries is traditionally an important but daunting task as many configuration knobs can be considered in parallel file system servers, clients and the I/O middleware. Without tuning, typical workloads stay behind the peak-performance by orders of magnitude. With considerable tuning effort a well fitting problem can yield good results: [4] reports 50% peak performance with a single 291 TB file. In [5] MPI-IO and HDF5 were optimized and adapted to each other, improving write bandwidth by 1.4x to 33x.

Many existing workloads can take benefit of a burst buffer as fast write-behind cache that transparently migrates data from the fast storage to traditional parallel file system. Burst buffers rely on flash or NVRAM to support random I/O workloads. For flash based SSDs many vendors offer high-performance storage solutions, for example, DDN Infinite Memory Engine (IME) [6], IBM FlashSystem [7] and Cray's DataWarp accelerator [8]. Using comprehensive strategies to utilize flash chips concurrently, these solutions are powerful and robust to guarantee availability and durability of data for many years.

The integration of Cray DataWarp burst buffer into the NERSC HPC architecture [9] increased the I/O performance of Chumbo-Crunch simulator by 2.84x to 5.73x, compared to Lustre. However, for the sake of efficient burst buffer usage, the serial simulator workflow had to be split into single stages (i.e. simulation, visualization, movie encoding), which then were executed in parallel. The research group at JSC uses DDN IME burst buffer [10] and GPFS to identify requirements for the next HPC generation. The main purpose is to accelerate the I/O performance of the NEST ("NEural Simulation Tool"). The preliminary IOR experiments show, that I/O performance can be increased upto 20x. BurstFS [11] uses local NVRAM of compute nodes, instead of dedicated remote machines. An elaborated communication scheme interconnects the distributed NVRAM and provides a contiguous storage space. This storage is allocated at beginning and exists for the lifetime of the job. In the experiments, BurstFS outperforms OrangeFS and PLFS by several times.

In [12], a user-level InfiniBand-based file system is designed as intermediate layer between compute nodes and parallel file system. With SSDs and FDR Infiniband, they achieve on one server a throughput of 2 GB/s and 3 GB/s for write and read, respectively.

The usage of DRAM for storing intermediate data is not new and ram-drives have been used in MSDOS and Linux (with tmpfs) for decades. However, offered RAM storage was used as temporary local storage and not durable and usually not accessible from remote nodes. Exporting tmpfs storage via parallel file systems has been used mainly for performance evaluation but without durability guarantees. Wickberg and Carothers introduced the RAMDISK Storage Accelerator [13] for HPC applications that by flushes data to a backend. It consists of a set of dedicated nodes that offer in-memory scratch space. Jobs can use the storage to prefetch input data prior job execution or as write-behind cache to speedup I/O. A prototype with a PVFS-based RAMDISK improved performance of 2048 processes compared to GPFS (100 MB/s vs. 36 MB/s for writes). Burst-mem [14] provides a burst buffer with write-behind capabilities by extending Memcached [15]. Experiments show that the ingress performance grows up to 100 GB/s with 128 BurstMem servers. In the field of big data, in-memory data management and processing has become popular with Spark [16]. Now there are many software packages providing storage management and compute engines [17].

The Kove XPD [3] is a robust scale-out pooled memory solution that allows to aggregate multiple Infiniband links and devices into one big virtual address space that can be dynamically partitioned. Internally, the Kove provides persistency by periodically flushing memory with a SATA RAID. Due to the performance differences, the process comes with a delay, but the solution is connected to a UPS to ensure that data becomes durable in case of a power outage. While providing many interfaces, the XPD does not offer a shared storage that can be utilized from multiple nodes concurrently.

3 XPD KDSA API

The XPD KDSA API is a low-level API that allows to send and receive data using write/read calls by utilizing RDMA. Data can be transferred synchronously or asynchronously, additionally, memory can be pre-registered for use with the Infiniband HCA. Since registration of memory is time consuming, for unregistered memory regions, the system may either use an internal (pre-registered) buffer and copy the user's data to the buffer, or for larger accesses it registers the memory, performs an RDMA data transfer and then unregisters the memory.

To address an XPD volume as a virtual address space, the XPD uses a connection specifier in the form: <local_address>/<server>.<link>:<volume ID>. Multiple volumes and client or server links can be aggregated by adding them with a +, data is then striped across these volumes/links. Similar to parallel file systems, this allows to scale the number of connections with the requirements. Upon connecting to an XPD, a client spawns a thread per volume to drive the

I/O, flags can control its behavior. To improve latency, this thread can use spin locks to wait for requests and transfer the data or it conserves CPU time by only becoming active upon events. The latter option is chosen as default for our driver.

4 XPD-MPIIO-Driver

The driver[1] is implemented as a shared library and usable with any MPI. It can be selected at startup of an application using LD_PRELOAD with the shared library. All implemented routines check the file name for the prefix "xpd:". Without the prefix, they route the accesses to the underlying MPI. Thus, files can be selectively stored on XPD volumes.

The file driver implements important functions utilizing the relaxed consistency semantics offered by MPI-IO: MPI_File_open, close, delete, get_position, get_size, preallocate, read_at, write_at, read_at_all, write_at_all, read, write, seek, set_size, set_view and sync. Collective read/write are calling the independent counter part. The selection is inspired by the needs of HDF5 and IOR. Note that the driver does not cache any I/O on the client side.

The implementation comes with a few limitations: Since we do not know the memory regions, the KDSA calls for unregistered memory are used implying overhead as described above. During the open/close the Infiniband connections to the XPD's are established and destroyed. This causes additional overhead but offers the freedom to choose the volumes on a file basis. Partial support for file views as needed by NetCDF4/HDF5 is provided.

Internally, the file driver uses the shared memory space provided by one or multiple XPD volumes. It records the actual file size at the beginning of this memory region but cannot grow beyond the aggregated size of the volumes. Each process tracks its view of the file size and exchanges this information upon file close or flush as needed by MPI-IO semantics. The data space is not initialized with zeros, which is an issue if files are written in a sparse format. Since for many use cases, the file is completely overwrite, this is not a show stopper – for instance, with fill-values, NetCDF/HDF5 initializes the data regions. A formatting tool is contained in the repository that initializes file size (alternatively call MPI_file_delete()) or completely zeroes memory regions.

5 Test Setup

5.1 Testsystems

The tests with the XPD were run on Cooley, the visualization cluster of Mira on ALCF. It provided three XPD's with a total of 14 FDR connections and is connected to a GPFS file system. Each node is equipped with one FDR HCA.

---

[1] **The code is available as open source.** http://github.com/JulianKunkel/XPD-MPIIO-driver.

To investigate the difference between XPD and other state-of-the-art HPC systems, we run some benchmarks on Cooley's GPFS and many on DKRZ's supercomputer Mistral. Mistral hosts 3000 compute nodes each equipped with an FDR interconnect and a Lustre storage system with 54 PByte capacity. The peak transfer rate of the file system we used is 450 GiB/s[2]. When we conducted our measurements, the phase 2 storage system was almost unused by other users.

5.2 Benchmarks

As our primary benchmark, IOR [18] is used varying access granularity, processes-per-node, nodes, XPD connections and access pattern (random and sequential). In all cases MPI-IO with independent I/O is measured. IOR is used with a transfer size equal to the access granularity and 20 GiB of data per XPD connection (and volume)[3]. To synchronize the measurements the inter-phase barriers were turned on (IOR option -g). For the Lustre benchmarks we were trying to reuse the XPD parameters wherever possible. Collective buffer was enabled for write operations smaller than 512 KiB, we configured MPI-IO to use one aggregator per node and, in all cases the number of stripes was twice as much as the number of nodes.

Finally, to measure performance of individual operations to investigate variability, the sequential benchmark `io-modelling` is used[4] It uses a high-precision timer and supports various access patterns on top of the POSIX interface.

6 Evaluation

The goal of our evaluation is to systematically investigate the scaling behavior of the Kove XPD's. The following experiments are conducted: (1) scaling clients for 14 connections; (2) scale-out performance on 14 nodes with increasing number of connections; (3) variability of performance; Additionally, a comparison to DKRZ's Lustre system is made and some results are obtained on Cooley's GPFS system.

Since the storage capacity is rather small (files up to 100 GiB have been accessed) compared to the speed of the tests, the time for open/close are investigated explicitly in experiment (4). In average across all conducted experiments, the time of open/close reduces the reported performance of the XPD by 10%. However, for production runs, larger files and capacities are assumed, reducing this overhead. Therefore, the performance reported subsequently in this paper is reported without the open/close time.

Note that on the XPD sequential and random I/O behave similarly due to the DRAM storage and, thus, we usually report random performance.

---

[2] http://www.vi4io.org/hpsl/2016/de/dkrz/lustre02.

[3] The memory capacity of the XPD's is shared amongst all users, therefore, we had access to 14 volumes each 20 GiB.

[4] https://github.com/JulianKunkel/io-modelling.

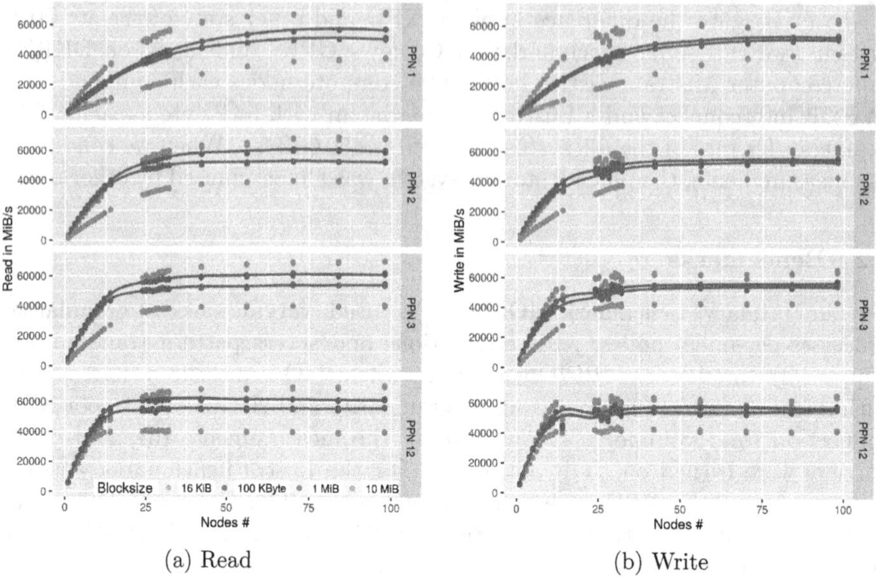

(a) Read (b) Write

Fig. 1. Performance overview: varying client node count and PPN. The graph contains fitting curves for 100 KiB and 1 MiB blocks.

6.1 Scaling the Number of Clients

In this first experiment, the maximum number of available volumes and IB links available are used (14).

Figure 1 shows the achieved performance for 1 to 98 client nodes and 1 to 12 processes per node (performance between 3 and 12 PPN is between the measurements). Under optimal conditions, the performance should increase linearly from 1 to 14 nodes as each is equipped with one IB FDR HCA and then it should saturate the network. Assuming roughly 6 GiB/s throughput for the FDR link, 84 GiB/s of performance should be observable.

Observations: (1) read/write behave mostly symmetrically, i.e., good read performance implies good write performance; (2) performance increases nearly with the number of client nodes and then saturates, but with PPN = 1 it scales beyond 14 client nodes; (3) for small access granularities, the workload is dominated by the latency of IB and the compute overhead, thus, it improves beyond 14 client nodes and using more PPN; (4) for large access granularities, a high percentage of peak is achieved quickly. Overall, 14 nodes with 12 PPN saturate at least 50% of the available network throughput and 24 clients reach almost peak; (5) performance of 100 KByte accesses is higher than for 1 MiB in many cases. This is due to the pre-registered memory region inside the KDSA library. This buffer is used for small accesses but not for 1 MiB. Therefore, the overhead for memory registration is added which slows down the I/O.

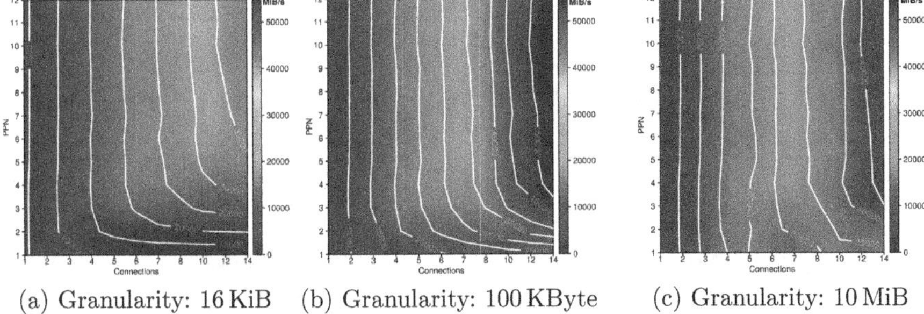

(a) Granularity: 16 KiB (b) Granularity: 100 KByte (c) Granularity: 10 MiB

Fig. 2. Read performance with variable connections and PPN. Isolines for multiples of 5000 MiB/s are shown.

6.2 Scale-Out with Multiple Connections

To show the scale-out behavior, the performance when varying PPN and the number of XPD connections has been measured for the fixed configuration of 14 client nodes (that should theoretically be able to saturate all XPD connections). Figure 2 shows a heat-map for different block granularities. This gives us also another perspective to investigate scaling behavior for variable PPN. In the best case, performance increases linearly with the number of connections and is constantly at a high level for variable numbers of PPN.

Observations: (1) for large accesses, the performance isolines show that about 25 GB/s are achievable per connection up to 5 connections regardless of the PPN; (2) starting with 6 connections, multiple PPN are needed to drive I/O and the scaling is not optimally any more. Still, as seen in Fig. 1, more PPNs and about 24 client nodes would increase throughput to 60 GiB/s; (3) smaller granularities also yield good performance with PPN = 1, but the hill like structure shows that multiple PPNs are necessary to drive the latency bound I/O. Overall, the system scale well when increasing the number of XPD connections and servers.

6.3 Performance Variability

The variability of access time has been investigated. When re-running an experiment, the overall performance of the repeated run should exhibit a similar performance behavior. Since each experiment takes at least several seconds to complete, we additionally investigated the runtime of repeatedly invoking the same I/O call.

A comparison of the runtime of the three repeats for each individual configuration ($\frac{min-max}{max}$) reveals the variability when re-running an experiment. On the XPD, the arithmetic mean value of variability is 1.23% for read and 1.78% for write accesses, albeit the mean runtime of an experiment was only about 10s. Thus, on average, when repeating an experiment, performance can be 1.8% worse than in the best case. Across the experiments, Lustre varies about 5% for read and write although its runtime is longer and, thus, less variation is to be

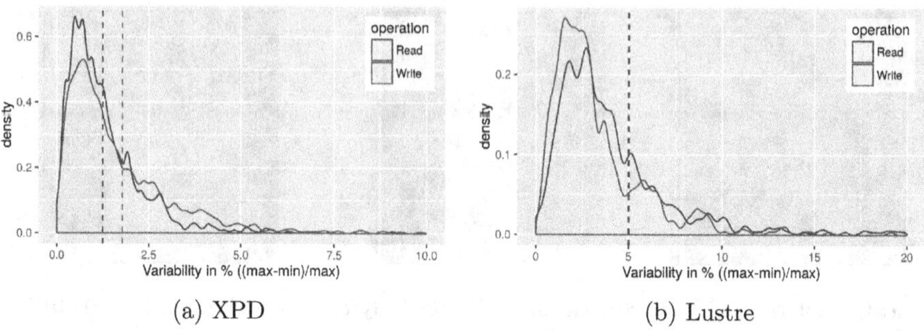

(a) XPD (b) Lustre

Fig. 3. Density of the variability range across all conducted experiments (span across three repeats each).

Table 1. Variability test: mean performance in MiB/s over the runtime

Size	Type	Read			Write		
		XPD	GPFS	Lustre	XPD	GPFS	Lustre
16 KiB	seq	707.8	659.8	522.0	709.8	533.0	778.0
100 k	seq	1653.8	1139.2	1082.2	1773.3	611.7	927.7
1 MiB	seq	1837.3	1062.5	996.2	1768.2	629.8	965.9
10 MiB	seq	3401.7	928.3	994.3	3274.3	742.3	916.9
16 KiB	rnd	676.8	1.2	1.5	600.4	71.7	20.6
100 k	rnd	1538.5	4.7	9.2	1636.1	346.7	80.6
1 MiB	rnd	2052.6	29.6	49.2	1967.1	184.6	157.6
10 MiB	rnd	3456.6	301.2	277.6	3335.6	430.0	352.1

expected. The density (similar to a fine-grained histogram) for all experiments is shown in Fig. 3.

Performance Variability with Individual I/Os. This experiment is conducted measuring timing of 10,000 individual I/Os with a single process on Cooley's XPD and GPFS, and on DKRZ's Lustre. The density plots of measuring these results is shown in Fig. 4. This graph shows the qualitative difference between the file systems. The mean performance for each experiment is shown in Table 1, i.e., the average performance when timing a complete run; naturally, a few very slow operations lead to a significant reduced mean performance.

Observations: As suggested by comparing application runs, the XPD's performance does not vary much between individual I/Os, i.e., the observed runtime always forms a group. While some reads in the optimized sequential I/O can perform as fast as on the XPD – i.e., with wire speed, most operations do not and, obviously, random I/O from parallel file systems is significantly slower. Actually, for sequential reads, in combination with caching, the read-ahead and

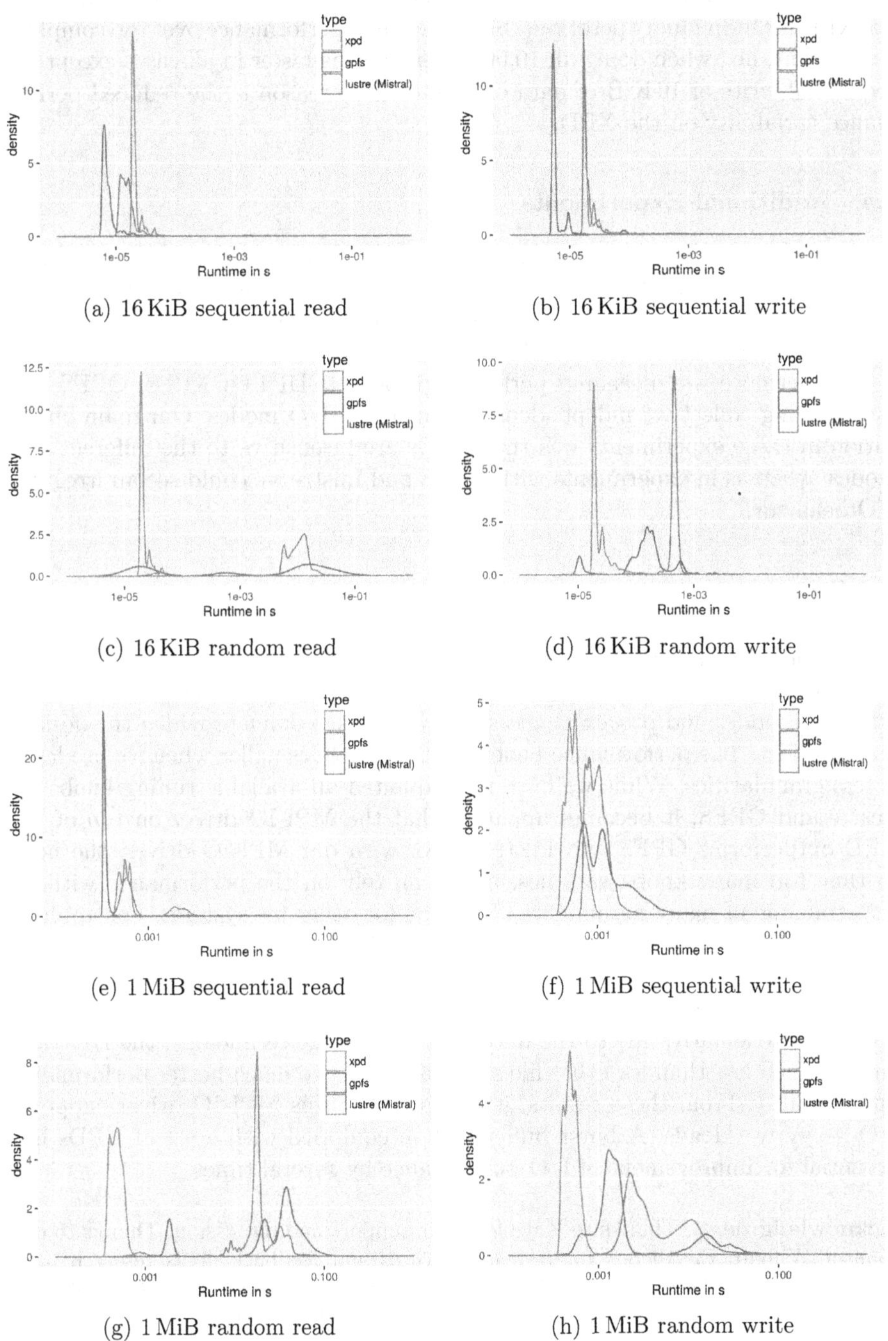

(a) 16 KiB sequential read

(b) 16 KiB sequential write

(c) 16 KiB random read

(d) 16 KiB random write

(e) 1 MiB sequential read

(f) 1 MiB sequential write

(g) 1 MiB random read

(h) 1 MiB random write

Fig. 4. Density of timing individual I/O operations

write-behind strategy of Lustre and GPFS can result in faster performance than the XPD for individual operations. Still, the mean performance over the complete experiment, i.e., when doing all 10,000 operations is faster in all cases except for sequential write of 16 KiB of data on Lustre. The reason is the reduced performance variability on the XPD.

6.4 Additional Experiments

Besides, we investigated open/close behavior of XPDs, and could create a linear model for prediction of open/close times. For example, our model says that for NN = 500 nodes and PPN = 12 an open time will be about 2.5 s. On Lustre using the same parameters we observed open times around 0.7 s.

Furthermore, we measured performance of NetCDF4 on XPDs, GPFS and Lustre using collective, independent, and chunked I/O modes. Our main observation in these experiments was that XPDs are insensitive to the different I/O modes, whereas in experiments with GPFS and Lustre we could see an irregular I/O behavior.

7 Summary

Storage on XPDs significantly outperforms our Lustre system in the small-blocks random I/O benchmarks. In this case and in contrast to XPD, the increasing number of nodes and processes accessing the storage don't provided the desired scaling effect. The performance benefit of the XPD is smaller when we use large access granularities. While we have not exploited all available tuning knobs for Lustre and GPFS, it becomes apparent that the MPI-IO driver on top of the XPD outperforms GPFS and Lustre. Also, with our MPI-IO driver, the need to tune too many knobs vanishes, users can rely on the performance without changing one of many parameters as needed for other file systems. For application relevant workloads using NetCDF, XPD is relatively insensitive to various settings of the I/O method and chunking. It simply scales with the number of processes and nodes up to a rather predictable throughput of 4 GiB/s per client node. In particularly, due to the nature of the storage technology, the I/O variance is much less than for other file systems leading to much better performance predictability. From these results, it appears that this MPI-IO driver supports I/O heavy workloads. A burst buffer system equipped with a set of XPDs has potential for improvement of I/O performance by several times.

Acknowledgment. Thanks to Kove for their support and discussion. Thanks to our sponsor William E. Allcock for providing access and feedback. This research used resources of the Argonne Leadership Computing Facility, which is a DOE Office of Science User Facility supported under Contract DE-AC02-06CH11357.

References

1. Liu, N., Cope, J., Carns, P., Carothers, C., Ross, R., Grider, G., Crume, A., Maltzahn, C.: On the role of burst buffers in leadership-class storage systems. In: Proceedings of the 2012 IEEE Conference on Massive Data Storage (2012)
2. Romanus, M., Parashar, M., Ross, R.B.: Challenges and considerations for utilizing burst buffers in high-performance computing (2015). arXiv preprint: arXiv:1509.05492
3. KOVE: about xpress disk (xpd) (2015). http://www.hamburgnet.de/products/kove/Kove-XPD-L3-4-datasheet.pdf
4. The HDF Group: A Brief Introduction to Parallel HDF5. https://www.alcf.anl.gov/files/Parallel_HDF5_1.pdf
5. Howison, M., Koziol, Q., Knaak, D., Mainzer, J., Shalf, J.: Tuning HDF5 for Lustre file systems. In: Workshop on Interfaces and Abstractions for Scientific Data Storage (IASDS 2010), Heraklion, Crete, Greece, 24 September 2010 (2012)
6. DDN: Worlds's most advanced application aware I/O acceleration solutions. http://www.ddn.com/products/infinite-memory-engine-ime14k
7. IBM: Flash Storage. http://www-03.ibm.com/systems/storage/flash
8. Cray: CRAY XC40 DataWarp Applications I/O Accelerator. http://www.cray.com/sites/default/files/resources/CrayXC40-DataWarp.pdf
9. Ovsyannikov, A., Romanus, M., Straalen, B.V., Weber, G.H., Trebotich, D.: Scientific Workflows at DataWarp-Speed: Accelerated Data-Intensive Science using NERSC's Burst Buffer (2016)
10. Schenck, W., El Sayed, S., Foszczynski, M., Homberg, W., Pleiter, D.: Early evaluation of the "Infinite Memory Engine" burst buffer solution. In: Taufer, M., Mohr, B., Kunkel, J.M. (eds.) ISC High Performance 2016. LNCS, vol. 9945, pp. 604–615. Springer, Cham (2016). doi:10.1007/978-3-319-46079-6_41
11. Wang, T., Mohror, K., Moody, A., Sato, K., Yu, W.: An ephemeral burst-buffer file system for scientific applications. In: Proceedings of the International Conference for High Performance Computing, Networking, Storage and Analysis, SC 2016, Piscataway, NJ, USA, pp. 69:1–69:12. IEEE Press (2016)
12. Sato, K., Mohror, K., Moody, A., Gamblin, T., de Supinski, B.R., Maruyama, N., Matsuoka, S.: A user-level infiniband-based file system and checkpoint strategy for burst buffers. In: 2014 14th IEEE/ACM International Symposium on Cluster, Cloud and Grid Computing (CCGrid), pp. 21–30. IEEE (2014)
13. Wickberg, T., Carothers, C.: The RAMDISK storage accelerator: a method of accelerating I/O performance on HPC systems using RAMDISKs. In: Proceedings of the 2nd International Workshop on Runtime and Operating Systems for Supercomputers, p. 5. ACM (2012)
14. Wang, T., Oral, S., Wang, Y., Settlemyer, B., Atchley, S., Yu, W.: BurstMem: a high-performance burst buffer system for scientific applications. In: 2014 IEEE International Conference on Big Data (Big Data), pp. 71–79. IEEE (2014)
15. Jose, J., Subramoni, H., Luo, M., Zhang, M., Huang, J., Wasi-ur Rahman, M., Islam, N.S., Ouyang, X., Wang, H., Sur, S., et al.: Memcached design on high performance RDMA capable interconnects. In: 2011 International Conference on Parallel Processing, pp. 743–752. IEEE (2011)

16. Zaharia, M., Chowdhury, M., Das, T., Dave, A., Ma, J., McCauley, M., Franklin, M.J., Shenker, S., Stoica, I.: Resilient distributed datasets: a fault-tolerant abstraction for in-memory cluster computing. In: Proceedings of the 9th USENIX Conference on Networked Systems Design and Implementation, p. 2. USENIX Association (2012)
17. Zhang, H., Chen, G., Ooi, B.C., Tan, K.L., Zhang, M.: In-memory big data management and processing: a survey. IEEE Trans. Knowl. Data Eng. **27**(7), 1920–1948 (2015)
18. Loewe, W., McLarty, T., Morrone, C.: IOR Benchmark (2012)

HetFS: A Heterogeneous File System for Everyone

Georgios Koloventzos[1(✉)], Ramon Nou[1], Alberto Miranda[1], and Toni Cortes[1,2]

[1] Barcelona Supercomputing Center (BSC), Barcelona, Spain
{georgios.koloventzos,ramon.nou,alberto.miranda,toni.cortes}@bsc.es
[2] Universitat Politècnica de Catalunya, Barcelona, Spain

Abstract. Storage devices have been getting more and more diverse during the last decade. The advent of SSDs made it painfully clear that rotating devices, such as HDDs or magnetic tapes, were lacking in regards to response time. However, SSDs currently have a limited number of write cycles and a significantly larger price per capacity, which has prevented rotational technologies from begin abandoned. Additionally, Non-Volatile Memories (NVMs) have been lately gaining traction, offering devices that typically outperform NAND-based SSDs but exhibit a full new set of idiosyncrasies.

Therefore, in order to appropriately support this diversity, intelligent mechanisms will be needed in the near-future to balance the benefits and drawbacks of each storage technology available to a system. In this paper, we present a first step towards such a mechanism called HetFS, an extension to the ZFS file system that is capable of choosing the storage device a file should be kept in according to preprogrammed filters. We introduce the prototype and show some preliminary results of the effects obtained when placing specific files into different devices.

1 Introduction

Storage devices have shown a significant evolution in the latest decade. As the improvements in the latencies of traditional hard disk drives (HDDs) have diminished due to the mechanical limitations inherent to their design, other technologies have been emerging to try and take their place. For instance, NAND-based solid state drive (SSD) technology has been extremely successful in improving I/O latency and bandwidth, and this has led to SSD devices often being incorporated into the storage stack as a caching tier for HDD-based storage systems, and also to being used as the principal data repositories. This, in turn, has forced any major applications that were bound by access times (such as databases [3]), to change in order to adapt to this new technology. Nevertheless, completely replacing HDDs by more efficient SSDs can be economically prohibitive due the larger cost per capacity of the latter. More importantly, however, NAND-based SSDs have a limited number of write cycles and, in fact, recent researches on

R. Nou and A. Miranda—The authors contributed equally to this work.

J.M. Kunkel et al. (Eds.): ISC High Performance Workshops 2017, LNCS 10524, pp. 691–700, 2017.
https://doi.org/10.1007/978-3-319-67630-2_49

long-term SSD usage in data warehouses have proved that, after intensive usage, the SSDs degrade so much that response times may equal those of HDDs [5,6].

In addition to SSDs, Non-Volatile Memory (NVM) technology is currently being researched as a better alternative. The different NVM technologies being explored typically exhibit faster I/O latencies than SSDs, which are closer to those of DRAM rather than to NAND-based devices. As such, current research efforts are focusing on whether these devices should be used as an extension of DRAM or included as an additional (persistent) caching layer to the storage stack [14].

Moreover, despite the recent advancements in SSDs and NVMs, the technological development of HDDs has not stopped. For instance, hard drives featuring an Helium-filled enclosure were recently introduced to the market since the gas density allows for more platters and a higher rotational speed of up to 19,000 rpms [22]. Shingled Magnetic Recording (SMR) [1] is also starting to find its way to customers, since it allows for a higher track density and increased capacity at similar cost.

Thus, in the near future, file systems will need to cope with a myriad of storage devices, each with particular performance and capacity characteristics, and each suitable to certain types of I/O workload. Current file systems, however, typically distribute data into available devices by placing them into a hierarchy according to performance, and using prefetching and multi-tier caching algorithms to reduce I/O latency.

This, however, typically disregards other considerations such as extending the life of devices such as SSDs through wear leveling, or tailoring a file's data distribution according to the usage that applications make of it. For instance, software engineers typically rely on writing to a file as barrier or as an atomic operation, a usage which is crucial for the resilience and for synchronization of applications [4]. This access pattern can represent a significant disadvantage for SSDs since it will wear the medium faster. Similarly, the OS libraries are primarily read dominant [2,19] and could be classified according to how often they are accessed, placing the rarely-used into an HDD for cold storage and the more commonly used ones into an SSD for improved performance. Multimedia files i.e., RIFF format, can be split. The first part with all the information of the file in a fast medium and the rest that accessed mostly sequentially to a rotating one. Lastly, intra-file formats could also be exploited by placing each file section into the storage device more suitable for the expected access patterns. Therefore, in order to support the diversity in storage media, file systems will need to provide intelligent algorithms that (1) appropriately quantify and model the benefits and drawbacks of each available storage device; (2) capture the more typical patterns that applications use to access data; and (3) use this information to create a tailored dynamic data distribution that optimizes the usage of the available hardware.

In this paper, we present *HetFS*, an extension to the ZFS file system that includes a component to capture information about file usage, and a simple decision making mechanism that uses this information to decide, according to a user-provided classification, the storage device where a file should be placed. We introduce the *HetFS* prototype and show some preliminary results measured by applying different precomputed file distributions to the kernel's boot process. The results offer an insight to the expected ZFS overhead added by the new mechanisms and showcase the potential benefits of such distributions. Please note that these modifications are meant as a first step towards a more complex feedback loop where *HetFS* will automatically capture file usage information and will use this information (allowing some degree of tuning from the user) to produce a data distribution that is optimized w.r.t. a file's more common access patterns and the features of the available storage devices.

The remainder of the paper is organized as follows: Sect. 2 describes the modifications made to ZFS in order to capture usage information and implement the user-provided file distributions. Section 3 describes our experiments regarding boot times with different file distributions. Related work is discussed in Sects. 4, and 5 concludes with our findings.

2 Heterogeneous File System

This section discusses the modifications done to ZFS in order to support the *HetFS* file forwarding mechanism. We chose to implement *HetFS* as an extension of ZFS[1] because this file system offers facilities to manage both the physical and the logical layers [16]. While historically file systems have been constructed on top of a single physical device, ZFS manages physical storage by means of storage pools (or *zpools*), which can be created using multiple and heterogeneous devices such as HDDs, SSDs, NVM or even tapes. A zpool describes the physical characteristics of the storage devices that compose it (called *vdevs*), and acts as an arbitrary data store from which file systems can be created. By leveraging this feature as an extension of ZFS, *HetFS* is able to produce a file classification based on access patterns and later use this information to guide requests to a specific storage device within a zpool.

2.1 File Classification

File classification is done by modifying the ZFS Posix Layer (ZPL), which is the ZFS layer responsible for interfacing between the VFS and the underlying ZFS data management layers. This layer still has enough semantic information about which file is being accessed by a `read()` or `write()` operation, and also offers enough detail to allow us to track the access to individual data blocks. Thus, we include a red-black tree in the ZPL where each node contains two separate linked lists for read and write requests.

The information traced is inserted into the red-black tree by a specialized kernel thread after a request has returned without errors, in order to not interfere much with it. Currently, the data consists of the file name, the offset of the

[1] Given that ZFS is proprietary software, we used a fork of OpenZFS [11] named ZFS on Linux (ZoL) [24]. For clarity we will keep referring to it as ZFS.

request, the length, and the type, that are extracted from the request. We also capture the time when the request arrived, and use this information to merge small requests into bigger ones if the current captured time is close to the previously stored one, and also if the offset is contiguous to the previous one. This approach gives us an insight on how files are accessed from applications, and also allows us to track if particular part of a file is accessed more which will help us to assess the access patterns for each individual file in future research.

Currently, the analysis of the collected information is done post-mortem, and the final decision of the available vdevs should store a particular file is left to the user. This decisions can be communicated to *HetFS* by means of a custom *procfs* interface with some pre-configured characteristics. In the future the operating system will conduct an automated analysis of these information to make an informed decision on which storage medium a file should be placed. If a manual decision has been made the analysis will not be taken into consideration.

2.2 Device Selection

Files can be typically classified by their access patterns: for instance, multimedia files are most likely to be accessed sequentially, and documents created from word processors follow complex internal structures which makes parts of the file more likely to be accessed with different frequencies and patterns than others. This means that the former would benefit from a ZFS vdev optimized for sequential access, whereas the latter would benefit from a ZFS vdev optimized for random accesses. Other files, like bitmaps, indexes, and even the file system's metadata would be better stored in a ZFS vdev that could benefit from byte addressability (e.g. NVM).

In order to forward I/O requests to the desired vdev, we modify the ZFS Block Allocation mechanism to use the analyzed information produced by the file classification mechanism, which is conveyed to *HetFS* through the aforementioned *procfs* interface. Information about the chosen vdev for a file is encoded into the ZFS equivalent of VFS' i-nodes, so that it can be propagated to all the necessary ZFS layers, and is then used to allocate *ZFS block pointers* into the appropriate vdev. Since the standard ZFS Block Allocation strategy relies on dynamic striping to maximize bandwidth, we modify the vdev selection algorithm to simply choose the device encoded into the file. In the future, however, this selection will also consider other factors like the vdevs performance, their optimal access mode as well as any limiting features. We also leverage existing code [23] by the ZFS team to place metadata into SSDs and extend it to several vdevs.

Note that, currently, a user or system administrator could decide to move files that need a lower access latency to a SSD for faster I/O bandwidth. If these files were write-intensive, it would decrease the durability of the SSD but the file would actually be served faster. These kinds of compromises would need to be decided either by the administrator or automatically by system wide policies. For example, if durability of an SSD is pursued, moving files that are accessed scarcely and sequentially to an HDD will give us a better life expectancy. In the future, *HetFS* should move files dynamically to appropriate vdevs in response to changes made by the administrator to pursue certain system-wide optimization goals. For instance, *HetFS* could decide to move files that have not been accessed for a certain period of time to a network storage system, which could be represented by another "device" in the ZFS pool. At default, operating system will analyze patterns and will be able to choose between storage media. A file that more than 50% is accessed contiguous will be sent to HDD. If more random access patterns emerge or even byte accesses the file could be sent to a SSD or NVRAM respectively. If a system administrator has created a rule about a file, the automatic decision will not be calculated.

3 Evaluation

This section describes our experiments when testing how several file distributions differently affect the boot process of the Linux kernel. Our experiment platform is a bare metal machine running Ubuntu 16.04 with Linux kernel 4.4.0–21. It is equipped with a processor Intel(R) Core(TM)2 Quad CPU Q9300 @ 2.50 GHz with 4 cores. It also has 8 GB RAM in 4 modules of 2 GB. For storage we have a Seagate BarraCuda at 250 GB with 7200 rpm and 8 MB cache connected with SATA 3.0 Gb/s and a Samsung SSD 850 at 250 GB with 512 MB cache.

3.1 Boot Time

We use *HetFS* to choose in which media to store different boot files in order to see how it affects the booting time of our test machine. We decided to use the boot time because it is a straight forward experiment that heavily involves the underlying file system. Also boot time is crucial when a new system is deployed. Having a simple performance experiment helps us measure if our approach to store files into specific storage media adds a reasonable overhead.

For each experiment, we rebooted the machine 100 times and write the output of systemd-analyze to a file. In Fig. 2 there are the boxplots of the median, best and worst total booting times for each run. First we did the experiment with the ZoL [24] version 0.6.5.6 (which is the one that can now be found in the Ubuntu 16.04 repositories), to measure the time of a stable run. Second we run ZoL with 0.7.0-rc3 and commit "935550f" since this is the commit before our code was introduced. This experiment is done in order to see if any major differences have been introduced between the ZFS versions. The third experiment is run by storing only the files that are read during the boot process in the SSD (labeled **RO** in the figure). The fourth experiment, which is labeled **RO+META** in the figure, is a set up where all files that are read during boot time and all ZFS metadata of every file is stored to the SSD. Finally, we add a fifth experiment where all the files and the metadata are stored in the SSD (labeled **RW+META**). All measurements were done by the systemd-analyze [18] command version 229. The systemd-analyze command returns the time spent in the kernel as well as the time spent in initrd before normal system userspace is reached. A userspace time is also provided which is the time normal system userspace took to initialize.

Figure 1 depicts our results. First of all, we can observe some differences between the 2 versions of ZFS which evidence changes between the versions. For instance, ZFS 0.7 has a 15% performance hit on kernel time but a speed up on userspace time of 27% when compared to ZFS 0.6. Nevertheless, this results in a less than 1% degradation to the total boot time. Placing only the read files in an SSD creates a 2% overhead at kernel time and an 8% overhead to userspace time, which sets the overhead of *HetFS* around 4%, but with a better expected SSD lifetime. In contrast, the results for the fourth run where also the ZFS metadata is stored in the SSD are significantly different: the kernel time is almost identical to the ZoL 0.7 baseline, but userspace time yields a 43% speedup. Overall, *HetFS* obtains a final 10% boost, which demonstrates that placing the file system's internal metadata into an SSD can significantly affect performance (and decrease the expected SSD lifetime as well). The final run, where all the data is stored in the SSD, obtains an improvement of a 20% with respect to the plain ZFS, which is to be expected since no data is stored in the slower HDD. Overall the results show that our approach of acquiring the data has a low impact at the responding time of the machine.

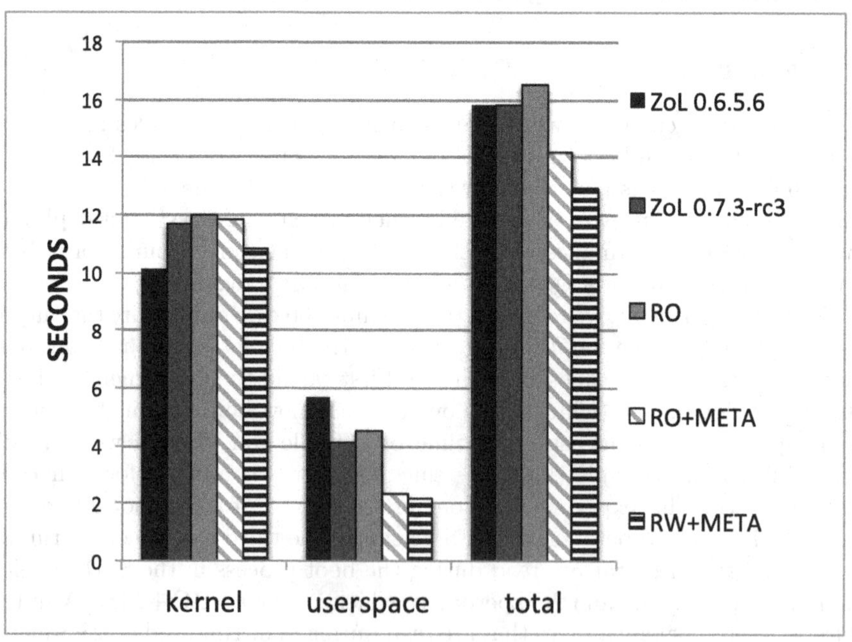

Fig. 1. Mean boot time using different configurations.

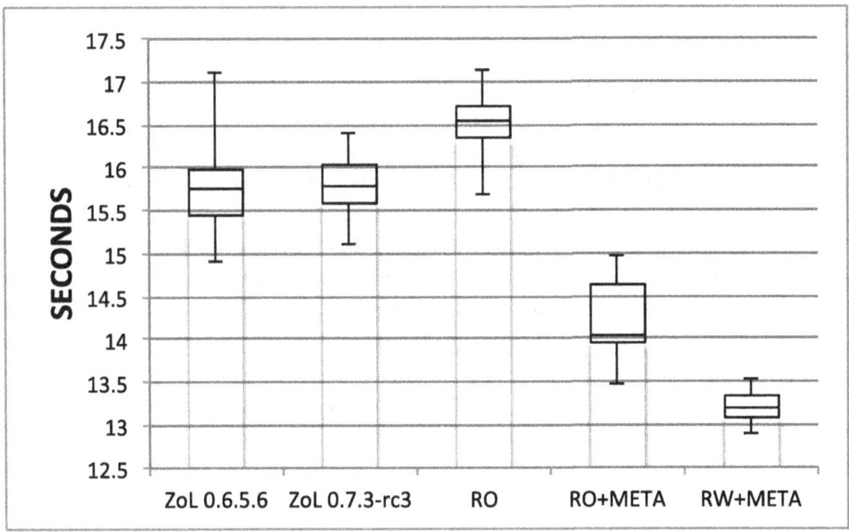

Fig. 2. Median, worst and best boot time for each run.

3.2 Write Requests

As is apparent from the previous section, significant performance gains can be expected from placing boot files into an SSD. Nevertheless, in order to better understand how much stress the SSD received, we also measured how many I/O requests ended up going to this media, along with the total count and size of the writes operations issued. The results are shown in Table 1. We observe that, since the boot process is not write-intensive, using the SSD to its full capability for storing also the ZFS metadata does not represent a significant load, since only 3 MB are requested to be written in the device (**RO+META**). Nevertheless, using the SSD to store exclusively read-only data results in only a 5% drop in performance when compared to a standard ZFS installation, but with significantly less data written to the SSD (1 MB/28 requests vs 2 MB/139 requests, respectively). Moreover, the worst scenario for an SSD is, as expected, to move all the data to it, which increases the total size of the writes to 3.3 MB, but with a 1.22x speedup when compared to standard ZFS.

Table 1. SSD writes vs. speedup

	ZFS 0.7.3	RO	RO+META	RW+META
Total size	2 MB	1 MB	3 MB	3.3 MB
# of requests	139	28	162	200
Speedup	1x	0.95x	1.11x	1.22x

4 Related Work

Research on hybrid or heterogeneous file systems is divided between how such a system will improve the performance of specific application and designs from scratch. There are numerous examples on specific application optimization, particularly in databases [3,7–9,14,21]. In contrast, our approach treats all applications equally unless the user specifies otherwise.

Hybrid file systems from scratch have their fare share of research. Combo [13] is a Windows-based file system. They achieved file separation because they are looking for free large contiguous parts for storing a file. This approach lacks the ability to automatically change medium based on access patterns. Conquest [20] achieved to mix HDDs and NVMs, but requires special host hardware which ours does not need. A new form of hybrid file system from scratch called N-hybrid was proposed in [10]. N-hybrid utilizes an SSD as a write-through cache for recently used files. Storing a file in a specific medium is possible in N-hybrid but only at the request level. If a file is requested in big chunks, it will be placed in an HDD. Our approach curates files not only by access patterns but also by user needs.

Extending the life of SSDs has also been an issue in recent years. Typically, either an HDD [17] or a NVM-enabled device [15] is used as a caching media at a higher stack level to protect the SSD from writes. Rather than setting up a hierarchy of storage devices, we try to achieve less SSD wearing by statically analyzing the file access patterns, and creating a file distribution that attempts to optimally forward I/O requests to the available devices, instead of just limiting the access to SSD.

Similarly to our work, Oracle has published a white paper [12] where they discuss how to achieve a hybrid storage system within the proprietary ZFS file system. They describe applications that would benefit from this facility but do not discuss any results, performance or otherwise. Instead, our approach focuses in the file system level and how it orchestrates where the files would be stored. Moreover, our work will engulf all storage media and it will make informed decisions based on access patterns on where a file should be placed.

5 Conclusions and Future Work

In this paper, we presented an extension to ZFS aimed to allow system administrators and/or normal users to specify which storage device belonging to a zpool to use to store specific files (e.g. HDDs, SSDs, NVMs or others). Moreover, this extension is presented to the user as a file system with a single mount point. We introduce two separate mechanisms: one for capturing information about file usage, and another that can use this information to decide the placement of individual files. An administrator could use these mechanisms to counteract the drawbacks of one medium with benefits from others, by actively defining which files should be placed in which device.

The experiments done with *HetFS* conclude that the overhead introduced by the mechanisms implemented is low, and different benefits can be achieved depending on the metric considered. For example, it is possible to reduce nearly 100% the number of writes going to an SSD, which helps with wear-leveling but at the same time somewhat impacts performance, or only move certain number of files to the SSD to have different ratios of performance improvement. Nevertheless, given that different devices have different behaviors, and different I/O workloads have different constraints, these decisions should be taken by automatic mechanisms that can adapt, learn and decide the best placement for a certain target metric.

Thus, the modification presented is a first step to incorporate more advanced or automatic techniques that can take this kind of decisions. Our future research lines are to rely on these mechanisms to automatically detect data access patterns, and define optimization algorithms that are able to use this information to decide the appropriate vdev for a certain file. This algorithms should accurately model a device characteristics and combine this information to target predefined optimization goals (e.g. SSD wear should be reduced by 25% but performance should not drop below 5%). Moreover, placement of file fragments can also be helpful for internally complex files. For example, headers of files that are usually read and written once could be stored in an HDD, whereas the heavily-accessed parts of a database index would benefit from being in NVM. With *HetFS*, we lay the foundation for developing such a system.

Acknowledgments. The research leading to these results has received funding from the European Community under the BIGStorage ETN (Project 642963 of the H2020-MSCA-ITN-2014), by the Spanish Ministry of Economy and Competitiveness under the TIN2015-65316 grant and by the Catalan Government under the 2014-SGR-1051 grant. To learn more about the BigStorage project, please visit http://bigstorage-project.eu/.

References

1. Aghayev, A., Shafaei, M., Desnoyers, P.: Skylight–A window on shingled disk operation. Trans. Storage **11**(4), 16:1–16:28 (2015)
2. Atlidakis, V., Andrus, J., Geambasu, R., Mitropoulos, D., Nieh, J.: POSIX abstractions in modern operating systems: the old, the new, and the missing. In: Proceedings of the Eleventh European Conference on Computer Systems, EuroSys 2016, pp. 19:1–19:17. ACM, New York (2016)
3. Canim, M., Mihaila, G.A., Bhattacharjee, B., Ross, K.A., Lang, C.A.: SSD bufferpool extensions for database systems. Proc. VLDB Endow. **3**(1–2), 1435–1446 (2010)
4. Harter, T., Dragga, C., Vaughn, M., Arpaci-Dusseau, A.C., Arpaci-Dusseau, R.H.: A file is not a file: understanding the I/O behavior of apple desktop applications. In: Proceedings of the Twenty-Third ACM Symposium on Operating Systems Principles, SOSP 2011, pp. 71–83. ACM, New York (2011)
5. Jung, M., Kandemir, M.: Revisiting widely held SSD expectations and rethinking system-level implications. In: Proceedings of the ACM SIGMETRICS/ International Conference on Measurement and Modeling of Computer Systems, SIGMETRICS 2013, pp. 203–216. ACM, New York (2013)

6. Klimovic, A., Kozyrakis, C., Thereska, E., John, B., Kumar, S.: Flash storage disaggregation. In: Proceedings of the Eleventh European Conference on Computer Systems, EuroSys 2016, pp. 29:1–29:15. ACM, New York (2016)
7. Koltsidas, I., Viglas, S.D.: Flashing up the storage layer. Proc. VLDB Endow. **1**(1), 514–525 (2008)
8. Lee, S.-W., Moon, B., Park, C.: Advances in flash memory SSD technology for enterprise database applications. In: Proceedings of the 2009 ACM SIGMOD International Conference on Management of Data, SIGMOD 2009, pp. 863–870. ACM, New York (2009)
9. Liu, X., Salem, K.: Hybrid storage management for database systems. Proc. VLDB Endow. **6**(8), 541–552 (2013)
10. No, J.: NAND flash memory-based hybrid file system for high I/O performance. J. Parallel Distrib. Comput. **72**(12), 1680–1695 (2012)
11. OpenZFS, January 2017. http://open-zfs.org/wiki/Main_Page
12. Oracle. Deploying Hybrid Storage Pools with Oracle Flash Technology and the Oracle Solaris ZFS File System, pp. 1–17, August 2011
13. Payer, H., Sanvido, M.A., Bandic, Z.Z., Kirsch, C.M.: Combo drive: optimizing cost and performance in a heterogeneous storage device. In: First Workshop on Integrating Solid-state Memory into the Storage Hierarchy, vol. 1, pp. 1–8 (2009)
14. Pelley, S., Wenisch, T.F., Gold, B.T., Bridge, B.: Storage management in the NVRAM Era. Proc. VLDB Endow. **7**(2), 121–132 (2013)
15. Qiu, S., Narasimha Reddy, A.L.: NVMFS: a hybrid file system for improving random write in NAND-flash SSD. In: 2013 IEEE 29th Symposium on Mass Storage Systems and Technologies (MSST), pp. 1–5, May 2013
16. Rodeh, O., Teperman, A.: zFS: a scalable distributed file system using object disks. In: Proceedings of the 20th IEEE/11th NASA Goddard Conference on Mass Storage Systems and Technologies (MSS 2003), MSS 2003, pp. 207–218. IEEE Computer Society, Washington, DC (2003)
17. Soundararajan, G., Prabhakaran, V., Balakrishnan, M., Wobber, T.: Extending SSD lifetimes with disk-based write caches. In: Proceedings of the 8th USENIX Conference on File and Storage Technologies, FAST 2010, p. 8. USENIX Association, Berkeley (2010)
18. systemd-analyze, January 2017. http://manpages.ubuntu.com/manpages/xenial/man1/systemd-analyze.1.html
19. Tsai, C.-C., Jain, B., Abdul, N.A., Porter, D.E.: A study of modern Linux API usage, compatibility: what to support when you're supporting. In: Proceedings of the Eleventh European Conference on Computer Systems, EuroSys 2016, pp. 16:1–16:16. ACM, New York (2016)
20. Wang, A.-I.A., Kuenning, G., Reiher, P., Popek, G.: The conquest file system: better performance through a disk/persistent-RAM hybrid design. Trans. Storage **2**(3), 309–348 (2006)
21. Xu, Q., Siyamwala, H., Ghosh, M., Suri, T., Awasthi, M., Guz, Z., Shayesteh, A., Balakrishnan, V.: Performance analysis of NVMe SSDs and their implication on real world databases. In: Proceedings of the 8th ACM International Systems and Storage Conference, SYSTOR 2015, pp. 6:1–6:11. ACM, New York (2015)
22. Yang, J., Tan, C.P.H., Ong, E.H.: Thermal analysis of helium-filled enterprise disk drive. Microsyst. Technol. **16**(10), 1699–1704 (2010)
23. ZFS Development Team. Rotor vector allocation (small records favour SSD)
24. ZoL: ZFS on Linux, January 2017. http://zfsonlinux.org/

Scientific Applications Performance Evaluation on Burst Buffer

George S. Markomanolis(✉), Bilel Hadri, Rooh Khurram, and Saber Feki

Supercomputing Core Laboratory, King Abdullah University of Science and Technology, Thuwal, Kingdom of Saudi Arabia
georgios.markomanolis@kaust.edu.sa

Abstract. Parallel I/O is an integral component of modern high performance computing, especially in storing and processing very large datasets, such as the case of seismic imaging, CFD, combustion and weather modeling. The storage hierarchy includes nowadays additional layers, the latest being the usage of SSD-based storage as a Burst Buffer for I/O acceleration. We present an in-depth analysis on how to use Burst Buffer for specific cases and how the internal MPI I/O aggregators operate according to the options that the user provides during his job submission. We analyze the performance of a range of I/O intensive scientific applications, at various scales on a large installation of Lustre parallel file system compared to an SSD-based Burst Buffer. Our results show a performance improvement over Lustre when using Burst Buffer. Moreover, we show results from a data hierarchy library which indicate that the standard I/O approaches are not enough to get the expected performance from this technology. The performance gain on the total execution time of the studied applications is between 1.16 and 3 times compared to Lustre. One of the test cases achieved an impressive I/O throughput of 900 GB/s on Burst Buffer.

Keywords: DataWarp · I/O · Burst Buffer

1 Introduction

While the computational power of new supercomputers is increasing significantly, I/O throughput is not increasing with the same rate. The humorous statement by computer engineer Ken Batcher that "a supercomputer is a device for turning compute-bound problems into I/O-bound problems" is becoming more genuine, since I/O subsystems, are typically slow compared to others parts of a supercomputer. This is mainly due to the well-known performance gap that keeps outspreading between the computing components (focusing more on the speed) and the storage devices (focusing more on the capacity of storage and less on performance). Thus, any new technology that promises a boost in I/O performance is becoming popular among the HPC-related research groups. The real world engineering applications demand reduction in the total time to solution, not just on the compute time, especially in cases where I/O is a significant part

J.M. Kunkel et al. (Eds.): ISC High Performance Workshops 2017, LNCS 10524, pp. 701–711, 2017.
https://doi.org/10.1007/978-3-319-67630-2_50

of the whole execution time. Optimizing the I/O is a complex process as the layers of data storage increases in modern supercomputers. In order to achieve better performance, it is harder but crucial to understand the signature of I/O during the execution of the application.

Burst buffer is a new I/O technology that adds a layer between the compute nodes and the standard parallel file system, for more details see [1]. In this paper, we are reporting the I/O performance of six applications on Burst Buffer technology in its Cray implementation DataWarp [2]. These applications are taken from various scientific disciplines, namely: computational fluid dynamics, combustion, climate and earth sciences. In addition to the real applications, two synthetic benchmarks are also studied. The performance of these six test cases is compared to Lustre parallel filesystem. For more information on start working with Burst Buffer and how the MPI I/O aggregators work, see [1].

2 Related Work

National Energy Research Scientific Computing Center (NERSC) have done significant work through NERSC Burst Buffer Early User Program [3]. They have shown cases where the Burst Buffer achieves better performance than Lustre. Moreover, they have identified various challenges to achieve better performance. We experienced similar challenges, and that is why in a following section we provide instructions for better utilization of the resources. In [4] the researchers evaluate the DataDirect Networks (DDN) Infinite Memory Engine (IME). For their experiments, they used IOR [5] which is designed to measure parallel file system I/O performance at both the POSIX and MPI-IO level, and the NEural Simulation Tool (NEST) applications, where they showed that IME has better I/O performance than GPFS file system. The main contribution of this paper is to report our experience on the Burst Buffer performance on a wide range of applications at large scale.

3 Burst Buffer

We used in our experiments the Shaheen II XC40 system [6], which includes richly layered data storage architecture. The primary data storage solution is a Lustre Parallel file system with a usable storage capacity of 17.2 PB delivering around 500 GB/s of I/O throughput. The Cray Sonexion 2000 installation is configured using 72 Scalable Storage Units (SSU) and144 Object Storage Services (OSS) connected to the XC40 via 72 LNET router service nodes. ShaheenII is also composed of 268 Cray DataWarp (DW) accelerator nodes hosting a total of 536 Intel P3608 SSD cards. Each Burst Buffer node provides aggregated peak write/read bandwidth 6 GB/s and 10 GB/s respectively. The combination provides an aggregate Burst Buffer capacity of 1.56 PB to Shaheen users. This fast middle storage layer provides up to three times the performance of the Lustre parallel file system and it is connected directly to the compute nodes through Aries interconnection. The IOR benchmark was launched using all 268 DataWarp

execution of the model, without reserving compute resources. For the case that we save the data to one single file, we use PnetCDF. One significant problem with the measurement of I/O performance on WRF is the calculation of the I/O bandwidth through the reported time from the output file. However, sometimes it was quite difficult to understand why the performance is not efficient. We followed different approaches to investigate the situation. The first one, and more direct, is to activate the debug option on WRF to report all the routines that are called, to break down the I/O time, where we observed thousand smaller I/O calls that could decrease the performance.

Although the latest Cray Environment CNL 6.X is not available to us, which will fix some performance issues, we tried to increase the collective buffering to investigate any improvements and use the CrayPAT instrumentation tool to examine the I/O on DataWarp. For the sake of simplicity, some of the commands/outputs include only the information that is required. We use 64 MPI I/O aggregators for the restart files, and change the size of collective buffering to 32 MB, while the default is 8 MB.

In Table 1 we present the performance data from CrayPAT regarding the I/O performance while writing the restart file with default collective buffering 8 MB. The average achieved I/O bandwidth is 1.4 GB/s per MPI process, and each of them writes almost 4.4 GB, and totally we have 46,960 I/O calls of 8 MB each. However, the collective buffering is changed to 32 MB and the average I/O bandwidth is 1.98 GB/s with totally 12,028 I/O calls. Thus, the size of collective buffer is also important depending on the application, and in this case the I/O bandwidth was improved by 41.4%.

Table 1. Measuring WRF I/O with CrayPAT for the restart file with default collective buffer size

Write MBytes	Write rate (MB/s)	Writes	Bytes/call	Filename/PE
369,720	1,437	46,690	8,303,272	Total - wrfrst_d01
4,448	1,371	560	8,328,689	pe.584
4,456	1,390	562	8,313,976	pe.528

The CrayPAT results are not in agreement with WRF output because CrayPAT measures the I/O per MPI aggregator, but WRF reports the total time of the collective I/O, including the data communication.

From the CrayPAT analysis, Lustre achieved a peak performance of 65 GB/s while a peak of 82 GB/s was reached using Burst Buffer. According to the WRF output report timings, we have the results of Fig. 1 where the I/O write performance of Burst Buffer increases while we increase the number of DataWarp nodes and we always use 144 OSTs for Lustre I/O. The DataWarp performance gets closer to the Lustre, but not better than it. However, reading the input file on DataWarp is more efficient than Lustre and the total execution time is shorter. If we compare the total execution time which is presented in Fig. 1 on

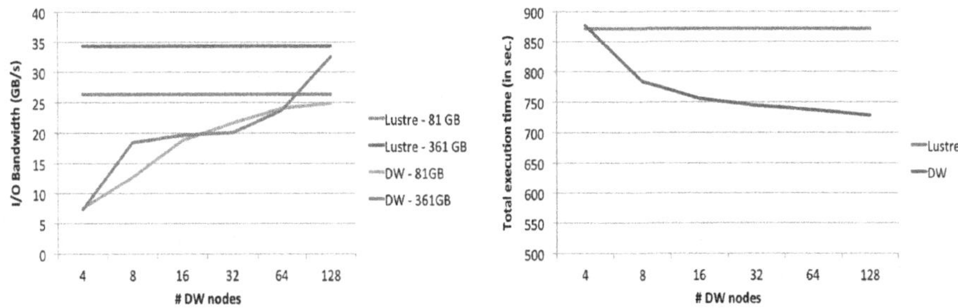

Fig. 1. DataWarp vs Lustre on WRF I/O performance

right side, then the Burst Buffer is faster than Lustre for almost all the cases, with maximum improvement of 16%. In WRF there is significant computation duration which is not influenced from DataWarp.

4.3 NGA

This case study is benchmarking a code on a turbulence partially premixed flames at high Reynolds number. The NGA code [11] can perform large-eddy simulation (LES) and direct numerical simulation (DNS). The benchmark used is this study is the Bunsen flame at a Reynolds number Re = 11,200 using 2.8 Billion grid points requiring around 25 runs of 24 h using 1024 nodes with 32,768 cores. Typically, in production mode, the checkpointing is performed several times daily, generating each time a solution file of approximately 560 GB. Figure 2 shows the results using different DataWarp nodes, Burst Buffer demonstrated with up to 3.75 times performance improvement with 32 nodes when compared to Lustre. Overall, this achieves up to 25% decrease of the complete simulation if regular checkpointing are performed. According to our experience, DataWarp requires a significant amount of data to stress the SSDs, more DW nodes we use, more data we need for the cases that the I/O is not optimized for such technologies.

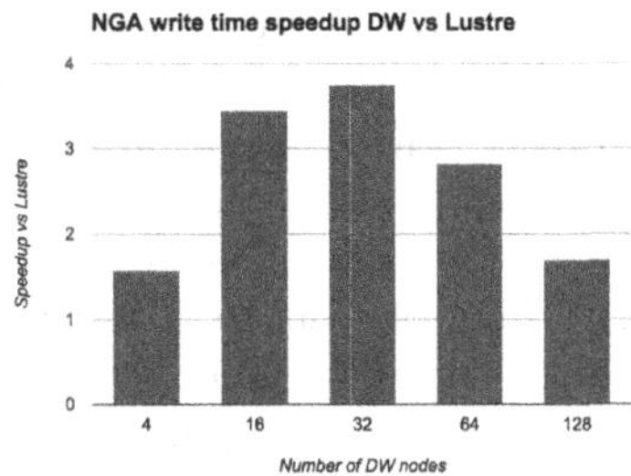

Fig. 2. Write time speedup on Burst Buffer compared to Lustre using different DataWarp Nodes

4.4 ATLIB

Natural migration [12] computes an image according to the equation

$$Image(x) = \sum_{s}^{N}\sum_{r}^{N}[G(s,x,t) * G(r,x,t)] \cdot G_1(s,r,t),$$

where s and r, respectively, denote seismic data source and receiver coordinates, and x denotes image coordinates. The Green's functions $G(s,x,t)$, and $G(r,x,t)$, and the scattered data $G_1(s,r,t)$ are precomputed and stored in a single file with more than 86 GB of size. Within the file, there are N = 5297 Greens functions; each is a 3D volume in time and 2D space. The implementation of natural migration is a hybrid MPI/OpenMP code distributed such that each MPI process runs on a socket with 16 OMP threads. The algorithm does N^2 data accesses to the Green's functions for computing the image. The time convolution ($*$) and dot-product ($\cdot$) operations in the equation above are computationally cheap compared to the IO cost for retrieving the Green's function off disks. Therefore, the performance of the natural migration algorithm is I/O bound. Optimization of such algorithm is necessary considering that the equation above is applied repeatedly for different geophysical parameters.

An equal amount of work is given to each MPI process in the scalability aspect of this performance analysis. Our experiments show that the performance of the code gets worse when the number of MPI processes/Lustre clients is increased. This performance degradation, however, dramatically improves by increasing the Lustre stripe count. As an example, the execution time on 100 nodes is around 452 s versus 930 s while using 250 nodes with a stripe count of 4. By increasing the stripe count to 10, the execution time on 250 nodes is significantly reduced to 505 s. Figure 3 on the left shows the same kind of performance analysis but using DataWarp Burst Buffer. The number of DataWarp nodes is the equivalent of stripe count in Lustre. Similarly, we notice that the performance on DataWarp improves while increasing the number of DataWarp nodes up to 40 nodes. However, increasing it to 100 just hits the performance significantly with any of the node counts used in this study. This could be explained by the difference of the underlying file system putting together the pool of allocated SSDs and its limited scalability in comparison to Lustre parallel file system in its current version. Nonetheless, DataWarp Burst Buffer technology provides good performance benefits of up to 34% for small to medium size runs (50, 100 and 250 nodes) as shown in Fig. 3, right side. Performance degradation is noticed on higher node counts (500 and 1000), and gets worse and worse as the number of I/O clients is increased. While we scale to 2649 compute nodes (to read all the sources with one execution) and 144 I/O clients, we could achieve similar performance to 50 compute nodes, which is quite efficient.

4.5 NAS Parallel Benchmarks Block Triagonal I/O

The NAS Parallel Benchmarks (NPB) [13] are constituted by a set of applications/benchmarks with a scope to evaluate the performance of parallel

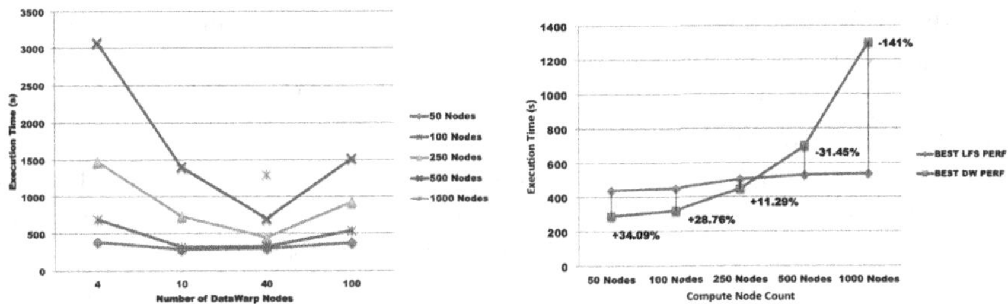

Fig. 3. Execution time per iteration of ATLIB on Burst Buffer and comparison with Lustre

supercomputers. In this study, we use the NAS Parallel Benchmarks Block-Tridiagonal (BT) I/O [14] to evaluate the I/O bandwidth on the available DataWarp installation. BT I/O presents a block-tridiagonal partitioning pattern on a three-dimensional array across a square number of processes. Each process handles multiple Cartesian subsets of the entire data set, and they increase with the square root of the number of processes participating in the computation. Multiple global arrays are consecutively written to a shared file by appending one after another. The number of global arrays can be adjusted, more information is provided in [15] For our experiments, we compile NPB v3.3.1 with Cray-MPICH v7.4.2, Cray compiler v8.5.2, and Parallel-NetCDF 1.7.0. We are interested in studying the I/O performance of various file formats and one of them is Parallel NetCDF (PnetCDF). Thus we chose an implementation of BT I/O which employs this format [16]. For the experiments that take place on Lustre, we always use the maximum amount of OSTs, which is 144. In Fig. 4, we compare results from Lustre and DataWarp. We have two categories of experiments for Lustre; one is with 128 compute nodes (using 32 cores per node) because this is also the maximum number of compute nodes that are used for the DataWarp experiments. The second one is with 512 compute nodes because we can achieve the peak performance on Lustre, and increasing the number of nodes does not provide any gain of the performance. For DataWarp we achieve maximum performance with 128 compute nodes and while we scale, we increase the problem size. We start with 400 GB of PnetCDF file with 2 DataWarp nodes. After numerous experiments we found a sweet spot at 51 TB i.e. 256 DataWarp nodes. From the results in Fig. 4, left side, we observe that DataWarp is at least three times faster than Lustre, achieving close to 90 GB/s, which corresponds almost to the ratio of IOR performance between DataWarp and Lustre. We achieved the maximum performance by applying 8 MPI aggregators per DataWarp node.

However, it is important to know if the I/O bandwidth is efficient as compared to the optimal performance. From IOR results we know that the maximum I/O bandwidth per DataWarp nodes for write, is around 5.7 GB/s. Thus we can extrapolate and calculate the I/O bandwidth efficiency to obtain the results of Fig. 4, right side. The I/O efficiency starts a bit over 50% with 2 DataWarp nodes and falls under 10% with 256 DataWarp nodes which mean that the I/O bandwidth is not scalable in this case. Thus, with this benchmark, DataWarp is three times better than Lustre, but the I/O pattern does not utilize optimally the DataWarp. As we use 128 compute node, and we have 8 MPI I/O aggregators per DataWarp node, with 16 DataWarp nodes, we have totally 128 MPI I/O aggregators, which means one per compute node. Increasing further the DataWarp nodes, we have more than one MPI I/O aggregator per node. Thus, there is some network contention and the performance is decreased.

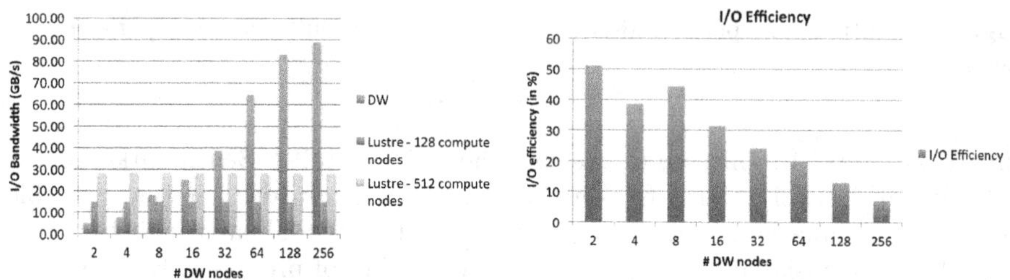

Fig. 4. NAS BT I/O on DW

From Darshan data, Fig. 5, it is clear that while we increase the size of the output file from 400 GB (left side) to 3.2 TB (right side), there are more write calls and so more seek operations, while more than 85% of the total execution time, is I/O. This hurts both filesystems, but DW is constituted by SSDs drives which are faster as also the increase of the MPI I/O aggregators can improve the performance according to [1].

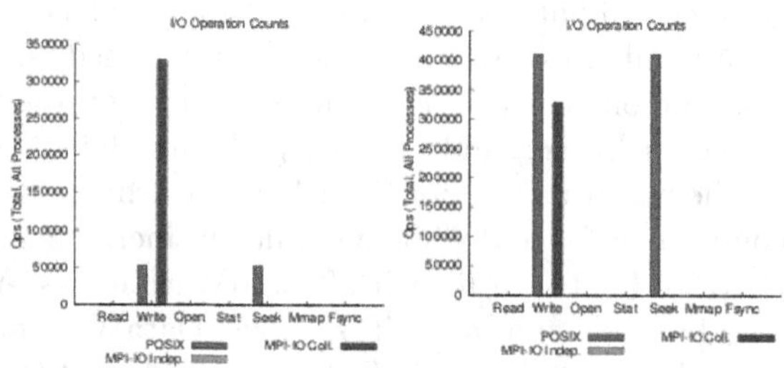

Fig. 5. Comparison of DataWarp and Lustre for NAS BT IO

4.6 Parallel IDX Benchmark

The IDX format provides efficient, cache oblivious, and progressive access to large-scale scientific data by storing the data in a hierarchical Z (HZ) order [17]. The HZ order is calculated for each data sample using the spatial coordinates of that sample. In order to study large datasets a parallel version of IDX, called

PIDX [18], was developed. To achieve high scalability with PIDX, the developers of the framework did implement the total I/O procedure in three phases. Initially, we have the restructuring; blocks of data are created to optimize the layout for I/O. In the continuation, we have the in-core reorganization of data in a read-friendly format following by the data aggregation to optimize disk access. During data restructuring, there is high utilization of the network between the participated processes, and only a subset of them have the required data to participate in next phase. Then, HZ encoding is applied locally on all processes of phase 1. Afterward, the data aggregation occurs, and the data are written to many IDX files. The data aggregation is constituted by steps, in which the first one, data are gathered to aggregators using one-sided MPI communication, and then each aggregator writes its IDX file. This method combines an aggregation strategy that the final phase does not create contention because it creates multiple files. In this work, we use a PIDX tutorial that the developers include in the distribution and they call it *checkpoint_simple*. It reproduces the I/O in the case that we integrate PIDX in a real application. In order to produce an average I/O workload per MPI process, that could correspond to a real application, we declare in our experiment that each MPI process handles 64 MB of data, so all together the 32 cores, are saving 2 GB of data in a file. Moreover, the 64 MB per process are constituted by 32 variables. In Fig. 6 we present the results using 144 OSTs on Lustre and 16 to 256 DataWarp nodes.

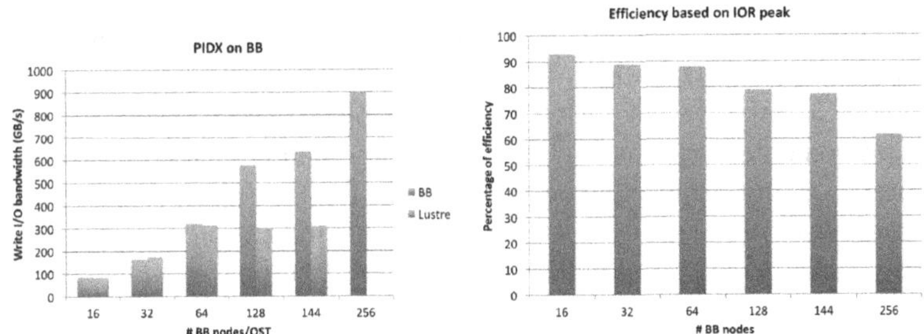

Fig. 6. Comparison of DataWarp and Lustre for PIDX

Moreover, we use 256 compute nodes for 16 DataWarp nodes, till 1024 compute nodes for 256 DataWarp nodes. For 256 compute nodes, we save 512 GB files, and the global domain is $20 \times 8 \times 2048 \times 512$, while for 1024 compute nodes, we save 2 TB files, and the global domain is $2048 \times 2048 \times 2048$. The requested size of I/O per MPI process remains 64 MB for all the experiments. Although, till 64 DataWarp nodes, the Burst Buffer and Lustre have similar write I/O performance, for more DataWarp nodes, Burst Buffer is scaling while Lustre does not. More accurate for 256 DataWarp nodes, Burst Buffer, achieves 900 GB/s which is three times faster than Lustre's peak, 300 GB/s. All the experiments took place in non dedicated mode and peak performance can be influenced. The right part of Fig. 6 shows the PIDX I/O efficiency based on IOR peak results.

Till 144 DataWarp nodes, the I/O efficiency is above 75%, and it drops a bit more than 60% for 256 DataWarp nodes. As we scale on the system, and with regard to the phase of PIDX that utilizes the network, if the system is busy the results can vary because of the Aries network on XC-40. Thus, we believe that some experiments could be better with dedicated mode and newer compute node Linux which will be available on this system in a few months. From the results we understand that PIDX is an efficient I/O library and it is quite scalable. Thus, it is evident that we need to adapt our I/O approach.

5 Conclusions and Future Work

With the continuous and fast growth of the computational power, the I/O in scientific applications becomes a more significant performance bottleneck. We have evaluated the impact of different file system configurations including the newly added I/O layer of Burst Buffer with various scientific applications. A performance improvement is noted in all case and a correlation between the best balance between the number of compute and DataWarp nodes was identified in some of these cases.

The modified NAS BT benchmark with PnetCDF obtained 3 times better performance than Lustre. The serialized I/O in the Fluent software is also evaluated, and a performance gain of 20% with Burst Buffer was observed. The NGA application had a significant I/O performance improvement, which led to 25% total execution time improvement. ATLIB was studied with various combinations of DataWarp and compute nodes and its performance improved by 34%. PIDX achieved 900 GB/s, which is a significant result since this a benchmark could provide a faster I/O solution for real applications by using its API. For future improvements, we consider modifying the open source codes to integrate PIDX library or any other efficient I/O library for DataWarp, such as LibHIO [19]. Moreover, we foresee the need for an auto-tuning tool for optimizing I/O operations on DataWap to alleviate the burden of tuning so many parameters from end users.

Acknowledgment. For computer time, this research used the resources of the Supercomputing Core Laboratory at King Abdullah University of Science & Technology (KAUST) in Thuwal, Saudi Arabia.

References

1. Markomanolis, G.S.: Getting started with the burst buffer. doi:10.6084/m9.figshare.4871738
2. Cray: XC-40, datawarp applications I/O accelerator. http://www.cray.com/sites/default/files/resources/CrayXC40-DataWarp.pdf
3. Bhimji, W., Bard, D., Romanus, M., Paul, D., Ovsyannikov, A., Friesen, B., Bryson, M., Correa, J., Lockwood, G.K., Tsulaia, V., Byna, S., Farrell, S., Gursoy, D., Daley, C., Beckner, V., Straalen, B.V., Trebotich, D., Tull, C., Weber, G., Wright, N.J., Antypas, K., Prabhat: Accelerating science with the NERSC burst buffer early user program. Cray User Group (2016)

4. Schenck, W., El Sayed, S., Foszczynski, M., Homberg, W., Pleiter, D.: Early evaluation of the "Infinite Memory Engine" burst buffer solution. In: Taufer, M., Mohr, B., Kunkel, J.M. (eds.) ISC High Performance 2016. LNCS, vol. 9945, pp. 604–615. Springer, Cham (2016). doi:10.1007/978-3-319-46079-6_41
5. IOR: test. www.csm.ornl.gov/essc/io/IOR-2.10.1.ornl.13/USER_GUIDE
6. Hadri, B., Kortas, S., Feki, S., Khurram, R.: Overview of the KAUST's Cray X40 system – Shaheen II. Cray User Group (2015)
7. ANSYS: Ansys® academic research, release 17.0, fluent, ansys inc.
8. Ansys: External flow over a formula-1 race car (2016)
9. Skamarock, W.C., Klemp, J.B., Dudhia, J., Gill, D.O., Barker, D.M., Duda, M.G., Wang, X., Powers, J.G.: A description of the advanced research WRF version 3. NCAR Technical Note NCAR/TN-475+STR (2008)
10. Morton, D., Nudson, O., Stephenson, C.: Benchmarking and evaluation of the weather research and forecasting (WRF) model on the Cray XT5 (2009)
11. Desjardins, O., Blanquart, G., Balarac, G., Pitsch, H.: High order conservative finite difference scheme for variable density low mach number turbulent flows. J. Comput. Phys. **227**(15), 7125–7159 (2008)
12. AlTheyab, A., Lin, F.C., Schuster, G.T.: Imaging near-surface heterogeneities by natural migration of backscattered surface waves. Geophys. J. Int. **204**, 1332–1341 (2016)
13. Bailey, D.H., Barszcz, E., Barton, J.T., Browning, D.S., Carter, R.L., Dagum, L., Fatoohi, R.A., Frederickson, P.O., Lasinski, T.A., Schreiber, R.S., Simon, H.D., Venkatakrishnan, V., Weeratunga, S.K.: The NAS parallel benchmarks-summary and preliminary results. In: Proceedings of the 1991 ACM/IEEE Conference on Supercomputing (Supercomputing 1991), pp. 158–165. ACM, New York (1991)
14. Wong, P., Van der Wijngaart, R.F.: NAS parallel benchmarks I/O version 2.4 (2003)
15. Liao, W.K.: Design and evaluation of MPI file domain partitioning methods under extent-based file locking protocol. IEEE Trans. Parallel Distrib. Syst. **22**(2), 260–272 (2011)
16. Northwestern University: Benchmarking MPI-I/O with PnetCDF on NAS parallel benchmark BT. #benchmarks (2013). http://cucis.ece.northwestern.edu/projects/PnetCDF/#benchmarks
17. Pascucci, V., Frank, R.J.: Global static indexing for real-time exploration of very large regular grids. In: Proceedings of the 2001 ACM/IEEE Conference on Supercomputing (SC 2001), p. 2. ACM, New York (2001)
18. Kumar, S., Vishwanath, V., Carns, P.H., Summa, B., Scorzelli, G., Pascucci, V., Ross, R.B., Chen, J., Kolla, H., Grout, R.W.: PIDX: Efficient parallel I/O for multi-resolution multi-dimensional scientific datasets. In: CLUSTER (2011)
19. Los Alamos National Security: Libhio, a library intended for writing data to hierarchical data store systems (2016). https://github.com/hpc/libhio

JULEA: A Flexible Storage Framework for HPC

Michael Kuhn(✉)

Universität Hamburg, 20146 Hamburg, Germany
michael.kuhn@informatik.uni-hamburg.de
https://wr.informatik.uni-hamburg.de/

Abstract. JULEA is a flexible storage framework that allows offering arbitrary client interfaces to applications. To be able to rapidly prototype new approaches, it offers data and metadata backends that can either be client-side or server-side; backends for popular storage technologies such as POSIX, LevelDB and MongoDB have already been implemented. Additionally, JULEA allows dynamically adapting the I/O operations' semantics and can thus be adjusted to different use-cases. It runs completely in user space, which eases development and debugging. Its goal is to provide a solid foundation for storage research and teaching.

Keywords: Flexible storage framework · High performance computing · Parallel file system · Object store · Key-value store

1 Introduction

File systems are typically monolithic in design: They support a single storage backend, a single interface and a single set of semantics. While this design has benefits with regards to portability, it is too inflexible for research and teaching. It makes it hard to try new algorithms and approaches because they often require changes to many different components of the file system.

There are two majors problems caused by this: On the one hand, many specialized solutions are created that try to solve a particular problem [11,19,21]. While these are often based on existing file systems, the code is seldom contributed back because it does not meet the original design goals; this makes it hard to maintain these approaches in the long term. On the other hand, it is necessary to have a more or less complete understanding of the file systems due to their complex design. This is especially problematic in the context of shorter projects and presents an unnecessary hurdle for young researchers and students to gain experience with file systems.

A possible solution for these problems is a flexible storage framework that is extensible using plugins for its application-facing interface, its storage backend and its internal behavior, that is, its semantics. This provides the flexibility required to support the many different use-cases found in HPC.

Many applications do not access the file system directly but instead rely on high-level libraries to perform I/O efficiently. This is especially common in scientific applications where exchangeability of data is a primary concern; libraries for

J.M. Kunkel et al. (Eds.): ISC High Performance Workshops 2017, LNCS 10524, pp. 712–723, 2017.
https://doi.org/10.1007/978-3-319-67630-2_51

self-describing data formats such as NetCDF and HDF5 are widely used there. An exemplary software stack is shown in Fig. 1a. Applications only directly interface with NetCDF, which depends on HDF5 and so on. Due to the complex interplay of different components and optimizations in this stack, performance issues are a common occurrence. One of the reasons are the strict POSIX semantics that are typically provided by the underlying parallel file system and forced upon the upper layers [18].

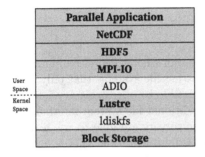

Parallel Application
NetCDF
HDF5
MPI-IO
User Space
ADIO
Kernel Space
Lustre
ldiskfs
Block Storage

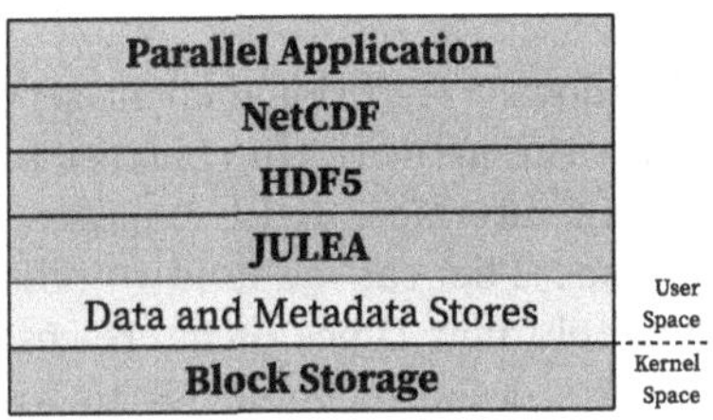

(a) I/O stack commonly found in HPC (b) Proposed I/O stack with JULEA

Fig. 1. Current HPC I/O stack and proposed JULEA I/O stack

Multiple projects are currently investigating possibilities of eliminating this problem by integrating the I/O libraries and file systems more closely [5,12]. Providing such an interface natively could have many benefits but is hard to achieve with current file systems. There are also approaches to combine technologies from the HPC and big data fields and use object stores instead of full-fledged file systems [3,13]. Additionally, there has been research regarding alternative file system interfaces [2,17] and to allow the file systems semantics to be adapted according to the applications' requirements [1,9,19].

While some of these approaches can use existing storage systems and extend them according to their goals, many need to implement basic functionality from scratch because they do not fit within the architecture of existing solutions.

The main contribution of this paper is JULEA, a flexible storage framework that can be used to rapidly prototype new approaches in research and teaching. Therefore, it provides basic storage building blocks that are powerful yet generic enough to support parallel and distributed storage use-cases. This kind of flexible functionality requires well-defined and well-documented plugin interfaces with common requirements in mind. To make it more accessible to developers, readability is favored over performance and there is a clear separation of functionality. It is possible to run it without system-level access to enable easy large-scale experiments on supercomputers, where such access is typically not available.

The resulting software stack is shown in Fig. 1b. All functionality is provided in user space to ease development and debugging. Existing I/O libraries like

MPI-IO or HDF5 can be adapted to make use of JULEA's functionality. Alternatively, applications can interface directly with JULEA, which manages data and metadata storage.

This paper is structured as follows: Sect. 2 presents JULEA's goals and design in detail; this includes the general architecture and different components. The implementation's current status is shown in Sect. 3. Some preliminary evaluation results are displayed in Sect. 4. Related work is presented in Sect. 5. Finally, the paper is concluded and future work is presented in Sect. 6.

2 Design

JULEA follows a traditional client-server design where clients communicate with servers via the network. In contrast to existing file systems that only provide a single client interface, JULEA makes it possible to offer arbitrary interfaces to applications. This can be used to offer traditional file system interfaces as well as completely new types of interfaces. The servers are able to use a multitude of existing storage technologies to foster experimentation; this is achieved by supporting multiple backends. To facilitate rapid prototyping, both clients and backends are easy to implement and exchange. Additionally, JULEA supports dynamically adaptable semantics for all I/O operations. This allows clients to support a wide range of use-cases, such as the very strict POSIX semantics as well as the more relaxed MPI-IO semantics.

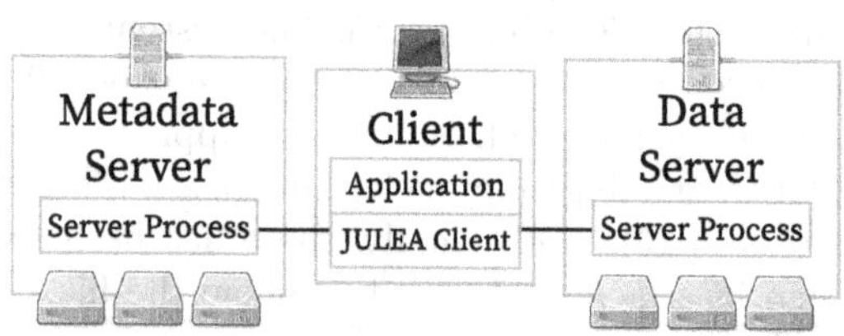

Fig. 2. JULEA's main components

Figure 2 shows the main components of JULEA's design. An application can use one or more JULEA clients to talk to the storage servers. While applications can directly use JULEA's clients, it is also possible to adapt I/O libraries to make use of them; for instance, this could be used to provide an appropriate MPI-IO module or HDF5 plugin. JULEA's servers are split into data and metadata servers, which allows tuning the servers for their respective access patterns.

2.1 Clients

Clients are completely unrestricted regarding the interface they provide. Traditional file systems typically offer a single interface that can not be changed easily due to it being interwoven with the rest of the file system architecture. Therefore, it is often only possible to add extensions to these existing interfaces, which limits the amount and degree of experimentation.

Because JULEA will be implemented in user space, arbitrary interfaces can be provided. This is typically problematic for kernel space file systems, whose client interfaces are restricted by the VFS. Clients can either be directly used by applications or offer interfaces to be used by high-level I/O libraries.

2.2 Backends

To allow backends to be optimized for different use-cases and access patterns, they are separated into data and metadata backends and are used by data and metadata servers, respectively. While data backends are meant to serve large streaming I/O, metadata backends should excel at small random accesses. Data backends manage objects and their interface is therefore very close to popular object stores and file systems. Metadata backends manage key-value pairs with an appropriate interface for this use-case.

To define an appropriate interface for the data backends, interfaces of existing file systems (such as Lustre and OrangeFS), object stores (such as Ceph's RADOS) and I/O interfaces (such as MPI-IO) have been taken into consideration. The resulting functions supported by data backends are as follows:

- **create**: Creates an object given by its name.
- **open**: Opens an object given by its name.
- **delete**: Deletes an object.
- **close**: Closes an object.
- **status**: Returns an object's modification time and size.
- **sync**: Syncs an object to the underlying storage device.
- **read**: Reads data of a given length from an object at the specified offset.
- **write**: Writes data of a given length to an object at the specified offset.

The create and open functions return an object handle on success that can then be used with all other functions. The delete and close functions destroy the object handle. In contrast to POSIX's `stat`, the status function only returns very basic information to be able to support a wide range of data backends.

As for the data backends, existing database (such as SQLite and MongoDB) and key-value (such as LevelDB and LMDB) solutions have been investigated to define a common interface for all metadata backends. This resulted in a common set of functions that are offered by metadata backends:

- **batch_start**: Starts a batch that can include put and delete operations.
- **batch_execute**: Executes a batch.
- **put**: Stores a value for a given key.
- **delete**: Delete a key-value pair for a given key.
- **get**: Returns the value for a given key.
- **get_all**: Returns all values.

- **get_by_prefix**: Returns all values for keys starting with a given prefix.
- **iterate**: Iterates over a multi-value result.

Batches allow aggregating multiple put and delete operations to improve performance; this functionality is also commonly found in current database systems. While the get function returns the value for a single key, the get_all and get_by_prefix functions can return multiple values. For this reason, the iterate function allows iterating over the respective results.

Data and metadata backends support namespaces to allow multiple clients to co-exist and not interfere with each other. Additionally, they support initialization and finalization functions to set up and destroy necessary data structures.

2.3 Semantics

JULEA allows many aspects of its operations' semantics to be changed at runtime. Several key areas of the semantics have been identified as important to provide opportunities for optimizations and are briefly described below. Even though it is possible to mix the settings for each of these semantics, not all combinations might produce reasonable results. Semantics templates make it possible to easily emulate existing semantics such as POSIX.

- The *atomicity* semantics can be used to specify whether or not it is possible for clients to see intermediate states of operations. These are possible because large operations usually involve several servers. If atomicity is required, some kind of locking has to be performed to prevent other clients from accessing data that is currently being modified.
- The *concurrency* semantics can be used to specify whether concurrent accesses will take place and, if so, how the access pattern will look like. This allows handling different patterns appropriately without the need for heuristics to recognize them. Depending on the level of concurrency, different algorithms might be appropriate for operations such as locking or metadata access.
- The *consistency* semantics can be used to specify if and when clients will see modifications performed by other clients and applies to both metadata and data. This information can be used to enable client-side read caching whenever possible.
- The *ordering* semantics can be used to specify whether operations are allowed to be reordered. Because there can be a large number of operations, the additional information can be exploited to optimize their execution.
- The *persistency* semantics can be used to specify if and when data and metadata must be written to persistent storage. This can be used to enable client-side write caching whenever possible.
- The *safety* semantics can be used to specify how safely data and metadata should be handled. It provides guarantees about the state of the data and metadata after the execution of operations has finished.

For more in-depth information about JULEA's semantics, please see [8–10].

3 Implementation

The design discussed in the previous section has been implemented within the JULEA project, which is freely available.[1] It is written in modern C11 code and features only two mandatory dependencies (GLib [6], libbson [14]) to make it easily portable. The code uses the GNU Lesser General Public License (LGPL 3.0 or later) to allow proprietary clients and backends in addition to the available open source ones.

While the clients are provided in the form of shared libraries that can be linked into the application, the server is a specialized program that can function as both a data and metadata server. The shared libraries are written in such a way as to allow applications to use multiple clients at the same time. Backends are also built as shared libraries and can be loaded by the clients and servers.

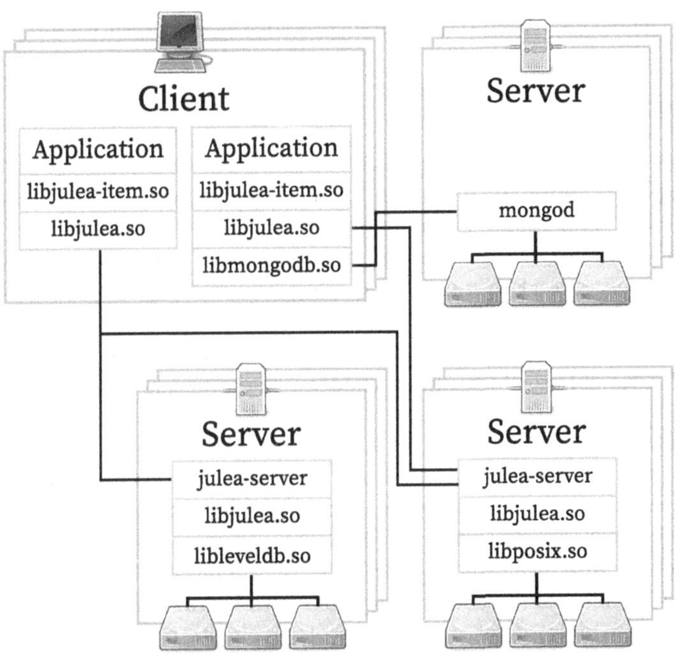

Fig. 3. JULEA's architecture with two applications using different configurations

Figure 3 shows two exemplary uses of JULEA. Both applications use JULEA's item client (`libjulea-item.so`) that provides an easy-to-use cloud-like I/O interface. For the application on the right side, JULEA has been configured to use its client-side MongoDB metadata backend (`libmongodb.so`) and its server-side POSIX data backend (`libposix.so`). JULEA's core library

[1] https://github.com/wr-hamburg/julea.

(`libjulea.so`) automatically loads all required client-side backends at runtime. The client forwards all requests to the core library, which in turn forwards them to the appropriate servers. For the application on the left side, JULEA has been configured to use its server-side LevelDB metadata backend (`libleveldb.so`) and its server-side POSIX data backend (`libposix.so`). In this case, no additional client-side backend has to be loaded. Both configurations are completely transparent for the application and provide the same functionality.

JULEA's flexibility results in a high number of possible configurations: In addition to the data and metadata backends being configurable, the semantics can be set for batches of operations. To facilitate easy verification and performance evaluation, JULEA contains extensive test and benchmark suites.

Additionally, JULEA includes miscellaneous utilities (a command line interface for creating, listing and deleting objects and key-value pairs; a tool for manipulating JULEA's configuration; a tool to gather server statistics) and proof-of-concept codes (a FUSE file system using JULEA). This makes it easy to achieve fast results with JULEA and provides insight into its internals.

3.1 Clients

Clients provide interfaces that can be used by applications or other I/O libraries. They are typically required to use their own, separate namespaces to not interfere with each other. This makes it possible to use multiple clients on top of the same JULEA installation. For instance, the item client would manage all its data and metadata within the `item` namespace while the POSIX client would use the `posix` namespace. This provides flexibility that is currently not available with many existing file systems. Currently, JULEA contains the following clients from which applications and libraries can choose depending on their requirements:

- The *object* client provides direct access to JULEA's data store and is able to access arbitrary namespaces. It provides abstractions for single-server and distributed objects that can be used by other clients; this allows other clients to focus on their respective functionalities.
- The *kv* client provides direct access to JULEA's metadata store and is able to access arbitrary namespaces. It provides an abstraction for key-value pairs. As with the object client, this allows other clients to make easy use of this functionality.
- The *item* client provides a cloud-like interface that supports collections and items. Collections are the top-level entity and can contain only items, which results in a relatively flat hierarchy. Both collections and items can be listed using iterators. Items can be distributed over the available data servers using JULEA's distributions; the client makes use of the object client's distributed object abstraction and the kv client's key-value abstraction to achieve this.
- The *posix* client implements a POSIX file system using the FUSE framework on top of JULEA. It currently uses the item client but will be migrated to the object and kv clients.

3.2 Backends

Backends determine how data and metadata operations are handled. They are completely transparent from the client point of view and can be exchanged using the configuration. Backends can be either client-side or server-side, which causes them to be loaded and used by JULEA's clients and servers, respectively. Due to the standardized backend interface, additional backends can be implemented easily. JULEA already contains the following backends:

- The *posix* server-side data backend provides compatibility with existing POSIX file systems. Due to using a full-featured file system as the data backend, certain functionalities – such as path lookup and permission checking – can be duplicated within the I/O stack depending on the used client.
- The *gio* server-side data backend uses the GIO library that provides a modern, easy-to-use VFS API supporting multiple backends of its own, including POSIX, FTP and SSH. It is mainly intended as a proof of concept and allows experimenting with GIO's more exotic backends.
- The *lexos* server-side data backend uses LEXOS to provide a light-weight data store. LEXOS has been designed and implemented in [16] and only provides basic I/O operations suited for an object store.
- The *null* server-side data backend is intended for performance measurements of the overall I/O stack. It excludes the influence of underlying storage hardware by returning dummy information and discarding all incoming data. Operations are still sent to the appropriate servers to allow measurements of JULEA's network components.
- The *leveldb* server-side metadata backend uses LevelDB for metadata storage. Due to JULEA's metadata interface and LevelDB's interface being very similar, the backend is a relatively thin wrapper.
- The *mongodb* client-side metadata backend uses MongoDB and maps key-value pairs to documents using appropriate indexes to speed up operations. In contrast to server-side backends, the connections to the MongoDB servers are handled by the MongoDB C driver [15].

4 Evaluation

JULEA's performance heavily depends on the used data and metadata backends. For this reason, this section will focus on some general performance aspects. The *local* results have been generated on a desktop machine (Intel Xeon E3-1225v3) with a consumer SSD (Samsung SSD 840 EVO). The *remote* results have been measured with two dual-socket nodes (Intel Xeon X5650) with an HDD (Seagate Barracuda 7200.12) that are connected via Gbit Ethernet; one node has been used as a client and one node has been used as a server.

Table 1 shows performance results for the posix and null data backends as well as the leveldb and mongodb metadata backends. The local and remote results

Table 1. Performance of different data and metadata backends

Storage	Backend	Operation	Perf. (local)	Perf. (remote)
Data	POSIX	Create	19,500 ops/s	3,600 ops/s
		Delete	29,500 ops/s	4,300 ops/s
		Status	39,500 ops/s	4,500 ops/s
	NULL	Create	49,000 ops/s	5,500 ops/s
		Delete	49,500 ops/s	5,000 ops/s
		Status	49,500 ops/s	4,900 ops/s
Metadata	LevelDB	Put	41,500 ops/s	4,300 ops/s
		Delete	43,000 ops/s	4,300 ops/s
	MongoDB	Put	7,500 ops/s	1,400 ops/s
		Delete	8,000 ops/s	1,500 ops/s

differ significantly because the remote results are limited by the Ethernet network's high latency.[2] While the posix data backend already shows satisfactory throughput, the null data backend shows the maximum throughput of JULEA's current implementation. The performance difference is even more pronounced when looking at the metadata backends: While the leveldb metadata backend almost achieves the maximum throughput possible, the mongodb one is significantly slower. Is is important to note that these numbers were generated using JULEA's built-in benchmark suite by simply using a different configuration file via the `JULEA_CONFIG` environment variable. Additionally, the benchmark suite currently uses only a single thread, that is, performance is likely better in real-world applications using multiple threads.

Table 2 shows performance results of different safety semantics when using the leveldb metadata backend. As mentioned previously, the safety semantics can be used to specify how safely data and metadata should be handled. The *none* setting provides no guarantees and does not even check whether the data has reached the servers; the *network* setting (which is the default) guarantees that data has reached the servers; the *storage* setting guarantees that data has been written to persistent storage. The safety semantics is handled implicitly by the storage framework but clients are free to override it. This can be used to considerably decrease overhead depending on applications' safety requirements.

Even though the presented results only highlight a few key aspects of JULEA's design, it can be seen that the framework is able to handle a multitude of different use-cases due to its flexibility. Adding new backends requires only a small amount of code[3] and is easy due to JULEA's clearly defined plugin architecture. Moreover, being able to adapt the semantics allows satisfying different requirements and tuning performance according to them.

[2] The network's round-trip time is 0.110ms, which results in a maximum of 9,090 ops/s.

[3] The existing backends are between 200 and 400 lines of code each.

Table 2. Performance of the LevelDB backend with different safety levels

Safety	Operation	Perf. (local)	Perf. (remote)
None	Put	225,000 ops/s	62,000 ops/s
	Delete	197,000 ops/s	59,500 ops/s
Network	Put	41,500 ops/s	4,300 ops/s
	Delete	43,000 ops/s	4,300 ops/s
Storage	Put	29,500 ops/s	3,800 ops/s
	Delete	31,000 ops/s	3,900 ops/s

5 Related Work

OrangeFS (formerly known as PVFS) is a user-level parallel file system [4,7]. Its Trove layer abstracts the underlying storage technologies and currently supports arbitrary POSIX file systems for data and BDB for metadata. There are currently projects to allow using LMDB and Cassandra for metadata. The metadata backend to use has to be specified at configure time; JULEA allows configuring the metadata backend using its configuration file. Additionally, JULEA's backends do not have to be integrated into the storage framework but can be built externally.

Ceph has gone through different underlying storage technologies [20]. In the past, it used EBOFS, a custom low-level object store. Current versions support arbitrary POSIX file systems but due to requirements regarding extended attributes only XFS, btrfs and ext4 are properly supported. Future versions will also support BlueStore, a custom file system built specifically for Ceph.

Lustre is a kernel file system and only provides a POSIX interface. There is work underway to establish DAOS, which is based on Lustre and offers interfaces for containers, key-value pairs, multi-dimensional arrays and blobs [12]. This will be used to provide an HDF5 interface directly on top of these interfaces. DAOS's approach is very similar to JULEA but has different goals. While DAOS is meant to be a production exascale storage system, JULEA's goal is to provide a convenient framework for research and teaching that can be used to evaluate the functionality and performance of new concepts. These concepts can then be integrated into production systems if deemed successful.

6 Conclusion and Future Work

JULEA provides a flexible storage framework and contains all the necessary building blocks to facilitate rapid prototyping and evaluation of different storage technologies. It has few dependencies and can be used without system-level access, making it a good candidate for research and teaching.

While the basic storage framework and some initial backends have been finished, more work remains to be done. First, to investigate the potential benefits of separating metadata and data of high-level data formats, we will implement an HDF5 VOL plugin that makes use of JULEA. While the actual data (datasets) will be stored using the data backend, everything else will be handling by the metadata backend, enabling efficient access to structural namespace information and attributes. We expect this approach to provide interesting insights because the current I/O stack causes HDF5 metadata access to be handled by the file systems' data servers, which are usually not tuned for these specific access pattern. Second, we will further extend JULEA's backend support. Specifically, we will add a data backend for Ceph's RADOS. This will allow both easy integration of JULEA into existing Ceph environments and facilitate comparison of different approaches found in RADOS and JULEA's distribution functionality. These additional data and metadata backends will lead to further improvements to JULEA's backend interface, which will allow it to remain stable in the foreseeable future and provide a reliable base for third-party backends.

References

1. Al-Kiswany, S., Gharaibeh, A., Ripeanu, M.: The case for a versatile storage system. Operating Syst. Rev. **44**(1), 10–14 (2010). http://doi.acm.org/10.1145/1740390.1740394
2. Albadri, N., Watson, R., Dekeyser, S.: TreeTags: bringing tags to the hierarchical file system. In: Proceedings of the Australasian Computer Science Week Multiconference, Canberra, Australia, 2–5 February 2016, p. 21 (2016). http://doi.acm.org/10.1145/2843043.2843868
3. BigStorage: Storage-Based Convergence Between HPC and Cloud to Handle Big Data (2017). http://bigstorage-project.eu/. Accessed Mar 2017
4. Carns, P.H., Ligon III, W.B., Ross, R.B., Thakur, R.: PVFS: A parallel file system for linux clusters. In: 4th Annual Linux Showcase and Conference, Atlanta, Georgia, USA, 10–14 October 2000. https://www.usenix.org/conference/als-2000/pvfs-parallel-file-system-linux-clusters
5. ESiWACE: Centre of Excellence in Simulation of Weather and Climate in Europe (2017). https://www.esiwace.eu/. Accessed Mar 2017
6. GLib: GLib Reference Manual (2017). https://developer.gnome.org/glib/. Accessed Mar 2017
7. Gu, P., Wang, J., Ross, R.: Bridging the gap between parallel file systems and local file systems: A case study with PVFS. In: 2008 International Conference on Parallel Processing, ICPP 2008, 8–12 September 2008, Portland, Oregon, USA, pp. 554–561 (2008). http://dx.doi.org/10.1109/ICp.2008.43
8. Kuhn, M.: A semantics-aware I/O interface for high performance computing. In: Kunkel, J.M., Ludwig, T., Meuer, H.W. (eds.) ISC 2013. LNCS, vol. 7905, pp. 408–421. Springer, Heidelberg (2013). doi:10.1007/978-3-642-38750-0_31
9. Kuhn, M.: Dynamically adaptable I/O semantics for high performance computing. In: Kunkel, J.M., Ludwig, T. (eds.) ISC High Performance 2015. LNCS, vol. 9137, pp. 240–256. Springer, Cham (2015). doi:10.1007/978-3-319-20119-1_18
10. Kuhn, M.: Dynamically adaptable I/O semantics for high performance computing. Ph.D. Thesis, Universität Hamburg (2015). http://ediss.sub.uni-hamburg.de/volltexte/2015/7302/

11. Kuhn, M., Kunkel, J.M., Ludwig, T.: Dynamic file system semantics to enable metadata optimizations in PVFS. Concurrency Comput. Pract. Experience **21**(14), 1775–1788 (2009). http://dx.doi.org/10.1002/cpe.1439
12. Lofstead, J.F., Jimenez, I., Maltzahn, C., Koziol, Q., Bent, J., Barton, E.: DAOS and friends: a proposal for an exascale storage system. In: Proceedings of the International Conference for High Performance Computing, Networking, Storage and Analysis, SC 2016, Salt Lake City, UT, USA, 13–18 November 2016, pp. 585–596 (2016). http://dx.doi.org/10.1109/SC.2016.49
13. Matri, P., Costan, A., Antoniu, G., Montes, J., Pérez, M.S.: Týr: blob storage meets built-in transactions. In: Proceedings of the International Conference for High Performance Computing, Networking, Storage and Analysis, SC 2016, Salt Lake City, UT, USA, 13–18 November 2016, pp. 49:1–49:12 (2016). http://dl.acm.org/citation.cfm?id=3014970
14. MongoDB, I.: Libbson: A BSON utility library (2017). https://github.com/mongodb/libbson. Accessed Mar 2017
15. MongoDB, I.: Libmongoc: A high-performance MongoDB driver for C (2017). https://github.com/mongodb/mongo-c-driver. Accessed Mar 2017
16. Schröder, S.: Design, Implementation, and Evaluation of a Low-Level Extent-Based Object Store. Master's Thesis, Universität Hamburg (2013)
17. Seltzer, M.I., Murphy, N.: Hierarchical file systems are dead. In: Proceedings of HotOS 2009: 12th Workshop on Hot Topics in Operating Systems, 18–20 May 2009, Monte Verità, Switzerland (2009). http://www.usenix.org/events/hotos09/tech/full_papers/seltzer/seltzer.pdf
18. Stender, J., Kolbeck, B., Hupfeld, F., Cesario, E., Focht, E., Hess, M., Malo, J., Martí, J.: Striping without sacrifices: Maintaining POSIX semantics in a parallel file system. In: Proceedings of the First USENIX Workshop on Large-Scale Computing, LASCO 2008, 23 June 2008, Boston, MA, USA (2008). http://www.usenix.org/events/wiov08/tech/full_papers/stender/stender.pdf
19. Vilayannur, M., Nath, P., Sivasubramaniam, A.: Providing tunable consistency for a parallel file store. In: Proceedings of the FAST 2005 Conference on File and Storage Technologies, 13–16 December 2005, San Francisco, California, USA (2005). http://www.usenix.org/events/fast05/tech/vilayannur.html
20. Weil, S.A., Brandt, S.A., Miller, E.L., Long, D.D.E., Maltzahn, C.: Ceph: A scalable, high-performance distributed file system. In: 7th Symposium on Operating Systems Design and Implementation (OSDI 2006), 6–8 November 2006, Seattle, WA, USA, pp. 307–320 (2006). http://www.usenix.org/events/osdi06/tech/weil.html
21. Wright, C.P., Spillane, R.P., Sivathanu, G., Zadok, E.: Extending ACID semantics to the file system. TOS 3(2), 4:1–4:42 (2007). http://doi.acm.org/10.1145/1242520.1242521

Delivering LHC Software to HPC Compute Elements with CernVM-FS

Jakob Blomer(✉), Gerardo Ganis, Nikola Hardi, and Radu Popescu

European Organization for Particle Research (CERN), Geneva, Switzerland
{jblomer,ganis,nhardi,rpopescu}@cern.ch

Abstract. In recent years, there was a growing interest in improving the utilization of supercomputers by running applications of experiments at the Large Hadron Collider (LHC) at CERN when idle cores cannot be assigned to traditional HPC jobs. At the same time, the upcoming LHC machine and detector upgrades will produce some 60 times higher data rates and challenge LHC experiments to use so far untapped compute resources. LHC experiment applications are tailored to run on *high-throughput computing* resources and they have a different anatomy than HPC applications. LHC applications comprise a core framework that allows hundreds of researchers to plug in their specific algorithms. The software stacks easily accumulate to many gigabytes for a single release. New releases are often produced on a daily basis. To facilitate the distribution of these software stacks to world-wide distributed computing resources, LHC experiments use a purpose-built, global, POSIX file system, the CernVM File System. CernVM-FS pre-processes data into content-addressed, digitally signed Merkle trees and it uses web caches and proxies for data distribution. Fuse-mounted files system clients on the compute nodes load and cache on demand only the small fraction of files needed at any given moment. In this paper, we report on problems and lessons learned in the deployment of CernVM-FS on supercomputers such as the supercomputers at NERSC in Berkeley, at LRZ in Munich, and at CSCS in Lugano. We compare CernVM-FS to a shared software area on a traditional HPC storage system and to container-based systems.

1 Introduction

Computing for High-Energy Physics (HEP) collider experiments benefits from its embarrassingly parallel workload. HEP software processes so-called "events". Events represent the data that a particle detector captured as a result of particle collisions; they can be processed independently from each other. In the case of the CERN Large Hadron Collider (LHC) this is reflected in the experiments' *high-throughput computing* (HTC) infrastructure, the World-wide LHC Computing Grid (WLCG) [1]. A federation of some 170 globally distributed data centers contributes resources in the form of commodity, Linux-based x86_64 servers. A *middleware* presents these resources as one coherent batch and data management system to hundreds of individual physics research groups. The aggregated amount of resources in WLCG, approximately half a million cores and one

J.M. Kunkel et al. (Eds.): ISC High Performance Workshops 2017, LNCS 10524, pp. 724–730, 2017.
https://doi.org/10.1007/978-3-319-67630-2_52

exabyte of storage, is comparable to a large supercomputer. Yet the computing environment comes closer to a typical Big Data installation than to an HPC system. Compute resources are considered as a set of independent CPU cores. A typical compute job runs for a few hours on a particular core. It has access to 2 GB to 4 GB memory, node-local scratch space, a GbE Internet connection to access central databases and to read and write data, and a standard Linux environment with a few custom system software packages. Substantial success was made in porting compute intensive simulation codes to special architectures found on supercomputers, including KNL and PowerPC systems [6]. Still, the use of supercomputers has been a manual, labor intensive task. A lack of bridging on the systems level between HTC and HPC worlds prevents LHC experiments to integrate supercomputers in a seamless and automated way into the general pool of resources. Custom approaches tailored to individual HPC centers are carried out in order to stage input data, write out output data, integrate with the supercomputer's job manager and to deliver codes to compute nodes. In this contribution, we will discuss the distribution of large software stacks to HPC resources.

2 Software Distribution in High-Throughput Computing

In the traditional HPC world, the distribution of codes is usually not a problem. Applications are carefully optimized, often statically linked binaries tailored to run on a specific supercomputer. They are either sent together with the compute job definition or they can reside on a shared cluster file system. In the HTC world, compute jobs can potentially be executed on any of the hundreds of the world-wide distributed data centers, whose compute nodes run different flavors of Linux with different sets of pre-installed libraries. Therefore, LHC experiments have long developed a discipline of bundling all the dependencies (compilers and system libraries) together with the application software. Overall, a single LHC software release consists of the order of ten gigabytes and hundred thousand files. New releases are produced on a daily basis.

Size and volatility of the LHC experiment software combined with the large number of compute nodes makes it difficult to use containers for software distribution. Instead, LHC experiments and other scientific collaborations use CernVM-FS, a purpose-built, global file system to provide a shared software area for compute nodes around the world. CernVM-FS pre-processes data into content-addressed, digitally signed Merkle trees and it uses web caches and proxies for data distribution. [2,3] Fuse-mounted [10,16] files system clients on the worker nodes provide access to the entire repository of precompiled software under the `/cvmfs` directory. Currently, LHC experiments provide close to half a billion (small) files in CernVM-FS.

The client loads and caches on demand only the tiny fraction of files and file meta-data needed at any given moment. This way, most data and meta-data requests are served from the compute nodes' local caches, with cache hit rates well over 99%. A typical cache hierarchy comprises some 100 MB in the worker node RAM, 10 GB on the worker node hard disk, and 50 GB on a handful of web proxies within the data center. Caching is key to CernVM-FS' ability to scale a very meta-data intensive workload—up to the MHz range of meta-data requests per node—to tens of thousands of nodes.

3 Aspects of HPC Computing Environments

For traditional HPC storage systems, such as Lustre and GPFS, the high meta-data load from LHC software is challenging. Storage of tens of millions of small files easily exceeds the user's inode quota. The synchronization of such a large number of files into the supercomputers storage system, for instance through *rsync* invocations on the login nodes, is error-prone and time consuming. At runtime, meta-data servers can easily become overloaded.

Another problem with copying software from CernVM-FS into a shared location is that its contents are often not relocatable. The supercomputer's systems team either need to create a symbolic link on the compute nodes from `/cvmfs` into the actual location or binaries and scripts need to be post-processed after copying. For one of the LHC experiments, this post-processing affected tens of thousands of files. [18]

The straight deployment of CernVM-FS on supercomputers, on the other hand, is often difficult because

1. restrictive policies for compute nodes prevent the deployment of the CernVM-FS client,
2. compute nodes might not have outgoing Internet connectivity, which is needed to populate the caches from central CernVM-FS servers,
3. compute nodes might lack local hard disks, removing a key caching layer of CernVM-FS.

The following sections discuss these obstacles. It is worth noting that binaries can be pre-compiled or cross-compiled for a variety of destination platforms and placed on CernVM-FS beforehand. In one instance, the software pre-compiled by gcc for standard x86_64 nodes even ran 20% faster compared to the same code compiled by Cray's compiler. [8]

3.1 File System Interface

Binary files containing the scientific codes have to reside on a "real" file system ready to be loaded by the operating system kernel. This is different from data, which can in principal also be accessed from applications through user-level libraries. CernVM-FS clients are based on the *Fuse* file system toolkit (cf. Fig. 1). Fuse is a kernel level file system that forwards all calls to a user-level module. Thus errors in the file system code do not cause kernel crashes. Although part of the Linux kernel, many supercomputers disable Fuse on the compute nodes.

On such systems, individual applications can access `/cvmfs` by means of the CernVM-FS connector for *Parrot* [15]. Parrot provides virtual file systems

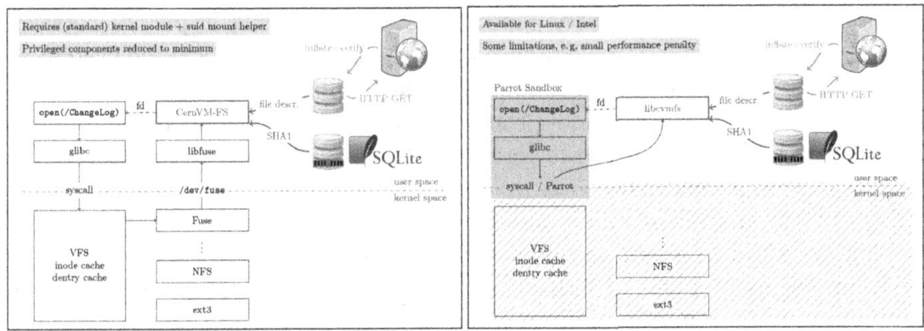

Fig. 1. CernVM-FS file system options. Left hand with Fuse upcalls to user space, right hand in pure user space with Parrot.

for Linux processes using `ptrace`-level sandboxing (cf. Fig. 1). As such, Parrot requires no special privileges but it also introduces a performance penalty. We found that the performance penalty is negligible for most compute tasks. Some HPC centers, however, reported problems with certain multi-core applications and with direct GPU access caused by the `ptrace` sandboxing. [8]

We are currently investigating Cray's Data Virtualization Service (DVS) [14] to provide network file systems to compute nodes. DVS can provide NFS volumes to compute nodes, and as such it can provide an NFS exported CernVM-FS mount point to compute nodes. In our experience, an NFS server providing `/cvmfs` scales up to a few thousand cores. Caching within DVS, however, could increase the scalability.

3.2 Local Cache Space

Much of CernVM-FS' scalability relies on the presence of node-local caches that satisfy most data and meta-data requests. When local hard disks are missing, the CernVM-FS client's cache can be placed on a cluster file system and shared by all the compute nodes. In contrast to a plain copy of the `/cvmfs`, in the CernVM-FS cache data format files are deduplicated and file meta-data is stored in larger blocks of typically a few hundred thousand files. The load from CernVM-FS clients accessing a cache on a shared file system is therefore much smaller than compute nodes directly loading software from a shared file system. At one supercomputer, the running time of codes with a shared cache on GPFS was more than three times shorter than running the software from a plain shared software area on GPFS due to inode cache thrashing in GPFS in the latter case. [17]

Even when exploiting the CernVM-FS cache format, however, millions of small files can end up on GPFS or Lustre and thousands of files can be opened concurrently by the compute nodes. To avoid the "many small files" pattern altogether, the CernVM-FS cache can be provided as a loopback device on the cluster file system. This requires one file per compute node, typically between one and ten gigabytes in size. The files are formatted with a local file system so that compute nodes are able to mount them as loopback devices. Because there is only a single file for every node, the parallelism of the cluster file system can be exploited and all the requests from CernVM-FS circumvent the cluster file system's meta-data server(s).

In our view, an efficient cache management requires flexibility in the CernVM-FS client in order to adapt to node size, network characteristics, and the storage technologies at hand. To this end, we created a plug-in interface to the client's cache subsystem so that customized cache algorithms can be independently developed and deployed. Many options are conceivable, for instance tapping burst buffers or a fully decentralized cache algorithm among the compute nodes [4]. For now, we provide a *tiered cache manager* and an *in-memory cache manager*. The two cache managers can be combined, allowing for a small hot set kept in the compute nodes' RAM and a larger warm set on a shared file system. Scale tests of these uncommon cache configurations are underway.

3.3 Internet Access

On a local cache miss, CernVM-FS clients reach out to a web server on the Internet to fetch data and populate the cache. HPC compute nodes often do not have access to the Internet but only dedicated *login nodes* have Internet connectivity.

We developed a "cache preloader" in order to pre-populate the entire content of a CernVM-FS directory tree from a login node into a location internal to the supercomputer, so that content becomes visible to the compute nodes. The cache preloader makes use of the Merkle trees to efficiently keep the data area on the shared file system synchronized. After an initial synchronization run, only change sets need to be transferred. Even for directories with hundreds of millions of files, incremental synchronization runs usually finish in a few seconds up to a few minutes. The cache preloader can furthermore prune the directory tree so that only relevant parts (for instance: the latest software versions) are copied.

4 Practical Examples

In recent years, various groups in the high-energy physics community acquired grants to run on HPC systems in the U.S. and in Europe. These included some Leadership Class Facilities such as Titan at the Oak Ridge National Lab and Mira at the Argonne National Lab. Almost all of these efforts made content from CernVM-FS available on supercomputers in one way or another. Table 1 provides an overview of code distribution approaches by different groups.

Table 1. Examples of code distribution on supercomputers used by LHC experiments.

#	HPC System	Loc	CernVM-FS Deployment
3	Piz Daint	CH	Fuse client with loopback cache [8]
4	Titan	US	Rsync of `/cvmfs` into GPFS [13]
9	Mira	US	Custom binaries [6]
20	Stampede	US	Rsync of `/cvmfs` [9]
33	HPC2	RU	Standard fuse client [11]
40	SuperMUC	DE	Parrot client with preloaded cache [17]
72	Edison	US	Shifter, parrot client with preloaded cache (tested) [7]
73	Archer	UK	Rsync of `/cvmfs` [18]
389	NEMO	DE	OpenStack virtual machines (tested) [12]

5 Related Work

A tool chain around the Shifter container system [5] was developed in order to copy the `/cvmfs` tree into a container. The content was deduplicated and compressed on a squashfs loopback device in order to reduce the size of the final container image to "only" a few hundred gigabytes. The main drawback of this approach is the time of some 24 hours it takes to produce the images. Containers in general are a promising approach to provide a commodity Linux environment on compute nodes. They can be combined with application delivery by CernVM-FS so that the container images remain small and manageable.

A utility called *uncvmfs* has been used to provide a more efficient copy of the `/cvmfs` tree. With uncvmfs, files are deduplicated by means of hardlinks. Unlike the CernVM-FS cache format, directories and symbolic links are not grouped into larger blocks, preserving many of the scalability issues of plain copies of the `/cvmfs` tree.

6 Summary

We have shown several options to approach code distribution of typical HTC applications onto supercomputers. While software stacks for LHC experiments are particularly large and volatile, we believe that typical Big Data applications will face similar challenges as HPC centers become more open for non-traditional workloads. While there are a number of successful efforts to use HPC resources in LHC computing, a generally applicable and automated approach to code distribution would be highly desirable. Beyond the scope of code distribution, using HPC resources for HTC workloads raises several other open questions, such as the integration into experiments' global data management, job management, and identity federation systems.

References

1. Bird, I., et al.: LHC computing grid: Technical design report. Technical report LCG-TDR-001, CERN (2005)
2. Blomer, J., Aguado-Sanchez, C., Buncic, P., Harutyunyan, A.: Distributing LHC application software and conditions databases using the CernVM file system. J. Phys. Conf. Ser. **331**, 042003 (2011). http://iopscience.iop.org/article/10.1088/1742-6596/331/4/042003/meta
3. Blomer, J., Buncic, P., Meusel, R., Ganis, G., Sfiligoi, I., Thain, D.: The evolution of global scale filesystems for scientific software distribution. Comput. Sci. Eng. **17**(6), 61–71 (2015)
4. Blomer, J., Fuhrmann, T.: A fully decentralized file system cache for the CernVMFS. In: Proceedings 10th International Conference on Computer and Communications Networks (ICCCN), August 2010
5. Canon, S., Jacobsen, D.: Shifter: Containers for hpc. In: Proceedings of the Cray User Group (2016)
6. Childersa, J.T., Gerhardt, L.: Developments in architectures and services for using high performance computing in energy frontier experiments. In: Proceedings 38th International Conference on High Energy Physics (ICHEP 2016) (2016)
7. Fasel, M.: Using nersc high-performance computing (hpc) systems for high-energy nuclear physics applications with alice. J. Phys. Conf. Ser. **762**, 012031 (2016). IOP Publishing
8. Filipcic, A., Haug, S., Hostettler, M., Walker, R., Weber, M.: Atlas computing on cscs hpc. J. Phys. Conf. Ser. **664**, 092011 (2015). IOP Publishing
9. Gardner, R.: Xsede integration. In: US ATLAS Physics Support, Software and Computing Technical Planning Meeting (2016)
10. Henk, C., Szeredi, M.: Filesystem in Userspace (FUSE). http://fuse.sourceforge.net, http://fuse.sourceforge.net/
11. Mashinistov, R.: Panda @ nrc ki. Talk at the PanDA Workshop (2016)
12. Meier, K., Fleig, G., Hauth, T., Janczyk, M., Quast, G., von Suchodoletz, D., Wiebelt, B.: Dynamic provisioning of a hep computing infrastructure on a shared hybrid hpc system. J. Phys. Conf. Ser. **762**, 012012 (2016). IOP Publishing
13. Nilsson, P., Panitkin, S., Oleynik, D., Maeno, T., De, K., Wu, W., Filipcic, A., Wenaus, T., Klimentov, A.: Extending atlas computing to commercial clouds and supercomputers. PoS, p. 034 (2014)
14. Sugiyama, S., Wallace, D.: Cray dvs: Data virtualization service. In: Cray User Group Annual Technical Conference (2008)
15. Thain, D., Livny, M.: Parrot: an application environment for data-intensive computing. Scalable Comput. Pract. Experience **6**(3), 9–18 (2005)
16. Vangoor, B.K.R., Tarasov, V., Zadok, E.: To FUSE or Not to FUSE: performance of user-space file systems. In: Proceedings of the 15th USENIX Conference on File and Storage Technologies (FAST 2017) (2017)
17. Walker, R.: Hep software on supercomputers. In: Talk at the CernVM Users Workshop (2016)
18. Washbrook, A.: Processing lhc workloads on archer. In: Talk at GridPP35 Conference (2015)

Scaling the EOS Namespace

Andreas J. Peters, Elvin A. Sindrilaru, and Georgios Bitzes(✉)

CERN IT, Geneva, Switzerland
Georgios.bitzes@cern.ch

Abstract. EOS is the distributed storage system being developed at CERN with the aim of fulfilling a wide range of data storage needs, ranging from physics data to user home directories. Being in production since 2011, EOS currently manages around 224 petabytes of disk space and 1.4 billion files across several instances.

Even though individual EOS instances routinely manage hundreds of disk servers, users access the contents through a single, unified namespace which is exposed by the head node (MGM), and contains the metadata of all files stored on that instance.

The legacy implementation keeps the entire namespace in-memory. Modifications are appended to a persistent, on-disk changelog; this way, the in-memory contents can be reconstructed after every reboot by replaying the changelog.

While this solution has proven reliable and effective, we are quickly approaching the limits of its scalability. In this paper, we present our new implementation which is currently in testing. We have designed and implemented QuarkDB, a highly available, strongly consistent distributed database which exposes a subset of the redis command set, and serves as the namespace storage backend.

Using this design, the MGM now acts as a stateless write-through cache, with all metadata persisted in QuarkDB. Scalability is achieved by having multiple MGMs, each assigned to a subtree of the namespace, with clients being automatically redirected to the appropriate one.

1 Introduction

The EOS project [1] started in 2011 to fulfill the data storage needs of CERN, and in particular storing and making available the physics data produced by the LHC experiments. Being developed and in production since 2011, EOS is built upon the XRootD [8] client-server framework, supports several data access protocols (XRootD, gsiftp, WebDAV, S3), and currently manages around 224 petabytes of disk space with 1.4 billion files across several instances.

Recently, the scope of EOS has expanded to additionally serve as the backend for user home directories and a file syncing service, CERNBox [3], as the future replacement to the AFS [2] service provided by CERN IT.

The gradual growth in the total number of files stored on EOS has revealed certain scalability limitations in the original design of the namespace subsystem. In this paper, we describe the legacy implementation and its shortcomings,

J.M. Kunkel et al. (Eds.): ISC High Performance Workshops 2017, LNCS 10524, pp. 731–740, 2017.
https://doi.org/10.1007/978-3-319-67630-2_53

discuss our new implementation based on a separate highly-available metadata store exposing a redis-like interface, and present some preliminary performance measurements.

2 Architectural Overview

An EOS instance is composed of several distinct components:

- The File Storage nodes (FSTs) are responsible for handling the physical storage — in a typical deployment, each FST manages several tens of hard drives.
- The Metadata Manager (MGM) is the initial point of contact for external clients, handles authentication and authorization, and redirects clients to the appropriate FSTs on both reading and writing.
- The Message Queue (MQ) handles inter-cluster communication between the MGM and the FSTs, delivering messages such as heartbeats and configuration changes.

The component this paper focuses on is the MGM, and in particular its namespace subsystem which stores all file metadata and among other things is responsible for translating logical paths to the physical locations where the files reside within the cluster.

Example 1. Sample namespace entry representing `/eos/somedir/filename`.
Inode number: `134563`
Name: `filename`
Parent directory inode: `1234`, meaning `eos/somedir`
Size: `19183 bytes`
File layout: `2 replicas`
Physical replica 1: `Filesystem #23`, meaning `fst-1.cern.ch:/mnt34/`
Physical replica 2: `Filesystem #45`, meaning `fst-2.cern.ch:/mnt11/`
Checksum: `md5-567c100888518c1163b3462993de7d47`

In the process of developing a better namespace implementation, and for the sake of being able to run experiments and measurements easily, we moved the namespace subsystem into a separate plugin. The rest of the MGM code uses a standard interface to talk to it, thus facilitating an easy way of replacing it without affecting the rest of the code.

Making the namespace more scalable involved some changes to the above architecture; namely, the addition of a new highly-available database component, as well as enabling the use of multiple MGMs for load-balancing. These changes are described in more detail in later sections.

3 The Legacy In-Memory Namespace

One of the primary goals of EOS from the beginning has been to deliver good and consistent performance. This includes being able to fully exploit the underlying hardware in terms of I/O and network performance of the FSTs, as well as perform low-latency metadata operations on the MGM.

The initial design includes a namespace implementation where all metadata lives in-memory on the MGM, and is persisted on-disk in the form of a changelog. In more detail:

- During MGM boot, the entire namespace is reconstructed in-memory by replaying the on-disk changelog.
- File lookups require no I/O operations, as all metadata is retrieved from memory. Entries are stored in a dense hash map (provided by the Google SparseHash library), keyed by the inode number, and consume approximately 1kb of memory each.
- For metadata updates, the memory contents are modified and an entry is appended to the changelog, which is fsynced periodically.
- A background thread compacts the changelog on regular intervals, thus purging out-of-date entries which have been superseded by newer ones. This process ensures the size of the changelog remains under control, and stays proportional to the total size of the instance, and not to the entire history of operations on it.

While this solution has proven reliable and effective, it has several important limitations:

- The total size to store the entire namespace of an instance cannot exceed the physical RAM available on the head node, since everything is stored in-memory.
- Replaying the changelog after a reboot can take a long time, upwards to one hour for some of our larger instances.
- The use of a single head node represents a scalability bottleneck, as well as a single point of failure.

The effects of long boot time can however be mitigated by employing optional active-passive replication, through which is possible to have a slave MGM on hot standby that can be manually promoted to master, in case the current one fails. During normal operation, the master MGM performs continuous one-way synchronization of its changelog towards any configured slaves.

4 The New, Scalable Namespace

One of the more promising ideas for replacing the legacy namespace has been to store all metadata on a redis [4] instance, a datastore well-known for its high performance and flexibility. We implemented a namespace plugin which used redis for metadata persistence — what made it unsuitable for our use-case was the need to accommodate very large datasets. Redis poses the requirement that the total data stored is smaller than the physical RAM of the machine hosting it.

A different idea has been to use an embeddable, on-disk key-value store such as RocksDB [5] directly on the MGM. This solves both major issues of the legacy design:

- No need for unreasonable amounts of RAM on the MGM, since the contents can be retrieved from disk when needed. This is certainly much slower than a memory lookup, but we can mitigate the effects by adding a caching layer for hot entries.
- Initialization time is nearly instantaneous even for datasets spanning several terabytes.

While such a design would solve all immediate problems we faced, an important downside remained. The MGM would still represent a scalability bottleneck and single point of failure, and losing it would result in the entire cluster becoming unavailable, requiring manual intervention.

Our final design combines the two ideas above. We implemented a highly available distributed datastore, QuarkDB, which supports and exposes a small subset of the redis command set, using RocksDB as the storage backend and translating all redis commands into equivalent RocksDB key-value transactions.

The MGM encodes all metadata in a redis-compatible format using a combination of `STRING`, `HASH`, and `SET` redis commands, serialized with protocol buffers [6].

To minimize the impact of an extra network roundtrip between the MGM and QuarkDB for most metadata operations, the MGM caches hot entries locally under a Least-Recently-Used eviction policy. As we shall see later in the measurements, there is no performance loss compared to the in-memory implementation for cached read operations, which is usually the dominating access pattern in terms of frequency.

Using the above architecture, it now becomes possible to spread the client load by employing multiple MGMs, having each responsible for a subtree of the namespace. In this regard, each MGM essentially acts as a write-through cache for all metadata which is persisted on QuarkDB. To simplify the management and deployment of multiple MGMs, the configuration setup moves from being stored in files locally on an MGM, to being centrally managed in QuarkDB.

5 Designing QuarkDB, a Highly Available Datastore

5.1 Choosing a Storage Backend and Access Protocol

As mentioned earlier, the goal of QuarkDB is to serve as the namespace metadata backend for EOS. In order to avoid the time-consuming task of re-implementing the low-level details of a database, we leverage the RocksDB library, a highly-performant embeddable datastore based on the log-structured merge-tree data structure. We made this choice based on the fact that RocksDB is open source, actively maintained, and used across several important projects already.

We chose the Redis Serialization Protocol, the same one used in the official redis server, based on its simplicity of use and implementation and the fact that there already exist tools compatible with it. (e.g. `redis-cli`, `redis-benchmark`).

5.2 Redis Data Structures Stored in RocksDB

The next step was to decide on a way to translate between redis operations and RocksDB key-value transactions. We implemented the following simple encoding scheme:

- Each redis key is associated to a key descriptor stored in RocksDB, which is its name prefixed by the letter "d", containing its type (whether a `STRING`, a `HASH`, or `SET`) and size. This allows to detect errors, for example when the user attempts to use an existing `HASH` like a `SET`.
- The contents of a `STRING` are stored in a key containing its name prefixed by the letter "a".
- Each element in a `HASH` or `SET` is stored in its own RocksDB key: the key name concatenated with the symbol "#" plus the element name, prefixed by the letter "b" or "c", depending on whether it's a `HASH` or a `SET`.

To make things more clear, the following example shows the steps performed during a lookup using the `HGET` redis command.

1. The client issues `HGET mykey myelement`. In this context, the client is an EOS MGM.
2. The key descriptor for `mykey` is retrieved by looking up `dmykey` in RocksDB.
3. If the key descriptor does not exist, an empty reply is returned. If the key descriptor is not associated to a `HASH` but some other data structure, an error is returned.
4. A lookup for `bmykey#myelement` is done in RocksDB, and the contents are returned to the client. If the lookup finds no result, it means there's no `myelement` within `mykey`, and an empty reply is returned.

Listing the contents of a container works in a similar way – after retrieving the key descriptor, a range scan is performed with the appropriate prefix, which returns all elements in the corresponding hash or set.

5.3 Introducing High Availability

To prevent QuarkDB from becoming the single point of failure, we implemented native quorum-consensus replication based on the Raft [7] consensus algorithm:

- The QuarkDB cluster is able to tolerate losing some nodes without any impact on availability, provided that a majority (or *quorum*) remain online. In a typical deployment with 3 replica nodes, as long as at least 2 out of 3 nodes are alive and connected to each other, the cluster is fully operational.

- Replication is semi-synchronous, meaning that clients receive an acknowledgement to a write as soon as it has been replicated to a quorum of nodes.

Raft works by essentially replaying a series of operations towards a database (called the *state machine* in Raft terminology), ensuring they are identical across all nodes and are applied with an identical order. In our case, the state machine is represented by the class which translates redis commands into RocksDB transactions, and is mostly separate from the consensus logic – this way, QuarkDB can be run in standalone mode as well, without having to pay for the high overhead of consensus in case high availability is not needed.

5.4 Ensuring Correctness

Since QuarkDB is to become a critical component of every EOS instance, ensuring correctness has been of paramount importance, especially given that implementing distributed consensus correctly can be quite tricky. QuarkDB is being written following the spirit of Test Driven Development (TDD), which has resulted in a large suite of unit, functional, and stress tests. This is in addition to several internal assertions that detect possible inconsistencies between the nodes, so as to further reduce the risk of the replicas getting out of sync and opting to crash early instead.

6 Preliminary Measurements

6.1 Test Setup

We used three identical bare-metal machines running CERN CentOS 7 with dual-socket Intel Xeon E5-2650 v2 at 2.60 GHz, providing a total of 32 cores on each machine.

6.2 QuarkDB Performance

Performance depends heavily on whether pipelining is used, that is if the client sends multiple commands at the same time without waiting for an acknowledgement of the previous ones. This amortizes the roundtrip latency and allows for certain optimizations, such as batching several responses to the client using a single `write()` system call.

All measurements were taken using the **`redis-benchmark`** tool with keyspacelen of 10 million – this ensures the load is spread over a large set of keys.

Ping Throughput. `PING` is a redis command to which the server simply replies with `PONG`. This test is useful to verify that the machinery handling network sockets and threads is efficient: QuarkDB is able to reach a peak of 1.6 million pings per second (Fig. 1).

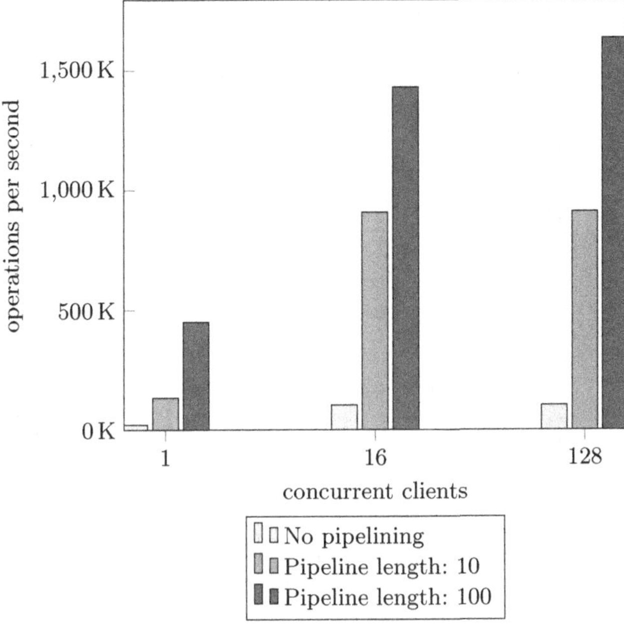

Fig. 1. QuarkDB PING throughput

Standalone Mode. Write performance reaches a peak of around 105 thousand operations per second using the `SET` command (Fig. 2). Each write was 200 bytes in size. Read performance reaches a peak of 320 thousand operations per second (Fig. 3).

Replicated Mode with Raft Consensus. Write performance reaches a peak of 9000 operations per second – the major limiting factor here is the Raft journal into which all write operations must be serialized (Fig. 4). Read performance is identical as in standalone mode (Fig. 3), since in our implementation reads go directly to the state machine, without passing through the raft journal.

6.3 EOS Measurements

There is currently a major limitation in how EOS handles writes into the namespace: certain locks prevent multiple clients from performing concurrent updates, resulting in low parallelism and limited use of pipelining towards QuarkDB.

We are in the process of fixing this limitation – even so, the performance achieved in replicated mode is still several times higher than what we currently see in production (20 Hz file creation rate). The goal is to eventually reach and surpass the rates achieved by the in-memory namespace.

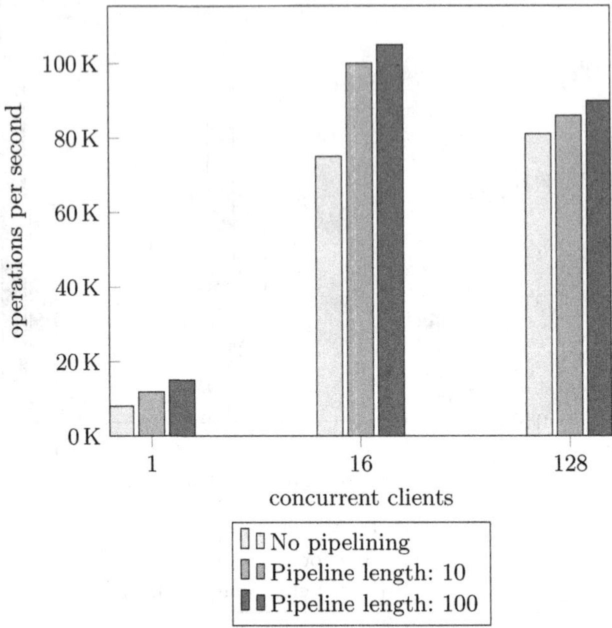

Fig. 2. QuarkDB write performance in standalone mode, SET command, 200 bytes

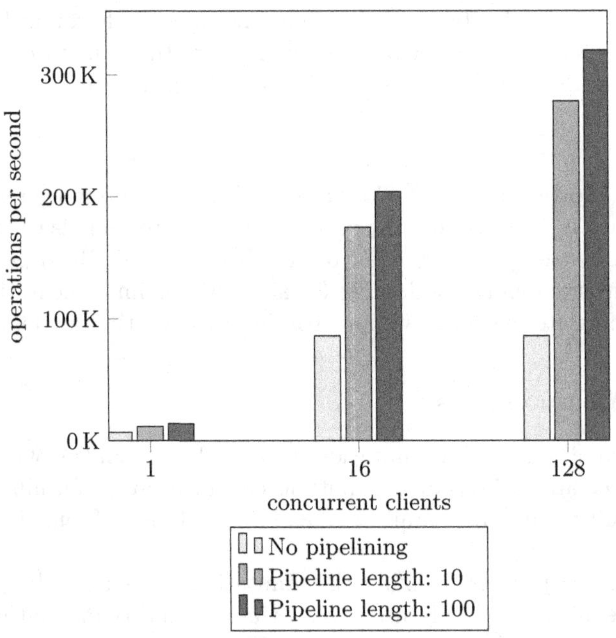

Fig. 3. QuarkDB read performance, GET command

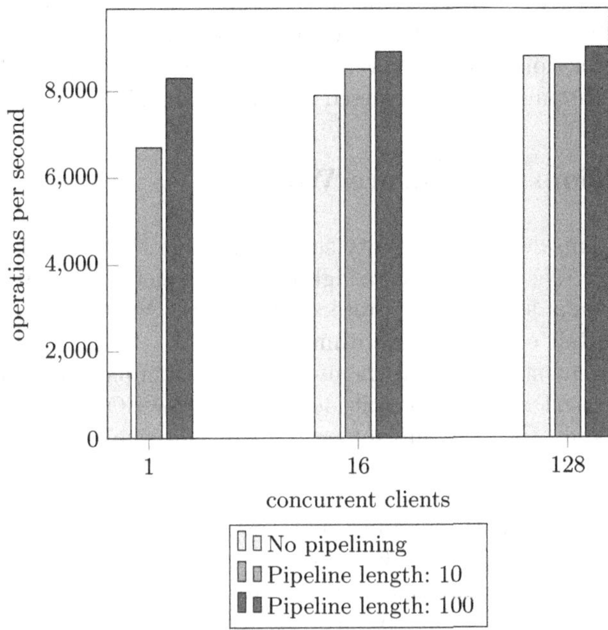

Fig. 4. QuarkDB write performance in Raft mode, SET command, 200 bytes

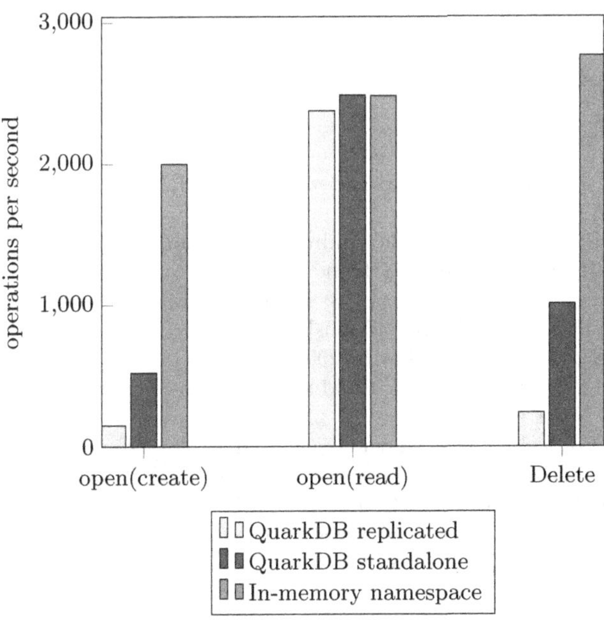

Fig. 5. End-to-end operations towards EOS

Measurements were taken using our custom load-testing tool through the XRootD file access protocol. It's important to note that operations such as file creation and deletion result in several key writes towards QuarkDB, which is why these measurements are presented separately (Fig. 5).

7 Conclusions and Future Work

We set out to improve the scalability shortcomings in the original design of the EOS namespace. We implemented a highly available metadata server component based on the redis serialization protocol, the RocksDB embeddable key-value store, and the Raft consensus algorithm.

Our measurements show that the new namespace implementation is capable of offering the next order of magnitude of scaling for EOS, ready to meet the data needs of the LHC experiments and CERN as a whole. Future work could improve on the design in several areas:

- Implementing automatic sharding in QuarkDB to overcome the inherent bottleneck imposed by the serial Raft log.
- Adding automatic and transparent failover to the MGM layer. An MGM failure could be made detectable by the rest, thus transferring its responsibilities and assigned namespace subtree to a different node, automatically and with minimal impact on availability.
- QuarkDB could be made to additionally serve as a highly available message queue, replacing the current one and removing one of the few remaining single points of failure in EOS.

References

1. Peters, A.J., Janyst, L.: Exabyte scale storage at CERN. J. Phys. Conf. Ser. **331**(5), 052015 (2011). IOP Publishing
2. Howard, J.H.: An overview of the Andrew file system. Carnegie Mellon University, Information Technology Center (1988)
3. Mascetti, L., et al.: CERNBox+ EOS: end-user storage for science. J. Phys. Conf. Ser. **664**(6), 062037 (2015). IOP Publishing
4. Sanfilippo, S., Noordhuis, P.: Redis (2009)
5. Borthakur, D.: Under the Hood: Building and Open-Sourcing RocksDB. Facebook Engineering Notes (2013)
6. Varda, K.: Protocol Buffers. Google Open Source Blog (2008)
7. Ongaro, D., Ousterhout, J.K.: In search of an understandable consensus algorithm. In: USENIX Annual Technical Conference (2014)
8. Dorigo, A., et al.: XROOTD-A highly scalable architecture for data access. WSEAS Trans. Comput. **1**(4.3), 348–353 (2005)

Erratum to: Performance Portability Analysis for Real-Time Simulations of Smoke Propagation Using OpenACC

Anne Küsters[1](✉), Sandra Wienke[2,3], and Lukas Arnold[1]

[1] JSC, Forschungszentrum Jülich GmbH, Wilhelm-Johnen-Straße, 52428 Jülich, Germany
a.kuesters@fz-juelich.de

[2] IT Center, RWTH Aachen University, Seffenter Weg 23, 52074 Aachen, Germany

[3] JARA-HPC, 52074 Aachen, Germany

Erratum to:
Chapter "Performance Portability Analysis for Real-Time Simulations of Smoke Propagation Using OpenACC" in: J.M. Kunkel et al. (Eds.): High Performance Computing, LNCS 10524, https://doi.org/10.1007/978-3-319-67630-2_35

The ORCIDs of the second and third authors were incorrect in the original version of the paper. The ORCIDs have been corrected.

The updated online version of this chapter can be found at
https://doi.org/10.1007/978-3-319-67630-2_35

J.M. Kunkel et al. (Eds.): ISC High Performance Workshops 2017, LNCS 10524, p. E1, 2017.
https://doi.org/10.1007/978-3-319-67630-2_54

Author Index